USA

BUSINESS

**World Trade Press
Country Business Guides**

ARGENTINA Business
AUSTRALIA Business
CHINA Business
HONG KONG Business
JAPAN Business
KOREA Business
MEXICO Business
PHILIPPINES Business
SINGAPORE Business
TAIWAN Business
USA Business

The Portable Encyclopedia For Doing Business With the United States

Karla C. Shippey, J.D. James L. Nolan, Ph.D.
Alexandra Woznick Edward G. Hinkelman

Carlsmith Ball Wichman Case & Ichiki
Duane H. Zobrist, Esq.
Nancy M. Beckner, Esq. Stephen L. Bradford, Esq.
Anna Elento-Sneed, Esq. Patrick H. Jones, Esq.

Dean W. Engel William T. LeGro
Christopher Mahon Robin E. Kobayashi, J.D.
Marty Olmstead Max Donner

Ernst & Young • The East West Group Inc. • International Monetary Fund
CIGNA Property and Casualty • The Exhibit Review • Foreign Trade
The NAFTA Research Institute • Magellan[sm] Geographix

Series Editor: Edward G. Hinkelman

WORLD TRADE PRESS ®

Resources for International Trade

1505 Fifth Avenue
San Rafael, California 94901
USA

Published by World Trade Press
1505 Fifth Avenue
San Rafael, CA 94901, USA
Tel: (415) 454-9934
Fax: (415) 453-7980
USA Orderline: (800) 833-8586
E-mail: WorldPress@aol.com

Cover and book design: Brad Greene
Illustrations: Eli Africa
Cartoons: Robert Mankoff
Maps: Magellan℠ Geographix
Desktop design and publishing: Peter G. Jones
Charts and graphs: David Baker
Copyeditor: Michael Levy
Proofreader: Christopher J. Forshay

Permission to reprint copyrighted materials has been given as follows: Excerpts from *1994 Worldwide Corporate Tax Guide* and *1994 Worldwide Personal Tax Guide,* copyright © 1994 by Ernst & Young, reprinted with permission of Ernst & Young. Export, import, and transportation statistics from *Foreign Trade,* copyright © 1994 by Defense & Diplomacy, Inc., reprinted with permission of the publisher. Cartoons reproduced with permission, copyright © Robert Mankoff from The Cartoon Bank, Inc., Hastings-on-Hudson, New York. "Foreign Investment," "Business Entities & Formation," and "Business Law" by Duane H. Zobrist and Stephen L. Bradford, copyright © 1995 Carlsmith Ball Wichman Case & Ichiki, reprinted with permission of the law firm. "Labor" by Duane H. Zobrist, Anna Elento-Sneed, and Patrick H. Jones, copyright © 1995 Carlsmith Ball Wichman Case & Ichiki, reprinted with permission of the law firm. "The US Tax System: A Broad Brush," "Relief from Double Corporate Taxation," "Relief from Double Personal Taxation," "Nonresident Alien (NRA) Status," and "Special Tax Considerations" by Duane H. Zobrist and Nancy M. Beckner, copyright © 1995 Carlsmith Ball Wichman Case & Ichiki, reprinted with permission of the law firm. Excerpts from *CIGNA Ports of the World* (15th ed.), copyright © 1994 CIGNA Property and Casualty Co., reprinted with permission from CIGNA Property and Casualty Companies. "Capital Transactions" and "Gold" reproduced from *Exchange Arrangements and Exchange Restrictions Annual Report 1994,* copyright © 1994 International Monetary Fund, reprinted with permission from IMF, Washington, DC, USA. Maps from MGExplorer™ subscription service, copyright © Magellan℠ Geographix, Santa Barbara, CA, USA.

Library of Congress Cataloging-in-Publication Data
USA business : the portable encyclopedia for doing business with the
    United States / Karla C. Shippey ... [et al.] ; contributors,
    Auerbach International ... [et al.].
        p. cm. — (World Trade Press country business guides)
    Includes bibliographical references and index.
    ISBN 1-885073-01-1
        1. United States—Economic policy—1993- —Handbooks, manuals,
    etc. 2. United States—Commercial policy—Handbooks, manuals, etc.
    3. Investments, Foreign—Government policy—United States—
    —Handbooks, manuals, etc. 4. United States—Economic
    conditions—1981- —Handbooks, manuals, etc. 5. United States—
    —Foreign economic relations—Handbooks, manuals, etc.   I. Shippey,
    Karla C., 1957-   .   II. Auerbach International.   III. Series.
HC106.82.U83 1995
658.8' 48' 0973—dc20   95-7680
                                                         CIP

Printed in the United States of America

ACKNOWLEDGMENTS

We owe many leaders in the international business community a debt of gratitude. Hundreds of trade and reference experts have brought this book to life. We are indebted to numerous international business consultants, reference librarians, travel advisors, consulate, embassy, and trade mission officers, bank officers, attorneys, global shippers and insurers, and multinational investment brokers who answered our incessant inquiries and volunteered facts, figures, and expert opinions. To all these many individuals, named and unnamed, we extend our thanks.

This publication would not have been possible without the professional talents of many researchers, authors, and editors. Topping the list is attorney Duane H. Zobrist of the law firm of Carlsmith, Ball, Wichman, Case & Ichiki, whose publication "Businessman's Legal Guide to Doing Business in the United States" formed the basis of four chapters in this book. We owe a tremendous debt to attorneys Nancy M. Beckner, Stephen L. Bradford, Anna Elento-Sneed, and Patrick H. Jones, and to all the behind-the-scene assistants at the Los Angeles and Honolulu offices of that firm, who pulled, shaped, and expanded that material per our specifications; and to Carlos Valderrama, Director of Latin American Operations, for his patient and efficient coordination of that extensive effort.

The cultural materials show the significant impact of author and human resources consultant Dean Engel, senior partner in The East West Group Inc., a consulting firm that develops cross-cultural strategies for clients operating worldwide. International trade consultant Dean C. Alexander, Director of The NAFTA Research Institute, Washington, DC, reviewed the NAFTA article and made sure that we had the current facts.

Legal author Robin E. Kobayashi analyzed US import and export policies and sifted through often conflicting procedural data to get to the hard facts. Author Christopher Mahon delved into US industries and opportunities. For assistance with US communications, we turned to Max Donner, Telecommunications Agent, Optimisers, Sausalito, California, a consultant, professor, and analyst in international telecommunications. Long-time news journalist Marty Olmstead took her pad on assignment, compiled all the business slang she heard, and then had to figure out what her sources meant.

We were in stitches over the dozens of cartoons supplied for reprint consideration by the charming and artistic Robert Mankoff from the Cartoon Bank in Hastings-on-Hudson, New York. We found helpful allies in Steve Fahrbach, Doug Crawford, and Rick Wood of Magellan[sm] Geographix, who worked with us on both black and white and color maps.

The ever-obliging Barry Tarneff of CIGNA Property and Casualty Co. has once again supplied us with transportation information—this time on US ports. In our search for trade fair information, we discovered Mary K. Bucknell of The Exhibit Review, Beaverton, Oregon, who amassed all the trade fair listings, and Meredith Hunt, Resource Center Manager at the Trade Show Bureau, Denver, Colorado, who supplied information on US trade fair sites. As a start on finding important addresses, publisher Leslie Mackenzie of Grey House Publishing offered her firm's "Directory of Business Information Services," a resource not to be missed when compiling an extensive trade and business library.

For gathering US flight times in handy chart form, we thank Maggie Condon of Travel Advisors, Mill Valley, California. A hearty thank you also to Cassie Arnold of Ernst & Young, San Francisco, for promptly obtaining the most current tax information from that firm's publications.

We relied heavily on the reference librarians and resources available at the libraries of the University of California at Berkeley, San Francisco Public Library, San Rafael Public Library, Marin County Civic Center Library, and Marin County Law Library. Of particular note, reference librarian Gail Lockman at the San Rafael Public Library answered our many oblique inquiries—always with a smile.

Special thanks to Mela Hinkelman, whose patience, understanding, generosity, and support made this project possible.

DISCLAIMER

We have diligently tried to ensure the accuracy of all of the information in this publication and to present as comprehensive a reference work as space would permit. In determining the contents, we were guided by many experts in the field, extensive hours of research, and our own experience. We did have to make choices in coverage, however, because the inclusion of everything one could ever want to know about international trade would be impossible. The fluidity and fast pace of today's business world makes the task of keeping data current and accurate an extremely difficult one. This publication is intended to give you the information that you need in order to discover the information that is most useful for your particular business. As you contact the resources within this book, you will no doubt learn of new and exciting business opportunities and of additional international trading requirements that have arisen even within the short time since we published this edition. If errors are found, we will strive to correct them in preparing future editions. The publishers take no responsibility for inaccurate or incomplete information that may have been submitted to them in the course of research for this publication. The facts published are the result of those inquiries, and no warranty as to their accuracy is given.

Contents

Introduction

The United States of America (the USA, or, more commonly, just the US) is the world's largest economy and the largest international supplier and consumer of a wide range of goods and services. It is strategically situated with the Atlantic Ocean to the east, the burgeoning Pacific Rim to the west, and the rapidly awakening economies of Latin America to the south, and maintains close ties with industrial Canada to the north. A major, if often reluctant, player on the international scene, the US exercises substantial influence in global politics and markets. It has been the dominant economy in the world since World War II. However, the US has been coping with a maturing economy after its prolonged postwar period of rapid growth. Battered by deficits and the dislocations of economic and social restructuring during recent years, the country is caught between the fragile certainty of its status in the old political and economic world order and its as yet unclear new international role in the evolving 21st century. Although some argue that the US is a giant in decline, it remains rich and dynamic, offering opportunities that continue to draw people and businesses from across the globe.

The US is still subject to uncomfortable fluctuations in its economy, the most recent coming with the recession in 1990–1992. But the country has been able to avoid a repetition of the surging inflation and high interest rates that plagued it during the late 1970s and early 1980s, making it a more stable and attractive place to do business. Although interest rates are rising, inflation in 1994 fell below 3 percent for the third year in a row, while growth in the economy rose by 4 percent. And despite a lack of notable successes on the home front, the US administration has spearheaded two major trade initiatives with the signing and ratification of the North American Free Trade Agreement (NAFTA) in 1993 and the General Agreement on Tariffs and Trade (GATT) in 1994. Its prominent role in these agreements should serve to keep the US at the forefront of international trade and open its vast markets even further in future years.

The US is an intriguing market and one well worth investigating from a number of perspectives. For buyers, the US can offer a wide variety of raw materials and intermediate, high-tech, and consumer products at a wide range of quality and price points. It is a major producer of electronics and machinery, of transportation products—in particular, automotive and aircraft products—minerals and timber products, and agricultural products and processed foods, among many others. So far-reaching is the US economy that its top export—electrical machinery—accounts for less than 8 percent of total exports. The US is also the world's top service economy, offering many innovative technical and professional services that are either unsurpassed or simply unavailable elsewhere.

From the seller's perspective, the US is also the world's top importer, a hungry consumer of a wide range of goods, from raw materials to goods of the lowest to the highest state-of-the-art technology, but most especially of components and finished consumer goods. US consumers are among the world's most affluent. Always receptive to foreign products, the US is likely to become an even more avid buyer of outside goods and services as the new world economy develops. This new economy should also work to the benefit of foreign manufacturers looking to take advantage of US industrial capacity and high-skill production capabilities. Although other producers may be able to outcompete its industries on either price or quality in specific areas, the US still remains the top contender in terms of productivity in a wide variety of industrial areas, and its trained workforce still outshines and outnumbers that of any other country.

For investors, the US remains the world's broadest and deepest financial market, one that operates with relatively few restrictions. And for investors interested in establishing new firms or in acquiring existing operations, the US has one of the most liberal foreign investment frameworks in the world. Home to some of the world's dominant corporate

giants, the US has never relied on state-run operations to build its influence. And although the US is a
highly regulated operating environment, in recent
years it has deregulated many of its industries to a
significant degree, opening even more opportunities.

People in the US are caught in a fluid situation in
which the old principles no longer hold out the same
promise of solutions to current problems, yet the
next step remains unclear. This is an environment
that requires great care and alertness, but it also offers many options and opportunities. Probably more
so than at any time in the past, the US is a complex
and challenging—as well as compelling—place in
which to do business.

USA Business was designed by businesspeople
experienced in international markets to give you an
overview of the way things actually work and what
current conditions are in the US. It will give you the
head start you will need in order to evaluate and operate in US markets. It also tells you where to get
more information in greater depth.

The following chapter discusses the main elements of the country's **Economy**, including its development, present situation, and the forces directing its future prospects. **Current Issues** explains the
top concerns affecting the country and its next stage
of development. The **Opportunities** chapter presents
discussions of major areas of interest to importers
and exporters. The chapter also clarifies the nature
of government procurement processes. **Foreign Investment** details attitudes, policies, incentives, regulations, procedures, and restrictions.

Foreign Trade presents information on what and
with whom the US trades. **Trade Agreements** outlines US trade legislation and special opportunities
within its trade framework. **Foreign Trade Zones**
discusses the advantages of operating through the
hundreds of FTZs that exist in the US to promote
foreign trade. The **Import Policy & Procedures** and
Export Policy & Procedures chapters delineate the
nature of US trade: current policy and the practical
information—nuts and bolts procedural requirements—necessary to trade with it. The **Industry
Reviews** chapter outlines the 12 most prominent industries in the US and their competitive positions
from the standpoint of a businessperson interested
in taking advantage of these industries' strengths (or
exploiting their weaknesses). **Trade Fairs** provides
a comprehensive listing of major trade fairs in the
US, complete with contact information, and spells
out the best ways to maximize the benefits offered
by these events.

Business Travel offers practical information on
travel requirements, resources, internal travel, local
customs, and ambiance, as well as comparative information on accommodations and dining in New
York, Los Angeles, Washington DC, Chicago, Miami,

and Houston—the main business venues in the US.
Business Culture provides a user-friendly primer on
local business style, mind-set, and negotiating practices, plus numerous other tips designed to improve
your effectiveness, avoid inadvertent gaffes, and generally smooth the way for doing business in the US.
Demographics presents basic statistical data needed
to assess the US market, while **Marketing** outlines
resources, approaches, and specific markets.

Business Entities & Formation discusses recognized business entities and registration procedures
for operating in the US. **Labor** assembles information on the availability, capabilities, and cost of labor in the US, as well as terms of employment and
business-labor relations. **Business Law** interprets the
structure of the US legal system, providing a digest
of substantive points in commercial law prepared
with the help of international legal authorities. The
Financial Institutions chapter outlines the workings
of the US financial system, including banking and financial markets, and the availability of the financing
and services needed by foreign businesses. **Currency & Foreign Exchange** explains the workings
of the US foreign exchange system. **International
Payments** is an illustrated, step-by-step guide to using documentary collections and letters of credit.
Taxation provides the information—on tax rates, tax
provisions, and tax status of foreign operations and
individuals—needed to evaluate a venture in the
country. **Transportation & Communications** gives
current information about accessing the US physically, by phone, and by other means.

The **Business Slang Dictionary** is a unique resource consisting of 275 entries focusing specifically
on US idiomatic business usage to provide
businesspeople with the means for interpreting business in the US. More than 1,200 **Important Addresses**
include contact information for US official agencies;
business associations; financial, professional, and
service firms; transportation and shipping agencies;
media outlets; and sources of additional information
to enable businesspeople to locate the offices and
help they need to operate in the US. Full-color, up-
to-date **Maps** aid the business traveler in getting
around in the major business centers in the US. This
volume is cross-referenced and indexed to provide
ease of access to the specific information needed by
busy businesspeople.

USA Business gives you the information you
need, both to evaluate the prospect of doing business in the US and to actually begin doing it. It is
your invitation to this fascinating society and market. Welcome!

Economy

OVERVIEW

The United States of America (the USA, or, simply, the US) is the largest economy, largest trading nation, third largest population, and fourth largest in area in the world. In political and military terms, since the collapse of the Soviet Union, the US is also the world's only remaining superpower. A relatively young nation, the US became the world's first modern representative democracy and the model for many subsequent ones. Having also had the good fortune to occupy an immense territory rich in resources at a time of rapid advances in industrial, transportation, and communications technology, the US has been able to develop economies of scale in serving large domestic and overseas markets. There are those who argue that the US is already past the height of its influence, but by many measures this huge, affluent nation continues to be one of the world's foremost.

With 9.159 million square km (3.536 million square miles) of land area, the US falls behind only Russia, Canada, and China in physical size. At the end of 1994 it had an estimated population of 261.4 million (behind China and India, and just ahead of

CONTENTS

Indonesia). The US population, growing at about 1 percent per year, is expected to hit 275.3 million in the year 2000. Overall population density is about 28.5 persons per square km (74 per square mile), but this figure represents vast open areas where population can be measured by square km per person as well as urban areas (such as parts of New York City) with densities as high as 20,321 person per square km (52,429 per square mile). Overall, the US was about 75 percent urban and 25 percent rural in 1990 (it was 70 percent urban and 30 percent rural as recently as 1960). New York City—its most populous—has a population of 7.3 million, while the New York consolidated metropolitan statistical area (CMSA) is the country's largest megalopolis with 19.7 million people.

The roughly rectangular contiguous US is about 4,800 km (3,000 miles) from east to west and 2,400 km (1,500 miles) from north to south. The nation has 19,812 km (12,383 miles) of coastline fronting on the Atlantic Ocean, the Gulf of Mexico, and the Pacific Ocean (including Alaska and Hawaii). To the north, it shares a 6,415-km (3,987-mile) common border with Canada, plus an additional 2,475-km (1,538-miles) frontier between Alaska and Canada. The US southern border with Mexico runs 3,110 km (1,933 miles).

The geologically old Appalachian Mountain range runs parallel to the US east coast, while the Sierra and the Rocky Mountains lie in a north-south direction along the west coast and inland, respectively, forming between them the arid Great Basin. The vast central plain drained by the Mississippi-Missouri-Ohio River system stretches from the Appalachians to the Rockies. Running from near the Canadian border in the north to the Gulf of Mexico in the south, the Mississippi River is 3,765 km (2,340 miles) long. Lake Superior, one of the five Great Lakes shared with Canada, is the second largest lake in the world (81,786 square km, or 31,700 square miles). Altitude varies from Denali Peak-Mount McKinley in Alaska (at 6,193 m, or 20,320 feet, the highest point in North

ECONOMY GLOSSARY

agricultural sector The portion of the economy involved in production of food and other organic commodity resources; it includes farming and ranching; fishing, hunting, and trapping (as economic rather than recreational pursuits); and forestry.

balance of payments A statement identifying all the economic and financial transactions between all public, private, corporate, and individual entities of one nation with those of other nations within a specific time period. Transactions include all transfers of ownership of anything having economic value measured in money from residents of one country to those of another.

balance of trade The difference between a country's imports and exports during a specific period.

constant dollar An economic measure in which the value of the currency is adjusted to exclude the effects of inflation over a period of time in order to compare underlying trends (also known as "real" dollars).

current dollar An economic measure consisting of the nominal value of the currency at a given point in time that does not take the effects of inflation into account.

direct foreign investment Purchase of actual assets by persons from another country. In the US direct foreign investment is defined as the ownership of at least a 25 percent interest by foreigners in a US firm; however, the US Department of Commerce may consider foreign ownership of more than 10 percent as foreign influenced, and therefore constituting direct foreign ownership.

gross domestic product (GDP) A measure of the market value of all goods and services produced within the boundaries of a nation, regardless of the ownership of the assets used to produce it. GDP excludes receipts from that nation's business operations in foreign countries, as well as the share of reinvested earnings in foreign affiliates of domestic companies.

gross national product (GNP) A measure of the market value of all goods and services produced by the labor and property of a nation. GNP includes receipts from that nation's business operations in foreign countries as well as the share of reinvested earnings in foreign affiliates of domestic companies.

industrial sector The portion of the economy involved in the processing and production of goods; it is generally considered to include manufacturing, mining, and construction.

inflation Loss of purchasing power of money, caused by the growth of the amount of money in circulation which, if the supply of goods falls, stays the same, or increases at a slower rate, leads to an increase in prices.

merchandise trade The export or import of goods; excludes trade in invisibles (services).

per capita GDP A measure of national income derived by dividing GDP by the population in a country; per capita GDP is not equivalent to mean per capita income, which may be either substantially lower or higher than per capita GDP.

portfolio investment Purchase of a minority holding in an enterprise, usually through acquisition of securities; this investment can be made on either a permanent or temporary basis by either domestic or foreign investors. In the US foreign portfolio investment is defined as the holding of less than a 25 percent share of a company.

sector A subdivision of the economy. Can refer to: a) public (government owned) versus private (owned by individuals) sectors; b) agricultural, industrial, and service sectors; or c) different industries within a sector, such as the financial sector versus the retail sector.

services sector The portion of the economy involved in the provision of services rather than actual goods; the services sector generally includes advertising and public relations; data processing; security services; domestic and household services; repair services; restaurant and lodging; entertainment; health care and hospital services; education; legal, accounting, architectural, and other professional services; personal services; nongovernmental social services; and governmental services.

total trade A trade measure for a particular period that includes: a) both imports and exports of goods or b) imports and exports of goods and services.

America), to 86 m (282 feet) below sea level in Death Valley, California.

Climatic Conditions and Resources Although it lies primarily within the temperate zone, the US encompasses a wide range of topographies and climatic conditions. The extremes of Hawaii—a volcanic tropical archipelago—and Alaska—a vast mountainous arctic and subarctic wilderness—add to the variety of conditions found in the US. Outside of largely arid Alaska and tropical Hawaii, roughly 15 percent of the US may be classified as arid (receiving less than 25 cm, or 10 inches, of annual precipitation), while another 25 percent is semiarid (with 25 to 50 cm, or 10 to 20 inches, per year). Most of the rest is split more or less equally between zones receiving 50 to 100 cm (20 to 40 inches) and 100 to 150 cm (40 to 60 inches) of annual precipitation; some areas regularly receive even more.

Some 35.8 percent of land is classified as pasture or rangeland, 28.5 percent as croplands (6.6 percent of which is irrigated), 26.5 percent as forest, 5.2 percent as developed, and 4 percent as other. Some 20.9 percent of all land in the US is owned by federal agencies.

The US is rich in natural resources, including large and commercially exploitable deposits of coal, copper, lead, molybdenum, phosphates, uranium, gold, iron, mercury, nickel, potash, silver, tungsten, and zinc. A major source of oil, natural gas, and coal, the US is both the world's largest producer and largest consumer of petroleum products. However, its diminishing oil reserves rank ninth in the world and account for only about 2.5 percent of total reserves. This is cause for concern in a physically large nation dependent on fossil fuels to support its energy intensive economy and elevated lifestyle. The US is the world's largest grower (and exporter) of wheat, corn (maize), soybeans, cotton, tobacco, and meat. It is second in rice. US territorial waters are also among the richest worldwide. The country also produces large amounts of commercial timber.

The People of the US The US prides itself on being a nation of immigrants, with the majority of its people tracing their ancestry to waves of immigration from Europe during the 18th, 19th, and early 20th centuries. In 1992 Whites made up 76.8 percent of the population, followed by African-Americans (11.3 percent), Hispanics (8.6 percent), Asians (3 percent), and Native Americans (0.8 percent). In 1990 roughly 20 percent of the population was foreign-born, and by 1992, immigration accounted for 33 percent of total population growth. In some states such as California—the state ranking first in population with 31 million as of 1993—non-Whites are expected to constitute a majority by the year 2000. This growing diversity mimics the situation at the end of the 1800s and the beginning of the 1900s, but with the differ-

ence that it includes far more immigrants of non-European origin.

Although the US has no official language, English is the language of record, business, and general usage. Many other languages are spoken in specific communities, with Spanish being the most common, reflecting the rapid growth of the Hispanic community. In 1990, 13.8 percent of the population five years of age or older spoke a language other than English. The immigrant population is also increasingly young, while the population at large is rapidly aging: the average age of 30 years in 1980 rose to 33 years in 1991.

Some 81 percent of the population considers itself to be Christian—56 percent Protestant and 25 percent Roman Catholic. Next largest is the nonreligious group at 11 percent of the population, followed by the Jewish religion (2 percent), while others—including Sikhs, new religionists, Hindus, Buddhists, and Muslims as the main groups—together represent 6 percent.

HISTORY OF THE ECONOMY

Settlement and Independence

When Europeans first began to establish permanent settlements along the east coast in the 16th century, the area that became the US was populated by a wide variety of low-density Native American groups. The Spanish settled the southern ranges of the area, and the French the northern zone. However, the most intensive settlement was by British colonists along the Atlantic coast, beginning in 1607. There were also relatively short-lived Dutch, Swedish, and Russian colonies.

The original British colonies were established as commercial ventures, religious refuges, or both. Most British settlers in the US were farmers, laborers, and craftspeople displaced by the British Enclosure Movement that forced large numbers of people off the land. Black indentured servants first arrived in 1619 and Black slavery was legally recognized in the British colonies in 1650. As European settlement developed, the settlers came into increasing conflict with the Native American occupants, resorting to more and more violent means to subdue and evict them.

In accordance with the prevailing mercantilist economic theories of the day, the colonies served as producers of precious metals and raw materials, as dumping grounds for excess population, and as captive markets for the manufactures of the parent country. The US colonies managed to conduct a wide range of primary and commercial activities, but were generally prevented from accumulating capital or developing strategic industries. By the 1700s the developing middle class and the local elite in the port cities were clamoring for a greater role in government, trade, and industry. Britain began imposing taxes on many imported materials to underwrite the cost of maintaining garrisons in the colonies. These troops, used to fight those of other European nations—primarily France—and their Indian allies, turned increasingly to police functions after the French withdrawal from Canada in 1763.

Hostilities broke out in 1775, and the colonies declared independence from Britain in 1776. Following a series of haphazard campaigns in which the colonists were saved from defeat by intermittent timely victories that turned British public opinion against the expensive prolonged war, the rebels—with the help of French forces—narrowly defeated the British expeditionary forces in 1781. After operating ineffectively as a confederacy of independent states, the colonies met in 1786 to draft a constitution, which went into effect in 1789. US expansion inland grew, as did seaborne commercial ventures, leading to conflicts with Native American groups on the one hand and with European nations on the other.

The US was able to remain viable largely because the broad Atlantic Ocean protected it from the European great powers and because those powers were embroiled in their own continental wars. During this period the Spanish withdrew from the southern US, as their own Latin American colonies battled for independence. French settlement along the lower Mississippi River lasted until 1803, when Napoleon sold French possessions to the US in the Louisiana Purchase, doubling the size of the new nation. In the final act of the prolonged de facto war for independence from Europe, the US fought with Britain in 1812. Peace was declared as a by-product of the Treaty of Ghent which settled European conflicts in 1814. By 1823 the US was sufficiently established to issue the Monroe Doctrine, declaring that it would fight any European power seeking to intervene in New World affairs.

A Growing Nation

In the 1830s the US dispossessed the last of the organized Native American groups east of the Mississippi River. The Santa Fe Trail was established in 1821 to open trade with Mexico; the first trips by settlers to the far west were made over the Oregon Trail in 1836 and the California Trail in 1841. Operating under the slogan of "manifest destiny"—a belief that the US was destined to control the entire North American continent—the nation came into conflict with Britain on the north and Mexico on the south and west. This tension almost led to another war with Britain, but a treaty was signed in 1842 to define the eastern portion of the boundary with Canada, followed by another in 1846 settling the western boundary.

In 1846 the US annexed Texas, precipitating hostilities with Mexico. The war lasted until 1848, and

the victorious US seized most of the remainder of the western territory it now occupies. In 1848 gold was discovered in the newly acquired California, leading to a rapid influx of settlers that helped open overland routes and settle the west coast. This period also marked the initial wave of Asian immigration to the US; these immigrants, primarily from China, came to work in the gold fields, remaining to establish a permanent presence in the place they called the Gold Mountain.

Throughout this period, conflict grew between the industrial northern states and the agrarian southern ones over federal versus local authority, centering around the issue of Black slavery. The Civil War began in 1861 when 11 southern states attempted to secede from the US. This fratricidal conflict raged until 1865, with federal troops occupying many portions of the south until 1877. Around this time, the US also seized the Hawaiian Islands, purchased Alaska from Russia, and helped fend off an attempt by Britain and France to move into Mexico. Conflicts between encroaching settlers and native populations also increased in frequency and intensity in western territories where the Indian Wars, which—along with the cowboy legend—have become a definitive part of US folklore, were carried out intermittently but implacably. By 1900 most native peoples were confined on reservations as wards of the federal government.

Looking Outward

According to historian Frederick Jackson Turner, the frontier, which had shaped US actions and national character, closed in 1890—meaning that there were no more wide open spaces left to conquer in the contiguous US. In the 1890s the still-growing US began to take a broader view of its position in the world. In 1898 it went to war with Spain, seizing Puerto Rico as well as the Philippines and Guam to open a foothold in East Asia. And in 1903 the US encouraged Panama to break away from Colombia so that a treaty could be signed with the new state, thus allowing construction of the Panama Canal (which opened in 1914). This period saw a general expansion of US commercial and political interests in Latin America and the Pacific, with the US intervening militarily in Mexico, Haiti, and China.

The US, which had previously remained somewhat aloof from European affairs, entered World War I in 1917. At the war's end in 1918, the US attempted to exercise a role in the establishment of a League of Nations. However, neither the European powers nor an isolationist US Congress and public were ready for the experiment. Following the postwar boom, the worldwide economy collapsed. The Great Depression—a period of massive worldwide economic collapse—resulted in the 1930s. Largely responsible for extricating the US and much of the rest of the world

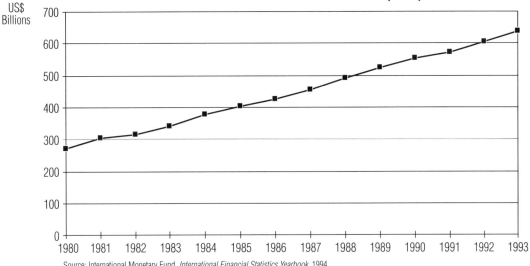

United States Gross Domestic Product (GDP)

Source: International Monetary Fund, *International Financial Statistics Yearbook,* 1994

from the Depression, a new wartime economic push developed as the US engaged in World War II, fighting Germany in Europe and Japan in the Pacific. The US, entering the ongoing war at the end of 1941, emerged at its end in 1945 as the strongest political, military, and economic power in the world. Its industrial might was unrivaled, and US home territory—distant from the fighting—had escaped unravaged. As the only power with an intact economic base, the US became even more of a world leader and set about helping to reconstruct some of the battered states. It would subsequently become allied with both Germany and Japan, trading more with them than with any but its closest geographic neighbors, Canada and Mexico, and with Britain, its one-time parent.

A full adjustment to a peacetime economy was prevented by the start of the Cold War between the US and the USSR-led eastern Communist bloc. Almost as soon as World War II was over, the new superpowers began fencing. Their maneuvers included an atomic weapons buildup, the militarization and cordoning off of Central Europe, and the Korean War (1950–1953), which resulted in an increasing US commitment in East Asia. The role that the US assumed—that of global policeman—led to a military buildup in Southeast Asia, beginning in earnest in 1964 and continuing until public outcry and a general lack of military success led to a US withdrawal in 1975. In the post-Vietnam era, the US has been involved in other confrontations, including a series of brushfire wars in the Western Hemisphere and elsewhere, the most recent of which was the Persian Gulf War in 1991. A rapprochement with China in the 1970s and the collapse of the USSR in the late 1980s and early 1990s—with the subsequent end of the Cold War—

have left the US without a traditional antagonist or a clear international role after 50 years as a principal actor in a Cold War world.

Domestic Social Changes

Preceding the public protests against the Vietnam War were the US civil rights protests of the 1950s and 1960s. Most were directed toward improving opportunities for minorities, primarily African-Americans, who, despite the enactment of legal protections following the Civil War, had continued to occupy a second class position in society. In the intervening years, other minority claimants have become increasingly vocal in demanding improved treatment, leading to a more diverse—but less coherent—body politic, a phenomenon with which the US must learn to deal more effectively in the immediate future.

Economic Development

The industrial revolution in the US began by the early 19th century with the use of waterpower to produce textiles with technology pirated from Britain. Mechanics—local US artisans, inventors, and tinkerers—developed a spate of technological innovations and applications. Nevertheless, the majority of the US population and economy was supported by subsistence farming, a situation that continued into the 20th century.

In a country as large and as isolated from the rest of the civilized world as the US, transportation was more of an issue than production. Little market development could occur in the absence of a functioning transportation infrastructure. US entrepreneurs—often using foreign capital, on which they later defaulted—first built roads and canals and then railroad and steamship lines. Many innovations connected with rail and powered ship transport were developed in the US, as were numerous subsequent transport innovations, including the production automobile and airplane. Such innovations were made possible by the production of the first commercial oil well in 1859, which, within a half century, would provide the primary fuel for transport and industry. The first consumer oriented automobile, the Ford Model T, rolled off the assembly line in 1908, serving as a model for subsequent mass production.

To unite the widespread US, communications were also essential. One of many innovations promoted by founding father Benjamin Franklin was a national postal service. The telegraph was developed in 1844, with transatlantic service instituted in 1858 and transcontinental service in 1861. The first telephone exchange opened in 1878, and although radio was not developed in the US, television was invented there in 1927; the first commercial TV service was offered in 1951. Motion pictures, developed in 1894, led to the merger of the communications and entertainment industries in a distinctive US fashion. The US also pioneered in satellite communications.

As a developing country, the US was a follower rather than an innovator in terms of finance and business structure throughout most of the 19th century. During that period it experienced unregulated, cutthroat capitalism, replete with booms and busts, panics, and the manipulative activities of industrial and financial giants known as "robber barons." In an attempt to rein in predatory, anti-competitive practices, Congress passed a series of regulatory laws, beginning with the Sherman Antitrust Act in 1890, to regulate some of the perceived abuses. In 1906 it passed one of the first pieces of consumer protection legislation—the Pure Food and Drug Act—to correct market abuses.

The US also led the world with one of the first environmental measures, the creation of national forests in 1891 (Yellowstone had already been designated a national park in 1872, inaugurating a program to preserve the country's natural wonders). In another US innovation, Woolworth's opened the first mass market concept store—the five-and-ten-cents store—in 1879, adding to the contribution of Sears Roebuck in developing direct marketing via catalogue sales. Advertising and modern marketing may also be considered quintessentially US developments.

Recent Developments

In recent years the US economy has been undergoing a transformation that is partially worldwide and partially unique to the US. Burdened by the stress of trying to run both an ambitious social investment program at home and a costly military venture in Southeast Asia, while at the same time

garrisoning much of the rest of the world, the energy-dependent US was dealt a body blow during the 1970s by shocks within the global oil market, upsetting the delicate equilibrium of its national economy. Reacting to a perceived waning international political role in the early 1980s, the US undertook a massive military buildup and instituted a huge domestic tax cut; its economy surged ahead. However, the increased activity came at the cost of skyrocketing budget deficits.

By the end of the 1980s, the overextended US economy was forced to lower expectations and radically prune operations. In the 1990s, many entities continue to undergo restructuring and layoffs, and this trend is extending to sharp cutbacks in the public sector as well as in private industry. The situation has been exacerbated by the dissolution of the Soviet Union, leaving the US as the only remaining superpower, but largely unable to project that power or exert the influence it feels should accrue to its status.

As a result, the US is torn by conflicting tendencies: it is trying to become more internationally oriented while at the same time threatening to retire into the isolationism that periodically afflicts it. The major change in direction signaled by the November 1994 US elections indicate uncertainty about exactly what role the US should take in future internal as well as international relations. However, most factions acknowledge that the international role of the US will have to be a broad one, as evidenced by the passage in late 1993 of the North American Free Trade Agreement (NAFTA) and of the General Agreement on Tariffs and Trade (GATT) in late 1994. However, the difficulties experienced in securing passage of these agreements highlight the prevailing uncertainty.

SIZE OF THE ECONOMY

The US gross domestic product (GDP) is roughly 50 percent larger than that of Japan, the next largest economy in the world. In 1993 US GDP was US$6.378 trillion, up 3.6 percent in real terms from 1992's US$6.038 trillion. According to preliminary figures, the economy grew at a rate of 4 percent in 1994, reaching about US$6.633 trillion. The Organization for Economic Cooperation and Development (OECD) projects 3.1 percent growth for the US economy in 1995, falling to a sluggish 2 percent in 1996, while the US Federal Reserve Board is predicting 1995 growth between 2 and 3 percent.

Growth in the US economy has begun to slow as it matures. Although GDP grew almost tenfold in current dollar terms between 1964 and 1993, with a compound annual growth rate (CAGR) of 7.9 percent, it grew at only a 2.65 percent CAGR on a real basis figured using constant dollars. Conventional wisdom among economists holds that the US economy can sustain steady annual real growth of only about 2.5 percent without experiencing inflation and other detrimental dislocations. However, despite the current surge in GDP growth—it grew at a 4.5 percent rate during the fourth quarter of 1993—the feared problems of capacity and labor shortages and wage and inflationary pressures have yet to emerge. This has caused some observers to question the continued applicability of such historically derived empirical rules.

Per capita GDP—the GDP divided by the population—is often used as a measure of individual national income. Preliminary figures place it at US$25,443 for 1994. Per capita GDP was US$24,696 in 1993, up from US$23,637 in 1992. This represents a gain of 4.5 percent in nominal terms, but only about 1.5 percent in real terms after netting out inflation. Between 1980 and 1993 the real annual CAGR was 1.2 percent above the inflation rate and about 0.25 percent above the population growth rate. This remainder represents real growth, due largely to increased productivity.

In 1993 the World Bank reported that the US ranked seventh in the world in terms of per capita gross national product (GNP). (Switzerland, Luxembourg, Japan, Denmark, Norway, and Sweden had higher per capita GNP, while Iceland, Germany, and Kuwait ranked just below the US on this measure; Mozambique had the lowest per capita GNP.) However, when the figures were adjusted for price levels the US ranked second worldwide (behind Luxembourg and ahead of Switzerland). In general, US prices for energy, housing, and food are much lower than those in other high-income nations, and although people in the US pay more for health care, this is primarily because health care is subsidized by governments elsewhere to a greater degree.

As an indication of actual distributions of income, US per capita GDP was US$23,637 in 1992, while actual disposable personal income was calculated as US$18,177. However, median income was US$30,786, more than two-thirds higher. When the 1992 income distribution is divided into quintiles, the lowest fifth (below US$16,900) received 3.8 percent of total income, the next quintile (below US$30,000) 9.4 percent, the third (below US$44,200) 15.9 percent, the next (below US$64,300) 24.1 percent, and the top quintile 46.8 percent, or nearly half of all income. Some 14.5 percent were considered to have incomes that placed them below the government's established poverty level. In contrast, about 11 percent of the population had incomes greater than US$75,000.

In mid-1994 median family net worth—actual assets less debts, counting cash, savings, and investments and equity in cars, houses, and other property—was US$23,519. However, half of all families in the US had net financial assets (cash, savings, and investments) of less than US$1,000, and 40 percent had negative net worth (debts exceeding assets).

CONTEXT OF THE ECONOMY

As recently as the turn of the 20th century, the US was just beginning to emerge as a developed economy, and as recently as the late 1980s, the country was considered to have lost the struggle for economic supremacy after Japan surpassed the US as measured by a variety of economic indices. During this latter period, many observers argued that the US should adopt Japan's more structured, focused, and government-directed cooperative economic model in place of the traditional undirected competitive market model used in the US. However, in the early 1990s, as Japan's economy hit the doldrums and undertook restructurings that had been faced somewhat earlier by the US economy, the calls to follow the Japanese model are becoming less strident and frequent.

Small versus Large Business The US economy is marked by the general tenet that any individual has the right to start a business venture and an opportunity to succeed with it. There is a strong tradition of independent, small, local businesses operated largely by middle class entrepreneurs. The actual number of lower class individuals who have started successful businesses with few resources is very small, and most of the extremely rich people in the US acquired their money through inheritance rather than entrepreneurialism. Nevertheless, the strong tradition of middle class entrepreneurialism is justified to a greater extent than in many other national economies. And while many businesspeople must in fact rely on favors, personal relationships, and contracts from larger entities to become established, the ethos that continues to hold is that—rather than influence—individual effort, value, and quality of service determines success in a generally impartial market. The lore and practice of US business is laced with language reflecting this individual struggle; sports and military analogies and metaphors are often used to express this competitive aspect.

Conventional wisdom in the US holds that most businesses are small and most employment is created by those small operations. In 1991, 26 percent of the labor force was employed by small businesses with fewer than 20 persons and 29 percent by operations with between 20 and 100 employees: thus, a total of perhaps 55 percent of the workforce was employed by what may be considered small businesses. Some 24 percent of US firms were medium-sized, employing between 100 and 500 persons, and about 27 percent were employed by large firms with more than 500 employees. In 1993, 10.3 million persons—about 8 percent of the workforce—were self-employed, representing the ideal of the small entre-preneurial businessperson. While some self-employed persons are well-paid professionals in private practice, the average reported income for the self-employed has been within the lowest quintile in recent years. And although some small operations subsequently become large, successful, and famous, many more fail or struggle along with marginal returns. It is the large firms that serve to establish the standards for compensation, benefits, and general business and employment practices.

Large corporations exercise a considerable influence on US business affairs, but usually it is the organization—rather than the individual heading it—which is vested with this authority. Despite a tendency to focus on personalities, the founding fathers of the great US corporations have generally ceased to wield the sort of absolute power attributed to the heads of such enterprises in the past (or elsewhere in the world at present). Few industries or markets today can be run as fiefdoms.

By the same token, because of its history and modern development, the US has many huge public bureaucracies, but no real state-run industries. Even such so-called "natural monopolies" as utilities—with a few exceptions such as the Tennessee Valley Authority (TVA) and a few other regional power authorities—and the remnants of some private railroad companies taken over by the government are generally operated by regulated but independent private companies. The US government is famous for breaking up its telephone communications monopoly in 1983, requiring that competitors be given access to the monopoly's facilities. Although some argue that the government does not regulate stringently enough, others contend that regulation serves to punish the most successful businesses—and the truth probably lies somewhere in between these extreme positions.

Fiscal and Trade Deficits A significant aspect of the US business environment is found in the looming deficits in trade and the federal budget. The US federal government has run a budgetary deficit every year since 1969 (and during several years before that as well). This deficit peaked at US$289.3 billion—25 percent of revenues—in 1992, and may well go higher in future years. The US has also had an increasing merchandise trade deficit every year since 1976. This deficit was US$166.3 billion in 1994—14 percent of total trade and the highest level to date. These linked phenomena, awesome because of their magnitude in any given year, are even more frightening because they are cumulative. The US had a budgetary deficit on the order of US$1 trillion in 1980; by 1994 this had risen to around US$4 trillion. Many other countries have operated and continue to operate in the face of growing budgetary deficits, but the prospect is unnerving to many in the US and even more so to many in the international community.

The problem is not merely the level of debt, but the apparent inability of the government to control it. A steadily growing portion of the obligation consists of the interest on the public debt which must be issued to carry the deficit, and there exist many entitlement programs that represent a growing portion of the total budget, adding to the deficit. Becoming, moreover, belligerent over its trade deficit, the US has been taking its partners to task for what it considers a lack of reciprocity in their less-than-open markets. However, the US becomes equally defensive when outsiders lecture it on its massive budgetary deficit.

Despite all of these problems, the US is one of the world's largest, most efficient markets. It remains the quintessential international market for securities as well as for most goods and services, one in which there are generally far fewer barriers and more due process protections than exist in almost any other market. Markets in the US are usually both broad and deep and—lapses and pockets of inefficiency notwithstanding—generally serve as the models for most comparable systems elsewhere.

THE UNDERGROUND ECONOMY

Although few in the US would characterize it as such, the country has a tax system in which compliance is largely voluntary—individuals and entities rather than officials are largely responsible for administering its provisions. There exist severe penalties for noncompliance, but the audit rate is relatively low, and the Internal Revenue Service (IRS) estimates that thousands of taxpayers fail each year to pay what they owe. More than the harshness of the tax laws themselves, it is the complexity of compliance with the tax codes and the myriad of regulations that tend to keep some entities operating outside of the system. Many of these parties evade a portion of their taxes, while others simply ignore the tax collector altogether. In addition to those who work informally for cash without official record of their employment—"off the books"—and are thus illegal, there are those who operate outside the system because their activities themselves are criminal. Estimates of total income from all such underground activities are imprecise and vary widely, but many tend to cluster around a figure of 10 percent of the GDP.

Corruption and Ethical Standards

With thousands of local, state, and federal offices, bureaucracies, and overlapping jurisdictions enforcing a myriad of rules, official corruption does exist in the US, but it is relatively infrequent and usually circumspect. The US enacted the Foreign Corrupt Practices Act, which bars US businesspeople who are operating abroad from making payments to obtain considerations, and although this has exposed US representatives to ridicule as being naive, disingenuous, or both, it represents a generally accepted national standard of conduct. Foreign businesspeople operating in the US are expected to behave accordingly. There are relatively few cases of blatant demands for under-the-table payments, kickbacks, or other considerations, and although such cases surface periodically, they do not represent standard operating procedure. It helps that there is no accepted cultural tradition or context that prescribes or supports such behavior.

However, there does exist a wide range of opinion about what constitutes acceptable behavior in a given instance, with periodic reevaluation of specific types of actions. For example, most relevant studies conclude that illegal alien workers in the US mostly fill jobs that citizens are unwilling to take and generally contribute more in revenue to the economy than they take away in cost of services used. Nevertheless, the hiring of undocumented workers is a sensitive issue and is illegal under US laws, although many niches and even entire sectors of the economy rely heavily on such labor. Since the Clinton administration took office in 1993, several of its candidates for appointment to prominent positions were disqualified because they had employed undocumented aliens, or had failed to pay required taxes on workers who were otherwise legal.

The specific issue is of relatively minor importance, but the discussion of it did serve to raise awareness and generate public debate, reassessing and reinforcing what the acceptable standards were

regarding such behavior. The active and largely independent press and other media in the US can usually be counted on eventually to report such public and private misdeeds. Although often conducted in an inquisitorial atmosphere that mystifies outsiders, the periodic raising of such issues helps to control corruption, malfeasance, and misuse of public office. It should also be noted that the US is an extremely litigious society, and any whiff of improper conduct can be enough to land a party in the courts. The US is also largely unique in its constitutional provision that allows for the impeachment of elected officials (which can result in trial and removal) for offenses committed.

Crime

The US has developed an international reputation for crime, much of which is viewed as an extension of its violent Wild West frontier and gangster heritage. Generally the US does have fewer restrictions on and higher possession and use rates of firearms, both in the general and the criminal populations. Consequently, there are higher homicide rates and higher rates of the use of firearms in the commission of crimes, as well as more accidents involving firearms. In recent years, the US public has consistently listed crime as one of the country's top problems, based largely, many would argue, on the extensive coverage that crime receives in the media.

Although between 1983 and 1992, reported crime rose by 19 percent based on total incidents and by 9.4 percent on a per capita basis, crime has actually been either stable or falling since 1990. Violent crime represents only 13 percent of total crime, with crimes against property representing the bulk of offenses. Crime is also highly localized, with metropolitan area crime representing nearly nine-tenths of the total.

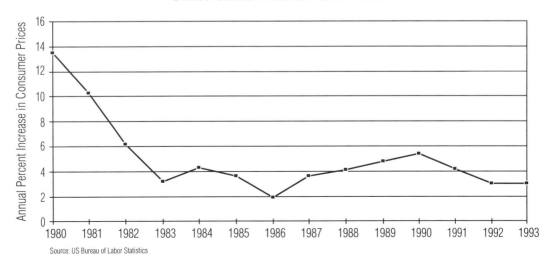

United States Inflation: 1980–1993

Source: US Bureau of Labor Statistics

Foreign businesspeople visiting the US should be at least as observant and careful as they would be in questionable situations at home. However, if they remain alert and avoid potentially dangerous situations, their odds of being a crime victim are relatively remote.

Much street crime in the US is related to trade in and use of illegal drugs. Although drug use has generally fallen and stabilized in recent years, it remains a social and economic problem of substantial proportions, which official programs have done little to abate. Despite a perception of permissiveness among many outsiders, US laws—especially those covering possession, use, and intent to distribute controlled substances—can be quite harsh, and outsiders should avoid even the appearance of having anything to do with drugs or other illegal behavior.

Of even greater importance than the elevated level of local crime associated with drugs is the erosion of standards. Although the drug trade is particularly troublesome and violent, the US has a wide range of other problems with organized crime, not only in the operation of vice and other illegal activities, but also in attempts to take over otherwise legitimate businesses. Such efforts are usually aimed at obtaining higher profit margins by cutting corners in regulated areas. Waste disposal, the distribution of various products, and construction have been frequently infiltrated and used by organized crime. Other businesses have been approached or acquired as a means of concealing and laundering the proceeds of illicit operations. Organized crime also runs loan-sharking operations that lend funds at usurious rates. Foreign businesspeople, however, will generally not come into direct contact with the operations of organized crime and are advised to steer clear of any activities with hints of criminal involvement.

Intellectual Property Rights

The US is one of the bastions of intellectual and industrial property rights. It subscribes to the Berne and Paris Conventions regarding copyright and industrial property rights, respectively; has its own strong statutory protections of such rights; and is an international crusader for the extension of such rights in other countries lacking such protections or enforcement of existing protections. This fierce stance is conditioned by the fact that US businesses annually lose revenues estimated as high as US$23 billion—US$10 billion alone in pirated computer software—and therefore have a huge interest in curtailing unauthorized use. US import laws are strict regarding counterfeit goods brought into the US, and the authorities have exerted extensive pressure on foreign governments and businesses that fail to live up to US standards in this area, often threatening retaliatory trade sanctions. Some non-US jurisdictions, especially in the developing world, see this as cultural and economic imperialism, denying them the benefits of advances that should be available to all. This point of view is somewhat easier to see with respect to pharmaceuticals than it is for pirated videotapes, but the US draws no such distinctions. Although this superior US attitude can make outsiders angry, foreign businesspeople must be aware of the emphasis that the US places on compliance with the intellectual and industrial property protections.

United States Consumer Price Index 1980–1993

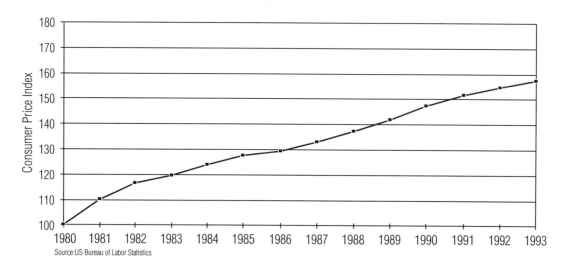

Source: US Bureau of Labor Statistics

INFLATION

Inflation in the US was a minor consideration between the end of World War II and the late 1960s. However, during the 1970s and early 1980s it became a preoccupation as it surged to levels seldom seen in US history. Although inflation was damped down to minimal levels during the late 1980s and early 1990s, concern that it could arise again in the mid-1990s has led the Federal Reserve Board to impose repeated rises in key interest rates in the hopes of squeezing out incipient inflation. Some observers worry that the Fed has been overly zealous in its efforts and that it could choke off US economic recovery and growth.

US consumer prices rose by an average 4.9 percent annually from 1960 through 1993, with a low of a 1 percent rise in 1961 and 1962 and a high of 13.5 percent in 1980. Despite concerns over high inflation, consumer prices actually topped 10 percent in only four of the last 35 years. Inflation averaged 2.4 percent during the 1960s, 7.1 percent during the 1970s, 5.5 percent during the 1980s, and 3.9 percent thus far during the 1990s, holding officially at 3 percent in 1992 and 1993, and falling to 2.8 percent in 1994. Consumer inflation rates are predicted to reach 3.5 percent in 1995, for the longest stretch of stable inflation in decades. Many economists have argued that the way in which rises in consumer prices are calculated serves to exaggerate inflation measures, suggesting that real inflation is even lower, by perhaps 0.5 percent.

In another related inflation measure, during the 15 years between 1979 and 1993, the purchasing power of the dollar fell by 49.5 percent, which amounts to an implicit annual rate of inflation of 3.3 percent.

Since the mid-1970s, US inflation rates have been somewhat lower than the composite rate reported by the OECD. Until recently, US rates have generally fallen well below those in the UK and France, while remaining generally higher than those in Germany and Japan.

To control inflationary pressures in the economy during the late 1970s and early 1980s, the US Federal Reserve Board altered its traditional policy of attempting to put a brake on inflationary pressures by controlling prices (that is, interest rates) by switching to controlling supply (that is, overall growth of the money supply). The operation ultimately succeeded, but in the process short-term interest rates swelled to greater than 20 percent, choking off US economic activity. Since the mid-1980s, the Federal Reserve has eased its strict management of the money supply and returned to its focus on interest rates. During 1994 and early 1995, the Fed grew concerned that rapid growth in the economy would reignite inflation. Consequently, the Fed raised short-term interest rates seven times by a total of 3 percentage points, doubling those rates to 6 percent.

The consensus among economists is that such actions are necessary to keep inflation in check. However, others note that despite sharp increases in the reported statistics, the economic recovery in the US has been somewhat narrow and localized, with little evidence of the shortages in labor, materials, and productive capacity that usually herald inflation. These observers worry that continuation of the Fed's aggressive policy could serve to choke off recovery. Following the most recent rise in January 1995, the Fed seems to have decided that evidence of slowing in the economy will allow it to maintain rates at the current level or perhaps even allow it to lower them slightly in the future.

LABOR

The US labor force is large and generally well-trained. It is among the world's foremost in terms of skilled high-tech workers, as well as dominant in many other specialized areas. Since 1950 the US workforce has doubled in size, growing at an average annual rate of 1.6 percent. In 1993 the US population 16 years of age and older—those considered as potentially eligible for employment—numbered 195 million, of whom 129.5 million persons were counted as active participants or active aspirants to participate in the workforce. Of the 65.5 million (33.6 percent of the relevant population) not participating in the labor force, varying percentages were estimated to represent those who voluntarily do not work, those involved in unpaid (and thus uncounted domestic work), students, discouraged workers who have given up actively trying to find formal jobs, and those involved in the informal underground or illicit economy.

As of the third quarter of 1994, the workforce numbered 131 million, of whom 113.9 million were involved in nonfarm employment (21 percent in the production of goods and 79 percent in the production of services), 7.9 million were unemployed, and an additional 66 million were listed as being outside the labor force.

Education and Training Education in the US is in the hands of state and local jurisdictions, but all maintain a requirement that those between the ages of 6 and 16 be involved in schooling. In 1990, 25 percent of the population had not completed high school, 30 percent had a high school diploma, 19 percent had some college, 6 percent had an associate (two-year college) degree, 13 percent had a baccalaureate (four-year degree), and 7 percent had an advanced degree. Although many segments of the population place a high value on education, recognizing it as an important avenue to future success, in recent years support for education has lagged well behind expenditures in other sectors. There is growing concern that the rapid expansion of immigrant populations lacking in basic English and skills, as well as populations emigrating from cultures which do not emphasize education, will result in a further decrease of attendance and support of education in the US. However, despite this lessening emphasis on education, the US remains a world leader in higher and technical education and advanced research conducted within academia.

In 1990 slightly more than 25 percent of workers reported having had some job training, although only 17 percent of the total reported actually using this training in their work. One-third of those with such training received it at work through their employer. Some 45 percent of all training programs were paid for by employers, 29 percent by the employee, and 26 percent by a governmental unit or program. Because of the general availability of basic education as well as the US leadership in higher education, and despite complaints by employers regarding deteriorating standards among those entering the job market, an abundance of workers can generally be found at all skill levels.

Distribution and Growth of the Workforce Although men still predominate, women are playing an ever larger role in the US workforce. In 1993, 75 percent of eligible males and 58 percent of females were directly involved in the workforce. In the same year, 54 percent of the active workforce consisted of men and 46 percent were women. Trends indicate that these proportions could be reversed early in the 21st century, with women actually outnumbering men by a significant number. Of the 129.5 million US workforce, 1.5 million represented members of the armed forces stationed in the US (1.2 percent), while civilian agricultural workers numbered 3.1 million (2.4 percent), civilian nonagricultural employees were 116.2 million (89.7 percent), and the unemployed were 8.7 million (6.7 percent).

By economic sector, 2.6 percent of the workforce was employed in farming, forestry, and fishing; 22.9 percent in industry—mining, construction, and manufacturing; and 74.4 percent in services (transportation, communications, and utilities; financial services; commerce; other services; and government). By occupation, 27 percent were managerial or professional personnel; 31 percent were technical, sales, or administrative support personnel; 14 percent were involved in other service occupations; 11 percent were in skilled production, craft, or repair positions; 14 percent were unskilled or semiskilled operators, fabricators, or laborers; and 3 percent were involved in farming, forestry, fishing, or related service positions.

For the period 1992 to 2005, total employment is projected to increase by 22 percent, to around 147.5 million. Growth is anticipated be strongest in the services sector, led by health care, business services, education, and social services. Employment is expected to fall by about 3 percent in manufacturing and by 1 percent in mining—the only areas which are projected to experience actual contraction. However, most employment areas are expected to lag behind overall growth. The best projected job growth is for professional specialties, service occupations, technical and support personnel, administrators, transportation (especially trucking), construction, marketing and sales, and semiskilled to skilled personnel.

Unemployment The US enjoys relatively low unemployment. Unemployment in the US is greater than that in many newly developed Asian nations, but equivalent to or less than that in most developed nations, and far below that in most developing and formerly communist nations. Official unemployment in the US was 6.9 percent in 1993, down from 7.4 percent in 1992. Unemployment fell to 5.4 percent at year-end 1994, well below the 6 percent level considered by most US economists to represent full employment and the lowest unemployment figure since 1990. During the past 30 years, US unemployment has ranged from a low of 3.5 percent in 1969 to a high of 9.7 percent in 1982. In 1993 when US unemployment was 6.8 percent, unemployment was as low 2.5 percent in Japan and as high as 11.8 percent in France among the OECD countries.

Many observers note that the manner in which unemployment statistics are calculated can severely understate real employment because it includes only those persons classified as actively seeking work. Given the fact that one-third of the potential working population is listed as outside the workforce, there is ample room for doubt that all of these individuals really prefer not to work. Conventional statistics also fail to account for those working part-time or at low paying jobs who would prefer to be working full-time or at higher paying jobs which they have been unable to obtain.

With restructuring and downsizing, massive layoffs by traditional large scale corporate employers have occurred, and many of those put out of work have been unable to find comparable replacement employment. Many have taken lower paying jobs with fewer benefits. In previous recessions, unemployment has generally been a phenomenon confined largely to blue collar—that is, unskilled and semiskilled production—workers, and such workers have generally obtained similar employment again when the economy improved. The current situation marks the first time that white collar—skilled and semiskilled service—workers have made up the majority of the unemployed. Several hundred thousand jobs have been lost since economic restructuring began in earnest during the late 1980s, and many of these jobs are not expected to return no matter how strong the economic recovery becomes.

In 1993 the average duration of unemployment was 18 weeks, but 20 percent were out of work for longer than 27 weeks, with others becoming discouraged and dropping out of the statistics. Of those unemployed and actively seeking work during that year, roughly 55 percent had involuntarily lost an existing job, while 10 percent had voluntarily left their previous job; 25 percent were reentering the job market following an absence, and 10 percent were new entrants to the job market.

In 1993 unemployment was 12 percent in farming, forestry, and fishing; 7 percent in mining; 14 percent in the bellwether construction industry; 7 percent in manufacturing; 5 percent in transportation, communication, and utilities; 8 percent in commerce; 4 percent in financial services; 6 percent in personal services; and 3 percent in the public sector (government). By occupation, unemployment was 3 percent among managerial and professional personnel; 5 percent among technical, sales, and administrative support personnel; 8 percent among service occupations; 8 percent among skilled production, craft, and repair personnel; 10 percent among operators, fabricators, and laborers; and 8 percent among farmers, foresters, and fishing and related service personnel. As always, unemployment was highest among the least skilled, least educated segments of the population.

The Role of Unions After a flurry of activity during the 1970s, unions have generally been on the defensive since the beginning of the 1980s. During much of this latter period, the federal administration was generally seen as pro-business and less sympathetic to unions. In 1981 President Ronald Reagan dismissed nearly 13,000 members of the Air Traffic Controllers Union after an illegal union walkout; the action crippled that union and was viewed as a challenge to organized labor. As the country has moved more toward the right, organized labor has been perceived as obstructionist and has lost some of its traditional political influence, as well as the unquestioning support of its remaining members.

About 80 percent of organized labor is affiliated with the American Federation of Labor-Congress of Industrial Organizations (AFL-CIO), which acts as a coordinating body for member unions, much as labor confederations do in many other countries. The AFL-CIO does not intervene directly in specific labor disputes of individual member unions. Several large bodies of organized workers operate as independent unions. In absolute numbers, membership in unions affiliated with the AFL-CIO has declined over a 15-year period by less than 2.25 percent (from 13.6 million in 1979 to 13.3 million in 1993). However, this represented a decline from 12.8 percent of the total workforce to 10.3 percent of the workforce during these years. Since 1930, union participation has risen to as high as 35.5 percent of the workforce (1945) and to a numerical high of 19.8 million—21.9 percent of the workforce—in 1980.

As an indication of union strength and activity, the number of work stoppages has been dwindling since reaching a high point during the mid-1970s. Between 1964 and 1993, the number of work stoppages rose as high as 424 in 1974, but fell to a low of 35 in 1993. The number of workers idled by stoppages reached a high of 2.5 million in 1971 and fell to a low of 118,000 in 1988 (a total of 182,000 workers

Structure of the US Economy - 1992

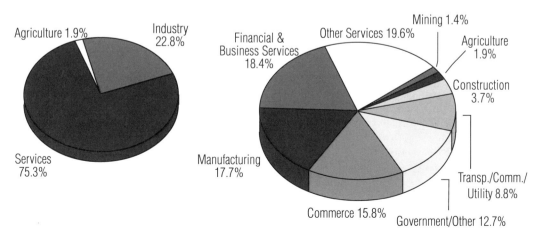

Note: Totals may exceed 100 percent due to rounding. Source: US Bureau of Economic Analysis, *Survey of Current Business*

went out on strike in 1993). In 1993 negotiated collective bargaining settlements resulted in wage increases averaging 3 percent during the first year and 2.4 percent annually over the life of the agreement, with union-produced agreements covering 2.1 million workers.

Much of organized labor strenuously opposed the passage of NAFTA because of members' fears that they would lose jobs. Not only was labor unable to defeat the measure, but despite threats to work against legislators voting for it few (if any) congressional losses in the 1994 elections could be attributed to labor opposition. Labor is also on the defensive because businesses are asserting their right to permanently replace striking workers. Nevertheless, even in an extended period of decline, labor unions remain influential in the US. Federal procedures governing union activity and administered by the National Labor Relations Board (NLRB) guarantee due process and protect the rights of workers to unionize.

Wages and Benefits In general, US workers have one of the highest standards of living in the world, supported by substantial wage levels. Following a period of declining productivity during the 1970s and 1980s, US workers have begun to justify their compensation to a greater degree through increasing productivity during the 1990s. Between 1980 and 1992, the US labor productivity index rose by 12.6. During the same period, the Japanese productivity index rose by 40.9 and the UK index rose by 13.6, while the German and French productivity indices fell by 6.9 and 10.9, respectively. Although US output per hour rose at less than the average of these countries, its unit labor costs also rose less rapidly than those of any other country except Japan, resulting in an overall productivity rate above the average.

In 1993 the average hourly base wages of US workers were US$10.83, up 2.4 percent from 1992's US$10.58. Preliminary reports for the third quarter of 1994 placed this figure at US$11.13. Up more than 60 percent in current dollar terms from US$6.66 in 1980, the average hourly rate actually fell by 5 percent in terms of constant 1982 dollars, from US$7.78 in 1980 to US$7.39 in 1993.

In 1993 average hourly rates in the mining industry were US$14.60; US$14.35 in construction; US$11.36 in manufacturing; US$13.64 in transportation, communications, and utilities; US$11.71 in wholesale and US$7.29 in retail trade; US$11.32 in financial services; and US$10.81 in other services. On a constant dollar basis from 1980 through 1993, the largest positive change was in financial services, which gained 14.2 percent in real terms, and other services, which gained 7.9 percent. All other categories saw net losses in real terms, ranging from a minimal 1.6 percent loss for wholesale trade to a 15.7 percent loss for construction workers.

As of the third quarter of 1994, the preliminary figure for the average weekly earnings of US workers was US$384.85. In 1992 average annual wages and salaries (including bonuses, tips, and in-kind payments) were US$28,665, up 5.5 percent from the previous year. Total annual compensation (including wages and salaries; employer contributions to social insurance, private, and other welfare funds; director's fees; jury fees; and similar payments) averaged US$34,536, up 5.8 percent from 1991 and 20 percent higher than wages alone. By sectors, farmers and retail trade personnel earned the lowest annual salaries and wages (US$15,925 and US$17,406, respectively), while utility personnel, communications workers, and miners earned the highest wages and salaries (US$42,998, US$42,076, and US$42,032, respectively).

In addition to cash compensation, US employers customarily supply a variety of benefits to their workers. Except for federal and state government employees and a few other limited exceptions, all employees and employers must participate in the US Social Security system, a retirement and social insurance plan. Concerns about the long-term viability of this system are well-founded: current benefits are funded by current contributions rather than by general revenues or an actual trust fund, and the number of workers paying into the program is falling while the number of beneficiaries is rising rapidly. By itself, social security generally does not provide adequate benefits for a comfortable retirement. However, it is the only universal, direct, federally mandated benefit. Employees and employers share the cost of contributing to the program, figured on a percent of wages up to a relatively high specified cap.

Among other common benefits offered during the early 1990s were paid vacation, unpaid family leave, medical insurance, life insurance, and retirement and savings plans. Some firms also offer various other employee perquisites, such as parking, educational assistance, travel accident insurance, severance pay, relocation allowances, recreation facilities, bonuses not tied to production, childcare, flexible benefit plans, reimbursement accounts for childcare or medical benefits, long-term care insurance, wellness programs, and various other types of employee assistance programs.

Workweek The standard US workweek is considered to be 40 hours. However, in 1993 the average number of hours actually worked was calculated at 34.5, based on total payrolls which include part-time as well as full-time workers. However, a subsidiary measurement showed manufacturing personnel as working an average 42-hour week including an average of 4.6 hours of overtime for eligible personnel. Employers may offer and even require such overtime work, as long as it is reimbursed at a rate of one-and-a-half times the regular hourly rate. During the last 30 years, the average workweek reached a low of 34.3 hours in 1991 and a high of 38.8 in 1965.

Many industries paying on an hourly basis have mandatory overtime, and many salaried workers—especially managerial and professional workers—are often expected to put in far more hours than those regularly scheduled. Nonfarm child labor is prohibited below the age of 14, and limits exist on the number of hours and times that those between the ages of 14 and 18 may work. Because of economic pressures as well as greater diversity within the workforce, part-time and flexible work schedules are becoming both more prevalent and accepted.

ELEMENTS OF THE ECONOMY

Traditionally an agricultural and then later an industrial power, the US is now moving further into more sophisticated and value-added services as its economy matures. In 1992 an outsized 75.3 percent of US GDP was produced by the services sector, while the industrial sector accounted for 22.8 percent and the agricultural sector for only 1.9 percent. These percentages have changed noticeably since 1980, when services accounted for 66.9 percent and industry and agriculture for 30.6 and 2.5 percent, respectively. Between 1980 and 1992 the dollar value of agriculture production grew by 75.1 percent, industry by 22.7 percent, and services by 38.1 percent, all in real terms.

Agriculture

Farming and Ranching The US began largely as a subsistence farming country, shifting slowly to greater production of cash crops. In the 1990s, US agriculture has been almost exclusively oriented toward cash crops, many for export to international markets. However, between 1974 and 1993, the number of farms in the US had dropped by nearly 9 percent to 2.1 million. By 1987, total farm holdings had fallen to 380 million hectares (964 million acres), down 5 percent from 1974, and the amount of cropland harvested was down 11 percent to 616 million hectares (282 million acres). In 1987, nearly half of total farm acreage was held by large farms of more than 787 hectares (2,000 acres), while only 3.5 percent was held by small family farms with fewer than 40 hectares (100 acres). Between 1980 and 1992, farm employment fell 6.8 percent to 3.3 million. With the average age of farmers in the US at 53 in 1994, the US Department of Agriculture (USDA) is predicting that 500,000 farmers will retire by the year 2002. As farms merge, farm employment could shrink to 1.5 million within 10 years.

In 1993 US government farm support payments were US$16 billion. One of the provisions of GATT calls for the lowering or phasing out of many such subsidies, which could make US agriculture an even less attractive investment (although other producers, particularly those in the European Union (EU), are expected to lose more competitiveness as even more extensive subsidies are dropped). Even without this outside pressure, internal budgetary concerns are likely to shrink farm subsidies. Further indication of the pressures experienced by US agriculture is provided by the fact that, between 1990 and 1993, prices paid by farmers for inputs rose by 11 percent, while prices received for outputs fell by 6 percent.

Despite these negative indicators, the US remains the most productive agricultural economy in the world. In 1992 cash receipts from US farm production were US$171 billion, with the largest shares coming from cattle (22 percent), dairy products (12 percent), and corn (9 percent). As of 1993 the US had not had a trade deficit in agricultural products since records have been kept.

Exports of US agricultural products have grown only moderately in recent years. However, the USDA predicts total exports of a record US$48.5 billion on record volume in fiscal 1995. Agricultural products are subject to sharp price fluctuations due to world supply and demand (for example, US agricultural exports fell to a low of US$26.2 billion in 1986 from a previous high of US$43.5 billion in 1981). Agricultural exports have also been falling as a percent of total exports, constituting only 10 percent of exports in 1992, down from 18 percent in 1980. Agricultural imports grew steadily to US$24.6 billion in 1992. However, agricultural imports have also fallen as a percentage of total imports to 4.6 percent in 1992 (two-thirds of what they were in 1980).

In 1992 the top US agricultural exports were animal products; oilseeds; vegetables, fruit, and nuts; feed grains; wheat; cotton; protein meal; vegetable oils; rice; and other feed grains. In 1992 the top agricultural import products were vegetables, fruit, and nuts; sugar; vegetable oils; coffee; meat; natural rubber; cocoa; tobacco; and spices.

Fishing In 1991 US fisheries were the sixth largest in the world, accounting for a catch of 5.5 billion metric tons of landed live weight—5.7 percent of the total world catch. Between 1970 and 1992, the landed catch roughly doubled to 9.6 billion pounds, while the value of the catch grew sixfold to US$3.7 billion. At the same time, fisheries employment grew by only 6 percent to 364,000. Aquaculture grew ninefold to US$273.5 million between 1970 and 1992. The US supplies about 60 percent of its consumption of marine products. In 1991 US exports of fisheries products amounted to US$6.2 billion, while imports were at US$9.4 billion.

Industry

Manufacturing and industry—including mining, construction, and manufacturing—accounted for 22.8 percent of US GDP in 1992. The role of basic industry in the US economy has diminished, falling from a 30.6 percent share of GDP in 1980 to the 22.8 percent noted in 1992. In that year, manufacturing represented 77.6 percent of the total industry sector, while the important construction sector accounted for 16.2 percent of the category. Mining fell to 6.2 percent in 1992, less than half its share in 1980.

Mining Despite US wealth in extractable natural resources, mining has been falling in importance as a constituent of GDP for some time. The steepest drop in mining output between 1980 and 1991 was in oil and natural gas production, which was down by 25 percent to US$66.7 billion, due to a combination of reduced production and lower prices. This was followed by a 10 percent drop in coal production to US$12.2 billion. However, nonmetallic products rose by 31 percent to US$7.2 billion, and metallic products rose by 30 percent to US$5.7 billion. Actual production of these nonfuel products rose between 1980 and 1993 by 25 percent to 31.6 million metric tons. Nevertheless, total mining employment has been falling, dropping by 5.1 percent since 1992 to 599,000 in 1993.

Construction Construction is often used as an indicator of general US economic activity. In a country where nearly two-thirds of households are occupied by owners, consumer optimism to a large extent determines the rate and nature of new construction, which in turn significantly influences output in such other industries as materials and furnishings. The building industry also influences a wide variety of downstream service businesses and is often one

of the best predictors of economic activity both nationally and locally.

New construction put in place rose from US$100.7 million in 1970 to US$470.1 million in 1993 in current dollars. In real terms, the increase is on the order of 36.5 percent, to US$402.3 million in 1987 dollars. The current dollar value of construction contracts rose from US$151.8 billion in 1980 to US$267.2 billion in 1993. By one measure there were 544,200 construction firms in the US employing more than 5 million workers in 1987. Using a different measure there were 7.2 million total employees in the construction industry in 1993.

Manufacturing Manufacturing has been one of the strengths of the US economy since the 19th century. However, current concerns are that the US is losing its edge to lower-wage producers overseas. Despite these worries—which are justified, especially for lower-tech commodity products—US manufacturing remains large and strong. Exports of US manufactured goods more than doubled to US$2.795 trillion between 1977 and 1989, and employees involved in export production have risen from 12.8 percent of the manufacturing workforce in 1980 to 15.5 percent in 1989. In fact, in 1992 exports of US manufactured goods represented a growing 17.4 percent share of such exports worldwide. The US held a 20 percent share of 1992 world exports of machinery, 19 percent of transportation equipment exports, 17 percent of chemicals, 10 percent of basic manufactures (semimanufactured and intermediate products), and 18 percent of miscellaneous manufactures (mostly consumer nondurables)—an indication of a still vibrant manufacturing sector.

The top 10 manufacturing industries by value of production in 1991 were food products (14 percent),

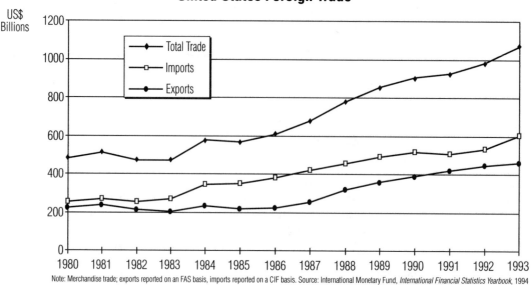

United States Foreign Trade

Note: Merchandise trade; exports reported on an FAS basis, imports reported on a CIF basis. Source: International Monetary Fund, *International Financial Statistics Yearbook*, 1994

transportation equipment (13 percent), chemical products (10 percent), industrial machinery and equipment (9 percent), electrical equipment (7 percent), petroleum and coal products (6 percent), fabricated metal products (6 percent), printing and publishing (5 percent), primary metals products (5 percent), and paper products (5 percent). Together, these top 10 manufactured product categories accounted for 74 percent of total manufacturing output.

In 1987 there were 368,900 manufacturing establishments, employing a total of 18.9 million workers. Between 1963 and 1987 the total number of manufacturing businesses grew by 20.3 percent and employment grew by 16.7 percent. In 1987, 66 percent of these businesses employed fewer than 20 persons, 24 percent between 20 and 100, 9 percent between 100 and 1,000, and somewhat less than 1 percent more than 1,000 workers.

Services

In recent decades the services sector has been confirmed as the core of the US economy. Although a significant portion of the US service sector is involved in providing highly sophisticated, high-value-added specialized services, a far greater percentage consists of low-skill, low-wage positions. With the restructuring of the US economy, many people accustomed to higher-wage jobs in industry or in more skilled areas of the service sector are having to take available jobs in lower-wage services. Along with the sector's contribution to GDP, employment in services has risen from a 62 percent share of employment in 1970 to 74 percent in 1993.

Utilities, Transportation, and Communications US prominence, both in industry and in lifestyle, is underwritten by the abundant provision of energy. Total energy production in the US rose by 58.5 percent to 65.8 quadrillion British thermal units (Btu) between 1960 and 1993. Of 1993 energy production, coal supplied 31 percent, petroleum 22 percent, natural gas 32 percent, and other sources (including nuclear) 14 percent. Energy consumed in the US in 1991 was equivalent to 2,727 million metric tons, up 14 percent since 1980, or 10,798 kg on a per capita basis, up 13 percent. The 1991 total consumption figure represents almost 25 percent of total world consumption, and the per capita figure is 5.3 times average per capita world consumption. Production of electricity rose by 29 percent during the same period to 3.041 billion kilowatt hours (kWh), representing nearly 26 percent of total world production in 1991. In 1992 the US utility industry contributed 2.9 percent of total GDP, up from 2.6 percent in 1980.

The US transportation industry is well developed, although coverage and organization differ from elsewhere in the world. Over-the-road transport is well developed, although rail transport is somewhat less developed due to an emphasis on surface road transport during the past 50 years. The US does not have a national flag airline, but is served by a number of competing private firms. Because of the distances involved, air traffic is heavy. However, major US airlines have been operating at a deficit during recent years. The US is a major supplier of aircraft as well as of services; it is also one of the major buyers of specialized aircraft, especially smaller commercial and general aviation aircraft. Meanwhile, US shipping has fallen behind that of many other nations, both in production and tonnage carried. Transportation contributed US$193.8 billion for 3.2 percent of GDP in 1992, down from a 3.8 percent share in 1980. Between 1990 and 1992, transport revenues were down 7.5 percent and income down by 10.8 percent.

The US is a premier developer and provider of communications services worldwide. Its domestic industry has become more fragmented and competitive since the deregulation of the monopoly telephone company in 1984. During 1992, total communications industry revenues were up by 6 percent and income was up by 18 percent, so that in that year, communications contributed 2.7 percent of GDP.

Combined employment in the utilities, transportation, and communications sector was 8.5 million in 1993, up 59 percent since 1970 and up 30 percent since 1980. In 1989, 67 percent of the workforce in this sector was involved in export services, up from 5 percent in 1980.

Wholesale and Retail Commerce In 1993 US wholesale and retail trade accounted for roughly 16 percent of GDP, 21 percent of total service sector income, and 28 percent of service employment. Such commerce employs more people than any other sector except for the catchall category other services. Wholesale distribution accounts for about four-fifths of income but far less of personnel. The numerous workers involved in retail trade constitute the front line—and generally the least skilled and most poorly paid—shock troops of the economic army. Between 1980 and 1989, employees involved in export sales rose to about 6 percent of the total.

Financial Services This category covers services involved in finance, insurance, and real estate—some of the fastest-growing areas of the US economy during the past two decades. It employs only one-fifth as many people as the category other services, but it trails that category's GDP contribution by only 7 percent and surpasses the contribution of all other service categories combined, as well as that of the manufacturing sector. Although the country is receiving more competition in this area from overseas providers, the US remains the dominant supplier of financial services and innovations worldwide.

Government and Other Services Other services includes such specific services as advertising; repairs to structures, equipment, and vehicles; computer and related services; security; private household domestic service providers; hotels and restaurants; entertainment; health and hospitals; education; legal, accounting, and other professional services; and nongovernmental social services. This category is the largest contributor to GDP of any specific category, providing nearly 20 percent of GDP in 1992 (up from 14 percent in 1980). It also employs 35 percent of all workers in the US economy, up from 26 percent in 1970.

In 1992 government accounted for about 13 percent of GDP, but less than 5 percent of the workforce. These employees were about one-third federal and two-thirds state and local level. Their total numbers have risen by 29 percent since 1970, but by less than 8 percent since 1980. Despite a general perception that government has grown inordinately, the rate of growth of government since 1970 is less than that of the total workforce (52 percent), other services (105 percent), financial services (102 percent), commerce (65 percent), transportation (59 percent), construction (50 percent), or mining (30 percent). In fact, during the same period, the only sectors with lower growth were those experiencing negative growth: agriculture (down 11 percent) and manufacturing (down 6 percent).

TRADE

The US is the world's premier trading nation, with a total volume of trade far larger than that of its nearest competitors, Japan and Germany. The US is also the world's largest importer of a whole range of products, from raw materials to finished high-value-added

technical products and consumer goods. And although the country imposes many rigorous standards and procedures on its trade, it is generally among the most welcoming of nations to the products of others, maintaining what are among the lowest tariffs and fewest absolute restrictions of any industrialized country in the world. Although relatively few imports require permits, virtually all US exports require licensing. In most cases this is a pro forma requirement, and the US government provides numerous resources to businesses interested in exporting goods and services from the US.

Import regulations, while strict, generally allow a wide range of goods into the country at relatively low tariff rates with relatively few restrictions. In 1970, 35 percent by dollar value of all imports for consumption were admitted duty free. In that year, total duties paid were equal to 6.5 percent of the value of all imports, and the level of such payments has gone no higher since that year. Duties paid as a percent of the value of dutiable imports came to 10 percent, again the highest level since then. In 1993, 41 percent of all imports by dollar value were admitted duty free, while duties paid as a percent of total import value were 3.2 percent, and duties paid as a percent of the value of dutiable imports fell to 5.4 percent. Under the terms of GATT, remaining tariffs are to be lowered by 40 percent over a phase-in period lasting as long as six years for certain product categories.

Size of US Trade In 1964 US total merchandise trade was valued at US$46 billion: US$25.7 billion in exports and US$20.3 billion in imports, for a balance of trade surplus of US$5.4 billion, or 11.7 percent of the total. By 1994 total merchandise trade had mush-

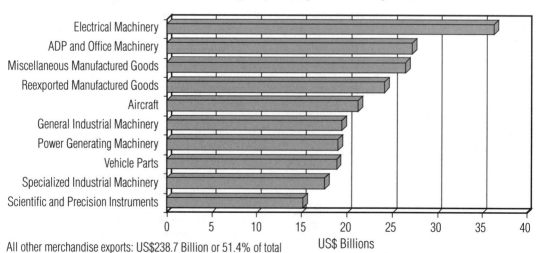

United States Leading Exports by Commodity - 1993

All other merchandise exports: US$238.7 Billion or 51.4% of total
Total 1993 merchandise exports: US$464.8 Billion
Source: US Bureau of the Census, *US Merchandise Trade*

roomed to US$1.172 trillion. Exports had grown to US$502.8 billion and imports to US$669.1 billion, for a balance of trade deficit of US$166.3 billion, or 14.2 percent of the total trade. Trade was equal to 7.1 percent of US GDP in 1964; by 1993 it had more than doubled to 17.7 percent. Although nearly 70 percent of the US economy—the world's largest—consists of domestic consumer purchases, it is likely to become increasingly international and trade oriented in future years.

Most US trade statistics have traditionally reported merchandise trade, or trade in goods. In mid-1994 the Department of Commerce (DOC) shifted its reporting to include trade in services as well. In 1993 merchandise trade amounted to US$1,046.3 billion, while services trade was at US$312.8 billion, which represents 30 percent of merchandise trade by dollar value and 23 percent of the total trade in goods and services. In relative terms, exports of goods increased in value by 3.75 percent from 1992 to 1993, while exports of services grew by 4.6 percent. Imports of goods grew in value by 9.9 percent, while those of services rose by 6 percent. (Note: these figures are computed on a somewhat different balance of trade basis, so they do not correspond exactly to the trade figures presented elsewhere.)

Exports US exports are quite diversified. Although known primarily as an exporter of industrial and high-tech products, the US is also the world's foremost exporter of agricultural products, contributing 62 percent by dollar value of world exports of corn (maize), 32 percent of wheat, 60 percent of soybeans, 17 percent of rice, 21 percent of cotton, and 13 percent of tobacco. In 1992 grain and feed exports were the largest category at 33 percent.

However, exports of such primary products— including minerals and other mining products—accounted for only 7 percent of total US merchandise exports by dollar value in 1993, with the combined categories of fruit and vegetable product exports as the only agricultural products to rank within the list of top 20 exports. Some 93 percent of exports (by dollar value) consisted of manufactured goods, led by electrical machinery at 7.9 percent of total exports. Together the top 10 export product categories accounted for 48.8 percent—nearly half—of total exports, as well as for all categories representing more than 3 percent of total exports.

Reexports of manufactured goods were ranked as the fourth largest export category in 1993, accounting for more than 5 percent of all exports by value. Such reexports were also one of the fastest-growing categories, rising by more than 15 percent between 1992 and 1993. In fact, only apparel and telecommunications equipment among core exports grew at a faster rate. This indicates that the US is playing a larger role as a trade intermediary rather than simply as an end user market, as was the case in the past.

Imports Long a major exporter of agricultural and other commodity resource products, the US has in recent years become a major importer—and in some cases a net importer—of many such products, particularly petroleum products. The US has come to rely on overseas supplies of energy, particularly crude oil, to an increasing degree. In 1970 US net energy consumption by value included 8.6 percent imports. This rose to 20.1 percent in 1993. In 1993 energy imports were almost five times energy exports, with crude oil representing two-thirds of such imports (exports consist primarily of higher-value re-

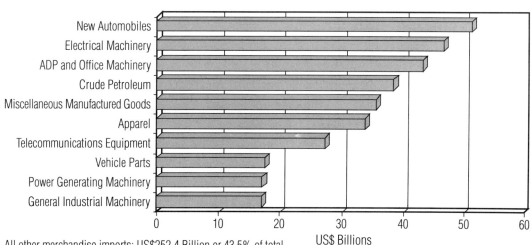

United States Leading Imports by Commodity - 1993

All other merchandise imports: US$252.4 Billion or 43.5% of total
Total 1993 merchandise imports: US$580.5 Billion
Source: US Bureau of the Census, *US Merchandise Trade*

fined specialty products). Among agricultural products, only the category of miscellaneous agricultural products—ranked 23rd among all imports—represents more than 1 percent of total imports.

Among manufactured goods, new vehicles represented the largest single category of imports—8.8 percent by value in 1993. (Total vehicle-related imports—including trucks and parts—were US$79 billion, 13.6 percent of all imports.) Together, the top five categories of imports—new vehicles, electrical machinery, ADP and office machines, crude petroleum, and miscellaneous manufactured goods—account for nearly one-third of total imports. The top 25 categories represent almost four-fifths of total merchandise trade imports by value.

Trading Partners In 1993 Canada remained the largest trade partner for the US, accounting for 18.8 percent of total trade. Canada was followed by Japan with 18.3 percent, Mexico (6.7 percent), China (5.6 percent), Germany (4.9 percent), and Taiwan (4.4 percent). Together these top six trade partners represented two-fifths of all US merchandise trade, and all trade partners accounting for a share of at least 4 percent of such trade. The top 10 trading partners—including the UK, South Korea, France, and Italy—accounted for 51.4 percent of total trade, while the top 20 represented 65.6 percent, nearly two-thirds of all trade. Thus, US trade may be seen as somewhat undiversified, focusing on a relatively few countries. However, there are relatively few countries large enough to sustain a major trade relationship with the US, and the US does maintain trading relationships that are important to both parties with many other countries, although they are not carried out on a scale large enough to rank very high. In 1992 US trade with the countries of the EU represented 20 percent of the total, with OPEC representing 6 percent, and developing countries 31 percent.

Canada, Japan, and Mexico have long been the top three partners for both export and import trade. In 1993 Canada bought US$100.2 billion of US export goods, while providing US$113.6 billion of imports to the US (about 80 percent of Canada's total exports). Japan accounted for US$110.4 billion in US imports, but bought only US$47.9 billion worth of US exports. The huge trade imbalance between the US and Japan continues to expand and constitute a source of friction between them. Mexico bought US$41.6 billion of US exports while selling US$40.7 billion in imports to the US. The UK, Germany, Taiwan, South Korea, France, the Netherlands, and Singapore round out the list of the top 10 purchasers of US exports, which account for 67.7 percent of total US exports.

In 1993 the US bought US$264.7 billion worth of imports—43.9 percent of total merchandise imports—from its top three suppliers: Canada, Japan, and Mexico. Its fourth largest supplier was China,

which sold it US$33.7 billion worth, or 5.6 percent of imports—up 23 percent in value from the preceding year. If the list is expanded to the top 13 import suppliers—Germany, Taiwan, the UK, South Korea, France, Italy, Singapore, Malaysia, and Hong Kong—it covers 75.9 percent of total US imports. This list of the top 13 supplier countries also fails to include any country (other than Mexico) that is a major supplier of crude oil.

FOREIGN PARTICIPATION IN THE ECONOMY

From its beginnings, the US has generally welcomed foreign investment in its economy. Throughout much of the 19th century, this stance was conditioned by a need for capital and technology unobtainable at home. Because of the country's size, large domestic economy, and geographic distance from most overseas investors, the US generally had little fear of being overwhelmed by foreign participation, at least among those connected with investment.

The US has experienced many periods during which it has pulled back from the international sphere politically, and it has discriminated against foreign labor, but seldom against foreign capital. A recent exception began during the 1970s, when dislocations brought on by sharp price rises for petroleum products led to fears that the US economy would be swamped by foreign influences. These fears built during the 1980s, when public outcry arose over a wave of Japanese successes in US sales in such areas as automobiles and electronics and subsequent investment in US properties. The high-profile acquisitions made by Japanese investors served to ignite an antiforeign backlash at a time when the US economy was attempting to cope with dislocations and the US dollar was weakening against other currencies. In reality, investment by the British and Dutch historically has exceeded that of the Japanese, and investment by Canadians, Germans, and the French have also been prevalent.

In 1973 the US government became aware that because of the lack of prohibitions and formal approval procedures, it had no means of tracking foreign investment in the US. This led to the enactment of a series of laws designed not to formally review or generally deny foreign investment, but to require disclosure of it to allow official monitoring. Federal agencies generally define a direct foreign investment as a holding of more than 25 percent of a US entity, although the Department of Commerce (DOC) has used a figure as low as 10 percent to assess some enterprises as being foreign-influenced (generally holdings of less than 25 percent are considered portfolio investments).

Although there is no formal investment review,

the US does place certain limits on foreign investment in specific areas. For example, a foreign national may not serve on the board of a US bank without prior approval from the Comptroller of the Currency (COC); the Federal Communications Commission (FCC) prohibits foreign ownership of more than 20 percent of a US broadcasting entity; foreign interests may own no more than 25 percent of domestic shipping or airline firms; and foreign entities are not eligible for certain benefits, such as leasing, grazing, or water rights on federal lands. US professionals and others representing foreign official entities are also required to register as agents of foreign governments. However, a 1975 attempt to require prior approval for foreign acquisitions of the securities of US firms was beaten back on the grounds that it would interfere with market operations. Recently, a proposal calling for registration and disclosure of foreign buyers and sellers of US securities has resurfaced and been opposed by those who see US financial markets becoming less attractive to overseas operators.

Real wages in the US remained stagnant throughout much of the 1980s, making US operations cheaper for multinational firms from high-wage countries, primarily in Europe. Foreign firms have also been eager to utilize US high-tech capabilities and extend their bases from which to serve the US market. This latter point has been of special concern to firms from countries threatened with a loss of access to US markets because of protectionist barriers against their products. More recently, some feared that they would be excluded following the passage of NAFTA. And, finally, the economy began to trend upward again in 1993 in both the US and much of Europe, making expansion a more attractive prospect.

However, throughout the 1980s and early 1990s, US-based foreign-owned manufacturing operations averaged a return on equity well below that of comparable US-owned firms. Many economists have explained this by referring to artificial transfer pricing designed to shift profits away from US tax authorities and back to the home country; however, this is now seen as a relatively minor element. Of far greater importance was the fact that during the 1980s many foreign firms new to the US were unfamiliar with doing business there, and—of even greater importance—many overpaid for assets while at the same time financing their acquisitions at high prevailing interest rates. Observers argue that the shakeout period for such operations is ending and that foreign-owned US operations are likely to become more competitive within the next few years. Another element that should help overall performance is the sale and removal from the books of some of the less viable purchases.

Size of Foreign Participation In 1992 the market value of all foreign-owned assets in the US was US$2.724 trillion. Some US$2.281 trillion of this represented foreign private assets, which dwarfed the US$443 billion in foreign government assets (accounting for less than 15 percent of the total). Direct investment accounted for about 30 percent of the foreign private investment component, while the remainder represented the market value of foreign portfolio investment (basically holdings of US securities). In 1993 cumulative direct foreign investment in the US was US$445.3 billion (measured at cost). This figure was more than five times the amount in 1980 (US$83 billion) and more than 100 times 1960's level of US$4.1 billion.

During 1992, actual direct foreign investment was US$13.5 billion. This included a total of 690 separate investments, including 360 buyouts of existing firms (three-quarters of investment by value), and 330 start-ups of new ventures (only one-fourth by value).

In 1991 US affiliates of foreign firms held US$1.744 trillion in assets in the US, had US$1.174 trillion in sales, and employed 4.8 million workers. Between 1977 and 1991, employment of manufacturing workers in the US by foreign owners grew by 244 percent, while during the same period US-owned firms were laying off a total of 3.9 million workers. Using only their US sales and assets, more than 100 of the top foreign-owned multinational US operations would be eligible for inclusion in the Fortune 500 list of the largest US companies. In 1993 US operations of foreign-owned multinationals produced roughly 20 percent of total US output—up from 4 percent in 1977.

Since 1980 there has been a generally steady increase in foreign activity in US securities markets. In 1993 net foreign portfolio investment in US securities reached nearly US$112 billion. Roughly 20 percent of this was in US government treasury securities, 33 percent was in US government agency securities, 27 percent was in corporate bonds, and 20 percent was in stocks. However, contrary to the investment pattern indicated by these holdings, more than four-fifths of all foreign trading activity was in US government securities, while an additional 10 percent was in stocks, with the rest evenly split between corporate bonds and US government agency securities. Foreigners trade government securities, but buy bonds, stocks, and agency securities to hang onto.

Origin of Foreign Investment In 1992 Japan held the largest share of cumulative direct foreign investment in the US. Its 23.1 percent share narrowly beat out the UK, which had a 22.6 percent share. Reports for the first half of 1994 indicated that renewed investment by British firms (and disinvestment by Japanese firms) had moved the UK ahead of Japan once again as the top foreign investor in the US. In 1992 the Netherlands was the third largest foreign investor with a 15 percent share, followed by Canada (9 percent), Germany (7 percent), and Switzerland (5 percent).

Other European countries accounted for a total of 10 percent, while investments from all other countries represented a total of only about 8 percent.

These figures represent a substantial realignment of foreign investment in the US. As recently as 1980, the largest shares were held by the Netherlands (23 percent), the UK (17 percent), Canada (15 percent), Germany (9 percent), and Switzerland (6 percent), with other European countries representing 11 percent. Japan was a relative newcomer to US investing, holding slightly less than 6 percent of foreign direct investment in the US.

In 1993 the largest foreign portfolio investors in US securities were Japan (29 percent), the UK (27 percent), Canada (9 percent), the Netherlands Antilles (4 percent), and France (2 percent). Together, these five nations accounted for more than 70 percent of total net holdings. The UK was the most active participant in US financial markets, accounting for 36 percent of total foreign portfolio trading during the year, followed by Japan (17 percent), Canada (6 percent), the Netherlands Antilles (4 percent), and France (4 percent), for a combined total of 67 percent of foreign trading volume.

Areas of Foreign Investment Manufacturing operations have remained the US sector that is most attractive to foreign investors, although various services are gaining rapidly. In 1992, 38 percent of cumulative direct foreign investment was in manufacturing, 16 percent in commerce, 11 percent in finance and insurance, and 9 percent in petroleum. Together, investment in these industries accounted for about three-fourths of all direct foreign investment. (In 1980, nearly half of such investment was concentrated in manufacturing, more than one-fifth was in commerce, and investments in petroleum and finance and insurance each neared 15 percent. Direct foreign investment in other areas was negligible.)

In 1992 manufacturing continued to be the top priority of foreign investors, with nearly a 40 percent share of investment in that calendar year. However, real estate was next in line—despite its poor showing in that year—with a 14 percent share. Other investments included general services (11 percent), finance (9 percent), and commerce (6 percent), with 16 percent in other miscellaneous areas. Notable recent foreign investments have been in the areas of electronics, software, pharmaceuticals, specialty chemicals, baby foods, and metals. There have also been several divestitures of large real estate holdings bought at elevated price levels during the late 1980s.

US Overseas Investment Since the 19th century US investors have been active in other countries. In 1992 total US-owned assets overseas were valued—at current market prices—at US$2.113 trillion (almost 30 percent less than the US$2.725 trillion of foreign investment in the US). The US government owned foreign assets valued at US$150 billion while US privately owned assets were US$1.963 trillion. US overseas private investment was about 40 percent in direct investments and 60 percent in portfolio investments, compared to foreign-owned investment in the US, which was 30 percent in direct and 70 percent in portfolio investment.

In 1992 cumulative US direct overseas investment was valued at US$486.7 billion on a cost basis, almost half of which was invested in Europe. On an individual country basis, the top target for US investors was the UK (16 percent), followed by Canada (14 percent), Germany (7 percent), Switzerland (6 percent), Japan (5 percent), Bermuda (5 percent), France (5 percent), the Netherlands (4 percent), Australia (3 percent), and Brazil (3 percent), or 68 percent of the total US overseas investment.

In 1980 the resulting total net purchases of US portfolio investment—noncontrolling holdings of securities—overseas came to US$3.1 billion; the total dollar volume of US overseas portfolio transactions was US$53.1 billion, two-thirds of which involved equity shares and one-third debt securities. In 1993 US overseas net portfolio purchases rose to a record US$128.6 billion on a total volume of US$2.39 trillion. Some 72 percent of total volume was in bonds and 28 percent in stocks, although final net purchase holdings were 47 percent bonds and 53 percent stocks. In 1993 the top five investment targets of US overseas portfolio investors were the UK (47 percent of total net purchases), Canada (15 percent), Hong Kong (4 percent), Japan (3 percent), and France (2 percent). Together, these markets accounted for 71 percent of all US overseas portfolio investment.

GOVERNMENT ECONOMIC DEVELOPMENT STRATEGY

Unlike many other countries in which the government assumes a major role in directing economic activity—and such a system is found in many industrialized, market oriented economies—the US prides itself on allowing the market to work independently. Periodically, there are calls for a greater government role in the economy, but to date these have been shouted down in favor of less regulated markets.

However, the US is hardly the home of pure unfettered capitalism, and has not been since the late 19th century. Government regulation and oversight of operations and markets has grown steadily during the past 100 years, so that the US economy is among the most heavily regulated in the world. Although operations within the areas delimited by the rules are generally free and open, the rules are voluminous and extensive. However, the unwritten rules of business in the US—as is the case in any country—are implicitly understood by the participants and govern activity to a greater degree than do formal rules. It is often difficult for outsiders to absorb the unwritten rules, and virtually impossible for them to follow all of the written ones.

The situation is made even more complex by the layers of rules instituted by the 50 separate US states and their numerous local jurisdictions. Although the US Constitution states that federal authority is paramount over that of states and localities (at least in the areas allocated to the federal government), the states retain wide discretion to enact and enforce their own codes. Many US states have engaged in bidding wars with each other in offering incentives to attract desirable economic investment. Some states are finding that onerous regulations and high tax rates add to the cost of doing business and cause them to lose new—and in some cases, existing— investment to states with fewer restrictions. The large, economically important states of California and New York are prime examples of states burdened by such regulations and taxes.

The aim of the system is not to make doing business more difficult; in fact, the stated aim is to accommodate and ensure equivalent access for a wide variety of constituencies. However, the result is often that operations become more complicated. The system of representative democracy used in the US is somewhat inelegant, allowing for ponderous bureaucracies, a wealth of regulation (some of it extremely detailed), and a means of operating that encourages mutual dealing and special interest influence. In general, this results not in garden variety corruption, but in a web of special provisions for special interests. These are seldom blatant, but they do serve to give some parties advantages over others in their operations. It can be argued that the effect of such distortions is almost random. Nevertheless, they add yet another level of complication to doing business in the US.

POLITICAL OUTLOOK FOR THE ECONOMY

As noted, the US historically has wavered between extremes of internationalism and isolationism, with isolationism being generally more prevalent. These cycles can be of shorter or longer duration. For example, the US remained largely inwardly focused for most of the 19th century, but in the period of the late 1880s through the early 1900s, it took a larger role in international affairs as a newly emerging industrial power. The US again pulled back during most of the period between 1910 and 1940, emerging as a major world power by the close of World War II. The failure to prevail in the conflict in Vietnam during the 1960s and 1970s and the country's inability to manage events in the Middle East led to a more recent pullback in the late 1970s. This was followed by a renewed period of outward focus during the 1980s. Thus far in the 1990s the direction remains unclear.

Worldwide economic restructuring, complicated by fallout from the economic excesses of the 1980s, has led countries and firms to retrench. This situation is made even more complex by the alteration of political forces following the collapse of the USSR, and the emergence of small, often belligerent nation states no longer effectively held in check by great power patrons. On the one hand, the policymakers and people of the more developed economies (such as the US) recognize that the as yet undeveloped structure of the new economic order is likely to be more international in scope than in the past. On the other hand, uncertainty over the structure and direction of this newly developing order is leading many to a defensive posture that favors isolationism and reaction.

Within the US the furor over NAFTA and GATT (both of which almost failed to pass the US Congress) is indicative of these contrasting pulls. A coalition of unlikely political allies on both the left and the right united over different concerns in attempts to defeat ratification of these treaties. On the right, there has been a worry that internationalization would lead to reduced national economic and political sovereignty as well as a loss of US jobs to lowerwage workers overseas. On the left, the sovereignty issue has taken a somewhat different path. There has been concern that internationalization would allow other countries with less stringent labor and environmental regulations to cause such regulation in the US to be reduced: the existing US regulations would be made untenable through competition, or US regulations could be challenged directly as anticompetitive restraints of trade.

For both the left and the right, the primary fear seems to be that the new order will not sustain the preexisting order and that certain constituencies will be losers under the new regime. Those on the other side of the argument maintain that the underlying conditions have already changed; that the existing system cannot be maintained; and that forward-looking agreements will help hasten the development of the new system while positioning the US to take advantage of its opportunities.

The dramatic victory of the out-of-power Republicans in taking over the US Congress and many statehouses in the November 1994 elections argues that there exists a strong reservoir of isolationist sentiment within the country. Many analysts argue that the sentiment expressed in this recent election is not so much an endorsement of any particular viewpoint or program, but one of frustration at the inability of US deliberative bodies to act in the face of these current challenges. In the climate of uncertainty that exists, the next national election in 1996—when the president as well as all members of the lower House of Representatives and one-third of the members of the upper Senate will be up for reelection—could signal an equally radical redirection if the recently elected body is unable to convince the public that it has been able to act effectively to shore up the situation.

To a certain degree, the outcome also depends on whether the US economy sustains its recent gains. The Republican loss of the presidency in the 1992 election is largely traced to dissatisfaction with a recessionary economy. Although the numbers have improved substantially in the last two years, the quality and breadth of the recovery continues to be questioned by many analysts. As firms restructure, job losses in the hundreds of thousands among higher paying manufacturing and corporate service positions have led to a significant loss not only of those positions, but also their attendant benefits and job security. This in turn has led to greater anxiety and less optimism—and less purchasing power— among the US consuming public. On one side, proponents look to internationalization to provide the ability to recoup economic leadership. On the other side, opponents see internationalization as the coup de grace of the existing economy.

THE INTERNATIONAL ROLE OF THE US

The US is a member of most international and multilateral economic, political, and trade organizations. The US is a charter founding member and permanent member of the executive governing Security Council of the United Nations (UN), and it participates in virtually all of the UN's various subagencies. However, it is sometimes at odds with specific agencies of the UN, as well as with the body itself. In the 1980s, the US resigned from the UN Education, Scientific, and Cultural Organization (UNESCO) because of a perceived anti-Western tone, and the US has withheld its payment of general dues and specific assessments to protest UN policies of which it did not approve.

The US is also a charter member of the International Bank for Reconstruction and Development (IBRD, or the World Bank), the International Monetary Fund (IMF), and the IMF's International Finance Corporation (IFC). It is a member of the OECD, and one of the Group of Seven (G-7), a caucus consisting of the leaders of the world's major developed industrial economies (the other six members in the G-7 are Canada, France, Germany, the UK, Italy, and Japan).

Significant trade agreements to which the US subscribes include GATT, soon to be superseded by the World Trade Organization (WTO). The US is also a sponsor and member of NAFTA, as well as of Asia Pacific Economic Cooperation (APEC)—designed to lead to a pan-Pacific Rim trading organization. It is also an organizer of the Summit of the Americas, designed to lead to a similar body linking the nations of North and South America in a trade pact. The US adheres to such international commodity agreements as Multi-Fiber Arrangement (MFA)—a series of bilateral agreements to govern international trade in textiles. A founding member of the Organization of American States (OAS), the US also sponsored the Caribbean Basin Initiative (CBI). It is also a charter member of the North Atlantic Treaty Organization (NATO), a mutual defense pact which is in flux as it searches for a format and a role in the current changed environment. Many specific provisions of more general agreements are negotiated and placed in effect through the means of bilateral agreements between the US and individual countries. Most of these contain fairly standard provisions, although there may be individual variation. Other agreements are multilateral.

Current Issues

THE LOSING BATTLE
TO STAY OUT OF DEBT

The twin deficits—fiscal and trade—are perhaps the most pressing issue for the US today, although many there have yet to recognize or acknowledge it. One school of economic thought holds that because the US essentially owes the funds to itself, the fiscal budget deficit in particular should be of little concern. As long as the economy generates enough funds to handle its necessary expenditures and to keep current on its obligations so that others remain willing to lend to it, there is no real problem. Virtually no modern enterprise—from the nuclear family to the largest multinational firm, not to mention national governments—has enough hard assets to satisfy all of its obligations at any given point in time. However, this viewpoint ignores the fact that the economy is increasingly global, and that the US is heavily reliant on outside sources of funds to keep the system going.

In December 1994 the world was treated to a demonstration of this problem on a slightly smaller scale in Mexico. Mexico has based its bid to move from the developing world into the more stable developed world on a strong currency, open markets, and the internationalization of its economy. The currency element is particularly important for countries that have had a legacy of severe inflation in recent years. The fallout from this attempt to maintain a strong currency has been the accumulation of rapidly rising trade deficits and the use of foreign reserves—acquired primarily from foreign investors—to subsidize the trade deficits. When the cost of doing so became too high in late December, Mexico had to

devalue its currency, resulting in a hemorrhage of the foreign funds that had been sustaining the Mexican economy. The panic selling of Mexican securities further undermined the peso. Recovery will be difficult, because Mexico has lost the confidence of many international investors.

Although the US is the world's largest economy and the dollar is an international reserve currency, its basic situation is not all that different form Mexico's. If entities of whatever size spend more than they earn and borrow to subsidize their spending, eventually they will run out of creditors, and it can take only a nudge to send remaining creditors scrambling for the exits. Many overseas creditors are becoming increasingly anxious about the growing size of US deficits and the apparent inability of the US to balance its books.

The Looming Deficits The real problem comes when the situation becomes a structural problem instead of a cash flow problem. Once the cumulative deficit reaches a critical mass relative to the underlying economy, this can occur even in the absence of other changes in the system.

In the 15 years from 1980 through 1994, GDP has grown by almost 145 percent while the annual budget deficit has grown 280 percent, and the cumulative budget deficit has increased from one-third of GDP to more than 70 percent of GDP. And these computations ignore rapidly rising off-budget expenditures, projected at US$281 billion in 1994.

During the same period, the annual trade deficit more than doubled. This trade imbalance is having an increasingly large effect because the chronic deficit is a material factor in decreasing purchasing power and in the falling value of the dollar. Thus, US maneuvering room is considerably decreased, and the difficulty is beginning to look more and more like a structural problem.

However, to put things into perspective, Japan has also been running a budget deficit since 1992. In 1994 Japan's budgetary deficit was 5.7 percent of its GDP, almost double the US budget deficit of 2.9 percent of GDP. Nevertheless, Japan continued to amass record trade surpluses with the US.

Debt The US has become the world's largest debtor nation, with the annual payments on the federal portion of the debt alone amounting to nearly US$300 billion in 1994. This points up the fact that the US relies heavily on outside financing—largely through the sale of US government securities—for more than one-quarter of its borrowing needs. The role of foreign capital in sustaining US government deficits also ignores the role that foreign funds play in nonfederal public financing—which accounts for 20 percent of total public borrowing. And this does not even touch on the borrowings of the even more rapidly growing private sector, including both businesses and individual consumers. As other large economies—such as Germany and Japan—require more capital to service deficits, they will be less willing to lend to the US. Some economists worry that a worldwide capital shortage could arise over the next few years.

The huge appetite of public issuers can also crowd out private borrowing by soaking up available capital, resulting in credit shortages, higher rates, and eventually a choking off of private activity. In recent years, this has been avoided by increased expansion of the money supply, but such creation of money contributes to decreases in the value of the currency. The low savings rate in the US (less than 3 percent) adds to the level of concern.

The Political Outlook The Clinton administration was elected in 1992 on a populist platform which included a provision for reducing taxation on the middle class. After taking office, the president shifted policy toward deficit reduction, ruling out even token tax cuts. Since 1990 the rate of growth of the annual federal fiscal deficit has been easing somewhat, although it was heading upward again in 1994.

The 1994 midterm elections saw public discontent with a lack of accomplishment, which has been interpreted by domestic politicians as requiring a retreat from deficit reduction in favor of tax reduction. Theoretically, both could be accomplished to some extent by cutting expenditures. However, the magnitude of the cuts necessary to actually have an effect on the deficit as well as on taxes paid is not considered to be politically feasible. Some observers contend that the political will to reduce spending enough to fund either program is lacking, and based on recent history, it is difficult to refute this argument. Hence, domestic and foreign analysts are bracing for worsening fiscal deficits for the foreseeable future.

In early 1995 the House of Representatives passed a constitutional amendment calling for a balanced federal budget by a wide margin. However, observers were unsure whether there were enough votes to pass the proposal in the Senate. Even if passed, the amendment would require ratification by the states and would not require concrete action for several years. Many economists have opposed the amendment, arguing that it would hamper effective government response to economic problems. However, many other observers argue that because of the hard political decisions required to balance the budget, Congress will be unable to summon the necessary courage without the discipline imposed by such an amendment. Whatever the outcome, the consensus is that it will take a long time before any results are noticeable.

The Trade Deficit The issue of the trade deficit has also remained intractable. Although US exports have surged in recent years, US consumers continue to buy even more goods and services from overseas than it sells abroad. The US has tried to pressure various trading partners, particularly in East Asia, to open their markets to a greater extent and make purchases of US goods and services a priority in order to help reduce the huge trade imbalances posted with those countries. However, the recovering economy has made US consumers more optimistic and thus willing to pay even higher prices for desired foreign goods.

While the North American Free Trade Agreement (NAFTA) has increased total trade, it has also resulted in a widening of the US trade deficit with its main trading partner, Canada, and a sharp reduction in its surplus with its number three partner, Mexico. The 1994 year-end collapse of the Mexican peso has worsened fears that the ailing Mexican economy will have major impacts on the US economy. The signing of the Uruguay Round of the General Agreement on Tariffs and Trade (GATT) is also expected to lead to higher near-term trade deficits before its full effects eventually eliminate trade distortions and promote greater trade.

The US reported that its merchandise trade deficit grew to US$166.3 billion—a new record high—in 1994. Sources in the US are expecting an improvement in 1995 as overseas economies improve, resulting in increased purchases of US exports, while imports into the US are expected to fall as the domestic economy slows down. However, the Organization for Economic Cooperation and Development (OECD) has predicted that the situation will not turn around before 1996, postponing the effective opportunity to reduce the US trade deficit problem. And no matter how favorable the trends become with respect to either the fiscal or trade deficits, such market-based changes remain unlikely to be of sufficient magnitude to reduce the twin problems without substantive policy intervention. Such intervention is more likely to exacerbate than improve the situation over the near term. Over the intermediate to long term, the continued success of the US economy will depend on its ability to figure out a way to deal with these difficult problems.

SYSTEMIC CHANGE: THE LACK OF CONSENSUS

The Social Fragmentation of the US Observers both at home and abroad complain that the US lacks a collective sense of purpose and that it is without leaders of a stature equivalent to those of the past. The US has largely lost whatever national consensus it had as recently as 25 years ago. Many would argue that the internal splits that developed in the body politic during the intense public debate over the Vietnam War in the 1960s and 1970s resulted in the demise of the fragile—and some would say false—consensus that had previously existed. The current lack of leadership should be seen not so much as a lack of able people, but as a fragmentation of interests that prevents leaders from rallying sufficient support to back any broad policy, program, or ideology.

Once before, during the US Civil War in the 1860s, the US was faced with a cleavage among major segments of its people. In that instance, unity was enforced by military means. However, at that time, the differences were predominantly and clearly ideological in nature—involving the primacy of federal versus state authority and the moral and economic issue of slavery—as well as between an industrializing North and an agrarian South with different needs and perceptions. Even though size and economic dominance clearly lay with the North, it took four long years of extremely bloody fighting to subdue the South, and even longer to reconstitute the union.

Relatively straightforward ideological and economic models no longer apply in the current US situation. At present, there are no clearly defined ideological questions, and appeals to ideology have served to blur rather than clarify the issues. Nor is there any clear preponderance of any economic model, other than the as yet vague assertion of internationalism, to direct the attempts at adjustment.

The world's economy no longer consists of the sum of essentially separate local economies, which generally remained largely insulated from international fluctuations. The traditional explanations of how those separate economies functioned and interacted have become less useful in explaining the current emerging global economy. However, the structure of the new world economy has yet to become clear. In the interim, individuals, enterprises, and nations are experiencing severe dislocations and confusion. Given its size and importance, the US is on the front lines of this struggle to adapt and make sense of these changes.

In this period of uncertainty, the US has seemed to splinter into a series of increasingly smaller interest groups, none of which has emerged as having a dominant model or ideology around which the country in general could coalesce. Similar phenomena involving political (and military) rather than economic causes can also be observed among breakaway republics and would-be statelets around the world. Instead of struggling to define inclusive systems or ideologies, many groups have been more interested in underscoring their differences. In effect, few minorities have been able to advance their own programs, but many have succeeded in being able to veto the proposals of others, leading to an

"And on my left is 'The Great Fantino,' who takes the position that the deficit will disappear by magic."

increasingly partisan, tense, and ineffective stand-still.

The Myth of the Melting Pot People in the US have traditionally maintained a core of shared values, identities, and myths that have united the country's otherwise divergent, geographically separated populations into a nation. In recent decades, this sense of similarity and unity of purpose has been eroding, leading to fragmentation and a lack of direction and consensus in the national psyche.

Unlike some other nations which are either culturally homogeneous or consist primarily of a limited number of distinct ethnic groups, which have a long history of interaction and adaptation to a similar social and natural environment, the US has always been a nation of more or less recent immigrants with all the lack of homogeneity and accepted patterns of doing things that this implies. The concept of the US as a "melting pot"—the idea that dissimilar peoples were magically absorbed by the body politic and transformed into "Americans," a unique people with a common world view—is enshrined in US lore. The melting pot has always been more myth than reality. However, two strong trends have traditionally helped to perpetuate this idealized view and allowed the nation to function as if the myth were largely true.

First, many immigrants came in groups to specific geographic areas which became noted as ethnic enclaves, perpetuating this self-selection. For example, the upper Midwest, with its high concentration of groups of Scandinavian origin, remains connected with that part of the Old World in the popular mind, both locally and nationally.

Immigrants were often able to remain in enclaves populated largely by those with a similar culture, heritage, and language, allowing them to get by with limited contact with many of their nonethnic neighbors. Such contact was often mediated by culture brokers who learned the ways of the mainstream culture and served as interpreters and middlemen. These brokers translated the concepts of one group for the members of the other, allowing each to think that they understood and were understood by the other while allowing each to retain many of its own views and prejudices. Such boundaries were more difficult to maintain in urban areas, where physical distance among different groups was minimal. However, until well into the 20th century, the US was largely a spread-out, low-density rural society, allowing for perpetuation of the myth.

Second, although immigrants came to the New World for many reasons and under many circumstances—with the glaring exception of Blacks imported against their wills as slaves—most came for economic opportunity, personal freedom, or both. With the cost and difficulty of travel, most of these people were effectively leaving their homelands forever and, as a consequence, were forced to totally immerse themselves in and identify with their new country. This break with the old and need to commit to the new made for an allegiance to the new country no matter how strong the memories of the old. This shared set of motives and shared experience of being cut off from the old and thrown into new circumstances allowed them to identify with common goals. The lack of a generally accepted strategy for coping with an often unfamiliar environment led to similar ways of dealing with the challenge which reinforced this convergence. Such convergence allowed the development of at least an overlay of common assumptions, even when it remained somewhat superficial.

Nevertheless, many US citizens, even those whose families have been in the country for generations and with no real ties to their place of ancestral origin, continue to think of themselves as "hyphenated Americans"—for example, Irish-Americans, German-Americans, Polish-Americans—having some other ethnic or national allegiance.

Recent Pressures During recent decades, the circumstances and assumptions on which social consensus was based have changed, as has the environment in which that traditional adaptation functioned. The confusion being experienced at present has been worsened by the US assumption of the role of standard-bearer of the Western world, a role thrust upon a largely unready US following World War II. Although individuals from the US have always been involved in international affairs, particularly in trade, the majority of people in the US have traditionally stayed close to home, nursing a rather parochial view of the world and having little contact with people unlike themselves.

In the post-World War II era, the US somewhat reluctantly assumed a much larger global role. The past 50 years have been conditioned by the international role of the US as the primary anticommunist antagonist in the Cold War. During this period, the country tried to live up to that role as it was perceived. The US was simultaneously trying to grow into an economy different in kind and in magnitude from any that had existed before; enjoy the fruits of that growth; and extend that way of life to much of the rest of the world—whether the world wanted it or not. At the same time, the US was bruised by the real and perceived rebuffs from those who preferred to do things their own way. The burdens of these multiple tasks and expectations finally proved too much to sustain for the set of shared precepts that constituted the US identity. The internal contradictions among the various parts of the US national image have become even more apparent with the demise of the Soviet bloc both as a credible military threat and—even more importantly—as an ideological opponent.

The Scapegoating of Immigrants At least part of the perceived cause of the current fragmentation of consensus in the US is the heavy influx of immigrants into the US in recent decades. Although this is more a contributing factor than a core cause of social fragmentation—the real problem having more to do with the global shift in economic relations than with internal social relations—it does serve as a major factor around which US articulation of its current plight forms. The US has always had immigrants, and there have been periods in the past during which the immigrant population was larger, more foreign, and more threatening to the integrity of the existing system than at present. Yet the US is currently experiencing a sense that today's immigrants are somehow more numerous, more foreign, and more threatening than at any time in the past.

When the economy was more certain and growing and there was a steady need for unskilled and semiskilled labor, immigration was uncontrolled and actively promoted. But with the current lessening demand for low-skill labor, changes in traditional labor and employment patterns—including massive layoffs and general economic and social uncertainty—there is less room in the system or in the popular mind for immigrants. Some 60 percent of respondents currently state that the US should curtail immigration.

Despite strong indications that immigrants seldom take jobs away from nationals and that they contribute more in productivity and payments than they cost in services provided, there is a tendency to make them scapegoats. Many blame them for unemployment and for being too much of an expense for citizens to bear. It should be noted that immigrants tend to cluster in a few states—California, Florida, New York, and Texas—where they may make up a disproportionate part of those in need of social services.

Because of this, there is a considerable backlash against more recent immigrants and a tendency to portray them as more culturally foreign. Because the bulk of more recent immigrants are from Asia and Latin America, many argue that different cultural and linguistic backgrounds are being represented in greater volume at present. (Before 1960, 80 percent of immigrants came from Europe; in the 1980s, the European share fell below 10 percent.)

It can be argued convincingly that the level of discomfort experienced by US nationals in the face of more recent immigration—including illegal immigration—has more to do with the degree of change occurring in the US than it does with the "otherness" of the scapegoated groups. The problems—of absorbing unprepared immigrant children into an educational system already stretched thin; of pro-

viding housing when a shortage of inexpensive housing has already reached crisis proportions; and of providing health, social, police, judicial, and prison services when the costs of services are rising and the language barrier is virtually insurmountable—are not inconsequential. However, they are little different either in degree or kind from those faced by the US in 1900, when immigration to the US peaked at levels nearly double those of today. The main difference is that 90 years ago, the economy was growing rapidly and needed basic labor. Today it is growing slowly and requires a different set of expensive skills rather than simply additional manpower.

Breaking Out of Gridlock There are no easy answers to these quandries. As long as divisive fractional entities continue to derail the proposals of other groups, little overall progress can be expected. The developing conservative consensus alleged to be evidenced by the 1994 elections may provide the impetus for the beginnings of a turnaround. However, the attempts of those newly in power to capitalize on their victory as a sign of a particular brand of conservatism is likely to result in even greater fragmentation. Any consensus is likely to be postponed until the structure of the emerging world economy becomes somewhat clearer. The US will have to solve the riddle of how to reincorporate its various warring segments into a functioning whole if it is to continue in anything like its past form. Alternately, it will have to find other forms that do the work of the existing, now-outmoded system. Either way, great risks and perhaps even greater opportunities await.

COMPETITIVENESS, PROTECTIONISM, AND GLOBALIZATION

People in the US, like those elsewhere, operate with a series of different, sometimes mutually contradictory precepts. In many instances, the specific concepts used in separate contexts and thus seldom come into conflict with each other. However, these different principles can cause confusion when they meet head-on in new circumstances. This is especially true at times, such as the present, when changing conditions require a reevaluation of accepted ways of doing and explaining things.

The Myth of the Cowboy The US has long idealized the pioneer, a "rugged individualist" with a can-do, competitive spirit. So strong is this ideal that even in a country in which the economy is largely determined by large cooperative, corporate ventures operating in a strict and narrow framework of rules and expectations, the image of the cowboy—who works alone, is fearless and independent, and fights and beats all adversaries—continues to animate people in the US.

Another related part of this self-reliance is a less admirable tendency toward isolationism. People in the US can be extremely insular, parochial, suspicious, and distrustful of outsiders. The history of the US is filled with periods during which the country held itself aloof from the international community. People in the US have often been fearful of cooperative action, especially when it meant surrendering individuality, authority, sovereignty, or any consideration of the immediate personal or national interest to outsiders. People in the US can be extremely generous on their own, but resist the leadership or demands of others.

Many of the instances in which the US has withdrawn have involved periods of rapid, far-reaching change. There are many in the US who would like to withdraw in the face of the current onslaught of changes. The attempt to control what is largely uncontrollable and hold off change by slavishly following old strategies is a constant in human history. However, as the US economy has grown larger and more prominent, and as advancing transportation and communication technologies have shrunk the effects of distance and forced the US to take part in world affairs, isolation has become even less effective. This retreat is also particularly ironic in a country that has always boasted about how it invented itself in a New World by breaking with the outmoded patterns of the past.

The Costs of Protectionism In today's global economy, the US desire to avoid change sometimes takes the form of protectionism, in which the idea of competitive advantage (doing what you do best) and comparative advantage (letting others do what they do best rather than trying to do it yourself) are largely denied in an attempt to hang onto domestic employment, sourcing systems, and sovereignty, no matter what the cost.

An example of the failure of such protectionism was the push to save jobs in the US leatherworking industry in the late 1970s, an attempt which flew in the face of the economics involved. US tanners and shoemakers wanted protectionist tariffs imposed on overly competitive inexpensive footwear coming into the US from Brazil and the Caribbean (such products now come primarily from China). The US shoe industry went so far as to argue that because it produced military footwear, it was a strategic industry, the demise of which would make the US militarily weaker because it would be dependent on overseas providers of combat boots.

This demand ignored the fact that the profits of US ranchers depended largely on the extra revenues from the sale of unprocessed hides (primarily to Brazil) rather than from the sale of meat alone. Because of increasingly stringent environmental regulations and the fact that tanning is a polluting industry, there

remained only a limited domestic market for raw hides. Furthermore, the overall cost structure made traditionally produced US footwear highly uncompetitive in both international and domestic markets.

While there were perhaps 60,000 jobs in the US leatherworking industry, there were roughly 500,000 in the ranching industry and another 500,000 in the US wholesale and retail footwear and leather goods industry. There was also a shortage of both labor and capital available to the US tanning and shoe industries at terms that would make them economically viable. Thus, job protection for these workers could have resulted in job loss for several times as many other US workers in the ranching and retail shoe industries, plus a shortage of a basic product and high prices for the US consuming public.

Other effects of such actions were also ignored: the processing countries would be deprived of employment and sales, and therefore of much-needed hard currency. They would thus be unable to import goods and services from other US industries, leading to additional secondary ill effects.

Choosing Between Staying Separate and Staying Competitive Similar stories could be told regarding such protected commodities as sugar, peanuts, and cotton or intermediate and finished products as varied as textiles and apparel and iron and steel. Although the special interest minority did not prevail in the leatherworking instance, the example demonstrates not only the flaws in the protectionist argument, but also the role of interest groups in US social, political, and economic life. As previously noted, small special interest splinter groups are often able to veto majority interests. This is true especially if such groups are concentrated and organized.

One of the challenges facing the US as a world power at the end of the 20th century is how to keep its sense of identity while at the same time developing a new role as part of the emerging world system. Ultimately, it may have to choose between a continuing independent role and economic success through greater incorporation into the new system. Protectionism may soon become a luxury that the US will be unable to afford if it is to remain competitive in the new world economy.

Opportunities

OPPORTUNITIES FOR IMPORTING FROM THE US

The US exports a vast array of goods and services to a wide variety of customers. It is especially competitive in producing goods that rely on high-tech manufacturing processes. It is less competitive in more basic industries—such as textile and apparel manufacture—that are labor intensive. The US trades with about 180 countries, opening the way for wide-ranging trade contacts.

Three factors tend to make trade negotiations with US companies a buyer's market, that is, one in which supply often exceeds demand and sales terms tend to favor the purchaser: (1) US manufacturers must compete with generally lower-cost producers in emerging economies; (2) the need to reduce the US trade deficit can lead US exporters to reach for sales on terms less favorable than they would otherwise accept; and (3) in certain areas of the US economy—such as the agricultural and automotive sectors—the domestic market is largely saturated and US firms must look to exports if they wish to grow at a rate greater than that of the underlying domestic economy, which has slowed since the high growth 1950s and 1960s. An additional consideration is that many US individuals and companies are increasingly interested in investing abroad. If subsidiaries of US companies can be set up in your country, opportunities for importing parts from the US to build and service the overseas outlets usually follow (as may chances to export the resulting product back to the US).

The following section describes US exports and reexports as areas of opportunity for importing from the country.

ANALYTIC AND OPTICAL INSTRUMENTS

Opportunities for importing precision instruments will depend on the technical sophistication and the specific needs of the consumers, that is, on whether the instruments are to be used for complex or simple procedures. For example, Japan imports US analytic instruments for highly specialized applications in research and development. Other countries import US analytic and optical instruments for less sensitive applications, such as for basic environmental testing and for measurements related to meeting government regulations. Manufacturers in the US are world leaders in the production of high-tech instruments with the flexibility required in manufacturing processes to supply other countries with a wide array of analytic and optical instruments. Popular exports include portable analytic instruments for on-site environmental analysis, industrial quality control systems, and information and laser technology. The US is also a major supplier to many industries—such as chemicals producers, clinical laboratories, health care providers, pharmaceutical companies, semiconductor manufacturers, and telecommunication services—that need analytic instruments specifically designed for their unique requirements.

Some Hot Items:
analytic instruments
- capillary electrophoresis instruments
- chromatographs
- DNA/protein sequencers
- portable analytic instruments
- scanning microscopes

optical instruments and components
- bar code scanners
- binoculars
- lasers
- laser printers
- laser surgical instruments
- optical microscopes

CHEMICALS

Manufacturers who need inorganic chemicals such as chlorine, caustic soda (sodium hydroxide), and soda ash, and such organic chemicals as primary petrochemicals, among many others, will find plentiful supplies in the US. Chlorine and caustic soda make up 80 percent of all US inorganic chemical shipments. Soda ash—used in the manufacture of glass, toothpaste, powdered soaps, and laundry detergents—accounts for 15 percent of industry shipments. The US has huge deposits of soda ash, and mines in Wyoming are the primary source worldwide of easily extractable product.

Organic chemicals are used by the paper, housing, packaging, automotive, pharmaceutical, paint and ink, fertilizer, and a virtually unlimited range of other industries. Petrochemicals are the precursors of plastics, fibers, elastomers, fertilizers, and chemical intermediates, which in turn provide the main

constituents of numerous consumer goods. Many firms throughout the US process these chemicals to prepare them for use as specified by particular industrial buyers, working with those industries to improve the performance of the chemicals provided.

Some Hot Items:
inorganic chemicals
- acids
- chlorine
- caustic soda (sodium hydroxide)
- industrial gases
- soda ash

organic chemicals
- benzene
- butadiene
- methanol
- propylene
- thylene
- toluene
- xylene

COMPUTERS

The US plays a leading role in the development and production of innovative and sophisticated computer products for nearly every market—individuals, private and public businesses, and academic institutions. The basic trends in the industry involve linking different areas of technology together into a single network and producing computers with greater power that come in more compact packages at reduced cost.

Computers are not only increasing efficiency in the workplace, they are also changing the way in which work is done. The introduction of computers to the business world has altered both the methods for producing goods and the means of processing trade information. Importers of US computers should be concerned with acquiring, along with the computer equipment needed for an intended use, the training necessary to implement and employ the sophisticated technology. Firms in the US can provide not only the products, but also the installation and training. Computer development and manufacturing in the US are on the cutting edge, especially in software, and US companies have a great deal of experience in successfully introducing computers into work environments.

Some Hot Items:
- computer aided design (CAD) systems
- computer storage devices
- keyboards
- mainframe computers
- modems
- monitors

- multimedia systems
- network management software
- personal computers
- personal computer software
- portable computers (laptop, notebook, handheld)
- supercomputers
- telecommunications software

ELECTRONIC COMPONENTS

As worldwide demand for electronic components increases, the US is working to maintain its competitive edge through strategic alliances among manufacturers to share the costs of production and gain economies of scale. US firms are also emphasizing the establishment of long-term relationships with suppliers and improvements in customer relations.

Current trends in the electronic components industry can benefit the potential importer of US products. Despite a fiercely competitive global market—particularly from the Japanese electronics industry—US electronic components producers have retained a leading position in the international marketplace, especially in the production of integrated circuits. Of the world's top 10 manufacturers of microprocessors, 6 are headquartered in the US, including Intel, the world's largest semiconductor company.

Some Hot Items:

boards
- circuit boards

passive components
- capacitors
- coils
- connectors
- relays
- resistors
- switches
- transformers

semiconductors
- analog integrated circuits
- discrete semiconductors
- logic integrated circuits
- memory integrated circuits
- microcomponent integrated circuits
- optical semiconductors

ENVIRONMENTAL TECHNOLOGIES AND SERVICES

The US is the world's largest producer and consumer of environmental goods and services, accounting for about 40 percent of the US$200 billion world market. An estimated 7,000 to 10,000 US companies are involved in the international environmental technologies and services market, including firms providing consulting, engineering, and design and manufacture of equipment and integrated systems. The US is a major exporter of environmental pollution control equipment in general and air pollution control equipment in particular.

Some Hot Items:

services
- analytic services
- construction
- design and engineering
- environmental consulting
- off-site services
- remediation
- transportation of hazardous wastes

technologies
- air pollution control equipment
- hazardous and toxic waste technologies
- pollution prevention technologies
- solid waste recycling systems
- water and wastewater processing systems

FOOD AND BEVERAGES

Importers can acquire a wide range of food and beverage products from the US. The processed food and beverage industry is, in fact, the largest manufacturing sector in the US economy. In 1993 production was valued at more than US$400 billion. Exports consistently outnumber imports, and with the domestic market becoming saturated, US producers are searching for ways to export an ever-increasing number and volume of products.

The most popular export items are value-added goods: food and beverage items that appear in retail outlets prepackaged and consumer-ready. These require sophisticated preparation, manufacturing, and packaging processes. In some areas, domestic consumer preferences have shifted from more expensive brand-name products to less expensive private label and generic goods. Importers of food products from the US might investigate such generic products as a money-saving option. The US also produces and exports lower value-added commodity products such as meat, poultry, bulk wheat, and other grains.

Some Hot Items:
- bakery products (fresh and frozen)
- barley
- beer
- brandy
- bread
- cakes
- cattle
- cereal
- chewing gum
- chocolate products
- chickens

- coffee (roasted)
- cookies
- corn
- crackers
- dairy products
- eggs
- fats
- fish (canned, frozen, and fresh)
- flour
- fruits (fresh, frozen, preserved, and dried)
- macaroni
- meats
- melons
- nuts
- oats
- oils
- oilseeds
- potato chips
- preserved fruits
- rice
- rye
- soft drinks
- sorghum
- spaghetti
- sugar
- syrup
- tobacco
- tomatoes
- turkey
- vegetables (fresh, canned, frozen, and dried)
- wheat
- whiskey
- wines

LEATHER HIDES

The US is the world's largest exporter of hides, 90 percent of which are from cattle. However, the supply of cowhides depends on the consumption of beef because hides are produced as a by-product of the meatpacking industry. Some of the largest US tanning facilities are operated by meatpacking firms, often adjacent to the packing plants. More than half of the cowhides tanned are used by the footwear industry, but leather also serves as the primary raw material for manufacturers of many other products, including saddles, clothing, hats, gloves, luggage, wallets, furniture, furnishings, and automotive upholstery. Countries on the Pacific Rim buy a substantial portion of US leather hide exports.

Some Hot Items:
- calf leather
- cowhides
- split leather
- wet-blue leather

MEDICAL, SURGICAL, AND DENTAL EQUIPMENT

The medical equipment and supplies industry is among the top-performing industries in the US because of the huge demand from US health care professionals, researchers, and regulators. Medical professionals in the US are well trained and provide a high level of health care. The quality of the equipment they purchase matches this professional expertise. In 1993 the US supplied 52 percent of world output of such products, and 23 percent of US output was exported. Common US exports include such lower level products as needles and syringes, opthalmic instruments and appliances, stethoscopes, percussion hammers, sphygmomanometers, and tensimeters. Many US firms can also provide, and may even help to develop, instruments to meet the specifications of the buyer.

Not all medical equipment sold is new. The sale of used and refurbished medical equipment—particularly such high-end items as magnetic resonance imaging (MRI) equipment and computed tomography (CT) scanners—represents a growing business. The US Food and Drug Administration (FDA) has set standards to ensure that used and refurbished equipment is safe and effective for intended uses.

Health care information systems are also growing in popularity. These systems include computer monitoring devices for patients, typically those in intensive care units; programs that record and track financial information; and units that collect and analyze data from medical equipment and instruments.

Some Hot Items:
dental equipment
- amalgams
- cements
- dental chairs
- dental hand instruments
- drills
- plaster
- sterilizers

surgical and medical instruments and supplies
- bandages
- blood pressure measuring devices
- catheters
- clamps
- drains
- hypodermic needles
- implantable devices
- laparoscopic devices
- prosthetics
- stethoscopes
- suture needles
- syringes
- wheelchairs

other
- magnetic resonance imaging equipment
- opthalmic goods
- pacemakers
- patient monitoring systems
- ultrasonic scanning devices
- X-ray apparatus and tubes

METALWORKING EQUIPMENT

US producers of metalworking equipment have turned to exports in the face of tough foreign competition. Consequently, a large number of producers are modifying their designs and manufacturing processes to comply with requirements for certification under the International Standards Organization (ISO). They are also retooling to produce equipment calibrated to the metric system, which is required elsewhere in the world. Japan and Germany are still the world's largest producers of machine tools, but a resurgent US has moved into third place, surpassing Italy. Exports from the US have tripled since 1983. The US typically exports its products to the industrializing countries of the Pacific Rim, China, and Latin America. It supplies the automotive, construction, and fabricated metal industries with tools and dies, machine tools, and robotic systems.

Some Hot Items:

metal cutting
- drilling and boring machines
- grinding, polishing, buffing, lapping, and honing machines
- home workshop machine tools
- lathes
- milling machines
- robots for drilling, cutting, grinding, polishing, and similar functions
- screw and thread machines
- saws and sawing machines

metal forming
- die-casting and extruding machines
- headers
- knurling and beading machines
- punching, shearing, and bending machines
- pressing machines
- robots for metal forming
- spinning, spline, rolling, and winding machines

other
- dies
- jigs
- welding equipment

PHARMACEUTICALS AND RELATED PRODUCTS

Firms in the US are among the most innovative, competitive players in world pharmaceutical markets. US manufacturers are striving to increase exports. However, their efforts have been hampered by the need to keep prices of drugs relatively low. In response to complaints from the US public, domestic government leaders, and foreign governments, 10 leading pharmaceutical companies have agreed to keep their price increases commensurate with the general rate of inflation. Another of the industry's major concerns remains effective enforcement of intellectual property rights, the violation of which costs millions of dollars in sales and revenues annually.

The best US export customers are the EU, Canada, Mexico, and Japan. China, Russia, and the republics of the former Soviet Union offer potentially good markets, depending on whether licensing agreements can be secured and whether those countries develop their own pharmaceutical production. Potential importers should note the US trend toward increased use of over-the-counter and generic drugs. The US—long on the on the cutting edge of science in providing medical breakthroughs—can also be expected to continue to be in the forefront in the development of new and improved products in the fight against local and global epidemics, from malaria to AIDS.

Some Hot Items:

- clinical chemistry products
- herbal products
- infectious disease tests
- over-the-counter drugs
- pharmaceuticals
- vaccines

TELECOMMUNICATIONS

The US is a dominant supplier of network telecommunications equipment to large corporations and national governments. Exports are primarily targeted at developing countries, such as China and Mexico. The US is a strong supplier of privately owned telecommunications equipment with a high level of sophisticated technology, including voice processing and video conferencing equipment. In addition to such products, the US is a leading provider of cellular radio telephones and fiber optics equipment. The fastest growth areas in telecommunications equipment are in high-speed data communications and video traffic, applications that require greater bandwidth and packet switching technologies. In an industry marked by continually changing technology, setting and meeting equipment standards is a growing concern for US manufacturers exporting products for use in countries that do not adhere to the US norms.

Some Hot Items:

- audio and visual studio equipment
- cable television equipment
- cellular radio telephones
- closed-circuit television equipment
- facsimile machines
- fiber optics equipment
- fixed and mobile radio systems
- radio transmitters, transceivers, and receivers
- signal switches (central office switches, packet switches, mobile telephone switches, microwave switches, data communication switches)
- transmission equipment (multiplexing equipment, repeaters, line conditioning equipment)

TEXTILES

The US textile industry—traditionally labor intensive—has had to find innovative means to compete with countries with lower labor costs. To this end, US companies have introduced technology to reduce manufacturing costs in areas such as knit fabrics. The US also leads the world in the development and production of high-tech man-made fibers, such as acrylics, nylon, and spandex. New technology has also been adapted to improve customer service and shipping procedures. In 1993 the American Textile Partnership (AMTEX) was formed, in part to create electronic communication linkages among wholesale and retail companies throughout the textile industry for the purposes of facilitating product manufacturing processes and meeting consumer demand. Potential importers of US textiles may wish to contact AMTEX and the US Department of Commerce (DOC) for referrals to textile industry associations and individual companies. The DOC supports a comprehensive export development program, which includes seminars held domestically and trade shows and missions abroad.

Some Hot Items:

- acrylic fiber
- broadwoven fabrics
- carpeting
- cotton
- curtains
- high-performance fabrics (fire retardant fabrics, protective fabrics, sports apparel, skiwear, and other similar products)
- knit fabrics
- nylon
- polyester
- rayon
- spandex
- spun yarns
- wool

TOYS

Although the US toy industry has experienced stiff competition at home from foreign-made products, its exports have actually doubled since 1989. A large percentage of these exports represents high value-added video games. Substantial numbers of dolls and toy parts are also exported to US subsidiaries located abroad for assembly and packaging. Although big name US toy companies dominate this export market, smaller companies are also active, especially those producing innovative specialty or educational toys.

Some Hot Items:

- action figures
- balloons
- balls
- board games
- carriages and strollers
- checkers and checkerboards
- chessmen and chessboards
- construction sets
- dolls and accessories
- dollhouses and furniture
- kites
- marbles
- models and model kits
- paint sets
- puzzles
- rocking horses
- science kits (microscopes, chemistry sets, and similar products)
- stuffed toys
- toy cars and trucks
- toy guns (particularly air rifles and pistols)
- video games

VEHICLES AND PARTS

In the past decade, the US has made significant improvements in the quality of its motor vehicles and parts. Both large auto manufacturers and supply companies have upgraded their products and strategies. As domestic market saturation increases, companies are looking for export opportunities; consequently, many are working to enhance the international appeal of their products in terms of quality and price. Special considerations include the production of vehicle parts that can be used in a range of different models and of vehicles that are less polluting.

Some Hot Items:

vehicles
- buses

- heavy-duty trucks
- light trucks
- passenger cars

vehicle parts
- air conditioning equipment
- automotive stampings
- body frames
- bumpers
- brakes
- camshafts
- carburetors
- chassis (automotive and truck)
- clutches
- electrical equipment
- exhaust systems

- filters (oil, fuel, and air)
- fuel systems
- horns
- lighting equipment
- piston rings
- pistons
- power steering equipment
- radiators
- shock absorbers
- steering mechanisms
- storage batteries
- transmissions (automatic and standard)
- valves
- wheel alignment equipment
- wheels

OPPORTUNITIES FOR EXPORTING TO THE US

Although the sheer size of the US economy makes it the largest trading nation in the world, and although it is in many ways a consumer-driven society, the large trade deficit that opened up in the US during the 1980s has made the country more protective of its domestic manufacturers as they struggle to maintain their share of world markets. Nevertheless, the US consumer still looks for the highest quality goods at the lowest possible price, opening the door to opportunities for overseas firms to export products to the US. High labor costs in the US make its domestic markets vulnerable on grounds of cost to imports from countries with low labor and overhead costs. In addition to motor vehicles and parts, the US imports a great deal of machinery, clothing and footwear, and agricultural products, among others.

CONSTRUCTION MATERIALS AND EQUIPMENT

To meet the demands of a huge domestic construction industry, the US imports substantial quantities of materials. Of particular note are imports of cement, ceramic wall and floor tiles, and plumbing fixtures—all of which far outnumber US exports of similar products. Flat glass and gypsum products are also major import categories, but exports of these usually exceed imports. Plastic materials are becoming more widely used in plumbing—not only for pipes, but also for sinks, tubs, and other fixtures—and there is a growing trend toward plumbing mechanisms that conserve water. Although the overall percentage of the US population that can afford to purchase a home has fallen during the past 15 years, more than 1 million new housing starts are made each year. The US office building construction market has declined, following the boom in the 1980s. Government construction projects have grown modestly through the 1990s; such projects depend largely on the availability of public funds for infrastructure repair and improvement. A substantial market also exists for remodeling of and improvements to existing structures.

Some Hot Items:
- aerial work platforms (hydraulic, electric, and truck or carrier mounted)
- airport construction machinery
- backhoes
- bathtubs
- blades for graders, scrapers, bulldozers, and snow plows
- cement
- bulldozers
- ceramic wall and floor tile
- concrete mixers
- cranes
- dredging machinery
- excavators
- flat glass
- flush tanks
- insulation materials
- kitchen sinks
- plumbing fixtures
- power shovels
- road construction and maintenance machinery
- roofing equipment
- spas and hot tubs
- toilets

ENVIRONMENTAL EQUIPMENT

US demand for air pollution control and solid waste treatment and disposal technologies is ex–

pected to continue to grow. In the US the chemical and allied products, petroleum and coal, paper and allied products, and the primary metals industries account for 75 percent of all money spent on environmental equipment. The US is the world's largest producer and consumer of environmental goods, exporting far more than it imports. To break into this market, exporters to the US will have to offer products and services that match or exceed those already available domestically. Opportunities also exist for supplying parts to US firms for use in such equipment. Although considered a world leader in environmental regulation, the US has not taken the lead in drafting international standards. Equipment standards tend to be fragmented, differing from industry to industry and state to state. Efforts are now underway in the US to rectify this situation, making compliance across state boundaries easier for an overseas supplier seeking to enter US markets coast to coast.

Some Hot Items:
air pollution control
- catalytic reducers
- electron beam controls
- electrostatic precipitators
- fabric filters
- mechanical collectors
- scrubbers

solid waste recycling
- compactors
- hazardous waste cleanup technology
- hazardous waste management systems
- incinerators
- landfill lining systems
- transportation vehicles
- waste conversion technology

water pollution control
- biological treatments
- chlorination
- chemical recovery or removal systems
- filters

FOOD AND LIVE ANIMALS

In 1993 US companies imported US$20.8 billion worth of processed foods and beverages. There will always be a large US demand for imported food products because of the immense size of the market. The demand for imports depends somewhat on the availability of domestically produced items, which in turn is affected by such factors as local weather conditions, labor difficulties, and pest infestations. For example, the 1994 rise in agricultural imports reflected the crop losses occasioned by the devastating floods in the Midwest the previous year. Imports arrive in the US from many countries across Europe,

Asia, North and South America, and Oceania. Canada (with 17.6 percent of the import market), Thailand (6.3 percent), France (5.2 percent), Australia (5.2 percent), and Mexico (4.9 percent) together account for nearly 40 percent of all food and related product imports. A particularly attractive growth opportunity is the export of ethnic specialty foods to the US for sale to the country's burgeoning immigrant population as well as to meet the trend among mainstream US consumers for more eclectic food products.

Some Hot Items:
- alcoholic beverages
- beer
- cereal
- cheese
- chocolate and cocoa products
- coffee (roasted)
- cookies and crackers
- dry, condensed, or evaporated products
- fish and seafood (canned, cured, fresh, or frozen)
- flour
- fruits (fresh or frozen)
- meat products
- nuts and seeds (salted and roasted)
- pickles
- rice
- salad dressings
- sauces
- soft drinks
- sugar (raw cane)
- specialty foods (canned or frozen)
- tea
- vegetable oil
- vegetables (fresh or frozen)

FOOTWEAR

The US imports the vast bulk of the footwear sold in its domestic markets. Nearly 76 percent of men's casual (nonathletic) and dress footwear sold in 1993 was imported, topped by imports of women's footwear, which amounted to 90 percent of sales. More than 1 billion pairs of nonrubber shoes and 565 million pairs of athletic shoes were imported in 1993. Annual per capita consumption of all kinds of footwear stands at 5.65 pairs. Although the US imports footwear from more than 90 countries, only a few provide substantial portions of imported goods. For nonrubber footwear, imports come primarily from China, with smaller market shares being held by goods made in Brazil, Indonesia, Taiwan, Korea, Italy, Thailand, Spain, and Hong Kong.

The trend in the US has been away from brand name footwear and toward products selected for functionality and comfort, as well as for style. Styles have shifted away from an athletic look to an outdoor look. Water resistant leathers predominate, and the demand for lightweight hiking and waterproof boots, outdoor crosstrainers, and sport sandals is on the rise. However, consumers have come to expect the same comfort features in all types of shoes—such as padded linings and insoles—that made athletic shoes so popular a decade ago.

Some Hot Items:
- athletic shoes
- dress and casual shoes for men and women
- hiking boots
- sandals
- slippers

FURNITURE

Furniture makers in the US produce most of the output for domestic market consumption. However, about 14 percent of home furniture and 7 percent of office furniture is imported from abroad. Household furniture imports come mostly from Taiwan, Canada, Italy, China, and Mexico. Canada supplies 50 percent of the US imported office furniture market.

The largest category of imported household furniture is made of wood; this is followed in popularity by metal and upholstered items. Home entertainment furniture is a growth area, spurred by the introduction of high-tech electronic entertainment centers with four or more electronic components, plus speakers and accessories that are sold as complete packages. Home and office furniture demands are generally determined primarily by construction markets, although office furniture manufacturers must consider the added factor of the frequent changes within the office environment necessary to keep up with technology and government labor laws and regulations. In addition, customer service and timely delivery are often more important to the success of office furniture importers than for firms that export home furniture to the US.

Some Hot Items:
- bed frames
- computer workstation furniture
- ergonomic chairs
- home entertainment furniture
- home office furniture
- mattresses
- sofa beds
- upholstered chairs and sofas
- wooden tables and chairs

HOUSEHOLD AUDIO AND VIDEO EQUIPMENT

About 70 percent of the US domestic household audio and video equipment market is supplied by imports. Products such as videocassette recorders (VCRs), digital audiotape recorders (DATs), and camcorders are made largely by a few companies in Japan and South Korea. Almost no VCRs, camcorders, tape players, recorders, radios, phonographs, or compact disc (CD) players are produced in the US. Household audio and video equipment arrive primarily from Japan, Mexico, Malaysia, South Korea, and China. Foreign suppliers are slowing down their recent policy of opening manufacturing facilities in the US, preferring instead to operate in the developing and low-cost labor economies of Mexico and East Asia.

The CD player has become the dominant component in virtually every audio system sold to US consumers, including both high-end component sets and low-end transportable "boom boxes." Sales of color televisions and videocassette recorders continue to set records, and growth potential can also be found in big-screen television, projection television, and home theater products. High-definition television is just being introduced into the US market.

Some Hot Items:
- amplifiers
- automotive loudspeakers and stereo systems
- big-screen televisions
- camcorders
- color televisions
- CD players (single and multi-disc)
- loudspeakers
- radios
- receivers
- "surround sound" technology in home theaters
- tape recorders
- videocassette recorders

HOUSEHOLD APPLIANCES

Overall, the US imports about 20 percent of its household appliances. However, imports supply 50 percent of the domestic market for several categories of small appliances, primarily because of the high labor content of these appliances. Major household appliances—including refrigerators and freezers, water heaters, dishwashers, clothes washers and dryers, and kitchen ranges and ovens—must meet new energy efficiency standards set by the US Department of Energy (DOE) in order to be sold in the US. Refrigerators and freezers must be free of chlorofluorocarbons (CFCs) in accordance with environmental regulations. The leading suppliers of appliances to the US are Mexico, China, Japan, South Korea, and Taiwan, in descending order.

Some Hot Items:
- air conditioners
- clothes washers and dryers
- coffee, espresso, and cappucino machines
- direct heating equipment
- dishwashers
- food processors
- freezers
- kitchen ranges and ovens
- refrigerators
- steam irons
- water heaters
- vacuum cleaners

JEWELRY

US demographics favor the jewelry industry. The older ranks of the baby boom generation have reached the ages of 45 to 54, while many more are 35 to 44 years of age; persons in these age groups are the top purchasers of jewelry. In addition to demographics, the US acceptance of the General Agreement on Tariffs and Trade (GATT) treaty is expected to have a very positive effect on jewelry imports by substantially lowering tariffs on these products. Although the jewelry market is not as large as other consumer markets, the US imports about 50 percent (US$3.5 billion) of its precious metal jewelry and about 32 percent (US$640 million) of its costume jewelry. Italy, Thailand, Hong Kong, and Israel are the leading suppliers of precious metal jewelry imports, and most costume jewelry imports are brought in from South Korea, China, and Taiwan.

Some Hot Items:

jewelry
- bracelets
- earrings
- necklaces
- pins
- rings

precious metals
- gold
- silver

LEATHER GOODS

Imports of leather products brought into the US increased about 6 percent in 1993, reaching nearly US$13.9 billion. Developing countries, including China, accounted for 71 percent of that total. (China itself was the dominant supplier by far, accounting for 41 percent of the total.) Suppliers in most developing countries maintain a substantial cost advan-

tage over US producers because leather goods are labor intensive products. Leather apparel, including shoes, accounts for the majority of imports. Although the US is the world's largest exporter of raw hides, it also imports about US$738 million worth of raw hides from more than 70 countries, including Argentina, Italy, the UK, Brazil, Uruguay, and Thailand.

Some Hot Items:
- belts
- gloves
- handbags
- jackets
- luggage
- shoes

LUBRICANTS AND FUELS

The US population relies heavily on automobiles, trucks, and airplanes, all of which require fuel and lubricants. These products are also sold for industrial, residential, and commercial use. Consequently, the domestic demand is immense. Imports supply 12 percent of the petroleum products consumed in the US market.

The demand for these products is expected to continue to increase through at least 1998. However, many companies are implementing fuel conservation programs, and the rise in total consumption is likely to be less than the growth of the US economy. An increase in the price of raw materials and in taxes on gasoline is also likely to act as a brake on consumer demand. The use of jet fuel is expected to increase at a faster rate than gasoline.

Some Hot Items:
- automotive gasoline
- automotive lubricants
- diesel fuel
- distillate fuel oils
- jet fuel
- kerosene
- machinery lubricants
- residual fuel oils

MACHINE TOOLS

The US market for machine tools is defined by technology and fluctuations in demand. Older machine tool technologies are on the decline, and new machine technologies are rising, especially those that involve electrical discharge machine (EDM) cutting and laser technology. The demand in the automotive industry will continue to increase, but demand is fading in the defense industry. The US imports about 40 percent of the machine tools purchased in the domestic market, with Japan and Germany supplying the largest share.

Some Hot Items:
- die-casting and extruding machines
- dies
- drilling and boring machines
- grinding, polishing, buffing, lapping, and honing machines
- jigs
- milling machines
- lathes
- punching, shearing, and bending machines
- pressing machines
- robotics
- screw and thread machines
- saws and sawing machines
- spinning and thread rolling machines

SPORTING AND RECREATIONAL GOODS

The US imports roughly 30 percent (about US$2.7 billion) of the sporting goods and recreational equipment consumed domestically. The US welcomes these products for two main reasons. First, market demand is high because of the growing popularity of health and fitness programs for all ages and sectors of the population. Second, the industry is labor intensive, so most sporting equipment can be produced more cheaply outside the US. Taiwan, China, and South Korea are the leading suppliers of US sporting goods. Less developed countries, such as China and Thailand, have recently been increasing their share of this import market. Exercise and fitness equipment, along with in-line roller skates, are among the fastest-growing product lines. Other sports with increasing participation rates include bowling, fishing, darts, and golf.

Some Hot Items:
- baseballs
- basketballs
- billiard and pool equipment and supplies
- bowling balls
- camping equipment and supplies
- darts and dartboards
- fishing tackle and equipment
- footballs
- golf equipment (bags, balls, carts, and clubs)
- hunting equipment, including sporting arms
- rowing machines
- skates (ice, roller, and in-line roller)
- skin diving equipment
- skis and skiing equipment (snow skiing, water skiing, and ski machines)
- soccer balls and equipment
- stair climbers
- stationary bicycles
- step aerobic machines

- tennis rackets and balls
- treadmills
- weights (lifting machines and free weights)

TOYS

Like sporting goods, toys can be produced much more cheaply outside the US. Consequently, nearly 70 percent of toys purchased in the US are imported. Traditional toys—such as dolls, toy trucks and automobiles, and small balls—will always be in demand, but video games continue to represent one of the largest growth areas. Video games account for 30 percent of all toy imports. Potential exporters should note that the US has stringent safety regulations for many toys.

Some Hot Items:
- action figures
- board games, puzzles, and models
- dolls and doll accessories
- electronic games and toys, including video games
- science kits (microscopes, chemistry sets, and similar items)
- toy guns
- toy musical instruments
- toy trains, planes, and automobiles

VEHICLES AND PARTS

The US imports more than US$62 billion worth of motor vehicles and more than US$24 billion worth of automotive parts and accessories. Four wheel drive sport vehicles, minivans, and light trucks are especially popular. As for automotive parts, automobile manufacturers are looking for more modular assemblies—systems of integrated components that can be installed into a vehicle as a complete separate unit—as well as common parts, those which are interchangeable between more than one model. The greatest opportunities in the US market are for products with features that address the efficiency, environmental, and safety concerns of US consumers, preferably for a competitively low price.

The US is also a strong market for bicycles. Cycling is on the rise and is becoming more competitive, as reflected in the growing number of bicycle routes, trails, and lanes being developed in many communities throughout the nation. About 42 percent of the bicycles purchased in the US are imported. The dynamics of the market changed and widened with the introduction of the mountain bike, prompting sales in a new sector and actually shortening the time within which many consumers sought replacements; this replacement cycle dropped from 5 to 3 years. This effect has leveled off with saturation of the market, but it demonstrates the potential opportunities in the US market for the sale of innovative and improved products. Japan and Taiwan supply the US with about 83 percent of the bicycles imported.

Some Hot Items:

automotive parts
- body components and frames
- brake systems and parts
- electrical equipment
- engines and parts
- steering systems and parts
- transmissions, drive assemblies, and parts
- wheels and parts

vehicles
- bicycles (mountain and racing)
- buses
- light trucks
- minivans
- passenger cars

OPPORTUNITIES FOR GROWTH

BUSINESS SERVICES

Demand for professional services—including accounting, advertising, auditing, bookkeeping, legal, management, and public relations services—will continue to increase, resulting in higher receipts and employment. Many companies have decided to focus on their principal activities, contracting with outside specialists to perform ancillary back office and other business activities. Opportunities are increasing for foreign firms to invest and specialize in such activities. However, because US practitioners represent the state of the art in many of these service areas—in both primary and backup services—US professional services firms are extremely competitive in the global marketplace.

One particular opportunity for foreign firms (as well as investors) is in the area of international trade consulting. As trade grows, there has been an explosion in the number and range of consultants serving the marketplace. The number of consultants has been increasing since the 1980s, when consulting grew constantly at double digit rates. As US economic interests focus more on exports, the need for consultants in international trade will grow.

CONSTRUCTION SERVICES

Many of the world's largest foreign construction contractors have entered the US market, but few have made significant inroads, except in limited specialized submarkets. In fact, most of these foreign contractors have bought US construction companies, although some of the largest of them have been establishing their own US operations. Foreign-owned construction firms won about US$8.9 billion in US construction contracts in 1992, down 28 percent from 1991 and 43 percent lower than the record US$15.5 billion in contracts secured in 1990. However, this slide is linked to the general slowdown in US construction and a lessened foreign participation in the US real estate sector during the early 1990s. As new construction activity picks up in the mid-1990s, opportunities should increase proportionally. Foreign-owned companies accounted for only about 4 percent of all construction contracts awarded in the US during 1992. Most of these foreign entrants are based in the UK, Germany, and Japan, although nearly a dozen other nations are represented.

ELECTRONIC INFORMATION SERVICES

Electronic information services will continue to grow in the US. The US government is encouraging the implementation of the National Information Infrastructure—known colloquially as the federal information superhighway—to connect homes, businesses, government agencies, universities, and medical facilities to a broadband communications network capable of offering video, voice, and data transmission. As things currently stand, most of the revenues in electronic information services come from business users of information for financial management, research, marketing, purchasing, and general business administration. Users of scientific, technical, and professional information are also important customers. The trend for the future will be to link more and more online users together, across professional disciplines, within the country as well as internationally. More foreign investment exists in electronic information services than in other related fields, such as data processing, network, and computer professional services.

ENERGY RESOURCES

The US energy market continues to provide solid opportunities for foreign investors because of perpetually strong demand. In fact, the overall economic well-being of the US depends on its ability to satisfy this demand for energy. While relying primarily on coal, crude oil, and natural gas, the US is also at the forefront in exploring renewable energy resources such as solar photovoltaic, wind, and geothermal energy.

Coal provides about 40 percent of US electricity. Foreign-affiliated producers accounted for approximately 24 percent of US coal production in 1991. European companies have become increasingly interested in US coal because the privatization of power generation in the UK and the elimination of production subsidies in such large traditional supplier countries as the UK and Germany may create substantial export opportunities for US coal over the long term.

The US produces about 6.7 million barrels of oil a day. Although an enormous amount, this represents a decline of about 200,000 barrels compared with 1993 average production. Consequently, US oil companies are looking to overseas exploration to replace dwindling reserves. As the demand for energy increases in many areas of the world, particularly in China and the rest of the Asia-Pacific region, opportunities for international petroleum companies to explore, develop, and produce crude oil and—to a lesser extent, given existing pricing structures—natural gas should increase rapidly. Thus, investment opportunities in US oil companies depend not only on the immense US demand for energy, but also on a growing global demand that is expected to drive up prices and returns.

Natural gas production will continue to be a priority for the US. Increased dependence on foreign oil, together with environmental concerns, have focused attention on plans to use natural gas to supply a greater portion of US energy requirements.

FINANCIAL SERVICES

The US financial system is the largest and most sophisticated in the world. The US offers a variety of formats, most of which are open to foreigners for use and investment.

The number of foreign bank offices in the US rose steadily throughout the past two decades, reaching 747 by the end of 1992; the number of foreign bank offices fell slightly to 720 in 1993. Nearly one-half of the offices are located in New York City, with most of the rest being located in California, Illinois, and Florida. Institutions from Japan, Canada, France, and the UK have the largest presences both in assets and number of banking offices in the US. Assets of foreign bank offices in the US have increased significantly in recent years, rising from US$198 billion in 1980 to US$865 billion in 1992, representing approximately one-fourth of US total banking assets.

The domestic financial environment has opened up opportunities for foreign financial institutions. The US savings and loan scandal of the 1980s and high US debt levels have lessened consumer confidence in US financial services. Opportunities are also growing in the financing and facilitation of international trade. Although some foreign banks have pulled back from US markets, others are taking the opportunity to expand their services.

Opportunities also exist in the huge, highly competitive US securities markets. Foreign interest in this sector has been tempered recently, following an inrush of outside firms into the market in the late 1980s and early 1990s. However, considerable opportunity exists for long-term players in the world's premier financial market.

INSURANCE

Foreign insurers will continue to expand in the largely unrestricted US insurance market. In 1991 foreign-owned insurers had sales of US$72.9 billion, up sharply due primarily to major foreign acquisitions of large US firms, from US$62.6 billion in 1990. Foreign-owned insurers also captured more than 11 percent of the US premium market. The US is the largest insurance market in the world, accounting for roughly one-third of premiums worldwide.

The US life insurance industry is financially sound, and long-term prospects for standard insurance and annuity products are good. By contrast, property and casualty firms—the other major sector of the insurance industry—have been particularly vulnerable recently. Hurricanes in the eastern US; floods in the Midwest; and earthquakes, fires, floods, and civil unrest in California have all hurt an industry whose ability to raise premiums is limited by overcapacity. However, as success in the industry is coming to depend more on ability to access capital, large overseas firms should find an increasing role in US markets.

The future of the US health insurance industry is still uncertain. Although government leaders and private citizens agree that health care reform is essential—because health care costs continue to rise at a rate far greater than inflation and are consuming an ever-greater portion of the domestic budget—the political battles for reform continue, and the exact impact they will ultimately have on health insurance companies remains unpredictable.

MANUFACTURING

Two main areas in the US manufacturing sector are creating the majority of opportunities for foreign investors who can sell the products themselves or sell the technological procedures by which the products are manufactured.

The US will continue to supply consumers with a vast array of manufactured goods, including automobiles and parts, computers, metalworking equipment, medical and dental tools and supplies, information and telecommunications equipment, and processed foods and beverages. Because much of the domestic market is saturated and affected by an increasing flow of imports, opportunities for growth in the US manufacturing sector will depend on how well its export operations are able to meet the consumer needs of developing countries, particularly those in Southeast Asia, Latin America, the countries of the former Soviet Union, and, especially, China. Those US companies that can supply those countries with manufactured goods of appropriate quality, features, and price levels—or the machinery to manufacture such goods—will represent a good opportunity for foreign investors.

Compared with workers in much of the rest of the world, the US worker enjoys a high rate of pay. Consequently, US manufacturers are often uncompetitive in more labor intensive products. For those products (like clothing) and, in fact, for all manufactured products, US companies are interested in technology that enables them to increase worker productivity. Foreign investors should find significant opportunities with such technology.

REAL ESTATE DEVELOPMENT

Although the real estate market itself has moved rather slowly in the opening years of the 1990s, the structure of the market has changed greatly with the growing popularity of real estate investment trusts (REITs). Those who traditionally invested in real estate can also invest in these securities—mostly organized along the same lines as mutual funds—that finance and hold real estate assets.

The real estate market is still recovering from the excesses of the market in the late 1980s. Center city office buildings continue to have a high vacancy rate (17.2 percent on average nationwide and ranging as high as 34 percent in some major markets during the third quarter of 1994). Investors have changed their tactics from trying to create a market for real estate, as was the case in the 1980s, to using demographics to identify and predict the market. Construction projects can be expected to follow such targeted approaches to a greater extent than in the past.

The continual increase in the use of technology will affect real estate ventures. Many industrial and office spaces have become technologically obsolete and will have to be either replaced or renovated. The trend toward greater dispersal of commercial office functions away from central city districts and closer to suburban areas is also providing a new area of opportunity.

Opportunities also exist in apartment buildings (a monthly turnover approaching 10 percent can make these a good investment), nursing homes (the age 55 and over group is the fastest growing sector of the US population), neighborhood shopping centers, and industrial warehouses (new technology for storing and shipping goods requires new buildings). Overinvestment in hotels resulted in overcapacity and a drop in prices, which hit a low point in the early 1990s. However, lodging is on the verge of an investment turnaround based on current, more realistic price levels. Other real estate opportunities may be seen in areas of the country—such as the Southwest—that have the greatest job growth.

PUBLIC PROCUREMENT

OPPORTUNITIES

US international procurement policy is rooted in the Buy American Act (BAA) of 1933, which was enacted as a response to a similar British policy during the Great Depression. The act basically required that all manufactured and nonmanufactured goods purchased for public use be produced in the US. However, since World War II the procurement policy of the US has been moving in the direction of greater openness. As part of the Tokyo Round of GATT, the Agreement on Government Procurement (AGP) was signed in Geneva in 1979 and incorporated into US law in 1981. As part of GATT-related attempts to lower or eliminate non-tariff barriers, the agreement attacked exclusionary public procurement policies. Many of the basic regulations that apply to public procurement in the US are set out in the Federal Acquisi-

tion Regulation (FAR). The 1994 Federal Acquisition Streamlining Act was designed to simplify acquisition procedures used by the federal government.

Purchases for the US government are made by (1) the Department of Defense (DOD), (2) civilian agencies, and (3) the General Services Administration (GSA). The GSA purchases information services, construction services, and office and transportation supplies for all units of the US government. The DOD and the civilian agencies purchase goods and services specific to their needs. The DOD is, by far, the largest US governmental purchaser of goods and services. In volume of procurements, it is followed, in descending order, by the Department of Energy (DOE), the GSA, the National Aeronautics and Space Administration (NASA), the Veterans Administration (VA), the Department of Transportation (DOT), and the Department of Agriculture (USDA).

Among the staggering array of goods and services that the US government purchases each year are the items found on the following abbreviated list.

- abrasive cleaning and sandblasting equipment
- accounting, calculating, and other office machines
- adhesives
- aerial delivery containers
- agricultural implements, supplies, and equipment
- air conditioning and air purification equipment
- aircraft parts—engines, fuel system components, etc.
- aircraft maintenance and repair equipment
- aluminum and aluminum alloys
- appliances
- athletic clothing and footwear
- atlases and maps
- audiovisual equipment
- baking and kitchen equipment
- bandages and surgical dressings
- barber shop equipment
- batteries
- beds, bedding, mattresses, and related items
- books and pamphlets
- boxes
- brooms and brushes
- cabinets
- cable
- cameras and photographic equipment
- cement
- chemicals
- cleaning compounds and preparations
- clothing
- communication equipment
- computers
- concrete
- construction services
- containers
- cutlery and flatware
- cutting and forming tools for metalworking
- data processing equipment
- demolition equipment
- dishes
- drafting instruments and tables—surveying and mapping
- earth moving and excavating equipment
- electrical supplies and lighting fixtures
- engines and engine parts
- fabrics
- fans
- fencing
- film
- filters
- fire control equipment
- flags and pennants
- food and beverages
- footwear—leather and rubber
- fuels and oil
- furnaces and heating equipment
- furniture
- garbage disposal machines
- generators
- glass
- highway maintenance equipment
- inks
- infrared equipment
- instruments—chemical analysis, electrical and electronic measuring and testing, medical, dental, navigational, and optical
- laboratory equipment and supplies
- laundry equipment
- luggage and leather goods
- machine tools
- medicine, medical supplies, and medical equipment
- metals and metalworking equipment
- military arms, ordnance, ammunition, munitions, and equipment
- mirrors
- nets
- office equipment, furniture, and supplies
- packaging materials
- paints
- paper
- pens—fountain and ballpoint
- personal safety equipment
- pest control agents
- prefabricated buildings
- protective equipment—chemical, biological, and radiological
- radar equipment
- radio communications equipment
- radios, television sets, and sound reproducing equipment
- recording equipment—audio and video
- refrigeration equipment
- roofing materials
- rope, twine, and cordage
- rubber fabricated materials
- safety glasses
- scaffolding equipment
- services—air cargo, architectural consulting, design, janitorial, management, technical, engineering, and translation
- stationery and supplies
- structural steel
- tile
- tobacco products
- tools—hand and power
- tripods
- vacuum cleaners

- vehicles and parts
- veterinary supplies and equipment
- watches
- welding equipment
- wire—electrical and nonelectrical
- wood products
- X-ray equipment

PUBLIC PROCUREMENT PROCESS

Businesses interested in selling goods to the US government should contact individual agencies directly for information on procedures and the types of goods that may be needed. Each military and civilian agency publishes its own separate publication to guide potential suppliers. There are also a number of general publications available from the US Government Printing Office (GPO) including: *Commerce Business Daily* (CBD), *Federal Acquisition Regulations* (FAR), *Selling to the Military, Standard Industrial Classification Manual,* and the *US Government Manual.*

US Government Printing Office (GPO)
Superintendent of Documents
Washington, DC 20402-9371, USA
Tel: [1] (202) 512-1800
Fax: [1] (202) 512-2250

Procurement contracts are also available from state and local government agencies, most of which purchase through a centralized authority which distributes supplies to various departments. For potential opportunities, a suppliers should contact the state and local agencies directly and request information on the types of contracts available and the purchasing process. Most state and local agencies also produce periodic publications that include procurement contract bid opportunities or publish bid notices in local newspapers.

Issues Common to Most Agencies

Although it is important to work with individual agencies, each of which may have its own special requirements, there are considerations and procedures that will be common to all areas of federal government procurement; these are set forth below.

Identify commodities and contacts. Check the list of goods and services purchased by procurement officials to determine what government agencies are buying. This can be done by contacting the agencies directly or by monitoring the *Commerce Business Daily* (CBD). The CBD is a daily government publication that lists all federal procurement requisitions of an amount estimated to be greater than US$25,000. However, note that some specialty programs and requisitions involving national security issues may not be listed.

List your firm on bidders' lists. Send your company's capability statement to any agency you think could be a potential customer. Use the statement to provide prospective clients with a written summary of your capabilities and a business card. The summary should consist of a brochure or a 1- or 2-page narrative specifying what you are selling, where you are located, plus a listing of previous customers as references; be sure to include addresses and phone numbers for your references. Items you are selling should be identified by standard industrial classification code numbers; these are listed in the *Standard Industrial Classification Manual.*

Market aggressively. Once a buying office has received your capability statement, follow up with a telephone call and, if possible, make an appointment to visit the office or meet with a representative. Professionalism and timeliness are key factors to stress in marketing. Call your contacts periodically to remind them of your products and services and to keep on top of changes in personnel, needs, or procedures. Find out how often your service or product is purchased; how many firms are on the bid list; and how often the bid list is rotated. Try to find a need and fill it, or create a need and sell it. The idea is to be needed and to be the first supplier in the mind of the purchasing officer when a need arises.

Small Purchases

Small purchases may provide a "foot in the door" for businesses seeking government contracts for the first time. Small purchases involve simplified purchasing procedures, which decrease administrative costs and increase the opportunities for small business concerns to obtain a fair proportion of government contracts. The simplified acquisitions threshold, below which all procurements are defined as small purchases, has recently been raised to US$100,000 from US$25,000. Note that purchases of goods and services by the US government below this US$100,000 level are reserved for firms defined as small businesses. However, if at least two small businesses cannot be found to compete for the contract, other options will be considered.

Large Purchases

In large government procurement purchases, two methods are used to award contracts. Each method has its advantages and prerequisites. The CBD synopsis will specify which contracting method is being used by the government, and the solicitation package sent to potential contractors will provide additional instructions for submitting bids or proposals. The two types of contracting methods are sealed bids and contracts by negotiation.

Sealed Bids Many procurement contracts are assigned through the sealed bid system, which is a highly structured method of contracting that requires companies to prepare and submit written competitive bids. These bids are then opened publicly, all at one time. The law mandates certain conditions for acceptance of a bid, which include not only the amount of the estimate, but also the business history of the bidder, the bidder's record of performance and solvency, and the bidder's hiring practices—that is, compliance with all labor, affirmative action, and antidiscrimination laws. All of this information must be presented in writing; the sealed bid system does not allow for additional discussion and negotiation with the bidder. Sealed bidding can be used only if a government agency can provide potential bidders with definitive specifications and sufficient lead time for preparation of the bid.

Contracts by Negotiation The contracts by negotiation process is designed to provide flexibility in filling procurement requirements when sealed bidding is not feasible. It allows agencies to select alternative methods for finding suppliers and acquiring goods and services at fair and reasonable prices. The advantage of this negotiation process is that agencies and suppliers can reconsider proposals, discuss alternative approaches, and arrange more flexible contract arrangements.

Tips for Winning Large Procurement Contracts Review the functions of the government agencies and target those that will most likely be interested in your products or services. Request from the targeted agencies any information that they can send you regarding their purchasing procedures and the office (and, if possible, the person) responsible for processing purchases and finding potential suppliers. Also search federal, state, and local government directory listings for contact information on purchasing offices.

Prepare to market your product and services to potential purchasers by doing your homework—learning everything you possibly can about the needs of the consuming agencies. Obtain from the agencies or from public records, if available, information on past contract awards, quantities, and costs for similar products or services. Review the financial status, business and hiring policies, production efficiency, and other features of your own operation to ensure that it can qualify as a government supplier.

Market your business directly to potential purchasers and agencies. In addition, give your company a competitive edge by exhibiting at trade shows and sending representatives to procurement conferences. Keep up with government and trade publications, and consider contributing articles or columns on industry trends and innovations to get your name known. Join professional associations and civic organizations for the opportunities such groups offer to meet people in government and industry. Purchasing offices often use trade publications, conference

directories, and membership lists of organizations to identify potential procurement sources.

FOREIGN TRADE ZONES

Foreign trade zones (FTZs) are areas established under US jurisdiction, usually at a port of entry, that are officially considered outside US Customs territory. In practical terms this means that merchandise can be landed, stored, handled, and otherwise manipulated in an FTZ without being subject to US Customs requirements and duties until it leaves the FTZ for official entry into the US. Items that are reexported following storage or manipulation in the FTZ and that never officially enter US territory pay no duties or taxes. Thus, FTZs offer many opportunities to international traders—both importers and exporters—doing business with the US. In 1994 there were 202 FTZs and 269 approved FTZ subzones—zones operated by and for a single firm—in the US.

Goods may remain in the FTZ for an unlimited time, and goods may even be transferred from a customs bonded warehouse to an FTZ for further storage after the warehouse holding period limit has expired. Traders can save on shipping and transport costs because they can ship merchandise in one form to save costs, altering or repackaging it to reduce the duty owed prior to Customs entry. Goods may also be processed and upgraded to meet requirements of various federal regulatory agencies prior to entry. The posting of a bond for storage, manipulation, or manufacture is not required for goods in an FTZ, nor are bonds required for licenses, permits, or other documents missing at the time of arrival: you may keep your merchandise in the FTZ until the necessary entry documents or copies are obtained. Even goods in excess of quotas may be held in an FTZ until the next quota period, and goods subject to a quota may, under certain circumstances, be changed or manufactured in the FTZ into an item which is not subject to a quota. Goods may also be stored in an FTZ while awaiting an advance classification opinion from Customs; samples from the shipment may be withdrawn in order to obtain such a ruling.

Traders can use negotiable warehouse receipts as collateral to borrow on goods stored in an FTZ. Goods may be sold or auctioned directly from the FTZ; if title to the goods is transferred before entry into US Customs territory, the purchaser becomes responsible for the payment of duties and excise taxes when they are entered. Goods may be exhibited for an unlimited period without bond; sales—both retail and wholesale—may be made from such stock. Goods in an FTZ are under the protection of federal laws, and security is usually considered superior to many other port and warehouse facilities. Foreign and domestic merchandise may be brought into the zone for combination into a new article, on which only the duty attributable to the imported portion is due. Items related to the transport and handling of goods—such as ship stores, aircraft supplies, and maintenance equipment and supplies—can be brought in and released as needed. Invoices do not have to be complete until your goods are sold and withdrawn from the FTZ.

These are only some of the possibilities offered by FTZs. For a more detailed discussion of FTZs and procedures for using them, refer to the "Foreign Trade Zones" chapter.

Foreign Investment*

INVESTMENT CLIMATE AND TRENDS

Roots of US Policy Toward Foreign Investment

Foreign investment has played an integral role in the development of the US since its earliest days as a nation. Capital from Europe funded much of the infrastructure and industry of the new country following its independence, and foreign investment continued vigorously throughout the 19th century. English bondholders funded the construction of the Erie Canal in 1817, and British, French, and Dutch interests financed the era of railroad expansion across the US during the 1880s. By the turn of the century, Scottish, English, French, German, and other investors had acquired substantial real estate holdings in Florida, Iowa, Maine, New York, Pennsylvania, Texas, and other states as they speculated in US agricultural, ranching, and oil properties.

World War I changed the European creditors into debtors. Many European countries liquidated their US investments accumulated during the preceding century to pay for wartime supplies of US wheat, cotton, oil, munitions, and other commodities. More-over, following World War I and through the close of World War II (between 1918 and 1945), the US experienced a period of economic nationalism, during which foreigners and foreign investment became targets for political attack. The Trading with the Enemy Act, which provides for confiscation and retention of enemy alien property, was enacted during World War I, invoked again in World War II, and technically remains in effect today. This statute currently serves as the basis for the Foreign Assets Control Regulations and the Transactions Control Regulations, which regulate trade and investment with Cuba, North Korea, Vietnam, Libya, Iran, Iraq, and other nations that have limited or no diplomatic relations with the US.

Following World War II, the US entered into a series of bilateral agreements (Standard Bilateral Treaties of Friendship, Commerce, and Navigation, or FCN treaties), which provide that business entities operating in the US that are owned or controlled by citizens of the foreign signatory will have the same rights as entities controlled by US citizens. The US has FCN treaties with a number of countries, including Japan, Germany, France, the Netherlands, and Italy.

Attraction or Protection—The Seesaw Principle

Although the US experienced significant growth in its overseas investments following World War II, it developed a chronic balance of payments deficit during the 1960s. At that time, the nation began taking steps to limit outflows of US capital and to encourage inflows of foreign capital through such measures as the imposition of an excise tax on US purchases of foreign securities and the promotion of sales of US securities to foreign purchasers. Voluntary restraints and a series of regulations and controls on direct investment by US citizens and corporations outside of the US followed in the late 1960s.

---

* By Duane H. Zobrist and Stephen L. Bradford. Copyright © 1995 Carlsmith Ball Wichman Case & Ichiki. Reprinted with permission of that law firm.

During the early 1970s, US securities and properties became increasingly attractive to foreign purchasers because of the generally depressed prices of US corporate securities and the decline of the value of the dollar in international exchange markets. A dramatic rise in foreign investment in the US during 1973, coupled with reports of several large acquisitions by foreign interests, provoked the concern of US citizens over whether US natural resources could fall completely under foreign control. Within three or four years, Japanese investors had sunk more than US$200 million into investments in the tourist industry in Hawaii and into agricultural land in the Midwest, while Canadian and British interests had accomplished multimillion dollar takeovers of oil, tobacco, and other US industry leaders, sparking public concern and leading to investigative and protective actions by the US Congress. Preliminary government studies indicated that information about foreign investment was generally inadequate. Because it lacked specific regulations covering most foreign investment and maintained no currency restrictions on the repatriation of investment funds, the US had not collected data on foreign investment in any systematic fashion.

Legislative inquiries resulted in the passage of such bills as The Foreign Investment Study Act of 1974 (FISA) and The International Investment Survey Act of 1976 (IISA), along with the establishment by the president of the Committee on Foreign Investment in the United States (CFIUS) in 1975. The purposes of FISA, IISA, and CFIUS were primarily to provide the federal government with authority to collect data for regular statistical surveys and to provide analyses of that information for government and public use. Disclosure requirements were added by subsequent legislation in the late 1970s. While stressing that US policy continued to support an open investment policy and fair and nondiscriminatory treatment of foreign investors, the US put in place the means to follow and potentially to regulate such investment.

In the 1980s, the world market witnessed another surge in foreign direct investment in the US. Several factors contributed to this increase:

- Deregulation of domestic capital markets and cross-border financial transactions by major industrial nations, especially Japan, France, and Italy.
- Continued liberalization of regulations on foreign direct investment in financial and insurance services.
- Depreciation of the US dollar since the mid-1980s.
- Desire by foreign multinational corporations to enter the large US market through cross-border mergers and acquisitions.

- Threat of additional US import restrictions and voluntary export restraints, factors that may have encouraged multinational enterprises to make strategic acquisitions and to establish US facilities in several industries—for example, Japanese investments in the automotive assembly and the ferrous metal industries.

Free Trade Trends During the late 1980s and early 1990s, the US government generally pursued investment and trade policies designed to promote a free world market. In November 1993, the US became a signatory to the North American Free Trade Agreement (NAFTA). Under NAFTA, Canada, Mexico, and the US established a free trade area in which tariff and non-tariff barriers to trade in goods and services will be virtually eliminated; conditions of fair competition within the free trade area will be promoted; investment opportunities within the free trade area will be increased; intellectual property rights will be protected and enforced; and a framework for further cooperation to enhance the free trade objectives of the agreement will be created. (Refer to the "Trade Agreements" chapter for further details about NAFTA.)

One year later, in November 1994, the US signed a pledge to pursue a similar trade accord with 17 other Pacific Rim countries participating in the Asia Pacific Economic Cooperation forum (APEC). The signatories to this APEC Accord pledged to cooperate in creating a free trade zone among them in removing tariff and non-tariff barriers within the next 25 years. In December 1994, the US and 33 other countries meeting at the Summit of the Americas agreed to create a Free Trade Area of the Americas, setting 2005 as the deadline for completing negotiations.

Central to President Clinton's international economic agenda was the US ratification of the General Agreement on Tariffs and Trade (GATT) Uruguay Round in December 1994. Key provisions of the Uruguay Round of GATT will reduce and equalize tariffs around the world; ease the access of service firms such as accounting, banking, and advertising companies into global markets; strengthen enforcement of copyright and similar laws to enhance worldwide protection of intellectual property rights; cut certain agricultural subsidies; and create the World Trade Organization as the successor to GATT. (Refer to the "Trade Agreements" chapter for further discussion of GATT.)

However, President Clinton's international economic agenda now faces opposition from a Congress controlled by leaders of the opposing US political party. In addition, the highly publicized surge in foreign investment in the US during the late 1980s has caused some US politicians to use foreign investment as a scapegoat for the trade deficit that the US runs with its trading partners. Political observers anticipate that those who question more liberal trade policies and who link those trade policies with foreign investment will continue to voice opposition to such investment. Thus far, new foreign investment in the 1990s is well below the levels reached in the late 1980s (attributable in large part to recessions affecting Europe and Japan), but direct and portfolio foreign investment is expected to remain both an important factor in the US economy as well as a significant political issue during the next few years.

LEADING FOREIGN INVESTORS

Size of Foreign Investment According to preliminary estimates by the US Department of Commerce (DOC), new foreign investment increased sharply in 1993 after declining during 1989 through 1992. Outlays by foreign investors for the acquisition and establishment of US business enterprises made directly and through existing US affiliates in 1993 reached US$26.2 billion, representing an increase of 71 percent from US$15.3 billion in 1992. The total assets of US businesses acquired or established by foreign direct investors in 1993 amounted to US$97.1 billion, up from US$35.7 billion in 1992. (These numbers are based on filings made by US business enterprises that had total assets of more than US$1 million or that owned at least 200 acres of US land in the year during which they were acquired or established, and differ from figures derived using other sources and methods.)

Origin of Foreign Investment The United Kingdom (UK), Japan, the Netherlands, Canada, France, and Germany have been the dominant sources of foreign direct investment in the US. Together, these countries accounted for roughly 90 percent of the new foreign investment made from 1985 to 1991. Japanese direct investment more than doubled, and French investment increased by more than 50 percent during this period.

However, UK investment increased substantially during 1993, reflecting in part the recent economic recovery in the UK, while Japanese investment in the US continued to drop. In 1993, European countries accounted for US$17.1 billion, or 65 percent, of total investments. Of that amount, US$9 billion was from the UK, US$3.1 billion was from Germany, and US$1.5 billion was from the Netherlands. Canadian investment of US$4 billion constituted 15 percent of total investments. Japanese investment was US$1.8 billion, down from US$2.9 billion in 1992, and only a fraction of its peak level in 1990, when Japanese firms held US investments of US$19.9 billion. The decline in Japanese investment has been attributed to a sluggish economy and reduced corporate profits in Japan, disappointing returns from prior US investments (mainly in high-dollar value real estate transactions),

and continued reluctance among banks to finance new investments.

Sectors of Foreign Investment Of the US industrial sectors in which businesses were acquired or established by foreigners in 1993, manufacturing (at US$12.4 billion) was the largest target. Other sectors of the economy that experienced substantial new investment were chemicals (US$5.7 billion), machinery (US$2 billion), and metals, food, and related products (US$1.4 billion). Services accounted for US$3.9 billion in foreign investment outlays, primarily in the motion picture and television, computer service, and hotel industries.

INVESTMENT POLICIES AND VEHICLES

In general, a foreign business operating in the US is free from many of the governmental licensing and other restrictions common in other countries. The federal government does not require registration of capital, and foreign investors may freely remit profits, dividends, interest, borrowed funds, or other income from the US to their home countries or to third-party nonresidents. One notable exception is that a Treasury Department license is required for the repatriation of capital to certain countries— including North Korea, Vietnam, Kampuchea, and Cuba—or to the nationals of such countries.

Disclosure Requirements

Although no limits are imposed on direct investment, federal statutes do require that foreign individuals and enterprises file reports and returns with various US government agencies in connection with investments made in the US . (*See* the "Regulatory Agencies and Committees" section of this chapter.) These filings include financial returns to the Internal Revenue Service (IRS) and reporting information to agencies—including the DOC—that study the domestic impact of foreign investment. The stated purpose of these federal statutes is to compile data, not to restrain or deter direct foreign investment in the US.

Forms of Investment

Foreign individuals and enterprises can invest or engage in business in the US in several basic ways: through direct investment in a US business enterprise; acquisition of debt or equity securities; and acquisition through other investment vehicles, such as real estate investment trusts (REITs) and third-country corporations. Investment structures may also combine one or more of the forms identified above. In addition, foreign individuals should consider the application of US gift and estate taxes in structuring their US investments. (Refer to the "Taxation" chapter.)

Direct Investment Foreign direct investment is generally defined by the DOC as the acquisition of at least 10 percent of the voting interest or control of a US business enterprise. The nonresident alien or foreign corporation that directly invests or conducts business in the US will be subject to the same tax regime as any other US business. (Refer to the "Taxation" chapter.)

One advantage of a direct investment is that it may be relatively simple to implement and, in the case of a portfolio investment, relatively risk-free—that is, the investor is not directly undertaking business activities that are likely to create third-party claims, which could place other assets at risk. Furthermore, to the extent that the foreign investor can structure the investment so as to earn tax free interest or tax free capital gains, the US tax liability may be minimized or entirely eliminated.

The most common method of foreign direct investment has been acquisition of the shares of an existing US corporation or formation of a new US corporation. Foreign interests that are contemplating investments in several lines of business in the US should consider creating a holding company, with separate subsidiaries for each investment or enterprise undertaken.

Partnerships Conducting business through a US partnership can offer significant flexibility, particularly under the current US income tax structure. For US tax purposes, a partnership is not recognized as a separate taxable entity. Unless the partnership agreement provides otherwise, all partners share profits and losses equally. Although the partnership must compute taxable income and file a US tax return, the return is filed for information purposes only and the partnership, as a separate entity, does not pay a tax. Instead, income, deductions, and losses are passed through the partnership to the partners and are taken into account with similar items that a partner derives from other sources. For this reason, foreign partners who have other US effectively connected income may find the partnership form of business beneficial. Participation in a partnership generally enables the investor to apply partnership losses and deductions against such other income (subject to limits such as the passive activity loss rules) in computing the investor's US taxable income. Also, the partnership form eliminates the double tax effect of the corporate form of investment in which tax is first imposed on corporate income and then imposed again through withholding on the dividend to the foreign investor.

When a partnership is engaged in a US trade or business, its foreign partners will also be treated as engaged in that US trade or business and will be subject to US tax at the graduated tax rates on their share of partnership income effectively connected with the US. A foreign investor in a US partnership is required to file a US income tax return. Foreign investors in a limited liability company (LLC) that is characterized according to government definitions as a partnership rather than as an association taxable as a corporation may also benefit from the flow-through tax treatment of a partnership. Foreign corporations that become partners in a US enterprise must consider the application of the branch profits tax and the second tier dividend withholding tax rules. (Refer to the "Business Entities & Formation" and "Taxation" chapters for more detailed information.)

Investment Through Debt Securities Investment through the use of debt instruments has become increasingly popular in recent years. As a result of the elimination of the US withholding tax on portfolio interest, the obligations of certain US firms which meet the statutory portfolio investment requirements can be sold in international markets without imposition of the US withholding tax. To avoid paying the withholding tax, foreign investors must remember to furnish Form W8 to the issuer of the debt. A close watch should also be kept on the IRS proposal to require foreign investors in US securities to obtain taxpayer identification numbers. If this requirement is adopted, a foreign investor failing to comply may become subject to the withholding tax on interest and dividend payments—currently assessed at a 31 percent rate. Opponents of this proposal claim it will dampen foreign investment, but the position of the IRS is that issuance of a taxpayer identification number will ensure compliance with US tax laws and will increase the efficiency of what is now a burdensome paperwork procedure for verifying whether an investor is in fact exempt from withholding.

Mortgage investments are also becoming more prevalent. With such investments, the repayment of principal and interest is secured by one or more parcels of real estate or through the guarantee of a federal agency, such as the Government National Mortgage Association (GNMA).

A variety of unique and interesting investment vehicles—some of which may include conversion features and profit participation—are attracting growing numbers of investors. Although in most instances these investments are geared toward the passive investor, certain principles applicable to these arrangements may also be available in the context of a closely held enterprise. In some situations, parties who might otherwise consider the establishment of a partnership or joint venture might reconsider whether the investment could be structured through the use of debt instruments having some type of profit participation feature. Note that if the investment is in US real property, the participating debt will be considered a US real property interest (USRPI) and must be reported under the Foreign Investment in Real Property Tax Act of 1980 (FIRPTA).

Other Investment Structure Options Among other investment structure options are the use of REITs (securitized interests in a pool of real estate assets) and the use of third-country corporations. For many years, foreign investors who were not residents of a treaty country found that investing in the US by means of third-country corporations with more favorable treaty benefits was highly advantageous. The Netherlands and the Netherlands Antilles were popular choices. Recent US tax law and treaty changes have substantially reduced the potential for taking advantage of treaty benefits afforded to third-country corporations. Furthermore, current US tax policy is strongly focused against such "treaty shopping."

RESERVED AND RESTRICTED INVESTMENT ACTIVITIES

For the most part, foreign interests may own unlimited equity in a US business enterprise. Moreover, under NAFTA, Canada, Mexico, and the US have each agreed to treat investors from the other signatories no less favorably than its own investors with respect to the establishment, acquisition, expansion, management, conduct, operation, and sale or other disposition of investments.

However, foreign investors are subject to US laws that regulate transactions made within the US, regardless of whether made by US or foreign parties. In addition, certain investments that affect vital national resources or security interests may be prohibited, including the following.

- **Radio Communications** Foreign ownership may not exceed 20 percent in domestic radio communications.
- **Domestic Air Transportation** Foreign ownership may not exceed 25 percent in companies engaged in domestic air transportation, nor may foreign interests control more than one-third of the board of directors of such companies. Under NAFTA, a US air carrier must be under the actual control of US citizens. (Non-citizens may own and control foreign air carriers that operate between US and foreign points.) In addition, shipping vessels bearing a US flag must be wholly owned by US citizens or by domestic corporations controlled by US citizens.
- **Banking and Insurance** A multitude of federal and state regulations limit the foreign ownership of banks and insurance companies in the US.
- **Energy Resources** Energy resource enterprises—such as hydroelectric power compa-

nies or facilities that utilize nuclear materials—are subject to federal licensing restrictions on foreign involvement. Similarly, foreigners are ineligible for federal mining claim grants, nor may foreigners own oil or mineral leases, unless their home countries offer reciprocal rights to US citizens.

- **National Security** The US Department of Defense (DOD) and related agencies may impose restrictions on foreign participation in projects related to national security or involving access to classified information.
- **Nuclear Materials** Under NAFTA, a foreigner may not obtain a license to transfer, manufacture, produce, use, or import any facilities that produce or use nuclear materials.
- **Land Ownership** Limits on foreign ownership of land in the US arise most frequently in connection with agricultural land. The Agricultural Foreign Investment Disclosure Act of 1978 requires foreigners to provide certain information about investments in US agricultural land. Moreover, state disclosure laws may impose requirements similar to those imposed under federal law. Certain other federal statutory provisions—such as the Trading with the Enemy Act—may also limit a foreigner's ability to own or lease land in the US. In addition, foreign investors may be ineligible to obtain certain rights—such as water and grazing rights on federal land—and other federal benefits may be available only to landowners who are US citizens. In addition to federal limitations, some states impose restrictions on either the ownership or the inheritance of land by foreigners. Among some of these states, such limitations are further applied to aliens who are general partners in partnerships that own real property. The laws of some states may also limit or regulate indirect land ownership by foreign interests, such as acquisition of an interest in a limited partnership that owns land or of stock in a corporation that owns real property.

NON-TAX INVESTMENT INCENTIVES

Although the US federal government imposes certain import and export restrictions, as well as duties, quotas, and controls, its official policy is generally to encourage and promote free trade. Thus, the US continues to participate in GATT trade barrier reduction negotiations, and together with Mexico and Canada, it has created one of the world's largest free trade areas through NAFTA. The Clinton administration has also demonstrated its intent to continue

REGULATORY AGENCIES AND COMMITTEES

Foreign investors should be aware of the following federal agencies and committees that specifically review foreign acquisitions of US businesses. (*See* the "Useful Addresses" section of this chapter for information on contacting these groups.)

The Committee on Foreign Investment in the United States (CFIUS) The Exon-Florio provisions of the Omnibus Trade and Competitiveness Act of 1988 authorize the president of the US to investigate certain foreign acquisitions of US businesses and, if certain conditions are met, to block or require divestment of those transactions that may threaten or impair the national security of the US. The president has delegated to CFIUS the authority to determine when a proposed transaction warrants review, to conduct investigations, and to submit recommendations to approve, block, or divest transactions.

The parties to a proposed acquisition have no legal duty to file notice of the transaction with CFIUS. However, unless a notice is filed, the transaction will remain subject to government action indefinitely, including possible divestment, at the direction of the president. Unfortunately, no comprehensive list of criteria currently exists for determining whether a proposed transaction poses a significant threat to national security. Moreover, unlike Hart-Scott-Rodino antitrust filings, there is no minimum threshold exclusion for small transactions in connection with notice filings made pursuant to the Exon-Florio provisions. Therefore, any transaction that would result in foreign control of a US business engaged in interstate commerce that may conceivably be construed to threaten the national security of the US is potentially subject to review.

International Trade Commission (ITC) This commission determines, among other things, whether dumped or subsidized imports have caused, or threaten to cause, material injury or retardation to an identifiable US industry.

Agricultural Stabilization and Conservation Service (ASCS) Pursuant to the Agricultural Foreign Investment Disclosure Act of 1978 (AFIDA), as amended, reports of a foreign acquisition or transfer of any interest—other than a security interest—in US agricultural land must be filed with the ASCS office in the county where the land is located within 90 days of the acquisition. A foreign party will be deemed in violation of the AFIDA and subject to significant penalties if it fails to submit any required report, neglects to keep the information up-to-date in any submitted report, or submits a report that is incomplete or contains false or misleading information.

Although all reports filed under AFIDA are available for public inspection, a foreign investor who desires anonymity under AFIDA can achieve such through the establishment of three successive tiers of ownership between the investor and any US agricultural land. AFIDA grants to the US secretary of agriculture the authority to inquire as to the identity of the first three tiers of ownership over US agricultural land, but provides no authority for obtaining information regarding a fourth level owner.

US Commerce Department's Bureau of Economic Analysis The International Investment Survey Act of 1976 (IISA) requires that initial, quarterly, annual, and five-year benchmark reports, forms, and questionnaires be filed with the Bureau of Economic Analysis concerning a foreign party's ownership of 10 percent or more of the voting stock of a US corporation or of an equivalent interest in an unincorporated US "business enterprise," defined to include any ownership of US real estate. The failure to file any of the forms required by IISA may result in substantial fines, one year's imprisonment, or both.

Information collected pursuant to IISA is intended to be confidential for analytical and statistical purposes only. Nevertheless, foreign individuals may have justifiable concern for the confidentiality of any information supplied on IISA reporting forms. Forms BE-13 and BE-12 require the identification of the name and country of each party in the ownership chain of a foreign parent back to its "ultimate beneficial owner," defined as the first party, proceeding up the ownership chain beginning with the foreign parent, which is not more than 50 percent owned or controlled by another party. Because of concerns for the privacy of individual investors, recent amendments to the IISA regulations allow foreign parties to preserve anonymity by providing that when the ultimate beneficial owner of a business enterprise is an individual, only the individual's country of location need be revealed, not the individual's name.

Because the reporting requirements under IISA are

fairly complex and require substantial accounting analysis, they should be prepared and completed by a foreign investor's accountants and reviewed by legal counsel to determine that the substantive requirements of the Act have been met.

Internal Revenue Service (IRS) The Foreign Investment in Real Property Tax Act of 1980 (FIRPTA) added to the Internal Revenue Code (IRC) a new section that imposes a tax on certain dispositions of US real property interest (USRPI) by foreign investors. Motivated by concern over the ability of the US to collect this tax, the US government introduced a withholding tax system by adding Section 1445 to the IRC. In general, Section 1445 requires the transferee of a USRPI to withhold the lesser of 10 percent of the amount realized on the disposition or the transferor's maximum tax liability—that is, the maximum amount determined by the IRS that the transferor could owe on its gain from the sale, plus any prior unsatisfied withholding tax liability against the transferor's interest.

Note that the withholding of tax under Section 1445 does not excuse the foreign transferor from filing a US tax return, nor does it modify the transferor's liability for the full amount of the tax due. It simply ensures that the US government will be assured of receiving at least a portion of the tax to which it deems it is entitled.

The reporting provisions considered most troublesome to many foreign investors are those that require the disclosure of the personal identity of a foreign investor who holds US real property directly or indirectly through one or more holding entities. Foreign persons desiring to retain their anonymity may apply for an exemption from the reporting requirement of the Act by providing the IRS with such security as the IRS determines necessary to ensure payment of the putative US taxes that would be owed with respect to any disposition of a US real property interest. (Refer to the "Taxation" chapter for further discussion.)

Other Federal Agencies Foreign investors may deal with a number of additional government agencies depending on the nature and scope of their business endeavors. These may include the Federal Trade Commission (FTC) and the Department of Justice (DOJ), the Food and Drug Administration (FDA), the Occupational Safety and Health Administration (OSHA), the Environmental Protection Agency (EPA), the Equal Employment Opportunity Commission (EEOC), the Federal Communications Commission (FCC), and the Interstate Commerce Commission (ICC), among others. (Refer to the "Business Entities & Formation" chapter for a description of what these agencies regulate.)

the work toward a global free trade environment by concentrating its efforts on the implementation of the objectives of the APEC accord and by strongly supporting the proposed Free Trade Area of the Americas.

Foreign Trade Zones Pursuant to the Foreign Trade Zones Act of 1934, the US has designated special foreign trade zones that serve as secured areas outside of customs territories for the purpose of attracting and promoting international trade and commerce. Foreign exporters can forward their products to these zones to be held for an unlimited period while awaiting favorable market conditions in the US or in neighboring countries without being subject to customs entry, payment of duties, or posting of bonds.

Products lawfully brought into foreign trade zones may be stored, sold, exhibited, broken up, repacked, assembled, distributed, sorted, graded, cleaned, mixed with other foreign or domestic products, or otherwise manipulated. The resulting products may thereafter be either exported or transferred into US customs territory. Customs duties are pay-

able only on those products actually transferred from the zone into customs territories of the US. Products manufactured or produced in the US may also be taken into a foreign trade zone and, provided that their identity is maintained in accordance with certain regulations, returned to US customs territory free of quotas, duty, or tax, even if such products (subject to certain restrictions) have been combined with or made part of other products while in the zone. (Refer to the "Foreign Trade Zones" chapter for a further discussion of foreign trade zones.)

Tariff and Non-Tariff Elimination Under NAFTA A crucial goal of NAFTA is the elimination of import duties on goods that originate within North America. The treaty accomplishes this goal over a 15-year period, with duties removed on key categories of goods—such as computers and most automobiles—as of January 1, 1994, the effective date of the agreement. In addition, NAFTA eliminates many non-tariff restrictions among the signatories, including import licenses and quotas (although industries such as automobile and automobile parts, agriculture, textiles, and energy are exempted). (Refer to the "Trade Agreements" chapter for further details on NAFTA.)

State and Local Government Incentives Various state and local governments offer incentives from time to time to attract foreign investment. These are often negotiated for a particular project rather than standard statutory programs. Such incentives usually involve forgiveness or reduction of taxes for a specified period of time and may even include the issuance of tax free, tax advantaged, or publicly guaranteed debt to underwrite the investment. The nature of the incentives thus offered and the level of competitiveness of a particular jurisdiction depends on a wide range of individual circumstances, including the type and size of the proposed investment and current local conditions.

AVAILABILITY OF LOANS AND CREDIT

There is no legal or policy discrimination, either in the credit market or the capital market, between domestic and foreign businesses or between domestic and foreign investors. The US is the world's largest and most sophisticated financial market, and resources are readily accessible. However, financial institutions in the US may require documentation to be presented to comply with US standards and may charge a premium for services and funds. Although procedures are generally up to international standards, US financial practices and customs may differ from those in other countries. A foreign enterprise should obtain professional advice before seeking to finance business operations in the US.

The capital and credit markets in the US are large and sophisticated, and new financing techniques are constantly emerging. Commercial banks are the leading suppliers of credit, but many other sources are available. The more common means of financing available in the US include loans from banks and commercial finance companies, the issuance of commercial paper (by large recognized international entities), stock and bond financing, and loans from and equity investments by insurance companies and pension funds. (Refer to the "Financial Institutions" chapter.)

REAL ESTATE—COMMERCIAL AND INDUSTRIAL SPACE

Key Real Estate Team Members When developing a workable business plan, identifying an appropriate site, designing, constructing (if necessary) the required facility, and managing operations, foreign business firms locating in the US will need the assistance of an effective team of consultants. Of prime importance are accounting and legal advisors well-versed in real estate and tax laws and practices of the home country, as well as applicable US state and federal laws.

Another key member of this consultant team is the real estate broker. A broker can gather market information, locate potential sites, and advise principals in the negotiation of lease or purchase agreements. Real estate prices can vary dramatically across the US, and brokers in the US maintain and have access to detailed market data specific to their locale. Brokers should be able to provide information tailored to the particular price, size, location, labor, and marketing needs of the foreign business to be established. Brokerage firms that participate in so-called multiple listing services can introduce their clients to properties that are listed through other brokerage firms as well as their own listings, thereby providing their clients with a wider spectrum of market options. Brokers work according to commission arrangements that typically are based on the dollar value of the transaction.

Whether the foreign business is outfitting an existing space for its purposes (known as "tenant improvement" work) or is constructing space according to its specific needs (known as "build-to-suit" work), its principals will need the services of a licensed, bonded, and insured architect and a general contractor. Engineers (structural, mechanical, and civil), soil consultants, and space planners also are critical members of the real estate team. The nature, scale, and location of the project may dictate a need for many other professionals, such as a public relations and marketing consultant, acoustician, traffic analyst, and government lobbyist. Investors should be particularly careful to assess potential environmental problems. Property owners may become responsible for environmental damage even if they do not initiate the problem. Depending on a foreign investor's degree of familiarity with development matters, the investor may choose to have a real property project coordinated by an architect or general contractor acting as a project manager, or by a consultant who serves expressly as the project manager.

Owning Versus Leasing Property Foreign investors will need to decide whether to own or lease real estate for their business purposes. In making this determination, foreign businesspeople should consider certain limitations—such as those imposed under AFIDA and the Trading with the Enemy Act—on direct foreign ownership of US land described in the "Reserved and Restricted Investment Activities" section earlier in this chapter. Foreign investors may also not be able to obtain certain rights such as water and grazing rights on federal land, and other federal benefits may be available only to landowners who are US citizens.

In addition, certain states may restrict either the ownership or the inheritance of land by foreigners. In these state jurisdictions, such limitations may also apply to aliens who are general partners in a partnership owning real property because of the nature of a general partner's interest in the property of the partnership. The laws of some states may also limit or regulate indirect ownership of real property by alien interests, such as through ownership of an interest in a limited partnership that owns land or of stock in a corporation owning such property.

Depending on the nature of the transaction, lease terms may be negotiated to be long enough—for example, 99 years—to give the foreign lessee an interest that, for financing and other purposes, approximates ownership. In determining the appropriate length of a lease, the investor should consider the length of the business needs, the anticipated rent increases over the term of the lease, and the growth potential of the real estate market in the chosen location.

Title Insurance Standard business practice in the US dictates that purchasers of real estate, especially for commercial purposes, buy title insurance. A title insurance company researches local government land records to advise a prospective purchaser of past ownership interests, uses, and claims relating to the parcel of land in question. The company then issues an insurance policy guaranteeing the policy purchaser title to the property as stated in the policy description. The cost of the title insurance policy (which generally includes the cost of the research) is based on the dollar size of the transaction.

USEFUL ADDRESSES

Agricultural Stabilization and Conservation Service (ASCS)
PO Box 2415
Washington, DC 20013, USA
Tel: [1] (202) 720-5237, 720-3467
Fax: [1] (202) 720-5816

Association of Foreign Investors in US Real Estate
700 13th St. NW, Suite 950
Washington, DC 20005, USA
Tel: [1] (202) 434-4510
Fax: [1] (202) 434-4509

Committee on Foreign Investment in the United States (CFIUS)
15th St. and Pennsylvania Ave., NW
Main Treasury Building, Room 5100
Washington, DC 20220, USA
Tel: [1] (202) 622-1860

Customs Service NAFTA Info Line
Tel: [1] (202) 927-1692
Automated service that will send information directly to your fax machine.

SPACE AVAILABILITY AND COSTS

The US is in an interim phase with respect to real estate markets: it has just about worked through the glut of the late 1980s but has yet to begin the next up cycle. Substantial overbuilding during the boom years of the 1980s left the country with an oversupply of many types of commercial real estate. Many foreign investors also overpaid for properties across the real estate spectrum during that frenzied period, and several have been in the process of divesting themselves of their less successful purchases. Although prices have fallen considerably since the top of the market, few would currently characterize them as having fallen to bargain levels. Moreover, some available properties may no longer be suited for their intended uses given technological change during the past five years.

Nevertheless, persistent high vacancy rates have served to reduce rental rates in many markets across the US. During the third quarter of 1994, central business district commercial real estate vacancy rates averaged 17.2 percent nationwide, ranging from a high of 34.3 percent in Dallas to a low of 11.4 percent in Boston, among the major markets. This was slightly higher than non-central business rates, which averaged 17 percent nationwide and ranged from 25.4 percent in Los Angeles to 8.9 percent in the Bellevue, Washington area. Because of this now chronic situation, rental rates have generally been trending downwards, ranging from US$166.41 per square meter (US$15.46 per square foot—US real estate is quoted per square foot) in Houston to US$351.01 per square meter (US$32.61 per square foot) in Washington, DC for central business district commercial rental space in the third quarter 1994; average rates for major markets were around US$237.88 per square meter (US$22.10 per square foot). Similar space outside the central business district in the same markets ranged from US$156.08 per square meter (US$14.50 per square foot) in Houston to US$257.04 per square meter (US$23.88 per square foot in West Los Angeles; the average in third quarter 1994 was about US$207.10 per square meter (US$19.24 per square foot). Actual construction costs are generally estimated to be at least four to five times the level of rents.

Department of Commerce
Bureau of Economic Analysis
International Investment Division
1441 L St. NW
Washington, DC 20230, USA
Tel: [1] (202) 606-9805

Department of Commerce
Foreign Trade Zones Board
Main Commerce Bldg.
Washington, DC 20230, USA
Tel: [1] (202) 482-2862 Fax: (202) 482-0002

Department of State
Investment Affairs
Main State Building
Washington, DC 20520, USA
Tel: [1] (202) 647-1128
Fax: [1] (202) 647-0320

Department of the Treasury
Office of Foreign Assets Control
Main Treasury Bldg.
Washington, DC 20220, USA
Tel: [1] (202) 622-2510
Fax: [1] (202) 622-1657

Internal Revenue Service (IRS)
1111 Constitution Ave., NW
Washington, DC 20224, USA
Tel: [1] (202) 622-5000
Tel: (800) 829-1040 (taxpayer assistance and info)
Tel: (800) 829-3676 (tax forms and publications)
Fax: [1] (202) 622-8393

International Trade Administration
Trade and Economic Analysis
Main Commerce Bldg.
Washington, DC 20230, USA
Tel: [1] (202) 482-5145
Fax: [1] (202) 482-4614

Office of US Trade Representative (USTR)
600 17th St., NW
Washington, DC 20506, USA
Tel: [1] (202) 395-3230
Fax: [1] (202) 395-3911

US International Trade Commission
500 E St., SW
Washington, DC 20436, USA
Tel: [1] (202) 205-1000
Fax: [1] (202) 205-2798

Foreign Trade

INTRODUCTION

The USA, is a vast country with a wealth of resources. Although during the past 25 years or so it has shifted farther away from industrial and more toward service production, it remains a formidable producer and supplier on a worldwide scale of agricultural and industrial raw materials and intermediate and finished goods, and it is the world's foremost supplier of services. At the same time that the nation continues to play a major role as an exporter, the US—the world's largest economy—is also its number one consumer of imported products. Its total volume of international trade ranks it above every other country in the world, challenged only by Japan and Germany, respectively the world's second and third largest trading nations. (However, total US trade is 1.75 times that of Japan and 1.8 times that of Germany.) Since the 1960s, this propensity to trade—and consume—has also led the US to become the world's largest debtor nation, a status that continues to be fed by massive merchandise trade deficits.

CONTENTS

Statistical Note In an attempt to internationalize and standardize coverage as much as possible, we have used the CIF basis (cost, insurance, and freight, meaning that insurance and transport costs are added to the base value of the goods) for reporting trade statistics. This measure is becoming more generally accepted by international economists and is the one adopted for primary reporting by the International Monetary Fund (IMF) in its publications. The rationale for this is that the effective cost of an import is its landed cost; the added costs must be accounted for somewhere in the process; and these costs are usually borne by the importer. However, most US government entities—including the Bureau of the Census, which compiles official trade statistics—report FOB (free on board) or customs value figures which do not include the shipping charges included in the CIF figures. This decision was made on the grounds that such costs are for services rather than for goods; shipping charges do not constitute part of the base cost of the items imported; and comparisons with the cost of similar goods become difficult if these other costs are included. Exports are almost universally reported on an FOB or FAS (free alongside ship) basis, which eliminates consideration of the shipping costs, also on the grounds that such costs are usually borne by the importer. The addition of shipping costs to imports almost invariably results in larger overall trade figures and—because the additions are applied asymmetrically, that is to import values only—either larger balance of trade deficits or smaller surpluses. Some figures use available US government sources which report FOB values.

SIZE OF FOREIGN TRADE

Merchandise Trade

As measured by merchandise trade, US foreign trade has grown from a relatively modest US$46 billion in 1964—7.1 percent of gross domestic product (GDP)—to US$1.068 trillion in 1993 (16.7 percent of

US Exports by Commodity
(in US$ billions)

Commodity	1993	1992	% Change
Agricultural Commodities			
Vegetables and fruit	$6.0	$5.7	5%
Wheat	4.7	4.5	4
Soybeans	4.6	4.5	2
Corn	4.5	5.0	−10
Meat and preparations	4.3	4.2	2
Animal feeds	3.5	3.6	−3
Manufactured Goods			
Electrical machinery	$36.6	$32.1	14%
ADP equipment	27.1	27.0	0
Airplanes	21.3	26.3	−19
General industrial machinery	19.5	18.5	5
Power generating machinery	19.1	18.0	6
Vehicle parts	19.0	16.8	13
Spec. industrial machinery	17.6	16.7	5
Scientific instruments	15.2	14.4	6
Telecom equipment	13.1	11.2	17
Organic chemical	11.1	11.0	0
Plastic chemical	10.7	10.3	4
Airplane parts	9.5	9.4	1
Nonmonetary gold	9.0	4.1	119
Other chemicals	6.8	6.3	3
Paper and paperboard	6.5	6.3	3
New cars to Canada	6.4	5.9	8
Metal manufactures	6.0	5.5	9
Textile yarn, fabric	5.9	5.8	2
Medicinal chemicals	5.7	5.4	6
Records and magnetic media	5.3	4.9	8
New cars (other)	5.0	5.1	−2
Clothing	4.8	4.1	17
Trucks	4.2	3.7	14
Printed materials	4.0	3.8	5
Inorganic chemicals	3.8	3.3	15
Mineral Fuel			
Petroleum preparations	$3.9	$4.0	−3%
Coal	3.2	4.4	−27
Selected Commodities			
Cork, wood, lumber	$5.8	$5.3	9%
Cigarettes	3.9	4.2	−7
Metal ores, scrap	3.3	3.5	−6
Pulp and waste paper	3.0	3.9	−23
Total, including others	**$464.8**	**$448.2**	**4%**

Source: Foreign Trade magazine

GDP). In 1994 preliminary figures indicate that trade was US$1.172 trillion (17.7 percent of GDP). This represents a compound annual growth rate (CAGR) of 11 percent, significantly higher than the 7.9 percent overall CAGR for the total economy as measured by GDP during the same period. Although growing rapidly and becoming an increasingly important component of the national economy, international trade remains less critical to the overall US economy than it is in many other major world economies. In comparison with the 1992 level of trade registering at 16.3 percent of GDP for the US, Japan's total trade that year represented 15.2 percent of GDP, China's 40.2 percent, France's 46.2 percent, Germany's 60 percent, and Taiwan's 76.9 percent. For such countries as Singapore and Hong Kong, which exist primarily for and because of trade, 1992 foreign trade represented, respectively, 266 percent and 246 percent of GDP, pointing up their roles as reexporters and traders par excellence. However, more than four-fifths of the US economy remains firmly focused on domestic markets. Indeed, the huge size of this domestic market is one of the prime attractions for outsiders seeking to do business in the country.

Total US foreign (merchandise) trade topped 10 percent of GDP in 1973, largely due to the sharp rise in the prices paid for imported oil following the embargo initiated by the Organization of Petroleum Exporting Countries (OPEC) in that year. Trade rose to a high of 17.8 percent of GDP in 1980, again in response to a second round of oil price shocks in 1979. It eased back to 14 percent in 1983 as world oil prices began the fall that would bring them to levels below one-third of their 1980 peak price. Trade as a percentage of US GDP has been creeping up since 1987.

While the rate of growth in US foreign trade has actually slowed, at the same time, it has become a larger constituent of overall GDP. The CAGR for trade was 11 percent during the 30 years between 1964 and 1993. This rate slowed to a still rapid, but much lower 6.3 percent during the 10 years from 1984 through 1993. Total merchandise trade has grown steadily since 1964, falling below the previous year's total only in 1982 and 1985. Trade shrank by 7.9 percent in 1982, responding to high interest rates and recessionary conditions in the US and abroad. In 1985 trade dropped by a modest 1.6 percent, largely the result of weakening oil prices and a strengthening dollar that reduced outflows at the same time that the nation's exports were becoming more expensive.

This overall growth in trade disguises differential growth of exports and imports. Between 1964 and 1993 exports grew by 1,709 percent while imports grew by 2,872 percent, almost 40 percent faster. The CAGR during this period was 10.5 percent for exports and 12 percent for imports. However, during the 10 years from 1984 through 1993 the CAGR for exports fell to 7.1 percent and for imports to 5.7 percent, with the surge in imports falling behind the growth of exports for the first time since the 1960s. Despite continued export strength in 1994, preliminary figures indicate a resurgence of import buying during the year.

Exports topped US$100 billion in 1975, roughly four times the level of 10 years earlier. Imports topped US$100 billion in 1974, up by more than 50 percent from the previous year's level due primarily to outlays for oil. Coincidentally, 1975 was the last year in which the US had a surplus merchandise balance of trade position. Both exports and imports have grown steadily in an almost uninterrupted fashion since 1964, falling below the previous year's dollar value only in 1975, 1982, and 1991, all of which represent periods of economic recession.

Trade in Services

In 1980 industry and manufacturing accounted for 29.1 percent of US GDP, while commodities (agriculture and mining) represented 6.6 percent and services 64.3 percent. By 1991 these percentages were 24.8 percent for industry, 3.5 percent for agriculture, and 71.7 percent for services, with both commodity and industrial production losing ground to services. Until recently the US government disaggregated international trade in services from its reports of foreign trade, restricting these reports to merchandise trade. However, as the US becomes more of a service economy, the service component of international exchange has been increasing in importance, and in 1994 the government announced that it would begin including services in total trade figures. Because the US has a favorable balance of trade in services, when trade in services is included in the calculation, the overall balance of trade situation is improved. If total trade is calculated using a services component, the US is able to forestall recording a trade deficit until 1983, whereas it has been in the red since 1976 if deficits are figured using only merchandise trade.

During the past several years, there has been an incremental shift toward services as a percentage of total trade. In 1980 trade in services—consisting of services and net investment income—accounted for 30.6 percent of total trade, while in 1992 services had increased to 33.9 percent. The 30.6 percent share of service trade in 1980 represents the lowest level of trade in services since that year; the highest level of service trade in the last 30 years was 37.4 percent in 1990.

In 1993 total trade in services was US$312.8 billion, figured on a payments basis, up 5.2 percent from the previous year and representing 23 percent of total trade. (These figures, which use assumptions different from those presented in the immediately

US Imports by Commodity
(in US$ billions)

Commodity	1993	1992	% Change
Agricultural Commodities			
Vegetables and fruit	$5.7	$5.7	0%
Meat and preparations	2.8	2.7	4
Live animals	1.5	1.4	7
Coffee	1.4	1.6	-13
Tobacco	1.0	1.0	0
Vegetable oils	0.9	1.0	-10
Manufactured Goods			
Electrical machinery	$46.8	$39.7	18%
ADP equipment	43.1	36.4	18
Clothing	33.8	31.2	8
Telecom equipment	27.3	25.8	6
New cars from Japan	21.6	20.8	4
Vehicle parts	17.7	15.8	12
Vehicles from Canada	17.6	13.9	27
Generating machinery	17.1	15.9	8
Industrial machinery	17.0	15.5	10
Spec. industrial machinery	13.5	11.8	14
New cars (other)	12.0	11.6	3
Toys and sporting goods	11.6	10.7	8
Trucks	10.1	9.8	3
Organic chemicals	9.3	9.4	-1
Iron and steel mill products	9.0	8.3	8
Paper and paperboard	8.6	8.0	8
Scientific instruments	8.5	7.6	12
Textile yarn, fabric	8.4	7.8	8
Metal manufactures	7.6	6.7	13
Furniture and parts	6.2	5.5	13
Gem diamonds	5.1	4.1	24
Plastics chemicals	4.8	4.3	12
Photographic equipment	4.3	3.8	13
Medicinal chemicals	4.1	3.8	9
Plastic articles	3.9	3.5	11
Mineral Fuel			
Crude oil	$38.4	$38.6	-1%
Petroleum preparations	10.8	11.3	-4
Selected Commodities			
Fish and preparations	$5.8	$5.7	2%
Cork, wood, lumber	5.6	4.0	40
Metal ores, scrap	3.0	3.3	-9
Pulp and waste paper	1.9	2.1	-10
Total, including others	**$580.4**	**$532.7**	**9%**

Source: Foreign Trade magazine

Top US Exports by Commodity – 1993

Commodity	US$ (billions) 1993	Percentage of of total trade	Percentage change 1992–1993
1. Electrical machinery	$36.6	7.9%	13.7 %
2. ADP and office machines	27.2	5.9	3.4
3. Miscellaneous manufactured goods	26.5	5.7	−1.8
4. Reexported manufactured goods	24.2	5.2	15.2
5. Airplanes	21.3	4.6	−19.0
6. General industrial machinery	19.5	4.2	5.4
7. Power generating machinery	19.1	4.1	6.1
8. Vehicle parts	18.9	4.1	13.2
9. Specialized industrial machinery	17.6	3.8	5.4
10. Scientific instruments	15.2	3.3	5.5
11. Telecommunications equipment	13.1	2.8	17.0
12. New cars	12.3	2.6	5.1
13. Organic chemicals	11.1	2.4	0.9
14. Plastics feedstocks	10.7	2.3	4.9
15. Airplane parts	9.5	2.0	1.1
16. Nonmonetary gold	9.0	1.9	119.5
17. Miscellaneous chemicals	6.8	1.5	7.9
18. Paper and paperboard	6.5	1.4	3.2
19. Vegetables and fruit	6.0	1.3	5.3
20. Miscellaneous metal manufactured goods	5.9	1.3	7.3
21. Fabric and yarn	5.9	1.3	1.7
22. Wood and lumber	5.8	1.2	9.4
23. Medical chemicals and drugs	5.7	1.2	7.5
24. Records and magnetic media	5.3	1.1	10.4
25. Apparel	4.8	1.0	17.1
Total exports	**$464.8**		**3.7%**

Top 5 exports—29.2% of total exports

Top 10 exports—48.6% of total exports

Top 25 exports—74.1% of total exports

Source: US Bureau of the Census

Note: Exports are reported on an FAS basis

preceding text, tend to understate services trade and overstate merchandise trade to some extent and are presented to indicate the order of magnitude and rate of growth of trade in services.) The components included in calculating services trade include travel costs (US$98.2 billion in 1993, up 5.2 percent from 1992), passenger fares (US$27.9 billion, up 1.1 percent), other transportation costs (US$47.6 billion, up 3 percent), royalties and licensing fees (US$25.2 billion, up 1.2 percent), other private services (US$87 billion, up 12.1 percent), direct defense expenditures (US$23.6 billion, down 4.4 percent), and US government services (US$2.3 billion, unchanged). Of these, travel paid for by foreign nationals represents the largest category (31.4 percent of service trade in 1993), while other private services—such as legal, accounting, financial, consulting, medical, marketing, and other personal, technical, and business services—represent the next largest and fastest growing category (27.9 percent and 12.1 percent, respectively).

EXPORTS

Agricultural and Other Commodity Exports

Although the US is a noted innovator and supplier of high value-added, high-tech products, the

Top US Imports by Commodity – 1993

Commodity	US$ (billions) 1993	Percentage of total trade	Percentage change 1992–1993
1. New cars	$51.3	8.8%	12.5%
2. Electrical machinery	46.7	8.0	17.6
3. ADP and office machines	43.2	7.4	18.7
4. Crude oil	38.4	6.6	−0.3
5. Miscellaneous manufactured equipment	35.5	6.1	7.9
6. Apparel	33.8	5.8	8.3
7. Telecommunications equipment	27.3	4.7	5.8
8. Vehicle parts	17.6	3.0	11.4
9. Power generating machinery	17.2	3.0	8.2
10. General industrial machinery	17.1	2.9	10.3
11. Specialized industrial machinery	13.5	2.3	16.4
12. Toys, games, and sporting goods	11.6	2.0	8.4
13. Footwear	11.2	1.9	9.8
14. Petroleum preparations	10.8	1.9	−4.4
15. Trucks	10.1	1.7	3.1
16. Organic chemicals	9.3	1.6	−1.1
17. Iron and steel products	9.0	1.6	8.4
18. Paper and paperboard	8.6	1.5	7.5
19. Fabric and yarn	8.4	1.4	7.7
20. Scientific instruments	8.4	1.4	10.5
21. Miscellaneous metal manufactured goods	7.6	1.3	13.4
22. Furniture and parts	6.3	1.1	14.5
23. Miscellaneous agricultural products	6.2	1.1	5.1
24. Fish and fish preparations	5.8	1.0	3.6
25. Vegetables and fruit	5.7	1.0	0
Total imports	**$580.5**		**7.9%**

Top 5 imports— 31.7% of total imports

Top 10 imports—6.5% of total imports

Top 25 imports—79.3% of total imports

Source: US Bureau of the Census
Note: Exports are reported on an FOB customs value basis

nation grew up as a colony serving as a source of basic commodities, and became a significant manufacturing power only late in the 19th century. However, by the early 1990s, agriculture and mining had fallen to a combined share of only 3.5 percent of GDP, down from a 6.6 percent share as recently as 1980. Agriculture alone fell below 2 percent of GDP for the first time in 1991. Nevertheless, in 1993 the US—the world's top producer—grew 11.8 percent of the world's wheat and accounted for 31.8 percent of global exports of the commodity. The nation was also the number one producer of corn (maize), growing 36.3 percent of the world's supply (61.8 percent of total exports worldwide); 44.8 percent of soybeans

(59.7 percent of total exports); 19.6 percent of cotton (21.2 percent of total exports); and 8.5 percent of tobacco (12.7 percent of total exports). Although the US produces only 1.5 percent of all milled rice in the world, it is still the second largest grower (behind Thailand) and in 1993 accounted for 17.4 percent of total exports worldwide. The US is also the top producer of meat in the world, accounting for 16.9 percent of total production in 1993. The nation also ranks sixth in fisheries production.

The US is also among the top three producers worldwide of all 5 categories of mineral fuels; of 5 of 7 categories of nonmetallic minerals; and 5 of 12 categories of metals. With respect to mineral fuels, in

1990 the US produced 24 percent of the world's natural gas, 20 percent of its coal, and 12 percent of its crude petroleum. Among nonmetals, it produced 51 percent of the world production of mica, 29 percent of phosphate rock, 20 percent of sulfur, and 14 percent of gypsum. Among metals, it produced 48 percent of all molybdenum, 18 percent of copper, 15 percent of lead, 14 percent of gold, 13 percent of silver, and 12 percent of mercury. In the same year, the US exported US$4.6 billion worth of mineral fuels, US$3.4 billion worth of nonmetallic minerals, and US$10.6 billion worth of metals.

Despite this strong performance, US exports of agricultural and mining products combined accounted for only 12.4 percent of exports in 1985 (manufactured goods accounted for 82.5 percent). By 1993 commodity exports had fallen to only 7 percent, with manufactured goods rising to 91.2 percent of total exports according to the US Bureau of the Census. In 1993 the only commodity products among the top 25 export product categories were nonmonetary gold (ranked 16th, it represented an anomaly, gold not having appeared among the top 25 products for many years), vegetables and fruit (19th), and wood and lumber (22nd), which is actually considered a semimanufactured product. The quantities and dollar values of many of these products have grown, but some have either plateaued or fallen below their levels of 10 to 15 years ago. Although commodities production and exports are expected to continue to be strong, they will also assuredly continue to decline as a percentage of total GDP and exports.

Industrial and Manufactured Exports

As previously noted, high value-added industrial and manufactured goods represent the core of US export oriented production. In 1993 the top US export was electrical machinery, followed—among the top five export categories—by automatic data processing (ADP) machinery and equipment, miscellaneous manufactured goods, reexports of manufactured goods, and airplanes. In fact, one has to look as far down as 13th on the list (organic chemicals, themselves manufactured intermediate products) and 14th (plastics chemical feedstocks, another example of intermediate products) before one gets to the first category of non end-user manufactured products. Of the top 25 categories of exports, 16 represented finished manufactured goods, while only three represented commodity products—and even those could be argued to represent semimanufactured goods. The remaining six product categories represent intermediate processed products, such as paper and paperboard, fabric and yarn, and various categories of chemical products.

Service Exports

Although services account for a dominant and growing portion of US GDP, and exports of services are an increasingly important element of US international trade, service exports have not been the focal point of such trade. Because they do not require formal customs entry, services have been understandably difficult to track. Prior to fiscal 1995 (which began in July 1994), the US statistics on trade in services were divorced from standard merchandise trade figures; they were added in on a quarterly basis, almost as an afterthought, as a residual category of "intangibles" used to balance the accounts. Statistics on US foreign trade now report an explicit services component in monthly estimates.

In 1993 total service exports were at US$184.8 billion, up 4.6 percent from 1992. Travel costs accounted for US$57.6 billion (up 6.1 percent from 1992), passenger fares US$16.4 billion (down 2.9 percent), other transportation US$23.1 billion (up 1.8 percent), royalties and licensing fees US$20.4 billion (up 2.5 percent), other private services US$54.9 billion (up 7.6 percent), direct defense expenditures US$11.4 billion (up 5.5 percent), and US government sales of services US$800 million (down 11.1 percent).

The US remains the dominant provider of many technical and professional services worldwide. Not only do US-based multinational firms retain US professionals to facilitate, conform, and report their far-flung international operations in accordance with US practice, but foreign private and, increasingly, government entities are using such US providers to upgrade their own operations. Although few if any nations follow US procedures exactly, many international standards as based on US-derived practices. The US remains dominant in such areas as business law, accounting, financial innovation, business consulting, and marketing.

Export Products

Although in 1993 the top 10 export product categories accounted for 48.6 percent of total merchandise exports, US exports are relatively diversified. In that year the top US product export was electrical machinery, accounting for 7.9 percent of the total, with the next category—ADP machinery and equipment—representing 5.9 percent of the total. The top dozen product categories all represented manufactured goods, generally sophisticated in nature. The top 25 categories accounted for 74.1 percent of the total, with item number 25—clothing—representing 1 percent (item number 24—records and magnetic media—was 1.1 percent). If the top 30 products are included, 79 percent of all exports are covered and, beginning with product number 30—meat and meat preparations—each subsequent category represents no more than 0.9 percent of the total.

Leading US Exports to Major Countries (1993 in US$ millions)

Canada

Parts and accessories of motor vehicles	$10,921
Motor vehicles	6,668
Internal combustion piston engines and parts	3,861
ADP machines	3,367
Thermionic, cold cathode, photocathode valves	3,238
Electrical machinery	1,947
Special purpose vehicles	1,914
Electrical switching apparatus	1,739
Telecommunications equipment	1,738
Measuring, checking, analyzing, and controlling instruments	1,718

Japan

Aircraft and associated equipment	$2,833
Rough wood	1,898
ADP machines	1,872
Thermionic, cold cathode photocathode valves	1,843
Unmilled corn	1,533
Parts for ADP machines	1,432
Fish (fresh, chilled, or frozen)	1,273
Tobacco and tobacco products	1,267
Measuring, checking, analyzing, and controlling instruments	1,235
Fresh and frozen meat	1,228

Mexico

Parts and accessories of motor vehicles	$4,269
Telecommunications equipment	1,592
Electricity distribution equipment	1,376
Electrical machinery and apparatus	1,342
Electrical switching apparatus	1,120
Thermionic, cold cathode, photocathode valves	1,103
Measuring, checking, analyzing, and controlling instruments	1,000
Internal combustion piston engines	892
Manufactures of base metal	840
Parts for ADP machines	830

China

Aircraft and associated equipment	$2,229
Motor vehicles	615
Telecommunications equipment	603
Measuring, checking, analyzing, and controlling instruments	322
Specialized machinery	314
Fertilizers	292
Wheat	274
Oil (not crude)	242
ADP machines	167
Heating and cooling equipment	160

Source: Foreign Trade magazine

Leading US Imports from Major Countries (1993 in US$ millions)

Canada

Motor vehicles	$18,377
Special purpose motor vehicles	7,578
Parts for motor vehicles	6,435
Paper and paperboard	5,736
Crude oil	4,996
Wood, simply worked and railway sleepers of wood	4,928
Natural gas	3,245
Aluminum	2,020
Internal combustion piston engines	1,742
Oil (not crude)	1,677

Japan

Motor vehicles	$21,952
ADP machines	9,703
Thermionic, cold cathode, photocathode valves	6,466
Motor vehicle parts	6,078
Telecommunications equipment	5,538
Parts for ADP machines	4,478
Internal combustion piston engines	3,679
Electrical machinery	2,801
Toys and sporting goods	2,752
Sound recorders and TVs	2,535

Mexico

Crude oil	$4,244
Motor vehicles	3,084
Parts for motor vehicles	2,350
Electricity distribution equipment	2,287
Television receivers	1,589
Telecommunications equipment	1,350
Electrical switching apparatus	1,348
Internal combustion piston engines	1,011
Electrical machinery	970
Vegetables	943

China

Footwear	$4,519
Baby carriages, toys, games, and sporting goods	4,459
Women's/girls' coats and capes	2,222
Articles of apparel of textile fabrics	1,599
Trunks, suitcases, vanity cases, briefcases	1,321
Men's/boys' coats, jackets	1,126
Plastic articles	969
Telecommunications equipment	917
Radiobroadcast receivers	913
Miscellaneous manufactured articles	912

Source: Foreign Trade magazine

In 1993 the top 10 exports represented 48.6 percent and the top 25, 74.1 percent of total exports, versus 47.1 percent and 71.8 percent respectively in 1990, indicating that the main exports have been accounting for somewhat more of total trade. There were several changes in the position of specific product categories in the rankings, but only four products were substituted, all in the rankings between 15th and 25th. Nonmonetary gold, medical chemicals, records and magnetic media, and clothing displaced corn, metal ore and scrap, cigarettes, and coal from the top 25 in 1993. Between 1992 and 1993, exports of seven of these top product categories increased by more than 10 percent: nonmonetary gold by 119.5 percent, clothing by 17.1 percent, telecommunications equipment by 17 percent, reexported manufactured goods by 15.2 percent, electrical machinery by 13.7 percent, vehicle parts by 13.2 percent, and records and magnetic media by 10.4 percent. Only two of the top 25 product categories decreased between 1992 and 1993: airplanes and miscellaneous manufactured goods, by 19 percent and 1.8 percent, respectively. (All comparisons are between current dollar values; constant dollar comparisons would show a somewhat different picture.)

Reexports

Because it is both such a large exporter of its own finished products as well as such a huge end-user market, the US has not been noted as a intermediate trader dealing in reexports. However, between 1990 and 1993, reexports grew by 38 percent in volume, from 4.7 percent to 5.5 percent of total export value, and rising from fifth to fourth place among all categories of exports. In 1993 reexports of manufactured goods represented 94.6 percent of all reexports, while those of agricultural products were at 3.5 percent, mineral fuels 0.3 percent, and other products 1.6 percent.

IMPORTS

Agricultural and Other Commodity Imports

With its vast land area and wealth of natural resources, the US has long been self-sufficient in—and a major exporter of—a wide variety of agricultural and commodity products. Once a net supplier of energy products to the world, the US has become increasingly dependent on foreign sources of energy since the 1950s. In 1993 crude petroleum was the fourth largest import, accounting for 6.6 percent of all merchandise imports on an FOB basis; prepared petroleum products were the 14th largest import category with a 1.9 percent share of imports. In recent years, this energy component has fallen somewhat: as recently as 1990, crude petroleum occupied

second place among all imports, was 14 percent higher in current dollar value, and accounted for 8.8 percent of total merchandise imports; prepared petroleum products were down by nearly one-third in dollar value, from eighth place and a 3.3 percent share in 1990. However, the long-term trend has been for such imports to grow in size and importance. Most observers both at home and abroad see US dependence on overseas energy imports as a glaring structural weakness in the US economy.

Despite the high level of energy imports adding to the category, US imports of agricultural and mineral products combined accounted for only 15.1 percent of imports in 1985 (while manufactured goods accounted for 81.5 percent). By 1993 commodities had fallen to 10.8 percent, with manufactured goods rising to 85.3 percent of exports, according to the US Bureau of the Census. The general dependence on imported energy has kept the share of such primary extractive products from falling more precipitously in the face of increased consumer demand and industrial imports of manufactured goods.

Aside from energy imports, relatively few primary products are to be found among the top imports to the US. Nevertheless, the US is a major importer of many types of such products, and a relatively small market share in the US is often equivalent to a major share elsewhere. Such imports include categories of miscellaneous agricultural products (23rd among the top imports, with a 1.1 percent share), fish and fish preparations (24th, 1 percent share), fruit and vegetables (25th, 1 percent), wood and lumber (26th, 1 percent), and diamonds (27th, 0.9 percent).

Industrial and Manufactured Imports

Some 23 of the top 30 US import product categories represent industrial or manufactured products. Of these, six categories clearly represent primarily intermediate manufactured products—organic chemicals, iron and steel products, paper and paperboard, fabric and yarn, plastic chemical feedstocks, and medical chemicals—while four are basically durable and nondurable consumer products intended for end users—new cars; clothing; toys, games, and sporting goods; and footwear. Most of the remainder represent capital goods to be used in producing other articles or processing other commodities, or areas of mixed consumer and industrial usage.

Service Imports

The US, with its relatively nonrestrictive rules of doing business, allows a broad range of service imports. Many US-based entities have welcomed expertise from overseas vendors, either on grounds of cost effectiveness where foreign providers offer better terms for equivalent services—notable recent examples would include engineering and computer programming—or in order to come up to speed on foreign operating norms and rules where there are few, if any, domestic sources for the information.

In 1993 service imports were at US$128 billion, up 6 percent from the previous year and representing 17.8 percent of total imports calculated on a payments basis. That rate of growth was faster than the rate for service exports (4.6 percent) for the same period, but 1993 service imports were only 69 percent as large in dollars. Travel costs, the largest single component, accounted for US$40.6 billion (up 7.5 percent from 1992); passenger fares, US$11.4 billion (also up 7.5 percent); other transportation, US$24.5 billion (up 4.2 percent); royalties and licensing fees, US$4.8 billion (down 4 percent); other private services, US$32.1 billion (up a stunning 20.7 percent); direct defense expenditures, US$12.2 billion (down 12.2 percent); and US government purchases of services, US$2.3 billion (up by a marginal 1.9 percent). The surge in imports of other private services in particular indicates the internationalization of US business, while the drop in defense expenditures denotes the somewhat reduced rate of overseas military spending in the post-Cold War era.

Import Products

In 1993 the top 10 import product categories accounted for 56.5 percent of total merchandise imports. In that year, the top product imported into the US was new cars, accounting for 8.8 percent of the total, with the second and third categories—electrical machinery and ADP machinery and equipment—representing respectively 8 percent and 7.4 percent of the total. These top three accounted for slightly less than one-quarter of the merchandise import total, while the top 25 categories represented 79.3 percent of the total. If the top 30 products are included, 83.4 percent of all exports are covered, and beginning with product number 27—diamonds—each subsequent product category represents no more than 0.9 percent of the total. In 1993 the top 10 imports represented 56.5 percent and the top 25, 79.3 percent of total exports, versus 55.2 percent and 73.9 percent respectively in 1990, indicating that the main imports are accounting for somewhat more of total trade.

There were several changes in the position of specific product categories in the rankings, some of which moved up or down by as many as four rank positions, but no product types were substituted. Between 1992 and 1993, imports of nine product categories increased by more than 10 percent: ADP and office machinery and equipment grew 18.7 percent; electrical machinery 17.6 percent; specialized industrial machinery 16.4 percent; furniture and parts 14.5 percent; miscellaneous metal manufactures 13.4 percent; new cars 12.5 percent; vehicle parts 11.4 per-

cent; scientific instruments 10.5 percent; and general industrial machinery 10.3 percent. Only three of the top 25 product categories decreased between 1992 and 1993: petroleum preparations (down 4.4 percent), organic chemicals (down 1.1 percent), and crude oil (down a marginal 0.3 percent). (All comparisons are between current dollar values: constant dollar comparisons would show a somewhat different picture.)

TRADE PARTNERS

In 1992, 58.7 percent of US foreign trade was with the countries of the Organization for Economic Co-operation and Development (OECD), consisting of 24 of the world's major Western economies, Japan, and some smaller, but generally more developed Western oriented nations. Trade with the members of the European Union (EU)—Belgium, France, Germany, Luxembourg, Italy, the Netherlands, Denmark, Ireland, the UK, Greece, Spain, and Portugal—accounted for 20.1 percent of total trade, while that with the nations of Central and Eastern Europe was 0.6 percent. Trade with China represented 3.4 percent, while that with the members of the OPEC totaled 5.6 percent. Trade with other developing countries was 31.5 percent; with those of Africa, 2.5 percent; with nations of the Americas, excluding Canada, 14.8 percent; with Southwest Asian countries, 3.3 percent; and with East Asian countries, 19.7 percent. (Note that these percentages will total to considerably more than 100 percent, due to overlapping coverage within different groupings.) Among these groupings, the US had trade surpluses only with the EU, Eastern and Central Europe, and the Middle East.

In 1993 Canada was the top US trading partner, accounting for roughly 20 percent of total merchandise trade. Japan ranked second, with 14.8 percent, followed by Mexico (7.7 percent), the UK (4.6 percent), and Germany (4.5 percent). Together, these top five trading partners accounted for 51.6 percent of all trade with the US. If the list is extended to include the top 10 trading partners—Taiwan, China, South Korea, France, and Singapore, in that order—it covers 67.7 percent of trade and encompasses all US trading partners with a share greater than 2 percent of total merchandise trade. When the roster is extended to the top 25 trading partners, it includes 86.8 percent of all trade. Thus, with the top 1, 5, 10, and 25 partners accounting respectively for roughly one-fifth, one-half, two-thirds, and seven-eighths of the nation's trade, the US is actually quite concentrated—and relatively poorly diversified—in terms of its international economic relationships.

Some countries moved by several places in the rankings between 1992 and 1993, but only Russia and

Turkey joining the list of the top 35 trade partners. Although there were relatively few substitutions or ranking changes in the list of major trading partners in 1993, some changes in magnitude were noteworthy. Among the top 35 countries, trade with no fewer than six grew by more than 20 percent: trade with Russia grew 84.6 percent, Malaysia 31.8 percent, India 28.3 percent, Switzerland 26.2 percent, China 21.8 percent, and Turkey 20.5 percent. Trade with eight nations increased by between 10 and 20 percent: trade with the Philippines increased by 19.2 percent, Singapore by 16.5 percent, Indonesia by 16 percent, Canada by 13 percent, Israel by 12.6 percent, the UK by 12.2 percent, the Dominican Republic by 11.1 percent, and Argentina by 10.9 percent. Trade with 11 countries grew by less than 10 percent. However, trade with the remaining 10 countries in the list declined by as much as 23.4 percent (Italy), 18.4 percent (Saudi Arabia), and 14.9 percent (Spain).

Most of the same names appear separately on the lists of major purchasers of US exports and suppliers of US imports, but there are also many asymmetrical relationships. For some time, Canada, Japan, and Mexico have remained the top three US trading partners in both exports and imports, together accounting for 40.8 percent of exports and 43.9 percent of imports. (However, although Japan occupies the same relative position on both lists, it sells more than twice as much to the US as it buys.) Following the top three, the order changes relative to sales and purchases. The UK is the number four purchaser of US exports, but China is the number four supplier of imports to the US, although it buys only enough US products to rank 13th. In 1993 Germany and Taiwan were, respectively, 5th and 6th on both lists, with Saudi Arabia occupying slot number 16 on both, and South Africa bringing up the rear at position number 35 on both. Several countries—Argentina, Turkey, Russia, Chile, and Egypt—are found only among the top 35 buyers of US exports because their sales to the US fall below the cutoff point. Conversely, several countries—Nigeria, Angola, Kuwait, and Norway, all primarily suppliers of oil—sell enough products to the US to rank them but fail to make enough purchases of US goods to be included among the top 35 export buyers.

Among buyers of US exports, the top five purchaser countries account for 54.3 percent of total merchandise sales, the top 10 for 70.2 percent, the top 25 for 88.8 percent, and the top 35 for 93.4 percent. For imports into the US, the top five seller countries account for 50.6 percent of total sales, the top 10 for 65.4 percent, the top 25 for 85.3 percent, and the top 35 for 91.2 percent. The US relies on a somewhat more diversified group of suppliers than it does for buyers, but US overseas trade still remains remarkably concentrated among a relatively few

Top US Import Sellers – 1993

Country	US$ (billions) 1993	% of total trade	% change 92–93
1. Canada	$113.6	18.8%	12.1%
2. Japan	110.4	18.3	11.0
3. Mexico	40.7	6.7	13.4
4. China	33.7	5.6	23.0
5. Germany	29.4	4.9	–0.7
6. Taiwan	26.3	4.4	1.9
7. United Kingdom	22.4	3.7	8.2
8. South Korea	17.8	2.9	2.3
9. France	15.7	2.6	2.6
10. Italy	13.8	2.3	7.8
11. Singapore	13.0	2.2	12.1
12. Malaysia	10.9	1.8	28.2
13. Hong Kong	10.0	1.7	–2.9
14. Thailand	9.0	1.5	13.9
15. Venezuela	8.7	1.4	1.2
16. Saudi Arabia	8.4	1.4	–25.7
17. Brazil	8.0	1.3	–1.2
18. Switzerland	6.2	1.0	6.9
19. Indonesia	5.9	1.0	25.5
20. Netherlands	5.7	0.9	3.6
21. Nigeria	5.6	0.9	5.7
22. Belgium-Lux.	5.6	0.9	16.7
23. Philippines	5.2	0.9	13.0
24. India	4.9	0.8	19.5
25. Sweden	4.7	0.8	–4.1
26. Israel	4.5	0.7	15.4
27. Australia	3.5	0.6	–12.5
28. Colombia	3.3	0.5	6.4
29. Spain	3.2	0.5	0
30. Dominican Rep.	2.7	0.4	12.5
31. Ireland	2.6	0.4	13.0
32. Angola	2.2	0.4	–8.3
33. Norway	2.0	0.3	0
34. Kuwait	2.0	0.3	566.7
35. South Africa	1.9	0.3	5.5
Total imports	**$603.4**		**8.9%**

Source: International Monetary Fund, Direction of Trade Statistics Yearbook, 1994

Top US Export Buyers – 1993

Country	US$ (billions) 1993	% of total trade	% change 92–93
1. Canada	$100.2	21.6%	11.1%
2. Japan	47.9	10.3	0.2
3. Mexico	41.6	9.0	2.5
4. United Kingdom	26.4	5.7	15.8
5. Germany	18.9	4.1	-10.8
6. Taiwan	16.2	3.5	6.6
7. South Korea	14.8	3.2	1.4
8. France	13.3	2.9	-8.9
9. Netherlands	12.8	2.8	-6.6
10. Singapore	11.7	2.5	21.9
11. Hong Kong	9.9	2.1	8.8
12. Belgium-Lux.	9.4	2.0	-6.0
13. China	8.8	1.9	17.3
14. Australia	8.3	1.8	-6.7
15. Switzerland	6.8	1.5	51.1
16. Saudi Arabia	6.7	1.4	-6.9
17. Italy	6.5	1.4	-25.3
18. Malaysia	6.1	1.3	38.6
19. Brazil	6.0	1.3	5.3
20. Venezuela	4.6	1.0	-14.8
21. Israel	4.4	0.9	7.3
22. Spain	4.2	0.9	-23.6
23. Thailand	3.8	0.8	-5.0
24. Argentina	3.8	0.8	18.7
25. Philippines	3.5	0.8	29.6
26. Turkey	3.4	0.7	25.9
27. Colombia	3.2	0.7	-3.0
28. Russia	3.0	0.6	42.8
29. Indonesia	2.8	0.6	0
30. Egypt	2.8	0.6	-9.7
31. Ireland	2.7	0.6	-3.6
32. Chile	2.6	0.6	-8.3
33. Sweden	2.3	0.5	-17.8
34. Dominican Rep.	2.3	0.5	9.5
35. South Africa	2.2	0.5	-8.3
Total exports	**$464.8**		**3.7%**

Source: International Monetary Fund, Direction of Trade Statistics Yearbook, 1994

countries. Of course, relatively few countries have economies that are large enough either to provide or consume amounts of goods and services substantial enough to register on this scale.

Among the top 35 buyers of US goods, sales grew by more than 20 percent to six countries between 1992 and 1993: Switzerland by 51.1 percent, Russia by 42.8 percent, Malaysia by 38.6 percent, the Philippines by 29.6 percent, Turkey by 25.9 percent, and Singapore by 21.9 percent. Sales to four countries grew by between 10 and 20 percent, most notably—because of the larger share of sales absorbed by them—to Canada by 11.1 percent and to the UK by 15.8 percent. Sales to eight countries grew by less than 10 percent (Japan bought only about US$100 million more in 1992 than in 1993, for a percentage change of only 0.2 percent). Sales to Indonesia remained essentially flat. Sales to 16 countries declined by as much as 25.3 percent (Italy), 23.6 percent (Spain), 17.8 percent (Sweden), and 14.8 percent (Venezuela). Of greater note because of the magnitude of their consumption of US products, purchases by Germany fell by 10.8 percent, while those of France and the Netherlands declined respectively by 8.9 and 6.6 percent.

BALANCE OF TRADE

Riding the wave of its preeminent position in the world following World War II, the US posted surplus trade and current account balances throughout the 1950s and 1960s, consistently exporting both more goods and services than it imported. This situation began to reverse itself in the 1970s as the rate of growth of the maturing US economy slowed at a time when the economies of many overseas countries were growing at a more rapid rate and becoming more competitive. The cumulative costs of trying to fund massive simultaneous domestic and foreign programs, rising international inflation, and sharply higher energy prices also began to take their toll. By the late 1970s, US merchandise trade had fallen into an apparently chronic structural deficit position.

There have been merchandise trade deficits in 21 of the past 30 years, with an unbroken chain of them since 1976. The red ink peaked at US$159.6 billion in 1987 calculated on an FOB basis (US$170.3 billion on a CIF basis). From this high, it fell to US$73.8 billion (FOB) in 1991 or US$85.7 billion (CIF) in 1992. The merchandise trade deficit registered US$132.5 billion (FOB) and US$138.5 billion (CIF) in 1993. Preliminary figures for 1994 showed a cumulative record high merchandise trade deficit of US$166.2 billion (although the trade deficit in both goods and services was a somewhat less awesome US$108 billion). During 1994 exports and imports exhibited strong growth, and both reached new record highs:

Top US Trade Partners
Total Trade – 1993

Country	US$ (billions) 1993	% of total trade	% change 92–93
1. Canada	$213.8	20.0%	30.0%
2. Japan	158.3	14.8	7.5
3. Mexico	82.3	7.7	7.6
4. United Kingdom	48.8	4.6	12.2
5. Germany	48.4	4.5	–4.7
6. Taiwan	42.5	4.0	4.4
7. China	42.5	4.0	21.8
8. South Korea	32.6	3.1	1.9
9. France	29.0	2.7	–3.0
10. Singapore	24.7	2.3	16.5
11. Italy	20.3	1.9	–23.4
12. Hong Kong	19.9	1.9	2.6
13. Netherlands	18.5	1.7	–3.6
14. Malaysia	17.0	1.6	31.8
15. Saudi Arabia	15.1	1.4	–18.4
16. Belgium-Lux.	15.0	1.4	1.3
17. Brazil	14.0	1.3	1.4
18. Venezuela	13.3	1.2	–5.0
19. Switzerland	13.0	1.2	26.2
20. Thailand	12.8	1.2	7.6
21. Australia	11.8	1.1	–8.5
22. Israel	8.9	0.8	12.6
23. Indonesia	8.7	0.8	16.0
24. Philippines	8.7	0.8	19.2
25. India	7.7	0.7	28.3
26. Spain	7.4	0.7	–14.9
27. Sweden	7.0	0.7	–9.1
28. Colombia	6.5	0.6	1.6
29. Ireland	5.3	0.5	3.9
30. Argentina	5.1	0.5	10.9
31. Dominican Rep.	5.0	0.5	11.1
32. Russia	4.8	0.4	84.6
33. Turkey	4.7	0.4	20.5
34. Chile	4.3	0.4	7.5
35. South Africa	4.1	0.4	–2.4
Total trade	**$1,068.2**		**6.6%**

Source: International Monetary Fund, Direction of Trade
Statistics Yearbook, 1994

US$502.8 billion for exports (up 10 percent from 1993), but and even stronger US$669.1 billion for imports (up 13.5 percent from 1993).

The total merchandise trade deficit for 1993 was up 31.6 percent from 1992. In 1993 the largest US deficit position with an individual country was US$62.5 billion with Japan, followed by China (US$24.9 billion), Canada (US$13.4), Germany (US$10.5 billion), and Taiwan (US$10.1 billion). In contrast, surplus positions were not only fewer, but were also much smaller, the largest being with the Netherlands (US$7.1 billion), Australia (US$4.8 billion), and Belgium-Luxembourg (US$3.8 billion). In 1993 the US ran trade deficits with 22 of its top 35 trading partners, accounting for 96 percent of the total merchandise trade deficit for the year. Through November 1994, the US deficit with Japan was US$65.6 billion, 11 percent higher than in 1993. For the same period, the US deficit with China reached a record high of US$30 billion. Of even greater concern than the figures for specific countries is the cumulative effect of 18 years of growing deficits. In 1994 the trade deficit with Japan reached a new record high, but the most alarming development was the rapidity of growth in the trade deficit with China.

The current account balance includes the merchandise trade balance as well as the net balance of trade in services, overseas investment income, and private and public unilateral transfers. Trade in services has remained in a solid surplus position since 1964, growing at a CAGR of 16.75 percent. Net investment income has been positive throughout the same period as well, although it has declined since peaking at US$32.9 billion in 1981. Performance by services and net investment income received has helped to ameliorate the more inclusive negative current account balance, which registered a surplus in 14 of the past 30 years (versus only nine years of surpluses in the balance of merchandise trade during the same period). This current account deficit bottomed out at US$163.4 billion in 1987.

During most of past 100 years, the US has imported low-value raw materials and intermediate goods while exporting a broad range of products—from commodities to high value-added items. During the past 50 years, this mix has shifted toward high-value goods. However, beginning in the 1960s and coming to full fruition during the 1980s, overseas competitors have become able to produce comparable, and in many cases, superior products on both technical and price grounds. This competition reduces demand abroad for US high value-added goods as well as boosts domestic demand for competing goods. This can be seen in the level of success enjoyed by Japan in the automotive arena (although many automobile imports represent units assembled abroad, often using US parts, by US subsidiaries or contract operations, nevertheless automobiles represent the largest single import category), as well as by Asian producers of machine tools, electronics, steel products, and ships.

As the US economy has matured, it has built up a high overhead factor which serves to make US goods less competitive on price internationally. Part of this overhead is due to the high wage levels needed to support a high standard of living, but other factors such as physical size, organizational infrastructure, and mandated programs contribute significantly to the overall burden. The US propensity to consume has exacerbated the trade imbalance. Private consumption accounts for about two-thirds of US GDP, and the large and generally affluent US market, with its generally high standard of living and high disposable income, is a lodestone for consumer products producers worldwide. Relatively low US import barriers have served to reinforce this influx of goods.

Over the past 30 years, the deficit-surplus position averaged 9.6 percent of total merchandise trade. During this period, surpluses averaged 5.3 percent of trade, ranging from a high of 15.4 percent of trade (in 1964) to a low of 0.6 percent (in 1973). For the same period, deficits averaged 11.3 percent of trade, with a high of 24.5 percent (in 1986) and a low of 0.4 percent (in 1976). Between 1983 and 1990, the deficit was greater than 10 percent of trade, rising above 20 percent of trade from 1984 through 1987. The deficit fell as a percent of trade in 1991 and 1992, but again rose to double-digit levels (12.7 percent) in 1993, a trend that continued in 1994 (14.2 percent).

The trade deficit has become a growing source of unease, both at home and abroad. The US has ex-

erted pressure on trading partners with whom it has run a consistent and growing deficit either to boost their imports of US goods or reduce their exports to the US. Despite a general philosophy that supports free trade, the US has raised "temporary" barriers in cases involving specific goods, categories of goods, and countries. Sectors that have been hit especially hard by overseas competition have called for anti-dumping investigations, arguing that the prices charged by foreign sellers on certain imports into the US are below those charged in the home market or even below cost in that home market and constitute unfair predatory pricing. The US steel industry has been a frequent filer of such petitions. The US has also negotiated voluntary restraint agreements, such as one under which Japanese automakers have agreed to limit their exports of vehicles to the US below a stated number of units each year. The US has similarly limited imports of certain machine tools from Japan and Taiwan. These Asian nations, with their huge and chronic trade surpluses with the US, have been specific targets of US protectionists, as has China. Domestic producers of certain agricultural commodities, particularly dairy products and sugar, have also been heavily protected against foreign import competition.

TRADE POLICY

In general, US policy supports free and open trade. During the past several years, the US has espoused free trade, arguing against trade barriers abroad and serving as a usually strong proponent of international bilateral and multilateral trade agreements, such as the North American Free Trade Agree-

United States Leading Trade Partners

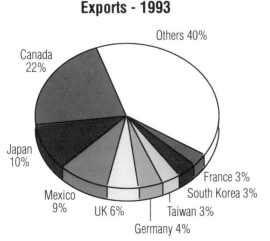

Exports - 1993
Others 40%
Canada 22%
Japan 10%
Mexico 9%
UK 6%
Germany 4%
Taiwan 3%
South Korea 3%
France 3%

Total 1993 merchandise exports: US$464.8 billion

Imports - 1993
Others 35%
Canada 19%
Japan 18%
Mexico 7%
China 6%
Germany 5%
Taiwan 4%
UK 4%
South Korea 3%

Total 1993 merchandise imports: US$603.4 billion

Note: Figures rounded to nearest whole percent. Source: *International Monetary Fund, Direction of Trade Statistics Yearbook*, 1994.

ment (NAFTA) with Canada and Mexico and the General Agreement on Tariffs and Trade (GATT). The US calls for a level playing field in international trade, a system in which all national entities have free access to international markets. Official policy holds that the US can grow out of its deficit position, increasing the volume and terms of trade in an environment in which such access exists for all participants. Such positions also call for each national entity to develop its areas of competitive advantage without the distortion of artificial barriers and for optimization of consumer choice and competitive pricing.

However, even free trade is not truly free, and entry procedures can be onerous. (Refer to the "Import Policy & Procedures" and "Trade Agreements" chapters.) A strong protectionist streak also exists in the US which has been rekindled and reinforced by US loss of predominance across a wide range of basic industrial production areas. The US argues that while it has generally opened its markets to other nations, many of these nations have failed to reciprocate and maintain closed, exclusionary markets biased against US goods. In general, it is true that the US market is more open than that of most other nations of the world. Nevertheless, there exist significant barriers to entering goods into the US. These include tariff and non-tariff barriers, quotas, administrative restrictions, and subsidies of some national products. Subsidies represent a practice that the US rails against in other regions, particularly—in the US view—with regard to agricultural and aircraft subsidies in the EU. This attitude is somewhat disingenuous, because the US operates the world's largest and most extensive agricultural support program—which pays its farmers not to grow certain crops, agrees to buy other domestically produced products at a guaranteed rate for government stockpiles, and restricts entry of some imported commodities.

As trade deficits persist and grow, the US has proposed a framework approach to bilateral trade negotiations—primarily with Japan—arguing that US imports by product type should have market shares in Japan equivalent to Japan's market shares in the US for similar products. To US negotiators this seems only equitable. To the Japanese it represents artificially managed trade and a loss of national political and economic sovereignty and consumer freedom.

Trade barriers can be raised by specific Congressional legislation, by determination of individual cabinet secretaries following procedures established by law, by the US Trade Representative (USTR), or by the regulatory arms of various governmental agencies. Trade barriers can be tariff barriers involving duty rates designed to impede imports by taxing them at a level that makes them uncompetitive in the US market; antidumping rulings and countervailing duties; or a variety of non-tariff barriers. The non-tariff barriers can include quotas, licensing, and other similar rules, as well as voluntary restraint agreements.

The US signed the Uruguay Round of GATT in late 1993, which was ratified by the US Congress in late 1994 after battles involving domestic partisan politics. Policy on such issues is in the midst of a somewhat chaotic review. There are conflicting pulls between protectionist and free trade elements in the public and the government, and elected leaders have no clear mandate from which to proceed. Although the trend seems to point toward a general long-term liberalization of trade, the near-term outlook remains uncertain.

MEMBERSHIP IN INTERNATIONAL ORGANIZATIONS

The US is a member of virtually all international economic, political, and trade organizations, and it is the mainstay—if not the actual initiator—of many of them. The US is a charter founding member of the United Nations as well as of virtually all of its various subagencies, although it has withdrawn officially or from active participation in some. For example, the US withdrew from the United Nations Educational, Scientific, and Cultural Organization (UNESCO) on the grounds that the organization had become anti-Western; tentative moves to rejoin in 1995 were shelved following the rise to power of neo-isolationists in the US Congress.

The US is also a charter founding member of the International Bank for Reconstruction and Development (IBRD, the World Bank), the IMF, and the International Finance Corporation (IFC). It is a member of the OECD, and is one of the Group of Seven (G-7), a semiformal caucus consisting of the leaders of the world's major economies (membership includes Canada, France, Germany, Great Britain, Italy, Japan, and the US).

Significant trade oriented agreements and organizations to which the US subscribes include GATT and its successor entity, the WTO. The US is also a member of NAFTA, as well as of Asia Pacific Economic Cooperation (APEC). The country is also a signatory to the Multi-Fiber Arrangement (MFA), covering international trade in textiles, as well as several other international commodity agreements.

The US also belongs to various largely political regional bodies, such as the Organization of American States (OAS) and the North Atlantic Treaty Organization (NATO).

Trade Agreements

INTRODUCTION

The legal foundation for US trade is fairly complex, and numerous governmental agencies have responsibilities with respect to it. The President, through the executive branch office of the US Trade Representative (USTR), proposes and negotiates trade agreements, which must be authorized and then ratified by the Congress. Other government agencies with specific responsibilities for aspects of trade include such wide ranging bodies as the cabinet level Departments of Agriculture, Commerce, Defense, Labor, State, and Treasury, and such agencies and regulatory bodies as the Agency for International Development (AID), the Civil Aeronautics Board (CAB), the Federal Aviation Administration (FAA), the Federal Communications Commission (FCC), the Federal Power Commission (FPC), the Federal Trade Commission (FTC), the Foreign Agricultural Service (FAS), the Food and Drug Administration (FDA), the Consumer Products Safety Commission (CPSC), the Foreign Claims Settlement Commission (FCSC), and the International Trade Commission (ITC), among others.

Although there is really no such thing as free trade—all trade being heavily regulated and controlled even when it is not specifically restricted or taxed—the US generally supports the idea of free trade, at least on a theoretical level. And despite its many limitations that cause overseas exporters to the US to argue otherwise, the US remains one of the world's freest, most open markets. The gap between US theory and practice on trade is not so much because of obstructionist intent or anti-trade bias, but rather because of the voluminous regulations of the many discrete agencies and the host of bureaucratic procedures involved in entering products into the US. Thousands of products and commodities—more than 40 percent—may actually be imported duty free and with few if any restrictions under the general tariff provisions established in the Harmonized Tariff Schedule of the United States (HTSUS). And through special trade agreements, the US has also established favorable—and in some cases, extremely favorable—trade conditions with specific countries and associations of countries. In many cases goods normally subject to duty may be entered duty free or at reduced rates as long as the imports satisfy the often fairly simple conditions of these programs, usually having to do with the origination of the products in the beneficiary country.

The legal framework of US trade law includes the Tariff Act of 1930 (the Hawley-Smoot Act), which provides the basis for tariffs. Other important legislation includes the Trade Act of 1974 (Section 301 of which provides the basis for sanctions against trade partners for unfair trade practices); the Trade Agreement Act of 1979 (which implemented the Tokyo round of the General Agreement on Tariffs and Trade (GATT)); the Export Administration Act of 1979; the Export Trading Company Act of 1982; the Tariff Act of 1984; the North American Free Trade Agreement Act of 1993 (NAFTA implementation), and the General Agreement on Tariffs and Trade Act of 1994 (GATT implementation).

The importation of a number of products into the US is either prohibited or restricted. These include such heavily regulated products as firearms,

CONTENTS

alcoholic beverages, foods, drugs, and live animals, to name a few. Entry of products such as these requires compliance with specific documentation, quota, licensing, and other restrictions imposed by separate regulatory agencies in addition to standard Customs procedures. For example, alcoholic beverages are subject to federal and state licensing as well as Internal Revenue Service excise taxes in addition to Customs requirements and duties. Even products eligible for special treatment under the various agreements discussed below must comply with any and all other requirements in addition to those imposed by the terms of the agreement under which they seek entry. Cross-border transactions and transfers can be quite complicated. (Refer to the "Import Policy & Procedures" and "Export Policy & Procedures" chapters.)

International trade agreements are usually based on the reciprocal extension of trade privileges between the nationals of sovereign entities. The US Congress routinely grants negotiating authority to undertake such dealings to the President, who operates through the USTR. Specific agreements must then be ratified by the Congress. Many such trade negotiations are conducted on a "fast track" basis in which the resulting agreement and its implementing legislation must be voted on by Congress as it stands without any amendments. Such authority requires that the process be concluded within a specified period of time.

MOST-FAVORED NATION STATUS (MFN)

MFN status represents what has come to be seen as the norm in bilateral trade relationships between countries rather than the special preferential status the name implies. Under MFN status both parties agree not to extend to any third party nation any trade preferences which are more favorable than those available under the agreement concluded between them, unless they simultaneously make the same provisions available to each other. MFN status is reciprocal, with each party agreeing to grant the status to the other. MFN must be negotiated on a separate basis with each and every country. The US requires that all such agreements include provisions for national security exceptions, intellectual property rights protections, a dispute settlement framework, a plan for mutual trade promotion, and various other safeguards. In 1992 US$193.9 billion (37 percent) of total US imports for consumption (US$523.3 billion) consisted of products imported duty free from MFNs, with imports from MFN sources growing at nearly twice the rate of total imports.

Because of the cumulative availability of such provisions to all parties, MFN effectively becomes the international standard. Because of this, the withholding of MFN status becomes a punitive, political act generally reserved only for outlaw states. In fact, even such states as Iran, Iraq, and Libya formally enjoy MFN status, although other US trade sanctions apply to these countries. The US currently withholds MFN status from only a handful of Communist and formerly Communist countries, including Cuba, North Korea, and Vietnam, and bilateral negotiations are underway with both Vietnam and North Korea. An international trade war was narrowly avoided in mid-1994 when the US renewed MFN status for the People's Republic of China after having threatened to allow China's MFN status to lapse. The threat was based on disagreements over China's human rights record, which had been linked to MFN renewal because of domestic political considerations.

Despite the assumption that because MFN status requires equivalent treatment no greater preferential treatment is allowed, international law and practice recognizes that specific countries may make additional arrangements granting special preferences to other nations without violating MFN precepts. Such arrangements include free trade areas between two or more countries and commodity-specific and/or country-specific preferences. International canons approve such arrangements provided that the agreement contains explicit rules of origin specifying limits to the benefits and that the special rate preferences are achieved by lowering internal rates among the participants rather than by raising external tariffs.

THE GENERALIZED SYSTEM OF PREFERENCES (GSP)

GSP programs have been set up by many industrialized nations to assist developing nations by granting selective waivers or reductions of tariffs on imports of products from developing nations. GSP programs in the US, Japan, Canada, and European Community (EC) countries promote growth in and exports from developing countries while also reducing the cost to national consumers of many imported products. More than 4,400 products from some 146 beneficiary entities are eligible for duty free entry under the GSP program.

The US GSP program was established by Title V of the Trade Act of 1974, which authorizes the President to grant duty free treatment to eligible products imported from designated beneficiary developing countries. Title V went into effect on January 1, 1976. Its initial term was 10 years, but the program has since been modified and extended and appears to have become a permanent fixture of US foreign trade policy. In 1993 imports under GSP (US$19.5 billion) were 3.3 percent of total US imports for consumption (US$589.2 billion). However, GSP imports grew at almost two-and-a-half times the rate of total imports.

Eligible Countries There are 117 independent countries, 26 non-independent countries and territories, and three associations of countries treated for customs purposes as single entities eligible for GSP treatment. In addition, 36 of the beneficiary countries, primarily in sub-Saharan Africa, have been designated for special treatment as least developed countries. The current definitive listing is published annually in the Federal Register and can also be found in General Note 4 of the current year's edition of the HTSUS.

Countries excluded as ineligible for GSP treatment include:

* Socialist countries that are not members of GATT or the International Monetary Fund (IMF);
* Members of the Organization of Petroleum Exporting Countries (OPEC), or other countries withholding supplies of vital commodities from trade or otherwise raising the price of such commodities through artificial manipulation;
* Countries that fail to grant reciprocal treatment to the US, especially if they grant preferential treatment to other developed countries;
* Countries that have nationalized property belonging to US citizens without due process and appropriate compensation;
* Countries failing to take adequate steps to prevent traffic in illegal drugs; or
* Countries supporting or granting sanctuary to terrorists.

The list of eligible and ineligible countries is subject to change by Executive Order. The President may waive any of the above criteria in order to grant eligibility to a certain country or category of countries if such is deemed to be in the national interest.

Eligible Products The many products eligible for GSP treatment include a wide range of manufactured and semi-manufactured products, as well as certain agricultural, fishery, and industrial products. Raw materials and similar unprocessed commodities are not generally eligible, although even basic processing qualifies many commodities as semi-manufactured. The USTR is responsible for publishing the complete list of eligible products by HTSUS classification number in the Federal Register each year.

The HTSUS—the document used to classify imports and assign tariff rates on all categories of products imported into the US—includes designations of GSP eligibility. In the HTSUS, items eligible for GSP status are designated with an "A" or an "A*" in the Special Rates of Duty column. "A" indicates that the

---

BASIC GSP REQUIREMENTS

There are seven basic requirements for importing goods duty free under the GSP:

1. The product must be imported from a designated beneficiary developing country (BDC).
2. The product must be on the GSP eligible products list.
3. The product must be entirely grown, produced, or manufactured in the BDC, or it must be primarily the product of the BDC with a minimum of 35 percent of its value coming from the cost of materials and/or direct costs of processing in the BDC.
4. Proper documentation, including a certified United Nations Conference on Trade and Development (UNCTAD) Certificate of Origin Form A, must be submitted in addition to normal customs entry documentation.
5. The product must be imported directly from the BDC to the US.
6. The importer must formally request GSP status.
7. The product must meet the competitive needs limitations, which can be used to limit preferential treatment for specific products from particular countries.

GSP rules exist in addition to regular Customs regulations and procedures, and GSP imports remain subject to all regular Customs requirements such as those governing packing, marking, and labeling, and restrictions and prohibitions on products imported.

---

article can be imported duty free from any beneficiary developing country (BDC). An "A*" means that the article cannot be entered duty free when imported from certain specified BDC's (due to the competitive needs limitations discussed below). Products imported from designated least developed countries are not subject to the restrictions imposed by "A*" status. The most recent, definitive listing of ineligible products from specific countries may be found in the Federal Register and in General Note 4(d) of the current year's HTSUS.

Approximately 2,750 product categories are eligible for entry duty free under the terms of the GSP program, and that these categories often include multiple individual product types, which will all be eligible. Questions concerning the correct tariff classification of items and their GSP status can be addressed to the US Customs Service Classification and Valuation Division.

This office is empowered to issue formal and binding rulings on the classification and GSP status of specific products to individual importers. To make a determination the office requires a complete description of the goods; methods of production or manufacture; specifications and analyses; quantities and costs of the component materials (eligible value added in the BDC is discussed below); proposed shipping route; prospective HTSUS number; and value of proposed shipment. Rulings can take from one to three months. As much data as possible should be included in order to expedite the process. Informal rulings may also be obtained from a local US Customs office, but such rulings are advisory in nature and are not binding. Definitive rulings on GSP status that are of general interest are published in the weekly US Customs Service publication, Customs Bulletins and Decisions.

Listing and Delisting Procedures Eligibility lists are updated annually. At the beginning of each calendar year the USTR prepares a list of countries and products ruled eligible for GSP treatment based on various established criteria. The USTR forwards the list and any recommendations to the President, who makes the final decision based on these criteria and other policy considerations. The USTR must then publish a list of eligible and ineligible countries and products, including any changes in eligibility of countries, products, or specific products from particular countries in the Federal Register within 60 days of the end of the preceding calendar year (that is, by March 1st).

Because no changes officially take effect until the date of publication, products ruled ineligible may continue to enter the US under the terms of the GSP program until official publication. Conversely, after this date products ruled ineligible will not be allowed preference even if they were contracted for and shipped before the deadline. If any doubt exists as to a product's or source's pending future status under GSP, the shipment should be scheduled to arrive at a US port by mid-February to be assured of receiving preferential treatment. In most instances, such products will still be allowed entry but at full duty rates.

Country of Origin and the Value-Added Requirement To be eligible for GSP, a minimum proportion of the components that contribute to the product's finished value must be grown, produced, or manufactured in the BDC. This country of origin requirement is designed to prevent the granting of preferential treatment to products which actually originate elsewhere and receive only insubstantial processing in the eligible country without substantially benefiting that BDC. An item meets the country of origin requirement if:

- It is 100 percent grown, produced, or manufactured in the BDC; or
- It is primarily a product of the BDC with at least 35 percent of its US appraised value coming from the direct costs of BDC materials and processing. This 35 percent of value stipulation constitutes the value-added requirement.

The qualifying value-added requirement enables some goods not wholly produced in the BDC to meet the country of origin requirement for eligibility. Non-eligibility in this situation generally indicates that the cost of imported materials and components is greater than 65 percent. Alternatively, if goods imported into the BDC for incorporation into the final product meet the US Customs requirements for substantial transformation, their value can be added to the cost of BDC materials and processing to make up the 35 percent minimum specified. Substantial transformation usually involves operations such that the processed materials are transformed into a different HTSUS classification.

The 35 percent of value can be composed entirely of the cost of the BDC materials, of the BDC processing operations, of the substantially transformed materials, or any combination of these elements. In practice, the majority of GSP imports are either wholly the product of the BDC or easily meet the 35 percent minimum with their domestic materials or processing alone. Reliance on the substantial transformation rule comes into play only in relatively rare cases.

The value-added requirement necessitates determining the actual costs of domestic materials and processing. In most cases the seller is responsible for making the determination and certifying the results on the appropriate forms. The seller must be prepared to document the costs of materials and processing to ensure that the merchandise meets the requirement. Customs has detailed rules as to what can and cannot be included in the costs being applied to the value-added calculation. Note that the regulations specify direct costs of processing only, so that the 35 percent figure cannot be inflated by adding overhead items to qualify a product.

Appraised Value Customs determines the appraised value—on which the 35 percent value-added requirement is calculated—only at the time of entry and does so somewhat arbitrarily. Nor will Customs give advance rulings on valuation as they will on pre-entry classification and rates of duty.

In general, the appraised value is either the FOB (free on board) or FAS (free alongside ship) value of the goods, which include the costs of transport from the factory to the shipping point. However, to qualify an item for GSP status, the BDC value-added portion of the appraised value must be greater than 35 percent of the item's value ex-works, or at the factory door, which excludes these additional domestic transport costs. Unless the product is one for which Customs has already established a standard value, importers should avoid situations in which the value-added figure is close to the 35 percent requirement.

Documentation In addition to the normal documentation necessary for making a US Customs entry, those claiming GSP treatment must submit an UNCTAD Certificate of Origin Form A, which is also used by other nations offering GSP programs as well as the basis for items subject to other US trade agreements. In most cases the seller will have the responsibility for obtaining, filling out, and certifying Form A. To be accepted by US Customs, Form A must be certified by a designated official authority in the BDC.

To insure duty free treatment, Form A should be submitted along with the usual required documentation at the time of entry. Goods may usually be entered in the absence of this document, but the importer must be prepared to submit it to Customs on demand within a specified period of time. If, when requested, it is not delivered within this period—usually 60 days—the district director will consider the GSP duty free claim as abandoned and levy duties on the goods accordingly.

Direct Importation To be eligible for GSP status, a product must have been "imported directly" into the US, meaning that it has been:

- Shipped directly from the BDC to the US; or
- If, when shipped from a BDC to the US through another country, it does not enter into the commerce of that country, and the invoices, bills of lading, and other documents show the US as the final destination; or
- If, when shipped through another BDC's free trade zone, the product does not enter into the commerce of that third country, is altered only in ways that do not constitute a manufacturing process, and the importer obtains a second Country of Origin Form A from the certifying authority in the BDC maintaining the free trade zone that states what operations were performed there.

GSP Request The importer must formally request GSP treatment. This is accomplished by prefixing the letter "A" to the HTSUS number for each article on the entry document for which GSP status is claimed.

Competitive Needs Limitations The purpose of the US GSP program is to make eligible products competitive in US markets, but not to the point that they seriously undersell comparable US goods. To protect domestic industry, an overly competitive product from a specific country loses its eligibility

at least temporarily. Known as the competitive needs limitation, this requires that imports into the US of any specific article from any single country:

- Must not represent more than 50 percent of the total imports to the US of that article during the previous year; or
- Must not exceed an amount set annually based on a dollar value adjusted in proportion to the US gross national product (GNP). The original amount set in 1976 was US$25 million, and the figure has increased annually in proportion to cumulative growth in the GNP.

If either of these limits is reached during the calendar year, the product from that country loses eligibility during the next year. The current list of ineligible products is published in the Federal Register and in General Note 4(d) of the HTSUS.

A country's product can regain eligibility the following year if the volume of imports of the product from the country on a non-preferential basis during the year falls below the levels established by the competitive needs limitations. However, in some cases the USTR may decide not to reinstate an item from a particular country because it is considered to have become competitive even without the GSP benefits. This determination may also be made if the USTR judges that with preferences the item will likely become ineligible again the following year.

Competitive needs limitations apply to a relatively small number of imports: the 1994 list of articles ineligible under this provision includes about 975 product categories from 18 countries. The nations primarily affected were India and Brazil, as well as several other countries located primarily in South America and Southeast Asia. Specific questions about GSP eligibility or procedures may be referred to either the Trade Policy Staff Subcommittee at the Office of the US Trade Representative or the GSP Program Manager in the Duty Assessment Division at Customs.

Import Sensitivity A number of articles are ineligible for GSP treatment because they are "import sensitive;" that is, their importation is or could potentially be harmful to domestic industry. Such items have included various categories of footwear; textiles and apparel; watches; electronic products; certain glass, steel, and iron products; ball bearings; and plywood.

Import sensitive products are specifically excluded from GSP status either by the legislation or by a later Executive Order. Very few items lose GSP eligibility because of import sensitivity. However, determinations of import sensitivity are subjective and decisions are usually made on a case-by-case basis.

GATT AND THE WTO

The General Agreement on Tariffs and Trade, known generally as GATT, is designed to provide a standard framework for global trade. Founded in 1947 with 23 members, GATT has passed through 8 series of negotiations, known as rounds and named after the location in which the opening session of each round was held. The most recent is the Uruguay Round, begun in 1986. Initially this round was to have been completed by 1990, but was extended as the agreement became more ambitious and more difficult to conclude.

The Uruguay Round finally came to include an overall tariff reduction of 38 percent—higher than the less ambitious reduction originally targeted—the reduction of nontariff barriers, and the integration of the series of bilateral Multi-Fiber Arrangements (MFA) into a single multilateral agreement that has the effect of phasing out quotas. The final agreement also included provisions on services, intellectual property rights (IPR), and subsidies. The final document proposed the adoption of the provisions and an agreement to submit to the authority of a newly created body, the World Trade Organization (WTO), which will have the authority to hand down binding decisions in trade disputes.

Signed in December 1993 by 124 member countries, the agreement was ratified by the US Congress in December 1994. By that point, some 36 countries had already ratified the agreement, although major trading economies had postponed their votes to see how the US would act. Subsequent to US ratification, Canada and Japan also ratified the agreement. Action by the European Community countries remained somewhat in question, but most observers were expecting them to fall in line eventually. By the time of the US ratification vote, 22 countries outside GATT, including China, Russia, and Taiwan, had applied for membership.

Effects The agreement is expected to facilitate international trade through increased outsourcing of intermediate products and parts, allowing various producers to achieve greater economies of scale by removing artificial barriers to sources and markets. The US has calculated that the reduction in tariffs worldwide will amount to a saving of US$744 billion. But although the US is expected to gain US$122 billion in increased export sales and reduced import costs during the first 10 years of GATT, it is also expected to lose US$40 billion in reduced tariff collections. Because US law requires that any reduction in revenues be made up either by offsetting reductions in expenditures or new sources of revenue, this prospect has caused concern both in domestic political circles and in an international community worried by huge US deficits.

GATT is also on record as promoting international free trade and opposing regional trade blocs that may lead to preferential treatment among members at the expense of nonmembers. This would theoretically include such bodies as the EC, NAFTA, Mercosur, APEC, and various similar regional trade pacts.

Provisions The Uruguay Round final agreement consists of more than 20,000 pages of text, so that the actual extent of its provisions are expected to remain unclear for some time. In general, GATT calls for the replacement of absolute quotas, which bar imports of quota items above a threshold level, with tariff rate quotas, which allow in essentially unlimited quantities but at higher duties. Eventually the levels on such tariff rate quotas are supposed to be reduced as well.

Other notable provisions involve strengthened intellectual property rights (IPR); the elimination of local content requirements; an agreement to remove national health and safety regulations as barriers to international trade; and conventions regarding the opening of service industries.

Of major importance to many developed as well as developing countries are the provisions involving trade in textiles and apparel. Currently regulated under the Multi-Fiber Arrangement which strictly limits imports by major consuming nations, such as the US, fiber, cloth, and garment exports and imports are to be deregulated over a period of 10 years. US domestic producers were unhappy over the loss of protection and their representatives even held up the ratification vote on GATT. However, exporting countries have been even less satisfied, arguing that the lengthy phase-out period harms them in their efforts to build up their industrial base. The Uruguay Round agreement also calls for limitations on voluntary restraint agreements; changes in how antidumping charges are calculated, assessed, and resolved; limits on government subsidies to various industries and activities; and an agreement to revisit the area of free trade in services.

Industrial signatory countries are to eliminate tariffs on a variety of products, including beer, distilled spirits, construction equipment, farm machinery, medical devices, furniture, paper products, pharmaceuticals, steel, and toys. Tariffs on chemicals are to be phased out over a 15-year period, with some strategic exceptions allowed. Tariffs are to be lowered on electronic products such as semiconductors and pharmaceuticals, with both expected to receive added protection under IPR provisions. Under these new IPR rules, trademarks will be protected for 7 years, patents for 20 years, and copyrights for 50 years. Official research and development (R&D) subsidies will also be limited to no more than 75 percent for basic research and 50 percent for applied research.

One of the most important sectors to the US and various other countries, particularly those in the EC, is agriculture. This is also the issue that took the longest to resolve. Tariffs on agricultural products are to be reduced 36 percent by developed countries and 24 percent by developing countries. Agricultural subsidies, currently estimated at US$160 billion per year, are to be reduced by 21 percent over 6 years, as are quotas. The US is to drop its strict absolute quota protections on peanuts, sugar, and dairy products, converting them to tariff rate quotas, with rates to be further reduced over time. Despite hefty US farm support programs, the country is expected to benefit more than many of its competitors which, it argues, maintain even higher agricultural subsidy levels.

Areas of Disagreement Specific areas excluded from GATT due to a failure of the major parties to reach agreement include aircraft, entertainment, financial services, shipping, steel, and telecommunications. The main antagonists over most of these issues have been the US and the EC. The US has vehemently protested what it views as heavy subsidies given to the Airbus consortium by EC governments. By limiting such subsidies, the US also seeks to forestall the entry into the international aircraft market as producers of such potential rivals as Japan and China.

The US was also angered by EC refusals to open many entertainment markets—particularly cinema and television programming—on the grounds of national cultural sovereignty, and a failure to lower regulatory barriers to allow full participation in financial service markets. As it is, several US service providers have pointed out that although US practitioners, such as attorneys, may be allowed into more countries under the terms of GATT, they may still be excluded from operating in many specific areas of business that are reserved for national professionals.

However, the US itself bars foreign professionals from practicing within its territory, although it does allow foreign professional consultants affiliated with US firms and does not prohibit foreign citizens from practicing provided they can pass its certification procedures. With some limited exceptions and subject to reciprocal accords, US professionals must generally be licensed in each of 50 separate state jurisdictions in order to practice across state lines, an insurmountable barrier even for US nationals. In general, the US has agreed to open its professional service markets only to the extent that it receives reciprocal concessions from other countries.

The dominant US telecommunications industry was displeased at the failure to reach an accord on opening that market globally. The struggling US shipping industry did not receive the kinds of help that it wanted in its struggle with lower cost international competition, nor did the hard-pressed US steel industry receive many concessions. The complaints of the US textile industry have already been noted.

The WTO Designed along the lines of such independent international bodies as the World Bank and the IMF, the WTO will conduct future trade policy negotiations among GATT signatories and be responsible for adjudicating disputes. The WTO will operate through a bureaucracy and three-judge panels which will arbitrate specific disputes in secrecy. Unlike GATT, which required consensus and in which the loser could simply veto an unfavorable verdict, WTO decisions may be appealed, but the final results are to be binding. Nations failing to conform their practice and laws to WTO rulings may have compensating sanctions levied against them. Any signatory may withdraw from the WTO, but this is expected to have major repercussions as the body becomes more established.

This potential loss of sovereignty under the WTO was among the main reasons for opposition to the treaty in the US, which fears that as the world's largest trading nation it could become the focus of invidious unfavorable rulings by countries otherwise too weak to obtain concessions from it. Others worry that US labor, environmental, and consumer protection measures could be challenged as anticompetitive, resulting in a lowering of international standards to the lowest common denominator rather than an elevation of overall standards.

GATT and the WTO will become separate organizations, with GATT being phased out as new business is shifted over to the WTO. In reality the two will overlap for some time because the WTO is not ready to begin functioning. As of the end of 1994, it did not even have a president. The US pushed the candidacy of Carlos Salinas de Gotari, the retiring president of Mexico, while the EC nominated Renato Ruggiero, a former Italian prime minister. South Korea's Trade Minister Kim Chul Su was also a candidate, favored by several Asian countries. Because the official must elected unanimously, the need for compromise may dictate that none of these candidates will be acceptable to specific portions of the membership. Hence the potential exists for a messy and divisive fight.

A subsidiary issue concerns the fear that influential countries such as the US would resign from GATT as soon as the WTO was constituted. This would leave several ongoing disputes without resolution and deprive GATT of the financial and moral support of its dominant members during the transition period. As of year-end 1994, the US had provisionally agreed to stay in GATT for at least one year.

THE NORTH AMERICAN
FREE TRADE AGREEMENT (NAFTA)*

NAFTA has created an economic bloc consisting of the US, Canada, and Mexico, which in 1993 had a combined gross domestic product (GDP) greater than US$6.5 trillion. The agreement is designed to open up markets and reinforce the effects of freer competition among its signatories. Implementation of NAFTA creates cross-border opportunities in trade, operations, investment, and various services. In addition, it covers other subjects that affect business in the region, such as intellectual property rights, technical standards, and labor and environmental issues. Specifically, the agreement calls for the gradual elimination of tariff and non-tariff barriers in a variety of areas and removes numerous impediments to investment, such as performance requirements and exclusionary approval procedures.

Although it is difficult to attribute all of the increased trade among the three partners to the effects of NAFTA, the consensus among observers is that the pact has had a major influence during its first partial year of existence. As of mid-year 1994, US exports to Mexico were up 17 percent and those to Canada up 10 percent. US imports from these two partners were up 17 percent and 11 percent, respectively, and indications were that these rates of growth were continuing to accelerate during the fall of 1994. In the first half of the year the US's trade surplus with Mexico fell by 44 percent, and its deficit with Canada increased by 55 percent. According to various estimates, jobs created in the US because of NAFTA numbered between 100,000 and 130,000, while those certified as lost due to the accord officially numbered only 12,700. Other observers argue that this job loss figure severely understates the true effect because official certification of job losses as NAFTA-related is difficult to achieve. According to the US Department of Labor more than 30,000 applications were received. The American Federation of Labor-Congress of Industrial Organizations (AFL-CIO), the umbrella organization for organized labor in the US, calculated that the actual number of displaced workers was more than 47,000.

Praise for the agreement has not been universal. Observers note that the 20 separate NAFTA multilateral commissions have been slow to begin functioning, nor has the new North American Development Bank started making loans as projected. The US focus and consensus on trade has been interrupted by domestic political concerns, and prospective new NAFTA partners are concerned about their chances for joining the pact any time soon. (In December 1994 the NAFTA parties did extend a formal invitation to Chile to apply for membership.) Canada has also raised doubts about what it fears is a US attempt to establish a "hub-and-spoke" arrangement in which the much larger US becomes the primary intermediary for direct international trade, parceling out the benefits secondhand to its junior partners. And while large Mexican companies are experiencing a boom in business, small Mexican businesses report that they are operating under unaccustomed severe competitive pressures.

Concern also exists that NAFTA could become divisive. As an agreement offering preferential treatment to specified partners on a regional basis, it runs counter to the thrust of GATT, which is designed to reduce trade barriers internationally instead of on a limited basis. As such NAFTA could provoke a rise in competing, regionally-based organizations. Many outsiders already see the EC as such an exclusionary bloc, while the proposed APEC free trade zone composed of the Pacific Rim countries, and Mercosur in Latin America could also become such exclusionary trading blocs. NAFTA members have stated that they are interested in including new members, with the idea that the agreement's preferential provisions could ultimately be extended to all the countries of the Americas and beyond.

Rules and Principles

Competition NAFTA requires the parties to adopt, maintain, and enforce rules against anticompetitive business practices. Government enterprises—federal, state, provincial, and local—will be required to abide by NAFTA nondiscrimination principles when exercising their authority, including the granting of licenses. NAFTA includes specific rules on government and private monopolies, including prohibitions against discrimination. Moreover, a trilateral trade and competition committee will review laws within the framework of the principles of free trade.

Dispute Resolution NAFTA provides several methods for the resolution of disputes. The NAFTA Trilateral Trade Commission will monitor trade relations among the parties and establish bilateral or trilateral panels of private sector trade experts to resolve specific disputes. If the recommendations regarding the resolution of particular disputes are not carried out, the aggrieved nation is authorized to withdraw "equivalent trade concessions." NAFTA provides for the establishment of special panels to review antidumping and countervailing duty cases as well as special provisions for resolving disputes involving environmental and health issues. These panels will analyze whether actions taken are consistent with the member's domestic laws to ensure

---

* Prepared in consultation with Dean C. Alexander, LL.M, J.D., Director, The NAFTA Research Institute, Washington, DC; Co-editor, NAFTA Law and Policy Series, Martinus Nijhoff Publishers; President, Septacontinentaux Corp., Bethesda, Maryland.

fair administration and guard against any weakening of standards. NAFTA also encourages resolution of private commercial disputes through alternative dispute settlement procedures, and the resolution of investment disputes through international arbitration.

Government Procurement NAFTA eliminates such discriminatory practices as requiring the use of domestic purchasers or suppliers in government procurement. The agreement opens a significant portion of the government procurement market to nondiscriminatory bidding. The mechanisms for the liberalization of this area are NAFTA's national treatment principle, most-mavored nation treatment, and predetermined, transparent procedures.

NAFTA covers federal government agencies, departments, and enterprises in each contracting nation. The agreement applies to federal government procurement of goods and services if the amount exceeds US$50,000 (US$25,000 if for goods only) and to federal construction projects valued at US$6.5 million or more. NAFTA is also applicable to procurement by federal state-run enterprises exceeding US$250,000 in goods and services and construction projects valued at US$10 million or more. Mexico will phase in these NAFTA procurement provisions over a transition period; they became effective in Canada and the US immediately. NAFTA recognizes that modifications of government rules are necessary, particularly with respect to state and provincial level government procurement.

Intellectual Property Rights NAFTA provides a high standard of protection for copyrights (including sound recordings), patents, trademarks, trade secrets, plant breeders' rights, industrial designs, and integrated circuits (semiconductor chips). Copyright provisions provide protection for 50 years. The agreement's patent protection provisions safeguard inventions in many areas, including pharmaceuticals and agricultural chemicals. NAFTA provides for strong enforcement, including provisions for damages, injunctive relief, and due process.

Investment NAFTA's coverage of investment issues includes ownership of tangible and intangible property, contractual rights, and both minority and majority interests in business and other types of investments such as securities and real estate. NAFTA significantly reduces the need for prior foreign government approval of investments. The agreement also provides for the elimination of various investment distortions, including the requirements that foreign investors use domestic suppliers; export a given amount of product; limit imports to a certain percentage of exports; or require the transfer of technology. Furthermore, NAFTA prohibits discrimination against investors who seek to acquire, establish, or operate a business in the member countries. Under NAFTA the members agree to eliminate screening of new foreign investments in most sectors and to limit the nature of official review in takeovers of existing enterprises.

Investments in a NAFTA country by a party from another NAFTA country are protected from arbitrary and uncompensated expropriation. NAFTA establishes procedural guidelines for the resolution of investment disputes through arbitration, including binding international arbitration. If a country expropriates the property of a national of another member country, the agreement provides for the full repatriation in foreign currency of the investors' profits, royalties, and capital as well as for fair compensation to the injured party.

Despite its comprehensive scope with regard to investment, the agreement contains some country-specific exceptions to the principles of national treatment and most-favored nation treatment, and upholds certain performance requirements. NAFTA does not cover investment in maritime concerns, government sponsored technology consortia, and research and development programs.

Market Access NAFTA covers numerous areas relevant to market access, including tariffs, quotas, and import licenses. Most significantly, the NAFTA countries have agreed to remove most import and export restrictions. Under specified circumstances each NAFTA nation may establish restrictions directly related to health, safety, and welfare as long as these are not designed as barriers to market entry. Under NAFTA drawbacks are to be phased out by 2001, with new mechanisms to cover items that remain subject to duties in the free trade area in order "to avoid the 'double taxation' effects of the payment of duties in two countries."

The NAFTA parties have also agreed not to impose additional customs user fees. The US eliminated customs user fees on items of Canadian origin at the beginning of 1994, and the US and Mexico have agreed to eliminate merchandise processing fees on goods originating from their respective countries by mid-1999. Along similar lines, NAFTA provides that Mexico will eliminate its performance-based customs duty waiver program. Following the preexisting US-Canada Free Trade Agreement (CFTA) provisions, Canada will eliminate such existing duty remission programs by 1998. Finally, NAFTA deals with various other issues, including export taxes, other export measures, and duty free temporary admission of goods.

Tariffs NAFTA provides for the gradual elimination of tariffs on US, Mexican, and Canadian products by the member states based on the Harmonized Commodity Description and Coding System (HS) classification. The reduction in tariffs will occur at different stages on a variety of products. Some tariffs were eliminated when the agreement became effective, while tariffs on other products will be removed over periods of five or 10 years. Tariffs on some sensitive products will not be completely re-moved for 15 years. Tariffs on US–Canadian trade will continue to follow CFTA provisions.

Rules of Origin Two explicit and strict rules of origin mechanisms are established under NAFTA: tariff-shift and value-content. Tariff-shift rules require that all non-NAFTA inputs must be transformed into a product with a different HS chapter heading or tariff item number from that under which they were admitted. Under NAFTA value-content rules, a set percentage of the value of the product must be of North American origin. This rule is often used in conjunction with a tariff-shift requirement, although some goods with non-NAFTA inputs are subject to the value-content rule as an alternative to the tariff-shift test. In addition a de minimis rule allows NAFTA origin treatment for items containing as much as 7 percent non-NAFTA content.

Rules of origin are strict and rather complex, requiring substantial documentation of North American content in order to obtain NAFTA duty free status. These provisions are intended to prevent non-member states from using a NAFTA partner as a minor processing, transshipment, or export platform center in an effort to obtain NAFTA benefits.

NAFTA establishes specific rules of origin for various trade sectors. For example, light trucks and passenger vehicles ultimately will have to demonstrate 62.5 percent North American content to obtain preferential treatment. NAFTA provides for the imposition of a 60 percent North American content requirement on other vehicles following a phase-in period. In the textiles sector, NAFTA requires that eligible garments be made from North American fabric and yarn. Finally, in order for computers to qualify under NAFTA, the motherboard (accounting for 20 to 40 percent of the value of a computer) must be manufactured in North America.

Technical Standards NAFTA affirms the rights of each party to adopt, apply, and enforce its own standards designed to promote safety and protect people, animals, plants, and the environment. However, NAFTA stipulates that standards-related measures must provide both national treatment and most-favored nation—that is, neutral—treatment for all members. The agreement establishes procedures for determining whether such requirements are being complied with and enforced even-

NAFTA: CERTIFICATE OF ORIGIN

To qualify goods for NAFTA treatment, an importer makes a declaration directly on the import documentation, requesting NAFTA treatment based on a valid NAFTA Certificate of Origin. The actual certificate must be presented to Customs on request. However, if the certificate is found to contain inaccurate information, the importer will be required to submit a corrected declaration and pay any additional duties as required.

A NAFTA Certificate of Origin is a uniform, printed form used in all NAFTA countries. It is completed and signed by the exporter, who must then provide it to the importer (and customs officials of the exporting country, if requested). An exporter who is not also the producer of the goods may nevertheless complete a NAFTA Certificate of Origin on the basis of any of the following:

1. The exporter's knowledge that the goods meet the origination rules.
2. The exporter's reasonable reliance on the written statement of the producer that the goods meet the origination rules.
3. The producer's completed NAFTA Certificate of Origin

for the goods, signed and voluntarily provided to the exporter.

A NAFTA certificate might cover a single importation of goods, or multiple importations of identical goods, or multiple shipments of more than one type of goods. The last of these three, the NAFTA Certificate of Origin for multiple shipments, is a blanket certificate; it applies to the various goods specified in the certificate imported within a designated 12-month period. The blanket certificate will remain valid for NAFTA preference claims made up to four years from the date the certificate was signed. This delayed date of validity allows a person who initially imports goods within the 12-month period—but then fails to enter them into the country for use within that time—nevertheless to claim NAFTA treatment after the 12-month expires period but within the four-year period.

Even if NAFTA treatment is not requested at the time of importation, it may still be requested up to one year after that date. The importer and exporter must provide copies of the NAFTA certificate to their respective customs administrations on request.

handedly. Moreover, NAFTA encourages agreements between governments and private organizations for conformance and mutual acceptance of test results and certification procedures. Finally, NAFTA generally requires that changes in standards-related measures be subject to a public notice procedure.

Goods and Services

Agricultural Products Under NAFTA, Mexican tariffs on certain sensitive products originating in the US and Canada will be phased out over as long as 15 years. All US and Mexican non-tariff barriers—such as licensing—will be converted to either tariff-rate quotas or ordinary tariffs during a phase-in period. CFTA provisions will continue to govern US–Canadian trade in agricultural products.

Automotive Products NAFTA is intended to liberalize and integrate the North American automotive sector by reducing barriers, increasing competitiveness, creating employment opportunities, and reducing prices paid by consumers. Mexican tariff and non-tariff restrictions on foreign sales to and participation in the Mexican market will be phased out over a 10-year period. Adjustments to US Corporate Fuel Economy rules will enable Mexican-produced parts and vehicles exported to the US to be classified as approved domestic products. US–Canadian automotive issues will continue to be covered by provisions of the CFTA.

Energy Implementation of NAFTA immediately reduced trade and investment restrictions in many areas of the Mexican energy market. While retaining the national monopoly in the core energy production sector, it allows firms to negotiate supply contracts directly with Mexican natural gas and basic petrochemicals entities. The Mexican State Electricity Commission (CFE) and utilities in the US and Canada will also be able to negotiate power purchase and sales contracts. The US–Canadian energy sector will continue to be governed by the provisions of the CFTA.

Environment NAFTA added environmental provisions that had not been a part of the CFTA. The agreement will create a series of mutual standards, protections, and procedures as well as many opportunities for environmental equipment firms and services. NAFTA's trade liberalization should in particular increase US exports of control and mitigation technology to Mexico and Canada.

Existing environmental accords, such as the Montreal Protocol on Substances that Deplete the Ozone Layer, have primacy over conflicting NAFTA provisions. NAFTA also encourages the upgrading of environmental standards in the three member nations. The agreement requires the maintenance of stringent health, safety, and environmental standards, requiring national treatment for investments. Environmental impact assessments must be made

for such investments. The NAFTA parties established the North American Commission on Environmental Cooperation in September, 1992, to "set in motion a process for sustained, long-term effective trilateral environmental cooperation."

Financial Services NAFTA provides a comprehensive approach to the regulation of providers of various financial services. The agreement contains definitive liberalization commitments and transition periods for the opening of markets. A key benefit of the agreement is that those involved in transactions in one member country will be able to use the same financial service providers for both domestic and international operations and allow foreign member operations in one country to process their financial materials in their home country. NAFTA also stipulates the need for transparency in applications procedures for the creation of financial institutions. Finally, the financial services sector will be subject to NAFTA's dispute settlement mechanism. Specific US–Canadian financial services commitments made under CFTA are incorporated into NAFTA. Mexico will permit financial firms organized according to NAFTA's requirements to be established in Mexico under certain market share limits, with these limits to be eliminated by the year 2000.

Sanitary and Phytosanitary Measures This section of NAFTA focuses on the establishment and enforcement of standards for the protection of human, animal, and plant life, as well as standards for health risks due to animal pests or plant diseases, food additives, or food contaminants. While providing that each NAFTA country may establish its own sanitary and phytosanitary rules, the agreement stipulates that such regulations must be based on scientific principle and risk assessment and must be applied only to the extent necessary to meet the country's chosen level of protection. Such regulations may not be designed to restrict trade. NAFTA generally requires public notice prior to the adoption or modification of such measures, while calling for member nations to work toward the eventual establishment of harmonized standards.

Services NAFTA improves access to Canada's US$250 billion services market, opens Mexico's largely closed US$146 billion services market, and further opens the US$4.5 trillion US services market to providers from the other member countries. The agreement liberalizes trade-related services by extending the basic principles of national treatment and most-favored nation treatment to this sector. NAFTA also eliminates the requirement that a service provider establish a local presence and resident status. Nevertheless, some restrictions on services remain, including various state, provincial, or federal reservations, non-discriminatory quantitative restrictions, licensing and certification requirements, denial of benefits to specific firms, and basic exclusions and reservations.

Among the key service sectors affected by NAFTA are: accounting, advertising, architecture, management and business consulting, construction, engineering, enhanced telecommunications, environmental services, health care management, land and property management, and aspects of law, medicine, and tourism. Although domestic maritime services are not covered by NAFTA, reference is made to the goal of maintaining relatively open international shipping markets. NAFTA excludes aviation but does cover specialty air services such as aerial mapping and surveying.

Telecommunications While NAFTA does not open basic telecommunications services, such as local and long-distance telephone services, it does open up services such as advanced data-processing and other enhancements. Specific rules on access to and use of public telecommunications networks are set out in the agreement, and NAFTA establishes an impetus toward future compatibility of interoperable telecommunications services in the US, Mexico, and Canada. However, it does not require contracting parties to provide or operate telecommunications networks or services for other contracting parties.

Textiles and Apparel NAFTA covers a wide range of products, including fibers, yarns, textiles, and clothing. The member states have agreed that NAFTA should have primacy over other existing textile agreements, and specific NAFTA provisions result in an effective increase of certain quotas, reserving the increase for suppliers from member countries. The signatories will immediately remove—or phase out over a maximum period of 10 years—customs duties on textiles and apparel that satisfy NAFTA rules of origin. Under NAFTA, the US will initially remove import quotas on such goods produced in Mexico, and will gradually remove import quotas on other Mexican textiles and apparel that do not meet NAFTA rules of origin. Both Canada and Mexico will phase out tariffs on apparel over 10 years and tariffs on other textile products over eight years.

NAFTA minimally increases most quotas on textiles and apparel by 2 percent per year for five years. The agreement does permit the use of unilaterally imposed tariff or quota increases should serious damage to domestic markets results from the greater volume of imports. NAFTA provides strict rules of origin, including provisions covering yarn and fiber content, and establishes tariff rate quotas on many products. Finally, more extensive textile and apparel labeling requirements are applicable under NAFTA.

Transportation NAFTA removes barriers to various land transport services and establishes a framework for compatible land transport technical and safety standards. Member nation charter and tour bus operators will acquire full access to regular bus routes in the signatory countries by the end of 1996. Because the Mexican market was the most restricted, most NAFTA provisions deal with opening it to US and Canadian firms. Although land transport was not specifically covered in the CFTA, reciprocal access between the two nations had been relatively more open.

NAFTA will allow foreign member bus and trucking firms to carry international passengers and cargo throughout the bloc on a phased in schedule. However, the agreement does not obligate NAFTA countries to remove restrictions on foreign member truck carriage of internal domestic cargoes. Mexico will allow US and Canadian firms to be the sole owners and operators of various transportation and port facilities used by firms handling their own cargo or firms handling other companies' cargo. Finally, NAFTA provides for the harmonization of operating and safety standards within a 3- to 6-year period. These include drivers' licenses, equipment standards, and the standards relevant to the transport of dangerous goods.

NAFTA Supplemental Agreements

The US, Mexico, and Canada agreed to supplemental accords to NAFTA on issues of labor, environmental, and import surges. These supplemental accords were designed to ensure enforcement of domestic environmental laws and workplace standards. The accords prohibit the signatories from lowering existing labor or environmental standards, although members are allowed to make such standards more stringent unless the motivation is to restrain trade. All states or provinces of the member countries remain free to enact even more stringent measures. In addition, the process of consultation, evaluation, and dispute settlement is to be opened to public comment. Access to the justice system and due process rights are to be extended to environmental and labor issues, and new administrative remedies have been added to existing formal legal procedures. The accords provide for the establishment of multilateral commissions to evaluate and settle disputes on labor and environmental issues.

Import Surges NAFTA contains several provisions safeguarding a country's industry and workforce against import surges. A bilateral safeguard mechanism permits a "snap-back" to pre-NAFTA or most-favored nation tariff rates for as long as four years if increased imports from Mexico are a substantial cause of or threaten serious injury to a US domestic industry. A global safeguard mechanism allows the imposition of tariffs or quotas on imports from Mexico or Canada, or both, as part of a multilateral safeguard action when imports from either or both countries threaten or cause injury to a US domestic industry. In addition, sensitive agricultural products are handled with tariff-rate quotas, under which higher most-favored nation tariffs become effective above a specified level of imports. Sensitive textile and apparel products are also covered by special provisions.

OTHER TRADE AGREEMENTS

The Agreement on Trade in Civil Aircraft

The Agreement on Trade in Civil Aircraft provides for the duty free importation of complete new or used aircraft for civil use. To be eligible, the importer must file a written statement with US Customs accompanied by documentation as required by the Secretary of the Treasury stating that the import is for use in US domestic civil aviation and that the product has been approved either by the US Federal Aviation Administration (FAA) or by the corresponding authority in the exporting country. Such exporting country certifications are accepted only if the FAA has previously certified that these overseas authorities enforce standards in conformance with and at least as stringent as those in effect in the US. In practice, only aircraft meeting these criteria—at present only those from countries with an established aerospace industry—are allowed to be imported into the US. Civil aircraft include all aircraft other than those purchased for use by the US Department of Defense or the US Coast Guard.

The Automotive Products Trade Act

The Automotive Products Trade Act provides for the duty free import of completed motor vehicles—cars, trucks, and similar vehicles—and original equipment for them from Canada. The products must originate in Canada. Such products can only be imported by a Department of Commerce (DOC) approved US manufacturer. In order to be approved, manufacturers must have produced at least 15 completed vehicles in the US during the previous 12 months and possess installed capacity to produce 10 or more completed vehicles per 40-hour week. The DOC publishes its list of approved manufacturers in the Federal Register.

The Caribbean Basin Initiative

The Caribbean Basin Initiative (CBI) is a program providing for duty free or reduced duty entry of merchandise from designated beneficiary countries or territories. This program, established by the Caribbean Basin Economic Recovery Act (CBERA), began in 1984 and has no expiration date. Designated beneficiaries include: Antigua and Barbuda, Aruba, the Bahamas, Barbados, Belize, Costa Rica, Dominica,

the Dominican Republic, El Salvador, Grenada, Guatemala, Guyana, Haiti, Honduras, Jamaica, Montserrat, the Netherlands Antilles, Nicaragua, Panama, St. Kitts and Nevis, Saint Lucia, Saint Vincent and the Grenadines, Trinidad and Tobago, and the British Virgin Islands. In 1993 US$6.6 billion of goods were entered duty free under the provisions of the CBI out of US$10.1 billion of total US imports from CBI nations, up from US$1.5 billion in duty free imports in 1992.

Merchandise must be imported directly into the US from the beneficiary country. At least 35 percent of the appraised value of eligible items must be derived from substantial operations performed on them within one or more beneficiary countries. Work performed in US controlled areas—the Commonwealth of Puerto Rico and the US Virgin Islands—may be included for up to 15 percent of this required 35 percent total. The US Secretary of the Treasury may require that specific products be wholly derived from the exporting country. Eligible products may be imported in bond into Puerto Rico for processing and removed afterwards without paying additional duty. Importers must be prepared to submit a generic UNCTAD Certificate of Origin Form A obtained from the exporter to US Customs to document eligibility of the product ("GSP" is to be crossed out and "Caribbean Basin Initiative" substituted on this form).

Many sugar, syrup, and molasses products are ineligible for special treatment under the CBI because of the overriding restrictive quota status of such items. A somewhat broader range of such products as well as beef and veal products originating from the following islands are restricted: Antigua and Barbuda, Montserrat, the Netherlands Antilles, Saint Lucia, and Saint Vincent and the Grenadines. Many textile products subject to international quota agreements are excluded. However, handloomed fabrics and textile articles produced by cottage industries as well as traditional folkloric handicraft textile products may be imported duty free if they are certified as such in accord with arrangements between the US and the specific beneficiary country. Watches and watch parts originating in countries subject to trade restrictions with the US but processed in a beneficiary country are ineligible.

Some leather articles—including handbags, luggage, flat goods, work gloves, and leather apparel—that were not designated as GSP eligible as of August 5, 1983 are eligible for entry at reduced rates of duty if otherwise in compliance with the provisions of the CBI.

Questions regarding eligibility and procedures under the CBI may be addressed to the Office of Trade Operations at the US Customs Service.

The US-Israel Free Trade Area

The US-Israel Free Trade Area is an agreement providing for duty free entry into the US of eligible products originating in Israel. This agreement was authorized in the Trade and Import Act of 1984 and implemented by the US-Israel Free Trade Area Implementation Act of 1985 and Presidential Proclamation 5365 on August 30, 1985. It became effective on September 1, 1985. As of January 1, 1995 all items previously eligible for import at a reduced rate under the agreement were scheduled to become duty free.

Most articles are eligible for special treatment under the program provided that they are grown, produced, or manufactured in Israel and are imported directly into the US from Israel. The cost or value of the materials and the direct costs of processing the article must constitute at least 35 percent of the appraised value of the product (up to 15 percent of the 35 percent may represent US-derived cost or value of items transmitted to Israel for processing). Third country content may be included if it is substantially transformed in Israel, usually by transformation into another HTSUS category.

Importers must be prepared to submit a generic UNCTAD Certificate of Origin Form A obtained from the exporter to US Customs to document the eligibility of the entry ("GSP" is to be crossed out and "Israel Free Trade Area Agreement" is to be substituted on this form).

Questions regarding eligibility and procedures under the US-Israel Free Trade Area Agreement may be addressed to the Trade Policy Staff Subcommittee at the Office of the US Trade Representative.

The Andean Trade Preference Act

The Andean Trade Preference Act (ATPA) is a program providing for the duty free entry of merchandise from the following designated beneficiary countries: Bolivia, Colombia, Ecuador, and Peru. The program was established on December 4, 1991 and is scheduled to expire on December 4, 2001. In 1993 US$400 million in goods were admitted duty free from ATPA beneficiaries out of a total of US$5.3 billion in imports from ATPA countries.

Most products from beneficiary countries are eligible for duty free entry into the US. However, products excluded from preferential treatment include textiles and apparel articles subject to existing textile agreements; some footwear; certain tuna products; petroleum products; watches and watch parts originating in countries subject to US trade restrictions; various sugar products; and rum and tafia.

Eligible products must be grown, produced, or manufactured in a beneficiary country and be imported directly into the US from that country. The cost or value of the materials and the direct costs of processing the article in one or more ATPA beneficiary countries or in countries designated under the CBI must constitute at least 35 percent of the appraised value of the product (up to 15 percent of the 35 percent may represent the cost or value of US inputs), and third country content may be included if it is substantially transformed in a beneficiary country.

Importers must be prepared to submit a generic UNCTAD Certificate of Origin Form A obtained from the exporter to US Customs to document the eligibility of the entry ("GSP" is crossed out on this form and "Andean Trade Preference Act" substituted).

Questions regarding eligibility and procedures under the ATPA may be addressed to the Office of Trade Operations at the US Customs Service.

The Compact of Free Association

The Compact of Free Association is a program providing duty free entry into the US of merchandise from the designated freely associated Pacific states of the Marshall Islands and the Federated States of Micronesia. Established by Section 242 of Presidential Proclamation 6030 on September 28, 1989, it became effective on October 18, 1989 and has no expiration date.

Duty free treatment is available for most products. However, excluded product categories include textile and apparel articles subject to existing textile agreements; footwear; handbags, luggage, flat goods, work gloves, and leather apparel not eligible for GSP treatment as of April 1, 1984; watches and watch parts; buttons of acrylic or polyester resins; and certain tuna and skipjack products. As with GSP status, duty free treatment may be lost in a particular calendar year if the value of articles exported to the US by a freely associated state equals or exceeds either a dollar amount established by an administrative procedure or when the value of exports from the particular state equals 50 percent of the total value of US imports of that article. Products denied special treatment under these determinations may still be imported at standard duty rates. In subsequent years duty free treatment is reestablished if the imports fall within the guidelines specified.

Eligible products must be grown, produced, or manufactured in the freely associated state and be imported directly into the US from that state. The cost or value of the materials and the direct costs of processing the article in the beneficiary country must constitute at least 35 percent of the appraised value of the product (up to 15 percent of the 35 percent may represent US cost or value), and third country content may be included if it is substantially transformed in a beneficiary country.

Importers must be prepared to submit a generic UNCTAD Certificate of Origin Form A obtained from the exporter to US Customs to document the eligibility of the entry ("Compact of Freely Associated States" is substituted for "GSP").

Questions regarding eligibility and procedures under the Compact of Free Association may be addressed to the Office of Trade Operations at the US Customs Service.

Products of US Insular Possessions

Under narrowly specified conditions, watches and watch parts can be imported duty free or at reduced duty rates from the insular possessions of the US: the US Virgin Islands, American Samoa, and Guam. The Secretaries of the US Department of Commerce and the US Department of the Interior set the annual quantities to be so imported and allocate their distribution among the insular possessions. Final allocation of eligible quantities is made by territorial officials through a system of credits based on the total wages paid by industry producers in the specific territory during the previous year. In practice, it is difficult for new producers to take advantage of these benefits or for third parties to sell their products to existing producers for incorporation into the finished eligible product.

Countries Subject to US Trade Restrictions

The US maintains restrictions on trade with Cuba, Iran, Iraq, Libya, North Korea, and the Federal Republic of Yugoslavia (Serbia and Montenegro). These restrictions generally prohibit direct and indirect commercial transactions with these countries, including the importation of articles from or the exportation of articles to public or private entities or individuals. Restrictions can be instituted or lifted on short notice. These restrictions are administered by the Office of Foreign Assets Control at the Department of the Treasury.

Prospective Trade Bodies and Agreements

Asia Pacific Economic Cooperation Founded in 1989, Asia Pacific Economic Cooperation (APEC) is an informal working group of 18 Pacific Rim nations. APEC is in the process of establishing a prospective trade agreement covering member nations, of which the US is one. As yet, there exists no formal agreement, much less a legal commitment. However, at their annual conference in Indonesia in November 1994, the members endorsed an accord calling for "free and open trade and investment" throughout the region. The accord calls for the elimination of internal trade barriers by developed country members by 2010 and by developing country members by 2020. The group opposes protectionism and the creation of exclusionary regional trading blocs while promoting the expansion of trade. The accord also goes on record as supporting rapid implementation of the provisions of GATT; harmonization of international product testing and safety standards; simplification of customs procedures; and development of an international dispute resolution system.

Observers note that although the accord is long on generalities and short on specifics and definitions, it is remarkable that the diverse participants were able to reach a consensus on any agreement. Many of the lesser developed countries lobbied for an even longer phased and gradual introduction for any significant provisions, and others disagreed on the implications of definitions to be used and questioned the intentions of some of the other members. In particular, some members questioned the good faith of the US, fearing that the country could try to turn the organization into a forum for advancing its own agenda at the expense of the interests of some of the other members.

Together the APEC member countries account for 42 percent of total world trade, 52 percent of world GDP, and 38 percent of world population. Members include Australia, Brunei, Canada, Chile, China, Hong Kong, Indonesia, Japan, Malaysia, Mexico, New Zealand, the Philippines, Papua New Guinea, Singapore, South Korea, Taiwan, Thailand, and the US.

The Americas Free Trade Agreement The Summit of the Americas, held in Miami in December 1994, resulted in the pledge of 34 New World governments to construct an Americas Free Trade Zone encompassing the entire western hemisphere by 2005. The conference agreed to pursue economic integration involving free trade along the lines of NAFTA. Among the issues discussed were investment, services, intellectual property rights, dumping, subsidies, illegal immigration, and Cuba—the only nondemocratic state left in the hemisphere and the only one not represented at the gathering. Some 23 pacts already exist among the various participants, and one goal is to harmonize these into a single agreement encompassing the US$13 trillion combined economy and 850 million people of the hemisphere.

Existing pacts include NAFTA, the Andean Group, the Central American Common Market, and the Caribbean Common Market. Mercosur—covering Brazil, Argentina, Paraguay, and Uruguay—went into effect on January 1, 1995, and is expected to form the basis for Alcsa, a proposed South American free trade zone. A customs union, like the EC, rather than a free trade zone per se, this new body could erect barriers to trade with outsiders. Some Latin Americans have expressed concerns that Brazil, the largest economy in Latin America, could attempt to dominate the new body, excluding others and turning the region into a captive market for itself. However, the lack of progress in expanding NAFTA membership makes them fear that they may have to accede to such Brazilian dominance if no better offers are forthcoming.

Although the US, Canada, and Mexico extended an invitation to Chile to join NAFTA at the summit and scheduled formal negotiations to begin in May 1995, many observers worry that the weakened Clinton administration may not be able to deliver on the invitation. A new Republican-dominated Congress may be unwilling to give the President fast track negotiating authority, especially if the Democrats insist on linking labor and environmental issues to the trade deal, as was the case with NAFTA. And although the Latin nations do not wish the US to take the entire lead, many summit participants have expressed doubts that the independent Organization of American States (OAS) is not strong enough to stage manage the negotiations necessary to complete the pact.

VOLUNTARY RESTRAINT AGREEMENTS

These include agreements between the US and exporting nations designed to keep their exports of specified products below certain negotiated levels. These are usually undertaken to avoid threatened trade sanctions by the US to more formally limit imports of goods that are thought to harm domestic industries. The most noteworthy voluntary restraint agreement is between the US and Japan covering US imports of Japanese automotive products. The agreement is designed to keep Japanese automobile imports below a certain market share level. In recent years rising prices and alternate sources of the types of models that drove the sales of Japanese cars have cut into the Japanese share of the US market, making the voluntary restraint agreements moot in some years. The steel industry was also subject to a series of voluntary restraint agreements between 1984 and 1993. These involved import surge control arrangements designed to go into effect if imports of specific types of products originating overseas surpassed specified levels.

The US remains ready and willing to invoke such arrangements if it determines that imports constitute a hazard to domestic industries. This is particularly true for politically sensitive industries, such as automobiles and steel. Most countries have preferred to enter into such agreements rather than provoke such a large customer, especially if the alternative is seen to be an open trade war. The US also retains the option of instituting unilateral measures including antidumping actions and countervailing duties to achieve the same ends.

INTERNATIONAL COMMODITIES AGREEMENTS

The US is a party to or is affected by a number of international agreements governing the export, import, and marketing of various commodities. Most of these agreements involve limits on production and sales by producer nations in order to maintain orderly markets and international price levels or by major consumers to regulate supply and price. The most famous producer organization is the Organization of Petroleum Exporting Countries (OPEC), which during the 1970s and early 1980s was able to exert considerable control over international petroleum prices. As other sources of supply have come on line and as member nations have violated their OPEC-imposed production limits, the cartel has been able to exercise less control. The US is not a member of OPEC and provisions in the country's trade legislation bar concessionary treatment for its members and those of similar organizations banding together to control the price and supply of such commodities.

The Multi-Fiber Arrangement The most important of these international commodity agreements for the US is the Arrangement Regarding International Trade in Textiles, generally known as the Multi-Fiber Arrangement (MFA). Contrary to most such agreements which seek to limit production, the MFA governs the international marketing of textiles and textile products by establishing strict import quotas. Initially instituted under the auspices of GATT, the MFA was passed by the US in 1974. It consists of a framework of bilateral agreements between the US and individual textile-producing countries specifying the annual levels of imports to be allowed into the US and how these quotas are to be allocated. Such quotas protect the US domestic textile and apparel industries by limiting the influx of outside, usually cheaper products, while assuring the specific international producers of a predetermined share of the US import market. Nevertheless, foreign producers clamor against limits on their goods, and US consumers pay a substantial price—calculated at US$310 per year per family—to maintain the domestic industries.

Currently the US has in effect 40 such bilateral agreements governing approximately 80 percent of US textile and apparel import volume. These regulate imports from such important textile producers as China and Hong Kong. Because the limits imposed by the MFA are so strict, trade in textile products can be difficult due to the extensive compliance requirements established. Attempts by some producers to circumvent assigned quotas, primarily by reexporting through third countries and trying to claim origin in these countries, has made enforcement oversight even more rigid. As part of the

Uruguay Round of GATT, such MFA agreements are to be phased out over a 10-year period. Through NAFTA, the US has already extended preferential treatment to Mexico by expanding its quotas for many regulated textile products.

Other Commodities Agreements Other international agreements include the International Coffee Agreement (with 60 members, headquartered in London), the International Jute and Jute Products Agreement (27 members, headquartered in Bangladesh), the International Natural Rubber Agreement (38 members, headquartered in Kuala Lumpur), the International Tropical Timber Agreement (41 members, headquartered in Yokohama), the International Wheat Agreement (36 members, headquartered in London), the International Sugar Agreement (with 33 members, headquartered in London), and the International Cocoa Agreement (40 members, also based in London).

The heyday of the international commodity agreement—the 1960s through the 1970s—seems to have passed, with various instabilities leading to the collapse of many of the organizations seeking to promote or enforce these agreements. Of these organizations, only the International Coffee Organization has seriously attempted to regulate its product through export quotas. The US withdrew from the organization in 1993, and the remaining members have since tried to organize it as a producer cartel, but have had little success. Two organizations—the natural rubber and the cocoa organizations—have attempted to maintain buffer stocks to smooth out fluctuations in supply and demand. The cocoa agreement—from which the US withdrew in 1993—has been extended until 1998, with the members agreeing to convert from their ineffective buffer stock arrangement to one of production quotas and market promotion. The remaining commodity agreements have no specific arrangements for regulating their respective products. Although it has been little more than an observer, the US remains a member of the agreements governing wheat, tropical timber, jute, and natural rubber.

USEFUL ADDRESSES

Private Organizations

NAFTA Research Institute
4410 Massachusetts Ave. NW, Suite 324
Washington, DC 20016, USA
Tel: [1] (202) 298-4574
Fax: [1] (202) 686-2828

US Chamber of Commerce
International Division
1615 H Street, NW
Washington, DC 20062
Tel: (202) 463-5460 Fax: (202) 463-3114

Government Agencies

Customs Service
Classification and Valuation Division
1301 Constitution Ave. NW
Washington, DC USA 20229
Tel: [1] (202) 482-6990

Customs Service
Duty Assessment Division
1301 Constitution Ave. NW
Washington, DC USA 20229
Tel: [1] (202) 482-6990

Customs Service
NAFTA Help Desk
1301 Constitution Ave. NW, Rm. 1325
Washington, DC 20229, USA
Tel: [1] (202) 927-0066
Fax: [1] (202) 927-0097

Customs Service
Office of Trade Operations
1301 Constitution Ave. NW
Washington, DC 20229, USA
Tel: [1] (202) 927-0300, 927-6724
Fax: [1] (202) 927-1096

Department of Commerce
Trade Information Center
14th St. and Constitution Ave. NW
Washington, DC 20229, USA
Tel: (800) USA-TRADE (toll-free in the US only)

Department of the Treasury
Office of Foreign Assets Control
Main Treasury Bldg.
Washington, DC 20220, USA
Tel: [1] (202) 622-2510
Fax: [1] (202) 622-1657

Office of the US Trade Representative
Trade Policy Staff Subcommittee
600 17th St. NW
Washington, DC 20506, USA
Tel: [1] (202) 395-3230, 395-3204
Fax: [1] (202) 395-3911

Publications & Resources

GATT: What It Is, What It Does
The Uruguay Round
Annual Report by the Director
FOCUS (newsletter)
Information and Media Relations Division, GATT
Centre William Rappard
Rue de Lausanne, 154
CH-1211 Geneva, Switzerland
Tel: [41] (22) 739-5208, 739-5308
Fax: [41] (22) 739-5458
These are free publications; a catalog with a listing of publications for purchase and GATT distributors worldwide is also available from this address.

North American Free Trade Agreement (NAFTA)
NAFTA, the North American Free Trade Agreement:
A Guide to Customs Procedures
Guide to the Caribbean Basin Initiative
Harmonized Tariff Schedule of the US (HTSUS)
Uruguay Round of Multilateral Trade Negotiations

US Government Printing Office
Superintendent of Documents
Washington, DC 20402
Tel: [1] (202) 512-1800
Fax: [1] (202) 512-2550

NAFTA Flash Facts
Department of Commerce
Tel: [1] (202) 482-2264
Delivers a wide range of short documents on
NAFTA via an automated fax retrieval system

NAFTA Info Line
Customs Service
Tel: [1] (202) 927-1692
Delivers a wide range of short documents on
NAFTA via an automated fax retrieval system

Economic Bulletin Board (EBB)
Tel: [1] (202) 482-1526
Modem (300/1200/2400 bps): [1] (202) 482-3870
Modem (9600 bps): [1] (202) 482-2584, 482-2167
Telnet: ebb.stat-usa.gov
Computer bulletin board service operated by the
Department of Commerce.

Foreign Trade Zones

INTRODUCTION

Foreign, or free, trade zones (FTZs) are secured areas located within the US but legally outside US Customs territory. The zones are set up in a way that resembles a public utility serving all users. Their purpose is to attract and promote international trade and commerce. In essence, they allow companies to operate in the US without first having to enter their goods through Customs and pay the applicable duties.

FTZs are usually located at or near US Customs ports of entry, at industrial parks, or at terminal warehouse facilities. There are also foreign trade subzones located in the zone user's authorized private facility; subzones are designated special-purpose facilities established by companies that cannot operate effectively at existing public zone sites. Since the 1970s the utilization of FTZs has increased dramatically. Between 1970 and mid-1994 the number of approved zones increased from 10 to 202. In addition, some 269 subzones operated by specific firms have been approved since 1963 (some are no longer active; others have been approved but never activated). Between 1970 and 1991 the value of goods entering zones and subzones increased from around US$100 million to more than US$75 billion. An up-to-date list of the dozens of US FTZs and subzones can be obtained from the office of the National Association of Foreign Trade Zones. (*See* "Useful Contacts" at the end of this chapter for the address of this office.)

Regulation of FTZs is administered nationally by the Foreign Trade-Zones Board, which consists of members representing each FTZ district. This board reviews and approves applications to establish, operate, and maintain FTZs. It generally authorizes intended operations if it determines that they will not be detrimental to the public interest. It is important to note that although FTZs are legally outside the Customs territory of the US, other federal laws—such as the Federal Food, Drug, and Cosmetic Act, as well as laws affecting public health, immigration, labor, welfare, and income tax—apply to products and establishments within such zones.

USE OF FTZS

Any company involved in the international trade of merchandise can use US FTZs. The specific advantages and disadvantages for using FTZs may depend on the specific circumstances of the firms and their transactions. One of the primary advantages for companies organized in the US is that they can bring foreign products into an FTZ, combine them with domestic products, and reexport the new composite product without paying any duties. This use of an FTZ avoids the need to pay the customs duties and any taxes that would be owed if foreign products were entered into the US, processed, and then exported.

Another advantage—especially for foreign companies but for US firms as well—is that they can bring products into an FTZ and hold them there without paying the usual customs duties and taxes until they are officially entered into the US. When the importer judges market conditions to be optimal for the particular goods, all or part of the shipment can then be officially entered into US Customs territory, at which time normal customs duties and taxes become payable. Also, the importer only has to pay for those goods that are actually delivered into US Customs territory; whatever remains is allowed to be kept in the FTZ indefinitely.

Merchandise in an FTZ may be stored, tested, sampled, relabeled, repackaged, displayed, repaired, manipulated, mixed, cleaned, assembled, manufactured, salvaged, destroyed, and processed. However, certain activities, such as the manufacture of fire-arms or the refining of certain oil products, are prohibited or restricted by law. Certain other activities, such as retail sales of merchandise within an FTZ, may only be conducted under permit. The many advantages to using FTZs can be grouped into three basic categories:

Money Saving Options Businesses can use FTZs to save money on their operations. First, no duty is owed on goods held in an FTZ until actual entry of those goods into US Customs territory. Merchandise which has not officially entered US Customs territory may also be exported from an FTZ free of duty and tax. While in a zone, merchandise need not be covered by customs bond or subject to US duty or excise tax.

Insurance on goods held in an FTZ is generally cheaper than on similar merchandise held outside a zone. Some users of FTZs have negotiated reductions as large as 40 percent on cargo insurance rates when imported merchandise is shipped directly to an FTZ, thus avoiding the potential for pilferage at intervening ports. Furthermore, the insurable value of merchandise held in an FTZ need not include the added cost of the duty payable on the merchandise.

The use of an FTZ for manipulation of goods can result in substantial savings. Shipping and transport costs can be reduced by delivering goods in bulk to an FTZ and then repacking them in individual containers. Merchandise from countries subject to a high duty rate may qualify for a lower rate if the merchandise is substantially transformed in the FTZ to constitute a new and different article of commerce.

Merchandise that is eventually destined for US consumption may be manipulated or manufactured in the FTZ to obtain the lowest possible duty on the imported goods. For example, goods shipped in bulk may be dried in an FTZ prior to entry, thus saving duty on the portion lost through evaporation or shrinkage. Other allowable processing might involve cleaning (to save duty on dirt or culls removed) and inspection and sorting for damage or contamination. Importers may also destroy goods prior to entry to avoid duty, request a reduced duty rate for recoverable waste removed in processing, and count goods to ensure that the quantity matches the invoice amount so as to avoid paying duty on missing articles. A product can also be processed into an article that has a lower duty rate. Also, duty on merchandise withdrawn from a zone is paid at the rate in effect at the time of actual withdrawal; therefore, if duty rates are scheduled to decrease, such timed release can provide a significant benefit over immediate entry.

Customs duties are not owed on labor, overhead, and profits attributed to production operations conducted in an FTZ. If the same production operations were done overseas, the value of the labor, overhead, and profit attributable to them would be included in the total assessed value of the goods for the purpose of assessing duties owed. Such savings may create incentives to undertake activity in a US FTZ rather than in a foreign country.

Efficiency FTZs can make international trade more efficient and convenient. Customs procedural requirements are reduced to a minimum by processing shipments through an FTZ. Unlike goods stored in a Customs bonded warehouse, which are subject to a holding limit, goods may remain in the FTZ for an unlimited amount of time, and goods may be exhibited without bond for an unlimited amount of time. While in an FTZ, goods may be sold or auctioned (after which import is the responsibility of and duty is payable by the new owner). Goods can be shipped from one FTZ to another without customs duties being owed. Customs security requirements provide added protection against theft, and goods are also covered by federal laws: it is a federal crime to steal merchandise from an FTZ.

Activities Within an FTZ Goods can be subjected to a wide range of operations in an FTZ. Parts made in the US may be combined with goods originating abroad; products made in different countries can be used to process articles made in third countries; and foreign-made goods can be packaged using packaging materials made in the US. This flexibility may allow an importer to gain a price advantage over wholly foreign or wholly domestically produced items; to avoid sending domestic materials abroad for processing and then reimporting them; and to ensure that items will meet US product standards prior to actual importation. Goods can be fully manufactured in an FTZ. Since 1980 the actual manufacture of goods in FTZs has increased dramatically, with manufacturing representing about 85 percent of all FTZ activity in 1991.

Typical Activities in and Products Traded Through FTZs

Activities which typically take place in FTZs, and the products corresponding to those activities, include the following:

- Assembling autos and trucks by combining domestic and foreign components.
- Displaying, inspecting, and storing carpets originating in Russia, India, and the Middle East.
- Displaying goods of US and foreign firms in international trade marts.
- Manufacturing earth moving equipment.
- Manufacturing motorcycles, jet skis, and all-terrain vehicles for import or export.
- Manufacturing a wide range of office equipment, including copiers, computers, and printers.

- Processing flavor and fragrance products for import or export.
- Processing gasoline, jet fuel, and synthetic natural gas for import or export.
- Producing industrial and agricultural chemicals for import or export.
- Producing pharmaceuticals for import or export.
- Assembling television sets and microwave ovens.
- Storing and repacking merchandise for export.
- Testing, repairing, warehousing, and scrapping electronic components.
- Unpacking, inspecting, testing, repacking, storing, and destroying items as diverse as lacquerware, jewelry, musical instruments, mechanical or electronic parts, toys, carpet sweepers, perfume, videocassette recorders, computers, flight controls, needlepoint, liquor, optical frames, and jade carvings.

PROCEDURES FOR USING FTZS

Definitions of Key Participants in an FTZ

Procedures for using FTZs involve certain key people or organizations: the district director, the grantee, the operator, and the user.

The District Director has jurisdiction over a district containing one or more FTZs. In addition to having other duties as an officer of the US Customs Service, this person is in charge locally of the FTZ as the resident representative of the Foreign Trade Zones Board. The district director may call on local representatives of other government agencies for advice in matters pertaining to the operation, maintenance, and administration of zones.

The Grantee The organization—sometimes a corporation, sometimes a municipality—to which the use of an FTZ is granted. For example, in New York City, the city is the grantee of the John F. Kennedy International Airport FTZ, while the grantee of the San Francisco FTZ is the quasi-independent San Francisco Port Commission.

The Operator A corporation, partnership, or individual that operates a zone or subzone under the terms of an agreement with the zone grantee. The operator of an FTZ may be the same entity as the grantee. In Seattle, for example, the Port of Seattle Commission is both the operator and the grantee. The operator is responsible for supervising all operations as required by law and regulations, including: admissions, transfers, removals, recordkeeping, manipulation, manufacturing, destruction, exhibition, physical and procedural security, and conditions of storage in the zone.

The User Any corporation or person who brings merchandise into or out of an FTZ. A user pays the grantee or operator rent on facilities as well as for storage, handling, promotion, and similar services.

Users may be permitted by the grantee to construct their own buildings or facilities in which to conduct their own specialized activities, or users may occupy and utilize existing facilities. The user of an FTZ works closely with the operator.

Admission of Merchandise into an FTZ

Merchandise may be admitted into a zone only upon application (Customs Form 214—Application for Foreign Trade Zone Admission and/or Status Designation), submitted to the district director, who issues the permit. The application includes statistical information (Customs Form 214-A) for transmittal to the Bureau of the Census, unless the applicant has made prior arrangements for the direct transmittal of statistical information to that agency. The applicant also submits, with the application, two copies of an examination invoice that meets legal requirements, evidence of the right to make entry, and a release order for the carrier. Exceptions to the procedure outlined by Customs Form 214 are available for merchandise temporarily deposited, merchandise in transit, or domestic merchandise admitted without permit.

Once an application has been properly executed, including selection of the desired zone status for the merchandise (note: a discussion of the types of zone status follows), and all other requirements have been fulfilled, the district director issues a permit for admission of merchandise to the FTZ.

Merchandise may also be admitted to a zone under a blanket application covering more than one shipment of merchandise. A blanket application may cover shipments which arrive under one transportation entry or shipments destined for the same zone applicant on a given business day. Some kinds of shipments presented for admission to a zone require special treatment or consideration. For example, imports which arrive in the US by mail, and for which a formal entry would normally be required, may be admitted to an FTZ under foreign or zone-restricted status upon approval by the district director.

Except for direct delivery goods—that is, merchandise delivered to a zone without prior application and approval, typically goods involved in ongoing operations or goods owned by the operator of the FTZ—all merchandise covered by a Customs Form 214 may be retained for Customs examination at the place of unlading, in the zone, or at another location designated by the district director. The district director may authorize release of the merchandise without examination. If a physical examination is conducted, the Customs officer will note the results of the examination on examination invoices.

Merchandise of every description may be admitted into a zone unless prohibited by law. If there is a question as to whether the merchandise may be admitted, the FTZ district director may permit the temporary deposit of the merchandise in the zone pending a final determination of its status. Any prohibited merchandise that is found within a zone will be disposed of in the manner provided for in the laws and regulations applicable to that merchandise.

Status of Merchandise in an FTZ

The exportation, entry, classification, and appraisement of merchandise transferred from an FTZ is affected by the status of the merchandise in the zone. Merchandise is classified in one of five categories as described below.

Privileged Foreign Status Prior to any manipulation or manufacturing process which would change its tariff classification, an importer may apply to the district director to give imported merchandise in the zone privileged foreign status. The merchandise is classified and appraised, and duties and taxes are determined as of the date the application is filed. However, such taxes and duties are payable only when the merchandise is transferred out of the zone and into US Customs territory.

Privileged Domestic Status Privileged domestic status, which may be approved upon application to the district director, is available for merchandise which is: the growth, product, or manufacture of the US on which all internal revenue taxes, if any, have been paid; previously imported merchandise on which all internal revenue taxes have been paid; or merchandise previously admitted free of duty. Privileged domestic merchandise may be returned to US Customs territory free of duty and taxes.

Zone-Restricted Status Merchandise transferred to a zone from US Customs territory for storage or for the purpose of satisfying a legal requirement for exportation may be given zone-restricted status. Such merchandise cannot be returned to the customs territory for consumption unless the FTZ board rules specifically that its return is in the public interest. Zone-restricted merchandise may not be manipulated or manufactured in a zone. However, it may be destroyed there.

Nonprivileged Status Nonprivileged status is a residual category for merchandise which has neither privileged nor zone-restricted status. Often it consists of waste recovered from manipulation or manufacture of privileged foreign merchandise within a zone. Merchandise with nonprivileged status, which would otherwise be inadmissible into US commerce, may be transformed in an FTZ into merchandise that is admissible into US commerce. After the merchandise is admitted to a zone, nonprivileged status may be changed to privileged or zone-restricted status at the option of the zone user, if the merchandise subsequently qualifies for that status.

Articles of Mixed Status Because manipulation and manufacture are permitted in an FTZ, articles transferred to Customs territory may be composed in part of, or derived in part from, merchandise that is privileged and nonprivileged, whether of foreign, domestic, or composite origin. The articles are appraised according to the status of the merchandise of which they are composed or derived, as noted above.

Inventory and Related Matters for Merchandise in the FTZ

The operator of the FTZ is responsible for maintaining inventory control and recordkeeping systems capable of accounting for all merchandise admitted to a zone; for producing accurate and timely reports and documents as required; for identifying shortages and overages of merchandise in a zone in sufficient detail to determine the quantity, description, tariff classification, zone status, and value of the missing or excess merchandise; for providing all information necessary to make entry for merchandise being transferred to the US Customs territory; and for providing an audit trail of Customs forms from initial admission through manipulation, manufacture, destruction, or transfer of merchandise from the zone. Although directly responsible for the maintenance of admission documents, for the inventory of the merchandise, and for the security of the merchandise, the operator may authorize zone users to maintain individual inventory control and recordkeeping systems.

Handling of Merchandise in an FTZ

Prior to any action, the user must file an application (or a blanket application) with the district director for permission to manipulate, manufacture, exhibit, or destroy merchandise held in the zone. (In the case of a subzone, the operator and the user generally are the same party.) The approved application—Customs Form 216—is retained in the operator's recordkeeping system. The district director will approve the application unless: the proposed operation is deemed to be in violation of specific laws or regulations; the place designated for its performance is not suitable to allow for the maintenance of the identity or status of the merchandise, or for safeguarding the value of the product generated; the district director is not satisfied that the destruction requested would be effective; or the executive secretary of the FTZ board has not granted approval of a new manufacturing operation.

The district director is authorized to approve a blanket application for a period of up to one year for continuous or repetitive operations. The district director may disapprove any blanket application, revoke any previously approved blanket application, or require the user to file an individual application.

If an approved application is subsequently rescinded by the district director for any reason, the applicant or grantee may appeal the ruling. The rescission shall remain in effect pending the decision on the appeal.

The operator must report the results of an approved manipulation, manufacture, exhibition, or certification of destruction unless the district director chooses to supervise the operation. The district director may permit destruction to be done outside the zone, in whole or in part, at the risk and expense of the applicant, if proper destruction cannot be accomplished within the zone. Any residue from destruction within a zone determined to be without commercial value may be removed to US Customs territory for disposal.

Transfer of Merchandise from an FTZ

General Rules for Transfer, Imports, and Exports With the exception of some domestic merchandise, no merchandise may be transferred from a zone without the appropriate Customs permit on the appropriate entry or withdrawal form or other document. The district director may authorize transfer from a zone without physical supervision or examination by a Customs officer. Once a permit is issued, the district director will authorize delivery of the merchandise to the operator, who then releases the merchandise to the importer or the carrier.

Except in the case of articles entered for use in a zone, merchandise for which a Customs permit for transfer to US Customs territory has been issued must be physically removed from the zone within five working days of the issuance of the permit. At the request of the operator, the district director may extend this period for good cause. Merchandise awaiting removal within the required time limit will be segregated or otherwise identified by the operator as merchandise that has been for all practical purposes transferred to Customs territory. It may not be further manipulated or manufactured in the zone.

Entry of foreign merchandise which is to be transferred from a zone, removed from a zone for exportation or transportation to another port, or imported for consumption or warehouse, must be made using the required Customs forms and must be accompanied by all necessary entry documentation. If the district director if satisfied that presentation of those documents would be impractical, presentation of an invoice and supporting documentation may be waived. In that case, the person making entry or the operator either files invoices and supporting documentation with the district director or maintains and makes those records available for examination by Customs on demand.

Only the importer of record has the right to make entry; the importer of record is the owner or purchaser of the goods, or—when designated by the owner, purchaser, or consignee—a licensed customs broker. A zone operator who is not the owner or purchaser or who does not otherwise qualify as a party with a financial interest in the merchandise may not make entry for merchandise from the zone. Merchandise held in a zone may be exported directly out of a zone. Merchandise transferred directly to US Customs territory from the zone for exportation at the port where the zone is located will be made under an entry for immediate exportation.

Entry for Warehouse Merchandise with privileged foreign status or composed in part of merchandise with privileged foreign status may not be entered for warehouse from a zone. Merchandise with nonprivileged foreign status containing no components that have privileged foreign status may be entered for warehouse in the same or at a different port. Foreign merchandise with zone-restricted status may be entered for warehouse in the same or at a different port only for storage pending exportation, unless the FTZ board has approved alternate disposition. Merchandise may not be placed and may not remain in a customs bonded warehouse after five years from the date of importation of the merchandise.

Transfer of Merchandise Between FTZs Merchandise may be transferred from one FTZ to another. The operator of the transferring zone must provide the operator of the destination zone with the documents tracing the history of the merchandise being transferred.

Estimated Removals When merchandise is manufactured or otherwise changed in a zone (other than by packing), the district director may allow the person making entry to file an entry on Customs Form 3461 based on estimated removals of merchandise during a calendar week. If actual removals are to exceed the estimate for the week, the person making entry must file an additional form to cover the additional units before they may be removed from the zone. When estimates exceed actual removals, the excess merchandise will not be considered to have been entered to US Customs territory. Such weekly entry procedures allow Customs to control entry while permitting the manufacturer to maintain an efficient flow of materials entered.

FURTHER READING

US Customs Foreign Trade Zone Manual
Superintendent of Documents
United States Government Printing Office (USGPO)
Washington, DC 20402-9325, USA
Tel: [1] (202) 512-1800
Fax: [1] (202) 512-2250

USEFUL ADDRESSES

US Customs Service
1301 Constitution Ave. NW
Washington, DC 20229, USA
Tel: [1] (202) 622-2000
Fax: [1] (202) 927-1393

US Customs Service
Office of Cargo Enforcement and Facilitation
Inspection and Control
1301 Constitution Ave. NW, Room 4141
Washington, DC 20229, USA
Tel: [1] (202) 927-0510, 927-1770
Fax: [1] (202) 927-1442

Foreign Trade Zones Board
US Department of Commerce
Main Commerce Bldg.
Washington, DC 20230, USA
Tel: [1] (202) 482-2862
Fax: [1] (202) 482-0002

National Association of Foreign-Trade Zones
1735 Eye St. NW, Suite 506
Washington, DC 20006, USA
Tel: [1] (202) 331-1950
Fax: [1] (202) 331-1994

Import Policy & Procedures

INTRODUCTION

As a result of major changes during the last two decades in the structure of the global economy, the US has largely recognized that liberal trade policies are on balance good for domestic consumers, workers, and businesses alike. The encouragement of imports has generally led to the vitalization of economies in other countries and, in return, greater demand for US products. In addition, imported products offer US consumers a wide range of choices of products to buy, while the competition between foreign and US products helps keep domestic prices down. Because US imports have outpaced exports during the last two decades, the current US focus is on increasing exports and opening new markets abroad for US products. Nevertheless, the US remains one of the world's top import markets. (Refer to the "Opportunities" chapter for export and import prospects.)

This section discusses US policies and procedures for importing into the country. Such information is useful to persons seeking to sell goods and services to the US; to firms that decide to establish a manufacturing facility or other operation in the US; to foreign investors who are considering an interest in an entity located in the US; and to persons in the US who are seeking to import from sources outside the country. (Refer to the "Marketing" chapter for a discussion of sales channels in the US and the "Business Entities & Formation" chapter for information on establishing a company in the US.)

CONTENTS

IMPORT POLICIES

Government Regulation

The US Customs Service, an agency within the Department of the Treasury, has principal authority for enforcing and administering the Tariff Act and other laws governing imports and the corresponding regulations, as well as for enforcing related laws and regulations of other government departments and agencies—including the US Department of Agriculture (USDA), the Internal Revenue Service (IRS), the US Food and Drug Administration (FDA), the Environmental Protection Agency (EPA), the Department of Transportation (DOT), and the Consumer Product Safety Commission (CPSC), to name a few. Customs is charged with such diverse activities as assessing and collecting duties, taxes, and fees imposed on imports; administering some navigation laws and treaties; enforcing inspection, quarantine, and other entry requirements imposed by the other government agencies that regulate imports; and protecting against criminal importing activities—smuggling, entries in violation of intellectual property rights, fraudulent entries, and the like.

The authority of the US Customs service extends to the nation's 50 states, the District of Columbia, Puerto Rico, and the Virgin Islands. Headquartered in Washington, DC, the Customs Service administers laws locally through seven regions (headed by regional commissioners), which are divided into districts (headed by district or area directors), and further divided into ports of entry (headed by port directors). (Refer to the "Transportation & Communications" chapter for information on ports of entry.)

Today, Customs is no longer a paper-intensive operation with a focus on the physical inspection of imported goods. Under the Customs Modernization Act (Mod Act), which became effective January 1, 1994, Customs is on its way to becoming more fully automated, with an emphasis on post-entry audits, electronic filings, advance compliance, and shared responsibility between the importer and Customs with respect to the valuation and classification of goods. The Mod Act has highlighted Customs' role as an enforcement oriented agency. Despite this more cooperative approach and streamlined procedures, penalties are stiffer today than ever before, and mitigation may also be more difficult to achieve.

Given the maze of tariff laws and regulations, of which up to 90 percent are expected to be revised because of the passage of the Mod Act, and the threat of penalties, sanctions, and forfeiture, the system can be confusing, especially regarding restricted products. However, the majority of imports can pass through with relative ease, provided the importer exercises a lot of care and patience. The best way to facilitate the process is to hire a customs broker; at least 97 percent of the goods that enter the US are cleared through Customs by brokers. (Refer to the "Important Addresses" chapter for a list of customs brokers.)

Assessment of Duties

Before goods will be cleared through US Customs, the importer is required to pay any customs tariffs due. Import tariffs are assessed against goods in accordance with the assigned classification under the Harmonized Tariff Schedule of the United States (HTSUS). Of the more than 10,000 classifications in the HTSUS, most are subject to interpretation—that is, an import could conceivably fall into more than one classification and thus could be assessed one of several different duty rates at the discretion of Customs. If the HTSUS classification is unclear, an importer can obtain a ruling from the US Customs Service. (*See* "Advance Tariff Classification" in this chapter for additional information.)

Rate of Duties All goods imported into the US are dutiable or duty-free as provided in the HTSUS. The US assesses an ad valorem, specific, or compound tariff against dutiable goods. Most common is the ad valorem rate, which is a percentage of the value of the merchandise, such as 5 percent ad valorem. A specific rate is a specified amount per unit of weight or other quantity, such as 5.9 cents per dozen. A compound rate is a combination of both an ad valorem rate and a specific rate, such as 0.7 cents per kg plus 10 percent ad valorem.

Rates of duty on imports may vary depending on the country of origin, the type of product, and other factors as listed in the HTSUS. With the exception of preferential duties available as a result of specific treaties, the US applies tariffs on a nondiscriminatory basis for countries granted most-favored nation (MFN) status. Most merchandise is dutiable under MFN rates (see the "General Column" under Column 1 of the HTSUS). Full, or "statutory," rates apply to merchandise from countries that have not been extended MFN status (see Column 2 of the HTSUS). Free rates and exemptions may also be provided (see Columns 1 and 2 of the HTSUS).

A frequently applied exemption is the Generalized System of Preferences (GSP), which allows duty free or reduced tariff treatment for certain merchandise imported from more than 140 beneficiary developing countries. Other exemptions include personal exemptions, exemptions for articles for scientific or other institutional purposes, and exemptions for returned goods of US origin.

Under the North American Free Trade Agreement (NAFTA), tariffs are lowered or eliminated on most imports from Canada and Mexico. The US also has separate trade agreements with Canada; the 24 countries and territories of the Caribbean Basin Initiative; Bolivia, Colombia, Ecuador, and Peru; Israel; and the Marshall Islands and the Federated States of Micronesia. (Refer to the "Trade Agreements" chapter for further details.)

Liability for Duties The liability for the payment of duties is fixed at the time the goods are entered for consumption or warehousing. The person or firm named on the entry documentation is the party with the obligation to pay all such duties. If the goods are entered for warehousing, this liability may be transferred to any party who purchases the goods and subsequently withdraws them from the warehouse. Duties cannot be prepaid before entry, but the periodic payment of duties is authorized by the Mod Act.

The Mod Act has created a five-year statute of limitations for the collection of unpaid duties. The US government must initiate suit or action to collect unpaid duties within five years after the date of the alleged violation or, in the case of fraud, after the date the fraud is discovered. This period is interrupted and extended for any time during which the person is absent from the US or the property is absent or concealed.

Surety To import into the US, the importer must post a bond with Customs to guarantee payment of any additional monies owed, such as potential duties, taxes, and penalties. Bonds can be obtained through US bond companies, although they usually will not sell a bond unless a customs broker is taking care of the entry. A customs broker may permit an importer to use the broker's bond. A cash bond may also be posted, but this is often impractical for the average importer.

Antidumping and Countervailing Duties The Department of Commerce (DOC), the International Trade Commission (ITC), and the US Customs Service all play a role in enforcing antidumping and countervailing duty laws. Antidumping duties (ADs) are assessed on imported merchandise of a class or kind that is sold to purchasers in the US at a price less than its fair market value. Fair market value of merchandise is the price at which it is normally sold in the manufacturer's home market. Countervailing duties (CVDs) are assessed to counter the effects of subsidies provided by foreign governments for merchandise that is exported to the US. These subsidies cause the prices of such merchandise to be artificially low, creating unfair competition with domestically manufactured goods and thus resulting in economic injury to US manufacturers.

In response to claims by US producers that foreign sellers are dumping products into the US market at less than fair market value, the DOC will investigate the situation. During the investigation, the DOC has discretion to require a cash deposit or bond to cover the potential AD or CVD liability. The DOC may even order that entry of the goods into the country be suspended until the investigation is completed.

If the DOC finds that dumping or subsidization has occurred, it may impose higher tariffs on those products. For example, the DOC has imposed higher tariffs on flat-rolled steel from 19 countries, including Germany, Canada, Japan, France, and the UK, and it has raised tariffs on imported roses from Columbia and Ecuador. The DOC orders imposing ADs or CVDs are published in the Federal Register, at which point Customs will usually collect only cash deposits—no bonds—to cover these duties.

Drawback Drawback is a refund of 99 percent of all ordinary Customs duties and internal revenue taxes. It enables US manufacturers to compete in non-US markets without having to include in their costs (or subsequently in their sales prices) the duty paid on imported merchandise. Antidumping and countervailing duties are nonrefundable on a drawback claim. Three types of drawback are provided for under the Mod Act: direct identification, substitution, and nonconforming merchandise.

Direct identification drawback provides a refund of duties paid on imported merchandise that (1) is not used and is either exported or destroyed under Customs supervision; or (2) is partially or totally consumed in the manufacture of an exported article. The importer must be able to demonstrate—through properly kept records—the identification of the merchandise from import to export or destruction. If the goods are not used in the US, drawback is available only if they are exported or destroyed within three years of the date of importation. If used in a manufacturing process, the articles must be exported within five years from the date of importation.

Substitution drawback is a refund of duties paid on designated imported merchandise when substituted articles are exported or destroyed under Customs supervision. "Substituted articles" are goods manufactured or produced using substituted domestic or imported merchandise of the same kind and quality as the designated imported merchandise. An article is of the same kind and quality if it is commercially interchangeable in a specific manufacturing process. Drawback is allowed only if (1) the imported materials are used in a manufacturing process within three years after receipt by the manufacturer; (2) the domestic materials (of the same kind and quality as the imported materials) are used in a manufacturing process within three years of receipt of the imported materials; and 3) if the materials are used in manufacturing, the articles are exported within five years of the date of importation of the designated material.

Nonconforming merchandise drawback is a refund of duties on exportation or Customs-supervised destruction of merchandise rejected as nonconforming. This drawback is available for merchandise that does not conform to a sample or specifications, was shipped without the consignee's consent, or is determined to be defective as of the time of importation. Drawback may be claimed for such goods, provided that duties were paid, the goods were entered or withdrawn for consumption, and the goods are returned to Customs for exportation or destruction within three years after Customs released them.

The Mod Act created new penalties for submission of false drawback refund claims. For violations based on negligence, the drawback claimant is subject to an initial penalty not to exceed 20 percent of the loss of revenue for a first-time violation. Subsequent violations will elicit higher penalties. For violations based on fraud, the maximum penalty is three times the actual or potential loss of revenue. For information regarding the legal aspects of drawback, contact the Drawback Section of the Office of Trade Operations at the Customs Service.

User Fees and Taxes

Merchandise Processing Fee Each shipment is subject to a merchandise processing fee. The schedule for "formal entries" (those valued at more than US$1,250) fixes different fees ranging from US$21 to US$400 per entry, with an ad valorem rate of 0.19 percent. The fee for "informal entries" (those valued at less than US$1,250) is US$2 for automated entries, US$5 for manual entries not prepared by Customs, and US$8 for manual entries prepared by Customs. The cutoff value for informal entries (US$1,250) is set by Customs regulation, but the Mod Act has raised the statutory cap from US$1,250 to US$2,500, and the Customs Service is likely to follow suit as soon as new regulations can be promulgated. Also note that some products—such as textile and apparel items—are either not eligible for informal entry or have much lower cutoff values. Under the terms of NAFTA, such processing fees are to be phased out for shipments from member countries.

Harbor Maintenance Fee The harbor maintenance fee is an ad valorem fee assessed on cargo imports and admissions into foreign trade zones (the secured free trade areas legally outside US Customs territory). The fee is 0.125 percent of the value of the cargo and is paid quarterly, except for imports that are paid at the time of entry.

Excise Taxes Some imports are subject to US internal revenue excise or consumption taxes. The most common are wine, beer, tobacco, perfume, and petroleum products.

Product-Specific Restrictions, Quotas, and Licenses

Before certain goods may be imported, the importer or exporter must obtain the prior approval of the particular US government agency that controls importation of the product. The importation of items that are considered to affect adversely the US economy and security, consumer health and well-being, and domestic plant and animal life may be prohibited or at least restricted. Restrictions include limits on the ports where the products may be entered; requirements that the products be specially treated, labeled, or processed as a condition of release; limits on the routing, storage, or use of the products within the US; and license and quota requirements.

Quotas Many products are controlled by import quotas. An import quota is a quantity control on imported merchandise for a fixed time. Quotas are established by congressional legislation, as well as by agency directives and presidential proclamations authorized by law. Customs administers quotas, but has no authority to change them. There are two types of quotas.

Tariff-rate quotas allow the entry of a specified quantity of a product at a reduced rate of duty during a given period. Quantities entered in excess of a tariff-rate quota are subject to higher duty rates. Examples include milk and cream (not concentrated); anchovies; mandarin oranges; certain olives; tuna fish; brooms made of broom corn; certain textiles assembled in Guam; certain textiles from Canada; and certain sugars, syrups, and molasses.

Absolute quotas allow only a specified quantity of a product to enter the US during a quota period. Goods brought to the US in excess of an absolute quota may be exported or warehoused for entry in a subsequent quota period. Examples include certain ethyl alcohol; condensed or evaporated milk and cream; certain butter substitutes and butter mixes; animal feeds containing milk or milk derivatives; certain chocolate products; ice cream; peanuts; certain cheddar cheeses; certain cottons and cotton waste; certain sugar blends; and textile articles from some countries.

Licensing, Permits, Prior Authorization The following classes of products are difficult to import because of stringent regulatory requirements imposed by one or more US governmental agencies.

Arms and Armaments Highly regulated by the Bureau of Alcohol, Tobacco and Firearms (BATF). The BATF issues import licenses and imposes stringent restrictions on the types of arms permissible.

Alcoholic Beverages Highly regulated, also by the BATF. The BATF requires import permits and compliance with extensive labeling and product fill and identity standards. Imports are also subject to other federal, state, and municipal alcohol regulations. A federal excise tax is payable at entry.

Dairy Products Highly regulated by the FDA and the USDA. Various entry and notification procedures—in addition to quota, license, permit, and quarantine restrictions—apply, depending on the specific product and its point of origination.

Drugs, Biological Materials, and Vectors Highly regulated by the FDA, USDA, and the US Public Health Service Centers for Disease Control (CDC). Requirements vary depending on the product, but generally include import permits, entry notification, detailed entry documentation, and foreign manufacturer and product registration. The FDA further imposes extensive requirements for drug quality and drug producing establishments.

Endangered or Threatened Species and Related Products Highly restricted by international treaty and various US and foreign endangered species laws. The restrictions are enforced by the US Fish and Wildlife Service (FWS) and include restricted ports of entry, licenses, permits, detailed import and export documentation, prior Customs notification, port of entry inspection, and recordkeeping requirements apply.

Hazardous Wastes Highly regulated by the EPA. These materials may be imported for very limited purposes and under a specific agreement between the EPA and the equivalent agency of the exporting country.

Insects Highly restricted under regulations enforced by the USDA, CDC, and FWS. Permits and special packaging requirements apply.

Livestock Highly regulated by the USDA. Restricted ports of entry, quarantines, permits, veterinary certificates, and importer's declarations required.

Meat and Meat Products Highly regulated by USDA. Import and quarantine restrictions, port inspections, veterinary certification, and import permits apply.

Motor Vehicles Stringent US Department of Transportation (DOT) safety standards and EPA emission-control standards apply.

Poultry and Poultry Products Highly regulated by the USDA. Import restrictions, port inspections, product certification, plant certification, and import permits apply.

Radioactive Materials and Nuclear Reactors Highly regulated by the Nuclear Regulatory Commission (NRC); the import of these materials and items must be authorized and licensed by the NRC.

Textiles and Textile Products Subject to complex quota restrictions, US Customs country-of-origin declarations, labeling requirements, and flammability standards.

Toys Highly regulated by the US CPSC. Strict safety standards, defect reporting requirements, recordkeeping rules for electrical toys or articles, and extensive marking and labeling requirements apply.

Wildlife and Pets Highly regulated by the FWS, CDC, USDA, and FDA, depending on the species. Various controls on port of entry, quarantine regulations, prior entry notifications, license and permit requirements, import and export documentation, and recordkeeping requirements apply, depending on the species.

Mandatory Technical Standards Many products sold in the US, whether foreign- or domestic-made, are subject to government-imposed standards of quality and safety. A person who imports into the US any product that is subject to mandatory technical standards must first obtain certification showing that the products are in conformance. The certification must be presented with the merchandise at the time of entry into the US, and a performance bond must be posted to guarantee compliance with mandatory standards. Examples of products requiring certification are:

- Automobiles and automotive equipment,
- Boats and boat equipment,
- Ceramic products,
- Electric household products,
- Electronic products,
- Lighting and lighting fixtures,
- Liquors and wines,
- Medical appliances and instruments,
- Radiation-producing products, and
- Radio and television products.

For information on the most current standards, contact the agency or department regulating the product. (*See* "Useful Addresses" at the end of this chapter for contact information.)

ATA Carnets

The US is a signatory to the international ATA—meaning "Admission Temporaire-Temporary Admission"—Carnet Convention and recognizes ATA Carnets through a program established by the Customs Cooperation Council in conjunction with the International Chamber of Commerce (ICC) in Paris. Under this convention, a single customs document allows expeditious, temporary, duty free entry of professional equipment, commercial samples, advertising materials, and goods intended for use at trade shows and exhibitions. The carnet serves as a guar-

antee against the payment of customs duties that may become due in the event that the temporarily imported articles are not in fact reexported. Consumable goods (food and other agricultural products), disposable items, or postal traffic cannot be entered under a carnet.

Under an ATA Carnet, acceptable goods may be brought into the US personally by travelers or shipped to them by air or sea, and the goods may remain in the US for as long as one year. Customs officials at the port of entry will set the actual time limit based on information provided by the shipper. Costs associated in obtaining a carnet include (1) a basic processing fee ranging from US$120 to US$250, depending on the shipment value; and (2) security, usually 40 percent of merchandise value, in the form of a certified check or surety bond. It takes five working days to obtain a carnet (expedited service is available at extra cost). Exporters may also submit an ATA Carnet application electronically. For information on obtaining an ATA Carnet in the US, contact the US Council of the International Chamber of Commerce:

US Council of the ICC
1212 Ave. of the Americas
New York, NY 10036
Tel: [1] (212) 354-4480
Fax: [1] (212) 944-0012
ATA Helpline: (800) ATA-2900 (in the US only)

Temporary Importation Under Bond (TIB)

If an ATA Carnet has not been obtained, certain goods which are either not imported for sale or for sale on approval may be admitted into the US duty free, under bond, for exportation within one year from the date of importation. The bond is generally set at double the estimated duties. With the exception of automobiles and automobile parts brought in for show purposes, the one-year period for exportation may be extended for additional periods, provided that the total period does not exceed three years. Entry under bond and any extensions are approved by the district or port director where entry is sought.

Marking

Country of Origin Generally, all products must be clearly labeled with the English name of the country in which the article was manufactured or produced. The marking must be conspicuously placed on the article and must be legible, indelible, and as permanent as the nature of the article permits. If the products are not properly labeled at the time of importation, a marking duty equal to 10 percent of the customs value of the products may be assessed.

This marking is not required for more than 85 classes of articles, including works of art, cigars and cigarettes, flowers, buttons, eggs, certain papers,

IMPORTABLE GOODS UNDER TIB

The following classes of goods may be entered under Temporary Importation Under Bond (TIB):

- **Articles processed in the US and exported.**
  - Certain merchandise to be repaired, altered, or processed in the US.
  - Articles of special design solely for temporary use in manufacturing or producing articles for export.
- **Models, samples, and advertising materials.**
  - Women's apparel imported by manufacturers solely as models.
  - Articles imported by illustrators and photographers solely as models to illustrate catalogs, pamphlets, or advertising matter.
  - Merchandise samples solely for taking orders (must comply with any quotas).
  - Articles solely for examination with intent to reproduce (except photoengraved printing plates); motion picture advertising films.
  - Articles solely for testing, experimental, or review purposes. (If items are destroyed during the process, Customs must receive proof of destruction to satisfy TIB requirements.)
  - Automobiles and automobile chassis, cutaway portions, and other parts brought for show purposes (allowed entry only if reciprocal privileges are granted to similar US articles).
- **Items for use in competitions or exhibitions.**
  - Automobiles, motorcycles, bicycles, airplanes, airships, balloons, boats, racing shells, and other vehicles and craft, and related equipment for a nonresident's use in a specific race or other contest.
  - Animals and poultry for breeding, exhibition, or competition for prizes, and related equipment.
  - Theatrical scenery, properties, and apparel brought in by proprietors or managers of theatrical exhibitions for use in such exhibitions.
  - Works of fine arts, drawings, engravings, photographic images, and philosophical and scientific apparatus brought in by professional artists, lecturers, or scientists for use in exhibitions and illustration, promotion, or encouragement of art, science, or industry in the US.
- **Items transported into US for a temporary purpose.**
  - Filled or empty compressed gas containers or other articles for covering or holding merchandise during transportation and suitable for reuse for that purpose.
  - Railroad equipment brought into the US for emergency situations.
  - Professional equipment, tools of trade, repair components, and camping equipment for nonresidents traveling temporarily in the US.

nails and screws, rope, shingles, lumber and certain articles of wood, sugar, vegetables, nuts, and fruit. Many of the exempt articles are difficult or impossible to mark or would be harmed by the marking. However, with few exceptions, the outermost containers in which these articles ordinarily reach the ultimate purchaser in the US must be marked with the English name of the country of origin. The few exceptions from marking either the product or the container are made for duty free US fishery products, products of US possessions, products exported and returned to the US, and articles valued at US$5 or less and passed without entry. Exporters should contact Customs to find out whether an article is exempt from marking.

If marked articles are to be repacked in the US after release from Customs, the importer must certify on entry that the country-of-origin marking will not be obscured or that the repacked containers will be properly marked. If the articles are sold to others who repack them, the importer must notify the repacker of the marking requirements. Failure to comply with certification requirements may result in penalties and/or additional duties.

Special Marking Requirements Separate from the county-of-origin marking requirements are special marking or labeling requirements for certain articles. For example, only certain modes of marking—

such as die-stamping, etching, cast-in-mold lettering, or engraving—are allowed for iron and steel pipe and pipe fittings; manhole rings; frames, or covers; compressed gas cylinders; knives, clippers, shears, safety razors, and surgical instruments; pliers and pincers; and vacuum containers. Other examples of special marking requirements include:

- Dishwashers, refrigerators, and other appliances, must be clearly marked to show annual energy expenditure.
- Textile products must be clearly marked with information on fiber content.
- Clock and watch movements must be clearly marked to show the name of the country of manufacture, the name of the manufacturer or purchaser, and the number of jewels, if any.
- Gold and silver ingots or bars must be clearly marked to show purity.
- Hazardous substances must be clearly marked with information on proper handling and disposal.
- Alcoholic beverages must include a health warning on the labels stating that (1) women should not drink alcoholic beverages during pregnancy because of the risks of birth defects, and (2) consumption of alcoholic beverages impairs a person's ability to drive a car or operate machinery and may cause health problems.

It is recommended that the specific relevant government agency be contacted for any special marking or labeling requirements. (*See* "Useful Addresses" at end of this chapter for contact information.)

False Impression US law provides that no entry is allowed for articles that bear a name or a mark calculated to mislead the public regarding the article's country of origin or the article's description. That is, the article must not be marked with the name of a locality other than the place where it was in fact manufactured, and it must not bear a name or a mark, including a trademark, words, or other symbols, that falsely identify the article. Articles that violate this law are subject to seizure and forfeiture. Anyone who deliberately removes, obliterates, covers, or alters the required markings after release from Customs is subject to fines and possibly imprisonment.

Countertrade

There are no government regulations on countertrade, which is an umbrella term for several types of trading arrangements under which the seller accepts goods or other instruments of trade as partial or entire payment for products. One of the most common forms of countertrade is counterpurchase, in which an exporter agrees to purchase a quantity of unrelated goods or services from a country in exchange for and approximately matching in value the goods sold to that country.

Civil and Criminal Fraud Laws

The US government has enacted civil and criminal fraud laws to discourage persons from evading the payment of duties. The civil statute under the Tariff Act of 1930 (19 USC 1592) provides that any person who by fraud, gross negligence, or negligence enters, introduces, or attempts to introduce merchandise into the US by means of any material and false written or oral statement, document, or act, or by any material omission, will be subject to a monetary penalty. Under certain circumstances, the person's merchandise may be seized by Customs to ensure payment of the penalty, and the merchandise may be forfeited if the penalty is not paid.

The criminal statute (18 USC 542) also provides for sanctions against persons presenting false information to Customs officers. It provides for a maximum of two years' imprisonment, a fine of US$5,000, or both, for each violation involving an importation or attempted importation. Other federal laws include the Money Laundering Control Act of 1986 and the Anti-Drug Abuse Act of 1988, in which penalties include imprisonment for up to 20 years for each offense and fines of up to US$500,000.

The Mod Act imposes additional criminal and civil penalties for presenting forged or altered documents to Customs at entry or for otherwise violating arrival, entry, clearance, or manifest requirements. These penalties extend to the electronic transmission of false or altered data or manifests to Customs (19 USC 1436). The act also establishes monetary penalties for fraudulent submission of a false drawback claim, the amounts of which increase with repeated violations. These penalties become effective on implementation of the nationwide automated drawback selectivity program (19 USC 1593A).

IMPORT PROCEDURES

In an international transaction, the seller and buyer must comply with two sets of requirements: the export regulations of the country from which the goods are shipped, and the import regulations of the country to which the goods are delivered. This discussion focuses on the second step: bringing the goods into the US—from preshipment packaging, through entry, to post-entry procedures.

Preshipment Inspection

There is no US requirement for preshipment inspection. Importers may choose to have an import shipment inspected or tested before it is sent to them. For an organization that can arrange for inspections and testing, contact:

Societe Generale de Surveillance
International Quality Services
Division of US Testing Company, Inc.
701 Lee St.
Des Plaines, IL 60016 USA
Tel: [1] (708) 296-8300
Fax: [1] (708) 635-8414

Packing the Goods

Packing Procedures Packaging is an extremely important stage in any import transaction. The goods should be packed in a way that will permit Customs officers to examine, weigh, measure, and release the goods promptly. Orderly packing and proper invoicing will speed up the clearance of goods through Customs if the importer:

- Invoices the goods in a systematic manner.
- Shows the exact quantity of each item of goods in each box, bale, case, or other package.
- Puts marks and numbers on each package.
- Shows those marks or numbers on the invoice opposite the itemization of goods contained in the package that bears those marks and numbers.

To the extent possible, a container should hold only one type of product. If different articles of different values are all packed together, the delay and confusion at Customs is likely to be increased. If goods are packed in a systematic manner, Customs may be satisfied with examining samples of the shipment. But if various goods are shipped in a single container, the entire shipment is likely to be examined.

The inspection process can also be expedited if an importer has requested advice from Customs on the packing standards. Customs is authorized to inspect packaging, as well as the goods imported, for narcotics hidden in the cargo (with or without the knowledge of the importer or shipper). This inspection may even involve stripping the container and physically examining the packaging and cargo. Compliance with recommended packing standards can minimize the delay, labor costs, and potential risk of damage from unloading and reloading the goods at a Customs inspection station. For example, the goods might be shipped on pallets or in consolidated units that can be moved quickly by forklift, or they might be arranged so as to leave sufficient aisle space for fast access by inspectors.

Commingling Commingling refers to the packaging together of articles subject to different rates of duty in such a manner that Customs cannot readily ascertain—by sampling, verification of the packing list or entry documentation, or evidence of acceptable testing—the quantity or value of each class of articles. Customs has discretion to assess com-

---

10 TIPS FOR CLEARING US CUSTOMS FASTER

1. Prepare the invoice carefully. Include all information required by Customs, all information that would be shown on a detailed packing list, and—to the extent possible—an exact description of each article contained in each individual package.
2. Submit a neatly typed invoice. Keep data within the proper columns. Allow sufficient space between lines.
3. Mark and number each package so it can be identified with corresponding marks and numbers on the invoice.
4. Mark the goods (or container) with the name of the country of origin in a legible, permanent, and conspicuous manner and in compliance with any special requirements prescribed by US law.
5. As appropriate, comply with US laws for the import of specially regulated products, such as foods, drugs, cosmetics, alcoholic beverages, radioactive materials, and hazardous wastes.
6. Carefully label products in accordance with US laws that require disclosure for the protection of the ultimate consumer.
7. Consult with US Customs to develop packing standards for the imported articles.
8. Notify all appropriate US agencies in advance of the expected arrival time at the port of entry.
9. Establish reliable security procedures during storage and transport of the goods to avoid tampering by smugglers. (The minimum penalty for the importation of undeclared controlled substances found in a shipment is US$500.)
10. File Customs documents electronically by shipping on a carrier that participates in the Automated Manifest System or by transmitting through the National Customs Automation Program (NCAP) as it becomes available.

---

mingled articles at the highest rate of duty applicable to any part of the commingled lot, unless the consignee or the consignee's agent physically segregates the articles under Customs supervision and at the risk and expense of the consignee.

If goods must be shipped in commingled form, the importer should check the HTSUS notes for the particular components involved to determine whether a provision has been made for tariff treatment of the commingled articles. If no provision is made, the importer may still avoid assessment of duties at the highest rate by furnishing satisfactory proof that (1) the commingling was not done for the purpose of avoiding the payment of lawful duties, and (2) the portion of the shipment classified at the highest tariff rate is commercially negligible in value, cannot be segregated without excessive cost, and will not be segregated before manufacture or other use. If the proof is satisfactory, the articles will be subject to duties at the tariff rate applicable to the material that is present in the greatest quantity.

Commercial Invoices

Information Required All commercial shipments and all goods with commercial value must be accompanied by a commercial invoice unless the importer or broker is transmitting the document electronically. The commercial invoice must provide the following information, as required by the Tariff Act:

1. Port of entry to which the merchandise is destined.

2. Shipment identification; if the merchandise is or will be sold, the time, place, and names of the buyer and seller; if consigned, the time and origin of the shipment, and the names of the shipper and receiver.

3. Detailed description of the merchandise, including the commercial name by which each item is known, the grade or quality, and the marks, numbers, and symbols under which it was sold by the seller or manufacturer to the trader in the country of exportation, together with the marks and numbers of the packages in which the merchandise is packed.

4. Quantities, in weights and measures.

5. Purchase price of each item, if sold or agreed to be sold; price should be stated in the currency of the sale.

6. Value for each item, if the merchandise is shipped for consignment; value should be stated in the currency of the usual transaction. (If there is no value, the price—in the currency that would have been received or acceptable—for the merchandise if sold in the ordinary course of trade and in the usual wholesale quantities in the country of exportation.)

7. Kind of currency.

8. All charges on the merchandise, itemized by name and amount, including freight, insurance, commission, cases, containers, coverings, and cost of packing. If not otherwise included, all charges, costs, and expenses incurred in bringing the merchandise from alongside the carrier at the first US port of entry. The cost of packing, cases, containers, and inland freight to the port of exportation need not be itemized by amount if included and identified in the invoice price. Required information must appear on an attachment, if not presented on the original invoice.

9. All rebates, drawbacks, and bounties, separately itemized, allowed on the exportation of the merchandise.

10. Country of origin.

11. All goods or services furnished for the production of the merchandise, and not included in the invoice price.

Format Requirements The commercial invoice and all attachments must be in English or accompanied by an accurate English translation. Unless transmitted through the National Customs Automation Program (NCAP) or the Automated Broker Interface (ABI), the invoice must be signed by the seller, shipper, or an authorized representative.

Each invoice must state in adequate detail what merchandise is contained in each individual package. It must also set forth in detail, for each class of merchandise, every discount from list or other base price that has been or may be allowed in fixing each purchaser price or value. If the invoice or entry does not disclose the weight, gauge, or measure of the merchandise necessary to ascertain duties, the importer must pay expenses incurred by Customs to ascertain this information before Customs will release the merchandise.

When more than a single invoice is included in the same entry, each invoice with its attachments must be numbered consecutively by the importer on the bottom of the face of each page, beginning with the number one. If the invoice is more than two pages, the numbers must be sequential, beginning with the number one for the first page of the first invoice and continuing in a single series of numbers spanning all invoices and attachments included in a single entry. For example, if a single entry includes two invoices, the first having one page and the second having two pages, the numbering at the bottom of the pages must be as follows: Inv. 1, p. 1; Inv. 2, p. 2; Inv. 2, p. 3.

Any information required on an invoice may be set forth on the invoice or on an attachment. If merchandise listed on the documents is sold while in transit, the importer must file the original invoice plus a resale invoice or a statement of sale showing the price paid for each item by the purchaser, along with the entry, entry summary, or withdrawal documentation.

Special Requirements There are various special invoice requirements related to the way the goods are shipped and to the particular types of goods shipped.

With respect to the way goods are shipped, the general rule is that a separate invoice is required for each shipment. That is, a single invoice should cover no more than one distinct shipment from one consignor to one consignee shipped by one commercial carrier. Exceptions are made for assembled and installment shipments. A single invoice may cover merchandise that has been assembled for shipment to one consignee by one commercial carrier, provided that the original bills or invoices covering the merchandise and showing the actual price paid or agreed to be paid are attached to the invoice for the assembled shipment. Installment shipments covered by a single order or contract and shipped from a single consignor to the same consignee may be included in a single invoice if all of the installments arrive at the port of entry within 10 consecutive days.

Any costs for assists in production must be indicated on the invoice if not included in the invoice price. "Assists" include such items as dies, molds, tooling, printing plates, artwork, engineering work, design and development, and financial assistance provided by the buyer of imported merchandise and used to produce the goods that are then exported to the buyer in the US. The invoice must state the value of all assists known to have been used, the name of the supplier, if known, and whether the assists were supplied without cost or on a rental basis. If the assists were invoiced separately, a copy of that invoice must be attached.

Special information is required on invoices for approximately 50 classes of goods. These include many textiles and textile articles, beads, various minerals, earthenware and crockery, plastic bags, footwear, fur products, glass products, gloves, machinery, motion picture films, rubber products, watches, and wood products. The US importer should advise the exporter of these special requirements before the invoice is prepared. (*See* 19 CFR 141.89 for up-to-date details.)

When tariffs are assessed based on the value of the imported goods, the invoice must additionally state information about the rate of exchange. Generally, the only rate of exchange that may be used for converting foreign currency for Customs purposes is the rate proclaimed or certified according to US law (*see* 31 USC 5151). If more than one exchange rate has been certified for the currency of the country from which goods are being imported, the invoice should show the exchange rate used to convert the US dollars into the foreign currency and, if several rates are used, the percentage of the currency to which each rate was applied. In addition, the invoice must separately state the rate (or combination of rates) used in the payment of costs, charges, or expenses, if different from the rates used in the payment for the merchandise. Finally, if the dollars have not been converted at the time the invoice is prepared, the invoice must state that no conversion has occurred, and it must give the rate or combination of rates that will be used or indicate that the rates to be used are unknown. No statements on the rates of exchange are required for merchandise unconditionally free of duty or subject only to a fixed rate of duty independent from the value of the articles.

Pro Forma Invoice

If a commercial invoice is not filed at the time of entry, Customs may conditionally release the merchandise provided that the importer produces a pro forma invoice. A pro forma invoice is a statement similar to the invoice but usually prepared by the importer to specify the goods purchased or otherwise acquired. Before the goods will be released based on a pro forma invoice, the importer must post bond for the production of the commercial invoice. Liability under that bond will arise if the importer fails to file the commercial invoice with the district port director of Customs within 120 days from the date of entry. An invoice needed for statistical purposes must generally be produced within 50 days from the date the entry summary must be filed.

Although a pro forma invoice is not prepared by the exporter, it provides the exporter with a general idea of the information needed for entry purposes. For this reason, the importer should carefully prepare the pro forma invoice to explain with sufficient accuracy the information that the importer will need from the exporter in order to clear US Customs efficiently. A fairly detailed pro forma invoice may take on added significance for an importer who needs to present it to Customs because a commercial invoice is unavailable. In such event, Customs processing will be less burdensome if the pro forma invoice contains sufficient data for examination, classification, and appraisal of the goods.

Frequent Errors in Invoicing

For an importer to avoid difficulties, delays, and possible penal sanctions, foreign sellers and shippers must exercise due care in the preparation of invoices and other entry documents. Each document must contain all the information required by law or regulations, and every statement of fact contained in the documents must be true and accurate. Any inaccurate or misleading statement of fact in a document presented to a Customs officer in connection with an entry, or any omission of required information, may result in delays in the release of the merchandise, the detention of the goods, or a claim against the importer for forfeiture value. Even if an inaccuracy or omission was unintentional, the importer may be required to prove that exercise of due diligence and the absence of negligence to avoid sanctions, with resulting delay in obtaining possession of the goods and in closing the transaction.

It is particularly important that all statements relating to merchandise description, price, or value and to the amounts of discounts, charges, and commissions be truthfully and accurately set forth. It is also important that the invoices set forth the true name of the actual seller and purchaser of the goods or, if the goods are not shipped for sale, the true name of the actual consignor and consignee. It is important, too, that the invoice reflect the true nature of the transaction pursuant to which the goods were shipped to the US.

The following common omissions and inaccuracies should be avoided:

- The shipper assumes that a commission, royalty, or other charge against the goods is a so-called "nondutiable" item and omits it from the invoice.
- A foreign shipper who purchases the goods and resells them to a US importer at a delivered price shows on the invoice the cost of the goods when purchased (before resale) instead of the delivered price.
- A foreign shipper manufactures goods partly with the use of materials supplied by the US importer, but invoices the goods at the actual cost to the manufacturer without including the value of the materials supplied by the importer.
- The foreign manufacturer ships replacement goods to a customer in the US and invoices the goods at the net price without showing the full price less the allowance for defective goods previously shipped and returned.
- A foreign shipper sells goods at list price less a discount, but invoices them at the net price, failing to show the discount.
- A foreign shipper sells goods at a delivered price, but invoices them at a price FOB (free on board) the place of shipment, omitting the subsequent charges.
- A foreign shipper indicates in the invoice that the importer is the purchaser, but in fact the importer is an agent paid on commission for the sale or is a party who will share in the proceeds of the sale when posted to the joint account of the shipper and consignee.
- Invoice descriptions are vague because they list products by part numbers, truncated descriptions, or coded identifications only or articles that are in fact distinct from each other are together in a single description.

Right to Make Entry

Entry by Importer Merchandise arriving in the US by commercial carrier must be entered by the owner or purchaser; by the owner's or purchaser's authorized regular employee; or by the licensed customs broker designated by the owner, purchaser, or consignee. US Customs officers and employees are not authorized to act as agents for importers or for-

warders of imported merchandise, although they may give reasonable advice and assistance to inexperienced importers.

Entry by Exporter Entry of goods may be made by a nonresident individual or partnership, a foreign corporation through an agent or representative of the exporter in the US, a member of the partnership, or an officer of the corporation. The surety firm guaranteeing any Customs bond required from the nonresident individual or organization must be incorporated in the US. In the case of a foreign corporation, a resident agent must be authorized to accept service of process on the corporation's behalf in the state where the port of entry is located.

Documents Evidencing Right to Make Entry Every entry must be supported by a form evidencing the right to make entry. If the goods are entered by the owner, evidence of ownership is all that is required. In most instances, entry is made by a person or firm that is certified by the carrier bringing the goods to the port of entry and that is considered the "owner" of the goods for customs purposes. The document issued by the carrier is known as a "Carrier's Certificate." For goods consigned "to order," the bill of lading (properly endorsed by the consignor) may serve as evidence of the right to make entry. An air waybill may be used for merchandise arriving by air. In certain circumstances, entry may be made by means of a duplicate bill of lading or a shipping receipt.

Ordinarily, the authority of an employee or agent—including a partner or corporate officer—to make entry for the employer or principal is most satisfactorily established by a Customs power of attorney. If entry is made by a customs broker, the importer or exporter should give a Customs power of attorney to the broker, who may then present it to Customs. Any person named in a Customs power of attorney must be a resident of the US authorized to accept service of process on behalf of the party that issued the power of attorney. Either the applicable Customs form or a document using the same language as the form is acceptable. References to those acts that the issuer has not authorized the agent to perform may be deleted from the form or omitted from the document. A power of attorney from a foreign corporation must be supported by documents showing the authority of the corporation. Once submitted to Customs, the power of attorney to accept service of process becomes irrevocable with respect to Customs transactions duly undertaken.

If the broker is acting pursuant to a Customs power of attorney for an exporter, the broker may request that the exporter additionally execute an owner's declaration, which in turn must be supported by a surety bond providing for the payment of any increased or additional duties found due. An owner's declaration executed in a foreign country is acceptable, but it must be executed before a notary public and must bear the notary's seal. Notaries public can be found in US embassies worldwide as well as in most larger consulates.

Tariff Classification

The two most important factors affecting the dutiable status of imported goods are the tariff classification under the Harmonized Tariff Schedule of the United States (HTSUS) and, if ad valorem rates of duty are applicable, appraisement of the value of the goods. When an entry is filed, importers must always provide the classification and valuation, even if the goods may enter duty free. This information is used for statistical purposes in addition to determining the dutiable status of the goods.

Tariff Classification The Mod Act has charged importers with the responsibility, shared with US Customs, of using due diligence in selecting the proper tariff classification for imported goods. That is, an importer should take all reasonable steps to ascertain the correct HTSUS classification for the goods, including becoming familiar with the HTSUS, hiring a broker, seeking advice from Customs, and even requesting an advance ruling from Customs. If a customs broker is hired, the importer has a legal duty to furnish the broker with sufficient information to enable the broker to classify and appraise the merchandise correctly. At the entry of a product, Customs is responsible for correcting and fixing the final classification and appraisal. If Customs determines that the importer failed to use reasonable care in making the original classification, resulting in misclassification or undervaluation of the merchandise, Customs may impose a monetary fine against the importer.

The HTSUS is organized into 22 sections, which in turn are divided into a total of 99 chapters, that classify merchandise into broad product categories. It indexes everything from ice and snow, to broccoli, to 3-(N-Ethylanilino) propionic acid, to zippers, to skeet targets. In addition to listing the general rates of duty payable on classified goods, it indicates special duties that apply under trade agreements, duty free treatment for imports from certain countries, and temporary reductions or increases in duty rates dependent on diplomatic relations and trade initiatives. The HTSUS can be obtained from a regional office of the US Government Printing Office or from the national headquarters.

Advance Tariff Classification An exporter, importer, or importer's customs broker may obtain advance information on any matter affecting the dutiable status of merchandise by writing either the district director at the port of entry or the Office of Regulations and Rulings at US Customs. However, the information obtained from this informal procedure is not binding with regard to tariff classification.

To obtain a binding tariff classification ruling— one that can be relied on for placing and accepting orders for the merchandise—the exporter, importer, or importer's customs broker may write any Customs district director. The written ruling request must be accompanied by:

- The names, addresses, and other identifying information of all interested parties and the manufacture identification code, if known.
- The names of the ports where entry will be made, if known.
- A description of the transaction, such as "a prospective importation of [type of merchandise] from [name of country]".
- A statement that, to the importer's knowledge, no issues on the commodity are pending before Customs or any court.
- A statement of whether classification advice on the same product has previously been sought from a Customs officer, and if so, the name of the officer and the advice given.

To avoid delays, a request for advance tariff classification should be as complete as possible. It should include a detailed description and sample of the product. If a sample cannot be submitted because of the nature of the product, the foreign seller may instead provide photographs, drawings, and other data that fully describe the product and its use. The product should be presented in the same packaging and with the same labels, brochures, and pamphlets as it will have when imported. Also helpful are cost breakdowns of the component materials, a description of the principal use of the goods, and information as to commercial, scientific, or common designations.

Valuation of Goods An importer is required to use reasonable care in providing the accurate transaction or other value for the merchandise. When the goods are presented for entry, US Customs will review the value declared and will approve or change the value for purposes of calculating duties.

Generally, the importer should provide the transaction value for the goods (19 CFR 152.103). The transaction value is the price actually paid or payable for the merchandise when sold for exportation to the US, excluding international freight, insurance, and other CIF (cost, insurance, and freight) charges, plus amounts for the following if not already included in that price:

- The packing costs—including charges for containers, packing material, and labor— incurred by the buyer.
- Any selling commission incurred by the buyer.
- The value of any assist (*see* "Special Require-

ments" under the "Commercial Invoices" section earlier in this chapter), prorated to account for the portion used in the imported merchandise.

- Any royalty or license fee that the buyer is required to pay as a condition of the sale—but not including charges for the right to reproduce originals or copies of artistic or scientific works, models, and industrial drawings; model machines and prototypes; and plant and animal species.

- The proceeds, accruing to the seller, of any subsequent resale, disposal, or use of the imported merchandise.

The importer may exclude as CIF charges the costs, charges, and expenses of transportation, insurance, and related services incident to shipment of the goods from the country of exportation to the US. The cost of transporting the goods after importation is also excludable, as are reasonable costs incurred for preparing the goods for use in the US—such as charges for construction, assembly, maintenance, or technical assistance. The importer may additionally exclude from the transaction value any amounts payable as customs duties and US taxes, including excise taxes.

In those rare instances in which the transaction value does not accurately reflect the true value of the goods, Customs may not accept it for purposes of determining duties. For example, the transaction value of the merchandise may be significantly lower than the true value if the buyer has made an extremely good bargain (perhaps because use of the goods is restricted, or the parties to the transaction are related). In such cases, Customs will apply special valuation rules as follows, in order of preference: 1) transaction value of identical merchandise; 2) transaction value of similar merchandise; 3) deductive value; and 4) computed value. The rules for applying these valuation methods are set forth in 19 CFR 152.104 et seq. An explanation of these methods can also be obtained from Customs. (*See* "Useful Addresses" at the end of this chapter for contact information.)

Entry Process

Informal Entry A limited number of items may be imported by informal entry—an expedited process in which Customs releases the items after the importer presents a declaration of informal entry on an appropriate customs form and pays any taxes or duties owed. A Customs officer may even accept an importer's commercial invoice that contains the declaration of informal entry in lieu of the official form. If the items are imported for sale, or pursuant to a purchase or an agreement to purchase, the importer must provide Customs with a commercial invoice for the transaction or, in the absence of an invoice, an itemized statement of value. Informal entry is allowed for the following (*see* 19 CFR 143.21):

Items of Minimal Value Shipments, installment shipments, and partial consignments of merchandise valued at no more than US$1,250 (the statutory cap has been raised to US$2,500 by the Mod Act, with possible raising of regulatory levels to follow), unless an exception applies. Exceptions are made for nearly all commercial shipments of textile fibers and products regardless of value and for shipments valued at more than US$250 of the following: billfolds and other flat goods, feathers, feather products, artificial and preserved flowers and foliage, footwear, fur articles, gloves, handbags, headwear, hat braids, leather articles, luggage, millinery ornaments, pillows, cushions, miscellaneous plastic or rubber articles, rawhides, skins, toys, games, sports equipment, and trimmings. Customs must approve installments (*see* 19 CFR 141.82) and partial consignments (*see* 19 CFR 141.51).

Personal Articles Certain household and personal effects.

Educational Materials Books and other items imported by libraries and certain similar institutions.

Temporary Trade Admissions Certain tools of trade, occupation, and employment; implements and instruments; professional books; commercial travelers' samples; theatrical scenery, properties, and effects; and motion picture films.

Unique Value Items Merchandise which Customs has determined is so unique that its value cannot be declared and which is not imported for sale or to pursue a purchase or agreement for purchase.

Reimports Products of the US valued in the aggregate at no more than US$10,000 and imported for repair or alteration before reexportation or imported after having been rejected or returned for credit by a foreign purchaser to the US seller.

A Customs officer may require articles otherwise eligible for informal entry to be entered through the formal consumption or appraisement process. Customs also has discretion to require an importer to consolidate individual shipments into a single one that requires formal or appraisement entry.

Formal Entry When a shipment subject to formal entry requirements reaches the US, the importer of record—that is, the importer, exporter, or agent, employee, or other representative designated in the entry documents—files entry documents for the goods with the district or port director at the port of entry. The entry documents are as follows:

- *Entry Manifest,* Customs Form 7533; or Application and Special Permit for Immediate Delivery, Customs Form 3461; or other form of merchandise release required by the district director.

- *Evidence of right to make entry.*
- *Commercial invoice* or, if a commercial invoice cannot be produced, a pro forma invoice.
- *Packing lists* if appropriate.
- *Other documents* necessary to determine merchandise admissibility.

Imported goods are not legally entered into the US until Customs authorizes delivery of the merchandise and the importer of record pays the estimated duties. In addition to Customs requirements, importers may have to meet inspection, quarantine, marking, labeling, and other requirements of other agencies that control the importation of particular commodities. (*See* "Product-Specific Restrictions, Quotas, and Licenses," "Marking," and "Useful Addresses" in this chapter for more details and contact information.) The importer of record is responsible for arranging for the examination, inspection, transport, and release of the goods.

The importer of record is responsible for entry arrangements and should make them in advance of the arrival of the shipment. The importer should select the port of entry where duties and documentation are to be filed with Customs and should ensure that the goods arrive there. Goods may be entered for consumption or warehouse at the port of arrival, or they may be transported in-bond to a different port, where they will be subject to the same conditions as at the port of arrival. If the goods arrive at a port other than where they will be entered, the importer is responsible for transporting the shipment to the port of entry or making other arrangements. The importer may be able to take advantage of various options to ease the entry process, including entry by electronic transmission of documents and payments, by special permit for immediate delivery, or through the mails. Goods may also be placed in a foreign trade zone (FTZ), in which event they are not entered at the customhouse.

Entry for Consumption A majority of the goods imported into the US are entered for consumption through a two-step process: (1) the filing of entry documents when the goods arrive; and (2) the filing of documents for duty assessment and statistical information after Customs has released the shipment.

First, when the goods arrive at the port of entry—which is often the same as the port of arrival—and are submitted to Customs, the importer of record presents sufficient documentation for the Customs official to release the goods. From the date the shipment arrives at the port of entry, the importer of record has five working days to file the entry documents at the location specified by the district or area director, unless an extension is granted.

The entry must be accompanied by evidence that the importer of record has posted a bond with Customs to cover any potential duties, taxes, and penalties that may become due. A bond may be obtained through a resident US surety company or may be posted in the form of US funds or certain US government obligations. With permission from Customs, it may also be posted electronically. A customs broker that is acting as the importer of record for a shipment may offer a bond obtained by the brokerage for this purpose.

After satisfactory entry documents and evidence of a bond are presented for the shipment, Customs may examine the merchandise or waive examination. If no legal or regulatory violations are noted, Customs will release the shipment for importation into the US. However, the entry is not completed until the importer of record files with Customs additional documents—including the entry summary—that contain information for duty assessment and statistical purposes. (*See* "Post-Arrival Procedures" later in this chapter.)

Entry for Warehouse If an importer prefers to postpone release of the goods from Customs, the importer may request to have the goods placed in a Customs-bonded warehouse under a warehouse entry. Perishable goods, explosive substances, or prohibited importations may not be placed in a bonded warehouse. However, certain restricted articles that cannot be released for import may be warehoused.

Goods may stay in a bonded warehouse for up to five years from the date of importation. At any time during that period, the warehoused goods may be reexported without payment of duty, or they may be withdrawn and entered for consumption in the US on payment of the duty in effect on the date of withdrawal. If the goods are destroyed under Customs supervision, no duty is payable.

While the goods are in the bonded warehouse, they may, under Customs supervision, be cleaned, sorted, repacked, or otherwise changed, as long as the process does not amount to manufacturing. The goods may then be exported without the payment of duty or withdrawn for consumption in the US on payment of the requisite duty.

Electronic Entry Any entry may be accomplished electronically through one of two systems, depending on availability: the Automated Broker Interface (ABI) program; or the National Customs Automation Program (NCAP). To file by means of the ABI, an importer must work through a customs broker authorized to use this program. The NCAP—which was created by the Mod Act and is being phased in with expected completion for all ports by 1999—will allow importers to file documentation and declarations; to post bonds; and to pay duties, fees, and taxes electronically. An importer filing through NCAP will be able to transmit information for a single entry or for a statement that covers all entries or warehouse withdrawals made during a calendar month. To participate in one of these programs, an importer or broker should request information from Customs.

Immediate Delivery For shipments of certain merchandise, an importer may obtain expedited release of a shipment for immediate delivery by filing for a special permit on Customs Form 3461. The application must be made before the merchandise arrives at the port of entry. If the goods are shipped on a carrier that participates In the Automated Manifest System, the carrier may receive a conditional release authorization after leaving the foreign country and up to five days before arrival in the US. On approval of the application, Customs will release the shipment expeditiously following arrival. The importer must then file, on paper or electronically, an entry summary and the estimated duties within 10 working days of the release.

Items that may be released through the special immediate delivery permit are described in detail in 19 CFR 142.21, and generally include the following:

- Merchandise arriving from Canada or Mexico, if approved by the district director and if a bond is on file;
- Fresh fruit and vegetables for human consumption arriving from Canada and Mexico and removed from the area at the border to the importer's premises within the port of importation;
- Shipments consigned to or for the account of any agency or officer of the US government;
- Articles for a trade fair;
- Merchandise subject to tariff-rate quotas and some goods subject to absolute quotas;
- Some merchandise released from a Customs-bonded warehouse under special permit; and
- Merchandise released by specific authorization from Customs Headquarters.

Appraisement Entry Merchandise that has not been appraised—or that has changed substantially in value—prior to arrival at Customs may be imported by appraisement entry under certain conditions. In general, appraisement entry is available for merchandise damaged during transport and before release by Customs as well as for household and personal effects used abroad; tools of a trade; secondhand articles; articles not part of a commercial transaction; and overages or dock accumulations that are not identified with a particular shipment. Application for this entry is made on Customs Form 7501 and must be accompanied by any bills or statements of cost relating to the merchandise and possessed by the importer, plus a declaration with respect to the inability to provide further information on the value of the articles for purposes of making a formal entry. The importer is responsible for paying any expenses for cartage, storage, or labor incurred because of an appraisement entry.

Mail Entry There are definite advantages to using the mails to import merchandise into the US. For duty free merchandise valued within the informal entry limits, importers who use the mails do not have to file entry documents. If duties are owed on a parcel valued within the informal entry limits, a Customs officer will prepare the entry documentation for the merchandise, and the duties (plus a Customs processing fee of US$5 and a nonrefundable postal fee of US$3.25) will be collected by the letter carrier on delivery of the parcel to the addressee.

If the merchandise value exceeds US$1,250, the importer must prepare and file a formal Customs entry accompanied by a commercial invoice. Each mailed package containing an invoice or statement of value should be marked on the address side "Invoice Enclosed." If the invoice or statement cannot be enclosed within the sealed package, it may be securely attached to the package. Failure to comply with these requirements can delay clearance through Customs.

Packages other than parcel post—such as letter class mail, commercial papers, printed matter, and merchandise samples—must bear on the address side a label (Form C1, provided by the Universal Postal Union) and the endorsement "May be Opened for Customs Purposes Before Delivery" or similar words that clearly waive the privacy of the seal and indicate that Customs officers may open the parcel. Parcels not labeled or endorsed in this manner and found to contain prohibited merchandise or merchandise subject to duty or tax are subject to forfeiture. All packages and merchandise imported by mail are also subject to the marking and labeling requirements—including country-of-origin marking—that would otherwise be imposed by law if the items had been imported through other means. If Customs examines an article and finds that these requirements have not been met, the article is considered undeliverable and will be returned to the country of origin.

If Customs examines a package and finds no dutiable articles, it will endorse the package as having passed duty free. If the package contains dutiable articles, it will bear a red adhesive Treasury Department envelope containing Customs Mail Entry Form 3419 and instructions for the addressee on filing.

The importation by mail of certain merchandise is subject to the control of agencies other than Customs or is otherwise restricted or prohibited. For example, packages that contain plants, plant products, soil, plant pests, plant material used for packing, animals or animal meats, and other products are subject to agricultural quarantine inspection by the USDA. Similarly, containers of hazardous, caustic, or corrosive substances, viruses, serums, and similar articles are subject to the inspection of various government agencies. In general, mailed packages are subject to seizure and forfeiture if they contain prohibited items, such as alcoholic beverages, lottery materials, obscene matter, and articles in violation of intellectual property laws (*see* 19 CFR 145.51 et seq.).

Post-Arrival Procedures

Unentered Goods If entry documentation is not filed or is still incomplete within five working days after merchandise has arrived at the port of entry, the shipment is subject to provisions regarding unclaimed or abandoned merchandise. The carrier of the goods is required to notify a bonded warehouse that the merchandise has remained unentered, and the warehouse will arrange transport at the risk and expense of the consignee of the goods. An importer then has six months to complete the entry before Customs will dispose of the goods. However, Customs has discretion to arrange for the immediate disposal of perishables, explosives, goods that may depreciate in value substantially, or articles whose value is disproportionately small relative to the cost of storage. Such unentered goods may be sold at public auction, destroyed, or transferred to a federal, state, or local government agency. Surplus proceeds from the sale of unentered goods are forwarded to the US Treasury.

Inspection Before Release of Goods Before release of the goods, the district or port director of Customs may waive examination or may inspect the goods to determine their value and compliance with invoicing, marking and labeling, and importation requirements. Customs may examine the shipment to ensure that it contains no prohibited articles—including illegal narcotics—and that the numbers of articles match the invoiced quantities. Some types of goods, such as food and beverages for human consumption, must be examined to determine whether they meet the requirements of other US laws. Certain goods, such as textiles and textile products, are subject to more intensive inspection because they are considered trade-sensitive products.

Customs officers will ascertain the quantities of goods imported, will allow for shortages under specified conditions, and will assess duty on any excess. The invoice for the goods must state the quantities in metric terms. In ascertaining the quantity of goods dutiable by net weight, a deduction is made from the gross weight for just and reasonable tare, which is an allowance for a deficiency in the weight or quantity of the merchandise to account for the weight of the box, cask, bag, or other receptacle containing the merchandise.

Detained Merchandise Customs must decide whether to admit a shipment within five working days following the date the merchandise is presented for examination. Goods not released within that time are considered detained. No later than five working days after goods are detained, Customs will issue a notice of detention to the importer or other party with an interest in the goods. The notice will describe any additional information needed to accelerate disposition. If Customs has not made a final determination on admissibility of detained merchandise within 30 days after it is presented for examination, the goods are presumed excluded. An importer may file a protest if goods are excluded. If Customs denies the protest or takes no action on the protest within 30 days, the importer may bring suit in the US Court of International Trade. Customs will then have the burden of proof in showing that it had good cause for not reaching an admissibility decision.

Seizure of Merchandise Under the Mod Act, the following items may be seized by Customs and forfeited:

- Merchandise that constitutes contraband or a controlled substance or that is stolen, smuggled, or clandestinely imported;
- Merchandise that fails to comply with any applicable prohibition or restriction based on health, safety, or conservation;
- Merchandise offered without a required authorization of a US agency;
- Merchandise subject to intellectual or industrial property rights protection;
- Merchandise intentionally marked with a false country of origin;
- Merchandise for which the importer has received written notice that previous importations of identical merchandise from the same supplier had marking violations; and
- Merchandise accompanied by counterfeit documents.

Entry Summary Documentation An importer must file entry summary documentation and deposit the estimated duties on imported goods within 10 working days after Customs releases them. These items may be filed at the time of entry, but the law allows this subsequent filing period so as to avoid delays in clearing Customs. During this period, the importer is permitted to make changes in order to reconcile actual import data with the data initially provided to Customs at the time of entry. The entry summary documentation that must be filed is as follows: (1) the entry package returned to the importer, broker, or an authorized agent after the merchandise is released; (2) an entry summary on Customs Form 7501; and (3) any other invoices and documents necessary for Customs to make a final assessment of duties, to compile statistics, or to determine whether all import requirements have been satisfied. The paperwork usually required in this process can be reduced or eliminated if the importer, broker, or agent uses the ABI or NCAP electronic filing system.

Liquidation

Liquidation Procedure Liquidation is the point at which the Customs determination of the rate and amount of duty becomes final for most purposes. Liquidation is accomplished by posting a notice of entry on a public bulletin board at the customhouse. The notice may indicate that the merchandise is liquidated as entered, which means that Customs has accepted the entry summary documentation as submitted by the importer. An importer may also be given an advance notice on Customs Form 4333A stating the rate and amount of duty. This form is not the actual liquidation, and an importer has no right to protest the duty assessed until the notice is posted. Time limits for filing a protest start to run as of the date the notice of entry is posted.

If Customs determines that an entry cannot be liquidated as entered, it will change the entry to reflect what is believed to be the correct classification and duty rate. Such a change may result in a rate of duty more favorable to an importer, in which event the importer will be issued a refund for any duties overpaid at the time of entry. Customs may also determine that a correction is needed that results in a higher rate of duty. In this situation, the importer will be given advance notice of the proposed duty rate advancement and an opportunity to validate the claim for a free rate or more favorable rate of duty. If the importer does not respond to the notice, or if the response is found to be without merit, Customs will liquidate the duty in accordance with the entry as corrected, and the importer will be billed for the additional duty.

At the time of entry, the importer may declare an intent to provide relevant data about the entry for reconciliation purposes when that information becomes available at a later date. The importer will then be allowed to submit reconciliation documentation for the entry, even after liquidation has occurred. However, importers must exercise this reconciliation right with prudence because, by law, importers have a responsibility to use reasonable care in making an entry so that Customs can rely on the accuracy of the information and can streamline the entry and liquidation process. If Customs believes that an importer has failed to use reasonable care in classifying and valuing merchandise and presenting entry data, Customs has discretion to impose a penalty in an amount commensurate to the level of culpability it assesses.

Protests Within 90 days after liquidation, an importer may file a protest of the liquidation on Customs Form 19 and may claim an adjustment or a refund. To apply for a ruling from Customs Headquarters, the importer must also file a request for fur-

ther review with the protest application. The same Form 19 can be used for this purpose, or the further review request can be filed separately, provided it is submitted within 90 days of liquidation. Further review is at the discretion of Customs Headquarters, and it is usually denied if a response has previously been given to a protest or inquiry about the same issue in the same transaction. If a protest is denied, an importer has the right to litigate the matter by filing a summons with the US Court of International Trade within 180 days after the denial.

Finality of Liquidation Although for most purposes the dutiable status of goods is finalized at the time of liquidation, the status is not absolutely settled until the time for protest has elapsed and any filed protest has been decided. In general, any entry is supposed to be liquidated within one year of the date the entry is initially made, but this period may be extended in one-year increments. However, the total time is not allowed to exceed four years from the date of entry.

Liquidation may be suspended, if required by law or court order. Such a suspension remains in effect until the issue is resolved. Customs must give notice of any extensions and suspensions to the importers, surety companies, and customs brokers that are parties to the transaction. After removal of a suspension, the entry must be liquidated within six months from the date of the notice of removal.

Recordkeeping

Substantial recordkeeping is required for entries of imported merchandise, and Customs is authorized to make reasonable audits of the records required. A list of the records that should be retained is available from Customs. The records primarily include entry declarations, documents, and electronic data related to entry activities that are kept in the ordinary course of business.

The effect of the Mod Act may be to emphasize the importance of keeping complete, accurate, and well-organized records, in that although the act reduces paperwork demands on importers at the time of entry, it extends the authority of Customs to demand production of documents at a later date. Persons involved in nearly every phase of importing are required to keep the import records related to each entry for five years from the date of entry. A party filing a drawback claim must retain records of the claim for three years from the date of entry.

A party who fails to comply with a lawful demand for records may be subject to substantial administrative penalties. However, these penalties are discretionary and may be reduced or eliminated on proof of mitigating circumstances, such as the loss of records during a disaster or prior submission of the materials to Customs.

FOREIGN TRADE ZONES

Foreign (or free) trade zones (FTZs) are secured areas within the US geographically but legally outside US Customs territory. Their purpose is to attract and promote international trade and commerce. The Foreign Trade Zones Board authorizes the establishment of these areas based on a showing that the intended operations will not be detrimental to the public interest. Although US Customs has no jurisdiction in the FTZs, other US laws—such as the Federal Food, Drug, and Cosmetic Act—are applicable to products and establishments within the zones.

Foreign exporters planning to expand or open new US outlets may forward their goods to a US FTZ. The goods can be held there for an unlimited period while awaiting a favorable market in the US or nearby countries without being subject to US Customs entry, payment of duty, tax, or bond. Merchandise lawfully brought into FTZs may be stored indefinitely, exhibited, broken up, repacked, assembled, distributed, sorted, graded, cleaned, mixed with foreign or domestic merchandise, or otherwise manipulated or manufactured. (Refer to the "Foreign Trade Zones" chapter for additional discussion.)

USEFUL ADDRESSES

Government Agencies

Bureau of Alcohol, Tobacco & Firearms
Department of the Treasury
650 Massachusetts Ave. NW
Washington, DC 20226, USA
Tel: [1] (202) 927-7777, 927-8500
Fax: [1] (202) 927-7862

Centers for Disease Control (CDC)
Office of Biosafety
1600 Clifton Rd. NE
Atlanta, GA 30333, USA
Tel: [1] (404) 639-3883

Consumer Product Safety Commission (CPSC)
Office of Compliance
Division of Regulatory Management
5401 Westbard Ave.
Bethesda, MD 20207, USA
Tel: [1] (301) 504-0400, 504-0500, 504-0580

Customs Service
1301 Constitution Ave. NW
Washington, DC 20229, USA
Tel: [1] (202) 927-6724, 927-1000
Fax: [1] (202) 927-1393
Quota Branch: [1] (202) 927-5850

Customs Service
Drawback Section, Office of Trade Operations
1301 Constitution Ave. NW
Washington, DC 20229, USA
Tel: [1] (202) 927-0300
Fax: [1] (202) 927-1096

Environmental Protection Agency
401 M St. SW
Washington, DC 20460, USA
Tel: [1] (202) 260-2090, 260-2080
TSCA Information Hotline: [1] (202) 554-1404
Office of Pesticide Programs: [1] (703) 305-7090

Federal Communications Commission (FCC)
1919 M St. NW
Washington, DC 20554 USA
Tel: [1] (202) 632-7106, 632-7000
Fax: [1] (202) 653-5402
Enforcement Division: [1] (202) 418-1170

Federal Trade Commission (FTC)
Division of Enforcement
6th and Pennsylvania Ave. NW
Washington, DC 20580 USA
Tel: [1] (202) 326-2996, 326-2000

Food and Drug Administration (FDA)
Center for Drug Evaluation and Research (HFD-8)
5600 Fishers Lane
Rockville, MD 20857, USA
Tel: [1] (301) 594-1012

Food and Drug Administration (FDA)
Center for Devices and Radiological Health
Division of Small Manufacturers Assistance
5600 Fishers Lane
Rockville, MD 20857, USA
Tel: [1] (301) 638-2041, (800) 638-2041

Food and Drug Administration (FDA)
Center for Food Safety and Applied Nutrition
200 C St. SW
Washington, DC 20204, USA
Tel: [1] (202) 205-5241/2

Food and Drug Administration (FDA)
Division of Enforcement, Imports Branch
200 C St. SW
Washington, DC 20204, USA
Tel: [1] (202) 205-4726

Foreign Trade Zones (FTZ) Board
Main Commerce Bldg.
Washington, DC 20230, USA
Tel: [1] (202) 482-2862
Fax: [1] (202) 482-0002

International Trade Administration (ITA)
14th St. and Constitution Ave. NW
Washington, DC 20230, USA
Tel: [1] (202) 482-2000
Fax: [1] (202) 482-5933

Interstate Commerce Commission (ICC)
12th St. and Constitution Ave. NW
Washington, DC 20423, USA
Tel: [1] (202) 927-5350, 927-6000
Fax: [1] (202) 927-5728

US Department of Agriculture (USDA)
14th St. and Independence Ave. SW
Washington, DC 20250, USA
Tel: [1] (202) 720-8732, 720-2791
Fax: [1] (202) 720-2166

US Department of Agriculture (USDA)
Animal and Plant Health Inspection Service
(APHIS)
Federal Building
6505 Belcrest Rd.
Hyattsville, MD 20782, USA
Plant Protection and Quarantine: [1] (301) 436-8645
Veterinary Services: [1] (301) 436-7885

US Department of Agriculture (USDA)
Food Safety and Inspection Service (FSIS)
Import Inspection Division
Rm. 3715, Franklin Ct.
Suite 3700-W
Washington, DC 20250-3700, USA
Tel: [1] (202) 501-7515

US Department of Commerce (DOC)
Main Commerce Bldg.
14th St. and Constitution Ave. NW
Washington, DC 20230, USA
Tel: [1] (202) 482-2000
Fax: [1] (202) 482-4576

US Department of Defense (DOD)
Office of International Economics & Policy
The Pentagon, Rm. 4B-938
Washington, DC 20301-2100, USA
Tel: [1] (703) 697-3248, 697-5737
Fax: [1] (703) 695-0054

US Department of Energy (DOE)
Consumer and Public Liason
1000 Independence Ave. SW, CP-60
Washington, DC 20585, USA
Tel: [1] (202) 586-5373, 586-5000
Fax: [1] (202) 586-0539

US Fish and Wildlife Service (FWS)
1849 C St. NW
Washington, DC 20240, USA
Tel: [1] (202) 208-3100, 208-5634
Fax: [1] (202) 208-6965
Permits office: [1] (202) 358-2104, (800) 358-2104

US Department of Transportation (DOT)
Office of Hazardous Materials Standards
400 Seventh St. SW
Washington, DC 20590, USA
Tel: [1] (202) 366-0656
Fax: [1] (202) 366-3753

Publications

Importer's Manual USA
World Trade Press
1505 Fifth Ave.
San Rafael, CA 94901, USA
Tel: [1] (415) 454-9934, (800) 833-8586
Fax: [1] (415) 453-7980

Harmonized Tarriff Schedule of the US (HTSUS)
Importing into the United States
Global Trade Talk
Publications of the Customs Service available from:
US Government Printing Office
Superintendent of Documents
Washington, DC 20402, USA
Tel: [1] (202) 512-1800
Fax: [1] (202) 512-2550

Export Policy & Procedures

OVERVIEW

Exports are seen as an engine of growth for the US economy. Between 1986 and 1990, US merchandise exports contributed more than 40 percent to the rise in the US gross national product (GNP). In 1990 alone nearly 84 percent of growth in the US GNP was due to exports, and in 1994 merchandise exports reached a new record high of US$502.8 billion.

The increase in US exports has resulted in hundreds of thousands of new jobs. The US Department of Commerce (DOC) estimates that for every US$45,000 in export sales, an additional US job is created—more than double the rate of job creation by domestic sales.

The US government heavily favors exports over imports as a matter of policy and provides as much assistance as possible, at little or no cost, to US-based firms seeking to expand their export business. Basic government policy in this regard holds that meeting and beating innovative competitors abroad can help US companies keep the edge they need at home. Today, many US firms are occasional exporters; many of these want exporting more fully integrated into their marketing plans. Others export regularly to one or two markets and want to expand into additional countries. Even more have never exported but are considering overseas sales as a potentially significant part of their future business.

In 1993 the top five export markets for US goods were Canada, Japan, Mexico, the UK, and Germany. Overall, the international market is more than four times larger than the US market, and growth rates in many overseas markets far outpace those in the domestic US market.

The following section discusses US export policy and the procedures for exporting from the country. This information is useful for those interested in purchasing goods and services from US companies, expanding their current operations in the US to serve export markets, establishing an enterprise in the US that will supply foreign markets, or investing in an export business located in the US.

EXPORT POLICIES

Government Agencies

The DOC, with 68 district and branch offices in cities throughout the US, provides export counseling and directs companies toward other government and private sector entities offering export services. Most of the information and programs of interest to US-based exporters are concentrated in the DOC's International Trade Administration (ITA), of which a subdivision—the US and Foreign Commercial Service (US&FCS)—maintains a network of international trade specialists in the US as well as commercial officers in foreign cities to help US companies doing business abroad.

Each DOC district office offers information about:
- International trade opportunities abroad,
- Foreign markets for US products and services,
- Services to locate and evaluate overseas buyers and representatives,
- Financial aid to exporters,
- International trade exhibitions,
- Export documentation requirements,
- Foreign economic statistics,
- US export licensing and foreign nation import requirements, and
- Export seminars and conferences.

EXPORTING GLOSSARY

CFR (cost and freight) A pricing term indicating that the cost of the goods and freight charges are included in the quoted price; the buyer arranges for and pays insurance.

CIF (cost, insurance, and freight) A pricing term indicating that the cost of the goods, insurance, and freight are included in the quoted price.

CPT (carriage paid to) and **CIP (carriage and insurance paid to)** Pricing terms indicating that carriage, or carriage and insurance, are paid to the named place of destination. They apply in place of CFR and CIF, respectively, for shipment by modes other than water.

EMC (export management company) A private firm that serves as the export department for several producers of goods or services, either by taking title or by soliciting and transacting export business on behalf of its clients in return for a commission, salary, or retainer, plus commission.

ETC (export trading company) A firm similar or identical to an export management company.

FAS (free alongside ship) A pricing term indicating that the quoted price includes the cost of delivering the goods alongside a designated vessel.

FCA (free carrier to named place) Replaces the former term "FOB named inland port" to designate the seller's responsibility for the cost of loading goods at the name shipping point. May be used for multimodal transport, container stations, and any mode of transport, including air.

FOB (free on board at named port of export) A pricing term indicating that the quoted price covers all expenses up to and including delivery of goods on an overseas vessel provided by or for the buyer.

freight forwarder An independent business that handles export shipments for compensation.

General Agreement on Tariffs and Trade (GATT) A multilateral trade agreement aimed at expanding international trade. Its main goals are to liberalize world trade and place it on a secure basis thereby contributing to worldwide economic growth and development. GATT is the only multilateral instrument that lays down agreed-upon rules for international trade. The organization that oversees the agreement—formerly also known as GATT, but now called the World Trade Organization (WTO)—is the principal international body concerned with negotiating the reduction of trade barriers and improving international trade relations.

general license Licenses, authorized by the US Bureau of Export Administration, that permit the export of nonstrategic goods to specified countries without the need for a validated license. No prior written authorization is required and no individual license is issued. There are over 20 different types of general licenses.

Generalized System of Preferences (GSP) An international program under which the members allow imports of merchandise from developing countries to enter duty free or at reduced tariff rates as a means of encouraging economic growth.

individual validated license (IVL) Written approval by the US Department of Commerce granting permission for the export of a specified quantity of products or technical data to a single recipient. IVLs also are required, under certain circumstances, as authorization for reexport of US-origin commodities to new destinations abroad.

legal kilo *See* legal weight.

legal weight The total weight of the merchandise and its own packaging, but excluding exterior containers or packing materials. The legal weight of canned vegetables would include the vegetables and the can, but not the crate and wrappings for shipping.

North American Free Trade Agreement (NAFTA) A free trade agreement among Canada, the US, and Mexico. The objectives of NAFTA are to eliminate barriers to trade, promote conditions of fair competition, increase investment opportunities, provide protection for intellectual and industrial property rights, and establish procedures for the resolution of disputes.

Other government agency sources of assistance include the Department of State, which has a diverse staff capable of providing US exporters with trade contacts, and the US Small Business Administration (SBA), which provides free counseling to potential and current small business exporters. Various individual state economic development agencies, departments of commerce, and other agencies often provide valuable assistance especially relevant to exporting products from the particular state. (*See* the "Useful Addresses" section at the end of this chapter, and the "Important Addresses" chapter and the end of this book for contact information.)

Exports Requiring Licenses

For reasons of national security, foreign policy, or short supply, the US controls the export and re-export of goods and technical data through two types of export licenses: general licenses and individual validated licenses (IVLs). Except for US territories and possessions and, in most cases, Canada, all items exported from the US require one of these export licenses. The general license is applicable to the export of all goods that do not require an IVL. Fundamentally, an IVL is needed for weapons, high-tech products that have the potential of being used against the US or its allies, and goods in short supply in the US. There are also special licenses that are used if certain criteria are met, for example, distribution, project, and service supply.

Several agencies of the US government are involved in the export license procedure. The agency that administers IVLs is the DOC's Bureau of Export Administration (BXA).

US Tariffs on Exports

There are no export tariffs in the US. The US applies tariffs only to imports.

Quality Standards

US goods prepared for export must conform to foreign standards and certifications systems in the destination market. For example, electrical standards in many foreign countries differ from US electrical standards. Similarly, many kinds of equipment must be engineered in the metric system for integration with other pieces of equipment or for compliance with the standards of a given country.

Adoption of ISO 9000, a series of voluntary international quality standards, has virtually become a prerequisite for doing business internationally. The National Institute of Standards and Technology (NIST) provides information on US and international voluntary standards, government regulations, and conformity assessment procedures for nonagricultural products. For more information, contact the National Center for Standards and Certification Information.

NIST receives notifications of proposed foreign technical regulations from the General Agreement on Tariffs and Trade (GATT) Secretariat, which may affect trade. Information on these proposed standards can be obtained by contacting the NIST GATT Hotline. For information on the latest European Community (EC) directives and draft recommendations, contact the NIST EC Hotline. For assistance in the metric conversion process, contact the NIST Metric Program office. (*See* "Useful Addresses" for contact information.)

Import Preferences for US Exports

The US is a signatory to a number of international treaties and conventions, under which the members are accorded special tariff treatment and trading preferences. (Refer to the "Trade Agreements" chapter for further discussion of these agreements.) Some of these treaties include the following:

GATT Trading Status The US holds most-favored nation (MFN) status under GATT. Among GATT members, MFN status requires nondiscriminatory trade treatment. An important benefit for US exporters stemming from the Tokyo Round Trade Agreements, completed in 1979, was the opening of many foreign government procurement orders to US suppliers. The 1991 Uruguay Round of multilateral trade negotiations, signed in 1994, benefited the US with a substantial market access agreement covering tariffs and non-tariff measures, and improvement in GATT to cover trade in such new areas as services, intellectual property rights, and trade-related investment measures.

North American Free Trade Agreement (NAFTA) NAFTA provides for the elimination of tariff and non-tariff barriers in trading among Canada, Mexico, and the US.

Other Trade Agreements The US has bilateral trade agreements guaranteeing reciprocal MFN status with non-GATT nations, including Hungary and Romania. Bilateral and multilateral trade agreements are also in force with a number of countries to protect intellectual property rights and to facilitate trade and business arrangements.

Customs Benefits for Exporters

Drawback of Customs Duties US firms that import materials or components that they process or assemble for reexport may obtain drawback refunds of all duties paid on the imported merchandise, less 1 percent to cover Customs costs. This practice encourages US producers to export by allowing them to compete in foreign markets without the handicap of including in their sales prices the duties paid on imported components. Under existing regulations, several types of drawback rules are of interest to US manufacturers:

NAFTA: IMPACT ON EXPORTING TO CANADA & MEXICO

For most trade among Canada, Mexico, and the US, the 1994 North American Free Trade Agreement (NAFTA) either eliminates customs duties immediately or phases them out over 5 to 10 years, with the phase-out of tariffs on a few sensitive articles occurring over 15 years. The NAFTA countries may agree to a faster tariff phaseout for particular goods at a later date.

In general, tariffs are eliminated or reduced only on goods defined as originating in a NAFTA country. Duty rates also vary depending on where the goods were produced. An understanding of the complex NAFTA rules of origin is therefore essential to determining whether goods will qualify for non-tariff or reduced tariff treatment. The rules of origin are the same whether goods are transported into or out of the US. (Refer to the "Import Policies & Procedures" chapter for a brief discussion of these rules.)

An importer in Canada or Mexico may claim NAFTA benefits for goods imported from the US. Goods that qualify for NAFTA treatment can be imported from the US duty free or at a reduced tariff. To qualify goods for NAFTA treatment, the importer makes a declaration directly on the import documentation that requests NAFTA treatment based on a valid NAFTA Certificate of Origin (a uniform, printed form used in all NAFTA countries). It must be completed and signed by the exporter, who then provides it to the importer (and to Customs officials in the exporting country, if requested). The importer must present the certificate to customs agents of the importing country. If the certificate is found to contain inaccurate information, the importer will be required to submit a corrected declaration and to pay any additional duties as required.

Refer to the "Trade Agreements" chapter for further discussion of NAFTA.

- If articles manufactured in the US with the use of imported merchandise are exported, the duties paid on the imported merchandise used may be refunded as drawback (less 1 percent).
- If both imported merchandise and domestic merchandise of the same kind and quality are used to manufacture articles, some of which are exported, the duties paid on the imported merchandise are refundable as drawback, regardless of whether that merchandise was actually used in the exported articles.
- If articles of foreign origin were imported for consumption, are kept in the same condition as when imported, and before being "used" in the US are exported or destroyed under Customs supervision within three years of the date of importation, then duties that were paid on the imported merchandise (less 1 percent) are refundable as drawback. Incidental operations on the merchandise, such as testing, cleaning, repacking, or inspection, are not considered to be "uses" of the article.

For more information, contact the US Customs Service Entry Rulings Branch.

US Foreign Trade Zones (FTZs) US exporters can also benefit from the customs privileges of US Foreign Trade Zones. These zones are domestic US sites that are considered to be outside US Customs territory and are available for activities that might otherwise be carried on overseas to avoid US entry and duty requirements. For export operations, FTZs provide accelerated export status with respect to applications for excise tax rebates and customs drawback. For import and reexport activities, no customs duties, federal excise taxes, or state or local ad valorem taxes are charged on foreign goods moved into FTZs unless and until the goods—or products made from them—are moved into customs territory. This means that the use of FTZs can be profitable for operations involving foreign dutiable materials and components being assembled or produced in the US for reexport. Moreover, no quota restrictions ordinarily apply within the FTZs. Information about FTZs is available from the zone manager, any local DOC district office, or from the Office of the Executive Secretary, Foreign Trade Zones Board.

Free Ports, Free Trade Zones, and Bonded Warehouses To encourage and facilitate international trade, more than 300 free ports, free trade zones, and similar customs-privileged facilities are operating in more than 75 foreign countries, usually in or near seaports or airports. Bonded warehouses can also be found in many of these same locations. Goods can be stored in a bonded warehouse for a certain period without duties being assessed. Once goods are released into a country, they are subject to duties. However, if they are reexported from the country, no tariffs are imposed, although the exporter will be liable for storage and similar costs related to warehousing and transporting the goods.

Foreign Sales Corporations (FSCs) To reduce US federal income tax on export-related income, a US exporter can set up a foreign sales corporation (FSC). An FSC is a corporation set up in certain foreign countries or in a US possession (other than Puerto Rico) to obtain a corporate tax exemption on a portion of its earnings generated by the sale or lease of export property and the performance of some services. The tax incentive provided by an FSC is in the form of a permanent exemption from federal income tax for part of the export income attributable to the offshore activities of the FSC. The tax exemption can be as large as 15 percent on gross income from exporting, and the expense can be kept low through the use of intermediaries who are familiar with and able to carry out the formal requirements. For more information, contact a local office of the Internal Revenue Service (IRS).

Import Barriers to US Exports

US Export Regulations US exporters are subject to the Export Administration Regulations (EARs), violations of which carry both civil and criminal penalties. Export controls are administered by the BXA. Whenever there is any doubt about how to comply with export regulations, DOC officials or qualified professional consultants should be contacted for assistance. The EARs are available by subscription from the US Government Printing Office. Subscription forms may also be obtained from local DOC district offices or from the DOC Office of Export Licensing.

Antidiversion Clause The US government requires a destination control statement on shipping documents to help ensure that US exports go to legally authorized destinations only. Under this requirement, the commercial invoice and bill of lading or air waybill for nearly all commercial shipments leaving the US must display a statement notifying the carrier and all foreign parties that the US material has been licensed for export to certain destinations only and may not be diverted contrary to US law. Exceptions to the use of the destination control statement are (1) shipments to Canada intended for consumption in that nation, and (2) shipments made under certain general licenses. Advice on the appropriate statement to be used is available from the DOC, the DOC district office, an attorney familiar with trade matters, or the freight forwarder.

Antiboycott Regulations The US has an established policy of opposing restrictive trade practices or boycotts fostered or imposed by foreign countries against other countries friendly to the US. This policy is enforced by the Department of the Treasury. In accordance with these laws, US persons are prohibited from participating in foreign boycotts or from taking actions that further or support such boycotts.

Antitrust Laws The US antitrust laws reflect the nation's commitment to an economy based on competition. They are intended to foster the efficient allocation of business resources by providing consumers with goods and services at the lowest price

that well-run business operations can profitably offer. Various foreign countries—such as Canada, the UK, Germany, Japan, and Australia, to mention only a few—also have their own antitrust laws, with which US-based firms must comply when exporting to such nations.

Most restraints on trade in the US are judged either as "per se violations" or by a "rule of reason." A per se violation is one that is deemed illegal by its mere existence, such as price-fixing agreements and conspiracies, divisions of markets by competitors, and certain group boycotts and tying arrangements. The rule of reason requires proof that (1) certain acts occurred, and (2) such acts had an anticompetitive effect. Under the rule of reason, various factors are considered, including business justification, impact on prices and output in the market, barriers to entry, and market share of the parties. For exports by US firms, there must be a "direct, substantial and reasonably foreseeable" effect on the domestic or import commerce of the US or on the export commerce of a US party before an activity may be challenged under either the per se or the rule of reason test.

Foreign Corrupt Practices Act (FCPA) The FCPA makes it unlawful for any US person or firm to offer, pay, or promise to pay (or authorize any such payment or promise) money or anything of value to any foreign official (or foreign political party or candidate for foreign political office) for the purpose of obtaining or retaining business. It is also unlawful to make a payment to any person while knowing that all or part of the payment will be offered, given, or promised directly or indirectly to any foreign official (or foreign political party, candidate, or official) for the purposes of assisting the person or firm in obtaining or retaining business. (Refer to the "Business Law" chapter for further details.)

US Food and Drug Administration (FDA) Requirements The FDA enforces US laws intended to assure the consumer that foods are pure and wholesome, that drugs and devices are safe and effective, and that cosmetics are safe. An item intended for export must generally meet FDA requirements. However, if the item meets the specifications of the foreign purchaser, is not in conflict with the laws of that country, and is properly labeled, it is exempt from the adulteration and misbranding provisions of the US Federal Food, Drug, and Cosmetic Act. If the exporter thinks the product is covered by the FDA, information on requirements can be obtained from the FDA.

Environmental Protection Agency (EPA) Regulations The EPA's involvement in exports is limited to hazardous waste, pesticides, and toxic chemicals. The EPA has no authority to prohibit the export of such products, but it has established a notification system to inform officials of a foreign government that materials of possible human health or environmental concern will be entering their country. An exporter of hazardous waste, unregistered pesticides, or toxic chemicals should contact the EPA Office of International Activities.

Import Regulations of Foreign Governments Import documentation requirements and other regulations imposed by foreign governments vary from country to country. Many governments require consular invoices, certificates of inspection, health certifications, and various other documents. These requirements also vary depending on the type of product exported. Agricultural and pharmaceutical products are typically subject to requirements—often including testing, labeling, and government agency approval procedures—stricter than products not intended for human or animal consumption.

Antidumping and Countervailing Tariffs Under GATT, an importing country may assess antidumping and countervailing tariffs against US exports that are found to have unfairly flooded the market in the importing country with goods priced below market value.

Export Quotas Products that are particularly competitive often face quotas that limit the amount of sales to foreign countries. Quotas are usually fixed by the importing country or by multilateral and bilateral trade restraint agreements with other countries. For example, a Generalized System of Preferences (GSP) quota is fixed by an importing country on the basis of the GSP established under GATT. An importing country may limit the number of items that can be brought into the country with favorable GSP tariff treatment. Once that number has been admitted, tariffs on additional imports of the product rise to the rates set under GATT.

Service Exports

World trade in services, which has been growing at an average rate of 5 percent a year, now constitutes approximately 20 percent of overall world trade. In some countries, the share is much higher: Spain has reported a 39 percent share, and Austria a 36 percent share. The US is a leading exporter of services, particularly business services that are highly innovative, specialized, or technologically advanced. Services accounted for 23 percent of the combined merchandise and services trade in the US in 1993. Unlike the trade in goods, the US trade in services has registered surpluses every year for decades.

Typical Service Exports The following sectors in the US have particularly high export potential:
- *Construction, design, and engineering* The experience and technological advances of the US construction industry, as well as special skills in operations, maintenance, and management make US firms competitive in international projects.

- *Banking and financial services* US financial institutions are competitive internationally, particularly when offering account management, credit card operations, collection management, and other services they have pioneered.
- *Insurance services* US insurers offer services ranging from underwriting and risk evaluation to insurance operations and management contracts in the international marketplace.
- *Legal and accounting services* US firms typically aid other US firms operating abroad through their international legal and accounting activities and also serve foreign firms in their business operations.
- *Computer and data services* The US computer services and data industries are competitive in marketing new technologies, computer operations, data manipulation, and data transmission.
- *Teaching services* The US education sector offers a large variety of cutting edge services for foreign purchasers, particularly in areas such as management, motivation, and the teaching of operational, managerial, and theoretical issues.
- *Management consulting services* US management consulting firms and other US firms that are willing to sell their particular management skills have found success in overseas markets.

For more information on opportunities and operations of services abroad, contact the International Trade Administration Office of Services Industries and Finance. For information about specific industry sectors, contact the Office of Technology and Aerospace Industries; the Office of Basic Industries; or the Office of Textiles, Apparel, and Consumer Goods.

Exporting Services versus Products There are many differences between the export of services and products. In deciding whether to export services, products, or some of both, an exporter should consider some of these important distinctions, including:

1. Services are less tangible than products. Providing a sample of a service is difficult; thus, a precise description of the service offered is more difficult to give than it is for a product. The description of a service must also be carefully honed to be as exact as possible, because no visual representation can be given; a product sample narrows the sale—what you see is what you get.

2. Intangibility of services makes financing difficult. Since the value of services is more difficult to monitor, financial institutions with international experience are frequently less willing to provide financial support for service exports than for product exports. Customer complaints and refusals to pay can also be more troublesome to assess because of the subjective qualities related to the provision of services; payment can often hinge on how pleased a client is with the services performed.

3. Services are often more time dependent than products. Frequently, a service can be offered only at a specific time, and as that time passes, the need for an unused or delayed service is reduced or lost.

4. Selling services is more personal than selling products. Selling services requires direct involvement with the customer, which requires greater cultural sensitivity.

5. Services are more difficult to standardize than products. Service activities must frequently be tailored to the specific needs of the buyer, which often necessitates the service client's direct participation and cooperation in the service delivery.

EXPORT PROCEDURES

Parties to an export originating in the US must comply with two sets of requirements: the export regulations of the US and the import regulations of the country to which the goods will be delivered. Thus, the foreign buyer must meet the import regulations of the importing country which may include import documentation, declarations, and licenses; this discussion focuses on the first step: sending the goods out of the US.

Exporting from the US requires the proper form of export license and can involve an enormous amount of documentation. The exporter should keep in mind that even if help is received with the license and documentation from others, such as banks, freight forwarders or consultants, the exporter remains responsible for ensuring that all statements in applications and documents are true and accurate.

Methods of Exporting and Channels of Distribution

The most common methods of exporting are indirect selling and direct selling. In indirect selling, an export intermediary such as an export management company (EMC) or an export trading company (ETC) usually assumes responsibility for finding overseas buyers, shipping products, and getting paid. For a US company—particularly a smaller firm inexperienced in foreign trade—the principal advantage of indirect exporting is that it provides a way to penetrate foreign markets without the complexities and risks of direct exporting.

Direct selling involves the US producer dealing directly with a foreign buyer. This approach has the advantages of including more control over the export process, having a potential for higher profits, and allowing a closer relationship to the overseas buyer and marketplace. However, the US company must spend more time, personnel, and corporate resources than with indirect exporting.

The paramount consideration in determining which method to use is the level of resources a company is willing to devote to its international marketing effort. Other important factors to consider are the size of the firm, the nature of its products, previous export experience and expertise, and business conditions in the selected overseas markets.

Export Licenses

The EAR sets forth the procedure for obtaining export licenses. There are basically two types of export licenses: the general license and the IVL. As a rule, export procedures for products shipped under a general license are less complicated than those for products shipped under an IVL.

General License The general license is a broad grant of authority by the US government to all US exporters for a large number of product categories. No application is required to obtain a general license; the law grants this license automatically. An exporter must simply be aware that the product is covered by general license—that is, the product is not covered by any specific exemption requiring an IVL or other special authorization.

There are more than 20 different types of general licenses, each represented by a symbol. They include:

General license BAGGAGE Authorizes individuals leaving the US for any destination to take with them as personal baggage the following items: personal effects, household effects, vehicles, and tools of a trade, provided that certain conditions concerning these items are met.

General license CREW Authorizes members of a crew on an exporting carrier to export personal and household items among their effects.

General license GATS Aircraft on Temporary Sojourn: authorizes the departure from the US of foreign registry civil aircraft on temporary sojourn in the US and of US civil aircraft for temporary sojourn abroad.

General license GCG Shipments to Agencies of Cooperating Governments: authorizes the export of commodities for official use of any agency of a cooperating government within the territory of the cooperating government.

General license G-COCOM Authorizes exports to Coordinating Committee on Multilateral Exports (COCOM) participating countries, for use or consumption in those countries, of commodities that the US may approve for export to controlled countries with only notification to the COCOM governments, as well as commodities within the China "Green Zone."

General license GCT Authorizes exports to eligible countries of all "A" level commodities with some exceptions. Exports are allowed only when intended for use or consumption within the importing country, reexport among and consumption within eligible countries, or reexport in accordance with other provisions of the EAR.

General license G-DEST Shipments of Commodities to Destinations Not Requiring a Validated License: the majority of items exported fall under this general license.

General license GIFT Authorizes the export of gift parcels by an individual in the US.

General license GIT In Transit Shipments: authorizes the export from the US of commodities that originate in one foreign country and are destined to another foreign country.

General license GLR Return or Replacement of Certain Commodities: authorizes the return or repair of commodities and the replacement of parts.

General license GLV Shipments of Limited Value: authorizes a "single shipment" of a commodity when the shipment does not exceed a specified value limit.

General license G-NNR Non-Naval Reserve: authorizes the export of petroleum.

General license GTDA Technical Data: authorizes exports to all destinations of technical data that are in the public domain and generally available.

General license GTDR Authorizes the export of technical data to free world destinations when the information does not qualify under GTDA and an IVL is not required.

General license G-TEMP Authorizes the temporary export of commodities and software for temporary use abroad for a period generally not to exceed 12 months.

General license GTF-US Goods Imported for Display at US Exhibitions or Trade Fairs: authorizes the export of commodities that are (1) imported into the US for display at an exhibition or trade fair, and (2) either entered under bond or permitted temporary free importation under bond providing for their export and are being exported in accordance with the terms of such bond.

General license GUS Shipments to Personnel and Agencies of the US Government: authorizes the export of commodities and software for personal or official use to any destination.

General license PLANE STORES Authorizes the export of aircraft of US or foreign registry departing from the US with usual and reasonable kinds and quantities of commodities necessary to support the operation of an aircraft, provided the commodities are not intended for unlading in a foreign country and are not exported under a bill of lading as cargo.

General license SAFEGUARDS Authorizes exports to the International Atomic Energy Agency (IAEA) and the European Atomic Community (EURATOM).

General license SHIP STORES Authorizes the export of usual and reasonable kinds and quantities of the commodities to support the operations of a vessel, provided the commodities are not intended for unlading in a foreign country and are not exported under a bill of lading as cargo.

For more information, contact the Bureau of Export Administration.

IVL The IVL is a specific grant of authority from the US government to a particular exporter to export a specific product to a specific destination on a specific occasion if a general license is not available. The licenses are granted on a case-by-case basis either for a single transaction or for many transactions within a specified period of time. For most products requiring an IVL, the exporter must apply to the DOC for this export license. One exception to the ordinary IVL procedure is made for munitions, which require a Department of State application and license. Other exceptions are listed in the EAR.

Determining Which License to Use The first step in complying with the export licensing regulations is to determine whether a product requires a general license or an IVL. The determination of the license, a three-step procedure, is based on what is being exported and its destination. The procedure is as follows:

1. Determine the destination. Check the schedule of country groups in the EAR (14 CFR Part 770, Supp. 1) to see under which country group the export destination falls.

2. Determine the export control commodity number (ECCN). All dual-use items (items used for both military and civilian purposes) are in one of several categories of commodities controlled by the DOC. To determine which ECCN applies to a particular commodity, see the Commodity Control List in the EAR (15 CFR Part 799.1, Supp. 1).

3. Determine which destinations require an IVL. Refer to the specified ECCN in Part 799.1 of the EAR. Look under the paragraph "Validated License Required" to check which country groups require an IVL. If the country group in question is not listed, no IVL is required. If it is listed, an IVL is required unless the commodity meets one of the technical exceptions cited under the ECCN.

For information and assistance in determining the proper license, contact a local BXA district office or the headquarters office in Washington, DC. To request a preliminary, written commodity classification opinion, contact the Office of Technology and Policy Analysis at the Bureau of Export Administration.

Shipments Under a General License If a general license is appropriate, the exporter is not required to complete a specific application. However, the exporter must determine whether a destination control statement is required. (*See* the "Antidiversion Clause" section in "Export Policies" of this chapter for further discussion of this statement.)

If the shipment is valued at more than US$2,500 or requires a validated export license and is not destined for a country with which the US has restricted trade, the exporter must complete a shipper's export declaration (SED). The SEDs are used by US Customs to indicate the type of export license being used and to keep track of what is exported. They are also used by the Bureau of Census to compile statistics on US trade patterns.

Shipments Under an IVL If an IVL is required, the US exporter must prepare a Form BXA-622P, "Application for Export License," and submit it to the BXA. The applicant must follow the instructions on the form carefully. In some instances, technical manuals and support documentation, such as the international import certificate and the statement of the ultimate consignee and purchaser, must also be included. The most common mistakes in filling out the application are:
- Failing to sign the application.
- Handwriting, rather than typing, the application.
- Responding inadequately to section 9b of the application, which requires a description of the commodity or technical data being exported. These descriptions often are not specific enough to satisfy the Bureau. As necessary, the applicant should attach additional material to explain the product fully.
- Responding inadequately to section 12 of the application, in which the end use of the products or technical data is to be described. The applicant should answer this section with specific details.

If the application is approved, a Validated Export License is mailed to the applicant. The license contains an export authorization number that must be placed on the SED. Unlike some goods exported under a general license, all goods exported under an IVL must be accompanied by an SED.

The final step in complying with the IVL procedure is recordkeeping. The exporter must keep records of all shipments licensed under an IVL for at least five years.

Preparing Products for Export

Selecting and preparing a product for export requires not only product knowledge but also knowledge of the unique characteristics of each market being targeted. Before the sale can occur, a product may need to be modified to satisfy buyer tastes or needs in foreign markets.

Product Preparation Considerations Some key considerations include the following:
- What product should the firm offer abroad?
- What requirements will the product satisfy?
- Should the firm modify its domestically

marketed product for sale abroad? Should it develop a new product for the foreign market?
- What specific features—design, color, size, packaging, brand, warranty, and so on—should the product have?
- What specific services are necessary abroad at the presale and postsale stages?
- Are the firm's service and repair facilities adequate to give prompt attention to both an expanding market and to overseas customers?

Product Adaptation To achieve success in a foreign market, a product may have to be modified in order to conform it to foreign government regulations, geographic and climatic conditions, buyer preferences, or standard of living. A product may also need to be modified to facilitate shipment or compensate for possible differences in engineering or design standards.

Foreign government product regulations are common in international trade and are expected to expand in the future. These regulations can take the form of high tariffs or of non-tariff barriers, such as regulations or product specifications. Detailed information on such regulations is available from the country desk officers of DOC's International Economic Policy (IEP) unit.

Engineering and Redesign Fundamental aspects of a product may require redesign. For example, electrical standards in many foreign countries differ from US electrical standards. It is not unusual to find phases, cycles, or voltages that would damage or impair the operating efficiency of equipment designed for use in the US.

Similarly, many kinds of equipment must be engineered in the metric system for integration with other pieces of equipment or for compliance with the standards of a given country. The US is virtually alone in its adherence to a nonmetric system, and US firms that compete successfully abroad have found metric measurement a vital detail in selling to overseas markets. Even instruction or maintenance manuals should take care to give dimensions in centimeters, weights in grams or kilos, and temperatures in degrees Celsius.

Branding, Labeling, and Packaging Some of the considerations that an exporter should undertake regarding the branding and labeling of products are:
- Are international brand names important to promote and distinguish a product? Conversely, should local brands or private labels be employed to heighten local interest? Can labels be produced in official or customary languages if required by law or practice?
- Does information on product content and country of origin have to be provided?
- Are weights and measures stated in the local unit?

- Must each item be labeled individually?
- Are local tastes and knowledge considered?

A US company may find that building international recognition for a brand is expensive, and piracy of the company's brand names and counterfeiting of its products are widespread in some countries. Protection for brand names varies from one country to another, and in some developing countries, barriers to the use of foreign brands or trademarks may exist. It may be a costly and lengthy process to register a trademark, copyright, or patent, delaying entry into the market by several years.

Installation An exporter should also consider the ease of installing the product overseas. If technicians or engineers are needed overseas to assist in installation, it is wise to preassemble or pretest the product before shipping in order to minimize the time in the field. If a product is sent disassembled, there may be savings in shipping costs, but there also may be a delay in payment because completion of the sale is contingent on the delivery of an assembled product. If trained personnel are not sent to install the product, all product information, such as training manuals, installation instructions, and parts lists, will need to be provided in the local language. It is also advisable to provide a quickly accessible line of communication—telephone, fax, or other—for customer service if you do not have a representative on site.

Warranties In some instances, the US company should include a warranty on the product, particularly if the buyer is likely to expect a specific level of performance and a guarantee that it will be achieved. However, consumer expectations for warranties vary from country to country depending on the level of development, competitive practices, activism of consumer groups, local standards of production quality, and other similar factors. If a warranty is not expected, the exporter generally need not provide one; otherwise, production costs may be higher than a competitor's. Exporters should keep in mind that servicing warranties is more expensive and troublesome in foreign markets. It is usually desirable to arrange warranty service locally with the assistance of a representative or distributor.

Servicing Of special concern to foreign consumers is the service the US company provides for its products. Service after the sale is critical for some products, especially if the product's technology is complex. US exporters who rely on a foreign distributor or agent to provide service must take steps to ensure an adequate level of service. (*See* the "After-Sales Service" section later in this chapter.)

Selling the Product

Pricing Proper pricing is usually the most problematic element for an exporter when trying to complete a sale and make a profit. The traditional components for determining proper pricing are costs, market demand, and competition.

Costs Many new exporters calculate their export price by the cost-plus method, in which the exporter starts with the domestic manufacturing cost and adds administration, research and development, overhead, freight forwarding, distributor margins, customs charges, and profit. However, the net effect of this pricing approach may be that the export price escalates to an uncompetitive level.

A more competitive method of pricing for market entry is marginal cost pricing, in which the direct, out-of-pocket expenses of producing and selling products for export are considered to be a floor beneath which prices cannot be set without incurring a loss.

In addition to production costs, overhead, and research and development, other costs—such as business travel, international postage, telephone calls, translation costs, consultant fees, freight forwarder costs, and product modification—should be allocated to domestic and export products in proportion to the benefit derived from those expenditures.

Market Demand Demand in the foreign market is a key to setting prices. For most consumer goods, per capita income is a reasonably good gauge of a market's ability to pay. In most lower per capita income markets, simplifying the product to reduce selling price may be an answer. Pricing should also accommodate wild fluctuations in currency and the relative strength of the dollar, if possible. The exporter should consider who the main customers will be; if products are intended for expatriates or the upper class of a developing country, a high price may work even though the average per capita income is low.

Competition Exporters should evaluate the competition's prices in each export market they intend to enter. When a particular foreign market is being serviced by many competitors, the exporter may have little choice but to match the going price or even go below it in order to establish market share. If the exporter's product or service is new to a particular foreign market, it may actually be possible to set a higher price than is normally charged domestically.

Quotations and Pro Forma Invoices Many export transactions begin with the receipt of an inquiry from abroad, followed by a request for a quotation or a pro forma invoice. A quotation describes the product, states a price for it, sets the time of shipment, and specifies the terms of sale and terms of payment. The description should include the following points:
- Buyer's name and address.
- Buyer's reference number and the date of inquiry.
- Listing of the requested products and brief descriptions.

- Price of each item. It is advisable to indicate whether the items are new or used and to quote in US dollars to reduce foreign exchange risk.
- Gross and net shipping weight, in metric units when appropriate.
- Total cubic volume and dimensions of products when packed for export, in metric units when appropriate.
- Trade discount, if applicable.
- Delivery point.
- Terms of sale.
- Terms of payment.
- Insurance and shipping costs.
- Validity period for the quotation.
- Total charges to be paid by the customer.
- Estimated shipping date to the factory or US port. It is preferable to give the US port.
- Estimated date of shipment arrival.

Sellers are often requested to submit a pro forma invoice with or instead of a quotation. Pro forma invoices are not requests for payment, but are essentially quotations in an invoice format. In addition to the above items, a pro forma invoice should include a statement certifying that the pro forma invoice is true and correct and a statement describing the country of origin of goods.

It is important that price quotations state explicitly that they are subject to change without notice. If a specific price is agreed upon or guaranteed by the exporter, the precise period during which the offer remains valid should be specified.

Terms of Sale It is important that a common understanding exist regarding the delivery terms, such as free on board (FOB) or free alongside ship (FAS). Confusion over terms of sale can result in a lost sale or a loss on a sale. The exporter should be familiar with the terms and definitions as contained in *Incoterms 1990.* This booklet can be obtained from International Chamber of Commerce (ICC) Publishing. The more common terms of sale can be found in the "Export Glossary" section of this chapter.

After the Sale

When preparing to ship a product overseas, the exporter needs to ensure that the merchandise is packed correctly so that it arrives in good condition; labeled correctly to ensure that the goods are handled properly and will arrive on time and at the right place; documented correctly to meet US and foreign government requirements, as well as proper collection standards; and insured against damage, loss, and pilferage and, in some cases, delay.

Freight Forwarders The international freight forwarder acts as an agent for the exporter in moving cargo to the overseas destination. The freight forwarder can assist with an order from the start by

10 KEYS TO EXPORT SUCCESS

1. Before starting an export business, obtain qualified expert counseling and develop a master international marketing plan that clearly defines your goals and objectives and identifies the problems you anticipate, plus potential solutions.

2. If necessary, secure a commitment from top management to overcome the initial difficulties and meet the financial requirements of exporting.

3. Take sufficient care in selecting overseas distributors, because they will generally operate much more independently than their domestic counterparts.

4. Establish a basis for profitable operations and orderly growth, and do not simply rely on unsolicited trade leads.

5. Devote continuing attention to your export business, even if your domestic market is also booming.

6. Treat international distributors on an equal basis with domestic counterparts by offering such things as institutional advertising campaigns, special discount offers, sales incentive programs, special credit term programs, and warranty offers that are appropriate to their situation.

7. Do not assume that a given market technique and product will automatically be successful in all countries.

8. Be willing to modify products to meet regulations or cultural preferences in other countries.

9. Print service, sale, and warranty messages in locally understood languages.

10. Provide readily available servicing for the product, because an otherwise successful product may acquire a bad reputation if it lacks the necessary service support.

advising the exporter of the freight costs, port charges, consular fees, cost of special documentation, and insurance costs, as well as the freight forwarder's handling fees—all of which help in preparing price quotations. The freight forwarder may also recommend the type of packing for best protecting the merchandise in transit and can arrange to have the merchandise packed at the port or placed into containers.

When the order is ready to ship, the freight forwarder will review the letter of credit, commercial invoices, packing list, and other documents to ensure that everything is in order for exit, entry, and transport purposes. The freight forwarder can also reserve the necessary space on board an ocean vessel, if the exporter desires.

When the cargo arrives at the port of export, the freight forwarder may make necessary arrangements with customs brokers, if the exporter has not already done so, to ensure that the goods comply with customs export documentation regulations. The freight forwarder may also have the goods delivered to the carrier in time for loading, may prepare the bill of lading, and may prepare any specially required documentation. After shipment, the freight forwarder will send all documents directly to the customer or to the paying bank if requested by the exporter.

Packing In packing an item for export, the shipper should be aware of the demands that transport puts on a package, namely, breakage, weight, moisture, and pilferage. Because proper packing is essential in exporting, the buyer often specifies packing requirements.

One popular method of shipment is the use of containers obtained from carriers or private leasing concerns. These containers vary in size, material, and construction, and can accommodate most cargo. Refrigerated and liquid bulk containers are readily available as well.

Labeling Specific markings and labeling are used on export shipping cartons and containers to meet shipping regulations, ensure proper handling, conceal the identity of the contents, and help receivers identify shipments. The overseas buyer usually specifies which export marks should appear on the cargo for easy identification by receivers. Exporters need to put the following markings on cartons to have the products shipped:

- Shipper's mark,
- Country of origin (USA),
- Weight (in pounds and kilos),
- Number of packages and size of cases (in inches and centimeters),
- Handling marks (international pictorial symbols),
- Cautionary markings, such as "This Side Up" or "Use No Hooks" (in English and in the language of the country of destination),
- Port of entry, and
- Labels for hazardous materials (universal symbols adapted by the International Maritime Organization).

Documentation Exporters should seriously consider having the freight forwarder handle the formidable amount of documentation that exporting requires, because freight forwarders are specialists in this process. Documentation must be precise. Slight discrepancies or omissions may prevent US merchandise from being exported, result in US firms not getting paid, or even result in the seizure of the exporter's goods by US or foreign government customs.

The following documents are commonly used in exporting; which ones are actually used depends on the requirements of both the US government and the government of the importing country:

- *Commercial Invoice* A bill for the goods from the buyer to the seller.
- *Bill of Lading* A contract between the owner of the goods and the carrier.
- *Consular Invoice* A document required by some nations to control and identify goods entering the country.
- *Certificate of Origin* A signed statement specifying the country from which the goods originated; required by some nations before entry is allowed.
- *Inspection Certification* A certificate required by some purchasers and countries to attest to the specifications of the goods shipped.
- *Dock Receipt and Warehouse Receipt* Receipts used to transfer liability when an export item is transported by the domestic carrier to the port of embarkation and left with the international carrier for export.
- *Destination Control Statement* A statement which is included in the commercial invoice, ocean or air waybill of lading, and the SED notifying the carrier and all foreign parties that the item may be exported only to certain destinations.
- *Insurance Certificate* A certified statement of the type and amount of coverage, required only if and when the seller provides insurance.
- *Shipper's Export Declaration (SED)* A document submitted to US Customs and used to control exports and compile trade statistics. It must be filed for shipments by mail valued at more than US$500, for shipments by means other than mail valued at more than US$2,500, and for any shipments covered by an IVL, regardless of value.
- *Export License* A general license or an IVL.
- *Export Packing List* A statement that itemizes the material in each individual package; indicates the type of package; shows the individual net, legal, tare, and gross weights and measurements for each package; and shows the shipper's and buyer's references. The packing list is usually attached to the outside of a package in a waterproof envelope marked "Packing List Enclosed."

Shipping The export marks should be added to the standard information shown on the domestic bill of lading and should show the name of the exporting carrier and the latest permissible arrival date at the port of export. The exporter should also include instructions for the inland carrier to notify the international freight forwarder by telephone on arrival.

International shipments are more and more often being made on through bills of lading under multimodal contracts. The multimodal transport operator takes charge of and responsibility for the entire movement from factory to the final destination.

When determining the method of international shipping, the exporter may find it useful to consult with a freight forwarder. The exporter should also consider the cost of shipment, delivery schedule, and foreign buyer's accessibility to the shipped product. Although air carriers are more expensive, their cost may be offset by lower domestic shipping costs and faster delivery times.

Before shipping, it is advisable to check with the foreign buyer about the destination of the goods in case the buyer wants the goods shipped to a free trade zone or a free port, where the goods will be exempt from import duties.

Insurance Export shipments are usually insured by cargo insurance against loss, damage, and delay in transit. For international shipments, the carrier's liability is frequently limited by international agreements, and the coverage is substantially different from domestic coverage. Arrangements for cargo insurance may be made by either the buyer or seller, depending on the terms of sale. Exporters are advised to consult with international insurance carriers or freight forwarders for more information.

Damaging weather conditions, rough handling by carriers, and other common hazards to cargo make marine insurance important protection for US exporters. If the terms of sale make the US firm responsible for insurance, it should either obtain its own policy or insure cargo under a freight forwarder's policy for a fee. If the terms of sale make the foreign buyer responsible, the exporter should make sure via examination of documentation (not assume or even take the buyer's word) that adequate insurance has been obtained. If the buyer neglects to obtain coverage or obtains too little, damage to the cargo may cause a major financial loss to the exporter.

Payment for Exports

Several basic methods are in common use for receiving payments for products sold abroad. (Refer to the "International Payments" chapter for details.) Major factors that influence the choice of the payment method include the length of the relationship with the buyer, the buyer's financial history, foreign exchange conditions, and the ease of accessing the various payment methods. Ranked in order from most secure to least secure for the exporter,

the basic methods of payment are:

1. Cash in Advance The shipper is relieved of collection problems. Receipt via wire transfer allows for immediate use of the money. Payment by check, even before shipment, may result in a collection delay. On the other hand, advance payment creates cash flow problems and increases risks for the buyer.

2. Letter of Credit Additional security in the form of a bank's promise to pay the exporter is added to that of the foreign buyer when the exporter has complied with all the terms and conditions of the letter of credit.

3. Documentary Collection or Draft Used when the buyer is concerned that the goods may not be sent if the payment is made in advance. Here, documents are required to be presented before payment is made. A draft, sometimes called a bill of exchange, is analogous to a foreign buyer's check and sometimes carries the risk that it will be dishonored.

4. Open Account The exporter bills the customer, who is expected to pay under agreed terms at a future date. It is a convenient method of payment and may be satisfactory if the buyer is well established, had demonstrated a long and favorable payment record, or has been thoroughly checked for creditworthiness. But the absence of documents and banking channels makes legal enforcement of claims difficult to pursue. In addition, collection abroad can be difficult and costly to the exporter, and receivables may be harder to finance, since drafts or other evidence of indebtedness are unavailable.

5. Credit Cards Accepted by many exporters of goods that are sold directly to the end user. International credit card transactions are typically placed by telephone or fax, methods that tend to facilitate fraudulent transactions.

6. Other Alternative payment mechanisms may include such methods as consignment sales, third country foreign currency, and countertrade and barter.

Financing Export Transactions

Being able to offer good payment terms is often necessary to make a sale. Exporters should be aware of the many financing options open to them so that they may choose the one that is most favorable for both the foreign buyer and the US seller.

Factors to Consider in Financing An exporter may need (1) preshipment financing to produce or purchase the product or to provide a service, or (2) postshipment financing of the resulting account or accounts receivable, or both. In making decisions about financing, the following factors are important to consider:

1. The need for financing to make the sale. In some cases, payment terms favorable to the buyer make a product more competitive. In other cases, the exporter may need financing to produce the goods that have been ordered or to finance other aspects of a sale, such as promotion and selling expenses, engineering modifications, and shipping costs.

2. The cost of different methods of financing. Interest rates and fees vary. The total costs and their effect on price and profit should be well understood before a pro forma invoice is submitted to the foreign buyer.

3. The length of time financing is required. Costs increase with the length of terms. Different methods of financing are available for short, medium, and long terms.

4. The risks associated with financing the transaction. The greater the risks associated with the transaction—whether they actually exist or are only perceived by the lender—the greater the costs to the exporter and the more difficult financing will be to obtain.

Extending Credit to Foreign Buyers A useful way to determine the appropriate credit period is to look at the normal commercial terms in the exporter's industry for internationally traded products, because foreign buyers generally expect to receive similar terms. With few exceptions, normal commercial terms range from 30 to 180 days for off-the-shelf items like consumer goods, chemicals, and for other industrial raw materials, agricultural commodities, and spare parts and components. Custom-made or higher-value capital equipment may warrant longer repayment periods. It may be necessary to make an allowance for longer shipment times, because foreign buyers are often unwilling to have the credit period start before they receive the goods.

Foreign customers are frequently charged interest on credit periods of a year or longer, but infrequently on short-term credit (up to 180 days). Most exporters absorb interest charges for short-term credit unless the foreign customer pays after the due date.

Exporters should also determine whether they incur financial liability should the foreign buyer default.

Use of Commercial Banks If the exporter already has a loan for domestic needs, then the lender already has experience with the exporter's ability to perform and would generally be more willing to provide financing for export transactions if there is reasonable certainty of repayment. When a lender wishes greater assurance than is afforded by the transaction, a government guarantee program may enable the lender to extend credit to the exporter.

For a US company that is new to exporting or is a small- or medium-sized business, it is important to select a bank that is committed to dealing with companies of that size. The exporter should also determine: (1) if there are charges for confirming a letter of credit, processing drafts, and collecting payment;

(2) whether the bank has foreign branches or correspondent banks; (3) whether the bank can provide buyer credit reports; (4) whether the bank has experience with US and state government financing programs that support small business export transactions; and (5) what other services, such as trade leads, are provided by the bank.

Other Private Sources The following are other avenues of financing:
- Export intermediaries, such as ETCs and EMCs, which can help finance export sales.
- Foreign buyers, who may make down payments or make progress payments as goods are completed to reduce the need for financing from other sources.
- Suppliers who may be willing to offer terms to the exporter, such as accepting assignment of a part of the proceeds of a letter of credit or a partial transfer of a transferable letter of credit, if they are confident that they will receive payment.
- Factoring by the exporter, which is the discounting of a foreign account receivable that does not involve a draft. The exporter transfers title to its foreign accounts receivable to a factoring house (an organization that specializes in the financing of accounts receivable) for cash at a discount from the face value.
- Forfaiting, which is the selling, at a discount, of longer-term accounts receivable or promissory notes of the foreign buyer.
- Confirming, which is a financial service in which an independent company confirms an export order in the seller's country and makes payment for the goods in the currency of that country. For the exporter, confirming means that the entire export transaction from manufacture to end user can be fully coordinated and paid for over time. Confirming is more common in Europe than in the US.

Government Assistance Programs Several federal government agencies, as well as a number of state and local agencies, offer programs to assist exporters with their financing needs. Some are guarantee programs that require the participation of an approved lender; others provide loans or grants to the exporter or a foreign government.

The Export-Import Bank of the United States (Eximbank) is the US government's general trade finance agency, offering numerous programs to address a broad range of needs. (*See* "Useful Addresses" in this chapter for contact information.)

Other agencies fill various market niches. The US Department of Agriculture (USDA) offers a variety of programs to foster agricultural exports. The SBA offers programs to address the needs of small exporters. The Overseas Private Investment Corporation (OPIC) provides specialized assistance to

US firms through its performance bond and contractor insurance programs. The Agency for International Development (AID) provides grants to developing nations that can be used to purchase US goods and services. (*See* "Useful Addresses" for contact information.)

After-Sales Service

Along with quality and price, service is a critical factor to the success of any export sales effort, especially with regard to consumer durables but with some consumables as well. Service includes the prompt delivery of a product, courteous dealings by sales personnel, a localized user manual or service manual, ready access to a service facility, and knowledgeable, cost-effective maintenance, repair, or replacement.

Among the many options for the delivery of service to foreign buyers are:

- A high-cost option, in which the product is returned to the manufacturing or distribution facility in the US for service or repair. The foreign buyer incurs a high cost and loses the use of the product for an extended period, while the seller must incur the export cost of the same product a second time to return it.
- A joint venture or other partnership arrangement for the exported good, in which the overseas partner may have a service or repair capability in the markets targeted. The cost of providing this service should be negotiated into the agreement.
- The use of local service facilities for goods sold at retail outlets. This option requires front-end expenses to identify and train local service outlets; costs are expected to be recouped over the long run.
- A warranty and service program, which lists authorized local warranty and service centers. This option involves administrative, training, and supervisory overhead costs.

USEFUL ADDRESSES

Government Agencies

Agency for International Development (AID)
Department of State Building
320 21st St. NW
Washington, DC 20523, USA
Tel: [1] (202) 647-1850
Fax: [1] (202) 647-1770

Customs Service
Entry Rulings Branch, Room 2107
1301 Constitution Ave. NW
Washington, DC 20229, USA
Tel: [1] (202) 566-5856

Department of Agriculture (USDA)
14th St. and Independence Ave. SW
Washington, DC 20250, USA
Tel: [1] (202) 720-8732, 720-2791
Fax: [1] (202) 720-2166
 Foreign Agricultural Service (FAS)
 Tel: [1] (202) 720-7115
 Fax: [1] (202) 690-2159

Department of Commerce (DOC)
14th and Constitution Ave. NW
Washington, DC 20230, USA
Tel: [1] (202) 482-2000
Fax: [1] (202) 482-4576

Department of Commerce (DOC)
Bureau of Export Administration (BXA)
14th St. and Constitution Ave. NW
Washington, DC 20230, USA
Tel: [1] (202) 482-2721
 Export Licensing Information
 Tel: [1] (202) 482-4811
 Office of Antiboycott Compliance
 Tel: [1] (202) 482-4550
 Office of Export Licensing, Exporter Counseling Division
 Tel: [1] (202) 482-5247
 Office of Technology and Policy Analysis
 Tel: [1] (202) 482-4188

Department of Commerce (DOC)
Foreign Trade Zones Board
Main Commerce Bldg.
Washington, DC 20230, USA
Tel: [1] (202) 482-2862
Fax: [1] (202) 482-0002

Department of Commerce (DOC)
International Trade Administration (ITA)
Office of Trade Development
14th and Constitution Ave. NW
Washington, DC 20230, USA
Tel: [1] (202) 482-1461
 Office of Basic Industries
 Tel: [1] (202) 482-5023
 Office of Services Industries and Finance
 Tel: [1] (202) 482-3575
 Office of Technology and Aerospace Industries
 Tel: [1] (202) 482-1872
 Office of Textiles, Apparel, and Consumer Goods Industries
 Tel: [1] (202) 482-5225

Department of Commerce (DOC)
International Trade Administration (ITA)
US and Foreign Commercial Service (US&FCS)
14th and Constitution Ave. NW
Washington, DC 20230, USA
 Office of Domestic Operations
 Tel: [1] (202) 482-4767
 Office of Export Promotion Services
 Tel: [1] (202) 482-6220
 Office of International Operations
 Tel: [1] (202) 482-6228

Department of State
Main State Bldg.
2201 C St. NW
Washington, DC 20520, USA
Tel: [1] (202) 647-3686, 647-4000
    Bureau of Economic and Business Affairs
    Tel: [1] (202) 647-7575
    Fax: [1] (202) 647-5713

Department of the Treasury
Main Treasury Bldg.
15th St. and Pennsylvania Ave. NW
Washington, DC 20220, USA
Tel: [1] (202) 622-2000

Environmental Protection Agency (EPA)
Office of International Activities
401 M St. SW
Washington, DC 20460, USA
Tel: [1] (202) 260-4870
Fax: [1] (202) 260-9653

Export-Import Bank (Eximbank)
811 Vermont Ave. NW
Washington, DC 20571, USA
Tel: [1] (202) 566-8990
    Export Assistance Hotline
    [1] (202) 566-8860, (800) 424-5201

Food and Drug Administration (FDA)
5600 Fishers Lane
Rockville, MD 20857, USA
Tel: [1] (301) 443-1544, 443-3170
Fax: [1] (301) 443-5930

Government Printing Office (GPO)
Superintendent of Documents
Washington, DC 20402, USA
Tel: [1] (202) 512-1800
Fax: [1] (202) 512-2550

International Trade Administration (ITA)
Office of International Economic Policy
14th and Constitution Ave. NW
Washington, DC 20230, USA
Tel: [1] (202) 482-3022

National Institute of Standards and Technology
(NIST)
National Center for Standards and Certification
Information
Route I-270 and Quince Orchard Rd.
Gaithersburg, MD 20899, USA
Tel: [1] (301) 975-4040
Fax: [1] (301) 926-1559
    GATT Hotline: [1] (301) 975-4041
    EC Hotline: [1] (301) 921-4164

National Institute of Standards and Technology
(NIST)
Metric Program Office
Route I-270 and Quince Orchard Rd.
Gaithersburg, MD 20899, USA
Tel: [1] (301) 975-3690
Fax: [1] (301) 975-1416

Office of the US Trade Representative (USTR)
600 17th St. NW
Washington, DC 20506, USA
Tel: [1] (202) 392-3230
Fax: [1] (202) 395-3911

Overseas Private Investment Corporation (OPIC)
1100 New York Ave.
Washington, DC 20527, USA
Tel: [1] (202) 336-8799
Tel: [1] (800) 408-9859

Small Business Administration (SBA)
Office of International Trade
409 Third St. SW, Suite 6100
Washington, DC 20416, USA
Tel: [1] (202) 205-6720
Fax: [1] (202) 205-7272

Publications

A Basic Guide to Exporting
World Trade Press
1505 Fifth Ave.
San Rafael, CA 94901, USA
Tel: [1] (415) 454-9934, (800) 833-8586
Fax: [1] (415) 453-7980

*Business America: The Magazine of International
Trade*
Government Printing Office (GPO)
Superintendent of Documents
Washington, DC 20402, USA
Tel: [1] (202) 512-1800
Fax: [1] (202) 512-2550
*Monthly publication of the US Dept. of Commerce,
with information on US export policy, trade
opportunities for US exporters, listings of
international trade exhibitions.*

Incoterms 1990
ICC Publishing, Inc.
156 Fifth Ave.
New York, NY 10010, USA
Tel: [1] (212) 206-1150
Fax: [1] (212) 633-6025

Electronic Resources

Economic Bulletin Board (EBB)
Tel: (202) 482-1526
Modem (300/1200/2400 bps): [1] (202) 482-3870
Modem (9600 bps): [1] (202) 482-2584, 482-2167
Operated by the Department of Commerce.

National Trade Data Bank (NTDB)
National Technical Information Service (NTIS)
5285 Port Royal Road
Springfield, VA 22161, USA
Tel: [1] (703) 487-4650
Fax: [1] (703) 321-8547
*A monthly two CD-ROM set from the Dept. of
Commerce with over 90,000 documents relating to
US foreign trade.*

Industry Reviews

INTRODUCTION

This chapter describes the status of and trends in major US industries. It also lists key contacts for finding sources of supply, developing sales leads, and conducting economic research. We have grouped industries into 12 categories. Some smaller sectors of commerce are not detailed here, while others may overlap into more than one area. If your business even remotely fits into a category, do not hesitate to contact several of the organizations listed; they should be able to assist you further in gathering the information you need. General trade organizations, which may also be very helpful (particularly if your business is in an industry not directly covered), are listed in the "Important Addresses" chapter at the end of this book.

Each section has two segments: an industry summary and a list of useful contacts. The summary gives an overview of the range of products available in a certain industry and describes the ability of that industry to compete in worldwide markets. The con-

tacts include government departments, trade associations, publications, and trade fairs that can provide information specific to the industry. Addresses and telephone and fax numbers for each are listed in the "Important Addresses" chapter, in the sections indicated. An entire volume could likely be devoted to each area, but such in-depth coverage is beyond the scope of this book; our intent is to give you a basis for your own research.

We highly recommend that you peruse the "Trade Fairs" and "Important Addresses" chapters, where you will find additional resources including a variety of trade promotion organizations, chambers of commerce, business services, and media outlets.

AGRICULTURAL PRODUCTS, PROCESSED FOODS, AND BEVERAGES

At the turn of the century, close to a million of the largest US farms (17 percent of all US farms) supplied half of the nation's agricultural output. Today, the 76,000 largest farms (less than 4 percent of present US farms) account for half of US farm output. This trend toward larger and fewer farms is expected to continue. Large scale production techniques have resulted in tremendous increases in the amount of production. Farm and ranch products were valued at about US$250 billion in 1993; processed food and beverage products were valued at about US$404 billion.

To a large extent, the economic growth in the agricultural sector has been achieved without regard to environmental abuses, a situation now recognized as deleterious to long-term productive capacity and hazardous to persons who live and work in farming areas. The US Environmental Protection Agency (EPA) is attempting to prevent further abuses and to promote environmental awareness. For example, this agency has adopted extensive employer requirements for training and protecting workers who handle pesticides. Efforts are also being made to protect water supplies from contamination by pesticide runoffs.

The US agricultural industry is entering a new era of international trade. The North American Free Trade Agreement (NAFTA) and the Uruguay Round of the General Agreement on Tariffs and Trade (GATT) will generate opportunities for US agricultural exports and imports. For the first time in many decades, US foreign policy is being defined in large part by economic and trade priorities, not by Cold War objectives, which have in the past put foreign policy at odds with foreign trade. These developments are encouraging many US growers to look beyond domestic markets for the first time.

Farm and Ranch Products

In 1994 much of the agricultural industry in the US was recovering from devastating floods in 1993 that severely affected nine Midwestern states. Although nearly 15 percent of the commercial-sized farms in those states were still financially vulnerable during 1994, the industry as a whole was expected to recover fully in 1995. In fact 1994 crop production is expected to increase by 5 to 10 percent, and animal products appear to be reaching a record level of production. An estimated US$42.5 billion worth of US agricultural products were expected to be exported in 1994, matching 1993 levels. This amount represents only 17 percent of total US agricultural output. In comparison, 1993 agricultural imports into the US were valued at US$24.5 billion, slightly more than half the level of exports.

Products US crops produced for commercial sale include various grains for human consumption—such as wheat, rye, and rice—and for animal feed—such as corn (maize), oats, barley, and sorghum. Other important corps grown on US farms include cotton, tobacco, sugar, oilseeds, fats, oils, a vast assortment of vegetables and fruit, nuts, hay, and seeds. Ranch products include cattle, hogs, sheep, chickens, turkeys, and dairy products such as milk, cheese, and eggs, to name a few.

Competitive Situation US agriculture is in an expansion mode, fueled by greater consumer and investment spending, which in turn is overcoming stagnant net exports and smaller increases in government expenditures. Strong growth in average personal income and lower unemployment rates typically support rising consumer demands for food and fiber. Given these trends, US ranchers are anticipating that US consumers will purchase larger quantities of meat, which will then boost both grain and livestock prices.

In 1994 bulk exports—such as wheat, flour, and coarse grains (about 80 percent of which represent corn)—were expected to decline, while high value exports—primarily livestock, dairy, and poultry

products—were expected to increase. The greatest change has been in the production and export of processed and prepared consumer foods. Consumer oriented exports—including everything from snack foods to meats, fruit, and vegetables—now account for more than one-third of US agricultural exports, up from 14 percent only a decade ago. In 1994 US exports of major summer fruits attained record levels as markets in Mexico and several Asian countries expanded.

Both NAFTA and the most recent GATT agreements are expected to boost US agricultural exports and farm income. NAFTA is already serving to expand agricultural exports to the growing Mexican market, as well as a reciprocal trade of imports into the US, particularly of flowers, vegetables, and fruits. The GATT Accord will reduce trade tariffs and eliminate numerous other trade barriers in 117 nations around the globe. Although GATT calls for the phasing out of agricultural subsidies, other major producers benefit from such payments to a greater extent than do US producers, which should give US farmers an edge in the future.

Processed Foods and Beverages

The processed food and beverages industry sector is the nation's largest manufacturing sector in terms of dollar value. In 1993 the value of this sector's shipments reached an estimated US$404 billion, an increase of more than 2 percent over 1992. Some 6 percent of the US domestic market was supplied by imports, but exports remained higher than imports: US$24.3 billion versus US$21 billion. Both NAFTA and a successful conclusion of the Uruguay Round of GATT will serve to boost food and beverages exports.

Products The US food and beverages industry produces a vast array of items. These include meats, poultry, and dairy products; preserved or frozen fruits and vegetables; grain mill products such as flour, cereal, and milled rice, and prepared flour mixes and doughs; dog and cat food; bakery products such as bread, cakes, cookies, crackers, and frozen baked goods; sugar and confectionery products, including chewing gum, chocolate, and other cocoa products; salted and roasted nuts and seeds; fats and oils; beverages such as wines, brandy and brandy spirits, distilled and blended liquors, malt beverages, bottled and canned soft drinks, and bottled, canned, or frozen fruit juices; flavoring extracts and syrups; canned and cured fish, fresh or frozen prepared fish; roasted coffee; potato chips and similar snacks; manufactured ice; and macaroni and spaghetti noodles.

Food and beverages are divided into two groups: higher value-added industries and lower value-added industries. The higher value-added industries manufacture retail-ready, packaged, consumer brand-name products, of which at least 40 percent of the industry shipment value is added through sophisticated manufacturing. This includes items such as processed fruits and vegetables, alcoholic beverages, ready-to-eat meals, bakery items, and candy products. Lower value-added items include meat, poultry, seafood, most dairy products, and grain-based intermediate products. Exports of higher value-added products increased significantly in 1993.

Competitive Situation Most industry analysts consider the US food and beverages processing sector to be mature and well-developed. Over the years, this industry has shown its resilient nature as it has adjusted to domestic and international trends. Emphasis on R&D has increased quality and production efficiency as the industry attempts to stay current with medical and technological developments, supporting the gradual growth of the industry in both US and global markets.

The nature of the domestic market continues to change, and competition within it is intensifying. An expanding immigrant population, originating mainly from South America and Asia, is having a notable effect on the industry as it taps into these domestic growing markets. To succeed in them, the industry must produce foods and beverages that appeal to the taste standards of different cultures. In other areas of the market, households are becoming smaller, single parent families are an increasingly common phenomenon, and the percentage of older people in the population also continues to rise. The food and beverage industry must provide products tailored to the needs of older and smaller households to compete with consumer trends to save time and effort by eating in restaurants instead of preparing homecooked meals.

Since 1985 the sale of private label food and beverages has been slowly increasing. Private label products, also referred to as generic or store brand items, are goods labeled with a store name or without any manufacturer's name. These goods are offered, usually at cheaper prices, as alternatives to brand name products. Modern manufacturing technologies, quality control, and improved packaging can be used just as easily by a private label as by a national brand, and many consumers perceive little quality difference between the two. However, growth in private label commodities is limited, primarily because private label manufacturers cannot afford to invest in new product development and advertising without raising prices, which they are reluctant to do. Nevertheless, private label products add a competitive factor to the food and beverage market, serving to keep manufacturers of name brand products constantly aware of the need to provide high quality and innovative goods within a price range that is competitive with less costly generic goods.

Over the next five years, the US processed food and beverages industry is likely to continue its slow expansion. Several sectors—such as alcoholic beverage companies, brewers, and winemakers—may have to contend with increased federal excise taxes, which may be used to finance health-related programs. Some sectors—the US tobacco in particular—have already felt the pinch of increased federal excise taxes imposed to fund such programs.

With domestic markets growing only slowly, many US food and beverage processors are concentrating on exports. As US firms become more skillful in cultivating overseas customers, and as the international economy improves, exports are likely to increase substantially. Exports of higher value-added food and beverages to Canada, Japan, Mexico, Germany, and the UK represented about 57 percent of the 1993 export total, and Mexico has recently emerged as a significant market for US higher value-added US products.

Wood and Paper Products

The US wood products industry is concentrated mostly in the Pacific Northwest and the Southeast. To a lesser degree, it is also established across the Midwest, Northeast, and Appalachian regions. The industry provides wood products mainly to the construction industry, but it also supplies raw materials to manufacturers of furniture, cabinets and fixtures, wood chips, and pallets and skids. In recent years, the industry has been severely hurt by government restrictions on logging.

The US paper and allied products industry is recognized worldwide as a high-quality, high-volume, low-cost producer that benefits from having a large consumer base, a modern technical infrastructure, adequate raw materials, and a highly skilled labor force. It ranks eighth among US manufacturing industries in the value of its shipments, and third in sales of nondurable goods.

In 1993 the domestic industry attained a wastepaper recovery rate of nearly 42 percent, surpassing its 1995 goal of 40 percent. Recycled paper constituted nearly 31 percent of fiber used at domestic paper and paperboard mills in 1993, up from 29 percent in 1992. Environmental spending for new and expanded recycling facilities is expected to accelerate as additional overseas markets develop for such products.

Products US wood and paper suppliers offer raw and processed materials. Wood products include lumber, hardwood veneer and plywood, softwood veneer and plywood, and reconstituted panel products. Paper products include wood pulp, printing and writing papers, sanitary tissue, industrial-type papers, containerboard, and boxboard.

Competitive Situation In 1993 production of lumber and wood products remained flat or declined in most product sectors. However, the value-added sectors—such as millwork and paneling—registered minor gains. The value of wood product exports rose in 1993 to US$7.1 billion, an increase of more than 15 percent over 1992 exports. Nearly all of this increase was the result of higher prices, the volume of exports remaining essentially flat. US imports of solid wood products increased in 1993 to about US$7.7 billion; Canada is the major supplier of solid wood products to the US, with softwood lumber the main commodity. Softwood lumber imports increased to make up for tight 1993 domestic supplies. Trends in imports will depend on the level of restrictions placed on forest lands in the US.

Despite an increasing trade deficit in 1993, reflecting soft prices for US paper and allied products, shipments of paper and allied products are expected to grow at an average annual rate of more than 2 percent through 1998. Exports are expected to grow faster than domestic sales, resulting in positive trade balances for this industry for years to come. Significant technological, structural, and organization changes should keep the US industry highly competitive in both domestic and international markets.

Government Agencies

Animal and Plant Health Inspection Service (APHIS)
PO Box 96464
Washington, DC 20090
Tel: (202) 720-2791, 720-2511

Bureau of Alcohol, Tobacco and Firearms (BATF)
650 Massachusetts Ave. NW
Washington, DC 20226
Tel: (202) 927-7777, 927-8500

Center for Food Safety and Applied Nutrition
200 C St. SW
Washington, DC 20204
Tel: (202) 205-5850 Fax: (202) 205-5025

Consumer Product Safety Commission (CPSC)
Washington, DC 20207
Tel: (301) 504-0100, 504-0580 Fax: (301) 504-0124

Department of Agriculture (USDA)
14th St. and Independence Ave. SW
Washington, DC 20250
Tel: (202) 720-8732, 720-2791

Federal Grain Inspection Service (FGIS)
PO Box 96454
Washington, DC 20090
Tel: (202) 720-8732, 720-5091

Food Safety and Inspection Service (FSIS)
14th St. and Independence Ave. SW
Washington, DC 20250
Tel: (202) 720-8732, 720-9113

International Trade Administration (ITA)
14th St. and Constitution Ave. NW
Washington, DC 20230
Tel: (202) 482-2000

US Fish and Wildlife Service (FWS)
1849 C St. NW
Washington, DC 20240
Tel: (202) 208-3100, 208-5634

Trade Associations

American Association of Food Distribution
28-12 Broadway
Fair Lawn, NJ 07410
Tel: (201) 791-5570 Fax: (201) 791-5222

American Farm Bureau Federation
225 Touhy Ave.
Park Ridge, IL 60068
Tel: (312) 399-5700

American Forest and Paper Association
1250 Connecticut Ave. NW, 2nd Fl.
Washington, DC 20036
Tel: (202) 463-2700 Fax: (202) 463-2785

Food Marketing Institute
800 Connecticut Ave. NW
Washington, DC 20006
Tel: (202) 452-8444 Fax: (202) 429-4519

Grocery Manufacturers of America
1010 Wisconsin Ave. NW
Washington, DC 20007
Tel: (202) 337-9400 Fax: (202) 337-4508

National Association of Convenience Stores
1605 King St.
Alexandria, VA 22314
Tel: (703) 684-3600

National Food Processors Association
1401 New York Ave. NW
Washington, DC 20007
Tel: (202) 639-5900

National Grocers Association
1825 Samuel Morse Drive
Reston, VA 22090
Tel: (703) 437-5300

National Licensed Beverage Association
4214 King St. West
Alexandria, VA 22302
Tel: (703) 671-7575, (800) 441-9894
Fax: (703) 845-0310

National Soft Drink Association
1101 16th St. NW
Washington, DC 20036
Tel: (202) 463-6732

United Fresh Fruit and Vegetable Association
727 N. Washington St.
Alexandria, VA 22314
Tel: (703) 836-3410 Fax: (703) 836-7745

Publications

Agriculture Outlook
(11 issues/year)
US Department of Agriculture
Superintendent of Documents
Washington, DC 20402
Tel: (202) 512-1800 Fax: (202) 512-2550

Bakery Production and Marketing
(14 issues/year)
Cahners Publishing
455 N. Cityfront Plaza Dr.
Chicago, IL 60611
Tel: (312) 222-2000 Fax: (312) 222-2026

Beverage Industry
(Monthly)
Stagnito Publishing
1935 Shermer Road, Suite 100
Northbrook, IL 60062
Tel: (708) 205-5660 Fax: (708) 205-5680

Beverage World
(Monthly)
Keller International Publishing Corp.
150 Great Neck Road
Great Neck, NY 11021
Tel: (516) 829-9210 Fax: (516) 829-5414

Candy Industry
(Monthly)
Advanstar Communications, Inc.
7500 Old Oak Blvd.
Cleveland, OH 44130
Tel: (216) 826-2866 Fax: (216) 819-2651

Chilton's Food Engineering
(Monthly)
Chilton
Chilton Way
Radnor, PA 19089
Tel: (215) 964-4225 Fax: (215) 964-4251

Farmer's Digest
(10 issues/year)
PO Box 624
Brookfield, WI 53008
Tel: (414) 782-4480 Fax: (414) 782-1252

Food Processing
(13 issues/year)
Putnam Publishing
301 Erie St.
Chicago, IL 60611
Tel: (312) 644-2020

Prepared Foods
(13 issues/year)
Cahners Publishing
455 N. Cityfront Plaza Dr.
Chicago, IL 60611
Tel: (312) 222-2000 Fax: (312) 222-2026

Progressive Grocer
(Monthly)
263 Tressor Blvd.
Stamford, CT 06901
Tel: (203) 977-7600 Fax: (203) 977-7645

Pulp and Paper
(Semimonthly)
Miller Freeman Publications
600 Harrison St.
San Francisco, CA 94107
Tel: (415) 905-2200 Fax: (415) 905-2232

Supermarket Business
(Monthly)
Howfrey Communications
1086 Teaneck Rd.
Teaneck, NJ 07666
Tel: (201) 833-1900 Fax: (201) 833-1273

Wood Technology
(Bimonthly)
Miller Freeman Publications
600 Harrison St.
San Francisco, CA 94107
Tel: (415) 905-2200 Fax: (415) 905-2232

Trade Fairs

Refer to the "Trade Fairs" chapter for complete listings, including contact information, dates, and venues. Trade fairs with particular relevance to this industry include the following, which are listed under the headings given below:

Agriculture, Horticulture & Fishing
- National Cattlemen's Assn. Convention & Trade Show
- United Fresh Fruit & Vegetable Assn. Annual Convention & Exposition

Food, Beverages & Hospitality
- Food & Dairy Expo
- International Boston Seafood Show
- International Exposition for Food Processors
- International Fancy Food & Confection Show
- International Meat Industry Convention & Expo
- Produce Marketing Assn. Annual Convention and Exposition
- Sea Fare International
- US Food Export Showcase

Forestry & Woodworking
- Forest Products Machinery & Equipment Expo
- Wood Technology Clinic & Show
- Woodworking, Machinery & Furniture Supply Fair

ELECTRICAL, ELECTRONIC, COMPUTER, AND TELECOMMUNICATION PRODUCTS

The electronics, computer, and telecommunications industries are becoming increasingly interdependent. Innovations in the electronics industry tend to be transferred almost immediately to the computer industry, but—because they often require new standards and huge capital investments—somewhat later to the telecommunications industry.

Although the fundamental natures of electrical and electronic products are related scientifically, business opportunities for electrical products are different from those for electronic products. Standard electrical products—transformers and electric lighting components, for example—are primarily dependent on the construction markets and industrial production. In comparison, electronic products serve the booming computer and telecommunications industries, which in turn are invading nearly every sector of the global economy.

Computers

Computer technology is used in all sectors of the US economy. Buyers range from government, academic, and business institutions to individual personal consumers. The 1980s marked the age of personal computing. Mainframe computer power was harnessed into desktop models suitable for businesses, schools, and homes. This trend will continue, and the distinction between powerful workstations and personal computers has begun to blur. In the 1990s the race is on to provide every consumer with personal access to a vast array of interactive information and entertainment services—known as "infotainment"—which will provide opportunities in a potentially lucrative world market. Although the computer equipment and software sectors are dominated by several large corporations, there is ample opportunity in this exploding market for the individual entrepreneur.

Computer Equipment

Computer equipment is produced by international corporations—such as Apple, IBM, Hewlett Packard (HP), and Digital Equipment (DEC)—and by more than 3,000 smaller corporations that manufacture personal computers and supply parts and services to the industry. In 1993 US production of computers, computer peripherals, and computer parts was valued at US$56.3 billion with exports valued at US$27 billion. The Asia-Pacific region accounted for 30 percent of the exports, while the European Union (EU) accounted for 44 percent.

Market demand in the US continues to grow faster than US production. In 1993 roughly 58 percent of the US demand for computers was served by imports. The Asia-Pacific region provides 70 percent of the imports, and the EU accounted for 15 percent.

Products US-made computers come in all sizes—supercomputers, mainframes, midrange computers, workstations, and personal computers (including portable laptop, notebook, and handheld models). Other types of computer equipment produced by US firms include computer kits assembled by the purchaser; computer storage devices (such as magnetic and optical disk drives and tape storage units); and computer peripherals (such as printers, plotters, graphics displays, and other input/output (I/O) equipment).

Competitive Situation The US competes with Japan and Western Europe for the greater share of the world computer market. The top 100 computer companies worldwide account for the major share of the international market for information equipment and services. Their sales expanded at a healthy rate of almost 10 percent in 1992, of which the share held by US suppliers remained steady at 61 percent.

US companies should continue to play a critical role as suppliers of information systems, networking equipment, and interactive services to global markets. They have enormous opportunities for growth in the infotainment market. However, they also face strong competition in this area from a broad range of both domestic and foreign firms, some of which have greater experience in consumer electronics and communication technologies. In an effort to promote the development of electronic information systems, the US government has passed the High-Performance Computing and Communications Initiative to furnish financial aid to scientists and academic researchers. It has also formulated plans for a National Information Infrastructure (also known as the federal information superhighway) and has begun to liberalize export policies in response to the opportunities.

Many leading US computer equipment suppliers have moved aggressively into software and computer services as price competition in hardware has intensified and profits have dwindled. US manufacturers are expected to restructure their operations to meet the significant challenges in the complex infotainment market during the next five years.

Computer Software and Networking

The US remains by far the largest single-country market for packaged software, holding a 45 percent share. In 1992 US vendors supplied 74 percent of the world packaged software market. Even in Western Europe and Japan, where domestic vendors hold strong positions, the US supplied 60 percent of this market. In 1992, 6 of the 10 companies with the largest worldwide software revenues were from the US. In general, US software companies are young, competitive, innovative, and entrepreneurial, and they continue to have good opportunities for increased sales worldwide.

Because growth in many international markets will exceed that in the US, international sales are an increasingly important factor in sustaining the revenue levels attained by US software vendors. Ongoing price wars and new products will no doubt spur global sales.

Products The computer software and networking sectors are divisible into three industries: computer programming services, prepackaged software, and computer integrated systems (CIS) designs. An abundance of prepackaged software is available to serve almost every need of the average computer user: from application tools (including data access and retrieval, data management, data manipulation, and design and development programs), to application solutions (programs that perform specific industry or business functions), to systems software (operating systems, operating system enhancements, and data center management software). Included among CIS designs are computer aided design, computer aided manufacturing, and computer aided engineering (CAD/CAM/CAE) systems. Firms that specialize in CIS designs generally focus on four major areas: mechanical processes; electronic design automation; geographic information systems; and architectural, engineering, and construction. It is possible to run CAD/CAM/CAE software on mainframes, workstations, personal computers, and network servers.

Competitive Situation US companies are extremely competitive in computer software and networking, although Japanese and European suppliers are making advances in some areas. Although a number of US computer equipment companies have restructured and reduced employment, software and networking production continues to expand.

Software development was one of fastest growing sectors of the US economy in 1993, increasing 12.6 percent to US$32 billion. Price wars among computer firms are continuing, particularly with regard to software for personal computers. As a result, analysts predict that personal computer software prices will continue to fall over the next few years. Lower margins may cause this market to consolidate and may encourage software vendors to reevaluate their business strategies. Competition from software developers in the developing world is also a growing factor in moving certain programming operations offshore.

Multimedia and virtual reality are emerging markets, with a handful of US companies at the forefront. Multimedia combines video, animation, still pictures, voice, music, graphics, and text into a single system and blurs the lines between several previously distinct products and industries: computers, software, consumer electronics, communications, publishing, and entertainment. Virtual reality programs allow users to interact with three-dimensional, computer-generated environments. The primary market for multimedia and virtual reality is entertainment, but the software is now being tailored to business applications, which are creating a secondary market.

No longer a niche market, today's CAD/CAM/CAE users range from the engineer designing aerospace parts to the homeowner remodeling a bathroom. The typical customers are professional designers. US vendors supplied more than two-thirds of the 1993 world CAD/CAM/CAE market, followed by Asian firms with 20 percent, and European companies with 10 percent.

Software suppliers are increasingly using legal forms of protection—including trade secret, patent, and contract law—to supplement copyright protection. During the past decade, several court cases have addressed the scope of copyright protection for computer programs in the US. Generally, court decisions have protected the products of software manufacturers while still allowing freedom of research.

Electrical and Electronic Products and Components

Efficiency is the guiding principle for the electrical and electronic products industries. The electricity market—domestic industries and households—is demanding more efficient means of generating electricity to save costs and to combat environmental pollution. The electronics market is demanding more power on a smaller surface at less cost.

Electrical and Renewable Energy Equipment

US manufacturers supply approximately 75 percent of the domestic demand for electrical equipment. Exports are shipped primarily to Canada and Mexico. Imports arrive primarily from Japan, Canada, and Mexico.

Products Electrical products manufactured in the US include: transformers for utility and housing markets; switchgear products such as switches, fuses, panelboards, distribution boards, and circuit breakers; motors, generators, and motor control products for industrial and small appliance use; and electric lighting and wiring equipment. Renewable energy electrical equipment produces electricity from resources that can be replenished or regenerated by natural forces. Manufacturers of this equipment produce such items as solar photovoltaic cells and turbines for wind energy.

Competitive Situation The sale of electrical products is dependent on industrial production, the state of the construction industry, and the demand for replacement of products. Thus, US markets for many electrical products experienced some setbacks during the recession, when new home construction fell off and consumers delayed their purchases of new and replacement home appliances and similar products. However, stabilizing economic conditions are encouraging developers to build and consumers to replace their older machines.

Certain trends in government and industry policies are also having visible effects on this industry. The Department of Energy and the EPA have started a voluntary, industry-driven collaborative program, called Motor Challenge, to produce electric motors in an effort to save money for US industries as well as to reduce carbon emissions. The US government has also urged manufacturers of electric lighting and wiring equipment to utilize metric measurements so that their products are more readily accepted in foreign markets.

The US is a world leader in providing renewable energy electrical equipment. The trade situation in solar photovoltaics has become extremely competitive since 1980, when the US commanded 84 percent of the world market. Its share of trade in this area has declined to about 30 percent, with increased production and competition from Japan, several European countries, India, Australia, Brazil, and China. The US continues to lead the world in other renewable energy sources, such as wind and geothermal energy.

Electronic Components

Electronic components are the fundamental building blocks for the electronics industry; demand for them comes primarily from the computer, telecommunications, instrumentation, medical equipment, and transportation industries. In 1993, sales of electronic components grew to almost US$81 billion, a significant improvement over the 1992 level of US$73 billion.

In 1993, 31 percent of the US electronic components and accessories demand was filled by imports, while the US exported 25 percent of its electronics component production. Canada and Mexico provided the largest markets for US suppliers.

Products US-manufactured electronic products include semiconductors, electron tubes, printed circuit boards (PCBs), passive components (such as capacitors, resistors, coils, and transformers), and connectors. The industry also manufactures microcomponent integrated circuits (ICs)—such as microprocessors, microcontrollers, microperipherals, and digital signal processors—and semiconductor manufacturing devices. Consumer electronics include color televisions, videocassette recorders, and audio compact disc players.

Competitive Situation Worldwide competition in the electronic components industry is fierce, driven by an extremely high demand for electronic products. In 1993 growth in semiconductor demand outpaced the growth of production capacity worldwide.

US firms face strong competition from companies in Japan and other countries that are turning out technologically sophisticated products. Although US firms frequently are the first to introduce a new product, the Japanese often have been able to refine the manufacturing process and produce large quantities at relatively low prices. For less sophisticated products, US suppliers have difficulty competing with such countries as South Korea, Malaysia, and Taiwan, where production costs are low.

With respect to microcomponent integrated circuits, US companies held more than 80 percent of the world microprocessor market in 1993. Three of the top five (and 6 of the top 10) microprocessor manufacturers are located in the US. Intel, the leading US producer, has been the world's largest semiconductor company for some time.

In consumer electronics, color television sets, videocassette recorders, and audio compact disc players continue to drive a strong US market. Within the next few years, new consumer products—such as high-definition television (HDTV), interactive multimedia, and handheld computers—will enter the US market in force. These products will be based on developing technologies and will require increasing quantities of electronic parts, including sophisticated semiconductors and other advanced components. Many will use digital technology, a field in which US suppliers hold the lead.

Telecommunications Equipment

Telecommunications equipment is used in more than 90 million households and 25 million businesses throughout the US. In 1993 US production of telecommunications equipment was valued at more than US$35 billion. About 25 percent of the domestic demand was supplied by imports, 65 percent of which arrived from East Asia; Japan alone accounted for about one-third of the US telecommunications imports. Canada and Mexico continued to rank near each other as the largest export markets for US telecommunications equipment, followed by the EU. The overall trade deficit in telecommunications is narrow, although the trade deficit is larger for equipment used by individual consumers than for more sophisticated network/transmission equipment.

Products The US telecommunications industry produces sophisticated network products such as switching and transmission equipment. It also manufactures telephones; facsimile machines; fixed and mobile radio systems; cellular radio telephones; radio transmitters, transceivers, and receivers; fiber optics equipment; satellite communications systems; closed-circuit and cable television equipment; and studio (audio and video) equipment.

Competitive Situation US firms are the dominant suppliers of network products to large telecommunication corporations, particularly highly sophisticated items and software intensive products such as video conferencing systems. However, US companies are vulnerable in the area of customer premises equipment—such as telephone sets, telephone answering machines, and facsimile machines—which can be manufactured in Pacific Rim countries at lower cost. To compete, some US telecommunications suppliers have established their own manufacturing operations overseas.

The outlook for telecommunications equipment production and sales in the US through 1998 is increasingly positive, with shipments forecast to grow an average of 2 to 4 percent per year. The challenge for the industry through the 1990s will be to add more intelligence to switching and transmission facilities, enabling full interconnection between differing technologies. Markets continue to grow for cellular radiotelephone systems and fiber optics, industries in which the US is very competitive. The US manufacturers also dominate world markets for most satellite ground equipment, due in part to a 10-year edge in technology and experience in a deregulated market.

Government Agencies

Consumer Product Safety Commission (CPSC)
Washington, DC 20207
Tel: (301) 504-0100, 504-0580 Fax: (301) 504-0124

Federal Communications Commission (FCC)
1919 M St. NW
Washington, DC 20544
Tel: (202) 632-7106, 632-7000

International Trade Administration (ITA)
Office of Computers and Business Equipment
14th St. and Constitution Ave. NW
Washington, DC 20230
Tel: (202) 482-0572

International Trade Administration (ITA)
Office of Microelectronics, Medical Equipment and Instrumentation
14th St. and Constitution Ave. NW
Washington, DC 20230
Tel: (202) 482-2587

International Trade Administration (ITA)
Office of Telecommunications
14th St. and Constitution Ave. NW
Washington, DC 20230
Tel: (202) 482-4466

National Telecommunications and Information Administration
Main Commerce Bldg.
Washington, DC 20230
Tel: (202) 482-1551 Fax: (202) 482-1635

Technology Administration
14th St. and Constitution Ave. NW
Washington, DC 20230
Tel: (202) 482-0137

Trade Associations

ABCD: The Microcomputer Industry Association
450 E. 22nd St., Suite 230
Lombard, IL 60148
Tel: (708) 268-1818

American Electronics Association
5201 Great American Parkway, Suite 520
Santa Clara, CA 95054
Tel: (408) 987-4200

Computer and Business Equipment Manufacturers Association
1250 Eye St. NW
Washington, DC 20005
Tel: (202) 737-8888

Computer and Communications Industry Association
666 11th St. NW, Suite 600
Washington, DC 20001
Tel: (202) 783-0070

Electronic Industries Association
2001 Pennsylvania Ave. NW
Washington, DC 20006
Tel: (202) 457-4900

Information Industry Association
555 New Jersey Ave. NW, Suite 800
Washington, DC 20001
Tel: (202) 639-8260 Fax: (202) 638-4403

Information Technology Association of America
1616 North Fort Myer Dr., Suite 1300
Arlington, VA 22209-3106
Tel: (703) 522-5055 Fax: (202) 525-2279

Interactive Multimedia Association
3 Church Circle, Suite 800
Annapolis, MD 21401
Tel: (410) 626-1380

International Communications Industry Association
3150 Spring St.
Fairfax, VA 22031
Tel: (703) 273-7200 Fax: (703) 278-8082

National Association of Broadcasters
1771 N St. NW
Washington, DC 20036
Tel: (202) 429-5300 Fax: (202) 429-5350

North American Telecommunications Association
2000 M St. NW, Suite 550
Washington, DC 20037
Tel: (202) 296-9800 Fax: (202) 296-4993

Software Publishers Association
1730 M St. NW, Suite 700
Washington, DC 20036
Tel: (202) 452-1600

Software Publishers Association
1730 M St. NW., Suite 700
Washington, DC 20036
Fax: (202) 223-8756

Tele-Communications Association
858 S. Oak Park Road, Suite 102
Covina, CA 91724
Tel: (818) 967-9411

Publications

Cellular Marketing
Communications
Global Communications
Satellite Communications
(All monthly)
Cardiff Publishing Company
6300 South Syracuse Way
Englewood, CO 80111
Tel: (303) 220-0600

Chilton's Electronic Component News
(Monthly)
Chilton
Chilton Way
Radnor, PA 19089
Tel: (215) 964-4225 Fax: (215) 964-4251

Computer Industry Almanac
(Annual)
225 Allen Way
Incline Village, NV 89451
Tel: (702) 831-2288 Fax: (702) 831-8610

Computerworld
(Weekly)
IDG
375 Cochituate Rd., Box 9171
Framingham, MA 01701
Tel: (508) 879-0700 Fax: (508) 875-8931

Datamation
(24 issues/year)
Cahners Publishing
275 Washington St.
Newton, MA 02158-1630
Tel: (617) 964-3030 Fax: (617) 558-4506

EDN (Electronic Design Engineering)
(26 issues/year)
Cahners Publishing
275 Washington St.
Newton, MA 02158-1630
Tel: (617) 964-3030 Fax: (617) 558-4470

Electronic Design
(Fortnightly)
Penton Publishing
San Jose Gateway, Suite 354
2025 Gateway Plaza
San Jose, CA 95110
Tel: (408) 441-0550

Electronic News
(Monthly)
Chilton
Chilton Way
Radnor, PA 19089
Tel: (215) 964-4225 Fax: (215) 964-4251

Electronic Products
(Monthly)
645 Stewart Ave.
Garden City, NY 11530
Tel: (516) 227-1300 Fax: (516) 227-1444

InfoWorld
(Weekly)
IDG
155 Bovet Rd., Suite 800
San Mateo, CA 94402
Tel: (415) 572-7341, (800) 227-8365 Fax: (415) 696-8765

MacWeek
PCWeek
(Weekly)
Ziff-Davis
1 Park Ave.
New York, NY 10016
Tel: (415) 243-3500 Fax: (415) 243-3650

Network World
(Weekly)
161 Worcester Rd.
Framingham, MA 01701
Tel: (508) 875-6400 Fax: (508) 820-3467

Telecommunications Reports
Business Research Publications, Inc.
1333 H St. NW, 11th Fl. West
Washington, DC 20005
Tel: (202) 842-3006

Voice Processing Magazine
(Monthly)
Advanstar Communications
3721 Briar Park
Houston, TX 77042
Tel: (713) 974-6637 Fax: (713) 974-6272

Trade Fairs

Refer to the "Trade Fairs" chapter for complete listings, including contact information, dates, and venues. Trade fairs with particular relevance to this industry include the following, which are listed under the headings given below:

Construction & Building Materials
- A/E/C Systems

Computers & Communications
- CAD & Engineering Workstations '95 & Business Graphics '95
- Cellular Telecommunications Industry Assn. Winter Meeting & Exposition
- Comdex/Fall, Comdex/Spring
- DECUS Interoperability/Open Systems Shows
- Enterprise Computing Solutions Exposition & Conference
- Image World Chicago featuring Video Expo and The CAMMP Show
- International Conference & Exposition on Multimedia and CD-ROM
- International Wireless Communications Expo
- MacWorld Expo
- Network + Interop
- Network World Unplugged
- Networks Expo
- New Media Expo
- OS/2 World Conference & Exhibition
- PC Expo
- Supercomm 95
- UNIX Expo
- Windows World 95

Electronics & Engineering
- Electro
- Instrument Soc. of America International Conference and Exhibition
- Southcon, Midcon, Northcon, Wescon
- National Design Engineering Show & Conference
- Nepcon

- Surface Mount International

Entertainment & Amusements

- Electronic Entertainment Expo
- Lighting Dimensions International
- SBCA Satellite Show
- Video Software Dealers Assn. Annual Convention

Office Products & Systems

- National Office Machine Dealers Assn.
- National Office Product Assn.'s Annual Convention & Exhibit
- Office Systems & Business Show
- World Workplace

FURNITURE

The US furniture industry is divided into two categories: household furniture and office furniture. About two-thirds of the furniture produced in the US is for household use. The household furniture industry is heavily dependent on the construction market and the price of lumber. The office furniture industry is significantly affected by trends in office furnishings, such as the increased need to develop furniture that accommodates computers in the workplace.

Household Furniture

In 1993 shipments by the US household furniture manufacturing industry rose by 5 percent, topping US$22.2 billion. Rising home sales and residential construction have contributed to this gain, signalling some of the economic recovery that furniture producers have long awaited. During the next five years, household furniture shipments are expected to increase 3 to 5 percent annually.

The US furniture industry showed a fairly large trade deficit in 1993, despite the efforts of manufacturers to focus on exports. From 1989 through 1993, US furniture exports increased by almost 150 percent, while imports rose by only 25 percent. However, further inroads into overseas markets have slowed because of the generally slow recovery from recession worldwide: the 1993 the increase in US furniture exports was only 5 percent, compared with a 17 percent increase in 1992. However, US furniture imports rose by 14 percent, creating a US$2.3 billion trade deficit, equaling the deficit posted in 1989.

US furniture makers ship 47 percent of their exports to Canada. Other notable export markets include Mexico, Saudi Arabia, Japan, and the UK. Most US furniture imports are from Taiwan, but significant quantities also arrive from Canada, Italy, China, and Mexico.

Four of the top ten residential furniture manufacturers are located in North Carolina. Two of the top ten—which are also two of the top three—are located in Michigan. The remaining four of the top ten manufacturers are located in Virginia, Connecticut, and Ohio.

Products The industry manufactures all types of furniture for home use. More than 40 percent of the 1993 shipments consisted of wood furniture. Upholstered furniture accounted for 30 percent, metal furniture for 10 percent, mattresses and bedsprings for 14 percent, and miscellaneous furniture products for 4 percent. These ratios have remained fairly constant over the last decade.

Competitive Situation In 1993 the profits of furniture companies were squeezed as a result of dramatic increases in lumber prices. Labor costs were also higher than in some competing countries. To add to their difficulties, furniture manufacturers have also been confronted with stricter environmental controls on their plant operations. The EPA is currently developing a control technique guideline for volatile organic compound emissions for the wood furniture and kitchen cabinet industries, as required by the Clean Air Act Amendments of 1990. Furniture plants are facing significant costs to meet the new standards, and a number of plants may be forced to close; other companies that are unable to fund such costs may find it more feasible to consolidate with a larger company that can afford the costs.

Nevertheless, the outlook for the US furniture industry in the second half of the 1990's is at least moderately promising. Foreign markets have become increasingly important to US makers of household furniture, and attempts to liberalize world trade through international agreements are taking on added significance. Developments under both GATT and NAFTA should enhance international trade in furniture by reducing tariffs. Recovery in the industry is already apparent from the increases shown in shipping and employment levels.

US furniture manufacturers are also making an effort to remain at the forefront of consumer trends in the US to compete with the growing number of imports. In this regard, one of the largest growth markets in the industry is for home entertainment furniture, now being offered in conjunction with audio and visual equipment manufacturers to provide complete home entertainment centers.

Office Furniture

The US office furniture industry grew significantly in the 1970s, as partitioned workstations, computer technology, and ergonomic equipment became more popular in the office environment. Demand was high for modern furniture engineered to buffer sound and to cater to the data entry and processing age. That demand leveled out in the 1980s, and at the same time, the country's economic growth slowed and unemployment rates rose. Companies began to restructure and downsize their operations, often laying off workers and closing offices.

Presently, the US office furniture industry is recovering from the economic recession of 1990-1991. In 1993 shipments for the industry increased about 5.9 percent to slightly more than US$8 billion. Exports and imports each amounted to slightly less than 7 percent of the industry's shipments. Canada is the chief trading partner of the US, consuming 35 percent of all exported US office furniture and supplying 50 percent of all such furnishings imported into the US.

Office furniture in the US is manufactured and sold by a relatively small number of firms. Although no listing exists of the exact number of companies, many of them belong to the Business and Institutional Furniture Manufacturers Association, which boasts 125 domestic manufacturer members, 70 supplier members, and several international members. Six firms have cornered 60 percent of the sales in terms of US dollar value. However, 60 percent of the association members have revenues of less than US$1 million each, indicating that a large number of small firms are in operation.

Products The US office furniture industry produces chairs, desks, tables, file cabinets, storage units, and systems furniture. Approximately 25 percent of the products are made from wood, and 75 percent are made of nonwood materials.

Competitive Situation Today's market environment for office furniture is competitive, and the industry is concerned with cost containment and operating efficiencies during its recovery from the tough first half of the 1990s. Emphasis is being placed on product quality, customer service, and timely delivery. A number of manufacturers have begun to acquire or merge with other office furniture companies in order to expand their market opportunities and to strengthen their financial resources.

Industry analysts are forecasting future growth as the economy recovers. Companies are expected to start making office furniture acquisitions that had been postponed during the recessionary years. Office furniture manufacturers are attempting to anticipate the fast-paced changes taking place in technology and are designing furniture to meet the demands of the high-tech office environment, especially in the service industries. Much of the growth in this industry is expected to come from supplying small- and medium-sized companies, many of which are just beginning to develop their high-tech facilities.

Government Agencies

Consumer Product Safety Commission (CPSC)
Washington, DC 20207
Tel: (301) 504-0100, 504-0580 Fax: (301) 504-0124

International Trade Administration (ITA)
Office of Textiles, Apparel and Consumer Goods Industries
14th St. and Constitution Ave. NW
Washington, DC 20230
Tel: (202) 482-3737

Trade Associations

American Furniture Manufacturers Association
PO Box HP-7
High Point, NC 27261
Tel: (919) 884-5000

International Furnishings and Design Association
107 World Trade Center, Box 58045
Dallas, TX 75258
Tel: (214) 747-2406

National Forest Products Association
1250 Connecticut Ave. NW, Suite 200
Washington, DC 20036
Tel: (202) 463-2700

National Home Furnishings Association
PO Box 2396
High Point, NC 27261
Tel: (919) 883-1650

The Business and Institutional Furniture Manufacturer's Association
2680 Horizon Drive SE, Suite A-1
Grand Rapids, MI 49546
Tel: (616) 285-3963

Publications

Forest Industries
(Monthly)
Miller Freeman Publications
600 Harrison St.
San Francisco, CA 94107
Tel: (415) 905-2200 Fax: (415) 905-2232

Furniture Design and Manufacturing
(Monthly)
Delta Communications Inc.
400 N. Michigan Ave.
Chicago, IL 60611
Tel: (312) 222-2000 Fax: (312) 222-2066

Furniture/Today
(Weekly)
Cahners Publishing Company
PO Box 2754
High Point, NC 27261
Tel: (919) 605-0121 Fax: (919) 605-1143

The Furnishings Digest
Mann, Armistead, & Epperson, Ltd.
121 Shockoe Slip
Richmond, VA 23219
Tel: (804) 782-3297

The Furniture Quarterly
Wheat, First Securities, Inc.
PO Box 1357
Richmond, VA 23211
Tel: (804) 782-3297

Wallcoverings, Windows and Interior Fashion
(Monthly)
Publishing Dynamics Inc.
15 Bank St., Suite 101
Stamford, CT 06901
Tel: (203) 357-0028

Trade Fairs

Refer to the "Trade Fairs" chapter for complete listings, including contact information, dates, and venues. Trade fairs with particular relevance to this industry include the following, which are listed under the headings given below:

Construction & Building Materials
- Builders Show
- Construction Specifications Institute Annual Convention and Exhibit
- National Assn. of the Remodeling Industry

Forestry & Woodworking
- Forest Products Machinery & Equipment Exposition
- Wood Technology Clinic & Show
- Woodworking, Machinery & Furniture Supply Fair

Furnishings & Interior Design
- International Casual Furniture Market
- Lightfair International
- Neocon 95
- Restoration 95

Gift Shows
- Boston Gift Show
- California Gift Show
- Chicago Gift Show
- Florida International Gift Expo
- Green! Gift Show
- International Gift & Accessories Market
- National Country Collectibles Show
- New York International Gift Fair
- San Francisco International Gift Fair

Merchandising
- International Home Furnishings Market
- Transworld Housewares & Variety Exhibit
- Variety Merchandise Show, Mid-Year Variety Merchandise Show

Office Products & Systems
- National Office Product Assn.'s Annual Convention & Exhibit
- Office Systems & Business Show
- World Workplace

HEALTH PRODUCTS AND EQUIPMENT

The health products industry is related to health and medical services in general; aspects of fitness and cosmetics are discussed under this heading as well. The US supplies health products and equipment in four areas: drugs and pharmaceuticals, medical and dental instruments and supplies, cosmetics and toiletries, and fitness equipment. In 1993, the health care industry employed more than 10 million people, including 2.8 million professionals: 2 million nurses, more than 650,000 doctors, and 150,000 dentists. Expenditures on health care in the US were expected to rise by more than 12 percent in 1994 to exceed US$1 trillion for the first time, which would amount to more than 16 percent of the gross domestic product (GDP). The industry is currently facing the threat of a restructuring of national health care, the effects of which are as yet uncertain.

Cosmetics

In 1993 cosmetics industry shipments increased by more than 4 percent to US$18.8 billion. Exports grew about 14 percent, accounting for roughly 7 percent of total product shipments. As a result, the industry enjoyed a trade surplus of about US$480 million. Prospects for exports of US products look most promising in Latin American and the Asia-Pacific region, especially in China and Japan.

The cosmetics industry is recognizing that globalization and meeting the different and constantly changing demands of consumers around the world are the keys to competing in the global marketplace. Cosmetics and toiletries companies and their suppliers are becoming increasingly international through company acquisitions, consolidations, and reorganizations.

Products The cosmetics industry produces a range of shaving preparations, fragrances, hair preparations, dentifrices, and other cosmetics. Other products include perfumes, colognes, makeup, body powders, creams, and lotions, deodorants, hair coloring preparations, tonics and scalp conditioners, home permanent kits, manicure preparations, mouthwashes, toothpastes, shampoos, suntan lotions, pre-moistened towelettes, and other toilet preparations.

Competitive Situation Demographics, environmental issues, globalization, and the economy are the factors that continue to shape the cosmetics industry. The heavy influence of demographics is evident in several industry trends. As the nation's elderly population grows, the demand is increasing for cosmetics with mild formulations, softer makeup colors, and treatments for aging skin. Similarly, lines of cosmetics designed to meet the needs of various ethnic groups have become an important and growing segment of the industry, a segment also recognized as having significant global market potential.

As consumers worldwide become better educated and as the global cost of living rises, there is a growing market for cosmetics scientifically proven to simultaneously medicate and beautify. This trend can be easily seen, for example, in the large variety of medicated and protective sunscreen products now pouring onto the market. Many cosmetics firms have also branched out to develop entire lines of products designed to improve the user's whole body and mind, often offered with programs developed for different needs from dieting to enhancing a person's lifestyle. Heightened consumer awareness about environmental issues is increasing the demand for new types of ingredients in cosmetics, and growth opportunities are promising for ingredient suppliers.

Drugs and Pharmaceuticals

US manufacturers furnish nearly half of the major pharmaceuticals marketed worldwide. In 1993 the value of shipments from this industry reached US$69 billion. The EU remains the largest importer of US pharmaceuticals, purchasing nearly 50 percent of all US exports. Approximately 12 percent of the US domestic market is supplied by imports. The US pharmaceutical industry will continue to grow, although some changes are expected in order to accommodate the needs of the US health and medical services industry as national health care reform is implemented.

Products Pharmaceuticals industry products can be grouped into four main categories: (1) pharmaceutical preparations intended for human and veterinary consumption; (2) medicinal chemicals, their derivatives, and processed botanical drugs and herbs; (3) diagnostic substances used with equipment for testing blood samples and bodily fluids; and (4) biologicals, which include bacterial and virus vaccines, toxoids, and analogous products as well as serums, plasmas, and other blood derivatives for human or veterinary use. Pharmaceuticals accounted for nearly 80 percent of industry shipments in 1993, while medicinals and botanicals barely topped 10 percent. The production of diagnostics and biologicals is relatively small, reflecting the relative magnitude of markets for these items.

Competitive Situation The US remains the most competitive and innovative player in world drug and pharmaceutical markets. However, the industry is facing considerable change as a result of price discounting, weak foreign economies, increased use of generic and over-the-counter drugs, increasing international competition, and the prospect of tighter governmental controls under health care reform. As a result, many firms are restructuring to merge research and development with manufacturing and to consolidate some of the industry's largest companies. To remain competitive internationally, the industry must overcome such obstacles as price controls, inadequate patent and copyright protection and enforcement, and foreign regulations on marketing and R&D. As rapid technological advances create new products to serve increasing market demands, government regulations are becoming more stringent to protect consumers from untested or false claims of the beneficial effects of such products.

Several smaller sectors of the industry are experiencing significant growth and are becoming more competitive in domestic and overseas markets. In this arena, demand for herbal products—once on the fringe of the market in the early 1960s—is on the rise, having taken a more mainstream role in the biomedical market sector. The diagnostic substances industry is now characterized by intense competition, and firms at the forefront must maintain high levels of innovative technology and must be able to keep up with rapid, dynamic change. Biotechnology has revolutionized the health and medical services industry by providing products that are faster, cheaper, and more accurate than those available in the past. Increasing numbers of home-test kits are available, outpacing growth in laboratory and hospital diagnostic products. In the biologicals sector, the vaccine market is still relatively small, but it has been boosted with the emergence of innovative research technologies. Vaccine companies are striving to develop new vaccines—particularly for AIDS and malaria—while at the same time improving current vaccines.

Fitness Equipment

The exercise and fitness sector, now the largest part of the sporting goods industry, has grown quickly since the late 1980s. Domestic demand grew at an estimated compound annual rate of 14 percent from 1988 to 1993. Shipments reached US$1.8 billion in 1993. Imports were virtually unchanged at US$381 million in 1993, while exports decreased an estimated 1 percent to about US$180 million.

Products Fitness equipment includes such products as cross-country ski machines, treadmills, stair climbers, stationary exercise bicycles, and weightlifting equipment.

Competitive Situation The long-term outlook for the US fitness equipment industry will be affected by demographic trends, industry restructuring, and the growth of exports. Many individuals of the baby boom generation are reaching a stage in life when they would expect to slow down and curb their physical activities. However, doctors and medical research have pointed out the need for continued fitness as a key preventive step for many ailments and conditions. Participation levels remain strong in most activities. Another positive factor will be the increased wealth of the baby boom generation, which also is reaching the age at which disposable income is highest. As a result, this generation is likely to begin purchasing higher quality fitness equipment for themselves and for their children.

Medical and Dental Instruments and Supplies

The US medical and dental instruments and supplies industry is a diverse and technologically dynamic field. Despite the slow growth in the domestic economy and buyers' resistance in a cost-conscious health care environment, the value of shipments by the US medical equipment and supplies industry rose more than 8 percent in 1993. This increase was partly due to strong overseas demand for US medical equipment. Large industries are the major players in the US medical and dental equipment and supplies industry, but the field also supports many small and medium-sized firms.

Products Medical and dental instruments and supplies manufactured in the US include (1) surgical and medical instruments, such as syringes, clamps, hypodermic and suture needles, stethoscopes, laparascopic devices, catheters and drains, and blood pressure measuring devices; (2) surgical appliances and supplies ranging from sutures and bandages to wheelchairs, prosthetics, and implantable devices; (3) dental equipment and supplies for dentists, dental laboratories, and dental colleges, such as dental hand instruments, plaster, drills, amalgams, cements, sterilizers, and dental chairs; (4) X-ray apparatus and tubes; (5) electromedical equipment, such as pacemakers and patient monitoring systems, and diagnostic products, such as ultrasonic scanning devices and magnetic resonance imaging equipment; and (6) ophthalmic goods, such as eyeglasses, sunglasses, and contact lenses.

Competitive Situation US medical and dental equipment manufacturers continued to be very active in the US$81 billion global market, supplying 52 percent of the 1993 world output. Exports continued to be a significant contributor to the US medical and dental equipment and supplies industry, accounting for 23 percent of the 1993 industry shipments.

Demographic trends, primarily the aging of populations, in the large Japanese and Western European export markets as well as in the US, will continue to be the primary influence upon demand for surgical appliances and supplies. Other factors contributing to the increase in demand for medical equipment abroad are the upgrading of health care systems and the creation of a single market in Europe.

Markets for ambulatory aids—wheelchairs, prosthetics, and other orthopedic aids—will be robust as cost-cutting pressures faced by hospitals and nursing homes favor products which afford long-term care patients the opportunity for greater mobility and capacity for self-care. Emerging areas of dentistry include periodontal diagnosis and laser treatment, which allows for less bleeding and shorter healing time. The US ophthalmic goods industry is an import sensitive sector. The highly labor intensive industry relies heavily on foreign suppliers. Although overseas suppliers have cornered the market for frames and low-end sunglasses, the US is a leader in lens technology, high-end sunglasses, and contact lenses.

Government Agencies

Consumer Product Safety Commission (CPSC)
Washington, DC 20207
Tel: (301) 504-0100, 504-0580 Fax: (301) 504-0124

Department of Health and Human Services
200 Independence Ave. SW
Washington, DC 20201
Tel: (202) 619-0257, 690-6867

Food and Drug Administration
Center for Drug Evaluation and Research
5600 Fishers Lane
Rockville, MD 20857
Tel: (301) 295-8012 Fax: (301) 443-2763

Food and Drug Administration
Small Manufacturers Assistance
5600 Fishers Lane
Rockville, MD 20857
Tel: (301) 443-6597 Fax: (301) 443-8818

Food and Drug Administration
Center for Devices and Radiological Health
12720 Twinbrook Parkway
Rockville, MD 20857
Tel: (301) 443-4690 Fax: (301) 443-3193

Food and Drug Administration (FDA)
5600 Fishers Lane
Rockville, MD 20857
Tel: (301) 443-1544, 443-3170

International Trade Administration (ITA)
Office of Microelectronics, Medical Equipment and Instrumentation
14th St. and Constitution Ave. NW
Washington, DC 20230
Tel: (202) 482-2587

Trade Associations

Aerobics and Fitness Association of America
15250 Ventura Blvd., Suite 310
Sherman Oaks, CA 91403
Tel: (818) 905-0040 Fax: (818) 990-5468

American Dental Trade Association
4222 King St. W.
Alexandria, VA 22302
Tel: (703) 379-7755 Fax: (703) 931-9429

American Health Care Association
1201 L St. NW
Washington, DC 20005
Tel: (202) 842-4444 Fax: (202) 842-3860

American Pharmaceutical Association
2215 Constitution Ave. NW
Washington, DC 20037
Tel: (202) 628-4410 Fax: (202) 783-2351

American Running and Fitness Association
4405 East-West Highway
Bethesda, MD 20814
Tel: (301) 913-9517 Fax: (301) 913-9520

Cosmetic, Toiletry and Fragrance Association
1101 17th St. NW
Washington, DC 20036
Tel: (202) 331-1770

Health Industry Manufacturers Association
1200 G St. NW, Suite 400
Washington, DC 20005
Tel: (202) 783-8700 Fax: (202) 783-8750

National Association of Chain Drug Stores
PO Box 1417
Alexandria, VA 22313
Tel: (703) 549-3001 Fax: (703) 836-4869

National Sporting Goods Association
1699 Wall St.
Mount Prospect, IL 60056
Tel: (708) 439-4000 Fax: (708) 439-0111

Nonprescription Drug Manufacturers Association
1150 Connecticut Ave. NW
Washington, DC 20036
Tel: (202) 429-9260

Pharmaceutical Manufacturers Association
1100 15th St. NW
Washington, DC 20005
Tel: (202) 835-3400 Fax: (202) 835-3414

World International Nail and Beauty Association
1221 N. Lake View
Anaheim, CA 92807
Tel: (714) 779-9883

Publications

Aesthetics World Today
(Quarterly)
Aestheticians International Association
4447 McKinney Ave.
Dallas, TX 75205
Tel: (214) 526-0752

Athletic Business Magazine
(Monthly)
1846 Hoffman St.
Madison, WI 53704
Tel: (608) 249-0186 Fax: (608) 249-1153

Drug and Cosmetic Industry (DCI)
(Monthly)
Edgell Communications, Inc.
7500 Old Oak Blvd.
Cleveland, OH 44130
Tel: (216) 826-2839 Fax: (216) 891-2726

Health News Daily
FDC Reports
5550 Friendship Blvd., Suite 1
Chevy Chase, MD 20815
Tel: (301) 657-9830 Fax: (301) 986-6467
Note: Also publish The *Pink Sheet* and *The Green Sheet* (on pharmaceuticals), *The Grey Sheet* (on medical devices), and *The Tan Sheet* (on non-prescription and nutritional industries)

International Drug and Device Regulatory Monitor
(Monthly)
Newsletter Services
1545 New York Ave. NE
Washington, DC 20077
Tel: (202) 529-5700

Jenks Health Care Business Report
Managed Health Care News
Advanstar Communications
PO Box 10460
Eugene, OR 97440-2460
Tel: (800) 949-6525

Pharmaceutical Executive
(Monthly)
Advanstar Communications
859 Willamette St.
Eugene, OR 97440
Tel: (503) 343-1200

Proofs:The Magazine of Dental Sales and Marketing
PennWell Publishing Co.
1421 S. Sheridan
Tulsa, OK 74112
Tel: (918) 835-3161

Trade Fairs

Refer to the "Trade Fairs" chapter for complete listings, including contact information, dates, and venues. Trade fairs with particular relevance to this industry include the following, which are listed under the headings given below:

Health & Beauty
- Beauty & Barber Supply Institute, Inc. Annual Convention
- Big Show Expo: The Beauty & Business Expo
- HBA Global Expo
- Natural Products Expo
- Pharmaceutical Industries Exposition & Conference

Medical & Dental
- Abilities Expo
- American Academy of Dermatology Annual Meeting
- American Academy of Family Physicians Scientific Assembly
- American College of Cardiology Annual Scientific Session
- American College of Surgeons Clinical Congress
- American Dental Assn. Annual Meeting
- American Hospital Assn.
- American Lung Assn./American Thoracic Soc. International Conference
- American Soc. of Clinical Oncology
- Annual Meeting of the American Academy of Ophthalmology
- International Vision Expo & Conference West
- Medical Design & Manufacturing West
- National Home Health Care Exposition
- Radiological Society of North America

Security & Safety
- International Security Conference & Exposition
- National Safety Council Congress & Exposition

Sporting Goods, Recreation & Travel
- National Sporting Goods Assn. World Sports Expo
- Super Show

HOUSEHOLD APPLIANCES AND PRODUCTS

In 1993 shipments of US-made appliances increased 3 percent in real terms, to a record US$17.7 billion in current dollars. For the industry as a whole, imports constitute 20 percent of the domestic market, reflecting the strong hold that US firms have on domestic markets for major appliances. However, in several categories, imported small appliances have captured more than 50 percent of the domestic market because production of these items is labor intensive, with the result that imported products made with lower labor costs can undercut the prices of comparable US-made appliances.

Products The US household appliance industry produces cooking equipment, refrigerators, freezers, water heaters, furnaces, laundry equipment, housewares, fans, vacuums, and small home appliances.

Competitive Situation Five major corporations dominate the US appliance industry and produce complete lines of basic, major household appliances: Whirlpool, General Electric, White Consolidated Industries, Maytag, and Raytheon. These well capitalized, well established companies offer state-of-the-art major appliances of high quality at low prices because competition among them is intense. They are able to maintain a high volume of production, invest heavily in capital improvements, and operate successfully in a market open to foreign producers. Because this is a mature industry and these appliances are built to last for years, most sales of major appliances are for new housing, kitchen remodeling, and replacements.

The National Appliance Energy Conservation Act of 1987 set national efficiency standards for several categories of major household appliances, including refrigerators and freezers, water heaters, dishwashers, clothes washers and dryers, and kitchen ranges and ovens. Standards have been updated and revised and have taken effect or will take effect in the mid-1990s for most major appliances. Energy efficiency and chlorofluorocarbon use remain major issues facing the appliance industry. For more than 50 years, chlorofluorocarbons (CFCs) have been used as coolants in refrigerators and freezers, as well as in the production of foam insulation. However, as evidence mounts of the damaging effects of CFCs on the earth's protective layer of atmospheric ozone, the US has pledged to halt CFC production by 1996 under the Montreal Protocol of 1987.

Government Agencies

Consumer Product Safety Commission (CPSC)
Washington, DC 20207
Tel: (301) 504-0100, 504-0580 Fax: (301) 504-0124

Department of Energy (DOE)
1000 Independence Ave. SW
Washington, DC 20585
Tel: (202) 586-5000, 586-5575

International Trade Administration (ITA)
Office of Textiles, Apparel and Consumer Goods Industries
14th St. and Constitution Ave. NW
Washington, DC 20230
Tel: (202) 482-3737

Trade Associations

Air-Conditioning and Refrigeration Institute
1501 Wilson Blvd., 6th Fl.
Arlington, VA 22209
Tel: (703) 924-8800

Associated Builders and Contractors
729 15th St. NW
Washington, DC 20005
Tel: (202) 637-8800

Associated General Contractors of America
1957 E St. NW
Washington, DC 20006
Tel: (202) 393-2040

Association of Home Appliance Manufacturers
20 N. Wacker Drive
Chicago, IL 60606
Tel: (312) 984-5800

National Association of Home Builders
15th and M Streets NW
Washington, DC 20005
Tel: (202) 822-0233

National Housewares Manufacturers Association
6400 Shafer Court, Suite 650
Rosemont, IL 60018
Tel: (708) 292-4200 Fax: (708) 292-4211

Publications

Air Conditioning, Heating & Refrigeration News
(Weekly)
Business News Publishing Company
755 West Big Beaver Rd., Suite 1000
Troy, MI 48084
Tel: (313) 362-3700 Fax: (313) 362-0317

Appliance
(Monthly)
Dana Chase Publications, Inc.
1110 Jorie Blvd., CS 9019
Oak Brook, IL 60522-9019
Tel: (708) 990-3484 Fax: (708) 990-0078

Appliance Manufacturer
(Monthly)
5900 Harper Road, Suite 105
Solon, OH 44139
Tel: (216) 349-3060 Fax: (216) 498-9121

Construction Review
(Bimonthly)
US Government Printing Office
Superintendent of Documents
Washington, DC 20402
Tel: (202) 512-1800 Fax: (202) 512-2550

Consumer Electronic and Appliance News
(Monthly)
Kasmar Publications
3821 W. 226th St.
Torrance, CA 90505
Tel: (408) 294-6390

Trade Fairs

Refer to the "Trade Fairs" chapter for complete listings, including contact information, dates, and venues. Trade fairs with particular relevance to this industry include the following, which are listed under the headings given below:

Furnishings & Interior Design
- International Casual Furniture Market
- Lightfair International
- Neocon 95
- Restoration 95

Merchandising
- ASD/AMD National Trade Show
- Gourmet Products Show Including Bed, Bath & Linen
- International Home Furnishings Market
- National Hardware Show
- National Merchandise Show
- Supermarket Industry Convention & Educational Exposition
- Transworld Housewares & Variety Exhibit
- Variety Merchandise Show, Mid-Year Variety Merchandise Show

INDUSTRIAL MACHINERY

Most US production machinery sectors posted improved performance in 1993, reflecting better conditions in the US economy. Performance in six machinery sectors in which shipments had declined in 1992—particularly manufacturers of farm, oil and gas, and textile machinery—turned around in 1993. However, 1993 shipments continued to decline for manufacturers of papermaking machinery still suffering from aftereffects of the 1991 recession and printing trades machinery (reflecting slow growth in the publishing industry).

Improvement in the overall performance of the industrial machinery sectors was brought about by several beneficial economic factors, both general and specific. General factors included a gradually improving US economy, lower interest rates which stimulated capital spending, continued technological improvements, and increased exports. Specific factors affected only particular industries: floods in the Midwest boosted the demand for construction equipment, and the mandatory phaseout of chlorofluorocarbon (CFC) refrigerant production by 1995 encouraged retrofit and replacement in industrial air conditioning and refrigeration systems.

Products US industrial machinery manufacturers offer the following kinds of equipment: air conditioning, refrigeration, and heating equipment; construction machinery—such as loaders, crawler tractors, cranes, paving equipment, backhoes, and trenchers; farm equipment; food products machinery; mining machinery; oil and gas field machinery; packaging equipment; paper manufacturing machinery; printing trades machinery; and textile machinery.

Competitive Situation Production machinery exports rose 5 percent in value in 1993 and constituted 34 percent of total shipments. All sectors participated in the gain with the exception of oil and gas field machinery and printing machinery, both of which declined by 2 percent. Manufacturers are focusing on opportunities in Asia, Latin America, the republics of the former Soviet Union, and Central Europe. Expanding opportunities in Mexico received particular attention in preparation for the implementation of NAFTA. Success abroad was aided by the availability of competitive financing, the US dollar's lower value, and joint international arrangements. Imports into the US rose faster in 1993 as the US economy strengthened. A summary of the competitive situation for each sector follows.

Specialized Machinery

Air Conditioning, Refrigeration, and Heating Equipment Steady growth is expected in both domestic and international markets. In the domestic market, demand for retrofits and replacements will increase because of the mandatory phaseout of chlorofluorocarbon refrigerant production by the end of 1995. US manufacturers are leaders in design and production of equipment that uses alternative refrigerants.

Construction Machinery Intense competition has encouraged manufacturers to hold down overhead costs by closely monitoring inventories of raw materials, components, replacement parts, and completed machines. For many companies, dealer stocks must often be depleted before increases in plant production are authorized. The US construction machinery industry will continue to be highly competitive because it is in the process of adopting global production strategies to hedge against changes in comparative produc-

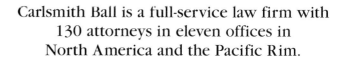
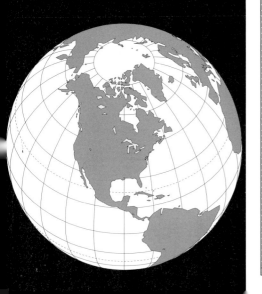

tion costs. Outlays of US government funds for financing mass transit, repairing the nation's bridges and roads, and rebuilding areas hit by natural disasters have also been dependable revenue sources for this industry, although this may change in the developing era of more restrained government spending.

Farm Equipment The US is no longer the dominant force in world grain markets. Alternative uses for crops may expand farm production marginally, but for the foreseeable future, farmers and the farm machinery industry face a contracting market. The farm equipment market is largely a replacement market, and within any five-year span, technological innovations have been minimal and therefore not a common reason for purchasing new equipment. Imports supply 26 percent of the domestic market, while 29 percent of the US industry's production is exported. To reduce inventories, the farm machinery industry is moving into a low inventory distribution or "build to order" system of production.

Food Products Machinery Such machinery made in the US has earned a worldwide reputation for quality, performance, value, reliability, and superior control systems. Food quality and sanitation in the US are without equal because of the high standards set by food companies, trade associations, and government regulatory agencies. The industry supplies specialized machinery for all kinds of food and beverage processing. Exports accounted for about 34 percent of 1993 US food machinery shipments, while imports supplied 25 percent of the domestic market.

Mining Machinery To retain its competitive edge in world markets, the US mining machinery industry is reducing production and inventory costs. Computers have been introduced to monitor the needs on production lines for raw materials and components, to track inventories, and to generate maintenance schedules for each major mining machine installed. Half of the US mining machinery production is exported, while 32 percent of the domestic market is supplied by imports.

Oil and Gas Field Machinery Growth in the sales of oil and gas field machinery are dependent on the exploration and development budgets of petroleum companies. A 1993 slump in world oil prices kept a damper on the market for field machinery. At the same time, markets are expanding for offshore drilling equipment and products for the prevention and containment of oil spills. The US petroleum equipment industry is a leading supplier of the most advanced petroleum equipment in the world. The value of imports is about 1 percent of the value of exports, which total nearly US$4 billion. US suppliers are expected to continue aggressively marketing their advanced equipment to assist many foreign countries to recover more petroleum from deep and difficult geologic formations,

particularly in the Russian Republic.

Packaging Machinery Production of packaging materials, containers, supplies, and services totals about US$80 billion a year. New materials, packaging designs, and techniques are constantly being developed. In the packaging machinery industry, US equipment has earned an international reputation for high quality, functional engineering, and well designed construction, including excellent control systems and electronics, reliability, and good value. Exports of finished machines continued to improve, especially machines for labeling, filling, closing, sealing, cartoning, and wrapping. Imports supply 24 percent of the domestic market.

Paper Manufacturing Equipment Four years of recession in the worldwide pulp and paper industries have caused three years of falling shipments for US paper machinery manufacturers. The paper machinery industry has a long history of boom-bust cycles, and it is expected to experience better times during the remainder of the decade. US-based suppliers have established a strong competitive position in this market segment. The spread of free market economics around the globe is fostering a greater demand for information and, hence, for the machinery to produce newsprint and other papers. Indeed, paper prices skyrocketed in late 1994 due to a lack of capacity, arguing for a sharp rise in shipments of equipment in 1995 and 1996. A number of firms are also finding developing markets for machinery to handle recycled paper production.

Printing Trades Machinery Shipments by the printing trades industry declined in 1993, reflecting sluggishness in the printing and publishing industries, which have been slow to recover from the national economic recession. Although in terms of employment, printing and publishing is the third largest industry in the US, many companies have downsized and cut back on capital expenditures. General economic recovery is expected to improve prospects for printing and publishing, and hence for suppliers of printing trades machinery. However, this industry is also facing increased competition from more accessible and affordable electronic media. Many industry observers expect printing equipment orders to be limited over the long run by a shift in overall spending away from print media.

Textile Machinery Markets for textile machinery largely depend on consumer trends. Thus, textile machinery for the production of knit and fleece products have been in particularly strong demand because of a shift in consumer preference toward casual clothing. Demand for denim and cotton fabric-making equipment has also grown, as has the demand for quality control equipment, such as for fiber testing and monitoring. Half of the US textile machinery produced is exported. However, imports are extremely high, making up 71 percent of domestic consumption. To expand sales, US companies are taking the lead in developing computerized systems and process controls for fiber-to-fabric processes, knitting, finishing, and yarn preparation. They also are at the forefront in offering energy efficiency and pollution-control features on textile machinery.

Government Agencies

Department of Energy (DOE)
1000 Independence Ave. SW
Washington, DC 20585
Tel: (202) 586-5000, 586-5575

Environmental Protection Agency (EPA)
401 M St. SW
Washington, DC 20460
Tel: (202) 260-2090, 260-2080

International Trade Administration (ITA)
Office of Materials, Machinery, and Chemicals
14th St. and Constitution Ave. NW
Washington, DC 20230
Tel: (202) 482-0575

Technology Administration
14th St. and Constitution Ave. NW
Washington, DC 20230
Tel: (202) 482-0137

Trade Associations

Air-Conditioning and Refrigeration Institute
1501 Wilson Blvd., 6th Fl.
Arlington, VA 22209
Tel: (703) 924-8800

American Mining Congress
1920 N St. NW, Suite 300
Washington, DC 20036
Tel: (202) 861-2800 Fax: (202) 8610-7535

National Association of Manufacturers
1331 Pennsylvania Ave. NW
Washington, DC 20004
Tel: (202) 637-3000

National Printing Equipment and Supply
Association
1899 Preson White Drive
Reston, VA 22091
Tel: (703) 264-7200

Packaging Machinery Manufacturers Institute
1343 L St. NW
Washington, DC 20005
Tel: (202) 347-3838

Petroleum Equipment Institute
PO Box 2380
Tulsa, OK 74101
Tel: (918) 494-9696

Publications

Air Conditioning, Heating & Refrigeration News
(Weekly)
Business News Publishing Company
755 West Big Beaver Rd., Suite 1000
Troy, MI 48084
Tel: (313) 362-3700 Fax: (313) 362-0317

American Papermaker
MacLean-Hunter Publications
57 Executive Park S., Suite 310
Atlanta, GA 30329
Tel: (404) 325-9153

American Printer
(Monthly)
Maclean Hunter Publishing
29 N. Wacker Dr.
Chicago, IL 60606
Tel: (312) 726-2802 Fax: (312) 726-2574

Chilton's Industrial Maintenance & Plant Operation
(Monthly)
Chilton
Chilton Way
Radnor, PA 19089
Tel: (215) 964-4225 Fax: (215) 964-4251

Construction Equipment
(Monthly)
Cahners Publishing Company
1350 E. Touhy Ave.
Des Plaines, IL 60018
Tel: (708) 635-8800 Fax: (708) 390-2690

Farm Equipment Guide
(Monthly)
Heartland Communications Group
1003 Central Ave.
Fort Dodge, IA 50501
Tel: (515) 955-1600 Fax: (515) 247-2000

Foodservice Equipment and Supplies Specialist
(13 issues/year)
Cahners Publishing Company
1350 E. Touhy Ave.
Des Plaines, IL 60018
Tel: (708) 635-8800

Industrial Product Bulletin
(Monthly)
Gordon Publications
301 Gibraltar Dr.
Morris Plains, NJ 07950
Tel: (201) 292-5100 Fax: (201) 898-9281

Industry Week
(Semimonthly)
Penton Publishing
1100 Superior Ave.
Cleveland, OH 44114
Tel: (216) 696-7000 Fax: (216) 696-8765

Machine Design
(28 issues/year)
Penton Publishing
1100 Superior Ave.
Cleveland, OH 44114
Tel: (216) 696-7000 Fax: (216) 696-0177

Mechanical Engineering
(Monthly)
American Society of Mechanical Engineers
345 E. 47th St.
New York, NY 10017
Tel: (212) 705-7722

Metal Fabricating News
(Quarterly)
PO Box 1178
Rockford, IL 61105
Tel: (815) 965-4031

Mine and Quarry Trader
(Monthly)
Allied Publications
PO Box 603
Indianapolis, IN 46206
Tel: (317) 297-5500 Fax: (317) 299-1356

Modern Materials Handling
(14 issues/year)
Cahners Publishing
275 Washington St.
Newton, MA 02158-1630
Tel: (617) 964-3030 Fax: (617) 558-4402

New Equipment Digest
(Monthly)
Penton Publishing
1100 Superior Ave.
Cleveland, OH 44114
Tel: (216) 696-7000 Fax: (216) 696-8765

Oil, Gas, and Petrochem Equipment
(Monthly)
PennWell Publishing Company
1421 S. Sheridan St.
Tulsa, OK 74101
Tel: (918) 835-3161 Fax: (918) 831-9497

Packaging
(Monthly)
Cahners Publishing Company
1350 E. Touhy Ave.
Des Plaines, IL 60018
Tel: (708) 635-8800

Packaging Digest
(Monthly)
Delta Communications, Inc.
455 N. Michigan Ave., Suite 1300
Chicago, IL 60611
Tel: (312) 222-2000

Paper Industry Equipment
(Annual)
Hatton-Brown Publishers, Inc.
225 Hanrick St., Box 2268
Montgomery, AL 36104
Tel: (205) 834-1170

Plant Engineering
(19 issues/year)
Cahners Publishing
1350 E. Touhy Ave.
PO Box 5080
Des Plaines, IL 60017
Tel: (708) 635-8800 Fax: (708) 390-2636

World Industrial Reporter
(Monthly)
Keller Industrial Publishing Corp.
150 Great Neck Rd.
Great Neck, NY 11021
Tel: (516) 829-9210

Trade Fairs

Refer to the "Trade Fairs" chapter for complete listings, including contact information, dates, and venues. Trade fairs with particular relevance to this industry include the following, which are listed under the headings given below:

Construction & Building Materials
- A/E/C Systems
- Builders Show
- International Air-Conditioning, Heating & Refrigerating Exposition

Environmental & Energy
- Offshore Technology Conference & Exhibition
- SPE Annual Technical Conference & Exhibition
- Waste Expo

Machinery & Manufacturing
- Autofact
- CMM International
- Fabtech International Exposition & Conference
- International Control Engineering Exposition & Conference
- International Programmable Controllers
- Metalform 95
- National Manufacturing Week
- National Plant Engineering and Maintenance Show & Conference
- Westech Advanced Productivity Exposition
- Eastech Advanced Productivity Exposition

Mining & Gemology
- SMME Annual Meeting & Exhibit

Packaging & Materials Handling
- Flex Expo
- Midpak '95
- Southern Packaging Exposition
- Western Packaging Exposition

Textiles
- Industrial Fabric & Equipment Exposition
- World Educational Congress for Laundering & Drycleaning

INDUSTRIAL MINERALS, CHEMICALS, AND MATERIALS

The status of and trends in the industrial minerals, chemicals, and materials industries varies depending on the individual product. Each major sector is discussed below. The common thread throughout these industries is the increasing effort to cut costs, increase productivity, and adapt to comply with environmental regulations.

Products Industrial minerals, chemicals, and materials produced in the US include such products as cement; coal; inorganic chemicals; metals—such as aluminum, copper, iron, gold, lead, silver, steel products, titanium, and zinc; minerals—such as boron, clays, phosphate rock, potash, salt, sand and gravel, and soda ash; petrochemicals—such as benzene, butadiene, ethylene, methanol, propylene, toluene, and xylene; crude petroleum and natural gas; refined petroleum products—such as gasoline, kerosene, distillate fuel oils, residual fuel oils, and lubricants; plastics and rubber; and soaps and detergents.

Competitive Situation The competitive situation for each of the main industry groups follows.

Specific Materials

Cement The US is a huge net importer of cement because of the sheer size of the domestic market, limited domestic capacity, and high domestic cement prices that are higher than world cement prices. About 55 percent of the cement shipped in the US in 1993 was consumed in residential and commercial building construction. Public works construction—including such projects as streets, highways, and water and waste systems—consumed about 42 percent of the cement shipped in the US.

Coal The US is the world's second largest supplier of coal, ranking behind Australia. Coal consumption is expected to continue to expand, despite the fact that such expansion is already beginning to conflict with costs required to ameliorate the environmental effects of coal use. If emissions are taxed or otherwise limited, the coal industry is expected to bear the brunt of any such penalties.

Inorganic Chemicals Inorganic chemicals include such chemicals as chloralkalis, industrial gases, acids, salts, inorganic compounds, and rare-earth metal salts. They are most commonly used as processing aids in the intermediate manufacturing processes for chemical and nonchemical products, and are seldom part of the final product. The major consumers of inorganic chemicals are the paper, housing, packaging, automotive, pharmaceutical, paint and ink, and fertilizer industries. Demand for these products is sensitive to developments within these industries and the health of the country's economy. In 1993, imports supplied 22 percent of the domestic market for inorganic chemicals, a 9 percent decline from 1992 levels. Exports in 1993 showed an increase. Over the long term, the current distribution of these commodities product suppliers is expected to continue, with minimal changes in the relative markets.

Metals and Minerals Increases in US motor vehicle sales in 1994 translated into higher demand from the auto industry for steel, aluminum, other metals, and glass made from glass sand. Reauthori-

zation of funding for the federal highway and mass transit programs will mean increased demand for stone, sand, and gravel, but this is expected to be offset, at least in part, by the continuation of a weak market in commercial building, especially of office buildings, hotels, and motels. US minerals trade declined in 1993, reflecting the sluggish world economy, with exports slipping farther than imports.

The US steel industry is reducing costs to meet the challenge of increased competition at home and abroad. Recent contract agreements with the United Steelworkers of America traded representation on the board and job security for improvements in productivity.

The US aluminum industry, a modern and efficient producer of high-quality products with an international competitive advantage, is looking forward to continued growth in its market. The automotive sector could provide the next large volume market, perhaps exceeding the phenomenal growth resulting from the introduction of the aluminum beverage can. New fuel economy standards could hasten the increase of aluminum use, as could the introduction of aluminum intensive electric powered cars.

Petrochemicals Petrochemicals are the precursors of plastics, fibers, elastomers, fertilizers, and chemical intermediates that are the raw materials for numerous consumer and industrial products. The US petrochemical industry faces growing competition in its export markets from the Gulf Cooperation Council and Pacific Rim countries, despite rising world demand projected to grow at an annual rate of 3.3 percent from 320 million metric tons in 1992 to 575 million metric tons by 2010. Analysts predict that the combined share of world consumption by the US, Western Europe, and Japan will drop from 71 percent to 63 percent during that period, not so much due to reduced consumption among the populace in these regions as because the rest of the world is expected to experience a greater proportional rise in per capita consumption.

Crude Petroleum and Natural Gas Increased dependence on foreign oil, together with environmental concerns, has focused attention on the use of natural gas to supply a greater portion of US domestic energy requirements. Less than 1 percent of US production of crude petroleum and natural gas is exported, while 36 percent of the US domestic market is supplied by imports. Independent producers account for a significant percentage of crude oil and natural gas reserves and for an estimated three-quarters of annual well completions.

Refined Petroleum Products Motor gasoline will continue to dominate US petroleum consumption throughout the decade, but its share of the transportation industry's demand for fuel is expected to decrease slowly as jet fuel and diesel fuel increase their shares. Motor gasoline is being increasingly taxed and regulated to meet emission and composition requirements. Imports supply 12 percent of the refined petroleum products consumed in the US market.

Plastics The US remains a major net exporter of plastics. Sales to Canada and Mexico accounted for about one-third of total US exports in 1992. Imports supplied 9 percent of the domestic market in 1993, and 21 percent of US production was exported. General purpose thermoplastics are usually manufactured in large quantities using well established technology. In contrast, specialty plastics are specifically developed to meet extreme environmental conditions and involve significant up-front research and development costs. Material substitution (that is, plastic for metal, wood, or glass) as a major growth factor is declining, but new applications are emerging for convenience and safety features. The favorable cost, low weight, and versatility of newer plastic materials will also make them more attractive to the auto industry.

Rubber The US now ranks first in the world in production of synthetic rubber, producing about 26 percent of total world output in 1992. Synthetic rubber materials fall into two broad categories: general purpose materials and specialty elastomers. The most common general purpose materials are widely used in the production of tires and industrial rubber products. In contrast, specialty elastomers are used for applications in which resistance to extreme environmental conditions or considerations of weight and volume are important. Growth prospects for the domestic synthetic rubber industry remain mixed, reflecting the industry's dependence on tire manufacture. However, exceptionally high growth rates for high-value elastomers are expected through the end of the decade. Imports supplied 15 percent of the domestic market in 1993, while US companies exported 22 percent of their 1993 production.

Soaps and Detergents The soaps and detergents industry is focusing to a greater degree on international markets. Developing countries offer good prospects for US exports because of the close correlation between rising standards of living in such countries and growth in consumption of soaps and detergents. New product lines, marketing strategies, and research and development expenditures will continue to reflect the environmental concerns of both the industry and consumers.

Government Agencies

Bureau of Land Management
1849 C St. NW
Washington, DC 20240
Tel: (202) 208-3100, 501-5717

Bureau of Mines
810 7th St. NW
Washington, DC 20241
Tel: (202) 208-3100, 501-9649

Federal Energy Regulatory Commission (FERC)
825 N Capitol St. NE
Washington, DC 20426
Tel: (202) 208-0200, 208-1371

International Trade Administration (ITA)
Office of Materials, Machinery, and Chemicals
14th St. and Constitution Ave. NW
Washington, DC 20230
Tel: (202) 482-0575

Trade Associations

American Mining Institute
1920 N St. NW, Suite 300
Washington, DC 20036
Tel: (202) 861-2800 Fax: (202) 861-7535

American Petroleum Institute
1220 L St. NW
Washington, DC 20005
Tel: (202) 682-8000

Chemical Manufacturers Association
2501 M St. NW
Washington, DC 20037
Tel: (202) 887-1100

Independent Petroleum Association of America
1101 16th St. NW
Washington, DC 20036
Tel: (202) 857-4722

National Glass Association
8200 Greensboro Dr.
McLean, VA 22102
Tel: (703) 442-4890

Rubber Manufacturers Association
1400 K St. NW
Washington, DC 20005
Tel: (202) 227-5558

Society of Plastics Industry
1275 K St. NW, Suite 400
Washington, DC 20005
Tel: (202) 371-5200 Fax: (202) 371-1022

Publications

Adhesives Age
(Monthly)
Argus Business
6151 Powers Ferry Road., NW
Atlanta, GA 30339
Tel: (404) 955-2500 Fax: (404) 955-0400

Advanced Materials and Processes
(Monthly)
ASM International
Materials Park, OH 44073
Tel: (216) 338-5151 Fax: (216) 338-4634

American Metal Market
(Daily)
Chilton Publishing Company
825 Seventh Ave.
New York, NY 10019
Tel: (212) 887-8580 Fax: (212) 887-8522

Chemical Business (Monthly)
Chemical Marketing Reporter (Weekly)
Schnell Publishing Company
80 Broad St., 23rd Fl.
New York, NY 10004
Tel: (212) 248-4177 Fax: (212) 248-4901

Chemical Week
(Weekly)
Chemical Week Association
888 Seventh Ave.
New York, NY 10019
Tel: (212) 621-4900 Fax: (212) 621-4949

Iron Age
(Monthly)
Hitchcock Publishing Company
191 S. Gary Ave.
Carol Stream, IL 60188
Tel: (708) 665-1000

Metal Bulletin
220 Fifth Ave.
New York, NY 10001
Tel: (212) 213-6202

Metals Week
McGraw-Hill Publications
1221 Ave. of the Americas
New York, NY 10020
Tel: (212) 512-2823

Minerals Today
(Bimonthly)
US Bureau of Mines
US Department of the Interior
Washington, DC 20241
Tel: (202) 501-9358

Mining Engineering
(Monthly)
8307 Shaffer Parkway
Littleton, CO 80127
Tel: (303) 973-9550 Fax: (303) 973-3845

Modern Plastics
(Monthly)
McGraw-Hill, Inc.
1221 Ave. of the Americas
New York, NY 10020
Tel: (212) 512-6267, (800) 257-9402 Fax: (212) 512-6111

Oil and Gas Journal
(Weekly)
PennWell Publishing Co.
PO Box 1260
Tulsa, OK 74101
Tel: (918) 835-3161

Randol Buyers Guide
Randol International Limited
18301 West Colfax Ave. #T1B
Golden, CO 80401
Tel: (303) 271-0324 Fax: (303) 271-0334
Gives information on mines and the mining industry

Rubber Directory and Buyer's Guide
Rubber and Plastics News
Plastics News
Crain Communications
1725 Merriman Rd., Suite 300
Akron, OH 44313
Tel: (216) 836-9180

Trade Fairs

Refer to the "Trade Fairs" chapter for complete listings, including contact information, dates, and venues. Trade fairs with particular relevance to this industry include the following, which are listed under the headings given below:

Chemicals & Plastics
- Chem Show '95
- Plastics/USA 95

Environmental & Energy
- Hazmacon
- Hazmat
- Offshore Technology Conference & Exhibition
- Oilheat Business & Industry Exposition
- SPE Annual Technical Conference & Exhibition
- Waste Expo

Mining & Gemology
- SMME Annual Meeting & Exhibit

Textiles
- World Educational Congress for Laundering & Drycleaning

SERVICE INDUSTRIES

Service industries operate in all sectors of the economy. They support corporations in the day-to-day conduct of business and individuals in the planning of leisure-time activities. Trends in the industry are tied to changing demographics in the domestic market and an increasing ability to become involved in international business transactions.

Equipment Leasing

There are four types of businesses that lease equipment: banks and their affiliates; manufacturers' subsidiaries; independent or nonaffiliated lessors, for whom leasing is the major source of revenue; and diversified financial services organizations, such as insurance companies, pension trusts, or other entities for which leasing is an additional revenue source. These business lease all kinds of equipment and services—agricultural equipment, aircraft, computers, construction equipment, containers, electrical power tools and machines, fresh and salt water transportation equipment, industrial and manufacturing equipment, materials handling equipment, medical equipment, office furnishings, office machines, telecommunications equipment, and trucks and trailers. Computers replaced aircraft as the largest leasing sector by value in 1992.

Expansion of equipment leasing depends largely on the overall growth rate of the economy. The development of a global presence is an incentive for leasing companies looking to expand their markets, but the international expansion of mainstream leasing companies will remain limited in the immediate future.

Financial Services

Commercial banks, savings institutions, and credit unions were expected to increase assets a modest 1 percent to nearly US$5 trillion in 1994, reversing a slight decline in 1993. These financial institutions had benefited from a widening of the spread between interest rates charged for loans and paid on deposits. However, many deposits continue to be diverted from savings to alternative investments, especially mutual funds and common stocks. Banks and savings institutions are responding to this trend by becoming full service institutions that provide independent savings plans, commercial and consumer lending, mortgage lending and mortgage servicing, insurance, and securities investments.

The late 1980s were especially difficult times for financial institutions. These years were marked by bank failures and sharply rising deposit insurance costs. Although the industry has greatly recovered, legislators and regulators feel increasing pressure to address many of the problems that still affect the commercial banking industry. Most important among these issues is the need to expand the opportunities for risk diversification for banks by removing the boundaries separating the banking, securities, and insurance businesses.

Like all industries, financial service institutions have been affected by changing technology. In particular, the use of automated teller machines (ATMs) has risen significantly, resulting in a drop in branch operating costs.

Trade finance is a growing field. Because the economic growth of the US increasingly depends on exports and because there is some risk associated with international trading, the ability to finance exports is becoming more important to US businesses. Such trade financing is expected to become as important to small and medium-sized businesses, which are entering the export arena in increasing numbers, as it has traditionally been to large businesses.

Professional Services

Professional services include accounting, auditing, and bookkeeping services; legal services; management and other consulting services; and advertising and public relations. A continuing trend toward using computers and specialized software has resulted in increased productivity, reduced costs, and improved turnaround time. US professional services firms are extremely competitive and have an advantage—sometimes based on cost, at other times based on expertise or reputation—In many sectors internationally. Professional service firms in the US, Japan, and Europe are all aggressively pursuing contracts in the EU, the largest regional market outside the US. Opportunities are also opening in Central Europe, the countries of the former Soviet Union, and in East Asia. Demand for professional services will continue to increase throughout the 1990s, but at a slower rate during the latter half of the decade. A major force behind this growth will continue to be the increased use of computers, integrated systems, and other high-tech equipment.

Retail Services

The retail trade sector is one of the major sources of jobs in the US economy, consistently accounting for about 21 percent of all non-farm jobs in the private sector. Retail establishments are primarily engaged in selling merchandise for personal or household consumption. Total retail sales, estimated at nearly US$2.1 trillion, or 33 percent of GDP in 1993, are expected to grow to more than US$2.2 trillion in 1994, an increase of about 7 percent, largely due to price increases.

The retail customer of the 1990s is significantly different from the customer of a decade ago. Retail strategies are being reassessed in view of the changing demographics and new buying patterns. The most significant demographic changes in the country include (1) the declining importance of households composed of married couples, (2) an increase in the number of people living alone, and (3) the projected surge in the number of teenagers and young adults during the next five years. Analysts point out that the customer of the 1990s is looking for genuine value, coupled with superior and differentiating customer services.

Retail stores and marketing techniques are changing. Sales at regional supermalls have fallen while retail sales at smaller community shopping centers have increased. New marketing techniques include electronic retailing through interactive television and catalog marketing.

Travel Services

The travel industry is a large and growing sector of the US economy. Probably no country in the world has a greater comparative advantage in tourism than the US. International visitor arrivals to the US have grown at an annual rate of more than 8 percent since 1988. Total travel spending in the US, including that by international visitors, was expected to grow 5.7 percent in 1994, following an increase of 4.8 percent in 1993. A weak US dollar and economic recovery in many areas of the world should serve to extend this trend through 1995 and perhaps beyond. Overall 1994 travel expenditures amounted to nearly 6 percent of the US GDP.

Travel services form a diverse and complex industry, composed of segments from the transportation, retail, and service industries. Most expenditures on travel are in the following categories: transportation by airplane, bus, train, ship, and taxi; transportation by rented vehicle, such as by car or camper (including the accompanying expenditures on gasoline); lodging; food service; amusement and recreational services; general retail and merchandise store purchases; and passenger transportation arrangements.

Travel has become an integral part of life in the US and should grow steadily during the 1990s. However, the travel industry will be challenged to find new ways to attract travelers as competition increases for their discretionary dollars. A trend toward smaller families allows for greater flexibility in the type and timing of travel, and also may contribute to discretionary income. However, the ebbing of the baby boom, delayed childbearing, and an older population will radically change the travel industry.

The professional travel industry in the US is highly fragmented and specialized, with even the largest participants controlling shares on the order of perhaps only 5 percent of the overall market. This situation changed somewhat in 1994 with the sale of the US operations of Thomas Cook to American Express, although this consolidation is not expected to have a major impact on service delivery in the industry. Of greater potential impact was the decision in early 1995 by major US airlines to put caps on commissions paid to travel agents. Traditionally, travel agents in the US have provided their services free to consumers, receiving their compensation from commissions paid by the service providers— airlines, hotels, car rental agencies, and the like. If the sharply reduced commissions proposed by the airlines hold, travel agencies may have to start charging the end users, which is expected to have a substantial effect on their business.

Competitive Situation The competitive situation of US service industries applies mostly to the professional services. The most important professional services are discussed below.

Accounting

Demand for accounting services will continue to increase, but in a climate in which both accounting firms and their clients are trying to reduce costs and improve efficiency. Clients reduce costs by having their own in-house staffs prepare supporting documents, insurance information, or tax records, and by hiring outside bookkeeping service and payroll firms. In an effort to improve efficiency, accounting firms will continue to reduce workforce and may restructure to change the prevailing partnership format. Merger activity may still be seen among the top tier "Big Six" and the second tier accounting firms. At the same time, the accounting profession is changing. Accountants, for example, are being asked to look beyond the numbers and evaluate the larger picture, looking into such issues as the quality of corporate planning or confronting problems associated with legal and ethical issues.

Advertising and Public Relations

The advertising industry in the US is the largest in the world, accounting for more than 40 percent of all advertising expenditures globally. The industry consists of three elements: advertisers, media, and advertising agencies. Cable television is the fastest-growing advertising medium in the US, and its increased popularity has caused the advertising rates of the major US television networks to fall. Expansion abroad by US advertising agencies will continue to be stifled by various factors. There is a growing trend for countries to restrict the advertising of certain products, particularly tobacco and alcoholic beverages. Also, some advertising industry executives are concerned that consumers—who, as a whole, have suffered from the economic decline of the early 1990s—may begin to attach even greater importance to price than to brand loyalty, which would tend to make their services less valuable. In view of these restrictions on traditional advertising, many firms interested in overseas expansion are looking more towards public relations—a new concept in many areas of the world—in order to achieve recognition in new markets.

Law

Competition in the legal services sector continues to increase, not only because it is necessary to reduce costs, but also because over the last 20 years, the number of lawyers in the US has tripled to almost 800,000. Consequently, law firms have been forced to operate more like businesses than like personal service counselors. Many now use previously unheard-of corporate management techniques, such as identifying profitable niche markets, packaging firm services to target markets, advertising these services to specific markets, and closely tracking delivery costs.

Foreign operations of US law firms have increased faster than the domestic operations of these firms, due primarily to the expansion of the international marketplace. New markets in Central Europe and the former Soviet Union have created an extremely competitive environment for multinational law firms. The People's Republic of China, Hong Kong, and Taiwan appear to be the next major markets of opportunity. Many firms are also looking toward Latin America in light of increasing trade interest in that region.

Management and Other Consulting

In the management and public relations services sector, the number and range of consultants in the marketplace is exploding. Another specialty area experiencing rapid growth is facilities management or "outsourcing." Many companies have decided to focus on their principal activities and hire external specialists to perform ancillary business activities.

Government Agencies

Commodity Futures Trading Commission
2033 K St. NW
Washington, DC 20581
Tel: (202) 254-6387

Federal Reserve System, Board of Governors
20th and C Sts. NW
Washington, DC 20551
Tel: (202) 452-2266, 452-3215

Internal Revenue Service (IRS)
1111 Constitution Ave. NW
Washington, DC 20224
Tel: (202) 622-5000, (800) 829-1040

Travel and Tourism Administration
Main Commerce Bldg.
Washington, DC 20230
Tel: (202) 482-1904 Fax: (202) 482-4279

Trade Associations

American Advertising Federation
1400 K St. NW, Suite 1000
Washington, DC 20005
Tel: (202) 898-0089 Fax: (202) 898-0159

American Bankers Association
1120 Connecticut Ave. NW
Washington, DC 20036
Tel: (202) 663-5186

American Bar Association
750 N. Lake Shore Dr.
Chicago, IL 60611
Tel: (312) 988-5000

American Council of Life Insurance
1001 Pennsylvania Ave. NW
Washington, DC 20004
Tel: (202) 624-2000 Fax: (202) 624-2319

American Financial Services Association
919 18th St. NW, 3rd Floor
Washington, DC 20006
Tel: (202) 296-5544

American Hotel and Motel Association
1201 New York Ave.
Washington, DC 20005
Tel: (202) 289-3100

American Institute of Certified Public Accountants
1211 Ave. of the Americas
New York, NY 10036
Tel: (212) 575-6200

American Rental Association
1900 19th St.
Moline, IL 61265
Tel: (309) 764-2475 Fax: (309) 764-1533

American Society of Association Executives
1575 Eye St. NW
Washington, DC 20005
Tel: (202) 626-2723 Fax: (202) 626-8825

American Society of Notaries
918 16th St. NW
Washington, DC 20006
Tel: (202) 955-6162 Fax: (202) 955-6163

American Society of Travel Agents (ASTA)
1101 King St., Suite 200
Alexandria, VA 22314
Tel: (703) 739-2782 Fax: (703) 684-8319

American Wholesale Marketers Association
1128 16th St. NW
Washington, DC 20034
Tel: (202) 463-2124, (800) 783-6242
Fax: (202) 467-0559

Association of American Publishers
220 East 23rd St.
New York, NY 10010
Tel: (212) 689-8920

Direct Marketing Association
11 West 42nd St.
New York, NY 10036
Tel: (212) 768-7277 Fax: (212) 719-5106

Equipment Leasing Association of America
1300 N 17th St., Suite 1010
Arlington, VA 22209
Tel: (703) 527-8655 Fax: (703) 527-2649

International Association for Financial Planning
2 Concourse Parkway, Suite 800
Atlanta, GA 30328
Tel: (404) 395-1605

National Association of Realtors
430 North Michigan Ave.
Chicago, IL 60611
Tel: (312) 329-8200

National Association of Wholesaler Distributors
1725 K St. NW, Suite 710
Washington, DC 20006
Tel: (202) 872-0885

National Restaurant Association
1200 17th St. NW
Washington, DC 20036
Tel: (202) 331-5900 Fax: (202) 331-2429

National Retail Federation
100 West 31st St.
New York, NY 10001
Tel: (212) 244-8780

Printing Industries of America
100 Daingerfield Road
Alexandria, VA 22314
Tel: (703) 519-8100

Travel Industry Association of America
1133 21st Ave. NW, Suite 800
Washington, DC 20036
Tel: (202) 293-1433

Publications

ABA Journal
(Monthly)
American Bar Association
750 Lake Shore Dr.
Chicago, IL 60611
Tel: (312) 988-5991 Fax: (312) 988-6014

Accounting Today
(Biweekly)
Faulkner & Gray
11 Penn Plaza, 17th Fl.
New York, NY 10001
Tel: (212) 967-7000 Fax: (212) 967-7155

Advertising Age: The International Newspaper of Marketing
(Weekly)
Crain Communications, Inc.
220 E. 42nd St.
New York, NY 10017-5806
Tel: (212) 210-0100 Fax: (212) 210-0111

Adweek
(Weekly)
BPI Communications
1515 Broadway
New York, NY 10036
Tel: (212) 536-5336 Fax: (212) 944-1719

American Banker
One State Street Plaza
New York, NY 10004
Tel: (212) 943-6700

American Demographics
(Monthly)
Dow Jones Inc.
PO Box 68
Ithaca, NY 14851
Tel: (607) 273-6343, (800) 828-1133
Fax: (607) 273-3196

Best's Review, Life/Health Insurance Edition
Best's Review, Property/Casualty Insurance Edition
(Monthly)
A.M. Best Co., Inc.
Ambest Road
Oldwick, NJ 08858
Tel: (908) 439-2200 Fax: (908) 439-3296

Business Insurance
(Weekly)
Crain Communications Inc.
740 Rush St.
Chicago, IL 60611-2590
Tel: (312) 649-5286 Fax: (312) 280-3174

Business Marketing
Crain Communications Inc.
740 Rush St.
Chicago, IL 60611-2590
Tel: (312) 649-5260 Fax: (312) 649-5228

Chain Store Age Executive With Shopping Center Age
(Monthly)
Lebhar-Friedman, Inc.
425 Park Ave.
New York, NY 10022
Tel: (212) 756-5000

Chilton's Distribution
(Monthly)
Chilton
Chilton Way
Radnor, PA 19089
Tel: (215) 964-4225 Fax: (215) 964-4251

Direct Marketing
(Monthly)
Hoke Communications
224 Seventh St.
Garden City, NY 11530
Tel: (516) 746-6700 Fax: (516) 294-8141

Discount Merchandiser
(Monthly)
Schwartz Publications
233 Park Ave. S.
New York, NY 10003
Tel: (212) 979-4860 Fax: (212) 474-7431

International Advertiser
(Bimonthly)
International Advertising Association
342 Madison Ave.
New York, NY 10017
Tel: (212) 557-1133

Journal of Global Marketing
(Quarterly)
The Hayworth Press, Inc.
10 Alice St.
Binghamton, NY 13904-1580
Tel: (607) 722-9678, (800) 342-9678
Fax: (607) 722-1424

Journal of Marketing (Quarterly)
Marketing News (Biweekly)
American Marketing Association
250 S. Wacker Dr., Suite 200
Chicago, IL 60606
Tel: (312) 648-0536 Fax: (312) 993-7542

Mergers & Acquisitions: The Journal of Corporate Venture
(Bimonthly)
MLR Publishing Company
229 S. 18th St.
Philadelphia, PA 19103
Tel: (215) 790-7000 Fax: (215) 790-7005

National Underwriter, Life & Health/Financial Services Edition
National Underwriter, Property & Casualty/Risk & Benefits Management
(Weekly)
National Underwriter Company
505 Gest St.
Cincinnati, OH 45203
Tel: (513) 721-2140 Fax: (513) 721-0126

Public Relations News
(Weekly)
Phillips Business Information
1201 Seven Locks Rd.
Potomac, MD 20854
Tel: (301) 424-3338 Fax: (301) 309-3847

Restaurant Business
(18 issues/year)
Restaurant Business Magazine
633 Third Ave.
New York, NY 10017
Tel: (212) 592-6200 Fax: (212) 592-6509

Stores
(Monthly)
National Retail Federation, Inc.
100 W. 31st St.
New York, NY 10001
Tel: (212) 244-8780

Travel Trade
(Weekly)
Travel Trade Publications
15 W. 44th St.
New York, NY 10036
Tel: (212) 730-6600 Fax: (212) 730-7020

Wall Street Journal
(Daily)
Dow Jones, Inc.
200 Liberty St.
New York, NY 10281
Tel: (212) 416-2000 Fax: (212) 416-3299

Trade Fairs

Refer to the "Trade Fairs" chapter for complete listings, including contact information, dates, and venues. Trade fairs with particular relevance to this industry include the following, which are listed under the headings given below:

Business Services & Marketing
- Europe-California Business to Business Expo
- Exhibit Industry Conference and Exposition
- Exhibitor Show '95, The National Conference on Trade Show Marketing
- International Selling & Marketing Expo
- Licensing Show
- Motivation Show
- POPAI Marketplace
- Specialty Advertising Assn. International SA/Showcase

Food, Beverages & Hospitality
- International Hotel/Motel & Restaurant Show

- Las Vegas International Hotel, Restaurant and Gaming Exhibition
- NAFEM Educational Exhibition
- NAMA National Convention and Trade Show
- Restaurant and Hotel-Motel Show

Merchandising
- Premium Incentive Show/Meetings & Incentive Travel Expo

Sporting Goods, Recreation & Travel
- Pow Wow 95

TEXTILE AND LEATHER PRODUCTS

All segments of the US textile industry are concerned with reducing costs and improving efficiency, as the competition from countries with lower production costs continues. The country's expertise in high technology has helped the textile industry in its struggle to compete, but the industry still remains labor intensive and thus at a disadvantage with respect to many low-wage producing nations worldwide.

Textiles

In 1993 total shipments for the textile industry were valued at more than US$67 billion. Exports increased for 4 straight years from 1989 to 1992, with the value of exports rising from US$2.8 billion to US$4.5 billion. Export levels also rose in 1993, but they showed the effects of difficult economic times, with only 7 percent of all shipments exported. Imports supplied 9 percent of the domestic market.

The advent of NAFTA has liberalized US access to the growing Mexican textile market. The agreement mandates that, with a few exceptions, North American fabric made from yarn of North American origin must be used in manufacturing textile and apparel products to qualify for NAFTA benefits. However, while it makes the Mexican market more accessible to US producers, NAFTA also raises quota allowances in the US market for Mexican producers.

Products The textile industry provides spun yarn products, broadwoven and knit fabrics, floor coverings, and man-made fibers—such as acrylic, nylon, polyester, spandex, and rayon.

Competitive Situation In the 1980s textile firms attempted to offset the labor cost advantage held by low-wage countries in East Asia and elsewhere by significantly increasing capital expenditures on the latest production technology. When profits fell during the recession in 1990, investment purchases were cut back. Rising profits and improved cash flow have recently permitted greater capital investment on machinery, software, and systems. This has resulted in the efficiency gains that US textile firms need to remain somewhat competitive internationally. For the textile industry, ongoing adjustment to a dynamic, rapidly changing business environment will involve the development of a flexible and highly trained work force, along with improved customer service and vendor-customer relations.

Apparel and Fabricated Textile Products

Total shipments of US apparel and fabricated textile products were valued at US$65.4 billion in 1993. Imports were valued at US$35.4 billion, or 37 percent of domestic demand. Exports were valued at US$5.5 billion. Shipments in apparel products increased slightly, due to a sharp rise in consumer spending for clothing. Shipments in fabricated textile products also increased, due to an increase in housing sales and gradually improving economic conditions.

Products Apparel products include all kinds of clothing for men, women, and children: coats, jackets, suits, shirts, trousers, neckwear, work clothing, blouses, dresses, and underwear. Fabricated textiles include curtains and draperies, home furnishings, textile bags, canvas and related products, automotive and apparel trimmings, banners, flags, sleeping bags, nondisposable diapers, fishing nets, parachutes, and seat belts, among others.

Competitive Situation The apparel industry is made up of a few large companies and many small and medium-size firms. The apparel and fabricated textile products industry is labor intensive. Low-wage developing countries enjoy a significant cost advantage over US producers. In 1993 major US companies produced an estimated 70 percent of their sales in domestic plants. They are continuing to shift sourcing outside the country, most recently to the Caribbean, Central America, and South America. To compete in the market, the industry is also investing in the latest technology to increase productivity. Recent technological advances in this industry have occurred in computer aided design to increase efficiency in product design and in instruments meant to improve the safety, health, and worker efficiency. However, despite improvements in technology, manufacturing processes in this industry will of necessity remain labor intensive.

Leather and Leather Products

In 1993 total US production of leather and leather goods was valued at US$8.7 billion. Exports were valued at about US$1.38 billion. Imports increased about 6 percent to US$13.9 billion, which represented about two-thirds of domestic consumption. Most of both production and consumption consists of leather footwear, which accounts for 45 percent of the value of industry shipments. The leather tanning and finishing industry shipped US$2.5 billion worth of goods, with the US exporting slightly more goods than it imported. Exports were worth US$758 million, while imports were valued at US$738 million.

Products The leather and leather products industry produces footwear, gloves and related items, luggage, handbags, small personal leather and flat goods, and leather wearing apparel. It also includes the leather tanning and finishing sectors.

Competitive Situation The production of leather goods is a labor intensive industry. Suppliers in most developing countries maintain a substantial cost advantage over US producers because they pay far lower wages. China is the dominant supplier, accounting for a growing 41 percent share of US imports.

In comparison, the leather and tanning industry is not as labor intensive because it merely prepares the raw materials for later transformation into leather goods. The US is somewhat more competitive in leather and tanning and today ranks as the world's largest raw hide exporter. The supply of cattlehides depends heavily on the demand for meat, because cattlehides are a by-product of the meatpacking industry. Between 1982 and 1987, the US tanning industry experienced considerable contraction and consolidation, with the number of companies declined by 10 percent, from 342 to 308.

Government Agencies

Consumer Product Safety Commission (CPSC)
Washington, DC 20207
Tel: (301) 504-0100, 504-0580 Fax: (301) 504-0124

International Trade Administration (ITA)
Office of Textiles and Apparel
14th St. and Constitution Ave. NW
Washington, DC 20230
Tel: (202) 482-5078

Trade Associations

American Apparel Manufacturers Association
2500 Wilson Blvd., Suite 301
Arlington, VA 22201
Tel: (703) 524-1864

American Association for Textile Technology
PO Box 99
Gastonia, NC 28053
Tel: (704-824-3522

American Textile Manufacturers Institute
1801 K St. NW, Suite 900
Washington, DC 20006
Tel: (202) 862-0500

Industrial Fabrics Association International
345 Cedar Building, Suite 800
St. Paul, MN 55101
Tel: (612) 222-2508

Leather Industries of America
1000 Thomas Jefferson St. NW
Washington, DC 20007
Tel: (202) 342-8086

Luggage and Leather Goods Manufacturers of America
350 Fifth Ave., Suite 2624
New York, NY 10118
Tel: (212) 695-2340

Publications

Apparel Industry Magazine
Shore Communications
180 Allen Road, Suite 300-N
Atlanta, GA 30328
Tel: (404) 252-8831

Bobbin Magazine
(Monthly)
Bobbin Blenheim Media Corp.
1110 Shop Rd.
Columbia, SC 29202
Tel: (803) 771-7500 Fax: (803) 799-1461

CDB Interior Textiles
(Monthly)
Columbia Communications
370 Lexington Ave.
New York, NY 10017
Tel: (212) 532-9290 Fax: (212) 779-8345

Nonwoven Industry
(Monthly)
Rodman Publishing
17 S. Franklin Turnpike
Ramsey, NJ 07446
Tel: (201) 825-2552 Fax: (201) 855-0553

Textile World
(Monthly)
Maclean Hunter Publishing Company
29 N. Wacker Dr.
Chicago, IL 60606
Tel: (404) 847-2770 Fax: (404) 252-6150

Women's Wear Daily
Fairchild Publications
7 West 34th St.
New York, NY 10001
Tel: (800) 247-6622

Trade Fairs

Refer to the "Trade Fairs" chapter for complete listings, including contact information, dates, and venues. Trade fairs with particular relevance to this industry include the following, which are listed under the headings given below:

Apparel, Accessories & Jewelry
• Fashion Accessories Expo
• Imprinted Sportswear Show
• International Fashion Boutique Show
• International Footwear Expo
• International Kids Fashion Show
• National Bridal Market
• Western Shoe Associates International Buying Market
• Women's & Children's Apparel Market
• Women's, Children's, and Men's Markets
Textiles
• Bobbin Contexpo: The Apparel Show of the Americas
• Bobbin Sho: AAMA Convention
• Industrial Fabric & Equipment Exposition

TOOLS AND INSTRUMENTS

The tools and instruments industry continues to serve an expanding market. Specific trends depend on the sector of the economy in which the tools and instruments are used. Products may be used, for example, in the automotive, construction, production machinery, electronics, computer, and telecommunications industries.

Metalworking Equipment

Shipments of metalworking equipment rose 9 percent in 1993 above those in the previous year, to about US$23 billion. An unusually large capital spending program by firms in the US automotive industry resulted in a significant increase in the shipments of such metalworking equipment. Much of the increase occurred in the tool and die and machine tool industries. The tool and die industry accounts for about one-half of total shipments for the metalworking group. Shipments should continue to be high. In order to compete with manufacturers in developing countries, which have lower labor costs, US manufacturers must put newer and more productive equipment into their plants and automate wherever possible. These two tactics will continue to create more business for the metalworking equipment industry.

Products The metalworking equipment industry produces machine tools for cutting and forming metal. It also supplies dies, jigs, fixtures, industrial molds, power-driven hand tools, welding equipment, and robotics.

Competitive Situation Exports of metalworking equipment were up 13 percent in 1993, reaching US$4.2 billion, and were expected to gain an additional 11 percent in 1994. Prime markets for higher exports include the industrializing countries of the Pacific Rim, China, and Latin America. NAFTA will speed investment in Mexico that is likely to spur capital equipment purchases. Canada and Mexico have typically ranked as the first and second largest metalworking export markets for US manufacturers.

As one of the few industrialized countries in the world with an expanding economy in 1993, the US was the target of increased market competition. In spite of the weak US dollar, imports grew significantly as the US market became the "only game in town." Imports of metalworking machinery climbed by roughly 15 percent between 1992 and 1993, to US$5.2 billion and were expected to grow an additional 15 percent in 1994.

The US is the third largest producer of machine tools in the world, behind Japan and Germany. The US machine tool industry is composed of a large number of small firms and a handful of large corporations that have machine tool divisions. The average machine tool company has annual sales of US$7.5 million. More than half of the businesses employ 10 to 50 employees; they are typically family owned or closely held.

In the tool and die industry, the number of operating establishments has remained remarkably stable over the past several decades, especially considering the large declines in some related industries. The small companies of this industry are generally flexible and resilient. But despite the stability in the overall number of establishments, there is usually a relatively high rate of business closings in bad times and new start-ups in good times.

Industrial and Analytical Instruments

Industry shipments of industrial and analytical instruments were expected to rise about 4 percent in real terms in 1994, to about US$36.1 billion in current dollars—with the growth rate expected to be about the same as in 1993. The US trade surplus is expected to widen, after narrowing in 1993, as exports increase 6 percent to US$10.7 billion and imports expand 7 percent to US$5.6 billion.

Products Industrial and analytical instruments include: (1) laboratory apparatus and furniture, analytical instruments, and optical instruments and lenses (optical microscopes, binoculars, lasers other than laser diodes, astronomical instruments, optical components, and sighting, tracking, and fire control equipment); (2) measuring and controlling instruments (including automatic controls for regulating environments), display and process control instruments, fluid meters, and counting devices; and (3) instruments to measure electricity.

Competitive Situation In the laboratory apparatus and furniture division, modest growth in shipments is expected to continue for the foreseeable future, supported by such trends as growing interest in life sciences, biotechnology, medical research and testing, and environmental protection. The trade surplus in analytical instruments grew about 1 percent in 1993 to US$1 billion. The pharmaceutical and biotechnology, petrochemical, and environmental sciences industries are all using increasing amounts of high-performance analytic instruments, both for laboratory and on-site testing. In the optical instruments and lenses division, price cutting by optics companies in Japan, South Korea, Taiwan, Singapore, and Europe has increased competitive pressure on US firms. Japan is the major foreign supplier of optical instruments to the US.

The market for measuring and controlling instruments, which often measure and regulate environments, should remain flat because of the lack of any significant change in the construction industry. Demand for process control instruments is increasing along with growth in the oil, gas, chemical, and phar-

maceutical industries of developing countries. Japanese imports of fluid meters and counting devices, which are often used in automotive panels, have placed competitive pressure on US domestic suppliers. Measuring and controlling devices include aircraft engine instruments, physical properties testing and inspection, nuclear radiation detection and monitoring devices, and meteorological instruments. Exports of these devices accounted for a healthy 40 percent of US shipments in 1993, as they had for at least five years, while imports declined to their lowest level since 1989. Leading export markets were Japan, Canada, and Germany, in that order.

Electrical test and measuring instruments are not designed to measure large voltage flows, but rather to measure electrical flows in products such as semiconductors, printed circuit boards, and communications equipment. With a trade surplus of about US$2 billion in 1993, the US is especially competitive in the more advanced test and measuring instruments, and has licensed much of the lower-end technology to regions such as China and India, where labor costs less and/or there are import quotas. The US will remain a leader in electrical test and measuring instruments, although competition is increasing from Europe in communications test equipment and from Japan in automated test equipment.

Government Agencies

Consumer Product Safety Commission (CPSC)
Washington, DC 20207
Tel: (301) 504-0100, 504-0580 Fax: (301) 504-0124

International Trade Administration (ITA)
Office of Energy, Environment and Infrastructure
14th St. and Constitution Ave. NW
Washington, DC 20230
Tel: (202) 482-5225

International Trade Administration (ITA)
Office of Services, Industries, and Finance
14th St. and Constitution Ave. NW
Washington, DC 20230
Tel: (202) 482-5261

International Trade Administration (ITA)
Office of Materials, Machinery, and Chemicals
14th St. and Constitution Ave. NW
Washington, DC 20230
Tel: (202) 482-0575

International Trade Administration (ITA)
Office of Microelectronics, Medical Equipment, and Instrumentation
14th St. and Constitution Ave. NW
Washington, DC 20230
Tel: (202) 482-2587

Trade Associations

American Hardware Manufacturers Association
931 N. Plum Grove Road
Schaumburg, IL 60173
Tel: (708) 605-1025 Fax: (708) 605-1093

Equipment Manufacturers Institute
10 S. Riverside Plaza, Suite 1220
Chicago, IL 60606
Tel: (312) 321-1480

Fabricators and Manufacturers Association
International
833 Featherstone Road
Rockford, IL 61107
Tel: (815) 399-8700 Fax: (815) 399-7279

International Electrical Testing Association
221 Red Rocks Vista Drive
Morrison, CO 80465
Tel: (303) 467-0526

Publications

American Machinist
Penton Publishing Co.
826 Broadway
New York, NY 10003
Tel: (212) 477-6420

Chilton's Hardware Age
Instrumentaion & Control Systems
Instrumentation & Automation News
(Monthly)
Chilton
Chilton Way
Radnor, PA 19089
Tel: (215) 964-4225 Fax: (215) 964-4251

Hardware Trade
(Bimonthly)
Master Publications
225 E. Cheyenne Mountain Blvd.
Colorado Springs, CO 80906

Intech
Instrument Society of America Services, Inc.
PO Box 12277
Research Triangle Park, NC 27709
Tel: (919) 549-8411

Machine Design
1100 Superior Ave.
Cleveland, OH 44114-2543
Tel: (216) 248-1125

Robotics World
Communication Channels, Inc.
6151 Powers Ferry Road NW
Atlanta, GA 30339
Tel: (404) 955-2500

Trade Fairs

Refer to the "Trade Fairs" chapter for complete listings, including contact information, dates, and venues. Trade fairs with particular relevance to this industry include the following, which are listed under the headings given below:

Electronics & Engineering
- Instrument Soc. of America International Conference and Exhibition
- National Design Engineering Show & Conference

- Nepcon
- Surface Mount International

Machinery & Manufacturing
- Autofact
- Fabtech International Exposition & Conference
- Metalform 95
- National Manufacturing Week
- National Plant Engineering and Maintenance Show & Conference

Medical & Dental
- Abilities Expo
- American Academy of Dermatology Annual Meeting
- American College of Cardiology Annual Scientific Session
- American College of Surgeons Clinical Congress
- American Dental Assn. Annual Meeting
- American Hospital Assn.
- American Lung Assn./American Thoracic Soc. International Conference
- American Soc. of Clinical Oncology
- Annual Meeting of the American Academy of Ophthalmology
- International Vision Expo & Conference West
- Medical Design & Manufacturing West
- Radiological Society of North America

Merchandising
- National Hardware Show

TOYS, SPORTING GOODS, AND PHOTOGRAPHY EQUIPMENT

The toys, sporting goods, and photography equipment industries are all affected by the changing demographics and available discretionary income of consumers. As industries, they must compete with countries with lower production costs for labor intensive products.

Photography Equipment

Photography equipment product shipments increased almost 2 percent in 1993 to about US$19.5 billion. Some 29 percent of the domestic market was supplied by imports. About 18 percent of products shipped were exported. Asia supplies 71 percent of US imports, with Japan alone accounting for 61 percent of imports.

Products Photography equipment includes still and motion picture cameras, photo finishing equipment, photocopy and microfilm equipment, sensitized film, photographic paper, and prepared photographic chemicals.

Competitive Situation The industry's diverse array of products for consumers, businesses, and industry has helped it to sustain itself during recent periods of sluggish demand. Current growth is driven by some of the industry's most competitive products, such as single use cameras and high-end copiers. New products—cameras, films, and items that incorporate electronic imaging—also stimulate demand. But growth patterns have been affected by generally soft economies in the US and in many foreign markets, and by increased competition for disposable personal income from consumer electronics products and other leisure goods and services.

US companies continue to dominate the market for copier models with speeds above 90 copies per minute (CPM), but their share of the market for 70 to 90 CPM machines declined to 60 percent in 1992 from 72 percent in 1990. A similar market share decline occurred in the midrange segment, down to 36 percent from 44 percent during the same period.

In consumer photography, there has been growth in the market for the 35-mm lens shutter (LS) cameras, but sales of the 35-mm single lens reflex (SLR) cameras declined nearly 20 percent. Imports supply the entire US market for 35-mm SLRs. The most popular film format continues to be 35-mm, which accounts for nearly 90 percent of all film sold in the US. The most popular film speed is 200 ISO, with 43 percent of the market, while the 24 exposure roll represents 74 percent of retail unit sales. The single use camera has become one of the fastest-growing products in the photographic industry, with sales up 24 percent to about 26 million units in 1993, following a 40 percent surge in 1992.

Sporting Goods

Product shipments of US sporting goods reached about US$7.3 billion in 1993. Some 31 percent of the domestic market, or about US$2.7 billion worth of goods, was supplied by imports; 20 percent of the total products shipped, or about US$1.5 billion worth of goods, were exported.

Products The sporting goods and athletic equipment industries produce equipment for archery, bowling, billiards, fishing, golf, gymnastics, physical fitness, tennis, winter sports, and team sports.

Competitive Situation The production of many sporting goods products is labor intensive, so US sporting goods firms have moved production from the US to countries where the cost of labor is lower. However, US manufacturers produce much of the highest-quality golf equipment in the world and export much of it to Japan, the top export country for sporting goods. Canada has been the second largest foreign market for US sports equipment. Exercise and golf equipment make up an important part (about 46 percent) of US exports of sports equipment to Canada. Opportunities for US exports of sports equipment will be opening up in Latin America and East Asia. In particular, the demand for US sports equipment is expected to increase in Mexico. NAFTA reduces high tariffs on sports equipment.

Certain demographic trends are affecting the industry. The baby boom generation is reaching its age of its highest disposable income and is expected to begin purchasing high-quality sporting goods for themselves and their children. Although a number of baby boomers may be slowing down because of age, they are also being encouraged by the medical establishment to stay active and fit, which should result in continued use of sporting goods.

Toys

Industry shipments for the toy industry in 1993 were valued at about US$4.2 billion. Three-quarters of all toys sold in the US are manufactured, either wholly or partly, overseas. However, exports are playing an increasing role in the profitability of US toy companies. While imports have increased 35 percent and US product shipments rose 13 percent since 1989, exports have almost doubled. Three product categories accounted for almost half of all US toy exports: video games, toys without spring mechanisms, and doll and toy parts, primarily for assembly elsewhere and reexport to the US.

In recent years, the popular press has discussed the trend in the industry to go back to producing "basic" toys, but this is something of a misconception because these industry staples (or "basic" toys) never really go out of style.

Products Toy products include video games, dolls, action figures, construction sets, board games, and puzzles.

Competitive Situation Although the major toy companies appear to dominate the export market, many small companies have realized the positive aspects of exports, particularly small specialty toy manufacturers producing high-quality educational and wooden toys. But the major companies still make greatest impact. With the announcement that Nintendo and Silicon Graphics are joining forces to produce three-dimensional video games, the US video game industry could experience tremendous growth over the next five years. Video games now rank first in both exports (21 percent of total US toy exports) and imports (30 percent of total US toy imports).

Two major factors affect the demand for toys: disposable personal income and the number of children between the ages of 5 and 14. Although the number of children under 5 years of age will drop between 1994 and 1998, those in the 5 to 14 age group will rise at slightly more than 1 percent compounded annually during the same period. Long-term disposable income is also expected to increase at a rate of about 2.5 percent annually.

The passage of the Uruguay Round of GATT is expected to enhance international trade in toys, and NAFTA will also increase US trade with Canada and Mexico, which are now the two largest export markets for US toys.

A growing concern for the toy industry is the necessity for meeting new government safety standards. Increasingly, manufacturers must add warning labels on toys intended for children three to six years of age if those toys contain small parts. There are also provisions requiring choking hazard warning labels for balloons, marbles, and small balls.

Government Agencies

Consumer Product Safety Commission (CPSC)
Washington, DC 20207
Tel: (301) 504-0100, 504-0580 Fax: (301) 504-0124

International Trade Administration (ITA)
Office of Consumer Goods
14th St. and Constitution Ave. NW
Washington, DC 20230
Tel: (202) 482-0337

Trade Associations

Hobby Industry Association of America
319 East 54th St.
Elmwood Park, NJ 07407
Tel: (201) 794-1133

International Minilab Association
2627 Grimsley St.
Greensboro, NC 27403
Tel: (919) 854-8088 Fax: (919) 854-8566

National Golf Foundation
1150 South US Highway One
Jupiter, FL 33477
Tel: (407) 744-6006 Fax: (407) 744-6107

National Sporting Goods Association
1699 Wall St.
Mount Prospect, IL 60056
Tel: (708) 439-4000 Fax: (708) 439-0111

United Ski Industries Association
8377-B Greensboro Dr.
McLean, VA 22102
Tel: (703) 556-9020

Publications

Action Sports Retailer Magazine
(Monthly)
Miller Freeman Publications
31652 Second Ave.
S. Laguna, CA 92677
Tel: (714) 499-5374

Athletic Business Magazine
(Monthly)
1846 Hoffman St.
Madison, WI 53704
Tel: (608) 249-0186 Fax: (608) 249-1153

Industrial Photography
Photographic Processing
Photographic Trade News
(Monthly)
PTN Publishing
445 Broad Hollow Rd.
Melville, NY 11747
Tel: (516) 845-2700 Fax: (516) 845-7109

NGSA Retail Focus
(Monthly)
National Sporting Goods Association
1699 Wall St.
Mt. Prospect, IL 60056
Tel: (708) 439-4000 Fax: (708) 430-0111

Photo Business
(Monthly)
BPI Communications
1515 Broadway
New York, NY 10036
Tel: (212) 764-7300 Fax: (212) 536-5351

Playthings
Geyer-McAllister Publications, Inc.
51 Madison Ave
New York, NY 10010
Tel: (212) 689-4411

Sporting Goods Business
Gralla Publications
1515 Broadway
New York, NY 10036
Tel: (212) 869-1300

Sports Trend
Shore Communications Inc.
Suite 300, N Building
180 Allen Rd. NE
Atlanta, GA 30328
Tel: (404) 252-8831

Toy and Hobby World International
A4 International Publications
41 Madison Ave.
New York, NY 10010
Tel: (212) 685-0404

Trade Fairs

Refer to the "Trade Fairs" chapter for complete listings, including contact information, dates, and venues. Trade fairs with particular relevance to this industry include the following, which are listed under the headings given below:

Merchandising
- American International Toy Fair
- Toy Show

Photography
- International Exposition of Professional Photography & National Industrial Conference
- Photo
- Photographic Convention & Trade Show
- Prolab

Sporting Goods, Recreation & Travel
- Action Sports Retailer Trade Expo—West
- DEMA Trade Show
- National Sporting Goods Assn. World Sports Expo
- NSPI's International Expo
- SIA Ski & Sports Show
- Sport Fishing Expo
- Super Show

VEHICLES AND VEHICLE PARTS

The motor vehicle and parts industry is a key component of the US economy. It is dominated by the Big Three vehicle manufacturers—General Motors, Ford, and Chrysler. The entire industry accounts for a substantial percentage of direct and indirect employment and industrial output in the US. An estimated 6.7 million persons were employed directly and in allied automotive industries in the US in 1991. Auto manufacturing employed nearly one-fifth—an estimated 1.2 million—of these. Manufacturers of motor vehicles and equipment generated annual shipments valued at US$236 billion in 1992, nearly 16 percent of all shipments in the durable goods industries and 8 percent of all product shipments in the manufacturing sector. Excluding related services and nondurables (such as the US$103 billion spent for gasoline and oil), purchases of vehicles and vehicle parts represent 5 percent of the public's total consumption expenditures.

Vehicles

After suffering large financial losses in the late 1980s, the US auto industry has been propelled on a painful, but generally beneficial, path to reduce operating expenditures through improvements in manufacturing technology and productivity and reductions in overhead expenses. In 1982 productivity was 22 vehicles per worker. By 1992 it had grown to 30 vehicles per worker. Quality has also improved. US buyers have finally begun to recognize the improved quality, pricing, and fuel economy of Big Three vehicles.

In 1992 total net sales and revenue rose for the first time since 1989, and the US had an estimated trade deficit in motor vehicles of US$43 billion in 1993, 12 percent higher than in 1992. As has been the case for many years, most of the auto deficit is the result of trade with Canada and Mexico—where General Motors, Ford, and Chrysler operate plants producing vehicles for the US market—and with Japan.

In 1992 the US ranked second to Japan in producing passenger cars, light trucks, and commercial motor vehicles. For that year, US production was 9.7 million units, 20.7 percent of the world's total output (Japan's share was 26.7 percent, or 12.5 million units). Japan's industry has been hurt recently by the relationship of the yen to the dollar and by US competitive pricing. In South Korea and Mexico, motor vehicle production has shown strong growth, each having nearly tripled its share of the world market since 1986, reaching 1.7 million units and 1.1 million units, respectively, in 1992.

Products The US manufacturers produce passenger cars, light trucks, and medium- and heavy-duty trucks.

Competitive Situation The US market for new passenger cars and light trucks is essentially saturated. There is little prospect that annual growth on a long-term basis will be much more than 1 to 2 percent. Despite, or perhaps because of, this situation, competition in the US among foreign and domestic manufacturers is growing even more intense. In 1993 US purchasers could choose from among 31 major domestic and foreign manufacturers offering 337 separate car and 143 separate light truck models, almost all of them superior in most respects to previous models. Moreover, virtually all of today's new vehicles were developed and brought to market more quickly than in the 1980s and were manufactured more efficiently and with less negative impact on the environment.

General Motors, Ford, and Chrysler have initiated several jointly funded product and manufacturing technology research projects under the umbrella of the United States Council for Automotive Research (USCAR). Instead of focusing on the design or production of specific vehicles, USCAR pursues the developments of generic, fundamental technologies to bring vehicles to the market sooner and at less cost to customers and the environment. In 1993 President Clinton proclaimed a major new undertaking involving the US government and industry to develop, within 10 years, a new generation of vehicles having up to three times greater fuel efficiency than now exists and more efficiency in manufacturing.

The industry continues its research and development of vehicles that will not contribute to environmental pollution. It hopes to develop engines that run on alternative fuels, including ethanol and methanol mixtures combined with gasoline, liquid natural gas, and liquid petroleum gas. The Big Three and the US Department of Energy are also researching improved battery storage technology designed to make the introduction of electric cars feasible. This is difficult: the first vehicles to market would cost from US$6,000 to US$10,000 more than comparable gasoline engine vehicles, and the need to replace the battery storage system at the end of three or four years could add another US$5,000 or more to the cost. The automakers' quest for environmentally friendly vehicles with improved fuel economy and less pollution has led to the development of production materials that are significantly lighter and recyclable. Composite materials, a mix of plastics with glass and carbon fibers or other substrates, are being used increasingly as substitutes for metal.

The domestic market in 1993 continued to exhibit what well may be a fundamental shift toward light trucks (sport utilities, minivans, and pickups) and away from station wagons and sedans. The strength of the light truck market segment was responsible for most of the growth in the overall motor vehicle market; light trucks supplied 38 percent of the US market in 1993.

The battle for the US market will exert some limited downward pressure on prices. However, more stringent safety, environmental, and fuel economy regulations may well be introduced and, if so, are likely to increase manufacturer costs and raise prices more rapidly than the average rate of inflation. Producers will thus have additional impetus to maximize manufacturing productivity and keep costs under control. Labor relations will become increasingly important to the industry. This is especially true since vehicle assembly operations are becoming more vulnerable to system-wide disruption by local strikes.

Virtually all competitive, high-volume vehicle and parts manufacturers worldwide have become significant players in the US market, and more are coming. Both BMW and Mercedes-Benz are planning to operate vehicle assembly plants in the US, in 1995 and 1997, respectively. South Korea's Kia motors began establishing a West Coast sales network in 1993 and introduced its compact sedan in 1994, to be followed by a sport utility model. However, this intense competition has also forced some corporations to pull out of the market, including Great Britain's Sterling, France's Peugeot, and the former Yugoslavia's Yugo.

A sea change now appears to be underway in US export efforts, fostered perhaps by the realization that the US market is fully mature while many emerging foreign markets have the potential for exponential growth well into the next century. Contributing greatly to Detroit's export prospects is the development of models with heightened international appeal, notably greater product quality, and significantly improved price competitiveness because of more efficient manufacturing techniques and much more favorable exchange rates. US medium and heavy-duty truck exports, once marginal, now play an important role in the US automotive industry. All the major truck companies have either begun or plan to expand their export markets.

In spite of the high stakes and the large market, the environment is not completely competitive. Each one of the Big Three US automakers has agreed to a number of cooperative manufacturing and marketing ventures with Japanese automakers.

Automotive Parts

In 1993 the US automotive parts industry produced about US$100.9 billion worth of goods. The estimated 1993 trade deficit in automotive parts was US$3.7 billion, compared with a deficit of US$5.1 billion in 1992. The parts industry is now recovering from a period of increased losses since 1989, when major US suppliers saw a sharp drop in profits due to lack of demand, pricing pressures from Detroit, and foreign competition. However, the recovery has brought a new determination and success in improving manufacturing products and efficiency.

The automotive parts industry is divided into tiers. First tier firms deal with the motor vehicle manufacturers directly, while second tier firms in turn supply the first tier groups.

Products Automotive parts and accessories include automotive stampings, carburetors, pistons, piston rings, and valves; vehicular lighting equipment; storage batteries; engine electrical equipment; and motor vehicle parts and accessories. The industry has two primary sectors: original equipment (OE) suppliers, which produce parts for automakers; and aftermarket parts manufacturers, which produce replacement parts for vehicles.

Competitive Situation Increased global competition has transformed US parts firms into world-class suppliers in terms of cost structure, global manufacturing position, and trade performance. These firms have discovered that the competitive products they now are making as original equipment for domestic and foreign vehicles manufactured in the US and for the local retail aftermarket have excellent export potential. In addition, Japanese-owned vehicle manufacturers are increasing their reliance on US-made components for use in both their US and Japanese plants.

As automakers continue to reduce the number of first tier suppliers they deal with—in order to achieve greater leverage on price and supply issues—US parts producers are being asked to supply more modular units (systems of integrated components that can be installed into a vehicle as a unit). The industry also will see a move toward "commonization" of parts, as automakers work to achieve production flexibility and significantly lower costs by designing various car models with a high percentage of common parts. As a result, many small suppliers may go out of business in the coming years, and the US$60 billion to US$80 billion supplier industry will probably witness a number of mergers and acquisitions. The trade performance of the US automotive parts industry should continue to improve during the rest of the 1990s. It is likely that US suppliers will see continued increases in the volume of trade, especially with Mexico.

Also, NAFTA will provide US suppliers improved access to the growing Mexican market, as well as the opportunity to structure their overall North American manufacturing operations to maximize quality and international cost competitiveness. Successful completion and implementation of the Uruguay Round of GATT should afford US automotive parts suppliers increased market access to about 100 countries that are GATT signatories. The anticipated accessions of China and Taiwan to GATT should also help US parts producers to gain a stronger foothold in these markets, which are currently dominated by the Japanese.

Government Agencies

Consumer Product Safety Commission (CPSC)
Washington, DC 20207
Tel: (301) 504-0100, 504-0580 Fax: (301) 504-0124

Department of Transportation (DOT)
400 7th St. SW
Washington, DC 20590
Tel: (202) 366-4000, 366-5580

Environmental Protection Agency (EPA)
401 M St. SW
Washington, DC 20460
Tel: (202) 260-2090, 260-2080

Federal Highway Administration (FHA)
400 7th St. SW
Washington, DC 20590
Tel: (202) 366-4000, 366-0660

International Trade Administration (ITA)
Office of Automotive Affairs
14th St. and Constitution Ave. NW
Washington, DC 20230
Tel: (202) 482-0554

National Highway Traffic Safety Administration
(NHTSA)
400 7th St. SW
Washington, DC 20590
Tel: (202) 366-4000, 366-9550

Trade Associations

American Trucking Association
2200 Mill Road
Alexandria, VA 22314
Tel: (703) 838-1700 Fax: (703) 684-5720

Automotive Industry Action Group
26200 Lasher Road, Suite 200
Southfield, MI 48034
Tel: (313) 258-3570 Fax: (313) 358-3253

Automotive Parks and Accessories Association
4600 East-West Highway, 3rd Fl.
Bethesda, MD 20814
Tel: (301) 654-6664 Fax: (301) 654-3299

Automotive Service Association
1901 Airport Freeway, Suite 100
Bedford, TX 76095
Tel: (817) 283-6205 Fax: (817) 685-0225

Automotive Service Industry Association
25 Northwest Point
Elk Grove Village, IL 60007
Tel: (708) 228-1310 Fax: (708) 228-1510

National Automobile Dealers Association
8400 Westpark Drive
McLean, VA 22102
Tel: (703) 827-7407 Fax: (703) 821-7075

National Industrial Transportation League
1700 N. Moore St., Suite 1900
Arlington, VA 22209
Tel: (703) 524-5011

Publications

Automotive Industries (Monthly)
Chilton's Automotive Marketing (Monthly)
Chilton's Motor Age (Monthly)
Chilton
Chilton Way
Radnor, PA 19089
Tel: (215) 964-4225 Fax: (215) 964-4251

Automotive News
(Weekly)
Crain Communications
1400 Woodbridge
Detroit, MI 48207
Tel: (313) 446-6000

Ward's Auto World (Monthly)
Ward's Automotive International (Twice monthly)
Ward's Automotive Reports (Weekly)
Ward's Automotive Yearbook (Annual)
Ward's Communications
28 W. Adams St.
Detroit, MI 48226
Tel: (313) 962-4433 Fax: (313) 962-5593

Trade Fairs

Refer to the "Trade Fairs" chapter for complete listings, including contact information, dates, and venues. Trade fairs with particular relevance to this industry include the following, which are listed under the heading given below:

Automotive & Transportation
- Dealernews International Powersports Dealers Expo
- International Trucking Show
- Mid-America Trucking Show
- National Automobile Dealers Assn. Convention & Equipment Exposition
- SAE International Congress & Exposition
- Specialty Equipment Market Assn./ Auto International Assn.

Trade Fairs

INTRODUCTION

The US hosts a enormous range of trade fairs and expositions that will interest anyone seeking to do business in the country's huge, dynamic, and expanding economy. Whether the aim is to buy US goods or offer your own goods and services for sale in the US, you will almost undoubtedly find several trade fairs that suit your purposes. The US is also a major site for international trade fairs attended by companies from all over the world, attracting exhibitors and buyers from many other countries as well.

There are literally thousands of trade fairs held across the US every year; the number of US fairs has increased by a third, the number of attendees by 42 percent, and exhibitors by 30 percent, just since 1989. Exhibitions have increased their share of total marketing expenditures faster than any other major medium in the past 10 years. There is intense competition for both the attendee and exhibitor dollar, which has led to some industry shifts that are worth noting. Multimedia booth displays have become increasingly common. US trade fair attendees have come to expect eye-catching, sophisticated displays, so that tired or outdated-looking booths will likely be passed by, particularly at large fairs that have thousands of booths to choose from. Attendees have higher expectations from the personnel staffing booths as well. These attendees are more likely than in years past to have actual decision-making authority, and are interested in being able to have detailed discussions about the products or services being exhibited. The average attendee receives far more information on an everyday basis than even a few years ago, so a trade fair is an opportunity for higher-level, specific information gathering, not just to superficially survey the market. Some see a trend at US trade shows toward a more European approach of setting up booths that are designed as small business centers rather than simply as large presentations.

Trade fairs are held across the US in a wide variety of locations. The most popular site in recent years has been Chicago—the city is centrally located in the Midwest and boasts an enormous convention center built around the 2.5 million square foot McCormick Place. The other top 10 cities in 1994, according to statistics from the Trade Show Bureau, were New York City; Atlanta, Georgia; Las Vegas, Nevada; Dallas, Texas; Orlando, Florida; Anaheim, California; Washington, DC; and San Francisco, California. (Disney World and Disney Land, with extensive hotel and convention facilities, are located in Orlando and Anaheim, respectively.) The states seeing the most growth in the number of trade fairs hosted are Minnesota, Kansas, and Missouri, all located in the Midwest.

The listing of trade fairs in this section is designed to acquaint you with the scope, size, frequency, and length of the events held in the US as well as to give you contact information for major organizers. This list has been compiled with the generous assistance of *The Exhibit Review*. It is by no means comprehensive because of the vast number of trade fairs held in the US every year. Instead, we have tried to include most of the biggest fairs held on a regular basis in the US, most of which are not open to the general public. While every effort has been made to ensure that the information given is correct and complete as of press time, the scheduling of such events is in constant flux. Announced exhibitions may be canceled; dates and venues are often shifted. If you are interested in attending or exhibiting at a show listed here, we urge you to contact the organizer well in advance to confirm the venue and dates and to ascertain whether the event is appropriate for you. (*See* "Tips for Attending a Trade Fair," following this introduction, for further suggestions on selecting, attending, and exhibiting at trade fairs.) When you are deciding whether to participate in a trade fair—as an exhibitor or as an attendee—the information in this chapter will give a significant head start.

In order to give you the easiest possible access to this information, fairs have been grouped alphabetically by product category, and within product category, alphabetically by name. Product categories, with cross-references, are listed in a table of contents following the introduction. When appropriate, fairs have been listed in more than one category. The breadth of products on display at a given fair means that you may want to investigate categories that are not immediately obvious. Many exhibits include the machinery, tools, and raw materials used to produce the products associated with the central theme of a fair. Anyone interested in such items should review a wide range of listings.

The list gives the names and dates of 1995 events, along with frequency, site, and contact information, and a description. Even if the date has already passed for a show in which you are interested, you should be able to determine the approximate dates for the next one, based on the frequency. Most major shows are held on approximately the same dates either every year or every other year. Determination of the site is more difficult; some fairs are always held in the same location, while others move to a different site every year.

As you gather further information on fairs that appeal to you, do not be surprised if the names are slightly different from those listed here. Some large trade fairs include several smaller exhibits, and some use short names or acronyms. Dates and venues, of course, are always subject to change.

FOR FURTHER INFORMATION

If you are looking for current trade show listings in general, the quarterly publication *The Exhibit Review* is a valuable resource; it also provides a custom report service with updated listings of trade fairs in any country that the periodical covers. The majority of listings in *The Exhibit Review* are for US events, but the publication has been expanding its international coverage and now lists many outside the US as well. The Trade Show Bureau is a research and promotion organization for the exposition industry and has a wide range of publications and reports available which can help increase the efficacy of a trade fair for both attendees and exhibitors. The Bureau published a report in 1994 entitled "A Guide to the US Exposition Industry" which may be of particular interest.

If you are already traveling to a particular area you may want to contact the Visitors and Convention Bureau of that city or state to find out whether there are any shows of interest during or around the time of your visit. Other valuable sources of information include the US and Foreign Commercial Service Officers at US embassies, chambers of commerce in the US, other business organizations dedicated to trade between your country and the US, and the embassy or consulates of your own country located in the US. Professional and trade orga-

nizations in the US involved in your area of interest may also be worth contacting. The US Department of Commerce magazine *Business America* publishes an annual list in its mid-December issue of international trade fairs of interest to US exporters, including information on which are Commerce Department Certified Trade Fairs. (Refer to the "Important Addresses" chapter for US embassies, consulates, chambers of commerce, business organizations, and diplomatic missions located in the US, as well as trade organizations.)

USEFUL ADDRESSES

Publications

Annual Trade Show Directory
Trade Show and Convention Guide
Forum Publishing Company
383 E. Main St.
Centerport, NY 11721, USA
Tel: [1] (516) 754-5000

Business America
(Monthly)
US Government Printing Office
Superintendent of Documents
Washington, DC 20402, USA
Tel: [1] (202) 512-1800
Fax: [1] (202) 512-2550

Directory of North American Fairs, Festivals, and Expositions
Amusement Business
BPI Communications
49 Music Square West
Nashville, TN 37203, USA
Tel: [1] (615) 321-4250
Fax: [1] (615) 327-1575

The Exhibit Review
(Quarterly)
PO Box 5808
Beaverton, OR 97006-0808, USA
Tel: [1] (503) 244-8677
Fax: [1] (503) 244-8745

Trade Shows Worldwide
(Annual)
Gale Research
PO Box 33477
Detroit, MI 48232-5477, USA
Tel: [1] (312) 961-2242, (800) 877-4253
Fax: (800) 414-5043

Organization

The Trade Show Bureau
1660 Lincoln St., Suite 2080
Denver, CO 80264, USA
Tel: [1] (303) 860-7626
Fax: [1] (303) 860-7479

TIPS FOR ATTENDING TRADE FAIRS

Trade fairs can be extremely effective for making face-to-face contacts and sales or purchases, identifying suppliers, checking out competitors, and finding out how business really works in the host country. However, the cost of attending or exhibiting at such fairs can be high. To maximize the return on your investment of time, money, and energy, you should be very clear about your goals for the trip and give yourself plenty of time for advance research and preparation.

You should also be aware of the limitations of trade fairs. The products on display probably do not represent the full range of goods available on the market. In fact, some of the latest product designs may still be under wraps. While trade fairs give you an opportunity to make face-to-face contacts with many people, both exhibitors and buyers are rushed, which makes meaningful discussions and negotiations difficult.

These drawbacks can easily be minimized if you have sufficient preparation and background information. Allow several months for preparation—more if you first need to identify the fair that you should attend. Even under ideal circumstances, you should begin laying the groundwork a year in advance. Don't forget that exhibiting at or attending a fair in a foreign country means more complex logistics: numerous faxes and phone calls involving you, the show operator, and local support people, plus customs and transportation delays.

Participating in international trade fairs, particularly at the outset, should be considered a means of fulfilling long-term goals. At domestic fairs, you may exhibit on a regular basis with short-term sales and marketing goals. But at a foreign fair, it is often best to participate as a way to establish your company, make contacts for the future, and learn more about a market, its consumers, and products. New exporters may not generate high sales, but they often come away with information that assists them with future marketing and product development.

Selecting an appropriate trade fair

Consult the listings of trade fairs in this book to find some that interest you. Note the suggestions in this chapter for finding the most current calendars of upcoming fairs. Once you have identified some fairs, contact the organizers for literature, including a show prospectus, attendee list, and exhibitor list. Ask plenty of questions! Be sure not to neglect trade organizations in the host country, independent show-auditing firms, and recent attendees or exhibitors. Find out whether there are "must attend" fairs for your particular product group. Fairs that concentrate on other, but related, commodities might also be a good match. Be aware that there may be preferred seasons for trade in certain products.

Your research needs to cover a number of points:

Audience • Who is the intended audience? Is the fair open to the public or to trade professionals only? Are the exhibitors primarily foreigners looking for local buyers or locals looking for foreign buyers? (Many trade fairs are heavily weighted to one or the other; others may be so oriented to local activity that they may not be equipped to cater to international businesspeople.) Decide whether you are looking for an exposition of general merchandise produced in one region, a commodity-specific trade show, or both. Are you looking for a "horizontal"—one that covers a wide range of products—or a "vertical" show—one that covers those involved in the production and marketing of a narrow range of products through all stages of the process?

Statistics • How many people attended the fair the last time it was held? What were the demographics? What volume of business was done? How many exhibitors were there? How big is the exhibition space? What was the ratio of foreign to domestic attendees and exhibitors?

Specifics • Who are the major exhibitors? Are any particular publications or organizations associated with the fair? On what categories of products does the fair focus? Does the fair have a general theme or a changing theme? How long has the fair been in existence? How often is it held? Is it always in the same location, or does it move each

TIPS FOR ATTENDING TRADE FAIRS (cont'd.)

time? How much does it cost to attend? Are there any separate or special programs connected with the event, and do they require additional entrance fees? What does it cost to rent space?

Before you go

• If you have not already spoken with someone who attended the fair in the past, be sure to find someone who will give you advice, tips, and general information.

• Make your reservations and travel arrangements well in advance, and figure out how you are going to get around once you get there. Even if the fair takes place in a large city, do not assume that getting around will be easy during a major trade fair. If the site is in a small city or a less-developed area, the transportation and accommodation systems are likely to become overburdened sooner than in metropolitan areas.

• Will you need an interpreter for face-to-face business negotiations? A translation service to handle documents? Try to line up providers well in advance of your need for their services.

• For printed materials, pay attention to language barriers and make preparations that will help you overcome them. Assess your literature and decide what should be available in translation or in bilingual editions. Have the translation work done by a true professional, particularly if technical terms are used. Consider having a bilingual business card, and add the country and international dialing code information to the address and telephone number. Find out from the show organizers which countries will be represented, and prepare information in the languages of those countries as well, if necessary.

• Do you need hospitality suites and/or conference rooms? Reserve them as soon as you can.

• Contact people you would like to meet before you go. Organize your appointments around the fair.

• Familiarize yourself with the show's hours, locations (if exhibits and events are staged at multiple venues), and the schedule of events. Then prioritize.

While you are there

• Wear businesslike clothes that are comfortable. Find out what the norm is for the area and the season.

• Immediately after each contact, write down as much information as you can. Do not depend on remembering it. Several companies now make inexpensive portable business card scanners with optical character recognition (OCR) software to read the information into a contact management program.

• Qualify your prospects before launching into a full presentation. Are you dealing with the right person? Ask open-ended questions to find out his or her true interests.

• Consider arriving a day early to get fully oriented, confirm appointments, and rest up.

• It is common sense: make sure you take breaks, even if you have to schedule them. You'll end up having far more energy and being more effective.

After the fair

• Within a week after the fair, write letters to new contacts and follow up on requests for literature. If you have press releases and questionnaires, send them out quickly as well. Even better, send these leads back to your office while you are still at the fair so that your new contacts receive literature on their return home.

• Write a report evaluating your experiences while they are still fresh in your mind. Even if you don't have to prepare a formal report, spend some time organizing your thoughts on paper for future reference. Aim to quantify the results. Did you meet your goals? Why or why not? What would you do differently? What unforeseen costs or problems arose?

• With your new contacts and your experiences in mind, start preparing for your next trade fair.

If you are selling

• Familiarize yourself with import regulations for products that you wish to exhibit at the fair.

• Set specific goals for sales leads, developing product awareness, selling and positioning current customers, and gathering industry information. For example, target the numbers of contacts made, orders written, leads converted into sales, visitors at presentations, brochures or samples distributed, customers entertained, and seminars attended. You can also set goals for total revenue from sales, cost-to-return benefit ratio, amount of media coverage, and amount of competitor information obtained.

• Review your exhibitor kit. Is there a show theme that you can tie into? Pay particular attention to the show's hours and regulations, payment policies, shipping instructions and dates, telephone installation policies, security, fire regulations, and extra-cost services.

• Find out about the labor situation. Is it unionized, and what are the regulations? Will you have to hire your own workers to set up and break down the booth, or can the organizer or showcase facility provide them for you?

• Gear your advertising and product demonstrations to the expected target audience. Should you stress certain aspects of your product line? Will you need brochures and banners in different languages? Even if you do not need to translate the materials currently in use into another language, will you need to rewrite them for a different culture? Consider advertising in publications that will be distributed at the fair.

• Plan the display in your booth carefully; you will have only a few seconds to grab the viewer's attention. Secure a location in a high-traffic area—for example, near a door, a restroom, a refreshment area, or a major exhibitor. For banners use copy that is brief and effective. Focus on the product and its benefits. Place promotional materials and giveaways near the back wall so that people have to enter your area, but make sure that they do not feel trapped. If you plan to use videotapes or other multimedia, make sure that you have enough space. Remember to ascertain whether you will need special equipment or equipment designed for different electrical current. Such presentations may be better suited to hospitality suites, because lights are bright and noise levels high in exhibition halls.

• Attend to the details. Order office supplies and printed materials that you will need for the booth. Have all your paperwork—order forms, business cards, exhibitor kit and contract, copies of advance orders and checks, travel documents, and so on—in order and at hand. If you ordered a telephone line, obtain your own host-country compatible telephone or arrange to rent one. Draw up a schedule for staffing the booth.

• Plan and rehearse your sales pitch in advance, preferably in a space similar to the size of your booth.

• *Don't:* sit, read, smoke, eat, or drink in the booth; badmouth your competitors or complain about the show; ignore prospects while chatting with colleagues; stand with your back to the aisle or lean on booth furniture.

• If you plan to return to the next show, reserve space while you are still on-site.

If you are buying

• Familiarize yourself with customs regulations on the products that you seek to purchase and import into your own country or elsewhere. Be sure to get such information on any and all products in which you might be interested.

• Set specific goals for supplier leads and for gathering industry information. For example, target the numbers of contacts made, leads converted to purchases, seminars and presentations attended, and booths visited. Other goals might be cost-to-return benefit ratio, amount of competitor information gathered, and percentage of projected purchases actually made.

• List all the products that you seek to purchase, their specifications, and the number of units you plan to purchase of each.

• Know the retail and wholesale market prices for the goods in your home country and in the country where you will be buying. List the highest price you can afford to pay for each item and still get a worthwhile return.

• List the established and probable suppliers for each of the products or product lines that you plan to import. Include addresses and telephone numbers and note your source for the information. Before you go, contact suppliers to confirm who will attend and to make appointments.

TRADE FAIRS
TABLE OF CONTENTS

Note: These listings are based on information provided by The Exhibit Review, Beaverton, Oregon.

Trade Fair	Site/Date	Contact

AGRICULTURE, HORTICULTURE & FISHING

Trade Fair	Site/Date	Contact
Eastern Regional Nurserymen's Trade Show Annual January 10–13, 1995 Kiamesha Lake, NY Concord Resort Hotel	Complete line of horticultural goods, products and services, and educational sessions. Attendees include association members plus industry professionals. 6,000+ attendees; 665 booths	Horticultural Associates Inc. 24 West Rd., Suite 53 Vernon, CT 06066 Tel: (203) 872-2095 Fax: (203) 872-6596
Fish Expo Annual *October 1995 Seattle, WA Seattle Center	Latest in commercial fishing equipment and electronics specifically for the commercial fisherman, including vessels, machinery, refrigeration, insurance, and more. 24,000+ attendees; 768 exhibitors	Diversified Expositions PO Box 7437 Portland, ME 04112-7437 Tel: (207) 772-3005 Fax: (207) 772-5059
International Pet Expo Every 2 years *October 1995 Las Vegas, NV	Exhibits of pet care products, foods, equipment and services. 6,000 attendees; 600 booths	Western World Pet Supply Assn., Inc. 406 S. First Ave. Arcadia, CA 91006-3829 Tel: (818) 447-2222 Fax: (818) 447-8350
International Workboat Show Annual *December 1995 New Orleans, LA New Orleans Conv. Center	Trade show for the workboat trades, featuring equipment, electronics, boat building and repair, port and shoreside services, offshore services, engines, machinery. 12,000+ attendees; 700+ booths	Diversified Expositions PO Box 7437 Portland, ME 04112-7437 Tel: (207) 772-3005 Fax: (207) 772-5059
Mid-Am Horticultural Trade Show Annual January 19–21, 1995 Chicago, IL	A trade show with educational sessions. Attendees include association members plus industry professionals. 8,650+ attendees; 650+ booths	Mid-America Trade Show 1000 Rand Rd., Suite 214 Wauconda, IL 60084 Tel: (708) 526-2010 Fax: (708) 526-3993
Mid-Atlantic Nurserymen's Trade Show (Winter) Annual January 4–6, 1995 Baltimore, MD	Association trade show with all types of horticultural materials, including tools, equipment, and plant material. 6,500 attendees; 750 booths	Mid-Atlantic Nurserymen's Trade Show PO Box 314 Perry Hall, MD 21128 Tel: (301) 256-6474 Fax: (301) 256-2208
National Cattlemen's Assn. Convention & Trade Show Annual January 25–28, 1995 Nashville, TN	Exhibits of livestock, machinery, and animal health products directly related to beef cattle production. 5,000 attendees; 450 booths	National Cattlemen's Assn. PO Box 3469 Englewood, CO 80155 Tel: (303) 694-0305 Fax: (303) 694-2851
Pacific Horticultural Trade Show Annual September 1–2, 1995 San Diego, CA San Diego Conv. Center	Association trade show with educational sessions. Attendees include association members plus industry professionals. 7,000+ attendees; 725 exhibitors	California Assn. of Nurserymen 4620 Northgate Blvd., Suite 155 Sacramento, CA 95834-1123 Tel: (916) 567-1133 Fax: (916) 567-0505
Southern Nurserymen's Assn. Horticultural Trade Show & Convention Annual August 4–6, 1995 Atlanta, GA Georgia World Congress Center	A complete assortment of horticultural and lawn and garden products; attendees include association members plus industry professionals. 10,000 attendees; 1,250+ booths	Southern Nurserymen's Assn., Inc. 1000 Johnson Ferry Rd., Suite E130 Marietta, GA 30068-2100 Tel: (404) 973-9026 Fax: (404) 973-9097
United Fresh Fruit & Vegetable Assn. Annual Convention & Exposition Annual February 5–7, 1995 Anaheim, CA Anaheim Conv. Center	Exhibits of all items related to the produce industry, including seeds, packaging machinery and products, fresh produce, labeling, software, insurance, commodity groups, etc. 8,000 attendees; 375 exhibitors	Convention Mgmt. Group 3918 Prosperity Ave., Suite 102 Fairfax, VA 22031 Tel: (703) 876-0300 Fax: (703) 876-0904

Trade Fair	Site/Date	Contact

APPAREL, ACCESSORIES & JEWELRY

Trade Fair	Site/Date	Contact
Fashion Accessories Expo 3 times a year January 8–10, 1995 May 7–9, 1995 *Third date TBA New York, NY Piers 90 & 92	2,000+ lines of international and designer accessories, including fashion and fine jewelry, small leather goods, handbags, scarves, and hosiery. 14,000 attendees; 755 booths	Conference Mgmt. Corp. 200 Connecticut Ave. Norwalk, CT 06856-4990 Tel: (203) 852-0500 Fax: (203) 838-3710
Gem & Lapidary Dealers Assn. 2 times a year February 4–11, 1995 *September 1995 Tucson, AZ Holiday Inn City Center	Exhibits of wholesale gems and jewelry. 28,000 attendees; 400 booths	G.L.D.A. PO Box 2391 Tucson, AZ 85702 Tel: (602) 742-5455 Fax: (602) 544-0715
Imprinted Sportswear Show 6 times a year *January: Long Beach, CA *February: Tampa, FL *March: Philadelphia, PA *July: Chicago, IL *October: Dallas, TX *Other dates/locations TBA	Trade show with educational programs for T-shirt and activewear retailers, textile screen printers, embroideries, and sporting goods dealers. The show includes advertising specialties and graphic arts systems. 5,000+ attendees; 500+ booths	The Imprinted Sportswear Shows 13760 Noel Rd., Suite 500 Dallas, TX 75240 Tel: (800) 527-0207, (214) 239-3060 Fax: (214) 419-7855
International Fashion Boutique Show 5 times a year January 7–10, 1995 March 18–21, 1995 *Other dates TBA New York, NY	Seasonal marketplace attended by buyers from department stores, boutiques and specialty stores for women's apparel, accessories, footwear, jewelry, gifts. 30,000 attendees; 1,800 booths	The Larkin Group 100 Wells Ave. Newton, MA 02159 Tel: (617) 964-5100 Fax: (617) 964-0657
International Footwear Expo Every 2 years April 4–6, 1995 New York, NY The Piers	The show is geared toward footwear and related accessory firms. 12,000+ attendees; 500 exhibitors	International Expositions Mgmt. Group, Ltd. 50 Glen St. Glen Cove, NY 11542 Tel: (516) 674-0200 Fax: (516) 674-0288
International Kids Fashion Show 4 times a year January 15–18, 1995 March 19–22, 1995 *Other dates TBA New York, NY	A marketplace for manufacturers and retailers of children's apparel, accessories, footwear, and juvenile products to meet and do business. 20,000 attendees; 1,000 booths	The Larkin Group 485 7th Ave., Suite 1400 New York, NY 10018 Tel: (212) 594-0880 Fax: (212) 594-8556
JA International Jewelry Show 2 times a year February 5–7, 1995 July 23–26, 1995 New York, NY	Exhibits of fine jewelry, precious stones and watches. 10,000+ attendees; 1,400 exhibitors	Blenheim Fashion Shows Fort Lee Executive Park One Executive Drive Fort Lee, NJ 07024 Tel: (201) 346-1400 Fax: (201) 346-1532
Jewelers International Showcase 2 times a year *January 1995 *October 1995 Miami Beach, FL	Worldwide manufacturers and wholesalers exhibit jewelry-related products to jewelry trade buyers from the US, Caribbean, Latin America. 6,000 attendees; 400 booths	Jewelers International Showcase 13501 SW 128th St., Suite 114 Miami, FL 33186-5862 Tel: (305) 253-6160 Fax: (305) 255-0228
National Bridal Market 2 times a year April 22–25, 1995 October 14–18, 1995 Chicago, IL Chicago Apparel Center	Attendees are wholesale and retail merchandise buyers. 5,000 attendees	Merchandise Mart Properties, Inc. 470 The Merchandise Mart Chicago, IL 60654 Tel: (312) 527-7610 Fax: (312) 527-7998

Trade Fair	Site/Date	Contact
Western Shoe Associates International Buying Market 2 times a year February 21–23, 1995 August 13–15, 1995 Las Vegas, NV Las Vegas Conv. Center	Men's, women's and children's shoes and accessories and handbags. 9,000 attendees; 750 booths	Western Shoe Associates 1040 E. Wardlow Long Beach, CA 90807 Tel: (310) 427-5168 Fax: (310) 427-2541
Women's & Children's Apparel Market 5 times a year *January 1995 *April 1995 *Other dates TBA Dallas, TX	Designer, junior, missy, plus children's wear, intimate apparel, bridal accessories, shoes, activewear, sportswear, western wear, outerwear, large sizes, and maternity. 15,000+ attendees; 1,200 booths	International Apparel Mart—Dallas 2100 Stemmons Freeway Dallas, TX 75207 Tel: (214) 749-5468 Fax: (214) 655-6238
Women's, Children's, and Men's Markets 4 times a year January 13–17, 1995 June 2–6, 1995 August 25–29, 1995 November 3–7, 1995 Chicago, IL Chicago Apparel Center	Attendees are wholesale and retail merchandise buyers. 7,000 attendees	Merchandise Mart Properties, Inc. 470 The Merchandise Mart Chicago, IL 60654 Tel: (312) 527-7610 Fax: (312) 527-7998

ARTS, CRAFTS & HOBBIES

Art Buyers Caravan Annual September 16–18, 1995 Atlanta, GA	Fine and decorative art and picture framing. All media are represented. 10,000 attendees; 300 booths	Commerce Publishing Co. 330 N. Fourth St. St. Louis, MO 63102 Tel: (314) 421-5445 Fax: (314) 421-1070
Art Chicago 95 Annual *September 1995 Chicago, IL Navy Pier	Exhibition of fine arts, including paintings, sculpture, graphics, and works on paper. 20,000 attendees; 150 exhibitors	International Fine Art Expositions 3725 SE Ocean Blvd., Suite 201 Stuart, FL 34996 Tel: (407) 220-2690 Fax: (407) 220-3180
Chicago Craft & Creative Industries Show & Convention Annual July 21–24, 1995 Rosemont, IL O'Hare Exposition Center	Exhibits of craft supplies, including raw materials, ribbons, unpainted wood, paint supplies, baskets, needlework, floral, framing, supplies, notions, miniatures, and kits. 10,000 attendees; 1,300 booths	Offinger Mgmt. Co. PO Box 2188 Zanesville, OH 43702-2188 Tel: (614) 452-4541 Fax: (614) 452-2552
Hobby Industry of America Show Annual Jan. 29–Feb. 1, 1995 Anaheim, CA	For buyers. Exhibits include crafts, aromatics, art materials, ceramics, collector items, dollhouse miniatures, florals, framing materials, instructional videos, home and personal decor, and needle arts. 7,000 attendees; 1,660 booths	Hobby Industry of America PO Box 348 Elmwood Park, NJ 07407 Tel: (201) 794-1133 Fax: (201) 797-0657

AUTOMOTIVE & TRANSPORTATION

Dealernews International Powersports Dealers Expo Annual February 18–20, 1995 Cincinnati, OH Albert B. Sabin Conv. Center	An industry only show focusing on the wholesale and retail motorcycle market. 12,000 attendees; 500 exhibitors	Advanstar Expositions 201 E. Sandpointe Ave., Suite 600 Santa Ana, CA 92707-5761 Tel: (714) 513-8400 Fax: (714) 513-8481
International Trucking Show Annual June 29–July 1, 1995 July 25–27, 1996 Anaheim, CA	Attendees include for-hire fleet operators, owner-operators, private carriers, public utilities, rental, leasing firms, suppliers. 30,000 attendees; 600 booths	Independent Trade Show Mgmt. 1155A Chess Dr., Suite C Foster City, CA 94404 Tel: (415) 349-4876 Fax: (415) 349-5169

Trade Fair	Site/Date	Contact
Mid-America Trucking Show Annual March 23–25, 1995 Louisville, KY	Exhibits of all products and services related to the heavy-duty trucking industry. 40,000+ attendees; 702+ booths	Exhibit Mgmt. Associates, Inc. 3038 Breckenridge Lane, Suite 101 Louisville, KY 40220 Tel: (502) 458-4487 Fax: (502) 473-0574
National Automobile Dealers Assn. Convention & Equipment Exposition Annual February 11–14, 1995 Dallas, TX Dallas Conv. Center	Provides an annual marketplace for equipment, services, and supplies that the franchised new car dealer would utilize in the everyday operation of the dealership. 20,000 attendees; 2,000 booths	National Automobile Dealers Assn. 8400 Westpark Dr. McLean, VA 22102 Tel: (703) 827-7407 Fax: (703) 821-7075
SAE International Congress & Exposition Annual February 27–March 3, 1995 Detroit, MI Cobo Center	Industrial exposition with tech session program for suppliers of components, systems, materials, testing facilities, and parts to OEMs in the automotive industry. 35,000 attendees; 600+ exhibitors	Society of Automotive Engineers, Inc. 400 Commonwealth Dr. Warrendale, PA 15096 Tel: (412) 776-4841 Fax: (412) 776-0002
Specialty Equipment Market Assn./ Auto International Assn. Annual October 24–27, 1995 Las Vegas, NV Las Vegas Conv. Center	Specialty automotive, performance, and racing parts and accessories for import vehicles. Products include street performance, pickup, van, RV, off-road, race cars, sports trucks and imports parts and accessories. 22,000+ attendees; 3,400 booths	Epic Enterprises 8989 Rio San Diego Dr., Suite 160 San Diego, CA 92108-1647 Tel: (619) 294-2999 Fax: (619) 294-6699

BUSINESS SERVICES & MARKETING

Trade Fair	Site/Date	Contact
Europe-California Business to Business Expo Annual April 6–7, 1995 Anaheim, CA Anaheim Conv. Center	Exhibits from business services, finance, insurance, computers, health care, marketing, advertising, media, hospitality, communications, transportation, real estate, and manufacturing. 12,000 attendees; 350+ exhibitors	Expoforum 23011 Moulton Parkway, Suite E-10 Laguna Hills, CA 92653 Tel: (714) 453-0555 Fax: (714) 453-0570
Exhibit Industry Conference and Exposition Annual July 19–22, 1995 San Francisco, CA Moscone Conv. Center	The trade show for the corporate exhibit manager, with exhibits of products, services, resources, and display systems for trade show exhibitors. 5,000 attendees; 250 exhibitors	Convention Mgmt. Group 3918 Prosperity Ave., Suite 102 Fairfax, VA 22031 Tel: (703) 876-0300 Fax: (703) 876-0904
Exhibitor Show '95, The National Conference on Trade Show Marketing Annual February 13–19, 1995 Las Vegas, NV	Exhibits of exhibit design and production, installation and dismantling services, transportation, portable and modular exhibit systems. 3,500 attendees; 400 booths	Hall-Erickson, Inc. 150 Burlington Ave. Clarendon Hills, IL 60514 Tel: (708) 850-7779, (800) 752-6312 Fax: (708) 850-7843
International Selling & Marketing Expo Annual May 2–4, 1995 New York, NY Jacob Javits Conv. Center	Marketing show, featuring promotion, marketing, direct mail, and database marketing products and services and market research. 14,000+ attendees	Miller Freeman, Inc. 1515 Broadway New York, NY 10036 Tel: (212) 869-1300 Fax: (212) 768-0015
Licensing Show Annual June 20–22, 1995 New York, NY New York Hilton	International forum and marketplace for the licensing industry. 8,000 attendees; 200 booths	Expocon Mgmt. Associates, Inc. 363 Reef Rd. PO Box 915 Fairfield, CT 06430-0915 Tel: (203) 256-4700 Fax: (203) 256-4730
Motivation Show Annual September 19–21, 1995 Chicago, IL McCormick Place North	Incentive and premium products and services from major domestic and international companies. 37,000 attendees; 2,000 exhibitors	Hall-Erickson, Inc. 150 Burlington Ave. Clarendon Hills, IL 60514 Tel: (708) 850-7779 Fax: (708) 850-7843

Trade Fair	Site/Date	Contact
POPAI Marketplace Annual October 24–26, 1995 New York, NY Jacob Javits Conv. Center	Exhibition of products and services for point-of-purchase advertising. 9,000+ attendees; 400+ booths	Point of Purchase Advertising Institute 66 N. Van Brunt St. Englewood, NJ 07631 Tel: (201) 894-8899 Fax: (201) 894-0622
Specialty Advertising Assn. International SA/Showcase 2 annual locations Jan. 29–Feb. 3, 1995: Dallas, TX August 1–3, 1995: Chicago, IL	Exhibitors are importers, manufacturers, converters, and assemblers of specialty advertising products; attendees are wholesale level distributor members, qualified nonmembers. 14,000/5,000 attendees; 2,450/890+ booths	SAAI 3125 Skyway Circle North Irving, TX 75038 Tel: (214) 252-0404 Fax: (214) 659-0404

CHEMICALS & PLASTICS

Trade Fair	Site/Date	Contact
Chem Show '95 Every 2 years December 4–7, 1995 New York, NY Jacob K. Javits Center	Process and pollution control equipment, controls, instruments, supplies, materials, packaging equipment, component parts. 18,000 attendees; 700 exhibitors	International Exposition Co. 15 Franklin St. Westport, CT 06880-5903 Tel: (203) 221-9232 Fax: (203) 221-9260
Plastics/USA 95 Every 3 years September 12–14, 1995 Chicago, IL McCormick Place East	Exhibition of machinery, equipment, products and services for the plastics industry. 15,000 attendees; 500+ exhibitors	Hall-Erickson, Inc. 150 Burlington Ave. Clarendon Hills, IL 60514 Tel: (708) 850-7779 Fax: (708) 850-7843

COMPUTERS & COMMUNICATIONS

Trade Fair	Site/Date	Contact
CAD & Engineering Workstations '95 & Business Graphics '95 Annual April 24–28, 1995 Philadelphia, PA	Exhibits of the latest technology in computer graphics hardware, software, and peripheral products. 20,000+ attendees; 200 booths	National Computer Graphics Assn. 2722 Merrilee Dr., #200 Fairfax, VA 22031-4499 Tel: (800) 225-NCGA Fax: (703) 560-2752
Cellular Telecommunications Industry Assn. Winter Meeting & Exposition Annual February 1–3, 1995 New Orleans, LA	A marketplace for cellular telecommunications and related industries. 6,000 attendees; 700 booths	Dobson & Associates, Ltd. 1225 19th St., NW, Suite 310 Washington, DC 20036 Tel: (202) 775-3606 Fax: (202) 775-3604
Comdex/Fall Annual November 13–17, 1995 Las Vegas, NV Sands Expo & Conv. Center	Volume resellers and value adders of small computers, peripherals, software, etc. 175,000 attendees; 2,200 exhibitors	The Interface Group 300 First Ave. Needham, MA 02194-2722 Tel: (617) 449-6600 Fax: (617) 449-6953
Comdex/Spring Annual April 24–27, 1995 Atlanta, GA Georgia World Congress Center	Exhibits from worldwide manufacturers of small computer systems, peripherals, software, etc. 100,000 attendees; 1,100 exhibitors	The Interface Group 300 First Ave. Needham, MA 02194-2722 Tel: (617) 449-6600 Fax: (617) 449-6953
DECUS Interoperability/ Open Systems Shows 2 times a year May 16–18, 1995 *Other date TBA Atlanta, GA	Event focusing on digital platform and multiple platform environments with DEC related marketplace. 6,000+ attendees; 425 booths	Talley Management Group 875 Kings Hwy., Suite 200 W. Deptford, NJ 08096 Tel: (609) 384-6287 Fax: (609) 853-0411
Enterprise Computing Solutions Exposition & Conference Annual August 1–3, 1995 Chicago, IL McCormick Place	Exhibited technologies will include client/server computing, distributed databases, local and wide area networks, network management and interoperability, and open systems. 20,000+ attendees; 150+ exhibitors	The Interface Group 300 First Ave. Needham, MA 02194-2722 Tel: (617) 449-6600 Fax: (617) 449-6953

Trade Fair	Site/Date	Contact
Image World Chicago featuring Video Expo and The CAMMP Show 3 annual locations May 16–18, 1995: Chicago, IL Sept. 19–21, 1995: New York Dec. 12–14, 1995: Orlando, FL	Trade show and seminar program; exhibits are of video production, computer animation, graphics, multi-media, and presentation products and services. 7,000+/20,000/7,000 attendees; 150 to 200+ exhibitors	Knowledge Industry Publications, 701 Westchester Ave. White Plains, NY 10604 Tel: (800) 800-5474, (914) 328-9157 Fax: (914) 328-9093
International Conference & Exposition on Multimedia and CD-ROM Annual *March 1995 San Francisco, CA Moscone Conv. Center	Developers and buyers of multimedia and CD-ROM hardware, software, and titles discuss and announce standards for the industry and products for the marketplace. 12,600 attendees; 175 exhibitors	Reed Exhibition Companies 383 Main Ave. PO Box 6059 Norwalk, CT 06852-6059 Tel: (203) 840-4800 Fax: (203) 840-4804
International Wireless Communications Expo/Spring Annual April 25–27, 1995 Las Vegas, NV Sands Expo & Conv. Center	The exhibit hall showcases mobile and portable radios, paging equipment, cellular phones and accessories, test equipment, and more. 6,000 attendees; 325 exhibitors	Argus Trade Shows 6151 Powers Ferry Rd., NW Atlanta, GA 30339-2941 Tel: (800) 828-0420 Fax: (404) 618-0441
MacWorld Expo 3 annual locations Jan. 4–7, 1995: San Francisco Apr. 26–28, 1995: Washington Aug. 8–11, 1995: Boston, MA	A show for business, professional, governmental, and general users of Macintosh computers, their products, and services. Open to the public. 65,0000/TBA/49,000+ attendees 500+/TBA/400+ exhibitors	Mitch Hall Associates. 260 Milton St. Dedham, MA 02026 Tel: (617) 361-8000 Fax: (617) 361-3389
Network + Interop 2 annual locations Mar. 28–30, 1995: Las Vegas Sept. 27–29, 1995: Atlanta, GA	A leading networking summit, addressing the entire scope of network computing in a single comprehensive event. Open to the public. 65,000/65,000 attendees; 600/500+ exhibitors	Softbank Expo & Conference Co. 303 Vintage Park Drive Foster City, CA 94404-1138 Tel: (415) 578-6900 Fax: (415) 525-0194
Network World Unplugged Annual/new event April 11–13, 1995 New York, NY New York Hilton and Towers	Exhibition of products, services, computer hardware, and software relating to remote computing and wireless networking. 10,000 attendees; 120 exhibitors	World Expo Corp. PO Box 9107 Framingham, MA 01701-9107 Tel: (508) 820-8662 Fax: (508) 872-8237
Networks Expo 2 annual locations Feb. 14–16, 1995: Boston, MA Hynes Conv. Center Sept. 12–14, 1995: Dallas, TX Dallas Conv. Center	Exhibits of computer networking and connectivity, products, and services. 30,000+/39,000+ attendees; 365+/495+ exhibitors	Bruno Blenheim, Inc. Fort Lee Executive Park One Executive Drive Fort Lee, NJ 07024 Tel: (201) 346-1400 Fax: (201) 346-1532
New Media Expo Annual March 14–16, 1995 Los Angeles, CA Los Angeles Conv. Center	A wide variety of hardware platforms, communications gear, consumer electronics, and infotainment software. 20,000 attendees; 200 exhibitors	The Interface Group 300 First Ave. Needham, MA 02194-2722 Tel: (617) 449-6600 Fax: (617) 449-6953
OS/2 World Conference & Exhibition Annual July 18–21, 1995 Boston, MA Hynes Conv. Center	Exhibits feature OS/2 applications and development tools, multimedia, networking, and hardware products. 18,000 attendees; 250+ booths	Miller Freeman Inc. 600 Harrison St. San Francisco, CA 94107 Tel: (415) 905-2200 Fax: (415) 905-2239
PC Expo 2 annual locations June 20–22, 1995: New York Jacob Javits Conv. Center Oct. 3–5, 1995: Chicago, IL McCormick Place East	Displays of computer hardware and software, including portable computers, graphical user interface applications, networking, multimedia technologies, computer services and training. 98,999+/33,000+ attendees; 800+/230 exhibitors	Bruno Blenheim, Inc. Fort Lee Executive Park One Executive Drive Fort Lee, NJ 07024 Tel: (201) 346-1400 Fax: (201) 346-1532

Trade Fair	Site/Date	Contact
Supercomm 95 Annual March 20–23, 1995 Anaheim, CA Anaheim Conv. Center	Attracts a diverse audience of manufacturers, suppliers, users, and providers of telecommunications. 23,000+ attendees; 500 exhibitors	SMS & EJK 7315 Wisconsin Ave., Suite 450 N Bethesda, MD 20814 Tel: (301) 986-7800 Fax: (301) 986-4538
UNIX Expo Annual September 26–28, 1995 New York, NY Jacob Javits Conv. Center	Exhibits include UNIX/open systems products, software, hardware, application development tools, peripherals, services, publications. 35,000 attendees; 450 exhibitors	Bruno Blenheim, Inc. Fort Lee Executive Park One Executive Drive Fort Lee, NJ 07024 Tel: (201) 346-1400 Fax: (201) 346-1532
Windows World 95 3 annual locations April 24–27, 1995: Atlanta, GA August 1–3, 1995: Chicago, IL Sept. 12–14, 1995: Dallas, TX	Exhibits include enhancement packages, software tools, multimedia software and components, hardware systems, utilities; plus vendors for memory and machine upgrades, networking and other related products and services 100,000/20,000/10,000 attendees; 1,100/150+/100+ exhibitors	The Interface Group 300 First Ave. Needham, MA 02194-2722 Tel: (617) 449-6600 Fax: (617) 449-6953

CONSTRUCTION & BUILDING MATERIALS

A/E/C Systems 2 annual locations June 5–8, 1995: Atlanta, GA Georgia World Congress Center *October 1995: Chicago, IL Navy Pier	Principal exhibits are computer hardware and software for the construction industry, including scheduling, estimating, design and office, and project management systems. 10,000/30,000 attendees; 500/1,750 booths	A/E/C Systems, Inc. One Farron Dr. Chadds Ford, PA 19317 Tel: (215) 444-9690 Fax: (215) 444-9583
Builders Show Annual January 27–30, 1995 Houston, TX Astrodomain Complex	Annual convention and exposition for professionals in the home building industry. 60,000+ attendees; 1,000 booths	National Assn. of Home Builders 1201 15th St., NW Washington, DC 20005-2800 Tel: (800) 368-5242, (202) 822-0200 Fax: (202) 861-2104
Construction Specifications Institute Annual Convention and Exhibit Annual June 23–25, 1995 Minneapolis, MN	Exhibits of building products and services used in commercial construction. 10,000+ attendees; 1,025+ booths	Construction Specifications Institute 601 Madison St. Alexandria, VA 22314 Tel: (703) 684-0300 Fax: (703) 684-0465
International Air-Conditioning, Heating, Refrigerating Exposition Annual Jan. 30–Feb. 1, 1995 Chicago, IL McCormick Place	Products of manufacturers in the HVAC and refrigeration industry, including commercial, industrial, residential, and institutional applications. 34,000+ attendees; 1,000 exhibitors	International Exposition Co. 15 Franklin St. Westport, CT 06880-5903 Tel: (203) 221-9232 Fax: (203) 221-9260
Multi-Housing World/ Kitchen/Bath Industry Show Annual April 28–30, 1995 New Orleans, LA Earnest N. Morial Conv. Center	Products used in kitchen/bath construction and remodeling and any materials used in multi-housing residential construction. 25,000 attendees; 3,000+ booths	Miller Freeman, Inc. 13760 Noel Rd., Suite 500 Dallas, TX 75240 Tel: (800) 527-0207, (214) 239-3060 Fax: (214) 419-7985
National Assn. of the Remodeling Industry Annual February 23–25, 1995 Indianapolis, IN	Attendees include primary buyers of remodeling equipment, materials, and services from across the nation and abroad. 15,000+ attendees; 1,000 booths	PTN Publishing 445 Broad Hollow Rd. Melville, NY 11747 Tel: (516) 845-2700 Fax: (516) 845-7109
World of Concrete Annual January 11–13, 1995 New Orleans, LA Ernest N. Morial Conv. Center	An international exposition and conference on construction with seminars and live demonstrations. 20,000+ attendees; 850+ exhibitors	The Aberdeen Group 426 S. Westgate Addison, IL 60101 Tel: (708) 543-0870 Fax: (708) 543-3112

Trade Fair	Site/Date	Contact

ELECTRONICS & ENGINEERING

Electro Annual April 4–6, 1995 Edison/Somerset, NJ	Products include EDA tools; test, measurement and inspection instruments; production materials; active components, passive and electro-mechanical components. 25,000 attendees; 800 booths	Electronic Conventions Mgmt. 8110 Airport Blvd. Los Angeles, CA 90045 Tel: (310) 215-3976 Fax: (310) 641-5117
Instrument Soc. of America International Conference and Exhibition Annual October 2–5, 1995 New Orleans, LA	A marketplace and educational forum for manufacturers of industrial instrumentation, measurement, and control systems. 35,000 attendees; 725 booths	Instrument Soc. of America 67 Alexander Dr. Research Triangle Park, NC 27709 Tel: (919) 990-9209 Fax: (919) 549-8288
Southcon, Annual March 7–9, 1995: Atlanta, GA **Midcon**, Annual Sept. 12–14, 1995: Chicago, IL **Northcon**, Annual Oct. 10–12, 1995: Portland, OR **Wescon**, Annual Nov. 7–9, 1995: San Francisco	High-tech electronics exposition and conference for OEMs, focusing on product design; attendees include circuit and packaging designers, manufacturing, research and development engineers and managers, and purchasing personnel. 6,000/10,000/8,000/45,000 attendees; 250/350/340/1,300 booths	Electronic Conventions Mgmt. 8110 Airport Blvd. Los Angeles, CA 90045 Tel: (310) 215-3976 Fax: (310) 641-5117
National Design Engineering Show & Conference Annual March 13–16, 1995 Chicago, IL McCormick Place North	Exhibits of mechanical, electro-mechanical products, engineered materials, systems, services, CAD/CAM. 28,700+ attendees; 1,004 exhibitors	Reed Exhibition Companies 383 Main Ave. PO Box 6059 Norwalk, CT 06852-6059 Tel: (203) 840-4800 Fax: (203) 840-4804
Nepcon 2 annual locations Feb. 28–March 2, 1995: Anaheim, CA Anaheim Conv. Center June 13–15, 1995: Boston, MA Bayside Exposition Center	Exhibition on equipment and technology for the design, fabrication, assembly, packaging, and testing of printed circuits and electronic assemblies. 35,600+/14,900+ attendees; 300/375 exhibitors	Reed Exhibition Companies 383 Main Ave. PO Box 6059 Norwalk, CT 06852-6059 Tel: (203) 840-4800 Fax: (203) 840-4804
Surface Mount International Annual August 29–31, 1995 San Jose, CA San Jose Conv. Center	Show and conference devoted to surface mount component, circuit board printing, equipment, and user communities. 7,000 attendees; 300 exhibitors	Miller Freeman, Inc. 600 Harrison St. San Francisco, CA 94107 Tel: (415) 905-2200 Fax: (415) 905-2239

ENTERTAINMENT & AMUSEMENTS

Electronic Entertainment Expo Annual/new event May 11–13, 1995 Los Angeles, CA Los Angeles Conv. Center	Electronic entertainment software to target top level buyers, publishers, international rights owners, press, and the financial community. 35,000+ attendees; 450 exhibitors	Infotainment World/Knowledge Industry Publications 951 Mariner's Island Blvd. San Mateo, CA 94404 Tel: (415) 349-4300 Fax: (415) 349-7482
International Gaming Business Exposition Annual March 20–22, 1995 Las Vegas, NV Sands Expo & Conv. Center	National and international companies display products, services, and technologies available to the casino gaming industry. 5,000 attendees; 180 booths	Conference Mgmt. Corp. 200 Connecticut Ave. Norwalk, CT 06856-4990 Tel: (203) 852-0500 Fax: (203) 838-3710
Lighting Dimensions International Annual November 19–21, 1995 Miami, FL	Exhibits of lighting, sound, and special effects equipment for clubs, concerts, theater, television, theme parks, and film. 6,000 attendees; 650 booths	Events Production Group, Inc. 135 Fifth Ave. New York, NY 10010 Tel: (212) 677-5997 Fax: (212) 677-3857

Trade Fair	Site/Date	Contact
SBCA Satellite Show 2 annual locations Feb. 16–18, 1995: Phoenix, AZ July 27–29, 1995: Nashville, TN	Exhibition for the home satellite television industry featuring dishes, receivers and TV programmers. 6,000 at each attendees; 450 booths	Show Mgmt. & Services, Inc. 900 Jorie Blvd., Suite 220 Oak Brook, IL 60521 Tel: (708) 990-2070 Fax: (708) 990-2077
Video Software Dealers Assn. **Annual Convention** Annual *July 1995 Las Vegas, NV	Exhibitors include manufacturers of prerecorded video, accessory products and related media. 12,500 attendees; 350 booths	Video Software Dealers Assn. 303 Harper Dr. Moorestown, NJ 08057 Tel: (609) 231-7800 Fax: (609) 231-9791
Winter NAMM International **Music Market** Annual January 20–23, 1995 Anaheim, CA	Exhibition for the music industry, including musical instruments, accessories, stage lighting, and sound. 43,000 attendees; 800 booths	National Assn. of Music Merchants 5140 Avenida Encinas Carlsbad, CA 92008 Tel: (619) 438-8001 Fax: (619) 438-7327

ENVIRONMENTAL & ENERGY

Trade Fair	Site/Date	Contact
Hazmacon Annual April 4–6, 1995 San Jose, CA San Jose Conv. Center	Trade show featuring products and services for all aspects of hazardous materials management, with conference. 9,000 attendees; 250 exhibitors	SHO, Inc. 444 Castro St., Suite 1015 Mountain View, CA 94041 Tel: (415) 964-2050 Fax: (415) 964-2246
Hazmat 2 annual locations June 14–16, 1995: Philadelphia, PA Philadelphia Conv. Center November 7–9, 1995: Long Beach, CA Long Beach Conv. Center	Exhibition of products and services for hazardous materials management, pollution abatement and control, hazardous waste disposal, environmental management, emergency response, and environmental remediation. 10,000/12,000 attendees; 700 booths	Advanstar Exhibitions 800 Roosevelt Rd., Bldg. E, Suite 408 Glen Ellyn, IL 60137-5835 Tel: (708) 469-3373 Fax: (708) 469-7477
Offshore Technology **Conference & Exhibition** Annual May 1–4, 1995 Houston, TX Astrodome USA	Exhibitors are manufacturers and suppliers of technical products and services utilized in offshore resources, recovery, and development. 35,000+ attendees; 1,300+ exhibitors	Soc. of Petroleum Engineers PO Box 833836 Richardson, TX 75083-3836 Tel: (214) 952-9393 Fax: (214) 952-9435
Oilheat Business & Industry **Exposition, 25th Biennial** Every 2 years June 6–8, 1995 Boston, MA	Largest oilheat expo; exhibits of burners, boilers, furnaces, and related services, plus A/C and environmental products, water heaters, tank trucks, office equipment, computer systems. 10,000 attendees; 326 booths	New England Fuel Institute 20 Summer Street PO Box 888 Watertown, MA 02272 Tel: (617) 924-1000 Fax: (617) 924-1022
SPE Annual Technical **Conference & Exhibition** Annual October 22–25, 1995 Dallas, TX Dallas Conv. Center	Exhibiting companies represent manufacturers and suppliers of petroleum exploration, production, drilling and refining equipment and services. 9,000+ attendees; 400+ exhibitors	Soc. of Petroleum Engineers PO Box 833836 Richardson, TX 75083-3836 Tel: (214) 952-9393 Fax: (214) 952-9435
Waste Expo Annual April 26–28, 1995 Chicago, IL	For public officials and private companies; manufacturers and firms who buy equipment and services, recyclers, and waste processors; and waste-to-energy companies. 12,000 attendees; 450 booths	National Solid Wastes Mgmt. Assn. 1730 Rhode Island Ave., NW Washington, DC 20036 Tel: (202) 659-4613 Fax: (202) 296-7915

FOOD, BEVERAGES & HOSPITALITY

Trade Fair	Site/Date	Contact
Food & Dairy Expo Every 2 years October 14–18, 1995 Chicago, IL	Displays of products and services for the food, dairy, beverage, and pharmaceutical processing industries. 22,000 attendees; 550 exhibitors	Dairy and Food Industries Supply Assn. 6245 Executive Blvd. Rockville, MD 20852-3938 Tel: (301) 984-1444 Fax: (301) 881-7832

Trade Fair	Site/Date	Contact
International Boston Seafood Show Annual March 14–16, 1995 Boston, MA Hynes Conv. Center	Trade show for buyers from around the world, featuring the latest in seafood products and services. 18,000+ attendees; 720+ exhibitors	Diversified Expositions PO Box 7437 Portland, ME 04112-7437 Tel: (207) 774-0076 Fax: (207) 772-5059
International Exposition For Food Processors Annual *November 1995 Chicago, IL	Exhibition of the latest technology in food and beverage processing machinery and supplies. 25,000 attendees; 500 booths	Food Processing Machinery & Supplies Assn. 200 Daingerfield Rd., Suite 300 Alexandria, VA 22314 Tel: (703) 684-1080 Fax: (703) 548-6563
International Fancy Food & Confection Show 2 annual locations *March 1995: San Diego, CA San Diego Conv. Center July 9–12, 1995: New York, NY Jacob Javits Conv. Center	A trade show featuring gourmet and specialty foods, confections, beverages, cookware, and accessories. 30,300+/21,000+ attendees; 1,200/800+ exhibitors	Assn. Expositions & Services Div. of Reed Exhibition Companies 383 Main Ave., PO Box 6059 Norwalk, CT 06852-6059 Tel: (203) 840-4820 Fax: (203) 840-4824
International Hotel/Motel & Restaurant Show Annual November 11–14, 1995 New York, NY Jacob K. Javits Conv. Center	A broad spectrum of products and services used by the hospitality and restaurant industries; attendees are representatives from mass feeding, lodging, and health care industries. 62,500 attendees; 1,450 exhibitors	George Little Mgmt., Inc. 10 Bank St. White Plains, NY 10606 Tel: (914) 421-3220
International Meat Industry Convention & Exposition Every 2 years September 21–24, 1995 Chicago, IL McCormick Place	Food processing and distribution, environmental services, seasonings and ingredients, safety, packaging, slaughtering, transportation, sanitation, and laboratory testing. 7,000 attendees; 410 booths	Convention Mgmt. Group, Inc. 3918 Prosperity Ave., Suite 102 Fairfax, VA 22031 Tel: (703) 876-0300 Fax: (703) 876-0904
Las Vegas International Hotel, Restaurant and Gaming Exhibition Annual June 28–30, 1995 Las Vegas, NV Las Vegas Conv. Center	Exhibition of equipment, products, supplies and services for the hospitality and gaming industries. 6,000 attendees; 250 exhibitors	Corcoran Associates 33 N. Dearborn, Suite 505 Chicago, IL 60605 Tel: (312) 541-0567, (800) 541-0359 Fax: (312) 541-0573
NAFEM Educational Exhibition Every 2 years September 14–17, 1995 Las Vegas, NV Las Vegas Conv. Center	Attendees include owners, buyers, managers, other professionals in the food service and hospitality industry. Exhibitors are NAFEM members. 16,000+ attendees; 1,900 booths	National Assn. of Food Equipment Manufacturers 401 N. Michigan Chicago, IL 60611 Tel: (312) 644-6610 Fax: (312) 245-1080
NAMA National Convention and Trade Show Annual *1995 dates TBA Chicago, IL	Exhibits of food, beverage and general merchandise vending machines and products sold in them. 8,000 attendees; 650 booths	National Automatic Merchandising Assn. 20 N. Wacker Dr., Suite 3500 Chicago, IL 60606-3102 Tel: (312) 346-0370 Fax: (312) 704-4140
Produce Marketing Assn. Annual Convention and Exposition Annual October 13–17, 1995 San Diego, CA	Convention and trade show devoted to fresh fruits and vegetables. Includes professional development program of workshops and general sessions. 9,500+ attendees; 1,100 booths	Produce Marketing Assn. PO Box 6036 Newark, DE 19714-6036 Tel: (302) 738-7100 Fax: (302) 732-2409
Restaurant and Hotel-Motel Show Annual May 20–24, 1995 Chicago, IL McCormick Place	Attendees include food service and hospitality professionals from all 50 states and approximately 70 foreign countries. 101,000+ attendees; 1,800+ exhibitors	National Restaurant Assn. 150 N. Michigan Avenue, Suite 2000 Chicago, IL 60601 Tel: (312) 853-2525 Fax: (312) 853-2548

Trade Fair	Site/Date	Contact
Sea Fare International Annual September 20–22, 1995 Long Beach, CA Long Beach Conv. Center	International seafood exhibition, with exhibits from around the world. 9,000 attendees; 440 booths	Sea Fare Expositions, Inc. 850 NW 45th St. Seattle, WA 98107 Tel: (206) 547-6030 Fax: (206) 548-9346
US Food Export Showcase Annual May 7–10, 1995 Chicago, IL McCormick Place	Offers importing opportunities from US food manufacturers to overseas buyers. 35,000 attendees; 350 exhibitors	Convention Mgmt. Group 3918 Prosperity Ave., Suite 102 Fairfax, VA 22031 Tel: (703) 876-0300 Fax: (703) 876-0904

FORESTRY & WOODWORKING

Trade Fair	Site/Date	Contact
Forest Products Machinery & Equipment Exposition Every 2 years June 15–17, 1995 New Orleans, LA	Machinery and equipment for saw-milling, logging, harvesting, plywood panel and pallet manufacturing, treating, laminating, and processing. 10,000+ attendees; 350 booths	Southern Forest Products Assn. PO Box 641700 Kenner, LA 70064-1700 Tel: (504) 443-4464 Fax: (504) 443-6612
Wood Technology Clinic & Show Annual March 15–17, 1995 Portland, OR Oregon Conv. Center	Exhibits featuring log processing equipment, lumber and panel manufacturing equipment, process control, saws, knives, etc. 11,000 attendees; 1,000 booths	Forest Industry Exposition Group Miller Freeman Inc. 600 Harrison St. San Francisco, CA 94107 Tel: (415) 905-2200 Fax: (415) 905-2239
Woodworking, Machinery & Furniture Supply Fair Every 2 years September 5–8, 1995 Anaheim, CA	A biennial exposition featuring exhibitors from over 20 countries; 36 seminar sessions are available. 24,000 attendees; 550 booths	Marketing/Association Services, Inc. 1516 S. Pontius Ave. Los Angeles, CA 90025 Tel: (310) 477-8521 Fax: (310) (312) 6684

FURNISHINGS & INTERIOR DESIGN

Trade Fair	Site/Date	Contact
International Casual Furniture Market Annual September 14–18, 1995 Chicago, IL Merchandise Mart Expocenter	Attendees are wholesale and retail merchandise buyers. 7,000 attendees	Merchandise Mart Properties, Inc. 470 The Merchandise Mart Chicago, IL 60654 Tel: (312) 527-7610 Fax: (312) 527-7998
Lightfair International Annual May 23–25, 1995 Chicago, IL Navy Pier	For lighting designers, interior designers, architects, engineers, landscape architects, facility managers, developers, contractors. 11,000 attendees; 525 booths	AMC Tradeshows 240 Peachtree St. NW, Suite 2200 Atlanta, GA 30303 Tel: (404) 220-2215 Fax: (404) 220-3030
Neocon 95 Annual June 12–14, 1995 Chicago, IL The Merchandise Mart	Products and services include fixtures, lighting, HVAC, office furniture, textiles, elevators, fire protection systems. 50,000 attendees; 500 exhibitors	Merchandise Mart Properties, Inc. 470 The Merchandise Mart Chicago, IL 60654 Tel: (312) 527-7610, (800) 677-6278 Fax: (312) 527-7998
Restoration 95 Every 2 years *1995 dates TBA Boston, MA Hynes Conv. Center	Products and services of interest to conservators, curators, architects, interior designers, artisans, and specialty contractors. 7,500+ attendees; 175+ exhibitors	E. Glew International 10 Tower Office Park Woburn, MA 01801 Tel: (617) 933-9699 Fax: (617) 933-8744

GIFTS & STATIONERY

Trade Fair	Site/Date	Contact
American Stationery Fair Annual/new event July 5–14, 1995 Atlanta, GA Atlanta Market Center	Fair is dedicated solely to stationery products in response to an expressed need from retailers and manufacturers. 50,000 attendees; 500+ booths	Atlanta Market Center 240 Peachtree St. NW, Suite 2200 Atlanta, GA 30303 Tel: (404) 220-2232, (800) ATL-MART Fax: (404) 220-3030

Trade Fair	Site/Date	Contact
Boston Gift Show 2 times a year March 25–29, 1995 July 22–26, 1995 Boston, MA Bayside Exposition Center	Stationery, gourmet products and foods, toys, general gifts, floral items, decorative and personal accessories, tabletop, crafts, souvenirs, jewelry. 13,000 attendees; 590 exhibitors	George Little Mgmt., Inc. 2 Park Ave., Suite 1100 New York, NY 10016-5748 Tel: (212) 340-9216 Fax: (212) 685-6598
California Gift Show 2 times a year *January 1995 July 1995 Los Angeles, CA	Stationery, tabletop, general gift, gourmet, decorative accessories, jewelry and fashion accessories, souvenirs, international products, and US contemporary crafts. 40,000 attendees; 3,150 booths	AMC Tradeshows 1933 S. Broadway, Suite 111 Los Angeles, CA 90007 Tel: (213) 747-3488 Fax: (213) 747-6182
Chicago Gift Show 2 times a year Jan. 29–Feb. 2, 1995 July 30–Aug. 3, 1995 Chicago, IL McCormick Place North	China, glass, giftware, stationery, tabletop products, games, floral items, gourmet products, home furnishings, toys, jewelry, folk art, clothing, crafts, accessories. 21,000 attendees; 1,100 exhibitors	George Little Mgmt., Inc. 10 Bank St. White Plains, NY 10606 Tel: (914) 421-3200
Florida International Gift Expo Annual January 29–31, 1995 Tampa, FL Tampa Conv. Center	Trade show for buyers of giftware, decorative accessories, souvenir, novelty and resort glassware and tabletop, collectibles, floral, apparel and fashion accessories, fine and fashion jewelry, stationery, and gourmet products. 9,000+ attendees; 650+ booths	AMC Trade Shows 240 Peachtree St. NW, Suite 2200 Atlanta, GA 30303 Tel: (404) 230-2206 Fax: (404) 220-2442
Green! Gift Show 2 times a year January 11–20, 1995 July 5–14, 1995 Atlanta, GA Atlanta Market Center	Juried, environmentally friendly exhibits range from stationery products, to decorative accessories, to toys for children and adults, to body and bath products, and more. 50,000 attendees	Atlanta Market Center 240 Peachtree St. NW, Suite 2200 Atlanta, GA 30303 Tel: (404) 220-2200, (800) ATL-MART Fax: (404) 220-3030
International Gift & Accessories Market 2 times a year January 11–20, 1995 July 5–14, 1995 Atlanta, GA Atlanta Market Center	For buyers of gift and gift-related merchandise and featuring: The National Country Collectibles Show; Bed, Bath & Linen; High Design; The Green Gift Show; Atlanta Tabletop Show and American Stationery Fair. 40,000 attendees; 2,000+ exhibitors	Atlanta Market Center 240 Peachtree St. NW, Suite 2200 Atlanta, GA 30303 Tel: (404) 220-2200 Fax: (404) 220-3030
National China, Glass & Collectibles Show Annual January 7–10, 1995 Washington, DC Washington Conv. Center	Buyer show of traditional giftware, decorative and personal accessories, stationery, gourmet, floral items, jewelry, souvenirs, crafts, collectibles, glass, and related tabletop items. 11,500 attendees; 475 exhibitors	George Little Mgmt., Inc. 10 Bank St. White Plains, NY 10606 Tel: (914) 421-9221
National Country Collectibles Show 2 times a year January 14–18, 1995 July 8–12, 1995 Atlanta, GA Atlanta Market Center	Exhibits include wall decor and lamps; early American and French country furniture; English and French country accessories, Americana and primitive folk art; pottery and stoneware. 50,000 attendees; 550+ booths	Atlanta Market Center 240 Peachtree St. NW, Suite 2200 Atlanta, GA 30303 Tel: (404) 220-2204, (800) ATL-MART Fax: (404) 220-3030
National Stationery Show Annual May 20–23, 1995 New York, NY Jacob K. Javits Conv. Center	Buyer show of greeting cards, postcards, note paper, social stationery, and related products. 25,000 attendees; 1,500 exhibitors	George Little Mgmt., Inc. 10 Bank St. White Plains, NY 10606 Tel: (914) 421-3200

Trade Fair	Site/Date	Contact
New York International Gift Fair 2 times a year January 22–26, 1995 August 13–17, 1995 New York, NY Jacob K Javits Conv. Center	Buyer show of general giftware, tabletop and housewares, decorative and personal accessories, museum gifts, crafts, contemporary design products, juvenile products, and floral products. Incorporates: Accent On Design, American & International Crafts, Floral & Garden Accessories, Just Kidstuff, Handmade in the USA, New & Distinctive Resources, The Museum Source. 45,000 attendees; 2,200 exhibitors	George Little Mgmt., Inc. 10 Bank St. White Plains, NY 10606 Tel: (914) 421-3200
San Francisco International Gift Fair 2 times a year January 14–18, 1995 August 5–9, 1995 San Francisco, CA Moscone Conv. Center	The gift fair will feature a broad range of products in 10 divisions, incorporating Design Focus, Crafts Focus with Accent on Design West, American & International Crafts West, Museum Source and Just Kidstuff West. 32,000 attendees; 2,000 exhibitors	Western Exhibitors 2181 Greenwich St. San Francisco, CA 94123 Tel: (415) 346-6666, (914) 421-9271 Fax: (415) 346-4965

HEALTH & BEAUTY

Trade Fair	Site/Date	Contact
Beauty & Barber Supply Institute, Inc. Annual Convention Annual August 10–13, 1995 Las Vegas, NV Conv. Center	Exhibition of products and services for the beauty and barber industry, including shampoo, conditioners, tools, equipment, and other related products and services. 12,000 attendees; 1,000 booths	BBSI 271 Route 46 W., Suite F209 Fairfield, NJ 07004 Tel: (201) 808-7444 Fax: (201) 808-9099
Big Show Expo: The Beauty & Business Expo 2 annual locations Apr. 23–25, 1995: Philadelphia Oct. 29–31, 1995: New York	Ethnic traveling beauty and business exposition, with classes, seminars, and exhibits for beauty shop owners, managers, and beauticians. 7,000/17,000 attendees; 100/175 booths	Big Show Expo 1841 Broadway New York, NY 10023 Tel: (800) 223-0886, (212) 757-7589 Fax: (212) 757-3611
HBA Global Expo Annual May 2–4, 1995 New York, NY Jacob Javits Conv. Center	Trade show for the cosmetic, fragrance, toiletry, and non-prescription drug industries. 6,000 attendees; 180 exhibitors	Blenheim Fashion Shows Fort Lee Executive Park One Executive Drive Fort Lee, NJ 07024 Tel: (201) 346-1400 Fax: (201) 346-1532
Natural Products Expo 2 annual locations March 10–13, 1995: Anaheim, CA September 15–18, 1995: Baltimore, MD	Exhibits of natural, organic and environmentally sound products . 16,000/8,500 attendees; 900/700 exhibitors	New Hope Communications 1301 Spruce St. Boulder, CO 80302 Tel: (303) 939-8440 Fax: (303) 939-9559
Pharmaceutical Industries Exposition & Conference Annual March 28–30, 1995 New York, NY Jacob K. Javits Conv. Center	Exhibits of plant and laboratory equipment and services for the pharmaceutical and cosmetic industries. 6,600+ attendees; 500+ exhibitors	Reed Exhibition Companies 383 Main Ave. PO Box 6059 Norwalk, CT 06852-6059 Tel: (203) 840-4800 Fax: (203) 840-4804

MACHINERY & MANUFACTURING

Trade Fair	Site/Date	Contact
Autofact Annual November 14–16, 1995 Chicago, IL	Attracts manufacturing professionals involved in CAD, CAM, CAE, CIM, robotics, artificial intelligence, vision sensors, machine tools, etc. 20,000 attendees; 300 booths	Society of Manufacturing Engineers 1 SME Dr., PO Box 930 Dearborn, MI 48121 Tel: (313) 271-1500 Fax: (313) 271-2861

Trade Fair	Site/Date	Contact
CMM International Annual August 28–31, 1995 Chicago, IL McCormick Place	Exhibits include converting equipment, materials, supplies, and services. 32,000+ attendees; 3,700 booths	Blenheim Trade Shows 1110 Shop Rd. PO Box 1986 Columbia, SC 29202 Tel: (803) 771-7500 Fax: (803) 799-1461
Fabtech International Exposition & Conference Every 2 years October 9–12, 1995 Chicago, IL	SME Expositions span the spectrum of traditional manufacturing processes and extend to the most advanced computer integrated manufacturing (CIM) systems. 20,000 attendees; 425 booths	Society of Manufacturing Engineers 1 SME Dr., PO Box 930 Dearborn, MI 48121 Tel: (313) 271-1500 Fax: (313) 271-2861
International Control Engineering Exposition & Conference Annual March 13–16, 1995 Chicago, IL McCormick Place North	International exposition of control products and systems for discrete parts and process manufacturing. 15,600+ attendees; 110 exhibitors	Reed Exhibition Companies 383 Main Ave. PO Box 6059 Norwalk, CT 06852-6059 Tel: (203) 840-4800 Fax: (203) 840-4804
International Programmable Controllers Annual May 8–11, 1995 Detroit, MI Cobo Conv. Center	Leading conference in the US for all forms of industrial control systems, with exhibits of technologies for plant floor automation. 33,000+ attendees; 185 exhibitors	ESD Ann Arbor Conference Center 2350 Green Rd, Suite 190 Ann Arbor, MI 48105 Tel: (313) 995-4440 Fax: (313) 663-7835
Metalform 95 Annual March 12–15, 1995 Rosemont, IL	Exhibits of mechanical and hydraulic power presses, press brakes, coil and sheet feeding equipment, safety equipment, die components, tooling, lasers, welding, finishing, and assembly. 17,000 attendees; 300 booths	Precision Metalforming Assn. 27027 Chardon Rd. Richmond Heights, OH 44143 Tel: (216) 585-8800 Fax: (216) 585-3126
National Manufacturing Week Annual March 13–16, 1995 Chicago, IL McCormick Place	All-encompassing manufacturing and engineering event. Exhibits include product design, control engineering, process manufacturing, plant engineering, maintenance, and more. 41,900+ attendees; 1,820 exhibitors	Reed Exhibition Companies 383 Main Ave. PO Box 6059 Norwalk, CT 06852-6059 Tel: (203) 840-4800 Fax: (203) 840-4804
National Plant Engineering and Maintenance Show & Conference Annual March 13–16, 1995 Chicago, IL McCormick Place East	Focus is on electrical equipment, HVAC, instruments and controls, mechanical power transmission, fluid handling, pollution control, buildings and grounds, material handling, computers/software, and maintenance equipment/supplies. 19,900+ attendees; 730 exhibitors	Reed Exhibition Companies 383 Main Ave. PO Box 6059 Norwalk, CT 06852-6059 Tel: (203) 840-4800 Fax: (203) 840-4804
Westech Advanced Productivity Exposition Annual March 27–30, 1995 Los Angeles, CA **Eastech Advanced Productivity Exposition** Annual May 23–25, 1995 West Springfield, MA	Exhibits include machinery, equipment, products, supplies, and services relating to all areas of product manufacturing for any industry. Open to the public. 30,000/17,000 attendees; 580/580 booths	Soc. of Manufacturing Engineers 1 SME Drive, PO Box 930 Dearborn, MI 48121 Tel: (313) 271-1500 Fax: (313) 271-2861

MEDICAL & DENTAL

Abilities Expo 4 annual locations Mar. 10–12, 1995: Tampa, FL Apr. 21–23, 1995: Anaheim, CA June 16–18, 1995: Edison, NJ Aug. 11–13, 1995: Rosemont, IL	Conference and exposition of products and services for the disabled, health care professionals, and rehab professionals. 10,000 attendees at each show; 300 booths at each show	Expocon Mgmt. Associates, Inc. 363 Reef Rd. PO Box 915 Fairfield, CT 06430-0915 Tel: (203) 256-4700 Fax: (203) 256-4730

Trade Fair	Site/Date	Contact
American Academy of Dermatology Annual Meeting Annual February 4–9, 1995 New Orleans, LA	Medical meeting with exhibits for professionals in the field of dermatology. 13,000 attendees; 700 booths	American Academy of Dermatology PO Box 4014 Schaumburg, IL 60168-4014 Tel: (708) 330-0230 Fax: (708) 330-0050
American Academy of Family Physicians Scientific Assembly Annual September 21–24, 1995 Anaheim, CA	Scientific meeting and trade show for family physicians. 15,000 attendees; 390 exhibitors	American Academy of Family Physicians 8880 Ward Pkwy Kansas City, MO 64114 Tel: (816) 333-9700 x3200 Fax: (816) 333-0303
American College of Cardiology Annual Scientific Session Annual March 19–22, 1995 New Orleans, LA	Firsthand information about pharmaceutical products, medical devices, equipment, and services related to cardiovascular health care. 25,000 attendees; 430 booths	American College of Cardiology Meeting Services Dept. 9111 Old Georgetown Rd. Bethesda, MD 20814-1699 Tel: (301) 897-2693 Fax: (301) 897-9745
American College of Surgeons Clinical Congress Every 3 years October 22–27, 1995 New Orleans, LA	Conference and trade show for physicians and surgeons. 20,000 attendees; 350 booths	American College of Surgeons 55 E. Erie St. Chicago, IL 60611 Tel: (312) 664-4050 Fax: (312) 440-7014
American Dental Assn. Annual Meeting Annual October 4–8, 1995 Las Vegas, NV	Exhibits include dental materials, instruments, equipment, therapeutics, and related services. 30,000 attendees; 1,000 booths	American Dental Assn. 211 E. Chicago Ave. Chicago, IL 60611 Tel: (312) 440-2581 Fax: (312) 440-2707
American Hospital Assn. Annual August 21–23, 1995 San Francisco, CA Moscone Center	Hospital-related products and services, including medical equipment, pharmacy, food service, furniture, insurance, marketing, facility design and construction, and more. 6,500 attendees; 400 exhibitors	American Hospital Assn. 1 North Franklin St. Chicago, IL 60602 Tel: (312) 280-6000 Fax: (312) 280-6462
American Lung Assn./ American Thoracic Soc. International Conference Annual May 22–24, 1995 Seattle, WA	Exhibits of pharmaceuticals, equipment and devices designed for diagnosis, treatment of lung disease, pulmonary research; medical publications. 9,000+ attendees; 325 booths	Talley Mgmt. Group 875 Kings Hwy., Suite 200 W. Deptford, NJ 08096 Tel: (609) 384-6287 Fax: (609) 853-0411
American Soc. of Clinical Oncology Annual May 20–23, 1995 Los Angeles, CA Los Angeles Conv. Center	Association convention with exhibits. 14,000 attendees; 620 booths	Bostrom Mgmt. 435 N. Michigan Ave., Suite 1717 Chicago, IL 60611-4067 Tel: (312) 644-0828 Fax: (312) 644-8857
Annual Meeting of the American Academy of Ophthalmology Annual Oct. 29–Nov. 2, 1995 Atlanta, GA	Ophthalmic devices and services, including equipment, instruments, educational materials, lasers, pharmaceuticals, contact lenses. 20,000 attendees; 1,800 booths	American Academy of Ophthalmology 655 Beach St. San Francisco, CA 94109 Tel: (415) 561-8500 Fax: (415) 561-8576
International Vision Expo & Conference West Annual October 27–29, 1995 Anaheim, CA Anaheim Conv. Center	Exhibits feature products and services for the vision correction industry. 10,000 attendees; 350 exhibitors	Assn. Expositions & Services Div. of Reed Exhibition Companies 383 Main Ave., PO Box 6059 Norwalk, CT 06852-6059 Tel: (203) 840-4820 Fax: (203) 840-4824
Medical Design & Manufacturing West Annual January 10–12, 1995 Anaheim, CA Anaheim Conv. Center	Exhibits of components, materials, equipment, systems, and services for medical OEMs. 10,000 attendees; 700 booths	Canon Communications 3340 Ocean Park Blvd., Suite 1000 Santa Monica, CA 90405 Tel: (310) 392-5509 Fax: (310) 392-4920

Trade Fair	Site/Date	Contact
National Home Health Care Exposition Annual November 15–18, 1995 Atlanta, GA Georgia World Congress Center	This rapidly growing trade show features a myriad of products and services for the health care industry. 34,500 attendees; 3,200 booths	SEMCO Productions 1130 Hightower Trail Atlanta, GA 30350 Tel: (404) 998-9800 Fax: (404) 642-4715
Radiological Society of North America Annual Nov. 26–Dec. 1, 1995 Chicago, IL McCormick Place	Scientific assembly with exhibits of new radiological equipment and services, plus updates of new applications of existing products. 56,000+ attendees; 550 exhibitors	RSNA 2021 Spring Rd., #600 Oak Brook, IL 60521 Tel: (708) 571-2670 Fax: (708) 571-7837

MERCHANDISING

Trade Fair	Site/Date	Contact
American International Toy Fair Annual February 13–20, 1995 New York, NY Jacob Javits Conv. Center	Buyer show with exhibits of all types of toys, games, and holiday decorations. 20,000+ attendees; 1,600+ exhibitors	Toy Manufacturers of America 200 Fifth Ave., Room 740 New York, NY 10010 Tel: (212) 675-1141 x209 Fax: (212) 633-1429
ASD/AMD National Trade Show 2 times a year/2 locations *March/August 1995: Las Vegas, NV *May/October 1995: Atlantic City, NJ	A buying show, featuring a variety of general merchandise, including close-outs, government surplus, sporting goods, hardware, toys, photo/sound equipment, and apparel. 27,000/5,000 attendees; 3,000/400 booths	ASD/AMD National Trade Shows 2525 Ocean Park Blvd. Santa Monica, CA 90405-5201 Tel: (800) 421-4511, (310) 396-6006 Fax: (310) 399-2662
Gourmet Products Show Including Bed, Bath & Linen Annual April 30–May 3, 1995 Las Vegas, NV Las Vegas Conv. Center	Exhibition of gourmet products, plus bedding, bath, and linen products for the home. 9,000 attendees; 800 exhibitors	George Little Mgmt., Inc. 577 Airport Blvd., Suite 440 Burlingame, CA 94010-5270 Tel: (415) 344-5171 Fax: (415) 344-5270
International Home Furnishings Market 2 times a year April 27–May 5, 1995 October 19–27, 1995 High Point, NC	Exhibits of residential case goods, upholstery, gift and decorative accessories, lighting, and floor covering. 55,000 attendees; 1,700 booths	International Home Furnishings Marketing Assn. PO Box 5687 High Point, NC 27262 Tel: (919) 889-0203
International Jewelry Fair/ General Merchandise Show 2 times a year April 8–11, 1995 November 3–7, 1995 New Orleans, LA Ernest N. Morial Conv. Center	Buyer show with all types of jewelry and general merchandise. 10,000 attendees; 1,000+ booths	Helen Brett Enterprises 1988 University Ln. Lisle, IL 60532-4182 Tel: (708) 241-9865 Fax: (708) 241-9870
National Halloween, Costume & Party Show Annual March 24–28, 1995 Rosemont, IL Rosemont Conv. Center	Attendees include retail and wholesale buyers and decisionmakers for items sold for costume parties and Halloween. 30,000 attendees; 2,000 booths	Transworld Exhibits Inc. 1850 Oak St. Northfield, IL 60093 Tel: (708) 446-8434, (800) 323-5462 Fax: (708) 446-3523
National Hardware Show Annual August 13–16, 1995 Chicago, IL McCormick Place Conv. Center	Exhibits feature hardware, lawn and garden, outdoor living, housewares, building supply, DIY, automotive products, and retail technology. 70,000 attendees; 3,000 exhibitors	Assn. Expositions & Services Div. of Reed Exhibition Companies 383 Main Ave., PO Box 6059 Norwalk, CT 06852-6059 Tel: (203) 840-4820 Fax: (203) 840-4824
National Merchandise Show Annual September 9–12, 1995 New York, NY Jacob Javits Conv. Center	General merchandise trade show featuring more than 90 merchandise categories and 120,000 products in all price ranges. An order-writing show with buyers from the US and many foreign countries. 34,000 attendees; 2,700 booths	Miller Freeman, Inc. 1515 Broadway New York, NY 10036 Tel: (212) 869-1300 Fax: (212) 730-2952

Trade Fair	Site/Date	Contact
Premium Incentive Show/ Meetings & Incentive Travel Expo Annual May 2–4, 1995 New York, NY Jacob Javits Conv. Center	Incentive products and services, including incentive travel. This show is a product and idea showcase for premium incentive personnel to do their planning and buying. 14,000+ attendees; 1,000+ exhibitors	Miller Freeman, Inc. 1515 Broadway New York, NY 10036 Tel: (212) 869-1300 Fax: (212) 768-0015
Supermarket Industry Convention & Educational Exposition Annual May 7–10, 1995 Chicago, IL	Products, equipment, supplies, and services available to and through the supermarket industry, including grocery products, health and beauty aids, store design, data processing, advertising, and warehousing. 35,000 attendees; 1,000 exhibitors	Food Marketing Institute 800 Connecticut Ave., NW Washington, DC 20006 Tel: (202) 452-8444 Fax: (202) 429-4519
Toy Show Annual *January 1995 Las Vegas, NV Las Vegas Conv. Center	Open to all toy categories; the first major US market of the year. 10,000 attendees; 400 booths	International Expositions Mgmt. Group, Ltd. 50 Glen St. Glen Cove, NY 11542 Tel: (516) 674-0200 Fax: (516) 674-0288
Transworld Housewares & Variety Exhibit 4 times a year January 13–17, 1995 March 31–April 4, 1995 *Other dates TBA Rosemont, IL Rosemont Conv. Center	General merchandise trade show, with over 180 different product categories on display, designed to provide exhibitors and buyers with a marketplace in which to buy and sell consumer products. 40,000 attendees; 2,000 booths	Transworld Exhibits Inc. 1850 Oak St. Northfield, IL 60093 Tel: (708) 446-8434, (800) 323-5462 Fax: (708) 446-3523
Variety Merchandise Show Annual February 18–21, 1995 New York, NY Jacob Javits Conv. Center **Mid-Year Variety Merchandise Show** Annual June 10–13, 1995 New York, NY	General merchandise trade shows featuring more than 90 merchandise categories and 120,000 products in all price ranges. An order-writing show with buyers from the US and many foreign countries. 35,000 attendees; 2,800 booths	Miller Freeman, Inc. 1515 Broadway New York, NY 10036 Tel: (212) 869-1300 Fax: (212) 770-2952

MINING & GEMOLOGY

Trade Fair	Site/Date	Contact
Discovery Marketplace of Gems 2 times a year *January/February 1995 *September 1995 Tuscon, AZ Discovery Inn	Exhibit of gems, crystals, fixings, machines, lapidary equipment, and stones. Wholesale show. 7,000 attendees; 250 booths	Discovery Marketplace of Gems 1010 S. Freeway Tucson, AZ 85745 Tel: (800) 622-5871 Fax: (602) 620-0097
SMME Annual Meeting & Exhibit Annual March 6–9, 1995 Denver, CO Colorado Conv. Center	Exhibition of products and services related to the mining industry. 5,000 attendees; 375+ exhibitors	Soc. for Mining, Metallurgy & Exploration PO Box 625002 Littleton, CO 80162-5002 Tel: (303) 973-9550 Fax: (303) 979-3461

OFFICE PRODUCTS & SYSTEMS

Trade Fair	Site/Date	Contact
National Office Machine Dealers Assn. Annual August 23–26, 1995 Atlanta, GA Georgia World Congress Center	National convention with exhibition, for dealers only. Manufacturers will be exhibiting the latest products in the business equipment and systems industry. In conjunction with NOPA. 25,000+ attendees; 339 exhibitors	Nat'l Office Machine Dealers Assn. Exposition Services 12411 Warnall Rd. Kansas City, MO 64145 Tel: (800) 228-9772 Fax: (816) 941-4838

Trade Fair	Site/Date	Contact
National Office Product Assn.'s Annual Convention & Exhibit Annual August 23–26, 1995 Atlanta, GA Georgia World Congress Center	Exhibitors represent the full horizontal line of office supplies, accessories, machines, computer accessories, software, and retail furniture. Held in conjunction with NOMDA/LANDA. 25,700+ attendees; 562 exhibitors	NOPA Convention & Exhibit Dept. 301 N. Fairfax St. Alexandria, VA 22314 Tel: (703) 549-9040 Fax: (703) 683-7552
Office Systems & Business Show Annual February 1–3, 1995 Portland, OR Oregon Conv. Center	Exhibits of all types of office equipment, furniture, products, and supplies, from paper goods to electronics. 15,000 attendees; 500+ booths	Business Exhibitors Northwest 2107 N. Vancouver Portland,, 97227 Tel: (503) 287-7541 Fax: (503) 287-1926
World Workplace Annual/new event September 17–20, 1995 Miami Beach, FL	Products and services for all aspects of the work environment including office furniture, lighting, HVAC controls, carpeting, CAFM, telecommuni-cations, real estate, IAQ, and more. 7,000 attendees; 1,000	IFMA 1 East Greenway Plaza, Suite 1100 Houston, TX 77046-0194 Tel: (713) 629-6753 Fax: (713) 623-6124

PACKAGING & MATERIALS HANDLING

Flex Expo Annual *April 1995 Dallas, TX Dallas Conv. Center	Exhibition of flexible packaging materials, products, technology, and machinery. 10,000 attendees; 200 exhibitors	Blenheim Trade Shows 1110 Shop Rd. PO Box 1986 Columbia, SC 29202 Tel: (803) 771-7500 Fax: (803) 799-1461
Midpak '95 Every 2 years September 27–28, 1995 Minneapolis, MN Minneapolis Conv. Center	Expo offering a full range of machinery, products, and services for the packaging and handling industry. 6,000+ attendees; 500 booths	Technology Exchange, Inc. 14505 21st Ave. N., Suite 210 Plymouth, MN 55447 Tel: (612) 473-9192 Fax: (612) 473-9216
Southern Packaging Exposition Every 2 years May 9–11, 1995 Atlanta, GA Georgia World Congress Center	Exhibits of packaging machinery, equipment, materials, supplies, and contract packaging services. 10,000 attendees; 360 exhibitors	Reed Exhibition Companies 383 Main Ave. PO Box 6059 Norwalk, CT 06852-6059 Tel: (203) 840-4800 Fax: (203) 840-4804
Western Packaging Exposition Every 2 years October 17–19, 1995 Anaheim, CA Anaheim Conv. Center	Show focus is packaging machinery, equipment, materials, supplies, and contract packaging services. 29,000 attendees; 800 exhibitors	Reed Exhibition Companies 383 Main Ave. PO Box 6059 Norwalk, CT 06852-6059 Tel: (203) 840-4800 Fax: (203) 840-4804

PHOTOGRAPHY

International Exposition of Professional Photography & National Industrial Conference Annual July 28–Aug. 2, 1995 Rosemont, IL	Exhibition of photographic equipment, lighting, backgrounds, props, albums, frames; anything used by the professional photographer, either in a studio or on location. 6,500 attendees; 300 booths	Professional Photographers of America 57 Forsyth St., NW, Suite 1600 Atlanta, GA 30303 Tel: (404) 522-8600
Photo Annual November 3–5, 1995 New York, NY Jacob K. Javits Conv. Center	An annual international trade show and conference for professional photographers. Exhibits include current equipment, products, and services for professional photographers. 15,000 attendees; 275 booths	Conference Mgmt. Corp. 200 Connecticut Ave. Norwalk, CT 06856-4990 Tel: (203) 852-0500 Fax: (203) 838-3710

Trade Fair	Site/Date	Contact
Photographic Convention & Trade Show Annual February 9–12, 1995 Las Vegas, NV Las Vegas Conv. Center	International trade show for photo/video retailers, processors, finishers, school photographers, labs, and manufacturers. 20,000 attendees; 580 booths	Photo Marketing Assn. International 3000 Picture Pl. Jackson, MI 49201 Tel: (517) 788-8100 Fax: (517) 788-8371
Prolab Annual November 3–5, 1995 New York, NY Jacob K. Javits Conv. Center	An international conference and exhibition for photo lab and mini lab professionals. 5,800 attendees; 400 booths	Conference Mgmt. Corp. 200 Connecticut Ave. Norwalk, CT 06856-4990 Tel: (203) 852-0500 Fax: (203) 838-3710

PRINTING & PUBLISHING

Trade Fair	Site/Date	Contact
American Library Association (ALA) Annual Conference Annual June 22–29, 1995 Chicago, IL	Exhibits include library supplies, equipment, audiovisual materials and database services. 17,000 attendees; 1,100+ booths	American Library Assn. (ALA) 50 E. Huron St. Chicago, IL 60611 Tel: (312) 280-3227, (800) 545-2344 Fax: (312) 280-3224
Graphic Arts Expo Every 2 years/2 locations Mar. 9–11, 1995: Charlotte, NC *October 1995: Chicago, IL	Exhibits of the latest in equipment, products, and services for the graphic communications industry. 20,000/49,000 attendees; 240+/604 booths	Graphic Arts Show Company 1899 Preston White Dr. Reston, VA 22091-4367 Tel: (703) 264-7200 Fax: (703) 620-9187
Graphics Conference **Annual** November 3–5, 1995 New York, NY Jacob K. Javits Conv. Center	For illustrators, graphic designers, computer publishers, art/creative directors, production managers, owners, etc. 11,000 attendees; 175 booths	Conference Mgmt. Corp. 200 Connecticut Ave. Norwalk, CT 06856-4990 Tel: (203) 852-0500 Fax: (203) 838-3710
Gutenberg Festival Annual *May 1995 Long Beach, CA	Exhibits of color copying, desktop publishing, color separations, offset printing, prepress equipment, and finishing systems. 35,000 attendees; 1,100 booths	Gutenberg Expositions PO Box 11712 Santa Ana, CA 92711 Tel: (714) 921-3120 Fax: (714) 921-3126
Know Show: Graphic Communications Exposition Annual *January 1995 Cleveland, OH Cleveland Conv. Center	Exhibition of equipment, printing, and graphic design services. 14,000 attendees; 150 booths	Xpoco, Inc. 2930 Prospect Ave., E. Cleveland, OH 44115-2608 Tel: (216) 621-3144 Fax: (216) 621-3191
Special Libraries Assn. (SLA) Annual Conference Annual June 8–13, 1996 Boston, MA *Note:* 1995 conference is in Montreal, Quebec (Canada)	Exhibits include library automation software, CD-ROM, databases, optical publishing, information storage and retrieval, microfilms and microfilm equipment, specialized books and periodicals. Open to the public. 5,000 attendees; 400+ booths	Special Libraries Assn. (SLA) 1700 18th St. NW Washington, DC 20009 Tel: (202) 234-4700 Fax: (202) 265-9317
Visual Communications Expo Annual November 3–5, 1995 New York, NY Jacob K. Javits Conv. Center	Four shows running concurrently, focusing on visual communications; offering the latest technology, services, and supplies. Consists of Photo, Prolab, Graphics Conference and The Multimedia Conference. 35,000 attendees; 800 booths	Conference Mgmt. Corp. 200 Connecticut Ave. Norwalk, CT 06856-4990 Tel: (203) 852-0500 Fax: (203) 838-3710

SECURITY & SAFETY

Trade Fair	Site/Date	Contact
International Security Conference & Exposition 2 annual locations *Feb. 1995: Las Vegas, NV Aug. 29–31, 1995: New York	Exhibits of residential, commercial, industrial, and government security products, systems, and services. 5,500/8,500+ attendees; 305/335 exhibitors	Reed Exhibition Companies 383 Main Ave. PO Box 6059 Norwalk, CT 06852-6059 Tel: (203) 840-4800 Fax: (203) 840-4804

Trade Fair	Site/Date	Contact
National Safety Council Congress & Exposition Annual November 5–10, 1995 Dallas, TX	Sessions, products, and services geared toward the safety, health professional in private industry as well as government and community interests. 19,000 attendees; 800+ exhibitors	National Safety Council 1121 Spring Lake Drive Itasca, IL 60143-3201 Tel: (708) 775-2041 Fax: (708) 775-2310

SPORTING GOODS, RECREATION & TRAVEL

Action Sports Retailer Trade Expo—West 2 times a year February 12–14, 1995 September 8–10, 1995 San Diego, CA San Diego Conv. Center	Trade show for buyers of all types of outdoor merchandise. 18,000+ attendees	Miller Freeman, Inc. Retail Sports Network 31652 2nd Ave. S. Laguna, CA 92677 Tel: (714) 499-5374 Fax: (714) 499-4921
DEMA Trade Show Annual January 26–29, 1995 Las Vegas, NV	Exhibitors include manufacturers of equipment and accessories, major certifying agencies, clothing manufacturers, video, photography, books, art and jewelry, and travel destination representatives. 12,000 attendees; 1,200 booths	R.L. Gray, Inc. 10372 Crawford Canyon Rd. Santa Ana, CA 92705 Tel: (714) 744-5287 Fax: (714) 744-2657
National Sporting Goods Assn. World Sports Expo Annual July 16–18, 1995 Chicago, IL	Licensed products, active lifestyles, fitness, sports medicine, general sporting goods, team and institutional activewear, outdoor, retail systems, and athletic footwear. 25,000 attendees	National Sporting Goods Assn. 1699 Wall St. Mt. Prospect, IL 60056 Tel: (708) 439-4000 Fax: (708) 439-0111
NSPI's International Expo Annual October 18–20, 1995 Atlanta, GA	Exhibition for pool and spa industry, with related products and services. 13,000 attendees; 420 exhibitors	National Spa & Pool Institute 2111 Eisenhower Ave. Alexandria, VA 22314 Tel: (703) 838-0083 x158 Fax: (703) 549-0493
Pow Wow 95 Annual May 27–31, 1995 New York, NY Jacob Javits Conv. Center	Exhibits include travel, tourism, accommodations, restaurants, resorts, skiing and attractions. 5,000 attendees; 1,100 booths	Travel Industry Assn. Suite 450, 1100 New York Ave., NW Washington, DC 20005-3934 Tel: (202) 408-8422
SIA Ski & Sports Show Annual March 3–7, 1995 Las Vegas, NV	Exhibits of equipment, apparel, footwear, and accessories for snow skiing and other outdoor sports. 15,000 attendees; 500 booths	Ski Industries America 8377B Greensboro Dr. McLean, VA 22102 Tel: (703) 556-9020 Fax: (703) 821-8276
Sport Fishing Expo Annual July 19–22, 1995 Las Vegas, NV	Exhibition of fishing tackle and related equipment 10,000 attendees; 1,200 booths	American Fishing Tackle Mfgrs. Assn. 1250 Grove Ave., Suite 300 Barrington, IL 60010 Tel: (708) 381-9490 Fax: (708) 381-9518
Super Show Annual February 3–6, 1995 Atlanta, GA Georgia World Congress Center	Seventeen individual shows featuring activewear, bowling & billiards, cycle products, fitness, footwear, golf, imprint and apparel, licensed products, marine and water sports, team sports, trading cards, trophies. 105,000+ attendees; 10,000 booths	The Super Show Communications & Show Mgmt. 1450 NE 123rd St. N. Miami, FL 33161-6051 Tel: (305) 893-8771, (800) 327-3736 Fax: (305) 893-8783

TEXTILES

Bobbin Contexpo: The Apparel Show of the Americas Annual April 5–7, 1995 Miami Beach, FL Miami Beach Conv. Center	An international marketplace for manufacturers and contractors to examine and purchase machines, fabrics and trims, and services, and simultaneously, for contractors to provide production sourcing opportunities for manufacturers. 5,000 attendees; 275 booths	Blenheim Trade Shows 1110 Shop Rd. PO Box 1986 Columbia, SC 29202 Tel: (803) 771-7500 Fax: (803) 799-1461

Trade Fair	Site/Date	Contact
Bobbin Sho: **AAMA Convention** Annual September 12–15, 1995 Atlanta, GA Georgia World Congress Center	An international marketplace for sewn products manufacturers to examine newest trends in fabrics, fibers, and technology and to compare products and services of more than 90 categories of industry suppliers. 25,000 attendees; 800 booths	Blenheim Trade Shows 1110 Shop Rd. PO Box 1986 Columbia, SC 29202 Tel: (803) 771-7500 Fax: (803) 799-1461
Industrial Fabric & **Equipment Exposition** Annual Sept. 30–Oct. 2, 1995 Los Angeles, CA	Exhibits include machinery, equipment, tools, supplies, services, products, industrial fabrics, fiber and film, nonwoven products and machinery, test labs, consultants and trade publications 6,000 attendees; 300 booths	Industrial Fabrics Assn. International 345 Cedar St., Suite 800 St. Paul, MN 55101 Tel: (800) 225-4324, (612) 222-2508 Fax: (612) 222-8215
World Educational Congress **for Laundering & Drycleaning** Every 2 years June 9–12, 1995 New Orleans, LA Ernest N. Morial Conv. Center	Exhibits of equipment, supplies, and services used by dry cleaners, linen supply and rental firms, coin laundries and dry cleaners, industrial launderers and dry cleaners, and institutional laundries. 25,000 attendees; 500+ exhibitors	Riddle & Associates 1874 Piedmont Rd., Suite 360-C Atlanta, GA 30324 Tel: (404) 876-1988 Fax: (404) 876-5121

Business Travel

No small chapter could do justice to a country as large and diverse as the US. In area, it spans a continent. It ranks third in the world in population, and its citizens come from all over the planet. More languages, cuisines, art forms, and fashions can be found in the US than in almost any other nation. Traveling here is the only way to get an idea of how vast the US is—and one trip is not enough. Thankfully, this immense country is readily accessible to travelers, with generally excellent transportation, accommodations, communications, dining, entertainment, shopping, public health standards, and medical services.

NATIONAL TRAVEL OFFICES WORLDWIDE

Australia Level 59, MLC Centre, King & Castlereagh Sts., Sydney, NSW 2001, Australia; Tel: [61] (2) 233-4666 Fax: [61] (2) 232-7219.

Canada (Montreal) 1253 McGill College Ave., Suite 328, Montreal, Quebec H3B 2Y5, Canada; Tel: [1] (514) 861-5040 Fax: [1] (514) 861-5026.

Canada (Toronto) Suite 602, 480 University Ave., Toronto, Ontario M5G 1V2, Canada; Tel: [1] (416) 595-5082 Fax: [1] (416) 595-5211.

Canada (Vancouver) American Consulate General, 1095 West Pender St., Vancouver, BC V6E 2M6, Canada; Tel: [1] (604) 685-1930 Fax: [1] (604) 688-8087.

Germany Bethmannstrasse 56, D-60311 Frankfurt/Main, Germany; Tel: [49] (69) 92-00-36-17/18 Fax: [49] (69) 29-4173.

Italy American Consulate General, Via Principe Amedeo 2/10, 20121 Milano, Italy; Tel: [39] (2) 2900-2657/2658/2059 Fax: [39] (2) 659-5908.

Japan Kokusai Building, 3-1-1, Marunouchi, Chiyoda-ku, Tokyo 100, Japan; Tel: [81] (3) 3212-2424 Fax: [81] (3) 3216-2508.

Mexico Edificio Plaza Comermex, 402, Blvd. M. Avila Camacho #1, Col. Polanco Chapultepec, 11560 Mexico, DF, Mexico; Tel: [52] (5) 520-3010/2101/2244 Fax: [52] (5) 520-1194.

Netherlands American Consulate General, Museumplein 19, 1071 DJ Amsterdam, Netherlands; Tel: [31] (20) 575-5380, [31] (20) 664-7746 Fax: [31] (20) 575-5377.

South America Springfield Building, 8125 NW 53rd St., Suite 100, Miami, FL 33166; Tel: [1] (305) 526-2912/4 Fax: [1] (305) 526-2915.

United Kingdom American Embassy, 24 Grosvenor Square, London W1A 1AE, UK; Tel: [44]

(71) 495-4466 (Info.), [44] (71) 495-4336 (Admin.) Fax: [44] (71) 495-4377.

VISA AND PASSPORT REQUIREMENTS

Except for citizens of Canada, Mexico, and the 22 nations that participate in the Visa Waiver Pilot Program (VWPP), foreigners need to present valid passports and visas to US Immigration and Naturalization Service (INS) officials to enter the US. The best place to get a visa is at the US consulate or embassy in your home country, although you can also apply for one at the US consulate or embassy in the country where you are at the time.

Business Visitor Visa To obtain a non-immigrant Business Visitor (B-1) Visa, you need:

- An application form (Form OF-156), available without charge at all US consulates.
- A passport valid for travel to the US that has an expiration date at least six months beyond the time you intend to stay in the US.
- One photograph, 37 mm x 37 mm (1.5 inches square), full face, without head covering, against a light background.

The fee for a visa is generally about the same as the visa fee your home country charges to US citizens. The visa departments of US consulates are efficient and honest, so you do not need to hire someone to help you obtain a visa.

If you are coming to the US to do business with a US firm, it is a good idea to present the INS officer with a letter from the US company stating the purpose of your trip, your intended length of stay, and, if you cannot show proof of sufficient funds to pay your own expenses, the company's guarantee of your travel costs.

Your visa does not guarantee that you will be able to enter the country when you arrive in the US, but the general rule practiced by the INS is to let in nearly everyone; the exceptions are citizens of, or arrivals from, one of the few countries with which the US has poor relations—such as Cuba, Libya, Iran, Iraq, Vietnam, and North Korea. Even then, ineligibility may be waived. This list is subject to change as US political relationships change with these and other countries.

Your visitor visa also does not guarantee a period of stay in the US, but travelers are generally admitted for 90 days. The INS will authorize your entry when you arrive at the airport or border and at that time will tell you how long you may stay. You may also apply to extend your stay beyond the time granted. Your visitor visa does not allow you to become employed during your stay in the US.

Visa Waiver Pilot Program (VWPP)

The VWPP allows citizens of participating countries to travel to the US for pleasure or business for 90 or fewer days without a visa. Current participants include: Andorra, Austria, Belgium, Brunei, Denmark, Finland, France, Germany, Iceland, Italy, Japan, Liechtenstein, Luxembourg, Monaco, the Netherlands, New Zealand, Norway, San Marino, Spain, Sweden, Switzerland, and the UK.

You still must have a valid passport and must be a citizen (not merely a resident) of that country. You must show the INS officer a roundtrip ticket from a carrier that has agreed to participate in the VWPP, and you must also arrive in the US on that carrier. You must have proof of financial solvency and must agree to waive your rights to an exclusion or deportation hearing (Form I-94W). Canadian or Mexican citizens, or citizens of VWPP nations who enter at the Canadian or Mexican borders, are not required to present roundtrip tickets. Extension are not available under the VWPP.

Treaty Trader and Treaty Investor Visas

Yet another visa category is set aside for individuals who are citizens of the many nations with which the US has trade and navigation treaties and who are coming to the US to carry on substantial trade or to invest substantial sums. The Treaty Trader (E-1) visa and the Treaty Investor (E-2) visa have differing specific requirements, but the key word in each is "substantial." The trade must be sizable and continuing; the investment must generate significantly more income than is needed to provide the investor with a living or must have a significant adverse economic impact on the US. The visas are valid for as long as you maintain your status with the trade or investment enterprise. Begin your application for such visas in the normal manner at the US consulate or embassy in your home country or the country from which you wish to enter the US. Visa officials will provide you with the information and forms you need for these special visas.

IMMUNIZATION

The US does not require visitors to have any immunizations in order to enter the country.

CLIMATE

The US covers a vast area and has a wide variety of climates generally within the temperate and subtropical zones. In general, the weather moves from west to east, carried by prevailing westerly winds coming off the Pacific Ocean; the Atlantic Ocean exerts relatively little moderating influence on the weather of the eastern coastal areas. The Pacific

Ocean gives the West Coast a moderate climate with little variation, while the deserts, mountains, Great Plains, Midwest, the Great Lakes region, and the Atlantic Coastal Plain experience much greater extremes in temperature and precipitation. The Gulf of Mexico strongly influences the southeastern US, which is warmer and more humid than the rest of the country. Southern Florida experiences nearly tropical conditions and is only slightly influenced by weather patterns over the rest of the continental US. The six cities on which this chapter focuses are representative of their surrounding regions. Temperature ranges given are the average daily lows and highs.

New York New York is on the Atlantic Coastal Plain, which has a generally humid climate. Winter brings below-freezing temperatures, snow, and rain. The January temperature range is from -3°C to 4°C (27°F to 40°F). Spring can be beautiful, with moderate temperatures ranging in April from 6°C to 16°C (43°F to 60°F) and sunny skies punctuated by heavy rain. Summer is warm and muggy; July temperatures range from 20°C to 30°C (68°F to 85°F), and frequent thunderstorms drench the city. Fall is the best season to visit; October temperatures range from 10°C to 19°C (50°F to 66°F), humidity drops, and the skies clear.

Washington, DC The climate of Washington is similar to that of New York, except warmer. Winters are not as severe; there is less snow, more rain, and slightly higher temperatures. Spring is mild and wet, and it can be a beautiful time to visit. Washington summers are notoriously hot and muggy, and people spend most of their time trying to get out of the city or complaining about not being able to leave. As in New York, fall is considered the best time to visit.

Miami Located on the southeastern coast of the US, Miami has a subtropical climate that is best experienced in the winter, when humidity and rainfall are at their lowest levels. January temperatures range from 14°C to 24°C (58°F to 76°F). This is the season when northerners flock to Florida to get away from the ice and snow. By April, the temperature range is from 19°C to 28°C (66°F to 83°F), and the monsoon-like rains begin. Tropical thunderstorms are frequent during the summer, and temperatures in July range from 24°C to 32°C (75°F to 89°F). Rain peaks in September, and hurricanes are a perennial threat. Fall brings a drop in humidity and a lessening of rain (although hurricanes can still occur); temperatures cool down to between 22°C and 29°C (71°F to 85°F) in October.

Houston This large city on the Gulf of Mexico coastal plain is known for its often unpleasant, overly humid climate. Winter is probably the best time to visit; January temperatures range from 5°C to 17°C (41°F to 62°F) and humidity is fairly low. Spring warms up to an average 20°C (69°F) in April, but humidity and rainfall also increase. Summer is to be avoided if possible; humidity is very high, thunderstorms are frequent, and July temperatures range from 23°C to 34°C (73°F to 94°F); frequent heat waves can make it even hotter. Everything in Houston is air conditioned. In the fall humidity and rainfall decline somewhat and the average temperature drops to 21°C (70°F).

Chicago Situated on the edge of the Great Plains, Chicago is exposed to frigid winter temperatures and heavy snows sweeping south from Canada and west from the Rocky Mountains, as well as blistering summer heat waves coming off the plains. Overall, many consider Chicago's climate to be more pleasant than that of New York, Washington, DC, or Houston. January temperatures range from –7°C to 0°C (19°F to 32°F), and strong winds—giving rise to Chicago's nickname, "The Windy City"—can cause a windchill that makes it feel many degrees colder for days at a time. Spring is cool and rainy, and April temperatures range from 5°C to 19°C (41°F to 57°F); late spring is a good time to visit. Summers are warm and sunny, with July temperatures ranging from 20°C to 29°C (67°F to 84°F), although heat waves can bring extended periods of 38°C (100°F) temperatures. Fall is generally pleasant, with an October temperature range of 8°C to 17°C (47°F to 63°F).

Los Angeles This city's Mediterranean-style climate is typical of the southern California coast—moderate to hot temperatures with only slight seasonal variations, onshore sea winds, light rainfall, heavy summer coastal fog, and considerable sun year-round—all courtesy of the Pacific Ocean's controlling influence. Temperature and rainfall variations are slight compared to other US cities. January temperatures range from 7°C to 18°C (45°F to 64°F), and rainfall is at its highest level, although the yearly average is less than 38 cm (15 inches). For all practical purposes, Los Angeles is situated in a desert, and almost no rain falls from May through November. Spring temperatures are slightly higher than in winter, often reaching 21°C (70°F) or higher. Although summer fog usually burns off by noon, it helps to cool the city; July temperatures range from 17°C to 27°C (62°F to 80°F). Fall is almost as warm as summer, and heat waves caused by Santa Ana winds blowing across from the eastern deserts can raise temperatures above 38°C (100°F). San Francisco, 400 miles to the north, has cooler temperatures, more fog, and somewhat more rain, while San Diego, 120 miles to the south, is warmer and drier.

BUSINESS ATTIRE

The clothing that US businesspeople wear depends on the industry and region of the country. Businesspeople of both sexes in the East and Midwest tend to dress conservatively in dark colors, although you are more likely to see fashionable Italian suits in New York than in Chicago. Those in the financial sectors dress the most conservatively, right down to their pinstripes. Houston, despite its western orientation, is only slightly less conservative in dress, while Miami is more forgiving, if only because of the climate. Los Angeles and California in general are more casual, especially in the entertainment and high-tech industries, where, respectively, avant garde casual dress or sports shirts and jeans may be standard attire—and the CEO may be indistinguishable from a junior computer programmer. However, even in California business attire in the large and influential financial sector is fairly conservative. Keep in mind that, as a foreign businessperson, you are trying to make a good impression on a business culture that, for all its cosmopolitanism and its power in world trade, is often surprisingly provincial and insular; it is accustomed to depending on a huge domestic market and is often less familiar with foreign peoples and practices. Thus, even in liberal California, it is probably best to dress a little more conservatively than the people with whom you will be dealing.

AIRLINES

Nearly every nation in the world with a national airline has a route to at least one city in the US, most often one of the New York area's three international airports. However, if your ultimate destination is other than a major international airport in New York, Chicago, or Los Angeles, you may find it easier to fly one of the half-dozen or so major US airlines with international flights. American, United, Delta, TWA, Northwest, USAir, and Continental not only serve a wide expanse of the globe, but thoroughly cover the US itself, which makes connecting flights a simpler matter and enables you to check your baggage through to your ultimate destination more easily. (Refer to the "Important Addresses" chapters for contact information for US airlines.)

TIME CHANGES

The continental US spans four time zones: Eastern (EST), Central (CST), Mountain (MST), and Pacific (PST). Alaska (AST) and Hawaii (HST) add two more zones. New York, in the Eastern zone, is five hours behind Greenwich Mean Time (GMT); Chicago and Houston in the Central zone are six hours behind GMT; Phoenix and Denver (Mountain time) are seven hours behind GMT; the Pacific Coast—including Los Angeles, San Francisco, and Seattle—is eight hours behind GMT; Alaska is nine hours behind GMT; and Hawaii is 10 hours behind GMT. Most of the country (except Arizona and Hawaii) goes on daylight savings time on the first Sunday in April—advancing the clock one hour—and returns to standard time on the last Sunday in October.

When you are within a US time zone, you can determine what time it is in any city listed here by adding the number shown to the US time. If it is daylight savings time in the US city you are calling from, subtract one from the number shown.

	EST	CST	MST	PST
Auckland	+17	+18	+19	+20
Bangkok	+12	+13	+14	+15
Beijing	+13	+14	+15	+16
Frankfurt	+6	+7	+8	+9
Hong Kong	+13	+14	+15	+16
Jakarta	+12	+13	+14	+15
Kuala Lumpur	+13	+14	+15	+16
London	+5	+6	+7	+8
Manila	+13	+14	+15	+16
Seoul	+14	+15	+16	+17
Singapore	+13	+14	+15	+16
Sydney	+15	+16	+17	+18
Taipei	+13	+14	+15	+16
Tokyo	+14	+15	+16	+17

CUSTOMS ENTRY (PERSONAL)

US Customs requirements are fairly simple. You can bring in 200 cigarettes, 50 cigars, or 2 kg of tobacco; 1 liter of alcohol; and up to US$100 of duty free gifts. Meat or meat products, fruit, plants, and seeds are prohibited, as are illegal drugs.

FOREIGN EXCHANGE

The US dollar (US$) is freely convertible almost everywhere. There are 100 cents (¢) to the dollar. Coins come in denominations of 1 cent (penny), 5 cents (nickel), 10 cents (dime), 25 cents (quarter), 50 cents (half-dollar), and 100 cents (dollar). The half-dollar is uncommon, and the US$1 coin is rarely seen. Paper currency comes in denominations of 1, 2 (rare), 5, 10, 20, 50, and 100 dollars.

You cannot use any other currency in the US, and it is difficult to find banks that are able to exchange foreign currency. It is best to buy traveler's checks denominated in US$ before you leave for the US; the small amount you will lose in the exchange rate is nothing compared with the time, energy, and frustration you will encounter trying to find a place to change money—even in the world financial center of New York. Otherwise, you can change money at booths and bank branches at some major international airports—such as those in New York, Los Angeles, San Francisco, and Chicago—or at American Express and Thomas Cook outlets.

Traveler's checks in US dollars are widely accepted, although smaller establishments may not be willing to cash them. International credit cards, such as VISA and MasterCard (respectively, EuroCard and

Access), are also widely accepted, while American Express, Diners Club, and Discover are also common, although less widely accepted. Most banks belong to networks of 24-hour automated teller machines (ATMs) that accept bank cards and credit cards.

Banks in the US will not cash your personal check unless you have an account with that bank.

TIPPING

Tipping is institutionalized in the US. The Internal Revenue Service (IRS) assumes that workers in service industries—particularly hotel, restaurant, and taxicab businesses—receive tips and taxes them accordingly. Employers are required to withhold the taxes on these estimated tips from their often minimal hourly wages of such employees, which reduces the net pay and often means that your waiter, maid, or driver literally lives on these tips. However, even before the IRS began this widely reviled practice, you could expect a surly, even hostile, response if you didn't tip, or didn't tip enough, especially in urban areas.

Food servers generally receive 15 percent of the bill, and in expensive restaurants 20 percent is the norm. Taxi drivers, hairdressers, and bartenders also expect 15 percent. Tip porters and bellhops 50 cents or US$1 per bag, coat-checkers US$1, and airport van drivers US$1 or US$2.

ACCESS TO CITIES FROM AIRPORTS

New York City John F. Kennedy (JFK), LaGuardia, and Newark airports have easy access to the city through public transportation, airport shuttle, or taxi, and all have rental car agencies. From Manhattan, JFK is 24 km (15 miles); a taxi ride costs about US$40 and takes about 50 minutes. Airport buses from JFK to Manhattan cost about US$12. LaGuardia is 13 km (8 miles) from Manhattan; expect to pay about US$27 for a taxi fare. Newark is 26 km (16 miles) from Manhattan; taxi fare is about US$50 plus. All cab fares require you to pay any tolls and bridge and tunnel fares in addition to the basic fare. You can also take Carey Airport Express buses or Gray Line Air Shuttle minibuses from JFK and LaGuardia for US$8 to US$12. New Jersey Transit buses from Newark leave you at the Port Authority Bus Terminal in Manhattan for about US$7. Various hotel shuttle, van, and limousine services are also available.

Washington, DC Washington National, Dulles, and Baltimore/Washington (BWI) airports all serve the nation's capital. Washington National is located in the state of Virginia directly across the Potomac River from Washington DC, only 20 minutes and US$1.25 by subway from the city center. Taxi fare is about US$10; Washington Flyer buses cost about US$8; city buses also serve the airport, as do shuttle services from most major hotels. Dulles is less convenient but less crowded than National. It is also in Virginia, about 45 minutes and 41 km (26 miles) from the city, accessible by cab (US$45), Washington Flyer bus (US$16), or hotel shuttle. Lastly, BWI, in the state of Maryland, halfway between Washington DC and Baltimore, is 1 hour and 40 km (25 miles) from downtown. Cab fare should be about US$55, while the Airport Connection buses cost about US$15. All airports also have rental car agencies and limousine service.

Miami Miami International Airport is almost 10 km (6 miles) west of downtown. Cab fare to downtown is about US$15, to Miami Beach between US$17 and US$26. The SuperShuttle vans go to area hotels for US$7 and up, while public buses cost US$1.25 (exact change required). The airport also has car rental agencies and limousine services.

Chicago The third largest US city is served by O'Hare International Airport, one of the world's busiest. O'Hare is about 32 km (20 miles) northwest of downtown, making it a 30- to 60- minute taxi ride (depending on traffic) costing about US$25 to US$30. Continental Air Transport runs a van service to major hotels and charges about US$13 for the 60-minute trip. The Chicago Transit Authority's O'Hare Line trains leave the main terminal at O'Hare for downtown locations, charging US$1.50 for the 45-minute trip. Several carriers fly into Midway Airport, which is closer to downtown—about 10 km (6 miles). Public transport is difficult, but taxi service is available. The half-hour ride costs about US$20. Continental Airport Express serves major hotels; the cost is US$9.50, and advance reservations are required. There are also car rental agencies and limousine service at the airports.

Houston The country's fourth largest city is served by Houston Intercontinental Airport, 24 km (15 miles) north of downtown. During Houston's stand-still rush hour (or whenever there is rain, fog, or for any other reason, and sometimes for no reason at all), the trip can take more than an hour. Taxi fare is about US$30. Airport Express's shuttle service charges about US$12 to deliver you to any of its three downtown terminals. The city's express bus service charges US$1.20. And, of course, rental cars and limousine service are available at the airport.

Los Angeles The major airport serving the second largest US city is Los Angeles International Airport (affectionately called LAX), on the coast 40 km (25 miles) west of downtown and 16 km (10 miles) west of Beverly Hills. The taxi ride downtown takes from 30 minutes to one hour, depending on traffic. Ask for a flat fare rather than the more expensive metered fare; the ride should cost US$25 to US$30. The SuperShuttle charges about US$12 for a ride to downtown hotels, and slightly more to Beverly Hills; L.A. Top Shuttle's fares are about the same. Limousine service is also available. The sprawling Los Angeles area is also served by regional airports in Orange County, Burbank, Long Beach, and Ontario. Check for the airports and carriers that will put you closest to where you will need to be during your stay.

ACCOMMODATIONS

The US has a vast array of hotel and motel rooms and an equally vast range of prices. You can pay as little as US$20 a night for a basic motel room or as much as US$3,000 for a night in a major hotel's most luxurious suite. If you must have access to a wide range of business services and you need to impress the businesspeople you are meeting, a first class hotel is the place to stay.

But if all you need is a place to sleep and wash up, choose a moderately-priced or budget hotel, or a motel. Every town of any size has at least one motel, and they are common at major freeway intersections. In larger cities, they may be located along major highways, which often go right through the center of town. However, you will often find them in the suburbs and on the outskirts of cities. The rooms are generally clean, if small, with full-size beds, and usually have a TV and phone. Some rooms even have small kitchens, and there is often a restaurant nearby. Do not expect much in the way of service, and the helpful advice offered a foreign traveler will vary from marginal to none. A few chains, such as Motel 6, charge as little as US$25 a night, although most charge US$30 to US$60. In New York City, rates for the better motels, such as Best Western, climb to more than US$100. However, Best Western has thousands of motels in the US, and outside of the big cities or the most attractive vacation areas, rooms can cost as little as US$30. Note that virtually all lodging accommodations of whatever price and category in the US come with private bath.

When it comes to prices, hotels are like airlines. They offer a bewildering array of categories, packages, special promotions, and schedules, all subject to availability and restrictions. The rates quoted here are generally the absolutely lowest possible rates for a single or double occupancy (some hotels charge the same for single and double) room on the weekend, which some hotels consider as starting on Thursday and others on Friday. If you check in during the week, be prepared to pay more. Room rates vary considerably depending on the day of the week and time of the year. Moreover, when business is good, rates go up; when business is slow, rates come down. Advertised rates are often subject to change without notice. State and local taxes on hotel accommodations can also add significantly to the bill and are not always included in the rate quote.

Because such a wide range of lodging is available, visitors should look well beyond the limited sample of hotels listed here. The easiest way to travel in the US is to have your travel agent do most of the work for you. If you want to save as much money as possible with the least amount of confusion, ask your agent for a package that includes airfare and hotel, or airfare, hotel and car rental.

Note: Telephone numbers beginning with (800) are toll-free numbers which can only be used within the US (and sometimes Canada as well).

New York City

Doral Tuscany 120 E. 39th St., Manhattan; 121-room hotel in the Murray Hill district on the East Side. Offering a high level of service, excellent restaurant, fitness center. Business services include meeting rooms, secretarial, concierge, photocopiers, and audiovisual equipment. Rates: starting at about US$189. Tel: [1] (212) 686-1600 or (800) 22-DORAL Fax: [1] (212) 779-7822.

Grand Hyatt 109 E. 42nd St. at Park Ave., Manhattan; 1,400 small (by US standards) rooms. Glitz, glass, and chrome. Business services include meeting rooms, computers, photocopiers, secretarial, concierge, audiovisual equipment, and express checkout. Rates: starting at US$159. Tel: [1] (212) 883-1234 or (800) 228-9000 Fax: [1] (212) 697-3772.

Holiday Inn Crowne Plaza 1605 Broadway at W. 49th St., Manhattan; 770 rooms plus seven VIP floors in the Times Square area. Restaurant, health club with indoor pool. Business services include completely equipped and staffed business center, meeting rooms, secretarial, concierge, computers, photocopiers, audiovisual equipment, express checkout. Rates: starting at US$179. Tel: [1] (212) 977-4000 or (800) HOLIDAY Fax: [1] (212) 333-7393.

Paramount 235 W. 46th St., Manhattan; 110 small rooms. Room service until midnight, 24-hour brasserie, children's playroom. Business services include business center, meeting rooms, secretarial, concierge, photocopiers, express checkout. Rates: starting at US$99. Tel: [1] (212) 764-5500 or (800) 225-7474 Fax: [1] (212) 354-5237.

Washington, DC

Capitol Hilton 1001 16th St. at K St. NW; 549 large rooms near the White House. Rooms have minibar, two phones; VIP rooms have separate concierge and check-in; fitness center, restaurants. Business services include meeting rooms, secretarial, concierge, computers, photocopiers, audiovisual equipment, fax machines, translation, currency exchange, express checkout. Rates: starting at US$250. Tel: [1] (202) 393-1000 or (800) HILTONS Fax: [1] (202) 393-7992.

Grand 2350 M St. NW; 263 rooms near

Georgetown. Each room has three phones; restaurants, 24-hour room service, valet and dry cleaning, valet parking. Business services include meeting rooms, secretarial, multilingual concierge, computers, photocopiers, audiovisual equipment, currency exchange. Rates: starting at US$125. Tel: [1] (202) 429-0100 or (800) 848-0016 Fax: [1] (202) 639-5784.

Morrison-Clark Inn Massachusetts Ave. and 11th St. NW; 54 rooms near Convention Center and Metro Center. Restaurant, room service until 11 pm, complimentary breakfast. Business services include meeting rooms, secretarial, concierge, computers, photocopiers, audiovisual equipment. Rates: starting from US$125. Tel: [1] (202) 898-1200 or (800) 332-7898 Fax: [1] (202) 289-8576.

Watergate 2650 Virginia Ave. NW; 235 large rooms in the Watergate office-apartment-hotel complex adjacent to Kennedy Center. Restaurant, health club, 24-hour room service. Business services include meeting rooms, secretarial, concierge, computers, photocopiers, audiovisual equipment, fax machines, express checkout. Rates: starting from US $155. Tel: [1] (202) 965-2300 or (800) 424-2736 Fax: [1] (202) 337-7915.

Miami

Fontainebleau Hilton 4441 Collins Ave., Miami Beach; 1,200 rooms on 20 acres of beachfront. Health club, pool, whirlpools, tennis, 12 restaurants and lounges, 24-hour room service. Business services include meeting rooms, secretarial, photocopiers, audiovisual equipment, fax machines, express checkout. Rates: starting at US $180. Tel: [1] (305) 538-2000 or (800) HILTONS Fax: [1] (305) 531-9274.

Inter-Continental Miami 100 Chopin Plaza; 644 rooms in city center near financial district. Pool, auditorium, 24-hour room service. Business services include business center, meeting rooms, secretarial, concierge, computers, photocopiers, audiovisual equipment, fax machines, modem hookups in rooms. Rates: starting at US$199. Tel: [1] (305) 577-1000 or (800) 327-3005 Fax: [1] (305) 577-0384.

Radisson Mart Plaza 711 NW 72nd Ave.; 334 rooms next to Miami International Merchandise Mart. Complimentary breakfast on concierge level, restaurant, health club, tennis, racquetball, free airport shuttle. Business services include meeting rooms, concierge, photocopiers, audiovisual equipment, fax machines, modem hookups in rooms, printing. Rates: starting at US$149. Tel: [1] (305) 261-3800 or (800) 333-3333 (toll-free in US) Fax: [1] (305) 261-7665.

Sheraton Biscayne Bay 495 Brickell Ave.; 612 rooms downtown in financial district overlooking Biscayne Bay. Restaurants, pool, executive floor. Business services include business center, meeting rooms, concierge. Rates: starting at US$139. Tel: [1] (305) 373-6000 or (800) 325-3535 (toll-free in the US) Fax: [1] (305) 374-2279.

Chicago

Drake 140 E. Walton Pl.; 535 rooms near North Side on Gold Coast. Restaurants, 24-hour rooms service. Business services include meeting rooms, secretarial, concierge, computers, photocopiers, fax machines, audiovisual equipment, express checkout. Rates: starting at US$149. Tel: [1] (312) 787-2200 or (800) HILTONS Fax: [1] (312) 951-5803.

Executive House 71 E. Wacker Dr.; 475 rooms and suites with excellent city views near the Loop. Restaurant, nearby health club available, valet parking. Business services include business center, meeting rooms, foreign language telephone system, photocopiers, fax machines. Rates: starting at US$185. Tel: [1] (312) 346-7100 or (800) 621-4005 Fax: [1] (312) 346-1721.

Marriott Downtown 540 N. Michigan Ave.; 1,172 rooms near North Side, Water Tower, North Pier, gallery districts. Restaurants, 24-hour room service, health club, pool. Business services include business center, meeting rooms, secretarial, concierge, computers, photocopiers, fax machines. Rates: starting at US$179 (including breakfast for two). Tel: [1] (312) 836-0100 or (800) 228-9290 Fax: [1] (312) 836-6139.

Swissôtel 323 E. Wacker Dr. at Illinois Center; 625 large rooms (among the largest in the country) near the Loop, with spectacular views of lake and river. European flair, with one-fifth of staff and one-half of guests from Europe; restaurant. Business services include business center, meeting rooms, stock market quotation board, newswire, business library. Rates: starting at US$175. Tel: [1] (312) 565-0565 or (800) 65-GRAND Fax: [1] (312) 565-0540.

Houston

Allen Park Inn 2121 Allen Pkwy; 249 rooms in motor inn near downtown. Health club, 24-hour restaurant. Business services include meeting rooms, secretarial, photocopiers, audiovisual equipment. Rates: starting at US$79. Tel: [1] (713) 521-9321 or (800) 231-6310 Fax: [1] (713) 521-9321, ext. 350.

Hyatt Regency Houston 1200 Louisiana St.; 950 rooms and suites downtown. Revolving rooftop restaurant and three other restaurants, nearby health club, valet parking. Business services include business center, meeting rooms, secretarial, concierge, translation service, photocopiers, fax machines, telex, computer printers, modem hookups in rooms, express checkout. Rates: starting from US$149. Tel: [1] (713) 654-1234 or (800) 228-9000 Fax: [1] (713) 951-0934.

Omni Houston Post Oak Lane at Woodway Drive; 368 rooms in the Riverway Complex, West Houston. Restaurants, health club, tennis, 24-hour room service. Business services include meeting rooms, secretarial, concierge, photocopiers, audiovisual equipment, express checkout. Rates: starting at US$145.

HOTEL AND MOTEL TOLL-FREE NUMBERS

Note: These toll-free "800" numbers may only be used within the United States (and Canada in some cases).

Moderate motels and hotels

Best Western	(800) 528-1234
Clarion	(800) 252-7466
Comfort	(800) 228-5150
Days Inn	(800) 325-2525
Holiday Inn	(800) 465-4329
Howard Johnson	(800) 654-2000
La Quinta	(800) 531-5900
Quality	(800) 228-5151
Radisson	(800) 333-3333
Ramada	(800) 272-6332
Red Lion	(800) 547-8010

Expensive hotels

Embassy Suites	(800) 362-2779
Guest Quarters Suites	(800) 424-2900
Hyatt	(800) 327-0200
Marriott	(800) 228-9290
Novotel	(800) 221-4542
Omni	(800) 843-6664
Sheraton	(800) 325-3535
Stouffer	(800) 468-3571
Westin	(800) 228-3000

Luxury hotels

Four Seasons	(800) 332-3442
Hilton	(800) 445-8667
Inter-Continental	(800) 332-4246
Kempinski	(800) 426-3135
Leading Hotels of the World	(800) 223-6800
Meridien	(800) 543-4300
Nikko	(800) 645-5687
Ritz-Carlton	(800) 241-3333

Tel: [1] (713) 871-8181 or (800) THE-OMNI (toll-free in the US) Fax: [1] (713) 871-0719.

Westin Oaks and Westin Galleria Galleria Mall, West Houston; 900 rooms in two hotels at opposite ends of Galleria Mall. Restaurants, pool, access to ice skating, running, tennis, 24-hour room service. Business services include meeting rooms, secretarial, concierge, photocopiers, audiovisual equipment, express checkout. Rates: starting at US$125 (Oaks) and US$115 (Galleria). Tel: [1] (713) 960-8100 or (800) 228-3000 (toll-free in the US) Fax: [1] (713) 960-6553.

Los Angeles

Beverly Prescott 1224 S. Beverwil Dr., W. Los Angeles; 140 rooms, each with balcony overlooking Beverly Hills, Century City, Hollywood, Pacific Ocean. Restaurant, pool, health club, room service. Business services include meeting rooms, secretarial, concierge; executive suites have fax, computers, printers. Rates: starting at US$185. Tel: [1] (310) 277-2800 or (800) 421-3212 (toll-free in the US) Fax: [1] (310) 203-9537.

Inter-Continental Los Angeles 251 S. Olive St., 469 rooms in downtown, geared to business travelers. Restaurants, pool, health club. Business services include business center, meeting rooms, secretarial, concierge, computer/fax/modem capabilities in each room. Rates: starting at US$139. Tel: [1] (213) 617-3300 or (800)-327-0200 (toll-free in the US) Fax: [1] (213) 617-3399.

Le Mondrian 8440 Sunset Blvd., West Hollywood; 188 rooms on the Sunset Strip. Restaurant, fitness center, pool, jazz lounge. Business services include meeting rooms, secretarial, concierge, computer center, drafting tables, video editing equipment, photocopiers, audiovisual equipment. Rates: starting at US$99. Tel: [1] (213) 650-8999 or (800) 255-5168 (toll-free in the US) Fax: [1] (213) 650-5215.

New Otani 120 Los Angeles St.; 448 rooms in garden-like setting near Music Center, downtown. Japanese-owned, with excellent Japanese-style service, restaurant, health club. Business services include meeting rooms, secretarial, concierge, photocopiers, audiovisual equipment, express checkout. Rates: starting at US$118. Tel: [1] (213) 629-1200 or (800) 421-8795 Fax: [1] (213) 622-0980.

EATING

Many residents and visitors alike express dismay at much of what is called traditional American cooking. Although food is readily available and relatively affordable, it consists primarily of meat and starches, tends to be highly caloric, and is often unimaginative in its basic preparation. Travelers may have difficulty in finding less heavy fare while on the road, and those with special dietary needs—including vegetarians—may find that the average US restaurant is not equipped to cater to them. At the same time, US chefs have access to a large variety of fresh meats, vegetables, and fruits, and a traveler can usually find well-prepared daily specials. Many restaurants, particularly in urban centers, will oblige dietary needs if the traveler makes them known. Moreover, food in the US is extremely eclectic, and there are thousands of types from which to choose.

Of special interest are regional cuisines and the so-called new American restaurants that use traditional ingredients with new techniques and ingredients to concoct often stunning dishes. Regional tastes range from the seafood-based cooking of the East, West, and Gulf Coasts, to Southern cooking with its specialized offshoots of Louisiana Cajun and Creole cooking, to Southwest cooking flavored with Mexican specialties, to California cuisine emphasizing fresh and light ingredients presented in imaginative combinations. Barbecue—smoked meats prepared with a pungent sauce—is a national specialty. Foreigners should note that much US cooking incorporates corn (maize), the New World's indigenous grain. Although corn is widely used elsewhere in the world, in many areas it is not usually considered food; visitors from these regions should not be taken aback.

Ethnic foods have become widely accepted throughout the US, and with greater exposure has come higher quality. However, many of these foods have been altered to fit the tastes of the general US populace, making them only vaguely recognizable to a native. Nevertheless, authentic ethnic foods can be found, often at smaller restaurants that are slightly off the beaten path.

For those who want to sample the quintessential US cuisine, many chains offer varieties of fast food: food prepared quickly using standardized methods and portions for cheap and rapid consumption. In addition to the well-known hamburgers and French fries menu, US fast food now includes tacos, chicken, fish, pizza, and other specialties. The roots of such cuisine can still be explored in surviving independent local diners, drive-ins, and food stands that serve home-style burgers, fries, and milkshakes.

Domestic and imported beer is available throughout the country. The national beer brands are somewhat unexciting if serviceable, but the new trend toward local microbreweries is providing greater variety. Bourbon and other corn-based whiskies are US specialties. The US has a large and generally high-quality wine industry, although wine may not be on the menu in many restaurants. Soft drinks are readily available, and water—almost always served with any meal—is safe to drink.

The price ranges quoted do not include wine or other drinks, taxes, or tips.

New York City

New York is often referred to as the food capital of the world. There is probably no cuisine you cannot find somewhere in this city. Like everything else in New York, dining out can be intimidating, especially when you get the check. The priciest places will cost at least US$150 for two, not including wine, tax, or tips—if you can get in. If you are not a regular

or a celebrity, for example, you may not be able to get into "21" Club at any price. Lutece welcomes anyone, but you generally must make reservations a month in advance. Four Seasons may be the best restaurant in the nation, but plan far ahead and bring a gold card. The places we have listed are not on the "must" list to see and be seen in, but they are nonetheless superb. An expensive restaurant will cost at least US$100 for two, while one listed as moderate will cost at least US$70. However, New York has thousands of restaurants, diners, coffee shops, and street food vendors, all competing strongly for your dollars; you can hardly walk more than a block without finding a place to eat, and it is possible to eat well without going into debt.

An American Place New American cuisine. *Expensive:* cuisine from a leading chef. Reservations required; closed Sundays; major credit cards accepted. 2 Park Ave. at E. 32nd St. Tel: [1] (212) 684-2122.

Carnegie Delicatessen The epitome of New York delis. *Moderately priced:* communal tables, frantic pace, huge sandwiches. No reservations; open daily; no credit cards. 854 7th Ave. Tel: [1] (212) 757-2245.

Gotham Bar and Grill International cuisine. *Expensive:* highly creative. Reservations required; open every day; major credit cards accepted. 12 E. 12th St., between 5th Ave. and University Pl. Tel: [1] (212) 620-4020.

Louisiana Community Bar & Grill Cajun cuisine. *Moderately priced:* friendly service. Reservations required, open daily; major credit cards accepted. 622 Broadway, between Bleecker and Houston. Tel: [1] (212) 460-9633.

Periyali Greek cuisine. *Moderately priced:* reservations required; closed Sundays; major credit cards accepted. 35 W. 20th St. Tel: [1] (212) 463-7890.

Washington, DC

The nation's capital has numerous restaurants offering cuisines from around the world. Many are very expensive, where a dinner for two costs more than US$100, but many more are expensive (more than US$75) or moderate (more than US$40). And like any American city, Washington is full of inexpensive restaurants, delis, and fast food places.

Allegro International cuisine. *Moderately priced:* famous for business buffet lunch. Reservations advised; open daily for breakfast, lunch, and dinner; major credit cards accepted. 16th and K Sts. NW. Tel: [1] (202) 879-6900.

Bice Italian cuisine. *Expensive:* reservations advised; open daily, closed for lunch on Saturdays; major credit cards accepted. 601 Pennsylvania Ave. NW between 6th and 7th Sts.; enter on Indiana Ave. Tel: [1] (202) 638-2423.

La Colline French cuisine. *Moderately priced:*

inventive. Reservations advised; open daily for breakfast, lunch, and dinner; major credit cards accepted. 400 N. Capitol St. NW Tel: [1] (202) 737-0400.

Mr. K's Chinese cuisine. *Moderately priced:* highly regarded, regional cuisine—Cantonese, Szechuan, Peking, Hunan. Reservations advised; open daily; major credit cards accepted. 2121 K. St. NW. Tel: [1] (202) 331-8868.

Vidalia Southern cuisine. *Moderately priced:* a mix of the old and new South in a bright but soothing setting. Reservations required; open Monday through Friday for lunch and dinner, on Saturday for dinner; major credit cards accepted. 1990 M St. NW. Tel: [1] (202) 659-1990.

Miami

A dinner for two at a top Miami restaurant will cost at least US$85, but there are many excellent eateries in the expensive (more than US$70) and moderate (more than US$50) ranges, and the usual inexpensive and budget places.

Fish Market Seafood. *Expensive:* the region's best, with "executive service" lunch served in 30 minutes or it's free. Reservations advised; open weekdays for lunch and dinner, Monday through Saturday for dinner, closed Sunday; major credit cards accepted. 1601 Biscayne Blvd., in Omni International Hotel. [1] (305) 374-4399.

Joe's Stone Crab Seafood and American cuisine. *Moderately priced:* extremely popular, informal, noisy, big, crowded, supplied by restaurant's own fishing fleet; large portions; take-out available. No reservations, often long waits; open for lunch and dinner Tuesday through Saturday, closed mid-May through mid-October; major credit cards accepted. 227 Biscayne St., Miami Beach. Tel: [1] (305) 673-0365; (800) 780-CRAB.

Mark's Place International cuisine. *Expensive:* highly inventive. Reservations required; open weekdays for lunch, daily for dinner. 2286 NE 123rd St., North Miami Beach. Tel: [1] (305) 893-6888.

Mimosa Nouvelle continental with a seafood tilt. *Moderately priced:* Expressionist art in a Mediterranean setting in the La Voile Rouge Hotel; brunch served poolside. Reservations advised; open daily for lunch and dinner plus Sunday for brunch; major credit cards accepted. 455 Ocean Dr., Miami Beach. Tel: [1] (305) 534-8700.

Yuca Cuban cuisine. *Expensive:* reservations required; open every day for dinner, Monday through Saturday for lunch; major credit cards accepted. 177 Giralda Ave., Coral Gables. Tel: [1] (305) 444-4448.

Chicago

While not on the scale of New York regarding numbers of restaurants or diversity—or, thankfully, price—Chicago is a typical American big city when it comes to dining out: a wide selection of cuisines and prices, plus Chicago's own reputation for experimentation, casualness, and eccentricity. An expensive dinner for two will cost at least US$60, while a moderately priced restaurant will charge more than US$40.

Bistro 110 Bistro cuisine. *Moderately priced:* often prepared in wood-burning oven; Sunday brunch features live jazz. Reservations advised; open daily for lunch and dinner; major credit cards accepted. 110 E. Pearson St. Tel: [1] (312) 266-3110.

Charlie Trotter's Nouvelle cuisine. *Expensive:* adventuresome, very popular place. Reservations required; closed Sundays and Mondays; major credit cards accepted. 816 W. Armitage Ave. Tel: [1] (312) 248-6228.

The Eccentric French, Italian, English, and American cuisine. *Moderately priced:* extremely inventive; owned by talk show hostess Oprah Winfrey. No reservations; open daily; major credit cards accepted. 159 W. Erie. Tel: [1] (312) 248-6228.

The Pump Room American. *Moderately priced:* 1930s supper club, with old standby dishes as well as new offerings; Jackets and ties required in the evening; open daily for breakfast, lunch, and dinner plus Sunday brunch; major credit cards accepted. Omni Ambassador East Hotel,1301 N. State Pkwy. Tel: [1] (312) 266-0360.

Scoozi Provincial Italian cuisine. *Moderately priced:* huge menu, including pizza. Reservations required for lunch; open daily for dinner, Monday through Friday for lunch; major credit cards accepted. 410 W. Huron. Tel: [1] (312) 943-5900

Houston

While you can get various world cuisines in Houston, this city is a good place to sample southwestern and Mexican cooking. And you can do this at prices far less than in other big American cities. An expensive restaurant will charge upwards of US$80 for two, but you can get by for US$25 and up at moderately priced establishments. Texans are known for putting a weird, but fun, twist on everyday experiences, and Houston's restaurants are no exception.

Cadillac Bar Mexican cuisine. *Moderately priced:* fine cuisine. Reservations advised; open daily; major credit cards accepted. 1802 Shepherd at I-10 Highway. Tel: [1] (713) 862-2020.

Cafe Annie Southwestern cuisine. *Expensive:* with emphasis on mesquite-grilled meats; noisy, friendly, lively, disorganized. Reservations required; open Monday through Friday for lunch, Monday through Saturday for dinner; major credit cards accepted. 1728 S. Post Oak Blvd. Tel: [1] (713) 840-1111.

Great Caruso Continental cuisine. *Expensive:*

European opera house setting, singers perform Broadway songs; excellent food and service. Reservations required; closed Mondays; major credit cards accepted. 10001 Westheimer. Tel: [1] (713) 780-4900.

Ruggles Grill American cuisine. *Moderately priced:* Bistro style, down home, inventive food with attentive but unpretentious service. Reservations suggested; open Tuesday through Friday for lunch and dinner; Saturday for dinner; Sunday for brunch and dinner; closed Mondays; major credit cards accepted. 903 Westheimer. Tel: [1] (713) 524-3839.

Ruth's Chris Steak House Texas beef-based cuisine. *Expensive:* complete with oil company decor and stock market reports; very Texas. Reservations advised; open daily for dinner; major credit cards accepted. 6213 Richmond. Tel: [1] (713) 789-2333.

Los Angeles

No American city has a wider variety of ethnic groups and the resulting range of restaurants than Los Angeles. However, unlike more centralized New York, LA's restaurants are scattered over a huge urban area that is accessible only by car. Cuisines are adventurous, inventive, blended; anything goes. Smoking in indoor restaurants is prohibited, as in many California cities. An expensive dinner for two will cost more than US$75, while a moderately priced restaurant will charge at least US$40.

Ivy American cuisine. *Expensive:* with inventive, changing menu; business lunch favorite. Reservations required, with at least one-hour wait for dinner; open daily for lunch and dinner; major credit cards accepted. 113 N. Robertson Blvd. Tel: [1] (310) 274-8303.

Joss Chinese cuisine. *Moderately priced:* unusual. Reservations advised; open daily for dinner, Monday through Friday for lunch; major credit cards accepted. 9255 Sunset Blvd. Tel: [1] (310) 276-1886.

Locanda Veneta Italian cuisine. *Expensive:* best in town; very small trattoria. Reservations required; open Monday through Saturday for dinner, Monday through Friday for lunch; major credit cards accepted. 8638 W. 3rd St. Tel: [1] (310) 274-1893.

Citrus French-California cuisine. *Expensive:* bright, open setting, excellent food; chef's tasting menu a bargain as is the less expensive adjacent and related Citrus Bistro. Reservations advised; open Monday through Friday for lunch and dinner, Saturday for dinner, closed Sundays. 6703 Melrose Ave., West Hollywood. Tel: [1] (213) 857-0034.

A Thousand Cranes Japanese cuisine. *Moderately priced:* traditional service; Sunday buffet features live music. Reservations advised; open every day; major credit cards accepted. 120 S. Los Angeles St. in New Otani Hotel. Tel: [1] (213) 629-1200.

LOCAL CUSTOMS OVERVIEW

Residents of the US are less formal and ceremonial in business situations than people of other cultures. However, politeness and consideration in the US are largely the same as they are elsewhere, with some significant variations. In general, US citizens are tolerant of foreign ways, to a point. Here is a guide to help you adjust to US ways of doing business.

• *Treat a woman on your level of authority or expertise as your equal, the same as you would treat a man.* Despite continuing discrimination in the workplace, the status of women in US business has increased dramatically in the last 20 years and continues to improve. Businesswomen in the US have more authority and power than their counterparts virtually anywhere else in the world, and they do not take kindly to demonstrations of machismo. They do not expect and do not want to be regarded either as special or as unimportant. You have been granted a meeting with them because they are the people you need to meet, not because they are ornaments. Nor should you feel that you are somehow being insulted by being referred to a woman. Forget gender; open a door for someone as a gesture of politeness, not as a concession to the person's gender. If a US businesswoman is taking you to lunch, allow her to pay the check just as you would allow a male host. She expects to greet you with a handshake and will likely be offended by such out-of-place gallantries as trying to kiss her cheek or hand. Any attempt to categorize her by gender is dangerous, and sexually suggestive remarks will generate a cold response, if not a hostile retort. You are there to do business, not jeopardize your chances by offending your US counterpart.

• *As you should treat women, so should you treat members of other races* in the increasingly multiracial and multi-ethnic US business society. Again, discrimination continues among US residents, but as a society the US has committed itself to equality. The US is among the world's most cosmopolitan cultures, home to people from every country on earth. Tolerance is not merely appropriate: it is essential.

• *Be on time for your appointments.* Some cities, such as New York, Chicago, Los Angeles, and Houston, are held hostage to heavy traffic, and in such cases you may be granted 10 to 15 minutes of tardiness, but seldom more. If you cannot make your appointment on time, call ahead to advise your host, who can reschedule you and do something else with the time (US businesspeople are fanatical about not wasting time). If you are late, your meeting will be canceled, and you will have to reschedule.

• *The handshake is the universal greeting,* used by both men and women, whether on first introduction or in subsequent meetings. In some places, a handshake commits one's honor to the business relationship that begins at that point.

MAJOR US AIRLINES TOLL-FREE NUMBERS

The following toll-free numbers may be used—within the US only—to reach these major airlines. Also included is the main hub for each airline and the regions served.

Airline	800 Number	Main Hub
Alaska	(800) 426-0333	Seattle

Service area: Pacific coast, Mexico, Russia

American	(800) 433-7300	Dallas

Service area: Nationwide, Europe, Asia, Australia, South & Central America

America West	(800) 235-9292	Phoenix

Service area: Southwest, Nationwide

Continental	(800) 525-0280	Houston

Service area: Nationwide, Central & South America, East Asia

Delta	(800) 221-1212	Atlanta

Service area: North America, Europe, Asia

Hawaiian	(800) 367-5320	Honolulu

Service area: Hawaii, West Coast, South Pacific

Northwest	(800) 225-2525	St. Paul

Service area: North America, Asia

Southwest	(800) 435-9792	Dallas

Service area: Southwest, West Coast, Midwest

Tower Air	(800) 452-5531	New York

Service area: Limited US service, Israel, France, Brazil, India, other charter flights

TWA	(800) 221-2000	New York

Service area: Nationwide, Europe, Middle East

USAir	(800) 428-4322	Pittsburgh

Service area: Nationwide, Canada, Europe

United	(800) 241-6522	Chicago

Service area: Nationwide, Europe, Asia, South Pacific, Central & South America

• *The first words a US resident will utter* after introductions are often, "What do you do?" It is not meant as an insult or to be overly familiar, but is merely the standard opening line in virtually any conversation between strangers. The person is asking what your profession is; everyone does it, and you will find yourself developing a standard response without even thinking of it.

• *Business cards are not as significant* in the US as they are elsewhere, especially in Asia. You may offer your card, and it will be accepted, but do not expect the recipient to pay much attention to it or necessarily to receive one in return. Usually, you will be asked for your card only if the recipient expects to contact you at a later time.

• *People are direct in the US.* They speak directly, ask pointed questions, and expect direct answers. They are not schooled in the ceremonies of negotiation as practiced elsewhere in much of the world. By comparison with other cultures, US citizens may seem impolite, in a hurry, rough. On the other hand, when an someone says "yes," the answer usually is really "yes." The same goes for "no." New Yorkers are known for extreme directness, even rudeness, although they do not necessarily mean to be impolite, merely efficient. Midwesterners are also direct, but usually much more polite; and Californians are much more casual. They do not always mean what they say, particularly in Los Angeles, the City of Dreams, where "I'll get back to you on that" may well mean "you do not have a chance," the closest that US residents come to the Asian way of negotiating. Things may be somewhat more formal elsewhere in the country where manners and formality are often more important.

• *You may be invited to a "working breakfast"*—or, in corporate circles, a "power breakfast"—an increasingly popular business tradition. People in the US have decided the time devoted to eating breakfast is wasted if it does not also include business, so, as with the business lunch, the purpose of breakfast is to negotiate a deal over ham and eggs. Then you can close the deal over a power lunch.

• *Gift-giving is not as important in the US* as elsewhere, and may indeed present problems. It is better not to give a gift at all than to give the wrong one, or give it to the wrong person. A gift may be looked upon as trying to gain influence in an underhanded way. US laws actually prohibit US government employees from receiving gifts in the course of their jobs. Business firms often keep a close watch on such gift-giving. And because it is not a normal and accepted practice, gift-giving may embarrass both the recipient, who is not equipped to reciprocate, and others who did not bring gifts.

However, there are exceptions. One of the best gifts to give and receive is entertainment. It can be a drink at a nice bar, a fancy dinner, tickets to a show or a sports event, or a round of golf. However, allow your US hosts to make the first offer. This is the only way you can understand what is appropriate and what is frowned upon by that particular company. Anything too costly is likely to be embarrassing and is usually refused.

Gift-giving is traditional and accepted at Christmas, not only in families but also among business associates. Business-related gift-giving should generally be restricted to gifts that can be used in business: pens, calendars, planners, paperweights, and the like. Extravagance is an embarrassing mistake. Another exception might be your first meeting with a person who is very important to the success of your visit, or your final encounter after successful negotiations just before your departure. Here, the best gift is something modest (but not cheap or tasteless, such as an advertising or marketing trinket) that is unique to your home country: a local handicraft, your national beverage, or a descriptive book on your country. In these circumstances, do not expect your recipient to give you a gift immediately. Except at Christmas, reciprocation may come much later, if at all.

Again, be careful to treat women the same as men when it comes to gift-giving. Avoid giving personal gifts, such as perfume or clothing.

• *Smoking is becoming socially unacceptable in more and more places in the US. Always ask if you can smoke before you light up.* Smoking is prohibited by law on airplanes, in many restaurants, and in public places. Businesses often prohibit smoking in their buildings. Realize that it is likely that smoking will offend a nonsmoker, and offending your nonsmoking host is not a good way to do business.

DOMESTIC TRANSPORTATION

Air The US is well served by airline routes. Most cities of any size are served by at least one domestic airline. Larger cities have domestic and international service, but sometimes at different airports. Smaller cities may be served by only a single domestic airline, and small commuter lines serve even smaller towns. The largest US carriers have both international and domestic routes, which makes connecting flights easy. There is intense competition for customers, and one airline's price cuts are inevitably matched by its competitors. Each airline has one or more hubs, through which it routes many of its passengers, depending on their destinations. Wherever you want to go, at whatever time, you are almost certain to find a flight to suit your schedule. Nearly all major airlines offer reservations through toll-free "800" phone numbers, and the country's thousands of travel agents can do the same, generally at no charge.

Train When cars came along, and then planes, people in the US largely forgot about trains. Cars were more convenient for spread-out cities, while planes covered the vast distances between cities faster and more comfortably. The train remains a mainstay for travel in the Northeast, connecting Washington, Baltimore, Philadelphia, New York, and Boston. There is also service between the Northeast and Chicago, although western and transcontinental service is sparse and not recommended. The cost of a train ticket is usually less than that of flying between closer cities, especially along the Northeast corridor. Terminals are downtown, closer to your hotel than airports, and total travel time may be shorter than flying, if you include getting to and from airports and

CAR RENTAL TOLL-FREE NUMBERS	
(Note: These 800 numbers can only be dialed from within the US.)	
Alamo	(800) 331-1084
Avis	(800) 331-1212
Budget	(800) 527-0700
Dollar	(800) 800-4000
Hertz	(800) 654-3001
National	(800) 227-3876
Payless	(800) 237-2804
Thrifty	(800) 367-2277

baggage claim. There is also fast, efficient service between Los Angeles and San Diego, especially welcome when freeway traffic is congested for the 200 km (120 miles) between these cities. Amtrak, the national passenger railroad, serves 44 states and 500 cities; some cities receive only weekly service, while Washington gets more than 50 arrivals daily and New York more than that. Long distance train travel is far less comfortable than in Europe and is mainly for sightseers, not businesspeople on a tight schedule. Delays are common and amenities are minimal, while the cost may be higher than flying. You can call Amtrak toll-free nationwide at (800) 872-7245 for information and reservations. Amtrak offers the USA Railpass, good for unlimited travel for 15 days at a price of US$308 or 30 days for US$389. You can buy the pass at any Amtrak station when you show your valid foreign passport.

Car The spread-out nature of the US and the inconsistency in US domestic transportation systems means that eventually you will probably need to drive yourself. Outside the East Coast, cities are large and sprawling, generally have poor public transportation, and taxi fares that make a typical 32 km (20 mile) trip very costly and inconvenient, especially if you have to do it every day for a week. In dispersed cities such as Los Angeles and Houston, and to a lesser extent Miami, a car is a must (Washington and New York are somewhat more manageable by foot, taxi, or public transportation.)

To drive in the US, you need a valid driver's license issued by a country that is a signatory to the 1949 Geneva Motoring Convention. However, it is wise to get an international license in the event that a car rental agency asks for one.

It is very easy to rent a car in the US if you have a valid license and a major credit card. You can very often get a hotel and rental car package deal at very reasonable rates. Otherwise, any hotel will have information on car rental, as will all airports, which usually have vast fleets of rental cars parked near the

US TIME ZONES AND TELEPHONE AREA CODES

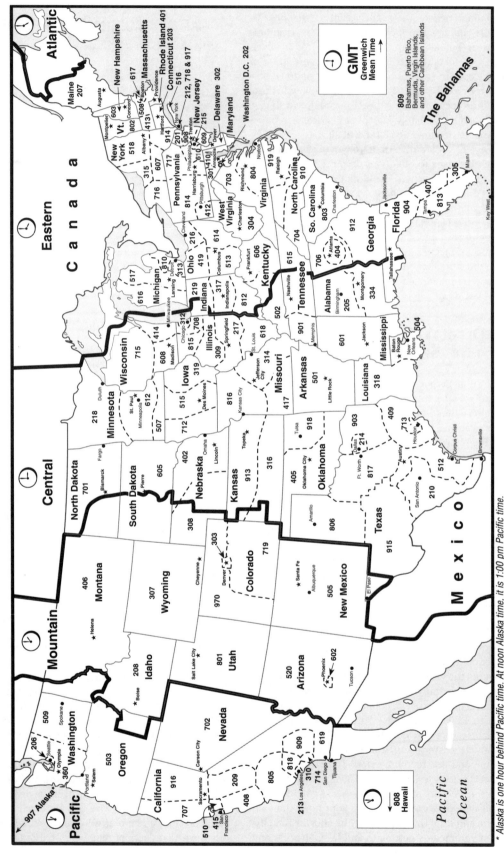

* Alaska is one hour behind Pacific time. At noon Alaska time, it is 1:00 pm Pacific time.

terminals or free shuttles to take you to your car. Some agencies in some cities can even provide a car phone that you can activate with your credit card.

Many cities are served by one or more limited access highways of the Interstate system, marked by a red, white, and blue shield bearing an "I" followed by a number. At times other than rush hours, traffic generally moves very quickly along these highways. However, it seems always to be rush hour on certain freeways in Los Angeles. Some states, mainly in the eastern US, have toll roads.

Motorists in the US drive on the right side of the road. Most states require drivers and passengers to wear seat belts. Driving while intoxicated is strictly illegal, and most states prohibit carrying open containers of alcohol in motor vehicles. City and state police are on the lookout for drunk drivers and for speeders. The metric system is generally not used for automobile speedometers and road signs; speeds are marked in miles per hour (mph). The national speed limit on highways is generally 55 mph (88 kph). However, in some states the speed limit is 65

mph (104 kph) in rural areas, and US drivers regularly exceed the speed limit in many places, especially the South, West, California, and even in the more crowded Northeast. Traffic in the fast lane may be traveling at 75 mph (120 kph) when possible, and 55 mph may be too slow even for the slow lane. During rush hour (about 7 to 9 am and 4 to 7 pm), traffic may come to a complete standstill due to a narrowing of the road (for example, from four to three lanes) or accidents. This in turn can lead to more accidents as drivers take their eyes off the road to look at the earlier accident.

Your rental car or contract should contain a notice describing what to do if you have an accident or a breakdown. Accidents usually receive prompt attention from police. If your car breaks down, look for a telephone—some highways have call boxes at regular intervals. If you are on a limited access highway or freeway and there is no phone, tie a handkerchief or scarf to the radio aerial or door handle, or leave your emergency flashing lights on, and wait for police. It is illegal and dan-

US DOMESTIC FLIGHT TIMES

Because distances are so great in the US, few businesspeople drive or take trains from one city to another. We have given approximate flight times between six major cities. Note that the direction one is traveling in can make a difference in flight time. In general, east-to-west flights take longer than west-to-east because of prevailing jet stream currents. It is also important to consider how many time zones you are crossing and in what direction. For example, a flight from Los Angeles to New York that leaves at 7:30 am L.A. time arrives in New York at 5:35 pm, so it effectively takes an entire day to fly from the west coast to the east coast. On the other hand, an 8:00 am flight from New York to L.A. lands at 10:45 am local time. See the map at left for time zone information.

Arrival Cities

Departure Cities	Chicago	Houston	Los Angeles	Miami	New York	Washington, DC
Chicago		2:40	4:25	3:00	1:55	1:45
Houston	2:30		3:30	2:20	3:15	2:45
Los Angeles	3:50	3:05		4:35	5:15	4:45
Miami	3:15	2:50	5:45		2:50	2:20
New York	2:25	3:55	5:55	2:55		1:10
Washington, DC	2:10	3:20	5:15	2:40	1:00	

Note: Times shown are elapsed time from take off to landing.

gerous to walk along one of these high-speed road-ways. Unaccompanied women especially should stay in the car with the doors locked until police arrive. Many national automobile associations have reciprocal arrangements with the American Automobile Association (AAA); before you leave, find out if your home automobile association participates in such a program and get details.

Car rental agencies will try to sell you collision insurance at high rates, that may amount to more than US$10 per day. Before you buy this overpriced insurance, check with your own insurance company to see if you are covered for rental cars in a foreign country. If you want to drop the car off in a city different from the one you rented it in, it is likely you will have to pay an additional charge, usually at least US$50, and often much more. However, many agencies will allow you to pick cars up and drop them off at different locations within the same metropolitan area.

Taxi In New York City, Washington, and Chicago, a taxi is the best way to get around. The main business districts of these cities are compact enough to keep the costs down. Buses and subways can be confusing, even frightening, to a newcomer, and driving a rental car is not advised, especially in New York: you will notice that many cars in New York have dents due to accidents on the congested streets. There is also some risk that the car will be vandalized or stolen. You can hail a cab from the street; the law requires licensed cab drivers to pick you up and deliver you to your destination by the shortest possible route. Taxis are usually required to post a consumer complaint telephone number in case of a dispute. You can also have your hotel or restaurant personnel call a cab for you. Note that unlicensed taxis—so-called gypsy cabs—operate in some larger cities. These taxis are not well regulated and are not recommended.

Because distances are so great in Miami, Houston, and Los Angeles, taxis can be prohibitively expensive. You can hail a cab from the street in Miami and Houston, but it can be difficult; it is best to phone for one. Los Angeles cab drivers do not cruise the streets as in the eastern cities; they respond only to phone calls. Have your hotel or restaurant personnel call a cab for you because different taxi companies serve different areas.

Public Transportation New York and Chicago have large and efficient subway and bus systems; Washington's bus system is excellent, and its subway is developing quickly. While you may find public transportation in these cities sufficient to meet your schedule, you may need more time than you can spare to learn how to get where you want to go. You will generally find your fellow passengers willing to help you. During rush hour the subway may be the most efficient way to get to your destination, particularly in New York, where rush hour surface traffic grinds to a halt. However, rush hour is when the subway is at its most crowded and intimidating. Miami's bus system is fair downtown and in Miami Beach, but slow elsewhere; its rail system is getting better. Houston's bus system is poor, and there is no subway or rail line. The Los Angeles bus system is vast but slow; its subway system has only begun to operate in recent years, so the available routes are quite limited. For these reasons, a rental car is the best choice in Miami, Houston, and Los Angeles.

HOLIDAYS

In perfect keeping with the country's overriding work ethic, there technically are no national holidays in the US. Each state legislature or governor decides which holidays will be observed. However, the states generally follow the federal holidays, which are otherwise binding only for the District of Columbia and federal employees. There are now 10 federal holidays, but only after much grumbling from the business community (not even Election Day is a federal holiday), which resents most of all the fact that many of these holidays fall on Mondays. This creates three-day weekends that impede business in two ways: workers not only do not work on Monday, but they often leave work early on the preceding Friday. On the other hand, the always pragmatic US merchants have made the best out of several holidays: no matter the emotional and historical significance of the day, they have turned them into giant promotional shopping days. Presidents' Day, Memorial Day, Labor Day, and the day after Thanksgiving are the country's biggest days for retail sales. Merchants look forward to Thanksgiving mainly because it is the unofficial opening of the Christmas buying season, when some stores ring up more than half of their yearly revenues.

The following list gives business and banking holidays.

Major US Holidays

New Year's Day	January 1
Martin Luther King Day	Third Monday in January
Presidents' Day	Third Monday in February
Memorial Day	Last Monday in May
Independence Day	July 4
Labor Day	First Monday in September
Columbus Day*	Second Monday in October

(*Also called Discovers' Day or Pioneers' Day)

Veterans Day	November 11
Thanksgiving Day	Fourth Thurs. in November
Christmas Day	December 25

When New Year's Day, Independence Day, or Christmas Day fall on a weekend, most businesses

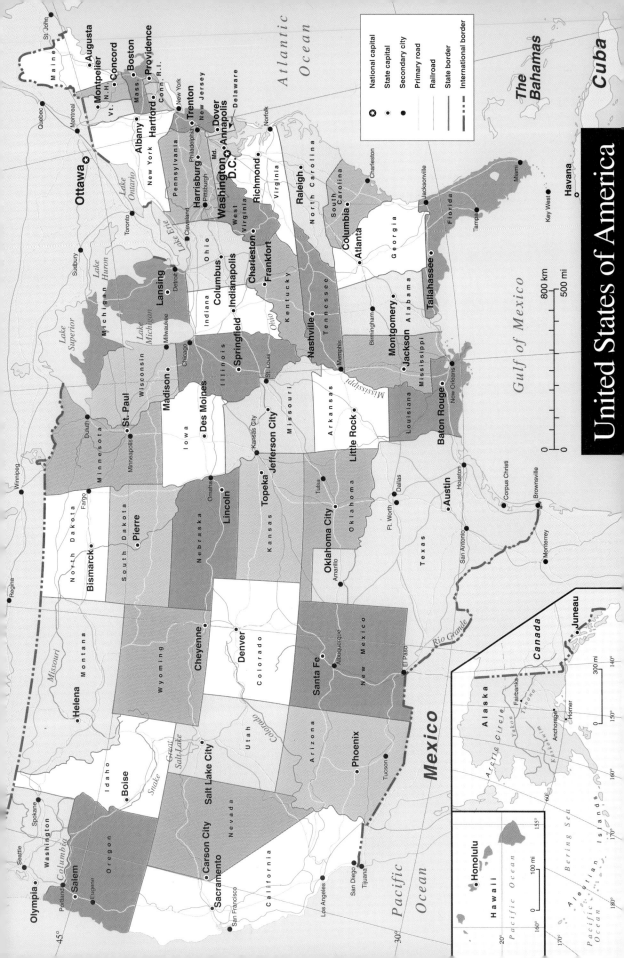

United States of America

Legend:
- National capital
- State capital
- Secondary city
- Primary road
- Railroad
- State border
- International border

800 km · 500 mi

500 mi · 800 km
0

Atlantic Ocean

The Bahamas

Cuba

Havana

Key West

Miami

Tampa

Jacksonville

Florida

Gulf of Mexico

Charleston

Columbia

South Carolina

Georgia

Atlanta

Tallahassee

Montgomery

Alabama

Jackson

Mississippi

New Orleans

Baton Rouge

Louisiana

Birmingham

Memphis

Nashville

Tennessee

Raleigh

North Carolina

Norfolk

Richmond

Virginia

West Virginia

Charleston

Frankfort

Kentucky

Charleston

Ohio

Columbus

Cleveland

Pittsburgh

Harrisburg

Pennsylvania

Philadelphia

Trenton

New Jersey

Dover

Delaware

Annapolis

Md.

Washington D.C.

New York

Albany

Hartford

Conn.

R.I.

Providence

Boston

Mass.

Concord

N.H.

Montpelier

Vt.

Augusta

Maine

St. John

Quebec

Montreal

Ottawa

Lake Ontario

Toronto

Lake Erie

Sudbury

Lake Huron

Lake Superior

Lake Michigan

Michigan

Lansing

Detroit

Milwaukee

Wisconsin

Madison

Chicago

Illinois

Indiana

Indianapolis

Springfield

St. Louis

Ohio

Missouri

Jefferson City

Kansas City

Topeka

Kansas

Des Moines

Iowa

St. Paul

Minneapolis

Duluth

Minnesota

Winnipeg

Regina

North Dakota

Bismarck

Fargo

South Dakota

Pierre

Nebraska

Lincoln

Omaha

Oklahoma

Oklahoma City

Tulsa

Amarillo

Arkansas

Little Rock

Mississippi

Dallas

Ft. Worth

Texas

Austin

Houston

San Antonio

Corpus Christi

Brownsville

Monterrey

Mexico

Rio Grande

El Paso

New Mexico

Santa Fe

Albuquerque

Colorado

Denver

Wyoming

Cheyenne

Montana

Helena

Missouri

Spokane

Seattle

Washington

Columbia

Olympia

Oregon

Salem

Eugene

Portland

Idaho

Boise

Snake

Nevada

Carson City

Sacramento

San Francisco

California

Los Angeles

San Diego

Tijuana

Great Salt Lake

Salt Lake City

Utah

Arizona

Phoenix

Tucson

Colorado

Pacific Ocean

45°

30°

Canada

Juneau

Alaska

Fairbanks

Anchorage

Homer

Yukon

Tanana

Kuskokwim

Arctic Circle

Bering Sea

Aleutian Islands

Pacific Ocean

300 mi
0

140°

150°

160°

170°

180°

Hawaii

Honolulu

Pacific Ocean

100 mi
0

20°

155°

160°

165°

170°

New York Metro

Westchester County

Passaic County
Paramus
Bergen County
Hackensack
Paterson
Fort Lee
Overpeck County Park
95
95
Tenafly Natural Park
Inwood Hill Park
Van Cortlandt Park
87
Bronx County
New York Botanical Garden
Bronx Zoo
Pelham Bay Park
The Bronx
95
Nassau Coun

New Jersey
Passaic
Teterboro Airport
1
George Washington Bridge
Hudson River
City College
Yankee Stadium
Columbia University
87
295
Ferry Point Park
Kings Point Park

Essex County
Branch Brook Park
Orange
95
Manhattan
Central Park
Randalls Island Park
La Guardia Airport
Queens County
East River
Kings Point Park

Hudson County
Lincoln Center For The Performing Arts
Lincoln Tunnel
Union City
Grand Central Station
Holland Tunnel
278
Queens Midtown Tunnel
Queens
Shea Stadium
Flushing Meadows Corona Pk.
Kissena Park
St. John's University
495
495

Newark
Jersey City
Liberty State Park
NY County
World Trade Center
Brooklyn Bridge
278
Forest Park
678
Aqueduct Race Track
27

Union
Newark International Airport
1
Port Newark
9
Newark Bay
New York
Kings County
27
John F. Kennedy International Airport

Lenape Park
Galloping Hill Park
Bayonne
Upper New York Bay
Prospect Park
278
Brooklyn Battery Tunnel

Union County
Linden
Richmond County
278
Staten Island
B r o o k l y n
Dyker Beach Park
Marine Park
27
Gateway National Jamaica Bay Rec. Area
Silver F Co. P

Middlesex County
Carteret
Perth Amboy
Great Kills Park (Gateway Nat'l Rec. Area)
Lower New York Bay
Coney Island Channel
Rockaway Inlet

Atlantic Ocean

Richmond County New York
Monmouth County New Jersey
Queens County New York

N

| | | 0 | | 5 mi |
| | | 0 | | 5 km |

—·—·—	State border
———	County border
———	Primary road
———	Secondary road
———	Railroad
- - - -	Tunnel
▢	Park
▢	Airport
95 1 27	Route marker

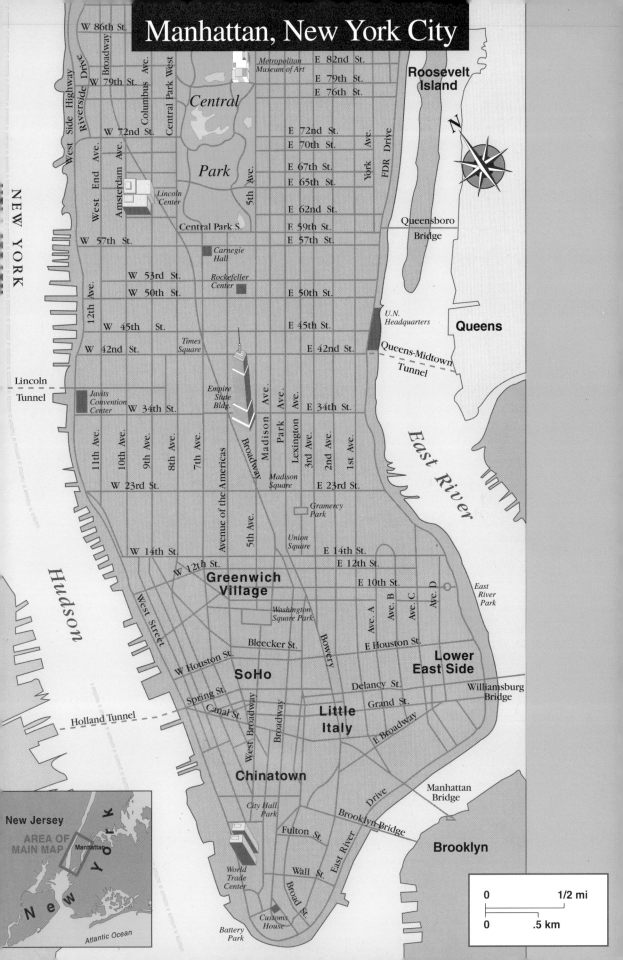

Manhattan, New York City

W 86th St.

W 79th St.

Broadway

Columbus Ave.

Central Park West

Riverside Drive

West Side Highway

Metropolitan Museum of Art

E 82nd St.

E 79th St.

E 76th St.

Central

Park

W 72nd St.

E 72nd St.

E 70th St.

E 67th St.

E 65th St.

E 62nd St.

York Ave.

FDR Drive

Roosevelt Island

West End Ave.

Amsterdam Ave.

Lincoln Center

E 59th St.

Central Park S.

5th Ave.

Queensboro Bridge

Queens

W 57th St.

E 57th St.

Carnegie Hall

W 53rd St.

W 50th St.

Rockefeller Center

E 50th St.

12th Ave.

W 45th St.

E 45th St.

U.N. Headquarters

W 42nd St.

Times Square

E 42nd St.

Queens-Midtown Tunnel

Lincoln Tunnel

Empire State Bldg.

Javits Convention Center

W 34th St.

E 34th St.

11th Ave.

10th Ave.

9th Ave.

8th Ave.

7th Ave.

Broadway

Madison Ave.

Park Ave.

Lexington Ave.

3rd Ave.

2nd Ave.

1st Ave.

W 23rd St.

Madison Square

E 23rd St.

Avenue of the Americas

5th Ave.

Gramercy Park

Union Square

W 14th St.

E 14th St.

E 12th St.

W 12th St.

Greenwich Village

E 10th St.

Ave. A

Ave. B

Ave. C

Ave. D

East River Park

Washington Square Park

Bleecker St.

Bowery

E Houston St.

Hudson

West Street

W Houston St.

SoHo

Spring St.

Canal St.

West Broadway

Broadway

Delancy St.

Grand St.

Little Italy

E Broadway

Lower East Side

Williamsburg Bridge

Holland Tunnel

Chinatown

City Hall Park

Fulton St.

Brooklyn Bridge

Drive

Manhattan Bridge

World Trade Center

Wall St.

East River

Broad St.

Brooklyn

Customs House

Battery Park

East River

N

New Jersey

AREA OF MAIN MAP

Manhattan

New York

Atlantic Ocean

NEW YORK

---

0   1/2 mi

0   .5 km

Washington, DC

Union Station

Senate Office Buildings

Supreme Court

Library of Congress

United States Capitol

House Office Buildings

Botanic Garden

3rd St.

North Capitol St.

New Jersey Ave.

New Jersey Ave.

1st St.

1st St.

New York Ave.

K St.

Massachusetts Ave.

National Gallery

National Archives

Nat'l Bldg Museum

Nat'l Museum of American Art

Nat'l Portrait Gallery

Ford's Theatre

F.B.I.

Dept. of Justice

Nat'l Museum of Natural History

Smithsonian Institution

The Mall

Independence Ave.

Southwest Frwy.

4th St.

7th St.

10th St.

12th St.

G St.

Washington Convention Center

H St.

6th St.

7th St.

9th St.

M St.

12th St.

Old Post Office

National Theatre

Nat'l Museum of American History

Constitution Ave.

Bureau of Engraving and Printing

O St.

Logan Circle

N St.

Vermont Ave.

14th St.

Treasury Building

Dept. of Commerce

The Ellipse

Washington Monument

P St.

17th St.

National Geographic Society

16th St.

I (Eye) St.

Lafayette Park

White House

Old Executive Offices

Corcoran Gallery

D.A.R.

O.A.S.

Reflecting Pool

Rhode Island Ave.

Connecticut Ave.

Dupont Circle

Pennsylvania Ave.

19th St.

World Bank

F St.

Virginia Ave.

Federal Reserve

Vietnam Veterans Memorial

Lincoln Memorial

DC War Memorial

Tidal Basin

Jefferson Memorial

Ohio Dr.

New Hampshire Ave.

22nd St.

23rd St.

GW University

Department of State

E St.

L St.

Washington Harbor

Watergate Hotel

Kennedy Center

29th St.

N St.

K St.

Roosevelt Bridge

Arlington Memorial Bridge

Potomac River

N

Metro Stations

1/4

1/2 mi.

0

Los Angeles Metro

Van Nuys

Burbank

Glendale

Pasadena

Rose Bowl

Colorado Blvd.

Balboa Blvd.

San Diego Freeway

170

Ventura Blvd.

101

134

Ventura Freeway

2

210

Eagle Rock

Santa Monica Mountains

405

Hollywood

Hollywood Freeway

Griffith Park

5

110

Hollywood Blvd.

Santa Monica Blvd.

Beverly Hills

Dodger Stadium

San Bernardino Fwy.

10

UCLA

Wilshire Blvd.

101

Downtown

Sunset Blvd.

2

Santa Monica Blvd.

Washington Blvd.

10

60

East Los Angeles

Santa Ana Fwy.

Santa Monica Freeway

La Cienega Blvd.

Adams Blvd.

USC

Culver City

Exposition Park

Luther King Jr. Blvd.

110

10

1

Santa Monica

90

La Brea Ave.

Slauson Ave.

Huntington Park

Bell

5

Venice Beach

Martin

Florence Ave.

The Forum

Inglewood

42

Manchester Ave.

Watts

710

Hollywood Park

Century Blvd.

South Gate

42

Downey

Los Angeles Intl. Airport

Lennox

Imperial Hwy.

Pacific

El Segundo Blvd.

Hawthorne

Lynwood

105

Ocean

Rosecrans Ave.

Lawndale

Compton

91

Sepulveda Blvd.

405

Gardena

Freeway

Figueroa St.

Alameda St.

Long Beach Blvd.

Atlantic Blvd.

Lakewood

Manhattan Beach

Artesia Blvd.

Western Ave.

91

Hawthorne Blvd.

Harbor

Carson St.

Carson St.

19

N

Redondo Beach

107

Carson St.

Carson

Avalon Blvd.

Wilmington Ave.

Long Beach Fwy.

Sepulveda Blvd.

Torrance

1

Crenshaw Blvd.

Vermont Ave.

710

110

Pacific Coast Hwy.

47

Rolling Hills

Ocean Blvd.

Long Beach

	Freeway
	Major highway
	Primary street
🛡	Interstate highway
🛡	US highway
🛡	Cal. State highway

5 mi.

5 km.

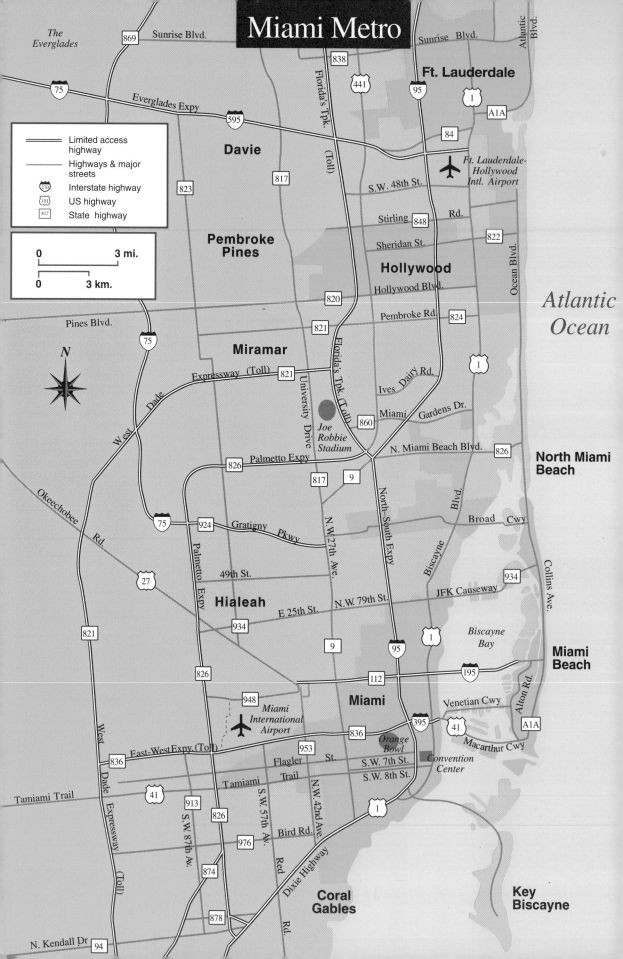

Miami Metro

The Everglades

Sunrise Blvd.

869

Sunrise Blvd.

Atlantic Blvd.

838

441

95

Ft. Lauderdale

1

A1A

75

Everglades Expy

595

84

Davie

Florida's Tpk. (Toll)

Ft. Lauderdale-Hollywood Intl. Airport

	Limited access highway
	Highways & major streets
210	Interstate highway
101	US highway
817	State highway

0   3 mi.

0   3 km.

823

817

S.W. 48th St.

Pembroke Pines

Stirling   848   Rd.

Sheridan St.

822

Hollywood

Ocean Blvd.

Hollywood Blvd.

Atlantic Ocean

820

Pines Blvd.

821

Pembroke Rd.

824

75

Miramar

Expressway (Toll)   821

1

University Drive

Florida's Tpk. (Toll)

Ives   Dairy Rd.

Miami   Gardens Dr.

860

Joe Robbie Stadium

N. Miami Beach Blvd.

826

North Miami Beach

N

826   Palmetto Expy

817   9

West   Dade

826   Palmetto Expy

Biscayne   Blvd.

Broad   Cwy

75   924   Gratigny   Pkwy

Okeechobee   Rd.

Palmetto Expy

49th St.

934

Collins Ave.

JFK Causeway

27

Hialeah

N.W. 27th Ave.

N.W. 79th St.

E 25th St.

934

1

Biscayne Bay

821

9

95

Miami Beach

826

112

195

948

Miami International Airport

Miami

395   1

Venetian Cwy

Alton Rd.

A1A

836

East-West Expy. (Toll)   836

Orange Bowl

Macarthur Cwy

41

953   St.

Flagler   Trail

S.W. 7th St.

Convention Center

Tamiami Trail

41

913   826

Tamiami   Trail

S.W. 57th Av.

N.W. 42nd Ave.

S.W. 8th St.

Dade   Expressway   (Toll)

976

Bird Rd.

1

Red   Rd.

Dixie Highway

S.W. 87th Av.

874

Coral Gables

Key Biscayne

878

N. Kendall Dr   94

Chicago Metro

Legend

Limited access highway	
Highways & major streets	
94	Interstate highway
14	US highway
88	State highway
State Border	

0 — 5 mi.
0 — 5 km.

N

Cook Rd.
Dundee Rd.
Rand Rd.
Northwest Hwy.
Elmhurst Rd.
Des Plaines River
Forest Preserve
Waukegan Rd.
Chicago River
Sheridan Road

Evanston
Northwestern University
Dempster
Skokie

Des Plaines
Northwest Tollway
Forest Preserve
Niles
Loyola University
Lincoln Park

O'Hare International Airport
Harlem Ave.
Irving Park Rd.
Chicago River
Lake Shore Dr.

York Rd.
Grand Ave.
Mannheim
Lake St.
Cicero Ave.
Milwaukee Ave.
JFK Expy.
North Ave.
DePaul Univ.
Lincoln Park Zoo

Oak Park
Grand Ave.
Fullerton
Washington Blvd.
St.
Sears Tower
Chicago

Wheaton
Dwight
D. Eisenhower Expy.
Roosevelt Rd.
Cicero
Berwyn
Ogden Ave.

West Tollway

Stevenson
Expressway
Dan Ryan Expy.
Michigan Ave.
Lake
Washington Park
Museum of Science & Industry
Jackson Park
Univ. of Chicago

La Grange Rd.
Midway Airport
Western Ave.
State St.
Shore
Chicago Skyway

Harlem Ave.
Cicero Ave.
Columbus Ave.
95th St.

Palos
Forest
Preserve

Oak Lawn
Tri-State Tollway

Argonne Nat'l. Lab.

Forest Preserve
Forest Preserve
159th St.

Calumet City

Illinois
Indiana

Hammond   **Gary**

Lake Michigan

North America

Russian
Republic

Chukchi Sea

Bering Strait

Arctic Ocean

Ellesmere Island

Greenland Sea

Icel

Reyk

Greenland (Den.)

Denm Se

Beaufort Sea

Alaska (US)

Yukon

Banks Island

Baffin Bay

Victoria Island

Baffin Island

Fairbanks ●

150°

● Anchorage

Gulf of Alaska

Mackenzie

● Whitehorse

Slave

Peace

Canada

Saskatchewan

Edmonton ●

Nelson

Churchill ●

Hudson Bay

Nuuk (Godthåb) ●

Davis Strait

Labrado Sea

Goose Bay ●

Newfoun

45°

● Vancouver

Quebec ●

St. Lawrence

Montreal ●

Halifa ●

● Seattle

Winnipeg ●

Ottawa ✪

Columbia

Missouri

Toronto ●

Boston ●

135°

Pacific Ocean

Salt Lake City ●

United States

● Denver

Detroit ●

Chicago ●

New York ●

● San Francisco

Colorado

St. Louis ●

Ohio

Washington DC ✪

Atlantic Ocean

30°

Los Angeles ●

● Tijuana

El Paso ●

Mississippi

Atlanta ●

New Orleans ●

The Bahamas

Rio Grande

Houston ●

Miami ●

Nassau ✪

Sa Dom

Tropic of Cancer

Monterrey ●

Gulf of Mexico

Havana ✪

Cuba

Haiti

Port-au-Prince

15°

Mexico

Guadalajara ●

Mexico City ✪

Jamaica

Kingston ●

D
R

Belize

Belmopan ✪

Honduras

Caribbean Sea

Colon

Guatemala

Guatemala ✪

Tegucigalpa ✪

Nicaragua

San Salvador ✪

El Salvador

Managua ✪

San José ✪

Panama ●

Costa Rica

Panama

Col

LEGEND

✪ Capital
● Major City

0 ———— 1000 km

0 ———— 500 mi

120° 105° 90°

75° 75°

close the previous Friday or the following Monday. When these holidays fall on a Tuesday or Thursday, it is also quite common for companies to close the day between the holiday and the weekend—relatively few offices are open the Friday after Thanksgiving.

BUSINESS HOURS

The typical US workday runs from 9 am to 5 pm, with a half-hour or an hour for lunch. There are a great many exceptions; many people on the Pacific coast are in their offices by 8 am or earlier. In some industrial cities, such as Detroit, plant shifts determine working hours for everyone, and office hours may run from 7 am to 3 pm to follow manufacturing work schedules (the next manufacturing shift begins at 3 pm and runs till 11 pm, with the so-called graveyard shift running from 11 pm to 7 am). Banks used to open at 10 am and close at 3 pm, but many are now open from 9 to 5 and often have Saturday morning hours as well. Some cities have tried to get employers to establish staggered work hours to relieve traffic congestion. Financial sector workers across the country usually start work when the New York Stock Exchange opens at 9:30 am EST, which means Los Angeles stock brokers begin work at 6:30 am PST, or earlier.

Most retail stores open between 9 am and 10 am and stay open until 5 or 6 pm six or seven days a week. Many are open 12 hours a day. Convenience stores are open very late, and many are open 24 hours, as are some restaurants, pharmacies, and supermarkets. Stores in shopping malls are generally open seven days a week and stay open into the evening.

COMMUNICATIONS

Telephones Telephone service in the US is generally first-rate. All US phone numbers have a three-digit area code followed by a seven-digit local number. When calling a number within the same area code, do not dial the area code. In some cities, however, the number you want to call may be far enough away to require that you dial a "1" before the seven-digit number; you will discover this if you dial the seven numbers and you hear a recording that tells you to dial a "1" first. This type of call, while not long distance, is still a toll call, meaning that you will be charged more than the base rate, although not the full long distance rates.

Some metropolitan areas have more than one area code. The Los Angeles and New York City regions each have five; Washington has one area code, its Maryland suburbs another, and its Virginia suburbs yet a third. Your hotel room should have a telephone book, which includes maps of area codes, or you can call Directory Assistance at 411 for numbers in the same area code, or 1 (area code) 555-1212 to obtain numbers in different area codes. For a listing of area codes across the US, refer to the "Important Addresses" chapter.

Finding a public phone that works can be a problem in some areas: they are favorite targets of vandals, and many public phones are old and broken down. If the phone is working, you are in luck. Because most US pay phones accept only coins, you are advised to use your credit card or phone card for calls lasting longer than a minute if you do not want to walk around with several dollars in change weighing you down. Each pay phone usually has an instruction chart for making credit card or collect calls, or you can simply dial "0" to reach an operator.

International Calls If possible, avoid direct dialing internationally from your hotel room; hotels usually impose a substantial surcharge on such calls. Instead, call the international operator in your own country and have your call charged to your home credit or phone card—this system is called Home Country Direct or World Connect. To reach the AT&T operator, dial "00"and ask the operator how to use the system. The system is also the best alternative if your hotel does not offer international direct dialing. Call the AT&T operator and give the country code, city code, and local number you are calling. The operator will connect you.

If the surcharge does not matter to you, simply dial the international access code (011), then the country code, then the area or city code, and finally the local number. For example, to call someone in Tokyo, Japan, dial 011-81-3 then the local number. If you want operator assistance—for collect calls, person-to-person calls, time and charges, or to use your calling card—the international access number is 01 rather than 011. (Note: These instructions are for AT&T long-distance service. If you do not hear "AT&T" when you dial 01, hang up and dial the AT&T access code—10ATT (10288)—before dialing 011 or 01.) (*See* "Useful Telephone Numbers" on the following page for access numbers to other long distance carriers.)

Calling Canada from the US is the same as calling long-distance within the US. Simply dial 1, then the area code and local number.

Fax, Telegram, and Telex Fax machines and services can be found in every city. Most large hotels offer fax services or can direct you to the nearest service. Many photocopy shops also offer fax services, and are listed in the yellow pages. You can send telegrams through Western Union and AT&T EasyLink, but since the advent of fax, telegrams have lost popularity in the US, except for sending money. Telex is considered outdated and is much less common in the US than elsewhere.

Post Office The US Postal Service picks up, sorts, and delivers a phenomenal amount of mail every day, most of it on time. The service offers overnight and two-day delivery at competitive prices, provides certified and registered mail services with proof of delivery, and generally can deliver a first class letter within two to five days anywhere in the country for 32 cents for the first ounce. At press time, a half-ounce airmail letter cost 50 cents, and an airmail postcard, 40 cents. International postal rates are expected to increase slightly in mid-1995. Most post office branches are open from 8 am to 5 pm weekdays. In larger cities, some are open on Saturdays.

If you need a parcel or important papers delivered on the same day or overnight, you may be better off with a courier service. The US has several large national and international courier services, plus thousands of local couriers, including many bicycle messengers who operate within congested urban areas. A listing of the toll-free numbers of some of the major courier services is given on the following page.

Foreign-Language Media The US does not have foreign-language newspapers or magazines that are easily accessible to travelers except in the largest multi-ethnic cities, such as New York, Washington, and Los Angeles. Even in those cities, you will have to search for newsstands that carry these publications. Many of the periodicals that are available have very narrow coverage and viewpoints. Spanish publications are the most available, but they are primarily oriented either towards Mexico or the US Hispanic community. Spanish radio and TV broadcasts are available in most large cities, while broadcasts in Asian languages are found along the West Coast, although they are much less common.

LOCAL SERVICES

The US is in the business of doing business, and every city has virtually every business service you may need, from phone to fax to copying to secretarial to delivery.

Offices The US has several large firms specializing in providing temporary offices for businesspeople. They can provide office space, furnishings, staff, communications systems, meeting rooms, secretarial services, phone answering, and even desktop publishing. You pay only for what you need. Some examples follow.

Alliance Business Centers	(800) 869-9595
HQ Business Centers	(800) 227-3004, Ext. 42
OmniOffices	(800) 331-6664

Housing Some firms specialize in obtaining temporary housing in apartments or condominiums for businesspeople at a cost far lower than hotels, with much greater convenience. One of the major companies offering such accommodations is Oakwood Corporate Housing; Tel: (800) 888-0808.

Mailing Addresses If you are going to be in one

city for an extended period, you may want to engage one of the mailbox services. For a small fee, these provide a mailing address, a private box, wrapping, packing, mailing, and mail forwarding services, access to courier services such as UPS or FedEx, photocopying, notary service, fax machines, and stationery supplies. They are listed in the Yellow Pages under "Mail Boxes" or "Mail Receiving."

Translation and Interpretation Services Many such companies provide a wealth of services, which may include written translation of any language in any subject, consecutive and simultaneous oral interpreters, desktop publishing, typesetting, graphics, or audiovisual adaptations. Others specialize in one or two languages, with Spanish, Chinese, and Japanese among the most common. Some perform their translation services by computer modem and fax within 24 or 48 hours. In addition, large cities have independent translation and interpretation services listed in the Yellow Pages of local phone books. New York City, Washington, Los Angeles, and San Francisco are particularly rich in these services.

Accredited Language Services .... (800) 755-5775
Ad-Ex .... (800) 223-7753
AT&T Language Line Services .... (800) 544-5721
Berlitz Translation Services .... (800) 367-4336
Berlitz Interpretation Services .... (800) 423-6756
Idem .... (800) 642-IDEM or 642-4336
The Language Lab .... (800) 682-3126

Printing Every US city has printers that offer overnight service for business cards and letterhead stationery. You can find photocopiers in pharmacies and even grocery stores, as well as in the large national chains such as Kinko's. All are listed in the Yellow Pages under "Copying" or "Printers."

Temporary Secretarial and Employment Services Most cities have many secretarial services firms that provide word and data processing, transcription, mail services, fax services, and many other office services, either in your office or in their own offices. These local firms, which you can find in the Yellow Pages of the local phone book under "Secretarial Services," are in addition to the large national firms that can also provide temporary workers in a wide variety of employment fields. These include accounting, legal, insurance, customer service, clerical, or administrative services. Look in the local yellow pages under "Employment Services" or "Employment Services—Temporary." Some of the companies that have offices in most major cities nationwide include Accountemps (accountants and bookkeepers a specialty), Adia Personnel Services, Kelly Temporary Services, Olsten Staffing Services, and Manpower Temporary Services.

STAYING SAFE AND HEALTHY

Despite what you see on television about crime, the US is generally a very safe place to visit. The crime rate in some cities may be high, but if you avoid the more dangerous neighborhoods and take some simple precautions, your chances of becoming a victim, particularly of violent crime, are extremely low. Ask at your hotel about the safety of nearby neighborhoods. Keep to well traveled, well lit streets, and try to avoid looking like a tourist—that is, lost, confused, and preoccupied. Walk and look as if you know what you are doing and where you are going. Avoid the display of valuable jewelry or cameras. Women should carry their purses on straps over their shoulders rather than in their hands and keep them close when in restaurants or walking on crowded streets. Everyone should keep money and important documents in the hotel safe, and consider using a moneybelt for the bulk of one's funds. When you rent a car, ask if the agency removes stickers that identify the car as rented: this is becoming a common practice in some areas. Consider parking on the street instead of in a parking garage if the garage does not have a good security system.

Public drinking water in the US is safe, and food is generally prepared under safe conditions. However, as a foreign visitor, you may experience occasional digestive upsets common to travelers everywhere in the world. Pharmacies and grocery stores are everywhere and offer everything you need for an upset stomach, headache, cold, or allergy. However, unlike in some countries, pharmacists cannot prescribe for you or sell prescription medications to you without a doctor's prescription.

Getting enough exercise is difficult when you are traveling, but the US has many health clubs. Many hotels that cater to businesspeople now provide exercise facilities; if yours does not, the concierge or desk clerk should be able to direct you to a nearby health club, oftentimes one where guests of the hotel receive a temporary courtesy membership or discount.

Several organizations offer a variety of medical assistance services to travelers.

Access America Travel insurance; multilingual 24-hour emergency travel, medical, legal assistance; medical referral, transportation, hospital payments. Tel: (800) 284-8300 (toll-free in the US only).

International SOS Assistance, Inc. Tel: (800) 523-8930; [1] (215) 244-1500.

Travel Assistance International 24-hour medical and personal emergency assistance; medical referral, transportation, payments. Tel: (800) 821-2828 (toll-free in the US only); [1] (202) 331-1609. Fax: [1] (202) 331-1588

Travel Guard International Tel: (800) 782-5151 (toll-free in the US only), [1] (715) 345-0505.

Worldcare Travel Assistance Association, Inc.

24-hour multilingual medical assistance, hospitalization coverage, payments. Tel: (800) 666-4993, 253-1877, 521-4822 (toll-free in the US only).

EMERGENCY INFORMATION

Dial 911 for police, fire, or ambulance in most cities and states. *Do not* dial this number unless you have a true, immediate emergency.

High-quality medical care is easily available nationwide. Most hotels have a doctor on call, or can direct you to a hospital or clinic. If you become ill while driving, stop at any roadside service station or store and ask for the nearest hospital; or look for roadside signs indicating directions to a hospital; or stop next to an emergency roadside phone and call the state police. While the quality of care available in the US is high, you must have proof of health insurance or ability to pay to be treated at many hospitals. You are strongly advised to find out whether your home health insurance carrier will cover you in the US; if not, consider purchasing temporary insurance. The list above gives contacts for a few companies offering such policies.

BEST TRAVEL BOOKS

There are hundreds, if not thousands, of books on travel in the US, its regions, states, cities, and recreation areas. Any well-stocked bookstore will have shelves filled with such books. We have focused on a few that do a good job of covering the immense diversity of the US. Keep in mind that the US is so big that no one book could ever thoroughly cover every region, state, and city, so although some of the information presented may be superficial, you can make up for that by obtaining more focused books in each area you visit.

Birnbaum's United States for Business Travelers 95, New York: HarperPerennial, 1994. ISBN 0-06-278152-9. 1,014 pages, US$14. Focuses on 42 top business travel destinations, each accompanied by a map. Lists business services available at hotels, and where to obtain other business services, as well as major tourist sights, entertainment and sports activities, shopping areas, and top dining spots. A lot of information in a small space. Birnbaum's also offers guides for a number of major US cities and a US guidebook for leisure travelers.

Fodor's USA 94: The Complete Guide to the Best of Everything in All Fifty States, New York: Fodor's Travel Publications, 1993. ISBN 0-679-02554-5. 1,072 pages, US$19. Tourist oriented, strong on sights, shopping, entertainment, dining. More than 100 maps. Organized by region rather than state or city, so information can be hard to find, but index is thorough and information is wide-ranging.

Frequent Travelers Guide to Major Cities, 1994, New York: Prentice Hall Travel, 1994. ISBN 0-671-87450-0. US$14.95. Geared to the business traveler, this book contains many detailed maps and useful telephone numbers.

Frommer's USA 1993–1994, New York: Prentice Hall Travel, 1993. ISBN 0-671-84704-X. 1,168 pages, US$19. Similar in tone and scope to the Fodor's guidebook. Frommer's also publishes city guides on most major US cities and some regions and states.

Taxi, Clinton, NJ: Middlegate, 1994. US$49.95 to US$79.95. CD-ROM and computer diskette products offering a range of metropolitan and street maps plus Zagat hotel and restaurant reviews for 20 cities in the US. Available in both IBM and Macintosh formats. Contact: Middlegate, Tel: (800) 439-8294 (toll-free in the US only) Fax: [1] (908) 735-0379.

Wall Street Journal Guides to Business Travel: USA & Canada, New York: Fodor's Travel Publications, 1991. ISBN 0-679-02176-0. US$50 (boxed set). City-by-city guide to the major business cities of Canada and the United States with maps, information on business services available, and other tips for the business traveler. Unfortunately, it has not been updated since 1991 and can be difficult to find.

The American Automobile Association (AAA) publishes maps and guidebooks that cover the entire United States. If you will be traveling much by car you should find out if your country's national automobile association has a reciprocal arrangement with AAA; if not, it may be well worth it to join. The guides and maps are free to members and can sometimes be purchased by nonmembers. Contact AAA, 1000 AAA Drive, Heathrow, FL 32746-5063.

Business Culture*

INTRODUCTION

At least some understanding of US business culture is an essential tool for an international trader doing business with a US businessperson. The role of business within the broader US culture is also an important, although often difficult, concept to grasp. An understanding of US culture will smooth the way in a business transaction and can make it not only beneficial but also enjoyable for both parties. The following discussion is designed to give a basic explanation of and a guide to US business culture to enable visitors to manage their relationships with US businesspeople more effectively.

Many of the values, beliefs, and behaviors are outlined in general terms in this chapter, which tends to suggest that US culture is homogeneous. No such claim is intended. As the fourth largest country in the world, with a population of more than 260 million, the US is one of the most diverse societies in the world. Although a majority of US residents are considered to be of European descent (a category that in fact

encompasses nationalities beyond Europeans), the country has substantial minority populations—Native Americans, African-Americans, Hispanics or Latinos, Asians, and Pacific Islanders. All of these peoples bring into the business arena their own languages, beliefs, and customs, making generalizations about the US businessperson difficult and, for the most part, useful only as guidelines against which to measure your own individual experiences. The diversity is striking, but so is the strong cultural identity of all these peoples with their country, the US.

BORN ON THE FRONTIER

From the beginning, the culture of the land has been divergent and vibrant, starting with the continent's earliest natives, and moving through waves of 16th and 17th century explorers and settlers, and then later colonizers principally from England, France, Spain, the Netherlands, Sweden, and Russia. To a large degree, the country has been populated by immigrants seeking a new and different life in a largely unfamiliar environment. Whether they landed in bustling turn-of-the-century cities or made their way to the great inland plains, these immigrants faced unknown frontiers; a pioneer ethos was central to early US society. As a result, the evolving culture came to value self-reliance, competition, individuality, and independence more than submission, sacrifice for the community, and cooperation. To this day, the archetype of US culture remains the stoical cowboy fighting against cattle thieves, standing against settlers who fenced in the ranges, calling a campfire "home," and living a hard, lonely existence in the saddle while exposed to harsh weather on the range. Despite the fact that relatively few US people actually lived under isolated frontier conditions and that much frontier activity was based on communal efforts, the individu-

* Prepared in consultation with Dean W. Engel, managing partner, The East West Group, Mill Valley, California, an organization specializing in cross-cultural communications for businesses operating globally.

alistic ideal persists in the national mythology.

The wild west pioneer days have passed, but the qualities of frontier life form a large part of what US people see as their self-image. The frontier roots of US culture can still be seen, for example, in the average US person's distrust of and resistance to any authority perceived as outside of oneself or one's chosen community. US people are generally skeptical of others—individuals, business entities, government at all levels—and treat those others as antagonists, particularly if the others have different interests, lifestyles, or business concepts. The subtleties and advantages of variation are sometimes lost in the US person's attempt to answer every question with a "yes" or "no"—rarely a "maybe." A phrase commonly heard in reference to how the average US person views the world is that everything is either black or white, with no shades of gray in between. The practical effect is that US persons tend to see opposites that separate various interests rather than similarities that might unite them. For example, the average US person may not be aware of the distinctions between European-style Socialism and Cuban Communism, tending to lump both of those political systems into one class, namely the opposite of democratic.

US SOCIETY VALUES, BELIEFS, AND BEHAVIOR

Candor

The US person is frank, outspoken, and candid. They have an opinion about nearly every topic, and there are only a few subjects that they are uncomfortable discussing. They see themselves as ambitious, hardworking, and energetic, and they take pride in their high standard of living and the important role of their nation in world affairs. Despite waves of racial and ethnic tension among the diverse groups that populate the US, the average US person tries to be friendly and outgoing when encountering visitors. They make friends and seem to establish a level of intimacy quickly, a process that takes a considerably longer time in many other cultures. These advances often surprise, and even mislead, visitors not only because of how rapidly they happen, but also because of uncertainty about the actual meaning of the relationship. Friendliness is a matter of courtesy, and from the US person's perspective a relationship remains superficial—among acquaintances—for the time it takes to develop a longer-lasting, trusting alliance. An invitation to "get together" or to "come by the house" is often meant symbolically, and therefore should be acted on with some discretion.

Individualism and Self-Reliance

The companion traits of individual freedom and self-reliance rank very high among the values of the average US person. The US culture glorifies the accomplishments of individuals, and constant battle is waged to retain as much freedom to express individual beliefs as possible within, and often despite, their society. The importance of being a member of a family, community, religious group, or organization is generally secondary to the preservation of individual rights and identity. Children are encouraged to express their own values and to choose their own careers and lifestyles; they are expected to leave home and become self-reliant; and they are urged to explore any opportunity that they fancy, even if it will take them far from home and community. A US person who has changed his or her lifestyle to reflect his or her own individual beliefs and needs may be respected, even if the change has meant that other commitments—whether to family, career, or community—have been abandoned. In the US, it is the individual who is singled out for both praise and blame.

This pervasive sense of the individual is puzzling to people from other cultures that see the individual as part of a family or community unit, emphasize collectivism and consensus, and prize the strength of the group over self-reliance and individuality. Many cultures equate individualism with self-indulgence and anarchy, and they react strongly against it. However, it is important to remember the reality underlying the national mythology of individualism and self-reliance: many US achievements are in fact the result of team efforts. Persons in the US are proven team-players, and the trend in some US companies is to use individual strengths by putting together teams of persons with various backgrounds to achieve specific results—such as the development of a quality control system, a recycling program, a new product, or a more efficient production line. In this respect, the US business arena is unique.

Freedom, Independence, and Democracy

US persons share a common belief in democracy, which they often equate with freedom, and many feel that freedom is not possible in the absence of democracy. Residents of the US are proud to live in the world's first constitutional democracy, the one that has provided the basic model for many subsequent democratic states. Each person in the US is guaranteed the right to liberty; freedom of speech, choice, and religion; and freedom from arbitrary authoritarianism.

While other cultures may seek the greater good for the society, valuing it above the rights of individuals, US persons are uneasy with the idea that individual rights should be curtailed for the greater good. The continuing debate in the US over the right of individuals to possess and use firearms—something few other developed nations allow—is an example of this struggle. US residents and foreigners within the US have relatively unlimited freedom to choose where they will live, what they will do, and with whom they will do it. They have comparable freedom to select a profession or type of business, invest in ventures, or choose among employers. Within the relatively broad limits of US slander and libel laws, individuals are free to criticize—openly and in the media—laws, government actions, and the actions of officials, private persons, or entities. If they choose, they may pursue their claims in a larger public forum or in the courts. If still dissatisfied, they may freely decide to leave the country, taking all of their belongings with them.

Freedom and independence underlie the concept that the US is a land of opportunity where risk taking is admired. The US culture takes pride in the bold entrepreneur who dares to build a revolutionary product or to offer a new service. Common US expressions include "reach for the stars," "take the risk," and "go for it." The element that is often missing in this image is the fact that far more enterprises fail than are successful. Indeed, freedom to choose one's own destiny independently also carries with it the freedom to fail. Legal safeguards exist to reduce the odds and the cost of failure, but individuals must still face the possibility and the consequences of failure as well as success. Fortunately, many find the resources to start again.

Competition

A natural result of the US focus on individualism, independence, and freedom is competition. The US populace is known for its competitive nature. Business jargon includes many metaphors and terms derived from sports and war to describe the US vision of business—and even life itself—as a competitive struggle. Although much daily activity is actually collaborative or cooperative in nature, the culture still holds competition and struggle in high esteem. Unfortunately, this value requires winners and losers, seldom allowing for a tie, much less a situation in which everybody wins. Naturally, a person prefers to be a winner, which usually means being aggressive to win out over others who also want to be winners, which therefore perpetuates and intensifies the competition.

Paradoxically, US parents teach their children and state publicly the noble sentiment that the quality of sportsmanship is more important than winning or losing ("it's not whether you win or lose, it's how you play the game"). In light of this idealized credo, the results of a recent survey of US businesspeople were not surprising: they ranked winning low on their list of values. Businesspeople in the US are certainly capable of compromise, but they seldom place compromise high in their ranking of desirable traits, nor do they often define compromise as a successful outcome. Winning remains an important, if semi-private, goal in business negotiations, and when winning becomes extremely important, competition can be harsh and unforgiving, and compromise difficult if not unlikely. (*See* "Negotiations" below.)

Equality and Justice

A basic precept in US culture is the notion of universal human rights and the equality of all people. In large measure, the US populace believes that in their land of opportunity, any individual can rise to a position of wealth, power, and influence. Even though there are many examples of continuing inequality among the peoples within the US, many of the residents still blame themselves rather than question the validity of their notion of equality. Other cultures find unusual the fervor with which US residents declare not only that all persons are created equal, but also that there is equal social, political, and economic opportunity for all. Whenever a situation contrary to the notion of equality arises within their own society, they enact laws or create policies designed to eliminate the perceived inequality.

In the minds of many, equality and justice are the same concepts, and there lies a thorn that has troubled US people for generations. To some extent, the laws and constitutions of the country can guarantee equal opportunities for all, but justice for all depends on the subjective treatment of each person by every other person. Some argue that there should be equality of outcomes and circumstances, as well, but this concept is dependent on justice, not equality. For this reason, it is virtually impossible to legislate and regulate individual degrees of success within the competitive US society. The situation is further complicated by the fact that the results of what is termed "inequality" can most clearly be seen in the gaps between certain socioeconomic, racial, and ethnic groups. This inequality in fact arises because of injustice, but few people—and the US person is no exception—are willing to admit to subjective injustice toward others.

Patriotism

Loyalty to the US, especially when dealing with foreign peoples, is a unifying aspect of the otherwise multicultural US community. In some regions of the US, patriotism is more intense than in others. Most residents of the nation will admit that, even though they may be critical of the US government or its policies, the US is at least a good place, if not the best place, to live.

It is important to understand that a US person

who is being critical of the country is usually comparing it to an ideal vision, not some other country or society. US persons have little fear in critiquing their nation; the constitution guarantees them freedom of speech, and they exercise that right freely in the belief that it will make their government more receptive to societal needs, not destroy it. This belief explains why failures and scandals within the government and private sector are searched out and publicized. It also accounts for the alacrity with which they will unify in the face of a perceived threat to their country or way of life.

Class

The US has often been called a classless society by outsiders, and insiders may say the same, believing that no barriers exist for a person who works hard enough. It is true that the US has no permanent, formal caste system and that someone from a humble background may become highly successful. On the other hand, it is also true that wealth opens most doors to positions of influence in the US, while many of those at or near the bottom never make it to the next level.

Different definitions of social class exist, but in the US, the upper class usually consists of those who have inherited significant wealth, are not dependent upon wage earnings, and are represented in the elite organizations of society. At the opposite extreme, the lower class includes those on public assistance, the uneducated and chronically unemployed, and poorly paid service, industrial, migrant, and other marginal workers. There is also an underclass of marginalized individuals who exist on the fringes of society and the economy.

The greatest social mobility in the US occurs within the middle class, which constitutes the bulk of the populace. Most US residents consider themselves to be middle class, and although specific statistical parameters are difficult to define, this perception is borne out by most analyses. The international visitor is likely to do business primarily with members of the upper-middle and middle class.

The upper-middle class includes well-paid and well-educated executives and professionals from both the public and private sectors. The middle class would include small business owners, teachers, farmers, ranchers, and white-collar and blue-collar workers who own their own homes and have enough disposable income to travel and buy a wide range of consumer goods. They tend to have at least a high school diploma and often some college education and encourage their children to gain a four-year degree. The lower-middle class consists largely of wage earners who may have no more than a secondary education and who own little if any property.

Religion: In God We Trust

The principle of religious freedom is enshrined in the First Amendment to the US Constitution, which protects both freedom of religion and freedom from religion, in the sense that no individual may be forced to adhere to a specific religion-based ethic. The majority of US citizens consider religion to be a private matter. Four-fifths of US people give their religious affiliation as Christian (either Protestant or Catholic), a substantial number say they are not religious, and smaller groups are adherents of religions as Judaism, Eastern Orthodox, Buddhism, Hinduism, and Islam.

The US emphasis on individualism carries over into religion, for members of religious organizations may, in most cases, maintain their affiliation even while openly espousing beliefs that directly contradict the dogma of their faith. It is a common belief that looking inward as well as outward for spiritual guidance reinforces self-reliance and encourages a questioning attitude toward authority. In turn, a person who does not automatically defer to authority may be more likely to devise new ways of solving problems and have more freedom to be spontaneous.

With the exception of the observance of religion-based national holidays, such as Christmas, the international businessperson is likely to find transactions unaffected directly by religion. A visitor is rarely expected to be aware of the religion of people with whom business is conducted and, as with most potentially charged topics, discussions of religion are best avoided as topics for conversation. However, if the subject comes up in a way that does not imply the superiority of one religion over another, the majority of US citizens will be interested in learning about the spiritual practices of others, for many are unfamiliar with practices other than their own. Although religion rarely plays an active part in business decisions, individual beliefs may in fact significantly affect decisionmaking.

US Education

In the US, students are usually taught to think inductively, to study a specific case or event, and then to generalize as to how the same events might be interpreted under different conditions. Rote learning is discouraged. Students are expected to be able to debate and successfully defend their arguments using linear logic, although they often do so from limited factual data. A premium is placed on correct answers, speedy problem-solving, quantifiable results, and verbal facility, which some argue comes at the expense of quality of thought. Immediate communication of thoughts tends to be valued more highly than deliberating until one has had time to examine the multiple facets of a problem and prepare a comprehensive response. Practical solutions that can be implemented quickly are preferred to more general breakthroughs or detailed analyses of data and options. The ability to be a team player is admired, although generally only if one can do so without sacrificing one's individuality.

Many critics complain that US students are poorly prepared, especially in analytical subjects such as science and math. However, despite the shortcomings of the US educational system, its universities remain the envy of much of the world. A degree, especially from a prestigious school, will open up doors that are closed to the majority and can make doing business much simpler and more lucrative for the graduate.

If you plan to hire US citizens to work in your business, you should consider where they went to school, not just what degree they hold. Keep in mind, however, that graduation from a large, well respected school is not a guarantee that a person has received an excellent education. In fact, research and other grant projects can take faculty away from teaching, resulting in classes run by supervised graduate students, particularly in the largest and often in the best-known, most prestigious campuses. A school of less prominence—particularly one that emphasizes specific fields of study—may actually produce better educated—and often better motivated—graduates.

US BUSINESS VALUES, BELIEFS, AND BEHAVIOR

The National Business Style

For many visitors, US business culture is unpredictable and confusing. On the one hand, US businesspeople are likely to begin to do business in almost any context—at parties, on airplanes, with relative strangers, on street corners. In this sense, they easily mix social and business concerns, gathering ideas and planning deals through relatively informal procedures. On the other hand, when they specifically meet to decide on the details of a transaction, social niceties and relationship or trust building amenities are kept to a minimum; they want to get down to business. Personal relationships are frowned on in most business contexts, family life is kept private, and business is conducted with heavy stress on efficiency and usually on formalities—written contracts, meeting rules of order, legal advice.

While individual personalities vary as much or even more than in other countries, the style of US business behavior can still be described in general terms. The international businessperson who operates in major cities such as New York, Chicago, or Los Angeles will likely find that business styles are similar to those in other large cities worldwide. Across the US, these urbanites may also seem to be

WHAT US BUSINESSPEOPLE VALUE

When asked to choose and rank the qualities and values they considered most important, a sample of US businesspeople listed, from most important to least important: freedom, independence, self-reliance, equality, individualism, competition, efficiency, time, directness, openness, aggressiveness, informality, future orientation, risk taking, creativity, and accomplishment.

It is interesting that US businesspeople mentioned winning, money, material possessions, and privacy last among their values, considering that their reputation abroad tends to center on these traits. While the accuracy of the relative rankings may be disputed, they denote tendencies that are generally valid. Most of these qualities can be summarized as being results oriented, that is, directed toward a quick decision, rapid action to implement the decision, and a satisfactory outcome within the shortest possible time frame. This orientation clashes with the precepts of other cultures that deliberative action requires substantial preparation time and that anything less would be impulsive and rash.

more like each other, but markedly different from US businesspeople in rural areas or small towns within the same region. However, these distinctions that are obvious to a native will not be particularly significant, and may not even be noticeable, to an outsider, whose main concern at least at first is simply to master business operations in a different time zone, language, and culture.

The style of the average US businessperson tends to be direct, informal, optimistic, short-term oriented, independent, competitive, vocal, analytical, and even confrontational. This style reflects the values primarily of US men of European ancestry, still the most likely to be holding top management positions, conducting large-scale international business dealings, and playing the dominant role in business culture throughout the US. The high value placed on the primacy of the individual, coupled with the nation's wealth and abundant resources and its long history of successful ventures, has created a people who feel entitled to everything that they can possibly achieve through their own efforts. They tend to be optimistic and somewhat materialistic (although most would consider an open admission of materialism to be improper and even shameful). In business, they might be highly competitive and fairly impersonal, although they might also be informal and collegial, having a well-developed sense of humor. For some US businesspeople, what appears to be spontaneity may actually be a practiced style, while many others are genuinely spontaneous and less constrained by formality and tradition.

US businesspeople are pragmatic and will often go along with the suggestions of others, especially if those ideas are clearly shown to be in the best interests of the US businessperson. Although they tend to trust others until they are given reason not to do so, they can turn against someone quickly for what may seem a minor infraction to the foreign observer. This is especially true in the area of ethics. For example, visitors should note that bribery and underhanded dealings are considered improper and are against the law in the US. Although corruption involving kickbacks and other gifts or under-the-table payments does happen, it is neither a common nor a culturally accepted practice. If discovered, it will result in the loss of the deal, scandal, and legal action.

Direct communication is highly valued in the US business community at all times, regardless of the situation surrounding a discussion. This directness is associated with the English language, which is known as a "low context" language: the content of a word varies little regardless of the context in which it is spoken. Thus, "no" means "no" whether it is shouted in a boardroom or whispered at a formal dinner. US businesspeople take pride in saying what they mean, and meaning what they say, and they expect the same of others. As a result, some confusion often arises when a US person meets with someone whose language is "high context" and whose words therefore have different meanings depending on where, when, and how they are spoken.

US businesspeople plan for success. They value education and often attend seminars and courses— on their own or company-sponsored—to update their technical and professional skills and to enhance the quality of their personal lives. They characteristically rebound fairly quickly from setbacks, which they may view as a learning experience rather than a failure. Entrepreneurs, for example, may start business after business, even in the face of several failures. Such flexibility and persistence has made the US a world leader in innovation.

National versus International Awareness

US businesspeople, especially those who have had little exposure to international operations, can be narrow-minded and nationalistic. This tendency is less strong in the current era than it was in the 1950s and 1960s, when the "Ugly American" was a common stereotype. Overall, people in the US are now more aware of alternate possibilities and the successes of other cultures. However, they still believe—like people of most cultures—that their culture is equal to any and

superior to most others. They will sharply defend their country against any perceived slur or criticism of its way of doing things. Nevertheless, they are also quick to criticize their own country and usually willing to discuss all but the most inflammatory issues with foreigners, provided that the visitor does not assume an arrogant, accusatory, or superior stance.

US persons who have had little experience in international negotiations may be startled by, or may react with humor toward, unfamiliar customs and styles of dress. They can be unintentionally insensitive to foreign concerns, because they often have little concept of alternate lifestyles and modes of doing business. Their reactions may occasionally reflect the extremes of suspicion or naive openness, especially if they have had little previous international exposure. (Of course, such behavior is not unique to US persons, but can be found in nearly every culture when encountering another with different values and beliefs.) To generate a more congenial reception, both parties should display some knowledge of the other's culture, respect for the differences, and willingness to find the uniting qualities and common concerns.

The initial cross-cultural reaction is most commonly followed not just by tolerance but genuine interest and curiosity; US persons tend to welcome new experiences. They may take great pains to make sure that their guest is comfortable and well taken care of, by which they mean included in activities, provided with requested services, entertained, and generally kept busy. They are usually generous hosts who will provide meals and entertainment for visitors, often in their own homes. While US businesspeople generally do not expect immediate reciprocity from a foreign guest, they do expect the same level of hospitality if they pay a visit to that person overseas.

Time is Money

An often heard US adage, "time is money" is a tenet of the US business community and colors the behavior of US society generally. This concept is seen in the language they use: US persons "save time" just as they save money. They also spend, invest, waste, lose, gain, and make time. For them, time is a commodity—and like all commodities, it is in limited supply and can be measured in terms of wealth. Attorneys, accountants, consultants, psychologists, psychiatrists, mechanics, and others who offer services that can be measured in terms of time also bill their clients in increments of time. Highly competitive US businesses reward employees who work long hours with minimal absences, the archetypal story being the one of an attorney who charged clients for 25 hours of work in a single day by working on a transcontinental flight, thereby gaining an extra hour of billable time. And many businesspeople feel obligated to arrive early or leave late from the office as a sign of their dedication.

The US businessperson's concept of time tends to result in business dealings that are short, focused, and direct. A few short questions may be asked at the beginning of a business meeting ("Do you want coffee?" "How was your flight?" "Have you enjoyed your time here so far?") with the expectation that the answers will be equally brief ("Yes, thanks, with cream." "Great, but a little bumpy." "Yes, the art museum here is fascinating."). Once this short introductory phase ends, the US businessperson will move directly into business issues. In doing so, they do not intend any disrespect; quite the contrary, they are trying not to "waste" anyone's time.

The pace of business—and life in general—is fast. In conversation, people interrupt each other with questions, finish each other's sentences, and respond so quickly that it seems impossible for them to have assimilated what others have said. This verbal and mental quickness (often referred to as "shooting from the hip"—another cowboy metaphor) is generally prized. Members of a business team may contradict each other openly, perhaps even debating points of view, suggesting alternatives, and contradicting senior members of the team.

Punctuality is important and lateness may be viewed in an extremely negative light, almost as if it were a moral flaw. If international businesspeople find that they will not be able to meet a timetable, the US parties should be informed as early and as directly as possible. US businesspeople place great emphasis on communication and time control. They expect to be kept informed constantly about the details on the progress of any mutual business undertaking, be it in planning, under negotiation, in process, or awaiting delivery. To a foreign businessperson who is used to greater autonomy in operations, these constant inquiries may feel like interference. It may even feel like distrust, as if the US party is checking on your mode of operations. However, it is primarily a matter of style rather than an attempt to second guess an overseas partner. To help smooth relationships, regular contact should be maintained; US businesspeople strongly dislike surprises and expect to be kept informed about any developments—good or bad.

Business Life versus Private Life

The line between business and private life is often unclear in US business circles. While US businesspeople may be uncomfortable when personal matters intrude into the business environment, many quite happily mix business with pleasurable social occasions outside of the office. They are ca-

"How can I sleep when people in other time zones are already up and making money?"

sual about inviting business clients and partners home for dinner, often on short notice. They may invite business acquaintances to spend the weekend at a country home or on a sports-oriented outing—attending a football game or going fishing, hunting, golfing, skiing or sailing. Business topics are likely to arise and negotiations continue in what is otherwise an informal atmosphere. The average US person will discuss business in the presence of family members and other friends, sometimes even asking for advice and comments from those not directly involved. Business relationships may also lead to personal ones.

Business entertaining is, of course, common to many cultures; it is usually intended to be part of the process of establishing a level of trust and preparing for a long-term business relationship. In many Asian cultures, for example, colleagues spend many nights socializing with each other or entertaining clients, but business deals are rarely sought or completed in that context. The distinction is that these cultures clearly separate their business and private lives. Socializing with business associates is aimed at creating a solid, enduring alliance, but it is not done at home or with family members, which would be considered an invasion of privacy.

An apparent paradox of the US business culture is that US businesspeople also tend to categorize and compartmentalize distinct elements, including the different aspects of their lives. The general feeling is that personal matters should not intrude into a business environment because the effect will be to lose the edge in the business relationship; cutthroat competition is not conducive to gaining allies, and doing business with persons you dislike means not having to worry about whether you might insult them. In fact, anyone who cannot leave work at the office and go home to other pursuits may be stigmatized in the US as obsessive—a "workaholic"—with skewed priorities and values.

Because of the undefined lines between US business and personal life, the best approach for a foreign businessperson who is invited into a social setting during a US visit is to follow the lead of the US colleague. If your US host brings up business, discuss your ideas, but don't be surprised if business concerns never arise. Time spent away from the office is highly valued, and most share the belief that once work is over, their time is their own and they are under no obligation to devote additional energy to business should they choose not to do so. To deal more successfully with a particular US partner, the visitor should look for the qualities that distinguish a US person who is "all business, all the time" from one who likes to relax outside the office; these qualities will be a clue to what you can expect, as well as to what is expected from you.

Business and the Family

Although most people in the US would argue for the importance of the family, family life may in reality become secondary to the demands of business. Child care is expensive and not yet readily available in the US, and the US educational system does not occupy children to the degree it does in most other developed countries. The composition of US families is changing, and this is having an impact on many US businesspeople.

In the current changing economy, significant numbers of adult children are unable to find work that will provide adequate income for them to establish their own households; therefore many are having to rely on their parents for support. In addition, improvements in medicine and the nation's demographic bulge from the baby boom generation have made the elderly the fastest growing sector of the US population. They, too, are often financially dependent on their working children and may live in the same household. Although these situations are common in many societies, they have been the exception rather than the rule in the US for at least most of the 20th century. To a large extent, US residents today have grown up in a nuclear family—two parents and a couple of children—and they are unprepared financially and emotionally for a return to the extended family.

At the other end of the spectrum, the number of single parent households—usually headed by women—is growing rapidly. While the stability and resources available to the nuclear family are not always the best, they are even more lacking for many single parent families. Inherent in single-parenting is the double stress of having to be the primary caregiver as well as the principal wage earner for the family. The majority of businesses still offer little, if any, assistance, support, flexibility, or programs to families in which all of the adults work, leaving no one to provide daily child care.

Informality

In comparison with other cultures, the US business culture is relatively informal. Although many cultures operate through careful adherence to formal procedures or through a hierarchy, US businesspeople are less concerned with formal levels of authority than they are with dealing with someone who has the necessary expertise and the ability to make a decision. They may well send a junior technician to a meeting with a senior foreign executive, not intending any slight, but because that junior technician has the expertise to best deal with the issues in question. On the other hand, if they are upset when their senior member is met by someone of lower rank, it's not because they are insulted, but because the foreign participant lacks the authority to make a commitment.

A general belief in equality before the law and—for many—before a divine presence tends to promote less formal relationships among US persons. Status differences that are reinforced elsewhere are often disregarded in the US. For example, the most powerful person in the room may be the most casually dressed. Senior officers may pride themselves in their camaraderie with subordinates and enjoy being considered "one of the gang" despite their rank. Executives are often careful to maintain at least the appearance of hands-on management and a consultative approach. Visitors should not take this appearance of equality and informality at face value; rather they should take their cues from the behavior of other people in the organization.

Many people in the US view formality as something artificial and burdensome, and they may even see it as evidence of insincerity, a moral flaw in US business. In the US, informality is a means of cutting through unnecessary constraints to gain results. It may include moving abruptly to the use of first names between negotiating parties, failing to follow established procedures, conducting business outside the office and in unusual ways and circumstances, or failing to dress to show wealth and power. These and other short-cuts may be disconcerting or even offensive to outsiders.

Foreigners should note that while some US businesspeople use informality as a tactic to throw their counterparts off balance, most genuinely engage in practices that they believe will put everyone at ease by making the atmosphere more relaxed and collegial. At the same time, the foreign visitor should not try to play a role that is inauthentic; while it may be useful to understand one's counterparts and to try to fit in, it is also useful to retain one's own style and equilibrium, even if these are strongly challenged by disorienting contrasts encountered in the US. For the most part, US culture prefers sincerity, with the result that both parties will end up uncomfortable—one because of the need to play a role, and the other because of the falsity of the role being played.

Optimism: The Half-Full Glass

US businesspeople are usually inclined to be optimistic. They will look at a situation and say that the glass is half-full rather than half-empty, meaning that the positive aspects outweigh the negative aspects and provide a foundation on which to build. Because most US businesspeople are basically optimistic and believe that they can exert control over their fate, they are likely to take an activist approach to solving problems. They are highly motivated to achieve their objectives and not constrained by fatalism. This view differs from that in cultures that consider business—and life—to be determined from the outside or by the events and traditions of the past. Actively working for a better future generally leads US residents to appear to have little time for the lessons of the past. This outlook also leads to constant tinkering with regulations, organizational structures, and programs, as well as to technological and organizational innovation.

People in the US generally expect to succeed simply by working hard and following the rules, an attitude that sometimes makes them appear either naive or lacking in empathy for those who fail. If success depends on individual effort and compliant behavior (that is, following the rules), then failure must be the result of an individual's shortcomings, and that individual's unfortunate fate is therefore deserved.

The optimism of the US populace has been tempered in recent years with the economic restructuring occurring in most US sectors. While people at lower income levels have typically had a somewhat less optimistic view of future prospects, for the first time in US history, people at all levels of income are uncertain about their futures. Corporate downsizing has shown that loyalty, effort, and observance of the rules provide no protection against dismissal from employment, even for middle and top managers. Younger generations are increasingly discouraged about whether they will be able to equal—much less surpass—their parents' standard of living. Older displaced workers are becoming unsure about maintaining what they now have. The dampening of optimism in the US is setting a tone of edginess and uncertainty, often making US businesspeople more wary in their dealings with others.

DOING BUSINESS IN THE UNITED STATES

What US Businesspeople Expect from Foreign Businesspeople

US businesspeople expect international visitors to be polite, cordial, and knowledgeable about business. All people, regardless of gender, age, race, class, business, or income category, are expected to be treated in the same professional manner. US businesspeople are particularly concerned about results, profits, fairness, winning, and collegiality, and they expect their foreign counterparts to be similarly oriented. Thus, when considering a deal, a US person will want to know that a foreign businessperson has a history of performing and completing agreements. Because the personal element is less important in US business, references and introductions generally play a smaller role in US business relations than in some other cultures. Nevertheless, these may be useful in establishing credibility with US businesspeople.

Reserve on the part of foreigners may be interpreted as disdain or aloofness by US businesspeople. Therefore, foreign businesspeople should try to counteract such impressions, such as by adopting a more direct style than in similar situations at home. An attitude of superiority on the part of foreign negotiators is inappropriate, as is any behavior that suggests discrimination. US businesspeople may unconsciously lecture others, but may be offended if given what appears to be a lecture by others. Foreigners should be honest and forthright—while also remembering to be diplomatic.

Topics of conversation to avoid include politics, sex, money, and religion, although these may be introduced in one form or another by the host. Note that subordinates, colleagues, and spouses of US businesspeople are likely to be knowledgeable and to express their own opinions; you are usually expected to listen to and seriously consider such opinions.

Approaches to Business

Foreign visitors who meet with US businesspeople may be startled to find that US colleagues and team members contradict each other openly and seemingly fail to defer to seniority or authority. In order to expand their comprehension, US businesspeople often imagine themselves in the role of their competitor or customer. They like to argue a position contrary to their own beliefs just to explore the ideas and viewpoints. They are willing to consider any technology or other

---

HOW US PERSONS SEE THE WORLD: SELECTED BELIEFS*

US culture, like every other culture in the world, is enormously complex and therefore is difficult to understand, let alone to describe in its entirety. There are, however, a number of key beliefs that characterize US culture, both by itself and in relation to other cultures.

American Cultural Beliefs	Beliefs in Many Other Cultures
Individual identity is acknowledged and seen as the primary way of defining "self." One usually chooses to join with others in a group, but it is not required to define oneself. Individuals take comfort in their ability to withdraw from the group when and if they so choose.	*Membership in one or more groups defines the individual.* People see and present themselves first in terms of family, village, religion, ethnic group, nationality, etc. In the absence of such group affiliation, the individual is unlikely to be comfortable with self or easily accepted by society.
Privacy is thought to be a natural state that everyone needs equally and a "right" to be guarded and guaranteed. Lack of privacy is a punishment that is usually reserved for inmates and young children.	*Being alone and therefore able to be singled out as an individual is not a good thing.* Privacy, which by definition is physical or mental self-exclusion, is unnatural, undesirable, and dangerous.
Competition among individuals and groups is encouraged and thought to be a basis for improvement and growth. An unwillingness to compete is seen as a sure sign of weakness. Individuals even compete with themselves for "personal bests."	*Cooperation is the basis for group success and, by extension, individual success.* Competition doesn't make sense in the absence of the concept of the individual, and is seen as leading to self-inflicted damage to the group.
Individual control over the environment and the circumstances of life is taken for granted. Fate and destiny have been replaced by hard work, good behavior, and the wonders of modern science. One's life is what one makes of it; there is no one to blame but oneself if things do not turn out for the best. All things are possible for all people.	*Fate and destiny define human lives.* They are reflected in one's birthright, heredity, family, social position, caste, and class. They are modified only by divine will as manifested in the pre-ordained blessings and disasters of nature as well as in divine responses to personal/community appeals and devotion.

* Copyright © 1995 Dean W. Engel, managing partner, The East West Group, Mill Valley, California, an organization specializing in cross-cultural communications for businesses operating globally.

means (no matter how unorthodox) that will give them greater control or further their goals. By the time they have finished discussing a topic, they have often made up their minds and are ready to proceed.

The joy of debate underlies the US businessperson's enthusiasm in greeting a stranger and warmth in hearing new ideas. This friendly, informal reception accorded to a foreign businessperson may signify nothing more than general cordiality and the US person's intention to participate in the particular meeting. It is not intended to convey acceptance or to create any implied contract. For this reason, failure to conclude an agreement in such a friendly atmosphere should not be taken as a radical change of heart or an insult toward the foreign visitor.

Perhaps most disconcerting of all, a US person may demand instantaneous feedback—an immediate reaction to an issue or a response to an often complex or crucial proposal. The US businessperson may even express frustration and impatience with an international visitor who does not have the authority or the willingness to make an independent, immediate decision. To an international visitor from a culture that is more formal, consultative, and hierarchical, this behavior appears impulsive and disorganized.

A foreign businessperson who understands the US approach to business and who prepares ways to meet it will find that a US businessperson can be, by turns, competitive and cooperative, and can make an enthusiastic business partner, even if sometimes a bit impulsive and naive. The tactics chosen will, of course, vary depending on the extent of the US person's experience in the international arena, but there are generally two keys to success: clarity of purpose and directness. At the outset of any discussion or meeting, a foreign person should be certain to state his or her purpose and to receive acknowledgment from the US party. Whether the meeting is to discuss ideas or to make a decision, the purpose should be clear from the start. Throughout the relationship, the foreign person should be as direct as possible. If a decision can be authorized only after deliberation by all the principals over time, that requirement should be expressly stated. Such a direct statement is likely to find more acceptance and respect in the US business community than the action of a foreign trader who subsequently refuses to follow through on a negotiated plan, claiming lack of authority.

Negotiations

By and large, people in the US are used to paying the asking price rather than haggling over items. Thus they have little cultural experience with bargaining. Nevertheless, you should not expect US people involved in business negotiations to accept your proposals as presented. It is important to realize that no matter how informal and friendly they may be, US businesspeople—like those elsewhere—deal with a view toward their own self-interest and not from altruism.

Do everything possible to minimize miscommunication. This is particularly important when cultural and linguistic differences exist between parties to the negotiation. Misunderstandings are easy under these conditions and must be guarded against. People in the US generally tend to trust people unless and until something occurs to indicate that they are not trustworthy. However, once that trust is broken, it may become virtually impossible to regain it. An essential requirement is that everyone should interpret the terms of the agreement in the same manner; otherwise simple misunderstandings can quickly escalate to become deal-breaking conflicts. Without mutual accord, an agreement may also be unenforceable, even in the courts.

Negotiating Style In general, US negotiating style is open and straightforward. Negotiators seldom resort to outright misrepresentation, although they may be highly selective in constructing their arguments and presenting their supporting data. They often rely on prepared financial projections, and you may not be able to sway them unless you can provide reasonable alternate sets of numbers that show how to gain the desired results by doing things your way.

Many foreign businesspeople who want to do business in the US perceive that US companies invariably demand the majority of the proceeds in exchange for their contributions—including innovations or technology, their ability to deliver, and their willingness to take risks.

If you are operating in their home office—or on their "turf"—let the US businesspeople set the tone. In general, most US business negotiations are informal and people tend to address each other by their first names. Although some individuals like to warm up by talking for several minutes about general matters, the majority of US businesspeople begin to discuss the specific issues almost immediately. However, because the US workforce is multicultural, significant differences may exist; visitors who are alert to these and willing to adapt their own behavior accordingly will facilitate communication.

The first rule of bargaining is to negotiate over issues, not positions. A party who takes a firm position tends to commit to defending that position and attacking contrary positions, deemphasizing the potential for a meaningful compromise or resolution. You should attempt to separate the personalities from the real issues in question. To do so, it is helpful to look behind the specific positions, try to discover what interests are being served, and rephrase alternatives that will satisfy the concerns of the other party. Above all, negotiators should strive to agree early on objective criteria to measure the results and effects.

Letting Everyone Win One of the goals in negotiating should be not only to get the best deal possible but also to achieve a deal that will not seem totally one-sided and unfair to the other party. Deals that are heavily unfavorable to one party are likely not only to unravel but also to spoil future prospects. To this end, it is desirable to avoid offending anyone, so far as is possible without compromising your own position and integrity. Therefore, if you are in a strong position, avoid dictating the terms to the other party. Rather, be magnanimous when possible. Let them know that you are sensitive to their interests. Also let them know what your best offer is. To do that, you must have decided the limits of your offer in advance.

If the other side is adamant and fails to bargain in good faith, one possible tactic is to refuse to attack their position or defend your own. Try to rephrase any attacks on you so that instead they are attacks on the basic problem, and try to find common elements that can be used to reformulate a different position. It may also be useful to work on less contentious issues first. In some instances, the central issue is overriding, and no resolution can be made until it is decided. In others, the parties can agree on certain side issues, which can bring them closer together and give them more of a stake in reaching a comprehensive solution so as not to lose the benefits already gained.

Always try to be sure that you and the opposition define and agree on the facts to the extent possible. Restate the argument to be sure that both parties agree on what has been said and proposed. Use the restatement to isolate specific issues for further discussion, setting aside points that are in agreement or are irrelevant to the main discussion. Acknowledge any contributions and concessions that the other side has made to you. Attempt to cast the optimal solution in terms of principles rather than advantages. Aim for fairness, pointing out ways in which your suggestions uphold fairness for the other side. Suggest alternatives and tradeoffs that you would be willing to make to achieve your main goals.

Techniques and Tactics The tactics and techniques you are likely to encounter in negotiating with US firms will vary widely depending on such factors as the personalities around the table, the company's business policies and international experience, and its commitment to making international deals. Some US negotiators will employ harsh tactics—known as "playing hardball"—aimed at pressuring what are seen as adverse parties in order to gain the supreme advantage in the relationship. For example, a company may start with a greatly exaggerated offer and then appear to give up substantial interests that in fact are fairly minor. Another hardball tactic is to use a negotiator who presents a harsh deal and one who

seems more willing to compromise, the intent being to gain the agreement of the prospective trading partner to what appears to be the best deal that the more helpful negotiator can convince the harsher one to accept. Such tactics are not, however, the best because not only will the parties tend to remain resentful and distrustful toward each other, but a US court may interpret such an agreement strictly against the powerful party so as to protect the powerless party. The better choice is to avoid pressure tactics and inequities in the negotiating process.

A basic consideration is the choice of the location for the talks. It is often preferable to meet at a neutral site—such as a hotel—that is seen neither as your territory nor theirs. Overseas visitors may be limited in the choice of a neutral meeting ground because virtually every venue in the US will be familiar to the US company. On the other hand, there may be some advantages to meeting in the US, even in the opposite party's offices, because the US negotiators may be more relaxed, less defensive, and more amenable to compromise; you can also leave more easily if the talks break down.

To avoid committing to a deal that is unfavorable, you should prepare for the negotiating session by deciding exactly which terms you prefer and which alternatives are totally unacceptable. You should consider your options in the event that the deal is not consummated, so that if you decide to leave the negotiations, you know where you are headed. Having confidence in your future will allow you to assert yourself strongly at the negotiating table and will show the other side that in the absence of compromise, you have other resources.

Directness and control are important negotiating tools in the US, which means that you should request what you feel is necessary in a forthright manner. If you need more time or a recess in the talks to study a proposal, consult with your associates, or deliberate over the negotiations, you should ask for a temporary break to regroup. It is appropriate simply to say that you are not prepared to discuss a particular point at that time. Each party at a negotiation should honor the reasonable requests of the other with regard to the process, and the extent of the respect shown at the negotiating table will indicate the trust and strength of the relationship created.

In a cross-cultural negotiation, the parties should be testing whether a long-term relationship is feasible. They should show their natural dispositions, structure time for relaxation, and approach multicultural differences with understanding, respect, and humor. It is as important to gauge your prospective trading partner as it is to cut the deal, and in the US both of these aspects often tend to occur rapidly and at the same time—during actual negotiations. This process therefore plays an extremely significant role in US business, and first impressions tend to be lasting ones.

Working with Women

More and more often, international businesspeople are finding that the US person across the negotiating table is a woman. About 60 percent of women in the US work outside the home for pay (compared to 75 percent of men), and some predict that by the year 2000 the number of women employed outside the home will actually exceed the number of men. Although women tend to have more education than men at virtually all levels, including post-high school advanced education, most hold lower-wage, so-called "pink collar" jobs, such as office assistant, mail clerk, and receptionist. In comparison to the number of men, there are still only a few women in the upper ranks of US business, although there are more in the US than in virtually any other country. The number of women in US business is growing, however, and the lines between acceptable occupations for women versus those for men are blurring as more and more of both genders cross over from what were once traditional occupations into nontraditional ones.

Despite many advances and greater acceptance of women at all levels in US business, many women feel that they are still not perceived as serious professionals in what remains a predominately male business environment. Moreover, they typically work longer hours than men for less pay; at home, they usually still have primary responsibility for domestic work and child rearing. A few, but slowly growing number, of US employers are developing family programs, child-care alternatives, job-share systems, and other benefits that will keep women on the job. Women in the US today want to be recognized for their professional contribution to the economy—both at home and outside the home.

In business dealings, no deference should be paid to the gender of the US businessperson. The same cultural characteristics are likely to be present, regardless of whether the US person is male or female. Thus, if a US businesswoman is friendly and informal when greeting a foreign visitor, that is simply a reflection of the style of doing business in the US; it is not a sexual statement. If a US woman seems abrupt and "businesslike," she is not adopting the style of a man, but merely the style of the US business of which she is a part. Many are quick to point out the different styles of women and men in doing business—women supposedly being more deliberative, collegial, and, diplomatic. But in the US, it is important to remember that these qualities define a personality, not a gender. Because US businesses tend to hire people who match the company policies and preferences, the personalities you

encounter—in both men and women—will be reflective of the way the company does business, not necessarily of any particular gender. The underlying rule is to treat a US businesswoman with professional business respect—not gender-based courtesy.

In fact, both women and men are protected by US laws against harassment and discrimination in the workplace. Harassment may be broadly defined, and to avoid potential legal claims, you should never make sexually oriented comments, nor act in such manner. A person of either gender who is visiting the US has a right to expect and demand respectful, professional behavior from US businesspeople. Conversely, any US person has a right to expect the same from foreign businesspersons.

Doing Business in Ethnic Communities

Many observers see the increasingly diverse US workforce as foreshadowing the global business community of the future. Moreover, changing US demographics are forcing US business toward greater diversity in a workplace that has traditionally been mostly White and male. Business has already been significantly affected by the participation of women and minorities, and their influence can only grow in the future. The growth of ethnic communities is seen as opening a vibrant new market for consumers who are not being reached by conventional products and marketing.

It is dangerous—and may well be offensive—to generalize about group traits, because generalizations tend to come from and lead to stereotypes. While stereotypes may have some basis in fact, facts often prove to be outdated, and stereotypes often become derogatory caricatures. They are usually of little use in understanding or dealing with specific representatives of any group and may actually hinder attempts to do so. The most valid approach may be one that allows the outsider to come to the table with as much knowledge but as few preconceptions as possible. As in any dealings with mainstream businesspeople, you must remain sensitive to the styles and concerns of others.

Terminology can be a touchy issue, and outsiders must be sensitive to terms which may carry negative connotations in various ethnic communities. For example, African-American is the current preferred usage, although Black is still generally acceptable; many other terms are not. Many with Latin ancestry currently prefer to be designated as Latino, rather than by the more traditional Hispanic. Because the Latino community is extremely diverse, it is preferable not to assign a specific national heritage—such as Mexican, Mexican-American, or Chicano—to an individual unless you know that the person claims that background and accepts the designation. While some indigenous North Americans are comfortable with the traditional misnomer of Indian, others prefer Native American.

Some Latinos (and Canadians) bristle at the use of the term American to describe US residents, arguing that all those from the New World are Americans and that people from the US have misappropriated it for their exclusive use. Some Native Americans argue that they alone should be entitled to use the term. Nevertheless, American is the common designation used—mostly without self-consciousness—in the US and in most of the non-Latin world to describe persons from the US. A large number of US persons indicate their heritage with a hyphenated designation, such as Greek-Americans, Japanese-Americans, or Egyptian-Americans.

Although numerous ethnically based subgroups exist in the US, many foreign visitors remark that US ethnic groups, no matter how differently they are viewed by the mainstream US populace, have been infused with US culture and have lost some of the characteristics of their own culture. Indeed, some minority businesspeople wish to be treated in the same manner as a members of the dominant group, preferring not to be singled out in any way. Others enjoy being recognized as special and unique, and thus distinct from mainstream US culture. Visitors are cautioned that while there may be many similarities due to tradition, language, and affiliation with the root cultures, US ethnic groups are likely to have values, beliefs, and behavior that may be significantly different from those of their overseas counterparts. Visitors must therefore be guided by their own intuition and by cues such as the individual's appearance—ethnic dress, accessories, hairstyling—by speech patterns, or by other distinctive mannerisms.

Many ethnic individuals have adopted—whether knowingly or subconsciously—the basic culture of mainstream US business. There may be variations, such as preferences for reciprocal hospitality and an almost ritualized exchange of compliments in greeting. Social and personal relationships may be more important and more highly developed than in mainstream culture. Business negotiations may be postponed until after a personal relationship has been established. Decisions may be made by the senior executive, with or without consultation with others, or may be consensual, requiring essentially unanimous agreement. Women may play a greater or lesser role from those generally found in mainstream culture. Variations among ethnic groups in the US can include the amount of eye contact; breadth of spacing—closeness or separation—between people; use of gestures; tone and loudness of voice; preference of formal or informal style; personal or impersonal transactions; and sense of time, opportunity, and control over one's destiny.

International visitors should be aware that the hiring of undocumented alien workers is against US law. Because immigration is a highly controversial issue in the US, it generally is not considered a safe topic for conversation.

Politics and the Businessperson

It is important for international businesspeople to be aware of political elements that have an impact on their businesses. State and local policies, such as local ordinances and the fees imposed on businesses to finance public services, may well have a more direct financial impact than national policies and election results. Conversely, local officials may be more willing to accommodate foreign businesspeople, waiving fees and taxes, even suspending or altering some regulations to gain benefits for the local economy. Foreigners need to evaluate their public relations in approaching the US because of the tendency—seen in all cultures—to resent the intervention or interference of outsiders.

In practical terms, the US has had a two-party political system for most of its history, with relatively few other parties achieving any influence. This differs from both the multiparty coalitions and single-party political systems found in many other countries. The US system also calls for fixed terms of office, so that transitions occur at specified times rather than more unpredictably as is the case in many other systems. The US political system also differs from that of many other countries in that power passes regularly and peacefully based on election results that are generally accepted by the electorate; there has not been a significant challenge to the legitimacy of the political system since the US Civil War in the 1860s.

In the 20th century, the Republican party has generally been considered the more conservative, more business-oriented one, while the Democratic party has been viewed as more liberal and interested in providing social services. Although the situation remains basically stable, the US political system and the two major parties are involved in trying to redefine themselves in order to manage rapid change and an increasingly apparent inability on the part of the traditional system to adapt effectively to new conditions. Corporate downsizing, an immense federal deficit, stagnant or falling prices in the real estate market, burgeoning immigration, an aging population, declining academic performance, rising crime, the realization that social service subsidies have grown enormously and have become a way of life for some people, and fears that the US is losing its competitive edge in world markets are merely some of the issues with which the system is straining to cope. As a sign of its concern over these and other issues, the 1994 electorate voted record numbers of inexperienced new electees into office, seeking innovative changes.

All persons over the age of 18 are eligible to vote, and registration is convenient and free. However, there is no requirement that people either register or vote. Large segments of the population feel dissatisfied with the choice of candidates and do not vote. Trends now becoming apparent in other parts of the world—economic instability, global competition, and growing religious fundamentalism—are moving domestic politics to the right in the US, leading the US populace to question even more of its political beliefs and structures.

Environmental and Health Concerns

Although it is still far from universal, there is a strong and increasing concern in the US over preservation of the environment. This may be enshrined in US law more than it is in US consciousness, but is also more stringently enforced than in many other countries. An international visitor who sets up operations in the US should be aware not only of all the regulations, but also of public norms and awareness. Good public relations may mean contributing to environmental organizations and using recycled materials or more environmentally friendly processes whenever possible. Public opinion can have a huge impact on the success of a business in the US. Citizens feel it is their right to pass judgment on business activities, and many will bring what they consider to be abuses to the attention of the media, enforcement agencies, or the courts.

On a more personal level, the use of tobacco products has become a sensitive issue in much of the US. Smoking is now prohibited by law on airlines and in most offices and indoor public spaces, as well as in some restaurants, especially in larger cities and on both coasts. Smokers must generally go outside the building or to designated areas to smoke. If you visit an office or a home and see no ashtrays, it is best to refrain from smoking inside or to ask whether smoking is permitted.

This focus on individual activities that affect the immediate environment around the individual can be extended to other personal activities in ways that can seem intrusive. People in the US can be highly health and allergy conscious—some obsessively so. Many expend a great deal of effort on exercise and diet, which is bemusing to many foreigners. Although many people in the US are substantially overweight, pay little attention to what they eat, and do not engage in physical activity, there is nevertheless considerable concern over diet and exercise. Health issues also top the list, and many will vocalize their adverse reactions to foods, perfumes, colognes, hairsprays, and other seemingly minor intrusions. Visitors should cautiously avoid heavy scents and

should be prepared for enthusiastic lectures and exhortations on these subjects. If you are asked whether you would like to participate in some particular dietary or exercise program, it is acceptable to decline politely.

The Legal System: When in Doubt, Sue

The US is a litigious society. Clogged dockets, the high cost of legal representation, concerns about arbitrary jury verdicts and massive liability awards, and a growing awareness that an adversarial system is counterproductive to rapid and appropriate results are all slowly moving the business community toward alternative dispute resolution (ADR) methods such as mediation and arbitration. However, visitors should realize that almost any activity can result in legal action—not only among the business participants, but also by end users of the products and services sold—and that many businesspeople in the US obtain legal advice before undertaking any transactions, no matter how minor.

Have your own US attorney examine any document before you sign it. The language of a contract tends to benefit the party who wrote it, and US courts can require parties to the contract to fulfill their promises and obligations or pay damages to cover the other party's losses—even if those amount to more than the original bargain. Although the use of mediators and other types of ADR is growing, it is not uncommon for a dissatisfied party to file suit in either state or federal court. US laws—which differ in the 50 states, not to mention the innumerable local jurisdictions and the federal system—are complex and likely to be substantially different from those in your home country. You could put yourself at a significant disadvantage if you do not have local counsel.

BUSINESS ETIQUETTE

Introductions

Although not necessary, having the name of, or an introduction to, a specific person in the firm you are contacting is helpful and reassuring. Most companies can refer you to someone within the firm who is able to deal with your inquiry. Likewise, it is preferable to set up appointments as far in advance as possible. However, US business is usually relatively informal, and many US firms are willing to schedule a meeting with you on short notice.

People in the US like to boast of the open, merit-based system in the country's business. In general, it is true that most US businesspeople are approachable without direct introductions or considerations being paid, and that people and ideas generally can advance through the system on their own merits.

However, access and advancement are neither guaranteed nor smooth. Some are never able to get the exposure necessary to have their proposals seriously considered; thus, even worthy proposals may be rejected. Nevertheless, the potential exists for outsiders to gain access to some of the most exalted businesspeople in the US. You may not be able to meet with the President of General Motors, but you are likely to be able to meet with an appropriate officer—if you are persistent and have a serious, reasonable idea to discuss.

People in the US place great stock in what is called networking. In reality, US businesspeople are relative newcomers to serious networking, which consists of informal personal contacts and referrals, an essential element of business in many other cultures. Nevertheless, US businesspeople have a different, more open approach to this useful tool. While a close personal relationship may be required in other cultures to gain a referral, only a tenuous connection is often required in US business culture for the caller to be passed on to others who may be able to offer help. It is always a good idea to ask those with whom you have any dealings if they can suggest anyone else with whom you should speak. Be sure to ask if you can use the person's name when contacting the referral.

Greetings

Very little physical contact occurs in most business interactions in the US. However, this may vary, depending on the person's background, the industry, the circumstances, and the degree of familiarity. Take your cue from the individuals that you meet. People usually greet each other by smiling and making eye contact. Firm handshakes are almost invariably given and received using the right hand. A weak handshake—described as a "dead fish" handshake—will convey a negative impression of uncertainty, lack of self-confidence, and even insincerity to a US party. It is unnecessary and inappropriate to forcefully squeeze the hand, but a quick firm grasp and a rapid but restrained up-and-down motion is desirable. Handshakes in the US usually do not continue for more than a couple of seconds. Other than shaking hands with the right hand, there is generally no prohibition or rule about using one hand or the other for any purpose, as is the case in some other cultures. Left-handed people in the US commonly eat and drink with that hand, and people may occasionally shake hands using both hands or only the left hand (particularly if the other hand is occupied or disabled).

Greetings usually include something along the lines of "Hello" or "Hi," often followed by "How are you?" The expected response is a brief one—such as, "Fine, thanks, and you?"—to which the first speaker says "Fine" or makes a similarly short reply. Other such greetings include phrases such as "How is business?" or "How is it going?" These ritualized greetings are seldom designed to elicit an honest or detailed response, and a literal response about your health, mental state, or business conditions will confuse the questioner. Although some US businesspeople may discuss innocuous topics such as the weather or some area of mutual interest, the greeting is often the only preparatory socializing that occurs before the discussion focuses on the business transaction at hand.

Beyond the handshake, physical touching in a greeting is not the norm—and it may even indicate a different type of relationship. Thus, while US men may sometimes embrace quickly—usually with a good thump on the back—they do not kiss when greeting each other because that would have homosexual overtones. It is acceptable for men and women or women and women to embrace, and even to brush their cheeks together or lightly kiss each other's cheeks. Most of the time, these more physical greetings are reserved for people who are already at least acquainted, if not long-standing friends.

Making Conversation

After a greeting, a common question for first-time acquaintances is "What do you do?" The appropriate answer is a brief description of one's profession, usually with a designation that clues the other person into the responsibility of your position—such as "I own a furniture import-export company" or "I am the director of international marketing for the ABC firm" or "I am a patent attorney for a software development company." US persons typically judge the apparent power and authority of a person based on such designations, while a title may often have relatively little significance to the US holder of the title.

Minimal physical contact is the rule when making conversation with a US businessperson. Businesspeople do not walk or sit casually arm in arm or hand in hand while discussing a deal—such contact implies an intimate relationship. Most US persons prefer to stand or sit at least an outstretched arm's length away from each other when talking. Some will spontaneously touch your arm or shoulder during a conversation, but many find such touching annoying and even offensive. On the other hand, failure to make frequent eye contact on meeting and during subsequent interaction—known colloquially as being "shifty-eyed"—may make people feel that you are untrustworthy. This may be particularly problematic for people from cultures in which direct eye contact is considered rude or disrespectful. In the US, it is interpreted as showing forthrightness and honesty as well as sincere interest in the conversation and the person.

Business may be discussed on virtually any occasion: during breaks in negotiating or training sessions, meals, parties, and sporting events (both spectator and participatory; golf in particular is often considered to be a business event, rather than a sport). Religion, politics, personal finances, and sex are generally considered topics too controversial for discussion among businesspeople. However, there may be many specific exceptions to this rule. The host may introduce an uncomfortable topic that requires your response. If possible, steer clear and change the subject. If you choose to discuss the subject, try to do so as diplomatically as possible. Current events and different ways of looking at or doing things in other countries are areas with potential for disagreement and misunderstanding. Although people in the US are usually genuinely interested in other viewpoints, those viewpoints can lead to discord, especially if they are presented in an outspoken or superior manner.

Conversations—usually more relaxed ones among friends rather than business discussions or casual social chatter—may include references to controversial topics, often in the form of jokes. Such conversations may occur in mixed company with the participation of various ethnic groups and persons of different gender. However, it is very difficult for an outsider to know exactly what the boundaries are and when such comments are appropriate. It is better not to actively participate on such occasions. Humor is generally appreciated. However, even if the topic is not obviously a touchy one, remember that humor often does not translate well into other languages and cultural contexts.

Gestures

Gestures are used to varying degrees by people in the US. They may be used freely and expansively, in a restrained manner, for emphasis, or unconsciously from nervousness. Shaking the head from side to side means no, while shaking up and down indicates agreement. Surprise may be shown by raising the eyebrows. People are beckoned by curling the index finger towards oneself with the palm upward. Uncertainty may be indicated by shrugging the shoulders. Holding the hand out with the palm facing forward means stop. Raising the hand and extending the index finger is a signal for attention; this gesture would be used, for example, to summon a waiter in a restaurant. However, shaking one's index finger at someone or pointing it directly at them can be considered as accusatory or challenging.

Many gestures that are considered rude or even obscene in other countries may be used innocently in the US with no untoward meaning. Foreigners should not be offended by such gestures unless the person making them is from a similar background and clearly intends disrespect. By the same token, the gesture that is objectionable throughout the US

is an upraised middle finger, which is considered obscene and challenging.

Business Interactions

Business Cards In the US, business cards are presented and exchanged informally and often pocketed or filed away without a glance or after only a cursory examination. This sort of behavior, which would be considered disrespectful if not actually insulting in some cultures, is standard in the US. In fact, many US businesspeople would view a break in a conversation to spend time looking at a business card as a form of rudeness, feeling that they should concentrate on the person rather than the card representing that person. An exception would be to verify a piece of information, such as a telephone number, while the person is present.

Business cards are usually kept for reference, so a well designed business card—striking but understated—that clearly identifies you and your company—in English—is crucial. An attractive brochure or folder that outlines the key services and benefits provided by your company and distributed with your business card may be even better. However, this type of handout should generally be confined to more formal business settings, because it could be considered inappropriate in an initial, casual contact. If you are going to be dealing with a group that uses a language other than English, it may be advisable to have materials prepared in that language, although in general, English is considered the language of business in the US.

Deference to Rank and Status Varying levels of deference may be shown to age, experience, and social or professional standing, depending on a person's personality and the corporate culture. Although it is becoming less common, some people will still stand when an older person enters or leaves a room, and some men will do so for women. Failure to do so is not necessarily considered disrespectful; rather it usually reflects the general informality that is characteristic of US business culture.

People in a business context may introduce themselves by first name only. To ask that a name be repeated is acceptable. Titles are seldom used and may be misleading. For example, the title of vice president may indicate that the person has considerable authority or merely that the company is free with honorifics. In general, US businesspeople are much less concerned with a person's relative rank in the organization than are people in many other cultures. However, they are sensitive to whether the person is in a position to deal with them. Junior executives may be as outspoken as, or more so than, their seniors. However, a junior person may also show deference to a senior person by ending a statement with a rising inflection that sounds like a question or leaning toward the superior.

Senior people in the US may be far from austere and removed from the rest of their company. They can be quite unassuming, friendly, and eager to greet you, speak with you, and see to your comfort—sometimes to the point of causing discomfort among visitors who are used to more formal and hierarchical behavior on the part of senior people. They may also be extremely informed and involved at relatively low levels of their operation. In US corporations, authority may be delegated to subordinates to a far greater degree than is common in many overseas firms. But no matter how egalitarian a senior executive may appear, it is always wise to remember that the person exercises considerable authority and should be treated with respect and circumspection. You may be able to take your cue from observing how the person's colleagues and subordinates interact with him or her. Of course, no matter what their rank or style, you should, of course, treat everyone you contact with respect and courtesy.

Despite presenting a relatively low-profile style, senior people in US firms may also take up more physical space with gestures, by placement of furniture, or by use of several personal belongings— such as a briefcase, notepad, and calendar planner. In larger firms, executive offices may even be in a separate area and may be quite lavish. A general rule of thumb in sizing up the degree of authority held by a US executive is to notice the number of windows in the office; corner offices are also often evidence of standing and power. However, these features are not always the best gauge of someone's authority, because some executives eschew these signs of power.

Timeliness Business appointments and meetings in the US usually begin on time, although everyone recognizes that last minute problems, delays in air flights or traffic, and any number of other minor or not-so-minor events can throw a schedule off. Keeping you waiting is usually not part of the US business game plan. You would take more of a risk by keeping them waiting, although a brief but sincere apology and explanation will usually mollify a US party unless the offense involves a substantial amount of time without justification. In general, you are allowed to be no more than 10 to 15 minutes late for an appointment before it will be canceled.

Personal Issues In the egalitarian, informal US, people are generally expected to take care of their own needs. Except in the wealthiest circles and the most formal of events, servants are absent. It is impolite to treat subordinates, such as junior people or assistants, as servant substitutes. For example, if coffee or tea is served during a meeting, guests may be expected to rise and refill their own cups.

Neatness is essential in business. Whether you wear blue jeans or an expensive European-cut suit, how you are dressed and groomed affects how you will be treated and how much value will be given to the service or product you are offering. Observe the US persons with whom you wish to do business and, without sacrificing your own style, consider modifying some of your customs to reflect their preferences. Some foreign businesspeople may wish to wear distinctive national garb, but most internationally oriented businesspeople conform to the accepted conservative suit-and-tie business uniform. This recognizable US business attire can make it easier for US businesspeople to identify with you.

People in the US often attempt to create an artificial distance around themselves in public, especially when little actual physical distance exists. An excellent example of this behavior in a business environment is seen in elevators. People in the US rarely conduct conversations in elevators, and generally avoid looking at or—especially—touching each other, no matter how crowded the space. If something unusual happens or someone makes a joke, everyone may chuckle, then revert to silence as if the event had not occurred. US elevators seldom have attendants, but to avoid moving about and jostling each other, the person inside closest to the control panel will often hold down the button that keeps the door open for entering or exiting passengers and will press appropriate floor buttons at the polite request of other riders.

Business Meals

In the US, business can be conducted at any meal, which might include breakfast; brunch (a mid-morning hybrid of breakfast and lunch); lunch; coffee (a snack taken anytime during the day, with or without coffee); drinks; dinner (the largest meal, usually eaten at night, but sometimes at midday); dessert; or a nightcap (drinks at the end of the day, with or without food). In some parts of the US, "supper" refers to an evening meal that is usually lighter than dinner. In some parts of the country, meals used specifically for discussing business have become known as "power breakfasts," "power lunches," and so forth.

US businesspeople may discuss business before the meal even begins, although some will take the time to discuss other topics in recognition of the social setting. Although the session involves eating, dining is usually of secondary importance. However, a somewhat different atmosphere is found at business meals designed to commemorate a successful deal, honor an employee, or otherwise celebrate an event. In this case, the meal may be impressively elaborate, the pace more stately, and the conversation less business-related.

A full meal in the US typically consists of appetizers, soup, salad, a single main course accompanied by vegetables and a starch, and dessert with coffee or tea. Bread is often served throughout the meal until dessert. The meal may be preceded by drinks or aperitifs, followed by after-dinner drinks, and accompanied by wine, although one or all of these may be omitted. Beer is considered somewhat declassé and is usually served only on less formal occasions. Many people throughout the US—particularly in smaller population centers and regions away from the coasts—abstain from drinking alcohol and are unfamiliar with wines. You may be offered iced tea, milk, soda, or any number of alternate beverages. Water is commonly provided and is a safe choice. (Note that in the US, water is virtually always safe to drink from both a social and a health perspective.)

A hosted business breakfast, lunch, or other occasion during which food or refreshments are offered—especially in an office, but even in a restaurant or hotel—is often served buffet-style. At a buffet, people line up and serve themselves from a central table, and then eat standing or seated with others. At most US business functions, random seating is the rule in the absence of name cards set at each place or an indication of the seating arrangement by the host. If you are unsure about how to eat an unfamiliar dish, such as an artichoke, it may be best to avoid it or order something else. You will seldom be pressed to consume a particular item, and unless you have been informed that a dish was especially prepared by someone who is present, you are under no obligation to partake (although trying at least a sample is considered polite).

With respect to alcohol and drug usage, control is imperative in business settings. No legitimate business occasions call for the use of illegal drugs; few business situations call for drinking, and virtually none for excessive drinking. Heavy or competitive drinking—never very common—has largely faded from the US business scene. Do not drink so much that it affects your behavior and perceptions. Sipping is preferable to quaffing. Not drinking alcohol at all is acceptable, and if pressed, you should be direct in your reason for abstaining.

Social Occasions and Invitations

Despite a disarming and informal manner, US businesspeople may be somewhat difficult to get to know as individuals, especially in a business setting governed by time pressures. If they want to broaden their acquaintance with you—or you with them—a social invitation may be appropriate. Social invitations can be as minor as an invitation to have a drink after work or more substantive, such as for a full dinner at a restaurant, club, or the host's home. In the US, people may invite business acquaintances to attend sports events, enjoy a ride, do some shopping or sightseeing, or even spend an entire weekend in a country or vacation home.

Invitations are seldom formal in the US, and may be issued in an offhand manner on short notice. It is usually not considered an insult to decline an invitation, especially on short notice, particularly if you have made other plans and are graceful in declining. A formal invitation is made by letter and marked "RSVP," indicating that you are expected to accept or decline. Try to do so as far in advance as is reasonable.

Although most US businesspersons will protest that rank is relatively unimportant, usually only people on roughly the same level of authority and wealth are invited to a social event. While a person may invite an immediate superior to dinner, it is unlikely that the invitation will include the superior's boss. On the other hand, a foreign junior businessperson might extend an invitation to a more senior US businessperson in order to reciprocate for courtesies extended.

A social invitation in the US can come from either a man or a woman and be extended regardless of the gender of the recipient. Such social invitations are generally not seen as improper, although a woman may choose to host a social event in a public place such as a restaurant, rather than at her home or in temporary lodgings while traveling. If you are invited out socially by a person of the opposite gender, you should interpret the invitation not as a proposal for intimate contact but simply as an opportunity to become better acquainted on a social level.

The person hosting the event usually covers the expenses, unless other cost-sharing options are discussed. If special transportation or other arrangements are required, you may be expected to pay the cost of getting to the actual event. Even if cost-sharing has not been raised, the invitee may offer to cover at least part of the bill, such as by paying for a round of drinks or a special appetizer. Moreover, it is usually considered polite to offer to pick up the tab, but in most cases the offer will be refused and it is impolite to insist—but if your offer is accepted, be prepared to follow through with good grace. As the invitee, you may also offer to leave the tip; if this is accepted, estimate the total bill and tip generously (the usual amount in restaurants is 15 percent, but for good food and service in a fancy place, 20 percent is common). Participants in less formal activities can "go Dutch," that is, split the cost equally or according to the charges that each party incurs. Finally, you may wish to host your own event and arrange in advance to have the costs charged to you so as to avoid any confusion over who will pay—restaurants and hotels are most obliging in this regard if you simply ask to prearrange payment.

In the Home

Home entertaining, with or without a meal, is quite common in the US. Gifts are not expected, although if you are invited to someone's home, especially for a meal, a bottle of wine, flowers, a unique condiment, or a small toy—if the hosts have children—would be appropriate. Chocolates or other confections or baked goods are also possibilities, although these may interfere with the host's planned menu or dietary requirements. Lavish gifts are seen as inappropriate.

When accepting an invitation to an informal occasion, you might ask if there is something in particular that you can bring for use during the occasion; for example, the host might ask you to bring something readily available, such as beer, to a barbecue. On some occasions, you may even be assigned an item to bring. Informal meals to which everyone contributes a dish or other comestible are generally referred to as "pot luck," meaning that there is no set menu and guests sample the various offerings contributed. Such requests that a guest contribute are intended to make the event more inclusive and participatory.

Some homes will be quite formal, while others will be extremely informal. The state of a host's housekeeping should not be interpreted as a reflection of how you are perceived; many people in the US consider it a mark of friendship to invite people into their homes without special preparation. Business is likely to be a topic of conversation, at least at the beginning. However, this is not the place to exchange business cards or to give a hard sell. To remove some of the awkwardness of the transition from business to social setting, you might try admiring the host's home, although not to excess. There is little danger that you will be offered some personal possession if you admire it—which is the custom in some countries—so have no fear in expressing interest in an item in order to get the conversation started.

If food is being served, the host may inquire about whether you have any special dietary considerations. In the absence of such an inquiry, be certain to mention to the host if you do have dietary limitations and be prepared to specify them if asked. If you are presented with something you would prefer not to eat, you are under no obligation to eat it, particularly if it is likely to make you ill or is contrary to your beliefs or dietary restrictions. On the other hand, unless there is a specific prohibition on an item, you would be advised to at least sample it out of courtesy to the host. Likewise, if you prefer not to drink alcohol, you should discreetly make this known. Although you are under no obligation to eat or drink what is offered, it is considered impolite to find fault with what is being served. It is also a good idea to refrain from smoking, unless others do so first.

In a private home or club, dessert, coffee, and other after-dinner drinks are frequently served away from the dining table. During this time, you are most likely to find people in a relaxed mood and willing to talk about something besides business. Such occasions are not expected to run into the late hours, and except in some urban areas, the US definition of late can seem surprisingly early to visitors of other cultures who are accustomed to late dinners and entertainment. In some more rural areas, meals can begin as early as 5 pm and the evening might be considered over by 8 pm. In urban areas, preliminaries generally begin between 6 and 7 pm and sometimes continue past midnight, although in most places the evening meal is usually served by 8 pm and events end around 11 pm.

Once the final offerings have been finished and the conversation has begun to lag, you should offer to leave. You will have to take your cues from your host as to whether the protestations that you stay are genuine or merely polite. Because people in the US are so informal, they may simply inform you when they are ready to end the evening. This is not intended as rudeness or a lack of hospitality, although many foreigners may be taken aback by such directness.

ADAPTING TO VARIED US BUSINESS ENVIRONMENTS

Large versus Small Firms

The distinct features of US business culture will vary, being in major part dictated by the size of the US business.

Large Firms Large businesses by nature are hierarchical; distribute authority across a wide range of functional, project, or geographical specializations; and strive for the highest financial return. They can also become highly involved in internal battles among different units. Their actions may be dictated by internal needs that have relatively little to do with the business at hand—and thus are that much more indecipherable to outsiders. The reaction time of large businesses is often quite long, but they can usually continue to operate for extended periods of time before they run out of momentum. Decisions can take months, because so many layers of the organization must be consulted. However, having reached a decision, corporations may then insist on an unrealistic time frame for implementation in order to make up for lost time.

What large businesses usually lack in flexibility and responsiveness, they may make up in depth of expertise and resources. As a result, some are able to operate quite efficiently and effectively despite their ponderous size and procedural handicaps. Their personnel may be either more or less capable: large organizations can afford to support less capable and redundant staff as well as to pay for the best people. Corporations are not necessarily the faceless, impersonal machines that they may seem. Each will have its own personality and culture. Corporations tend to select people who are much like the people who already work in them, and this can vary as well by functional specialization, industry, or location.

Small Firms Businesses that are smaller—especially entrepreneurial ones—are generally more accommodating, more emotionally driven, and quicker to act. Conversely, despite the lack of any formal structure that would separate the decisionmakers from those who do the actual work, they may actually have less flexibility because they lack resources, funds, or personnel needed to sustain new or different programs. Although capable of quick reactions, they may also be incapable of implementing change due to narrow vision. Smaller firms are usually more interested in growth and stability than they are in maximizing profits alone. Because of their smaller size and more limited resources, they cannot rely on reserves and momentum to carry them along: when things go bad, they can go bad quite rapidly.

Smaller firms may lack broad expertise, but because they generally cannot afford to support less-than-capable people, the personnel they do have are usually quite competent at their jobs. By the same token, small firms often cannot pay premium salaries, and their staffs may thus not be of the highest caliber available. Many small firms are family enterprises or have been created through the strenuous efforts of an entrepreneur. While there may be infighting, it is usually evident up-front in the clash of personalities rather than disguised, as is often the case in large firms.

Industry Differences

Although US business style is generally similar nationwide, international visitors find that US businesspeople behave somewhat differently depending on the industry in which they work. Most industries fall into one of a few style categories: formal, moderately formal, or informal. While keeping in mind the general cultural rules, international visitors must rely on their own observations to understand the application within a particular industry setting.

Garment executives may wear their company's trademark clothing—which might be suits or blue jeans—while certain professionals or salespeople may adopt the clothing style of their clients. Various businesspeople may instead choose to dress in a manner that is more formal than their clients, believing that it enhances their appearance of success and authority. Some companies permit their employees to "dress down"—that is, informally—some of the time, usually on Fridays or during the summer months. Dress is much less formal in manufacturing and similar firms where client contact is less important and formal dress less functional. Companies with large numbers of engineers, computer programmers, accountants, or architects may permit employees to leave their jackets on the coatrack all day, yet others may have a rule against the display of shirtsleeves in the office.

Financial, Professional, and Large Corporate Firms The term "Wall Street" refers to the financial offices near the New York Stock Exchange in New York City as well as to the entire US corporate financial industry: brokerage firms, law offices, accounting firms, insurance companies, banks, and investment companies who cluster in the financial districts of the nation's larger cities. To a slightly lesser extent, Wall Street standards also apply—at least to the upper levels—at large corporate firms nationwide. Business transactions at these levels are formal, and the substance of a transaction is primary. You may be greeted graciously or your reception may be impersonal and perfunctory, even in a prestigious firm with impressive offices. No insult is intended; it is "nothing personal—it's just business."

Attention focuses on the transaction, although there may be some genteel interpersonal interaction, especially at upper levels of management. You may find this to be equally true in the courts, in government offices, and in executive offices of major businesses and institutions. Visitors are advised to dress formally and to focus on the quality of the transaction.

In the top echelons of the US corporate and financial worlds, international standards of corporate attire that are accepted in cosmopolitan cities around the world apply. The dress code is usually unwritten, but deviations are rare. Most men wear conservative suits or sports jackets and trousers, along with long-sleeved shirts in white, blue, or an understated pattern. Patterned neckties are the norm. Shoes are minimally adorned and made of dark leather; dark socks are the norm.

Women wear skirted or (less frequently) trousered suits, ensembles of skirts or trousers with blouses, or dresses that often coordinate with jackets. Hem lengths vary from just above the knee to a few inches above the ankle. Shoes are worn with stockings. Most women executives wear little or no makeup and style their hair simply.

Extremes of fashion are generally not accepted. Accessories should be inconspicuous. Both genders should limit jewelry, keeping it understated and of good quality. Neatness is essential. Some US businesspeople use the quality of a businessperson's shoes and accessories to gauge informally the personality and authority of the person with whom they are dealing. These items should be of the best quality that you can manage.

Creative Businesses Typically, a creative organization would be an advertising and public relations, entertainment (filmmaking, multimedia, photography, theater, dance, museum, arts, music), design (graphic and other art, interior design, architecture), or other communications firm. Depending on the corporate culture, computer, scientific, and technology company employees as well as university staff may also behave like creative organizations. Creative workers often engage in role playing and brainstorming to solve problems. Ideas may roll out in rapid succession, in an apparently disorganized fashion.

These groups generally operate somewhat more informally than other businesses. Individuals may be more interested in taking time to establish a personal relationship with an international visitor before engaging in business negotiations. They often hold meetings over meals and, unlike many US businesspeople, are more likely to socialize frequently with their clients and colleagues. They are generally more accepting of customs and behavior with which they are unfamiliar; they may have traveled extensively. Visitors are often entertained and oriented to their surroundings. Most academics and scientists may be embarrassed by excessive deference or formality. Some of these organizations also lack the resources to be lavish hosts.

The style of dress in these organizations is less formal than that of business centers. These employees and entrepreneurs may enjoy considerable latitude regarding appearance. Both men and women tend to wear less formal, more functional, and more comfortable clothing, usually of good quality that is built to last. Most men wear sports jackets, slacks, and open-collared shirts, keeping a tie handy for meetings. A man with high status may have the authority to ignore tradition and be the only person at a meeting without a tie or jacket. Although standards are much more flexible than in the financial industry, women tend to dress in a similarly understated style in jackets, skirts, and blouses. A more relaxed approach is necessary. Fashion and unusual accents in dress are often admired. A disorderly—but clean—appearance may be intentional and carefully cultivated. Nevertheless, after dark, even these free spirits will usually don a jacket, a tie, or both.

Production Industries These include traditional manufacturing and other processing industries. Often these are subsidiaries of large corporations, and management will more closely reflect the culture typical of the large corporate setting. However, many are smaller, independent firms located in secondary centers. The approach is usually collegial, but focuses narrowly on the particular process and the industry. Visitors should be knowledgeable and prepared to discuss industry concerns in depth.

Dress is usually less formal, often not up to the level of international business in terms of attention to detail and appearance. In many industries, regular business attire is inappropriate to the shop floor, where work clothes—or at least shirtsleeves—are more common. Overdressing in such instances may be disconcerting—even forbidding—to the local businesspeople.

Retail Operations Depending on the specific sector, norms can vary widely for retail operations—from formal to creative to informal. Usually the focus is on the customer, and people in the industry dress up or down and behave in an attempt to accommodate the customer. Although less so than in many creative industries, retail is often heavily concerned with image. Behind this facade, retail personnel are often very narrowly focused on product and all the aspects necessary to move that product. Visitors should be attuned to these needs. If selling, a visitor should be prepared to offer solutions to the needs of people in this industry; if buying, visitors should expect the sellers to be prepared to speak to the visitor's needs.

Regional Differences

The US covers an immense amount of territory, far more than most overseas visitors can readily comprehend. General traits are likely to be more similar than different. However, regional differences do exist, although many may not be readily evident to an unfamiliar visitor who is already struggling with the overwhelming basic cultural, linguistic, and tempo differences, especially in larger cities, where most business is conducted. In part, these regional differences are influenced by variations in climate. Thus, offices in warm cities such as Atlanta, Houston, and Los Angeles are frequently more casual than those on the Eastern seaboard or in Midwestern cities such as Chicago. San Francisco and Boston tend to be more formal than Denver, Seattle, and St. Louis. In Hawaii, lawyers have been known to appear in court wearing brightly colored aloha shirts—attire that could result in contempt of court citations on the mainland.

Basically, urbanites from overseas are likely to feel more familiarity in larger US cities than smaller towns. The states along the Atlantic and Pacific Coasts—particularly New York and California—are generally considered to be more advanced in terms of trends and innovations than the rest of the country, while the semirural interior is considered to be far more conservative. Although many more subdivisions could be made, the US may be divided into five different regions: the Northeast, the South, the Midwest, the West, and outlying areas.

The Northeast This region covers the states along the Atlantic Coast from the Canadian border south to Washington, DC, extending west to include Pennsylvania. The region is best known for the Boston-Washington corridor, which forms a megalopolis centered around New York City, where the bulk of US financial firms and corporate headquarters are located. Connecticut, Massachusetts, Vermont, New Hampshire, Rhode Island, and Maine are collectively known as New England, and have a somewhat more formal and traditional style than brazen New York or politically obsessed Washington, DC. The states of New York, New Jersey, Pennsylvania, and Delaware are generally referred to as Mid-Atlantic states. The Northeast includes such urban centers as Boston, Philadelphia, and Washington, DC, as well as immense rural hinterlands. The style of business that foreigners are most likely to encounter is that of New York City, sometimes known as the Big Apple.

The aspects of New York's personality most often noted by foreign visitors—as well as by people from other parts of the US—is its high energy, frenetic pace, cold and even threatening demeanor, and sheer concentration of population. This density of population causes New Yorkers to construct behaviors to give themselves personal space. They may seem aloof, unfriendly, even hostile, and excessively concerned with structure. This style is largely designed to hold back the chaos that rushes in on every side. New Yorkers take pains never to seem to be surprised; this may make them appear to be unconcerned or jaded. They can, however, be quite friendly—if you can break through the protective shell they construct around themselves. But the fast pace can make it difficult to connect with them. In this environment, people may do business together for years without knowing much about each other's personal lives.

Boston has been characterized as an example of a very structured business culture based on formal oligarchic relationships developed over time by local elites; in many ways, Philadelphia resembles Boston more than New York. Doing business in Washington, though, may be the ultimate test of patience and diplomacy, given the special political and bureaucratic subculture that exists there. However, because the centers of government and business are kept largely separate in the US, unless one is doing business directly with the federal government, one is unlikely to make a pilgrimage to Washington, DC, in order to seek approvals to deal with a US counterpart. The business style found in smaller cities and towns and in rural areas of the Northeast is generally similar to that found in the rest of the country.

The South This broad area consists primarily of the states of the former Confederacy—Virginia, North and South Carolina, Georgia, Tennessee, Florida, Alabama, Mississippi, Arkansas, and Louisiana (Texas is considered more western)—plus bor-

der states such as Maryland, Kentucky, and West Virginia. Many businesses and factories have moved to the traditionally agrarian and rural southern states in search of lower costs, including less heavily unionized labor. Agriculture and other resource-based activities, such as forestry, remain significant factors in the economy of the region.

The pace is generally much slower in southern states than elsewhere in the country, although business in Atlanta—the business capital of the New South—can be nearly as fast-paced as in northern cities. The visitor may be greeted warmly and invited to the US host's home at the first meeting, but this display of southern hospitality does not necessarily indicate acceptance. Southerners can be very gracious, but they also tend to be conservative and somewhat suspicious of outsiders and different customs. The style may be either quite formal or extremely informal, quite diplomatic or extremely outspoken, depending on the individual and the situation. Most Southerners are quite interested in history, culture, and politics, and they like to discuss them, provided that such issues as race relations and the US Civil War are handled with delicacy, if at all.

Florida is part of the South in many ways, but in other respects it is more like New York or California because of its heavy Northerner retiree population and Miami's growing role as the US gateway to Latin America. Miami holds a unique place in US society. Its style of business is heavily influenced not only by New York but also by its large Cuban-dominated Latin community.

New Orleans is also of interest, both as a business center—it is an important US port for international commerce—and as a cultural experience that is uniquely American but with Continental and Caribbean accents.

The Midwest Also known as the Heartland, this vast area stretches from the Canadian border on the north to Texas on the south, and from the Pennsylvania border in the east to the Rocky Mountain states on the west. It is generally considered to include the states of Ohio, Indiana, Michigan, Illinois, Wisconsin, Minnesota, Iowa, and Missouri (sometimes known as the prairie states), plus North and South Dakota, Montana, Nebraska, Kansas, and Oklahoma (generally known as the plains states). The Midwest is best known for the industry centered around the Great Lakes and the cities of Chicago and Detroit; the plains states are the breadbasket of the US, famous for grain, cattle, and hog production; and the Mississippi River, which runs from north to south through the middle of the Midwest, is a major conduit of commerce and a center for processing industries. Because of the concentration of traditional heavy industry in its northern area, the Midwest is sometimes referred to as the Rust Belt. Widespread

OVERSEAS RESOURCES ON US CULTURE

In a world where media is available and less expensive than travel, a businessperson—whether from the US or of any culture—often gains a certain perception of other cultures through literature and film. Unfortunately, such portrayals of a culture are often inaccurate because of the tendency to dramatize and to focus on what sells instead of more mundane reality. Thus, the perceptions of a culture presented in film and literature are unreliable when a person needs to understand the country's business culture.

Instead of relying on suspect sources, observers of US business culture recommend that prospective foreign visitors to the US prepare by reading US newspapers, such as the *New York Times, Washington Post, Los Angeles Times, Miami Herald, Chicago Sun Times,* other big city dailies, or local papers from the area where they plan to do business. It may also be helpful to seek out trade publications and business magazines. Current television news programs—such as CNN, a cable network widely available overseas—can also suggest a sense of US business style, concerns, and attitudes.

For those who have no access to such materials or who are uncomfortable with English, there are many US oriented or sponsored organizations located overseas that can give prospective foreign visitors insight into, and a better feel for, US society. Firms, businesspersons, and business associations that are native to the foreign country but have had dealings with US businesses are often good sources. US businesses operate in many countries, and their employees may be amenable to those who wish to learn more about the US and to initiate a network of referrals. Requests to and consultation with the US embassy, consulates, and other government agencies, specifically those regulating the business in which you are interested, can be helpful sources on industry and regional variations from the general US business style. Home country banks with US operations or US bank branches in your country may have services that can advise you.

A wealth of books, audiocassettes, and videotapes about the US and its peoples can be found for rental, purchase, loan, or use in video stores, bookstores, and public libraries. A growing number and variety of materials are also available through online computer services, such as the Internet. For industry-specific information, trade associations and chambers of commerce in the US are also excellent sources.

Refer to the "Important Addresses" chapter for contact information on US publications, organizations, and bookstores.

---

pressures from US and global economic restructuring have resulted in industrial and urban decay in this area.

Even in its urban areas, the people of the Midwest tend to be conservative, actively religious, and family oriented. If you make eye contact as you walk down the streets of, for example, Lincoln, Nebraska, you will be met with open smiles and friendly greetings. If you are obviously an international visitor, you may also attract curious stares, but if you are lost or need help, the locals will generally be extremely friendly and helpful. Dress can be either casual or formal, depending on whether you are meeting with corporate executives, blue-collar workers, or farmers. In smaller Midwestern towns, women are more likely to be traditional homemakers than active in business.

The West From the Mexican border on the south, following the Rocky Mountains to the Canadian border on the north and extending westward to the Pacific Ocean, the West still reflects the spirit of the frontier. The West generally includes Wyoming, Colorado, and Idaho (the Rocky Mountain states); Texas, New Mexico, and Arizona (the Southwest); Nevada and Utah (the Great Basin); Washington and Oregon (the Pacific Northwest); and California. A category unto itself, California's populace strongly reflects elements of the US West and East Coast: its business activity increasingly rivals that of the US East Coast, and its cities serve as a gateway to Pacific Rim countries. With large urban centers in Los Angeles, San Jose, San Francisco, and San Diego, California has the largest population of any of the US states and a GDP equivalent to that of the eighth largest economy in the world; it is also one of the most dynamic, trendsetting centers of evolving US business—as well as popular—culture.

Many foreigners conjure up an image of the West's legendary cowboys and Indians when they think of the US. The traits of individuality, adaptability, and self-reliance that embody the frontier spirit continue to mark the US character, especially in the western part of the country. Honesty, integrity, directness, and independence are strongly valued. Some deals are still made on a handshake basis. This generally holds true from the boardrooms of Dallas and Houston (center of the US oil industry) to Denver (hub of the mountain states) to Phoenix (heart of the New Southwest) and on to Seattle, San Francisco, Los Angeles, and San Diego (gateways to the Pacific Rim and Mexico).

Western dress ranges from the informality of cowboy boots or running shoes with jeans to formal business suits to the avant garde, studied chic of Hollywood. The financial and business centers reflect the same style and methods as New York, although some argue that the pace is marginally slower—or more "laid-back." Latin American influence is pervasive in place names, architecture, food, design, dress, music, and language. Spanish has become an unofficial second language across the southern tier of the West, while Chinese and Japanese are becoming more prevalent along the Pacific Coast.

Outlying Areas The US extends beyond the 48 continental states to vast, sparsely populated Alaska in the northwest, Hawaii to the west, and such island possessions as Samoa and Guam in the Pacific and the Virgin Islands and Puerto Rico in the Caribbean. Alaska, the last frontier, has only recently been developed as a business venue and, with its pioneer ambiance, is more western than the West. Hawaii is multicultural and largely oriented toward East Asia, particularly Japan. Both the Pacific and Caribbean island possessions are small and relatively undeveloped, with an Asian flavor in the Pacific and an Afro-Latin Caribbean mixture in the Virgin Islands and Puerto Rico.

FURTHER READING

American Ways: A Guide for Foreigners in the United States, by Gary Althen. Yarmouth, ME: Intercultural Press, Inc., 1988. ISBN 0-933662-68-8. 171 pages.

The Concise Guide to Executive Etiquette, by Linda and Wayne Phillips. New York, NY: Bantam Doubleday, 1990. ISBN 0-385-24766-4. 205 pages, US$9.95.

Gestures: The Do's and Taboos of Body Language Around the World, by Roger E. Axtell. New York: John Wiley & Sons, Inc., 1991. ISBN 0-471-53672-5. 227 pages, US$9.95.

Merriam Webster's Guide to International Business Communications, by Toby D. Atkinson. Springfield, Mass.: Merriam-Webster, Inc., 1994. ISBN 0-87779-028-0. 327 pages, US$21.95.

Multicultural Management: New Skills for Global Success, by Farid Elashmawi and Philip R. Harris. Houston: Gulf Publishing Company, 1993. ISBN 0-8415-042-9. 234 pages, US$28.95.

Getting to Yes: Negotiating Agreement Without Giving In, by Roger Fisher and William Ury, with editor Bruce Patton. New York: Penguin Books, 1992. ISBN 0-14-006534-2. 161 pages, US$6.95.

Global Human Resource Development, by Michael J. Marquardt and Dean W. Engel. Englewood Cliffs, NJ: Prentice Hall, 1993. ISBN 0-13-357930-1. 320 pages.

Dynamics of Successful International Business Negotiations, by Robert T. Moran and William G. Stripp. Houston, TX: Gulf Publishing Company, 1991. ISBN 0-87201-196-8. 250 pages, US$27.50.

Demographics

AT A GLANCE

These statistics are compiled from a variety of authoritative sources, including the United Nations, the World Bank, the International Monetary Fund, and the United States Department of Commerce, Bureau of the Census.

POPULATION GROWTH RATE AND PROJECTIONS

Average annual growth rate (percent)

1960–70	1970–80	1980–90	1990–2000
1.27%	1.05%	0.93%	1.01%

Age structure of population (percent)

	1990	2025
Under 15 years old	21.7%	18.1%
15–64 years old	65.9%	61.4%
Over 64 years old	12.5%	20.4%

POPULATION BY AGE AND SEX, 1992
(Millions)

AGE	TOTAL	MALE	FEMALE
All ages	255.082	124.493	130.589
0–9	37.861	19.382	18.480
10–14	18.100	9.271	8.829
15–19	17.074	8.762	8.312
20–24	19.050	9.706	9.345
25–29	20.189	10.140	10.049
30–34	22.273	11.107	11.166
35–39	21.099	10.481	10.618
40–44	18.805	9.287	9.518
45–49	15.361	7.541	7.820
50–54	12.056	5.858	6.198
55–59	10.487	5.022	5.464
60–64	10.441	4.891	5.550
65 +	32.284	13.045	19.241
15 +	199.121	95.841	103.280

POPULATION

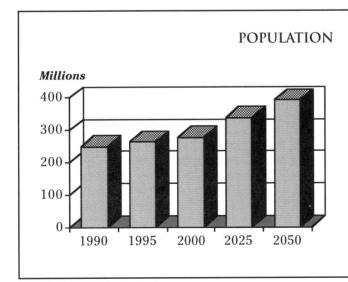

Millions

Male (1990)	121,239,000
Female (1990)	127,471,000
TOTAL	248,710,000

Population density
 per sq. km

1990	27.1
2000	28.6

Population distribution

	Urban	Rural
1970	68.6%	31.4%
1990	79.5%	20.5%

VITAL STATISTICS

Live births   **1990**   4.158 million

Birth rate (per 1,000 persons)
                    1982   15.9
                    1990   16.7

Infant mortality rate (per 1,000 live births)
                    1980   12.6
                    1990   9.2

Child mortality rate (per 1,000 births)
                    1980   2.5
                    1990   1.9

Registered deaths **1990**   2.148 million

Death rate (per 1,000 persons)
                    1980   8.8
                    1990   8.6

Life expectancy at birth (years)
        Overall   **1970**   70.8
        Overall   **1990**   75.4
        Male   **1990**   71.8
        Female   **1990**   78.8

Fertility rate (children born per women)
                    1970   2.48
                    1991   2.08
                    2010   2.12

Women of child-bearing age
(% of all women)
                    1970   52.2
                    1990   56.0

PRINCIPAL CITIES

(1992 census)

New York, NY	7,312,000
Los Angeles, CA	3,490,000
Chicago, IL	2,768,000
Houston, TX	1,690,000
Philadelphia, PA	1,553,000
San Diego, CA	1,149,000
Dallas, TX	1,022,000
Phoenix, AZ	1,012,000
Detroit, MI	1,012,000
San Antonio, TX	966,000
San Jose, CA	801,000
Indianapolis, IN	747,000
San Francisco, CA	729,000
Baltimore, MD	726,000
Jacksonville, FL	661,000
Columbus, OH	643,000
Milwaukee, WI	617,000
Memphis, TN	610,000
Washington, DC	585,000
Boston, MA	552,000
El Paso, TX	544,000
Seattle, WA	520,000
Cleveland, OH	503,000
Nashville, TN	495,000
Austin, TX	492,000
New Orleans, LA	490,000
Denver, CO	484,000
Oklahoma City, OK	454,000
Fort Worth, TX	454,000
Portland, OR	445,000
Long Beach, CA	439,000
Kansas City, MO	432,000
Virginia Beach, VA	417,000
Chattanooga, TN	416,000
Tucson, AZ	415,000

UNITED STATES CONSUMER PRICE INDEX

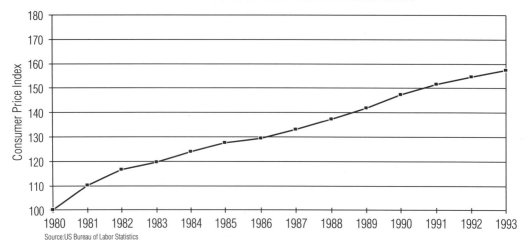

Source:US Bureau of Labor Statistics

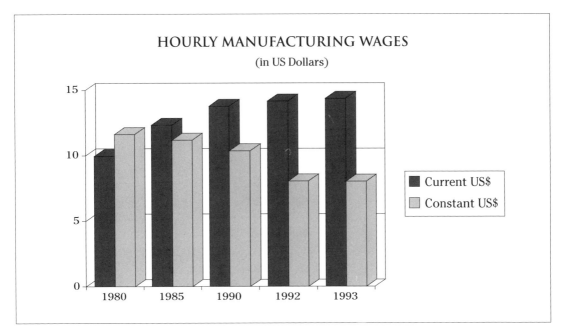

HOURLY MANUFACTURING WAGES
(in US Dollars)

Legend: ■ Current US$ □ Constant US$

NATIONAL INCOME

GNP per capita (1993): US$24,697

Average annual growth rate 1980–93:
5.3 percent current US$
1.3 percent constant US$

Income Distribution
(Percent share of incomes, 1992)

Lowest	20%	3.8%
Second	20%	9.4%
Third	20%	15.9%
Fourth	20%	24.1%
Top	20%	46.8%

PRICE INDEX BY CATEGORY
(1982–1984 = 100)

Category	1989	1990	1991
Food	105.6	132.4	140.9
Housing	109.8	140.0	155.7
Clothing	105.0	124.1	133.7
Other	105.4	122.8	131.5
Overall	107.6	130.7	144.5

AVERAGE ANNUAL RATE OF INFLATION

1970–80	1980–90	1992	1993
7.1%	5.5%	3.0%	3.0%

HEALTH

US Nutrition
Individual Daily Average Consumption

Calories

1970–1979	1980–1989	1990
3,300	3,500	3,700

% of Calorie Requirements

1970–1979	1980–1989	1990
132%	140%	148%

Health Expenditures
(as a percentage of GDP)

1970	7.4%
1980	9.2%
1990	12.2%
1991	13.2%

Tobacco Consumption
(kilos per capita in adult population)

1975	3.9
1990	2.4
2000 *(est.)*	1.6

COMMUNICATION CHANNELS

Daily newspapers

	Circulation (thousands)	Number of dailies
1980	62.2	9,620
1985	62.8	9,120
1990	62.3	11,471
1992	60.1	11,339

Televisions and Radios (millions of sets in use)

	Televisions	Radios
1980	76.0	78.6
1985	85.0	87.1
1990	92.0	94.4
1992	92.0	96.6

Telephones (percent of households with service)

1980	93.0
1985	91.8
1990	93.3
1993	94.2

MOTOR VEHICLES

(millions in use)

Type	1980	1985	1990	1992
Cars	121.601	131.864	143.550	144.213
Trucks	27.962	33.143	40.362	41.439
Motorcycles	5.694	5.444	4.259	4.065
Buses	0.539	0.593	0.627	0.645

ENERGY CONSUMPTION PER CAPITA

(million Btu)

1970	1980	1990	1993
327	334	326	326

EDUCATION

(degrees granted in millions)

Level	1980	1990	2000 (est.)
Elementary	28.2	31.1	35.7
Secondary	18.0	15.3	18.7
College	12.0	13.8	15.4
Total	58.3	60.3	69.8

Marketing

KEYS TO MARKETING IN THE US

Marketing in the US can be as simple as selling a product to a local retailer or as complex as establishing a company or even a national network of sales, distribution, and service centers. The US markets are relatively accessible to foreign businesses, from the smallest, independent operations to the largest of international giants. The major marketing problem is often the level of competition rather than difficulties with getting the product into the country as is often the case elsewhere. Of course, both explicit and hidden trade barriers exist, and some products—drugs, foods, arms and ammunition, and hazardous materials, to name a few—are subject to significant and complex government rules, regulations, and even prohibitions. Moreover, the litigious nature of US society demands caution on the part of an exporter to the US. Products must be designed, manufactured, and labeled in ways that will lessen the risks of devastating damages awarded to customers injured while using defective items. Proper advance planning is a necessity to successfully market in the US.

One key to successful entry into US markets is to keep initial costs as low as possible until you have established a toehold. This argues for careful test marketing. It is not necessary to spend a fortune on research to learn whether there is a market; it is easy to find that out from a variety of sources. This book is one, and others include your own embassy's commercial services, the US Department of Commerce, US trade associations, and state and local economic development agencies in the US. Private and public bookstores and publishing catalogs also offer volumes that collect and explain a wealth of information dealing specifically with marketing issues in the US.

Another key to success in US markets is to ensure that you deliver your product on time, if not earlier. Industrial and individual customers in the US place strong emphasis on timeliness. If promised goods are not delivered on schedule, a US company is likely to seek another source of supply, and if a product is not stocked in a store, a US customer will often purchase a competing item. Do not promise something that cannot be delivered, and always deliver on what has been promised.

Finally, an international trader must remember that a careful approach to marketing in the US can often make the difference between profit and disastrous losses, particularly if a market is saturated with a commodity product that costs all manufacturers roughly the same to produce and distribute. Development of a different product may seem to be a wise move in such a situation, but an innovative marketing plan and selling proposition may prove to be just as workable—and profitable—without the delay and expense inherent in altering the product and retooling for its production.

Marketing in the US requires that you:

- Evaluate the product and identify the customers most likely to purchase it (and how they will use it).
- Learn the characteristics of regional and other niche markets.
- Discover the best marketing channels for your product.

CONTENTS

- Find the right means of advertising.
- Tailor your product to overcome obvious and hidden trade barriers.
- Commit to exporting.

A review of the "Industry Reviews" and "Opportunities" chapters will be helpful in discovering the domestic competition and the opportunities for trading with US businesses. Helpful contacts—particularly trade associations, chambers of commerce, and government agencies—are listed in the "Important Addresses" chapter.

WHO WILL BUY?

The US is a country of more than 260 million people. Its markets are extremely diverse, with demands that range from the most basic to the most sophisticated products. Manufacturing, agriculture, forestry, mining, tourism, and services are all prominent sectors. Indeed, the question to ask is not "Is there a market?" but "What is the best market for the product or service in the US?" The answer to this question must be derived from an evaluation of the product or service's intended and potential uses, which in turn leads to identification of the most likely users. To sell a product or service successfully in today's crowded and competitive US consumer market, one must recognize the customers likely to use the product, determine the product attributes most likely to appeal to those customers, and tailor the merchandise, quality, packaging, and presentation accordingly.

Finding Customer Information

High-tech developments have made information on US markets and opportunities more accessible today than ever before. Product codes, scanners, and other electronic means allow for an ongoing, up-to-the-minute tally of sales information. This can then be utilized to study buying patterns to help introduce the products in the most effective way and to determine quickly whether a particular ad campaign has been effective. National, regional, and local demographic data is compiled by many public agencies—the US Census Bureau, economic development offices, trade associations, and universities, to name a few. Reports can also be obtained from private data service firms, which typically tailor the information to the needs specified by the client.

Many electronic (online) services—accessed by computer modem through telephone lines—carry current news, offer research sources, allow for input from subscribers, and provide for information exchange among the users of the system. Also available on line are databases, abstracts of publications, and sometimes the entire text of specific books, periodicals, or articles. More than 3,200 databases of raw data

on potential US markets are available on CD-ROM disks. Federal, state, and local government agencies may have online services listing opportunities for trading with US companies. For contact information, *see* "Useful Addresses" at the end of this chapter.

Utilizing Customer Information

Considering the avalanche of information available, the trick is knowing how to sort through it and what to do with it. The idea is to focus marketing efforts by analyzing the data in terms of the needs and preferences of potential customers and then formulating an effective sales strategy that will reach and appeal to these most likely buyers. The basic theory behind amassing information about consumer attributes is that their purchasing behavior can be predicted from an analysis of their general characteristics. Some marketers hire an information service company to generate, process, and distribute customer information about a particular market, often electronically. These companies commonly assist in developing information systems tailored to the needs of the particular marketing organization. By subscribing to such a system, a businessperson can review financial management, research, marketing, purchasing, and administrative information. Market research firms can carry this analysis a step further, performing a professional review of the data and advising the trader about markets that appear to be most lucrative. For a full package of services—market research, analysis, and advertising development and placement—an advertising company can be employed.

Regardless of whether one obtains the assistance of a professional in marketing, one should gain at least a general familiarity with, if not in-depth knowledge about, the types of customer information available and how to use it. Most of this information falls into four areas: demographics (customers' physical and environmental attributes), psychographics (what the customer thinks and values), buying patterns (what, where, and how often the customer buys and how much is spent), and media attraction (where they most often learn about what they buy). From a review of all of this data, a trader can begin to target the market for a particular product, but if any part of the picture is missing, the analysis becomes less accurate and more likely to go wrong. Thus, to predict who will buy a product or service, analysis of customer information should proceed as follows:

- Determine the demographics—the physical and environmental characteristics of potential customers: who they are in terms of such factors as age, education, geographical environment, earned income, and family status and structure.

- Add the psychographic data—as manifested by the customers' preferred lifestyles—to find out why they act the way the do, why they want a product or service, why they prefer one item over another, what they are likely to spend their money buying, and what will be most likely to influence their decisions.
- Mix in buying patterns to figure out how much purchasing power the potential customers have—how often they purchase a product, how much they spend, and where they go to buy it.
- Identify the media channels that appeal most to the potential customers in order to penetrate the market most efficiently—that is, to "get the biggest bang for the buck."

This research will ideally lead to an evaluation of the product itself to determine whether it is more than likely going to fit the intended market, that is, whether the product will satisfy the current needs of the primary buyers. It should suggest whether customers might consider the product a necessity or a luxury item (which in turn would indicate whether the product will sell regardless of its packaging and whether customers will make single or repeated purchases). Another factor that should become apparent is the frequency of purchases, which will help to determine how fast the customer base will have to grow to ensure the success of the business. The marketer should also look at the product in terms of trends seen in the market data in an effort to anticipate whether the product will have to be altered or the product line modified in order to meet the changing needs and desires of the targeted customers.

Trends in US Markets

The difficulty in assessing US markets is that they change at an increasingly rapid pace. A trader must keep aware of developing trends when evaluating current customer information: the anticipation of shifts in markets can be as important as knowing current customer needs. Large scale trends that affect US markets include the following.

Lifestyles in the US have become more diverse. Mass marketing of consumer products is almost a thing of the past in the US because of the diversity among today's consumers. The traditional US nuclear family—mom, dad, and 2.2 children—is decreasing in prevalence with the rise and recognition of the nontraditional family unit—which can be a household consisting of one person, unrelated persons, a same-sex couple, a single parent, or a childless married couple, as well as any combination of the above residing in a single dwelling for the purposes of sharing costs, child care, and camaraderie. Related to this trend is a rise in dual-earner families and in the number of women in the workforce, with the result that shopping patterns show a significant increase in the number of men and teenagers who are sharing responsibility for household buying decisions. Every new lifestyle offers a potential new market niche.

Households are smaller and more transitory. The decline of the nuclear family, coupled with the slowdown in US housing starts during the recession years of the early 1990s, has affected markets for businesses that have relied on buyers of new homes. Many households now occupy smaller spaces, including not only smaller new houses but also apartments, condominiums, townhouses, or mobile units (known as manufactured housing). The needs of these households—which also tend to be more transitory—have changed in accordance with their lifestyles, creating new market opportunities, such as for adjustable and collapsible furnishings, foldaway furniture, small cars, mini appliances, space organizers, and similar items. However, at the other end of the spectrum, the baby boom generation—now reaching middle age and settling into established career and family life—is also creating a somewhat increased demand for family housing that includes even more spacious floor plans that need to be filled with additional goods.

Population composition is more diverse than ever before. Ethnic and racial diversity in the US is expected to continue to increase, based largely on two factors. First, the US birth rate slowed during the 1970s, reflected in demographics showing fewer children and an aging population. The 1990s is being termed a "baby boomlet" generation because the birth rate has picked up, although it falls below the higher levels of the 1950s and 1960s. Nevertheless, this baby boomlet generation is 60 percent larger than the immediately preceding "baby bust" generation. Second, the population rate in the US continues to rise, fueled by increasing ethnic and immigrant cultures, particularly among younger generations. Assuming that these trends continue, the racial and ethnic diversity of the US will open substantial new multicultural markets to businesspeople who anticipate and prepare for the shift (and hamper those who fail to do so).

The big spenders are aging. The aging of the US population is a significant trend, creating immediate opportunities for marketing to the middle-aged and elderly. In the decade of the 1990s, the successful, high-income earning baby boomers will move into the 45- to 60-year-old age bracket, many as heads of households. At the same time, competition among producers of products aimed at the younger consumers is intensifying as that market segment begins to contract. Over the next two decades, baby boomers will represent a declining share of the US population, as the first of the baby boomlet children move from being teenagers into their thirties. Marketers who pay attention to the fluctuations in the US birthrate will have a clue to the rise and fall of markets from decade to decade and can anticipate those changes within their own marketing strategies, altering their product lines to appeal to the biggest spenders as they grow older and their needs and desires change with time.

Higher salaries are becoming more closely tied to higher education levels. Educational factors have also begun to play a more obvious role in customer buying patterns and purchasing power as the US shifts to a service oriented economy. Persons who have college and advanced degrees are commanding the highest salaries because of the specialized knowledge and skills they can offer to service industries. In contrast, less well educated persons, who tend to support labor intensive operations, are finding fewer long-term job opportunities and lower wages, thus decreasing their purchasing power. The effect of this trend is that markets are growing for the higher-income brackets, but faltering somewhat within the middle- and lower-income levels.

Customers are becoming increasingly aware of global, national, and regional environmental and social concerns. The trend among businesses and individual consumers alike is to buy products that are healthier and more environmentally friendly. Recyclable products, recycling systems, and products that eliminate or decrease environmentally harmful residues and by-products are in greater demand. Millions of consumers are turning toward reduced-fat diets, vitamin-mineral supplement plans, and alternative health food products. Funding for charities and non-profit institutions is an area of growing concern as government continues to reduce its support for many such programs, and product promotions in which businesses donate a percentage of the proceeds to a worthy cause are on the rise and showing favorable results. More companies are offering innovative programs—such as exercise clubs, stress reduction and health seminars, ergonomic equipment testing, on-site day care, and confidential counseling—to enhance the personal health and improve the quality of life for employees during the workday, in the hope of encouraging loyalty and better job performance.

Labor intensive production is being de-emphasized. Businesses and public organizations are not immune to changing purchasing requirements, although the pace of change is usually less rapid than in consumer markets. The demand is high for machinery, materials, and supplies that are laborsaving, environmentally sound, and energy efficient. Many businesses are attempting to reduce the number of employees by upgrading the technologies and procedures they use, either switching to high-tech systems or upgrading their equipment to incorporate the most recent technologies in an effort to retain a competitive edge. The use of temporary employees and independent contractors is on the rise, allowing businesses to reduce their space requirements, decrease the amount of equipment and supplies they need, and generally control their overhead and operating costs.

WHERE IS THE MARKET LOCATED?

After determining the primary applications of a product and its most likely customers, a marketer should review the regions of the US and identify the areas where the major users of the product are concentrated. From agricultural valleys and plains to bustling commercial centers and ports, the US holds outstanding opportunities for marketing both standard and innovative products to business and personal customers. More than 95 percent of the total land area of the US is rural, but nearly 80 percent of the population clusters in urban centers.

The trend in marketing has been away from a nationwide approach and toward customized regional and local plans. In this manner, merchandise can be targeted to selected audiences, and—if necessary—product content, packaging, labeling, and advertising can be tailor-made to appeal to certain segments of the US populace. However, regional marketing of modified products costs more than national promotion of a standardized product line. Therefore, regional markets must be carefully evaluated to ensure that marketing efforts are as efficient as possible in relation to the market penetration and returns to be achieved.

In researching geographic US markets, keep in mind that the US populace is quite mobile. Populations have always tended to shift, moving toward what at least appear to be better sources of opportunity and away from areas where opportunities are decreasing. Thus, when manufacturing industries in the Northeast and Midwest began to struggle in the 1980s and early 1990s, populations began to shift to the South and in the Mountain and Southwestern States (known as the Sunbelt), which people found inviting because of lower costs of living, expanding opportunities, especially in construction and high-tech industries, and more favorable climatic conditions.

For purposes of discussing the regional characteristics of US markets, the country has been divided into nine areas, although both broader and smaller, more finely honed divisions could be made. The regions and cities mentioned have populations ranging from at least 500,000 to several million. Many urban areas include several counties, some even cross state borders, and many are ringed by such extensive subsidiary settlement that the city and its surrounding suburbs have merged into what appears to be a continuous super-metropolitan zone.

New England

From the days when northeastern communities were first established as colonies of the British Crown, that section of the country has been called New England. Today, the region includes six states: Maine, New Hampshire, Vermont, Massachusetts, Rhode Island, and Connecticut. Much of New England consists of traditional small towns, rural landscapes, and forests and mountains. Its largest metropolitan area is Boston, an education center and site of the nation's oldest college (Harvard); and the metropolitan area of Hartford, Connecticut—home to the largest concentration of insurance firms in the US—now ranks as among the wealthiest in the US in terms of median income.

A number of qualities make this region an inviting place to live and work. Affordable housing is available in nearly rural areas that are only a short commute away from major services and business centers. The populace is enthusiastic about outdoor recreational activities, which vary with the season. Fishing, skiing, camping, biking, and sailing are popular among residents and draw thousands of tourists each year. The area also contains some of the sites that are most significant in early US history. Housing tends to be older than in most areas of the US, but New Englanders proudly preserve the homes, public buildings, and other historic sites, as well as the general ambiance of older times.

High-tech industry plays a substantial role in the region's economy, a development served by the many universities, colleges, and research laboratories located there. On the other hand, many of the labor intensive manufacturing industries (originally the mainstay of economic growth in this area) are moving out. Companies are turning toward service and trade opportunities, and a large number are looking to global trade connections to fuel their growth. In this respect, the relatively small state of Connecticut has established itself as one of the largest exporters in the US, with Canada as its biggest trading partner.

Mid-Atlantic

The Mid-Atlantic states—New York, Pennsylvania, New Jersey, Delaware, Maryland, Virginia, and West Virginia—extend from the northeastern US and the Canadian border southward along the Atlantic coastline; these states surround the nation's capital, Washington, DC. The largest market in this region—and in the entire country—is New York City, the financial and cultural capital of the US. But the nation's political capital and its environs—including the Maryland cities of Annapolis and Baltimore—are a close second in overall importance. Heavily populated areas extend outward in all directions from these cities. Nonetheless, within an hour's drive from

any of these large cities, the surroundings grade into more rural settings with clusters of smaller towns and rural areas.

Resorts and natural wonders—Niagara Falls and the Adirondack and Catskill Mountains—attract visitors to upstate New York. South of New York State, the countryside is covered with farms, pastures, and woods, inviting many hardworking city dwellers into the wilderness for weekend outdoor activities. The Atlantic seaboard tends to be the most populated and industrialized area of the US, with city leading to city from New York City south and west to Newark and Trenton (New Jersey), Philadelphia (Pennsylvania), Wilmington and Dover (Delaware), and on to Washington, DC. The waterfront is a major attraction in this area, offering both populated and quiet beach resorts, the casinos of Atlantic City (New Jersey), and several large resorts and pleasure boat harbors. The largest inland population centers are in Buffalo, Albany, and Rochester (New York), Harrisburg and Pittsburgh (Pennsylvania), Richmond and Norfolk (Virginia), and Charleston (West Virginia). These states are also famous for their many prestigious educational institutions, and many college communities are found there.

A widely diverse cultural population resides in the Mid-Atlantic states, sustained by the large numbers of immigrants that still pour into the US through the New York port of entry and the concentration of US and foreign businesses, diplomatic offices, and government agencies established there. This multicultural diversity is a factor in the gap between the well educated and poorly educated populations in these states, a persistent problem for which many local areas are trying to develop innovative solutions, including vocational and technical training programs integrated into lower level public schooling and curricula tailored to the area's job opportunities and needs. In many cities, these programs are showing success, helping to keep unemployment rates below the national average.

A unifying aspect to much of this region is the desire of the populace to preserve the past. The sites of the country's earliest European history can be seen throughout this region, and are reflected in rebuilt historical town centers, antique shops, and splendid restorations of 18th century town and country homes. In many cities and towns, modernization has been carefully planned and developed to keep alive the historical flavor important to the population here.

Many of the largest cities in the Mid-Atlantic region are undertaking massive revitalization programs, funded through public-private partnerships, to coax residents, businesses, and shoppers back to their city centers. The loss or reduction of many manufacturing industries—particularly steel—and a nationwide recession have all left behind many vacant, vandalized, and run-down sections. The economies of these areas are being strengthened and diversified with the growth of high-tech and service oriented firms, now operating side-by-side with leaner industrial and manufacturing companies. A significant number of medical, electronic, computer, robotics, and chemical research and technology facilities are located here.

New York's Buffalo and Rochester are gateways to Canada, benefiting from a tremendous export trade, particularly in high-tech products and publications. These cities are also the preferred sites for hundreds of Canadian companies because operating, labor, and occupancy costs are lower in western New York State. A large number of high-tech firms have moved research laboratories and manufacturing facilities into upstate New York, and automotive component manufacturing is a significant sector of Buffalo's diverse economy.

Southeast

In the Southeast, highly diverse populations and environments extend from North and South Carolina, through Georgia and Alabama, to the Gulf Coast peninsular state of Florida. The charm of the South is still apparent, not only in its relaxed, hospitable atmosphere, but also in restored homes, with carefully designed gardens and other features found throughout the Carolinas, Georgia, and Alabama and in such cities as Beaufort, Charleston, Savannah, Edenton, and Mobile. Raleigh, Durham, and Chapel Hill in North Carolina are long-established and well-respected educational centers, drawing students and teachers from across the nation, as well as the world. The modern bustling cities of Charlotte and Greensboro (North Carolina), Birmingham (Alabama), and Atlanta (Georgia) are among the largest urban centers in this region. Birmingham, in particular, sports the largest enclosed full-service shopping mall in the region, complete with more than 200 stores, as well as a hotel and numerous offices.

The population centers of Florida extend in a zigzag chain from the state's capital, Tallahassee, in the north, eastward to Jacksonville, south to Orlando (home of the largest group of amusement and entertainment parks in the US, including Disneyworld and the Epcot Center), southwest to Tampa/St. Petersburg, and southeast to Fort Lauderdale, West Palm Beach, and Miami. Although frequently battered by hurricanes, Florida's resilient population has nevertheless swelled at an enormous rate during the past decade, making it one of the fastest-growing states in the nation. This population shift has been caused largely by two factors: Miami is the gateway to the Caribbean and Latin America for trade and immigration, both of which are on the rise; and baby boomers are heading south for their middle age and retirement years, often in areas where they have vacationed for many years. Among Florida's greatest economic assets are its modern port cities, out of which shipping lines connect to every continent in the world. And one of its unique attributes, setting it apart even from other Southeast states, is its distinctly Latino and Caribbean flavor, particularly in Miami, where these cultures account for more than half of the population.

Fueled also by the migration of diverse businesses into the Southeast, the populations of this region are experiencing rapid growth. In the past, these states have been economically dependent on a narrow range of products, including tobacco, textiles, furniture manufacturing, and tourism. Nowadays, newly arriving companies are establishing general manufacturing facilities, high-tech and medical research and production laboratories, printing and publishing companies, and warehousing and distribution outlets. The expansion and modernization of port cities and transportation hubs have turned this area into a major shipping center. The primary draw seems to be the quality of life, as well as the availability and lower cost of labor; these states offer year-round temperate climates, rural areas within a short commute of major business centers, a multitude of outdoor recreational activities, and excellent college and graduate educational programs. Many of these recently established companies are emphasizing international trade, particularly in Atlanta (Georgia), which will host the 1996 Summer Olympics.

While the picture does seem rosy, many of the biggest cities are struggling with high vacancy rates and run-down buildings in their downtown areas—a result of recession and overbuilding. Plans to revitalize the downtown areas include everything from new development, to implementation of security and crime prevention programs, to promotion of cultural activities, especially during the evenings. Hands-on science and history museums are being constructed in some of these areas; sports arenas and convention centers are being developed; and downtown "greenbelts"—parks, waterways, sculpture gardens, and other public amenities—are being installed. To prevent unplanned development, some of these states have also restricted the conversion of agricultural lands for development.

Mississippi Valley

Also known as the Mid-South, this zone is comprised of the states of Kentucky, Tennessee, Arkansas, Mississippi, and Louisiana, the borders of which are partly formed by the Mississippi River, the longest in the US. At the mouth of the Mississippi, the port city of New Orleans is world-famous for its festivals, food, jazz and blues music, a warm unhurried lifestyle, and the Creole-French flavor of daily life. Upriver is the region—called the Deep South by many—where US country folk music and folklore still reign. Much of the area is still covered by cotton fields and evidence of Civil War battle-fields, and the distance between wealth and pov-erty is perhaps more pronounced than in any other region of the country. Arkansas, Kentucky, and Ten-nessee include extensive mountainous areas and offer a mixture of forested highlands and fertile ag-ricultural lowlands.

The largest urban center north of New Orleans is Memphis, Tennessee (also the site of Graceland, former home of early rock-and-roller Elvis Presley, and one of the most-visited sites in the US). Second-ary population centers include the cities of Shreve-port (Louisiana), Little Rock (Arkansas), Jackson (Mississippi), Nashville (home of Opryland USA) and Knoxville (Tennessee), and Lexington and Louisville (Kentucky). Each of these cities has its own set of distinctive characteristics: some focus on their ur-ban center, but others have a small town appeal, with many workers living in rural settings and quiet sub-urbs within short commuting distances. Many an-nual art, music, and dance festivals draw interna-tional crowds.

The economies of the cities throughout the Mis-sissippi Valley are no longer dependent on a few large industries—oil and gas, for example—but have di-versified into many areas, attracting businesses as varied as health care, telecommunications, and high-tech electronics. Many of these cities are located on strategic US crossroads, resulting in tremendous in-creases in warehouse and distribution services. The port at New Orleans is one of the most active in the world. This region also boasts a tremendous tourist trade, attractive to international visitors for its mu-sic, art, riverboats, and extensive sports and recre-ational facilities.

The Prairie States

The north midwestern region of the country is commonly referred to as the Prairie States—Illinois, Indiana, Ohio, Michigan, Wisconsin, and Minnesota. The region is characterized by rolling forested hills and lakes. All of these states border the Great Lakes, and the entire area is dotted with bodies of water, leftovers of glaciers that covered the region during the Ice Age. Populations are clustered into the mod-ern cities of Minneapolis/St. Paul and Duluth (Min-nesota), Detroit (Michigan), Milwaukee (Wisconsin), Chicago (Illinois), and Indianapolis (Indiana). Ohio has five important urban centers: Cleveland, Cincin-nati, Columbus, Dayton, and Toledo.

The harsh winter weather typical in these prai-rie states has resulted in an abundance of huge in-door developments, including modern convention centers, connected downtown centers, and some of the largest shopping malls in the world—including the Mall of America, the world's largest shopping mall in Bloomington, a few miles south of Minneapolis. Vast stretches of undeveloped woodlands, particu-larly along the border with Canada in Minnesota, attract a large seasonal influx of outdoors enthusi-asts—canoers, campers, and hunters. Vacation homes are popular in these states, with many resi-dents owning and maintaining both a city dwelling and a home on a lake where they spend summers commuting back to town.

Residents of the Prairie States subscribe to a get-the-job-done work ethic. They tend to have a con-servative outlook, tempered with enormous energy and growing international awareness. The great out-doors beckons, so work is completed efficiently, com-mute times are kept reasonable, and time for enjoy-ing the wonders of nature is treasured.

Agribusiness continues to take a significant role in the economies of the Prairie States, with farms, food-related businesses, and breweries among the largest employers. However, cities throughout the region continue to dominate many areas of US heavy industrial, automotive, and machinery production. These economies, like those in other regions of the country, are seeing increased diversification into service oriented industries, with particular empha-sis on high-tech electronics, health care, telecommu-nications, finance and banking, insurance, and retail and wholesale distribution. The Prairie cities are lo-cated on some of the nation's most active crossroads, with Chicago's O'Hare Airport ranking as the busi-est in the US in terms of passenger traffic. Freight companies have established hubs at many airports here, trucking and rail freight outlets are big busi-ness, and modern ports along the Great Lakes allow access for international shipping. A high concentra-tion of universities and vocational and technical schools, many supported through public-private partnerships, supply a well-trained workforce to businesses in this region.

The Great Plains

The central region of the US was once entirely covered by grassy plains, and hence the states there—Iowa, Missouri, Oklahoma, Kansas, Nebraska, and North and South Dakota—are often referred to as the Great Plains States, or, simply, the Plains. Much of this region contains immense expanses of flat farm-land, broken occasionally by clusters of buildings marking small, rural towns. However, there are ar-eas marked by rugged terrain (the Badlands of South Dakota being one) and mountains (the Ozarks in Missouri and northwest Arkansas) being particularly well known. Cities and towns tend to be separated by vast distances connected by fairly straight highways. The largest population centers lie along the rivers that run through the region. On the Missouri River, visitors will find Bismarck (North Dakota), Pierre (South Dakota), Omaha (Nebraska), and Kansas City (in Kansas on the west and in Missouri on the east); at the confluence of the Missouri and the Mississippi, St. Louis (Missouri); on the Platte, Kearney, Grand Island, and Lincoln (Nebraska); on the North Canadian, Oklahoma City; on the Arkansas, Tulsa (Oklahoma) and Wichita (Kansas); and on the James, Springfield (Missouri).

Perhaps more than any other region in the US, the Plains States have kept alive the traditions of the Wild West. Old West towns, living history museums, Indian camps, army forts, and pioneer trails are not only available for exploring, but are actively promoted. The National Cowboy Hall of Fame and the Eastern Heritage Center are found in Oklahoma City. The traveler who samples a buffalo steak in a South Dakota Black Hills diner can claim to have had the ultimate Western US tourist experience.

The economies of the Plains States are as varied as in the rest of the US. Agribusiness remains important, but service industries are experiencing booming growth. Wholesale and retail distribution, tourism, telecommunications, and telemarketing are mainstays. Manufacturing continues to be a major sector of the economy, but it has declined somewhat during the past decade as the orientation turned toward trade and service industries. This region supports a large number of well-known higher education facilities, offering a sizable, highly skilled pool of workers.

The Rocky Mountains

The Rocky Mountain—or just Mountain—region is named for its most obvious feature, which cuts a path from the Canadian border southward through the states of Montana, Idaho, Wyoming, and Colorado. The population centers and activities in these states generally focus on these mountains. Vast expanses are devoted to protected national parklands—the most famous perhaps being Yellowstone, Grand Teton, Rocky Mountain, and Glacier National Parks.

The largest Rocky Mountain urban center is Denver, Colorado, but many other cities in this region are also worth noting, including Colorado Springs (the site of the US Air Force Academy), Boulder (site of the University of Colorado), Cheyenne (Wyoming), Boise (Idaho), and Helena and Billings (Montana). Some of the most famous US ski resorts—Aspen, Vail, and Sun Valley, to name a few—are located in the Mountain States. During the summer, fly fishers populate the mountain streams—the South Platte near Colorado Springs, the Upper Fryingpan near Aspen, the Salmon in Idaho, the Flathead, Clark Fork, Bitter-

root, and Blackfoot in Montana, as well as around Jackson Lake in Wyoming.

Grit and determination characterize much of the population of the Mountain States; entrepreneurs are much in evidence. A few grizzled prospectors can still be found seeking gold, silver, and copper deposits, but more common are the specialized boutiques catering to tourists and the rich and famous in mountain resorts. Dude ranches are also popular attractions. An active, outdoor lifestyle attracts a young, affluent population.

Mining is out, high-tech is in, although the energy—mainly oil and natural gas—sector continues to be important, especially in Wyoming. Forestry and ranching continue to be mainstays in the economies of most of the Rocky Mountain states. Growth, particularly in Colorado's urban centers, has been spurred by an influx of computer, biotechnology, and telecommunication firms.

The Southwest

The arid, mountainous states of the US Southwest—Utah, Nevada, Arizona, New Mexico, and Texas—are in full bloom. Arizona and Nevada populations in particular are experiencing rapid growth, swelled by large numbers of baby boomers who are approaching middle or retirement age and are attracted to the sunny climate and relatively low cost of living. From Texas port cities along the Gulf of Mexico to the inland cities that creep out over the deserts from the shadows of mountain foothills, this area is characterized by a sense of the immensity of nature and the need to preserve it; much of it is still untamed territory despite the inroads of civilization.

Nevertheless, many modern metropolises are well established and continue to expand: Phoenix, Tucson, and Flagstaff (Arizona); Albuquerque and Santa Fe (New Mexico), Amarillo, Austin, Dallas, Fort Worth, San Antonio, and Houston (Texas), and Salt Lake City (Utah). Border crossings into Mexico, at such US locations as Brownsville, Laredo, Del Rio, El Paso, and Nogales, support large populations focusing on the continual and growing cross-border trade and traffic. The casino meccas of Nevada—Las Vegas and Reno—are year-round tourist attractions and bustling business centers, and the canyons of Utah and Arizona offer grand vistas for hikers and wild white-water rafting for the hardy. All of these states support fine universities that attract substantial student populations.

The country's largest Indian reservation—home to the Navajo nation—crosses from northeastern Arizona into neighboring northwest New Mexico, and members of dozens of Indian tribes live in or near the many reservations sprinkled throughout this region. Cowboy traditions are close to the hearts of native southwesterners, exemplified by the ten-gallon cowboy hats and string ties still commonly worn by ranchers and business executives alike. Some of the nation's foremost art centers are located in the Phoenix and Santa Fe areas, and authentic Native American art is displayed in many locations, from city galleries to roadside trading posts.

The economies of these states are nearly as diverse as their geographies, but one unifying factor is the growing tendency toward the development of service industries. Once heavily dependent on its oil and gas industry, the Texas economy is still the nation's largest energy supplier, but it has also branched into many manufacturing and service oriented industries—particularly high-tech companies in plastics, aircraft, electronics, telecommunications, semiconductors, robotics, and computers. Wholesale distribution centers have also relocated to Texas, taking advantage of the proximity to the Gulf and Mexico, and Texas ports are some of the most active.

Wholesale and retail distribution centers are also spreading around nodes found in Las Vegas, Reno, Phoenix, and Albuquerque, particularly in response to a surge in freight transportation industries in these areas. Salt Lake City is a significant center for computers, biotechnology, health care, and telecommunications. Light manufacturing, telemarketing, insurance, and entertainment businesses have also become significant contributors to these economies. Considerable construction and expansion—with an emphasis on infrastructure improvements—is underway to accommodate the businesses and people flocking to the wide open spaces of the Southwest.

The West Coast

The West Coast states of the US include Washington, Oregon, and California. These states, once considered the country's final frontier, are today often at the forefront of the nation's developing social fads, fashions, and political trends. They offer many well recognized, progressive public and private universities, and tremendous variations in climate—from perpetually rainy Seattle to arid, hot Los Angeles. The industrial and population centers are found in and around Seattle (Washington); Portland and Eugene (Oregon); and Sacramento, San Francisco, San Jose, Los Angeles, and San Diego (California). Residents and tourists throughout this region tend to spend their leisure time in outdoor recreational activities—hiking, boating, backpacking, and camping are popular in the many mountain national parks; a large number of rivers allow for fishing and river rafting; beach and coastal towns offer resorts with all manner of cold or warm water sports.

The populations in the West Coast region are far from homogenous. In fact, friendly rivalry, and sometimes stronger competition, is the norm among the region's population centers. Baby boomers have swelled the populations of Oregon and Washington in the 1990s, in part because of a population migration away from the more expensive and fast-paced life typical in California's still-growing metropolitan areas. Immigrant populations—particularly of Asian and Latino origins—account for a rapidly increasing percentage of the total.

Built on agriculture, forestry, and aerospace, the economies of the West Coast states have struggled with rough times in recent decades because of drought and severely changing weather patterns, government restrictions on deforestation, pest infestations, and cutbacks in military spending. Agribusiness, entertainment, and oil continue to be the mainstay of the economy, and aerospace companies are experiencing a hopeful rebirth by focusing their efforts in the private sector. Some of the most world-famous pockets of high-tech industries—electronics, semiconductors, computers, and telecommunications—are located here, including the renowned Silicon Valley, which is being rivaled by developing centers in Portland and Los Angeles. The service sector is experiencing the fastest growth and offers opportunities in areas as diverse as high-tech plastics and electronics; health care; transportation; import and export trade; finance and venture capital; insurance; product distribution; and environment technology. Port and border cities in this region serve as gateways to Mexico, Canada, and all the countries along the Pacific Rim.

"Growth management" has become a West Coast catchphrase, with many areas focusing on innovative ways to improve infrastructure and transit systems—the inadequacy of which becomes apparent when highway-bound commutes turn into nightmares because of crowded, sometimes storm-damaged and earthquake-collapsed freeways, that can take years to rebuild. For these reasons, telecommuting from home offices is becoming increasingly popular in many areas. On the average, the population has a fairly high technological awareness and adeptness. They also have a high sensitivity to the conditions of their urban centers, and for the most part the downtown areas remain attractive, vital hubs of activity for business and cultural events.

The Pacific

The two US Pacific states—Hawaii and Alaska—seem particularly diverse, especially when viewed in terms of climate, which ranges from the extremes of Arctic Alaska to those of lush, tropical Hawaii. Their major business and population centers are Honolulu (Hawaii), and Anchorage, Juneau, and Fairbanks (Alaska). Indigenous peoples and immigrants comprise much of Hawaiian and Alaskan populations, and their customs and cultures are in evidence throughout the areas. The populations in these states pride themselves on their adaptation to their distinctive environments—business in Hawaii may be conducted in colorful cotton, short-sleeved Aloha shirts, while Alaska residents have developed innovative ways of dealing with frigid temperatures, ice, wind, fog, and long hours of twilight and darkness.

Tourism plays a significant role in the economies of both Pacific states. Hawaii does a tremendous import-export trade, particularly with the Pacific Rim, while oil is the largest sector in Alaska. Transportation is a significant economic sector, with both states offering modern, deepwater ports and air transport hubs. Each state has its own agricultural, fishing, and ranching specialties. Hawaii and Alaska have also depended heavily on the defense sector, and they continue to rely on substantial military communities. Scientific communities are also particularly strong in these states, which offer significant natural phenomena for study—volcanoes, frozen tundra, glaciers, plus a vast array of unique wildlife.

FROM A TOEHOLD TO AN ESTABLISHED PRESENCE: US MARKETING CHANNELS

Entry into US markets can be accomplished through a variety of channels, which may be loosely classified as: those already established for trade promotion; those that involve a low level of investment in the US; and those that require a high-level of US investment. Depending on such factors as intent, financial and physical size, product line, and potential US markets, a company that wants to do business with the US might start with any one of these channels or might decide to use a combined approach. While there are advantages to being close to the markets, a significant presence in US markets can be attained and maintained rapidly and a relatively low cost without establishing any direct business presence there. The goal is to determine how to reach the primary users of a product through the most effective, cost-efficient means, and then learn how to gain their repeat business.

Overall, a trader must weigh the advantages of using existing channels against the advantages of starting from scratch. Presumably, the locals know the markets—where they are, what they need, and what they will buy. By doing business through a US distributor, an exporter can avoid having to wade through all of the details about the potential US markets. Test-marketing through a few US-based specialists can show the nature, location, and size of a market before heavy investment is made. On the other hand, marketing through someone else will mean a loss not only of profits but also of at least some control over the process. The exporter will have to rely on the US representative's investigation and marketing decisions, and sales might reflect the approach and reputation of the US distributor as much as the content and quality of the product. The exporter's product will probably be only one of many handled by the US distributor. Therefore, the selection of a distributor must be made carefully. Whether to allow exclusive representation may be an even tougher decision in light of the large and widespread US business and consumer markets.

1. Go electronic.

High-tech and interactive are the buzzwords of the 1990s, and marketers should take full advantage of the innovations rapidly being introduced to the US public. This may be as simple as signing up for an 800 or 900 telephone line—800 numbers are toll-free to the caller, while 900 numbers charge the caller for the call, and are considered by many to be a separate profit center. These can be used simply for taking orders or answering inquiries or can represent operations as complex as establishing a full-fledged telemarketing operation. Consider seeking orders and offering information by facsimile (fax) over the telephone lines. Advertise through an electronic online service—accessed via computer modem over telephone lines—many of which carry current news, allow for input from subscribers, and provide a type of networking among the users of the system. Consider interactive multimedia technology—which combines computer, telephone, and television technologies. These systems are fast becoming an at-home phenomenon and a potentially lucrative means of direct marketing. "Storeless" electronic shopping seems to be the wave of the future in many US market niches, especially to reach the many consumers who are no longer willing to spend their precious free time on daylong shopping trips.

Advantages Customers are attracted to electronic information services because of the massive amount of information that is potentially at their fingertips and the elimination of the time needed to travel to malls and wander through stores. Electronic systems offer the ability to reach large markets with little effort or cost. Customers can shop and receive information with little more effort than that involved in turning on a few devices. Opportunists can locate markets, peruse bulletin boards of desired products and services, and offer their own expertise and merchandise directly. Companies offering electronic information services can provide links in many foreign countries, although some barriers may have to be overcome, including language, governmental restrictions, licensing, and high-tech infrastructure issues.

Disadvantages Although they are growing rapidly, the use and application of these systems are still in a relatively early developmental stage. Many markets remain unexplored, and the majority of businesses and individual consumers are not connected to any online system. While the potential exists, it has not yet been realized to any significant degree. Because of the lack of developed standards, significant concerns have been raised with respect to protecting the security of the information on electronic systems (such as antivirus measures, encryption, and the misuse of credit card or other confidential information), privacy rights, and intellectual property rights in materials distributed. Because subscribers generally have free access to materials on the system, other issues—such as disclosure, misrepresentation, regulation of content, and fair competition—will need to be addressed in order to avoid abuses.

2. Exhibit at trade shows, regional fairs, and conventions.

This marketing channel is particularly useful for reaching private and pubic commercial entities; it may be less useful for reaching end users of the products or services, although this is not always the case. Consumers may attend these events, even in large numbers, but they often limit their activities to scooping up free promotional items, making few actual purchases. Nevertheless, do not ignore the retail sales that accrue directly and indirectly from these events. However, the main purpose of attending these events is to meet large potential customers and to secure contacts that will further the exporter's business—such as suppliers, distributors, and retail outlet owners—as well as to explore the various options and ideas offered by competitors and other exhibitors.

Advantages Products and new technologies can be demonstrated to potential customers and distributors. Hands-on testing by buyers increases product awareness and favorable perception, leading to a competitive edge. Contacts can be made on many levels, from the smallest businesses to the largest corporations, from local distributors and agents to foreign business representatives. Never underestimate the importance of the personal touch that can be conveyed through such direct interactions.

Disadvantages It may be necessary to wait before an appropriate fair takes place. Competition is usually intense, and form—hype or glitz—rather than substance—a serious, reasoned presentation—is often the key to success. Immediate sales may not even cover the costs of attending. The benefit to the business can only be seen over time and depends on whether the contacts at the event are in fact appropriate to the business.

3. Hire a merchant wholesaler or a commission wholesaler.

Wholesale channels in the US are geared toward the distribution of bulk commodities, capital goods, and consumer goods, with the exception of motor vehicles and parts. Wholesale distributors come in all sizes. Many distribute regionally, including across several states, and many others distribute nationally. Approximately 90 percent of all wholesalers are merchant wholesalers. The other types are sales offices or branches of manufacturers (which do not handle competing products) and commission wholesalers (including agents and brokers). Total sales of the entire wholesale industry were expected to top US$3.3 trillion in 1994.

A major distinction between merchant wholesalers and other types of wholesalers is that merchant wholesalers purchase goods outright, taking full title to them, and then reselling to retail and industrial users. Such merchant wholesalers often store, assemble, grade, package, and label the goods, allowing them to assess the quality and design that will be most appealing in highly competitive local consumer markets. In comparison, commission merchants (including agents and brokers) typically sell products to which the supplier retains title and responsibility; their markets tend to be retail outlets and merchant wholesalers.

Advantages If a product is sold to a merchant wholesaler, the supplier usually bears no further risk with respect to that product; the merchant wholesaler assumes all risks of ownership and sale (although the original seller retains product liability responsibility, a major concern in the litigation-prone US). Some merchant wholesalers offer value-added services, allowing a manufacturer to save on the cost of bringing a product to market: doing market research, applying bar codes, tracking products, servicing products, delivering to buyers, labeling, and packaging, among others. Thus, an overseas manufacturer can export goods to a US merchant wholesaler, who will in turn label and package the goods as required for sale in US retail markets.

Disadvantages To a large extent, a supplier loses control over the method and manner of marketing a product once it is transferred to a merchant wholesaler. Some control can be retained if the parties intend to form a long-term relationship. If each party has a history of doing business and a stake in maintaining the relationship, a supplier can exercise some leverage by withholding goods if unsatisfied with the wholesaler's marketing plans.

To avoid losing too much control, an exporter can work through a commission wholesaler. However, a commission wholesaler takes a percentage of the sales price as a fee for the sale, which may decrease the return to the exporter below acceptable levels unless the price charged to the consumer is raised (which could make the product uncompetitive). Moreover, the risk of damage or loss of value by other means before a product is sold remains with the exporter until the product is transferred to the ultimate purchaser.

4. Do direct marketing.

Avoid the costs of intermediaries by directly contacting likely business and consumer customers. This method is often chosen by firms that supply consumer products or specialized items for small niche markets. Through direct marketing, goods can be transferred more directly from a producer to individuals, industrial consumers, small boutiques, national or regional chain stores, large scale department stores, discount stores, and service-oriented firms.

In direct marketing, the trend is away from mass audience mailings to the use of sharply focused catalogs and brochures targeted at niche markets that are calculated to be receptive specifically to the products advertised. To this end, database marketing has become an extremely useful tool for reaching business, government, and individual customers. Databases offer the direct marketer computerized lists of thousands of potential customers that can be sorted into groups having the particular characteristics thought to be most likely to indicate interest in the product being sold.

Advantages Direct marketing is particularly easy for manufacturers that supply limited lines of consumer goods, because they can find sufficient sales through targeted marketing to particular types of specialty stores—for example, toy stores, sports outlets, jewelry stores, or clothing chains. This type of marketing is also useful in reaching buyers more likely to purchase from their homes—such as those facing harsh or extreme weather conditions, those

---

TIPS FOR CHOOSING A COMMISSION WHOLESALER

Seek out a commission wholesaler through:

- **Government services** Contact services available from your own government agencies for export trade promotion.

- **US trade associations** Request information from national and local trade associations in the US about commission wholesalers in a particular industry and region.

- **Trade fair contacts** Exhibit or visit regional and national industry-specific trade fairs, which are typically attended by hundreds of wholesalers.

- **Trade and telephone directories** Search the listings for commission wholesale services within the directories that cover the regions that seem most appropriate for marketing your products.

- **Newspaper and magazine listings** Research the services offered by reviewing the advertisements of those that promote themselves.

- **End users, retailers, wholesalers, industry experts, and exporters** Consult with your contacts in the industry. Ask customers and potential clients for recommendations and references to their preferred commission wholesalers.

Investigate your prospective wholesaler's:

- **Experience** Find a wholesaler in the business of distributing, selling, or servicing foreign goods in general. Test the wholesaler's knowledge about your type of product and about the region you want to target in particular. If you want to sell wool rugs, find a wholesaler who promotes floor coverings and textiles, not one who deals with toys. No matter how good their reputation, if it is in the wrong field, it will not help your reputation.

- **Financial status** Ask for and review financial data on the commission wholesaler's business. Request information from a credit bureau or service, such as Dun & Bradstreet.

- **Reputation** Check with the wholesaler's references, including other clients and bankers, about dependability, ease of working relationship, and service problems.

- **Strength** Find out whether the commission wholesaler is well established and has sufficient market penetration in the regions where you believe your product will sell.

- **Goals** Query the wholesaler's intentions with respect to international trade generally and your relationship in particular. If you want a long-term commitment, make sure the wholesaler wants one too.

- **Conflicts of interest** Be certain your commission wholesaler is going to devote sufficient promotion time to your products and that your product will compliment, rather than be in direct competition with, others sold by the wholesaler.

whose work or commute schedule leaves them with little time for shopping, those who find going to a local market a physical challenge, and those who are dissatisfied with the offerings available locally.

Disadvantages Direct marketing can be extremely difficult, because US businesses and consumers are virtually inundated with catalogs, advertising inserts, and other promotional materials—commonly derided as "junk mail." Many potential customers fight this deluge by demanding that their names be deleted from mailing lists and databanks. To compete using direct marketing, promotional materials must really fascinate the recipient. Moreover, for a widely varied product line, direct sales can be costly because of the need to reach a broader segment of the population. Direct marketing is usually not the best means of selling a complex product that requires explanation and requires the buyer to select from a variety of options. This type of marketing is also only as effective as the quality (in terms of the accuracy with which the potential customers have been selected) of the mailing lists used. That accuracy will decrease if the target market is small or consists of populations or businesses that tend to be transitory. Also, direct sales often require a great deal of customer service support and must accept a high level of returns because the customer cannot actually judge the product prior to delivery.

5. Bid on public projects or procurement contracts.

National, regional, state, and local official and government agencies purchase millions of dollars' worth of supplies, equipment, and services from the private sector every year, and the vast bulk of such procurement is open to bids from overseas suppliers. Civil and military agencies need everything from paper clips to heavy machinery. Many of these sales occur through a competitive bidding process. (Refer to the "Opportunities" chapter for discussion of the bidding process and a list of commonly sought items.)

Advantages A successful bid can advance a product's reputation in US markets. It can also result in new contacts in the private sector if the goods or services are open to public view.

Disadvantages If a bid is made and accepted, the goods or services must usually be delivered at the bid price within the specified period with few alterations or exceptions allowed. Making a bid may require considerable uncompensated preparation, including the completion of voluminous government forms detailing the company's history, financial condition, and products or services offered. Procedures for bidding are not standardized, varying widely among various officially buyers.

6. Establish a local representative office.

Setting up an office is relatively easy in most US locales, and the most difficult decision generally consists of where to locate the office. In the US, this type of office should be geared toward establishing contacts with business customers, wholesalers, government procurers, and the like. A small representative office is unlikely to impress or influence the average individual consumer.

Advantages The local office can offer prompt service with a personal touch, thus showing commitment to the customer. A carefully chosen representative can use personal charm and knowledge of local preferences to gain the desired contacts and contracts and to promote repeat business. In some industries, especially in high-tech, a local representative can provide on-site installation and consulting services. And unlike a wholesaler, who handles the products of many different companies, your local representative works exclusively for you.

Disadvantages Expenditures of funds and labor involved in finding, leasing, staffing, and outfitting a local representative office can be substantial; there are also usually a number of government regulatory requirements to meet—such as obtaining a state or local business license, registering the business or its name, or applying for a tax identification number. By establishing a physical office in the US, an overseas company has created the US business presence necessary for it to be held liable in a US lawsuit.

7. Enter into a joint arrangement with a local company.

A joint arrangement with a local company is one major avenue for deepening a business presence in the US without going all the way to establishing your own facilities there. Such an arrangement may include forming a corporation, partnership, franchise, or joint venture. (Refer to the "Business Entities & Formation" chapter for a description of the formalities and details of the various joint arrangement structures.)

Advantages A joint arrangement can take advantage of the strengths that a US ally has to offer, such as its local distribution network, marketing expertise, contacts, and an understanding of how to make the product fit the needs of the US market. It can allow the US ally to assume the responsibility for customer satisfaction and service locally.

Disadvantages As with any marriage, difficulties between the parties must constantly be worked out, and trust, honesty, and fairness are required. The contract must be carefully worded to protect against potential damages and disruption or dissolution of the arrangement. Consider a trial period of sufficient length—one or two years—before agreeing to any lengthier, more binding agreement.

8. Open your own US outlet.

Retailing in the US is oriented toward the sale of products for personal and household use. The trend in retailing in the 1980s and early 1990s was toward the superregional mall: a collection of three or more large-draw "anchor" stores (usually department or large specialty stores) and numerous smaller chain and individual outlets. Malls are often enclosed and sometimes two or three stories high. In recent years, sales at the super malls have been decreasing, and customers appear to be favoring smaller community shopping centers, neighborhood "strip" centers, and local markets. Specialty stores are showing strong growth. This trend bodes well for the exporter who wants to open up shop in the US through smaller outlets rather than depending on contracts with established retail buyers.

Advantages For products that are sold to known target markets, an exporter can market directly to consumers through a retail outlet, controlling the selling proposition and the prices by eliminating intermediaries. The ability to control the sales environment and the training of personnel can improve the quality of service and upgrade consumer goodwill and product and provider image by reducing the gap between the supplier and consumer.

Disadvantages Retail outlets typically sell to a targeted group, and the successful sale of a product depends on its appeal to that particular group. Competition with other retailers of similar products can be fierce; customers love to comparison shop and bargain hunt, making price, packaging, and presentation as important as content. Significant costs are inherent in establishing, maintaining, and staffing an independent retail operation, and there must be a sufficiently developed product line and an adequate supply of goods to stock an entire store. The sale of ancillary merchandise can boost sales, but also requires additional commitment.

9. Build a local manufacturing facility.

Many foreign companies have made significant investments in manufacturing facilities in the US, particularly in high-tech industries and automated or computerized facilities. However, most of these have involved large-scale production or assembly of big ticket consumer or industrial products.

Advantages The price of products can be kept competitive with domestically produced merchandise because of the lower import and transport costs needed to reach customers. Companies can take better advantage of the rapid high-tech developments in the US, and there is a large, available, highly educated and skilled workforce. On site facilities are generally more responsive to changes in local conditions than are remote locations.

Disadvantages Operations in the US will generally be expensive to set up and be subject to US labor, tax, and commercial laws. Companies may have to develop new management structures and train their foreign personnel to deal with culture shock, which they are sure to encounter in dealing with the average US resident. Given the added requirements, the cost structure of US operations—often quite high in comparison with other locations—must be carefully assessed.

ADVERTISING CHANNELS

A first-time advertiser in US markets will encounter an overwhelming array of potential advertising options. Telecommunications, print, and broadcast media are all well developed. The traditional pathways—newspapers, magazines, radio, and television—have each splintered into numerous alternatives on both the national and local levels. No longer is television monolithic: cable television is popular and accessible in most places in the US. It offers specialized sports, music, finance, news, and other stations (some of which feature "infomercials"—lengthy advertisements disguised as programming) in addition to general network programming. Satellite television makes hundreds of stations available from around the world. There are also the more familiar local, national, and foreign networks. There is public television, which usually has no commercials, but does announce the names of program sponsors.

Among newspapers, a customer can choose from among national, regional, and local daily newspapers; weekly and monthly news, trade, or specialty journals; community shopper papers; and papers targeted at particular occupations—such as the legal, medical, real estate, or accounting professions—or interest groups—various sports and other special interest groups. Magazines are becoming increasingly specialized and narrowly targeted as well. Thus, marketers face a challenging task in deciding which medium provides the best fit for a given product; the diverse opportunities may require considerable time and study to investigate and absorb.

An exporter seeking to advertise products or services in the US will face stiff competition from domestic advertisers. Although advertising spending varies widely by geography and the size and type of the company, the average US business spends little more than 3 percent of its annual revenues, at most, on advertising. Of that amount, the largest percentage is spent in reaching individual consumers. Less than 25 percent of advertising is targeted at business customers.

Newspapers and small regional news journals tend to be the least expensive advertising channels. Television advertising tends to be the most expensive, although it generally reaches the largest—although not always the most targeted—audience. Extreme variations in advertising costs are seen across the country, primarily because of regional differences in the level of media competition. In general, the more competition there is among the media companies, the lower the advertising costs (although overall high costs in urban areas affect prices for advertising there regardless of greater competition). Households in smaller population areas with fewer media options tend to be more costly to reach with advertising than those in large urban centers.

Print Media

Newspapers The US newspaper industry was hit hard by the nationwide economic slowdown in the early 1990s. With less disposable income to cover ever increasing personal expenditures, many customers have eliminated the purchase of some discretionary items, including newspaper subscriptions. Recovery has remained slow, with many papers showing little or no growth in circulation. Recent jumps in the cost of newsprint are also expected to hurt newspaper profits. However, the outlook for the next several years is still somewhat rosier: newspapers are expecting increases in circulation and advertising receipts as the nation's economy improves and consumer confidence returns. Although newspapers have a shrinking share of total media advertising expenditures, they are still one of the least expensive and quickest means of getting the word out to a relatively large market.

Newspapers are more dependent on advertising revenues than any other medium in the US. More than 1,500 daily newspapers are operating in the US, with total circulation of more than 60 million. Many newspapers are small, serving regional markets with circulations well below 50,000. Just a few newspapers are national in circulation, and the larger regional papers can be readily purchased in bookstores and newsstands across the nation. On an average weekday, an estimated 60 percent of adults (age 18 and older) in the US read at least one newspaper, although this figure may overstate the case. Sunday papers typically have a larger circulation than the weekday editions.

The trend among newspaper companies is toward regularly published special interest sections—such as daily, weekly, or other periodic grouped features on real estate, entertainment, food and cooking, home improvement, or some other specialty subject. Some newspapers with a circulation covering distinct geographic markets prepare special neighborhood sections for suburban readers. All of these developments offer marketers ways to more finely tune and target their advertising.

The larger companies are also offering database marketing and electronic services through which subscribers can request specific information. Advertisers are expected to benefit from these new services—particularly from database marketing, by which newspapers can deliver specific advertising information to groups selected based on demographic and lifestyle data. Businesses that seek nationwide advertising will appreciate the introduction of electronic data interchange systems, that is, networks through which an advertiser can purchase advertising in a number of newspapers at one time and receive a single invoice.

Magazines and Other Periodicals Much like newspapers, the US periodicals industry has suffered from recession and is now slowly recovering. In an effort to pick up the pace of growth, many periodical publishers have been discounting advertising rates and making special offers to attract advertising. The total number of periodicals operating in the US is well over 11,000, and foreign magazines are available in many locations as well. Most magazines are sold to the public by subscription and through a wide range of single-copy outlets—newsstands, bookstores, supermarkets, and other retail stores. However, subscriptions account for nearly 80 percent of total circulation.

It should be noted that periodicals have the reputation of being a secondary advertising medium, but in fact they can be extremely useful tools to focus on particular markets and special interest groups. In addition to general news magazines, periodicals can be found for a nearly unimaginable variety of specific facets of life: finance, investment, business, consumer sales, farm, gardening, agriculture, home improvement, design, entertainment, music, medicine, real estate, outdoor recreation, sports, education, children, computers, electronics, television, technology, science, telecommunication, fashion, literature, religion, art, aviation, cars, food, or health—to name but a fraction of the possibilities. A number of publishers also offer special editions of their products tailored to particular age or interest groups that would otherwise not purchase subscriptions.

New technologies have allowed periodical publishers to expand beyond the printed page into cross-media and multimedia products: fax services, electronic networks, CD-ROM databases, and videotext productions are increasing in popularity and offer immediate and interactive contact with the customer. Many US publishers are expanding into international markets; this gives the advertiser the advantage of distributing product and service information to targeted markets worldwide through a single source.

Television

Three major networks—ABC, NBC, and CBS—plus the newer, up-and-coming Fox network dominate traditional television broadcasting nationwide.

TWELVE TIPS TO BOOST YOUR SALES

Even after having some success in US markets, a trader needs to reevaluate regularly not only whether a product is selling, but whether it is being exposed to the most ideal market, or even reaching the intended market. These tips suggest ways to test the success of your market strategies and to explore new pathways.

1. Keep in contact with your most important customers and contacts.

Personal contact—by telephone or in-country visits—can be critical to building a commercial relationship. For many businesses in the US, telephone contact is considered sufficient, but a trip is a luxury to be undertaken once the relationship has been ongoing and lucrative. The US is highly oriented to communications, less to transportation. The executive with a 20-line phone, several telecommunication panels, several video screens, and a satellite hook-up is no joking matter.

2. Offer to demonstrate or send samples of your products.

If you supply US merchants, the value of a presentation—with or without your physical presence—can be a key to acceptance. This is a highly effective—and usually inexpensive—sales booster.

3. Distribute promotional catalogs, brochures, flyers, and technical data to potential buyers, libraries, educational institutions, and industry associations.

These potential customers will be able to evaluate the material on their own and will understand who you are when you approach them. Follow up the materials with telephone calls and additional promotional materials that focus on new releases and product improvements.

4. Respect language and cultural differences, and adapt your product and marketing as needed.

The profit motive generally operates across cultures, and the nationals of different countries often have many things in common. However, you must also recognize the substantial differences. A generic marketing program can fall flat and even build ill will in the process. What works in your country won't necessarily work in the US. Your products and marketing techniques need to be suited to your target market. They must also be in line with government regulations. Learn the differences, respect them, adapt to them, and avoid multimillion-dollar mistakes. It's not only a courtesy to your customers, it's a necessity to your success in making your exports competitive within the US.

Products may need to be modified for sale in different regions or to customers with diverse characteristics. National brands have been losing ground to goods tailored to regional markets—particularly from locally owned franchises and small local suppliers that know their customers well through personal experience. You can learn from this trend. Sometimes a slight variation in a product to reflect regional customer tastes and trends can mean all the difference to sales.

5. Focus your product promotion.

Concentrate your time, money, and efforts on a specific market or region, work to build lasting relationships and repeat business there, and then expand as your products gain their own reputation. Avoid wasting resources by targeting the most likely customers—for big spenders, look to retail and chain outlets; for low-income consumers, consider discount and large outlet stores; for high-tech and specialty items, contact industrial manufacturers and firms offering financial and commercial services. After successfully penetrating the most likely market and establishing a base, consider expanding your distribution into new markets.

6. Follow up on initial sales inquiries.

Pursue a lead. Establish a liaison for major accounts—a single person who will be responsible for working with a client from the start of a transaction, through delivery, to after-sales support.

7. Price your product to fit the market.

Don't get greedy and try to generate maximum profits. At the same time, don't underprice your merchandise. In the US, there are many bargain hunters, but there are also many who question the quality of products that come with a low price tag. Price your product to match the market.

8. Demand quality in product production.

Consumers in the US are used to having quality products, and they are used to returning items and demanding their money back when their purchase doesn't work, breaks, or otherwise doesn't live up to the intended purpose. Some of the most popular television shows and magazines test product quality and offer advice to consumers on best buys. If you offer a poor-quality product and someone finds out about it, you had better change your name the next time you try to market anything else.

9. Establish a direct feedback system.

From the start, you should have a plan in place to measure the effectiveness of your marketing efforts. This may be as simple as the collection of sales receipt data, brief surveys of new customers, or postcard customer registration forms. For tracking purchases of consumer goods, a number of electronic systems—usually using product codes and scanners—are available.

10. Promote repeat business.

Some companies are now sending personalized thank you notes, reminder cards, and holiday greetings to their more treasured or large-ticket item purchasers. Some electronic tracking systems offer the option of processing a customer's preferences and automatically issuing discounts, advertising, or special offers to the customer on the spot or through the mail.

11. Deliver on time.

If you don't, someone else will. Failure to deliver on time can destroy a carefully built reputation. If you are delivering to an intermediary, a delay in your delivery will also undermine that party's reputation and most likely will cost you future sales. There's not much you can do to make ships go faster or airlines schedule more flights, but you can try your best to have your products ready to package on time. If necessary, you can stockpile your products at a US facility. Do your best to avoid nasty interruptions at customs by finding the best possible freight forwarders and brokers. When you must (and can), forget the expense and deliver by a dependable courier service. The extra effort will go a long way toward establishing, fortifying, and expanding your reputation in the market.

12. Emphasize customer service.

Marketing becomes more effective if customers reached once return to buy again. Customer service is essential in developing repeat business; the treatment of your customers is as important as the quality of the product. Your representatives and personnel must be able to explain your product: what it is, what it will do, and how it operates. They must know not only the product, but also be able to relate to the customer. Your company's image is at stake.

Two additional proposed networks have been announced, but so far they have little programming and few affiliates. There are also many small, local private and public stations. The number of stations continues to grow, albeit slowly, because most available slots on the broadcast spectrum have been filled. Nevertheless, competition to draw and hold viewers is intensifying. The networks, which rely on advertising revenues (to a much greater extent than does cable television), have had a financially difficult decade and have had to streamline their operations in order to produce new programs while keeping advertising rates manageable. Manageable is a relative term, and advertising rates for television are much higher than for print media. However, marketers generally seem to agree that the power of television advertising is worth the price. More than 85 million US households watch an average of seven hours of television every day, and most viewers are remarkably familiar with the advertising slogans of many commercials.

Cable television is another area worth exploring. Although distribution is limited to the subscribers of a particular company, a large majority of the television viewing public prefers cable service to broadcast television's traditional antenna on the roof—because the quality of reception is good in any kind of weather and most cable companies provide a wider range of channels than are readily available over the airwaves. Nearly 60 million US households subscribe to basic cable services; this represents more than half of the households with televisions. That number is expected to increase and then level off at about 70 percent by the end of the decade. Unlike network television companies, cable companies have the advantage of earning revenue from subscriptions, not just advertising, with the result that their advertising rates are somewhat more affordable. The more important advantage to cable television is that it can appeal to niche audiences; the most common arrangement is for subscribers to take a basic set of channels and then select additional ones from any of several specific interest packages, such as a group of sports, educational, or movie stations. Thus, specific markets can be more easily targeted.

Radio

Radio advertising accounts for the smallest percentage of overall advertising expenditures in the US, perhaps because the overwhelming numbers indicate that the most constant listeners are teenagers, who have relatively less purchasing power and tend to buy a somewhat narrow range of goods. Nevertheless, the competition can be fierce for prime-time radio advertising slots—particularly during commute hours in urban centers because morning and evening "drive time" programs are very popular with listeners sitting on congested highways. In cities the airwaves offer music, foreign language, news, religious, and financial stations, while in the less populated regions the number of radio stations drops dramatically. Radio stations tend to poll the likes and dislikes of their listeners, and therefore targeted advertising on radio stations can be done relatively easily and accurately.

Other Advertising Formats

Promotions Nearly half of the advertising expenditures in the US go into promotions—which may be anything from a giveaway pen or notepad to cents-off coupons or price discounts for repeat purchases. Sales, price reductions, prizes, and frequent buyer discounts are common tools used to persuade potential customers to try a product and come back for more.

Billboards In many areas of the country, advertisers display their products on gigantic billboards, most often placed strategically along a highway or attached to the visible sides of buildings in a city center. The design and preparation of the huge billboard panels can be costly and time-consuming. The message must be seen, understood, and remembered by a passerby within the instant it takes to drive past it. Note that some communities have banned billboards as being unaesthetic and unsafe because they can be distracting to drivers.

Nontraditional Media Advertising through non-traditional media is, in fact, rapidly becoming a US tradition. Wherever there is a blank spot—on a shopping bag, a cash register receipt, a theater ticket, a baseball cap, the outside of a bus—there is an opportunity for sending a message to the buying public. The display space does not even have to stand still: some firms hire flatbed trucks to drive billboard-sized displays around city centers, adding further to urban sensory overload. US consumers find ads on the table tops of their favorite restaurants and at fast-food outlets, in the opening minutes of the vid-eotapes they watch, and on their milk and egg cartons, cereal boxes, and frozen waffle packages as they fix breakfast. The possibilities are virtually unlimited.

Marketing or Advertising Firms

Many firms offer product promotion services to assist foreign or domestic businesspersons in defining, locating, and breaking into the optimum US markets. Full-service advertising agencies have dominated this area for many years both in the US and abroad, and many work out of branch and subsidiary offices in foreign countries as well as in major cities within the US. Because agencies have the reputation of offering the services of highly skilled personnel and providing a complete marketing package, they also charge substantial fees. However, they are meeting some price resistance as competition intensifies from public relations, information service, and database firms. (Refer to the "Important Addresses" chapter for contact information.)

Public Relations Firms

A public relations (PR) firm can help a businessperson market a product by establishing and promoting an image that will best appeal to targeted buyers. A PR firm can build a client's reputation by arranging corporate sponsorships and community betterment projects, and can spread the word about a product, help with labor relations, or even lay the groundwork for obtaining financial assistance for the client company. After all, having the right image can mean the difference between success and disaster in the US market. Sometimes a well placed, well timed news release is all that is needed to attract the interest of the consuming public and start a flow of orders. For this reason, PR firms are kept on retainer to polish the image of most top US enterprises. This concept of boosting image recognition has also led to the trend of advertising designed to promote an image rather than a specific product.

FITTING THE PRODUCT INTO THE US MARKET

Import Barriers Tariffs, taxes, licenses and quotas do not constitute significant barriers to most products seeking a market in the US. More than half of the imports entered into the US for consumption enter duty free, and quotas and licenses apply to only a few specific items. (Refer to the "Import Policies & Procedure" chapter.) If import problems do arise, an exporter to the US can consider other ways of ameliorating the situation. For example, foreign trade zones can potentially offer a safe haven from which to survey the scene. (Refer to the "Foreign Trade Zones" chapter.) Another possibility is to establish a manufacturing facility to produce the products in the US.

Language and Cultural Differences The obvious market in the US consists of the majority English-speaking mainstream population, but this market is hardly as monolithic and homogeneous as it might initially seem. Immense and rapidly growing markets also exist in the US for products targeted to other groups. In most large commercial centers—New York, Chicago, Los Angeles, Miami, and San Francisco, to name a few—substantial markets exist for products that appeal to multicultural-multilingual populations, most notably among consumers who speak Spanish, various Asian languages, Italian, or French. To tap into a particular ethnic market within the US, businesses might target regions or cities where the population of that particular group is more concentrated, such as New Orleans for its French-speaking population, New York and the West Coast cities for Asian (and Spanish-speaking) groups, and the southwestern states for Spanish-speaking populations.

Outsiders should remember not to make the mistake that many US marketers have made by considering these ethnic target markets as homogeneous based simply on linguistic or generalized cultural affiliation. For example, the US Hispanic community varies considerably by geography and point of origin. In the Southwest, most Spanish-speakers are of Mexican origin. However, in New York, most are from Puerto Rico, and insiders consider people of Cuban origin to be very different from people from the nearby Dominican Republic. This situation becomes even more complicated when arrivals from various distinct South and Central American nations are taken into account. Perhaps people from abroad will be better attuned to such differences than are those in the one-size-fits-all US.

Product Labeling and Quality Requirements Strict laws and complex government agency regulations apply to many products marketed within the US, particularly those sold to consumers, health care institutions, restaurants, and the like. Information on these requirements can be obtained by contacting the relevant federal regulatory agency. Similarly, state regulatory agencies should be contacted in order to learn whether additional local requirements must be met before introducing a product into a market. Those interested in importing products into the US should note that while transparent, the requirements can be complex, stringent, and spread among numerous agencies, making compliance difficult. (Refer to the "Important Addresses" chapter for contact information on regulatory agencies.)

Measurements The overwhelming number of US consumers and businesses persist in avoiding the metric system, preferring the English measures that have been in common usage for hundreds of years: gallons, quarts, pints, cups, and fluid ounces; miles, yards, feet, and inches; pounds and tons; and so on. Likewise, US residents measure temperatures in Fahrenheit, not Celsius. Although use of metric measurements is growing slowly—and is even required for some official Customs requirements and paperwork—the metric system is still introduced—not widely used—only in US primary school grades and is used generally only by the scientific community. Products should therefore generally be labeled with the US equivalents to the metric measures.

LEARNING TO LOVE EXPORTING TO THE US: FIVE IN-HOUSE RULES

1. Eliminate as much guesswork as possible.

You cannot successfully export to the US by accident. You need a well-thought-out marketing plan, and you might find that the use of expert consultants represents time and money well spent. It is never simply a matter of saying, "Let's sell our product in the US." You need to know where and how you're going to market it. You need to find out whether your product needs to be changed to fit into the US market or to meet government requirements. You need to figure out how you are going to find a buyer or wholesaler. You need to have some idea of your target market, how to reach that market, how much you can expect to sell, and how many different products to introduce. A plan is the best way to uncover hidden traps and costs before you get overly involved and end up in a mess. You may see an opportunity, but you need to know how to exploit it successfully. To do that, you must plot, plan, and prepare.

2. Just go for it.

Planning is important and should never be forgotten, but sometimes the best plan is to use a shotgun approach—just blast away and see if you hit anything. You can narrow your options later. If your product is new to the market, there may be almost no preexisting marketing information, and you may essentially have no choice other than just to dive in.

3. Commit to exporting.

You must explicitly commit to exporting to the US. In light of the number of available media options and the diversity in US markets, your first entry could well flop. Success in marketing in the US may mean sticking with your desire to export, weathering the initial setbacks, adding the financial backing needed to try again, and just hanging on until you reach the critical level that allows your product to take off.

International marketing consultants report that many companies invariably cut their international trade budgets when the results in the first few months are anything less than wonderful: these cuts represent premature decisions and produce unnecessary failures. The hard fact is that exports do not bring in money as quickly as domestic sales. It takes time and persistence for an international marketing effort to succeed. You have to overcome many hurdles—personal, political, cultural, and legal, to name a few. It could take a few months or a year or more to see the first glimmers of success. Be patient, keep a close but not suffocating watch on international marketing efforts, and give your venture a chance to develop.

4. Avoid an internal tug-of-war.

The complex strategies, relationship building, and legal and cultural accommodations that export marketing require will mean that support and teamwork within your own company are crucial to the success of the venture. Allowing internal conflict to continue—between partners, divisions, or investors in your own company—over current intentions and plans domestically and abroad will amount to creating your own obstacles to exporting success.

5. Stick with exporting even if business booms at home.

Exporting is not something to allow to surface only when domestic markets falter and then to submerge when business at home increases. It is difficult to move into exporting. All up-front investment in relationships, financial ties, and management resources that export marketing entails will require that a clear commitment be made right at the start. Any other attitude is likely to doom the venture from the beginning; you might as well forget it. This aspect cannot be overemphasized: either take the long-range view or don't play at all. Decide that you are going to export and that exporting is going to be a significant part of your business.

USEFUL ADDRESSES

Government Statistical Sources

Bureau of Economic Analysis
US Department of Commerce
1401 K Street, NW
Washington, DC 20230, USA
Tel: [1] (202) 523-0777, 606-9900
Produces Regional Economic Information System in a variety of forms.

Bureau of Labor Statistics
441 G Street, NW
Washington, DC 20212, USA
Tel: [1] (202) 606-5888, 606-6378
Annual Consumer Expenditure Survey good source on household spending.

Internal Revenue Service
1111 Constitution Avenue, NW
Washington, DC 20002-6433, USA
Tel: [1] (202) 874-0700, 874-0410
Compiles data on annual aggregate income by source in all US counties.

National Center for Education Statistics
555 New Jersey Ave. NW
Washington, DC 20208, USA
Tel: [1] (202) 219-1839, 219-1828
Compiles the annual Digest of Educational Statistics.

National Center for Health Statistics
3700 East-West Highway, Room 157
Hyatsville, MD 20782, USA
Tel: [1] (301) 436-8500
The National Health Interview Survey is a continuing nationwide survey.

Bureau of the Census
Washington, DC 20233, USA
Tel: [1] (301) 763-4100
FastFax Tel: (900) 555-2FAX
Produces the annual Statistical Abstract of the US plus many other products.

US Postal Service
475 L'Enfant Plaza
Washington, DC 20260, USA
(202) 268-2000
Compiles residential and business delivery statistics by zip codes.

Commercial Organizations

Audit Bureau of Circulations
Compiles and verifies statements of readership circulation filed by publishers of more than 1,000 periodicals distributed in the US.

American Advertising Federation
1400 K St., Suite 1000
Washington, DC 20005, USA
Tel: [1] (202) 898-0089
Fax: [1] (202) 898-0159

American Entrepreneurs Association
2311 Pontius Avenue
Los Angeles, CA 90064-1809, USA
Tel: [1] (213) 479-3987

American Federation of Small Business
407 South Dearborn Street
Chicago, IL 60605-1111, USA
Tel: [1] (312) 427-0206

US Chamber of Commerce
1615 H Street, NW
Washington, DC 2007-4902, USA
Tel: [1] (202) 659-6000

Committee for Economic Development
477 Madison Avenue
New York, NY 10022-5802, USA
Tel: [1] (212) 688-2063

Public Relations Society of America
33 Irving Plaza
New York, NY 10003, USA
Tel: [1] (212) 995-2230

US Travel Data Center
1133 21st St. NW
Washington, DC 20036, USA
Tel: [1] (202) 293-1040
Compiles statistics on trip attributes, traveler
demographics, and buying patterns and offers the
Travel Market Report annually.

Publications

*Advertising Age: The International Newspaper of
Marketing*
(Weekly)
Crain Communications, Inc.
220 E. 42nd St.
New York, NY 10017-5806, USA
Tel: [1] (212) 210-0100
Fax: [1] (212) 210-0111

Adweek
(Weekly)
BPI Communications
1515 Broadway
New York, NY 10036, USA
Tel: [1] (212) 536-5336
Fax: [1] (212) 944-1719

American Demographics
Marketing Tools
Marketing Power
American Demographics
PO Box 68
Ithaca, NY 14851-0068
Tel: [1] (607) 273- 6343, (800) 356-0688
Fax: [1] (607) 273-3196
Besides these periodicals, American
Demographics offers many books on marketing in
the US, including Capturing Customers

Bacon's Directories
Bacon's Publishing Company
332 S. Michigan Ave., Suite 900
Chicago, IL 60604, USA
Tel: [1] (312) 922-2400
Publish media directories: Newspaper/Magazine,
Radio/TV, Media Alerts, Publicity Checker

NTC Business Books
4255 West Touhy Ave.
Lincolnwood, IL 60646-1975
Tel: [1] (708) 679-5500, (800) 323-4900
Fax: [1] (708) 679-2494
Offer a wide variety of books on marketing and
advertising in their catalog.

Standard Rate and Data Service
Macmillan Inc.
3004 Glenview Rd.
Wilmette, IL 60091, USA
Tel: [1] (708) 441-2234
Provide rate and data service for: Business
Publications, Community Publications, Consumer
Magazines, Newspaper Rates, Print Media, Spot
Radio

Business Entities & Formation*

FORMS OF BUSINESS ENTERPRISES

While businesses in the US may be organized in a number of ways, the alternatives most often used are sole or individual proprietorships, partnerships, corporations, joint ventures, and limited liability companies (LLCs). Investors also may enter into franchise or distributorship agreements. Each business form offers its own peculiar attributes, and the choice of the appropriate organizational structure for carrying out business activities or investments in the US depends on the objectives, degree of control desired, preferred tax treatment, anticipated duration of the investment, and other personal and business circumstances and preferences. (Refer to the "Taxation" chapter for a discussion of tax treatment.)

This chapter provides a general overview of the entities that are available and how they are most often used for transacting business in the US.

Corporations

Traditionally, the most common means used by a foreign business to undertake a US investment or business venture has been through a US corporation. The number of businesses operating as corpo-

rations in the US is more than double the number operating as partnerships. Although sole proprietorships far outnumber corporations in the US, foreign investors generally prefer corporations because proprietorships are run by individuals, and most of them start and stay small.

A corporation is organized in one state and then recognized in all 50 US states. It has substantially all of the legal rights of an individual and is responsible for its own debts. The primary advantages that the corporate entity may offer to its investors are: (1) each shareholder's liability is limited to the amount invested in the corporation; (2) ownership of shares in the corporation is readily transferable; and (3) legal continuity of the business is assured regardless of any shareholder's death or any change in management or ownership of the corporation. In the US, a company that has a few thousand dollars in capital generally may be incorporated under the same statutes as a company with millions of dollars in capital. However, larger companies with shares that are publicly issued and traded are subject to more stringent disclosure and reporting laws and regulations than companies with shares that are held by just a few investors. Legal counsel can advise foreign investors in deciding whether the corporate form of business is the most advantageous for their purposes.

Legal advice is also recommended in selecting a state in which to incorporate a business, because wide variations exist among state corporation laws—from the requirements of incorporation to the operation of the entity and to its dissolution. Some states have more stringent standards and requirements—such as director or incorporator qualifications, recordkeeping, and meeting requirements—than others, and taxes and incorporation fees will vary. The states that offer the most liberal incorporation laws—in particular, Delaware, New York, and Nevada—are quite popular with investors. Neverthe-

* By Duane H. Zobrist and Stephen L. Bradford. Copyright © 1995 Carlsmith Ball Wichman Case & Ichiki. Reprinted with permission of that law firm.

less, most state laws are broadly similar because a majority of states have adopted the Model Business Corporation Act with only minor variations.

The decision to incorporate in one state does not prevent a corporation from doing business in any other state; the corporation may even locate its headquarters in a state other than where it is incorporated. To qualify to do business in another state, an out-of-state corporation need only file certain documents with the proper authorities and pay the statutory fees. The cost of such qualification varies from state to state, like the cost of incorporation, but overall, these costs are not unduly burdensome.

With respect to specific incorporation procedures, each state has its own codified corporation laws detailing how a corporation may be organized. With few exceptions, federal law does not govern the incorporation of business enterprises in the US—the most notable exception being the establishment of a federally-chartered national bank. Generally, a state agency (usually the secretary of state's office) approves the name of the company and the charter or articles of incorporation (which, together with the corporate bylaws, set forth the rules and regulations by which the corporation will be governed). Thereafter, a minimum amount of capital must be paid into the corporation, and shares are issued to the owners (that is, the shareholders) of the corporation. The incorporation process typically takes one or two weeks, but may be longer in some states. Incorporation can cost less than US$100, although it can be substantially more—US$1,000 or even far more—if complex business and shareholder arrangements are needed.

In theory, shareholders hold ultimate corporate authority over policies and operational decisions, but their authority is usually exercised through a board of directors, which they elect. In many corporations, shareholders are only required to approve a few major corporate actions directly. For example, the shareholders may vote on amendments to the charter or articles of incorporation, increases in the authorized capital of the corporation, the sale of substantially all of the corporation's assets, a merger with another corporation, or the voluntary dissolution of the corporation, but on little else.

The corporate directors chosen by the shareholders in turn select officers, who conduct the company's daily operations. Typically, the following corporate officers are named: (a) a president or chief executive officer; (b) one or more vice presidents; (c) a treasurer or chief financial officer; and (d) a secretary. In many companies, one or more of the top corporate officers also are members of the board of directors.

The corporate bylaws constitute a set of rules that govern the procedures for shareholders' meetings, the selection of directors, the authority of di-

DETERMINING THE DEBT-EQUITY STRUCTURE OF A US CORPORATION

Investors in a new corporation should carefully compare the amount of capital (or equity) put into the corporation against the loans and other debt taken on by the corporation. The proportion of equity to debt is referred to as the debt-equity ratio of the corporation, and it indicates the company's financial strength based on its ability to satisfy its obligations. A corporation's debt-equity structure directly relates to its ability to meet its usual business needs and to service its debt.

There are also a several tax issues to consider in relation to the debt-equity ratio. If a corporation is too "thinly" capitalized—that is, the debts are disproportionate to the capital—the US tax authorities may treat as equity all or part of any shareholder loans to the corporation. As a result, when the corporation repays the loan, both principal and interest may be characterized as the payment of a taxable dividend to the shareholder. Federal tax laws contain a highly complex system of rules to cover most aspects of such arrangements, including the imputation of interest on related party loans, existence of original issue discount, timing of income recognition and interest deductions, limitations on the deductibility of interest paid or accrued to related foreign persons, treatment of "below-market" loans, issuance of debt instruments in exchange for property, and reallocation of income and deductions among related enterprises. These rules must be taken into account in determining the corporation's debt-equity structure.

In addition, the tax impact of interest payments, for both the US and the foreign investor's home country, requires careful scrutiny. If the investment is treated as a loan, the interest on a loan made by a foreign shareholder to a US corporation will usually be subject to the 30 percent flat tax on US source passive income, subject to reduction under specific existing bilateral treaties. Moreover, a US corporation's payment of interest to foreign shareholders may trigger taxable income in the shareholder's home jurisdiction even if the US corporation has no present benefit from the interest expense.

rectors and officers, and any other internal procedures required to be codified for the operation of the business. Shareholders and directors must usually meet at least once a year. However, shareholders or directors may take most actions, including those reserved for annual meetings, without actually holding a formal meeting in a physical location, provided they give unanimous written consent to the proposed action.

As long as a shareholder's only involvement is through holdings of the corporation's securities, or through independent, arm's length business dealings with the corporation—that is, dealings conducted at market prices and conditions that do not involve special considerations—the shareholder is generally not liable for acts of the corporation. The shareholder's sole responsibility is for fulfilling promises, if any, to contribute additional capital. However, directors and officers may be subject to liability if they are held to be seriously remiss in attending to their responsibilities for operating the corporation. Both directors' and officers' potential liabilities are often covered by insurance.

Corporations that trade their shares publicly must undergo rigorous regulatory scrutiny by the federal Securities and Exchange Commission of the United States (SEC) and, in some cases, by other regulatory authorities in the state where the corporation's securities are issued. Most corporations with publicly traded stock are required to file with the SEC periodic financial reports containing financial statements that have been audited by independent certified public accountants. Companies that do not trade their shares publicly generally have much less burdensome disclosure and reporting requirements. Nevertheless, they still may need to have independent certified public accountants prepare audited financial statements for purposes of obtaining bank financing and other credit.

Partnerships

The use of partnerships—particularly limited partnerships—has become increasingly popular with foreign investors, because the conduct of business through a US partnership can offer significant flexibility. A partnership arises from any agreement between two or more persons to unite their property, labor, skill, capital, or some combination of these resources to establish and carry on a business as co-owners for profit. Although parties may act in such a way as to imply that they have formed a partnership, it is advisable that they execute a written document—known as a partnership agreement—to define the rights and obligations of each partner. The organization and operation of a partnership is primarily governed by the statutory law of the state where the partnership is formed. Partnership law is generally standard throughout the US because most states have adopted, with minor revisions, both the Uniform Partnership Act and the Uniform Limited Partnership Act—which are model statutes developed by a national organization as prototypes for adoption at the discretion of the states. Because a partnership is essentially a contractual agreement, parties have a great deal of flexibility in using this form of organization and generally can adapt it in any way that best suits the particular needs of the partnership's business.

Foreign investors may find the partnership form of organization beneficial for certain types of investments—particularly for acquiring interests in real estate and projects for the exploration of natural resources—because, subject to certain limitations, this form of organization enables investors to apply partnership deductions or losses against other US effectively connected income in computing the partner's US taxable income. For US tax purposes, a partnership is not treated as a separate taxable entity. Unless the partnership agreement provides otherwise, all partners share profits and losses equally. Although the partnership must compute taxable income and file a return, the return is used for information purposes only. As a separate entity, the partnership does not pay income tax. Instead, the individual partners include in their own income tax returns their individual share of the partnership income, deductions, or loss—these items pass through to them from the partnership regardless of whether the items are in fact distributed. The partnership form also avoids the double tax effect of the corporate form of investment in which tax is imposed on corporate income and again on the dividend of after-tax profits to a foreign shareholder. However, foreign corporate partners must consider the branch profits tax. (Refer to the "Taxation" chapter.)

A partnership may be formed for a definite or an unlimited term. However, unless the partnership agreement specifies otherwise, the death or bankruptcy of a partner automatically dissolves the partnership. In addition, the sale of a partner's interest usually gives the other partners the right to terminate the partnership. In the case of a dispute among partners that cannot be resolved amicably, any partner may petition a court of competent jurisdiction to dissolve the partnership.

General Partnerships Two or more persons may form a general partnership by joining together as co-owners to carry on a business for profit. Normally, each general partner is actively engaged in the conduct of the partnership business. Unless stated otherwise in the partnership agreement—which, together with the applicable state statute, governs the management and operation of the partnership—each partner has the same rights, obligations, and authority as every other member of the partnership. Moreover, unless specifically prohibited by the partnership agreement, any partner may enter into contracts that are binding on the partnership. The principal drawback of a general partnership is that each partner has unlimited personal liability for all debts and obligations of the partnership, including those wrongfully incurred by another partner.

Limited Partnerships A limited partnership is distinguished from a general partnership in that only some of the partners have unlimited liability. While a limited partnership must have at least one general partner with unlimited liability, it may also have limited partners with liability limited to a specific amount set forth in the partnership agreement. However, limited partners may not participate in the active management of the partnership's business without jeopardizing their limited liability protection. The capital contribution of a limited partner may consist of cash or property, but usually not services. A limited partner may share in partnership profits to whatever extent is allowed in the partnership agreement.

Limited Liability Companies

Foreign investors interested in a relatively new business form in the US that has the beneficial characteristics of a partnership and a corporation may consider establishing a limited liability company (LLC) for small business purposes. An LLC is an unincorporated entity that offers the advantages of flow-through tax treatment and operational flexibility like a partnership, but with the corporate feature of limited liability for the owners. To obtain favorable tax treatment, the LLC generally must be characterized according to government definitions as a partnership rather than as an association taxable as a corporation. This form of business entity is generally available to any investor. However, professionals—such as accountants, attorneys, physicians, and others regulated under state business and professions codes—are often not allowed to form LLCs.

The characteristics of an LLC may in fact be more familiar to a foreign businessperson than to a US businessperson, because similar types of business entities have been available outside the US for many years. The LLC business form is a relatively recent development in the US. As of February 1995, all but four states—Hawaii, Massachusetts, Pennsylvania, and Vermont—had enacted statutes recognizing LLCs. Some states have adopted, in modified form, the Uniform LLC Act, based on a combination of the Revised Uniform Limited Partnership Act and the Model Business Corporation Act.

Under a typical state act, an LLC is formed by filing articles of organization with the state, which gives public notice of certain basic information about the company, such as its name, the date on which

the company is to dissolve, its purposes, and the address of its principal place of business and resident agent in the state. Operational rules for an LLC are contained in its operating agreement—the equivalent of a partnership agreement—which may be written or oral. Its affairs are dealt with by "managers" designated in the operating agreement, or in the absence of such a designation, by all members.

The typical state statute provides for dissolution of an LLC at the death, resignation, expulsion, bankruptcy, or dissolution of a member, unless the remaining members agree to continue the business of the LLC, or unless the operating agreement or articles of organization provide otherwise. State LLC law also usually provides that an individual's membership interest is the personal property of that individual and may be assigned in whole or in part. However, an assignment of a membership interest will not entitle the assignee to participate in managing the LLC or to become or exercise any rights of a member unless the remaining members consent or unless the operating agreement provides otherwise.

Joint Ventures

A joint venture—also abbreviated and known as a JV—is particularly useful to foreign investors planning to carry out a particular business transaction in the US for a limited period of time. JVs are often used when a project requires a pooling of skills, knowledge, or capital, which often can be better achieved through a coalition of several individuals or companies. Generally, the mutual rights and liabilities of joint venturers—the participants in joint ventures—with respect to their common enterprise are equivalent to those of partners, and the principles of law applicable to partnerships also apply to the joint venture. However, if the parties so desire, they may form their joint venture as a corporation. In such event, a corporation is formed to carry out a particular objective with the plan that the corporation will be dissolved and its assets distributed to its shareholders after completion of the project.

The corporate form of joint venture has certain tax disadvantages, including a second-level tax on the corporate earnings distributed to the joint venture shareholders. Moreover, the joint venturers are unable to deduct losses incurred by the joint venture during the course of the project; losses are taken into account at the corporate level. If the joint venture is a partnership, each joint venturer is taxed on its share of the joint venture's income and each participant may take its proportional share of losses and expenses as a deduction subject to certain limitations.

Branch or Representative Offices

Rather than incorporate a separate subsidiary in the US to handle business operations, a foreign corporation may prefer to operate in the US through a US branch. A branch normally consists of an office and employees or agents in the US. To qualify to transact business in a particular state, a foreign company that establishes a branch or a representative office generally must register with the government of that state. In the absence of treaty protection, the revenue earned through a branch office will be subject to the US federal branch profits tax. Investors should seek local legal advice on the specific advantages and disadvantages of operating as a branch office versus setting up a wholly or partially owned domestic entity.

Sole or Individual Proprietorships

The typical sole or individual proprietorship is an unincorporated business owned and operated by a single individual. Generally, the owner is actively engaged in the conduct of the business. However, the owner may lawfully employ as many workers as needed by the proprietorship to carry out its business activities. Because the individual proprietorship is not treated as a separate legal entity, the owner has unlimited personal liability for the debts and obligations of the business. A sole proprietor cannot limit such risk to a predetermined portion of the investment in the business. For this reason, a sole proprietorship is not typically used by owners of large businesses, but rather is most often used for small enterprises.

No special laws govern the organization or operation of sole proprietorships. Such matters are generally governed only by the state and local laws of contract, agency, tort, and licensing usually applicable to all business operations. Accordingly, the sole proprietorship offers the individual owner a great deal of flexibility, including the ability to make and implement policy without delay or formality.

The total profits of the sole proprietorship are taxed at the federal and state level as income to the owner at the owner's individual graduated tax rate. Similarly, all expenses and any losses of the sole proprietorship flow directly to the owner.

Franchises and Distributorships

Many business opportunities exist in the US for franchises or distributorships. Some of the most well-known US products and services—fast food restaurants, hotels, automobile dealerships, and car rental agencies, to name but a few—are sold through franchises or distributors. In the US, a franchise or distributorship is not a separate form of business entity, but rather a method of doing business.

A basic distinction between a franchise and a distributorship is that a franchisor exercises more control over the method of delivering the product or service than does a distributor. For this reason,

franchise arrangements are more closely regulated in the US than distributorships. In the common franchise arrangement, a company (the franchisor) typically owns a trademark, which it licenses others to use on condition that the licensee (the franchisee) will conform its business operations to the standards required by the franchisor. Adherence to such standards is generally required only to the extent that the products or services sold are associated with the trademark, allowing the franchisee at least some flexibility its business operations. The franchisor usually operates through a limited number of franchisees and often provides assistance to the franchisee in terms of organization, promotional activities, management training, marketing plans, and other business affairs. Because some franchise agreements can be extremely rigid and can tend to favor the franchisor, those interested in franchising should have agreements closely examined by legal counsel.

A distributorship may be set up to be similar to a franchise, although usually the company whose products a distributor sells exercises less control over business operations and provides less business support to its dealers. Thus, a supplier of goods or services may arrange with any number of companies to distribute those products or services. A common condition placed on an individual distributor is to sell a certain average amount of products or services within a designated time, but the methods used in fulfilling this obligation are often left to the individual distributor, particularly if the supplier does not license any trademark to the distributor. This method is particularly common in automobile and retail gasoline distribution.

Franchises can be advantageous to foreign investors who want to invest in US products with proven domestic markets and who wish to receive the kind of business support generally provided by a franchisor. Investors looking for greater independence may prefer a distributorship, precisely because it is subject to substantially less governmental regulation and supplier control. Foreign businesspersons offering products or services for importation into the US may consider establishing their own franchise or distributorship systems, although they should first conduct comprehensive market and legal research to determine the demand and feasibility of establishing a new franchise or distributorship line.

REGISTERING A BUSINESS

Savvy businesspeople—foreign and domestic alike—seek legal and accounting advice from professionals familiar with the local, state, and federal laws, regulations, and customs when first creating business

REGULATORY AGENCIES

Businesses in the US operate in a complex regulatory environment. Taken from the top, the president of the US has established cabinet positions, Congress in its turn has created various agencies and commissions, and state and local governments have also formed various agencies, all with supporting bureaucracies. Many of these agencies regulate business interests in the US.

For matters of federal law and regulation, contact the headquarters of the government agencies listed here. Many federal agencies, such as the IRS, have regional offices located throughout the US. The addresses and telephone numbers of the regional offices are available from the agency headquarters or can be found in local telephone directories under "Government" listings.

Environmental Protection Agency (EPA)
401 M St. SW
Washington, DC 20460, USA
Tel: [1] (202) 260-2090, 260-2080
Fax: [1] (202) 260-0500 (Enforcement)
The EPA enforces restrictions on emissions into the air and into public waste disposal systems.

Equal Employment Opportunity Commission (EEOC)
1801 L St. NW #10006
Washington, DC 20507, USA
Tel: [1] (202) 663-4900
Fax: [1] (202) 663-4912
The EEOC enforces laws prohibiting discrimination based on age, sex, religion, national origin, or race in hiring or other employment practices.

Federal Communications Commission (FCC)
1919 M St. NW
Washington, DC 20554, USA
Tel: [1] (202) 632-7106, 632-7000
Fax: [1] (202) 653-5402
The FCC regulates radio, television, and telecommunications systems.

Federal Trade Commission (FTC)
6th St. and Pennsylvania Ave. NW
Washington, DC 20580, USA
Tel: [1] (202) 326-2000, 326-2222
Fax: [1] (202) 326-2050
The FTC works in collaboration with the Department of Justice to enforce US antitrust laws by regulating commercial competition, mergers, and corporate acquisitions and to enforce laws designed to eliminate unfair practices and tendencies toward monopolization of any line of commerce.

Department of Justice (DOJ)
Antitrust Division
10th St. and Constitution Ave. NW
Washington, DC 20530, USA
Tel: [1] (202) 514-2410, 514-2007
Fax: [1] (202) 514-8123
The DOJ works with the Federal Trade Commission to enforce US antitrust laws and laws preventing unfair trade practices and monopolization.

Food and Drug Administration (FDA)
5600 Fishers Lane
Rockville, MD 20857, USA
Tel: [1] (301) 443-1544, 443-3170
Fax: [1] (301) 443-5930
The FDA, which is part of the Department of Health and Human Services, regulates pharmaceutical and food products and, with the FTC, enforces federal laws that require truth in labeling and advertising.

Internal Revenue Service (IRS)
1111 Constitution Ave. NW
Washington, DC 20224, USA
Tel: [1]   (202) 622-5000 (information),
           (800) 829-1040 (taxpayer assistance),
           (800) 829-3676 (tax forms and publications)
Fax: [1] (202) 622-8393
The IRS regulates the collection of taxes and implements the nation's tax policies.

Interstate Commerce Commission (ICC)
12th St. and Constitution Ave. NW
Washington, DC 20423, USA
Tel: [1] (202) 927-5350, 927-6000
Fax: [1] (202) 927-5728
The ICC regulates rail and road transportation involving more than one state, as well as oil and gas pipelines. State and local governments regulate insurance, land usage, building construction, and other areas of local interest.

National Labor Relations Board (NLRB)
1717 Pennsylvania Ave. NW
Washington, DC 20570, USA
Tel: [1] (202) 632-4950, 254-9392
Fax: [1] (202) 254-6781
The NLRB is responsible for monitoring relations between employers and unions.

Occupational Safety and Health Administration (OSHA)
200 Constitution Ave. NW
Washington, DC 20210, USA
Tel: [1] (202) 219-8151, 219-7162
Fax: [1] (202) 219-6064
Part of the Department of Labor, OSHA is responsible for establishing and enforcing detailed and complicated safety rules for businesses involved in interstate commerce.

REGULATORY AGENCIES (cont'd)

Securities and Exchange Commission (SEC)
450 5th St. NW
Washington, DC 20549, USA
Tel: [1] (202) 272-2650
Fax: [1](202) 272-7050
The SEC regulates the sale of securities and the accompanying disclosure requirements.

Small Business Administration (SBA)
409 3rd St. SW
Washington, DC 20416, USA
Tel: [1] (202) 205-6740, 205-7713
Fax: [1] (202) 205-7064
The SBA is the principal government advocate for small businesses and offers information and assistance on financial, investment, and management matters.

plans. With such assistance, business owners may be able to structure their companies to maximize government compliance while minimizing the cost and effort required for regulatory compliance.

Many government approvals and registrations are valid only for limited periods. Certain documents must be filed and certain fees paid on an annual or other periodic basis to keep registration in force. Investors and owners should record and make note of critical dates—such as expirations of approvals or filing deadlines—to ensure that all registrations and approvals remain current and valid. Once a business is established, its investors and operators will need to remain current on new legal and accounting developments that may impact their business plans and operations. (Refer to the "Important Addresses" chapter for partial listings of government agencies and legal and accounting firms.)

Basic Authorization and Application Procedures

Companies that wish to do business in the US must register for a federal tax identification number with the Internal Revenue Service (IRS). The federal tax identification number is used by the IRS to collect taxes from the company, income taxes withheld from the company's employees, social security withholdings, and federal unemployment tax contributions.

In addition to registering with the IRS, companies also may be required to register with a number of state agencies. Primary among these is the state's tax agency, which will collect any assessed taxes and fees for doing business within the state, usually including any state taxes on the sale of personal property and services. Any business with sales subject to the sales tax must apply to the state tax agency

for a seller's permit for each location maintained in the state. In certain circumstances, businesses may be liable for use tax, excise tax, and environmental and hazardous substance permits and fees with the state where they will do business. These permits and fees are usually handled by the office of the secretary of state in the individual states.

If a business will be paying wages or fees for services, registration with the state's labor department is usually required. Companies that register with the state department of labor often are issued employer registration numbers, which are used by the state to monitor the company's activities in the state. For example, a registration number may be used by the state to collect state unemployment taxes, monitor payment of workers' compensation benefits, or to administer other benefits that may be required by state law.

Company trademarks or service marks should be registered with both federal and state offices. Most counties, cities, and other localities also require firms to register and obtain a license to do business within their jurisdictions.

Procedures by Business Entity

In addition to the general procedures set forth earlier in this chapter, individuals starting a business should be mindful of the following procedures, which relate more specifically to whichever entity has been chosen and may be required in the specific state in which a business is to operate.

Sole Proprietorships A sole proprietorship can be established with few formalities. It is wise to take the following steps:

- File public notices of registration—such as fictitious business name or doing business as (dba) statements for the name of the enterprise—if required in connection with local licensing regulations.
- Obtain local business licenses, if required.
- Maintain proper financial books and records in accordance with federal and state tax requirements. (Independent audits are not required for the financial statements of a sole proprietorship, although financial institutions may require more formal records in connection with lending.)

Partnerships A few more decisions and steps are needed to establish a partnership than a sole proprietorship. Although these procedures will vary somewhat in accordance with the partnership law of the state where the business is formed, in general the following steps must be taken:

- Determine whether to form a general or limited partnership.

- Negotiate, prepare, and sign a written partnership agreement.
- Record in the office of the county clerk a statement of partnership that has been signed, acknowledged, and verified by two or more partners.
- If creating a limited partnership, comply with state laws that require the filing of certain information about the limited partnership with a state or county official and the publication of this information in a local newspaper. (For a general partnership, no information about the partnership agreement is required to be published.)
- File the statements required by state law to specify the partnership's address, principal place of business, and designated agent for service of process—that is, the person authorized to receive legal claims and actions made against the business.
- File public notices of registration—such as fictitious business name statements for the name of the enterprise—if required in connection with local licensing regulations.
- Obtain local business licenses.
- Maintain proper financial books and records in accordance with federal and state tax requirements, paying particular attention to the tax consequences of any partner's distributive share of partnership income or loss that is either from US sources or effectively connected with a US trade or business. (Refer to the "Taxation" chapter for a discussion of tax treatment.)

Corporations The requirements for incorporation vary from state to state, making the decision of where to incorporate nearly as complicated as the decision of whether to incorporate at all. Fortunately, a business that is incorporated in one state in the US is recognized as a corporation in any other state, although some state and local registration requirements may still need to be met to do business across state lines. The most common steps to be taken to incorporate a business in the US are as follows:

- Prepare and sign articles of incorporation pursuant to the requirements of the state of incorporation, which typically set forth:
  —the name of the corporation
  —the purposes, powers, and authorized capital of the corporation
  —the person designated as agent for service of process.
- Submit articles of incorporation and any other documents required to the secretary of state's office for legal review and filing, along with any required tax payments and filing fees.
- Prepare and sign bylaws of the corporation and any other organizational documents relating to

such matters as the election of corporate officers, issuance of stock, and authorization of important agreements and contracts.
- Obtain from federal and state securities agencies the appropriate permits or exemptions from registration.
- File a fictitious business name statement, if the corporation plans to transact business under a name other than the one stated in its articles of incorporation.
- Obtain local business licenses.
- Maintain proper financial books and records—including a corporate minute book—in accordance with federal and state business and tax requirements.

Joint Ventures Parties who desire to unite their resources in a joint venture should proceed as follows:

- Negotiate, prepare, and sign a written joint venture contract, which should include:
  — the designation of the joint venture parties
  — the contributions and obligations of each joint venturer
  — the purpose of the joint venture
  — the term of the venture
  — the process for distribution of profits and losses.
- Follow any other procedures for establishing either a partnership or corporate entity, as applicable.

Limited Liability Companies To form a limited liability company in the US, parties must follow the laws of the state where the company is being created. In general, the procedures are as follows:

- File a short form called "Articles of Organization" with the secretary of state's office.
- Decide whether a written operating agreement—which functions like a partnership agreement—is desired, and if so, negotiate, prepare, and sign such an agreement.
- Maintain proper financial books and records, and make all appropriate registrations as required for the operation of any business.

Branch or Representative Offices A foreign businessperson may open a branch or representative office in the US by completing the following:

- File requisite certificates and documents with the appropriate state and local government offices, such as: certificates of good standing—indicating that the corporation exists in good standing in the country of its incorporation—together with an English translation if needed; statements providing administrative information about the foreign corporation—usually

filed with the secretary of state's office; and possibly statements on the intended use of a fictitious business name.
- Maintain proper financial books and records and make appropriate filings as required for the operation of any business.

Franchises or Distributorships Persons who desire to do business through a franchise or distributorship should take the following steps to set up such an arrangement:

- Create the form of business organization under

which the franchisee or distributor will operate—that is, sole proprietorship, partnership, corporation, or limited liability company.
- In the case of a franchise, carefully review the franchisor's offering circular and other documents related to the franchise business.
- Negotiate, prepare, and sign a franchise or distribution agreement.
- Conduct business in accordance with the franchise requirements (if applicable) and the laws and regulations relating to the operation of any business.

US ANTITRUST LAWS: LEGAL RESTRICTIONS ON TRADE RESTRAINTS

How US Antitrust Laws May Apply to Foreign Entities

The US antitrust laws seek to encourage competition by prohibiting monopolistic practices and unreasonable restraints on trade in the US. When a foreign business entity sets up a US subsidiary, the foreign entity may become subject to US antitrust laws in at least three important ways. First, any agreements among foreign entities to share markets or fix prices are illegal under US antitrust laws if any consequences of those agreements are felt in the US. This is true even if such agreements are legal in the foreign countries where they were executed. Second, territorial or other trade restrictions in licensing agreements between foreign and US entities may conflict with US antitrust laws. Third, the acquisition of an existing US business by a foreign entity that already exports to the US or that already has either a fixed place of business in the US or a US subsidiary may constitute an unlawful combination, the effect of which would be to reduce competition. Before a foreign investor acquires a US business, it is therefore advisable to determine whether the filing of a pre-acquisition notification with federal antitrust authorities is necessary.

What Laws Apply

The primary US antitrust laws include the Sherman Antitrust Act, the Clayton Act, as amended by the Robinson-Patman Act and other acts, the Federal Trade Commission Act, the Hart-Scott-Rodino Antitrust Improvement Act, and the Exon-Florio provisions of the Omnibus Trade Act. The enforcement of the antitrust laws are within the province of the US Department of Justice (DOJ) and the Federal Trade Commission (FTC). Private litigants may also bring actions under US antitrust laws.

Seek Legal Advice

Prior to making an investment in or entering into an agreement with a US business, a foreign investor or business should obtain legal advice to ensure that the investment is consistent with US antitrust laws. These laws are designed to restrict mergers and acquisitions that may have the effect of substantially lessening competition in the US.

Because antitrust statutes in the US are written in broad and general terms, a review and analysis of recent US federal court decisions is strongly recommended to determine whether the structure of, or a specific provision of, a particular business transaction is permissible. Although federal courts attempt to be consistent, changes in economic and market conditions, the composition of the courts, and the philosophies of individual judges can produce different interpretations and constructions of the antitrust statutes. Because federal courts are constantly interpreting and construing the antitrust statutes and applying their interpretations to different facts, legal advice about antitrust issues depends heavily on the specific details of the transactions and the jurisdictions where they will occur.

Patent Considerations

The existence of a US patent can impact the application of US antitrust laws. US patents are commonly referred to as "negative monopolies" because they give the patent owner the right to preclude others from making, using, or selling the patented article or process. However, the rights granted to a patent owner are not exempt from US antitrust laws. Thus, improper use of patents or improper conduct by patent owners in violation of antitrust laws can result in substantial damage awards, fines, and even prison sentences.

TEN REMINDERS, RECOMMENDATIONS, AND RULES

1. Selection of the most appropriate form of entity is one of the most important decisions facing a new enterprise. Although selection of the proper entity format cannot assure the success of the venture, a wrong choice may contribute to a venture's failure.
2. Because the laws and regulations applicable to establishing and operating a business in the US are spread throughout federal, state, and local sources, advice from legal and accounting professionals familiar with the specific jurisdiction of interest is essential.
3. US laws and regulations and their interpretations are constantly changing. Businesspeople, foreign and domestic alike, find it helpful to belong to chambers of commerce, business associations, and other organizations that monitor legislative, judicial, and economic changes and make regular reports of their findings to their members.
4. The attitude of the federal government toward foreign investment in the US is generally one of laissez-faire: very little is done at the federal level to encourage or discourage such investment. However, on the state and local level attitudes may differ considerably. Some areas may be very supportive of foreign investment and actively solicit it, while other areas may be less encouraging and possibly resentful of foreign investment. Check the political, demographic, and economic conditions in your particular area of interest before proceeding to form a business entity.
5. If several investments or lines of business are contemplated, the creation of a holding company with separate subsidiaries for each investment or enterprise should be considered.
6. Any foreign individual or entity that conducts business in the US is required to obtain the same necessary permissions and registrations as a US person or entity before undertaking any business.
7. Foreign individuals and entities generally can own land in the US, subject to certain limitations and reporting requirements. (Refer to the "Foreign Investment" chapter for a discussion of reserved and restricted foreign investment activities.)
8. Depending on the nature of the investment and the desired business structure, tax matters may be very complex; all tax considerations should be evaluated as part of your decision-making procedure, not after the fact.
9. Political experts anticipate greater focus on immigration matters in the US, aimed principally at decreasing the flow of illegal immigration. Therefore, all foreign persons entering the US to pursue business opportunities should be careful that all immigration documents and approvals are in order and validly maintained. (Refer to the "Business Travel" chapter for a more complete discussion.)
10. Once your business entity is established, pay regular attention to the maintenance of business records, making and updating registrations and filings, and paying all taxes and fees required on time.

FURTHER READING

The preceding discussion is provided as a basic guide for those interested in doing business in the US. The resources described in this section provide additional information on business law, investment, taxation, accounting, and procedural requirements.

Doing Business in the United States, Ernst & Young. New York: Ernst & Young International, Ltd., 1994. Available in the US from: Ernst & Young, 787 Seventh Avenue, New York, NY 10019, USA; Tel: [1] (212) 773-3000. Also available in more than 120 other countries in which Ernst & Young maintains local offices. Provides an overview of the investment environment in the US, together with information about taxation, business organizational structures, business practices, and accounting requirements.

Doing Business in the United States, Price Waterhouse. Los Angeles: Price Waterhouse World Firm Limited, 1992, with 1993 supplement. Available in the US from: Price Waterhouse, 1251 Avenue of the Americas, New York, NY 10020, USA; Tel: [1] (212) 819-5000. Also available from local offices throughout the US. Covers the investment and business environment in the US and audit, accounting, and taxation requirements.

Investment in the United States, KPMG Peat Marwick, LLP. New York: KPMG Peat Marwick, LLP, 1994. Available in the US from: KPMG Peat Marwick, LLP, 345 Park Avenue, New York, NY 10154-0102, USA, Tel: [1] (212) 758-9700. Also available from Peat Marwick offices worldwide. Provides an overview of opportunities for international investors exporting to or from the US, structure of business entities, business and indirect taxation, taxation of individuals, labor regulations, the US banking system, and government controls.

Guia Legal Para Inversiones y Negocios en los Estados Unidos (Legal Guide to Investment and Business in the United States), Carlsmith Ball Wichman Case & Ichiki. Los Angeles: Carlsmith Ball Wichman Case & Ichiki. Available in Spanish in the US from Carlsmith Ball Wichman Case & Ichiki, 555 South Flower Street, 25th Floor, Los Angeles, CA 90071, USA, Tel. [1] (213) 955-1235 (Contact: Carlos J. Valderama). Also available from the firm's Mexico

City office and through CEMCAPSE, the Mexican publisher. Provides an overview of US business organizations, taxation, structuring of investments and business operations, investment regulations, banks and financing, importing and exporting, business regulation, intellectual property rights, labor relations, commercial transactions, product liability, and immigration.

Direct Investment in North America, Bureau of National Affairs International. Available in the US from: Bureau of National Affairs International, 1231 25th St., NW, Washington, DC 20037, USA; Tel: [1] (202) 833-7470. Monthly reference news and analysis service on topics relating to direct foreign investment in Canada, Mexico, and the US.

Martindale-Hubbell Law Directory, 121 Chanlon Road, New Providence, NJ 07974, USA; Tel: (800) 526-4902 (customer service). Annual directory of attorneys, services, suppliers, and consultants by state; provides biographical profiles and areas of expertise.

USEFUL ADDRESSES

Individuals or firms interested in establishing a business in the US should first contact the appropriate government regulatory agencies for information, forms, and tips on the legal requirements. (*See* the sidebar "Regulatory Agency" in this chapter.) In addition, much useful assistance and information is available from the secretary of state's office in each state, national and local chambers of commerce, state and local industrial or economic development offices, embassies, banks and other financial service firms, local consultants, legal and accounting firms, and other resident foreign businesses. Addresses and telephone numbers can be found in local telephone directories. In addition, the contacts that follow offer information and referrals to local resources. (Refer to the "Important Addresses" chapter for more complete listings.)

National Association of Development
Organizations
444 N. Capitol St. NW, #630
Washington, DC 20001, USA
Tel: [1] (202) 624-7806
Fax: [1] (202) 624-8813
Association of organizations located throughout the US that are interested in the local economic development; offers information on national and local development programs.

National Association of State Development
Agencies
750 First Street NE, #710
Washington, DC 20002, USA
Tel: [1] (202) 898-1302
Fax: [1] (202) 898-1312
Association of the directors of state economic development agencies: sponsors conferences and consulting services with emphasis on promotion of state and local business development.

National Association of Manufacturers
1331 Pennsylvania Ave. NW, #1500
Washington, DC 20004, USA
Tel: [1] (202) 637-3000, 637-3099
Fax: [1] (202) 637-3182
Association that represents interests of its members to US government offers information on legislative developments, and conducts programs on such business issues as labor relations, job safety and health, regulatory concerns, and consumer affairs.

National Development Council
3921 Albemarle St. NW
Washington, DC 20016, USA
Tel: [1] (202) 364-9641
Fax: [1] (202) 364-9648
Council established to assist low-income communities in expanding economic development, such as by seeking long-term financing and promoting increased employment opportunities.

US Chamber of Commerce
1615 H St., NW
Washington, DC 20062, USA
Tel: [1] (202) 659-6000, 468-5652 (publications), 463-5460 (international division)
Fax: [1] (202) 463-5836
Federation of businesses, trade, and professional associations and state and local chambers of commerce; maintains a business forecast and survey center and monitors legislation.

Labor*

INTRODUCTION

The relationship between employers and employees in the US is complex. Federal, state, and local governments frequently pass new laws and amend old laws to regulate the workplace. Federal and state courts constantly issue decisions that interpret and reinterpret the laws. Employers in the US must adopt personnel management systems that comply with all of these various laws and court decisions. Because the laws and rules constantly change, employers must keep track of the changes and modify their management systems to remain in compliance.

Employers in the US must also cope with demographic shifts in the labor force. While the labor force is still primarily comprised of educated White males, its composition is rapidly changing. New workers are increasingly female and non-White. Moreover, many of the new workers have lower skill levels, have received minimal education, and bring with them different cultural backgrounds and perceptions. These demographic shifts have resulted in conflicts between old and new workers, management and new workers, and additional laws that attempt to address the changes in the labor force.

This chapter provides basic information on the size and characteristics of the US labor force, as well as projections on the available labor pool for the next 5 to 10 years. The statistics provided in the chapter are estimates of national averages published by the US Department of Labor (DOL), Bureau of Labor Statistics, or the US Bureau of the Census. The actual number of workers available to a particular employer depends on the location of the worksite, the type of industry the employer is engaged in, and the type of job being offered, although in general labor availability is good in the US at all skill levels.

This chapter also includes general information on the employment laws, labor costs, and employment practices that companies must contend with if they employ workers in the US. Information on these topics is confined to federal laws, national averages published by the Bureau of Labor Statistics, and generally accepted practices. The specific laws, costs, and practices applicable to a particular employer also depend on the employer's location, industry, and job offerings.

CONTENTS

CHARACTERISTICS OF THE US LABOR FORCE

Population and Labor Force Growth

During the 1950s the population of the US grew at a rate of almost 1.9 percent per year. The population growth rate is expected to slow to 0.7 percent per year by the year 2000, when total population is

* By Duane H. Zobrist, Anna Elento-Sneed, and Patrick H. Jones. Copyright © 1995 Carlsmith Ball Wichman Case & Ichiki. Reprinted with permission of that law firm.

POPULATION GROWTH RATE
By Region

Area	1979–1992	1992–2005
West	30%	24%
Midwest	3%	7%
South	19%	16%
Northeast	4%	3%

expected to reach 276 million.

The slower growth rate of the population has been matched by an easing in the growth rate of the labor force. During the 1970s the US labor force grew at a rate of 2.9 percent per year. During the latter part of this century, the rate is expected to drop to 1 percent per year. By the year 2000 the US labor force is predicted to reach approximately 141 million and increase slowly to 151 million by the year 2005.

The actual growth in the US population and labor force may be higher, depending on the rate of immigration. The Bureau of the Census estimates that legal immigration into the US will be approximately 450,000 per year for the balance of the century. At this rate, legal immigration would add about 9.5 million people to the US population and 4 million to the labor force. If estimates of legal and illegal immigration are combined, the number of annual immigrants to the US increases to 750,000 people. At that rate, immigration would add 16.1 million people to the population and 6.8 million to the labor force.

Increases in the population and the labor force are not evenly distributed across the US. Recent immigrants, who are mostly from Latin America and Asia, have tended to settle in the South and West. Three states—California, Texas, and New York—together account for more than one half of all foreign-born residents. California will be particularly affected by immigration, with two-fifths of its population estimated to be either Hispanic or Asian by the year 2000. Primarily as a result of these immigration patterns, the South and the West have been and will continue to be among the fastest growing regions of the US in the latter part of this century.

Age, Sex, and Racial Composition of the Labor Force

Although the size of the US population and labor force are expected to grow slowly, the composition of the labor force is rapidly changing. Three important demographic shifts in the labor force account for this change.

Aging US Labor Force In 1970, 42 percent of the labor force were between the ages of 16 and 34, 40 percent were between 35 and 54, and 18 percent were 55 or older. By the year 2000, 38 percent of the labor force will be between the ages of 16 and 34, 51 percent will be between 35 and 54, and 11 percent will be 55 or older.

The increasing average age of the labor force is attributable to a sharp increase in the US birth rate between 1946 and 1961. Children born during this period (referred to as baby boomers) began entering the labor force in the mid-1960s. These workers dramatically increased the size of the labor force and decreased the average age of US workers. As the baby boomers have aged, the average age of the US labor force has risen correspondingly. Moreover, while previous generations of workers have tended to drop out of the labor force after age 55, baby boomers tend to remain in the labor force longer. As a consequence, the percentage of older workers (age 55 and older) is projected to grow twice as fast as the total labor force, accounting for 14 percent of the labor force by the year 2005.

Women in the Workforce The number of women in the labor force has increased dramatically and will continue to increase through the end of the century. In 1950 women comprised 29.6 percent of the US labor force. By 1979 their share had increased to 42 percent. By the year 2005 projections are that women will comprise 48 percent of the total labor force. The majority of these working women are married and come from families with children.

The rapid increase in the number of women working outside the home is due to social and economic factors: the slow growth in the US economy that has made two wage earner families necessary; increases in the number of single family households headed by women; advances in technology and infrastructure that have reduced the time and labor required for managing a home; and the women's liberation movement, which has redefined the role of women in US society. These factors have made women the fastest-growing segment of the US labor force. In fact between the years 1985 and 2000, two-thirds to three-fifths of all entrants into the US labor force will be women.

While most women workers still tend to be concentrated in traditionally female (or pink collar) jobs, which pay less than men's jobs, that pattern is changing. The number of women in traditionally male jobs is increasing rapidly, particularly in occupations requiring an advanced education. For example, in 1970 women comprised 18.5 percent of executives and administrators, 34.4 percent of technicians, and 44 percent of all professionals. By 1983 women comprised 32.4 percent of executives and administrators, 48.4 percent of technicians, and 48.1 percent of all professionals. This trend is expected to continue for the balance of the century.

Changing Racial Composition The racial composition of the US labor force is also changing. Immigration and higher birth rates will result in substantial increases in the number of African-American, Hispanic, and Asian workers. For example, in 1992 the racial composition of the labor force was 78 percent White, 11 percent Black, 8 percent Hispanic, and 3 percent Asian or other. By 2005 the racial breakdown will be 73 percent White, 11 percent Black, 11 percent Hispanic, and 5 percent Asian or other. The concentration of minorities will be far greater in many of the nation's major regional labor markets.

The increase in non-White and immigrant workers is even more evident in the racial composition of new workers. Blacks, Hispanics, Asians, and other racial groups will account for approximately 35 percent of all labor force entrants between 1992 and 2005. Hispanics alone are projected to add 6.5 million workers to the labor force. However, the largest share of the increase in the non-White labor force is expected to be among Black women.

Education Levels of the Labor Force

The US has a laissez-faire approach to education, and there are few national education standards or policies. Control over schools and educational curricula is delegated to local government systems and privately operated institutions. As a result, the type of education (subjects and skills) offered to students varies widely.

The amount of education received by students in the US also varies. Compulsory school attendance is limited to children from age 6 to 18 (16 in some states) and is divided into grammar, middle, and high school training. Students who successfully complete this process are generally able to read and write English, to compute with arithmetic and perform simple algebra, and to have a rudimentary knowledge of certain social and natural sciences. Many high school graduates seek advanced or specialized education at a college, university, or trade school. However, advanced education is neither required nor guaranteed in the US. Entrance to such schools is limited to a finite number of students, primarily those with the necessary financial resources to afford it or the ability to qualify for scholarships and financial aid.

Despite this hands-off approach to education, the US has produced a generally well-educated labor force. In 1993, 88 percent of US workers were high school graduates and 53 percent of workers had either some college education or a college degree. The trend toward higher educational attainment is expected to continue as the country's economy shifts toward the service and high-tech industries.

However, the trend toward higher education is not equally distributed among the US labor force. Primarily because of social and economic factors, non-White workers are less likely to have received the same level of education as White workers. For example, in 1993 approximately 11 percent of White workers had less than a high school education, as compared with 16 percent for Blacks and 38 percent for workers of Hispanic origin. At the other extreme of educational attainment, 28 percent of White workers were college graduates as compared with 17 percent for Blacks and 12 percent for workers of Hispanic origin.

Educational attainment of immigrants is even lower. Of adults who entered the US in the 1970s, approximately 25 percent had fewer than five years of schooling, as compared with 3 percent for native-born US citizens. Many of these new workers lack even the basic skills essential for employment. Moreover, language, attitude, and cultural conditioning may prevent them from taking full advantage of the jobs that will become available between now and the end of the century.

Impact of Demographic Shifts

The demographic shifts in the US labor force will have a significant impact on the work relationships between employers and employees. Areas that will be affected include the following.

Worker Productivity As mentioned earlier, baby boomers tend to remain in the workforce longer. These workers provide employers with a large pool of stable, educated, and skilled workers which, in turn, increases worker productivity. However, this increase in productivity will erode as the US economy shifts from a core manufacturing base to one primarily based on service with a mix of high-tech industries. As the

UNEMPLOYMENT RATES FOR WORKERS AGE 25–64

Education	1970	1980	1985	1990
Total	3.3%	5.0%	6.1%	4.4%
Less than a high school education	4.6	8.4	11.4	8.5
High school graduate	2.9	5.1	6.9	4.9
College 1–3 years	2.9	4.3	4.7	3.7
College 4 or more years	1.3	1.9	2.4	2.2

UNEMPLOYMENT RATES
For Persons Age 16 and Over by Race, in States with High Immigration

Race	National	Calif.	New York	Texas
Total	6.8	9.2	7.7	7.0
White	6.0	8.9	6.7	6.0
Black	12.9	14.9	12.9	14.0
Hispanic	10.6	12.4	12.9	8.9

economy changes, employers in low-growth industries will have to become increasingly efficient to remain competitive. Some employers are also beginning to offer training programs to increase worker productivity in high-tech systems, personal communications, time management, and similar skills.

Education and Skill Level of Workers As the economy shifts toward service and high-tech industries, the skills required for many of these new jobs will increase. However, a large proportion of new workers entering the labor force are expected to be undereducated immigrants or disadvantaged non-Whites. Thus, employers in the new industries may find it increasingly difficult to recruit qualified workers.

Unemployment Patterns Although unemployment in the US has been relatively low over the past 20 years, the unemployment rate among less educated workers is consistently higher than the na-

tional average.

Moreover, unemployment rates among non-Whites also tend to be higher than the national average. For example, in 1993 the national unemployment rate for the civilian noninstitutional population age 16 and over was estimated at 6.8 percent. However, the corresponding unemployment rate for Blacks was estimated at 12.9 percent and at 10.6 percent for persons of Hispanic origin. (*See* chart above.)

Areas of the US with high numbers of immigrants have also experienced higher than average unemployment. As shown in the above chart, the unemployment rate in 1993 for the civilian noninstitutional population age 16 and over was estimated at 9.2 percent in California, 7.7 percent in New York, and 7.0 percent in Texas. The unemployment rates are even higher for non-Whites in those states.

Preliminary estimates as of September 1994 show a similar pattern. Unemployment was estimated at 5.9 percent for the nation as a whole, 8.3 percent for California, 6.2 percent for New York, and 6.2 percent for Texas.

With the demand for more educated workers increasing and the demand for less skilled workers decreasing, the net result will be higher unemployment among less educated workers. Disadvantaged non-White US citizens and immigrants will also represent a disproportionately large share of the unemployed. Conversely, employers may find it more difficult and expensive to fill high-skill positions from a proportionately smaller skilled labor pool. This problem could become noticeable in the immediate future. At the end of 1994 the overall unemployment rate was 5.4 percent, below the 6 percent theoretical full employment rate traditionally accepted by

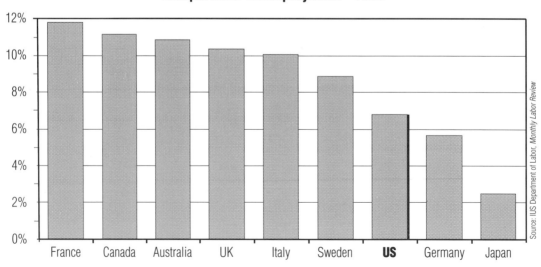

Comparative Unemployment - 1993

Source: US Department of Labor, *Monthly Labor Review*

Note: Calculated based on US labor force definitions, except for minimum age.

most US economists. If this level remains an accurate indicator, the economy will soon begin to feel the effects of competition for the limited pool of skilled workers.

Wages and Benefits The demographic shifts in the labor force may increase labor costs for many employers for several reasons. First, because wages and benefits in the US are generally linked to the number of years an employee works for a company (with more senior employees receiving higher wages and benefits), employers will be required to pay more in wages and benefits as the labor force ages.

Second, the increasing number of women in the labor force will create pressure on employers to provide additional benefits such as childcare services and flexible work hours. The federal government has already begun enacting employment laws designed to address the increased number of women in the work place. (*See* discussion of the Family and Medical Leave Act in the "Federal Labor and Employment Laws" section later in this chapter.)

Third, employers unable to find sufficient numbers of educated or skilled workers may be forced to hire less qualified employees, which would result in lower productivity. These employers may find it necessary to provide company paid education programs to train the less qualified applicants in the necessary skills.

Fourth, employers that wish to reduce the size of their existing workforces for productivity or economic reasons may find the process equally expensive. In the US, the general practice is to provide an employee whose job has been eliminated with a severance benefit designed to give the ex-employee a source of income while seeking alternative employment. The cost of the severance benefit increases with the length of employment, and sometimes takes into account the expected time it will take to find or retrain for a new job.

Finally, employers in new industries (especially high-tech companies) may find their pool of qualified workers shrinking, particularly if baby boomers are unable to retrain themselves in the new skills necessary for these jobs. Accordingly, wages and benefits for skilled workers may increase as competition rises among employers trying to attract qualified labor from a smaller pool.

While labor costs for many employers will increase, some employers may find that their labor costs remain stable. Employers who require unskilled labor will find an increasingly large pool of unemployed workers from which to hire. Without government action to increase the minimum wage (which was suggested by the Clinton Administration in early 1995, but was opposed by the majority party in Congress) or benefits required by law, the labor costs for such workers should remain relatively low.

Employee Morale As the labor force has become more diversified, conflicts between old and new workers have increased correspondingly. Older workers unable to adapt to technological changes have become increasingly more critical of employers that hire younger workers to fill new positions. Women entering the labor force—and particularly women in traditionally male jobs—have encountered resistance from male coworkers. Increasing numbers of non-White employees, especially those who speak little or no English, are experiencing cultural and linguistic communication problems with English-speaking employees. The apparent result of these changes has been a dramatic increase in the number of lawsuits—especially discrimination complaints—being filed against employers.

Employment Laws In the US, most employment laws are enacted to address perceived societal problems. As the US economy shifts to service and high-tech industries and the composition of the labor force changes, increasing political pressure will be brought to bear on government to enact laws to deal with the effects of the change. Some of the laws will be designed, like the Family and Medical Leave Act was, to encourage changes in employment practices that reflect changes in the labor force. Other laws—like those requiring workers to show proof of US residency—are intended to discourage changes in the make-up of the labor force. Regardless of the purpose, the ultimate result will be additional employment laws and changes in existing laws; employers will have to adapt to the changes in order to do business in the US.

HIRING, MANAGING, AND FIRING EMPLOYEES IN THE US

In the early 1900's, the relationship between an employer and employee was one of master and servant. The employer (the master) could freely determine hiring criteria for the employees (the servants) and could unilaterally set the terms and conditions under which those employees would work. The employer was also free to discharge an employee at any time, with or without advance notice and for any reason or no reason at all. Beginning in the 1930s, the federal and state governments began passing laws to regulate the relationship between employers and their employees. These laws regulate many areas of employment including the criteria that can be used by an employer in hiring, managing, and firing employees. During the last 20 years, federal and state courts have adopted judicial rules that further regulate employer conduct.

The following is a brief summary of the legal restrictions placed on employers in hiring, managing, and firing employees.

Hiring Employees

Equal Employment Opportunity Federal laws prohibit employers from making employment decisions on the basis of race, color, national origin, religion, age, sex, physical or mental disability, veteran status, or citizenship. However, it is against the law to employ aliens who are not authorized to work in the US. Some states additionally prohibit employers from making employment decisions on the basis of ancestry, marital status, sexual orientation, work-related injury, or arrest and court records. Employers who make decisions based on such protected classifications are said to be engaging in discrimination.

Because of the antidiscrimination laws, an employer may not hire or refuse to hire someone based on whether that person is within a protected classification. There are exceptions to this rule, but the exceptions are few and extremely difficult to apply to most employment situations. Accordingly, an employer in the US is expected to hire based solely on the applicant's qualifications for the job. Failure to comply with the antidiscrimination laws may result in government investigations, lawsuits, and fines.

Reasonable Accommodation of the Disabled In 1990 the US Congress enacted the Americans with Disabilities Act (ADA). This law prohibits employers from discriminating against individuals with physical or mental disabilities. It also requires employers to: (1) provide compensation, benefits, and working conditions to disabled employees equal to those provided to nondisabled employees; and (2) provide reasonable accommodation to applicants and employees whose disabilities would otherwise prevent them from performing the essential functions of their jobs. Failure to comply with the ADA may result in a federal government investigation, lawsuits, and fines.

The ADA is the most complex and comprehensive employment law enacted in the last 20 years. In essence, it forces employers to identify and document the essential functions of each job classification within the operation. The new law also restricts an employer's ability to question job applicants about their physical and mental abilities. As a consequence, more and more employers in the US are seeking professionals (attorneys, consultants, and physicians) to assist them in the selection and hiring of employees, adding an additional layer to the cost structure.

Verification of Legal Work Status Illegal immigration has been a source of concern in the US in recent years. A great deal of the controversy surrounding this issue centers around the belief that immigrants take jobs that would otherwise go to US citizens and overburden the country's social welfare services. The validity of these claims is in dispute, particularly because the overwhelming number of illegal workers hold low-paying jobs. (Refer to the "Current Issues" chapter for a further discussion of this question.) Nevertheless, as a consequence of this belief, increasing political pressure has been placed on the federal government to halt the flow of illegal immigrants into the country.

In 1986 Congress enacted the Immigration Reform and Control Act (IRCA). Under this federal law, all new employees are required to provide documentation that verifies their identity and proves that they are legally authorized to work in the US. Employers and new employees are also required to complete and retain a form (INS Form I-9) that certifies this information. Failure to comply with these procedures can result in a government investigation and fines.

In essence, IRCA shifts the burden for ensuring that illegal aliens are not employed in the US from the government to the employers. As noted above, legal and illegal immigration is expected to continue at the same rapid pace for the remainder of this century. If economic conditions do not improve—particularly in areas of the US where the economy remains weak and illegal immigration high—additional restrictions may be placed on employers to discourage the use of illegal aliens.

Written and Implied Employment Contracts In the US, it is common for an employer to inform a prospective employee about the wages, benefits, and working conditions to expect while employed by the company. Generally, this information is communicated in one of four ways.

First, some employers enter into written employment contracts with individual employees. Employment contracts are legally binding agreements between an employer and an employee. The contract specifies the exact terms and conditions under which the employee will work. Typically, these terms and conditions include provisions on the length of employment; the employee's duties, wages, and benefits; and the circumstances under which the employee can be discharged from employment. If one party to the contract fails to comply with a particular provision, the other party to the contract can take legal action to enforce the agreement.

Second, employers can enter into written employment contracts with groups of employees. These contracts—called collective bargaining agreements—can only be negotiated with a union certified by the federal government as the collective bargaining representative for the particular group of employees. (The process through which a place of employment becomes unionized and negotiates with a union is discussed later in this chapter in "Unions and Collective Bargaining in the US".)

Third, many employers prepare a summary of personnel policies and practices that is given to each newly hired employee. The written summary (often referred to as a personnel manual or an employee handbook) can be used as a mechanism for complying with employment laws requiring distribution of certain written information to employees. For example, if an employer adopts certain types of employee benefits— such as medical, pension, severance, or life insurance benefits—federal law requires the employer to establish a written plan that details the procedures used by the employer to administer the plan.

Court decisions indicate that a written summary may result in legal obligations for an employer, depending on the language used in the summary. As a result, many employers seek assistance from professional consultants or attorneys in preparing such documents.

Finally, some employers verbally communicate information to prospective employees about the terms and conditions of employment. Because of court decisions, an employer must be extremely careful about the verbal statements made to potential employees. Promises made to job applicants can result in legal obligations once the employees begin working for the company.

Managing Employees

Health and Safety Federal and state laws regulate the physical conditions under which employees must work. Most of these laws are designed to preserve minimum health and safety standards for employees (such as access to restroom facilities, provision of safety equipment, and access to medical attention in case of accidents). Employers should be careful to ascertain their responsibilities under any federal and state laws that apply to their particular industries. Failure to comply with health and safety laws could result in severe penalties and even closure of the business.

Relationships Between Coworkers In the US, supervisors and managers are considered the employer's representatives. Thus, any actions or statements made by supervisors and managers may be considered to represent the actions and statements of the employer. If a supervisor or manager takes an action or makes a statement that is unlawful, the employer may be held legally responsible for the supervisor's or manager's conduct. Therefore, employers need to provide carefully tailored training to supervisors and managers to ensure that the employers' interests are appropriately represented and policies properly carried out. This is particularly important if the supervisor or manager has the authority to make regulated employment decisions such as hiring, training, work schedules, wages, benefits, promotions, discipline, or terminations.

Employers are also responsible for ensuring that coworkers do not discriminate against one another in the workplace. Consequently, many employers adopt written policies that prohibit employees from discriminating against one another. These policies often identify the protected classifications and describe the procedures employees may utilize if they feel they are being discriminated against. As the US labor force becomes more diversified and disputes between employees of different racial and cultural backgrounds increase, written antidiscrimination policies will become an increasingly important part of management's efforts to minimize lawsuits and other legal actions against the company.

Harassment Harassment policies are directly related to the federal and state laws that prohibit discrimination. Harassment is generally defined as verbal or physical conduct against an employee based on the employee's membership in a protected class. Thus, an employer's antiharassment policy prohibits employees from harassing one another on the basis of protected classifications.

A particular type of harassment receiving special attention under federal and state laws is sexual harassment. A type of sex discrimination, it is strictly forbidden by law. Unwelcome sexual advances, requests for sexual favors, and other physical, verbal, or non-verbal conduct of a sexual nature constitute sexual harassment when: (1) submission to the conduct is made a condition of employment for an employee; (2) an employee's submission to or rejection of the conduct is used in making employment decisions affecting the employee; or (3) the conduct has the purpose or effect of interfering with the employee's work performance or creating an intimidating, hostile, or offensive working environment for the employee. Employers who engage in, or allow employees to be subjected to, sexual harassment may be heavily penalized under US laws.

Within the last five years, the number of sexual harassment cases in the US has risen dramatically. Part of the phenomenon is due to the increasing number of women in traditionally male jobs. As the two sexes interact in the workplace, conflicts have arisen over work practices and employee conduct. These conflicts often result in claims that one employee is harassing another. A number of sexual harassment cases have received extensive coverage in the US media. The publicity surrounding these cases has served as a catalyst for other employees to file sexual harassment charges against employers. Accordingly, employers in the US are also developing special policies and procedures to deal with this type of workplace conflict.

Work Rules and Discipline It is also common for employers in the US to establish work rules for employees, so that the employees know how to behave at work. There are two types of "work rules": (1) rules that set forth the procedures an employee must follow when performing a job; and (2) rules that set forth the type of conduct an employee is prohibited from engaging in during the course of a workday. Work rules are communicated verbally and in writing.

Not all employees will abide by the work rules established by the employer. However, corporal punishment, physical detention, or fines against such employees are generally unlawful in the US. If an employee violates a work rule, the practice is for the employer to notify the employee of the infraction verbally or in writing so that the employee will understand the problem and not repeat the infraction. Many employers adopt discipline systems to correct employees who commit infractions of work rules. Discipline systems vary from employer to employer. The most common means of discipline include written or verbal warnings, counseling for the employee, suspension from work without pay, and discharge.

Discharge

As previously noted, in the early 1900s, employers were free to discharge employees at any time, with or without notice, for any reason or no reason at all. Today, numerous federal and state laws restrict an employer's ability to discharge employees. US law also enables terminated employees to file legal actions (through government agencies, courts, or union grievance procedures) to overturn an employer's decision. To minimize the risk of legal challenges, many employers have adopted policies and procedures to guide their management in discharging employees. These policies and procedures generally address the following issues.

Reasons for Termination While there are many circumstances under which an employer might initiate discipline or discharge procedures, a common one is misconduct on the part of the employee. Misconduct may take many forms, including insubordination, excessive absenteeism or tardiness, poor work performance, violation of company policies, falsification of time cards or time records, and abuse of sick or personal leave. Although the law prohibits discipline and discharge for certain reasons, genuine misconduct on the part of the employee generally entitles the employer to take appropriate disciplinary action up to and including discharge.

Employers may choose to discharge employees because of economic conditions. Employees who are discharged from their employment because of lack of work are said to have been laid off or to have lost their employment because of a reduction in force (RIF). Again, while there may be legal ramifications for such economic layoffs, an employer is generally allowed to discharge employees because of lack of work.

Legal Restrictions For many years, the general rule regarding discharge of employees in the US has been known as the "at-will" rule. Under this rule,

unless there is an employment contract of definite duration (for an agreed time), an employee can be discharged at any time, for any reason, or for no reason at all. However, this general rule has been greatly modified by both legislation and judicial decisions.

The federal National Labor Relations Act (NLRA) prohibits an employer from discharging an employee because of the employee's union-related activities. In matters of discharge, federal and state laws have also been enacted that make discrimination against a variety of persons who are members of protected classifications unlawful.

More recent laws, including the Federal Worker Adjustment and Retraining Notification Act (WARN), have restricted the employer's right to lay off employees for economic reasons without giving notice. Under WARN's general rules, employers with more than 100 employees must give their employees 60 days' notice if either one of two events occurs: (1) a closure of a single site of employment or a facility that results in an employment loss of at least 50 employees (a plant closing); or, (2) a reduction in force that is not caused by a plant closing and that results in an employment loss of at least 33 percent of the employees and at least 50 employees (a mass layoff). Federal regulations detail the procedures to be taken to meet this notice requirement. Also, some states have enacted legislation requiring specific notice procedures for plant closings or layoffs. Employers should review state requirements when considering economic decisions involving the discharge of significant numbers of employees.

Another legal restriction on the ability of an employer to discharge an employee relates to employees with individual employment contracts. Typically, these contracts include provisions that outline how the employee may be discharged. Employees with such contracts may challenge a decision to discharge by arguing that the employer breached the contract by not following discharge procedures set forth in the contract. Legally, the question of whether an employer has properly followed discharge procedures in an employment contract is determined on a case-by-case basis.

With respect to employment without a formal contract, there has been a large increase in employee challenges to employer discharge actions. More and more former employees are alleging "wrongful discharge" by their employer, and court decisions have created several bases for these wrongful discharge lawsuits. First, almost every state in the US declares that a discharge from employment is unlawful if it violates public policy. For example, if an employer were to discharge an employee to prevent the employee from cooperating in a criminal investigation of the employer's questionable practices, the courts would probably find that this was unlawful because the reason for the discharge violated a clear public policy. Such public policy cases often involve so-called whistle-blowers who claim that they were discharged to prevent them from reporting violations of the law by their managers or their employer.

Another wrongful discharge theory is based on breach of an implied contract. Former employees may challenge their discharges by arguing that they had an implied contractual right to continue in their jobs or that an employer violated its own employment policies. These arguments are often supported with evidence of reliance on written company policies issued as personnel manuals or employee handbooks, allegedly creating implied contracts. Some employers have been successful in defeating such claims by including so-called disclaimer language in their manuals: explicit statements that the manual and the policies contained in it do not constitute a contract.

Finally, a few courts have declared that there is an implied covenant of good faith and fair dealing in the employment relationship. Under this theory, an employer may not lawfully discharge an employee if the discharge breaches the employer's duty to deal fairly and in good faith with its employees. This concept is vague, and many state courts have refused to recognize it as a viable theory in wrongful discharge cases.

In summary, the ability of an employer to discharge its employees is subject to a number of legal challenges. Employers should be careful to review employment contracts and the laws of the state in which they operate to determine which theories of wrongful discharge and which antidiscrimination statutes are in place.

Procedures for Involuntary Separations Because there are several legal theories available to employees to challenge employer discipline and discharge actions, employers in the US take special care to ensure that discharges are made fairly and in a non-discriminatory manner. Employers generally must document the actions they take to investigate and resolve difficulties with employees, including the steps they take in investigating employee conduct and in deciding whether the employee should be discharged. Some employers utilize a system known as progressive discipline, which means that the employer must first warn an employee about problems, then take increasingly stronger steps (for example, suspension) before discharging the employee. Such a system is not mandated by law, but these steps may be helpful in protecting against wrongful discharge challenges by former employees.

Employers are also careful to provide proper separation procedures (known as outprocessing) for employees who have been discharged; many employers adopt procedures to conduct exit interviews with employees leaving the company for any reason. In this interview, the employee is given a chance to discuss his or her experiences with the company. The exit interview gives an employer the opportunity to provide a final paycheck to an employee and to explain any postemployment benefits, including continued health coverage, that are available under federal law.

Voluntary Separations Employees may voluntarily resign or quit their employment under almost any circumstances. Employees who voluntarily resign are generally outprocessed in the same manner as employees who are involuntarily terminated.

In the US, employees may also retire from employment at a certain point. Although mandatory retirement at a certain age is generally unlawful in the US under both federal and state law, many employees who elect to retire receive retirement payments and other benefits provided by their employers. However, because the increase in the number of aging baby boomers and sharply rising costs are increasing the expenses of providing such benefits, within the next five years employers may be reconsidering the type of benefits provided to retirees.

Forums for Legal Challenges to Discipline and Discharge In the US employees utilize several different forums to challenge employer-imposed discipline or employer-initiated discharges. The following discussion outlines three types of procedures that employees follow to challenge such actions by the employer.

First, some employees seek private *arbitration* to determine the validity of the employer's decision to discipline or discharge. Arbitration clauses are increasingly common in individual employment contracts. Moreover, almost all union contracts include arbitration clauses, which commonly state that the employer must have "just cause" to take disciplinary or discharge actions. Arbitrators are usually selected by mutual agreement of the parties or are appointed by the American Arbitration Association. Arbitrations are relatively informal and can result in fairly quick resolution of employment disputes.

Second, to challenge discipline or discharge actions with which they do not agree, employees may raise a variety of *administrative complaints* to governmental agencies. Employees may approach agencies that handle claims of employment discrimination based on race, sex, age, and other protected classifications. At the federal level, the Equal Employment Opportunity Commission (EEOC) handles such complaints. The various states have their own administrative agency counterparts to the EEOC for similar complaints at the state level.

Employees may also approach state or federal

OVERVIEW OF WAGES IN THE US

Wages vary widely by industry, occupation, and geographic location. Some examples follow.

With respect to industry variations, private sector production or nonsupervisory employees as a whole averaged earnings of US$443.60 per week (US$11.09 per hour) as of May 1994. But by specific industry, such workers earned US$583.60 per week (US$14.59 per hour) in the construction industry; US$480.40 per week (US$12.01 per hour) in manufacturing industries; US$479.20 per week (US$11.98 per hour) in wholesale trade; US$441.20 per week (US$11.03 per hour) in services industries; and US$298.80 per week (US$7.47 per hour) in retail trade. For all of 1995 overall employment costs (wages, salaries, and benefits) rose by 3 percent. By sector, production employment costs rose by 3.1 percent, while those in the services sector rose by 2.9 percent; white collar costs rose by 3.2 percent and blue collar and service costs rose by 2.8 percent. The 1994 rise was the smallest since the government began keeping this statistic in 1981. Rises in employment costs have been slowing since 1989.

With respect to occupation, males holding full-time executive, administrative, and managerial positions as of March 1993 had median weekly earnings of US$817.48 (based on median annual earnings of US$42,509.00). Male machine operators, assemblers, and inspectors had median weekly earnings of US$459.31 (based on median annual earnings of US$23,884.00).

With respect to geographic location, average weekly pay of all workers in New York, NY, in 1992 was US$746.19 (based on annual average pay of US$38,802.00); in Dallas, TX, this figure was US$576.88 (based on annual average pay of US$29,998.00); in San Diego, CA, it was US$502.94 (based on annual average pay of $26,153.00).

In all industries, the unionization of the workforce also impacts wage rates. For example, as of 1993 full-time workers represented by unions had median usual weekly earnings of US$569.00; full-time workers not represented by unions had median usual weekly earnings of US$426.00.

administrative agencies with complaints about wages, administration of benefits, or alleged safety violations. Government agencies have a considerable amount of discretion in conducting investigations and have the ability to subpoena records and otherwise inquire into company operations. It is often mandatory that an agency determination be made before an employee is allowed to pursue an action in court.

Finally, former employees are increasingly resorting to *the courts* to challenge employer-initiated decisions to discharge. Employees may sue in federal and state courts, alleging unlawful discrimination, wrongful discharge, unlawful denial of wages or benefits, and related claims that range from negligence to defamation to invasion of privacy. Litigation in federal or state courts is an expensive and time-consuming procedure, regardless of whether the employer can prevail against the merits of the employee's claim. Once a lawsuit is filed, the employee challenging the discharge will have access to most company records concerning the decision to discharge the employee. Additionally, the employer, managers, and supervisors involved in the decision to discharge would probably be involved in pretrial depositions and other discovery.

Lawsuits are particularly dangerous for the employer, because some of the claims that may be brought in lawsuits open the possibility for the former employee to recover punitive damages. Punitive damages are designed to punish the wrongdoer and are, therefore, imposed in addition to compensatory damages, which are designed to compensate the injured party for the costs arising from the harmful conduct. The amount of punitive damages awarded depends on such factors as the egregiousness of the harm, the maliciousness of the conduct, and the employer's net worth and ability to pay.

WAGES AND BENEFITS OF EMPLOYEES IN THE US

The compensation package (wages and benefits) paid by employers to their employees is, like other aspects of the employment relationship in the US, complex and subject to changes that must be carefully monitored. These changes interact with larger changes in the labor force. For example, the increased role of women in the labor force has created the demand for flexible working hours, job-sharing arrangements, childcare benefits, and parental leave. These types of issues are already being addressed by both government and private sector actions, and employers operating in the US can expect such modifications to continue.

Legal Requirements for Wage Payments

General Hour Requirements Before wages can

be determined, an employer in the US first establishes the hours of work for employees. In setting work hours, several components are taken into account. First, federal law requires an employer to establish a workweek that consists of seven consecutive 24-hour days. Once the seven-day workweek is established, the employer then designates the workweek for each particular employee. Some state laws limit the total number of days an employee can work per workweek. Generally, most employers will schedule employees to work five days per workweek, with two days off for rest. However, depending on the state laws that apply to the employer, it may also be possible to establish a shorter or longer workweek for an employee.

Second, an employer generally establishes the total number of hours an employee will work each workday. Although few regulations govern the maximum number of hours an employee may work during a workday, there are "overtime" laws that require extra pay for employees who are required to work longer than eight hours in any particular workday. Consequently, many US employers establish eight hours as the normal workday for an employee. Other employers—especially those whose employees are primarily white-collar workers in major markets—establish a 7 or 7.5 hour workday with a paid lunch period.

Third, some state laws require employers to provide break periods for employees during the workday. These break periods are generally used as rest periods or meal periods by employees. Breaks are scheduled by employers for each employee in accordance with state laws.

Fourth, federal law and some state laws require employers to keep records of the time worked by employees during the workweek. Generally, these time records indicate the date the employee came to work, the time the employee reported to work, the time the employee completed work, and the total number of hours worked by the employee during the workweek. Employers who fail to maintain proper time records for their employees can be penalized under federal and state laws.

General Wage Requirements After the work hours for employees have been established, the employer can determine the wages that will be paid for work performed. As noted, wage rates are generally determined by a number of factors including the nature of the work performed, the wage rates paid by other companies in the same area for similar work, and the employer's own finances. However, there are also federal and state laws that must be taken into account.

Federal law requires employers to pay employees a minimum wage of US$4.25 per hour, and some states may require an even higher minimum wage. Federal law further requires an employer to pay overtime compensation to employees who work more than 40 hours per workweek. Overtime compensation is defined as 1.5 times the employee's regular rate of pay. Thus, if an employee is paid US$10.00 per hour and works 42 hours in one workweek, the employer would be required to pay that employee $430.00 for the week (US$10.00 per hour for the first 40 hours of work plus US$15.00 per hour for two overtime hours).

In addition to considering federal and state laws on wage rates, an employer also determines the

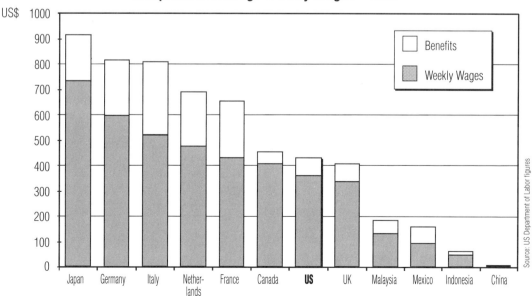

Comparative Average Weekly Wages - 1992

Source: US Department of Labor figures

method by which wages will be paid. The two most common methods are hourly wages and salaries. Hourly wages consist of a set wage rate that is paid to an employee for each hour of work. A salary, on the other hand, is a predetermined monthly or yearly sum of money that is paid to an employee for work performed regardless of the number of hours the employee actually works. Generally, salaries are paid to employees in higher level positions within the company (such as managers, professional employees, or high level administrators). Employers in some industries pay on a piecework basis, or by the task completed, although this is becoming less common.

The employer must also determine how often employees are paid, and on what dates. Some states specify the number of times an employee must be paid each month, such as semimonthly. (Most employers try to pay employees at least twice a month.) Payments are generally made through payroll checks issued by the employer or on behalf of the employer by a payroll service. Paychecks include statements that explain how the employee's pay for that pay period was calculated. For example, the pay statement would specify the number of hours worked during the payroll period, the number of overtime hours worked during the payroll period, and the total amount of pay earned by the employee. In addition, pay statements also specify whether deductions have been taken from the employee's earnings for items such as social security taxes, federal and state income taxes, and other amounts authorized by the employee.

Federal and state laws require employers to keep accurate records of all payments made to employees.

Child Labor Laws Federal and state laws restrict the employment of youths in a number of ways. Under federal law, the permissible jobs and hours of work, by age, in nonfarm work are as follows.

- Youths 18 years of age or older may perform any job for unlimited hours.
- Youths 16 and 17 years of age may perform any job not declared hazardous by the US Secretary of Labor, for unlimited hours.
- Youths 14 and 15 years of age may work outside school hours in various nonmanufacturing, nonmining, nonhazardous jobs under the following conditions: no more than 3 hours on a school day, 18 hours in a school week, 8 hours during a nonschool day, or 40 hours in a nonschool week. In addition, youths 14 and 15 years of age may neither begin work before 7:00 am nor work after 7:00 pm, except from June 1 through approximately September 1 (when the Labor Day holiday occurs), at which time evening hours may be extended until 9:00 pm.
- Children younger than 14 years of age may not be legally employed in regular nonfarm work.

As with other wage and hour provisions, child labor laws require detailed recordkeeping, and violations of these laws can result in civil and criminal penalties.

Prevailing Wage Laws for Government Contractors Companies that obtain contracts from the federal or state government must pay their employees in a manner regulated by the DOL or by the appropriate state agencies. The general term used for such compensation is the prevailing wage. Under the federal Davis-Bacon Act and its state counterparts, companies that obtain government contracts must pay their employees at least the wages set by government wage determinations for the type of work involved. Failure to comply with these regulations may result in civil and criminal penalties.

Overview of US Employee Benefits

In addition to wages, the other major component of compensation for employees in the US is employer-provided employee benefits. Federal and state laws require employers to provide certain basic employee benefits. In addition, employers commonly offer nonmandatory benefits to attract and retain qualified employees.

The type and quality of benefits vary from employer to employer, although some benefits are almost universally provided. In 1991, for example, 96 percent of medium-sized or large private US employers (that is, employers with more than 100 employees) provided paid vacation time to their workers; 92 percent provided paid holidays; and 67 percent provided paid sick leave. Benefits usually cost US employers an amount equal to between one-quarter and two-fifths of wage and salary costs. While total employment costs rose by 3 percent in 1994, the benefit cost component rose by 3.4 percent. However, this was down from the 4.6 percent rise in 1993.

Providing health care benefits to employees is an important and controversial issue in the US. As of 1991, 83 percent of medium-sized or large private US employers offered medical care insurance benefit plans to their employees; 51 percent required some employee contribution for self-coverage; and 67 percent required employee contribution for family coverage. With rising health care costs, the clear trend since 1980 has been that the percentage of employers that provide health care plans is decreasing, while employee contribution requirements and deductibles (that is, portions of medical bills that health care plans will not cover) are increasing.

Except for the benefits required by federal and state laws, there are no guidelines for determining other benefits a particular employer should offer its employees. Subject to competitive issues with regard to the ability to attract and retain employees, employers have complete discretion in establishing benefit programs. However, an employer may find it difficult to withdraw a benefit once it has been provided.

Common Benefits

The following sections briefly describe common types of employee benefits.

Social Security Benefits Social security benefits are required by federal law and are paid out to former employees who have paid in a minimum amount to the system, reached a certain age, and have retired from employment. The purpose is to provide retired employees with a source of income during their old age. Social security benefits are administered by the federal government and are financed through contributions made by employers and employees. These contributions are collected by the US Internal Revenue Service (IRS). Employer contributions are collected directly from the companies, while employee contributions are deducted from employee paychecks by employers and then forwarded to the IRS. Self-employed persons must make quarterly deposits of assessed contributions.

Unemployment Compensation Unemployment compensation benefits are required by the laws of all 50 states and are provided to employees who have been discharged from employment other than for cause. The benefits are administered by the state governments, but are financed through assessments levied on employers by both the federal and state governments. Federal unemployment tax assessments are collected by the IRS. State unemployment tax assessments are collected by the state's unemployment insurance department.

Workers' Compensation Insurance Workers'

COMMON BUSINESS HOLIDAYS

New Year's Day†	January 1
Martin Luther King Day	Third Monday in January
Presidents' Day	Third Monday in February
Memorial Day	Last Monday in May
Independence Day†	July 4
Labor Day	First Monday in September
Columbus Day*	Second Monday in October
Veterans Day	November 11
Thanksgiving Day†	Fourth Thurs. in November
Christmas Day†	December 25

† When these holidays fall on a weekend, many businesses close the previous Friday or following Monday. When they fall on a Tuesday or Thursday, businesses may close the day between the holiday and the weekend. Few offices are open the Friday after Thanksgiving.
*Also called Discovers' Day or Pioneers' Day.

compensation benefits are required by state laws for the purpose of reimbursing an employee for medical expenses incurred as a result of an illness or injury that arises out of the course and scope of employment. Workers' compensation benefits also provide an employee with partial wage replacement during the period of disability and inability to work. These benefits are generally provided through insurance policies financed totally by the employer.

Disability Benefits Disability insurance is intended to replace lost wage income for employees who suffer from a non-work-related illness or injury, or who are disabled by pregnancy and childbirth or other medical conditions. There are two types of disability insurance benefits. The first type—temporary or short-term disability insurance—is generally for employees whose disabilities last less than six months. The second type—long-term disability insurance—is generally for employees whose disabilities last six months or longer.

Some state laws require employers to provide temporary disability insurance benefits to their employees. In other states, disability insurance benefits are optional. The benefits are generally provided through insurance policies financed, in whole for short-term coverage or in part for long-term coverage, by the employer.

Apart from disability insurance benefits, federal and state laws require employers to provide a paid or unpaid leave of absence to disabled employees. Typically, these laws require the employers to allow the employees to return to the jobs they previously occupied, at the same wage rate and with the same benefits they previously earned.

Leave for Jury Duty Under federal and most state laws, citizens may be required to serve on federal and state juries. Quite often these federal and state laws require employers to grant an employee a leave of absence, with or without pay, during the period of jury duty. Once jury duty is completed, the employee returns to work at the same job with the same wage rate and benefits previously earned.

Leave for Military Duty Federal law requires employers to provide a leave of absence, with or without pay, to employees called to serve in the military, including the Military Reserves and the National Guard. Generally, such employees are away from work for only short periods of time (two weeks to three months). Employers must allow employees returning from such military duty to resume their original jobs, with the same wage rate and benefits previously earned.

Leave for Voting In the US, political elections are of great public importance, so much so that many voting laws require employers to allow employees to leave work for a short time so that they can vote in an election.

Medical Benefits Many employers provide some type of medical plan to their employees. There are generally two types of such medical plans: (i) indemnity insurance plans that reimburse employees for medical expenses they incur; and (ii) health maintenance organizations that allow member-employees to utilize the medical services provided by the organization. Medical plans can be financed in a number of ways. Some employers pay the entire cost of the employee's medical plan, while other employers finance the plan through company and employee contributions. However, because of the high and increasing cost of medical care in the US, fewer and fewer employers are able to totally fund medical plans for employees. At the same time, a number of employee organizations and politicians are attempting to pass new federal laws that would require employers to provide medical plans for their employees at company cost. Companies wishing to do business in the US should check carefully into this issue.

Although most employers are not required to provide a medical plan for their employees, federal law requires employers who do so to allow an employee who leaves employment (subject to certain limitations) to continue to participate in the employer's medical plan for a limited period of time. However, such employees are usually required to pay the full costs of their continued participation in the employer's medical plan.

Family Care Leave The US population is aging, and a growing number of employees are shouldering the burden of caring for aging parents, as well as for their own children. As a consequence, the US government enacted the Family and Medical Leave Act (FMLA) in 1993, and some states have adopted similar laws. In general, many employers are required to provide employees with unpaid leave for the birth or adoption of a child, for care of a parent, child, or spouse with a serious health condition, or for the serious health condition of an employee that prevents that employee from working. The FMLA covers employers with more than 50 employees, and the length of leave under this statute is generally a cumulative 12 weeks within any 12-month period. During the FMLA leave, the employee's job position, seniority, and benefits are protected.

Holidays In the US, there are several nationally recognized holidays (federal holidays). It is also common for states to adopt state-recognized holidays (state holidays) in addition to the federal holidays, and many cities observe additional holidays locally. A majority of employers observe these federal and state holidays by either: (1) allowing their employees to have the holiday off with pay; or (2) paying employees a premium wage (usually 1.5 times the regular hourly wage) for working on that day.

Vacations It is very common for employers to provide employees with a predetermined number of days of paid leave each year. The purpose of this leave is to allow the employee to rest and engage in recreation. Some employers provide employees with the same number of vacation days each year; others allow for the number of vacation days to increase commensurate with the length of employment. That is, an employee with one year of service may get five days of vacation, while an employee with five years of service may get 10 or more days of vacation.

Sick Leave Employers commonly allow employees limited amounts of paid sick leave each year. Sick leave is very similar to disability benefits; its purpose is to provide wages to employees who are disabled because of illness or injury. However, unlike disability benefits, sick leave is generally for very short periods of time (often a predetermined number of days per year). Furthermore, sick leave is usually paid by the employer out of general funds rather than through an insurance policy.

Life Insurance Life insurance is a benefit provided to an employee's surviving heirs in the event the employee dies. The benefit generally consists of a lump sum cash payment to the surviving heirs, the amount of which is determined by the wages earned by the employee immediately prior to the death. Life insurance benefits are obtained through insurance companies that assess monthly premiums for the benefit. These monthly premiums can be financed totally by the company, or paid through continued employer and employee contributions.

Pension Plans Although social security benefits provide retired employees with a source of income during their old age, the cost of living in the US exceeds the amount of social security benefits most retirees collect. Thus, many employers provide some type of company retirement or pension plan to supplement their social security benefits. These pension plans are financed through monthly payments made by the employer and/or employee during employment. Retirement and pension plans are regulated by the federal Employee Retirement Income Security Act (ERISA), which controls the establishment and operation of these plans.

The basic types of pension plans are defined benefit plans—usually paid for by the employer and offering a fixed benefit payment based on earnings during employment—and defined contribution plans—paid for by the employee and/or the employer and providing a variable benefit based on contributions.

Severance Plans Some employers adopt severance pay plans to supplement unemployment benefits paid to employees who are discharged from employment other than for cause. Severance pay plans are also regulated by ERISA.

UNIONS AND COLLECTIVE BARGAINING IN THE US

Labor unions in the US are organizations formed by employees to give them added clout in bargaining with employers regarding wages, hours, and working conditions. They are typically led by officers and representatives elected by the members. While unions do not enjoy the level of membership they once did in the US, they remain powerful, particularly in certain industries. The following discussion briefly describes unionization in the US and discusses some of the legal and practical considerations facing an employer confronted with a union-organizing effort or employing a unionized workforce.

Unionization in the US

The right to unionize and bargain collectively has been recognized in the US since the passage of the National Labor Relations Act (NLRA) in 1935. In recent decades, there has been a reduction in unionization in the private sector. In 1993 the proportion of private sector nonagricultural workers who were union members stood at 11.2 percent, less than one-third of the approximately 35 percent covered in the 1950s. By contrast, more than one-third of the public sector workers were union members in 1993, compared with 10 to 11 percent in the 1950s.

Moreover, the success of unions in winning employee elections has fallen over time. The proportion of elections in which workers voted to unionize fell from 72 percent in the early 1950s to about 50 percent from 1975 to 1990. Additionally, the number of workers eligible to vote in these elections has also fallen, reflecting the fact that union organizing drives have increasingly focused on smaller firms.

As previously noted, government statistics continue to show that wage rates for unionized employees generally exceed those of nonunion employees, often by as much as one-third. While collective bargaining generally produces an increase in wages and other compensation during the term of the agreement, such negotiated increases have been relatively modest in recent years. For example, in the fourth quarter of 1993 the government reported that the average wage increase arising from collective bargaining was 3 percent. However, this figure fell to 2.5 percent for the fourth quarter of 1994, less than the 3 percent rise in employment costs recorded for all of 1994.

The number and severity of work stoppages has fallen substantially along with the decrease in union representation. For example, in the decade of the 1970s, there were 289 work stoppages involving 1,000 or more workers; in the 1980s, there were only 83 such work stoppages, a reduction of 71 percent.

Despite these downward trends for unions, organized labor remains a significant force, especially in certain US industries and geographical areas. For example, in the construction industry in 1993, more than 400,000 workers were members of the Carpenters Union, more than 400,000 were members of the Laborers Union, and more than 300,000 were members of the Operating Engineers Union. Thus, while unions may not have the membership they once enjoyed, US employers must still be cognizant of the potential for union organizing efforts and understand the process of union organizing.

The Process of Unionization

The organizational process by which employees choose a union is normally initiated by the filing of a petition by the union to represent the employees. This petition is filed with the National Labor Relations Board (NLRB), the federal government agency responsible for monitoring relations between employers and unions. After a petition has been filed, the NLRB determines which employees are eligible to be represented by the union, and a secret ballot election is scheduled so that the employees may choose whether they wish to be represented by the union. Typically, the choice is between voting for or against union representation, but there are occasions when more than one union seeks to represent the same employees, in which case all unions will appear on the ballot, along with a "no union" option.

It is normal for there to be a period of campaigning by both the union and the employer before the election. The behavior of the employer and the union during an election campaign is subject to a variety of rules designed to ensure that the election is free and uncoerced. In practice, there are numerous restrictions concerning what an employer may do during the course of the campaign, while the union's ability to campaign is relatively unrestricted.

At the end of the campaign, a secret ballot election is conducted by the NLRB. If the union is able to obtain the votes of a simple majority (50 percent plus 1) of the eligible employees, the union prevails in the election. In the days following an election, both the union and the employer have the opportunity file any objections to the conduct of the election. Either side may allege that the other engaged in improper and illegal conduct that made the election unfair and thus the result of the election invalid. The NLRB then investigates such objections. There may be a formal hearing following the objections to determine their validity and, if objectionable conduct on the part of the winning side is found, the results of the election will be set aside and a new election scheduled. If there are no objections, or if the objections are determined to be without merit, the NLRB will certify the results of the election. If the union has won, the union and the employer then begin the process of collective bargaining.

Collective Bargaining with a Union

After a union has been certified to represent the employees, the process of negotiating the terms and conditions of employment for the employees begins. This process—known as "collective bargaining"—involves discussions between the employer and the union concerning all aspects of the employment relationship. The wages, hours, and working conditions of the employees must be negotiated, because these are considered to be mandatory bargaining subjects. Other mandatory bargaining subjects include benefits, employee work rules and assignments, and subcontracting of work.

In the negotiation process, there is no requirement that the parties must come to an agreement about any provision or that they accept any proposal. The law requires that both sides bargain in good faith—that is, they must demonstrate a sincere effort to reach common ground. The law obliges both the union and the employer to participate actively in collective bargaining deliberations, indicating their intention to reach agreement.

When the parties have agreed on all pertinent points in the negotiations, the agreement is put into writing in a document known as a collective bargaining agreement. A collective bargaining agreement typically includes provisions on the wages and benefits of employees, as well as discipline, discharge, grievance, and arbitration procedures. Such agreements must usually be ratified by the union membership.

If the parties cannot reach agreement after good faith bargaining, they may then resort to so-called economic weapons in an attempt to force the other side to accept their proposals. The principal economic weapon used by unions is a strike—that is, a refusal to work. Alternatively, an employer may institute a lockout—that is, a refusal to allow the employees to come to work. The NLRB has developed a number of rules concerning the use of legitimate economic weapons. For example, other unions are generally allowed to honor the striking union's picket line (by refusing to do business with the company that has been struck). However, secondary boycotts of the target company's products by third parties at the urging of the striking union are generally prohibited.

Administration of Collective Bargaining Agreements

Once a collective bargaining agreement is reached, the parties are required to adhere to its terms. Failure to follow the contract usually leads to disputes, known as grievances. Contracts normally contain a grievance procedure culminating in binding arbitration by an outside, independent arbitrator if the parties cannot reach agreement on their own. There is a well-developed body of arbitration law that provides guidance in evaluating the strength of each side's position.

One particular type of dispute arising under a contract cannot be settled by arbitration; union contracts often contain provisions known as no strike clauses, under which the union agrees that during the term of the agreement the employees will not strike. If the union or the employees breach this agreement by striking during the term of the agreement, the employer may sue the union in federal court to obtain an injunction ordering the employees back to work.

During the term of the agreement, the parties may, under certain circumstances, enter into interim bargaining over issues that were unresolved in the original negotiation or that need to be renegotiated. The rules governing midterm bargaining are complex, but as a general matter, once agreement is reached on an issue—such as the wage rate for the employees during the term of the agreement—this issue may not be revisited without the agreement of both parties to reopen discussions. Collective bargaining agreements often include "reopener" clauses when the parties anticipate that the agreement may have to be renegotiated during its term. The most common midterm reopener clause allows for renegotiation of wages.

When a collective bargaining agreement expires, the parties negotiate a new agreement. The process of good faith bargaining is renewed, and if no agreement is reached, the parties may resort to their economic weapons—strike or lockout. It is not uncommon for parties to bargain up to the last minute before a contract expires.

GOVERNMENT REGULATIONS: AGENCIES AND LAWS

The following is a brief summary of some of the labor and employment laws with which US employers must comply. The business addresses of the major federal government agencies regulating employment are also included.

The specific laws that apply to an employer will depend on the location of the employer's worksite, the type of industry, and the type of employees working for the company.

Federal Labor and Employment Laws

National Labor Relations Act (NLRA) The NLRA (29 USC 151 et seq) gives employees the right to organize, form, join, or assist labor organizations; to bargain collectively through representatives of their own choosing; to engage in concerted activities for collective bargaining, mutual aid, or protection; and to refrain from such activities. The law applies to all employers involved in labor disputes affecting interstate commerce. The law is enforced by a federal agency called the National Labor Relations Board (NLRB), which is responsible for overseeing union representation elections and processing unfair labor practice charges.

Railway Labor Act (RLA) The RLA (45 USC 151 et seq) applies to railroad carriers and air carriers, and it gives employees the right to organize and bargain collectively through representatives of their own choosing, or to refrain from joining a labor organization or participating in such activities. The provisions of the RLA are enforced by three agencies: the National Mediation Board (which handles railroad and air carriers), the National Railroad Adjustment Board (railroad carriers only) and the National Air Transport Adjustment Board (air carriers only).

Fair Labor Standards Act (FLSA) (29 USC 201 et seq) This act requires employers to pay a minimum wage to employees and to pay overtime compensation for work performed by employees in excess of 40 hours per workweek. It also regulates the employment of minors and requires employers to maintain extensive time records of hours worked by employees. The FLSA applies to all employers who have employees engaged in commerce. The US Department of Labor, Wage and Hour Division, is responsible for administering the FLSA.

Davis-Bacon Act This act (40 USC 276a et seq) requires employers to pay prevailing wages and benefits to various classes of laborers and mechanics as determined by the Secretary of Labor. The employers are also required to maintain payroll and fringe benefits records, submit weekly payroll reports, pay mechanics and laborers on the worksite once a week, and post the wage scales in a prominent place at the worksite. The act applies to all employers who have federal contracts or subcontracts of US$2,000 or more for any construction, alteration, or repair of public buildings or works that requires the use of mechanics or laborers. The US Department of Labor, Wage and Hour Division, is responsible for administering this.

Service Contracts Act (SCA) (41 USC 351 et seq) Similar to the Davis-Bacon Act, the SCA requires employers to pay prevailing wages and benefits to employees and to provide employees with notice of the compensation rates. The act also prohibits employers from requiring employees to work under unsanitary, hazardous, or dangerous conditions. The SCA applies to all employers having service contracts with the federal government in excess of US$2,500. However, there are some exclusions for certain categories of employees and contractors. Again, the US Department of Labor, Wage and Hour Division, is responsible for administering the SCA.

Title VII of the Civil Rights Act of 1964 Title VII (42 USC 2000e et seq) prohibits discrimination in employment on the basis of race, color, religion, sex, or national origin. This includes discrimination in recruitment, hiring, discharges, compensation, or other terms and conditions of employment. The statute applies to all employers engaged in an industry affecting commerce and having 15 or more employees. There are specific and narrow exemptions. Title VII is administered by a federal agency called the Equal Employment Opportunity Commission (EEOC).

Age Discrimination in Employment Act of 1967 (ADEA) (29 USC 621 et seq) This act prohibits discrimination on the basis of age against persons who are at least 40 years of age. This includes discrimination in recruitment, hiring, discharges, compensation, or other terms and conditions of employment. The statute applies to all employers engaged in an industry affecting commerce and having 20 or more employees. The ADEA is also administered by the EEOC.

Rehabilitation Act of 1973 This act (29 USC 701 et seq) requires federal contractors and subcontractors with procurement contracts in excess of US$10,000 to take affirmative action to employ and advance qualified individuals with disabilities. It also prohibits any program or activity receiving federal financial assistance from discriminating against qualified individuals with disabilities. A disabled individual is any person who: (a) has a physical or mental impairment that substantially limits one or more of such person's major life activities; or (b) has a record of such an impairment; or (c) is regarded as having such an impairment. The Rehabilitation Act is administered by the US Department of Labor.

Americans With Disabilities Act of 1990 (ADA) This act (42 USC 12101 et seq) prohibits discrimination against qualified individuals who are disabled. Unlike the Rehabilitation Act of 1973, which applies only to federal contractors, this act applies to private employers with 15 or more employees. A qualified individual with a disability is defined as a person with a disability who, with or without reasonable accommodation, can perform the essential functions of the employment position the individual holds or desires. The ADA is administered by the EEOC.

Equal Pay Act of 1963 In general, this act (29 USC 206(d)) pertains to all employers covered by the Fair Labor Standards Act. It prohibits employers from discriminating among employees on the basis of gender in the payment of wages. Basically, the law requires equal pay for equal work on jobs that require equal skill, effort, and responsibility and that are performed under similar working conditions.

Employee Retirement Income Security Act of 1974 (ERISA) (29 USC 1001 et seq) This act is a comprehensive statutory and regulatory scheme that governs the establishment and administration of pension and employee welfare benefit plans. The law includes both tax and labor provisions that set forth specific standards for participation, vesting, funding, and termination of pension plans. It also prescribes standards for the reporting and disclosure of plans to employees, and fiduciary responsibility for those administering the plans.

All employers with pension or employee welfare benefit plans are subject to ERISA. Under ERISA, the Secretary of Labor and individual plan participants or beneficiaries are authorized to file civil actions to enforce the law and to recover benefits due. The statute also provides for criminal penalties in cases of willful violation. Furthermore, a federal agency called the Pension Benefit Guaranty Corporation is responsible for overseeing the termination of pension plans and ensuring payment of benefits to participants and beneficiaries.

Consolidated Omnibus Budget Reconciliation Act of 1985 (COBRA) COBRA (PL 99-272) This act requires employers to make available continued coverage under their group health plans (which would include basic hospitalization, major medical, dental, vision, and prescription drug plans) to: (a) employees who lost their coverage because they left their jobs (due to either resignation or discharge) or shifted from full-time to part-time status; (b) spouses and other dependents of covered employees who lost their coverage because of the employee's death, divorce, legal separation, or eligibility for Medicare; and (c) children of covered employees who lost their coverage because they reached majority age and are no longer considered dependents. With certain exceptions, coverage must continue to be available for specified periods ranging from 18 to 36 months. Continued coverage is provided only to individuals who elect it (within a 60-day election period) and pay the necessary premiums. Employers are also required to provide employees and their spouses notice of their COBRA rights when the employers' plans become subject to the law, at the time the employees become eligible for the group health plan, and on the occurrence of a qualifying event. Except for churches and the federal government, employers with at least 20 employees are subject to the law.

Family and Medical Leave Act of 1993 (FMLA) This act (29 USC 2601 et seq) requires employers with 50 or more employees (who work within 75 miles of the worksite) to provide up to 12 weeks of unpaid leave per year to eligible employees for the following reasons: (a) the birth of a child and to care for such child; (b) the placement for adoption or foster care of a child; (c) to care for a spouse, child or parent with a serious health condition; or (d) a serious health condition that renders the employee disabled. Employees who have provided at least 1,250 hours of service over a 12-month period prior to the request for leave are eligible for this benefit. Employers are also required to maintain health benefits to employees on FMLA leave and guarantee reinstatement to returning employees in the same position or a similar position with equivalent pay, benefits, terms, and conditions of employment. The US Department of Labor is responsible for administering the FMLA.

Occupational Safety and Health Act (OSHA) This act (29 USC 651 et seq), requires employers to: (a) furnish each employee a place of employment free from recognized hazards causing or likely to cause death or serious physical harm; (b) comply with occupational safety and health standards set forth by the regulations promulgated under the law; (c) keep records as prescribed by the regulations (such as records of accidents, injuries, and deaths); (d) post notices informing employees of their protection and the employer's obligations under the law; and (e) refrain from discriminating against employees who exercise their rights under the act. All employers engaged in a business affecting commerce, including professional, agricultural, nonprofit, and charitable organizations, are covered by OSHA. This act is administered by the US Department of Health and Human Services and a federal agency called the National Advisory Committee on Occupational Safety and Health.

Immigration Reform and Control Act of 1986 (IRCA) The IRCA (8 USC 1103 et seq) is designed in part to control the unlawful employment of aliens in the US. The law: (a) makes it unlawful to hire, recruit, or refer for a fee unauthorized aliens; (b) requires those who hire, recruit, or refer for a fee individuals for employment, to verify both the identity and employment eligibility of such individuals; (c) makes it unlawful to continue to employ unauthorized aliens hired after November 6, 1986; and (d) makes it an unfair immigration-related employment practice to discriminate against individuals on the basis of citizenship. Two federal agencies, the US Department of Justice and the Immigration and Naturalization Service, are responsible for administering and enforcing this law.

Worker Adjustment and Retraining Notification Act (WARN) (29 USC 2101 et seq) This act requires employers to give 60 days' advance written notice of any plant closing or mass layoff to each affected employee (or to a representative of that employee); to the state dislocated worker unit (created under Title III of the Job Training Partnership Act); and the chief elected official of the unit of local government in which such closing or layoff is to occur. All employers with 100 or more full-time employees or employers with 100 or more employees who in the aggregate work at least 4,000 hours per week (exclusive of overtime) are subject to the act. The statute is administered and enforced through civil actions by employees, their representatives, or by the unit of local government affected by the closing or layoff.

USEFUL ADDRESSES

US Department of Labor Offices

Department of Labor (DOL)
200 Constitution Ave. NW
Washington, DC 20210, USA
Tel: [1] (202) 219-5000
Fax: [1] (202) 219-6161

Bureau of Labor Statistics
2 Massachusetts Ave. NE
Washington, DC 20212, USA
Tel: [1] (202) 606-5888
Fax: [1] (202) 606-7797

Employment and Training Administration
200 Constitution Ave. NW
Washington, DC 20210, USA
Tel: [1] (202) 219-6971
Fax: [1] (202) 219-6827

Employment Standards Administration
Fair Labor Standards Act Enforcement
200 Constitution Ave. NW, #S3516
Washington, DC 20210, USA
Tel: [1] (202) 219-7043
Fax: [1] (202) 219-4753

Employment Standards Administration
Wage and Hour Division
200 Constitution Ave. NW, #S3502
Washington, DC 20210, USA
Tel: [1] (202) 219-8305

Occupational Safety and Health Administration (OSHA)
200 Constitution Ave. NW
Washington, DC 20210, USA
Tel: [1] (202) 219-8151
Fax: [1] (202) 219-6064

Pension and Welfare Benefits Administration
200 Constitution Ave. NW
Washington, DC 20210, USA
Tel: [1] (202) 219-8921
Fax: [1] (202) 219-5362

Other Federal Agencies

Equal Employment Opportunity Commission (EEOC)
1801 L Street NW, #10006
Washington, DC 20507, USA
Tel: [1] (202) 663-4900
Fax: [1] (202) 663-4912

National Commission for Employment Policy
1522 K St. NW, #300
Washington, DC 20005, USA
Tel: [1] (202) 724-1545
Fax: [1] (202) 724-0019

National Labor Relations Board (NLRB)
1717 Pennsylvania Ave. NW, #701
Washington, DC 20570, USA
Tel: [1] (202) 632-4950
Fax: [1] (202) 254-6781

Business Law*

THE US LEGAL SYSTEM

CONTENTS

INTRODUCTION

The complex federal and individual state laws of the US are constantly subject to legislative change and differing judicial interpretations. Moreover, numerous federal and state agencies impose rules and regulations on trade and other business activity within the US, many of which affect foreign businesses operating in the country.

The information in this chapter is intended to summarize some of the important topics in US business law. Being a summary, it cannot convey all of the detail necessary to evaluate the issues involved in a specific proposed transaction or operation. This summary does not constitute legal advice, nor should it be used in place of legal advice from a licensed attorney. Be certain to review your business activities with an attorney familiar with international transactions as well as with the laws of the US and your own country. You should carefully investigate all current legal requirements which apply to your particular business activities, no matter how tangential they seem. (Refer to the "Important Addresses" chapter for a list of some law offices in the US.)

STRUCTURE OF GOVERNMENT AND LAWS

The US is a federal democratic republic, politically divided into 50 states. Each state is a sovereign government; this means that each state has its own legal system. The federal government has three branches: the executive branch consisting of the president, the vice president, and certain additional ministerial officers appointed by the president; a bicameral legislature consisting of the US Senate and the US House of Representatives (collectively, the

* By Duane H. Zobrist and Stephen L. Bradford. Copyright © 1995 Carlsmith Ball Wichman Case & Ichiki. Reprinted with permission of that law firm.

LEGAL GLOSSARY

acceptance An unconditional assent to an offer or one conditioned on minor changes that do not affect material terms of the offer. *See* Counteroffer, Offer.

acknowledgment The act of conferring legal authenticity on a written document, typically made by a notary public, who attests and certifies that the document is in proper legal form and that it is executed by a person identified as having authority to do so. Acknowledgment is also referred to as authentication.

agency The relationship between an agent and a principal. The agent represents and acts on behalf of the principal, who instructs and authorizes the agent to so act.

arm's length Without collusion, as if between self-interested and unrelated parties operating at parity.

counteroffer A reply to an offer that materially alters the terms of the offer. Example: a seller who accepts a buyer's offer on condition that the goods will be made of a different material has made a counteroffer. *See* acceptance, offer.

domicile The place where a party is living or located with no definite, present intention of moving away.

fiduciary obligation An obligation placed on a party (the fiduciary) entrusted to handle money or property for the benefit of another party. The fiduciary must act in good faith with due regard for the benefit of the other party.

good faith A legal standard implying honesty in fact in the conduct or transaction concerned, honesty of intention, or freedom from an intention to defraud, depending on the circumstances.

injunction A court order that either requires a party to do a specific act or prohibits that party from doing so. Injunctions can be granted on a permanent or temporary basis, pending resolution of a dispute.

jurisdiction A geographic area in which a court or legal body has the power and authority to act.

legal act An action intended to have and capable of having an effect that is specified by law, such as the creation, termination, or modification of a right given by law. Example: the signing of a power of attorney is a legal act because it gives lawful authority to an agent.

legal person An individual or entity recognized under law as having rights and obligations specified by law. Example: limited liability companies, corporations, and partnerships are entities recognized as legal persons.

negligence A failure to exercise reasonable care, which could result in legal liability for damages caused to others. *See* reasonable care.

negotiable instrument A written document transferable merely by endorsement or delivery. Example: a check or bill of exchange is a negotiable instrument.

offer A proposal that is made to a specific individual or entity to enter into a contract. The proposal must contain definite terms and must indicate the offeror's intent to be bound by an acceptance. Example: a buyer's order to purchase designated goods on certain delivery and payment terms is an offer. *See* acceptance, counteroffer.

power of attorney A written document by which one individual or entity (the principal) authorizes another individual or entity (the agent) to perform stated acts on the principal's behalf. Example: a principal may execute a special power of attorney (authorizing an agent to sign a specific contract) or a general power of attorney (authorizing an agent to sign all contracts for the principal).

privity The notion that in order to maintain an action on any contract, a connection or relationship should exist between the plaintiff and defendant as parties to the contract on which the action is being brought.

reasonable care The level of care that an ordinary, prudent person would exercise under the same circumstances. *See* negligence.

statute of frauds A law that requires designated documents to be in writing in order to be enforced by a court. Example: contracting parties may orally agree to transfer ownership of immovable property, but a court might not enforce that contract, and might not award damages for breach, unless the contract was written.

tort A legal wrong committed on a party or property based on a violation of some duty owed to the plaintiff when that duty is imposed by law and does not arise under a contract.

warranty A warranty is an affirmation of fact regarding the characteristics, safety, or suitability of a product. An express warranty is one that is explicitly stated. An implied warranty is inferred by law based on the circumstances of the transaction.

Congress); and a judiciary consisting of the US Supreme Court and the lower federal courts. The structures of the state governments are generally modeled on that of the federal government.

The Constitution of the US is the supreme law of the land. Pursuant to constitutional authority, federal and state legislatures enact and amend various civil, commercial, and other codes. These codes are supplemented by regulations issued by various government departments and agencies. The Supreme Court is empowered to invalidate the laws of Congress or the actions of the president and executive branch if they violate the Constitution.

The federal government has only those powers specifically given to it by the US Constitution. These powers are generally those that affect the welfare of the country as a whole, such as the power to control imports and exports, to regulate immigration, and to protect patents and copyrights. Some powers, such as those pertaining to the regulation and taxation of local business enterprises, are shared by the federal government with the 50 state governments, and all powers not enumerated for exercise by the federal government are reserved for the states to exercise. Each state government in turn can delegate certain of its powers to local governments,

usually governments of the state's counties and cities. In the event of a conflict between a federal law and a state or local law, the federal law will govern. As a result of the US federal system, any particular transaction may be governed solely by federal law, solely by state law, or perhaps both.

The US has also ratified numerous bilateral and multilateral international treaties and conventions that contain provisions affecting the transaction of business. Conflicts of law arising between treaties to which the US is a signatory and US federal law can be complicated to resolve, but generally Congress has the power to nullify, in whole or in part, a treaty commitment, and federal law can be found to supersede treaty provisions. (*See* "Conflicts of Law" and "Treaties" entries under the "Law Digest" in this chapter.)

BASIS OF THE LEGAL SYSTEM

The US legal system is based on the tradition of common law developed in England. The common law system differs from the civil law system (followed by most European and Latin American countries) in that law is not only codified in statutes made by the legislature, but also is made through interpretation

"It's a deal, but just to be on the safe side let's have our lawyers look at this handshake."

THE INTERNATIONAL TRANSACTION: BASICS OF A ONE-TIME SALE

When dealing internationally, you must consider the business practices and legal requirements of the country where the other party to your contract is located. Parties generally have the freedom to agree to any contract terms that they desire, but the laws of your country or the other country may require a written contract. In some transactions, the laws may even specify all or some of the contract terms. Whether a contract term is valid in a particular country is mainly of concern in case you have to seek enforcement. Otherwise, you have fairly broad flexibility in negotiating contract provisions. However, you should always be certain to come to a definite understanding with the other party on four basic issues: the goods (quantity, type, and quality); the time of delivery; the price; and the time and means of payment.

For a small, one-time sale, an invoice or a simple contract may be acceptable. For a more involved business transaction or an ongoing relationship, a formal written contract is preferable in order to define clearly the rights, responsibilities, and remedies of all parties. Contracts that involve capital goods, high credit risks, or industrial or intellectual property rights will require special protective clauses. In preparing such contracts, it is essential to obtain legal advice from a professional who is familiar with the laws and practices of both countries involved.

For a simple, one-time deal, you need to consider at least the following clauses:

Contract Date

Specify the date when the contract is signed. This date is particularly important if payment or delivery times are fixed in reference to it—for example, "shipment within 30 days of the contract date."

Identification of Parties

Name the parties, describe their relation to each other, and designate any persons who are authorized to act for each party. The persons designated should also be the ones who sign the contract. If a person is signing on behalf of a company, you should be certain of that person's authority—request a statement or corporate resolution if you are uncertain. A company will be bound to a contract in the US if the person signing has apparent authority.

Goods

Description Describe the type and quality of the goods. You may simply indicate a model number, or you may have to attach detailed lists, plans, drawings, or other specifications. This clause should be clear enough that both

parties fully understand the specifications and have no discretion in interpreting them.

Quantity Specify the number of units, or other measure of quantity, of the goods. If the goods are measured by weight, you should specify net weight, dry weight, or drained weight. If the goods are prepackaged and are subject to weight restrictions in the end market, you may want to ensure that the seller will provide goods packaged to comply with those restrictions.

Price Indicate the price per unit or other measure, such as per pound or ton, and the extended price.

Packaging Arrangements

Set forth packaging specifications, especially for goods that could be damaged in transit. At a minimum, this provision should require the seller to package the goods in such a way as to withstand transportation. If special packaging requirements are necessary to meet consumer and product liability standards in the end market, you should specify them also.

Transportation Arrangements

Carrier Name a preferred carrier for transporting the goods. You should designate a particular carrier if, for example, a carrier offers you special pricing or is better able than others to transport the product.

Storage Specify any particular requirements for storage of the goods before or during shipment, such as security arrangements, special climate demands, and weather protection needs.

Notice Provisions Require the seller to notify the buyer when the goods are ready for delivery or pickup, particularly if the goods are perishable or fluctuate in value. If your transaction is time-sensitive, you could even provide for several notices to allow the buyer to track the goods and take steps to minimize damages if delivery is delayed.

Shipping Time State the exact date for shipping or provide for shipment within a reasonable time from the contract date. If this clause is included and the seller fails to ship on time, the buyer may claim a right to cancel the contract, even if the goods have been shipped, provided that the buyer has not yet accepted delivery.

Costs and Charges

Specify which party is to pay any additional costs and charges related to the sale.

Duties and Taxes Designate the party that will be responsible for import, export, and other fees and taxes and for obtaining all required licenses. For example, a party may be made responsible for paying the duties, taxes, and charges imposed by that party's own country, since that party is best situated to know the legal requirements of that country.

Insurance Costs Identify the party that will pay the costs of insuring the goods in transit. This is a critical provision because the party responsible bears the risk if the goods are lost during transit. A seller is typically responsible for insurance until title to the goods passes to the buyer, at which time the buyer becomes responsible for insurance or becomes the named beneficiary under the seller's insurance policy.

Handling and Transport Specify the party that will pay shipping, handling, packaging, security, and any other costs related to transportation, which should be enumerated.

Terms Defined Contracts for the sale of goods most commonly use Incoterms—as defined by the International Chamber of Commerce in Paris—to assign responsibility for the risks and cost of transport. (Refer to the "International Payments" chapter for explanations of the Incoterms.)

Insurance or Risk of Loss Protection

Specify the insurance required, the beneficiary of the policy, the party who will obtain the insurance, and the date by which it will have been obtained.

Payment Provisions

In a one-time transaction, the seller will typically seek the most secure form of payment before committing to shipment, while a buyer will want the goods cleared through customs and delivered in satisfactory condition before remitting full payment. If payments cannot be made in advance, parties most often agree to use documentary credits. (Refer to the "International Payments" chapter for an explanation of such payments.)

Method of Payment State the means by which payment will be tendered—for example, delivery of a documentary letter of credit or documents against payment; prepayment in cash or traveler's checks; or credit for a specified number of days.

Medium of Exchange Designate the currency to be used—for example, US dollars, the currency of the non-US country of origin, or the currency of a third country.

Exchange Rate Specify a fixed exchange rate for the price stated in the contract. You may use this clause to lock in a specific price and ensure against fluctuating currency values.

Import Documentation

Designate the documents for exporting and importing that each party will be responsible for obtaining, completing, and presenting to customs. Shipment of the goods, and even the contract itself, may be made contingent on a party's having obtained in advance the proper licenses, inspection certificates, and other authorizations. (Refer to the chapters "Import Poli-

cies & Procedures" and "Export Policies & Procedures" for further discussion of these requirements.)

Inspection Rights

Provide that the buyer has a right to inspect goods before taking delivery to determine whether the goods meet the contract specifications. This clause should specify the party who will make the inspection—for example, the buyer, a third party, or a licensed inspector; the location where the inspection will occur—for example, at the seller's plant, the buyer's warehouse, or a receiving dock; the time at which the inspection will occur; the presentation of a certified document of inspection, if needed; and any requirements related to the return of nonconforming goods, such as payment of return freight charges by the seller.

Warranty Provisions

Limit or extend any implied warranties, and define any express warranties on property fitness and quality. The contract may, for example, state that the seller warrants that the goods are of merchantable quality, are fit for any purpose for which they would ordinarily be used, or are fit for a particular purpose requested by the buyer. The seller may also warrant that the goods will be of the same quality as any sample or model that the seller has furnished as representative of the goods. Finally, the seller may warrant that the goods will be packaged in a specific way or in a way that will adequately preserve and protect the goods.

Indemnity

Agree that one party will hold the other harmless from damages that arise from specific causes, such as the design or manufacture of a product.

Enforcement and Remedies

Time Is of the Essence Stipulate that timely performance of the contract is essential. In the US, inclusion of this clause allows a party to claim breach merely because the other party fails to perform within the time prescribed in the contract. Although common in US contracts, a clause of this type is considered less important in other countries.

Modification Require the parties to make all changes to the contract in advance and in a signed written modification.

Cancellation State the reasons for which either party may cancel the contract and the notice required for cancellation.

Contingencies Specify any events that must occur before a party is obligated to perform the contract. For example, you may agree that the seller has no duty to ship goods until the buyer forwards documents that secure the payment for the goods.

Governing Law Choose the law of a specific jurisdiction to control any interpretation of the contract terms. The

THE INTERNATIONAL TRANSACTION: BASICS OF A ONE-TIME SALE (cont'd.)

law that you choose will usually affect where you can sue or enforce a judgment and what rules and procedures will be applied.

Choice of Forum Identify the place where a dispute may be settled—for example, the country of origin of the goods, the country of destination, or a third country that is convenient to both parties.

Arbitration Provisions Arbitration can be used as an alternative to litigation for the resolution of disputes that arise. You should agree to arbitrate only if you seriously intend to settle disputes in this way. If you agree to arbitrate but later file suit, the court is likely to uphold the arbitration clause and force you to settle your dispute as initially agreed in the contract.

An arbitration clause should specify whether arbitration is binding or nonbinding on the parties; the country where arbitration will be conducted (which should be the US or another country that has adopted the UN Convention on Rec-

ognition and Enforcement of Foreign Awards or a similar convention); the procedure for enforcement of an award; the rules governing the arbitration, such as the UN Commission on International Trade Law Model Rules; the institute that will administer the arbitration, such as the International Chamber of Commerce (Paris); the law that will govern procedural issues or the merits of the dispute; any limitations on the selection of arbitrators (for example, a national of a disputing party may be excluded from being an arbitrator); the qualifications or expertise of the arbitrators; the language in which the arbitration will be conducted; and the availability of translations and translators if needed.

Severability Provide that individual clauses can be removed from the contract without affecting the validity of the contract as a whole. This clause is important because it provides that, if one clause is declared invalid and unenforceable for any reason, the rest of the contract remains in force.

by the courts. Under the doctrine of stare decisis, prior court interpretations of law will govern subsequent and similar cases. Review of court decisions is therefore an integral part of understanding the US law on any particular matter.

All US states have adopted English common law as their legal basis except Louisiana, which has a civil law system based on its French roots.

GEOGRAPHICAL SCOPE OF LAWS

This chapter describes US federal laws, which are national in scope and govern in all 50 states. Each state also has its own laws, including a commercial code, civil code, penal code, code of civil procedure, and code of criminal procedure. The state codes are generally similar to the federal ones, but can vary widely in details. Therefore, the laws of the particular state where you are doing business must always be checked for differences with the federal requirements.

PRACTICAL APPLICATION

Role of Legal Counsel

Because of the overlay and diversity of federal, state, and local business and tax laws and regulations across the US, attorneys and accountants play an important role in structuring and negotiating business transactions in the US. Foreign businesspersons may find that they are unaccustomed to the amount of responsibility given to attorneys in the conduct of business in the US. Attorneys in the US are gener-

ally considered to be a part of the business "team," not professionals sought out only when a problem arises.

The quality and cost of legal services can vary throughout the US, depending on the geographic area and practice specialty. For example, it would not be unusual for law firms in the major metropolitan cities of New York and Los Angeles with sophisticated and specialized business practices to charge substantially more than US$200 per hour. Nevertheless, businesspeople, domestic and foreign alike, may find it more cost-effective to retain such firms because of the high degree of legal familiarity, extra business services, and well-established reputations they can bring to their clients' affairs. For referrals based on location and area of expertise, contact the state and local bar associations (the licensing bodies and business groups for the practice of law), listings in *Martindale-Hubbell's Law Directory* (a national legal directory), embassies, and chambers of commerce. (Refer to the "Important Addresses" chapter.)

A growing number of law firms, particularly in major metropolitan areas, are specializing in international trade and investment and typically offer bilingual and bicultural services and offices abroad. Of recent significance is the passage of the North American Free Trade Agreement (NAFTA), which has created new opportunities for attorneys and law firms in Canada, the US, and Mexico by reducing restrictions on foreign service firms, mandating the creation of a dispute arbitration system, and increasing protection for intellectual and industrial prop-

THE US FOREIGN CORRUPT PRACTICES ACT

US business owners are subject to the Foreign Corrupt Practices Act (FCPA). The stiff penalties imposed under this act may make a US business owner reluctant to deal with a foreign company if there is even a hint of corrupt practice related to the transaction. The FCPA makes it unlawful for any US citizen or firm (or any person who acts on behalf of a US citizen or firm) to use a means of US interstate commerce (examples: mail, telephone, telegram, or electronic mail) to offer, pay, transfer, promise to pay or transfer, or authorize a payment, transfer, or promise of money or anything of value to any foreign appointed or elected official, foreign political party, or candidate for a foreign political office for a corrupt purpose (that is, to influence a discretionary act or decision of the official) for the purpose of obtaining or retaining business.

It is also unlawful for a US business owner to make such an offer, promise, payment, or transfer to any person if the US business owner knows, or has reason to know, that the person will give, offer, or promise directly or indirectly all or part of the payment to a foreign government official, political party, or candidate. For purposes of the FCPA, the term "knowledge" means both "actual knowledge"—the business owner in fact knew that the offer, payment, or transfer was included in the transaction—and "implied knowledge"—the business owner should have known from the facts and circumstances of a transaction that the agent paid a bribe, but failed to carry out a reasonable investigation into the transaction. A business owner should make a reasonable investigation into the transaction, for example, if the sales representative requests a higher commission on a particular deal for no apparent reason, if the buyer is a foreign government, if the product has a military use, or if the buyer's country is one in which bribes are considered customary in business relationships.

The FCPA also contains provisions applicable to US publicly held companies concerning financial recordkeeping and internal accounting controls.

Legal Payments

The provisions of the FCPA do not prohibit payments made to facilitate routine government action. A facilitating payment is one made in connection with an action that a foreign official must perform as part of the official's job. In comparison, a corrupt payment is made to influence an official's discretionary decision. For example, payments would not generally be considered corrupt if made to cover an official's overtime if such overtime is necessary to expedite the processing of export documentation for a legal shipment of merchandise or to cover the expense of additional crew to handle a shipment.

A person charged with violating FCPA provisions may assert as a defense that the payment was lawful under the written laws and regulations of the foreign country and therefore was not for a corrupt purpose. Alternatively, a person may contend that the payment was associated with demonstrating a product or performing a preexisting contractual obligation and therefore was not for obtaining or retaining business.

Enforcing Agencies and Penalties

Criminal Proceedings The US Department of Justice (DOJ) prosecutes criminal proceedings for FCPA violations. Firms are subject to fines of up to US$2 million. Officers, directors, employees, agents, and stockholders are subject to fines of up to US$100,000, imprisonment for up to five years, or both.

A US business owner may also be charged under other federal criminal laws. On conviction, the owner may be liable for one of the following: (1) a fine of up to US$250,000; or (2) if the owner derived pecuniary gain from the offense or caused a pecuniary loss to another person, a fine of up to twice the amount of the gross gain or loss.

Civil Proceedings Two agencies are responsible for enforcing the civil provisions of the FCPA: the DOJ handles actions against domestic concerns, and the Securities and Exchange Commission (SEC) files actions against issuers. Civil fines of up to US$100,000 may be imposed on a firm, or on any officer, director, employee, agent, or stockholder acting for a firm. In addition, the appropriate government agency may seek an injunction against a person or firm that has violated or is about to violate FCPA provisions.

Conduct that constitutes a violation of FCPA provisions may also give rise to a cause of action under the federal Racketeer-Influenced and Corrupt Organizations Act (RICO), as well as under similar state statutes if such exist in a state with jurisdiction over the US business.

Administrative Penalties A person or firm that is held to have violated any FCPA provisions may be barred from doing business with the US government. Indictment alone may result in suspension of the right to do business with the government.

Department of Justice Proceedings

Any person may request the DOJ to issue a statement of opinion on whether specific proposed business conduct would be considered a violation of the FCPA. The opinion procedure is detailed in 28 CFR Part 77. If the DOJ issues an opinion stating that certain conduct conforms with current enforcement policy, conduct in accordance with that opinion is presumed to comply with FCPA provisions.

erty rights. As a result, many US, Mexican, and Canadian attorneys and firms are establishing affiliations with each other to serve on a consultant, referral, or other basis.

Attorneys licensed to practice in foreign countries are generally permitted to act as consultants in the US, but may not practice law unless specifically licensed by the applicable state bar association or board.

Contracts

Contracts in the US can be complex and lengthy documents, especially for trade, investment, and real estate matters. The contract negotiation process is primarily a function of whether the parties have a prior working relationship and whether they can negotiate and operate on an equal basis. Contract language should be clear and understandable to the parties involved. Each party to a business contract should retain separate legal counsel so that the legal advice it receives is tailored to its particular needs and is not potentially compromised by the attorney having a conflict of interest between the two parties.

The Role of Notaries

In many countries notaries public are charged with preparing and registering legal documents and many such documents cannot take effect without such notarization. Notaries play a far more restricted role in the US, where their function is to authenticate signatures on documents, and little special training is required to become a notary. In the US attorneys usually perform the more technical functions allocated to notaries elsewhere.

Notaries public can usually be located through the telephone directory for a given location, and are commonly found in banks, real estate sales offices, and insurance and title companies. Some law firms have notaries who serve the clients of the firm. Referrals can usually be obtained from business associates if notarization is required. In many locales, a minimum fee is charged—usually around US$5.

Dispute Resolution

Resolving disputes through lawsuits in the US tends to be a costly, lengthy, and often acrimonious proposition. Certain industries, such as the construction trades and the medical insurance field, have increasingly utilized alternative dispute resolution (ADR) processes, such as arbitration and mediation, instead of litigation to resolve differences. Under arbitration, the parties to a contract agree in advance to submit their disputes to arbitration and agree on a method of selecting an arbitrator or arbitrators from an approved group of recognized authorities. Under mediation, an expert is available throughout the term of the contract to assist the parties in resolving their differences. The expert may have been previously identified by the parties in their contract or subsequently agreed to by the parties. Mediation can be used in conjunction with arbitration and for matters in any stage of litigation.

Business persons contemplating the use of ADR procedures should seek advice on the relative advantages and disadvantages in comparison with those of litigation. The ADR procedures can be, but may not necessarily be, less expensive and time-consuming than litigation. Parties using ADR procedures will need to designate in their contracts such matters as whether decisions by arbitration boards or mediators will be binding, whether information revealed and decisions made during ADR procedures remain confidential, and whether rules of procedure and evidence that govern in courts of law will also apply to their private dispute resolution hearings.

RELATED SECTIONS

Refer to the "Taxation" chapter for a discussion of tax issues in the US; "Business Entities & Formation" for a description of the business forms recognized in the US and the procedures involved in organizing them; "Labor" for employment rules and standards; and "Trade Agreements," "Import Policy & Procedures," and "Export Policy & Procedures" for discussions of various rules involved in trade.

LAW DIGEST

ACKNOWLEDGMENT

Each state has its own requirements relating to the certification of acknowledgment (or proof of writing) of documents, in particular for documents conveying title to real estate interests, wills, and other instruments establishing matters of inheritance. Generally, judges or presiding officers of any court, county or city officers, notaries public, or any other officer authorized by law to take acknowledgment or proof of execution may certify the identity of the person or persons signing the document, on receiving satisfactory evidence of that identity. The form of acknowledgment, including the placement of a seal, is generally specified by statute.

ALIENS

The US immigration laws divide all aliens desiring to enter the US into immigrant and non-immigrant categories. Immigrants are aliens who enter the US intending to reside there permanently. Aliens are generally presumed immigrants unless they can clearly establish their non-immigrant status. The key to this determination is not only the length of stay in the US, but the purpose of the visit and whether the alien intends to leave the US after such visit.

Non-immigrants are aliens who seek to enter the US for a temporary period, usually for one year or less, to engage in an activity authorized under the US immigration laws.

The US Immigration and Naturalization Service (INS) and US consular posts are the two main government agencies charged with the responsibility of processing the various types of visa applications.

Non-Immigrant Visas

Most non-immigrant visas are issued through the US consular posts around the world. Applicants may apply for visas at the consulate nearest to their place of residence or at a consulate outside of one's country of residence. Non-immigrant visas are generally issued for short periods of time and can authorize a single entry (that is, one trip) to the US or multiple entries. Subsequent to the expiration date of a non-immigrant visa, an extension of the visa must be obtained before the alien will be allowed to reenter the US. Non-immigrant visa categories include: B-1 business visitor visas, E visas for treaty traders and treaty investors, L-1 intracompany transferee visas, H visas for temporary workers, and O and J-1 visas for cultural and scientific exchange visitors.

B-1 Business Visitor Visas This visa type allows a visiting alien to engage in business activities in the US that are incidental to the alien's employer's trans-

action of international commerce or trade on a temporary basis. This would include the organization and establishment of a foreign employer's US office, temporary managerial consulting for an existing office, or attendance at professional conventions or trade shows. No productive employment is allowed; remuneration must be received from a foreign source. The B-1 visa category requires application to a US consulate; no special permission needs to be obtained from the INS in the US prior to the issuance of the visa. For many foreign nationals, the visa can be issued for a 10-year period and for an unlimited number of entries.

The B-1 visa normally permits a business visitor to enter the US for a maximum initial stay of six months in order to conduct limited business activities, and may be extended if necessary. The key condition of the B-1 visa category is that the alien cannot engage in gainful employment in the US. The alien applicant must be able to prove that the services performed in the US will principally benefit the foreign employer.

E Visas for Treaty Traders and Treaty Investors This type of visa is designed for a national of a country that has entered into a Treaty of Friendship, Commerce, and Navigation with the US. The E-1 visa may be issued to an individual alien (or to an employee of a foreign company of the same nationality as the treaty country) for entry into the US solely to carry on substantial trade between the US and the alien's home country. The E-1 status may be available to certain key alien employees of the trader. The E-2 visa is available to an individual alien (or to an employee of a foreign company of the same nationality as the treaty country) who is coming to the US solely to develop and direct a business enterprise as an investor of a substantial amount of capital. Certain key alien employees of the investor may also be granted E-2 status.

An alien who obtains either E-1 or E-2 status can be accompanied by his or her spouse and unmarried children under the age of 21 on derivative status visas. A spouse or child holding a derivative visa is not authorized to engage in employment in the US, unless that spouse or child has independently obtained a non-immigrant visa that permits employment.

The E category provides for an initial period of stay of one to five years depending on the country of nationality, and it may be extended almost indefinitely so long as the trade or investment continues. The E category visa applications are processed exclusively through the US consulates abroad; no separate applications need be filed or special permission obtained from the INS in the US prior to the issuance of the visa. Those persons qualifying for E visa status do not have to maintain a foreign residence, provided that such aliens do intend to leave the US when their period of stay, plus any authorized extension, expires.

L-1 Intracompany Transferee Visa This visa is available to an alien who, prior to the time of application for admission to the US, has been employed by a foreign employer for at least one of the three preceding years in an executive or managerial capacity or in a capacity that involves specialized knowledge, and who desires temporary admission to the US to render services to the foreign employer, or to a parent, subsidiary, affiliate, or branch of the foreign employer.

To obtain an L-1 visa, the US employer must first file a petition with the appropriate regional service center office of the INS with jurisdiction over the location where the alien will be employed. Once this petition is approved by the INS, it will be sent (by cable, if requested) to the appropriate US consulate abroad, where the alien applicant can obtain an L-1 visa to enter the US. An alien who obtains an L-1 visa can be accompanied by a spouse and unmarried children under the age of 21 on derivative status visas. These derivative visas do not authorize employment in the US.

Petitions are approved for three year periods. Extensions are allowed for the period during which the alien's services are required by the US employer, up to seven years for managers or executives or five years for employees with specialized knowledge.

H-1B Visas for Temporary Workers These visas are issued to persons seeking to enter the US to perform temporary labor or services in "specialty occupations." A specialty occupation is one requiring a minimum prerequisite of (1) theoretical and practical knowledge; and (2) the attainment of a bachelor's or higher degree in the specialty. If the US job requires a license, the alien must be appropriately licensed in the occupation of practice. The position to be filled by the alien can be permanent in nature, but the employer's intention must be to employ the alien in that position on a temporary basis. Likewise, the alien employee must intend to remain only temporarily in the US.

To obtain the H-1 visa, a US employer must file with the US Department of Labor an affirmation that states that the wages paid to, and the working conditions of, the alien meet certain standards and that notice of the filing has been posted or given to an applicable union. Once the application is approved by the Department, the US employer must then file a petition with the INS in order to secure permission to employ an alien professional or prominent person for a temporary period. Once the petition is approved, it is sent (by cable, if requested) to the appropriate US consulate abroad, where the alien can

obtain an H-1B visa to enter the US. The H-1B visa may authorize an alien's stay in the US for up to six years although petitions are approved in three-year increments.

H-2B Visas These are used by US companies to employ skilled or unskilled aliens in positions that are temporary in nature and for which unemployed US workers are not available. The US employer must intend to employ the aliens for a temporary period and the employer's need for the skills possessed by the aliens must also be temporary.

To obtain the H-2B visa, the US employer must obtain a labor certification from the US Department of Labor. A single request can cover one or more aliens filling the same position. The US employer must file with the INS the approved labor certification and a petition and must submit documents to show that the position is temporary. Following approval of the petition, the final step is to take the petition approval notice to the appropriate US consulate abroad to have the H-2B visa stamped into the alien's passport.

The initial period of stay granted under H-2B status is determined by the time that the temporary services are needed, which must be reasonable in terms of the duties to be performed and cannot be longer than an initial period of one year. The US company may request an extension of stay in increments of one year, but the alien cannot be continuously employed in the US for more than three years.

H-3 Visas These visas are used by US enterprises to bring aliens to the US for a temporary period to participate in an established company training program. The training program may provide classroom training, or a combination of classroom and on-the-job training, that is unavailable in the alien worker's home country. The H-3 visa category is utilized as a means of increasing the alien's knowledge and skills and thus enhancing the alien's contribution to a US employer's foreign operations.

The US employer must file a preliminary petition with the INS in order to bring alien employees to the US to participate in the training, which must consist of an established program available to other employees in similar positions. Once the preliminary petition is approved, the alien must take the approval notice to the appropriate US consulate abroad to obtain the H-3 visa. New regulations limit such training visas to a maximum limit of two years. However, an extension of stay up to the two year limit can be granted even if the employer originally requested less than the full two years.

H-4 Visas These visas are in the derivative status category that may be used by a spouse and unmarried children under the age of 21 of aliens who have been granted H-1, H-2, or H-3 visas. The spouse and children entitled to such status are not authorized to engage in employment in the US, unless they have independently obtained a non-immigrant visa that permits them to work.

O Visas This type of visa is available to aliens of "extraordinary" ability in science, art, education, business, or athletics, to their family members, and to certain additional individuals who are needed as assistants for the period of time necessary to participate in the event for which the alien was admitted.

J-1 Exchange Visitors Visa This visa category is used by foreign students, scholars, industrial and business trainees, international visitors, specialists, and others for entry under US government-approved exchange visitor programs for the purpose of cultural exchange and gaining experience in their respective fields while in the US.

Approval for J-1 exchange programs must be obtained from the US Information Agency (USIA). A US business may take advantage of a J-1 program by either applying to the USIA and receiving approval as a program sponsor (that is, applying under an in-house program) or applying in individual cases through another program sponsor who has been approved by the USIA (that is, applying under an umbrella program). The sponsor of the exchange visitor program is empowered by the USIA to issue a Certificate of Eligibility for each exchange visitor; the USIA's approval for each exchange visitor is not required. Once the Certificate of Eligibility is issued, the exchange alien must take the certificate to the appropriate US consulate abroad to apply for issuance of a J-1 visa. Family members of the exchange alien may enter the US under a related category J-2 visa. An exchange alien's spouse and unmarried minor children may accept employment in the US with INS authorization, but only if their compensation will be used for their own support and not that of the exchange alien.

The initial period of stay granted to an alien entering the US as an industrial or business trainee cannot exceed the length of the program, up to 18 months. Exchange aliens who enter the US as industrial or business trainees must be furnished on-the-job training to receive knowledge of US business techniques in their fields of endeavor within the standard number of working hours for the particular industry.

Permanent Residents

The US government has designated the groups to which immigration preference is given. For certain groups, such as immediate relatives of US citizens, no limitation is placed on the number of aliens who can immigrate. However, most groups are subject to an overall numerical limitation of 270,000 immigrant visas per year. Within this overall numerical limitation, four family-based and five employment-based groups are given preference for immigration to the US.

Under the Immigration Act of 1990, two immigrant visa categories are available specifically to foreign investors and businesspeople. The first category creates an immigrant visa for employment creation investors, that is, aliens who have established new commercial enterprises in the US. To qualify for this visa, the immigrant employer must employ five or more US citizens or permanent residents who are not related to the immigrant employer and must invest a minimum of US$500,000 to US$1,000,000. The second category creates an immigrant visa for aliens of extraordinary ability and certain multinational executives and managers.

ARBITRATION

In the written contracts or agreements between them, parties to a transaction may agree to submit any controversy arising out of their contract to arbitration by a board or group of recognized experts in the field, rather than to litigate their claims in court. States may have adopted the Uniform Arbitration Act, and organizations—such as the American Arbitration Association—have established rules and procedures governing the conduct of arbitration.

ATTACHMENT

Attachment is the legal process by which a plaintiff (the one bringing a legal action) obtains a court order to seize property of the defendant (the one against whom the plaintiff's action is brought) before a court finds a judgment in the plaintiff's favor. The purpose of attachment is to secure the payment of damages to the plaintiff in the event damages are awarded. Attachment may be granted when the plaintiff can show that (1) a cause of action exists; (2) it is probable the plaintiff will succeed on the merits of the case; (3) the plaintiff has demanded and would be entitled to a money judgment against one or more of the defendants; and (4) the defendant is a foreign corporation not qualified to do business in the state of action, or the defendant refuses to accept legal service or attempts to frustrate enforcement of a judgment in the plaintiff's favor.

COMMERCIAL TRANSACTIONS

The standards that govern commercial transactions are found principally in the laws of the various states, although specific federal statutes or treaties govern in certain areas. All of the states have adopted, in one form or another, the Uniform Commercial Code (UCC), which was produced as a model state statute through the joint efforts of the American Law Institute and the National Conference of Commissioners on Uniform State Laws. Moreover, the US has adopted and ratified the United Nations Convention on International Contracts for the Sale of Goods, which provides an additional set of rules that govern certain commercial activities in the US.

The Uniform Commercial Code

The UCC was promulgated as semipermanent legislation, with the intention that it would prove flexible enough to permit those engaged in commercial transactions to adapt its provisions to changing circumstances and methods of doing business, provided that certain basic principles relating to reasonableness and fair dealing are respected. Accordingly, the UCC in each state explicitly permits many of its provisions to be varied by agreement among the parties to a transaction.

The UCC currently contains the following 11 substantive articles: (1) General Provisions; (2) Sales; (2A) Leases; (3) Negotiable Instruments; (4) Bank Deposits and Collections; (4A) Funds Transfer; (5) Letters of Credit; (6) Bulk Sales; (7) Warehouse Receipts, Bills of Lading, and Other Documents of Title; (8) Investment Securities; and (9) Secured Transactions, Sales of Accounts, and Chattel Paper.

Article 1: General Provisions Article 1 concerns the purposes of the UCC, which are (1) to simplify, clarify, and modernize the law governing commercial transactions; (2) to permit the continued expansion of commercial practices through custom, usage, and agreement of the parties; and (3) to make uniform the law among various jurisdictions. This article sets forth rules providing that the UCC be liberally construed and applied; that parties can modify the provisions of the UCC by agreement; that remedies provided by the UCC should be liberally administered; and that every contract or duty within the UCC imposes an obligation of good faith in its performance or enforcement.

Article 2: Sales Article 2 applies to transactions in goods. It does not apply to transactions that create or modify only security interests, nor does it replace any other statutes relating to sales to consumers, farmers, or other specifically protected classes of buyers. Certain provisions of Article 2 apply only to the "sale of goods" as distinct from all "transactions in goods." The article sets forth rules regarding the formation and readjustment of contracts for the sale of goods; the general obligations and construction of such contracts; the passing of title; the rights of the seller's creditors; the rights of good faith purchasers; the performance of such contracts by sellers and buyers; and rules regarding breach, repudiation, excuse, and remedies for breaches of contracts.

Article 2A: Leases Article 2A codifies certain common law principles relating to the leasing of personal property. Among other things, this article regulates the formation and construction of lease contracts; the effect of and performance obligations relating to such contracts; and the remedies that may be pursued by either the lessor or the lessee in the event of a default under the lease contract.

Article 3: Negotiable Instruments Article 3 relates to negotiable instruments, such as checks, certificates of deposit, and notes. The article sets forth rules regarding the requirements and form of negotiable instruments; the liability of parties to negotiable instruments; the effect of transfers; the rights of holders; and procedures for presentation, notices of dishonor, protest, and the discharge of parties under such instruments.

Article 4: Bank Deposits and Collections Article 4 concerns banks and creates a uniform law regarding bank deposits and bank collections. The article includes rules and presumptions relating to the bank collection process; banks' liabilities and duties to customers; and banks' handling of documentary drafts.

Article 4A: Funds Transfers Article 4A governs certain wire transfer payments. Among other things, this article describes the significant characteristics of funds transfers; regulates the issuance and acceptance of payment orders; and normalizes the execution of payment orders and the payment obligations of the parties to the various funds transfers.

Article 5: Letters of Credit Article 5 provides a statutory framework for letters of credit and provides definitions of terms; fixes the responsibilities of parties; imposes warranties on those transferring or presenting drafts drawn under a letter of credit; provides for indemnities by banks; sets the time in which a bank must act on a draft; describes the conditions under which a bank may or must honor drafts; and provides for the transfer and assignment of proceeds of letters of credit. Many of these rules are the same as those adopted by the International Chamber of Commerce (ICC) with respect to documentary credits.

Article 6: Bulk Sales Article 6 concerns the transfer in bulk of a substantial portion of the materials, supplies, merchandise, or other inventory of certain business enterprises. This article covers only those enterprises having as their principal business the sale of merchandise from stock, including those that manufacture what they sell. Accordingly, enterprises that principally sell services are not subject to this article. The article in general requires the buyer to give creditors of the seller advance notice of the bulk sale so as to enable such creditors to assert their rights against the seller and the seller's assets prior to the sale. If the requirements of Article 6 are not met, the buyer could incur liability to the seller's creditors, generally to the extent of the purchase price paid to the seller.

Article 7: Warehouse Receipts, Bills of Lading and Other Documents of Title Article 7 deals with the transportation and storage of goods; the rights of parties storing goods at a warehouse; the rights of purchasers of warehouse receipts; the rights of pledgees of warehouse receipts; the rights of shippers against their carriers; the rights of purchasers of bills of lading; and the rights of pledgees of bills of lading. The article also specifies the commercial risks a party takes when accepting particular documents of title.

Article 8: Investment Securities Article 8 deals with the transfer of stock and other investment securities. The article sets forth certain rights and duties of the issuers of and the parties that deal with investment securities, both certified and uncertified.

Article 9: Secured Transactions, Sales of Accounts and Chattel Paper Article 9 applies to any transaction that is intended to create a security interest in personal property or fixtures—including goods, documents, instruments, general intangibles, chattel paper or accounts. It also applies to any sale of accounts or chattel paper. The article sets forth rules regarding the validity of security agreements; the rights and priorities of various parties; the filing system for the perfection of security interests; the limits of the secured party's protection against purchasers from the debtor; and the rights of the secured party upon the debtor's default. Article 9 facilitates the extension of credit secured by floating liens on accounts receivable, inventories, and other current assets.

The United Nations Convention on International Contracts for the Sale of Goods

Certain transactions of foreign businesspeople desiring to buy or sell goods in the US may be subject to and governed by the provisions of the United Nations Convention on International Contracts for the Sale of Goods (the Convention) rather than the UCC. The Convention applies to a transaction between a buyer and a seller if: (1) each has its place of business in a different nation; and (2) both nations have ratified the Convention and the ratification by each nation has taken effect. The provisions of the Convention are similar to, but sometimes differ from, those of the UCC. If they wish, parties otherwise governed by the Convention may opt out of its jurisdiction and may choose to be governed instead by the UCC. To date, approximately 30 nations have ratified the Convention.

CONFLICTS OF LAW

When a case or controversy arises in which the parties and their circumstances have significant relationships to more than one government or jurisdiction, the rules applied to determine which law will be followed are known as conflicts of law (or choice of law) rules. The conflicts of law rules do not resolve the controversy, but serve only to settle the issue of which law will be used to determine the controversy. Conflicts of law can occur between all forums, including the federal law of the US versus the law of one of its states, the law of one state versus the law of another state, and US federal law versus the law of another sovereign nation.

Federal Law Versus State Law

Under the Supremacy Clause of the US Constitution (Article VI), the states are required to give effect to the Constitution, statutes, and treaties of the US, and to authoritative decisions of the federal courts in areas of national law. Other major provisions of the Constitution that limit state power to encroach on federal matters include the Full Faith and Credit Clause (Article IV, Section 1), the Due Process Clauses (Fifth and Fourteenth Amendments), the Privileges and Immunities Clause (Article IV, Section 2), the Equal Protection Clause (Fourteenth Amendment), and the Commerce Clause (Article I, Section 8).

State Law Versus State Law

In determining whether to apply the laws of its state or the laws of another state, a court will characterize the issue between the parties to a particular body of law, such as torts, contracts, property, or some other field, and will apply the laws of its own state for that subject accordingly. The laws of the state for that body of law may in fact dictate that the laws of the other state govern. If state law does not dispose of the conflict, a court can consider factors such as: (1) the needs of interstate and international systems; (2) the relevant policies of the forum; (3) the relevant policies of the other interested states; (4) the protection of justified expectations; (5) the basic policies underlying the particular field of law; (6) the certainty, predictability, and uniformity of result; and (7) the ease in the determination and application of the law to be applied.

Often, to avoid the application of state conflicts of laws principals, the parties to a transaction may wish to designate in their agreement or contract which state law applies.

Federal Law Versus Foreign Sovereign Law

These conflicts fall into two categories: private international law (which relates to the rights of individuals in relation to individuals of another country) and law of nations (which concerns the rights between nations or between a nation and a citizen or subject of another nation). Generally, courts in the US are bound to regard applicable treaties and statutes as superior to the rules of international law, and may not declare a statute adopted by Congress or a declaration included in a treaty null and void merely on the grounds that it would violate principles of international law.

CONSUMER PROTECTION

Virtually every state has adopted some form of consumer credit protection legislation, such as the Uniform Consumer Credit Code. In some instances, the states have incorporated federal legislation by reference, such as the National Consumer Act and the federal Consumer Credit Protection Act.

The major federal acts that protect the rights of borrowers and consumers are: (1) the Truth-in-Lending Act (provisions of the Consumer Credit Protection Act), which deals with credit transactions, credit advertising, credit billing, and consumer leases; (2) the Equal Credit Opportunity Act, which prohibits discrimination against applicants for credit on the basis of race, color, religion, national origin, sex, marital status, or the like; (3) the Fair Debt Collection Practices Act, which provides that a debt collector may not use unfair or unconscionable means to collect or attempt to collect any debt; and (4) the Electronic Funds Transfer Act, which provides for the rights, liabilities, and responsibilities of participants in the electronic funds transfer system and for protection of individual consumer rights.

Federal and state laws generally require that contracts or agreements involving consumer credit or debt clearly disclose such items as the amounts of the loan or debt, together with all finance charges, late charges, other fees and allowances, and due dates. Such legislation also protects consumers against unfair or deceptive trade practices.

CONTRACTS

Contracts are governed by the common law developed in each state as modified by state statute. The common law elements of a contract in its simplest form are: (1) an offer; (2) an acceptance of that offer; and (3) transfer of payment or some item of value in connection with the offer and acceptance (known as consideration). Contracts may be orally made, but certain contracts must be in writing, such as contracts agreeing to make a future contract and sales of real estate and other property interests. Contracts may be voided (that is, considered to have no effect) if they were based, for example, upon a mistake of law or if they were entered into by someone

deemed to lack decision-making capability.

A party to a contract who has suffered due to the other party's failure to perform a contractual duty (referred to as a breach of contract) may choose to seek a remedy provided by law. The basic remedies include: (1) compensatory damages, which seek to "make good" the losses suffered by the plaintiff by requiring the defendant to pay the plaintiff money characterized as general, special, nominal, or punitive damages; (2) restitution, which is designed to prevent the defendant from profiting from the breach; (3) rescission, which attempts, to the extent possible, to "undo" the contract by putting the parties back where they were before the contract was formed—this is generally in cases where fraud, mutual mistake, or illegality was involved; (4) reformation of the contract, whereby the courts make the contract conform to the parties' intentions when the contract was entered into—generally used in cases of mistake or fraud; (5) specific performance, which compels the defendant to do what was promised, such as convey land or perform some unique and particular act; and (6) injunction, by which a court orders the defendant to act (by mandatory injunction) or not to act (by prohibitory or preventive injunction) in the way specified.

The courts of each state have developed their own body of contract law. For example, the California courts have determined that every contract governed by California law includes by implication the covenant of good faith and fair dealing in its terms. Some state legislatures have codified common law elements and expanded upon them. To create some uniformity among the states in the operations and judicial interpretation of commercial contracts, all states have adopted, in some form, the UCC. (*See* "Commercial Transactions" in this "Law Digest" section.) In addition, each state has adopted specific statutory provisions applicable to contracts based on the laws of that state—such as the New York law provision that an irrevocable offer that does not specify any period is irrevocable for a reasonable period (New York GOL § 5-1109).

CORPORATIONS

Organization Each state has its own codified corporation laws pursuant to which a corporation in the US may be organized. With few exceptions, federal law does not govern the incorporation of business enterprises in the US (except with regard to the establishment of a national bank). Generally, a state agency (usually the Secretary of State's office) approves the name of a company and approves the charter or articles of incorporation. The articles of incorporation, together with the corporate bylaws, set forth the rules and regulations by which the corporation will be governed. Thereafter, a minimum amount of capital must be paid into the corporation, and shares are issued to the owners (the shareholders) of the corporation.

Corporate Authority The ultimate corporate authority of the shareholders is usually exercised through a board of directors selected by them. Normally, direct approval by the shareholders is required for only a few major corporate actions, such as amending the charter or articles of incorporation; an increase in the authorized capital of the corporation; the sale of substantially all of the corporation's assets; a merger with another corporation; or voluntary dissolution of the corporation.

Corporate Management The corporate officers usually selected by the board of directors to direct the daily operations of the corporation consist of the following: (1) a president or chief executive officer; (2) one or more vice presidents; (3) a treasurer or chief financial officer; and (4) a secretary. One or more of the top corporate officers may also be members of the board of directors.

The corporate bylaws are drafted to govern shareholders' meetings, selection of directors, and the authority of directors and officers, as well as to establish many other internal procedures for the operation of the business. Shareholders' and directors' meetings are held regularly (at least annually) and at other times when needed. Most actions, including those taken at annual meetings, may be taken without an actual meeting provided there is unanimous written consent to the proposed action by the shareholders or directors, as the case may be.

Officers and directors may be subject to liability if they are seriously remiss in executing their responsibilities for the care of the corporation.

Shareholder Liability If a shareholder deals at arm's length with the corporation, respecting it as a separate entity, the shareholder generally is not liable for acts of the corporation and is responsible only for fulfilling the shareholder's promises, if any, to pay in additional capital.

Publicly Held Corporations Corporations that trade shares publicly must register and maintain filings with the US Securities and Exchange Commission (the SEC) and, in some cases, with other regulatory authorities in the state where the corporation's securities are issued. Most corporations with publicly traded stock are required to file periodic financial reports with the SEC containing financial statements audited by independent certified public accountants.

ENVIRONMENTAL QUALITY

National environmental policy has been defined primarily through legislative and administrative actions, rather than by judicial action. The key federal provisions are found in the National Environmental Policy Act (NEPA) and the Environmental Quality Improvement Act (EQIA). Under NEPA, EQIA, and other related statutes and their regulations, the federal government works with state and local governments to set standards and procedures designed to control pollution and generally improve the quality of the environment.

The Environmental Protection Agency (EPA) is the federal agency responsible for pollution control and which, among other things, enforces restrictions on emissions and noise into the atmosphere and the disposal of solid and hazardous wastes, radioactive material, toxic substances, and pesticides into the water and on the land. States typically have their own agency to manage environmental policy and pollution control.

FOREIGN INVESTMENT

Government Controls

The laws affecting foreign investment are diverse and complex, but a foreign business in the US is free from many of the governmental licensing and other restrictions found in other countries. Because the federal government has not imposed any exchange control requirements, there are no restrictions placed on the transfer of profits, dividends, interest, borrowed funds, income, or other funds from the US. The federal government does not require the registration of capital, nor does it restrict the repatriation of capital to nonresidents, except that a Treasury Department license is required for the repatriation of capital to certain boycotted countries (for example, North Korea and Cuba), or to nationals of such countries.

The amount of equity that a foreign person may own in a US business enterprise is, for the most part, unlimited. However, there are some enterprises, generally those involved with national defense or public welfare, for which federal law restricts the amount of non-US ownership and control. Some examples include:

Radio Communications Foreign ownership may not exceed 20 percent in domestic radio communications.

Domestic Air Transportation Foreign ownership may not exceed 25 percent in companies engaged in domestic air transportation, nor may foreigners control more than one-third of the board of directors of such companies. Shipping vessels bearing the flag of the US must be wholly owned by US citizens or by domestic corporations controlled by US citizens.

Banking and Insurance A multitude of federal

and state agencies regulate the operation of banks and insurance companies in the US, including restrictions on foreign ownership.

Energy Resources Energy resource enterprises, such as hydroelectric power companies and facilities which utilize nuclear materials, are subject to federal licensing restrictions on foreign involvement. Foreigners are not eligible for federal mining claim grants, nor may foreigners own oil or mineral leases, unless their home countries offer reciprocal rights to US citizens.

National Security The US Defense Department and related agencies impose restrictions on foreign participation in projects related to national security or involving access to classified information.

Land Ownership Regulation of foreign ownership of land in the US arises most frequently in connection with agricultural land. The Agricultural Foreign Investment Disclosure Act of 1978 requires foreigners to provide certain information regarding investments in US agricultural land. Moreover, there may be state law disclosure requirements similar to those imposed under federal law. Certain other federal statutory provisions, such as the Trading with the Enemy Act, may also limit a foreigner's ability to own or lease land in the US. In addition, foreign investors may be ineligible to obtain certain rights, such as water and grazing rights on federal land, and other federal benefits may be available only to landowners who are US citizens.

In addition to federal limitations on foreign ownership of US land, certain states impose restrictions on either the ownership or the inheritance of land by foreigners. In these state jurisdictions, such limitations may also apply to aliens who are general partners in a partnership owning real property because of the nature of a general partner's interest in the property of the partnership. The laws of some states may also limit or regulate indirect alien ownership of real property (for example, a limited partner's interest in a limited partnership which owns land or stock of a corporation owning such property).

Disclosure Requirements

Certain federal statutes require the filing of reports and returns with various US government agencies in connection with investments in the US by foreign individuals and enterprises. These filings include reporting information to agencies which study the domestic impact of foreign investment, and financial returns to the IRS.

The SEC Sections 13(d) and 13(g) of the Securities Exchange Act of 1934 require any person who directly or indirectly acquires beneficial ownership of more than 5 percent of any equity security registered with the SEC to file a report with the SEC within 10 days after such acquisition. The report discloses, among other things, the person's identity, residence, citizenship, and certain background information. In addition, reports must be sent to the issuer of the security and to the stock exchange through which the security is traded. These reports are applicable to foreign beneficial owners even if the shares are acquired outside the US.

Monetary Instruments The Currency and Foreign Transactions Reporting Act of 1970, as amended, requires all banks and financial institutions to comply with a variety of recordkeeping requirements. Federally insured banks must record the identities of persons having accounts with them and persons having signature authority on such accounts. They also must maintain microfilm and other reproductions of certain checks, drafts, and other monetary instruments. Certain domestic financial institutions are required to report domestic currency transactions, including the payment, receipt, and transfer of US currency and coins. Generally, the reporting obligation arises with respect to transactions involving US$10,000 or more. Substantial civil and criminal penalties may be imposed for any violations.

In addition, persons entering or leaving the US must file a customs declaration on Form 6059-B disclosing whether they are carrying US$10,000 or more in cash, travelers checks, money orders, negotiable instruments, securities, or other monetary instruments. If carrying such amounts, the person must also file Form 4790, which requires the disclosure of the name and address of the beneficial owner of the above items. The penalty for noncompliance can result in substantial fines and imprisonment for up to five years, plus the forfeiture of the amount of the funds involved.

The Federal Trade Commission (FTC) and Antitrust Division of the Department of Justice (DOJ) The Hart-Scott-Rodino Antitrust Improvements Act of 1976 (the Hart-Scott-Rodino Act) grants to the FTC and the Antitrust Division of the DOJ the authority to prohibit certain proposed business combinations—by merger or by the acquisition of stock or assets—which would have adverse competitive effects on US interstate commerce. The Hart-Scott-Rodino Act requires that prior notification and a waiting period be given to the FTC and the Antitrust Division of certain proposed business combinations in order to evaluate the competitive effects.

Basically, the Hart-Scott-Rodino Act contains three threshold tests, which must be met before parties to a proposed business combination are required to comply with the act's reporting and waiting period requirements. Regardless of which one of the threshold tests is met, one party to the proposed combination must have annual net sales or total assets of US$100 million or more and the other party must have annual net sales or total assets of US$10 million or more. In determining a person's total assets or net sales under these tests, all entities and persons affiliated with the acquired and acquiring parties must be included. Notwithstanding the foregoing, the Hart-Scott-Rodino Act's filing and waiting provisions generally do not apply to proposed combinations following which the acquiring entity will neither own the assets of the acquired corporation with a purchase price exceeding US$15 million nor hold voting securities conferring control over an acquired corporation which (together with all entities which it controls) has sales or assets of US$25 million or more. (*See* the"Monopolies and Restraint of Trade" entry in this "Law Digest" section.)

The Committee on Foreign Investment in the US (CFIUS) The Exon-Florio provisions of the Omnibus Trade and Competitiveness Act of 1988 authorize the president of the US to investigate certain foreign acquisitions of US businesses and, if certain conditions are met, to block or divest those transactions that the president determines may threaten to impair the national security of the US. The president has delegated to CFIUS the authority to determine when a proposed transaction warrants review; to conduct investigations; and to submit recommendations to approve, block, or divest transactions.

Although the parties to a proposed acquisition have no legal duty to file notice of the transaction with CFIUS, unless notice is filed, the transaction will remain indefinitely subject to government action, including possible divestment, at the direction of the president. There is currently no comprehensive list of criteria for determining whether a proposed transaction poses such a significant threat to national security. Moreover, there is no minimum threshold exclusion for small transactions in connection with notice filings made in accord with the Exon-Florio provisions, as is the case with the Hart-Scott-Rodino filings. Therefore, any transaction that would result in the foreign control of a US business engaged in interstate commerce at any level that may conceivably threaten the national security of the US is subject to review.

Investment in US Agricultural Land The Agricultural Foreign Investment Disclosure Act of 1978 (AFIDA), as amended, requires certain disclosures be made in connection with foreign investment in US agricultural land. The act requires any foreign party who acquires or transfers an interest in US agricultural land to file Form ASCS-153 within 90 days of the acquisition or transfer of any interest, other than a security interest, in US agricultural land. Form ASCS-153 requires, among other things, the disclosure of the legal name of the owner, purchaser, or seller of the land; a description of the land; the purchase price; and the purposes for which it is intended to be used.

If a party is not a foreign party at the time of the transaction but subsequently becomes a foreign party, certain reporting requirements are required. Similarly, if land is not agricultural at the time of the transaction but is subsequently converted to use as agricultural land, a report must be submitted not later than 90 days after the date on which the land is converted for agricultural purposes.

The Department of Agriculture's Stabilization and Conservation Service (ASCS) is charged with administering AFIDA, and reports are filed with the ASCS office in the county where the land is located. A foreign party will be deemed to be in violation of AFIDA if the party fails to submit any required report; fails to update any submitted report to account for any material changes in the transaction or property; or submits a report which is incomplete or contains false or misleading information. Significant penalties will be imposed by ASCS for failure to comply with AFIDA.

Although all reports filed under AFIDA are available for public inspection, a foreign investor who desires anonymity under AFIDA can achieve such through the establishment of three successive tiers of ownership between the investor and any US agricultural land; AFIDA grants to the US Secretary of Agriculture the authority to inquire as to the identity of the first three tiers of ownership of US agricultural land, but no authority for obtaining information regarding a fourth level owner.

Investments in US Business Enterprises and Real Estate The International Investment Survey Act of 1976 (IISA) requires that initial, quarterly, annual, and five-year benchmark reports be filed with the US Department of Commerce's Bureau of Economic Analysis concerning a foreign party's ownership of 10 percent or more of the voting stock of a US corporation or of an equivalent interest in an unincorporated US "business enterprise," which is defined to include any ownership of US real estate. Form BE-13 must be filed within 45 days after a foreign party's establishment of 10 percent or greater voting (or equivalent) interest in a US business enterprise, unless an exemption applies.

Other forms required by the provisions of IISA are: Form BE-607, Industry Classification Questionnaire; Form BE-14, Report by Intermediaries; Form BE-605, Quarterly Report; Form BE-15, Annual Report; and Form BE-12, Quinquennial Report. Exemptions are available for the quarterly, annual, and quinquennial reporting requirements based on the value of a reporting entity's total assets, annual sales, and net profit. The failure to file any of the forms required by IISA may result in a fine of up to US$10,000 and, if the offender is a corporation, any officer, director, employee, or agent of the corporation who knowingly participates in a violation of the act may be punished by a like fine, one year's imprisonment, or both.

Forms BE-13 and BE-12 require the identification of the name and country of each person in the ownership chain of a foreign parent back to its "ultimate beneficial owner," defined as the first party; it proceeds back through the ownership chain until it reaches a foreign parent not more than 50 percent owned or controlled by another party. Recent amendments to IISA regulations allow foreign parties to preserve their anonymity by requiring only the party's country of location and not the party's name when the ultimate beneficial owner is an individual.

Returns Required Pursuant to FIRPTA The Foreign Investment in Real Property Tax Act of 1980 (FIRPTA) added a new section to the Internal Revenue Code (IRC) which imposes a tax on certain dispositions of a US real property interest (USRPI) by foreign investors. Section 897 requires a foreign investor to take gain or loss from such a disposition into account as effectively connected with the conduct of a US trade or business. Section 1445 requires the transferee of a USRPI to withhold the lesser of 10 percent of the amount realized on the disposition or the transferor's maximum tax liability (that is, the maximum amount determined by the IRS that the transferor could owe on the gain from the sale plus any prior unsatisfied withholding tax liability as to the transferor's interest).

FIRPTA also created Section 6039C of the IRC which requires, in relevant part, that any foreign person holding a direct investment in a USRPI must file a return giving the person's name and address, a description of the USRPI held during the calendar year, and any other information the Secretary of the Treasury may prescribe by regulation. A foreign person is generally treated as holding a direct investment if the fair market value of the person's USRPI equaled or exceeded US$50,000 at any time during the year and the foreign person did not engage in a trade or business in the US at any time during the calendar year.

Reporting of Related Party Transactions Detailed IRS reporting requirements exist for 25-percent foreign owned domestic corporations and foreign corporations engaged in a US trade or business with respect to transfer pricing of transactions with related parties. Such filings require a description of how the reporting corporation is related to each related party and the transactions between the reporting corporation and each foreign related party. The identity of the direct and ultimate indirect 25-percent foreign shareholders must be disclosed, and significant penalties are imposed for failure to comply with the reporting requirements.

FOREIGN TRADE

Any product imported into the US is subject to dutiable or duty free entry in accordance with its classification within the Harmonized Tariff Schedule of the US (HTSUS). The HTSUS, which went into effect on January 1, 1989, is based on the International Convention on the Harmonized Commodity Description and Coding System, to which the US acceded on October 31, 1988. Under the US Constitution, duties on imported products may only be imposed by the federal government and cannot be imposed separately by any of the states.

Classification and Rate of Duty Classification and valuation are generally the two most important factors affecting the dutiable status of products imported into the US. The HTSUS classifies products by assigned numbers. Because some products might arguably be classified under more than one number, complex rules of interpretation must often be utilized.

The duties applicable to each HTSUS number are generally imposed on an ad valorem basis (that is, a percentage of the appraised value of the products). However, certain products are subject to either a specific rate (that is, a specified amount per unit of weight or other quantity) or a compound rate (that is, a combination of both an ad valorem rate and a specific rate).

Rates of duty in the HTSUS are divided into two columns. The first column is subdivided into "general" and "special" rates of duty. The second column generally lists higher rates of duty applicable to imports from certain communist countries. The general duty rate applies to most products imported into the US. However, special duty preferences are often available for imported products containing US components or originating from economically disadvantaged countries or countries having a special relationship with the US. Products originating in developing countries are often entitled to special duty preferences based on economic need. Many special duty preferences are standardized in the US Generalized System of Preferences (GSP) program for economically disadvantaged countries. Other specific trade agreements with nations such as Israel, Canada, and Mexico entitle products from these countries to special duty preferences based on close ties with the US.

Temporary Free Importations Certain types of products, when not imported for sale in the US, or for sale on approval, may be admitted into the US on a temporary basis without the payment of duty, provided that the foreign exporter or US importer posts a bond. The bond is posted in an amount which is usually double the estimated duties. Such products must be exported out of the US within one year from the date of importation under bond. Upon application to the district or port director, the one-year exportation limit may generally be extended for one or more additional periods. However, the total may not exceed three years.

Marking Unless specifically exempted under the US Customs laws, every individual imported product must be legibly marked in a conspicuous place with the English name of the country of origin. In addition to this general requirement, other government agencies besides the US Customs Service may have certain marking or labeling requirements. For example, the Food and Drug Administration (FDA) requires special markings on certain foods and medical products, and the FTC requires fiber content markings on most textile products.

Antidumping Duties Imported products that are sold in the US at less than fair value (that is, for less than is charged for the same product in its home country) and that may injure domestic producers of competing products are subject to duties beyond the duties otherwise decreed by the HTS. An antidumping duty will be imposed if the OC concludes that the dumped products are being sold in the US at less than fair value and the US International Trade Commission (ITC) concludes that the dumped products have caused, or threaten to cause, material injury or retardation to an identifiable industry within the US. The antidumping duty will be equal to the difference between the higher price charged for the products in the applicable foreign market and the price charged in the US.

Countervailing Duties Imported products that are sold in the US at less than fair value due to direct or indirect subsidies from foreign governments or other foreign entities and that may injure domestic producers of those products are subject to countervailing duties beyond the tariffs otherwise assessable under the HTS. As with antiduming duties, a countervailing duty will be imposed if the DOC concludes that the subsidized products are being sold in the US at less than fair value and the US International Trade Commission concludes that the subsidized products have caused, or threaten to cause, material injury or retardation to an identifiable industry within the US. The countervailing duty will be equal to the net amount of the subsidy provided by the foreign government or entity.

Quotas, Embargoes, and Other Restrictions In a limited number of situations, quotas, embargoes, and other restrictions may be imposed on certain imported products to protect or promote US agriculture; national security; public health, safety, and welfare; or other political or foreign policy priorities.

Tariff-Rate Quotas Tariff-rate quotas provide for the entry into the US of a specified quantity of a specified product at a reduced rate of duty during a given period. Although there is no overall limitation on the amount of the product that may be imported during the quota period, any quantity that exceeds the quota for the period will be subject to a higher duty rate. Because the quota status of a product subject to a tariff-rate quota cannot be determined in advance of its entry, the (reduced) quota rates of duty are ordinarily assessed on such products entered from the beginning of the quota period until it is determined that imports are nearing the quota level. The US Customs officials then require the deposit of estimated duties at the (higher) over-quota duty rate and report the time of official acceptance of each entry. Once a final determination of when a quota was filled is made, Customs refunds any excess charges or collects any additional charges, and all subsequent entries are made at the higher rate. Most tariff-rate quotas affect agricultural products.

Absolute Quotas Absolute quotas provide for the entry of a fixed quantity of specified products during the quota period. While some absolute quotas are global in scope, others are allocated to specified foreign countries. Imports of the quota products in excess of a specified quota may be reexported or detained for entry during a subsequent quota period. Certain products subject to absolute quotas are repeatedly filled at or shortly after the opening of the quota period. Accordingly, each of these quotas is officially opened at a specified time on the first day of the quota period so that all importers have an equal opportunity for the simultaneous presentation of entries under the quota. When the total quantity for which entries are filed at the opening of the quota period exceeds the quota, the merchandise is released on a pro rata basis (that is, the ratio between the quota quantity and the total quantity offered for entry). This method is intended to ensure an equitable distribution of the quota among importers.

Embargoes Embargoes are usually imposed for national security or foreign policy reasons. For example, embargoes have been imposed in recent years on products from North Korea, Kampuchea, Vietnam, Iran, and South Africa. As national and foreign policy considerations change, some countries are added to the embargo list while others are deleted.

Other Restrictions Other restrictions may prohibit or place quality or other controls on imported products, often due to public health, safety, and welfare concerns. These concerns may focus on such items as adulterated or dangerous food, drugs, livestock, wildlife, and insects. Other areas of concern may include consumer products, firearms, electronics, motor vehicles, biological materials, and radioactive and other nuclear materials.

Foreign Trade Zones Under the Foreign Trade Zones Act of 1934, the US has designated special foreign trade zones (free trade zones) that serve as secured areas outside of US customs territory for the purpose of attracting and promoting international trade and commerce. Foreign exporters can forward their products to such zones to be held for an unlimited period while awaiting favorable market conditions in the US or neighboring countries without having to enter the items, pay duties, or post bonds.

Products lawfully brought into these zones may be stored, sold, exhibited, broken up, repacked, assembled, distributed, sorted, graded, cleaned, mixed with other foreign or domestic products, or otherwise manipulated. The resulting products may be either exported or entered into the US. Customs duties are paid only on those products actually entered into the US. Products manufactured or produced in the US may also be taken into a foreign trade zone and, provided that their identity is maintained in accordance with certain regulations, returned to customs territory free of quotas, duty, or tax, even though such products (subject to certain restrictions) may have been combined with or made part of other products while in the zone.

INDUSTRIAL AND INTELLECTUAL PROPERTY RIGHTS

Patents

A US patent is a grant from the federal government to an inventor of the right to exclude others from making, using, or selling an invention in the US for a specific term of years. A patent application describing the invention in detail and stating specifically what the inventor believes is new and patentable is filed with the US Patent and Trademark Office in Washington, DC. Generally, a patent will be granted for the invention if the invention is novel, useful, and not obvious to a person of ordinary skill in the relevant art.

The two most common kinds of patents are utility patents and design patents. A utility patent, which expires 17 years from the date of grant by the US Patent and Trademark Office, may be obtained for the utilitarian or functional nature of a machine, an article of manufacture, a composition of matter, or a process. A design patent, which expires 14 years from the date of grant, may be obtained for the ornamental external appearance of an article of manufacture. Upon the expiration of a patent term, the right to exclude others also expires, and anyone may use the invention without permission.

A foreign patent does not protect intellectual property in the US. By reason of certain formal conventions and treaties to which the US and a number of countries are signatories, "owners" of intellectual property rights in such foreign countries may obtain certain benefits that could not otherwise be accorded to them by the intellectual property laws of the US. Although no international patent system exists today that provides a unified system of granting patents with unified standards of enforcement, significant steps have been made by many national governments toward simplifying the procedures for obtaining patent protection in foreign countries. This simplification is a result of multilateral and bilateral treaties and conventions executed between various countries. The major treaties and conventions are discussed below.

The International Convention for the Protection of Industrial Property (the Paris Convention) Some 88 countries, including the US, are members of the Paris Convention on patents, trademarks, service marks, industrial designs, utility models, and trade names. The Convention provides that each member country will accord foreign nationals the same patent rights that the member country's patent laws provide to its own nationals. While this provision guarantees that foreign applicants will be treated at least as well as domestic applicants in pursuing protection of their property rights, it does not require that member countries provide protections comparable to those available in the foreign applicant's home jurisdiction. Because each country is free to determine the scope of its own industrial property laws, nationals of country A may receive less favorable treatment in country B than is afforded nationals of country B in country A.

The "right of priority" provision of the Paris Convention provides that a patent owner who files an application in another member country may, within one year from the date of filing, apply for patent protection in any other member country and have the later application regarded as if it were filed on the same date as the first application, thus gaining priority. The earlier priority date obtained in this fashion may be necessary to avoid the printed publication bar imposed in the US.

The Paris Convention makes no substantive changes as to the patentability of an invention in a member country. Each country is free to apply its own substantive standards and make an independent determination of whether the invention is patentable under its national law. Accordingly, the Paris Convention, while facilitating the filing of patent applications in foreign countries, does not provide for an "international patent."

Patent Cooperation Treaty Currently subscribed to by 41 countries, including the US, this treaty went into force on January 24, 1978. The treaty establishes a single uniform application format (known as an international application) acceptable in each member state and also establishes a systematic procedure for processing such applications regardless of where filed. Once filed, the application triggers a search of the prior patents in the countries designated in the application by an international searching authority (which, for a US applicant, is the US Patent and Trademark Office). Under the Patent Cooperation Treaty, an applicant receives an official search report before being required to submit translations and national fees to foreign countries. The applicant has an extended period (20 months) after filing the international application to decide, on the basis of the search report, which of the designated countries to ask for patent protection.

The Patent Cooperation Treaty does not replace the Paris Convention and may be used in connection with the mechanisms of that convention. Like the Paris Convention, the Patent Cooperation Treaty makes no substantive changes as to the patentability of an invention in an individual member country. The extent to which a member country relies on the international search conducted pursuant to the Patent Cooperation Treaty is left to the discretion of the member country. The uniformly acceptable format of the international application may, however, reduce the costs of multiple foreign filings and expedite the overall processing of foreign patents.

Trade Secrets

No federal statutes in the US preclude the misuse of trade secrets. Rather, laws precluding the misuse of trade secrets have been enacted by individual states, and vary from one state to another.

Generally, a trade secret is any formula, pattern, device, or compilation of information used in a business, that gives the owner a competitive advantage in the business, and that has been maintained by its owner as a secret. In some states, trade secrets may include customer lists, sources of supply, pricing information, and other similar business information.

While the duration of patent protection is limited, trade secrets are protected for an indefinite period of time if continuously maintained as secrets. Matters of public knowledge or matters that are disclosed by goods in the marketplace are not trade secrets. Although a trade secret is usually known only to a particular business entity, it may be disclosed to employees employed in its use and to others who are pledged to secrecy.

Most states distinguish between trade secrets and "confidential or proprietary information," such as customer lists, which usually do not qualify as trade secrets. Most states will not prohibit the disclosure of confidential or proprietary information unless such disclosure is proscribed by written agreement.

Trademarks

A trademark is defined as "any word, name, symbol, or device, or any combination thereof, adopted and used by a manufacturer or merchant to identify its goods and distinguish them from those manufac-

tured or sold by others." Trademarks and service marks identify goods and services, respectively, as coming from a single source, and consumers rely on these marks to purchase goods (or services) with which they are familiar. In the US, rights in and to trademarks and service marks are acquired by the entity that first actually uses the mark in an ongoing business on goods or in connection with the performance of services.

Although a trademark or service mark need not be registered to be protected in the US, because rights are acquired by the mere use of a mark with goods or services, federal registration gives notice to unwitting infringers that a mark is owned. Registration of trademarks used in a particular state may be obtained by filing an application with such state. After a trademark has been used in interstate commerce, federal registration may be obtained by completing an application with the US Patent and Trademark Office. Such registration usually provides a clearer—although still rebuttable—case for ownership. Registration or renewals issued by the US Patent and Trademark Office prior to November 16, 1989, are granted terms of 20 years; those issued on or after that date are granted terms of 10 years.

Like patent rights, trademark and service mark rights acquired in one country do not extend to other countries. Provisions of the Paris Convention apply to rights in a similar fashion to that described for patents.

Copyrights

A copyright is a federally granted right to protect the expressions of an author or originator of a literary or artistic work from unauthorized copying or performance. A copyright automatically arises when a work is created. To maintain copyright protection, an appropriate notice should be placed on the work when published and copyright registration should be obtained from the US Copyright Office in Washington, DC. Such registration does not create the copyright, but serves to maintain the copyright protection already created. The copyright must be registered before a suit for copyright infringement can be brought, and it should be registered within three months after the first publication for maximum protection. For works created or first published on January 1, 1978, or later, the term of copyright protection in the US is the author's lifetime plus 50 years. The term of protection of certain works, such as works made for hire, is determined differently.

The US is a signatory to the following copyright conventions.

The Universal Copyright Convention The Universal Copyright Convention, sponsored by the United Nations, has been ratified by many countries in either or both of two versions: the Geneva Act of

LABOR LAW

Restrictive Labor Laws on Discipline or Discharge of Employees Federal and state legislation has restricted what had been, under the at-will doctrine, the absolute right of an employer to discharge employees. The federal National Labor Relations Act (NLRA) prohibits an employer from discharging an employee because of the employee's union-related activities. Federal and state laws have also been enacted which make discrimination against a variety of persons who are members of protected classifications unlawful.

More recent laws, including the Federal Worker Adjustment and Retraining Notification Act (WARN), have also restricted employers' right to lay off employees for economic reasons without giving notice. Under WARN's general rules, employers with more than 100 employees must give their employees 60 days' notice if either of two events occurs: (1) the closure of a single site of employment or a facility which results in an employment loss of at least 50 employees (a plant closing); or (2) a reduction in force that is not caused by a plant closing but which results in an employment loss of at least 33 percent of the employees and at least 50 employees (a mass layoff). The procedural details of the WARN notice requirement are specified in federal regulations. Some state legislation also affects notice requirements for plant closings or layoffs, and employers should review state requirements if considering such economic decisions.

Individual Employment Contracts Another legal restriction on the ability of an employer to discharge an employee relates to employees with individual employment contracts. Typically, these contracts include provisions which address how the employee may be discharged. Employees with such contracts may challenge a decision to discharge by arguing that the employer breached the contract by not following discharge procedures set forth in the contract. Legally, the question of whether or not an employer has properly followed discharge procedures in an employment contract is a question of fact that is determined on a case-by-case basis.

Wrongful Discharge Employees without formal employment contracts are more frequently challenging discharge actions. Former employees allege that they have been "wrongfully discharged" by their employer. Court decisions have created several bases for these wrongful discharge lawsuits. First, almost every state in the US declares that it is unlawful for an employer to discharge an employee if the discharge violates public policy. For example, if an employer were to discharge an employee in order to prevent the employee from cooperating in a criminal investigation of the employer's questionable practices, the courts would probably find that this discharge was unlawful because the reason for the discharge violated a clear public policy. Such public policy cases often involve so-called whistle-blowers, that is, former employees who claim that they were discharged to prevent them from reporting violations of the law by their managers or their employer.

Another wrongful discharge theory involves allegations of breach of an implied contract. A former employee may challenge a discharge by arguing that there was an implied contractual right to continue in the job and/or that the employer violated its own discharge policies. Claimants will often rely upon written company policies issued as personnel manuals to support such implied contract claims. Some employers have been successful in defeating such claims by including so-called disclaimer language in their manuals. Such language explicitly states that the manual and the policies contained therein do not constitute a contract.

Finally, some states have found that there is an implied covenant of good faith and fair dealing in the employment relationship. Under this theory, an employer may not lawfully discharge an employee if the discharge breaches the employer's duty to deal fairly and in good faith with its employees. This concept is vague, and many state courts have refused to recognize it as a viable theory for wrongful discharge. (Refer to the "Labor" chapter for recommendations on procedures for disciplining and discharging employees.)

1952 or the Paris Act of 1971. Basically, both the Geneva Act and the Paris Act provide that the unpublished works of citizens of any member country and works first published in a member country are protected in every other member country to the same extent as works initially published in the first member country. Both acts allow a contracting country to impose formalities and conditions for claiming copyright protection with respect to works first published in its territory or by its nationals. The general term of protection under the Universal Copyright Convention is mandated to be a minimum of the life of the author plus 25 years, although other terms of protection are possible under various exceptions to the general rule.

The Berne Convention The Berne Convention was formed by 10 signatory nations in 1886. However, the US did not become a signatory until 1989 because of incompatibility with US domestic law. Protection under both the Universal Copyright Convention and the Berne Convention is based on the general concept of "national treatment," which requires each member to provide the nationals of other member nations with the same level of copyright protection provided to its own citizens. The Berne Convention also requires that certain specified minimum rights be guaranteed under the laws of member states for works originating in other member states. Among these are the duration of the copyright for the life of the author plus 50 years and rights relating to translation, reproduction, public performance, broadcasting, adaptation, and arrangement.

INTEREST

State laws generally specify the maximum rate of interest which may be charged for a loan or forbearance of money, goods, or items. State provisions also typically define usury: the rate or amount of interest that exceeds the highest rate of interest allowed by law. The interest rate on short-term loans (30-day to 3-year terms) and medium-term business loans (three- to five-year terms) is often keyed to the "prime rate" or "reference rate" announced periodically by lending banks. This is usually defined as that rate of interest charged to commercial borrowers with the highest credit rating for unsecured loans having maturities of 90 days or less. The rate on long-term loans may be fixed at a specified rate for the full term of the loan or may vary (adjust, or float) according to some index as specified in the loan document.

JOINT VENTURES

A joint venture is an organization formed to carry out a particular business transaction for a limited time. This form is often used when a project requires a pooling of skills, knowledge, or capital that can be better achieved through a coalition of several individuals or companies. Joint ventures are often organized as partnerships or LLCs (see discussion below). Generally, the mutual rights and liabilities of joint venturers (that is, the participants in a joint venture) with respect to their common enterprise are those of partners or LLC members, and the principles of law applicable to partnerships or LLCs are applicable to the joint venture. However, a joint venture may be incorporated if the parties so desire. In such cases, a corporation is formed to carry out a particular objective, with the expectation that the corporation will be dissolved and its assets distributed in liquidation to its shareholders at the conclusion of the project.

The corporate form imposes a second level tax on the distribution of the joint venture's earnings to shareholders. The joint venturers are not allowed to deduct expenses or losses incurred by the joint venture during the course of the project. If the joint venture operates as a partnership or an LLC classified as a tax partnership, each joint venturer takes into account, for income tax purposes, that person's share of the joint venture's income, gains, losses, deductions, or credits.

LIMITED LIABILITY COMPANIES

A limited liability company (LLC) is an unincorporated entity that combines the advantages of flow-through tax treatment and the operational flexibility of a partnership with a corporation's limitation on liability for its owners. Nearly all states have adopted an LLC Act, some simply by modifying the Uniform LLC Act, based upon a combination of the Revised Uniform Limited Partnership Act and the Model Business Corporation Act.

Under the typical state act, an LLC is formed by the filing of articles of organization with the state. These provide the public with certain basic information concerning the company, such as its name, the date on which the company is to dissolve, its purposes, and the address of its principal place of business and resident agent in the state. Operational rules for an LLC are contained in its operating agreement—the equivalent of a partnership agreement—which may be written or oral. Its affairs are handled by managers designated in the operating agreement, or in the absence of such designation, by all members.

The typical state statute provides for dissolution of the limited liability company upon the death, resignation, expulsion, bankruptcy, or dissolution of any member unless the remaining members agree to continue the business of the LLC or unless otherwise provided for in either the operating agreement or the articles of organization. State LLC law also usually provides that a membership interest is the personal property of a member which, unless otherwise agreed, may be assigned in whole or in part. An assignment of a membership interest does not entitle the assignee to participate in the management of the affairs of the LCC or to become, or exercise any rights of, a member unless the remaining members either give their consent or provisions for such are included in the operating agreement.

Under the laws of some states, certain professionals, such as accountants, attorneys, physicians, and those regulated under state business and professional codes, may not form LLCs.

To obtain favorable tax treatment, the LLC generally must be characterized according to income tax definitions as a partnership rather than as an association taxable as a corporation.

MONOPOLIES AND RESTRAINT OF TRADE

US antitrust laws seek to encourage competition by prohibiting monopolistic practices and unreasonable restraints on trade. When a foreign corporation sets up a US subsidiary, the foreign corporation may become subject to US antitrust laws in at least three important ways. First, any agreements among foreign entities to share markets or fix prices are illegal under US antitrust laws if any consequences thereof are felt in the US. This remains true even if such agreements are legal in the foreign countries where they were executed. Second, territorial or other restrictions in licensing agreements between foreign and US entities may conflict with the US antitrust laws. Finally, the acquisition of an existing US business by a foreign corporation that already exports to the US or that already has either a fixed place of business in the US or a US subsidiary may constitute an unlawful combination that would reduce competition. Prior to the consummation of any acquisition, it may be necessary to file a preacquisition notification with federal antitrust authorities.

The US laws relevant to antitrust include: the Sherman Antitrust Act; the Clayton Act, as amended by the Robinson-Patman Act and other acts; the Federal Trade Commission Act; the Hart-Scott-Rodino Antitrust Improvement Act; and the Exon-Florio provisions of the Omnibus Trade Act. The enforcement of the antitrust laws is within the province of the US Department of Justice (DOJ) and the Federal Trade Commission. Private litigants may also bring actions under the antitrust laws.

The existence of a US patent can have an impact on an application of antitrust laws: US patents are commonly referred to as "negative monopolies" in that they give the patent owner the right to preclude others from making, using, or selling the patented article or process. However, the limited rights granted to a patent owner are not exempt from the antitrust laws of the US. Thus, improper use of patents or improper conduct by patent owners in violation of the antitrust laws can result in substantial damage awards, fines, and even prison sentences.

Some of the more common antitrust problems confronting businesses in the US today are outlined below.

Price Fixing

Horizontal Combinations Agreements or conspiracies made and formed among competitors for the purpose of or with the effect of raising, lowering, fixing, or stabilizing the price of a commodity involved in interstate commerce. These constitute an illegal and a per se violation of the antitrust laws.

Vertical Combinations Agreements among manufacturers, wholesalers, distributors, or retailers for the purpose of raising, lowering, fixing, or stabilizing the price of a commodity involved in interstate commerce. Such arrangements, subject to certain exceptions, are likewise illegal and constitute a per se violation of the antitrust laws.

Price Discrimination The unlawful consummation of two or more separate, contemporary sales to two or more different purchasers of commodities of like grade and quality for different prices where the result will be to lessen or adversely affect competition. Exceptions to the general rule allow sellers to meet bona fide competitive prices in the separate markets or to pass on the benefits of specific discounts received.

Suggested Resale Prices and Refusals to Deal A supplier may legally suggest the price at which its products may be resold and may also select the distributors through which it wishes to market its products. However, suppliers that attempt to establish and maintain resale prices by refusing to deal with distributors who will not adhere to the suggested resale price run significant risks of being held in violation of the antitrust laws.

Territorial and Customer Restrictions

Horizontal Restrictions or Allocations Such restrictions and allocations between competitors are illegal and constitute per se violations of the antitrust laws.

Vertical Restrictions or Allocations Although vertical territorial and customer restrictions between manufacturer and distributor are not per se illegal, not all such agreements are permissible. To determine whether a specific arrangement is permissible, a thorough examination of the effects the agreement will have on competition must be made. When such agreements are prompted by justifiable business reasons, promote interbrand competition, and are nonmonopolistic, they are generally considered permissible.

Market Allocations and Refusals to Deal In general, what can be accomplished by agreement can usually also be accomplished by a refusal to deal. Accordingly, the above discussion on vertical agreements equally applies to vertical territorial restrictions accomplished by refusals to deal.

Tying Arrangements A tying agreement exists when a seller requires the buyer to purchase a product the buyer does not want (the tying product) as a condition to obtaining a product the buyer does want (the tied product). In general, an antitrust violation results if four conditions are met: (1) the seller has sufficient economic power with respect to the tying product to restrain free competition for the tied product; (2) a substantial amount of commerce is affected; (3) the seller is not a small company; and (4) the seller is not trying to break into a new market or to protect goodwill. Sufficient economic power is presumed if the tying product is patented or a trade secret. Furthermore, use of a patented product in a tying arrangement will constitute patent misuse, and the owner of the patent will be denied relief in a patent infringement suit. Consequently, even if a tying arrangement would appear not to fit within one of the above exceptions, the arrangement should be avoided if a patent or trade secret is involved.

Patent Misuses The most common misuses of patents involve:

(1) The use of patented goods in a tying agreement (discussed above).

(2) The acquisition of exclusive patent rights by grant-back clauses. A typical grant-back clause requires as a condition of obtaining a patent license that the licensee convey back to the patent owner exclusive rights to any improvements on the original patent. The Antitrust Division of the DOJ takes the position that exclusive grant-backs are per se illegal. Although nonexclusive grant-backs may be permissible under some circumstances, they subject the parties to the agreement to significant risk of antitrust violations.

(3) The requirement of the payment of royalties after expiration of the patent. In the situation in which multiple patents are licensed, the question as to whether royalty payments must be reduced upon the expiration of each patent remains open.

(4) The attempt by the patent owner to enforce a patent known to be invalid. The key is that the patent owner must know of the invalidity; a good faith belief that the patent is valid, even if such is not the case, is a complete defense in a lawsuit for an antitrust violation.

PARTNERSHIPS

A partnership arises from any agreement between two or more persons to unite their property, labor, skill and/or capital in order to establish and carry on a business as co-owners for profit. Although such an agreement may be implied by the conduct of the parties, parties generally enter into a written agreement to define the rights and obligations of each partner. The organization and operation of a partnership is primarily governed by state statutory law. All states have adopted, with minor revisions, both the Uniform Partnership Act and the Uniform Limited Partnership Act (except for Louisiana, which has its own statute governing partnerships). Because a partnership is basically a contractual agreement, general common law principles of contract, agency, tort, and licensing that are normally applicable to all business operations apply to partnerships as well.

For tax purposes, a partnership is not recognized as an entity separate and distinct from its partners. Unless the partnership agreement provides otherwise, all partners share profits and losses equally. Although the partnership must compute taxable income and file a return, the return is filed for information purposes only, and the partnership, as a separate entity, does not pay taxes. Instead, the individual partners include in their own income tax returns the income, deductions, or losses that have been passed through to them proportionately by the partnership. Partners are taxed currently on all such earnings regardless of whether all funds were actually distributed to them. Partnerships enable investors to apply partnership deductions or losses to offset taxes on income from other sources.

A partnership may be formed for a definite or unlimited term. However, unless the partnership agreement specifies otherwise, the death or bankruptcy of a partner automatically dissolves the partnership. In addition, unless agreed otherwise, the sale of one partner's interest usually gives the other partners the right to terminate the partnership. The partners may also agree to limit the right to sell or transfer their interests. In the case of a dispute among partners that cannot be resolved amicably, any partner may petition a court of competent jurisdiction to dissolve the partnership.

General Partnerships A general partnership is formed by two or more persons joining together to carry on a business for profit as co-owners. Normally, each general partner is actively engaged in the conduct of the partnership business. Unless stated otherwise in the partnership agreement (which, together with the applicable state statute, governs the management and operation of the partnership), each partner has the same rights, obligations, and authority as every other member of the partnership. Moreover, unless specifically prohibited by the partnership agreement, any partner may enter into contracts that are binding on the partnership. Each partner in a general partnership also has unlimited personal liability for all of debts and obligations of the partnership, including those wrongfully incurred by another partner.

Limited Partnerships A limited partnership differs from a general partnership in that not all of the partners have unlimited liability. While a limited partnership must have at least one general partner who has unlimited liability, it may also have limited partners whose liability is limited to a specific amount set forth in the partnership agreement. A limited partner may not participate in the active management of the partnership's business without jeopardizing limited liability protection. The capital contribution of a limited partner may consist of cash or property, but usually not services. A limited partner may share in partnership profits to any agreed-upon extent. While usually no information about a general partnership agreement is required to be published, most states require certain pertinent information about limited partnerships be filed with appropriate state or county officials and/or published in a local newspaper.

PRODUCT LIABILITY

Under the laws of most states in the US, many claims that would be treated as contractual under foreign laws—particularly those of civil law jurisdictions—may be classified as torts. Professional malpractice and the liability of a carrier for damage to goods in transit are two examples. In the US, the same act may constitute both a breach of a contract and a tort. In such situations, the plaintiff need not choose between different bases of liability, as is the case in some countries, but instead may assert conflicting theories of recovery in the same action.

The law of product liability covers claims for property damage and/or personal injury arising out of the use of a product. The ultimate responsibility for injury or damage in a product liability case most frequently rests with the manufacturer. However, liability may also be imposed upon a retailer, wholesaler, lessor, and occasionally on a party wholly outside the manufacturing and distribution process.

The principal theories of recovery on which a product liability claim may be based are negligence, breach of warranty, and strict tort liability. Although differences exist among these three theories, four elements are common to each: (1) there must be a defect in the product; (2) the defect must have existed when the product left the defendant's control; (3) some injury or damage must have been sustained; and (4) there must be a causal relationship between the defect and the injury or damage. A plaintiff who fails to establish any one of these elements cannot prevail in a products liability claim.

Negligence If the claim is based on negligence, the plaintiff must establish, in addition to the above elements, that the defect resulted from the defendant's failure to exercise reasonable care under the circumstances. The duty to exercise reasonable care extends to the design, manufacture, distribution, and packaging of a product. In addition, a manufacturer is required to exercise reasonable care in preparing instructions concerning the proper use of a product and warnings about any dangers that might not be obvious to the expected user. However, the manufacturer or seller is not considered to be an insurer of its products and has no duty to produce accident-proof products. If the defect is one that could not have been prevented or discovered in the exercise of reasonable care, and no evidence is presented that the manufacturer was negligent in selecting suppliers of component parts, the manufacturer could not ordinarily be charged with negligence. Liability for negligence generally cannot be disclaimed.

Although traditionally a defendant was shielded from liability for negligence against everyone except the immediate buyer unless the product was deemed inherently or imminently dangerous, many states have substantially limited this so-called "privity" defense. In those states rejecting the notion of privity, a defendant can be held liable under a negligence theory to a remote plaintiff with whom there exists no contractual relationship, assuming a specific duty and breach thereof by the defendant can be established.

Breach of Warranty A breach of warranty action is entirely independent of the principles of negligence and, therefore, escapes many of the difficult problems of proof which arise in negligence cases. Basically, a warranty is an expressed or an implied affirmation of fact regarding the characteristics, safety, or suitability of a product. A warranty may be a basis for a product liability action if the warranty proves to be untrue and a party is injured as a result of reliance on the warranty. In many jurisdictions, a claim for breach of warranty is limited to plaintiffs in privity of contract with the defendant (that is, only the person who received the warranty and was injured as a result of the breach of warranty may recover for such a breach). Moreover, the statute of limitations for bringing a breach of warranty action begins to run from the time of sale of the product, rather than from the time of injury or damage, as is the case in actions based either on a negligence or strict tort liability theory.

Product liability litigation can arise from claims based on the breach of either an express or an implied warranty. Depending on the circumstances of a sale, a merchant is deemed by law implicitly to warrant that goods being sold are merchantable and, if there is reason for the merchant to know of any particular purpose for which the goods are required, that the goods are fit for such purposes. In some circumstances, implied warranties can be excluded by the language or actions of the parties.

Strict Liability In many states, a party injured by a defective product not only may sue for negligence and for the breach of an express or implied warranty, but may also bring an action of strict tort liability. Under the theory of strict tort liability, the plaintiff is relieved of the burden of showing that the seller or manufacturer failed to act reasonably in the design, production, or sale of its product. Nevertheless, strict liability does not equate to absolute liability; the plaintiff must still prove that the product was defective at the time it left the defendant's control. The privity defense is usually not available under the strict tort liability theory, and, therefore, remote defendants are susceptible to suit under this products liability concept. Strict tort liability generally cannot be disclaimed.

Transferability of Claims and Insurance In the vast majority of states, a corporation acquiring the assets of another corporation is not liable to one injured by a defect in a product previously sold by the transferor corporation unless: (1) there is an express or implied assumption of liability for debts; (2) there is fraud in the transfer; (3) the purchasing corporation is a mere continuation of the selling corporation; or (4) there is a consolidation or merger of the two corporations.

SOLE PROPRIETORSHIPS

No special laws govern the organization or operation of this form of business enterprise, in which an individual person is the direct owner of the assets of the business and is wholly responsible for its liabilities. Rather, the laws relating to sole proprietorships are the general state and local laws of contract, agency, tort, and licensing normally applicable to all business operations. The maintenance of financial books and records in accordance with federal and state tax laws and regulations is required, as is the case with all businesses.

TREATIES

Current information on the status of conventions and treaties to which the US is a party is available from the Treaty Affairs Section of the Office of the Legal Adviser, Department of State, Washington, DC 20520, USA in a pamphlet entitled *Treaties in Force* published annually. For changes, check the recent issues of the Department of State Bulletin and the CCH Congressional Index, published by Commerce Clearing House, which tracks the progress of treaties through the US Senate.

Some of the conventions and treaties to which the US is a signatory include the Berne Convention, General Agreement on Tariffs and Trade (GATT), International Convention for the Protection of Industrial Property, North American Free Trade Agreement (NAFTA), Patent Cooperation Treaty, United Nations Convention on International Contracts, and Universal Copyright Convention.

Financial Institutions

INTRODUCTION

The US financial system is the largest, most advanced, and one of the most open in the world. Although foreign financial entities must gain prior approval to offer financial services in the US and abide by all US regulations, they may operate within the US on an equal basis with all similar domestic financial institutions. Customers may deal with any financial institution that they choose and are free to negotiate agreements or change providers virtually at will. Foreign businesses and individuals have free access to financing through the system, may use any provider they choose, and can operate within the system with no special limitations. Foreigners may invest in, buy, sell, or trade any and all US securities, generally without restriction.

Although some elements of the financial industry argue that US technical rules and procedures inhibit international financial transactions and make the US a less competitive financial services market, the distortions—mostly having to do with reporting—caused by these rules are generally offset by the depth, breadth, and usually lower cost structure of doing business in US markets.

During the past 25 years, the US financial system has changed radically. It has become far more internationally oriented; has (hopefully) weathered the storms of developing world debt and domestic savings and loan debacles; survived disintermediation and the shift of top credits away from bank lending to the issuance of commercial paper; dealt with in-creased competition both from within and without; struggled with money market mutual funds, stock market booms and crashes, programmed trading, junk bonds, penny stocks, limited partnerships, financial futures, and derivatives; and absorbed a host of technological innovations that have changed how financial services are provided and business is done. Despite all this, the US financial system remains the envy of much of the world, offering major opportunities to do business both with it and through it.

THE BANKING SYSTEM

The US banking system consists of the Federal Reserve system (the equivalent of a central bank); commercial banks, including foreign banks; savings institutions; and credit unions. Although it is basically straightforward, the federally regulated system is complicated by the presence of 50 separate state jurisdictions, each with its own regulatory and operating variations.

The Federal Reserve System

The Federal Reserve system—known as the Fed—is not technically a central bank because its authority is divided. It is organized into 12 semiautonomous districts, the heads of which are elected locally to serve on the governing Federal Reserve Board along with presidential appointees. This combined board is responsible for setting monetary and credit policy, and although it is considered to be independent, it usually follows the policy lead established by the Department of the Treasury.

The Federal Reserve Board holds regular meetings to review and set policy, and can meet on call to deal with emergencies. Traditionally the Fed's board has met in secret, with only summary minutes being published later. However, in the past few years, the Fed has begun announcing its actions immediately after meeting because attempts to guess what the Fed was doing ("Fed-watching") were leading to even greater speculative behavior and market volatility.

Every nationally chartered bank must be a member of the Federal Reserve system and keep a required percentage of its funds (6 percent of its deposits) as an interest free reserve with its district Federal Reserve bank.

Federal Reserve Operations The Fed exercises control over money and financial markets using a limited range of indirect tools: open market operations, discount rates, reserve requirements, and margin requirements. Open market operations—consisting of the buying or selling of US government securities, usually on a short-term temporary basis, to either reduce or increase the amount of free cash in the system—are the most frequently used means of fine-tuning financial activity. (The sale of securities reduces cash in the system while the purchase of securities adds actual cash to the system, allowing banks to fund loans.) Most such transactions are conducted through repurchase agreements, which are agreements to buy and then resell securities over a specified period, often as short as overnight.

Another Fed tool for guiding policy is the setting of the discount rate, which is the rate at which the Fed lends to banks; all such loans must be secured by holdings of approved securities. Most such loans are on an overnight or other short-term basis, and the rate set for them is the so-called discount rate, the interest rate on which all others are ultimately based. Actual "discount window" lending is a relatively minor element in the US financial system, and any bank seeking access to it too frequently is likely to be examined by federal authorities as potentially unsound. The Federal Reserve system is the lender of last resort. However, access to such loans is considered a privilege rather than a right. The level of the discount rate signals the Fed's intentions, and it is used to set the Federal funds (fed funds) rate, the rate at which financial institutions lend to each other to manage cash balances and provide liquidity.

Reserve requirements represent the percentage of bank funds which must be held on deposit with the district federal reserve bank as a liquid reserve. Federal Reserve Regulation D (known as Reg D) sets these reserve requirements. Basically, reserves are a percentage of account balances held by the bank. Because banks use these acquired funds to fund lending, the maintenance of reserves limits a bank's ability to lend. Alterations in Reg D levels are extremely infrequent.

The Fed also uses the authority of Regulation T to set securities margin requirements. Margin requirements are the percentage of the purchase price which must be in cash in order for a buyer to purchase securities on credit. Lower margin requirements lead to more speculative behavior, while higher margin requirements dampen speculation by making credit less available. Reg T has stayed at 50 percent since 1974.

Until the early 1980s, Fed Regulation Q established ceilings on interest rates that could be paid by banks. These were quite low in comparison with market rates on large wholesale deposits (greater than US$100,000). During the 1970s, money market mutual funds enabled individuals to pool their funds to take advantage of the higher rates. As funds flowed from banks into money market funds, the banks clamored for authority to pay market rates, and Reg Q was repealed. However, a legacy of this phenomenon exists in the failure of conventional definitions of money to catch up to current reality. The Fed attempts to control monetary policy by managing the growth of M1 and M2—money supply figures based on liquid (demand) deposits. Money market funds are now used like demand deposits, but they are still accounted for as if they were illiquid time deposits. Transactions also occur much more rapidly due to new technologies, so the turnover rate (velocity) can accelerate the effects of growth even when growth is being restricted.

This means that the Fed is no longer looking at what it statistically thinks it is looking at, ultimately rendering its management actions less effective and more indirect than before. Some analysts argue that these limitations on the Fed's ability to manage policy are not such a bad thing: because the money markets have grown so large and interconnected, they believe that such intervention constitutes interference with the functioning of free markets.

The Fed also serves as a national clearinghouse for processing checks and for transfers of funds and US government securities among banks. Banks may choose to clear checks directly with other banks or through regional or other private clearing facilities. Nevertheless, most checks are cleared through the Federal Reserve system, which in 1991 handled a daily average of US$51 billion in checks. In the same year, the Fed processed an average daily volume of US$765 billion in direct electronic funds transfers (EFTs) and US government securities valued at US$474 billion. The Fed also operates an Automated Clearing House (ACH) for recurring payments and FedWire, the service which processes high-volume fed funds and government securities transfers.

Commercial Banks

Commercial banks provide the majority of financial transactions and services in the US. In the early 1990s, the US had about 13,000 commercial banks, down from a maximum of 31,000 such institutions in 1921, holding roughly US$3.7 trillion in assets—about three-quarters of the total within the banking system. These range from small community banks to huge multinational firms. From the 1950s until midway through the 1980s, US money center banks—the largest, full-service, internationally oriented banks, most of which are located in New York City—were dominant players in world financial transactions.

However, at the end of 1993, Citicorp, ranking only 29th, was the highest-ranking US bank. Indeed, only nine US commercial banks ranked among the top 100 in the world. (In addition to Citicorp, these were: Bank of America, NationsBank, Chemical, J.P. Morgan, Chase Manhattan, Bankers Trust, BancOne, and First Union, in descending order.) Between 1983 and 1988, the worldwide share of US commercial bank lending fell from 27 to 15 percent. By comparison, the share held by Japanese banks was 40 percent in 1988, although their dominance has fallen since then.

Commercial banks in the US can be either federally or state chartered; if federally chartered, the words "National" or "N.A." appear in their title. Federally chartered banks are regulated directly by the Comptroller of the Currency and must be members of the Federal Reserve system and the Federal Deposit Insurance Corporation (FDIC). The FDIC insures individual bank deposits up to a ceiling of US$100,000. The costs of this insurance have grown sharply, from 8.3 cents per US$100 of insured deposits in 1989 to 23 cents per US$100 in 1993. In early 1995, the Fed proposed dropping the rate for stronger institutions to 4 cents per US$100, largely because total FDIC reserves were approaching the congressionally mandated level of 1.25 percent of total industry deposits. State chartered banks are regulated by banking authorities in the specific state in which they are incorporated. Provided they meet certain standards, state chartered banks may apply for membership in the Federal Reserve system and the FDIC.

Banking in the US is still regulated based on the National Banking Act, which dates to 1863. This legislation specifies five areas of bank activity: deposit taking, foreign exchange trading, lending, issuance of notes, and negotiating or discounting promissory notes. More recent layers of regulation date to the 1930s and represent responses to abuses prior to the Great Depression. These strictures have become increasingly outmoded, and many have been effectively rendered moot by more recent developments.

Financial regulation is presently in a state of flux as regulators attempt to catch up with rapid changes in the industry. Overlaps in regulatory jurisdiction lead to even greater confusion. State chartered banks may have no oversight other than that exercised by state banking authorities, although if they participate in federal programs they must submit to the federal regulatory authority. State laws can also restrict certain activities of federally chartered banks. For example, no national bank can establish branches unless allowed by state law (states without branching are referred to as unit banking states). However, no bank may establish branches, even if allowed by state law, without prior approval from the Comptroller of the Currency. And although federal law technically prohibits interstate retail banking, it is being bypassed to a large extent, and some states allow banks from other states to operate branches in their jurisdictions on a reciprocal basis. Federally chartered commercial banks are regulated primarily by the Comptroller of the Currency. However, bank holding companies are regulated by the Federal Reserve, as are the US operations of foreign banks and offshore banks which deal in international transactions and operate as if they were not located in the US.

Commercial banks—sometimes known as full-service banks—are allowed to offer both deposit-taking and lending services, plus a wide variety of other banking services. They are also the source of the bulk of short- to intermediate-term lending for both businesses and individuals in the US.

The US commercial banking sector has been under pressure since the 1970s. Pushed to invest large volumes of petrodollars derived from oil price hikes during that decade, banks extended credit to a host of risky borrowers, including developing countries. The inability of many developing countries to service this debt threatened the US and the world banking establishment throughout the 1980s, and did not recede until the early 1990s, when there were improvements in debtor nation economies and more pressing financial problems elsewhere. Also, US banks became heavily involved in commercial real estate through real estate investment trusts (REITs), losing huge sums when prices sagged during the mid-1970s. As a result of all of this turmoil, the number of US commercial bank failures reached 206 in 1989—the highest level since the 1930s—before receding to 120 in 1992. The number of banks on the FDIC's problem list had fallen by half from its high point in 1987. Profitability has also been recovering, although bank performance prospects are considered to be relatively mediocre during the mid-1990s.

Although US banks pioneered the use of automated teller machines (ATMs) and have made credit cards almost universally accepted and available, they have done less well with such other technological innovations as debit cards and home banking, which have yet to gain acceptance.

Foreign Banks

Approximately 300 foreign banks operate in the US. At the end of 1993, these entities ran some 720 separate offices of all types, down from a high of 747 in 1992. About half of these offices are representative offices, which conduct no actual banking business. The remaining offices are organized as branches or agencies (accounting for about 70 percent of foreign bank assets in the US) or as incorporated US subsidiaries or offshore units of overseas banks (accounting for the remaining 30 percent of such assets). In 1992 foreign banks in the US controlled nearly one-fourth of total US commercial banking assets and provided roughly 36 percent of all bank loans.

About 64 percent of foreign bank operating units in the US represent agencies, which can pay drafts, make business loans, and provide trade financing, but may not take deposits or offer trust services. Agencies are exempt from loan limit and reserve requirements, meaning that they can often outbid full-service banks subject to such restrictions for business. Agencies operate based on the capital of the parent bank. Some 26 percent of foreign banks in the US are operated as subsidiaries: separately incorporated banks at least 25 percent owned by foreign entities. Subsidiaries, which can be either established or acquired by foreign interests, are allowed to operate in all areas in which full-service domestic banks can do business.

Few foreign banks operate US branches, the full-service offices which are subject to all local banking regulations and account for only 2 percent of foreign bank operations in the US. Foreign bankers wishing to compete in local full-service (including retail) markets usually find the subsidiary format more attractive, while those seeking primarily commercial and international business rely on agencies, which, as noted, are exempt from the some of the regulations applicable to full-service banks. About 5 percent of foreign banking business in the US is conducted by Edge Act or Agreement corporations (offshore banks). New York State Investment Companies account for the remaining 3 percent of the foreign US commercial bank operating presence. These specialized, state licensed operations can offer international wholesale commercial banking services, including short- to medium-term loans.

Slightly more than half of all foreign bank offices in the US consist of representative offices. These presences—authorized under the laws of the individual states—maintain contacts with US correspondent banks, undertake research and assess US business conditions, and serve as contacts for actual and potential US customers. However, they may conduct no business that earns a return or results in an obligation for the parent entity.

Roughly half of all foreign bank offices in the US are located in the city of New York, the effective capital of US business and finance. Most of the rest are located in California (the center of ties with the Pacific Rim), Florida (the seat of business with Latin America), or Chicago (the center of foreign business activity involving the US heartland). Banks from Japan, Canada, France, and the UK, in descending order, maintain the largest presences in the US.

As was the case among banks elsewhere, many foreign banks established themselves in the US in or-der to service their clients doing business there. In general, once approved, foreign banks are allowed to operate on the same basis as US banks, although there are some technical regulatory differences. The US may also choose to restrict certain banking operations if the home country fails to offer reciprocal concessions to US banks. Individual states may also impose their own requirements or even bar foreign branching or majority ownership of local financial institutions.

US Banking Overseas The US banking presence overseas has been contracting since the heyday of the US banking thrust abroad in the 1970s and early 1980s. Following the drubbing smaller banks took—primarily on loans to developing countries in the 1980s—fewer have been interested in international operations, most of which require doing things on a relatively large scale to provide real returns. Even many large, internationally oriented US banks have been dismantling their direct overseas presences as competition from even larger international banks has reduced the margins, but not the risks, on such overseas operations. At the beginning of 1993, 120 US banks maintained 774 overseas operations, down 15 percent from 916 in 1985. About three-quarters of these were conducted by national banks.

Offshore Banks

Known as Edge Act banks (after the legislation under which they were authorized) if federally chartered or as Agreement banks if state chartered, these institutions are physically located within the US, but are only authorized to conduct international transactions. Although chartered by the Fed, Edge Act banks are exempted from normal reserve requirements (as are foreign agencies), as well as from the usual prohibitions on interstate banking.

Savings Institutions

Savings institutions—savings banks and savings and loan associations (S&Ls), generally known collectively as thrifts—accept deposits from and extend credit primarily to individuals. Designed in the 1930s to promote individual home ownership, they exist to make residential mortgage loans and may also invest in commercial real estate. Federal savings banks may branch nationwide, and during the past 15 years, many financial institutions have acquired such businesses to establish a foothold in markets they could not otherwise enter. Thrifts may also be owned by nonfinancial entities and have been used by industrial and commercial firms to gain entry into financial businesses. In 1993 there were about 2,350 functioning independent savings institutions—down from 6,200 in 1965—holding assets of approximately US$1 trillion (roughly 20 percent of total US banking assets).

The savings industry's difficulties stem from the

BANKING ISSUES

Although the banking scene has changed radically in recent years, core banking regulation has remained much as it was in the 1930s. In the past, banks kept their loans, for better or worse, for the life of the loan. Now, many banks sell their business, using on the funds to relend, and relying on the fees generated rather than on interest earnings for a far greater percentage of their revenues. For example, most mortgage loans are sold to agencies such as the Federal National Mortgage Association (FNMA), with the originating banks keeping only the origination and servicing fees. Even securitization of relatively low dollar value, short-term receivables such as auto loans and credit card balances is growing, altering the underpinnings of the US banking business.

The implementation of stringent new requirements regarding capitalization (in conjunction with the guidelines of the Bank for International Settlements, or BIS) and asset risk ratings remains under discussion, with exemptions being sought for many small institutions as well as for top-tier large banks. Perennial issues involve federal authorization of interstate branching; the equitable distribution of responsibility for community development lending; reforms in the Federal Reserve system; credit reporting requirements; the development of a secondary market for small loans; and regulatory consolidation and standardization.

Other issues include removal of the existing limitations on banks wishing to offer insurance and securities products. Banks received a boost in this area in early 1995 when the US Supreme Court ruled that they should be allowed to offer annuities, traditionally a product reserved for the insurance industry. The court ruled that banks should be allowed greater flexibility in undertaking operations outside the traditionally defined areas of banking. Banks held roughly 20 percent of the annuity market in 1993.

The Financial Accounting Standards Board (FASB)—the rule-making body for the accounting industry, which issues dictates having the force of law—decided that banks should mark more of their assets, including securities and loans, to market value rather than carrying them at cost or face value, reserving for the difference. Full implementation of FASB standards was scheduled to be in place in 1995. However, elements of the rules—which would result in lower reported earnings for banks—remain under discussion. In January 1995, the Fed did vote to rescind an FASB rule concerning the method used to calculate interest on accounts, effectively giving banks a larger voice in such decisions.

fact that it borrows short-term to fund long-term mortgage lending. This was sustainable when interest and inflation rates remained low and stable. Even when long-term interest rates have remained higher than short-term rates—a situation that has not always held—the savings institutions have increasingly lost their source of low-cost funds as depositors fled the thrifts for higher yields elsewhere.

The situation in the industry reached crisis proportions in the mid-1980s, when regulators allowed savings institutions to move into riskier investments in hopes of salvaging their fortunes. Between ineptitude and fraud, the industry was almost annihilated. The government intervened to reorganize the industry in 1989 under the Financial Institutions Reform, Recovery, and Enforcement Act (FIRREA). This legislation created a new regulating agency, the Office of Thrift Supervision (OTS), placed the worst of the savings institutions under the Resolution Trust Corporation (RTC), charged with liquidating their assets, and abolished the effectively bankrupt Federal Savings and Loan Insurance Corporation (FSLIC), merging its remnants and functions into the larger and somewhat

better funded FDIC. Despite the lowering of rates paid by banks for FDIC insurance, thrifts are to continue to pay the highest rates. (Regulators have even discussed raising the rates thrifts pay to as much as 40 cents per US$100, which some observers argue would make them totally uncompetitive.) Figures for the cost of the S&L debacle depend on the source, with the worst-case scenario arguing that US$500 billion will ultimately be needed to salvage the thrift industry. Most estimates tend to cluster around US$300 billion, although by some accounts as much as US$200 billion has already been committed.

Unless they are directly involved in real estate, foreigners will not be able to access funds through savings institutions. However, foreign businesses may invest in savings institutions, although given the current unsettled state of this sector, they should seek professional advice before doing so.

Credit Unions

Authorized under separate legislation that exempts them from reserve requirements, FDIC membership, and certain other rules that apply to other banking institutions, credit unions are cooperative financial institutions that provide deposit-taking, transaction, lending, and certain other retail services to individual member customers. Credit unions may be either federally (96 percent) or state chartered. Federal credit unions are regulated by the National Credit Union Administration (NCUA) and insured by the Federally Insured Credit Unions (FICU) program, which provides deposit insurance at rates far lower than those charged by the FDIC. Credit unions argue that because of their record of solvency and their less risky investment profile—loans are often secured by either savings balances or paychecks from the sponsoring agency—they deserve to be relieved of burdensome requirements. This argument received a blow when a large, Washington, DC area credit union had to be taken over by regulators after its investments in risky derivative securities went bad in early 1995.

In 1993 roughly 13,000 credit unions held total assets of about US$288 billion, or slightly less than 6 percent of US banking sector assets; they accounted for about 13 percent of consumer lending and 7 percent of household savings. These entities are usually affiliated with large corporations and offer services to their employees. Credit unions derive most of their revenues from personal loans to their members and from holdings of short-term US government securities; they may not make commercial loans. Nor can they be accessed as a funding source by foreign businesses operating in the US (although nothing prevents qualifying foreign individuals from belonging to a credit union).

Bank Services and Operations

In the US, credit for periods of up to one year is usually offered by a commercial bank on an unsecured line of credit basis. The customer may draw down such sums up to the credit limit (line), repaying outstanding balances within specified periods. There is usually no charge except for the interest on the amounts actually used. Such lines are extended and canceled at the bank's discretion.

Under an advance line of credit, customers write their own loan, up to an agreed-upon total amount, obtaining cash for stipulated periods. This type of loan is discretionary and can be used as often and for as much or as little money as the client wishes, within the terms of the agreement. Under the more restrictive acceptance line of credit, the customer submits the bill for eligible transactions and the bank pays the third party, often using the goods shown on the bill as the security for the loan. Acceptance credits are somewhat less costly because of the greater control and collateral, but are less popular.

Intermediate-term financing covers periods of one year to as long as seven years, although specific institutions may lend only for shorter periods. It is generally provided through "term" financing, because the loan is for a specified period or term (it is also subject to stipulated terms, or conditions). Such loans are usually tied to the prime rate, the base rate that banks charge their business customers. Actual loans may be made at a higher prime plus rate for riskier ventures or at a lower prime minus rate for safer or better established ventures (or for those who can negotiate a better rate with the bank). Customers may sometimes obtain rates tied to the London Interbank Offering Rate (LIBOR) cost of funds rate often used in international transactions.

A loan with a maturity of more than one but less than three years will often be made on a revolving basis. Under this arrangement, the borrower may take as much as is needed of the agreed-upon limit and may also repay the outstanding balance at will within the limits of the agreement. No matter what the total amount of the credit facility, or loan, interest will only be charged on the outstanding balance, although an annual commitment fee—usually around 0.5 percent of the total limit—may be charged on the unused amount.

For loans of periods longer than three years, drawdown and repayment terms are generally arranged on a contractual basis. These can take any number of forms. Borrowers may arrange for a grace period during which payments are deferred until a future date; a self-liquidating amortization schedule in which a fixed payment is apportioned between interest and principal over the life of the loan; or a balloon payment in which some or all of the outstanding principal is paid as a lump sum to settle the loan at its maturity with intermediate payments covering only interest charges; or other arrangements. The loan contract usually requires that the borrower maintain certain financial ratios or other conditions designed to ensure that the enterprise remains viable to repay the bank's money. Borrowers may be required to provide some collateral or security for loans and often have to give the bank some level of access to and control over their operations in recognition of the bank's interest. (However, US banks are not allowed to take an equity interest in nonrelated businesses except as collateral for a loan, and then only on a temporary basis.)

Although other types of financial institutions may lend for periods longer than seven years, entities seeking long-term financing from banks usually must borrow on a regular term basis and roll the balances over at the end of the loan. Some banks may lend at fixed rates, but to protect themselves from interest rate fluctuations, most usually lend at floating rates (based on prime or LIBOR)—that is, on a cost-plus basis consisting of the current market rate adjusted periodically. Thus a rollover represents a gamble because the borrower could have to pay a substantially higher rate or accept more restrictive conditions when the loan comes up for renewal.

Commercial banks offer a broad range of services, including checking accounts; asset management accounts (transaction accounts in which free balances are swept into an interest-bearing account); issuing and negotiating letters of credit; lockboxes for receivables; making payments; account reconciliations; trust, custody, transfer, registration, and dividend and interest payment services; credit card services; foreign exchange; electronic funds transfers (EFTs); and some investment banking and investment management services, among others. Only the largest banks will offer a full range of services, and some will be more adept than others at particular transactions. However, in the overbanked US, even the smallest local bank maintains correspondent relationships with larger domestic and—directly or indirectly—international banks, enabling customers to access virtually any required service.

Banks are also among the most important sources of introductions for foreign businesspersons seeking to operate in the US. Although US businesspeople are generally less reliant on bank recommendations than are those in many other countries, a good bank reference can provide an important entree into US business circles or make the difference in concluding a transaction.

Financial Groups

Unlike some other countries where financial institutions are allowed to operate in any financial activity, the US maintains a separation between commercial banking and investment and merchant banking, at least in theory. A relic of the Great Depression, the National Banking Act of 1933—commonly known as the Glass-Steagall Act—prohibits commercial banks from operating in the securities industry or, as noted, from taking an ownership position in an outside firm. Thus, financial conglomerates incorporating a variety of types of financial institutions have been technically forbidden. However, over the last 15 years, many restrictions have been circumvented, eroding the separation between commercial and investment banking. Nonbank financial institutions have discovered ways to incorporate bank, nonbank, or near-bank (limited-service) subsidiaries, while banks have gained more leeway to operate in some areas of investment banking.

Approved, federally chartered bank subsidiaries have been allowed to underwrite and deal in asset-backed and municipal securities since 1987. This authority was provisionally extended to debt and equity securities in 1989. Such activities must be undertaken by independently capitalized subsidiaries, and no more than 10 percent of the subsidiary's total revenues may come from such activities. Roughly 30 large banks have been granted such authority by the Fed, about one-third of them foreign banks. An additional 17 foreign banks are allowed to conduct securities as well as commercial banking activities in the US based on prior exemptions. Although technically separate, bank subsidiaries may offer retail securities services directly to the bank's customers, allowing the banks to compete with nonbank financial institutions.

Development Banks

Many nations operate specific—often governmental or quasi-governmental—banking organizations designed to implement development and provide services to particular sectors of the economy. The US lacks such special banks, but does delegate certain development responsibilities to commercial banks and savings institutions through the requirement that they lend a certain portion of their funds to underserved, usually lower income, borrowers within their service areas. Other specialized programs that offer financing and services to particular target groups, such as the Small Business Administration (SBA), make aid available through guarantees to the commercial institutions that actually make the loans.

In some countries, such set-aside loans—which usually go to the industrial rather than the retail sector—are known as policy loans, because they support government development policy. An ongoing issue in the US is the complaint of the banks that they have been charged with undertaking such responsibilities at their own risk and cost—and can be penalized if they do not do so—while other financial service providers have been able to evade such requirements despite having been allowed to encroach on the traditional preserves of the banks.

The US is a participant in several international institutions that function as development banks, lending to other areas of the world. Such institutions as the International Bank for Reconstruction and Development (IBRD, or the World Bank) and the International Monetary Fund (IMF) are supranational financial institutions that lend primarily on a government level and are not accessed by individual borrowers. However, other international institutions may allow US-based firms to receive financing for the sale of goods or services to approved projects in beneficiary countries.

The Inter-American Development Bank (IDB) is the largest external funding institution for large-scale projects in Latin America. Founded in 1959, the IDB is underwritten by 46 member countries and obtains most of its funds through the sale of bonds in international markets. Only member country firms are eligible for procurement consideration; procurements include consulting services as well as sale of goods. The North American Development Bank (NADB) was formed through NAFTA to fund environmental cleanup projects along the US-Mexican border. The bank is to be funded initially by the US and Mexico, eventually issuing its own bonds. As of the beginning of 1995, it was still organizing and had yet to fund any projects.

NONBANK FINANCIAL INSTITUTIONS

A wide range of nondepositary financial institutions exist in the US. These include leasing, finance, factoring, and mortgage banking firms—all of which are involved in asset-based financing in one way or another—and insurance companies, pension funds, investment companies, commercial lending firms, and venture capital firms, as well as variations on these themes.

Asset-Based Finance Companies

Leasing Companies These firms finance the acquisition of equipment and personal property, retaining title to the goods and leasing them back to the users. Leasing can cover such wide-ranging types of capital goods as computer equipment, office furniture, trucks and automobiles, heavy equipment, machinery, cargo containers and railroad cars, and aircraft. A lease can be structured to allow the lessee to retain the item outright or to buy it by paying the residual value at the end of the lease, or the item may revert to the lessor. Such arrangements, known as financing leases, serve as a substitute for ownership of an item and are generally designed to cover its useful economic life. Operating leases provide short-term access to a piece of equipment for less than its useful economic life. Leasing companies are expanding their services to include such secondary products as insurance and maintenance contracts, and some are experimenting with securitization of their leases or owned property.

Leasing usually involves low or no up-front costs, and the resulting financing can be obtained for longer periods than direct purchase financing available from banks. Leasing generally costs about the same or only slightly more overall than a conventionally financed purchase. Leasing usually avoids or reduces the need for an initial capital investment and can free up capital for use elsewhere. In most financing leases, any tax benefits are passed through to the firm leasing the equipment.

Leasing activity was expected to grow to about US$129 billion in terms of value of goods leased in 1994, up about 3 percent from 1993. Such leasing accounts for nearly one-third of all business equipment purchases in the US. Foreigners are allowed to participate in and use the services of leasing companies without restriction.

Finance Companies Commercial finance companies usually offer funding secured by the equipment, inventory, or receivables of the borrower. Some finance companies are subsidiaries of manufacturing firms specifically designed to finance purchases of the company's products. Perhaps the largest and best-known such entity is the General Motors Acceptance Corporation (GMAC), which finances consumer purchases of General Motors vehicles. Personal finance companies usually fund small loans for purchases of items such as appliances that are below the lending minimums of most commercial banks. Personal finance companies also may deal with persons whose credit rating is below that accepted by banks.

Whether commercial, captive, or personal, finance companies charge a premium above that charged by bank, usually from 2 to 6 percentage points above what banks charge for comparable loans. This premium is due to the greater risks involved, the higher cost of funds to the finance company, and the often captive nature of the customer base. Applicants may have to submit to extensive evaluation procedures, often including audits for commercial clients. Potential customers may have to pay an application fee to cover the cost of this investigation, as well as an up-front commitment fee, which can amount to more than 1 percent of the loan amount; such fees are seldom returnable if the application is denied. Extensive monitoring continues during the life of the loan, and loan covenants are usually quite strict and more intrusive than bank loan provisions.

Lending may be on a revolving basis, with the borrower being allowed to draw down funds as collateral becomes available, with the specific loan being liquidated as the collateral is sold off. So-called floor plan loans are used to finance inventory, often specific big-ticket items, such as vehicles in a dealer's inventory. Finance companies may also discount installment sales receivables. Foreigners may generally participate in and use the services of finance companies without restriction, although the higher costs and greater restrictions may make this type of financing unattractive.

Factoring Companies Factoring companies, or, simply, factors, purchase the receivables of businesses, providing current cash at a discount in return for the business' future receipts. They usually buy the actual rights to the payments represented by the receivables and become responsible for collecting them rather than merely lending against the receivables. They also assume the risk if the debtor fails to pay; usually the factor has no recourse to the seller of receivables. Factors usually must notify the debtor of the purchase of the receivable and must mark invoices to that effect, instructing the debtor to pay the factor directly. In addition to the discount on the receivables, based on the imputed interest rate between the purchase and collection of the note, factors charge a fee based on a percentage of the net amount of the receivables bought. The actual cost to the seller can amount to 10 percent or more of the face value of the receivables sold. There are no restrictions on foreign participation in or use of the services of the factoring industry.

Mortgage Banking Companies These financial institutions are intermediaries that extend financing through mortgages on real property—including commercial, industrial, residential, and, in some cases, raw land or other development properties—packaging the resulting loans for sale to institutional investors. During the early 1990s when interest rates were falling and vast numbers of new mortgages were being originated (lending on properties for the first time) and existing mortgages were being refinanced at lower rates, mortgage bankers were extremely active. Despite its attractions, the mortgage banking business has remained relatively small and profitable because of the barriers to entry (a high level of both capital and expertise is needed) and its cyclicality, which is tied to xfluctuations in interest rate and real estate prices. Because of the need to know a specific market, mortgage banking also tends to remain fairly localized. There are no specific legal bars to foreign participation in or use of the services of the industry.

Insurance Companies

The US insurance industry—the largest in the world, accounting for nearly one-third of all premiums worldwide—is highly developed. Based on total assets at the end of 1993, 9 of the top 25 and 19 of the top 50 insurers worldwide were located in the US, including the second largest, Prudential Insurance (Japan's Nippon Life was the largest). US consumers are second in life insurance premiums paid and insurance in force, behind those of Japan, but first in property and casualty coverage. In addition to providing a wide variety of products and services, the insurance industry is also a major source of long-term funding to business operations at home and abroad. Insurance companies are large investors in mortgages, real estate, and other large, long-term, usually privately placed, capital investments. Unlike banks, insurers can take equity ownership positions in the firms in which they invest. They are also major investors in publicly traded government and private debt and equity securities.

Total insurance industry revenues were expected to rise by about 5 percent to US$720 billion in 1994, with premium revenues growing to US$565 billion and investment income remaining essentially flat at about US$155 billion. However, rising interest rates, the dismal 1994 performance of the US bond mar-

ket, problems with derivative instruments and mediocre stock market results suggest that growth in investment results may actually have been negative. About 55 percent of total industry revenues represent the roughly 1,700 life and health companies operating in the US, while the remaining 45 percent comes from the country's estimated 3,800 property and casualty companies.

In addition to unfavorable investment results, life and health insurers cut back somewhat on price increases in response to the national debate over increased government control of the largely private US health care system. Rising costs have further raised resistance to additional life and health price hikes. Several natural disasters during 1994 increased payouts by property and casualty insurers, prompting many to limit their underwriting and to press for rate relief. The US is generally overserved by insurers, and competition holds down rate increases, especially in property and casualty lines.

Life and health companies saw their major growth come from the sale of annuities and guaranteed interest contracts (GICs) to individual and corporate pension fund clients. Between 1990 and 1993, sales of annuities grew by an average of 5.7 percent annually, while those of traditional life insurance policies grew by only 2.6 percent. Life insurance assets were about US$1.79 trillion in 1993. Roughly 40 percent of this was invested in corporate bonds, 20 percent in government securities, 15 percent in mortgages, 10 percent in stocks, and the rest in miscellaneous investments (direct real estate holdings, policy loans, and other assets). Property and casualty insurers, with 1994 estimated assets of nearly US$690 billion, most of that in relatively short-term investments, have experienced most of their growth in individual lines—auto and home policies—while commercial lines business has remained relatively flat. One of the most rapidly growing areas is that of reinsurance, in which insurers resell some of their risks to outside insurers, often located abroad (captive reinsurers incorporated in Bermuda are among the most active in this area).

Industry Trends In recent years, the US insurance industry has been hurt by increased levels of self-insurance, larger firms having decided it is cheaper to handle their own insurance costs than it is for them to purchase outside coverage. Optimistic underwriting and pricing as well as unrealistic investment assumptions during the mid- to late-1980s also led to questions about solvency in the early 1990s. The National Association of Insurance Commissioners (NAIC), essentially an industry lobby, has set higher capitalization standards for insurers, resulting in improving balance sheets for US insurers. Many observers have viewed such attempts at self-regulation basically as ploys designed to retain the industry's exemption from federal antitrust laws—an exemption which allows it to share data and co-operate to a degree that would be considered collusive in other domestic industries.

Employment has been shrinking in the US insurance industry in recent years as it seeks to reduce costs. Many firms have consolidated to achieve greater capitalization and operating efficiencies, while at the same time there has been a trend toward specialization in lines of insurance written and diversification into noninsurance businesses, all in hopes of solving the problems of maturity, overcapacity, and threatened margins within in the industry.

The industry has also been affected by unfavorable judgments holding it liable for damages in environmental cases, and the nature of US tort liability law remains a negative for insurers. The industry has also been under pressure because of redlining, that is, discrimination in the pricing of or the refusal to write policies to less-than-prime clients. Finally, the recent official opening of the annuity business to banks has led to investigations of insurers who are alleged to have colluded to keep banks out of this rapidly growing area. Another trend causing unrest in the industry is the shift in the sale of insurance products through alternate, direct distribution channels from traditional delivery through a large network of high-cost agents.

Foreign Industry Presence In 1991 foreign insurers operating in the US had revenues of US$72.9 billion, or 11 percent of total industry revenues. In the same year, 1,396 foreign insurance companies (367 life and 1,029 other firms) with assets totaling US$302.9 billion (US$171.6 billion for life companies and US$131.1 billion for others) operated in the US. The largest representation was among firms from Canada, the UK, the Netherlands, and Switzerland, although activity by French and German firms has been growing. Foreign reinsurers have captured one-third of the US market, and between 1981 and 1991, foreigners invested US$16 billion in the US insurance industry. (However, three-fifths of this amount came in just three transactions: the buyout of the Farmers Group by Batus Inc. of the UK; the buyout of Fireman's Fund by Germany's Allianz; and the investment of US$1 billion in the Equitable Life Assurance Society by France's Axa Groupe.) Meanwhile, domestically owned US insurers are also expanding outwards, looking to pick up business in Europe, Asia, and Latin America.

The US insurance industry is relatively open to foreign operations, being limited mainly by its fragmented regulation; 50 separate state jurisdictions establish their own licensing, operating, and regulatory policies and procedures (there being no overall federal regulation). Some states are considered lax, while others are viewed as draconian.

Pension Funds

Only the commercial banking system holds more assets than do US pension funds. In 1993 US public and private pension funds held US$4.776 trillion in assets, up fivefold from US$949 billion in 1980. Slightly more than 70 percent of this was held in private pension plans. Privately sponsored pension plans in the US have grown from 311,100 plans covering 44.5 million participants in 1975 to 712,300 plans covering 76.9 million participants in 1990, or about 40 percent of US workers.

The traditional pension plan was a defined benefit plan, in which payouts were a percentage of the retiree's salary. However, by 1990 nearly 85 percent of plans were defined contribution, in which the benefits are based only on the investment performance of contributions. Many of these consist of personal Individual Retirement Accounts (IRAs) and 401(k) plans maintained by individuals. Larger plans manage their own assets (within limits prescribed by the federal Employee Retirement Income Security Act, or ERISA), although most—especially small private plans—delegate this responsibility to financial managers.

Pension plans invest in a wide variety of assets, from basic bank CDs to listed securities to large mortgage, real estate, and privately placed debt deals. Plans have the ability to invest in virtually any legal activity, and while most pension funds are invested conservatively in bonds and GICs, large plans often invest in a variety of higher-risk areas to diversify and bolster their returns. Such investments can include sending funds overseas and dealing with foreigners either at home or abroad. Foreign financiers are also eligible to manage US pension fund assets.

Commercial Lending Companies

These entities are authorized under New York state banking law to borrow and lend to businesses. Commercial lending companies can maintain credit balances, but may not accept deposits.

Trade Finance

Commercial banks are the primary source of trade finance and one of the few potential funding sources for import financing. However, individual countries often operate trade development banks or other institutions to help their own firms in exporting to the US. Many of these offer financing, guarantees, or insurance to US buyers of goods imported into the US. Those interested in exporting to the US should investigate any such programs available in their home countries. In the US a variety of governmental and quasi-governmental as well as private institutions exist to promote and fund exports from the US. These include the Export-Import Bank, the Private Export Funding Corporation

(PEFCO), Export Trading Companies (ETCs), the Overseas Private Investment Corporation (OPIC), the Commodity Credit Corporation (CCC), the Trade Development Agency (TDA), and the Agency for International Development (AID).

Export-Import Bank Known as the Eximbank, this institution is a federal government agency designed to encourage and finance US exports of goods and services. It exists specifically to counter trade subsidies offered by other countries to their national exporting firms, making US exports more competitive in overseas markets. Eximbank offers short-, intermediate-, and long-term loans at competitive market rates to buyers, sellers, or bank intermediaries when conventional funding cannot be secured through private sources. Eximbank services and loans are available to foreigners operating in the US with the stipulation that any and all goods financed must be of US origin. Programs provide loans, guarantees, working capital guarantees, and insurance.

Eximbank lending generally involves fixed rate loans at market rates. Loans can be made directly to foreign buyers of US capital goods or services, as well as to organized intermediaries—such as banks—lending to foreign buyers. The agency offers some special features to small businesses involved in overseas sales. The guarantee program offers repayment guarantees covering commercial and political risk to private financial institutions that lend to approved foreign buyers of US exports. The working capital guarantee program is designed to provide financing to small- and medium-sized firms operating in the US to produce and sell goods overseas. The program can also make guarantees to financial institutions that make working capital loans to such firms.

Operating through its subsidiary, the Foreign Credit Insurance Association (FCIA), the Eximbank offers coverage intended to allow US-based firms to compete for overseas sales by offering credit to buyers. Policies may also be available to financial institutions extending direct credit to such businesses. Specific policies cover short-term (up to 180 days) sales of parts, raw materials, and consumer goods and intermediate-term (up to five years) sales of capital goods. Policies can also be obtained to cover financing or operating leases of equipment to foreign lessees. Some sales of services are also insurable. Proceeds can be assigned to a financial institution, allowing the insured either to discount foreign receivables or use them as collateral. New or small businesses can obtain special coverage, including coverage of a higher percentage of the deal or discounted premiums.

Private Export Funding Corporation Formed in 1970 by a group of large domestic banks, PEFCO extends loans to foreign buyers to enable them to purchase US goods. All PEFCO loans are guaranteed by the Eximbank.

Export Trading Companies Authorized by the Export Trading Company Act of 1982, privately incorporated ETCs must engage exclusively in international trading activity, primarily to support domestic exports. An ETC may offer consulting, market research, marketing, advertising, product development, legal, communications, order processing, back office, and logistical services—including transportation and warehousing—foreign exchange trading, and trade finance. A ETC can take title to goods and act as a principal, agent, or broker on behalf of an exporting firm in international transactions. It may also provide insurance coverage for such transactions. These entities were modeled after Japan's dominant trading companies, which do all of these things and more. Although ETCs provide useful services, no ETC has approached the importance of the Japanese institutions.

Overseas Private Investment Corporation This wholly US government owned private corporation provides financial and other assistance to US-based private firms investing in developing countries. Its investment development department identifies and researches overseas investment opportunities, offers counseling, insures against a variety of political risks, and participates in financing. Projects must meet official policy goals and standards, have host country approval, and be commercially viable. It is expected that US investors—primarily small businesses—hold at least 25 percent of the equity in the venture. US based firms, including those with foreign participation and domestic-foreign joint ventures, are potentially eligible for OPIC assistance.

Commodity Credit Corporation The CCC is an independent government corporation controlled by the US Department of Agriculture. It provides financing for export production of US agricultural products. US-based operations with foreign participation are potentially eligible for assistance from the CCC, provided production is intended for export. Under the provisions of the Uruguay Round of the General Agreement on Tariffs and Trade (GATT), national subsidy programs such as the CCC are to be scaled back or abolished.

Trade and Development Agency The TDA was established to provide assistance to US firms interested in exporting to developing and middle income countries. It primarily identifies opportunities and offers technical assistance, but may also assist in arranging lending.

Agency for International Development The State Department's AID primarily offers support to developing countries, but it also serves as a conduit for international procurement opportunities for US-based firms interested in participating in its projects.

Underground Financial Operations

The highly developed US financial system offers a multitude of financial possibilities at almost all levels for virtually all borrowers and service-seekers. However, these may at times be somewhat difficult to access for foreign individuals and firms unless they are already experienced operators with established financial credentials in their home countries. While US institutions are able to deal with a wide range of customer needs and have few, if any, restrictions on dealings with foreign clients, many prefer to deal with a relatively narrow range of particular clients, leaving those who do not fit the current profile outside the system. Nevertheless, the formal US financial system offers opportunities for virtually all legitimate activity, and with proper preparation and perseverance, foreign businesspeople should be able to find the services they need (a referral from a home country bank to a US branch or correspondent bank is helpful).

The Informal Economy As a large economy, the US supports substantial informal and illicit underground economies. Nevertheless, such underground sectors do not play the role in the US that they do in many other countries with less developed economies and financial institutions. A significant underground barter and off-the-books, cash-based economy does exist, although its size is obviously difficult to estimate and it generally tends toward the financing of small transactions. Nevertheless, such activities are usually figured in the billions of dollars, not merely in operations but also in terms of tax revenues lost.

Informal financing arrangements are also common, especially among recent immigrants and in urban ethnic enclaves, where inhabitants have not yet become familiar with or acceptable to mainstream financial providers. Foreign businesspeople are unlikely to find such informal financing—which is at best quasi-legal, offering little or no guarantee or recourse in case of difficulties—to be useful or adequate for their needs. Some enterprising members of particular communities might wish to investigate these possibilities. However, it should be noted that a great deal of financial fraud is perpetrated on foreigners by their unscrupulous countrymen who use unfamiliarity with and distrust of US institutions by new arrivals to bilk them.

Organized Crime Organized crime in the US operates in many areas of vice and other illicit services, including loan-sharking: the lending of funds for terms as short as a few days, or even hours, at rates approaching several thousand percent on an annualized basis. It is unlikely that foreign businesspeople will find themselves in a situation to be offered such illegal loans, and they would be well advised to steer clear of such proposals should they arise.

The main element of the criminal underground economy is the wholesale funding of criminal activity, such as the narcotics trade, and the subsequent search by organized crime for ways to launder its illicit gains by passing them through a series of legal conduits. Federal law requires anyone entering the country to declare to US customs cash or negotiable instruments valued at more than US$10,000; no duty is levied on such imports, but they do thus become potentially traceable, and it is an offense to fail to declare such funds. US financial institutions must also report all cash transactions of US$10,000 or more. These measures are designed to hinder and track the movement of large sums of cash through the system in the laundering process. US operating procedures are usually standardized, well documented, and reasonably open; most financial dealings other than the most mundane and simple require formal contracts and the involvement of legal counsel and formal disclosures. Any dealings that involve a general lack of such formalities and disclosure should be approached with circumspection.

FINANCIAL MARKETS

Financial markets in the US are, by most measures, the most highly developed in the world. Although some other markets may have taken the lead in certain relatively narrow areas of specialization; others may operate using newer technology; and many may grumble over US dominance and its somewhat archaic ways of doing business, US financial markets represent the acknowledged standard in world capital and money markets. Non-nationals are accorded national treatment in US financial markets and can use or operate within these markets with no additional authorization other than that required for US individuals and businesses.

Equities Markets

Stock Exchanges The US equities markets are collectively the largest in the world; with a 1992 market value of US$4.758 trillion, they were double the size of runner-up Japan's. In fact, the combined market values of the second through tenth largest stock markets in the world barely surpassed the value of US markets.

The US has several different stock exchanges, many of which compete directly, but some of which specialize in particular securities or types of securities. The most important are located in New York City: the New York Stock Exchange (NYSE) and the American Stock Exchange (ASE, or, as it is more frequently known, the AMEX). Other much smaller regional exchanges are located in Boston, Philadelphia, Cincinnati, Chicago (the Midwest Stock Exchange—the survivor of a series of mergers of smaller exchanges since the 1940s), and San Francisco and Los

Angeles (the Pacific Exchange—stocks are generally traded in Los Angeles and options in San Francisco). These exchanges trade both debt and equity securities (bonds and stocks—although most bond trading occurs off the exchanges) and may deal in other financial instruments as well (for example, convertible bonds, warrants, preferred stocks, and options).

Stocks not listed on a formal exchange are traded in the over-the-counter (OTC) market consisting of a network of market makers (broker-dealers who handle specific stocks) operated by the National Association of Securities Dealers (NASD). This OTC market includes the National Association of Securities Dealers Automated Quotation system (Nasdaq), which reports current bid and ask prices, and the National Market System (NMS), a subset of more heavily traded issues that operates on a direct, real-time basis. The Nasdaq is currently the third largest market worldwide, after the Tokyo Stock Exchange.

The Securities and Exchange Commission (SEC), the federal agency that regulates securities markets, maintains Rule 394, which requires all trading of exchange listed securities to occur on an exchange. Some trades may be made off the exchanges under certain circumstances, in the so-called third market (the exchanges constituting the first market and the OTC the second market). A large amount of trading—more than 20 percent according to some estimates—occurs in this third market. However, with very few exceptions no security may be sold to the public unless it has been through the registration procedures of the SEC.

The Markets In 1980 the market value of trading on US stock exchanges was US$522 billion, 76 percent of which was conducted on the NYSE. By 1992 the value had risen fourfold to US$2.156 trillion, 82 percent of which was handled on the NYSE. Although other exchanges continue to serve specialized purposes, the dominance of the NYSE continues to grow among formal markets. Its daily average volume grew from 44.9 million shares in 1980 to 202.3 million shares in 1992. In early 1995 daily trading on the NYSE was in the neighborhood of 310,000 shares; trading on the Nasdaq was 300,000; on the AMEX, 26,000; and on other exchanges, a total of 35,000 shares.

Also called the Big Board, the NYSE traces its origins to 1792; it was formally organized in 1863, but not officially incorporated until 1971. The exchange has 1,366 memberships, known as seats, representing property interests which can be sold. In 1994 seats were selling for US$830,000. All trading on the NYSE must go through one of these members. The exchange allows seatholders to rent their seats to approved tenants (about 40 percent do so). The NYSE also instituted a category of limited memberships through which approved traders can access the market either electronically or physically, but not

in both ways; there are about 50 of these traders. The NYSE concentrates on the securities of larger, more established, and better capitalized firms. The second most important exchange, the AMEX, is descended from less patrician outdoor curb markets, which began to organize after World War I and incorporated in 1953. The AMEX generally deals in the securities of smaller, less well seasoned firms, although some of its listings represent large, established firms that prefer the somewhat less formal operating rules and lower listing costs of the AMEX. It also lists a large number of foreign stocks, especially Canadian stocks. The OTC market began to coalesce into a more formal entity in the late 1930s, when brokers were required to join the NASD, and debuted as a formal automated system in 1971.

In 1980 the NYSE listed 2,228 separate issues of 1,570 companies; some 33.7 billion shares were outstanding with a market value of US$1.243 trillion. By 1992 this value had increased to US$4.035 trillion, representing 115.8 billion shares outstanding in 2,658 issues from 2,089 companies. In early 1994, the NYSE listed more than 2,400 companies, including 159 foreign companies. By comparison, in 1980 the Nasdaq listed 3,050 separate issues from 2,894 companies. In 1992 the Nasdaq included 5,393 separate issues from 4,611 companies. In 1994 Nasdaq listed roughly 3,400 stocks on the NMS and an additional 1,300 on its SmallCap Stock Market. However, Nasdaq activity is relatively concentrated. In 1994 National Market stocks accounted for 87 percent of all Nasdaq trades by share volume and 97 percent by dollar value. By 1993 the number of shares traded was roughly equal on both the NYSE and Nasdaq, although the value of trades on the Nasdaq was only 60 percent of that on the NYSE.

There are about 50,000 unlisted stocks in the US. Perhaps 16,000 of these trade at least once during any given year, with the rest representing closely held stock that does not turn over. Theoretically any and all of these securities can be traded, although in practice many of them change hands only through inheritance or sale of the underlying enterprise.

Trading Systems Although between 70 and 80 percent of NYSE trading occurs using the Super Designated Order Turnaround (SuperDOT) system, which packages small orders and handles them automatically at prevailing prices, the core of business on the major exchanges still relies on an open outcry auction using what is known as the specialist system. Specialists are exchange-designated market makers who manage trade in specific stocks, buying and selling for their own accounts to maintain an orderly market. When the stock for which they are responsible falls, these specialists are obligated to buy for their own account in order to break that fall. They sell as it goes up, to prevent volatile, unsustainable price runups. In order to facilitate this function, they keep the official records of incoming buy and sell orders—known as "the book"—allowing them to manage the flow of trade and also—legally—to take advantage of this inside knowledge. About 430 NYSE members (roughly 30 percent of all members) serve as specialists.

Many observers feel that the specialist system is archaic and distorts the free functioning of markets. They argue that available technology would allow the elimination of specialist intermediaries in favor of automated trade matching. Proponents of the specialist system point to the fact that the specialists slowed the drop in the prices of their assigned stocks at great personal cost by buying during the crash of 1987, further arguing that they would have fulfilled their stated function had they not been overwhelmed by the volume and velocity of a decline reinforced by automated sell programs. Moreover, they note that the largely automated Nasdaq system broke down because individual broker-dealers with no direct obligation to buy their stocks simply ceased to trade as conditions worsened. This resulted in a lack of liquidity and a breakdown in the market for OTC stocks, many of which fell proportionally more in value than did NYSE issues. Others note that while the NYSE specialist-based system manages as much as 80 percent of its trades automatically through Super DOT, the Nasdaq handles only 60 percent of trades automatically through its Small Order Execution System (SOES) instituted in 1984.

The specialist system is well entrenched and is likely to dominate the exchanges for the foreseeable future. The DOT, and its current successor, the SuperDOT, were, after all, instituted not to enhance the functioning of the market, but to protect the exchange and the brokerage community, which had been unable to keep up with the paper flow before the advent of automation.

Stock Market Indices US financial markets are measured by a wide variety of indices. The main measure used for US equity markets is the Dow Jones Industrial Average (DJIA, or simply, the Dow). This includes a sample of 30 of the largest issues of major industrial and, increasingly, commercial firms listed on the NYSE. Despite being an extremely narrow indicator of market activity, it is the oldest and best-known such index, and the one that is generally used to gauge stock market movements.

The Standard & Poor's 500 Index (S&P 500) tracks 500 large, diversified—but primarily industrial—US stocks. As such, it is a broader indicator of stock market movement than the DJIA. An even broader measure, the NYSE Composite Index, includes substantially all the shares listed on that exchange. However, all these indices are biased toward the shares of larger companies to a greater or lesser extent. The AMEX index covers the fewer, generally smaller company stocks listed on that exchange and provides a different measure of activity focused on that sector of the market. The Nasdaq Composite Index reports changes in that mostly small- to medium-sized company market sector.

Additional indices include the Value-Line Index (covering a selection of the stocks of about 1,700 companies of differing sizes in a variety of sectors); the Russell 2000 Index (which focuses on small company stocks), and the broad-based Wilshire 5000 Index, which includes NYSE stocks (85 percent), AMEX stocks (3 percent), and the most active OTC Nasdaq stocks (12 percent).

There also exist variations and sectoral subindices for many of these major market indices, such as a separate Dow Jones Average for 20 Transportation Stocks, 15 Utilities Stocks, a more inclusive 65 Stock Composite Index, and the Dow's new Equity Market Index. Standard & Poor's and the NYSE also maintain separate industrials, transportation, and utilities indices, as well as a financials index. Also, S&P has an index of 400 intermediate, or midsized, companies. The Nasdaq has subindices covering industrials, insurance firms, and banks. All of these indices are proprietary in nature, maintained by different entities which license their use. All are widely reported, although the DJIA, followed by the S&P 500, is the most widely followed.

Each index is constructed somewhat differently. However, these differences are generally of a technical nature, and the indices generally track each other relatively closely. Nevertheless, different measures react with varying degrees of sensitivity and at different times to developing trends in the financial markets. For example, because the DJIA covers so few large, widely held, and heavily traded stocks, it can be affected noticeably by sharp but idiosyncratic movement in one or two of its component stocks, while the much broader NYSE index may show a more stable or even somewhat different underlying trend. Alternatively, strength in the Dow can mask weakness in the broader indices, as was the case during much of 1994.

Stock Market Performance During 1994 US stock market performance was relatively flat, rising by only 2.1 percent as measured by the Dow, which closed the year at 3,834.44. However, broader market measures showed declines: the S&P 500 fell by 1.5 percent, the NYSE Composite by 3.1 percent, and the NASDAQ Composite by 3.2 percent. The Russell 2000, which fell by 3.2 percent and the Wilshire 5000, down by 2.5 percent, tracked the other major indices more closely, although the AMEX Index fell by an outsized 9.1 percent.

Between 1970 and 1994, the Dow grew from 753.2 to 3,834.4, or 409 percent overall, at an average com-

CHANGES AND TRENDS

One major change in US financial markets in recent decades has been a shift from individual investors to institutional investors as the driving force. These large investors, dominated by pension funds and mutual funds which generally trade in blocks of 25,000 shares, control increasingly gargantuan pools of assets. Such trades now account for roughly half of the dollar value of exchange activity. In 1993 institutional investors accounted for 42 percent of activity on the NYSE—down from a high of 52 percent in 1988. In 1993, 24 percent of activity was made by NYSE members for their own accounts, which represent a different type of institutional activity, while 32 percent were trades by retail customers for their own accounts. Up until the late 1960s individual investors generally represented around 70 percent of trading. Institutional assets have increased from less than US$200 billion in 1975 to almost US$1.2 trillion in 1993.

Some of this change represents a shift from the ownership of individual stocks to holdings of pools of stocks through mutual funds. In 1991, 73.2 percent of US households held interest-earning assets through financial institutions (up from 71.8 percent in 1984, although the average value of such holdings fell by nearly 12 percent to US$3,607). Some 46 percent had checking accounts (down from 53.9 percent in 1984), and 20.7 percent held stocks or shares in mutual funds (up only marginally from 20 percent in 1984). Not only had the breadth of these holdings of financial instruments failed to expand significantly, but the average dollar value of such holdings had increased by only 6.5 percent in nominal terms to US$5,469.

However, households with IRAs or Keogh accounts (personal retirement plans similar to IRAs, designed to cover self-employment income) rose from 19.5 percent in 1984 to 22.9 percent in 1991. Of even greater importance was the fact that the value of assets held in these accounts—much of it in stocks or mutual funds—almost doubled to an average of US$11,638. This phenomenon is reinforced when the share of assets held by individuals indirectly through 401(k) plans and defined benefit pension plans is included. Nevertheless, the basic fact remains that individuals exercise direct control over relatively few of these assets, which are handled primarily in large blocks by institutional investment managers.

Other developments that have affected financial markets in the US have included leveraged buyouts (LBOs), market indexing, and programmed trading. The 1980s saw the rise of the leveraged buyout, in which one company took over another company with borrowed funds using the assets to be derived from the company taken over as collateral. There is still considerable debate over whether this trend was positive or negative for US business. The funds for such activity began to dry up in the early 1990s, so the question is currently somewhat moot.

Market indexing involved the dedication of investment funds to holdings that mimicked the indices, such as the S&P 500. Because large institutional investors represent such large pools of funds, they can generally do no better than the overall market on average. Maintaining an index fund saves on transaction and management costs, which can often pull managed fund results below market averages. A somewhat related issue was programmed trading, in which computerized programs dictated that securities held by institutional firms should be bought or sold based on their relationship to index futures contracts. Programmed trading has been faulted for distorting markets and for worsening the market crash of 1987. Many of the reforms instituted in the aftermath of the crash were aimed at limiting the impact of such programmed trading. However, within a couple of years, programmed trading had returned to a level equal to or above that during the pre-crash era without a definite effect having been established. The only sure arguments regarding programmed trading are that it results in greater volatility and that as a hedge it is largely ineffective.

pound annual growth rate (CAGR) of 6.7 percent during the 25-year period. Between 1984 and 1993, the Dow rose by a total of 198 percent in current dollar terms, while stock market indices in the next largest international markets (in descending order, as measured by size of stock market and in dollar terms) grew by 338 percent in Japan, 242 percent in Britain, 428 percent in France, 290 percent in Germany, 59 percent in Canada, 354 percent in Switzerland, and 553 percent in Hong Kong. By comparison, such emerging markets as Argentina grew by 983 percent, Chile by 1,747 percent, Mexico by 1,868 percent, and the Philippines by 1,909 percent, in dollars—and by even more in local currencies—during the same period, albeit from much lower bases.

The US market—the largest, most liquid, and most stable worldwide—reflects overall steady growth. However, this picture is considerably different in view of the fact that many of the recent gains during the 1980s (when the Dow rose threefold from 891 to 2,679) and from 1990 through 1994 (when it rose by more than an additional 1,000 points, or more than 40 percent) are largely wiped out when the underlying gains are reported on a constant dollar basis. This also demonstrates the fact that the US is a maturing economy experiencing generally moderate economic growth, and as such, the performance of its financial markets cannot be expected to seriously outstrip that of the underlying economy for extended periods. In fact, some observers, citing the example of Great Britain during the early 20th century, worry that an economy too reliant on secondary financial market activity unsustained by primary industrial and market growth is a sign of decline.

Types of Stock and Other Securities Unlike some other countries which may have multiple different classes of stock, often determined by whether or not the securities can be held by non-nationals, the US—with its open investment regime in which foreigners can buy or sell any securities—has relatively few different types of equity securities. The main difference is between common and preferred stocks. Other equity securities traded include rights, warrants, and American Depository Receipts (ADRs).

Common Stocks Common stocks constitute the vast majority of equity securities. These instruments represent a proportional share of ownership of the net assets of the corporation. Common stocks may or may not pay cash dividends, which are usually based on the level of profits (some firms elect to maintain payouts out of prior retained earnings even if not covered by current earnings). US corporations usually declare and pay dividends quarterly on a regular schedule, although they may declare special dividends at other times. Dividends may also be declared in additional shares of stock. Common stock carries with it limited liability, because shareholders cannot lose more than the value of their investment and are not liable for excess debt, losses, or judgments against the corporation. Common stock may be issued with a par value or with no par, or base, value; as a practical matter, this issue is of no concern to the shareholder.

In general, common stock is freely transferable and can be bought by anyone and sold to any willing buyer. Some stock issued or used for special purposes is known as restricted stock, which cannot be sold or otherwise transferred except under certain specified terms and circumstances. Common stock may be issued in different classes, usually as Class A and Class B stock. These classes may carry different rights in terms of voting and/or payouts, with the controlling class being available only to shareholders approved by the other holders of voting shares. The other class of shares allows outsiders to participate in the earnings and capital gains of the firm without rights in issues of corporate governance. The SEC frowns on such arrangements, which are not generally allowed by the rules of the NYSE, so that some corporations list their different classes of stock on other exchanges in order to maintain narrow control.

Preferred Stock Preferred stock functions much like a bond: while it represents a share of equity in the corporation, it has a fixed payout, and its price usually fluctuates based on the level of interest rates rather than on the change in value of the enterprise. Preferred stock par value is important because it establishes the level of the contracted payout. Preferred dividends must be paid before any common stock dividends. With cumulative preferred stock, dividends owed accrue until paid, so that all outstanding preferred dividends must be paid in full before any common stock dividends. Unlike bonds, preferred stocks have no maturity date and generally are permanent obligations of the corporation unless retired. Participating preferred stocks allow holders to share in additional special dividends if such are declared, while convertible preferred can be converted into shares of common stock at the holder's discretion under certain conditions. Preference stock generally refers to a senior issue of preferred which takes precedence over subsequent issues. In case of liquidation of the corporation, preferred shareholders would be paid off before common shareholders; however, in such cases there are seldom adequate remaining assets to satisfy such claims.

Rights and Warrants In case of new offerings of stock in the corporation, existing shareholders may be given an advance opportunity to buy these shares at market or sometimes at preferential prices. Such rights are usually issued in proportion to holdings, in order to allow existing shareholders the opportunity to maintain their relative level of ownership. Rights must be exercised within a specified period of time, and can usually be treated as transferable property which can be sold as a separate security.

Warrants, similar to rights, are usually included with stock or bonds as a "kicker," an extra benefit to attract interest in the main security. A warrant is a transferable security which allows the holder to buy additional shares of the underlying security at specified prices under stated conditions. Most warrants are for specific periods—usually 5 to 10 years—although perpetual warrants that never expire can be issued. Warrants are speculative securities: at the time of issue they are worthless, serving only as an incentive to those who think the security will gain value in the future.

American Depositary Receipts (ADRs) ADRs represent proxy securities of foreign firms traded on US markets. Many overseas firms choose not to list their stocks directly on US exchanges, or international settlement difficulties can make dealing in actual shares impractical. Instead, a US financial institution will create a secondary security representing actual shares of the foreign security physically held by and registered to it, hence the name "depositary receipt." This allows US investors to buy and foreign firms to sell securities of overseas companies in the US. The ADRs can be redeemed for actual shares of the foreign stock, although this is seldom done. In 1994 there were about 980 ADRs trading in the US. These securities are traded over-the-counter or listed on the exchanges. ADR issues must be registered with the SEC, and holders receive all applicable US protections.

Regulation Primary federal regulation of the US financial markets is the responsibility of the SEC. The 50 states also have analogous local regulatory bodies which may require additional compliance measures. Established by the Securities and Exchange Act of 1934, which was designed to prevent the abuses that brought on the 1929 market crash, the SEC has provided the model for most modern securities regulatory bodies worldwide. The SEC supervises private financial exchanges, investment companies, registered investment advisors, and the NASD and its members. In implementing the various pieces of federal securities legislation, the SEC establishes rules that regulate procedures and standards for a variety of activities. These include, among other areas, rules for: short selling, solicitations, rights distributions, confirmation procedures, margin credit arrangements, proxy solicitation, tender offers, net capital requirements for securities firms and broker-dealers, reserves, commissions, off-exchange trading, sales of unregistered securities, and shelf and active registrations.

In general, the SEC requires that firms issuing securities for sale in the US ensure that their holders receive audited financial information conforming to its specifications in a timely fashion; be allowed to effectively exercise voting privileges; and receive any and all applicable dividends and any other payouts, including stock dividends, splits, warrants, and rights. It operates primarily by requiring a high level of disclosure.

In the late 1930s, the SEC set up the NASD to serve as a self-policing industry association, to which it delegated the authority to manage the activities of those in the securities industry. Many observers consider the SEC to be understaffed, underfunded,

and inadequate to monitor the entire securities industry. It can initiate only civil cases (criminal cases must be developed by the Justice Department). Some observers argue that the decision of the SEC in the early 1970s to turn down regulatory responsibility for futures trading—leading to the formation of the Commodity Futures Trading Commission (CFTC)—cut the regulatory agency off from the most dynamic financial market development of recent decades, leaving it unable to manage effectively the course of markets. The issue of merging these agencies to unify securities regulation emerges periodically, with the latest attempt occurring in early 1995. However, most observers doubt that any action will take place.

In the late 1980s the SEC took on such issues as insider trading and market manipulation, resulting in some high-profile indictments and convictions that shook up the industry. However, despite the opportunity provided by the crash in 1987, the SEC made relatively few additional rules or suggestions for the future. In an attempt to brake excessive trading, the SEC established a set of so-called circuit breakers to slow down market moves, an arrangement whereby trading on the NYSE in particular would be temporarily halted to allow a cooldown period if the trading exceeded 50 points on the upside (the cap) or the downside (the floor). This procedure seems to be at least marginally effective in damping down volatility, although it has not faced any really serious challenges since its inception.

Registration Requirements US securities regulation is primarily designed to provide adequate disclosure and free and open access to markets for all participants. Thus, the sale of securities to the public is a rather complex process which often involves disclosure greater than that to which businesses in other countries are accustomed. Exemptions or reduced SEC registration requirements can be obtained for US, state, and local government and agency securities; those issued by individual banks, such as negotiable certificates of deposit (bank holding company securities must be registered); commercial paper and bankers' acceptances maturing in less than 270 days; and various other generally small and special purpose issues, as well as those that will not be sold interstate or through the mails. Private placements and the sale of certain securities to qualified institutional buyers and accredited persons (that is, to sophisticated investors having specified levels of capital), and of securities of a company that has issued less than US$1.5 million of securities in the preceding year, are eligible for limited registration procedures (Regulation A registrations).

The SEC has no authority to judge or certify the quality of an offering; it attests only that the offering meets all disclosure and procedural rules. For most securities, a detailed registration statement must be submitted to the SEC. Usually, the preparation of the registration statement entails prolonged negotiations and considerable effort on the part of the company, independent accountants and lawyers, and investment bankers—securities industry personnel who agree to sponsor and sell the offering for a fee and often for a consideration involving a part of the issue. The SEC conducts an extensive review and can request additional information. While this is going on, issuing firms are subject to a blackout or cooling off period during which they are barred from publicly discussing the proposed security or their firms. In addition to this federal procedure, many states require separate registration before any public offering can be made within their jurisdictions.

The registration process involves the preparation of a prospectus describing the company and its operations along with a considerable amount of both historical and pro forma projected financial data, as well as the identities and compensation for top officers and any holdings of greater than 5 percent of the securities of the company. Usually three years of audited existing financial data are required. These financial statements must be current within 135 days for US firms and within 180 days for foreign firms seeking to register in the US. Foreign firms are not required to submit financial data prepared in accordance with US generally accepted accounting principles (GAAP), but if such nonconforming data is submitted, it must be accompanied by a disclosure statement that reconciles the submitted data with US accounting standards. Some foreign firms balk at the amount of required financial data as well as the fact that it must be conformed to US accounting standards. This often calls for far greater financial disclosure than is considered appropriate in many foreign business settings. However, overseas business accounting standards often disclose more operations information than US businesses consider appropriate.

In 1983 the SEC approved shelf registration. This procedure allows major firms on which information is generally available to make an open registration of debt securities (and later of stocks as well) to be offered at the company's discretion. When the company is ready to issue the securities, it files specific current information and proceeds without the customary registration delays (and expense). This procedure is not available for initial public offerings of securities by companies that have not previously undergone a full registration, but is highly useful for firms interested in issuing additional securities.

SEC Rule 144A—instituted in 1990 and broadened in 1994—allows firms to use a less extensive and less time-consuming procedure for the registration of restricted securities that can only be sold to large institutional investors assumed to be more astute and better funded than the general public. Many foreign entities have used this procedure to gain access to US financial markets through private placements of such securities with US institutional investors without going to the trouble of making them available to the US public. Although this allows issuers to sell their securities quickly and easily, it does restrict them to a narrower niche of the market. Other issuers have found that this market can rapidly become crowded and is quick to shut down in the face of setbacks.

Reporting Requirements All companies registered with the SEC must file quarterly and annual reports with the SEC (where they become available for public examination), as well as notify the SEC within short specified time frames of material events affecting the corporation. These requirements apply to all companies with shares traded on an exchange and to companies traded over-the-counter once they reach a certain size and number of shareholders. Filings are made in English.

Firms incorporated in the US must file Form 10-K, an annual report describing company activities and financial results, within 90 days of the close of the fiscal year. The 10-K must include audited balance sheets and income, cash flow, and changes in shareholder equity statements prepared according to US GAAP. Less detailed unaudited quarterly reports (10-Qs) must be filed within 45 days of the close of each fiscal quarter. A Form 8-K must be filed within 15 days of certain events, such as a change in control, a major acquisition or divestiture, or some other material change in the company or its activities.

All corporations operating in the US—whether domestic or foreign—that wish to acquire more than 5 percent of an existing registered, publicly traded company through a formal tender offer for the company's shares must comply with standard SEC disclosure and procedural requirements. The acquisition of a minimum of 5 percent of any class of the securities of a publicly traded firm by any means, including open market or negotiated purchase, requires the buyer to file a public disclosure Form 13-D within 10 days of the event. The SEC can impose certain limitations or conditions on additional acquisition of the target firm by the acquiring firm, as can other regulatory agencies in cases involving regulatory interests or antitrust considerations.

Foreign-incorporated firms operating in the US—unless also separately incorporated in the US—can usually avoid filing 10-Ks and related documents, or, if unable to avoid filing them, do so based only on their US operations and not global activity. However, foreign firms operating in the US must file Form 20-F (a less detailed annual report) within 180 days of the close of the fiscal year. Not all of the material reported is required to meet US GAAP standards, although any data not following GAAP must include appropriate reconciliations. Foreign firms do not have to file quarterly reports unless such disclosure is required by the authorities in the home country; is filed for public disclosure in accordance with the requirements of a foreign stock exchange; or is routinely prepared for distribution to shareholders elsewhere. In any of these cases, the information would then be filed on Form 6-K.

The SEC has issued regulations to implement the adoption of the Electronic Data Gathering Analysis and Retrieval (EDGAR) system. All SEC filings, correspondence, and supplemental responses will have to be submitted in electronic form through direct transmission, on diskette, or on tape. This is to become mandatory in 1996 following a phase-in period. In a similar but unrelated instance of acquiescing to new technology, the SEC decreed that settlement (payment and transfer of title) of all securities trades would be required to occur in three business days, rather than the five-day period that existed previously, by June 1995. (The longer period was established when transfers required the physical delivery of funds and certificates, virtually all of which is now accomplished electronically through book entries.)

Listing Requirements For a security to be listed on a US exchange, the company must meet all SEC registration requirements and maintain its required filings of results. In addition, the company must submit detailed information, including audited past financial statements, to the listing entity and demonstrate a wide enough public distribution to ensure an active market for the securities. For the NYSE, the minimum standards for US-incorporated firms have included a threshold of 1.1 million shares outstanding with a market value of at least US$18 million in public hands; this must include either at least 2,000 shareholders, each with minimum holdings of 100 shares (called a round lot); or a total of at least 2,200 shareholders and average trading volume of at least 100,000 shares per month during the preceding six months. The company must own net tangible assets of at least US$18 million and have a pretax net income of at least US$2.5 million in its most recent fiscal year and at least US$2 million in each of the two preceding fiscal years; or a minimum total of US$6.5 million during the preceding three years, with at least US$4.5 million in one of the past two years.

Foreign firms must show a minimum of 2.5 million publicly held shares outstanding worldwide, with a minimum market value of US$100 million. Firms must have at least 5,000 nonaffiliated shareholders with minimum holdings of 100 shares apiece. Such firms must demonstrate international hard assets worth at least US$100 million and a total pretax income of at least US$100 million during the prior three years with at least US$25 million in each of

those three years. The NYSE reviews its standards frequently and its stated policy is to use them as guidelines rather than as firm requirements.

The NYSE charges an initial listing fee of US$36,800 and a per share charge beginning at US$14,750 for the first two million shares listed. Annual listing fees are US$1,650 per million for the first two million shares plus US$830 for each additional million shares. The NYSE delists firms if the number of shares outstanding in public hands falls below 600,000; the market value drops below US$5 million; or the number of public round lot shareholders is less than 1,200.

AMEX Requirements The AMEX maintains less stringent listing requirements, and charges lower fees. Domestic companies must have net tangible assets valued at US$4 million, and net operating income (before taxes and extraordinary items) of at least US$750,000 in the preceding fiscal year or in two of the three preceding years. A minimum of 500,000 shares must be publicly held by at least 800 nonaffiliated shareholders, each with a minimum holding of 100 shares; alternatively, it may have at least 1 million shares with at least 400 holders of 100 shares each. The share price must remain at a minimum of US$3 per share for an extended period prior to listing. International companies seeking an AMEX listing must show net tangible assets of at least US$25 million; earned income before taxes of at least US$30 million during the preceding three years, with a minimum of US$7.5 million in two out of the three preceding years; at least 1 million shares outstanding in public hands, with a minimum of 800 shareholders with at least 100 shares each; and publicly held shares with an aggregate market value of at least US$3 million.

Nasdaq Requirements Similar rules apply to both foreign and domestic firms seeking to list through Nasdaq. Companies must demonstrate that at least two licensed broker-dealers make a market in their security; a minimum of 300 nonaffiliated shareholders; and a minimum of 100,000 shares or ADRs outstanding. In order to list secondary securities such as rights or warrants, the underlying security must already be traded either through Nasdaq or on a formal exchange. Since 1991 listings through Nasdaq's SmallCap Stock Market require minimum assets of US$4 million and shareholders' equity of at least US$2 million when listed, and must subsequently maintain minimums of US$2 million in assets and US$1 million in capital and surplus to remain listed. Minimum bid prices must be at least US$3 per share and those requesting the listing must demonstrate that two dealers make a market in the stock.

To be included on the Nasdaq NMS, the stock must have at least 500,000 publicly held shares valued at a minimum of US$3 million; the share price must have been at least US$5 for the five trading days prior to application; and the firm must have had a net income of at least US$400,000 in net income and US$750,000 in revenues in the most recent year or in two of the three most recent fiscal years. Alternatively, NMS listing can be achieved by companies with at least a three year operating history; minimum net tangible assets of US$12 million; at least 1 million shares outstanding; and a market value of US$15 million for publicly held shares. Either way, the applicant must demonstrate that at least two broker-dealers have made an active market in the securities during the five days prior to the filing.

Securities that fail to meet even the relatively low requirements for inclusion in Nasdaq can still be traded (and, in fact, must be traded by at least two broker-dealers prior to their listing through NASDAQ). Many such issues, including so-called penny stocks (those priced under US$1), are low-priced, unseasoned, often speculative securities of small public firms that are traded through the so-called pink sheets (write-ups of the private National Quotation Board which give minimal price data and list broker-dealers). Since 1990 the NASD has operated the OTC Bulletin Board (OTCBB), an automated equivalent of the pink sheets, covering approximately 4,500 issues.

Securities Firms The NASD, to which all firms and individuals that operate as professionals in the US securities industry must belong, has a membership of about 52,000. At the end of 1993, the US had 11 of the top 25 securities firms worldwide as measured by capital. Although Japan's Nomura Securities ranked first, the second, third, and fourth largest (respectively, Goldman Sachs, Salomon Brothers, and Merrill Lynch) were all US firms. The number of US securities firms peaked in 1987—the year of the stock market crash—at 9,515; by 1993 this number had fallen by almost 20 percent to 7,705. As the number of securities firms contracted, the remaining ones required more capital to operate in the changing environment. In the late 1980s foreign—primarily Japanese—firms began to acquire stakes in US securities operations by injecting capital. At the same time, foreign securities firms including as Nomura, Nikko, Daiwa, and Yamaichi also began to establish direct presences in the US securities business. In the early 1990s, several large US financial companies that had acquired securities firms in the early 1980s, disappointed by the volatility of securities earnings and growing needs for capital, began to divest themselves of these subsidiaries. Securities industry revenues were US$19.8 billion in 1980, reaching US$90.7 billion in 1992.

To operate in the securities business, firms must be licensed, maintain minimum capital levels, and subscribe to the Security Investor's Protection Corporation (SIPC), which insures client balances against brokerage failure. Many firms maintain additional insurance to cover excess customer losses above the US$500,000 per account limit provided by the SIPC. Professionals must be licensed by and be members of the NASD. Except in limited situations, all transactions involving registered securities must go through a licensed broker, who must in turn operate through a member of the exchange on which the security is traded or through an NASD member who can access Nasdaq. The exchanges are formal, private entities, and those wishing to operate on them must purchase one of the limited number of seats on the exchange, or else go through a firm owning such rights.

Fixed brokerage commissions were deregulated in 1975, and over the last 20 years transaction costs in US markets have fallen to roughly half of those in most other securities markets. In practice, this has meant that institutional buyers can negotiate commissions based on their volume of business, although small accounts have less leverage to obtain lower-cost access. Securities firms have also worked out certain rebate or discount schemes to attract traders using what are known as soft dollars, offering free investment research and similar services. Although most individual investors have reaped fewer benefits from negotiated commissions, the move did open the way for the formation of discount brokerage houses that deal primarily with individuals, offering transactions without most of the add-on services (such as advice and research) provided by the large full-service firms (often called wire houses). Indirectly, these discounters also opened the way for commercial banks to get into the retail securities business.

Investment Banking Besides buying and selling securities, most larger securities firms also operate investment banking arms. Investment bankers generally provide financial expertise to companies interested in high-level financial transactions, such as initial public offerings (IPOs) of securities, mergers and acquisitions, and refinancing and restructuring. Large investment banks usually also run securities trading operations, both for customers and their own accounts; one of the main reasons investment bankers are hired to manage securities offerings (underwriting) is that they can place the resulting securities through their trading and brokerage operations. Because of the potential conflicts of interest between trading and underwriting units, such units are supposed to maintain procedural barriers that separate the activities of each. Financial operations that involve the firm's own capital and an equity stake in another firm are generally known as merchant banking. In 1993 securities firms underwrote an estimated US$37 billion of IPOs (shares of new companies) and US$41 billion in additional issues of stock for existing publicly traded companies.

The reforms instituted following the crash of 1929 resulted in the separation of investment and commercial banking in the US, with investment banks being denied the ability to accept deposits and commercial banks being precluded from underwriting or otherwise dealing in securities. This separation has continued on the books, but has been eroded in recent years. Since 1987 certain commercial banks have been allowed to broker and even underwrite securities through subsidiaries. By year-end 1992, more than 6 percent of all securities firm capital was held by such bank subsidiaries, and by mid-1993 bank subsidiaries were underwriting 5.5 percent of all investment grade corporate debt.

Debt and Money Markets

The debt and money markets often blend into each other, although in general they operate separately to fill different capital needs. The money market—defined as representing debt securities with maturities of one year or less—consists of US government and private securities (often referred to as paper and usually consisting of unsecured promises to pay). Also, money market securities are usually unregistered, while longer term securities must be registered with the SEC. Bonds are debt instruments with maturities of longer than one year, usually sold at the face value (par), although they may be sold at a premium (above face value) or a discount (below face value). Most bonds pay fixed interest (the coupon rate) semiannually. Adjustable or floating rate debt instruments pay a variable rate that is adjusted over the life of the bond according to an established procedure. Zero coupon bonds are sold at a deep discount, accrue imputed interest over the life of the instrument, and pay off the face amount at maturity, having made no cash payouts during the intervening period.

In 1993 total debt outstanding in the US amounted to US$15.9 trillion, 27.6 percent of which represented government debt, including federal, state, local and agency obligations (76 percent of this was federal debt). Of total debt, that of financial institutions represented 20 percent, private debt 50.1 percent, and foreign debt 2.3 percent. (In 1980 total US debt amounted to US$4.7 trillion, 22 percent of which was government debt, 12 percent financial, 61 percent private, and 4 percent foreign.) In 1993 average daily activity in the debt markets amounted to roughly US$247 billion worth of securities traded; however, of this amount, US government debt accounted for roughly 84 percent.

Money Markets Money markets exist primarily to provide liquidity for various participants in the economic system by allowing them to lend or obtain funds on a short-term basis. The mainstay of the money markets are US Treasury bills (known as T-bills). These securities, issued in minimum denominations of US$10,000, come with 3-, 6-, or 12-month maturities. The 3- and 6-month bills are sold at weekly auctions, with 12-month bills being sold monthly. T-bills are sold at a discount from the face value determined by auction and depending on prevailing interest rates in the money markets. The difference between the discount and the face value is the imputed interest, which can be quoted as a discount rate or as a bond equivalent yield.

Commercial Paper Commercial paper represents unsecured corporate promissory notes with maturities of less than 270 days, the cutoff point above which SEC registration is required. Because this debt is unsecured, many issuers back their commercial paper with bank lines of credit or standby letters of credit. Concerns periodically arise over the validity of such insurance, because given the huge outstanding amounts of such paper and the fact that so much of it is issued directly by financial firms, most observers doubt that such backup would be valid in a crisis situation. Commercial paper has increasingly become a means for large corporations to bypass bank lending by selling their debts directly in the money markets at costs substantially below that of funds from banks or other intermediaries, many of which must fund themselves through similar means. In 1980 US corporations issued US$122.4 billion worth of commercial paper; in 1993 US firms issued US$555.1 billion, an increase of 353 percent. About 70 percent of commercial paper is issued by financial firms.

In keeping with standard money market practice, most commercial paper is issued at a discount based on prevailing short-term interest rates, returning the full face amount at maturity. Many corporations place their own paper directly with investors, although a substantial amount—mostly that issued by nonfinancial corporations—is sold by brokers operating through major New York securities firms. Because institutional investors hold these short-term instruments to maturity, there is no active secondary market for commercial paper. Commercial paper is usually issued in large denominations, from US$100,000 to US$1 million. Only the best-known, most creditworthy firms are able to issue commercial paper.

Certificates of Deposit Certificates of deposit (CDs) are negotiable securities issued by commercial banks to depositors based on time deposits that the banks hold for them. Such deposits cannot be withdrawn before maturity without substantial penalties, giving the bank use of the funds for the term of the deposit. However, CDs can be traded in the secondary market to achieve liquidity. As exempt securities issued by financial institutions, CDs do not require SEC registration. CDs can have maturities of as much as five years, although most are for periods no longer than 6- to 18-months, and to be traded in the money markets must generally have less than one year to go to maturity. Many securities firms also package bank CDs for sale to their clients, making a market in the resulting securities.

Bankers' Acceptances Bankers' acceptances (BAs) consist of trade bills that the bank has guaranteed (accepted) for payment at a date in the future, usually from 1 to 6 months hence. As financial institution instruments, BAs do not require SEC registration, although they seldom have maturities beyond the 9-month ceiling for exemption from such registration. BAs can be discounted and resold by secondary market dealers for liquidity.

Additional Money Market Instruments There are a variety of other short-term money market instruments, including federal, state, and local government tax or revenue anticipation bills, notes, and certificates (TABs, TANs, TACs, RANs, etc.), as well as constantly evolving variants issued and traded by a wide range of market participants. The shortest of money market transactions involve the trading of federal funds among financial institutions. Other businesses and institutions can participate in the repurchase (repo) market: the short-term—often overnight—purchase of a security and its subsequent resale to the original seller at a price that takes into account the differing marginal interest rates between the two transactions.

Because of the institutional bias of the money markets, it is difficult for individuals to participate directly in them. But banks and brokerage firms offer cash management accounts and other mechanisms that allow individual and business clients to use the money markets. Hundreds of money market mutual funds also exist to enable individuals to take advantage of the benefits of these markets, although in 1991 only 4.2 percent of US households had such money market accounts.

Capital Markets In 1992, 589 entities with 1,462 separate corporate bond issues having a total face value of US$2,009 billion were listed on the NYSE, only one of the markets for trading such instruments. By comparison, in 1980 there were 70 percent more entities—1,045—with 3,057 separate bond issues listed—more than twice as many—but with a value of only US$602 billion, less than one-third the 1992 amount. One reason for this was that during the stock market boom of the 1980s, many firms shifted capital raising away from bonds toward what was at the time considered cheaper equity financing. Another reason was the general consolidation of firms, resulting in fewer issuers. In 1992, 58 percent of private sector bonds were issued by real estate or financial entities, 17 percent by manufacturing firms, 10 percent by utilities, 9 percent by communications firms, cent by utilities, 9 percent by communications firms,

3 percent by commercial firms, and 2 percent by other firms.

In 1980 US trading in foreign bonds was US$35.2 billion, with net purchases of US$1 billion. Thirteen years later in 1993, US trading in foreign bonds reached US$1.73 trillion, nearly 40 times as much, with net purchases of US$60.8 billion, more than 60 times the 1980 level. In 1980 foreign traders were involved in US bond transactions valued at US$123 billion, with net purchases reaching US$10.4 billion. By 1993 total foreign transactions involving US bonds were worth US$5.7 trillion, with net purchases of US$90.1 billion. The vast majority of foreign trading activity was in US Treasury securities (91 percent) followed by US government agency bonds (5 percent), with corporate bonds (4 percent) a distant third. In 1993 foreign trading in US debt instruments outstripped trading in US stocks by nearly 10 to 1, although nearly 20 percent of total foreign net purchases of US securities represented stocks. Conversely, three-quarters of US transactions involving foreign securities represented bond trades, while only slightly less than half of US net purchases were of foreign bonds. Often, US Treasury securities are used as an international store of wealth: they are readily available, generally as strong as any security, and easy to trade, given how open US financial markets are. Thus international activity involving bonds, especially US bonds, tends to be characterized by rapid turnover, with a huge dollar volume of extremely short-term (often overnight) transactions.

To investors, US bonds offer a wide array of nuanced possibilities. Within recent years, bearer bonds—those payable to the holder—have been replaced with registered bonds—those registered to the owner and most often held in book entry rather than physical custody certificate form—primarily as a result of the increasing computerization of financial transactions. Traditionally, the bondholder literally cut the sequentially numbered coupon off of the bond certificate and deposited it with a financial institution to receive the interest owed; now virtually all payments are made automatically through book transfers into the registered holder's securities or bank account. Bonds may include a call provision, which allows the issuer to pay them off at specified rates (usually at par or at a premium) after an established term if it so desires (usually if it can refinance them at a lower interest rate). Uncallable bonds are more secure, paying the same interest until maturity.

US Federal, State, and Local Government Securities US government securities, which account for the vast majority of federal debt, include: short-term T-bills (with maturities of 1 year or less), intermediate notes (with 1- to 10-year maturities, known as T-notes), and bonds (with 10- to 30-year maturities, known as T-bonds). Treasury securities (other than

T-bills) generally have minimum face values of US$5,000 with subsequent increments of US$1,000 and make fixed interest payments semiannually. They may be bought through most banks and all securities firms, as well as directly from the government through the district Federal Reserve banks, which act as agents for the US Treasury. Amounts to be borrowed are generally announced the week before the sale of the securities, allowing buyers to bid on specific issues. Large bidders set the actual prices paid, with smaller entities and individual bidders generally having their orders filled at the prevailing price thus established. US Treasury debt is guaranteed by the full faith and credit of the US federal government and is considered the safest financial investment that exists. Thus, US Treasury debt usually establishes a floor for interest rates on all other debt, which is considered to be riskier. Treasury securities are usually uncallable, although the Treasury has the authority to issue callable securities.

Federal Agency Debt A wide range of US government agencies are allowed to issue debt, which—while not formally backed by the government—is generally considered to include a moral obligation under which the US Treasury would not allow it to default. The primary issuing entity is the Federal National Mortgage Association (FNMA, known generally as "Fannie Mae"), a publicly owned, federally sponsored corporation that exists to provide liquidity to the financial system by buying mortgages from the institutions that originate them, thus allowing them to relend the funds. The government entity then holds the actual assets long-term, issuing securities based on this portfolio of private debt. The Government National Mortgage Association (GNMA, or "Ginnie Mae"), is a government-owned offshoot of FNMA that operates in a similar fashion to facilitate government mortgage lending. The Federal Home Loan Mortgage Corporation (FHLMC, or "Freddie Mac") provides a similar service for US savings institutions. These agencies package the individual mortgages they buy into pools (groups of similar types of mortgages with similar rates and maturities) and sell them to investors as debt securities. They offer investors a higher rate than is generally available in the general debt markets, although they are subject to substantial fluctuation due changes in interest rates.

Other federal agency debt includes that of the Student Loan Marketing Association (SLMA or "Sallie Mae"), which buys and packages guaranteed student loans; the Banks for Cooperatives and the Federal Intermediate Credit Banks of the Farm Credit Bureau, the Federal Land Banks, the Tennessee Valley Authority (TVA), the US Export-Import Bank, and the US Post Office. The securities of international organizations, such as the World Bank and the IDB, are also sold in the US, and non-resident foreign individuals and most foreign corporations receive special tax treatment on such securities acquired in US markets.

Debt of Other Government Entities State and local jurisdictions in the US also issue debt which is generally free of federal tax (US Treasury debt is exempt from state and local taxes, and depending on the specific agency and issue, federal government agency debt may carry some tax benefits). Such so-called municipal bonds are divided into general obligation and revenue bonds. Revenue bonds depend on income generated from the project financed to service the debt, while general obligation bonds are serviced out of the general revenues of the issuing entity and are thus considered to be safer because the entity has the power to levy taxes to increase those revenues. Most municipal bonds include a call provision, allowing the issuer to refinance at lower rates. Municipal issuers sold US$289 billion of long-term and US$46 billion of short-term bonds in 1993. Municipal securities have generally been considered safe, with few local entities having defaulted on their obligations since the Great Depression. However, during the 19th century, such sovereign entities regularly defaulted on debt. And, at the end of 1994, Orange County, California declared bankruptcy, placing the repayment of certain of its municipal securities in doubt.

Private activity bonds represent a hybrid municipal security issued by a municipal authority to finance a private business activity. These receive qualified tax exemptions based on the theory that the activity will generate indirect revenues within the jurisdiction and that the jurisdiction will only extend this status to worthy projects. Such issues must meet a variety of technical requirements, and depending on the project and the status of the investor, may or may not be tax-free.

Corporate Debt Securities Corporate bonds come in a variety of types, primarily distinguished by the nature of the security that backs them. Most are callable. The safest type is the mortgage bond, which is backed by specific hard assets; in certain circumstances, this pledge can be converted with bondholder approval to what is known as a prior lien bond, which allows the specific assets to be used to secure new credit while giving the mortgage bondholders first priority based on all other assets. With collateral trust bonds, a corporation backs the debt issue with a portfolio of other securities held in trust by a commercial bank; often these pledged securities are issued by a subsidiary of the parent corporation issuing the collateral trust bonds. Equipment trust bonds are secured by the equipment of the corporation, such as by the owned (not leased) aircraft of an airline corporation. Because the economic life of such assets is relatively short, the bonds often mature over a shorter period and may roll over into new securities backed by newer equipment. Debentures are the least secure bonds, backed only by the general remaining assets of the corporation. In reality these distinctions are of less importance to a buyer than the analysis of the corporation's ability to cover its interest and principle payments from current operations.

Some corporations issue convertible debt, which, under specified circumstances, can be converted into shares of common stock. This provision is a somewhat speculative incentive offered to purchasers of the security. Convertibility makes the security more difficult to analyze, but offers opportunities to the buyer.

Securities firms have various proprietary indices to track bond performance. Some of the main ones are maintained by Merrill Lynch and Lehman Brothers, but none has the same stature as the more generally followed stock indices.

High-Yield Debt Now known generally as junk bonds, such high-yield debt has traditionally referred to securities which were (1) unrated because the issuers either did not expect to secure a favorable rating or did not want to pay one of the rating services to rate the bond or (2) securities that had fallen in value ("fallen angels") due to unfavorable business events affecting the issuing corporation. Such a drop in value of the underlying debt, coupled with the fixed interest rate, results in outsized rates of return to the holder who buys at a discount, provided the firm does not default. Rating agencies—the main ones being Standard & Poor's and Moody's—are independent firms which examine the issue and the issuer and rate them according to the likelihood that the debt will be serviced and repaid. Only the highest rated debt (BBB or above for S&P and Baa or above for Moody's) can be held by most commercial banks and insurance companies, major institutional buyers of corporate debt securities.

Since the Great Depression, high-yield debt has compared favorably with rated debt in terms of default rates. During the early 1980s, investment firms began dealing in junk bonds and ultimately underwriting original issue junk bonds—securities that went unrated and carried a high interest rate, a deep discount relative to the coupon rate, or other unusual and speculative provisions. Such debt was used in increasingly speculative ways to fund mergers and acquisitions. In 1990 the junk bond market collapsed dramatically following the indictment of some of the major individuals and firms involved in it. The market has since recovered, but in 1993 of roughly US$938 billion worth of new corporate debt issued by US firms, only 6 percent represented original issue, high-yield debt.

Investment Companies and Mutual Funds

Known technically as investment companies and commonly as mutual funds—in some countries, the equivalent would be investment trusts—such firms were established under the Investment Company Act of 1940. Investment companies include face amount certificate companies (a rare form of investment company which issues certificates based on funds held); unit investment trusts (consisting of a firm which buys and packages a specific type of security—usually municipal or other types of bonds—which are held to maturity, paying out interest and principal repayments as received to the unitholders, but which are not traded during the life of the trust); and management companies, representing all other possibilities. Management companies may be diversified companies (which must hold securities—mutual funds) or nondiversified companies (usually venture capital firms or investment holding companies).

Mutual Funds The main varieties of mutual funds are closed-end and open-end mutual funds. These must hold at least 75 percent of assets in cash or equivalents (including receivables), government securities, securities of other investment companies, or other securities of independent firms. A mutual fund may hold no more than 5 percent of its total assets in the securities of a single issuer, nor may it own more than 10 percent of the voting securities of an issuer. Total mutual fund assets rose to US$2.1 trillion in 1994, of which roughly half were invested in short-term money market mutual funds, while slightly more than one-quarter was in equity mutual funds and slightly less than one-quarter was in bond mutual funds. At the end of 1993, there were more than 4,200 mutual funds with a total of 77 million shareholder accounts (the actual number of investors is much lower because of multiple accounts). In 1994, seven US mutual funds had assets greater than US$10 billion.

Closed-End Funds Closed-end funds consist of a fixed number of shares. No new shares are issued, and the value of the fund fluctuates based on the value of the securities held. Existing shareholders are allowed to sell their shares, which are usually listed on formal exchanges, and new shareholders can buy the shares in the same way. Unlike the otherwise similar unit investment trusts, which also have fixed capital and a fixed number of shares (units), closed-end mutual funds actively manage and trade their portfolios. Depending on a variety of factors, closed-end funds can trade at a premium above the net asset value (or NAV, the market value of the assets held by the fund divided by the number of shares) or a discount below that value. Many closed-end funds specialize in certain types of investments.

Open-End Funds An open-end mutual fund has a variable number of shares based on how many investors own it at any point in time. Additional shares are issued to new buyers, and the funds stand ready to redeem their shares at the net asset value of the underlying portfolio at the investor's discretion. Many mutual funds follow increasingly narrow investment strategies. The broadest categories are stock funds, bond or income funds, money market funds, and municipal funds. Funds that invest in international securities are one of the fastest-growing fund sectors in the US. In mid-1993 there were 209 global funds (those investing in both US and foreign securities) with assets totaling US$63 billion and 170 foreign funds (investing only in non-US securities) with assets totaling US$38 billion. This represented an increase from the previous year of 40 percent in both the number of such funds and in assets managed. Roughly half of all mutual fund assets held worldwide are held by US investors.

Fund Operations Funds are operated by managers who set investment policy and take as compensation a percentage based on total assets managed. Mutual funds can be sold directly or through securities firms, and may be no load (sold at net asset value, usually directly to the buyer) or load (sold with a percentage of up to 8.5 percent deducted from the amount invested that goes to the salesperson as a commission). Foreigners may buy or sell US mutual funds at will in the US. However, different regulatory environments make it difficult for US mutual funds to operate to service customers located overseas.

Mutual funds are regulated by the SEC. They must issue detailed prospectuses and operating reports, and they must follow narrow rules for accounting and valuation. States also have a variety of laws and regulations governing mutual funds. As greater numbers of new, often unsophisticated investors flocked to mutual funds when interest rates and returns fell in the early 1990s, the SEC called for even greater regulation and disclosure by mutual funds. These have included standardized means of calculating and reporting performance and expenses. The SEC has proposed direct sales of mutual funds without the requirement that the investor first be sent a formal prospectus (this method of sales is common in the UK). Another element of the mutual fund scene has been the rise of proprietary mutual funds run by commercial banks, which now control about 10 percent of all mutual fund assets.

Real Estate Investment Trusts Another specialized type of mutual investment fund is the REIT, which holds a portfolio of real estate properties or securities for its investors. Mortgage REITs lend to developers to build properties, while equity REITs own and operate income-producing properties. At the end of 1993, equity REITs made up 81 percent of the REIT market, with mortgage REITs and hybrids of the two types representing 11 percent and 8 per-

cent, respectively. Shares of REITs are usually listed and traded on major exchanges.

A REIT must be organized as a corporation; have fully transferable shares; a minimum of 100 shareholders; no more than 50 percent of their shares held by five or fewer individuals; invest 75 percent of assets in real estate; derive at least 75 percent of earnings from real estate; derive less than 30 percent of earnings from real property held for less than four years or securities held less than six months; and pay out at least 95 percent of taxable income as dividends. Generally REITs pay relatively high dividends compared with other investments, plus have the potential for capital appreciation if the underlying properties increase in value.

Annuities Annuities are popular, mutual fund–like investments operated by insurance companies, by mutual fund advisors working on behalf of an insurer, or—increasingly—by banks. The underlying basis of the annuity involves a contract between the insurer and the insured by which the insurer agrees to pay out sums to the buyer (the annuitant) during a period in the future, based on payments made in the present. A fixed annuity entails a future payment of a predetermined amount, while a variable annuity future payment is determined by the investment results of the insurer. Insurance annuities are a tax-advantaged investment, used by many people in the US to save for retirement.

Limited Partnerships An increasingly popular form of investment, this consists of a separate legal entity with a general partner, who manages the investment, and a series of limited partners—the investors—who provide the investment capital. Many of these investments are organized as master limited partnerships (MLPs), the partnership interests of which can be traded on exchanges. MLPs operate much like mutual funds. However, all income and expenses flow directly through to the individual partners, allowing the partners to deduct the expenses without having the receipts pass through a separate corporate structure.

Venture Capital Firms Venture capital firms are closed-end, nondiversified management companies that invest risk capital to develop companies. Such firms generally take an ownership position of some sort through equity or long-term debt arrangements and may offer technical or management expertise to the firms in which they invest. Most venture capital firms work to build an existing business with the idea of making a public offering of securities within a three to five year time horizon. Small Business Investment Companies (SBIC) are a similar type of quasi-public venture entity licensed by the federal Small Business Administration (SBA) to make long-term loans or equity capital available to small businesses that meet certain criteria.

In 1994 US venture capitalists raised a record US$4.2 billion in new capital, up 45 percent from the amount raised in 1993. This upsurge was based on resurgent initial public offerings markets in 1992 and 1993, when venture capitalists committed US$2.8 billion. However, the prospects for stock offerings fell somewhat in 1994. The 10 largest established US venture capital firms accounted for more than one-third of the capital raised, with some 88 other firms raising an average of US$30 million each. Large firms do the most business because most institutional investors (which contribute more than 40 percent of the funds for venture capital) must put large sums of their funds to work, and even exceptional small deals will usually not help a large institution's overall performance. However, state and local pension funds are now pushing venture capitalists to invest their funds in smaller businesses in the local area.

In 1992 venture capital firms invested 55 percent of their funds in expansions, 14 percent in bridge loans, 13 percent in early stage investments, 8 percent in start-ups, 7 percent in leveraged buyouts and acquisitions, and 3 percent in seed money projects. In that year, the largest areas of investment were software and related services (22 percent), health care (17 percent), communications (14 percent), biotechnology (10 percent), and consumer products (8 percent). Together these accounted for 70 percent of venture capital funding. In all, some 3,218 investments were made in 1,087 firms. In 1992 more than 550 US venture capital firms had international operations. While there are no reliable figures on foreign participation in the US venture capital market, there are no barriers to prevent such participation.

Futures and Options (Commodity) Markets

Futures Markets Futures trading was developed to hedge risks on fluctuations in the price of commodities. A futures contract consists of an agreement between two parties either to make or take delivery of a standard amount of a specific commodity, at a certain time, and at a specified price. Although there are theoretically any number of commodities upon which such contracts can be written, in practice, only established contracts for which adequate investor interest exists are codified for trading on the established exchanges. And although a core of futures traders are interested in hedging against adverse price moves of commodities in which they have a producer's or consumer's interest as part of their business, the bulk of futures business involves speculative bets against such price movements. In virtually all cases, the holder of the contract neither delivers nor accepts the actual end product, but rather closes out the contract for the implicit profit on it.

Futures activity is speculative and high-volume, sustained by the fact that margin requirements are very low—as little as 5 percent of the purchase price of the commodity. Because of this degree of leverage, a slight change in the price of the underlying commodity can result in a large percentage gain or loss that is much higher than the amount of cash actually invested. Some estimates put the aggregate losses on futures trading as high as six times the aggregate gains on such trades. The imbalance is caused by professionals who close out losing trades extremely rapidly, while allowing winning trades to build up.

The major futures exchanges are the Chicago Board of Trade (CBOT) and the Chicago Mercantile Exchange (known as the Merc). The New York Futures Exchange (NYFE) was founded as an attempt to extend the franchise of the NYSE and capture some of the developing trade in futures; however, the major activity remains in Chicago. Other exchanges include the New York Mercantile Exchange (MYM); the New York Coffee, Sugar, and Cocoa Exchange (CSCE); the New York Cotton Exchange (CTN); the New York Commodity Exchange (COMEX); the New York Financial Exchange (FINEX); the International Petroleum Exchange (IPE); the Kansas City Board of Trade (KC); the MidAmerica Commodity Exchange (MCE); and the Minneapolis Grain Exchange (MPLS). US futures activity is regulated by the federal Commodity Futures Trading Commission (CFTC), which operates through the various exchanges and through the National Futures Association (NFA) trade organization. US exchanges and investors can also trade contracts abroad in the UK, Canada, and Australia.

Commodities futures contracts are traded on grains and oilseeds; livestock and meat; food and fiber; and metals and petroleum. Contracts are quoted in cents per unit for a standard unit of quantity of the product. For example, oats contracts are available on the CBOT in contracts of 5,000 bushels, quoted as cents per bushel. However, the greatest futures activity occurs in financial futures which allow investors to speculate (or hedge) on the change in prices of various financial indices. The main ones include interest rate futures, currency futures, and financial index futures (including the S&P 500 Index, S&P Midcap 400 Index, Nikkei 225 Stock Average, GSCI, CAC-40 Stock Index, FT-SE 100 Index, and the All Ordinaries Index, many of which represent foreign market indices). A variety of other contracts are or have been traded, including such contracts as Euroyen time deposits, cheddar cheese, nonfat dry milk, frozen shrimp, and a utility stock index. There is also an active market in futures on option contracts.

In 1993 some 5.146 million futures contracts—nearly 60 percent of them representing financial and currency futures—were traded on US exchanges, up 245 percent from 1980 (financial and currency futures represented only 16 percent of trading in that year).

Assets controlled by US trading pools rose from US$675 million in 1980 to US$21 billion in 1993. US futures trading continues to grow rapidly, but represents an increasingly smaller portion of international futures trading. US traders account for substantial percentages of trading in several contracts in overseas exchanges, while foreign traders represent an increasingly large proportion of trading on US exchanges. In 1992 Globex (an international multiple exchange, screen-based electronic trading system) was inaugurated and in 1993 NYMEX-ACCESS (a New York based international electronic trading system) went on line. The CBOT is also readying plans to begin trading futures based on emerging market securities and currencies.

Options These contracts give the holder the right—but not the obligation—to either buy (call) or sell (put) a stipulated commodity at a specified price on or before the expiration date. The underlying product can be a security, a predetermined amount of a commodity, or even a futures contract. Because exercise of the option is at the discretion of the holder, it need not be exercised unless it will be profitable; if unprofitable, it is simply allowed to expire, with the only loss being the relatively small cost of purchasing the option. Conversely, those who write options can earn incremental revenue on their holdings at the risk of having to deliver them. Writing an option on a commodity that one already possesses is known as writing a covered option, while writing an option on something does not own is known as writing a naked option, and is more speculative. However, all options are considered highly speculative investments.

Unlike European options which can only be exercised on the expiration date, US, or American, options can be exercised at any time up through the expiration date. Most options are for a standard period, usually no more than eight months hence. Long-Term AnticiPation Securities (LEAPs) are written for periods as long as three years. Popular options contracts include those on the S&P 500, the NYSE Index, the Value Line Index, the S&P MidCap 400, the CBOE S&P 100, AMEX Major Market Index, the Institutional Index, and the Japan Index.

In 1992, 202 million options worth US$72.2 billion were traded on all exchanges in the US; of these, 11.6 million (16 percent) worth a total of US$50.1 billion at face value were exercised. The rest expired unexercised. In 1980, 97 million options worth US$45.8 billion were traded, with 4.9 million (5 percent) worth US$20.4 billion being exercised.

Prior to 1973 options were traded informally over-the-counter through so-called put and call brokers, who made markets in options. They are now traded on the AMEX, the NYSE, the Pacific Stock Exchange, the Philadelphia Stock Exchange, and the Chicago Board of Options Exchange (CBOE). All listed options are cleared through the Options Clearing Exchange (OCC), which matches puts and calls, allocating specific contracts on a random basis to the firms that participate in options trading. The CBOE is the US's and the world's largest options market; it handles 60 percent of all options traded in the US, 42 percent of all US equity options, and 92 percent of all US financial index options. Foreigners are free to operate through US options exchanges.

Swaps and Derivatives Options and futures are examples of derivatives, that is, secondary securities based on underlying commodities or other securities. These products include interest rate swaps, OTC customized options, forward foreign exchange contracts, and other types of instruments. Many are traded informally off-exchange, and although only institutional investors are allowed to operate with them, regulators periodically become concerned about the dangers they pose to the financial system. To date, regulators have ruled that these instruments are not true options (a regulatory determination that they represented options would force them to be traded through formal futures exchanges). The industry argues that this would result in their being forced into unregulated overseas markets. This perspective could be shaken by the 1994 experience of the bankruptcy of Orange County, California, brought on by excessive speculation using mortgage-based derivative instruments. However, while it has not suggested greater regulation of the actual markets, the SEC has called for greater disclosure by those investing in derivatives. The US remains the major source of such innovations.

FURTHER READING

Information on the US financial system is available from an extremely wide variety of sources. Within the US—and widely available elsewhere—one of the best, most current sources is the *Wall Street Journal,* which is published five days each week and covers US business in detail.

American Banker
One State Street Plaza
New York, NY 10004, USA
Tel: [1] (212) 943-6700

Barron's National Business and Financial Weekly
Dow Jones & Co., Inc.
200 Burnett Road
Chicopee, MA 01020, USA
Tel: [1] (212) 416-2700, (800) 628-9320
Fax: [1] (212) 416-2829

Institutional Investor
88 Madison Ave.
New York, NY 10022, USA
Tel: [1] (212) 303-3300

Investor's Business Daily
12655 Beatrice St.
Los Angeles, CA 90066, USA
Tel: [1] (310) 448-6000

Wall Street Journal
200 Liberty St.
New York, NY 10281, USA
Tel: [1] (212) 416-2000
Fax: [1] (212) 416-3299

USEFUL ADDRESSES

American Bankers Association
1120 Connecticut Ave. NW
Washington, DC 20036, USA
Tel: [1] (202) 663-5000
Fax: [1] (202) 828-4532

Credit Union National Association
805 15th St. NW
Washington, DC 20005, USA
Tel: [1] (202) 682-4200
Fax: [1] (202) 682-9054

Export-Import Bank of the United States
(Eximbank)
811 Vermont Ave. NW
Washington, DC 20571, USA
Tel: [1] (202) 566-2117

Federal Deposit Insurance Corporation (FDIC)
550 Seventeenth St. NW
Washington, DC 20429, USA
Tel: [1] (202) 393-8400
Fax: [1] (202) 835-0319

Federal Reserve System
Board of Governors
20th and C Sts. NW
Washington, DC 20551, USA
Tel: [1] (202) 452-3215, 452-3201
Fax: [1] (202) 452-3819

Futures Industry Association
2001 Pennsylvania Ave. NW, Suite 600
Washington, DC 20006, USA
Tel: [1] (202) 466-5460
Fax: [1] (202) 296-3184

International Bank for Reconstruction
and Development (World Bank)
1818 H St. NW
Washington, DC 20433, USA
Tel: [1] (202) 477-1234

National Association of Securities Dealers (NASD)
1735 K St. NW
Washington, DC 20006, USA
Tel: [1] (202) 728-8000

Securities and Exchange Commission
450 5th St. NW
Washington, DC 20549, USA
Tel: [1] (202) 272-2000, 272-2650
Fax: [1] (202) 272-7050

Securities Industry Association
120 Broadway
New York, NY 10271, USA
Tel: [1] (212) 608-1500

Security Traders Association, Inc.
One World Trade Center, Suite 5411
New York, NY 10048, USA
Tel: [1] (212) 524-0484

Treasury Department of the United States
Office of the Comptroller of the Currency
250 East E St. SW
Washington, DC 20219-0001, USA
Tel: [1] (202) 874-5000
Fax: [1] (202) 874-4950

Currency & Foreign Exchange

INTERNATIONAL PAYMENT INSTRUMENTS

As more of the overall US economic growth becomes linked with exports—which accounted for 65 percent of US economic growth in 1990—the issue of trade finance and international payments has taken on additional importance. With the acceptance of more stringent bank capital and reserve requirements under the 1990 Basel Accord Capital Adequacy Requirements, trade finance has also become somewhat scarcer. Banks provide the bulk of international payment financing and services in the US, followed by multinational firms that self-finance trade through internal international transfers. Roughly 6 percent is financed by US government official credits through export credit programs run by a variety of agencies, including the Commodity Credit Corporation, the Export-Import Bank, the Overseas Private Investment Corporation (OPIC), the Trade and Development Agency (TDA), and the Agency for International Development (AID).

The vast majority of trade financing is short-term (less than one year), while medium-term and long-term financing (generally as long as five years and longer than five years, respectively) are far less common and require separate arrangements.

The most familiar trade payment arrangements in the US are letters of credit (L/Cs) and documentary credits. Documentary credits—also known as bills of exchange (B/Es) for the negotiable instruments that are created—can be documents against acceptance (D/As) or documents against payment (D/Ps).

However, other possibilities exist, including open account, barter, and countertrade, most of which are short-term operations in practice. Additional techniques that may be used to facilitate the financing of trade include credit insurance, factoring, forfaiting, leasing, hedging, derivatives and commodity-linked instruments, and project financing, which is generally used for longer-term arrangements. The availability and cost of trade financing depends on the creditworthiness of the country and enterprise involved in the transaction; usually a firm cannot be accorded a credit rating higher than the country in which it operates.

Between 60 and 75 percent of all trade is short-term and uses L/Cs and D/Ps with terms between 90 and 180 days. These may be supported by such procedures as factoring (selling trade receivables to a factoring company to provide liquidity) and forfaiting (the purchase by a forfaiting company of such receivables at a discount), both of which are readily available from a variety of firms in the US. Open account arrangements involving purchases and sales on credit are usually reserved for well established, active business relationships.

US businesses generally shun barter and countertrade—arrangements whereby transactions are accomplished, respectively, through direct exchanges of goods or through linked transactions in which a sale is contingent on an equal and offsetting purchase—although some will engage in these types of transactions if it represents the only manner of dealing with some developing or formerly socialist economies that are starved for hard currency. In recognition that many smaller firms in developing countries rely on such payments from their buyers to be able to produce or otherwise acquire the goods to be sold, some US buyers may informally extend credit to their suppliers through partial or even substantial advance payments. However, in general, US purchasers demand a standard L/C or D/P arrangement.

Remaining, longer-term trade finance arrangements in the US have been heavily influenced by the Basel Accords. Because lenders must now support their operations with higher capital and with reserves based on the level of risk in their portfolios, credit guarantees are being more widely sought to lower the risk level of transactions and thus the required reserves. A growing trend toward privatization in developing countries has also raised the demand for riskier long-term project financing, as has the greater participation of smaller US firms in export markets. The US trade finance structure has traditionally been organized around the needs of large exporters. The increase in international activity among small- and medium-sized businesses which are often inexperienced in overseas operations has left both the principals and the financial sector scrambling to fill this demand.

CURRENCY

The currency in the US is the dollar. The symbol "$" is generally used both domestically and internationally, although "US$" may also be used to distinguish it from the 25 currencies of other countries worldwide that are denominated in local dollars. The US dollar is also known colloquially as the "buck" and sometimes as the "greenback." By convention international foreign exchange transactions are referenced in US dollars, the primary international reserve currency.

Dollars are issued as paper bills in denominations of US$1, US$2, US$5, US$10, US$20, US$50, and US$100. Although they do circulate and are legal tender, US$2 bills are extremely rare. Bills of US$50 and US$100 are not particularly common in everyday transactions. Many retail outlets refuse to accept these large denomination bills because of fear of increased incidence of robbery resulting from the presence of larger sums and fear of counterfeit bills, which are less readily detected by personnel unfamiliar with these larger bills. Large denomination bills may also have some stigma attached because they are often used in the illicit narcotics trade.

The US formerly issued bills in large denominations of US$500, US$1,000, US$5,000, US$10,000, and US$100,000, although the Bureau of Printing and Engraving (the agency of the US Treasury responsible for manufacturing paper currency) discontinued these large denomination bills in 1969. They remain legal tender, but are being withdrawn from circulation by the Federal Reserve. The largest bill, US$100,000, was never released for public circulation, but was issued as a special purpose money reserved for transactions between the US Treasury and its agent, the Federal Reserve System; the Treasury issues the currency, which is distributed and managed by the Federal Reserve.

The US officially went off the gold standard in 1933, switching to silver to back its currency. Silver certificates—redeemable for silver—were issued until the late 1950s, at which time all currency in circulation became Federal Reserve Notes, which are unsecured, full faith and credit monetary instruments, not redeemable for specie. All US bills are the same size and color (green) and have essentially the same design. Each bill has the denomination printed on all four corners on both sides, a portrait of a different former US president or statesman on one side, and a different scene on the reverse. Care should be exercised by foreign businesspeople who are accustomed to notes of different colors or sizes.

In July, 1994, the Department of the Treasury announced plans to redesign US currency in order to add anti-counterfeit security features. This will be the first major redesign effort since 1929. Actual designs are expected to be accepted by the end of 1995, with the first new US$100 bills to be issued in 1996; newly-designed smaller denominations will follow. The size, national symbols, and colors will remain the same, while the new features may include placing enlarged portraits slightly off-center, the addition of watermarks and microprinting, and changes in paper and ink. The Department has emphasized that they will not recall or demonetize any currency, and older bills will remain legal tender as long as they are in circulation.

The US dollar is divided into 100 cents. Coins are issued in denominations of 1 cent (a penny), 5 cents (a nickel), 10 cents (a dime), 25 cents (a quarter), 50 cents (a half-dollar), and 100 cents (a dollar). The coins are of different sizes, although the quarter and the dollar bearing the likeness of Susan B. Anthony are similar in size (and weight), which contributed to public resistance when this dollar coin was introduced in the late 1970s. Half-dollar coins are relatively rare; dollar coins are quite rare. Dollar coins were issued between 1971 and 1978 (the large Eisenhower dollar) and 1979 and 1981 (the smaller Susan B. Anthony dollar, subsequently withdrawn from circulation).

The 1-cent coin is made of copper and the 5-cent coin of nickel (hence its name). The 10-cent, 25-cent, and 50-cent coins were made of silver until 1965, when cupronickel-clad coins became standard. The US Mint, which produces all US coinage, also issues commemorative coins from time to time, as well as silver and gold eagle coins (respectively, one troy ounce of 0.999 fine silver or one-tenth, one-quarter, one-half, or one ounce of gold). All of these are legal tender, but none of these numismatic issues are circulated. Many vending machines in the US accept any denomination of coin (except the 1-cent penny), although some require a specific denomination to operate, usually a quarter.

Transactions that come to a fractional amount—usually because of added sales taxes—are rounded to the nearest whole cent, usually automatically or through the use of tables.

REMITTANCE AND EXCHANGE CONTROLS

The US maintains no exchange controls, restrictions on import or repatriation of capital or earnings, or other limits on the flow of funds into, out of, or within the country. (Repatriated funds are subject to the withholding of any US income taxes owed.) Foreign capital is admitted and treated the same as domestic capital. Furthermore, there is no required registration of foreign investment funds. The US does require all those entering and leaving the country to declare to US Customs any cash or other negotiable

GOLD TRANSACTIONS*

US citizens or residents may freely purchase, hold, and sell gold in any form, at home or abroad, except for certain gold transactions (e.g., imports or exports) involving Cuba, Haiti, Iraq, the Democratic People's Republic of Korea, the Libyan Arab Jamahiriya, Vietnam, and the Federal Republic of Yugoslavia (Serbia and Montenegro). Commercial banks may deal in gold bullion and gold coins, with the same exceptions. Treasury licensing for importers, exporters, producers, refiners, and processors of gold is not required, with the same country exceptions. Gold, but not counterfeit gold coins, may be freely imported, except from the countries mentioned above. US gold coins are legal tender at their face value.

Commercial imports of gold jewelry are free of quantitative restrictions but are subject to import duty at a rate of approximately 12 percent. There is no duty on gold ore, bullion, or coins. All forms of gold must be declared at the point of entry into the United States.

*Copyright © 1994 International Monetary Fund. Reproduced from Exchange Arrangements and Exchange Restrictions Annual Report 1994, with permission of the IMF, Washington, DC, USA.

bearer instruments cumulatively valued at more than US$10,000. No duty is payable on any amount of such funds imported or exported, but there are penalties for failure to declare such cash. This rule was instituted primarily to allow the government to track large sums of cash that may represent funds to be used in illicit transactions or in money laundering operations designed to disguise illicit funds. Banks in the US are also required to report transactions of US$10,000 or more, and US residents must also disclose (for tax purposes) any foreign accounts valued at US$10,000 or more. There are no limitations or restrictions on accounts denominated in any currency held by either residents or foreigners, although relatively few US financial institutions offer accounts denominated in currencies other than the US dollar.

The US allows the value of its currency to float relative to market factors. The US Treasury retains the option of intervening in foreign exchange markets to influence the relative value of the currency. However, the growing consensus is that foreign exchange markets are too large, active, and international in scope for any entity to effectively control the value of a currency. This trend has grown along with the rise in the proportion of US funds held overseas as Eurodollars (funds held outside the country and not subject to direct US control). It has become even more apparent as the Japanese yen (¥) and the German Deutschmark (DM) have gained strength as international reserve currencies during the past two decades. The US Treasury can influence international valuations to a certain extent by its policy statements—more than by its actions. This was the case in the latter half of 1994, when the US "talked down" the US dollar versus the yen, keeping the dollar below the 100-yen mark for much of the year in an attempt to force Japan to alter its trade policy and accept more US imports in order to reduce its huge trade surplus with the US.

Because there are no exchange controls, there is no black market in US currency within the country (although thriving black markets in US dollars do exist in countries with stringent currency controls). Business transactions will almost always be conducted through the financial system, and foreign exchange may be available at wholesale rather than retail rates, although the differential will generally be minor, except when compared with more unfavorable small retail transaction rates.

Although US wholesale foreign exchange markets are among the largest and most active in the world, foreign visitors to the US can expect to encounter some difficulty in finding outlets to exchange retail sums of foreign funds—either currency or foreign-denominated traveler's checks—for dollars. Except in the immediate border areas near Canada and Mexico and in international trade and tourist centers—primarily the major centers on each coast—few US outlets are familiar with or handle foreign currencies at all, especially less common ones. Branches of major banks may exchange foreign funds

for dollars. However, few US banks are even equipped to accept deposits in foreign funds, much less exchange them.

Exchange booths are operated at larger international airports (some airports are designated "international" more as a courtesy than as an indication of the range of available services or sophistication of operations) and some other urban locations. In general, traveler's checks will receive a somewhat better rate than cash, due to the problems involved in handling actual currency. Some more expensive hotels, retail outlets, and restaurants in major tourist and business centers that cater to foreign visitors may also accept payment in a currency other than US dollars or may exchange foreign funds for dollars.

The most secure method of obtaining dollars for a US trip is to purchase traveler's checks denominated in US dollars before leaving home. Major brands of traveler's checks—American Express, Bank of America, MasterCard, or Thomas Cook—are readily accepted by virtually all US outlets as well as by banks and hotels. Major credit cards are also generally accepted in payment for many purchases, and travelers may even be able to use them obtain a US dollar cash advance in the US (home country rules vary, as do charges—note that hefty interest rates are usually charged from the date of the advance). Billing will be in your home currency at the exchange rate effective on the date of purchase. Most credit card firms offer reasonable exchange rates, although the rates may not be as good as those that might be obtained elsewhere. Note that some outlets refuse to accept any credit cards, while others accept only one or a few, and yet others will attempt to get you to use a particular card even though they nominally accept others. Relatively few US outlets will insist

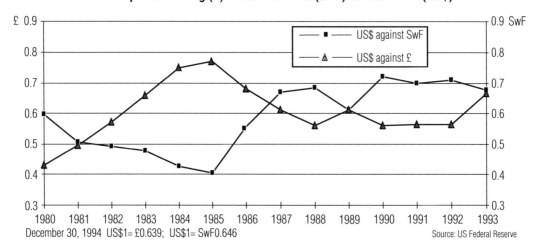

United States Foreign Exchange Rates – Year-End Actual
British pound sterling (£) and Swiss franc (SwF) vs. US dollar (US$)

December 30, 1994 US$1= £0.639; US$1= SwF0.646

Source: US Federal Reserve

on a surcharge or a lower discount for credit card purchases, as is common elsewhere (most US retail purchases are made at the fixed offering price rather than through negotiation).

A great deal of US consumer banking is now accomplished through automated teller machines (ATMs). Most banks operating ATMs belong to one or more ATM networks (CIRRUS and PLUS being the most common, along with STAR on the West Coast and NYCE in the New York area), and most networks also have international affiliations. Travelers may be able to use their home ATM cards (or credit cards) to access funds through these outlets (you will always have to know your personal identification number—PIN—and, in some cases, you must preregister for the service). Note that crime is a hazard at some US ATMs.

In virtually no case will a foreign personal check denominated in any currency be accepted. One exception to this rule is for an American Express cardholder, who may cash a personal check upon presentation of the card (terms and limits depend on whether the card is green, gold, or platinum), obtaining cash and traveler's checks at company outlets. Funds can also be wired through Western Union or American Express MoneyGram outlets. Terms and procedures vary, but both firms charge between 5 to 10 percent of the amount transferred; both offer an international network of outlets allowing you to have funds sent to you from your home country or from elsewhere within the US.

Foreign businesspeople can make advance arrangements for their home country banks to transfer funds for them to a US correspondent bank. Funds can also be sent directly to the recipient at a US address by certified check—preferably in US dollars—

which can be cashed at a US bank; by postal money order (available and redeemable at any US post office) within the US; or by international money order (obtained at a foreign bank and sent to you in the US). Specific rules vary and identification is required to cash these instruments.

FOREIGN EXCHANGE OPERATIONS

The US foreign exchange market is ultimately the responsibility of the US Treasury Department, which sets economic policies and issues currency and government instruments. Day-to-day operations are monitored and conducted through the Federal Reserve System. No specific license is required to deal in foreign exchange in the US, and most larger banks do so. Because the US dollar is a fully convertible international reserve currency—one which is considered an international store of wealth and one in which foreign exchange trading is conducted worldwide—it is actively traded both in the US and abroad. Other recognized reserve currencies include the Japanese yen (¥), the Deutschmark (DM), the British pound sterling (£), the French franc (F), the Swiss franc (SwF), and the Canadian dollar (Can$).

Foreign exchange is available in the spot (current) market for actual delivery in two business days or in the forward markets. (Foreign exchange can also be traded between the current and the next business days, known as "tom/next.") Forward market purchases are available with standard periods at 30, 60, and 90 days, with additional standard forward contracts at 90-day intervals extending as long as 450 days. However, most requirements for longer than 360 days are handled by rolling over into other contracts at the expiration of the initial contract.

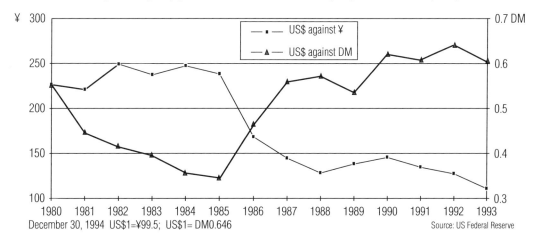

United States Foreign Exchange Rates - Year End Actual
Japanese yen (¥) and German Deutschmark (DM) vs. US dollar (US$)

December 30, 1994 US$1=¥99.5; US$1= DM0.646

Source: US Federal Reserve

Some institutions will arrange forward contracts for intermediate periods, usually by interpolating the rates between adjoining contracts. About 90 percent of all forward activity is for 90 days or less; usually an additional 9 percent is within 9 months (270 days), with longer contract periods representing less than 1 percent of total trading.

It is possible to deal in options on currencies (rights to buy or sell fixed amounts of currencies at predetermined prices at a point in the future) as well as options on currency futures. Swaps—buying spot and selling forward or selling spot and buying forward—and other derivatives are also available. Offshore and domestic bank trading operations are also involved in trading Eurodollars and other Eurocurrencies. The US has traditionally been an innovator in such markets.

RATES OF EXCHANGE

The US dollar floats on a more or less free, supply and demand basis against other currencies. It can change in value differentially with respect to various currencies, although international arbitrage generally keeps movements closely in line worldwide. At the end of 1994, the US dollar was equal to 0.6386 British pounds (or US$1.566 to the pound—the pound is usually quoted indirectly in pence because the British did not traditionally use a decimal system), 1.4015 Canadian dollars, 5.336 French francs, 1.549 German marks, 99.5 Japanese yen, or 1.308 Swiss francs.

The US dollar began to rise against other world currencies in the late 1970s as the US Federal Reserve System began to increase interest rates to dampen growth in the money supply and reduce inflation. This resulted in an inflow of investment to the US based on the higher returns available. The dollar reached a high (overvalued position) around the mid-1980s and then began its slide as lower interest rates made it less competitive with some other currencies. In the early 1990s, the dollar retreated even further against many other reserve currencies because of the massive outflow of US investment to other countries—especially to emerging markets—compounded by the chronic US trade deficit, resulting in even greater outflows. Between 1980 and the end of 1994, the US dollar rose 20.6 percent against the Canadian dollar and 26.3 percent against the French franc. During the same period, it fell 14.8 percent against the Deutschmark, 22 percent against the Swiss franc, 32.6 percent against the British pound, and 56.1 percent against the yen.

Some observers contend that the US dollar will strengthen as US investment funds return to the country, primarily from emerging markets, many of which dropped precipitously in the wake of the fall of the Mexican peso at the end of 1994. However, due to its close links with Canada and Mexico—respectively, the first and third largest trading partners of the US—some analysts fear that the US will be unable to tighten its policies enough to really realign its currency with respect to other major currencies.

FOREIGN RESERVES

The US has generally maintained healthy foreign reserves. Foreign reserves (including special drawing rights (SDRs), reserve positions with the International Monetary Fund (IMF), and foreign exchange, but excluding stocks of gold) were US$1.2 billion in 1964—less than 0.2 percent of GDP. Such reserves

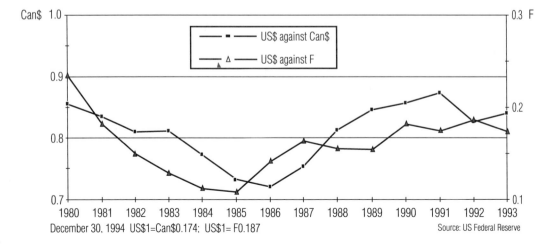

United States Foreign Exchange Rates – Year-End Actual
Canadian dollar (Can$) and French franc (F) vs. US dollar (US$)

December 30, 1994 US$1=Can$0.174; US$1= F0.187

Source: US Federal Reserve

did not rise above US$10 billion until 1980, when they grew sharply to US$15.6 billion (0.6 percent of GDP). Reserves grew steadily—with the exception of a drop in 1987—to a new high of US$72.3 billion in 1990 (1.3 percent of GDP).

As of year-end 1994, US foreign reserves stood at US$63.29 billion, up by nearly US$1 billion from the previous year. Foreign currency holdings traditionally represented a relatively minor element of total reserves until the mid-1980s, when they rose to around 50 percent of the total. Foreign currency reached a high of US$52.2 billion in 1990, 72 percent of total reserves, falling to 65 percent (US$41.22 billion) of total reserves in December 1994. Other foreign reserve positions included SDRs of US$10.04 billion; and US reserves with the IMF of US$12.03 billion. Gold reserves were valued at US$11.05 billion, largely unchanged from the previous year.

The US does a huge volume of international trade and receives major inflows of foreign funds invested in US securities. The US has used these funds to finance its trade deficits. There remains concern that unless the US budget and trade deficits begin to be brought under control, its securities could become less interesting to foreigners; the value of its currency could continue to weaken; and its comfortable reserve cushion could erode.

FURTHER READING

This discussion has been provided as a basic guide to currency with respect to the financial organization of the US. Those interested in current developments may wish to consult the *Wall Street Journal*, which covers economics, business, and finance in the US.

USEFUL ADDRESSES

Federal Reserve System
Board of Governors
20th and C Sts. NW
Washington, DC 20551, USA
Tel: [1] (202) 452-3215, 452-3201
Fax: [1] (202) 452-3819

International Monetary Fund (IMF)
700 19th St. NW
Washington, DC 20431, USA
Tel: [1] (202) 623-7100
Fax: [1] (202) 623-4940

Treasury Department
Foreign Exchange Operations
250 East E St. SW
Washington, DC 20219-0001, USA
Tel: [1] (202) 622-2650
Fax: [1] (202) 622-2021

Treasury Department
Office of the Comptroller of the Currency
250 East E St. SW
Washington, DC 20219-0001, USA
Tel: [1] (202) 874-5000
Fax: [1] (202) 874-4950

International Payments

International transactions add an additional layer of risk for buyers and sellers that are familiar only with doing business domestically. Currency regulations, foreign exchange risk, political, economic, or social upheaval in the buyer's or seller's country, and different business customs may all contribute to uncertainty. Ultimately, however, the seller wants to make sure he gets paid and the buyer wants to get what he pays for. Choosing the right payment method can be the key to the transaction's feasibility and profitability.

There are four common methods of international payment, each providing the buyer and the seller with varying degrees of protection for getting paid and for guaranteeing shipment. Ranked in order of most security for the supplier to most security for the buyer, they are: Cash in Advance, Documentary Letters of Credit (L/C), Documentary Collections (D/P and D/A Terms), and Open Account (O/A).

Cash in Advance

In cash in advance terms the buyer simply prepays the supplier prior to shipment of goods. Cash in advance terms are generally used in new relationships where transactions are small and the buyer has no choice but to pre-pay. These terms give maximum security to the seller but leave the buyer at great risk. Since the buyer has no guarantee that the goods will be shipped, he must have a high degree of trust in the seller's ability and willingness to follow through. The buyer must also consider the economic, political and social stability of the seller's country, as these conditions may make it impossible for the seller to ship as promised.

Documentary Letters of Credit

A letter of credit is a bank's promise to pay a supplier on behalf of the buyer so long as the supplier meets the terms and conditions stated in the credit. Documents are the key issue in letter of credit transactions. Banks act as intermediaries, and have nothing to do with the goods themselves.

Letters of credit are the most common form of international payment because they provide a high degree of protection for both the seller and the buyer. The buyer specifies the documentation that he requires from the seller before the bank is to make payment, and the seller is given assurance that he will receive payment after shipping his goods so long as the documentation is in order.

Documentary Collections

A documentary collection is like an international cash on delivery (COD), but with a few twists. The exporter ships goods to the importer, but forwards shipping documents (including title document) to his bank for transmission to the buyer's bank. The buyer's bank is instructed not to transfer the documents to the buyer until payment is made (Documents against Payment, D/P) or upon guarantee that payment will be made within a specified period of time (Documents against Acceptance, D/A). Once the buyer has the documentation for the shipment he is able to take possession of the goods.

D/P and D/A terms are commonly used in ongoing business relationships and provide a measure of protection for both parties. The buyer and seller, however, both assume risk in the transaction, ranging from refusal on the part of the buyer to pay for the documents, to the seller's shipping of unacceptable goods.

Open Account

This is an agreement by the buyer to pay for goods within a designated time after their shipment, usually in 30, 60, or 90 days. Open account terms give maximum security to the buyer and greatest risk to the seller. This form of payment is used only when the seller has significant trust and faith in the buyer's ability and willingness to pay once the goods have been shipped. The seller must also consider the economic, political and social stability of the buyer's country as these conditions may make it impossible for the buyer to pay as promised.

DOCUMENTARY COLLECTIONS (D/P, D/A)

Documentary collections focus on the transfer of documents such as bills of lading for the transfer of ownership of goods rather than on the goods themselves. They are easier to use than letters of credit and bank service charges are generally lower.

This form of payment is excellent for buyers who wish to purchase goods without risking prepayment and without having to go through the more cumbersome letter of credit process.

Documentary collection procedures, however, entail risk for the supplier, because payment is not made until after goods are shipped. In addition, the supplier assumes the risk while the goods are in transit and storage until payment/acceptance take place. Banks involved in the transaction do not guarantee payments. A supplier should therefore only agree to a documentary collection procedure if the transaction includes the following characteristics:

- The supplier does not doubt the buyer's ability and willingness to pay for the goods;
- The buyer's country is politically, economically, and legally stable;
- There are no foreign exchange restrictions in the buyer's home country, or unless all necessary licenses for foreign exchange have already been obtained; and
- The goods to be shipped are easily marketable.

Types of Collections

The three types of documentary collections are:
1. Documents against Payment (D/P)
2. Documents against Acceptance (D/A)
3. Collection with Acceptance (Acceptance D/P)

All of these collection procedures follow the same general step-by-step process of exchanging documents proving title to goods for either cash or a contracted promise to pay at a later time. The documents are transferred from the supplier (called the remitter) to the buyer (called the drawee) via intermediary banks. When the supplier ships goods, he presents documents such as the bill of lading, invoices, and certificate of origin to his representative bank (the remitting bank), which then forwards them to the buyer's bank (the collecting bank). According to the type of documentary collection, the buyer may then do one of the following:

- With Documents against Payment (D/P), the buyer may only receive the title and other documents after paying for the goods;
- With Documents against Acceptance (D/A), the buyer may receive the title and other documents after signing a time draft promising to pay at a later date; or

- With Acceptance Documents against Payment, the buyer signs a time draft for payment at a latter date. However, he may only obtain the documents after the time draft reaches maturity. In essence, the goods remain in escrow until payment has been made.

In all cases the buyer may take possession of the goods only by presenting the bill of lading to customs or shipping authorities.

In the event that the prospective buyer cannot or will not pay for the goods shipped, they remain in legal possession of the supplier, but he may be stuck with them in an unfavorable situation. Also, the supplier has no legal basis to file claim against the prospective buyer. At this point the supplier may:

- Have the goods returned and sell them on his domestic market; or
- Sell the goods to another buyer near where the goods are currently held.

If the supplier takes no action the goods will be auctioned or otherwise disposed of by customs.

Documentary Collection Procedure

The documentary collection process has been standardized by a set of rules published by the International Chamber of Commerce (ICC). These rules are called the Uniform Rules for Collections (URC) and are contained in ICC Publication No. 322. (See the last page of this section for ICC addresses and list of available publications.)

The following is the basic set of steps used in a documentary collection. Refer to the illustration on the following page for a graphic representation of the procedure.

(1) The seller (remitter, exporter) ships the goods.
(2) and (3) The seller forwards the agreed upon documents to his bank, the remitting bank, which in turn forwards them to the collecting bank (buyer's bank).
(4) The collecting bank notifies the buyer (drawee, importer) and informs him of the conditions under which he can take possession of the documents.
(5) To take possession of the documents, the buyer makes payment or signs a time deposit.
(6) and (7) If the buyer draws the documents against payment, the collecting bank transfers payment to the remitting bank for credit to the supplier's account. If the buyer draws the documents against acceptance, the collecting bank sends the acceptance to the remitting bank or retains it up to maturity. On maturity, the collecting bank collects the bill and transfers it to the remitting bank for payment to the supplier.

Documentary Collection Procedure

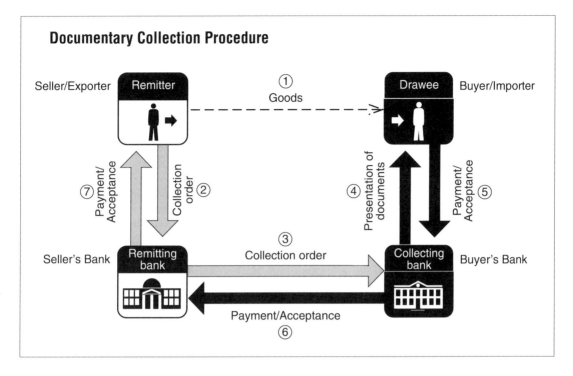

TIPS FOR BUYERS

1. The buyer is generally in a secure position because he does not assume ownership or responsibility for goods until he has paid for the documents or signed a time draft.

2. The buyer may not sample or inspect the goods before accepting and paying for the documents without authorization from the seller. However, the buyer may in advance specify a certificate of inspection as part of the required documentation package.

3. As a special favor, the collecting bank can allow the buyer to inspect the documents before payment. The collecting bank assumes responsibility for the documents until their redemption.

4. In the above case, the buyer should immediately return the entire set of documents to the collecting bank if he cannot meet the agreed payment procedure.

5. The buyer assumes no liability for goods if he refuses to take possession of the documents.

6. Partial payment in exchange for the documents is not allowed unless authorized in the collection order.

7. With documents against acceptance, the buyer may receive the goods and resell them for profit before the time draft matures, thereby using the proceeds of the sale to pay for the goods. The buyer remains responsible for payment, however, even if he cannot sell the goods.

TIPS FOR SUPPLIERS

1. The supplier assumes risk because he ships goods before receiving payment. The buyer is under no legal obligation to pay for or to accept the goods.

2. Before agreeing to a documentary collection, the supplier should check on the buyer's creditworthiness and business reputation.

3. The supplier should make sure the buyer's country is politically and financially stable.

4. The supplier should find out what documents are required for customs clearance in the buyer's country. Consulates may be of help.

5. The supplier should assemble the documents carefully and make sure they are in the required form and endorsed as necessary.

6. As a rule, the remitting bank will not review the documents before forwarding them to the collecting bank. This is the responsibility of the seller.

7. The goods travel and are stored at the risk of the supplier until payment or acceptance.

8. If the buyer refuses acceptance or payment for the documents, the supplier retains ownership. The supplier may have the goods shipped back or try to sell them to another buyer in the region.

9. If the buyer takes no action, customs authorities may seize the goods and auction them off or otherwise dispose of them.

10. Because goods may be refused, the supplier should only ship goods which are readily marketable to other sources.

LETTERS OF CREDIT (L/C)

A letter of credit is a document issued by a bank stating its commitment to pay someone (supplier/exporter/seller) a stated amount of money on behalf of a buyer (importer) so long as the seller meets very specific terms and conditions. Letters of credit are often called documentary letters of credit because the banks handling the transaction deal in documents as opposed to goods. Letters of credit are the most common method of making international payments, because the risks of the transaction are shared by both the buyer and the supplier.

STEPS IN USING AN L/C

The letter of credit process has been standardized by a set of rules published by the International Chamber of Commerce (ICC). These rules are called the Uniform Customs and Practice for Documentary Credits (UCP) and are contained in ICC Publication No. 400. (See the last page of this section for ICC addresses and list of available publications.) The following is the basic set of steps used in a letter of credit transaction. Specific letter of credit transactions follow somewhat different procedures.

- After the buyer and supplier agree on the terms of a sale, the buyer arranges for his bank to open a letter of credit in favor of the supplier.
- The buyer's bank (the issuing bank), prepares the letter of credit, including all of the buyer's instructions to the seller concerning shipment and required documentation.
- The buyer's bank sends the letter of credit to a correspondent bank (the advising bank), in the seller's country. The seller may request that a particular bank be the advising bank, or the domestic bank may select one of its correspondent banks in the seller's country.
- The advising bank forwards the letter of credit to the supplier.
- The supplier carefully reviews all conditions the buyer has stipulated in the letter of credit. If the supplier cannot comply with one or more of the provisions he immediately notifies the buyer and asks that an amendment be made to the letter of credit.
- After final terms are agreed upon, the supplier prepares the goods and arranges for their shipment to the appropriate port.
- The supplier ships the goods, and obtains a bill of lading and other documents as required by the buyer in the letter of credit. Some of these documents may need to be obtained prior to shipment.
- The supplier presents the required documents to the advising bank, indicating full compliance with the terms of the letter of credit. Required documents usually include a bill of lading, commercial invoice, certificate of origin, and possibly an inspection certificate if required by the buyer.
- The advising bank reviews the documents. If they are in order, the documents are forwarded to the issuing bank. If it is an irrevocable, confirmed letter of credit the supplier is guaranteed payment and may be paid immediately by the advising bank.
- Once the issuing bank receives the documents it notifies the buyer who then reviews the documents himself. If the documents are in order the buyer signs off, taking possession of the documents, including the bill of lading, which he uses to take possession of the shipment.
- The issuing bank initiates payment to the advising bank, which pays the supplier.

The transfer of funds from the buyer to his bank, from the buyer's bank to the supplier's bank, and from the supplier's bank to the supplier may be handled at the same time as the exchange of documents, or under terms agreed upon in advance.

Parties to a Letter of Credit Transaction

Buyer/Importer — Buyer — Issuing bank — Buyer's bank

Seller/Supplier/Exporter — Seller — Advising bank — Seller's bank

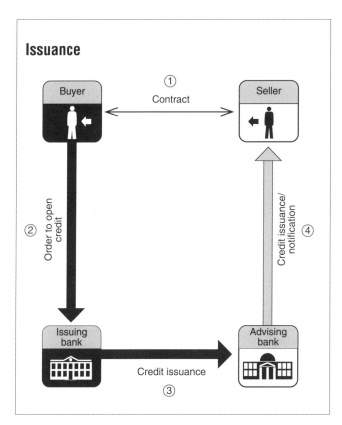

Issuance of a Letter of Credit

① Buyer and seller agree on purchase contract.
② Buyer applies for and opens a letter of credit with issuing ("buyer's") bank.
③ Issuing bank issues the letter of credit, forwarding it to advising ("seller's") bank.
④ Advising bank notifies seller of letter of credit.

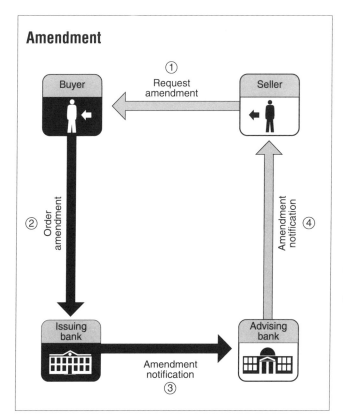

Amendment of a Letter of Credit

① Seller requests (of the buyer) a modification (amendment) of the terms of the letter of credit. Once the terms are agreed upon:
② Buyer issues order to issuing ("buyer's") bank to make an amendment to the terms of the letter of credit.
③ Issuing bank notifies advising ("seller's") bank of amendment.
④ Advising bank notifies seller of amendment.

Utilization

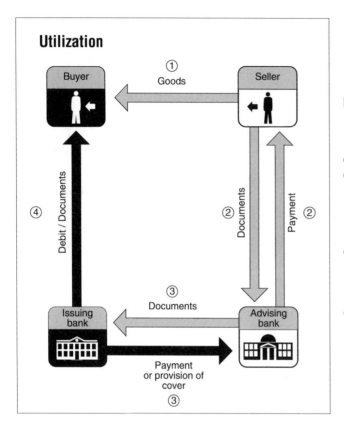

Utilization of a Letter of Credit

(irrevocable, confirmed credit)

① Seller ships goods to buyer.
② Seller forwards all documents (as stipulated in the letter of credit) to advising bank. Once documents are reviewed and accepted, advising bank pays seller for the goods.
③ Advising bank forwards documents to issuing bank. Once documents are reviewed and accepted, issuing bank pays advising bank.
④ Issuing bank forwards documents to buyer. Seller's letter of credit, or account, is debited.

COMMON PROBLEMS IN LETTER OF CREDIT TRANSACTIONS

Most problems with letter of credit transactions have to do with the ability of the supplier to fulfill obligations the buyer establishes in the original letter of credit. The supplier may find the terms of the credit difficult or impossible to fulfill and either tries to do so and fails, or asks the buyer for an amendment to the letter of credit. Observers note that over half of all letters of credit involving parties in East Asia are amended or renegotiated entirely. Since most letters of credit are irrevocable, amendments to the original letter of credit can only be made after further negotiations and agreements between the buyer and the supplier. Suppliers may have one or more of the following problems:

• Shipment schedule stipulated in the letter of credit cannot be met.
• Stipulations concerning freight cost are deemed unacceptable.
• Price is insufficient due to changes in exchange rates.
• Quantity of product ordered is not the expected amount.
• Description of product to be shipped is either insufficient or too detailed.
• Documents stipulated in the letter of credit are difficult or impossible to obtain.

Even when suppliers accept the terms of a letter of credit, problems often arise at the stage where banks review, or negotiate, the documents provided by the supplier against the requirements specified in the letter of credit. If the documents are found not to be in accord with those specified in the letter of credit, the bank's commitment to pay is invalidated. In some cases the supplier can correct the documents and present them within the time specified in the letter of credit. Or, the advising bank may ask the issuing bank for authorization to accept the documents despite the discrepancies found.

Limits on Legal Obligations of Banks

It is important to note once again that banks *deal in documents and not in goods.* Only the wording of the credit is binding on the bank. Banks are not responsible for verifying the authenticity of the documents, nor for the quality or quantity of the goods being shipped. As long as the *documents* comply with the specified terms of the letter of credit, banks may accept them and initiate the payment process as stipulated in the letter of credit. Banks are free from liability for delays in sending messages caused by another party, consequences of Acts of God, or the acts of third parties whom they have instructed to carry out transactions.

TYPES OF LETTERS OF CREDIT

Basic Letters of Credit

There are two basic forms of letters of credit: the Revocable Credit and the Irrevocable Credit. There are also two types of irrevocable credit: the Irrevocable Credit not Confirmed, and the Irrevocable Confirmed Credit. Each type of credit has advantages and disadvantages for the buyer and for the seller. Also note that the more the banks assume risk by guaranteeing payment, the more they will charge for providing the service.

1. Revocable credit This credit can be changed or canceled by the buyer without prior notice to the supplier. Because it offers little security to the seller revocable credits are generally unacceptable to the seller and are rarely used.

2. Irrevocable credit The irrevocable credit is one which the issuing bank commits itself irrevocably to honor, provided the beneficiary complies with all stipulated conditions. This credit cannot be changed or canceled without the consent of both the buyer and the seller. As a result, this type of credit is the most widely used in international trade. Irrevocable credits are more expensive because of the issuing bank's added liability in guaranteeing the credit. There are two types of irrevocable credits:

a. The Irrevocable Credit not Confirmed by the Advising Bank (Unconfirmed Credit) This means that the buyer's bank which issues the credit is the only party responsible for payment to the supplier, and the supplier's bank is obliged to pay the supplier only after receiving payment from the buyer's bank. The supplier's bank merely acts on behalf of the issuing bank and therefore incurs no risk.

b. The Irrevocable, Confirmed Credit In a confirmed credit, the advising bank adds its guarantee to pay the supplier to that of the issuing bank. If the issuing bank fails to make payment the advising bank will pay. If a supplier is unfamiliar with the buyer's bank which issues the letter of credit, he may insist on an irrevocable confirmed credit. These credits may be used when trade is conducted in a high risk area where there are fears of outbreak of war or social, political, or financial instability. Confirmed credits may also be used by the supplier to enlist the aid of a local bank to extend financing to enable him to fill the order. A confirmed credit costs more because the bank has added liability.

Special Letters of Credit

There are numerous special letters of credit designed to meet specific needs of buyers, suppliers, and intermediaries. Special letters of credit usually involve increased participation by banks, so financing and service charges are higher than those for basic letters of credit. The following is a brief description of some special letters of credit.

1. Standby Letter of Credit This credit is primarily a payment or performance guarantee. It is used primarily in the United States because US banks are prevented by law from giving certain guarantees. Standby credits are often called non-performing letters of credit because they are only used as a backup payment method if the collection on a primary payment method is past due.

Standby letters of credit can be used, for example, to guarantee the following types of payment and performance:

* repayment of loans;
* fulfillment by subcontractors;
* securing the payment for goods delivered by third parties.

The beneficiary to a standby letter of credit can draw from it on demand, so the buyer assumes added risk.

2. Revolving Letter of Credit This credit is a commitment on the part of the issuing bank to restore the credit to the original amount after it has been used or drawn down. The number of times it can be utilized and the period of validity is stated in the credit. The credit can be cumulative or noncumulative. Cumulative means that unutilized sums can be added to the next installment whereas noncumulative means that partial amounts not utilized in time expire.

3. Deferred Payment Letter of Credit In this credit the buyer takes delivery of the shipped goods by accepting the documents and agreeing to pay his bank after a fixed period of time. This credit gives the buyer a grace period, and ensures that the seller gets payment on the due date.

4. Red Clause Letter of Credit This is used to provide the supplier with some funds prior to shipment to finance production of the goods. The credit may be advanced in part or in full, and the buyer's bank finances the advance payment. The buyer, in essence, extends financing to the seller and incurs ultimate risk for all advanced credits.

5. Transferable Letter of Credit This allows the supplier to transfer all or part of the proceeds of the letter of credit to a second beneficiary, usually the ultimate producer of the goods. This is a common financing tactic for middlemen and is used extensively in the Far East.

6. Back-to-Back Letter of Credit This is a new credit opened on the basis of an already existing, non-transferable credit. It is used by traders to make payment to the ultimate supplier. A trader receives a letter of credit from the buyer and then opens another letter of credit in favor of the supplier. The first letter of credit is used as collateral for the second credit. The second credit makes price adjustments from which come the trader's profit.

OPENING A LETTER OF CREDIT

The wording in a letter of credit should be simple but specific. The more detailed an L/C is, the more likely the supplier will reject it as too difficult to fulfill. At the same time, the buyer will wish to define in detail what he is paying for.

Although the L/C process is designed to ensure the satisfaction of all parties to the transaction, it cannot be considered a substitute for face-to-face agreements on doing business in good faith. It should therefore contain only those stipulations required from the banks involved in the documentary process.

L/Cs used in trade with East Asia are usually either irrevocable unconfirmed credits or irrevocable confirmed credits. In choosing the type of L/C to open in favor of the supplier, the buyer should take into consideration generally accepted payment processes in the supplier's country, the value and demand for the goods to be shipped, and the reputation of the supplier.

In specifying documents necessary from the supplier, it is very important to demand documents that are required for customs clearance and those that reflect the agreement reached between the buyer and the supplier. Required documents usually include the bill of lading, a commercial and/or consular invoice, the bill of exchange, the certificate of origin, and the insurance document. Other documents required may be copies of a cable sent to the buyer with shipping information, a confirmation from the shipping company of the state of its ship, and a confirmation from the forwarder that the goods are accompanied by a certificate of origin. Prices should be stated in the currency of the L/C, and documents should be supplied in the language of the L/C.

THE APPLICATION

The following information should be included on an application form for opening an L/C.

(1) **Beneficiary** The seller's company name and address should be written completely and correctly. Incomplete or incorrect information results in delays and unnecessary additional cost.

(2) **Amount** Is the figure a maximum amount or an approximate amount? If words like "circa," "ca.," "about," etc., are used in connection with the amount of the credit, it means that a difference as high as 10 percent upwards or downwards is permitted. In such a case, the same word should also be used in connection with the quantity.

(3) **Validity Period** The validity and period for presentation of the documents following shipment of the goods should be sufficiently long to allow the exporter time to prepare his documents and ship them to the bank. Under place of validity, state the domicile of either the advising bank or the issuing bank.

(4) **Beneficiary's Bank** If no bank is named, the issuing bank is free to select the correspondent bank.

(5) **Type of Payment Availability** Sight drafts, time drafts, or deferred payment may be used, as previously agreed to by the supplier and buyer.

(6) **Desired Documents** Here the buyer specifies precisely which documents he requires. To obtain effective protection against the supply of poor quality goods, for instance, he can demand the submission of analysis or quality certificates. These are generally issued by specialized inspection companies or laboratories.

(7) **Notify Address** An address is given for notification of the imminent arrival of goods at the port or airport of destination. Damage of goods in shipment is also cause for notification. An agent representing the buyer may be used.

(8) **Description of Goods** Here a short, precise description of the goods is given, along with quantity. If the credit amount carries the notation "ca.," the same notation should appear with the quantity.

(9) **Confirmation Order** It may happen that the foreign beneficiary insists on having the credit confirmed by the bank in his country.

Sample Letter of Credit Application

Sender	**Instructions** **to open a Documentary Credit**
American Import-Export Co., Inc. 123 Main Street San Francisco, California	
Our reference AB/02	San Francisco, 30th September 19.. <small>Place / Date</small>

Please open the following [X] irrevocable [ ] revocable documentary credit	**Domestic Bank Corporation** Documentary Credits P.O. Box 1040 San Francisco, California
① Beneficiary Mexico Trading Corporation Paseo de la Reforma No 108, Piso 5 Col. Revolución 06030 Mexico, DF	④ Beneficiary's bank (if known) Mexico Commercial Bank Mexico City Main Office 11570 Mexico, DF
② Amount US$70,200.--	
③ Date and place of expiry 25th November 19.. in San Francisco	Please advise this bank [ ] by letter [X] by letter, cabling main details in advance [ ] by telex / telegram with full text of credit

Partial shipments	Transhipment	Terms of shipment (FOB, C & F, CIF)
[X] allowed [ ] not allowed	[ ] allowed [X] not allowed	CIF San Francisco

Despatch from / Taking in charge at	For transportation to	Latest date of shipment	Documents must be presented not later than
Mexico, DF	San Francisco	10th Nov. 19..	③ 15 days after date of despatch

Beneficiary may dispose of the credit amount as follows [X] at sight upon presentation of documents ⑤ [ ] after ....days, calculated from date of	[ ] by a draft due .... drawn on [ ] you [ ] your correspondents which you / your correspondents will please accept
against surrender of the following documents ⑥ [X] invoice (....3....copies) Shipping document [X] sea: bill of lading, to order, endorsed in blank [ ] rail: dublicate waybill [ ] air: air consignment note [ ]	[X] insurance policy, certificte (................ copies) covering the following risks: "all risks" including war up to [ ] Additional documents final destination in the USA [X] Confirmation of the carrier that the ship is not more than 15 years old [X] packing list (3 copies)
⑦ Notify address in bill of lading / goods addressed to American Import-Export Co., Inc. 123 Main Street San Francisco, California	Goods insured by [ ] us [X] seller
⑧ Goods 1'000 "Record players ANC 83 as per pro forma invoice no. 74/1853 dd 10th September 19.." at US$70.20 per item	

Your correspondents to advise beneficiary [ ] adding their confirmation [X] without adding their confirmation ⑨ Payments to be debited to our..U.S. Dollars...............account no 10-32679150
NB. The applicable text is marked by [X]
American Import-Export Co., Inc. Signature _____
E 6801 N 1/2 3.81 5000   For mailing please see overleaf

<small>This credit is subject to the «Uniform customs and practice for documentary credits» fixed by the International Chamber of Commerce. It is understood that you do not assume any responsibility neither for the correctness, validity or genuineness of the documents which will be remitted to you nor for the description, quality, quantity and weight of the goods thereby represented.</small>

TIPS FOR PARTIES TO A LETTER OF CREDIT

Buyer

1. Before opening a letter of credit, the buyer should reach agreement with the supplier on all particulars of payment procedures, schedules of shipment, type of goods to be sent, and documents to be supplied by the supplier.
2. When choosing the type of L/C to be used, the buyer should take into account standard payment methods in the country with which he is doing business.
3. When opening a letter of credit, the buyer should keep the details of the purchase short and concise.
4. The buyer should be prepared to amend or renegotiate terms of the L/C with the supplier. This is a common procedure in international trade. On irrevocable L/Cs, the most common type, amendments may be made only if all parties involved in the L/C agree.
5. The buyer can eliminate exchange risk involved with import credits in foreign currencies by purchasing foreign exchange on the forward markets.
6. The buyer should use a bank experienced in foreign trade as the L/C issuing bank.
7. The validation time stated on the L/C should give the supplier ample time to produce the goods or to pull them out of stock.
8. The buyer should be aware that an L/C is not failsafe. Banks are only responsible for the documents exchanged and not the goods shipped. Documents in conformity with L/C specifications cannot be rejected on grounds that the goods were not delivered as specified in the contract. The goods shipped may not in fact be the goods ordered and paid for.
9. Purchase contracts and other agreements pertaining to the sale between the buyer and supplier are not the concern of the issuing bank. Only the terms of the L/C are binding on the bank.
10. Documents specified in the L/C should include those the buyer requires for customs clearance.

Supplier

1. Before signing a contract, the supplier should make inquiries about the buyer's creditworthiness and business practices. The supplier's bank will generally assist in this investigation.
2. The supplier should confirm the good standing of the buyer's bank if the credit is unconfirmed.
3. For confirmed credit, the supplier should determine that his local bank is willing to confirm credits from the buyer and his bank.
4. The supplier should carefully review the L/C to make sure he can meet the specified schedules of shipment, type of goods to be sent, packaging, and documentation. All aspects of the L/C must be in conformance with the terms agreed upon, including the supplier's address, the amount to be paid, and the prescribed transport route.
5. The supplier must comply with every detail of the L/C specifications, otherwise the security given by the credit is lost.
6. The supplier should ensure that the L/C is irrevocable.
7. If conditions of the credit have to be modified, the supplier should contact the buyer immediately so that he can instruct the issuing bank to make the necessary amendments.
8. The supplier should confirm with his insurance company that it can provide the coverage specified in the credit, and that insurance charges in the L/C are correct. Insurance coverage often is for CIF (cost, insurance, freight) value of the goods plus 10 percent.
9. The supplier must ensure that the details of goods being sent comply with the description in the L/C, and that the description on the invoice matches that on the L/C.
10. The supplier should be familiar with foreign exchange limitations in the buyer's country which may hinder payment procedures.

GLOSSARY OF DOCUMENTS IN INTERNATIONAL TRADE

The following is a list and description of some of the more common documents importers and exporters encounter in the course of international trade. For the importer/buyer this serves as a checklist of documents he may require of the seller/exporter in a letter of credit or documents against payment method.

Bill of Lading A document issued by a transportation company (such as a shipping line) to the shipper which serves as a receipt for goods shipped, a contract for delivery, and may serve as a title document. The major types are:

Straight (non-negotiable) Bill of Lading Indicates that the shipper will deliver the goods to the consignee. The document itself does not give title to the goods. The consignee need only identify himself to claim the goods. A straight bill of lading is often used when the goods have been paid for in advance.

Order (negotiable or "shippers order") Bill of Lading This is a title document which must be in the possession of the consignee (buyer/importer) in order for him to take possession of the shipped goods. Because this bill of lading is negotiable, it is usually made out "to the order of" the consignor (seller/exporter).

Air Waybill A bill of lading issued for air shipment of goods, which is always made out in straight non-negotiable form. It serves as a receipt for the shipper and needs to be made out to someone who can take possession of the goods upon arrival—without waiting for other documents to arrive.

Overland/Inland Bill of Lading Similar to an Air Waybill, except that it covers ground or water transport.

Certificate of Origin A document which certifies the country of origin of the goods. Because a certificate of origin is often required by customs for entry, a buyer will often stipulate in his letter of credit that a certificate of origin is a required document.

Certificate of Manufacture A document in which the producer of goods certifies that production has been completed and that the goods are at the disposal of the buyer.

Consular Invoice An invoice prepared on a special form supplied by the consul of an importing country, in the language of the importing country, and certified by a consular official of the foreign country.

Dock Receipt A document/receipt issued by an ocean carrier when the seller/exporter is not responsible for moving the goods to their final destination, but only to a dock in the exporting country. The document/receipt indicates that the goods were, in fact, delivered and received at the specified dock.

Export License A document, issued by a government agency, giving authorization to export certain commodities to specified countries.

Import License A document, issued by a government agency, giving authorization to import certain commodities.

Inspection Certificate An affidavit signed by the seller/exporter or an independent inspection firm (as required by the buyer/importer), confirming that merchandise meets certain specifications.

Insurance Document A document certifying that goods are insured for shipment.

Invoice/Commercial Invoice A document identifying the seller and buyer of goods or services, identifying numbers such as invoice number, date, shipping date, mode of transport, delivery and payment terms, and a complete listing and description of the goods or services being sold including prices, discounts, and quantities. The commercial invoice is usually used by customs to determine the true cost of goods when assessing duty.

Packing List A document listing the merchandise contained in a particular box, crate, or container, plus type, dimensions, and weight of the container.

Phytosanitary (plant health) Inspection Certificate A document certifying that an export shipment has been inspected and is free from pests and plant diseases considered harmful by the importing country.

Shipper's Export Declaration A form prepared by a shipper/exporter indicating the value, weight, destination, and other information about an export shipment.

GLOSSARY OF TERMS OF SALE

The following is a basic glossary of common terms of sale in international trade. Note that issues regarding responsibility for loss and insurance are complex and beyond the scope of this publication. The international standard of trade terms of sale are "Incoterms," published by the International Chamber of Commerce (ICC), 38, Cours Albert Ier, F-75008 Paris, France. Other offices of the ICC are British National Committee of the ICC, Centre Point, 103 New Oxford Street, London WC1A 1QB, UK and US Council of the ICC, 1212 Avenue of the Americas, New York, NY 10010, USA.

C&F (Cost and Freight) Named Point of Destination The seller's price includes the cost of the goods and transportation up to a named port of destination, but does not cover insurance. Under these terms insurance is the responsibility of the buyer/importer.

CIF (Cost, Insurance, and Freight) Named Point of Destination The seller's price includes the cost of the goods, insurance, and transportation up to a named port of destination.

Ex Dock—Named Port of Importation The seller's price includes the cost of the goods, and all additional charges necessary to put them on the dock at the named port of importation with import duty paid. The seller is obligated to pay for insurance and freight charges.

Ex Point of Origin ("Ex Works" "Ex Warehouse" etc.) The seller's price includes the cost of the goods and packing, but without any transport. The seller agrees to place the goods at the disposal of the buyer at a specified point of origin, on a specified date, and within a fixed period of time. The buyer is under obligation to take delivery of the goods at the agreed place and bear all costs of freight, transport and insurance.

FAS (Free Alongside Ship) The seller's price includes the cost of the goods and transportation up to the port of shipment alongside the vessel or on a designated dock. Insurance under these terms is usually the responsibility of the buyer.

FOB (Free On Board) The seller's price includes the cost of the goods , transportation to the port of shipment, and loading charges on a vessel. This might be on a ship, railway car, or truck at an inland point of departure. Loss or damage to the shipment is borne by the seller until loaded at the point named and by the buyer after loading at that point.

GLOSSARY OF INTERNATIONAL PAYMENT TERMS

Advice The forwarding of a letter of credit or an amendment to a letter of credit to the seller, or beneficiary of the letter of credit, by the advising bank (seller's bank).

Advising Bank The bank (usually the seller's bank) which receives a letter of credit from the issuing bank (the buyer's bank) and handles the transaction from the seller's side. This includes: validating the letter of credit, reviewing it for internal consistency, forwarding it to the seller, forwarding seller's documentation back to the issuing bank, and, in the case of a confirmed letter of credit, guaranteeing payment to the seller if his documents are in order and the terms of the credit are met.

Amendment A change in the terms and conditions of a letter of credit, usually to meet the needs of the seller. The seller requests an amendment of the buyer who, if he agrees, instructs his bank (the issuing bank) to issue the amendment. The issuing bank informs the seller's bank (the advising bank) who then notifies the seller of the amendment. In the case of irrevocable letters of credit, amendments may only be made with the agreement of all parties to the transaction.

Back-to-Back Letter of Credit A new letter of credit opened in favor of another beneficiary on the basis of an already existing, nontransferable letter of credit.

Beneficiary The entity to whom credits and payments are made, usually the seller/supplier of goods.

Bill of Exchange A written order from one person to another to pay a specified sum of money to a designated person. The following two versions are the most common:

Draft A financial/legal document where one individual (the drawer) instructs another individual (the drawee) to pay a certain amount of money to a named person, usually in payment for the transfer of goods or services. Sight Drafts are payable when presented. Time Drafts (also called usance drafts) are payable at a future fixed (specific) date or determinable (30, 60, 90 days etc.) date. Time drafts are used as a financing tool (as with Documents against Acceptance D/P terms) to give the buyer time to pay for his purchase.

Promissory Note A financial/legal document wherein one individual (the issuer) promises to pay another individual a certain amount.

Collecting Bank (also called the presenting bank) In a Documentary Collection, the bank (usually the buyer's bank) that collects payment or a time draft from the buyer to be forwarded to the remitting bank (usually the seller's bank) in exchange for shipping and other documents which enable the buyer to take possession of the goods.

Confirmed Letter of Credit A letter of credit which contains a guarantee on the part of both the issuing and advising bank of payment to the seller so long as the seller's documentation is in order and terms of the credit are met.

Deferred Payment Letter of Credit A letter of credit where the buyer takes possession of the title documents and the goods by agreeing to pay the issuing bank at a fixed time in the future.

Discrepancy The noncompliance with the terms and conditions of a letter of credit. A discrepancy may be as small as a misspelling, an inconsistency in dates or amounts, or a missing document. Some discrepancies can easily be fixed; others may lead to the eventual invalidation of the letter of credit.

D/A Abbreviation for "Documents against Acceptance."

D/P Abbreviation for "Documents against Payment."

Documents against Acceptance (D/A) *See* Documentary Collection

Documents against Payment (D/P) *See* Documentary Collection

Documentary Collection A method of effecting payment for goods whereby the seller/exporter instructs his bank to collect a certain sum from the buyer/importer in exchange for the transfer of shipping and other documentation enabling the buyer/importer to take possession of the goods. The two main types of Documentary Collection are:

Documents against Payment (D/P) Where the bank releases the documents to the buyer/importer only against a cash payment in a prescribed currency; and

Documents against Acceptance (D/A) Where the bank releases the documents to the buyer/importer against acceptance of a bill of exchange guaranteeing payment at a later date.

Draft *See* Bill of exchange.

Drawee The buyer in a documentary collection.

Forward Foreign Exchange An agreement to purchase foreign exchange (currency) at a future date at a predetermined rate of exchange. Forward foreign exchange contracts are often purchased by buyers of merchandise who wish to hedge against foreign exchange fluctuations between the time the contract is negotiated and the time payment is made.

Irrevocable Credit A letter of credit which cannot be revoked or amended without prior mutual consent of the supplier, the buyer, and all intermediaries.

Issuance The act of the issuing bank (buyer's bank) establishing a letter of credit based on the buyer's application.

Issuing Bank The buyer's bank which establishes a letter of credit in favor of the supplier, or beneficiary.

Letter of Credit A document stating commitment on the part of a bank to place an agreed upon sum of money at the disposal of a seller on behalf of a buyer under precisely defined conditions.

Negotiation In a letter of credit transaction, the examination of seller's documentation by the (negotiating) bank to determine if they comply with the terms and conditions of the letter of credit.

Open Account The shipping of goods by the supplier to the buyer prior to payment for the goods. The supplier will usually specify expected payment terms of 30, 60, or 90 days from date of shipment.

Red Clause Letter of Credit A letter of credit which makes funds available to the seller prior to shipment in order to provide him with funds for production of the goods.

Remitter In a documentary collection, an alternate name given to the seller who forwards documents to the buyer through banks.

Remitting Bank In a documentary collection, a bank which acts as an intermediary, forwarding the remitter's documents to, and payments from the collecting bank.

Revocable Letter of Credit A letter of credit which may be revoked or amended by the issuer (buyer) without prior notice to other parties in the letter of credit process. It is rarely used.

Revolving Letter of Credit A letter of credit which is automatically restored to its full amount after the completion of each documentary exchange. It is used when there are several shipments to be made over a specified period of time.

Sight Draft *See* Bill of Exchange.

Standby Letter of Credit A letter of credit used as a secondary payment method in the event that the primary payment method cannot be fulfilled.

Time Draft *See* Bill of Exchange.

Validity The time period for which a letter of credit is valid. After receiving notice of a letter of credit opened on his behalf, the seller/exporter must meet all the requirements of the letter of credit within the period of validity.

FURTHER READING

For more detailed information on international trade payments, refer to the following publications of the International Chamber of Commerce (ICC), Paris, France.

Uniform Rules for Collections This publication describes the conditions governing collections, including those for presentation, payment and acceptance terms. The Articles also specify the responsibility of the bank regarding protest, case of need and actions to protect the merchandise. An indispensable aid to everyday banking operations. (A revised, updated edition will be published in 1995.) ICC Publication No. 322.

Documentary Credits: UCP 500 and 400 Compared This publication was developed to train managers, supervisors, and practitioners of international trade in critical areas of the new UCP 500 Rules. It pays particular attention to those Articles that have been the source of litigation. ICC Publication No. 511.

The New ICC Standard Documentary Credit Forms Standard Documentary Credit Forms are a series of forms designed for bankers, attorneys, importers/exporters, and anyone involved in documentary credit transactions around the world. This comprehensive new edition, prepared by Charles del Busto, Chairman of the ICC Banking Commission, reflects the major changes instituted by the new "UCP 500." ICC Publication No. 516.

The New ICC Guide to Documentary Credit Operations This new Guide is a fully revised and expanded edition of the "Guide to Documentary Credits" (ICC publication No. 415, published in conjunction with the UCP No. 400). The new Guide uses a unique combination of graphs, charts, and sample documents to illustrate the Documentary Credit process. An indispensable tool for import/export traders, bankers, training services, and anyone involved in day-to-day Credit operations. ICC Publication No. 515.

Guide to Incoterms 1990 A companion to "Incoterms," the ICC "Guide to Incoterms 1990" gives detailed comments on the changes to the 1980 edition and indicates why it may be in the interest of a buyer or seller to use one or another trade term. This guide is indispensable for exporters/importers, bankers, insurers, and transporters. ICC Publication No. 461/90.

These and other relevant ICC publications may be obtained from the following sources:

ICC Publishing S.A.
International Chamber of Commerce
38, Cours Albert Ier
75008 Paris, France
Tel: [33] (1) 49-53-28-28 Fax: [33] (1) 49-53-28-62
Telex: 650770

International Chamber of Commerce
Borsenstrasse 26
P.O. Box 4138
8022 Zurich, Switzerland

British National Committee of the ICC
Centre Point, New Oxford Street
London WC1A QB, UK

ICC Publishing, Inc.
US Council of the ICC
156 Fifth Avenue, Suite 820
New York, NY 10010, USA
Tel: [1] (212) 206-1150 Fax: [1] (212) 633-6025

Taxation

CONTENTS

CORPORATE TAXATION*

AT A GLANCE

Corporate Income Tax Rate (%)	35 (a)
Capital Gains Tax Rate (%)	35
Branch Tax Rate (%)	35 (a)
Withholding Tax (%)(b)	
Dividends	30 (c)
Interest	30 (c)(d)
Royalties from Patents,	
Know-how, etc.	30 (c)
Branch Remittance Tax	30 (e)
Net Operating Losses (Years)	
Carryback	3
Carryforward	15

(a) In addition, many states levy income or capital-based taxes. An alternative minimum tax is imposed (see "Taxes on Corporate Income and Gains").
(b) Rates may be reduced by treaty.
(c) Applicable to payments to nonresidents.
(d) Interest on certain "portfolio debt" obligations issued after July 18, 1984, and noneffectively connected bank deposit interest are exempt from withholding.
(e) This is the branch profits tax (see "Other Significant Taxes").

TAXES ON CORPORATE INCOME AND GAINS

Corporate Income Tax

US corporations are subject to federal taxes on their worldwide income, including income of foreign branches (whether or not the profits are repatriated). In general, a US corporation is not taxed by the US on the earnings of a foreign subsidiary until the subsidiary distributes dividends or is sold or liquidated. Numerous exceptions to this deferral concept may apply, resulting in current US taxation of some or all

* Note: This division is reprinted from Worldwide Corporate Tax Guide, 1994 edition, © Ernst & Young, courtesy of that firm. This material should not be regarded as offering a complete explanation of US taxation. Ernst & Young is a leading international professional services firm with offices in over 120 countries and throughout the US. Refer to "Important Addresses" chapter for the address and telephone number of the US headquarters of Ernst & Young.

THE US TAX SYSTEM: A BROAD BRUSH*

Tax planning plays an essential role in the foreign investor's development of a successful strategy for undertaking US business or investment. In the US, as in many other countries, tax liabilities for an individual depend on the structure selected for doing business—that is, whether a business is established as a taxable entity apart from the individual. In the international marketplace, tax planning requires a coordinated strategy that takes into account the tax laws of both the investor's home country and those of the federal, state, and local US jurisdictions where the foreign investor will do business or invest.

Taxes are levied in the US by federal, state, and local governments, each of which assesses several different taxes. State and local governments have their own tax legislation, subject to some constitutional limitations. Although there is no uniformity in state taxation, most state governments—but not all—levy income and/or franchise taxes, sales or gross revenue taxes, use taxes, property taxes, unemployment taxes, and death duties. Qualification and franchising fees are also imposed by most state governments. Moreover, many city, county, and other local governments impose taxes—such as ad valorem taxes—on personal and real property holdings and sales and use taxes on retail transactions. The most common taxes foreign investors will encounter in the US are as follows.

Income Taxes The largest source of federal tax revenue is the US income tax, imposed on the net income of corporations, individuals, trusts, and estates. Payment of this tax may be affected by treaty between the US and one or more other countries. Most states levy an income tax, but a few states and most localities do not.

Franchise Taxes Many states impose annual franchise taxes on companies incorporated in or doing business in the state. In essence, this tax is levied in exchange for the right to do business within the state. Most often it is based on the total capital of a business or on its net earnings.

Employment Taxes In addition to income taxes, the federal government imposes social security and other employment taxes on business entities and other employ-ers, as well as self-employed individuals. States also impose unemployment taxes. Employers must withhold federal and state income taxes and social security from employee wages.

Sales or Gross Revenue Taxes Sales or gross revenue taxes are based on the gross sales price of a transaction. These taxes constitute the largest revenue source for most state governments. Counties and cities may also levy similar taxes.

Most sales taxes are assessed on sales of tangible personal property for final use or consumption by the purchaser within the jurisdiction that imposes the tax. Sales for purposes of resale or further manufacture are often not taxed or are taxed at lower rates. In some states, leases of personal property are treated as continuing sales subject to sales or use taxes. Some states also impose gross revenue or excise taxes on gross income from renting a real property, providing hotel lodgings, selling services, and other income-producing activities that do not involve the sale of products or the lease of personal property.

Use Taxes A use tax is imposed on property acquired in one jurisdiction and brought into another state for use, storage, or consumption. The use tax is similar to a sales tax or gross revenue tax, which it usually complements to prevent taxpayers from avoiding sales or gross revenue taxes by purchasing property outside the state where the property will be used.

Property Taxes Most local governments below the state level impose an ad valorem tax on owners of real property and of some types of tangible personal property situated within the county, city, or other locality. The assessment is generally based on a percentage of the fair market value of the property. This tax is usually deductible from federal, state, and local income taxes.

Gift, Estate, Excise, and Miscellaneous Taxes The Federal and many state governments assess gift and estate taxes. Some states impose inheritance taxes or death duties. Special taxes are imposed on transactions related to specific products, such as tobacco, alcohol, and firearms.

---

* By Duane H. Zobrist and Nancy M. Beckner. Copyright © 1995 Carlsmith Ball Wichman Case & Ichiki. Reprinted with permission of that law firm.

of the foreign subsidiary's earnings.

Branches of foreign corporations generally are taxable on income that is effectively connected with a US trade or business. However, if the foreign corporation is resident in a country having an income tax treaty with the US, business profits are taxable by the US only to the extent the income is attributable to a permanent establishment in the US.

Rates of Corporate Tax

The following rates applied in 1994. A corporation's taxable income exceeding US$75,000 but not exceeding US$10,000,000 is taxed at 34 percent. Corporations with taxable income between US$335,000 and US$1,000,000 are effectively taxed at 34 percent on all taxable income (including the first US$75,000). Corporations with taxable income of less than US$335,000 receive partial benefit from the graduated rates of 15 percent and 25 percent that apply to the first US$75,000 of taxable income. A corporation's taxable income exceeding US$15,000,000 but not exceeding US$18,333,333 is subject to an additional tax of 3 percent. Corporations with taxable income in excess of US$18,333,333 are effectively subject to tax at a rate of 35 percent on all taxable income. These rates apply both to US corporations and to the income of foreign corporations that is effectively connected with a US trade or business.

Alternative Minimum Tax

The alternative minimum tax (AMT) is designed to prevent corporations with substantial economic income from using preferential deductions, exclusions and credits to substantially reduce or eliminate their tax liability. To achieve this goal, the AMT is structured as a separate tax system with its own allowable deductions and credit limitations. The tax is imposed at a flat rate of 20 percent on alternative minimum taxable income (AMTI). It is an "alternative" tax because corporations are required to pay the higher of the regular tax or AMT. To the extent the AMT exceeds regular tax, a minimum tax credit is generated and carried forward to offset the taxpayer's regular tax to the extent it exceeds the AMT in future years.

In general AMTI is computed by making adjustments to regular taxable income and then adding back certain nondeductible tax preference items. The required adjustments are intended to convert

preferential deductions allowed for regular tax (for example, accelerated depreciation on real estate) into less favorable alternative deductions that are allowable under the parallel AMT system. In addition, an adjustment based on adjusted current earnings can increase or decrease AMTI. Net operating losses and foreign tax credits may reduce AMT by up to 90 percent, compared to a potential reduction of 100 percent for regular tax purposes.

CAPITAL GAINS AND LOSSES

Capital gains are taxed at a maximum rate of 35 percent. In general, capital losses may offset only capital gains, not ordinary income. A corporation's excess capital loss may be carried back three years and for five years to offset capital gains in such other years.

Administration

The annual tax return is due by the 15th day of the third month after the close of the company's fiscal year. A corporation is entitled, upon request, to an automatic six-month extension to file its return. In general, 100 percent of a corporation's tax liability must be paid through quarterly estimated tax installments during the year in which the income is earned. The estimated tax payments are due on the 15th day of the 4th, 6th, 9th, and 12th months of the company's fiscal year.

Foreign Tax Relief

A tax credit is allowed for foreign income taxes paid or deemed paid by US corporations, but it is

RELIEF FROM DOUBLE CORPORATE TAXATION*

Corporations are subject to taxation in any jurisdiction—federal, state, and local—where they do business in the US. Corporations that "do business" in more than one state are generally taxed on net income from a particular state based on a weighted formula to apportion the corporation's income between its in-state and out-of-state activities. "Doing business" within a state is determined generally by the nature and extent of activities in the state. Passive investment, such as owning corporate stock, is usually not treated as doing business. Important factors considered include the following: the maintenance of an office, plant, or inventory within the state; the presence of employees and payment of wages within the state; or the sale of property or provision of services within the state.

In most cases, a three-factor ratio is used to apportion corporate income among the states where it does business. Generally, this ratio is computed by applying to total taxable income the average of the following fractions: (i) assets in the taxing state over total assets; (ii) payroll in the taxing state over total payroll; and (iii) income related to operations or activities in the taxing state over total income. Certain types of nonbusiness income are generally allocated to the state where the property producing the income is located or where the taxpayer's "corporate domicile" is located. For example, income from real property is allocated to the state where the property is located, but dividends are customarily allocated to the recipient's corporate domicile, provided such income is not part of the taxpayer's business income subject to apportionment. Some states, such as California, utilize a unitary method of taxation, which require the taxpayer to take into account income derived by other corporations, including foreign corporations, that have certain ownership, operational, and corporate structure relationships with each other and with the taxpayer.

* By Duane H. Zobrist and Nancy M. Beckner. Copyright © 1995 Carlsmith Ball Wichman Case & Ichiki. Reprinted with permission of that law firm.

limited to the US tax on the foreign-source portion of a company's worldwide taxable income. Separate limitations must be calculated based on various categories of income, including passive income, high withholding tax interest income, and dividend income from each foreign corporation in which the company holds a 10 percent or greater interest and all US shareholders hold a total interest of less than 50 percent. In addition, foreign tax credits, together with net operating loss deductions, may only reduce up to 90 percent of the AMT.

DETERMINATION OF TAXABLE INCOME

General

Income for tax purposes is generally computed according to generally accepted accounting principles, as adjusted for certain statutory tax provisions. Consequently, taxable income frequently does not equal income for financial reporting purposes.

In general, a deduction is permitted for ordinary and necessary trade or business expenses. However, expenditures that create an asset having a useful life longer than one year may need to be capitalized and recovered ratably.

Depreciation

A depreciation deduction is available for most property (except land) used in a trade or business or held for the production of income, such as rental property. Tangible depreciable property that is used in the US (whether new or used) and placed in service after 1980 and before 1987 is generally depreciated on an accelerated basis (ACRS). Tangible depreciable property that is used in the US and placed in service after 1986 is generally depreciated under a modified ACRS basis. In general, under the modified ACRS system, assets are grouped into six classes of personal property and into two classes of real property. Each class is assigned a recovery period and a depreciation method.

Alternatively, a taxpayer may elect to use the straight-line method of depreciation over specified longer recovery periods or the methods prescribed for AMT purposes, which would avoid a depreciation adjustment for AMT.

The cost of intangible assets developed by a taxpayer may be amortized over the determinable useful life of an asset. Certain intangible assets, including goodwill, going concern value, patents, and copyrights, may generally be amortized over 15 years if they are acquired as part of a business after August 10, 1993. A taxpayer may elect to apply this provision to all property acquired after July 25, 1991.

Tax depreciation is generally subject to recapture on the sale of an asset to the extent the sales proceeds exceed the tax value after depreciation. The amounts recaptured are subject to tax as ordinary income.

The following are the depreciation methods and recovery periods for certain assets.

Asset	Depreciation Method	Recovery Period (Years)
Commercial and industrial buildings	Straight-line	39(a)
Office equipment	Double-declining balance or straight-line	7 or 12
Motor vehicles	Double-declining balance or straight-line	5 or 12
Plant and machinery	Double-declining balance or straight-line	7 or 12(b)

(a) *31.5 years if placed in service before May 13, 1993.*
(b) *These are generally the recovery periods.*

Net Operating Losses

If allowable deductions of a US corporation or branch of a foreign corporation exceed its gross income, the excess is called a net operating loss. Net operating losses may be carried back 3 years and forward 15 years to offset taxable income in those years. Limitations apply in utilizing net operating losses of acquired operations.

Inventory Valuation

Inventory is generally valued for tax purposes at either cost or the lower of cost or market value. In determining the cost of goods sold, the two most common inventory flow assumptions used are LIFO and FIFO. The method chosen must be applied consistently. Uniform capitalization rules require the inclusion in inventory costs of many expenses previously deductible as period costs.

Dividends

In general, dividends received from other US corporations qualify for a 70 percent dividends-received deduction, subject to certain limitations. The dividends-received deduction is generally increased to 80 percent of the dividend if the recipient corporation owns at least 20 percent of the distributing corporation. Dividend payments between members of an affiliated group of US corporations qualify for a 100 percent dividends-received deduction. In general, an affiliated group consists of a US parent corporation and all other US corporations in which the parent owns, directly or indirectly through one or more chains, at least 80 percent of the total voting power and value of all classes of shares (excluding nonvoting preferred shares).

Consolidated Returns

An affiliated group of US corporations (as described in "Dividends" above) can elect to determine their taxable income and tax liability on a consolidated basis. The consolidated return provisions generally allow electing corporations to report the aggregate of group income and deductions in accordance with the requirements for financial consolidations. Consequently, the net operating losses of some members of the group can be used to offset the taxable income of other members of the group, and transactions between group members, such as intercompany sales and dividends, are generally deferred or eliminated until there is a transaction outside the group. Under certain circumstances, losses incurred on the sale of consolidated subsidiaries are disallowed.

Foreign Subsidiaries

Under certain circumstances, undistributed income of a foreign subsidiary controlled by US shareholders is taxed to the US shareholders on a current basis, as if the foreign subsidiary distributed a dividend on the last day of its taxable year. This may result if the foreign subsidiary invests its earnings in "US property" (including loans to US shareholders); earns certain types of income (referred to as "subpart F" income) including certain passive income and "tainted" business income, or has "excess passive assets" (in general, in excess of 25 percent of total assets).

Two other provisions restrict the deferral of tax on offshore income. The foreign personal holding company (FPHC) rules apply to foreign corporations with predominantly passive income that are closely held by US individual shareholders. The passive foreign investment company (PFIC) rules apply to foreign corporations with a high percentage of passive income or passive assets. The PFIC rules do not include a minimum threshold of ownership by US shareholders.

MISCELLANEOUS MATTERS

Foreign-Exchange Controls

The US currently has no foreign-exchange control restrictions.

Debt-to-Equity Rules

The US has thin capitalization principles under which the Internal Revenue Service (IRS) may attempt to limit the deduction for interest expense when a US corporation's debt-to-equity ratio is too high, If a US corporation is thinly capitalized, funds loaned to it by a related party may be recharacterized by the IRS as equity. As a result, the corporation's deduction for interest expense may be disallowed, and principal and interest payments may be considered distributions to the related party and be subject to withholding.

The US has no fixed rules for determining if a thin capitalization situation exists. A debt-to-equity ratio of 3:1 or less is usually acceptable to the tax authorities, provided the taxpayer can adequately serve its debt without the help of related parties.

However, a deduction is disallowed for certain "disqualified" interest paid on loans made or guaranteed by related foreign parties that are not subject to US tax on the interest received. This disallowed interest may be carried forward to future years and allowed as a deduction. No interest deduction is disallowed under this provision if the payer corporation's debt-to-equity ratio does not exceed 1.5:1. If the debt-to-equity ratio exceeds this amount, the deduction of "excess interest expense" is deferred. "Excess interest expense" is defined as the excess of interest expense over interest income, minus 50 percent of the adjusted taxable income of the corporation plus any "excess imitation carry forward."

The provision is generally effective for interest paid or accrued after July 10, 1989. For interest on guaranteed debt, the provision applies to interest paid or accrued after December 31, 1993.

Transfer Pricing

In general, the IRS may recompute the tax liability of related parties if, in its discretion, it is necessary to prevent the evasion of taxes or to clearly reflect income. Specific regulations require that related taxpayers (including US and foreign affiliates) deal among

OTHER SIGNIFICANT TAXES

The table below summarizes other significant taxes.

Nature of Tax	Rate (%)
Branch profits tax, on branch profits (reduced by reinvested profits and increased by withdrawals of previously reinvested earnings). The rate may be reduced by treaty	30
Branch interest tax, on interest expense paid by the branch (unless the interest would be exempt from withholding tax if paid by a US corporation); the rate may be reduced by treaty	30
Personal holding company (PHC) tax applies to a US or foreign corporation not meeting the definition of foreign personal holding company (FPHC) that satisfies a passive-income test, in addition to regular tax or alternative minimum tax; imposed on undistributed income	39.6
Accumulated earnings tax, penalty tax levied on a corporation (excluding an FPHC or a PHC) accumulating profits to avoid shareholder-level personal income tax; assessed on accumulated taxable income exceeding US$250,000 (US$150,000 for certain personal services corporations)	39.6
State and local income taxes, imposed by most states and some local governments	0 to 12
State and local sales taxes, imposed by many states and some local governments	Various
Payroll taxes	
Federal unemployment insurance (FUTA), imposed on first US$7,000 of wages	6.2
Worker's compensation insurance, varies depending on nature of employees' activities	Various
Social security contributions, imposed on	
Wages up to US$60,600 (for 1994), paid by	
Employer	7.65
Employee	7.65
Wages in excess of US$60,600 (for 1994; Medicare component), paid by	
Employer	1.45
Employee	1.45

TREATY WITHHOLDING TAX RATES

The following are US withholding tax rates for dividend, interest and royalty payments from the US to residents of various treaty countries.

Various exceptions or conditions may apply, depending upon the terms of the particular treaty.

In addition to the signed but unratified treaties mentioned in the above footnotes, the US has signed tax treaties with Argentina, Bangladesh, Israel, and Sri Lanka, but these treaties are not in force.

The US terminated its treaties with Aruba and the Netherlands Antilles effective January 1, 1988. However, under a modification of the US termination notice, Article VIII of the treaties, which exempts from US tax interest paid by US persons to corporations and residents of Aruba and the Netherlands Antilles, remains in force.

	Dividends %	Interest %	Patent and know-how Royalties %		Dividends %	Interest %	Patent and know-how Royalties %
Australia	15	10	10	Luxembourg	15/5 (a)	0	0
Austria	15/5 (a)	0	0	Malta	15/5 (a)	12.5	12.5
Barbados	15/5 (a)	5 (e)	5 (e)	Mexico	15/5 (a)(i)	15/10 (i)(j)	10
Belgium	15/5 (a)	15	0	Morocco	15/10 (a)	15	10
Canada	15/10 (a)	15	10	Netherlands	15/5 (a)	0	0
China	10	10	10	New Zealand	15	10	10
Cyprus	15/5 (a)	10	0	Norway	15	0	0
Czech Rep.	15/5 (a)	0	10	Pakistan	30/15 (a)	30	0
Denmark	15/5 (a)	0	0	Philippines	25/20 (a)	15	15
Egypt	15/5 a)	15	15	Poland	15/5 (a)	0	10
Finland	15/5 (a)	0	5	Romania	10	10	15
France	15/5 (a)	0	0	Russian Fed. (h)	10/5 (a)	0	0
Germany	15/5 (a)	0	0	Slovak Rep. (h)	15/5 (a)	0	10
Greece	30	0/30 (b)	0	Spain	15/10 (a)	10	10
Hungary	15/5 (a)	0	0	Sweden	15/5 (a)	0	0
Iceland	15/5 (a)	0	0	Switzerland	15/5 (a)	5	0
India	25/15 (a)	15	20/15 (c)	Trinidad and			
Indonesia	15	15	15	Tobago	30	30	15
Ireland	15/5 (a)	0/30 (b)	0	Tunisia	20/14 (a)	15	15
Italy	15/5 (a)	15	10	USSR (g)	30	0	0
Jamaica	15/10 (a)	12.5	10	United Kingdom	15/5 (a)	0	0
Japan	15/10 (a)	10	10	Nontreaty			
Korea	15/10 (a)	12	15	countries	30	30 (d)	30

(a) The withholding rate is reduced to 5 percent (10 percent in the case of Canada, Jamaica, Japan, Korea, Morocco, and Spain; 14 percent in the case of Tunisia; 15 percent in the case of India and Pakistan; and 20 percent in the case of the Philippines) if, among other conditions, the recipient is a corporation owning a specified percentage of the voting power of the distributing corporation.
(b) The exemption does not apply if the recipient controls directly or indirectly more than 50 percent of the voting power in the paying corporation.
(c) The rate is 20 percent through December 31, 1995, and 15 percent thereafter.
(d) Interest on certain "portfolio debt" obligations issued after July 18, 1984 and noneffectively connected bank deposit interest are exempt from withholding.
(e) These are the rates under a protocol to the treaty. The rates are effective from February 1, 1994. Before that date, the withholding rate for interest and royalties is 12.5 percent.
(f) A new treaty with Denmark was signed in 1980, but it has not yet been ratified.
(g) The US Department of Treasury has announced that the USSR treaty continues to apply to the republics comprising the Commonwealth of Independent States (CIS). As indicated in the above table, the US has entered into a tax treaty with the Russian Federation. The US has signed a treaty with Kazakhstan, but the treaty has not yet been ratified. It is negotiating a tax treaty with Ukraine.
(h) For dividends, interest, and royalties, the treaty applies to amounts paid on or after February 1, 1994. For other income, the treaty is effective for taxable periods beginning on or after January 1, 1994.
(i) The withholding rates for dividends and interest will be lowered, effective January 2, 1999.
(j) The 10 percent rate applies to interest on bank loans and on bonds or other securities traded on certain securities markets. The 15 percent rate applies to other interest.

themselves on an arm's length basis. Under the best-method rule included in the transfer-pricing regulations, the best transfer-pricing method is determined based on the facts and circumstances. Transfer-pricing methods that may be acceptable, depending on the circumstances, include uncontrolled price, resale price and profit-split. It is possible to reach transfer-pricing agreements in advance with the IRS.

If the IRS adjusts a taxpayer's tax liability, tax treaties between the US and other countries usually pro-

vide procedures for allocation of adjustments between related parties in the two countries to avoid double tax.

Related-Party Loans

Under treasury regulations, interest expense accrued on a loan from a related foreign lender must be actually paid before the US borrower can deduct the interest expense. The regulations generally apply retroactively to interest accrued after December 31, 1983.

PERSONAL TAXATION*

AT A GLANCE — MAXIMUM RATES

Income Tax Rate (%) 39.6
Capital Gains Tax Rate (%) 28*
Net Worth Tax Rate (%) 0
Estate and Gift Tax Rate (%) 55

Tax rate on long-term gains. The maximum rate of tax on short-term gains is 39.6 percent.

INCOME TAX — EMPLOYMENT

Who is Liable

US citizens and resident foreign persons are subject to tax on their entire income, regardless of source. US citizens and residents may, however, exclude up to US$70,000 of their foreign-earned income plus certain housing expenses if they meet certain qualifying tests and file a US tax return to claim the exclusion. Special rules discussed in Section L apply to nonresident foreign persons who work in the US.

A resident foreign person is subject to income tax on worldwide income under the same rules that apply to US citizens. In general, a nonresident foreign person is subject only to tax on US-source income. Residency for income tax purposes generally has no bearing on an individual's immigration status.

Generally, foreign nationals may be considered resident foreign persons if they are either lawful permanent residents ("green card" holders) or their physical presence in the US is long enough under a substantial presence test. Under the substantial presence test, a foreign national will be deemed to be a US resident if the individual:

- Was present in the US for at least 31 days during the current year; and
- Was considered to have been present for at least 183 days during a consecutive three-year test period, which includes the current year, using a formula weighted as follows:

Current year	100.00%
1st preceding year	33.33%
2nd preceding year	16.67%

Using this formula, an average of 122 days' presence during each of three consecutive years will cause a foreign national to be considered a US resident under the substantial presence test.

Among several exceptions to this test are the following:

- Days present as a qualified student, teacher, and/or trainee, or when a medical condition arose and prevented departure, are not counted.
- An individual might claim to be a nonresident of the US by virtue of having a "closer connection" (such as a tax home) in a foreign country.
- Income tax treaties may override internal US tax rules for dual residents.

The Internal Revenue Service (IRS) has issued regulations that require individuals to file a statement with the IRS setting forth the facts that prove their claim for exemption.

In certain circumstances, it may be beneficial for an individual to be considered a resident of the US for income tax purposes. An individual may make what is known as a "first-year election" in the year of arrival if certain conditions are met.

* Note: This division is reprinted from Worldwide Personal Tax Guide, 1994 edition, © Ernst & Young, courtesy of that firm. This material should not be regarded as offering a complete explanation of US taxation. Ernst & Young is a leading international professional services firm with offices in over 120 countries and throughout the US. Refer to "Important Addresses" chapter for the address and telephone number of the US headquarters of Ernst & Young.

Taxable Income

Gross Income In general, gross income is required to be segregated into three separate baskets as follows:

- Earned income: generally salary and earnings from active trades or businesses.
- Portfolio income: generally investment income, including interest, dividends, certain royalties, and gains from the disposition of investment property.
- Passive income: generally income from traditional tax shelter investments such as real estate.

In addition to cash payments, taxable salary generally includes all employer-paid items except qualifying moving expenses, medical insurance premiums, pension contributions to a nonqualified plan and, for individuals on short-term assignments, meals and temporary housing expenses. *(See* "Nonresidents" for additional information on the taxation of nonresidents.)

Deductions attributable to passive income may generally not be used to offset net income in another basket. For example, losses attributable to an individual's limited partnership investment in a real estate venture (which would correspond to passive income) may not shelter earned income or portfolio income; rather, such losses may be used only to offset income earned on other investments within the passive basket. Most unused deductions (losses) attributable to passive income may be carried over to subsequent years to be utilized when income is recognized in the same basket or against other basket income when the investment is sold in a fully taxable transaction.

Income Tax Rates

The applicable US tax rates depend on whether an individual is married or not and, if married, whether an individual elects to file a joint return with his or her spouse. Certain individuals also qualify to file as a "head of household."

The tax brackets and rates for 1994 are set forth in the following tables.

Married Filing Joint Return

Taxable Income Exceeding US$	Not Exceeding US$	Tax on Lower Amount US$	Rate on Excess US$
0	38,000	0	15
38,000	91,850	5,700	28
91,850	140,000	20,778	31
140,000	250,000	35,704.50	36
250,000	—	75,304.50	39.6

RELIEF FROM DOUBLE PERSONAL TAXATION*

In general, an individual who maintains a permanent home in a particular state and who has spent a specific period of time within the state is a resident of that state for tax purposes. The state of residence will tax that individual on net income from all sources, both within and outside the state. An individual who does not meet the specified residency requirement is taxed on income derived only from within the state. If the same income is taxed by another state, a credit for out-of-state taxes paid may be available in the individual's state of residence. Similar rules usually apply to income taxes imposed by local governments. States generally do not allow a credit for taxes paid to foreign countries.

* By Duane H. Zobrist and Nancy M. Beckner. Copyright © 1995 Carlsmith Ball Wichman Case & Ichiki. Reprinted with permission of that law firm.

Head of Household

Taxable Income Exceeding US$	Not Exceeding US$	Tax on Lower Amount US$	Rate on Excess US$
0	30,500	0	15
30,500	78,700	4,575	28
78,700	127,500	18,071	31
127,500	250,000	33,199	36
250,000	—	77,299	39.6

Single Individual

Taxable Income Exceeding US$	Not Exceeding US$	Tax on Lower Amount US$	Rate on Excess US$
0	22,750	0	15
22,750	55,100	3,412.50	28
55,100	115,000	12,470	31
115,000	250,000	31,039.50	36
250,000	—	79,639.50	39.6

Married Filing Separate Return

Taxable Income Exceeding US$	Not Exceeding US$	Tax on Lower Amount US$	Rate on Excess US$
0	19,000	0	15
19,000	45,925	2,850	28
45,925	70,000	10,389	31
70,000	125,000	17,852.25	36
125,000	—	37,652.25	39.6

The income brackets in these tables are indexed for inflation annually.

The preceding rates are used to compute an individual's regular federal tax liability. The US also imposes an alternative minimum tax (AMT) at a rate of 26 percent on alternative minimum taxable income up to US$175,000 and of 28 percent on alternative minimum taxable income over US$175,000. Its primary purpose is to prevent individuals with substantial economic income from using preferential tax deductions (such as accelerated depreciation), exclusions (such as certain tax-exempt income) and credits to reduce substantially or eliminate their tax liability. It is an alternative tax because, after an individual computes both the regular tax and AMT liabilities, the greater of the two amounts constitutes the final liability.

Some states, cities and municipalities also levy income tax. City and/or municipal income tax rates are generally 1 percent or less (although the rate in New York City is approximately 4.46 percent). State income tax rates generally range from 0 percent to 12 percent. Therefore, an individual's total income tax liability depends on the state in which the individual resides or works.

Deductible Expenses

Certain types of deductions, including amounts related to producing gross income, are subtracted to arrive at adjusted gross income. Alimony payments to a former spouse and qualifying unreimbursed moving expenses are among the most commonly claimed deductions in this category. Qualifying employer-reimbursed moving expenses are not included in income. Alimony (but not child support) must meet certain criteria to be deductible by the payer. For alimony to be deductible, it generally must be included in the recipient's gross income. A tax of 30 percent must generally be withheld (and remitted to the IRS) from alimony paid by a US citizen or resident to a nonresident foreign person's former spouse. Certain US income tax treaties may reduce the 30 percent withholding tax rate (tax treaties are listed in "Double Tax Relief and Double Tax Treaties").

Once adjusted gross income is determined, a citizen or resident foreign person is entitled to claim the greater of itemized deductions or a standard deduction. The amount of the standard deduction varies depending on the taxpayer's filing status. In 1994, the standard deduction was US$6,350 for married individuals filing a joint return, US$5,600 for the head of a household, US$3,800 for a single (not married) individual and US$3,175 for a married taxpayer filing a separate return.

Itemized deductions include:

- Medical expenses to the extent that they exceed 7.5 percent of adjusted gross income;
- Income and property taxes of states and localities;
- Foreign income taxes if a foreign tax credit is not elected;
- Certain interest expense;
- Casualty and theft losses to the extent they exceed 10 percent of adjusted gross income;
- Charitable contributions made to qualified US charities; and
- Unreimbursed employee business expenses and other miscellaneous itemized deductions, to the extent that the net total exceeds 2 percent of adjusted gross income.

Itemized deductions, other than medical expenses, casualty and theft losses, and investment interest expense, must be reduced by an amount equal to 3 percent of the taxpayer's adjusted gross income in excess of US$111,800 (US$55,900 for married individuals filing separately) for 1994. The adjustment, however, cannot reduce the deductible amount by more than 80 percent.

Personal Deductions and Allowances

Individuals who are not dependents of other taxpayers are entitled to deduct a personal exemption in arriving at taxable income. For 1994, each personal exemption was equal to US$2,450. US citizens and residents are generally entitled to claim an additional personal exemption for a spouse when a joint return is filed. However, if the spouse is a nonresident foreign person and a joint return is not filed, the taxpayer may claim this exemption only if the spouse has no US-source gross income and is not a dependent of another taxpayer. Additional personal exemptions may be claimed for each qualified dependent who is a US citizen or, in certain circumstances, a resident of the US, Canada, or Mexico for some part of the tax year. US income tax treaties may modify the preceding rules. Personal exemptions are phased out by 2 percent for each US$2,500 (or part thereof) by which the adjusted gross income exceeds US$167,700 (married persons filing jointly), US$139,700 (head of household) or US$111,800 (single persons). For married persons filing separately, the exemptions are phased out by 2 percent for each US$1,250 by which adjusted gross income exceeds US$83,850. (These thresholds applied in 1994.)

INCOME TAX — SELF-EMPLOYMENT

Who is Liable

The classification of self-employed individuals generally includes anyone who is in business to make a profit for himself or herself. *See* "Nonresidents" for discussion of special rules that apply to nonresident alien individuals.

Taxable Income

Self-employed individuals are entitled to the same deductions as employees, except that they may deduct directly related ordinary and necessary business expenses. However, special rules may apply to limit business deductions if a taxpayer's business activity does not result in a profit for 3 out of 5 years. In this situation, the activity may be classified as a hobby, and the expenses are deductible only if they qualify as itemized deductions. They may establish and take a deduction for contributions to their own retirement plans within special limitations.

DIRECTORS' FEES

In general directors' fees are considered to be earnings from self-employment. (*See* "Income Tax—Self-Employment.")

INVESTMENT INCOME

Dividend, interest, and capital gain income is considered portfolio income and, in general, is taxed at the ordinary rates. Certain types of interest income, such as interest on certain state and local government obligations, are exempt from federal tax, but may be subject to AMT. Special rules discussed in "Nonresidents" apply to nonresident alien individuals.

Net income from the rental of real property and from royalties is aggregated with other income and taxed at the rates set forth in "Income Tax—Employment."

RELIEF FOR LOSSES

Capital Losses

Capital losses are fully deductible against capital gains. However, net capital losses are deductible against other income only up to an annual limit of US$3,000. Unused capital losses may be carried forward indefinitely.

Passive Losses

In general, passive losses, such as those generated from limited partnership investments or rental real estate, may be offset only against income generated in the passive basket.

Limited relief may be available for real estate rental losses. For example, an individual who actively participates in the rental activity may use up to US$25,000 of losses to offset income in other baskets. The US$25,000 offset is phased out for taxpayers with adjusted gross income between US$100,000 and US$150,000, and special rules apply to married

individuals filing separate tax returns.

Disallowed losses may be carried forward indefinitely and used to offset net passive income in future years. Any remaining loss may be used in full when a taxpayer sells the investment in a transaction that is recognized for tax purposes.

CAPITAL GAINS AND LOSSES

Net capital gain income is taxed at ordinary rates except that the maximum rate for long-term gains is limited to 28 percent. Net capital gain is equal to the difference between net long-term capital gains over short-term capital losses. Long-term refers to assets held for more than one year. Short-term capital gains are taxed as ordinary income. (For the tax treatment of capital losses, *see* "Relief for Losses.")

Investors who hold qualified small business stock for at least five years may be entitled to exclude 50 percent of the gain realized on disposition of the stock.

US taxpayers, including resident foreign persons, may be able to defer some or all of the gain from the sale of a principal residence if a new principal residence is purchased or constructed within two years prior or subsequent to the sale of the old residence. The entire gain is deferred if the amount reinvested in a new home equals or exceeds the adjusted sales price of the old home.

If the US taxpayer or foreign person is age 55 or older, he or she may make a one-time election to exclude up to US$125,000 of the taxable gain on the sale of a principal residence (US$62,500 on each return for married taxpayers filing separately) if the taxpayer has owned and lived in the residence for at least three years during the five-year period ending on the date of sale. A one-year residency rule applies to certain disabled individuals.

NET WORTH TAX

No federal tax is levied on an individual's net worth. However, some states and municipalities impose a tax on an individual's net worth.

ESTATE AND GIFT TAXES

US estate and gift taxes are imposed at graduated rates from 18 percent to 55 percent on the value of property transferred by reason of death or gift. Generally, citizens and residents are entitled to a limited lifetime credit (currently US$192,800, which is the tax on taxable transfers of US$600,000), which may be applied against either estate or gift taxes. This credit is referred to as the unified credit. The benefits of the unified credit and graduated rates begin to phase out once cumulative taxable estate and/or gift transfers exceed US$10 million. Generally, transfers between spouses who are US citizens or from a non-US citizen to a US citizen spouse are not subject to estate or gift taxes. However, transfers from a US citizen to a non-US citizen spouse may be subject to estate or gift tax.

US estate and gift tax rules, like those of US income taxation, differ depending on whether a foreign national is considered to be a resident or nonresident foreign person. However, the distinction between residents and nonresidents differs from that under US income tax rules. For estate and gift tax purposes, a nonresident is a foreign national who is not a US citizen and whose "domicile" at the date of death is outside the US. A person's domicile is generally defined as the place the individual regards as his or her permanent home—the place where he or she intends to return, even after a period of absence.

Gift Tax

US citizens and resident foreign persons are subject to gift tax on transfers of all property, tangible and intangible, regardless of the location of the property. (*See* "Nonresidents" for a description of gift tax on transfers by nonresidents.) Tax is imposed on the fair market value of property on the date of the gift, at graduated rates determined by the individual's cumulative lifetime transfers.

Each year, a donor is entitled to exclude from gift tax gifts of present interests up to US$10,000 for each donee. A husband and wife may elect to have gifts made by one spouse considered as made one-half by each spouse. This "gift-splitting election" on these joint gifts increases the annual exclusion to US$20,000 for each donee. Gifts in excess of the annual exclusion are subject to taxes ranging from 18 percent to 55 percent. However, the unified credit may be used to offset this liability.

A US citizen or resident is exempt from gift tax on annual transfers of up to US$100,000 to a non-US citizen spouse.

Estate Tax

The estate of a US citizen or resident includes all property, tangible and intangible, regardless of location. (*See* "Nonresidents" for a description of estate tax on a nonresident's estate.)

Property transferred at death from a US citizen to a non-US citizen spouse generally is not excluded from the decedent's gross estate, unless the property is placed in a qualified domestic trust before the estate tax return is due. To be considered a qualified domestic trust, a trust must satisfy the following conditions:

- At least one trustee of the trust must be a US citizen or a domestic corporation, and no distribution from the trust may be made without a trustee's approval.

- The trust must meet the requirements prescribed by Treasury regulations.
- The executor must make an irrevocable election on the estate tax return.

Estate tax is levied on the property in the trust:

- If at any time the trust ceases to meet the above requirements;
- If the corpus is distributed prior to the surviving spouse's death, except in cases of hardship; and
- Upon the death of the surviving spouse.

SOCIAL SECURITY TAXES

FICA

Under the Federal Insurance Contributions Act (FICA), social security tax is imposed on wages or salaries received by individual employees to fund retirement benefits paid by the federal government. For 1994, the social security tax of 15.3 percent, which includes a 2.9 percent Medicare tax, was imposed on the first US$60,600 of annual employment income. However, there is no limit on wages subject to the Medicare portion of the social security tax. Half of the tax is withheld from the employee's wages, and half is paid by the employer.

SECA

Self-employment tax is imposed under the Self-Employment Contributions Act (SECA) on self-employment income, net of business expenses, of US citizens and resident foreign persons. For 1994 SECA tax was imposed at a rate of 15.3 percent, which includes a 2.9 percent Medicare tax, on self-employment income up to US$60,600. However, there is no limitation income subject to the Medicare portion of SECA tax. Self-employed individuals pay the entire tax but may deduct 50 percent as a trade or business expense on their federal income tax return. No tax is payable if net earnings for the year are less than US$400. If a taxpayer has both wages subject to FICA tax and income subject to SECA tax, the wage base subject to FICA tax is used to reduce the income base subject to SECA tax. SECA tax is computed on the individual's income tax return.

FUTA

Federal unemployment tax (FUTA) is imposed on employers' wage payments to employees. FUTA is imposed on income from services performed within the US regardless of the citizenship or residency of the employer or employee. The 1994 tax rate is 6.2 percent on the first US$7,000 of wages of each employee. Most states also have unemployment taxes that are creditable against the FUTA tax when paid. Self-employed individuals are not subject to FUTA tax.

ADMINISTRATION

The US system of tax administration is based on the principle of self-assessment. US taxpayers must file a tax return annually with the IRS and with the state and local tax authorities under whose jurisdiction they live if those governments impose an income or net worth tax.

On the federal return, taxpayers report income, deductions, and exemptions and compute the tax due. Taxes are generally collected by employer withholding on wages and salaries and by individual payment of estimated taxes on income not subject to withholding. Normally, tax due in excess of amounts withheld and payments of estimated tax must be paid with the return when filed. A taxpayer may elect to pay the additional 1993 tax attributable to the rate increase from 31 percent to a maximum of 39.6 percent in three installments. The first installment is due on April 15, 1994, the second on April 15, 1995, and the third on April 15, 1996. The taxpayer may also claim a refund of an overpayment of tax on the annual return. Substantial penalties and interest are usually imposed on a taxpayer when a return is not filed on time or when tax payments, including estimated payments, are not made by the applicable due dates.

Tax returns may be selected for an audit at a later date by the IRS or state auditors. Failure to provide adequate support for amounts claimed as deductions on the return may result in the disallowance of deductions and a greater tax liability, on which interest and/or penalties must be paid from the original due date. In general, taxpayers are required to maintain supporting documentation for at least three years after a return is filed.

US citizens and resident foreign persons file Form 1040, US Individual Income Tax Return, or one of the simplified forms such as Forms 1040A (for taxpayers with taxable income under US$50,000 who do not itemize deductions) or 1040EZ (for single filers with taxable income under US$50,000, no itemized deductions and no dependents). The due date for calendar-year taxpayers is normally April 15 (three and one-half months after year-end for fiscal-year taxpayers). Extensions to file tax returns may be obtained by filing a request with the IRS. However, an extension to file the return is not an extension to pay any tax due with the return. To prevent interest and penalties from being charged on unpaid tax, a calendar-year taxpayer should pay any tax due by April 15.

NONRESIDENTS

Taxation of Nonresident Aliens—General

In general, a nonresident foreign person is subject to US tax on income that is effectively connected with a US trade or business and on US-source fixed or determinable, annual or periodic gains, profits and income (generally investment income such as dividends, royalties, rental income, and so forth). US-source investment income is ordinarily taxed on a gross basis at a flat 30 percent rate of tax, whereas income effectively connected with a US trade or business is taxed after related deductions at the graduated rates of tax listed in "Income Tax—Employment." Portfolio interest and (generally) capital gains from the sale of stock in a US company are exempt from the 30 percent tax. Moreover, an election to tax rental income on a net basis is available. However, gains from sales of US real property interests are generally considered to be "effectively connected income," and special complex rules apply. (Generally, these gains are taxed at a minimum rate of 21 percent.)

A nonresident foreign person may not use the standard deduction instead of actual itemized deductions. Also, the types of itemized deductions a nonresident foreign person is allowed to claim are limited to casualty losses, charitable contributions made to qualified US charities, certain miscellaneous deductions, and state and local taxes imposed on effectively connected income. A nonresident is not allowed to claim an itemized deduction for medical expenses, taxes (other than state and local income taxes) or most interest expenses. In addition, a nonresident foreign person normally is entitled to only one personal exemption. Nonresidents are subject to the phaseout thresholds for both itemized deductions (*see* "Income Tax—Employment") and the personal exemption (*see* "Income Tax—Employment") according to their tax rate group.

Unmarried nonresident foreign persons are taxed under the rates for single individuals. Married nonresidents whose spouses are also nonresidents generally are taxed under the rates for married persons filing separately.

As discussed in the following paragraphs, nonresident foreign persons file special tax forms and are also subject to special US estate and/or gift tax rules.

Employment Income

In general, a nonresident foreign person who performs personal services as an employee in the US at any time during the tax year is considered to be engaged in a US trade or business. An exception to this general rule applies to a nonresident foreign person performing services in the US when:

- The services are performed for a foreign employer;
- The employee is present for no more than 90 days during the tax year; and
- Compensation for the services does not exceed US$3,000.

NONRESIDENT ALIEN (NRA) STATUS*

Foreign persons who are US income tax residents are subject to US tax on worldwide income and to various burdensome reporting and disclosure requirements. Nonresident foreign persons are taxed by the US on US-source and US effectively connected income only. Accordingly, a key tax planning consideration for a nonresident foreign person is to avoid inadvertent US residence. The US Internal Revenue Code (IRC) contains two basic tests to determine residency for income tax purposes in a particular year: (1) the lawful permanent residence or green card test; and (2) the substantial presence test.

The Lawful Permanent Residence Test According to the lawful permanent residence (or green card) test, an individual who is granted lawful permanent residency in the US in accordance with US immigration laws—and therefore holds a green card—is deemed to be a US resident for federal income taxation purposes.

The Substantial Presence Test An individual who is present in the US for 31 or more days during the current year and who has been present in the US for at least 183 days (using a weighted formula over a three-year period), is considered to be a US income tax resident for the current year, unless the person can qualify for the "closer connection" exception. Under the weighted formula, a non-immigrant whose presence in the US is limited to 121 days per calendar year will successfully avoid classification as a resident under the substantial presence test.

Closer Connection Exception An individual who is present in the US for more than 182 days during any one calendar year is automatically deemed to be a US resident for that year. If this automatic presumption does not apply, but an individual nevertheless meets the substantial presence test, a rebuttal to the residency presumption may still be made by proving that the person has a "tax home" in a foreign country and a closer connection to that other country than to the US.

If the individual has a US green card application pending, however, the closer connection exception will not apply.

To claim the closer connection exception, an individual must file a statement of the information and facts showing the individual's closer connection. The statement must be attached to the US income tax return or, if no return is otherwise required to be filed, the statement must be filed separately with the Internal Revenue Service Center, Philadelphia, PA 19255, on or before the due date for individual tax returns for the year to which the statement relates. If the statement is not filed on time, the individual may not be permitted to use the closer connection exception to avoid US tax liabilities.

Tax Treaty Residence Rules An individual entitled to the benefits of an income tax treaty with another country may be able to rely on the treaty rules for determining residence rather than the IRC tests. The federal tax authorities have recently issued regulations that allow a dual resident foreign person—that is, a person who is deemed to be a US resident under IRC rules but a resident of a treaty-partner country under US domestic law—to claim NRA status under the residency tiebreaker rules of the treaty for purposes of computing the foreign person's US income tax liability. However, a foreign person who relies on the residency tiebreaker rules of an applicable treaty is nevertheless considered a US tax resident for all other IRC purposes.

Special Allowances for Mexican and Canadian Commuters A foreign person who resides in Mexico or Canada is considered to commute regularly if that person commutes to a location of employment or self-employment in the US from the residence in Mexico or Canada on more that 75 percent of the work days during the working period at issue. In determining the number of days that such a commuter is present in the US, any day on which the round-trip commute takes place can be excluded.

* By Duane H. Zobrist and Nancy M. Beckner. Copyright © 1995 Carlsmith Ball Wichman Case & Ichiki. Reprinted with permission of that law firm.

These conditions are similar to those contained in many income tax treaties, although the treaties often expand the time limit to 183 days and increase or eliminate the maximum dollar amount of compensation.

If an employee does not fall under the above statutory exception or a treaty exception, all US-source compensation received in that year is considered effectively connected income (not just the amount exceeding the US$3,000 limitation or the dollar limitation of a treaty). This income includes wages, bonuses, and reimbursements for certain living expenses paid to or on behalf of the employee.

Compensation is considered to be from a US source if it is paid for services performed in the US. Where the income is paid or received is irrelevant in determining its source. If income is paid for services performed partly within the US and partly in a foreign country and if the amount of income attributable to services performed in the US cannot be accurately determined, the US portion is determined on a workday ratio basis.

Effectively connected income retains its character even if received before or after a US trade or business has ceased. Consequently, wages for services performed in the US and received during a year in which a nonresident foreign person has no US workdays are taxed at the graduated rates instead of the flat 30 percent rate.

States usually follow the federal tax treatment in determining whether a nonresident foreign person's income is subject to state taxation.

FICA tax is imposed on compensation for services performed in the US, regardless of the citizenship or residence of the employee or employer. Consequently, absent an exception, nonresident foreign person employees who perform services in the US are subject to FICA tax, even though they may be exempt from US income tax by a statutory rule or an income tax treaty provision. Certain categories of individuals are exempt from FICA tax, such as foreign government employees, exchange visitors in the US under a type-J visa, foreign students holding a type-F visa, and individuals covered under a social security totalization agreement between the US and another country. These agreements may provide relief from social security tax for qualifying short-term transferees, and they allow qualifying individuals to continue paying into the social security system of their home country. Totalization agreements are currently in effect with Austria, Belgium, Canada, Finland, France, Germany, Ireland, Italy, Luxembourg, the Netherlands, Norway, Portugal, Spain, Sweden, Switzerland, and the UK. An agreement with Greece became effective mid-1994. Negotiations are being conducted with the UK on a supplementary agreement. The agreements usually apply for a maximum period of five years.

An employer (US or foreign) is responsible for withholding US income or social security taxes from nonresident alien employees.

Self-Employment Income

In general, a nonresident foreign person who performs independent personal services in the US at any time during the tax year is considered to be engaged in a US trade or business.

Although subject to tax at the graduated rates, compensation paid to a nonresident foreign person for performing independent personal services in the US is subject to a 30 percent withholding tax. A nonresident foreign person must then file a US tax return to claim a refund of any amount overwithheld or pay any additional tax due. If compensation is exempt from US tax under an income tax treaty or if the amount paid is not greater than the personal exemption amount (US$2,450 in 1994), a nonresident foreign person may request exemption from withholding by preparing Form 8233, Exemption from Withholding on Compensation for Independent Personal Services of a Nonresident Alien Individual, and giving it to the withholding agent (payer). In addition, many US income tax treaties contain separate provisions affecting the taxation of independent personal services income.

Nonresident foreign persons are not subject to SECA tax.

Filing and Payment Procedures

Nonresident foreign persons with US gross income to report generally must file Form 1040NR, US Nonresident Alien Income Tax Return. This return is required even if a taxpayer has effectively connected income but no taxable income or if income is exempt under a tax treaty. However, nonresidents are not required to file Form 1040NR if they are not engaged in a US trade or business during the tax year and if any liability for tax on US-source investment (passive) income is satisfied by the 30 percent withholding tax.

If required, Form 1040NR is normally due on April 15 for nonresidents who had wages subject to withholding; otherwise, the due date is normally June 15. Extensions to file the return (but not to pay tax due) may be obtained by filing a request with the IRS.

Estate and Gift Taxes

Nonresidents are allowed a marital deduction only for transfers to spouses who are US citizens (*but see* "Estate Tax and Gift Taxes"). The general non-treaty rules are explained in the following paragraphs.

Gift Tax Foreign nationals who are not domiciled in the US generally must pay gift tax only on transfers of real property and tangible personal property located in the US. Intangible property, such as stocks and bonds, is generally exempt. The gift tax rates for nonresidents are the same as those for citizens and residents. (*See* "Estate and Gift Taxes.")

Nonresidents are allowed to give up to US$10,000 annually to each recipient with no gift tax consequences, but they may not split gifts with their spouse.

Real Estate Tax For US tax purposes, the estate of a nonresident includes only tangible, intangible and real property located within the US at the time of death. For this purpose, shares of US corporations and certain debt obligations of US residents are considered to be property located in the US. The estate tax rates are the same as those for citizens and residents. A unified credit of US$13,000 is allowed.

Application of US estate and gift tax rules may be modified if a nonresident foreign person is a resident of a country with which the US has entered into an estate and gift tax treaty. The US currently has estate and/or gift tax treaties with Australia, Austria, Denmark, Finland, France, Germany, Greece, Ireland, Italy, Japan, the Netherlands, Norway, South Africa, Sweden, Switzerland, and the UK.

DOUBLE TAX RELIEF AND TREATIES

Foreign Tax Credit

A foreign tax credit is the principal instrument used by US persons to avoid being taxed twice on their foreign-source income—once by a foreign government and again by the US. Generally, the foreign tax credit permits a taxpayer to reduce US tax by the amount of income taxes paid to a foreign government, subject to certain limitations.

The foreign tax credit is generally limited to the lesser of actual foreign taxes paid or accrued and US tax on foreign-source table income. Separate limitations must be calculated for several categories of income, including passive income and high-withholding-tax interest income. Income not separately categorized is included in an overall limitation category. For example, employment income (earned income) is included in the overall category. Under the separate limitation rules, only foreign taxes paid on a particular category of income are available for credit against US tax on foreign-source taxable income in that category. A foreign tax credit against AMT liability is allowed, but special rules limit the amount that may be used for alternative minimum tax purposes to 90 percent of AMT, computed before any AMT net operating loss deduction.

Tax Treaties

Special rules apply to nonresident foreign persons who are residents of countries that have income tax treaties with the US. For example, a treaty may reduce or eliminate the 30 percent tax rate applicable to dividends, interest and royalties. As mentioned previously, certain treaties also contain provisions that may be relevant in determining residency status. Treaties may also limit or eliminate the taxation of visitors who work in the US on short-term assignments or may provide exemption from tax for teachers, professors, trainees, students, and apprentices.

Even if a treaty provides for exemption from or a reduction of the 30 percent tax, this does not mean that the reduced rate automatically applies. Nonresident foreign persons must first claim their treaty benefits. For example, income tax withholding applies unless nonresident foreign person employees file a statement with their employer (foreign or US) stating the facts by which they qualify for exemption from US tax under an income tax treaty clause. Similarly, foreign students, teachers, and researchers must complete Form 8233 and file it with their US institution or employer. Treaty benefits for other types of income, such as royalties or interest, are obtained by filing Form 1001, Ownership, Exemption, or Reduced Rate Certificate, with the withholding agent (the payer). Generally, a separate Form 1001 must be filed for each type of income.

If applicable, the withholding agent must notify the nonresident foreign person of the gross amounts paid and taxes withheld by March 15 of the following year. This is done on Form 1042S, Foreign Person's US-Source Income Subject to Withholding. This form, when attached to the nonresident foreign person's US income tax return (Form 1040NR), provides proof to the IRS of amounts withheld.

The US double income tax treaties are set forth in the following list.

Australia	Hungary	Norway
Austria	Iceland	Pakistan
Barbados	India	Philippines
Belgium	Indonesia	Poland
Bermuda	Ireland	Romania
Canada	Italy	Russian Fed.
China	Jamaica	Slovak Rep.
Cyprus	Japan	Spain
Czech Rep.	Korea (South)	Sweden
Denmark	Luxembourg	Switzerland
Egypt	Malta	Trinidad & Tobago
Finland	Mexico	Tunisia
France	Morocco	USSR*
Germany	Netherlands	UK
Greece	New Zealand	

* The US honors the USSR treaty with the republics of the Commonwealth of Independent States (CIS) that have not concluded a separate treaty.

SPECIAL TAX CONSIDERATIONS*

DOMESTIC CORPORATIONS

Tax considerations in forming, operating, and even liquidating a corporation are numerous and complex. A brief survey of critical tax rules that affect corporations doing business in the US follows.

Distributions and Liquidations

A corporation that distributes appreciated property to its shareholders usually recognizes taxable gain on that distribution, just as if the corporation had sold the property at fair market value. This rule is generally applied regardless of whether the property is distributed as part of a liquidation of the corporation. Such application is a substantial change in prior US tax law, which often permitted tax-free liquidation of a corporation because the tax was paid by the shareholders on receipt of the liquidating distribution. Tax-free liquidation is now available only for the liquidation of a subsidiary in which the corporate parent owns at least an 80 percent interest. Tax-free liquidation of an 80 percent-owned subsidiary may not be available if the parent is a foreign corporation.

Accumulated Earnings

In addition to being liable for the income tax, nearly all corporations will be liable for the accumulated earnings tax—imposed at the rate of 39.6 percent—if the corporation is used so as to avoid tax liabilities to the shareholders by retaining earnings and profits beyond the reasonable needs of the business instead of distributing them. Thus, the accumulated earnings tax is a penalty tax for failure to distribute corporate earnings. This tax can be a significant concern for corporations that plan to retain profits in the US rather than distribute earnings to their foreign shareholders.

Personal Holding Companies

A somewhat similar penalty tax is imposed—also at the rate of 39.6 percent—on the "undistributed personal holding company income" of a corporation classified as a personal holding company. This tax focuses on companies—sometimes referred to as "incorporated pocketbooks"—that are organized to hold investment assets and income or to receive compensation for services performed by their shareholders. In general, a personal holding company is a closely held corporation with significant passive income, such as dividends, rents, interest, and royalties.

Special Deductions

In computing gross income, a corporation is entitled to deduct dividends received from most domestic corporations and dividends from certain foreign corporations. The deduction is normally 70 percent of the dividends. However, a deduction of 100 percent of dividends received is available for certain qualifying dividends received from members of the same affiliated group of corporations as the recipient corporation.

"Consolidated" Returns

An affiliated group of domestic corporations may elect to file a consolidated tax return. A typical consolidated group might consist of a parent company with one or more wholly owned first tier subsidiaries, which in turn may have second or third tier subsidiaries. The main advantage of consolidated reporting is that losses from one enterprise may be used to offset income from a separate enterprise, even if each enterprise is conducted by a separate corporation in the group. A consolidated group also makes it easier to transfer money and property within the group.

Tax-Free Organizations and Reorganizations

Corporations and their shareholders are permitted to undertake certain transfers or exchanges of property, stock, and sometimes securities without recognizing gain or loss, provided that such transactions are connected with the organization or reorganization of one or more corporations and provided that various technical requirements are met. For example, if two corporations merge and the shareholders of the disappearing corporation receive only stock of the surviving corporation, the reorganization can generally be structured so as to avoid tax liabilities to the merging corporations and their shareholders.

Exempt Organizations

Certain corporations and other organizations and trusts may be exempt from federal income tax. Exempt organizations include, but are not limited to, those organized and operated for religious, charitable, and educational purposes; business leagues and chambers of commerce; civic leagues organized to promote social welfare; and labor organizations. Such organizations are generally exempt from tax only with respect to income that relates to their exempt purposes. Thus, exempt organizations do pay federal taxes on unrelated business income and certain other activities.

---

*By Duane H. Zobrist and Nancy M. Beckner. Copyright © 1995 Carlsmith Ball Wichman Case & Ichiki. Reprinted with permission of that law firm.

US-OWNED ENTITIES IN FOREIGN COUNTRIES

The US federal tax laws contain a number of highly restrictive and complex rules relating to US persons who directly or indirectly organize and/or own foreign corporations, foreign partnerships, or foreign trusts. In general, these rules are intended to prevent US persons from moving income and assets offshore—that is, outside US jurisdiction—and thereby avoiding tax liabilities.

Some specific rules are discussed here because a foreign investor may be classified as a US resident foreign person and, thus, as a US person—by being present in the US for substantial periods or by obtaining a green card. Some of these rules may also affect the ability of a foreign investor to participate in or restructure a US business enterprise through a tax-free reorganization. In addition, these rules may adversely affect US persons who receive gifts or inheritances of foreign stock from nonresident foreign persons or who are beneficiaries of foreign trusts established by foreign persons.

Property Transfers

US federal tax laws often permit the organization and reorganization of US business enterprises without the recognition of taxable income, provided that certain technical requirements are met. In contrast, if a foreign corporation is a party to such an arrangement, the federal tax laws frequently require gain to be recognized if a US person directly or indirectly transfers property to a foreign corporation (an "outbound" transaction). The gain is taxable even if the transaction would have been tax free if completed with a domestic corporation. These rules may also apply to prevent US persons from avoiding tax on the repatriation of earnings and profits realized through a foreign corporation (an "inbound" transaction). A US person's transfer of property to a foreign corporation as a capital contribution or paid-in surplus may also be subject to an excise tax of 35 percent of the excess of the property's fair market value over adjusted basis plus any recognized gain.

Controlled Foreign Corporation (CFC)

Any foreign corporation is a CFC if more than 50 percent of its stock (by vote or value) is owned by US shareholders. A number of highly complex provisions require a US shareholder of a CFC to include some or all of the CFC's income in current taxable income, even if the corporation does not pay a dividend. These rules are intended to prevent a US person from using a foreign corporation to build up income offshore at low tax rates, particularly when a foreign corporation is not actively engaged in business in the jurisdiction where it is organized or is

engaging in related party transactions. In practice, however, the scope of the CFC rules is much broader. In addition to the imposition of tax, the CFC rules impose extensive reporting and disclosure requirements on US persons.

Foreign Personal Holding Company (FPHC)

If five or fewer US individuals own (directly or indirectly) more than 50 percent of a foreign corporation that earns significant passive income, the corporation may be treated as an FPHC. Even if no profits have been distributed to US shareholders of an FPHC, they are subject to a "deemed" dividend rule by which they must include in income their respective shares of the corporation's undistributed foreign personal holding company income. US individuals cannot insulate themselves from US tax liability by using intermediate foreign entities such as foreign trusts or other foreign corporations to hold the FPHC stock. The FPHC rules may be more burdensome than the CFC rules, because all of the FHPS's adjusted taxable income—not just some "tainted" income as for a CFC—is treated as undistributed foreign personal holding company income. The FPHC rules also impose extensive reporting and disclosure obligations on US shareholders.

Passive Foreign Investment Companies and Foreign Investment Companies

Two additional anti-avoidance measures are the passive foreign investment company (PFIC) rules and the foreign investment company (FIC) rules. It is possible for an entity to be classified as both a CFC and a PFIC.

PFICs Rules regarding PFICs are designed to prevent a US person from obtaining the benefit of the US tax deferral achieved as the result of owning stock in a foreign corporation which earns and retains passive income. If that corporation is not a CFC or an FPHC, a US person will not be subject to US tax on the earnings of that corporation until a dividend is actually paid or the shareholder sells stock of the corporation. Thus, a foreign corporation can retain and reinvest its earnings in various low-tax jurisdictions, and the earnings can grow virtually tax free. When a distribution is ultimately made, the amount available for distribution to shareholders will be greater. Even though a US person who receives a dividend will pay US tax on the distribution, that shareholder's after-tax return would be greater than if the corporation had distributed profits currently and the shareholder had paid US tax on the currently distributed dividends. The PFIC rules are designed to prevent a US person from achieving this tax advantage; they apply to a US person regardless of the degree of US ownership. Thus, for example, a US person owning less than 1 percent of a PFIC's stock would be subject to these rules, notwithstanding the fact that all other shares of the PFIC were owned by foreign persons.

Any foreign corporation is a PFIC if (1) 75 percent or more of its gross income for the year is passive, or (2) the average percentage of its assets (by value or, in some cases, by adjusted basis) which produce passive income or which are held to produce passive income equals or exceeds 50 percent. The PFIC rules impose an additional tax when a US person receives an "excess distribution" from a PFIC. This tax is called the "deferred tax amount" and is more or less designed to impose US tax as it would have been imposed had the PFIC distributed its earnings and profits as earned, plus an interest charge for having deferred payment of tax.

The PFIC rules provide a special mechanism called a "qualified electing fund" by which, in lieu of obtaining any deferral benefit, a US person can take into gross income the taxpayer's share of the fund's ordinary income and capital gain on a current basis. If a PFIC makes this election, its shareholders who are US persons will, in general, not be subject to the regular PFIC rules, which impose tax based on the deferred tax amount. If the US owner delays making the election so that the election is made after the first tax year in the US owner's holding period with respect to the PFIC, the US owner will be taxed under both the regular PFIC rules and the qualified electing fund rules unless special steps are taken to purge the PFIC of tax deferral benefits from the period prior to the election. These steps generally require the US owner to recognize taxable income as if the US owner had sold the PFIC stock or received an excess distribution.

FICs Like the PFIC rules, the FIC rules are also an anti-avoidance measure aimed at US persons who own stock in foreign corporations. The FIC rules treat all or part of a taxpayer's gain from the sale or exchange of stock in an FIC as ordinary income. An FIC is any foreign corporation that is (i) registered under the Investment Company Act of 1940, or (ii) engaged primarily in the business of investing, reinvesting, or trading in securities, commodities, or futures contracts at a time when 50 percent or more of its stock is owned directly or indirectly by US persons. Such a corporation can make an election to distribute at least 90 percent of its taxable income and provide certain notices to its shareholders in accordance with US Internal Revenue Service (IRS) requirements. If a corporation makes this election, its shareholders will not be subject to the FIC or PFIC rules.

Foreign Trusts, Estates, and Partnerships

If a US person transfers property to a foreign trust, a foreign estate, or a foreign partnership, the federal tax laws impose an excise tax equal to 35 percent of the excess of the fair market value of the property over the sum of the transferor's adjusted basis in the property plus the gain, if any, recognized on the transfer. In addition, when a US person transfers property to a foreign trust and there is a US beneficiary of any portion of the trust, that US person will be treated as the owner of the trust. Moreover, a number of adverse tax consequences can arise in the case of the US beneficiaries who receive distributions of accumulated trust income from a foreign trust which is not a grantor trust.

FOREIGN CORPORATIONS DOING BUSINESS IN THE US

Foreign corporations are treated much like US corporations for purposes of the tax imposed on taxable income effectively connected with activities in the US. However, there are a number of important differences between the tax treatment of domestic and foreign corporations, as noted below.

Consolidated Returns

A foreign corporation (except for certain Canadian and Mexican corporations) does not have the benefit of being included in a consolidated return.

Branch Profits Tax

A foreign corporation engaged in a US trade or business is subject to the branch profits tax. The effect of this tax is to treat the foreign corporation's US branch much like a US subsidiary of a foreign corporation for purposes of taxing repatriated branch profits and interest paid or deducted by the branch. A foreign corporation that does not reinvest its earnings for the year in a US trade or business or that reduces its investment in its US branch is treated as having made a distribution to its foreign parent. That "deemed" distribution may be subject to the branch profits tax if the branch has current or accumulated earnings and profits. A failure to reinvest or a reduction in investment is similar to the payment of a dividend by a US subsidiary to a foreign parent. Similar to the tax on dividends, the branch profits tax on this "deemed" repatriation of profits is a flat 30 percent. Special rules apply when a US branch is completely terminated so as to ameliorate the adverse effect of the branch profits tax.

The tax on interest paid by the branch is treated as paid by a US corporation and is subject to the normal 30 percent flat tax imposed on US-source interest income. In certain cases, interest deducted (but not paid) by the branch is treated as if it had been paid from a US subsidiary to its foreign parent, and it is taxed accordingly. An available income tax treaty may reduce the rate of tax to the rate imposed on the payment of dividends or interest under the treaty. For example, under the treaty between the US and Mexico, the rate is reduced to 5 percent with respect to the dividend equivalent amount and 10 percent in the case of interest. Some treaties preclude the application of the branch profits tax to the dividend equivalent amount; however, special anti-treaty shopping rules apply.

Accumulated Earnings and Personal Holding Company Taxes

Foreign corporations are subject to the US tax rules relating to the accumulated earnings tax and the personal holding company tax. However, these taxes are not applied to an FPHC or a PFIC. The personal holding company tax also does not apply to any foreign corporation if all of its stock is owned by nonresident foreign persons, whether directly or indirectly through other foreign persons, except when the corporation has income from certain types of personal service contracts.

Gain on Distributions

Foreign corporations are subject to US tax rules requiring gain to be recognized on distributions of appreciated property. However, application of these rules is limited, in the sense that gain recognized is generally taxed only to the extent that it would have been taxed on the outright sale of the property. Thus, for example, if a foreign corporation holds stock of a corporation listed on the New York Stock Exchange, the capital gain recognized by the foreign corporation on a distribution of that stock would not be subject to tax unless the gain were effectively connected with the corporation's conduct of a US trade or business.

US Real Property Investments

A foreign investor in US real property may have US tax consequences if disposition of that property is connected with US trade or business operations and if gain or loss is recognized. The investor will also be required to file an annual return with regard to the property. For futher discussion of the Foreign Investment in Real Property Tax Act (FIRPTA), refer to the "Business Law" chapter.

PARTNERSHIPS AND LIMITED LIABILITY COMPANIES

Foreign investors who are considering doing business in the US through a partnership or limited liability company (LLC) should keep in mind the following tax considerations. (Refer to the "Business Entities and Formation" chapter for further description of these business forms.)

- A partnership is usually not considered a separate taxpayer from the partners. This same rule applies to an LLC if it is treated as a partnership for tax purposes. For both of these business organizations, income, gains, and losses pass through to, and are taken into account by, the partners or members in computing their taxable income for the year. For example, if a partnership has both individual and corporate partners, each individual's share of partnership income is included on that partner's individual tax return and is taxed at the individual rates; each corporate partner will account for its share of income on its corporate tax return and will pay tax at its applicable corporate tax rate.

- The pass-through income rule applies even if the partnership does not distribute profits to the partners in any particular year. Conversely, if a partnership has losses for the year, a partner will usually not have taxable income from the partnership, even if the partnership distributes money or other property to that partner, provided that, for money distributions, the distribution does not exceed the partner's tax basis in the partnership interest.

- Although the partnership is not a taxpayer, it is required to file an informational tax return, which includes information regarding each partner's share of income, gain, or loss.

- Some partnership or LLC arrangements have characteristics similar to a corporation. Corporate characteristics include centralized management, limited liability of the partners or members, free transferability of interests in the entity, and continuity of life. A partnership or LLC with more than two of these characteristics is taxed as a corporation.

- Special tax rules apply to a publicly traded partnership (PTP). A PTP is taxed as a corporation unless 90 percent or more of its gross income consists of specific types of income, including interest, dividends, real property rents, gains from the sale of real property, income from exploiting minerals and natural resources, and gains from the sale of capital assets held to produce the foregoing types of income.

- Special withholding tax rules apply to a partnership that has foreign partners, including withholding on each foreign partner's distributive share of effectively connected US income. Such withholding tax applies even if the partnership makes no distributions to its foreign partners.

TRUSTS AND ESTATES

The tax rules applicable to trusts and estates are very complex. The following points present a brief overview of some basic US tax concepts applicable to the taxation of trusts and estates.

- Trusts and estates are generally considered taxpayers separate from the persons who create them and from the beneficiaries. Domestic US trusts and estates are subject to tax on their worldwide taxable income; however, in computing taxable income, they can ordinarily deduct distributions to beneficiaries and heirs (to the extent of distributable net income).
- The beneficiaries or heirs who receive such income distributions are directly taxed on the income.
- The tax rates applicable to domestic trusts and estates are the same as for individuals; however, those rates apply at lower taxable income levels. For example, in 1994 the maximum 39.6 percent tax rate applied to a trust's taxable income that exceeded US$7,500. In comparison, for an unmarried individual, the maximum rate did not apply until taxable income exceeded US$250,000.
- Some trusts—generally referred to as "grantor trusts"—are not separate taxpayers. Instead, the grantor (often the settlor) of the trust continues to be taxed on the income of the trust. A trust is classified as a grantor trust when the grantor or the grantor's spouse has certain powers over the trust or interests in the trust assets—such as the power to revoke the trust or the right to benefit from the income of the trust.
- A US person who transfers property to a foreign trust that has or acquires a US beneficiary will in most cases continue to be treated as the owner of the trust, even if the transferor has retained no powers over the trust or rights in the assets. This treatment means that the US transferor will continue to be taxed on the trust income.
- A US trust or estate that has foreign beneficiaries is subject to a number of special rules. The US fiduciary must generally withhold tax on distributions to foreign beneficiaries, although withholding is not required if the trust distributes income annually and the income is of a type that would not have required withholding if the beneficiary had earned the income directly. For example, interest earned on a bank account by a nonresident foreign person with no US trade or business is not subject to US tax. Accordingly, if a trust holds such a bank account and pays out the interest income annually to a nonresident foreign person beneficiary, the trustee is not required to withhold tax on the payments of that income to the beneficiary.

EXPORTING AND ROYALTY LICENSING TAX HINTS

Exports

In a properly structured transaction, a foreign person can sell inventory produced or manufactured outside the US to buyers in the US without the imposition of US tax. A foreign person can also purchase inventory from US manufacturers and distributors for resale outside the country without the imposition of US tax. In analyzing the US tax consequences of such transactions, the first issue is to determine whether the sales income will be treated as US-source income. The next step is to determine whether the income will be effectively connected with the conduct of a US trade or business. Finally, the foreign person must review any applicable income tax treaties that might provide additional protection from US taxation. Most such treaties prohibit the taxation of business profits unless the foreign person has a permanent establishment in the US, and many treaties allow some form of contact with the US without creating a permanent establishment.

US-Source Income Income from the sale of inventory is typically considered to be sourced at the location where title passes. Thus, even when US buyers are regularly solicited in the US so that the foreign seller is engaged in a US trade or business, if title to the property purchased by those buyers passes outside the US, the sales gains would generally not be US-source income and would not be subject to US taxation, unless the seller has an office or fixed place of business in the US to which the income can be attributed. Of course, if the foreign seller produces the inventory in the US, at least a portion of the income will be considered as derived from a US source, even if title passes outside the US.

If at least some sales income will be subject to US tax, the taxpayer may try to insulate the amount of gain that will come within the scope of the US tax jurisdiction. Whether such a technique will be successful depends on careful analysis by a specialist in US taxation. US tax authorities have broad powers to reallocate income and deductions among controlled businesses.

Royalty Licenses

If a foreign corporation earns income from royalties and the royalty income arises out of the use of property in the US, the income is considered derived from a US source. It is subject to the 30 percent branch profits tax, unless it is effectively connected with a US trade or business. This treatment applies even if the royalty is paid in a lump sum. However, if the payment is part of the price for purchasing the property that is creating the income, the sourcing rules for sales of property, instead of the royalty rules, apply (except when the payments are contingent). As with other types of passive income, tax on US-source royalty income may be reduced under an applicable income tax treaty.

In structuring licensing activities, foreign investors should note that the US tax authorities take a broad view of the royalty provisions and usually treat such income as derived from a US source no matter how many intermediary sublicensees may exist. Thus, if the ultimate sublicensee uses the property in the US, each intermediary sublicensee in the chain will have US source income.

Transportation & Communications

INTRODUCTION

The US boasts the most sophisticated freight transportation in the world, with state-of-the-art airport and port facilities, an incredibly extensive, high-quality road system, many major inland waterways, and a railway infrastructure which—following some difficult times—has become increasingly important in recent years. The most difficult freight transportation issues in the US involve choosing from the truly vast array of service and routing choices. The enormous physical size of the US, the wide distribution of important markets and supply centers throughout the country, and the high cost of labor in the transportation industries mean that shipping costs may add significantly to the cost of importing from or exporting to the US. It is therefore particularly important to make informed and intelligent decisions about the most appropriate means of transportation in a given situation.

The rapid move toward intermodal transport—along with deregulation of the airline, trucking, and rail industries—has resulted in even more bewildering choices and fees. An ocean carrier, for instance, may handle the logistics for door-to-door transport, contracting with other firms for land and/or air portions of the trip. Deregulation of the transportation industries and escalating labor and fuel costs have also led to confusing fee structures. Although it may be difficult to determine the cost of each leg of the journey, it can be all-important for purposes of cost comparison. And once straightforward transportation decisions are no longer simple. A shipment from Asia to the East Coast might have automatically been shipped through the Panama Canal to the nearest major port in previous years, but now it may be both cheaper and faster to ship to a West Coast port, then transport the goods by some combination of truck and rail to the ultimate destination. Domestic freight is also becoming increasingly controlled by integrated carriers; these took on 51 percent of domestic freight (by weight) in 1993, including express shipments.

Even more than in some other industries, time truly *is* money in transportation: differences of a few hours can have a major impact on overall costs. Considerations such as the efficiency of US Customs at a given port, how long it takes to shift containers from a ship to trains or trucks, and local road traffic congestion may have a strong influence on a shipper in choosing a port and inland transport—even though the time savings may amount to mere hours. One example of cost savings in higher priced forms of transport is found in the trend toward smaller, "just-in-time" deliveries to avoid the expense of warehousing stock. This trend has helped to increase US air cargo traffic dramatically.

Just as US business has become dependent on rapid, efficient transport of goods, it has also come to expect high-quality, rapid transmission of information. The array of choices and pricing structures in telecommunications is similarly dizzying, particularly compared with what is available in many countries where communications services are still highly regulated. It is true that competition has brought down costs of US telecommunications services for many, but in order to realize these savings, one may

TRANSPORTATION GLOSSARY*

bill of lading A document issued by a carrier to a shipper, signed by the captain, agent, or owner of a vessel, furnishing written evidence regarding receipt of the goods (cargo), the conditions on which transportation is made (contract of carriage), and the engagement to deliver goods at the prescribed port of destination to the lawful holder of the bill of lading. A bill of lading is, therefore, both a receipt for merchandise and a contract to deliver it as freight.

break bulk cargo Cargo which is shipped as a unit but which is not containerized. Examples are any unitized cargo placed on pallets, or in boxes.

charter A charter party or charter agreement is a lease or agreement to hire an airplane, vessel, or other means of conveyance to transport goods on a designated voyage to one or more locations.

common carrier By U.S. government regulation a common carrier publishes stated rates for carriage and must accept any passengers or goods for transport so long as space is available and the published rate is paid.

consolidation The combining of less than truckload (LTL) shipments of cargo from a number of shippers at a centrally located point of origin by a freight consolidator, and transporting them as a single shipment to a destination point. Consolidation of cargo often results in reduced shipping rates.

containerization The practice or technique of using a boxlike device (container) in which a number of packages are stored, protected, and handled as a single unit in transit. Advantages of containerization include: less handling of cargo, more protection against pilferage, less exposure to the elements, and reduced cost of shipping.

customs broker An individual or firm licensed by the U.S. Customs Service to act for importers in handling the sequence of customs formalities and other details critical to the legal and speedy exporting and importing of goods.

freight forwarder A person engaged in the business of assembling, collection, consolidating, shipping and distributing less-than-carload or less-than-truckload freight. Also, a person acting as agent in the trans-shipping of freight to or from foreign countries and the clearing of freight through customs, including full preparation of documents, arranging for shipping, warehousing, delivery and export clearance.

intermodal transport The coordinated transport of freight, especially in connection with relatively long-haul movements using any combination of freight forwarders, piggyback, containerization, air-freight, ocean freight, assemblers, motor carriers.

landbridge The movement of containers from a foreign country by vessel, transiting a country by rail or truck, and then being loaded aboard another vessel for delivery to a second foreign country. An example would be a container from Shanghai which arrives in the U.S. at Tacoma, Washington, and is carried by rail to New Jersey where it is shipped by ocean to London (water-rail-water operation).

roll-on, roll-off (Ro-Ro) A broad category of ships designed to load and discharge cargo which rolls on wheels. Broadly interpreted, this may include train ships, trailer ships, auto, truck and trailer ferries, and ships designed to carry military vehicles.

unitization The practice or technique of consolidating many small pieces of freight into a single unit for easier handling.

Warsaw Convention The informal name for The Convention for the Unification of Certain Rules Relating to International Carriage by Air, signed in Warsaw in 1929. An international multilateral treaty which regulates, in a uniform manner, the conditions of international transportation by air. Among other things it establishes the international liability of air carriers and establishes the monetary limits for loss, damage, and delay.

waybill A document prepared by a transportation line at the point of a shipment, showing the point or origin, destination, route, consignor, consignee, description of shipment and amount charged for the transportation service, and forwarded with the shipment, or direct by mail, to the agent at the transfer point or waybill destination.

have to devote a fair amount of time to research and to staying current with industry trends. Demands on the telecommunications infrastructure in the US—likely to be judged the most sophisticated in the world—are so heavy, along with technological advances so rapid, that service providers struggle to stay a step ahead of their customers.

AIR TRANSPORT

Spurred in part by the popularity of overnight and second-day delivery services, the 1980s were years of enormous growth for the air cargo industry in the United States. While growth has slowed somewhat since then, it continues at a steady pace. Early figures for 1994 showed a nearly 12 percent increase in the number of domestic shipments and 7 percent in air export shipments over the previous year. Many US airlines were caught off guard in the first half of 1992, during the Gulf War; passenger traffic fell and cargo volume continued to grow. Carriers and airports learned then that their capability and capacity for handling cargo had taken on a new importance and the upgrading of cargo facilities has become a much higher priority for many since then. For air cargo shipments worldwide over the next 20 years, Boeing Commercial Airplane Group forecasts an average growth of 6.5 percent, accompanied by an increase in international traffic: Boeing's prediction is that international shipments will represent 80 percent of total US revenue-ton-kilometers (RTKs) by 2013.

The United States has a large network of airports that handle both domestic and international cargo, but the industry has traditionally been dominated by the "Big Four": New York City's John F. Kennedy International (JFK), Los Angeles International (LAX), Chicago's O'Hare International (ORD), and Miami International (MIA). These four airports, plus FedEx's headquarters in Memphis, comprise five of the top seven cargo airports in the world, according to 1992 figures from Airports Council International. However, several factors have contributed to the growth of air cargo traffic at smaller airports in secondary markets in recent years: upgraded facilities; the growing importance of intermodal transport; new sorting facilities for the biggest air cargo handlers, FedEx and UPS; and the demand for just-in-time deliveries which obviate the need for large warehouse facilities. Some of the country's medium-sized airports, such as Portland (Oregon) International and Dulles International (in Washington, DC), have aggressively pursued upgrade projects which have attracted traffic and revenue. Compared with airports in large, congested cities, airports in secondary markets often find it easier to obtain federal funding, local support for expansion, and are also more likely to have access to land.

TOP US CARGO ARIPORTS

Airport	Metric Tons Cargo* 1993	% Change '92–'93
1. Memphis International	1,393,971	1.5%
2. John F. Kennedy International (New York, NY)	1,381,781	2.3
3. Los Angeles International	1,326,333	7.1
4. Standiford (Louisville, KY)	1,231,052	15.4
5. Miami International	1,178,691	17.6
6. Chicago O'Hare International	1,146,521	2.8
7. Newark International	696,751	18.5
8. Dallas/Ft. Worth International	757,619	4.8
9. San Francisco International	616,807	2.8
10. Hartsfield Atlanta International	614,758	12.7
11. Anchorage International	611,159	5.4
12. Indianapolis International	535,969	22.7
13. Dayton International	529,174	17.6
14. Oakland International	429,327	18.8
15. Philadelphia International	396,728	8.3

* Thousands of metric tons

Source: Airports Council International

Airports

New York/Newark The number one air cargo complex in the United States is the three-airport JFK International/LaGuardia/Newark system, managed by the Port Authority of New York/New Jersey. Almost all of the cargo business is at JFK or Newark, with JFK handling nearly 1.27 million metric tons (1.4 million short tons) in 1993—about 70 percent of the cargo moving through the New York metropolitan area. The area boasts the largest consumer market in the country, with about 17 million people, plus many more within range of local trucking companies. Also, JFK International can provide direct connecting flights to more domestic and international markets than any other US airport, making it a key transshipment point.

Lying 15 miles southeast of Manhattan, JFK International Airport occupies nearly as much land as the island of Manhattan. An extensive redevelopment program launched in the late 1980s has included a new air traffic control tower, a new parking garage, passenger and cargo facility upgrades, and a new quadrant roadway system. Nippon Cargo Airlines is constructing a US$40 million, 18,600 sq m (200,000 square foot) cargo terminal at JFK, and Japan Airlines is investing more than US$110 million in a 23,250 sq m (250,000 square foot) freight facility with an automated cargo handling system. Moreover, JFK is one of a limited number of airports equipped to handle live animal shipments (which it does at its VETPORT), and the Halmar/US Perishables Cargo Center is a US$31.5 million, 18,600 sq m (200,000 square foot) facility for temperature-sensitive shipments.

The top US carriers serving JFK are American, Delta, TWA, and United; virtually every other major and national US airline flies into JFK as well, as do more than 60 foreign flag lines. Although officially in second place to FedEx's home airfield of Memphis when ranked by cargo tonnage handled, JFK has long been the premier cargo airport in the US. However, the rising importance of Pacific Rim trade and growing competition from other East Coast airports has meant that the gap is closing quickly between JFK and Los Angeles International, with Miami following right behind.

Newark International Airport ranked seventh in 1993 in air cargo traffic, and in recent years its rate of growth has been tremendous—the amount of cargo handled in 1992 was up 21 percent from the previous year, and 1993 saw another 18.5 percent increase, with a significant portion of that from international business. Newark International's expanded handling facilities promise to continue to bring in new business. The brand-new 29,760 sq m (320,000 square foot) Southside Cargo Facility consists of 24,645 sq m (265,000 square feet) of warehouse space and 5,115 sq m (55,000 square feet) for offices. In addition, the Port Authority has been in negotiations with SAS and Continental to build a US$40 million, 270,000 square

foot cargo facility at the north end of the Newark airport; it could be finished as soon as 1997. The facility is expected to become a major alternative to European hubs. All major US airlines, a number of the nationals, a few regionals, and over a dozen foreign flag airlines fly into Newark.

Los Angeles Expanding Pacific Rim trade has helped Los Angeles International Airport (LAX) to increase moderately the amount of cargo handled in recent years. In 1993, LAX saw a 7.1 percent growth rate in air cargo, and the 1992 increase was 8.5 percent. As the premier gateway to Asia and the South Pacific, and like New York's JFK, LAX offers an enormous number of connections to airports throughout the US; about 50 foreign airlines fly into it. Because the immense, sometimes around-the-clock congestion on the roadways in the Los Angeles area has become a tremendous impediment to access for trucking companies, the airport is looking forward to the completion of a new freeway to ease the relentless traffic tie-ups.

Miami The rapid increase in Latin American trade has been a boon for Miami International Airport (MIA), which posted a 17.6 percent increase in cargo tonnage handled in 1993. Business with Latin America comprises three-quarters of Miami's international cargo business, and many of the smaller Caribbean, Central American, and South American countries use Miami as their sole US destination. Miami has become the major hub for moving cargo between the US or Europe and Latin American. Iberian Airlines, Lufthansa, and British Airways rely heavily on wide-body cargo flights to Miami, with connecting cargo service on smaller aircraft to South America.

US MAJOR AIR CARRIERS WITH INTERNATIONAL SERVICE

Airline	Main hub	Areas served	Ranking* 1993	FTKs* 1993
American	Dallas, TX	US, Europe, Asia, Australia, South and Central America	11	2,078
Continental	Houston, TX	US, Central and South America, East Asia	29	552
Delta	Atlanta, GA	North America, Europe, Asia	15	1,317
FedEx	Memphis, TN	Over 180 countries worldwide	1	5,630
Northwest	St. Paul, MN	North America, Asia	8	2,793
TWA	New York, NY	North America, Europe, Middle East	32	434
United	Chicago, IL	Europe, Asia, South Pacific, Central and South America	10	2,255
UPS	Atlanta, GA	Over 180 countries worldwide	26	597
USAir	Pittsburgh, PA	North America, Caribbean, Europe	45	227

* Millions of scheduled freight ton kilometers performed in 1993, as reported by the International Air Transport Association.
Source: Foreign Trade magazine

Miami's airport is undergoing a US$500 million renovation and development program for cargo facilities, replacing its original 50 year-old buildings. By 1997, Miami will have increased its warehouse space by nearly 3 million square feet, doubled its aircraft parking capacity enough to handle 80 wide-body freight planes, and have an annual handling capability of 3.653 million metric tons (4 million short tons) of cargo.

Chicago O'Hare International (ORD) has long been the busiest passenger airport in the US, handling more than 50 million passengers a year. American and United Airlines both have major hubs at O'Hare, and many other domestic airlines serve the airport, but only 17 foreign carriers—mostly European—fly into O'Hare. Because of Chicago's location in the Midwest, it has been an important transfer point for domestic passengers and cargo, but much less so for international flights. Although O'Hare posted a 12.9 percent increase in cargo tonnage in 1992, 1993 saw only 2.8 percent growth, while other smaller Midwestern airports, including Louisville, Indianapolis, Dayton, and Cincinnati, saw double digit growth.

Atlanta Hartsfield International Airport (ATL), the main hub for Delta Airlines, has seen enormous growth in its international business in recent years. Imports and exports are now a quarter of tonnage handled, compared to just 10 percent in the early 1980s; forecasters say that by the year 2000, that figure will grow to more than 50 percent. Airport management is targeting Latin America as the source of much of that increased business and would like to expand into handling more Asian flights as well.

Recent upgrades have given Hartsfield reason to expect continued success. A fifth runway will enable a phenomenal 100 total takeoffs and 100 total landings an hour. The first completely robotic cargo warehouse is operated at Hartsfield by Delta Airlines; it can handle more than 102,000 metric tons (112,500 short tons) of cargo annually. Twenty-four automated guided vehicles (AGVs) carry loads of up to 4,540 kilos (10,000 pounds) each between any of the 27 loading-unloading docks. The largest air cargo perishables facility in the world opened in 1992, with 3,900 sq m (42,000 square feet) of bonded, refrigerated warehouse space for such items as cut flowers, fruit, and vegetables; it also boasts 233 sq m (2,500 square feet) of freezer storage designed for meat and seafood products. An equine-livestock handling center is on-site as well, with space for pre-export examination, staff veterinarian offices, and many animal stalls.

Dallas/Ft. Worth Opened in 1974, the Dallas/Ft. Worth International Airport (DFW) was criticized for being too far from Dallas—32 km (20 miles) from downtown—unnecessary, and too expensive. But now the airport is the second busiest in the world (after Chicago's O'Hare), as measured by the number of passengers handled annually, and it was the eighth busiest cargo airport in the US in 1993, up from tenth place in 1992. Dallas' location, roughly equidistant from Los Angeles, Chicago, and New York, has given the city and its airport a solid advantage in attracting large distribution centers. Construction of a seventh runway began in 1994, and officials would like to build an eighth, which could raise overall air capacity for the entire nation by as much as 15 percent. Predictions call for the number of flights per day at DFW to increase from 2,200 to nearly 4,000 over the next several years.

Denver Originally hailed as the most modern, automated airport in the world, Denver International Airport (DIA) has turned into one of the biggest boondoggles in the history of the airline industry. It was to have opened just before Christmas 1993, replacing Stapleton International Airport; as it finally opened in early 1995, major airlines were announcing hefty surcharges on flights originating or terminating there in order to offset costs as much as five times those at the old airport. The 138 sq km (53 square mile) airport has been planned to handle 100 landings an hour, four times the capacity at Stapleton. The extra-long, well-spaced runways and the high-tech traffic controls have been designed to handle landings even under the severe weather conditions that often hit this Rocky Mountain city. In 1992, DIA managers were predicting a 25 percent jump in the amount of cargo handled in the first year of operation; it remains to be seen whether the up-to-the-minute facilities can overcome the steep costs of operating at this airport. Even with outmoded facilities, Stapleton International has seen healthy gains in the amount of cargo handled annually, up 7.8 percent in 1992 and 11.6 percent in 1993.

In late 1993 it became clear that the highly publicized automatic baggage handling system debuting at Denver International was crippled with enormous problems; the airport's opening was delayed several times. As time passed, other serious questions arose about the costs and management of the airport's construction. Many of these additional costs will be passed along to the airlines operating at DIA, who are, in turn, beginning to charge higher ticket and cargo prices. Flights into or out of DIA may cost as much as US$40 more than they did into Stapleton, and United Airlines is reportedly paying as much to DIA for annual operations as it is to all other airports in the US combined. United, Continental, UPS, and FedEx have long used Denver as a major hub; it remains to be seen whether higher operating costs will drive away either them or their customers in large numbers.

Air Carriers

Unlike many countries, the US does not have a national flag carrier—a number of competing private firms among the airlines classified by the Department of Transportation (DOT) as "majors" provide the majority of international and domestic service, and there are numerous other lines classified as national, medium regional, or small regional carriers. Of the 11 major carriers, 9 were among the top 50 air freight carriers worldwide in 1993, according to statistics from the International Air Transport Association.

The airline industry has been buffeted by major losses in the 1990s, following a period of upheaval during the 1980s as the US government deregulated most aspects of business operations. The cutthroat competition for passengers and cargo has led to relatively low prices, extremely complicated and variable pricing structures, and bankruptcy court for several carriers. A few major airlines, most notably Eastern and PanAm, have even gone out of business in recent years. Although the overall prognosis for the industry is somewhat rosier than a couple of years ago, few would doubt that more reorganization and consolidation will occur in the second half of the 1990s.

The 11 major US carriers consist of 7 airlines that provide both passenger and freight service internationally (American, Continental, Delta, Northwest, TWA, United, and USAir), 2 that provide passenger and freight service domestically (America West and Southwest), and 2 that are freight-only international carriers (FedEx and UPS). All of the majors serve a large number of points in the United States, most of them in every region. About 92 percent of the US total revenue passenger kilometers (RPKs) and 37 percent of the world's is comprised of the US majors' traffic. International cargo makes up 45 percent of the total cargo carried by the US majors.

Some other important US all-cargo carriers include: Airborne Express, Air Transport International, American International Air, Amerijet, Arrow, Atlas, Burlington Air Express, Challenge (Miami), DHL Airways, Emery Worldwide, Evergreen, Fine, Florida West, Martinaire, Million, Mountain Air Cargo, Northern Air Cargo, Omni Air Express, Patriot, Polar Air Cargo, Roadway Global Air, Trans Air Link, Wrangler, and Zantop. Many of these carriers provide service to a number of international points in addition to their US service.

WATER TRANSPORT

The US water transportation industry consists of deep sea transportation of US foreign trade and domestic cargo, as well as shipments of cargo in the Great Lakes, the St. Lawrence Seaway, the inland waterways, and local waters. General cargo operations are usually performed by vessels operating as common carriers in regularly scheduled liner service, while dry bulk cargoes more often move in specialized vessels and liquid bulk cargoes are carried in tankers and tank barges.

In 1993, 35.8 percent of US exports (by customs value) left the country on vessels, and 53.5 percent of US imports arrived by vessel (as compared with 29.1 percent of exports or 20.6 percent of imports departing or arriving, respectively, by air). When figured by weight, of course, there are substantially more goods shipped by vessel, since it is the transport mode of necessity for bulk commodities.

Ports *

The trend toward intermodal shipments and the growing importance of international trade to the US economy, particularly with Asia and Latin America, has had a major impact on ports, their facilities, and the services they offer. About 90 percent of all steamship general cargo is shipped in containers which can easily be transferred from ships to trucks, trains, barges, and sometimes airplanes. Ports like

TOP US CONTAINER PORTS

	City	Container* traffic 1993	% change 1992-1993
1.	Los Angeles, CA	415,714	1%
2.	Long Beach, CA	412,074	23
3.	New York, NY	331,796	4
4.	Seattle, WA	205,534	8
5.	Oakland, CA	193,642	6
6.	Charleson, SC	144,382	5
7.	Tacoma, WA	138,168	0
8.	Hampton Roads, VA	131,222	-2
9.	Miami, FL	119,668	4
10.	Savannah, GA	100,925	5
11.	Houston, TX	100,693	25
12.	Baltimore, MD	68,513	-6
13.	Port Everglades, FL	51,877	4
14.	Portland, OR	47,684	23
15.	New Orleans, LA	44,836	4

* Number of TEUs handled (twenty-foot equivalent units).

Source: Ports Imports/Exports Reporting Service

* Port facility information in this section is excerpted from Ports of the World (15th ed.), copyright © 1994 CIGNA Property and Casualty Co., reprinted with permission from CIGNA Property and Casualty Companies.

Tacoma, Washington, have risen from relative obscurity to become major players in the past 10 to 15 years because of strategic locations and upgraded facilities.

Four of the nation's busiest container ports are located on the West Coast: Los Angeles, Long Beach, Seattle, and Oakland. Ports along the Gulf Coast are seeing a major upsurge in business as traffic increases between the US and Mexico and the US and Latin America. Traditionally busy ports like San Francisco and Boston have lost a great deal of business because of an inability to provide efficient intermodal facilities and transportation links. The Port of New York/New Jersey—once the leading container port in the US despite high costs and inefficiency—has slipped to third place and is up against stiff competition not even envisioned a decade ago.

Pacific Coast Ports The Ports of Los Angeles and Long Beach have come to comprise the nation's top port area. Together they handle half of all cargo moving through West Coast ports, and half of all cargo unloaded at Los Angeles ports is destined for local delivery points. Both are deep water ports, which places them among the few Pacific ports that can handle the largest container ships; more than 30 container steamship lines call on the Port of Los Angeles regularly. Some of the access problems that have hurt New York in recent years are also becoming major issues in the Los Angeles area, although direct rail links to the terminals are now under construction. In northern California, the Port of Oakland continues to draw business away from San Francisco, which has struggled with poor access to interstate highways and rail lines, labor disputes, and outdated facilities. The San Francisco port operates at only 3 percent of its shipping capacity, and 92 percent of the container cargo in the Bay Area was handled by the Port of Oakland in 1994.

The main Pacific Northwest ports are in Portland, Oregon; Seattle, Washington; and Tacoma, Washington. Tacoma's growth in the last decade has made it the seventh busiest container port in the US. The port has a rail link, enabling it to shift merchandise from ships to trains in eight hours—a third of the time that the rival port of Seattle once needed for the same task. Seattle port managers have responded by improving their rail links and by spending over US$200 million to expand terminals and add more modern cranes and other equipment by 1998. Trade with Asia accounts for three-quarters of total revenues for the Port of Portland; half of its tonnage is from trade with Japan, while the balance is largely with Thailand, China, and Singapore. Automobile, bulk, and break bulk shipments comprise the majority of shipments, but containers are the fastest-growing sector, with a 24 percent increase in 1992 and a 10 percent increase in 1993.

Brief descriptions of the top Pacific Coast ports follow; other major ports include: Anchorage, Alaska; Portland, Oregon; Richmond, California; Sacramento, California; San Diego, California; San Francisco, California; and Stockton, California.

Los Angeles, California
Transportation Service—Truck, rail, and barge.
Cargo Storage—Covered: 167,400 sq m (1.8 million square feet). Open: 159 hectares (392 acres). Refrigerated and freezer storage: 4,000 sq m (43,000 square feet).
Special Cranes—Container, 37 with 36.3 metric ton (40 short ton) capacity.
Air Cargo—Los Angeles International Airport: 30 km (18 miles).
Cargo Handling—Port equipment handles liquid and dry bulk, containerized and general cargo. Chief commodities imported include machinery, petroleum, and chemicals. 19 tanker terminals and 2 Ro-Ro off-loading points are available at port.
General—Two new terminals, one for coal, the other for containers, are currently under construction as part of a major capital development program. Los Angeles enjoys a moderate climate with 51 cm (20 inches) of rain annually, most of which falls during winter months.

Long Beach, California
Transportation Service—Rail and truck.
Cargo Storage—Covered: 139,500 sq m (1.5 million square feet). Open: 304 hectares (750 acres). Refrigeration outlets available.
Special cranes—Heavy lift, 249.4 metric ton (275 short ton) capacity. Container, 26 with 40.6 metric ton (40 long ton) capacity.
Air Cargo—Long Beach Regional Airport: 8 km (5 miles), provides limited cargo connections; Los Angeles International Airport: 64 km (40 miles), offers more complete services.
Cargo Handling—Containerized, liquid, dry bulk, and general cargo can all be handled at port. Special equipment is also available for automobile, lumber, newsprint, fruit, salt, and cement handling. Seven ore and bulk terminals, six tanker terminals, and three Ro-Ro off-loading points are available in the area.
General—Average temperatures range from 12°C to 23°C (53°F to 74°F). Heavy rains can be expected during the winter months, with annual accumulation of approximately 51 cm (20 inches). A 60 hectare (147 acre) expansion of pier "J" was completed in late 1992.

Oakland, California
Transportation Service—Truck, rail, and barge.
Cargo Storage—Covered: 53,555 sq m (575,858 square feet). Open: 217 hectares (535 acres). Refrigerated: available in nearby private facilities.
Special Cranes—Heavy lift capacity, one with 450 long ton maximum. Container, 24 with 45.72 metric

ton (45 long ton) maximum.

Air Cargo—Oakland International Airport: 6 km (4 miles).

Cargo Handling—Containerized, bulk, and general cargo can all be handled by existing port equipment. Oakland's chief export commodities include synthetic resins, pulp, waste paper, fruits, and vegetables.

General—Temperatures range from 2°C to 37°C (36°F to 98°F), and rainfall averages 56 cm (22 inches) annually. Plans are under way to develop a new US$38 million container terminal. The port has nine container and two neo-bulk terminals.

Tacoma, Washington

Transportation Service—Truck, rail, and barge.

Cargo Storage—Covered: 260,400 sq m (2.8 million square feet). Open: 200 hectares (500 acres). Refrigerated Storage: 56,000 cu m (2 million cubic feet).

Special Cranes—Heavy lift, maximum 181.4 metric tons (200 short tons). Container, 12 with 45.4 metric ton (50 short ton) capacity.

Air Cargo—Seattle-Tacoma International Airport: 26 km (16 miles).

Cargo Handling—Liquid, dry bulk, containerized, and general cargo can be handled at port. Tacoma's chief commodities are lumber, logs, grains, bulk aluminum, and automobiles. One tanker terminal, two ore and bulk and two Ro-Ro off-loading points can be utilized for specialized needs.

General—Temperatures in Tacoma range from 1°C to 29°C (33°F to 85°F), and annual rainfall is approximately 99 cm (39 inches).

Seattle, Washington

Transportation Services—Truck, rail, and barge.

Cargo Storage—Covered: 154,380 sq m (1.66 million square feet). Open: 153 hectares (378 acres). Refrigerated: 9.7 cu m (345 cubic feet).

Special Cranes—Several floating cranes with 544 metric ton (600 short ton) capacity. Container, 26 with 46.3 metric ton (51 short ton) capacity.

Air Cargo—Seattle-Tacoma International Airport: 24 km (15 miles).

Cargo Handling—Containerized, bulk, and general cargo can all be handled by existing port equipment. Forestry, agriculture, and general containerized cargoes are the chief commodities through Seattle. One grain terminal and one Ro-Ro off-loading platform are available.

General—Seattle's temperatures range from 1°C to 29°C (33°F to 85°F), and rainfall averages 102 cm (40 inches) per annum. Seattle's expansion plans include the construction of additional chill warehouses.

Atlantic Coast Ports The Port of New York/New Jersey was long the premier port for both the Atlantic Coast and the United States. But in recent years the twin ports of Los Angeles and Long Beach have taken over the top spots, and since the mid-1980s New York/New Jersey has lost business to secondary cites because of high labor and land costs, expensive carrier service, roadway congestion, and poor rail links. Progress is being made on the latter, and pricing policies have been adjusted as well. The port continues to be served by more than 100 steamship lines, and efforts are being made to improve both facilities and the level of service. However, some problems endemic to the Port of New York/New Jersey cannot be addressed by the Port Authority, and the changed trade flow from Europe to more Asian and Latin American destinations has meant that some of the shift away from New York will be permanent. Still, the New York area is the largest US consumer market and its primary business center, making the port attractive to many shippers despite the cost and logistical hassles.

Charleston, South Carolina, is the main southeastern port; its proactive approach in upgrading facilities and seeking out market share has worked well. Charleston was the sixth busiest container port in the country in 1993, considered by many to be the most efficient, due to computerized customs clearance, modern cranes that cut loading and unloading time, and attractive shipping schedules. As much as 41 percent of Charleston's port business came from Northeast Asia at one time—that number has declined to 25 percent—but the Southeast Asian countries of Singapore, Malaysia, Thailand, and India are providing some of the replacement. Charleston is receiving intense competition from ports in both Savannah, Georgia, and Hampton Roads (Norfolk), Virginia. The latter has spent heavily in recent years for on-dock rail links and an aggressive marketing plan, while a nearby low-cost inland trade zone is another attractive lure to carriers.

A number of Atlantic and Gulf Coast ports—chief among them the port of Miami—are already reaping benefits of increased trade with Mexico, Latin America, and the Caribbean Basin. Venezuela alone accounts for 18 percent of Miami's business, and the port is seeing increased traffic from Chile and the west coast countries of South America.

Detailed summaries of facilities at the top Atlantic Coast ports follow; other major ports on the Atlantic include: Baltimore, Maryland; Boston, Massachusetts; Hampton Roads (Norfolk), Virginia; Philadelphia, Pennsylvania; Wilmington, Delaware; Jacksonville, Florida; Port Everglades, Florida; Richmond, Virginia; and Wilmington, North Carolina.

New York, New York

Transportation Service—Truck, rail, and barge.

Cargo Storage—Covered: 465,000 sq m (5 million square feet). Open: 932 hectares (2,300 acres).

Special Cranes—Heavy lift capacity, 544.2 metric tons (600 short tons). Container, 48 with 45.72 metric ton (45 short ton) capacity.

Air Cargo—John F. Kennedy (JFK) International

Airport: 16 km (10 miles). LaGuardia Airport or Newark International Airport: 24 km (15 miles).

Cargo Handling—Containerized, bulk, and general cargo can all be adequately handled through port. New York's major imports include machinery, petroleum, chemicals, and textiles. Specialized cargo handling is available at ore and bulk cargo berths, 39 tanker and 2 liquefied gas terminals and an orange juice concentrate facility. Some berths have Ro-Ro ramps.

General—New York experiences a four-season climate with temperatures ranging from –12°C to 35°C (10°F to 95°F). Rainfall averages 102 to 127 cm (40 to 50 inches) annually. The New York/New Jersey Port Authority is expanding its dockside rail facilities, and there is a major warehouse renovation program underway. A 6,510 sq m (70,000 square foot) perishable cargo center opened at JFK in 1992.

Charleston, South Carolina

Transportation Service—Truck, rail, and barge.

Cargo Storage—Covered: 190,820 sq m (2,051,829 square feet). Open: 177 hectares (437 acres). Refrigerated: 42,450 cu m (1.52 million cubic feet).

Special Cranes—Heavy lift capacity, 1 crane to 430.8 metric tons (475 short tons); 20 other container and gantry cranes with capacities ranging from 27.2 to 136 metric tons (30 to 150 short tons).

Air Cargo—Charleston International Airport: 19 km (12 miles).

Cargo Handling—Containerized, bulk, and general cargo are all adequately handled by existing port equipment. Ro-Ro loading areas are available at designated berths. Equipment is also available for handling wood and paper products.

General—Charleston's average annual temperature is 11°C (51°F). Winter temperatures will occasionally drop below freezing. Annual rainfall averages 132 cm (52 inches). Charleston has plans to add 419 m (1,373 linear feet) of berthing and 26 paved hectares (65 acres) for container storage at the Wando Terminal.

Miami, Florida

Transportation Service—Truck, rail, and barge.

Cargo Service—Covered: 55,800 sq m (600,000 square feet). Open: 81 hectares (200 acres). Refrigerated: 4,500 cu m (160,714 cubic feet).

Special Cranes—Heavy lift capacity, 2 cranes to 181.4 metric tons (200 short tons), 17 other container, gantry, and mobile cranes, with capacities ranging from 36.3 to 127 metric tons (40 to 140 short tons).

Air Cargo—Miami International Airport: 13 km (8 miles) west.

Cargo Handling—Handling equipment is adequate for general cargo traffic. Ro-Ro services are provided with eight off-loading platforms in the port area. Special equipment can be obtained for handling newsprint. All bulk cargo, nuclear products, and some specific chemicals are banned from the port.

General—Miami's new automated cargo clearance system is now operational. Temperatures range from 10°C to 35°C (50°F to 95°F). Annual rainfall averages 152 cm (60 inches). Rainstorms can cause flooding. Dredging is underway to increase the maximum draft for the port to 13 m (42 feet). Also, the port is planning to add two 50.8 metric ton (50 long ton) capacity cranes for their Lummus Island facility.

Hampton Roads (Norfolk), Virginia

Transportation Service—Truck, rail, and barge.

Cargo Storage—Covered: 180,420 sq m (1,940,000 square feet). Refrigerated: 11,620 cu m (415,000 cubic feet). Container storage for 33,900 units including 94 reefer outlets.

Special Cranes—Heavy lift capacity, 317.5 metric tons (350 short tons). Container, 21 with maximum 165.1 metric ton (182 short ton) capacity including Kone dual hoist cranes rated at 50 containers/hour.

Air Cargo—Norfolk International Airport: 13 km (8 miles). Patrick Henry International Airport: 16 km (10 miles) north.

Cargo Handling—Containerized, break bulk, general cargo, including fruit, and bulk cargo, can all be handled by existing cargo equipment. Specialized cargo handling is provided at 9 ore and bulk cargo facilities, 11 tanker terminals, 1 liquefied petroleum gas terminal and 5 Ro-Ro off-loading platforms. The port operates an inland facility in northern Virginia serviced by rail and truck. It is an intermodal container transfer facility handling 1,000 containers per month.

General—Temperatures range from –4°C to 29°C (25°F to 85°F) and the average rainfall is 61 cm (24 inches). Hampton Roads is continuing a modernization program, which includes the expansion of berths and facilities, channel dredging up to 18 m (60 feet) to handle deep draft colliers and improved coal handling facilities.

Savannah, Georgia

Transportation Service—Truck, rail, and barge.

Cargo Storage—Total warehouse: 223,200 sq m (2,400,000 square feet). Open: 371 hectares (916 acres). Refrigerated: 35,700 cu m (1,275,000 cubic feet).

Special Cranes—Heavy lift, maximum 158.7 metric tons (175 short tons); 14 other gantry and container cranes with capacities ranging from 31.7 to 90.7 metric tons (35 to 100 short tons).

Air Cargo—Savannah International Airport: 5 km (3 miles) from the Garden City Terminal, providing limited service.

Cargo Handling—Containerized, liquid, and dry bulk cargo can all be handled by existing port equipment. Six ore and bulk cargo terminals, seven tanker terminals, five Ro-Ro off-loading platforms and a liquefied gas terminal are available.

US PORTS

OF ENTRY

LEGEND

- ● PORT OF ENTRY
- ★ DISTRICT OFFICE (also Port of Entry)
- ★ REGIONAL HEADQUARTERS (also District Office and Port of Entry)
- —— STATE BOUNDARY
- ▬▬ DISTRICT BOUNDARY
- ▬▬ REGIONAL BOUNDARY
- ■ User Fee Airports

PRECLEARANCE STATIONS

NORTH CENTRAL REGION
Montreal
Toronto
Winnipeg
Calgary
Edmonton
Vancouver

SOUTHEAST REGION
Bermuda
Freeport
Nassau

PUERTO RICO – VIRGIN I.

AGUADILLA
MAYAGUEZ
GUANICA
PONCE
JOBOS
HUMACAO
SAN JUAN
FAJARDO
CHARLOTTE AMALIE
CRUZ BAY
CORAL BAY
CHRISTIANSTED
FREDERIKSTED

Included in Southeast

General—Temperatures average between 11°C and 27°C (51°F and 81°F). Winter temperatures can drop below freezing. Rainfall averages 124 cm (49 inches) per year. The Georgia Ports Authority has 891 hectares (2,200 acres) of waterfront property for development and expansion into the 1990s.

Gulf Coast Ports As a regional group, the major Gulf Coast ports have seen the most rapid growth in recent years, with Houston, New Orleans, and Gulfport all posting double digit increases in the number of containers handled annually. The orientation of these ports is largely toward Mexico, Central America, and South America, although all receive shipments from many other regions. The passage of NAFTA has already had a major impact on the amount of traffic between Mexico and the ports along the Texas, Mississippi, and Louisiana coasts.

While New Orleans has seen major increases in containerized shipments, it accounts for only about one-third of their business, with the rest primarily break bulk. New Orleans' approach is to continue to improve facilities that will accommodate a wide range of shippers and virtually any commodity, from steel to coffee to manufactured goods. Six major rail lines from all directions converge in New Orleans, the city is the gateway to the Mississippi River, and the port is well served by more than 50 common carrier truck lines.

Houston has the largest container facility on the Gulf Coast: Barber's Cut terminal, which is currently undergoing a US$90.3 million renovation. Most recent capital improvements have gone into the port's container services and rail access.

Details on facilities at the Ports of New Orleans and Houston follow; other major ports on the Gulf Coast include: Beaumont, Texas; Corpus Christi, Texas; Galveston, Texas; Gulfport, Mississippi; Lake Charles, Louisiana; Mobile, Alabama; Port Arthur, Texas; and Tampa, Florida.

Houston, Texas
Transportation Service—Truck, rail, and barge. LASH and Seebee service is also available.

Cargo Storage—Covered: 148,800 sq m (1.6 million square feet). Open: 154 hectares (380 acres). Refrigerated: 223,200 sq m (2.4 million square feet) located nearby.

Special Cranes—Heavy lift, 2 floating with 453.5 metric tons (500 short ton) capacity. Container, 11 with 40.6 metric ton (40 long ton) capacity.

Air Cargo—Hobby: 8 km (5 miles); and Intercontinental Airport: 64 km (40 miles).

Cargo Handling—Port equipment handles liquid, dry bulk, containerized, and general cargo. One dry bulk terminal with five grain elevators, 26 tanker terminals, two liquefied gas terminals, and two Ro-Ro platforms are available. Facilities are available to adequately handle more than 50 dry bulk cargoes.

General—Temperature extremes are 0°C to 38°C (32°F to 100°F). However, the overall climate is mild.

New Orleans, Louisiana
Transportation Service—Truck, rail, and barge.

Cargo Storage—Covered: 558,000 sq m (6 million square feet). Open: 1.21 million sq m (13 million square feet). Refrigerated: 34,410 sq m (370,000 square feet).

Special Cranes—Mobile cranes to 725.6 metric tons (800 short tons) capacity and floating cranes to 634.9 metric tons (700 short tons) for heavy lift. Container: 5.4 to 36.3 metric tons (6 to 40 short tons).

Air Cargo—New Orleans International Airport ("Moisant"): 16 km (10 miles).

Cargo Handling—Containerized, bulk, and general cargo can all be handled by existing port equipment. Iron and steel comprise 60 percent of general cargo imports. Six ore and bulk and five Ro-Ro platforms are available in the port area.

General—Semitropical climate exists, with flooding possible during the spring.

Inland Ports Inland ports are not heavily used by international shippers for several reasons. While some of the major ports on the Great Lakes and St. Lawrence Seaway are equipped to handle containers, the majority of the cargoes handled are domestic bulk shipments, and are largely tied to the steel making industry. Less than 3 percent of US imports (by customs value) arrive at Great Lakes ports, and a much smaller volume is exported from these ports. In addition, many of the Great Lakes and St. Lawrence Seaway ports may be inaccessible for several months in the winter because of ice. Ports along the Mississippi and other inland waterways are reached almost exclusively by barges operated by US companies.

The most important inland ports are at Albany, New York; Buffalo, New York; Chicago, Illinois; Cleveland, Ohio; Detroit, Michigan; Lake Superior, Minnesota; Erie, Pennsylvania; Green Bay, Wisconsin; Milwaukee, Wisconsin; and Toledo, Ohio.

Shipping Firms
The vast majority of international shipments to or from the US on oceangoing vessels are carried on foreign flag ships. Only about 4 percent of total cargo tonnage originating from or destined for the US in 1992 was carried on US-flag deep-sea vessels—although, measured by value instead of weight, this represented about 15 percent. This is due to the fact that most US-flag ships involved in foreign trade are engaged in liner service and carry comparatively higher-value cargo. There are a relatively small number of US-flag companies involved in international trade: American President Lines operates line-haul containerships and feeders in the Pacific Basin and the Persian Gulf, Lykes Bros. Steamship Co. operates routes worldwide, and Sea-Land Service serves

64 countries on five major container trade routes. However, many foreign-flag shipping lines serve US ports. Some of the largest are: Evergreen, Maersk, Hanjin, NYK Line, Hyundai Merchant, Orient Overseas, "K" Line, and Mitsui OSK Line.

OVERLAND TRANSPORT: TRUCKING AND RAILROADS

The US boasts the most highly developed network of roadways in the world, although development of roads and the trucking industry has been at the expense of railroads, which are sometimes less efficient, more expensive, and in poorer condition than those in many other countries. From the mid-1950s through the early 1970s, the US saw an intensive period of road construction as the interstate highway system was developed and many connecting state roads were built or greatly improved. The growing congestion of urban areas, the rising value of real estate, high construction costs, and environmental concerns have virtually put a stop to major road building projects in the US in the past two decades. The biggest current concerns with the US road and rail infrastructures involve the ongoing maintenance of existing facilities, particularly thousands of bridges across the country which have fallen into disrepair.

Trucking The trucking industry is the largest provider of US freight services when measured by revenues, in part because trucks tend to carry higher-value goods than do railroads or barge lines. The trucking industry has seen dramatic changes recently, and this will continue for the next few years. The major shifts are due to increased demand for shorter routes with more frequent, reliable service and to the increasing use of information technology to track both vehicles and shipments. Moreover, NAFTA is expected to have a broad impact as more Canadian, Mexican, and US carriers are permitted to make cross-border door-to-door deliveries all over North America. More and more trucking firms are handling the full spectrum of transportation logistics for both domestic and international shipments, either by providing the services themselves or by contracting with other firms.

The trucking industry is comprised of three main service categories: truckload (TL), less-than-truckload (LTL), and small package. The largest carrier market in terms of tonnage, TL freight is typically hauled directly from sender to receiver. As defined by the Interstate Commerce Commission (ICC), LTL traffic consists of shipments weighing less than 4,540 kilos (10,000 pounds), and it usually involves several steps: local pickup, sorting at a terminal facility, line-haul, sorting at a destination terminal, and local delivery. Small package service encompasses the

two- to seven-day ground service (long dominated by UPS) and the next-day delivery market, led by FedEx. The industry can also be divided into three other groupings: ICC regulated trucking, non-ICC intercity trucking, and non-ICC local trucking. The 53,000 ICC carriers account for nearly 30 percent of total annual revenues generated by the industry, non-ICC intercity a bit more than 30 percent, and non-ICC local about 40 percent.

Lines between businesses engaged in the trucking industry and other transportation services have blurred tremendously in recent years—air express carrier FedEx owns and operates an enormous truck fleet, while the package delivery giant United Parcel Service (UPS) was classified in 1993 by the Federal Aviation Administration (FAA) as a major air carrier. The LTL carrier Roadway Express joined the air freight industry in 1993 with their company called Roadway Global Air (RGA), and small package carrier Emery Worldwide has entered into an LCL-shipping partnership with CF Motor Freight. Even when long-haul shipments are by rail, air, or oceangoing vessel, most shipments are carried on trucks at some stage of the transport, so the trend is toward industry partnerships that make the transfer of goods onto and off of trucks ever more efficient. Trucking companies and railroads, once fierce competitors, have increasingly come to see each other as partners, as both sides recognize that one cannot survive without the other.

Railroads Both revenues and the amount of freight carried by rail lines declined in the early 1980s, but after a spate of mergers that quickly reduced the number of Class I line-hauling companies from 40 to 20 (and then to only a dozen by 1993), revenues and tonnage both began to rise again. Railroads are now offering significant competition to the trucking companies, particularly with the introduction of doublestack service in 1984, which has drawn business away from a number of the long-haul routes. Rail intermodal traffic more than doubled between 1980 and 1992, increasing from 3.1 million trailers and containers to 6.7 million. Hundreds of short line railroads, which own nearly a quarter of the 283,180 km (176,000 miles) of railroad track in the US, are also offering competition to the truckers, linking US ports to manufacturing sites and the major railroads.

Railroads in the US are still battling a negative image, since service was poor and rates inflexible for years. Government deregulation of pricing, improved attention to customer service, technological advances in logistics management, and the growth of intermodal transport have all given major boosts to the freight railroads, resulting in renewed interest in their services since the mid-1980s. Rail traffic and tonnage should continue to grow, albeit modestly, for the next several years; intermodal traffic is the fastest-growing area. The primary source of rail traffic is still bulk commodities, with coal accounting for 40 percent of total rail tonnage. Some of the other important commodities carried by railroads are: chemicals, lumber and wood products, paper, metallic ores, primary metal products, motor vehicles and parts, stone, clay, and glass.

At press time, the Santa Fe Pacific Corp. railroad was set to be acquired by Burlington Northern. If the deal is approved by the Interstate Commerce Commission (and the expectation is that the ICC will give it the go-ahead by the end of 1995), it will become the nation's largest railroad, with a 51,500 km (32,000 mile) unified route system that will link the Pacific Coast with the Gulf Coast and the Midwest. This transaction may also signal renewed interest in merging railroads: Union Pacific (UP) had originally been set to acquire Santa Fe, but the merger of its two rivals will take UP out of the top spot. However, freight rail service is already heavily concentrated in the hands of a few companies. More than 75 percent of revenue ton-kilometers (RTKs) generated by US railroads came from six railroads: Burlington Northern; Union Pacific; CSX Transportation; Norfolk Southern Corp.; and the Atchison, Topeka & Santa Fe Railway Company.

The increasing importance of foreign trade to the US economy and the passage of NAFTA are both having an impact on freight rail service in several areas; US railroads have been forging connections with Canadian and Mexican rail and barge lines in order to provide more seamless cross-border service. Within a few years rail and trucking companies based in any of the three North American nations will be permitted to market their own services and use their own equipment across borders. There are still some logistical and regulatory issues to resolve, particularly with regard to safety, but it will certainly mean increased options for anyone shopping for transportation services.

COMMUNICATIONS

Telecommunications

The US market offers businesses a wide array of services and equipment for telecommunications, so wide that many newly established US operations of foreign companies find the choices confusing and difficult to explain to their overseas counterparts. Selection of appropriate services and equipment is essential both for profitable operations and to provide US customers with the ease of communication they have come to expect from suppliers and business partners.

Telecommunications in the US, unlike in most countries, is completely managed by private com-

QUESTIONS WHEN SELECTING A LONG DISTANCE COMPANY

- Will the company agree in writing not to raise rates for a specific period?
- Does the company provide personal service 24 hours a day?
- Does the company refrain from offering employees enticements, such as frequent flier miles or contributions to special organizations, which are incorporated into higher rates?
- Does the company offer useful specialized services such as teleconferencing or foreign language services?
- Can the company provide good references?
- Is the bill easy to read and check?
- Does the company offer any support or point of contact in your headquarters country?
- Can the company explain the taxes paid for long distance and international service, and can it arrange for tax exempt certification if your company qualifies?
- Will the company agree in writing that it will not require subscription of all listed lines?
- Does the written rate sheet for your calling plan match the actual charges that appear on your bill?

panies; customers may choose and combine the offerings of different suppliers. Over the past 15 or so years, the US telecommunications industry has transformed from being the exclusive province of a few government-regulated companies—AT&T and the so-called "Baby Bells"—to the current environment of nearly unrestricted competition. An important exception is that in most areas only one company has a license to provide basic local telephone service; rates for this service are normally set by state government agencies. Since these local telephone companies are prohibited from offering long distance or international telephone services, all businesses use the services of at least two, and sometimes more, telephone companies.

Local Telephone Services Because the service area covered by local telephone companies is often determined by state lines, a metropolitan region like New York or Philadelphia that lies across more than one state line may be served by more than one company. (Some companies do serve more than one state, but this is most common in sparsely populated areas.) This can, of course, be somewhat confusing, since various local phone companies provide services that are similar, but not necessarily uniform, and rate structures can differ quite a bit. Local measured rate service provides access to other calling services and charges a small amount per minute for each local call. Charges typically range from US$0.01 per minute for calls within in the same city to US$0.35 for calls to cities more than 150 kilometers (93 miles) away. Local measured rate service typically costs about US$20 per month, per line. In general, businesses subscribe to one line for every two employees, but this figure varies greatly depending on the relative importance of telecommunications to a particular firm's operations. Telephone lines can be ordered only from the local telephone company and its authorized sales representatives.

Local phone companies also provide some special services for business customers. These include private line services (which connect offices in different locations with unlimited usage for a fixed monthly fee) and Wide Area Telephone Service (WATS, which provides local calling services to all callers at a given location for an hourly rate usually much lower than the per minute rate). Discount plans may be available, but are not automatic and should be requested whenever placing an order for new service.

Long Distance and International Services There are more than 1,000 providers of long distance services in the US. The three largest long distance telephone companies—AT&T, MCI, and US Sprint—serve 85 percent of the market and usually charge the highest basic rates. Other carriers may provide specialized services which focus on supporting particular types of customers, such as small businesses, educational institutions, or international organizations. These companies offer lower rates with comparable service, but often do not have nationwide networks of service centers to provide local support.

By far the largest long distance company is AT&T, and it was the sole long distance carrier in the US before deregulation in 1984. Because of numerous lawsuit settlements, referred to as consent decrees, there are some residual limitations on AT&T's offerings. The second largest long distance company is MCI, which offers a wide range of innovative marketing programs, but its network of microwave and satellite communications does not always meet the standards of customers who prefer state-of-the-art telecommunications transmission. In recent years MCI has entered into a marketing partnership with British Telecom. The third largest long distance company, US Sprint, offers a nationwide network of fiber-optic transmission facilities, but it lacks the capacity of its larger competitors. Subject to government approval, US Sprint is expected to enter into a marketing partnership with France Telecom and Deutsche Bundespost Telecom. Note that specific services of all these carriers and many smaller car-

riers are often available at lower cost from independent brokers.

While basic rates for long distance service in the United States are the lowest in the world, they are increasing rapidly. Between July 1993 and June 1994 alone, AT&T's basic rates increased by nearly 15 percent, and its largest competitors matched these price increases. The highest cost per minute for domestic long distance service charged by a major telephone company at the end of 1994 was US$0.38 per minute. The average per minute cost was US$0.22; specialized telephone companies frequently will offer rates of US$0.15 per minute or less. The rates for international service vary even more widely. For example, at the end of 1994 the highest published rate for a one-minute call from the US to Australia was US$3.10 with AT&T (from New York), compared with the lowest published rate of US$0.34 with ITS Passport (from San Francisco). Remember that relatively few consumers end up paying full list rates.

Companies with monthly telephone costs larger than US$1,000 might wish to consider choosing at least two long distance companies for different types of usage. Many carriers will be able to suggest a variety of programs and discount plans to help reduce costs and better serve a company's needs. There are over 100 commonly used plans offering various combinations of discounts for different types of calls, for calls to specific telephone numbers or areas, or for calls made during certain times of the day. New business operations should generally avoid discount programs that require a long-term commitment (so-called "term plans") because the field is so competitive that a firm may find it advantageous to change within only a few months to another carrier or a different program offered by the same carrier.

Mobile Telecommunications Services About 24 million people in the US are cellular telephone users, and the number is increasing rapidly. Every major metropolitan area in the US is served by two competing cellular telephone companies. Cellular telephone instruments cost between US$100 and US$600 to purchase, and monthly service charges range from US$20 to US$50. Per minute charges for both incoming and outgoing calls on cellular telephones average US$0.30, and the average cellular bill is US$58 per month. Lower rates are often available to business callers through specialized service providers who buy cellular service at volume discounts and then resell it. Each cellular telephone is assigned a telephone number similar to a fixed line number, from which the caller may make as well as receive calls. Normal service covers only a particular metropolitan area; calls placed to and received from outside that area involve a special service, called roaming, for which there is a substantial additional charge. New subscribers to cellular telephone ser-

SPECIALIZED TELEPHONE SERVICES

Local, long distance, and international carriers offer a wide range of specialized services. Many of these can also be provided by customer-owned telecommunications equipment, but may be available from telephone companies at a lower cost or with more flexible payment terms. Some of the most popular services are described below.

Hunt groups establish a series of telephone lines to which incoming calls will be delivered in succession, substantially reducing the chances that the caller will receive a busy signal.

Call forwarding allows another telephone number to receive all incoming calls until cancelled, without limiting the ability to make outgoing calls on the same line.

Busy call forwarding automatically routes incoming calls from one telephone line to another if the first line is busy.

Call return recognizes and stores the number of the last incoming call and calls it back when you dial a special code.

Call blocking prohibits calls from a particular telephone line to certain individual numbers or all numbers in a particular area. This is useful to control expenses from telephones frequently used by visitors or temporary workers.

Speed dialling automatically dials a pre-programmed telephone number with just one or two push-button commands.

Teleconference service (or three-party calling) allows three parties to speak with one another during the same telephone conversation.

Voicemail forwards incoming calls to a computer-operated digital recording system. The cost of voicemail service in the US is a fraction of what is charged in many other countries, often under US$5 per month for high-volume customers. As a result, many non-US companies choose to have all worldwide locations use one voicemail system located in the US and communicate with one another through that single system.

Telephone answering services provide personal handling of incoming calls made to a selected number or forwarded temporarily from an existing number. The person who answers will often handle simple matters, such as scheduling an appointment or ordering a publication. Average monthly costs range from US$50 (in small cities) to US$90 or more (in New York and Washington). This is particularly worthwile for companies that receive calls outside of the US office's regular business hours.

Operater assisted calls allow the caller to speak only to a particular individual at a number. It is usually far more expensive than dialing direct.

Toll-free 800 numbers are the most popular special service. The caller pays no charge, and the cost of the call is billed directly to the called party. It is also possible to automatically forward calls from a US toll-free number to an overseas location, and this can prove to be the most inexpensive way for a foreign company to set up a presence in the US.

Calling cards offered by local, long distance, and international carriers allow calls to be made with a special security code from any touch-tone telephone (including most public pay phones), then billed to the caller's home or office account. Pay phones themselves, because of large commissions charged by middlemen, are very expensive for long distance calls; moreover, since the largest coin accepted is US$0.25, they are not really practical for making long distance or international calls. Prepaid phone cards for use at pay telephones are gaining in popularity in the US, but have only recently come into vogue. They can be purchased at various convenience stores or from Western Union or from AT&T for US$5 to US$50, but may be difficult to find.

vices are usually prohibited from making international telephone calls until they have established a good credit record.

Paging is a much less expensive mobile communications service option and has gained favor in the past few years with a wide range of customers, from salespeople to schoolchildren—25 million people in the US now own pagers. This service allows callers with touch-tone telephones to signal the paging customer with the number at which he or she can be reached. The service costs about US$10 per month, with pager units priced from US$50 to US$100, although an alphanumeric pager that can display headline news, stock quotes, and other such brief messages will cost a bit more both to purchase and for the monthly service charge.

Directory Assistance The primary source of telephone number information in the US is the "white pages" listings in directories published by local telephone companies and by some private organizations (such as local chambers of commerce). These directories list all businesses and residences alphabetically by name at no charge—in fact, there is a charge to avoid being listed. "Yellow pages" directories are also published by local telephone companies and by various private concerns. These list commercial establishments, are organized alphabetically by type of product or service, and include many display advertisements. Businesses must pay to be listed, and the fees for the larger display ads can be quite substantial, but for some companies it may be the most effective—or even the only—form of advertising.

Local phone companies provide their own directories to customers free of charge, but directories for other areas must be purchased, often at prices of US$50 and up. Since most businesses maintain only a few directories in an office, operator assisted directory information service—at a fee—is frequently used. Local directory assistance provides telephone numbers within the same area code; this service is available throughout the US by dialing 411. There may be a charge, usually US$0.10 to US$0.50, for each request. For numbers in other area codes, the caller must dial 1, then the area code, then 555-1212. This will be a long distance call, typically charged at US$0.75. Another increasingly attractive option to maintaining a large library of directories or calling directory assistance is purchasing CD-ROMs that include business and/or residential telephone numbers and addresses for large regions of the country. Sets of several discs covering the entire US can be purchased for less than US$100. International directory assistance is also available, but rates may be US$3.75 or more for each request.

Automation New technologies are leading to rapid automation of many telecommunications services in the US. For instance, many organizations have replaced personal receptionists with automated systems which handle incoming calls with computer-managed prerecorded instructions, known as prompts. Some also have the ability to record the caller's voice (often referred to as voicemail systems); only specific personnel within the organization can then play back the caller's message. These systems typically can handle many incoming calls at one time, but usually require that the caller understand English and use a touch-tone phone. Generally these systems will automatically hang up if the caller is unable to respond properly to the prompts with a touch-tone phone, although some will eventually forward the call to a live person. This may be a concern for businesses less accustomed to conducting business in English, since almost all automated services presume that the caller has English language comprehension skills. However, some or-

ganizations that take a large number of calls from non-English-speaking customers (for example, international airlines or embassies) do offer instructions in two or more languages.

Billing Telecommunications services bill at different rates depending on the type of service and the time of day that calls are placed. Rates, usually calculated for minutes or fractions of minutes of use, almost always will be split into three different rate periods for domestic calls: standard (weekdays from 8 am to 5 pm), evening (weekdays from 5 pm to 11 pm), and night/weekend (weekdays from 11 pm to 8 am, all day Saturday, and Sunday until 5 pm). The rate periods for international calls differ greatly depending on the country being called. Many businesses regularly review their phone bills for unauthorized charges, which may be disputed. This is a wide practice, because telephone billing fraud in the US is estimated to be over US$500 million annually.

Taxes on local, long distance, and international telephone services are frequently as much as 20 percent of a total bill. They are assessed separately by local, state, and federal governments. The tax burden of international "800" (toll-free) service can be particularly heavy because although it qualifies for high direct taxation in the US, it cannot be deducted from the value-added taxes in the country where the call originates. A corporation also foregoes the higher tax deductions available in most countries outside the US. Foreign organizations that qualify for tax exempt status need not pay high direct telecommunications taxes. For example, common carriers (such as airlines and shipping companies) and nonprofit organizations (for example, chambers of commerce and national tourist organizations) are normally exempt from US telecommunications taxes.

Telecommunications Equipment Unlike in many other countries where the provision of some or all telecommunications equipment is a national monopoly, equipment in the US may be purchased from retailers and manufacturers. Most office equipment retailers will sell or lease the types of equipment required by a typical branch office operation. Service and maintenance, which may be provided by the same retailer or by a third party, can often cost more than the equipment itself.

The most basic type of telephone equipment, a key set, allows both incoming and outgoing calls. If an office expects to utilize more than 10 voice lines, it usually must choose between the Centrex service offered by the local telephone company or a specialized type of equipment called a private branch exchange (PBX). One of these will be necessary in order to transfer calls within the office, add third parties to calls, and make lines available for outgoing calls. Most such systems operate like an internal telecommunications network; in-house users dial added digits in order to call outside the office. Many PBXs also contain built-in computer programs which allow a company to reduce telecommunications expenses; for example, it can be used to convert a daytime voice line to a data line at times other than business hours. New PBX equipment costs thousands of dollars, but refurbished used equipment is available at a fraction of the cost of new equipment.

Fax equipment has also become essential for all businesses, but is particularly important for international businesses operating across many time zones and communicating with people who speaking various languages. Prices for fax machines range from US$250 to more than US$1,000, depending on transmission speeds and special features. International businesses should consider paying more for a memory feature, which can store 20 pages or more to be sent at a later time, when the recipient's fax line is available or when telephone rates are less expensive. Another possibility is to have a fax modem connected to or installed in a computer, which allows for a wide range of sending options, although it is generally less convenient to receive faxes via fax modem than on a traditional fax machine.

Electronic Information Services

Several different types of electronic information services are available in the US, for both voice and data. These range from simple calls to a prerecorded message to interactive databases which allow an individual to access information or execute a transaction. These services normally involve some combination of three types of charges: a monthly subscription fee, per minute or per message usage charges, and long distance telephone charges. Many businesses place orders and issue invoices using a service called electronic data interchange (EDI); the largest vendor of this service is GEISCO, a General Electric subsidiary.

Audiotext Services Most audiotext services require a touch-tone telephone and are accessed by dialing either an area code plus 976 followed by a four-digit number or 900 followed by a seven-digit number. The caller is then prompted to press codes on the telephone keypad in order to access particular types of information. Typical information available would include interest rates, flight schedules, or theater listings. Note that 900 and 976 calls can be quite expensive, and therefore access to them may be blocked in some offices.

Fax-on-Demand Services These are similar to audiotext services, but because they provide printed documents, the information provided can be far more specific and in-depth. The US government has become an enthusiastic provider of fax-on-demand; literally thousands of documents can be accessed in the US through various government agencies. Private companies may use fax-on-demand to provide potential customers with detailed product information for free; or if their product is the fax itself, they may charge customers, most often with a credit card. Depending on how the system is set up, either the company providing the fax or the customer receiving it may pay for the phone connection.

Online Services The number of online services available via computer modem has exploded in the 1990s. In most cases online services are available only to subscribers who pay basic subscriptions costing from US$10 a month to thousands of dollars a year. Fee structures may also be based on the time of day, the number of minutes online, the amount of information downloaded, the speed of the modem being used, and the actual files being accessed. In 1994 the number of online subscribers jumped by nearly 40 percent, and an estimated 6.3 million people are using an online service.

Companies like CompuServe, America Online (AOL), and Prodigy are aimed at the home, educational, and small business ser and provde comparatively little serious business information online. However, they are quite inexpensive (as little as US$10 a month for several hours of usage), have some useful services, provide electronic mail (widely known as E-mail) addresses, and give limited, but growing, access to the Internet. Services include access to online versions of some popular magazines, newspapers, and reference sources; travel reservation services; customer service for computer software; and Internet access with easy-to-use interfaces. Of the three major companies mentioned above, CompuServe, with a worldwide membership of 2.5 million, has the largest number of files of interest to a business user, but charges additional fees for access to many of them. America Online tripled its membership in 1994 to 1.5 million, largely due to its friendly interface and simple pricing structure. Prodigy is the first of the large online services to offer a World Wide Web (WWW) Internet browser, but it has lagged behind in attracting new subscribers; it is geared largely to home and school users, and is of less interest to the business user. Other similar but far less popular online services include GEnie (owned by General Electric) and Apple's eWorld.

Most online services are not themselves Internet service providers, although some may be accessed through the Internet. The most popular services give subscribers access to hundreds of databases, which may contain anything from citations from or the full text of articles to directory listings, from economic and financial data to legal texts. Knight-Ridder (formerly Dialog) and Nexis are very popular, although they can also be very expensive to use. Fees vary tremendousy and have been undergoing major restructuring (and fortunately, simplification), so it is difficult to make generalizations about costs. The interfaces allow very complex Boolean searching, but can be intimidating to the uninitiated, and at least some training is necessary in order to use them in a cost-effective manner. Another popular service, with a fee structure generally more acceptable to the occasional user, is Dow Jones News/Retrieval. This is the only online full text source for the *Wall Street Journal* and a number of other Dow Jones publications, and it provides access to a large number of foreign newspapers and business resources.

The Internet Not a service, but rather a vast network of computer networks, the Internet—variously known as the Information Superhighway, the Infobahn, or just the 'Net—has become *the* hot topic in the past couple of years. There may be vast research and commercial opportunities on the Internet, but its overwhelming size and complexity, coupled with a lack of authority or control, have led many to dub it "the Wild West of technology." No one actually owns the Internet, since it is comprised of 48,000 networks in 75 countries; an estimated 20 million people are on the 'Net today, compared with one million in 1988.

Because the Internet is loosely built around a US government research network, it originally flourished at research facilities and on university campuses, so businesses are relative latecomers. However, the number of commercial domains, or addresses, is now over 22,000, more than triple the number in 1991. Advertising and marketing on the Internet is a delicate matter, since it is strictly against "netiquette" to do mass mailings to Internet addresses: one company that recently did so was "flamed" by Internet users, that is, besieged by thousands of angry messages sent to the company Internet mailbox; the onslaught caused an entire network to crash. Even though the advertising cannot come to the users, the users can go to the ads. The challenge lies in drawing the users to the sites; one solution is creating what amounts to online shopping malls.

There are a number of ways businesses can connect to the Internet. The most popular is through the major commercial online services like AOL or CompuServe, but these companies provide only limited (albeit growing) access to many features like the World Wide Web (WWW), ftp, and telnet. Other services primarily provide Internet access, but may also have other files, databases and services available. Because their main emphasis is on Internet connections, these others may be the best choice for businesses who are looking for full access to the Internet. Delphi is the leading national provider of this type. Other companies, like Netcom or Alternet, will provid a full connection, some technical support, and perhaps user software, but few other services. These may be less expensive for heavy Internet users, but novices are probably better off getting their feet wet with the larger, more general online service providers.

Bulletin Boards There are thousands of computer bulletin board services (BBSs) across the country which allow the user to exchange information and computer shareware or freeware with others who have similar interests. Many of the most heavily used BBSs are locally based and geared to the leisure user, although there are some large commercial boards and smaller professionally oriented ones as well. The BBSs often provide limited access to the Internet, although sometimes just to E-mail. Subscription prices and user fees are usually quite low, particularly compared with national online services, but each BBS generally has a fairly narrow focus. Some of the national ones, like those run by US government agencies, are accessible either directly or through an Internet address.

USEFUL ADDRESSES

Government Agencies

Department of Transportation (DOT)
400 7th St. SW
Washington, DC 20590,USA
Tel: [1] (202) 366-4000

Federal Aviation Administration (FAA)
800 Independence Ave. SW
Washington, DC 20591, USA
Tel: [1] (202) 267-3111
Fax: [1] (202) 267-5047

Federal Communications Commission (FCC)
1919 M St. NW
Washington, DC 20554, USA
Tel: [1] (202) 418-0200
Fax: [1] (202) 632-0163

Federal Highway Administration (FHA)
400 7th St. SW
Washington, DC 20590, USA
Tel: [1] (202) 366-0660
Fax: [1] (202) 366-7239

Federal Maritime Commission
800 N. Capitol St. NW, 10th Fl.
Washington, DC 20573, USA
Tel: [1] (202) 523-5706
Fax: [1] (202) 523-4224

Federal Railroad Administration (FRA)
400 7th St. SW
Washington, DC 20590, USA
Tel: [1] (202) 366-0881
Fax: [1] (202) 366-7009

Interstate Commerce Commission (ICC)
12th St. and Constitution Ave. NW
Washington, DC 20423, USA
Tel: [1] (202) 927-5350, 927-6000
Fax: [1] (202) 927-5728

Maritime Administration
400 7th St. NW
Washington, DC 20590, USA
Tel: [1] 366-5807
Fax: [1] 366-3890

National Transportation Safety Board
490 L'Enfant Plaza East SW
Washington, DC 20594, USA
Tel: [1] (202) 382-6600

Publications

Air Transport World
600 Summer St.
Stamford, CT 06904, USA
Tel: [1] (203) 348-7531
Fax: [1] (203) 348-4023

World Trade
(Monthly)
17702 Cowan St.
Irvine, CA 92714, USA
Tel: [1] (714) 798-3500
Fax: [1] (714) 798-3501

Global Trade & Transportation
(Monthly)
North American Publishing Co.
401 N. Broad Street
Philadelphia, PA 19108, USA
Tel: [1] (215) 238-5300
Fax: [1] (215) 238-5457

Global Production & Transportation
(Monthly)
1319 Spruce St.
Boulder, CO 80302, USA
Tel: [1] (303) 939-8440
Fax: [1] (303) 939-0069

Journal of Commerce
(Daily)
110 Wall St.
New York, NY 10005, USA
Tel: [1] (212) 245-1616
Fax: [1] (212) 208-0206

Shipping Digest
51 Madison Ave.
New York, NY 10010, USA
Tel: [1] (212) 689-4411, (800) 309-3332
Fax: [1] (212) 683-7929

Pacific Shipper
K-III Directory Corp. Inc.
424 West 33rd St.
New York, NY 10001, USA
Tel: [1] (212) 714-3100 x171

US Business Slang Dictionary

A

ace in the hole/ace in the pocket/ace up one's sleeve An undisclosed advantage, usually one that will ensure success when revealed. "The new process we've developed is our ace in the hole—it will allow us to keep our costs so low that no one else will be able to match our bid for this project."

acid test The worst possible conditions that can be devised to test whether an idea or product might be successful. "Let's put this contract to the acid test. Give it to our attorney."

across the board Involving everything. "This contract has problems across the board. Every clause needs to be reworked."

advance Funds paid to someone before work is performed. "They insisted on an advance because our order is a custom design."

ahead of the game In the lead position. "We will be ahead of the game when we introduce this product at the end of the month. Our competitors are still working on the design of their model and haven't even started production yet."

air (to) a) To broadcast. "This commercial will air on seven West Coast television stations beginning tomorrow." b) To share or publicize. "Let's air that idea and see what others think about it."

appeal Attractiveness. "Our ads need more mass appeal."

art Photographs, illustrations, and other visual presentations used in publications and advertisements. "We'll have to redo the art for these ads. The appeal isn't broad enough."

asleep at the switch Neglectful or inattentive. "Let's take advantage of the trends now, while our competitor is asleep at the switch."

B

baby boomers The now middle-aged generation of the US population, which was characterized by a high increase in birth rate following World War

II. "Baby boomers represent a substantial market for our hair dye. We should be certain to target our advertising to them." The term "baby boomlet" refers to the generation born during a smaller surge in US populations that began in the 1980s and has continued into the 1990s as baby boomers began to have children.

backlog Work not yet completed or orders not yet filled. "What a backlog! I can't see my desk through all the papers!"

back burner Relatively insignificant position. "We should put this issue on the back burner for now and concentrate instead on completing this other project before the deadline."

back down (to) To yield. "This deal won't happen unless you back down on your demands."

back to square one (to the drawing board) To forget about ideas or approaches that are not working, return to the basic issue, and begin anew. "This advertising concept is not working; we need to go back to square one."

bail out (to) a) To help solve a problem. "Thanks for bailing me out. I'll pay you back for the loan as soon as the check from the buyer clears the bank." b) To abandon a failing project or product before losing more money, time, or labor. "I think we should bail out of the plan to make purple and green piano keys. It looks like a deadend."

bait and switch The practice of luring buyers by advertising an item for sale at a special price, then selling them a different item at a higher price. Often, the original item was never available. "The computer store advertised a laser printer for US$800, but when I got there, all they had were models for US$950. I was a victim of bait and switch tactics."

ballpark figure Rough estimate. "Even if you don't have all the numbers yet, could you give us a ballpark figure of the total cost?"

(the) ball is in your court Sports term meaning "The next move is up to you."

bat a thousand (to) To succeed in all aspects of a venture. In baseball, it means that a player makes a base hit every time at bat. "Everyone you asked to the meeting is coming. You're batting a thousand this week."

Beantown Boston, Massachusetts.

bear a) A person who believes stock market prices or activity will fall. See "bull." b) Someone who is gruff and generally difficult to deal with.

bells and whistles Extraneous but alluring features. "This contract has some interesting bells and whistles, but some of its basic terms are totally unreasonable."

bench strength Sports expression for access to talented people or other resources in depth. "This company has superb bench strength, particularly in the knowledge and skill of its top and middle managers."

best shot Superlative effort. "We'll give this deal our best shot. We really want it to work out."

Big Apple New York City, New York.

big cheese/big enchilada/big wig Person in charge. "You had better look busy. The Big Enchilada is coming down the hall." See "food chain."

Big Easy New Orleans, Louisiana.

biggest bang for the buck The best result in relation to the money spent. "For this product, the Midwest market gave us the biggest bang for the bucks. The ads we placed there were less expensive and received a larger response than the ones we placed on the East Coast."

Big Six (formerly Big Eight) The six largest US public accounting firms: Arthur Andersen & Co., Ernst & Young, Deloitte & Touche, KPMG Peat Marwick, Coopers & Lybrand, Price Waterhouse.

big-ticket items Large, costly items, such as cars, furniture, computers, or refrigerators.

bite the bullet Face reality in a losing situation. "I guess it's time to bite the bullet on this deal. I don't think it is going to happen, and I'd rather not spend any more time on it."

black hole An endeavor or a company that absorbs unlimited sums from investors with no hope of profits in the near future.

black knight A potential investor who attempts a hostile takeover of a corporation. "The controlling shareholders of our largest competitor are fighting a black knight." See gray knight. Opposite: white knight (a savior).

blue chip A well-known company with a solid history of profits or dividends. In poker, the blue chip is usually the most valuable. "My wealthy conservative aunt doesn't like surprises. She prefers blue chip stocks."

bogus A sham or something spurious or deceptive in nature. "This sales pitch has some basic flaws; it seems bogus to me."

boiler plate Standard contract provisions, often printed in small type and referred to as "fine print." "Let's use the first paragraphs of this form as boiler plate in all our manufacturing contracts."

boom A period of explosive economic growth, characterized by excess demand for goods and services, rising interest rates, and an optimistic public attitude. Opposite: bust.

boondoggle An undertaking that wastes money, time, or energy. "That idea was really a boondoggle. We should have put it to an acid test before we went to market."

bottom line a) Net profit of a business. "Our bottom line this year was US$2.4 million." b) The final or short answer to a question. "I'm tired of going back and forth on this issue. What's the lowest price you will accept? Give me your bottom line."

brainstorm (to) Creative session in which a group of people propose, discuss, and develop ideas. "I don't know what to do about the Bidley account. Let's call a meeting and brainstorm."

brand image Consumers' perception of a company's product. "If this proposed product lacks quality, our brand image could suffer, and consumer sales of all of our products could be affected."

brass tacks The basic issues. "All right, let's put aside all these details and get down to brass tacks."

break-even point The time when income equals the cost of doing business; in other words, neither profit nor loss is being made.

break the ice Overcome awkward barriers when first meeting someone. "Its important to have a good introductory line to help break the ice."

bring to the table Present issues or ideas. "We have four concerns to bring to the table when we meet with the client to negotiate this deal."

buck One US dollar.

buck the trend (to) To go against the conventional way of thinking. "I know the market is advancing, but I'm going to buck the trend and sell short."

bug Problem. In the computer industry, a malfunction, usually a logical error, in a program. "We need to eliminate all the bugs and get our production line running more smoothly."

bull a) A person who believes stock market prices or activity will increase. See "bear." b) A derogatory expression used for something one believes to be of no validity. "That argument is all bull."

bust A period of economic deflation. Opposite: boom.

buyout Acquisition of a company, or a division of a corporation, by an investor or group of investors formed for that purpose. "The XYZ Group was organized quickly so they could do a buyout of Transocean's freight division."

buy the farm To terminate or go out of business. "His shop was in such a poor location, that after just six months in business, he bought the farm."

by the numbers (by the book) According to the rules. "Let's not attract the attention of the Securities and Exchange Commission. Be sure to do everything by the numbers."

C

call one's bluff To insist that a person who has made a promise act so as to carry it out. "You say that you can deliver 500 ducks by Friday. I'm going to call your bluff, and if you actually make the delivery, I'll pay you double the wholesale market price."

can someone (to) To fire or dismiss ("axe") someone from a job. "That clerk got canned for losing the account."

cannibalize (to) a) To take something apart, salvaging what is useful and abandoning what is not. "The new owners have completely cannibalized the research and development department." b) To take sales away from one's own product with a new product. "The new model was a success except that it cannibalized the existing product."

cap (to) To limit. "Their salaries should be capped at US$60,000 a year for the next three years."

cash-strapped Short of liquid funds. "Craminex put so much money into research and development that now they're strapped for cash."

cash cow A company or product that generates more cash than it uses. "XYZ is a cash cow. Revenues are substantial, even though we haven't spent much on advertising."

CD-ROM Compact disk-read only memory. Technology allowing a large amount of material to be put on an optically-read disk. "We can get the whole series on CD-ROM and save the shelf space the books would need."

CEO Chief Executive Officer, usually the person in charge of a company. "When the CEO speaks, the rest of us act."

chain of command Hierarchy. "You should check with my boss. He's first in the chain of command, and has authority to give you a discount." See "food chain."

clean house (to) To review employees, usually with an eye to reducing personnel. "Our new supervisor thinks we're overstaffed and is looking to clean house."

clean up (to) To make a large profit quickly or to buy or sell something under very advantageous conditions. "I cleaned up on that sale. The buyer was so eager that I was able to sell the entire shipment for twice the list price."

close a deal Complete a transaction; reach final agreement on contract terms. "We finally closed a deal with our supplier. The bolts will be delivered next week."

clout power or political influence. "If you want to cut the red tape, you have to know someone with the right clout."

cold call (to make a) To make an unsolicited visit or call to a company or individual to sell a product. "It's hard to call up total strangers, but some of my cold calls have resulted in big sales."

collar (white, pink, or blue) A class of employees— white being salaried, generally office, employees; blue being employees typically paid on an hourly basis and who wear uniforms or work clothes; and pink being employees in occupations (such as nursing and clerical) traditionally held by women.

comeback Winning response. A term derived from sports, meaning that a losing team has been able to score enough points at the end of a game to become the victors. "That was a snappy comeback. You must have memorized the slang dictionary."

corner the market Control a particular market. "We have cornered the market. No other companies are selling this product."

corporate raider One who buys a company in the face of significant resistance from current owners, often breaking it up afterwards to pay for the purchase.

cover all the bases (to) To be complete. "With the addition of these two clauses, this contract seems to cover all the bases. Are you ready to sign it?"

cover up Conceal or obscure facts, usually for purposes of making a situation look better than it is.

crash course Accelerated instruction, usually covering only the essential information about a topic. "I need a crash course in US culture tonight so that I can feel confident when I meet our US supplier tomorrow."

crown jewel A company's most valuable asset. "The West Coast division is our crown jewel; they've posted top sales for the fifth year in a row."

cut a deal Agree on favorable terms to both parties. "Let's cut a deal. I'll buy 500 of these widgets at 40 percent of the list price, and I'll pay in advance on condition that you deliver by the end of the week."

cut and dried Standard or already arranged. "These terms are cut and dried, but we can make adjustments to these other items if you desire."

cut throat Ruthless. "The competition in computers is becoming cut throat."

cutting edge The forefront. "If you want to be on the cutting edge of fashion, you have to follow the trends in Paris and Milan."

D

deadend No exit or hope for success. "This project is a deadend. There's no chance it will turn a profit."

dead time Period of no business activity. "We had to pay for dead time last month while our computer system was down."

debug Fix errors. A term derived from the computer industry, in which software is commonly "debugged" before being marketed.

demo Demonstration; sample product. "We need to make some demos to show to potential buyers at trade fairs."

demographics Segments of the population, divided for marketing purposes into groups based on such factors as age, race, religion, gender, income, domicile, and home ownership. "We've looked at all the demographics, and I think we've identified our market niche."

deep-six Eliminate or forget about something. "Let's deep-six this idea. I see no profit in it."

doable Possible. "If you want to meet with all the company's principals next week, I think it's doable."

DOC US Department of Commerce.

dock (n) Loading platform or pier.

dock (to) (v) To reduce, to cut. "Charles has left work early every day this week, so I'm going to dock his pay."

dog and pony show Slightly derogatory metaphor for a presentation, promotion, or advertisement that is primarily intended merely to impress a client.

dog eat dog Ruthless competition. "It's a dog-eat-dog world out there. We've got to target the right market to survive."

DOT US Department of Transportation.

down Inoperable; broken. "Our computer is down."

downside The negative, less desirable alternative. "I like the idea of making them wonder, but on the downside, stalling too long could cost us the deal." See "upside."

downsize (to) To reduce operating costs, usually by laying off employees and restructuring the company. "I lost my job when the company decided to downsize its operations."

down time A period during which a business cannot operate. In relation to computers, the time during which a computer is inoperable. "We had some downtime last July when the dockworkers went on strike. We couldn't get the goods off the ships and onto the trucks."

draw a (the) line Fix a boundary. "This is taking too much time. We need to draw the line at two hours. Whatever it looks like at that time, goes to print."

E

eager beaver Employee who appears to be excessively hardworking, and often irritating to co-workers. "It seems that the new accountant is trying to take over all the new accounts in our office. That eager beaver has been working late every night just to make the rest of us look lazy."

earnest money Funds paid to make a contract binding.

eggs in one basket Holding the same investments without diversifying. Often heard in securities and investment sectors, but may have a more general application. "By concentrating on courses in taxation, that graduate has put all her eggs in one basket and now she has limited job opportunities."

eleventh hour At the last minute. "The dockworkers were supposed to go on strike at dawn. Lucky for us they negotiated all night and agreed on labor contracts at the eleventh hour, so our shipment should be unloaded today."

empower To give local or subordinate workers the authority to structure their jobs in hopes of gaining efficiency and improving employee morale.

E-mail (to) To send messages or documents by electronic mail, which is transmitted by computer through a central, national center. "Please E-mail this document to our supplier. I want it to get there as quickly as possible."

ETA Estimated Time of Arrival. "I'm on my way now. My ETA is 3 pm."

Eximbank Export-Import Bank of the US. A US export financing bank created by law to promote exports. Refer to "Financial Institutions" chapter for discussion of this institution.

even keel (to be on an) To be balanced and steady. "When this product was first introduced, sales were extremely high. Then they dropped by half. Now that we have reevaluated the market, sales are rising at a constant rate. I think we are finally on an even keel."

eye-opener An enlightening or surprising revelation. "The survey result was a real eye-opener. Who would have guessed that this product would sell in that market?"

eyes only, for your Private, confidential. "When you send the documents to me, be sure to label them for my eyes only. No one else should see them."

eye-to-eye Similar beliefs or viewpoints. "We get along well because we see eye-to-eye on most issues."

F

fallout Repercussions, usually negative. "We're going to get some fallout from that court decision on patent infringement."

fast buck Money quickly earned, often, but not necessarily, through questionable or even devious means. "We were able to turn a fast buck this time, even though we had to cut quality to do it."

fast track Quickest procedure or path to a desired result. "That employee has been promoted four times in just eight months. He is on the fast track to the executive suite."

fax Facsimile. A document transmitted over telephone lines.

FDA US Food and Drug Administration.

(the) Fed The Federal Reserve System. "If inflation keeps getting worse, we think the Fed will raise short-term interest rates again."

(the) Feds Any US federal government authorities. "Our shipment of baskets was held up by the Feds at the border, where they inspected every carton for illegal drugs, but of course didn't find any."

feel the pinch Aware of, and even suffering from, an unfavorable condition. "I seem to have less money to spend these days. I'm feeling the pinch of inflation."

fleece (to) To confuse another party, or to gain materially from another person's ignorance. "We could have fleeced that company on this deal, since the CEO had no background in this market, but our honesty will probably benefit us over the long term."

fly-by-night operation Shaky or shady business. "I think ABC Company doesn't hold up to scrutiny. Joe says it's a fly-by-night operation."

food chain Hierarchy. "In this corporate food chain, the CEO is at the top—like a shark—and I'm at the bottom—just one of the little fish."

fringe benefits Employee perquisites, such as discounts on company merchandise, expense accounts, or free parking.

front runner Candidate most likely to succeed. "Right now, the Harvard graduate is a front runner for the job."

frozen assets Property holdings that the owner is not permitted by law to sell or otherwise transfer. "During the Persian Gulf War, the US President froze Iraq's assets in the US."

G

game plan Method or approach. "We need to devise a game plan before we start marketing this new product."

gatekeeper Person, often a secretary, who controls access to a person. "The boss needs a good gatekeeper to keep him focused on the essentials."

get out from under (to) To be relieved from an obligation. "Let's just pay them off and get out from under that contract so we can move ahead."

GIGO Garbage In-Garbage Out. Results are only as good as the input. "I don't trust this analysis. After all, remember GIGO. If the initial concept is flawed, how can we really expect to profit from selling this product?"

go for broke (go for it) Take whatever risks are necessary. "This project could succeed or be a disaster. But we've thought through the alternatives, and this seems to be the best one. I think we should go for broke."

go-getter An ambitious person. Often one who works too hard to get ahead.

go public (to) Disclose information to the public. "We found a defect in the exhaust systems. I think we should go public with this information and recall the systems right away."

gold mine A very profitable business. "The Martin family doesn't have to worry about money any more. Their car dealership is proving to be a gold mine."

grapevine An informal network of communications that usually includes gossip. "I heard on the grapevine that you may have to sell your property in Honolulu." See "scuttlebutt."

gray knight A potential investor who makes a bid to take over a corporation but whose motives are unknown. "I just heard that a gray knight has entered into the acquisition negotiations. This will certain complicate our fight to keep our controlling shares, at least until we know the motives behind this latest offer."

gray market a) Unofficial marketing channels in which products are bought and sold in violation of restrictions and contractual rights imposed by the manufacturers. "That's a gray market because those brandname goods were made in the US, purchased overseas at prices lower than those available directly from the US manufacturer, reimported to the US, and sold as resale items." b) Segment of the population past the age of retirement (65), also known as senior citizens. "The gray market accounts for much of the cruise business out of Florida."

green card The official identification card for immigrants to the US who have been admitted as permanent residents and thus have the right to work in the US. "Anyone who applies for this job must have proof of US citizenship or a green card."

green technology Applications designed to clean up and preserve the environment. "This environmental engineering firm has developed a number of innovative green technologies that might work in our plants."

gut feeling Intuition. "I have a gut feeling that this is the person we've been looking for to take charge of this program for us."

H

haggle (to) To bargain. "Let's not haggle over the price of everything in your store. You must be able to cut me a deal on these few items if I buy this television at the asking price. What's the bottom line?" See "cut a deal" and "bottom line."

half the battle Partly completed (but not necessarily halfway). "Getting the names into the computer was only half the battle. Printing them onto mailing labels and then doing the mailing is next."

hammer out Negotiate, usually over final or detailed terms. "Now that we've agreed to the basic terms, we need to sit down and hammer out the details."

happy hour (cocktail hour) Usually late afternoon or early evening period (4 pm to 6 pm) when people socialize after work, often with alcoholic drinks and appetizers. "Let's continue this discussion over happy hour at the bar on the corner—it has reduced drink prices and free snacks."

hardball Overly strong or harsh approach. "Competition is intense in this area. We are going to have to play hardball to break into this market."

hard copy Tangible material printed from a computer, as opposed to copy that exists only on a disk.

hardware Computer equipment. See "software."

haves and have nots Persons who have a good standard of living and those who do not.

head honcho The person in charge. "If you want 60 percent off the price, you'll have to speak to the head honcho."

head hunter Job recruiter for executive posts. "We use a head hunter to fill all our top management positions."

hidden agenda Undisclosed concerns or intentions. "Something in that latest sales pitch made me wonder whether the company has a hidden agenda. We need to be cautious in agreeing to any deals with them. They might intend to put us out of business."

hired gun A person, generally from outside of an organization, who has specific expertise or is asked to perform a task that involves aggression or that is considered less than distasteful. "For this intense negotiating session, they brought in some hired guns. When I sat down at the table, I was facing a formidable row of attorneys—all from highly reputable and expensive firms."

hype (to) To promote, usually with exaggeration. "They're really hyping their new convertible as if no one's ever heard of a removable top for a car."

I

icon A computer command shown as a picture (or image) on the computer screen. "If you wish to print out your letter, just press the icon that looks like a printer."

ID Identification, usually personal. "I can accept your check, sir, but only if you have some ID with your picture on it."

in hock Indebted, financially or otherwise. "We are in hock to that other department; they lent us several employees to help us work through our backlog."

input Ideas. "I called this meeting because I would like some input from everyone about this new project."

INS US Immigration and Naturalization Service.

inside track Having knowledge or familiarity not commonly available to others. "The only person on the inside track around here is the secretary of the boss."

interface a) Meet or converse. "We need to interface over this issue to work out the details." b) Linkages between computer programs and uses.

IRA Individual Retirement Account.

IRS US Internal Revenue Service, which is the US government's taxing authority.

J

junk bond Wall Street term for bonds with a low credit rating, usually regarded as speculative investments.

jet lag Condition of exhaustion and/or disorientation caused by flying on an airplane through several time zones. "The flight to Miami from Munich gave me a bad case of jet lag, and I am still waking up on German time."

jump through hoops (to) To overcome obstacles, often ones that are tedious and unnecessary. "I had to jump through hoops just to get past the receptionist. Now I'll have to do the same thing to get past the office secretary."

K

kickback A hidden rebate given by a seller illegally or secretly as a payoff to secure a contract or order. "It seems odd that XYZ Limited chose another supplier, when our price for the same type of products was lower. Maybe there was a kickback involved."

kiss off (to) to abandon; walk away from. "That CEO hasn't returned any of my calls. I'm going to kiss off the idea of retailing through those stores."

knock-offs Copies of an original, often counterfeit or made without authorization. "The purses in this shipments are knock-offs. The logos duplicate the brand-labels of several fashion designers, and therefore entry is denied based on US trademark protection law."

know the ropes (score) Fully comprehend a situation. "After you have been here for a while, you'll get to know the ropes."

L

lay it on the table (lay it on the line; lay the cards on the table) To speak directly about the circumstances, to tell the facts about a situation. "The time has come for me to lay it on the table so that you can understand why I've been so cautious about this deal. Then maybe you can help me figure out what to do next."

light a fire To encourage development or action. "Sales have slowed in the past two months. I think we need to light a fire under our agents."

liquid Having immediate access to cash. "We have stayed liquid so that we would have the funds available to take advantage of the opportunity."

lock, stock, and barrel Everything; the entire holdings of a company. "Blue Bell Dairy doesn't exist as a separate company anymore. Swanberg bought the company lock, stock, and barrel."

long haul (run) A lengthy time. "Once we start, we will be in this for the long haul because we will have invested to much to stop before the project is completed."

loop, in the Informed about activity in the company or within one's circle. "She knows all about the proposed cutbacks. The boss keeps her in the loop." See "out of the loop."

loop, out of the Passed over or not given information that is circulated among others in one's circle. "Information about the pending sale should not be released generally. Until the sale is finalized, everyone but the managers should be kept out of the loop."

loose cannon Unpredictable person who has trouble maintaining self-control. "Dan's really a loose cannon. He can make a million-dollar deal one day, and then lose it the next by insulting the client."

M

make a killing Realize a large gain on a transaction. "We bought those widgets at half-price and sold them at double the market price. We sure made a killing!"

make or break A pivotal act that will cause success or failure. "This is our last attempt. It will either make or break this business."

Mickey Mouse Petty, trivial, or subordinate. "Let's move on to the important issues and get away from the Mickey Mouse stuff."

miss the market (to) To fail to buy or sell at a certain price, usually followed by a transaction with unfavorable terms. "When we decided to wait six months before purchasing those rolls of plastic, we missed the market. The price has tripled since then."

monitor Computer screen.

monitor (to) To watch or evaluate a situation. "Louise hasn't worked on this type of project before so I'm going to monitor her work for a while."

muddy the waters Cause confusion. "These extra issues are muddying the waters. We need to concentrate on the core issues."

N

network System of increasing contacts by sharing information and forming relationships; also used as a verb. "I'm going to that open house at the new store tonight. A lot of dealers will be there and I want to network."

nickel-and-dime (to) To attack a little, often inconsequential, piece at a time; to bring slowly to financial ruin. "At the rate we're negotiating, this deal may never close. The other party keeps arguing over small details, even though we haven't worked out the overall plan, yet. I think they're trying to nickel-and-dime us."

nitty gritty Necessary procedural details.

nose to the grindstone Work hard. "I kept my nose to the grindstone all week, and I have only three small deals to show for all that work."

nuke it Delete, eliminate, remove from consideration. "This idea will cost too much to develop. I think we should nuke it and concentrate on the other options."

nuts and bolts Basic, essential ingredients.

O

off the record Not made public or recorded; confidential. "I'll comment on that issue only if we are off the record."

online a) Hooked up to a computer or an information system. "We can go online to get the latest data." b) Operational. "The new factory is ready to go online next week."

out of it Unaware, often tired or depressed. "I feel out of it today. I finally closed the deal we've been working on for weeks, but I'm not even excited about it."

outsourcing A company's use of independent contractors or consultants to perform specific jobs, with the requirements and price of each contract separately negotiated. "To make our operations more cost-efficient, we are going to have to start outsourcing some of the work."

P

PBX Private business exchange. A telephone system used by small businesses and offices to route calls.

PIN Personal Identification Number. A security access code, usually selected by the user. "It seems like everything has PINs these days—from bank cards, to credit cards, to hotel room keys."

pitch Speech to a potential client or customer. "No wonder she's our best salesperson. You should have heard her pitch to the Carson Group." Also: to pitch a product is to promote it.

players Persons involved in a deal or transaction. "We certainly have the right mix of players for this project. Everyone has a past related success."

poison pill A corporate strategy designed to avoid hostile takeovers by reducing the desirability of the acquisition. "We need a poison pill right away to try to avoid losing our interests in this company. One option is to acquire some large debts. Any other ideas?"

pool (to) Combine separate talents or assets for the benefit of all parties. "Let's pool our resources. With your distributors and our agents, we should be able to corner the market on this product."

promo Promotional material. "Our promos include pens, notepads, coffee mugs, and t-shirts, all with the company name and logo in silver on a blue background. Do you like the design?"

puff up Inflate; make something appear better than it is in fact. "Those sales figures must be puffed up. It's hard to believe that a start-up company in this type of industry can be doing so well."

punch up Make more interesting. "The only way that this advertisement is going to appeal to a teenage crowd is if we punch up the copy with some younger generation lingo."

Q

quid pro quo Latin phrase meaning "this for that" and used in negotiations to mean exchanging a concession for a concession. "Hey, you can't expect something for nothing. Here's the quid pro quo on this deal."

quote Bids or estimates of cost, usually for a particular job or project. "Let's get some quotes on this project before we choose which firm to hire for the job."

R

R&D Research and Development.

rag trade/rag business The fashion apparel industry.

rain check (to take a) To postpone; to suggest rescheduling a meeting or appearance for a later date. "I can't get away from the office today. I'll have to take a rain check on lunch."

rally (to) To recover from a slump or decline. "Stock prices are rallying after the announcement that interest rates aren't going up again."

RAM Random access memory. Computer memory that can be written over and reused.

rank and file Employees who are not part of management.

rat race Life at a fast pace. "We moved to the country to get away from the rat race of the city."

red-eye Overnight flights, usually between the east and west coasts of the US. "I can make the meeting in New York tomorrow if I take the red-eye from Los Angeles tonight."

red flag A warning. "Every time I see an indemnity clause in a contract, it puts up a red flag; I review it very carefully and usually have to insist on changes."

red ink (in the red) Deficit or loss in business. "Our books are covered with red ink; we better start showing a profit soon or we will have to find new jobs."

reengineer Restructure or redesign; usually refers to the reorganization of a company's operating procedures.

rep Representative, usually in sales. "We have 42 reps operating in 20 states."

RFP Request for proposal. An invitation to bid on a job. "We just got an RFP from the Able Company on their new project. We need to put together a response right away."

road, on the Traveling. "I'll be on the road for the next two weeks, so we'll have to meet after I get back."

romance (to) Courting a company, making preliminary contacts and raising interest in forming a long-term business relationship. "We'll have to romance this company some more before we get a signed contract."

rolling in dough Wealthy; rich. "Don't be fooled by the jeans and raggy shirt. That guy is rolling in dough."

roll up one's sleeves (to) To get to work on a project immediately. "Now that we've agreed to the terms, I'll roll up my sleeves and get the contract written."

ROM Read only memory. Computer memory that can only be read and not reused or recorded over.

rubber check Negotiable instrument that is signed without sufficient funds to cover it, so it will "bounce" like rubber.

rule of thumb General guideline. "As a rule of thumb, you should make friends, not enemies."

S

save face Avoid injury or embarrassment; salvage a situation or reputation from potential destruction. "That accidental toxic spill could have been a major public relations disaster for our company, but we managed to save face by our immediate and controlled response."

SBA US Small Business Administration.

schmooze (to) To socialize; to converse with casually, particularly with potential business contacts. "I thought this deal would never go through, but all it took was a little schmoozing over dinner, and the client signed the contract."

scuttlebutt Rumor or gossip. "The scuttlebutt on Jim is that he threatened to quit if he didn't get that promotion."

seed money Funds used to start a company; risk capital; funds used for research and development. "Before we establish this company and start operating, maybe we better first find some seed money and research the market for the product."

set in stone Inflexible, unchangeable. "This deal is set in stone now. Changing it will be nearly impossible, and probably costly."

shark A lawyer. See also "black knight."

shot in the dark A guess. "I'm not sure what to do first, so let's take a shot in the dark and see where we end up."

Silicon Valley A region south of San Francisco—encompassing San Jose, Sunnyvale, Cupertino, and Palo Alto—famous for its concentration of high-technology companies, especially those that first worked with silicon chips.

sleeper Undervalued product or company with a huge but unrealized profit potential. "I think the Tidy Clam Finder is a sleeper. We just have to figure out the marketing strategy, and we'll be selling millions."

slush fund A company's account used for entertaining important clients and influential persons; may also refer to secret funds used for possibly improper purposes. "The slush fund is running a bit low since we've been dining out with the CEO and all the other officers of that corporation. We'd better close the deal soon."

smokeout A buyer's contractual condition that the seller disclose all or most of the details about a product or company before the purchase is completed.

skyrocket (to) To increase tremendously and quickly. "The sales of our newest product line have skyrocketed off the charts."

state-of-the-art The most current technology; the best available. "I love listening to music in Jane's studio. Her stereo system is state-of-the-art."

stay on top (to) To retain control and to be immediately informed. "We'll have to stay on top of this problem or we might lose more than a few clients."

stonewall (to) To be inflexible or refuse to acknowledge. "We haven't received their response to our proposal. I think they are stonewalling to see if we will offer more favorable terms."

straw bid A buyer's false offer to pay more than the buyer can afford. "MPC, Inc. offered to buy out our company for an outrageously high sum. I believe the offer is just a straw bid, particularly because MPC declared bankruptcy just six months ago."

suitor A company intending to acquire another concern, possibly under hostile conditions. "Have you heard that the giant conglomerate, Gifts, Inc., has become a suitor of Brassware, Ltd.?"

T

table (to) Place aside for consideration in the future. "I think we should table this idea for now. We need some more facts and figures to make an informed decision."

take it on the chin (to) To bear up under attack or stress; to withstand abuse or overwork.

talk turkey Discuss honestly. "Let's stop hinting around. I'm ready to talk turkey."

tap out (tapped out) Out of money. "I'd love to advance the money, but I'm tapped out."

TGIF Thank God It's Friday. "It's been a really rough week. TGIF. How about a relaxing dinner?"

thin ice Taking a risk. "You are on thin ice when you insult my business and then expect me to invest in your project."

Third Age Age 65 or older. People of age 65 or older are often called senior citizens.

throw light on Make clear. "I do not understand why the delivery was delayed so long. Could you throw some light on this for me?"

tight money Cash is hard to find; a restrictive monetary policy, and often high interest rates.

tip of the iceberg A small visible portion. "This little problem may be just the tip of the iceberg; there may be some major issues that we don't know about yet."

track record A company's history, including its policies, financial status, and performance record. "This company's track record for the past 10 years shows wise financial strategies and steady growth."

TRO Temporary restraining order. A legal term referring to a court order that restrains or prohibits certain actions for specific time. "That company's production is under a TRO until it complies with environmental laws."

turf Area of activity or influence.

turkey An embarrassingly unsuccessful performance, product, or person. "My broker sold me a real turkey. That stock dropped 10 points right after I bought it."

turnaround A company that successfully emerges from a period of financial problems. "I know they've had their difficulties, but Acme Co. is a classic turnaround case. It's really improving the bottom line." See "bottom line."

turnkey A project or product that is sold on the basis that it can begin to function as soon as it is delivered.

U

union shop Company or corporation in which all the employees are required to belong to a labor union.

upside The positive, favorable alternative. "A change in the location of our factory will be costly, but the upside is that the new factory will be closer to our distribution center and will save transport costs." See "downside."

upstream merger Subsidiary corporation merging with its parent. "We've been working for months on this upstream merger so that when the consolidation occurs, the employees will feel positively about the new chain of command." See "chain of command."

user-friendly Easy to operate or use. "I don't know anything about computers so I need a user-friendly software program."

V

venture capitalist An investor who supports new companies with money and other resources. "Those guys started their computer company on their own, but they were lucky enough to get money from a venture capitalist."

VIP Very Important Person. "A delegation of VIPs is arriving to meet with our CEO and the Board today."

virus A set of directives encoded into a computer software program intended to cripple or destroy totally the system of the user. "Every time I put a new diskette into my computer, my software checks for hidden viruses. One little virus could infect our entire network."

voice-over Speech of an unseen narrator on a television or radio commercial. "We'll show a picture of the new house with a voice-over by a person who sounds like a sincere lending officer."

W

waffle Fluctuation or equivocation. "I'm waffling on this question. I'm not sure what would be the best decision."

wave of the future A trend. "Global marketing is the wave of the future."

wet behind the ears/not dry behind the ears Inexperienced. "This is Tom's first marketing job, so he's still a little wet behind the ears."

white knight Person (or company) that rescues a corporation from a hostile takeover, either by making an equity investment in the target concern or by causing a friendly takeover. Opposite: black knight. See "gray knight."

whole hog Completely. "We need to saturate the market with these new ladders. Let's go whole hog in our sales efforts."

window dressing Making something look as attractive as possible. "Our fourth quarter financial statement needs some window dressing to show our shareholders the most optimistic outlook for next year."

Windy City Chicago, Illinois. (Also known as Chitown and the Second City.)

work this out Reach a conclusion or resolution. "Our goals are the same, so we should be able to work this out to benefit both of us."

world class Highest caliber. "This is a world-class company; it delivers only the finest quality service to its clients."

write-off A deduction claimed against taxable income, resulting in a tax savings.

WYSIWYG Acronym for "what you see is what you get." In computer terms, it means that the printout will look exactly like what is on the screen.

X

xerox (to) To photocopy, not necessarily on a Xerox brand machine. "I'm xeroxing copies for the whole staff."

Y

yo-yo Something with an unstable or constantly fluctuating nature. "He's a yo-yo. He changes his mind every time we talk."

Z

zap a) To eradicate, erase. "If you're finished reading that computer memo, please zap it. I don't want anyone else to see it." b) To send a message quickly, for example by E-mail.

Important Addresses

CONTENTS

INTRODUCTION

The following addresses have been gathered from a wide range of sources. We have attempted to verify each address at press time; however, it is likely that some of the information has already changed. Inclusion of an organization, product, or service does not imply a recommendation or endorsement.

Unless otherwise noted, all addresses are in the United States; the international country code for calling the US is [1] and is not shown in the US address listings. Area codes are given in parentheses, while non-US country codes are in square brackets. All US phone numbers consist of a three-digit area code and a seven-digit local number. For a listing of US area codes, states, and state abbreviations, see the list on the following pages. Refer to the chapter "Business Travel" for details on making telephone calls in the US.

US addresses usually follow fairly standardized formats. Names of buildings may be used, but are not common. The suite, office, or floor number is written following the street address, often on the same line. Some cities use directionals (i.e., NW, S, etc.) either before or after the name of the street. It is important to use them—mail delivery may be significantly delayed if this information is missing. The city is on the following line, followed by a comma and the two-letter state abbreviation. The postal or "zip" code is on the same line. The zip code is most often five digits, despite the post office's best efforts to get people to add the four-digit extension; however, if you have the full nine-digit code, use it.

A few common elements and abbreviations in US addresses are:

Ave.	Avenue	Hwy.	Highway
Bldg.	Building	Pkwy.	Parkway
Blvd.	Boulevard	Rd.	Road
Ct.	Court	Rm.	Room
Dr.	Drive	St.	Street
Fl.	Floor	Ste. or #	Suite

AREA CODES IN THE UNITED STATES

A selective list of area codes for states with more than one area code has been included below. It is impossible to give a full list of all area codes in use; however, virtually any US telephone directory will have a map and listing of major cities. You may also call the long-distance telephone operator for an area code. There are 50 states plus the District of Colombia (usually written simply as DC), where the national capital, Washington, DC, is located. The abbreviations given are in common usage, particularly for mail. For a map of US area codes, refer to page 214.

Because of the rapid increase in the number of telephone lines used for cellular telephones, modems, fax machines, and extra telephones, several new area codes are being added each year in the United States, particularly in large metropolitan areas. If a city has two area codes, the second code listed here is generally just for cellular phones and pagers.

State name	Abbreviation	City name	Area code(s)
Alabama	AL	Montgomery*	205
Alaska †	AK	Juneau*	907
Arizona	AZ	Phoenix*	602
Arkansas †	AR	Little Rock*	501
California	CA	Anaheim	714
		Los Angeles (central)	213
		Los Angeles (west and south), Long Beach	310, 562
		Berkeley, Oakland	510
		Pasadena	818
		Sacramento*	916
		San Diego	619
		San Francisco	415
		San Jose	408
		Santa Barbara	805
Colorado	CO	Denver*	303
Connecticut †	CT	Hartford*	203
Delaware †	DE	Dover*	302
District of Colombia †	DC	Washington	202
Florida	FL	Jacksonville, Tallahassee*	904
		Miami	305
		Orlando	407
		Tampa	813
Georgia	GA	Atlanta*	404
Hawaii †	HI	Honolulu*	808
Idaho †	ID	Boise*	208
Illinois	IL	Chicago	312, 630
		Springfield*	217
Indiana	IN	Indianapolis*	317
Iowa	IA	Des Moines*	515
Kansas	KS	Topeka*	913
Kentucky	KY	Frankfort*, Louisville	502
		Lexington	606
Louisiana	LA	Baton Rouge*, New Orleans	504
Maine †	ME	Augusta*, Portland	207
Maryland	MD	Annapolis*, Baltimore	410
Massachusetts	MA	Boston*	617

* State capital
† Only one area code in use for this state or district

State name	Abbreviation	City name	Area code(s)
Michigan	MI	Detroit	313
		Lansing*	517
Minnesota	MN	Minneapolis, St. Paul*	612
Mississippi †	MS	Jackson*	601
Missouri	MO	Kansas City	816
		Jefferson City*, St. Louis	314
Montana †	MT	Helena*	406
Nebraska	NE	Lincoln*, Omaha	402
Nevada †	NV	Carson City*, Las Vegas	702
New Hampshire †	NH	Concord*	603
New Jersey	NJ	Newark	201
		Trenton*	609
New Mexico	NM	Santa Fe*	505
New York	NY	Albany*	518
		Long Island	516
		New York City (Manhattan)	212, 917
		New York City (all except Manhattan)	718
		Rochester	716
		Syracuse	315
North Carolina	NC	Charlotte	704
		Raleigh*	919
North Dakota †	ND	Bismark	701
Ohio	OH	Cincinnati	513
		Cleveland	216
		Columbus*	614
Oklahoma	OK	Oklahoma City*	405
Oregon †	OR	Salem*	503
Pennsylvania	PA	Philadelphia	215
		Pittsburgh	412
		Harrisburg*	717
Rhode Island †	RI	Providence*	401
South Carolina †	SC	Columbia*	803
South Dakota †	SD	Pierre*	605
Tennessee	TN	Memphis	901
		Nashville*	615
Texas	TX	Austin*	512
		Dallas	214
		Houston	713, 281
		San Antonio	210
Utah †	UT	Salt Lake City*	801
Vermont †	VT	Montpelier*	802
Virginia	VA	Alexandria, Arlington	703
		Richmond*	804
Washington	WA	Olympia*	360
		Seattle	206
West Virginia †	WV	Charleston	304
Wisconsin	WI	Madison*	608
		Milwaukee	414
Wyoming †	WY	Cheyenne*	307

All addresses and telephone numbers are in the United States unless otherwise noted. The country code for the US is [1].

GOVERNMENT

GOVERNMENT AGENCIES

Department of Agriculture

Department of Agriculture (USDA)
14th St. and Independence Ave. SW
Washington, DC 20250
Tel: (202) 720-8732, 720-2791 Fax: (202) 720-2166

Animal and Plant Health Inspection Service (APHIS)
PO Box 96464
Washington, DC 20090
Tel: (202) 720-2791, 720-2511 Fax: (202) 720-3054

Center for Food Safety and Applied Nutrition
200 C St. SW
Washington, DC 20204
Tel: (202) 205-5850 Fax: (202) 205-5025

Federal Grain Inspection Service (FGIS)
PO Box 96454
Washington, DC 20090
Tel: (202) 720-8732, 720-5091 Fax: (202) 205-9237

Food Safety and Inspection Service (FSIS)
14th St. and Independence Ave. SW
Washington, DC 20250
Tel: (202) 720-8732, 720-9113 Fax: (202) 690-4437

Foreign Agricultural Service (FAS)
14th St. and Independence Ave. SW
Washington, DC 20250
Tel: (202) 720-8732, 720-9115 Fax: (202) 690-1595

Department of Commerce

Department of Commerce (DOC)
Main Commerce Bldg.
14th St. and Constitution Ave. NW
Washington, DC 20230
Tel: (202) 482-2000 Fax: (202) 482-4576

Bureau of Export Administration (BXA)
14th St. and Constitution Ave. NW
Washington, DC 20230
Tel: (202) 482-2000, 482-2721 Fax: (202) 482-2387

Economic Development Administration
14th St. and Constitution Ave. NW
Washington, DC 20230
Tel: (202) 482-2000, 482-5113 Fax: (202) 482-0995

Foreign Trade Zones Board
Main Commerce Bldg.
Washington, DC 20230
Tel: (202) 482-2862 Fax: (202) 482-0002

International Trade Administration (ITA)
14th St. and Constitution Ave. NW
Washington, DC 20230
Tel: (202) 482-2000 Fax: (202) 482-5933

National Institute of Standards and Technology (NIST)
Bldg. 101, #A1134
Gaithersburg, MD 20899
Tel: (301) 975-2000, 975-2762 Fax: (301) 869-8972

National Telecommunications and
Information Administration
Main Commerce Bldg.
Washington, DC 20230
Tel: (202) 482-1551 Fax: (202) 482-1635

Patent and Trademark Office
Washington, DC 20231
Tel: (703) 557-3158, 308-4357

Technology Administration
14th St. and Constitution Ave. NW
Washington, DC 20230
Tel: (202) 482-0137 Fax: (202) 482-4817

Travel and Tourism Administration
Main Commerce Bldg.
Washington, DC 20230
Tel: (202) 482-1904 Fax: (202) 482-4279

Department of Defense

Department of Defense (DOD)
The Pentagon
Washington, DC 20301
Tel: (703) 697-5737

Office of International Economics & Policy
The Pentagon, Rm. 4B-938
Washington, DC 20301-2100
Tel: (703) 697-3248 Fax: (703) 695-0054

Department of Education

Department of Education
400 Maryland Ave. SW
Washington, DC 20202
Tel: (202) 708-5366, 401-1576 Fax: (202) 401-0596

Department of Energy

Department of Energy (DOE)
1000 Independence Ave. SW
Washington, DC 20585
Tel: (202) 586-5000, 586-5575 Fax: (202) 586-4403

Consumer and Public Liaison
1000 Independence Ave. SW, CP-60
Washington, DC 20585
Tel: (202) 586-5373 Fax: (202) 586-0539

Federal Energy Regulatory Commission (FERC)
825 N. Capitol St. NE
Washington, DC 20426
Tel: (202) 208-0200, 208-1371 Fax: (202) 208-2106

Department of Health and Human Services

Department of Health and Human Services
200 Independence Ave. SW
Washington, DC 20201
Tel: (202) 619-0257, 690-6867 Fax: (202) 690-6274

Food and Drug Administration (FDA)
5600 Fishers Lane
Rockville, MD 20857
Tel: (301) 443-1544, 443-3170 Fax: (301) 443-5930

Food and Drug Administration
Small Manufacturers Assistance
5600 Fishers Lane
Rockville, MD 20857
Tel: (301) 443-6597 Fax: (301) 443-8818

Food and Drug Administration
Center for Devices and Radiological Health
12720 Twinbrook Parkway
Rockville, MD 20857
Tel: (301) 443-4690 Fax: (301) 443-3193

Social Security Administration
6401 Security Blvd.
Baltimore, MD 21235
Tel: (410) 965-8882, 965-7700 Fax: (410) 965-1344

Department of Housing and Urban Development

Department of Housing and Urban Development (HUD)
HUD Bldg.
451 7th St. SW
Washington, DC 20410
Tel: (202) 708-1422, 708-1420 Fax: (202) 708-0299

Department of the Interior

Department of the Interior
Main Interior Bldg.
1849 C St. NW
Washington, DC 20240
Tel: (202) 208-3100, 208-3171 Fax: (202) 208-5048

Bureau of Land Management
1849 C St. NW
Washington, DC 20240
Tel: (202) 208-3100, 501-5717 Fax: (202) 208-5902

Bureau of Mines
810 7th St. NW
Washington, DC 20241
Tel (202) 208-3100, 501-9649 Fax: (202) 501-3716

Fish and Wildlife Service (FWS)
1849 C St. NW
Washington, DC 20240
Tel: (202) 208-3100, 208-5634 Fax: (202) 208-6965

Department of Justice

Department of Justice (DOJ)
Main Justice Bldg.
10th St. and Constitution Ave. NW
Washington, DC 20530
Tel: (202) 514-2000, 514-2007 Fax: (202) 514-0468

Federal Bureau of Investigation (FBI)
10th St. and Pennsylvania Ave. NW
Washington, DC 20535
Tel: (202) 324-3000, 324-3691 Fax: (202) 324-4705

Immigration and Naturalization Service (INS)
425 Eye St. NW
Washington, DC 20536
Tel: (202) 514-4316 Fax: (202) 514-3296

Department of Labor

Department of Labor (DOL)
200 Constitution Ave. NW
Washington, DC 20210
Tel: (202) 219-5000, 219-7316 Fax: (202) 219-6161

Employment and Training Administration
200 Constitution Ave. NW
Washington, DC 20210
Tel: (202) 219-5000, 219-6871 Fax: (202) 219-6827

Occupational Safety and Health Administration (OSHA)
200 Constitution Ave. NW
Washington, DC 20210
Tel: (202) 219-8151, 219-7162 Fax: (202) 219-6064

Office of International Economic Affairs
200 Constitution Ave. NW #S5325
Washington, DC 20210
Tel: (202) 219-7597 Fax: (202) 219-5071

Department of State

Department of State
Main State Bldg.
2201 C St. NW
Washington, DC 20520
Tel: (202) 647-3686, 647-4000 Fax: (202) 647-0464

Bureau of Economic and Business Affairs
2201 C St. NW
Washington, DC 20520
Tel: (202) 647-7575 Fax: (202) 647-5713

Bureau of International Organization Affairs
2201 C St. NW
Washington, DC 20520
Tel: (202) 647-3686, 647-6400 Fax: (202) 647-6510

Bureau of Oceans and International Environmental and Scientific Affairs
2201 C St. NW
Washington, DC 20520
Tel: (202) 647-3686, 647-4000 Fax: (202) 647-0217

US International Development Cooperation Agency
Main State Bldg.
2201 C St. NW
Washington, DC 20523
Tel: (202) 647-1850, 647-9620 Fax: (202) 647-1770

Department of Transportation

Department of Transportation (DOT)
400 7th St. SW
Washington, DC 20590
Tel: (202) 366-4000, 366-5580 Fax: (202) 426-4508

Federal Aviation Administration (FAA)
800 Independence Ave. SW
Washington, DC 20591
Tel: (202) 366-4000, 267-8521 Fax: (202) 267-5047

Federal Highway Administration (FHA)
400 7th St. SW
Washington, DC 20590
Tel: (202) 366-4000, 366-0660 Fax: (202) 366-7239

Federal Railroad Administration (FRA)
400 7th St. SW
Washington, DC 20590
Tel: (202) 366-4000, 366-4043 Fax: (202) 366-7009

Federal Transit Administration (FTA)
400 7th St. SW
Washington, DC 20590
Tel: (202) 366-4000, 366-4043 Fax: (202) 366-3472

Maritime Administration
400 7th St. SW
Washington, DC 20590
Tel: (202) 366-4000, 366-5807 Fax: (202) 366-3890

National Highway Traffic Safety Administration (NHTSA)
400 7th St. SW
Washington, DC 20590
Tel: (202) 366-4000, 366-9550 Fax: (202) 366-2106

Office of Hazardous Materials Safety
400 Seventh St. SW
Washington, DC 20590
Tel: (202) 366-0656 Fax: (202) 366-3753

Department of the Treasury

Department of the Treasury
Main Treasury Bldg.
15th St. and Pennsylvania Ave. NW
Washington, DC 20220
Tel: (202) 622-2000

Bureau of Alcohol, Tobacco and Firearms (BATF)
650 Massachusetts Ave. NW
Washington, DC 20226
Tel: (202) 927-7777, 927-8500 Fax: (202) 927-7862

Customs Service
1301 Constitution Ave. NW
Washington, DC 20229
Tel: (202) 927-6724, 927-6724 Fax: (202) 927-1393

Internal Revenue Service (IRS)
1111 Constitution Ave. NW
Washington, DC 20224
Tel: (202) 622-5000, (800) 829-1040
Fax: (202) 622-8393

Other Federal Agencies

Agency for International Development (AID)
Main State Bldg.
2201 C St. NW
Washington, DC 20523
Tel: (202) 663-1449, 647-1850 Fax: (202) 647-1770

Commodity Futures Trading Commission
2033 K St. NW
Washington, DC 20581
Tel: (202) 254-6387, 254-8630 Fax: (202) 254-6265

Consumer Product Safety Commission (CPSC)
Washington, DC 20207
Tel: (301) 504-0500, 504-0580 Fax: (301) 504-0124

Environmental Protection Agency (EPA)
401 M St. SW
Washington, DC 20460
Tel: (202) 260-2090, 260-2080
Fax: (202) 260-0500 (Enforcement)

Export-Import Bank of the United States (Eximbank)
811 Vermont Ave. NW
Washington, DC 20571
Tel: (202) 566-8990 Fax: (202) 566-7524

Federal Communications Commission (FCC)
1919 M St. NW
Washington, DC 20544
Tel: (202) 632-7106, 632-7000 Fax: (202) 653-5402

Federal Trade Commission (FTC)
6th St. and Pennsylvania Ave. NW
Washington, DC 20580
Tel: (202) 326-2000, 326-2222 Fax· (202) 326-2050

Interstate Commerce Commission (ICC)
12th St. and Constitution Ave. NW
Washington, DC 20423
Tel: (202) 927-5350, 927-6000 Fax: (202) 927-5728

National Labor Relations Board (NLRB)
1717 Pennsylvania Ave. NW
Washington, DC 20570
Tel: (202) 632-4950, 254-8064 Fax: (202) 254-6781

Office of the US Trade Representative
600 17th St. NW
Washington, DC 20506
Tel: (202) 395-3230 Fax: (202) 395-3911

Overseas Private Investment Corp. (OPIC)
1100 New York Ave. NW
Washington, DC 20527
Tel: (202) 457-7200, 336-8799 Fax: (202) 408-9859

Securities and Exchange Commission (SEC)
450 5th St. NW
Washington, DC 20549
Tel: (202) 272-2650 Fax: (202) 272-7050

Small Business Administration (SBA)
409 3rd St. SW
Washington, DC 20416
Tel: (202) 205-6740, 205-7713 Fax: (202) 205-7064

US International Trade Commission (ITC)
500 E St. SW
Washington, DC 20436
Tel: (202) 205-2000, 205-1000 Fax: (202) 205-1819

US Postal Service (USPS)
475 L'Enfant Plaza SW
Washington, DC 20260
Tel: (202) 268-2020, 268-2284 Fax: (202) 268-6980

US Trade and Development Agency
State Annex 16
Washington, DC 20523
Tel: (703) 875-4357 Fax: (703) 875-4009

OVERSEAS DIPLOMATIC MISSIONS OF THE USA

The US maintains diplomatic missions in over 170 countries worldwide; following is a partial listing.

Argentina
Embassy
4300 Colombia
1425 Buenos Aires, Argentina
Tel: [54] (1) 777-4533, 777-4534
Fax: [54] (1) 777-3547, 777-0673

Australia
Embassy
Moonah Place
Canberra, A.C.T. 2600, Australia
Tel: [61] (6) 270-5000 Fax: [61] (6) 270-5970

Consulates General in Melbourne, Sydney, and Perth
Consulate in Brisbane

Austria
Embassy
Boltzmanngasse 16
A-1091 Vienna, Austria
Tel: [43] (1) 313-39 Fax: [43] (1) 310-0682

Consular Section
Gartenbaupromenade 2, 4th Fl.
A-1010 Vienna, Austria
Tel: [43] (1) 313-39 Fax: [43] (1) 513-4351, 310-6917

Belgium
Embassy
27 Boulevard du Regent
B-1000 Brussels, Belgium
Tel. [32] (2) 513 3830 Fax: [32] (2) 511-2725, 512-6653

Brazil
Embassy
Avenida das Nacoes
Lote Brasilia 3, Brazil
Tel: [55] (61) 321-7272 Fax: [55] (61) 225-9136;

Consulates General in Rio de Janeiro and Sao Paulo
Consulate in Porto Alegre
Commercial and Agricultural Offices in Belo Horizonte and Belem Para

Canada
Embassy
100 Wellington St.
Ottawa, ON K1P 5T1, Canada
Tel: [1] (613) 238-5335, 238-4470
Fax: [1] (613) 238-5720, 233-8511
(US mailing address: PO Box 5000
Ogdensburg, NY 13669-0430)

Consulates General in Calgary, Halifax, Montreal, Quebec City, Toronto, and Vancouver

Chile
Embassy
Codina Bldg.
Agustinas Santiago 1343, Chile
Tel: [56] (2) 671-0133 Fax: [56] (2) 699-1141, 697-2051

China (People's Republic of)
Embassy
Xiu Shui Bei Jie 3
Beijing 100600, PRC
Tel: [86] (1) 532-3831 Fax: [86] (1)532-3178,532-3297

Consulates General in Guangzhou, Shanghai, Shenyang, and Chengdu

Colombia
Embassy
Calle 38, No. 8-61
Apartado Aereo
Bogota 3831, Colombia
Tel: [57] (1) 320-1300 Fax: [57] (1) 288-5687, 285-7945

Consulate in Barranquilla

Czech Republic
Embassy
Trziste 15
118 01 Prague 1, Czech Republic
Tel: [42] (2) 536-641/6 Fax: [42] (2) 532-457

Denmark
Embassy
Dag Hammarskjolds Alle 24
2100 Copenhagen
Copenhagen O, Denmark
Tel: [45] 31-42-31-44 Fax: [45] 35-43-02-23, 35-42-01-75

Dominican Republic
Embassy
Corner of Calle Cesar
Nicolas Penson y Calle Leopoldo Navarro
Santo Domingo, Dominican Republic
Tel: [1] (809) 5412171, 541-8100
Fax: [1] (809) 686-7437, 688-4838

Egypt (Arab Republic of)
Embassy
North Gate 8
Kamal El-Din Salah St.
Garden City
Cairo, Arab Republic of Egypt
Tel: [20] (2) 355-7371 Fax: [20] (2) 357-3200, 355-4353

Finland
Embassy
Itainen Puistotie 14A
Helsinki SF-00140, Finland
Tel: [358] (0) 171931
Fax: [358] (0) 174681, 635332, 171573

France
Embassy
2 Avenue Gabriel
75382 Paris Cedex 08, France
Tel: [33] (1) 42-96-12-02, 42-61-80-75
Fax: [33] (1) 42-66-97-83, 42-66-48-27

Consulates General in Bordeaux and Strasbourg
Commercial Offices in Lyon and Nice

Germany (Federal Republic of)
Bonn Embassy
Deichmanns Aue 29
53170 Bonn, Fed. Rep. of Germany
Tel: [49] (228) 339-1 Fax: [49] (228) 339-2663, 334-649

Berlin Embassy Branch Office
Neustaedtische Kirchstrasse 4-5
10117 Berlin, Fed. Rep. of Germany
Tel: [49] (30) 238-5174 Fax: [49] (30) 238-6290

Consulates General in Frankfurt am Main, Munich,
Stuttgart, and Leipzig
Commercial Office in Dusseldorf

Greece
Embassy
91 Vasilissis Sophias Blvd.
10160 Athens, Greece
Tel: [30] (1) 721-2951, 721-8401
Fax: [30] (1) 645-6282, 721-8660, 723-7332

Consulate General in Thessaloniki

Hong Kong
Consulate General
26 Garden Rd.
Hong Kong
Tel: [852] 2523-9011 Fax: [852] 2845-1598, 2845-9800

American Trade Office
18th Fl., St. John's Bldg.
33 Garden Rd.
Hong Kong
Tel: [852] 2841-2350 Fax: [852] 2845-0943

India
Embassy
Shanti Path
New Delhi
Chanakyapuri-110021, India
Tel: [91] (11) 600-651 Fax: [91] (11) 687-2028, 687-2391

Consulates General in Bombay, Calcutta, and Madras

Indonesia
Embassy
Medan Merdeka Selatan 5, Box 1
Jakarta, Indonesia
Tel: [62] (21) 360-360 Fax: [62] (21) 386-2259, 385-1632

Consulates General in Medan and Surabaya

Ireland
Embassy
42 Elgin Rd.
Ballsbridge
Dublin 2, Ireland
Tel: [353] (1) 668-7122, 668-9612
Fax: [353] (1) 668-9946, 668-2840

Israel
Embassy
71 Hayarkon St.
Tel: Aviv, Israel
Tel: [972] (3) 517-4338, 517-4347 Fax: [972] (3) 663-449

Italy
Embassy
Via Veneto 119/A
00187-Rome, Italy
Tel: [39] (6) 46741

Commercial Section
Centro Cooperazione Internazionale
Piazzale Giulio Cesare
20145 Milan, Italy
Tel: [39] (2) 498-2241/3 Fax: [39] (2) 481-4161

Consulates General in Florence, Milan, and Naples

Japan
Embassy
10-5, Akasaka 1-chome
Minato-ku
Tokyo 107, Japan
Tel: [81] (3) 3224-5000
Fax: [81] (3) 3505-1862, 3589-4235

US Trade Center
7th Fl., World Import Mart
1-3 Higashi Ikebukuro 3-chome
Toshima-ku
Tokyo 170, Japan
Tel: [81] (3) 3987-2441
Fax: [81] (3) 3987-2447, 3987-2447

Consulates Generals in Naha, Okinawa, Osaka-Kobe,
and Sapporo
Consulates in Fukuoka and Nagoya

Korea (South)
Embassy
82 Sejong-Ro
Chongro-ku
Seoul, Rep. of Korea
Tel: [82] (2) 397-4114 Fax: [82] (2) 738-8845

Luxembourg
Embassy
22 Blvd. Emmanuel-Servais
2535 Luxembourg
Tel: [352] 460123 Fax: [352] 461401

Malaysia
Embassy
376 Jalan Tun Razak
50400 Kuala Lumpur, Malaysia
Tel: [60] (3) 248-9011 Fax: [60] (3) 242-2207, 242-1866

Mexico
Embassy
Paseo de la Reforma 305
Col. Cuauhtemoc
06500 Mexico, DF, Mexico
Tel: [52] (5) 211-0042
Fax: [52] (5) 511-9980, 208-3373, 207-8938
(US Mailing address: PO Box 3087, Laredo, TX 78044)

US Export Development Office
Liverpool 31
06600 Mexico, DF, Mexico
Tel: [52] (5) 591-0155 Fax: [52] (5) 566-1115

Consulates General in Ciudad Juarez, Guadalajara,
Monterrey and Tijuana
Consulates in Hermosillo, Matamoros, and
Nuevo Laredo

Netherlands
Embassy
Lange Voorhout 102
2514 EJ The Hague, Netherlands
Tel: [31] (70) 310-9209
Fax: [31] (70) 361-4688, 363-2985

Consulate General in Amsterdam

New Zealand
Embassy
29 Fitzherbert Terr.
Thorndon
Wellington, New Zealand
Tel: [64] (4) 472-2068 Fax: [64] (4) 472-3537

Consulate General in Auckland

Norway
Embassy
Drammensveien 18
0244 Oslo 2, Norway
Tel: [47] 22-44-85-50 Fax: [47] 22-43-07-77

US Information Office in Tromso

Peru
Embassy
PO Box 1991
Lima, Peru
Tel: [51] (14) 338-000 Fax: [51] (14) 316-682

The Philippines
Embassy
1201 Roxas Blvd.
Ermita, Manila 1000, The Philippines
Tel: [63] (2) 521-7116 Fax: [63] (2) 522-4361

Commercial Office
395 Senator Gil J. Puyat Ave.
Makati, Metro Manila, The Philippines
Tel: [63] (2) 818-6674 Fax: [63] (2) 818-2684

Consulate in Cebu

Poland
Warsaw Embassy
Aleje Ujazdowskie 29/31
Warsaw, Poland
Tel: [48] (2) 628-3041 Fax: [48] (2) 628-8298

US Trade Center
Aleje Jerozolimskie 56C
IKEA Building, 2d Floor
00-803 Warsaw, Poland
Tel: [48] (22) 21-45-15, 21-42-16, 625-4375
Fax: [48] (22) 21-63-27

Consulates General in Krakow and Poznan

Portugal
Embassy
Avenida das Forcas Armadas
1600 Lisbon, Portugal
Tel: [351] (1) 726-6600, 726-6659, 726-8670, 726-8880
Fax: [351] (1) 726-9109

Consulates in Ponta Delgada, Sao Miguel, and Azores

Russia
Embassy
Novinskiy Bul'var 19/23
Moscow, Russia
Tel: [7] (095) 252-2451/9
Fax: [7] (095) 956-4261

US Commercial Office
Novinskiy Bul'var 15
Tel: [7] (095) 956-4255, 255-4848, 255-4660
Fax: [7] (095) 230-2101, 224-1106

Consulates General in St. Petersburg, Vladivostok, and
Yekaterinburg

Saudi Arabia
Embassy
PO Box 94309
Riyadh 11693, Saudi Arabia
Tel: [966] (1) 488-3800 Fax: [966] (1) 488-3237

US Rep. to the Saudi Arabian US Joint Commission on
Economic Cooperation
(USREP/JECOR)
PO Box 5927
Riyadh, Saudi Arabia

Consulates General in Dhahran and Jeddah

Singapore
Embassy
30 Hill St.
Singapore 0617
Tel: [65] 338-0251 Fax: [65] 338-4550

Commercial Services and Library
1 Colombo Court
Unit #05-16, Colombo Ct. Building
North Bridge Road
Singapore 0617
Tel: [65] 338-9722 Fax: [65] 338-5010

South Africa
Embassy
877 Pretorius St.
PO Box 9536
Pretoria, Rep. of South Africa
Tel: [27] (12) 342-1048 Fax: [27] (12) 342-2244

Consulates General in Cape Town, Durban, and
Johannesburg

Spain
Embassy
Serrano 75
28006 Madrid, Spain
Tel: [34] (1) 577-4000 Fax: [34] (1) 577-5735

Consulate General in Barcelona
Consulate in Bilbao

Sweden
Embassy
Strandvagen 101
S-115 89 Stockholm, Sweden
Tel: [46] (8) 783-5300 Fax: [46] (8) 661-1964

Switzerland
Embassy
Jubilaeumstrasse 93
3005 Bern, Switzerland
Tel: [41] (31) 357-7011 Fax: [41] (31) 357-7344

US Trade Representative
Botanic Bldg.
1-3 Avenue de la Paix
1202 Geneva, Switzerland
Tel: [41] (22) 749-4111 Fax: [41] (22) 749-4885

Taiwan
The US does not maintain an embassy in Taiwan.
Unofficial commercial and other relations are
conducted through the American Institute in Taiwan.

American Institute in Taiwan
#7 Lane 134
Hsin Yi Road, Section 3
Taipei, Taiwan ROC
Tel: [886] (2) 709-2000, 709-2013
Fax: [886] (2) 702-7675

American Trade Center
Room 3207, International Trade Building
Taipei World Trade Center
333 Keelung Road, Section 1
Taipei 10548, Taiwan ROC
Tel: [886] (2)720-1550 Fax: [886] (2) 757-7162

Thailand
Embassy
95 Wireless Rd.
Bangkok, Thailand
Tel: [66] (2) 252-5040 Fax: [66] (2) 254-2990

Commercial Office
3d Fl., Towers Bldg., Tower A
93/1 Wireless Rd.
Diethelm 10330, Thailand
Tel: [66] (2) 255-4365-7 Fax: [66] (2) 255-2915

Consulate General in Chiang Mai
Consulate in Udorn

Turkey
Embassy
110 Ataturk Blvd.
Ankara, Turkey
Tel: [90] (312) 468-6110, 468-6128
Fax: [90] (312) 467-1366

Consulate General in Istanbul
Consulate in Adana

United Kingdom
Embassy
24/31 Grosvenor Sq.
London W1A 1AE, UK
Tel: [44] (71) 499-9000
Fax: [44] (71) 409-1637, 491-4022

American Trade Office
Regent Arcade House
19-25 Argyll St.
London W1V 1AA, UK
Tel: [44] (71) 287-2624 Fax: [44] (71) 287-2629

Consulates General in Belfast, Northern Ireland; and
Edinburgh, Scotland

Venezuela
Embassy
Miranda y Avenida Principal de la Floresta
PO Box 62291
Caracas 1060-A, Venezuela
Tel: [58] (2) 285-2222, 285-3111 Fax: [58] (2) 285-0366

Trade Office
Centro Plaza, Torre C, Piso 18
Los Palos Grandes
Caracas 1062, Venezuela
Tel: [58] (2) 283-2353, 283-2521
Fax: [58] (2) 284-5412

Consulate in Maracaibo

FOREIGN DIPLOMATIC MISSIONS IN THE USA

Embassy of Algeria
2811 Kalorama Rd. NW
Washington, DC 20008
Tel: (202) 265-2800 Fax: (202) 667-2174

Embassy of Argentine Republic
Economics and Trade Division
1901 L St. NW, Suite 640
Washington, DC 20036
Tel: (202) 265-4557, 387-2527 Fax: (202) 775-4388

Embassy of Australia
1601 Massachusetts Ave. NW
Washington, DC 20036
Tel: (202) 797-3000 Fax: (202) 797-3168

Embassy of Austria
3524 International Court NW
Washington, DC 20008
Tel: (202) 895-6700 Fax: (202) 895-6750

Embassy of the Commonwealth of the Bahamas
2220 Massachusetts Ave. NW
Washington, DC 20008
Tel: (202) 319-2660 Fax: (202) 319-2668

Embassy of the People's Republic of Bangladesh
2201 Wisconsin Ave. NW
Washington, DC 20007
Tel: (202) 342-8372 Fax: (202) 333-4971

Embassy of Belgium
3330 Garfield St. NW
Washington, DC 20008
Tel: (202) 333-6900, 625-7567 Fax: (202) 333-3079

Embassy of Belize
2535 Massachusetts Ave. NW
Washington, DC 20008
Tel: (202) 332-9636 Fax: (202) 332-6888

Embassy of the Republic of Bolivia
3014 Massachusetts Ave. NW
Washington, DC 20008
Tel: (202) 483-4410 Fax: (202) 328-3712

Embassy of Brazil
3006 Massachusetts Ave. NW
Washington, DC 20008
Tel: (202) 745-2700 Fax: (202) 745-2827

Embassy of Brunei Darussalam
2600 Virginia Ave. NW, Suite 300
Washington, DC 20037
Tel: (202) 342-0159 Fax: (202) 342-0158

Embassy of the Republic of Bulgaria
1621 22nd St. NW
Washington, DC 20008
Tel: (202) 387-7969 Fax: (202) 234-7973

Embassy of Canada
501 Pennsylvania Ave. NW
Washington, DC 20001
Tel: (202) 682-1740 Fax: (202) 682-7726

Embassy of Chile
1732 Massachusetts Ave. NW
Washington, DC 20036
Tel: (202) 785-1746 Fax: (202) 887-5579

Embassy of The People's Republic of China
2300 Connecticut Ave. NW
Washington, DC 20008
Tel: (202) 328-2500 Fax: (202) 234-3715

Embassy of Colombia
2118 Leroy Plaza NW
Washington, DC 20008
Tel: (202) 387-8338 Fax: (202) 232-8643

Embassy of Costa Rica
2114 S St. SW
Washington, DC 20008
Tel: (202) 234-2945 Fax: (202) 265-4795

Embassy of the Republic of Cote d'Ivoire
2424 Massachusetts Ave. NW
Washington, DC 20008
Tel: (202) 797-0300 Fax: (202) 483-8482

Embassy of the Republic of Cyprus
2211 R St. NW
Washington, DC 20008
Tel: (202) 462-5772 Fax: (202) 483-6710

Embassy of the Czech Republic
3900 Spring of Freedom St. NW
Washington, DC 20008
Tel: (202) 363-6315 Fax: (202) 966-8540

Embassy of Denmark
3200 Whitehaven St. NW
Washington, DC 20008
Tel: (202) 234-4300 Fax: (202) 328-1470

Embassy of the Dominican Republic
1715 22nd St. NW
Washington, DC 20008
Tel: (202) 332-6280 Fax: (202) 265-8057

Embassy of Ecuador
2535 15th St. NW
Washington, DC 20009
Tel: (202) 234-7200 Fax: (202) 667-3482

Embassy of the Arab Republic of Egypt
3521 International Ct. NW
Washington, DC 20008
Tel: (202) 895-5400 Fax: (202) 244-4319

Embassy of El Salvador
2308 California St. NW
Washington, DC 20008
Tel: (202) 265-9671

Embassy of Finland
3301 Massachusetts Ave. NW
Washington, DC 20008
Tel: (202) 298-5800 Fax: (202) 244-4319

Embassy of France
4101 Reservoir Rd. NW
Washington, DC 20007
Tel: (202) 944-6000 Fax: (202) 944-6116

Embassy of the Federal Republic of Germany
4645 Reservoir Rd. NW
Washington, DC 20007
Tel: (202) 298-4000 Fax: (202) 298-4249

Embassy of Ghana
3512 International Dr. NW
Washington, DC 20008
Tel: (202) 686-4520 Fax: (202) 686-4527

Embassy of Greece
2221 Massachusetts Ave. NW
Washington, DC 20008
Tel: (202) 939-5800 Fax: (202) 939-5824

Embassy of Guatemala
2220 R St. NW
Washington, DC 20008
Tel: (202) 745-4952 Fax: (202) 745-1908

Embassy of the Republic of Haiti
2311 Massachusetts Ave. NW
Washington, DC 20008
Tel: (202) 332-4090 Fax: (202) 745-7215

Embassy of Honduras
3007 Tilden St. NW
Washington, DC 20008
Tel: (202) 966-7702 Fax: (202) 966-9751

Embassy of the Republic of Hungary
3910 Shoemaker St. NW
Washington, DC 20008
Tel: (202) 362-6730 Fax: (202) 966-8135

Embassy of Iceland
1156 15th St. NW, Suite 1200
Washington, DC 20005
Tel: (202) 265-6653 Fax: (202) 265-6656

Embassy of India
2107 Massachusetts Ave. NW
Washington, DC 20008
Tel: (202) 939-7000 Fax: (202) 939-7027

Embassy of the Republic of Indonesia
2020 Massachusetts Ave. NW
Washington, DC 20036
Tel: (202) 775-5200 Fax: (202) 775-5365

Embassy of Ireland
2234 Massachusetts Ave. NW
Washington, DC 20008
Tel: (202) 462-3939 Fax: (202) 232-5993

Embassy of Israel
3514 International Dr. NW
Washington, DC 20008
Tel: (202) 364-5500 Fax: (202) 364-5610

Embassy of Italy
1601 Fuller St. NW
Washington, DC 20009
Tel: (202) 328-5500 Fax: (202) 238-5542

Embassy of Jamaica
1520 New Hampshire Ave. NW
Washington, DC 20036
Tel: (202) 452-0660 Fax: (202) 452-0081

Embassy of Japan
2520 Massachusetts Ave. NW
Washington, DC 20008
Tel: (202) 939-6700 Fax: (202) 328-2187

Embassy of the Hashemite Kingdom of Jordan
3504 International Dr. NW
Washington, DC 20008
Tel: (202) 966-2664 Fax: (202) 966-3110

Embassy of the Republic of Kenya
2249 R St. NW
Washington, DC 20008
Tel: (202) 387-6101 Fax: (202) 462-3829

Embassy of the Republic of Korea
2450 Massachusetts Ave. NW
Washington, DC 20008
Tel: (202) 939-5600 Fax: (202) 797-0595

Embassy of the State of Kuwait
2940 Tilden St. NW
Washington, DC 20008
Tel: (202) 966-0702 Fax: (202) 966-0517

Embassy of Lebanon
2560 28th St. NW
Washington, DC 20008
Tel: (202) 939-6300 Fax: (202) 939-6324

Embassy of Lithuania
2622 16th St. NW
Washington, DC 20009
Tel: (202) 234-5860 Fax: (202) 328-0466

Embassy of Luxembourg
2200 Massachusetts Ave. NW
Washington, DC 20008
Tel: (202) 265-4171 Fax: (202) 328-8270

Embassy of Malaysia
2401 Massachusetts Ave. NW
Washington, DC 20008
Tel: (202) 328-2700 Fax: (202) 483-7661

Embassy of Mexico
1911 Pennsylvania Ave. NW
Washington, DC 20006
Tel: (202) 728-1600 Fax: (202) 728-1712

Embassy of the Kingdom of Morocco
1601 21st St. NW
Washington, DC 20009
Tel: (202) 462-7979 Fax: (202) 265-0161

Embassy of the Netherlands
4200 Linnean Ave. NW
Washington, DC 20008
Tel: (202) 244-5300 Fax: (202) 362-3430

Embassy of New Zealand
37 Observatory Circle NW
Washington, DC 20008
Tel: (202) 328-4800 Fax: (202) 667-5227

Embassy of Nicaragua
1627 New Hampshire Ave. NW
Washington, DC 20009
Tel: (202) 939-6570 Fax: (202) 939-6542

Embassy of the Federal Republic of Nigeria
1333 16th St. NW
Washington, DC 20036
Tel: (202) 986-9400

Embassy of Norway
2720 34th St. NW
Washington, DC 20008
Tel: (202) 333-6000 Fax: (202) 337-0870

Embassy of Pakistan
2315 Massachusetts Ave. NW
Washington, DC 20008
Tel: (202) 939-6200 Fax: (202) 387-0484

Embassy of Panama
2862 McGill Terrace NW
Washington, DC 20008
Tel: (202) 483-1407 Fax: (202) 483-8413

Embassy of Paraguay
2400 Massachusetts Ave. NW
Washington, DC 20008
Tel: (202) 483-6960 Fax: (202) 234-4508

Embassy of Peru
1700 Massachusetts Ave. NW
Washington, DC 20036
Tel: (202) 833-9860 Fax: (202) 659-8124

Embassy of the Philippines
1600 Massachusetts Ave. NW
Washington, DC 20036
Tel: (202) 467-9300 Fax: (202) 328-7614

Embassy of the Republic of Poland
2640 16th St. NW
Washington, DC 20009
Tel: (202) 234-3800 Fax: (202) 328-6271

Embassy of Portugal
2125 Kalorama Rd. NW
Washington, DC 20008
Tel: (202) 328-8610 Fax: (202) 462-3726

Embassy of Romania
1607 23rd St. NW
Washington, DC 20008
Tel: (202) 332-4846 Fax: (202) 232-4748

Embassy of the Russian Federation
2650 Wisconsin Ave. NW
Washington, DC 20007
Tel: (202) 298-5700 Fax: (202) 298-5735

Embassy of Saudi Arabia
601 New Hampshire Ave. NW
Washington, DC 20037
Tel: (202) 342-3800 Fax: (202) 337-3233

Embassy of the Republic of Senegal
2112 Wyoming Ave. NW
Washington, DC 20008
Tel: (202) 234-0540 Fax: (202) 332-6315

Embassy of the Republic of Singapore
3501 International Place NW
Washington, DC 20008
Tel: (202) 537-3100 Fax: (202) 537-0876

Embassy of the Republic of South Africa
3051 Massachusetts Ave. NW
Washington, DC 20008
Tel: (202) 232-4400 Fax: (202) 265-1607

Embassy of Spain
2375 Pennsylvania Ave. NW
Washington, DC 20037
Tel: (202) 452-0100 Fax: (202) 833-5670

Embassy of the Democratic Socialist Republic
of Sri Lanka
2148 Wyoming Ave. NW
Washington, DC 20008
Tel: (202) 483-4025 Fax: (202) 232-7181

Embassy of Sweden
1501 M St. NW
Washington, DC 20005
Tel: (202) 467-2600 Fax: (202) 467-2699

Embassy of Switzerland
2900 Cathedral Ave. NW
Washington, DC 20008
Tel: (202) 745-7900 Fax: (202) 387-2564

Embassy of the Syrian Arab Republic
2215 Wyoming Ave. NW
Washington, DC 20008
Tel: (202) 232-6313 Fax: (202) 234-9548

Embassy of Thailand
1024 Wisconsin Ave. NW
Washington, DC 20007
Tel: (202) 944-3600 Fax: (202) 944-3611

Embassy of the Republic of Trinidad and Tobago
1708 Massachusetts Ave. NW
Washington, DC 20036
Tel: (202) 467-6490 Fax: (202) 785-3130

Embassy of Tunisia
1515 Massachusetts Ave. NW
Washington, DC 20005
Tel: (202) 862-1850 Fax: (202) 862-1858

Embassy of the Republic of Turkey
1714 Massachusetts Ave. NW
Washington, DC 20036
Tel: (202) 659-8200

Embassy of Ukraine
3350 M St. NW
Washington, DC 20007
Tel: (202) 333-0606 Fax: (202) 333-0817

Embassy of the United Arab Emirates
3000 K St. NW, Suite 600
Washington, DC 20007
Tel: (202) 338-6500 Fax: (202) 337-7029

Embassy of the United Kingdom
3100 Massachusetts Ave. NW
Washington, DC 20008
Tel: (202) 462-1340 Fax: (202) 898-4255

Embassy of Uruguay
1918 F St. NW
Washington, DC 20006
Tel: (202) 331-1313 Fax: (202) 593-0935

Embassy of the Republic of Venezuela
1099 30th St. NW
Washington, DC 20008
Tel: (202) 342-2214 Fax: (202) 342-6820

All addresses and telephone numbers are in the United States unless otherwise noted. The country code for the US is [1].

TRADE PROMOTION ORGANIZATIONS

WORLD TRADE CENTERS

This is a selective list of the many World Trade Centers Association members operating in the US. The WTC Association also has facilities in Baltimore, MD; Irvine, CA; Lexington, KY; Long Beach, CA; Madison, WI; New Orleans, LA; Norfolk, VA; Portland, OR; St. Paul, MN; and Tacoma, WA. Other cities have active WTC Associations, but facilities have not yet been built. For a more complete list, contact the WTC in New York.

World Trade Center Atlanta
240 Peachtree St. NW, Suite 2200
Atlanta, Georgia 30303
Tel: (404) 525-4144 Fax: (404) 525-4991

World Trade Center Boston
Executive Offices, Suite 50
Boston, MA 02210-2004
Tel: (617) 439-5001 Fax: (617) 439-5033

World Trade Center Chicago
One World Trade Center
929 Merchandise Mart Plaza
Chicago, IL 60654
Tel: (312) 467-0550 Fax: (312) 467-0615

World Trade Center Denver
1625 Broadway, Suite 680
Denver, CO 80202
Tel: (303) 592-5760 Fax: (303) 892-3820

World Trade Center Houston
1200 Smith, Suite 700
Houston, TX 77002-4309
Tel: (713) 651-2229 Fax: (713) 651-2299

Los Angeles World Trade Center
Greater Los Angeles World Trade Center Association
350 S. Figueroa St., Suite 172
Los Angeles, CA 90071
Tel: (213) 680-1888 Fax: (213) 680-1878

World Trade Center Miami
One World Trade Plaza
80 SW 8th St., Suite 1800
Miami, FL 33130
Tel: (305) 579-0064 Fax: (303) 536-7701, 530-0641

World Trade Center New York
The Port Authority of New York and New Jersey
One World Trade Center, Suite 35 East
New York, NY 10048
Tel: (212) 435-8385 Fax: (212) 435-2810

World Trade Center Portland
121 SW Salmon St., Suite 250
Portland, OR 97204
Tel: (503) 464-8888 Fax: (503) 464-8880

World Trade Center St. Louis
121 S. Meramec, Suite 1111
St. Louis, MO 63105
Tel: (314) 854-6141 Fax: (314) 862-0102

World Trade Center of San Francisco
110 Sutter St., Suite 408
San Francisco, CA 94104
Tel: (415) 392-2705 Fax: (415) 392-1710

World Trade Center Seattle
1301 Fifth Ave., Suite 2400
Seattle, WA 98101-2603
Tel: (206) 389-7301 Fax: (206) 624-5689

World Trade Center Washington, DC
6801 Oxon Hill Road
Oxon Hill, Maryland 20745-1120
Tel: (301) 839-2477 Fax: (301) 839-7868

GENERAL TRADE AND BUSINESS ORGANIZATIONS

American Association of Exporters and Importers (AAEI)
11 West 42nd St.
New York, NY 10036
Tel: (212) 944-2230 Fax: (212) 382-2606

American Society of International Executives
122 C St. NW, Suite 740
Washington, DC 20001
Tel: (202) 783-0051

The Brookings Institution
1775 Massachusetts Ave. NW
Washington, DC 20036
Tel: (202) 797-6105 Fax: (202) 797-6003

The Business Council
888 17th St. NW
Washington, DC 20006
Tel: (202) 298-7650 Fax: (202) 785-0296

Council of State Chambers of Commerce
122 C St. NW, Suite 330
Washington, DC 20001
Tel: (202) 484-8103 Fax: (202) 737-4806

Emergency Committee for American Trade
1211 Connecticut Ave. NW, Suite 801
Washington, DC 20036
Tel: (202) 659-5147 Fax: (202) 659-1347

Federation of International Trade Associations (FITA)
1851 Alexander Bell Drive
Reston, VA 22091
Tel: (703) 391-6108

Industrial Research Institute
1550 M St. NW
Washington, DC 20005
Tel: (202) 872-6350 Fax: (202) 872-6356

International Trade Council
PO Box 2478
Alexandria, VA 22305
Tel: (703) 548-1234

International Trade Facilitation Council
3144 Circle Hill Rd.
Alexandria, VA 22305
Tel: (703) 548-1234

International Traders Association
The Mellinger Company
6100 Variel Ave.
Woodland Hills, CA 91367
Tel: (818) 884-4400

National Association of Export Companies (NEXCO)
PO Box 1330, Murray Hill Station
New York, NY 10156
Tel: (212) 725-3311 Fax: (212) 725-3312

National Cooperative Business Association
1401 New York Ave. NW, #1100
Washington, DC 20005
Tel: (202) 638-6222 Fax: (202) 638-1374

National Customs Brokers and Forwarders Association of America (NCBFAA)
One World Trade Center, Suite 1153
New York, NY 10048
Tel: (212) 432-0050 Fax: (212) 432-5709

National Foreign Trade Council (NFTC)
1625 K St. NW
Washington, DC 20006
Tel: (202) 887-0278 Fax: (202) 452-8160

National Industrial Council
1331 Pennsylvania Ave. NW, #1500N
Washington, DC 20004
Tel: (202) 637-3053 Fax: (202) 637-3182

Small Business Exporters Association (SBEA)
4603 John Taylor Court
Annandale, VA 22003
Tel: (703) 642-2490 Fax: (703) 750-9655

US Chamber of Commerce
International Division
1615 H St. NW
Washington, DC 20062
Tel: (202) 463-5460 Fax: (202) 463-3114

United States Council for International Business
1212 Ave. of the Americas, 21st Floor
New York, NY 10026
Tel: (212) 354-4480 Fax: (212) 575-0327
*The US affiliate of the International Chamber of
Commerce (ICC)*

US Business and Industrial Council
220 National Press Bldg.
14th and F Streets NW
Washington, DC 20045
Tel: (202) 662-8744 Fax: (202) 662-8754

US CHAMBERS OF COMMERCE

*This is a selective list of chambers of commerce in
major US cities.*

Eastern Baltimore Area Chamber of Commerce
2 Dunmanway
Dunkirk Building, Suite 238
Baltimore, MD 21222
Tel: (301) 282-9100 Fax: (301) 282-9103

Greater Boston Chamber of Commerce
600 Atlantic Ave., 13th Floor
Boston, MA 02210-2200
Tel: (617) 227-4500

Chicago Association of Commerce & Industry
200 North LaSalle St.
Chicago, IL 60601
Tel: (312) 580-6900 Fax: (312) 580-0046

Greater Cincinnati Chamber of Commerce
and World Trade Association
300 Carew Tower
441 Vine St.
Cincinnati, OH 45202-2812
Tel: (513) 579-3143 Fax: (513) 579-3102

Cleveland Growth Association
200 Tower City Center
Cleveland, OH 44113
Tel: (216) 621-3300 Fax: (216) 621-6013

Columbus Area Chamber of Commerce
PO Box 1527
Columbus, OH 43216
Tel: (614) 221-1321 Fax: (614) 469-8250

Greater Dallas Chamber of Commerce
1201 Elm St., Suite 2000
Dallas, TX 75270
Tel: (214) 746-6739

Greater Detroit Chamber of Commerce
600 West Lafayette Blvd.
Detroit, MI 48226
Tel: (313) 964-4000 Fax: (313) 964-0531

Fort Lauderdale Area Chamber of Commerce
512 NE Third Ave.
Ft. Lauderdale, FL 33301
Tel: (305) 462-6000 Fax: (305) 527-8766

Greater Houston Partnership
1100 Milam St., 25th Floor
Houston, TX 77002
Tel: (713) 658-2416

Indianapolis Chamber of Commerce
320 N. Meridean St., Suite 928
Indianapolis, IN 46204
Tel: (317) 464-2200 Fax: (317) 464-2233

Jacksonville Chamber of Commerce
PO Box 329
Jacksonville, FL 32201
Tel: (904) 366-6600

Los Angeles Area Chamber of Commerce
International Commerce Division
404 South Bixel St.
Los Angeles, CA 90017
Tel: (213) 629-0602 Fax: (213) 629-0708

Greater Miami Chamber of Commerce
International Economic Development
Omni Complex
1601 Biscayne Blvd.
Miami, FL 33132
Tel: (305) 350-7700 Fax: (305) 3374-6902

New Orleans Area Chamber of Commerce
PO Box 30240
New Orleans, LA 70190
Tel: (504) 527-6900 Fax: (504) 527-6950

New York Chamber of Commerce
1 Battery Park Plaza
New York, NY 10004
Tel: (212) 493-7400 Fax: (212) 344-3344

Greater Philadelphia Chamber of Commerce
1234 Market St., Suite 1800
Philadelphia, PA 19107-3718
Tel: (215) 972-3990 Fax: (215) 972-3900

Phoenix Chamber of Commerce
34 West Monroe St., Suite 900
Phoenix, AZ 85003
Tel: (602) 254-5521 Fax: (602) 495-8913

Greater San Diego Chamber of Commerce
402 W. Broadway, Suite 1000
San Diego, CA 92101-3585
Tel: (619) 232-0124 x391 Fax: (619) 234-0571

San Francisco Chamber of Commerce
San Francisco World Trade Association
465 California St., 9th Floor
San Francisco, CA 94104
Tel: (415) 392-4511, x 801/822 Fax: (415) 392-0485

San Jose Chamber of Commerce
180 S. Market St.
San Jose, CA 95113
Tel: (408) 998-7000 Fax: (408) 286-5019

Greater Seattle Chamber of Commerce
Trade and Transportation Division
600 University Ave., #1200
Seattle, WA 98101
Tel: (206) 389-7307

District of Columbia Chamber of Commerce
1411 K St. NW, Suite 603
Washington, DC 20005
Tel: (202) 347-7201

Greater Washington Board of Trade
1129 20th St. NW
Washington, DC 20036
Tel: (202) 857-5900

STATE GOVERNMENT TRADE OFFICES

Each state has a trade office or commerce department.
A selective list follows.

California State World Trade Commission
1121 L St., Suite 310
Sacramento, CA 95814
Tel: (916) 324-5511 Fax: (916) 324-5791

Colorado International Trade Office
1625 Broadway, Suite 680
Denver, CO 80202
Tel: (303) 892-2850 Fax: (303) 892-3848

Connecticut Department of Economic Development
International Division
865 Brook St.
Rocky Hill, CT 06067
Tel: (203) 258-4200 Fax: (203) 529-0535

District of Columbia Office of International Business
1250 Eye St. NW, Suite 1003
Washington, DC 20005
Tel: (202) 727-1576 Fax: (202) 727-1588

Florida Department of Commerce
International Trade & Development
107 West Gaines St., Room 366
Tallahassee, FL 32399-2000
Tel: (904) 487-1399 Fax: (904) 487-1407

Georgia Department of Industry, Trade and Tourism
Division of Trade
PO Box 1776
Atlanta, GA 30301
Tel: (404) 656-3556 Fax: (404) 656-3567

Illinois Department of Commerce
International Business Division
100 West Randolph, Suite C-400
Chicago, IL 60601
Tel: (312) 814-7164 Fax: (312) 814-6581

Michigan Export Development Authority
1200 Sixth St.
Detroit, MI 48226
Tel: (313) 256-2004 Fax: (313) 256-1046

New Jersey Department of Commerce
and Economic Development
Division of International Trade
153 Halsey St., Fifth Floor
Newark, NJ 07100
Tel: (201) 648-3518 Fax: (201) 623-1287

New York Department of Commerce
International Division
1515 Broadway, 51st Floor
New York, NY 10036
Tel: (212) 827-6210 Fax: (212) 827-6263

North Carolina Department of Economic
and Community Development
430 North Salisbury St.
Raleigh, NC 27611
Tel: (919) 733-7193 Fax: (919) 733-0110

Ohio Department of Development
International Trade Division
77 South High St., 29th Floor
PO Box 1001
Columbus, OH 43266
Tel: (614) 466-2317 Fax: (614) 644-1789

Pennsylvania Department of Commerce
Bureau of Foreign Investment
486 Forum Building
Harrisburg, PA 17120
Tel: (717) 787-7190 Fax: (717) 234-4560

Texas Department of Commerce
PO Box 12728
Austin, TX 78711
Tel: (512) 472-5059 Fax: (512) 472-5059

AMCHAM OVERSEAS OFFICES

American Chambers of Commerce (AmChams) are
voluntary associations of business executives concerned
with US foreign trade and investment. AmChams
represent their members before governments, business
communities and the general public.

Argentina
AmCham in Argentina
Avenue Leandro North Alem 1110, Piso 13
1101 Buenos Aires, Argentina
Tel: [54] (1) 311-5420, 311-5126
Fax: [54] (1) 311-9076

Australia
AmCham in Australia—Sydney
Level 2, 41 Lower Fort St.
Sydney, N.S.W. 2000, Australia
Tel: [61] (2) 241-1907 Fax: [61] (2) 251-5220

AmCham in Australia—Adelaide
Level 1, 300 Flinders St.
Adelaide, S.A. 5000, Australia
Tel: [61] (8) 224-0761 Fax: [61] (8) 224-0628

AmCham in Australia—Melbourne
Level 1, 123 Lonsdale St.
Melbourne, Victoria 3000, Australia
Tel: [61] (3) 663-2644 Fax: [61] (3) 663-2473

AmCham in Australia—Brisbane
Level 23, 68 Queen St.
Brisbane, Queensland 4000, Australia
Tel: [61] (7) 221-8542 Fax: [61] (7) 221-6313

AmCham in Australia—Perth
Level 6, 231 Adelaide Terrace
Perth, W.A. 6000, Australia
Tel: [61] (9) 325-9540 Fax: [61] (9) 221-3725

Austria
AmCham in Austria
Porzellangasse 35
A-1090 Vienna, Austria
Tel: [43] (1) 319-5751 Fax: [43] (1) 319-5151

Belgium
AmCham in Belgium
Avenue des Arts 50, Boite 5
B-1040 Brussels, Belgium
Tel: [32] (2) 513-67-70/9 Fax: [32] (2) 513-79-28

Bolivia
AmCham of Bolivia
Casilla 8268
La Paz, Bolivia
Tel: [591] (2) 342-523 Fax: [591] (2) 371-503

Brazil
AmCham in Brazil—Rio de Janeiro
C.P. 916, Praca Pio X-15, Fifth Floor
20040 Rio de Janiero, RJ, Brazil
Tel: [55] (21) 203-2477 Fax: [55] (21) 263-4477

AmCham for Brazil—Salvador
Rua da Espanha 2, Salas 604-606
40000 Salvador, Bahia, Brazil
Tel: [55] (71) 242-0077, 242-5606
Fax: [55] (71) 243-9986

AmCham for Brazil—Sao Paulo
Rua Alexandre Dumas 1976
04717 Sao Paulo, SP, Brazil
Tel: [55] (11) 246-9199 Fax: [55] (11) 246-9080

Chile
Chilean-American Chamber of Commerce
Avenida Americo Vespucio Sur 80, 9 Piso
82 Correo 34
Santiago, Chile
Tel: [56] (2) 208-4140 Fax: [56] (2) 206-0911

China
AmCham in the People's Republic of China—Beijing
G/F, Great Wall Sheraton Hotel
North Donghuan Road
Beijing, PRC
Tel: [86] (1) 500 5566 x2271

AmCham in Shanghai
c/o Union Building, Suite 1804
100 Yanan Road, East
Shanghai 200002, PRC
Tel: [86] (21) 326-5800 Fax: [86] (21) 320-0203

Colombia
Colombian-American Chamber of Commerce
Apdo. Aéreo 8008
Calle 35, No. 6-16
Bogotá, Colombia
Tel: [57] (1) 285-7800 Fax: [57] (1) 288-6434

Colombian-American Chamber of Commerce—
Medellín
Apartado Aéreo 66655
Medellín, Colombia
Tel: [57] (4) 268-7491

Offices also in Cali and Cartagena

Costa Rica
Costa Rican-American Chamber of Commerce
c/o Aerocasillas, PO Box 025216
Department 1576
Miami, FL 33102-5216
Tel: [506] 20-22-00 Fax: [506] 20-23-00

Czech & Slovak Republics
AmCham in Czech and Slovak Republics
Karlovo Namesti 24
120 80 Prague 2, Czech Republic
Tel: [42] (2) 299-887 Fax: [42] (2) 291-481

Dominican Republic
AmCham in the Dominican Republic
Torre B.H.D.
Av. Winston Churchill, PO Box 95-2
Santo Domingo, Dominican Republic
Tel: [1] (809) 544-2222 Fax: [1] (809) 544-0502

Ecuador
Ecuadorian-American Chamber of Commerce
Edificio Multicentra, 4 P
La Niña y Avda. 6 de Diciembre
Quito, Ecuador
Tel: [593] (2) 543-512 Fax: [593] (2) 505-571

Ecuadorian-American Chamber of Commerce
F. Cordova 812, Piso 3, Oficina 1
Edificio Torres de la Merced
Guayaquil, Ecuador
Tel: [593] (4) 566-481 Fax: [593] (4) 563-259

Egypt
AmCham in Egypt
Cairo Marriott Hotel, Suite 1541
PO Box 33 Zamalek
Cairo, Egypt
Tel: [20] (2) 340-8888

El Salvador
AmCham of El Salvador
87 Avenue North, #720
Apartment A, Col. Escalón
San Salvador, El Salvador
Tel: [503] 23-3292 Fax: [503] 24-6856

France
AmCham in France
21 Avenue George V
F-75008 Paris, France
Tel: [33] (1) 47-23-70-28 Fax: [33] (1) 47-20-18-62

Germany
AmCham in Germany
Rossmarkt 12, Postfach 100 162
D-6000 Frankfurt/Main 1, Germany
Tel: [49] (69) 28-34-01 Fax: [49] (69) 28-56-32

AmCham in Germany—Berlin
Budapesterstrasse 29
W-1000 Berlin 30, Germany
Tel: [49] (30) 261-55-86 Fax: [49] (30) 262-26-00

Greece
American—Hellenic Chamber of Commerce
16 Kanari St., 3rd Floor
Athens 106 74, Greece
Tel: [30] (1) 36-18-385, 36-36-407
Fax: [30] (1) 36-10-170

Guatemala
AmCham in Guatemala
12 Calle-I-25, Zona 10
Edif. Giminis 10, Torre Norte
Nivel 12, Of. 1206
Guatemala, Guatemala
Tel: [502] (2) 353-372 Fax: [502] (2) 353-372

Honduras
Honduran-American Chamber of Commerce
Hotel Honduras Maya, Apdo. Pos. 1838
Tegucigalpa, Honduras
Tel: [504] 23-70-43 Fax: [504] 32-20-31

Honduran-American Chamber of Commerce
—San Pedro Sula
Centro Bella Aurora, Apdo. Postal 1209
San Pedro Sula, Honduras
Tel: [504] 654-0164

Hong Kong
AmCham in Hong Kong
1030 Swire House
PO Box 355
Central, Hong Kong
Tel: [852] (2) 526-0165 Fax: [852] (2) 810-1289

Hungary
AmCham in Hungary
Dozza Gyorgy ut. 84/A, Room 406
H-1064 Budapest, Hungary
Tel: [36] (1) 142-9108 Fax: [36] (1) 122-8890

India
American Business Council—India
U-50 Hotel Hyatt Regency
New Delhi 110 066, India
Tel: [91] (11) 688-5443 Fax: [91] (11) 688-5046

Indonesia
AmCham in Indonesia
The Landmark Center, 22nd Floor, Suite 2204
Jalan Jendral Sudirman I
Jakarta, Indonesia
Tel: [62] (21) 571-0800 x2222 Fax: [62] (21) 571-0656

Ireland
AmCham in Ireland
20 College Green
Dublin 2, Ireland
Tel: [353] (1) 679-3733 Fax: [353] (1) 679-3402

Israel
Israel-American Chamber of Commerce and Industry
35 Shaul Hamelech Blvd.
64927 Tel Aviv, Israel
Tel: [972] (3) 6952341 Fax: [972] (3) 6951272

Italy
AmCham in Italy
Via Cantu 1
20123 Milan, Italy
Tel: [39] (2) 86-90-661 Fax: [39] (2) 80-57-737

All addresses and telephone numbers are in the United States unless otherwise noted. The country code for the US is [1].

Ivory Coast
AmCham, Ivory Coast
01 BP 3394
Abidjan 01, Ivory Coast
Tel: [225] 21 67 66, 44 68 48 Fax: [225] 21 68 17

Jamaica
AmCham of Jamaica
The Wyndham Hotel
77 Knutsford Blvd.
Kingston 5, Jamaica
Tel: [1] (809) 926-7866/7 Fax: [1] (809) 929-8597

Japan
AmCham in Japan—Tokyo
Fukide Building, #2
4-1-21 Toranomon, Minato-ku
Tokyo 105, Japan
Tel: [81] (3) 433-5381 Fax: [81] (3) 436-1446

AmCham in Japan—Okinawa
PO Box 235
Okinawa City 904, Japan
Tel: [81] (98) 8935-2684

Korea (South)
AmCham in Korea
Room 307, Chosun Hotel
Seoul, Rep. of Korea
Tel: [82] (2) 753-6471, 6516 Fax: [82] (2) 755-6577

Malaysia
American Business Council of Malaysia
15.01 Lev 15th, Amoda/22 Jalan Imbi
55100 Kuala Lumpur, Malaysia
Tel: [60] (3) 248-2407, 2540 Fax: [60] (3) 242-8540

Mexico
AmCham in Mexico—Mexico City
Lucerna 78-4
Col. Juárez, Deleg. Cuauhtémoc
06600 México, DF, México
Tel: [52] (5) 724-3800 Fax: [52] (5) 703-3908
US mailing address: PO Box 60326, Apdo. 113, Houston,
TX 77205-1794

AmCham in Mexico—Guadalajara
Avda. Moctezuma #442
Col. Jardines del Sol
45050 Zapopan, Jal., México
Tel: [52] (3) 634-6606 Fax: [52] (3) 634-7374

AmCham in Mexico—Monterrey
Picacho 760, Despachos 4 y 6, Col. Obispado
Monterrey, N.L., México
Tel: [52] (83) 48-7141, 4749 Fax: [52] (83) 48-5574

Morocco
AmCham in Morocco
18, Rue Colbert
Casablanca 01, Morocco
Tel: [212] (2) 31-14-48 Fax: [212] (2) 31-66-07

The Netherlands
The AmCham in the Netherlands
Carnegieplein 5
2517 KJ The Hague, the Netherlands
Tel: [31] (70) 3-65-98-08/9 Fax: [31] (70) 3-64-69-92

New Zealand
The AmCham in New Zealand
PO Box 3408
Wellington, New Zealand
Tel: [64] (4) 727549 Fax: [64] (4) 993579

Nicaragua
AmCham of Nicaragua
Apdo. 202
Managua, Nicaragua
Tel: [505] (2) 67-30-99 Fax: [505] (2) 67-30-98

Pakistan
AmCham in Pakistan
NIC Building, Sixth Floor
Abbasi Shaheed Road
GPO Box 1322
Karachi 74000, Pakistan
Tel: [92] (21) 526-436 Fax: [92] (21) 568-3935

Panama
American Chamber of Commerce & Industry
of Panama
Apartado 168, Estafeta Balboa
Panama 1, Republic of Panama
Tel: [507] 69-3881 Fax: [507] 23-3508

Paraguay
Paraguayan-American Chamber of Commerce
Edif. El Faro Internacional P. 4
Asunción, Paraguay
Tel: [595] (21) 422-132-136 Fax: [595] (21) 422-135

Peru
AmCham in Peru
Avenida Ricardo Palma 836, Miraflores
Lima 18, Perú
Tel: [51] (14) 47-9349 Fax: [51] (14) 47-9352

The Philippines
AmCham in the Philippines
PO Box 1578, MCC
Manila, Philippines
Tel: [63] (2) 818-7911 Fax: [63] (2) 816-6359

Poland
AmCham in Poland
Pac Powstancow Warszawy 1
PL 00950 Warsaw, Poland
Tel: [48] (22) 026-39-60 Fax: [48] (22) 26-51-31

Portugal
AmCham in Portugal
Rue de D. Estafania 155, 5 Esq.
Lisbon 1000, Portugal
Tel: [351] (1) 57-25-61 Fax: [351] (1) 57-25-80

Saudi Arabia
American Businessmen of Jeddah
Hyatt Regency Jeddah
PO Box 8483
Jeddah 21482, Saudi Arabia
Tel: [966] (2) 685-3335 Fax: [966] (2) 685-1498

American Businessmen's Group of Riyadh
PO Box 3050
Riyadh 11471, Saudi Arabia 07045
Tel: [966] (1) 477-7341 Fax: [966] (1) 478-7682

Also has offices in Dhahran and at Dhahran Airport

Singapore
American Business Council of Singapore
Scotts Road, #16-07 Shaw Center
Singapore 0922
Tel: [65] 235-0077 Fax: [65] 732-5917

South Africa
AmCham in South Africa
PO Box 62280
Johannesburg, South Africa
Tel: [27] (11) 788-0265/6 Fax: [27] (11) 880-1632

Spain
AmCham in Spain
Avenida Diagonal 477
08036 Barcelona, Spain
Tel: [34] (3) 405-12-66 Fax: [34] (3) 405-31-24

AmCham in Spain— Madrid
Hotel Euro Building
Padre Damian 23
28036 Madrid, Spain
Tel: [34] (1) 458-65-59 Fax: [34] (1) 458-65-20

Sri Lanka
AmCham of Sri Lanka
c/o US Embassy
210 Galle Road
Colombo 3, Sri Lanka

Sweden
AmCham in Sweden
Box 5512
114 85 Stockholm, Sweden
Tel: [08] (6) 66-11-00 Fax: [08] (6) 62-74-57

Switzerland
Swiss American Chamber of Commerce
Talacker 41
8001 Zurich, Switzerland
Tel: [41] (1) 211-24-54 Fax: [41] (1) 211-95-72

Taiwan
AmCham—Kaohsiung
123-3 Ta-Pei Road, First Floor #1-1
Niao Sung Hsiang
Kaohsiung County 83305, Taiwan
Tel: [886] (7) 731-3712

AmCham in Taipei
Room 1012-Chia Hsin Building Annex
96 Chung Shan North Road, Section 2
PO Box 17-277
Taipei 104, Taiwan
Tel: [886] (2) 581-7809 Fax: [886] (2) 542-3376

Thailand
AmCham in Thailand
PO Box 11-1095
140 Wireless Road, Seventh Floor
Kian Gwan Building
Bangkok, Thailand
Tel: [66] (2) 251-9266 Fax: [66] (2) 255-2454

Turkey
Turkish-American Businessmen's Association
Fahri Gizdem Sokak 22/5
80280 Gayrettepe, Istanbul, Turkey
Tel: [90] (212) 274-2824-212 Fax: [90] (212) 275-9316

Turkish-American Businessmen's Association
Farabi Sok. 12/8
06680 Cankaya, Anakaram, Turkey
Tel: [90] (41) 28-06-89, 67-14-10
Fax: [90] (41) 67-27-44

Also has offices in Bursa, Izmir, and Gaziantep

United Arab Emirates
American Business Council of Dubai
Northern Emirates
International Trade Center, Suite 1610
PO Box 9281
Dubai, United Arab Emirates
Tel: [971] (4) 314-735 Fax: [971] (4) 314-227

United Kingdom
AmCham in the United Kingdom
75 Brook St.
London W1Y 2EB, UK
Tel: [44] (71) 493-03-81 Fax: [44] (71) 493-23-94

Uruguay
Chamber of Commerce Uruguay-USA
Calle Bartélome Mitre 1337
Casilla de Correo 809
Montevideo, Uruguay
Tel: [598] (2) 95-90-59 Fax: [598] (2) 95-90-59

Venezuela
Venezuelan-American Chamber of Commerce
and Industry
Torre Credival, Piso 10
2da. Avenida de Campo Alegre, Apdo. 5181
Caracas 1010A, Venezuela
Tel: [58] (2) 263-0833 Fax: [58] (2) 263-1829

FOREIGN BUSINESS ORGANIZATIONS IN THE USA

Argentina
Argentine-American Chamber of Commerce
10 Rockefeller Plaza, Tenth Fl.
New York, NY 10020
Tel: (212) 698-2238 Fax: (212) 698-2239

Asia
US-ASEAN Trade Council
425 Madison Ave.
New York, NY 10017
Tel: (212) 688-2755 Fax: (212) 371-7420

Asia Society
725 Park Ave.
New York, NY 10021
Tel: (212) 288-6400 Fax: (212) 517-8315

Asia Society
1785 Massachusetts Ave. NW
Washington, DC 20036
Tel: (202) 387-6500 Fax: (202) 387-6945

Australia
Australian-American Chamber of Commerce, Inc.
41 Sutter St., Suite 620
San Francisco, CA 94104
Tel: (415) 362-6168 Fax: (415) 394-5606

Austria
US-Austrian Chamber of Commerce, Inc.
165 West 46th St., Room 1112
New York, NY 10036
Tel: (212) 819-0117 Fax: (212) 819-0117

Belgium
Belgian-American Chamber of Commerce in the
United States
350 Fifth Ave., Suite 1322
New York, NY 10118
Tel: (212) 967-9898 Fax: (212) 629-0349

Brazil
Brazilian-American Chamber of Commerce in the
United States
22 West 48th St., Room 404
New York, NY 10036
Tel: (212) 575-9030 Fax: (212) 921-1078

Brazilian-American Chamber of Commerce
80 SW Eighth St., Suite 1800
Miami, FL 33130
Tel: (305) 579-9030 Fax: (305) 579-9756

China
US Office of China Chamber of International
Commerce
4310 Connecticut Ave. NW, Suite 136
Washington, DC 20008
Tel: (202) 244-3244 Fax: (202) 244-0478

Colombia
Colombian-American Association, Inc.
150 Nassau St., Suite 2015
New York, NY 10038
Tel: (212) 233-7776 Fax: (212) 233-7779

Denmark
Danish-American Chamber of Commerce
825 Third Ave.
New York, NY 10019
Tel: (212) 980-6240 Fax: (212) 754-1904

Ecuador
Ecuadorean-American Association, Inc.
150 Nassau St., Suite 2015
New York, NY 10038
Tel: (212) 808-0978 Fax: (212) 233-7779

All addresses and telephone numbers are in the United States unless otherwise noted. The country code for the US is [1].

Egypt
US-Egypt Chamber of Commerce
330 East 39th St., #32L
New York, NY 10016
Tel: (212) 867-2323 Fax: (212) 697-0465

Europe
European-American Chamber of Commerce
801 Pennsylvania Ave. NW
Washington, DC 20004
Tel: (202) 347-9292 Fax: (202) 628-5498

US Business Council S.E. Europe
1901 North Fort Meyer Drive, Suite 303
Arlington, VA 22209
Tel: (703) 527-0280 Fax: (703) 527-0282

Finland
Finnish-American Chamber of Commerce
380 Madison Ave., 24th Fl.
New York, NY 10017
Tel: (212) 808-9721 Fax: (212) 490-1041

France
French-American Chamber of Commerce
 in the United States
509 Madison Ave., Suite 1900
New York, NY 10022
Tel: (212) 371-4466 Fax: (212) 371-5623

Germany
German-American Chamber of Commerce
40 West 57th St., 31st Fl.
New York, NY 10019-4092
Tel: (212) 974-8830 Fax: (212) 974-8867

German-American Chamber of Commerce
104 South Michigan Ave., Suite 600
Chicago, IL 60603-5978
Tel: (312) 782-8557 Fax: (312) 782-3892

German-American Chamber of Commerce
One Park Plaza Building, Suite 1612
Los Angeles, CA 90010
Tel: (213) 381-2236 Fax: (213) 381-3449

German-American Chamber of Commerce
465 California St., Suite 910
San Francisco, CA 94104
Tel: (415) 392-2262 Fax: (415) 392-1314

Representative for German Industry and Trade
1627 Eye St. NW, Suite 550
Washington, DC 20006
Tel: (202) 659-9177 Fax: (202) 659-4779

Representative for German Industry and Trade
5555 San Felipe, Suite 1030
Houston, TX 77056
Tel: (713) 877-1114 Fax: (713) 877-1602

Representative for German Industry and Trade
3475 Lenox Rd. NE, Suite 620
Atlanta, GA 30326
Tel: (404) 239-9494 Fax: (404) 264-1761

Guatemala
Guatemala-US Trade Association
299 Alhambra Circle #207
Coral Gables, FL 33134
Tel: (305) 443-0343 Fax: (305) 443-0699

Greece
Hellenic-American Chamber of Commerce
29 Broadway, Room 1508
New York, NY 10006
Tel: (212) 629-6380 Fax: (212) 564-9281

India
India Chamber of Commerce of America
445 Park Ave.
New York, NY 10022
Tel: (212) 755-7181

Ireland
Ireland-United States Council for Commerce
551 Madison Ave., 11th Fl.
New York, NY 10022
Tel: (212) 248-0008 Fax: (212) 255-6752

Israel
American-Israel Chamber of Commerce
350 Fifth Ave., Suite 1919
New York, NY 10118-1988
Tel: (212) 971-0310 Fax: (212) 971-0331

American-Israel Chamber of Commerce
180 North Michigan Ave., Suite 911
Chicago, IL 60601
Tel: (312) 641-2937 Fax: (312) 641-2941

Italy
Italy-American Chamber of Commerce, Inc.
350 Fifth Ave., Suite 3015
New York, NY 10118
Tel: (212) 279-5520 Fax: (212) 279-5839

Japan
Honolulu-Japanese Chamber of Commerce
2454 South Beretania St.
Honolulu, HI 96826
Tel: (808) 949-5531 Fax: (808) 949-3020

Japanese Business Association of Southern California
345 South Figueroa St., Suite 206
Los Angeles, CA 90071
Tel: (213) 485-0160 Fax: (213) 626-5526

Japanese Chamber of Commerce and Industry
of Chicago
401 North Michigan Ave., Room 602
Chicago, IL 60611
Tel: (312) 332-6199 Fax: (312) 822-9773

Japanese Chamber of Commerce of New York, Inc.
145 West 57th St., Sixth Fl.
New York, NY 10019
Tel: (212) 246-8001 Fax: (212) 246-8002

Japan Productivity Center
1729 King St., #100
Alexandria, VA 22314
Tel: (703) 838-0414 Fax: (703) 838-0419

Korea
Korean Chamber of Commerce
3350 Wilshire Blvd., Suite 660
Los Angeles, CA 90010
Tel: (213) 480-1115 Fax: (213) 480-7521

US-Korea Society
725 Park Ave.
New York, NY 10021
Tel: (212) 517-7730 Fax: (212) 794-9761

Latin America
Council of the Americas
680 Park Ave.
New York, NY 10021
Tel: (212) 628-3200 Fax: (212) 517-6247

Houston Inter-American Chamber of Commerce
510 Bering Drive, Suite 300
Houston, TX 77057
Tel: (713) 975-6171 Fax: (713) 975-6610

Latin Chamber of Commerce
1417 West Flagler St.
Miami, FL 33135
Tel: (305) 642-3870 Fax: (305) 541-2181

Latin American Manufacturing Association
419 New Jersey Ave. SE
Washington, DC 20003
Tel: (202) 546-3803 Fax: (202) 546-3807

Pan American Society of the United States, Inc.
680 Park Ave.
New York, NY 10021
Tel: (212) 249-8950 Fax: (212) 517-6247

US Hispanic Chamber of Commerce
1030 15th St. NW, Suite 206
Washington, DC 20005
Tel: (202) 842-1212 Fax: (202) 842-3221

Mexico
Mexican Chamber of Commerce of Arizona
PO Box 626
Phoenix, AZ 85001
Tel: (602) 252-6448

Mexican Chamber of Commerce of the County of L.A.
125 Paseo de La Plaza, Room 404
Los Angeles, CA 90012
Tel: (310) 826-9898 Fax: (310) 826-2876

US-Mexico Chamber of Commerce
1211 Connecticut Ave. NW
Washington, DC 20036
Tel: (202) 296-5198 Fax: (202) 822-0075

Middle East
National Council on US-Arab Relations
1735 I St. NW, Suite 515
Washington, DC 20006
Tel: (202) 293-0801 Fax: (202) 293-0903

National US-Arab Chamber of Commerce
1825 K St. NW, Suite 1107
Washington, DC 20006
Tel: (202) 331-8010 Fax: (202) 331-8297

Northeast US-Arab Chamber of Commerce
420 Lexington Ave., Suite 2739
New York, NY 10017
Tel: (212) 986-8024 Fax: (212) 986-0216

US-Arab Chamber of Commerce
One World Trade Center, Suite 4657
New York, NY 10048
Tel: (212) 968-8024 Fax: (212) 968-0216

US-Arab Chamber of Commerce, Pacific
PO Box 422218
San Francisco, CA 94142-2218
Tel: (415) 398-9200 Fax: (415) 398-7111

Netherlands
Netherlands Chamber of Commerce
in the United States, Inc.
One Rockefeller Plaza, 11th Fl.
New York, NY 10020
Tel: (212) 265-6460 Fax: (212) 265-6402

Netherlands Chamber of Commerce
in the United States
233 Peachtree St. NE, Suite 404
Atlanta, GA 30303
Tel: (404) 523-4400 Fax: (404) 522-7116

Norway
Norwegian-American Chamber of Commerce
Upper Midwest Chapter
229 Foshay Tower
Minneapolis, MN 55402
Tel: (612) 332-3338 Fax: (612) 332-1386

Norwegian-American Chamber of Commerce
20 California St., Sixth Fl.
San Francisco, CA 94111-4803
Tel: (415) 986-0770 Fax: (415) 986-6025

Norwegian-American Chamber of Commerce
800 Third Ave., 23rd Fl.
New York, NY 10022
Tel: (212) 421-9210 Fax: (212) 838-0374

Peru
Peruvian-American Association
50 West 34th St.
New York, NY 10036
Tel: (212) 964-3855

The Philippines
Philippine-American Chamber of Commerce
711 Third Ave., 17th Fl.
New York, NY 10017
Tel: (212) 972-9326 Fax: (212) 867-9882

Philippine-American Chamber of Commerce
c/o Philippine Consulate
447 Sutter St.
San Francisco, CA 94108
Tel: (415) 433-6666

Puerto Rico
Puerto Rico Chamber of Commerce in the US
Box 899, Ansonia Station
New York, NY 10023
Tel: (212) 924-4731

Saudi Arabia
Saudi Arabian Council of Chambers of Commerce
and Industry
c/o Hamed Jared, Washington Representative
Embassy of Saudi Arabia
601 New Hampshire Ave. NW
Washington, DC 20037
Tel: (202) 342-3800 Fax: (202) 342-0271

Spain
Spain-US Chamber of Commerce
350 Fifth Ave., Room 3514
New York, NY 10118
Tel: (212) 967-2170 Fax: (212) 564-1415

Sweden
Swedish-American Chamber of Commerce
599 Lexington Ave., 42nd Fl.
New York, NY 10022
Tel: (212) 838-5530 Fax: (212) 755-7953

Swedish-American Chamber of Commerce
230 California St., Suite 602
San Francisco, CA 94111-4319
Tel: (415) 781-4188 Fax: (415) 781-4189

Switzerland
Swiss-American Chamber of Commerce
37 West 67th St.
New York, NY 10023
Tel: (212) 875-9688 Fax: (212) 873-2836

Trinidad and Tobago
Trinidad and Tobago Chamber of Commerce
c/o Trintoc Services, Ltd.
400 Madison Ave., Room 803
New York, NY 10016
Tel: (212) 759-3388 Fax: (212) 319-9677

United Kingdom
British-American Chamber of Commerce
52 Vanderbilt Ave., 20th Fl.
New York, NY 10017
Tel: (212) 661-4060 Fax: (212) 661-4074

British-American Chamber of Commerce
41 Sutter St., Suite 303
San Francisco, CA 94104
Tel: (415) 296-8645

INDUSTRY-SPECIFIC TRADE ASSOCIATIONS

ABCD: The Microcomputer Industry Association
450 E. 22nd St., Suite 230
Lombard, IL 60148
Tel: (708) 268-1818

Aerobics and Fitness Association of America
15250 Ventura Blvd., Suite 310
Sherman Oaks, CA 91403
Tel: (818) 905-0040 Fax: (818) 990-5468

Air-Conditioning and Refrigeration Institute
1501 Wilson Blvd., 6th Fl.
Arlington, VA 22209
Tel: (703) 924-8800

American Advertising Federation
1400 K St., Suite 1000
Washington, DC 20005
Tel: (202) 898-0089 Fax: (202) 898-0159

American Apparel Manufacturers Association
2500 Wilson Blvd., Suite 301
Arlington, VA 22201
Tel: (703) 524-1864

American Association for Textile Technology
PO Box 99
Gastonia, NC 28053
Tel: (704) 824-3522

American Association of Food Distribution
28-12 Broadway
Fair Lawn, NJ 07410
Tel: (201) 791-5570 Fax: (201) 791-5222

American Bankers Association
1120 Connecticut Ave. NW
Washington, DC 20036
Tel: (202) 663-5186

American Bar Association
750 N. Lake Shore Dr.
Chicago, IL 60611
Tel: (312) 988-5000

American Council of Life Insurance
1001 Pennsylvania Ave. NW
Washington, DC 20004
Tel: (202) 624-2000 Fax: (202) 624-2319

American Dental Trade Association
4222 King St. West
Alexandria, VA 22302
Tel: (703) 379-7755 Fax: (703) 931-9429

American Electronics Association
5201 Great American Parkway, Suite 520
Santa Clara, CA 95054
Tel: (408) 987-4200

American Farm Bureau Federation
225 Touhy Ave.
Park Ridge, IL 60068
Tel: (312) 399-5700

American Financial Services Association
919 18th St. NW, 3rd Floor
Washington, DC 20006
Tel: (202) 296-5544

American Forest and Paper Association
1250 Connecticut Ave. NW, 2nd Fl.
Washington, DC 20036
Tel: (202) 463-2700 Fax: (202) 463-2785

American Furniture Manufacturers Association
PO Box HP-7
High Point, NC 27261
Tel: (919) 884-5000

American Hardware Manufacturers Association
931 N. Plum Grove Road
Schaumburg, IL 60173
Tel: (708) 605-1025 Fax: (708) 605-1093

American Health Care Association
1201 L St. NW
Washington, DC 20005
Tel: (202) 842-4444 Fax: (202) 842-3860

American Hotel and Motel Association
1201 New York Ave.
Washington, DC 20005
Tel: (202) 289-3100

American Institute of Certified Public Accountants
1211 Ave. of the Americas
New York, NY 10036
Tel: (212) 575-6200

American Mining Congress
1920 N St. NW, Suite 300
Washington, DC 20036
Tel: (202) 861-2800 Fax: (202) 861-7535

American Mining Institute
1920 N St. NW, Suite 300
Washington, DC 20036
Tel: (202) 861-2800 Fax: (202) 861-7535

American Petroleum Institute
1220 L St. NW
Washington, DC 20005
Tel: (202) 682-8000

American Pharmaceutical Association
2215 Constitution Ave. NW
Washington, DC 20037
Tel: (202) 628-4410 Fax: (202) 783-2351

American Rental Association
1900 19th St.
Moline, IL 61265
Tel: (309) 764-2475 Fax: (309) 764-1533

American Running and Fitness Association
4405 East-West Highway
Bethesda, MD 20814
Tel: (301) 913-9517 Fax: (301) 913-9520

American Society of Association Executives
1575 Eye St. NW
Washington, DC 20005
Tel: (202) 626-2723 Fax: (202) 626-8825

American Society of Notaries
918 16th St. NW
Washington, DC 20006
Tel: (202) 955-6162 Fax: (202) 955-6163

American Society of Travel Agents (ASTA)
1101 King St., Suite 200
Alexandria, VA 22314
Tel: (703) 739-2782 Fax: (703) 684-8319

American Textile Manufacturers Institute
1801 K St. NW, Suite 900
Washington, DC 20006
Tel: (202) 862-0500

American Trucking Association
2200 Mill Road
Alexandria, VA 22314
Tel: (703) 838-1700 Fax: (703) 684-5720

American Wire Producers Association
1101 Connecticut Ave. NW, Suite 700
Washington, DC 20036
Tel: (202) 857-1155 Fax: (202) 429-5154

American Wholesale Marketers Association
1128 16th St. NW
Washington, DC 20034
Tel: (202) 463-2124, (800) 783-6242 Fax: (202) 467-0559

Associated Builders and Contractors
729 15th St. NW
Washington, DC 20005
Tel: (202) 637-8800

Associated General Contractors of America
1957 E St. NW
Washington, DC 20006
Tel: (202) 393-2040

Association of American Publishers
220 East 23rd St.
New York, NY 10010
Tel: (212) 689-8920

Association of Home Appliance Manufacturers
20 N. Wacker Drive
Chicago, IL 60606
Tel: (312) 984-5800

Automotive Industry Action Group
26200 Lasher Road, Suite 200
Southfield, MI 48034
Tel: (313) 258-3570 Fax: (313) 358-3253

Automotive Parks and Accessories Association
4600 East-West Highway, 3rd Fl.
Bethesda, MD 20814
Tel: (301) 654-6664 Fax: (301) 654-3299

Automotive Service Association
1901 Airport Freeway, Suite 100
Bedford, TX 76095
Tel: (817) 283-6205 Fax: (817) 685-0225

Automotive Service Industry Association
25 Northwest Point
Elk Grove Village, IL 60007
Tel: (708) 228-1310 Fax: (708) 228-1510

Chemical Manufacturers Association
2501 M St. NW
Washington, DC 20037
Tel: (202) 887-1100

Computer and Business Equipment Manufacturers Association
1250 Eye St. NW
Washington, DC 20005
Tel: (202) 737-8888

Computer and Communications Industry Association
666 11th St. NW, Suite 600
Washington, DC 20001
Tel: (202) 783-0070

Cosmetic, Toiletry and Fragrance Association
1101 17th St. NW
Washington, DC 20036
Tel: (202) 331-1770

Direct Marketing Association
11 West 42nd St.
New York, NY 10036
Tel: (212) 768-7277 Fax: (212) 719-5106

Electronic Industries Association
2001 Pennsylvania Ave. NW
Washington, DC 20006
Tel: (202) 457-4900

Equipment Leasing Association of America
1300 N 17th St., Suite 1010
Arlington, VA 22209
Tel: (703) 527-8655 Fax: (703) 527-2649

Equipment Manufacturers Institute
10 S. Riverside Plaza, Suite 1220
Chicago, IL 60606
Tel: (312) 321-1480

Fabricators and Manufacturers Association International
833 Featherstone Road
Rockford, IL 61107
Tel: (815) 399-8700 Fax: (815) 399-7279

Food Marketing Institute
800 Connecticut Ave. NW
Washington, DC 20006
Tel: (202) 452-8444 Fax: (202) 429-4519

The Gold Institute
1112 16th St. NW, Suite 240
Washington, DC 20036
Tel: (202) 835-0185 Fax: (202) 835-0155

Grocery Manufacturers of America
1010 Wisconsin Ave. NW
Washington, DC 20007
Tel: (202) 337-9400 Fax: (202) 337-4508

Health Industry Manufacturers Association
1200 G St. NW, Suite 400
Washington, DC 20005
Tel: (202) 783-8700 Fax: (202) 783-8750

Hobby Industry Association of America
319 East 54th St.
Elmwood Park, NJ 07407
Tel: (201) 794-1133

Independent Petroleum Association of America
1101 16th St. NW
Washington, DC 20036
Tel: (202) 857-4722

Industrial Designers Society of America
1142 E. Walker Rd.
Great Falls, VA 22066
Tel: (703) 759-0100 Fax: 9703) 759-7679

Industrial Fabrics Association International
345 Cedar Building, Suite 800
St. Paul, MN 55101
Tel: (612) 222-2508

Information Industry Association
555 New Jersey Ave. NW, Suite 800
Washington, DC 20001
Tel: (202) 639-8260 Fax: (202) 638-4403

Information Technology Association of America
1616 North Fort Myer Dr., Suite 1300
Arlington, VA 22209-3106
Tel: (703) 522-5055 Fax: (202) 525-2279

Interactive Multimedia Association
3 Church Circle, Suite 800
Annapolis, MD 21401
Tel: (410) 626-1380

International Association for Financial Planning
2 Concourse Parkway, Suite 800
Atlanta, GA 30328
Tel: (404) 395-1605

International Communications Industry Association
3150 Spring St.
Fairfax, VA 22031
Tel: (703) 273-7200 Fax: (703) 278-8082

International Electrical Testing Association
221 Red Rocks Vista Drive
Morrison, CO 80465
Tel: (303) 467-0526

International Franchise Association
1350 New York Ave. NW, #900
Washington, DC 20005
Tel: (202) 628-8000 Fax: (202) 628-0812

International Furnishings and Design Association
107 World Trade Center, Box 58045
Dallas, TX 75258
Tel: (214) 747-2406

International Minilab Association
2627 Grimsley St.
Greensboro, NC 27403
Tel: (919) 854-8088 Fax: (919) 854-8566

Leather Industries of America
1000 Thomas Jefferson St. NW
Washington, DC 20007
Tel: (202) 342-8086

Luggage and Leather Goods Manufacturers of America
350 Fifth Ave., Suite 2624
New York, NY 10118
Tel: (212) 695-2340

National Association of Broadcasters
1771 N St. NW
Washington, DC 20036
Tel: (202) 429-5300 Fax: (202) 429-5350

National Association of Chain Drug Stores
PO Box 1417
Alexandria, VA 22313
Tel: (703) 549-3001 Fax: (703) 836-4869

National Association of Convenience Stores
1605 King St.
Alexandria, VA 22314
Tel: (703) 684-3600 Fax: (703) 836-4564

National Association of Home Builders
15th and M Streets NW
Washington, DC 20005
Tel: (202) 822-0233

National Association of Manufacturers
1331 Pennsylvania Ave. NW
Washington, DC 20004
Tel: (202) 637-3000, 637-3099
Fax: (202) 637-3182

National Association of Real Estate Investment Trusts
1129 20th St. NW, Suite 705
Washington, DC 20036
Tel: (202) 785-8717 Fax: (202) 785-8723

National Association of Realtors
430 North Michigan Ave.
Chicago, IL 60611
Tel: (312) 329-8200

National Association of Securities Dealers
1735 K St. NW, Suite 9000
Washington, DC 20006
Tel: (202) 778-2244 Fax: (202) 778-2201

National Association of Wholesaler-Distributors
1725 K St. NW, Suite 710
Washington, DC 20006
Tel: (202) 872-0885

National Automobile Dealers Association
8400 Westpark Drive
McLean, VA 22102
Tel: (703) 827-7407 Fax: (703) 821-7075

National Food Processors Association
1401 New York Ave. NW
Washington, DC 20007
Tel: (202) 639-5900

National Forest Products Association
1250 Connecticut Ave. NW, Suite 200
Washington, DC 20036
Tel: (202) 463-2700

National Glass Association
8200 Greensboro Dr.
McLean, VA 22102
Tel: (703) 442-4890

National Golf Foundation
1150 South US Highway One
Jupiter, FL 33477
Tel: (407) 744-6006 Fax: (407) 744-6107

National Grocers Association
1825 Samuel Morse Drive
Reston, VA 22090
Tel: (703) 437-5300

National Home Furnishings Association
PO Box 2396
High Point, NC 27261
Tel: (919) 883-1650

National Housewares Manufacturers Association
6400 Shafer Court, Suite 650
Rosemont, IL 60018
Tel: (708) 292-4200 Fax: (708) 292-4211

National Institute of Government Purchasing
11800 Sunrise Valley Dr.
Reston, VA 22182
Tel: (703) 715-9400 Fax: (703) 715-9897

National Industrial Transportation League
1700 N. Moore St., Suite 1900
Arlington, VA 22209
Tel: (703) 524-5011

National Licensed Beverage Association
4214 King St. West
Alexandria, VA 22302
Tel: (703) 671-7575, (800) 441-9894 Fax: (703) 845-0310

National Printing Equipment and Supply Association
1899 Preston White Drive
Reston, VA 22091
Tel: (703) 264-7200

National Restaurant Association
1200 17th St. NW
Washington, DC 20036
Tel: (202) 331-5900 Fax: (202) 331-2429

National Retail Federation
100 West 31st St.
New York, NY 10001
Tel: (212) 244-8780

National Soft Drink Association
1101 16th St. NW
Washington, DC 20036
Tel: (202) 463-6732

National Sporting Goods Association
1699 Wall St.
Mount Prospect, IL 60056
Tel: (708) 439-4000 Fax: (708) 439-0111

National Tooling and Machining Association
9300 Livingston Rd.
Ft. Washington, MD 20744
Tel: (301) 248-6200 Fax: (301) 248-7104

Nonprescription Drug Manufacturers Association
1150 Connecticut Ave. NW
Washington, DC 20036
Tel: (202) 429-9260

North American Telecommunications Association
2000 M St. NW, Suite 550
Washington, DC 20037
Tel: (202) 296-9800 Fax: (202) 296-4993

Packaging Machinery Manufacturers Institute
1343 L St. NW
Washington, DC 20005
Tel: (202) 347-3838

Petroleum Equipment Institute
PO Box 2380
Tulsa, OK 74101
Tel: (918) 494-9696

Pharmaceutical Manufacturers Association
1100 15th St. NW
Washington, DC 20005
Tel: (202) 835-3400 Fax: (202) 835-3414

Printing Industries of America
100 Daingerfield Road
Alexandria, VA 22314
Tel: (703) 519-8100

Public Relations Society of America
33 Irving Plaza
New York, NY 10003
Tel: (212) 995-2230

Retail Bakers of America
14239 Park Center Dr.
Laurel, MD 20707
Tel: (301) 725-2149 Fax: (301) 725-2187

Rubber Manufacturers Association
1400 K St. NW
Washington, DC 20005
Tel: (202) 227-5558

The Silver Institute
1112 16th St. NW, Suite 240
Washington, DC 20036
Tel: (202) 785-0185 Fax: (202) 835-0155

Society for Marketing Professional Services
99 Canal Center Plaza, #320
Alexandria, VA 22314-1588
Tel: (703) 549-6117, (800) 292-7677 Fax: (703) 549-2498

Society of Plastics Industry
1275 K St. NW, Suite 400
Washington, DC 20005
Tel: (202) 371-5200 Fax: (202) 371-1022

Software Publishers Association
1730 M St. NW, Suite 700
Washington, DC 20036
Tel: (202) 452-1600

Tele-Communications Association
858 S. Oak Park Road, Suite 102
Covina, CA 91724
Tel: (818) 967-9411

The Business and Institutional Furniture
Manufacturer's Association
2680 Horizon Drive SE, Suite A-1
Grand Rapids, MI 49546
Tel: (616) 285-3963

Travel Industry Association of America
1133 21st Ave. NW, Suite 800
Washington, DC 20036
Tel: (202) 293-1433

United Fresh Fruit and Vegetable Association
727 N. Washington St.
Alexandria, VA 22314
Tel: (703) 836-3410 Fax: (703) 836-7745

United Ski Industries Association
8377-B Greensboro Dr.
McLean, VA 22102
Tel: (703) 556-9020

World International Nail and Beauty Association
1221 N. Lake View
Anaheim, CA 92807
Tel: (714) 779-9883

FINANCIAL INSTITUTIONS

REGULATORY AGENCIES AND PROFESSIONAL ASSOCIATIONS

American Bankers Association
1120 Connecticut Ave. NW
Washington, DC 20036
Tel: (202) 663-6000 Fax: (202) 828-4532

American Institute of Banking
1120 Connecticut Ave. NW
Washington, DC 20036
Tel: (202) 663-5153

Bankers Association for Foreign Trade
1600 M St. NW, Seventh Fl.
Washington, DC 20036
Tel: (202) 452-0952 Fax: (202) 452-0959

Credit Union National Association
805 15th St. NW
Washington, DC 20005
Tel: (202) 682-4200 Fax: (202) 682-9054

Export-Import Bank of the United States
811 Vermont Ave. NW
Washington, DC 20571
Tel: (202) 566-2117

Federal Deposit Insurance Corporation
550 Seventeenth St. NW
Washington, DC 20429
Tel: (202) 393-8400 Fax: (202) 835-0319

Futures Industry Association
2001 Pennsylvania Ave. NW, Suite 600
Washington, DC 20006
Tel: (202) 466-5460 Fax: (202) 296-3184

Independent Bankers Association of America
One Thomas Circle NW, Suite 950
Washington, DC 20005-5802
Tel: (202) 659-8111, (800) IBA-VIEW

International Bank for Reconstruction and
Development (IBRD or World Bank)
1818 H St. NW
Washington, DC 20433
Tel: (202) 477-1234

National Association of Securities Dealers Inc.
1735 K St. NW
Washington, DC 20006
Tel: (202) 728-8000

Securities and Exchange Commission
450 5th St. NW
Washington, DC 20549
Tel: (202) 272-3100

Securities Industry Association
120 Broadway
New York, NY 10271
Tel: (212) 608-1500

Security Traders Association, Inc.
One World Trade Center, Suite 5411
New York, NY 10048
Tel: (212) 524-0484

Treasury Department of the United States
Office of the Comptroller of the Currency
250 East E St. SW
Washington, DC 20219-0001
Tel: (202) 874-5000 Fax: (202) 874-4950

US Central Credit Union
7300 College Blvd., Suite 600
Overland Park, KS 66210-1880
Tel: (913) 661-3800 Fax: (913) 345-2628

All addresses and telephone numbers are in the United States unless otherwise noted. The country code for the US is [1].

BANKS

Federal Reserve System

Federal Reserve System
Board of Governors
21st and Constitution Ave. NW
Washington, DC 20551
Tel: (202) 452-3000

District No. 1
Federal Reserve Bank of Boston
600 Atlantic Ave.
Boston, MA 02106
Tel: (617) 973-3000

District No. 2
Federal Reserve Bank of New York
Federal Reserve PO Station
New York, NY 10045
Tel: (212) 720-5000

District No. 3
Federal Reserve Bank of Philadelphia
Ten Independence Mall
Philadelphia, PA 19106
Tel: (215) 574-6000

District No. 4
Federal Reserve Bank of Cleveland
PO Box 6387
Cleveland, OH 44101-1387
Tel: (216) 579-2000

District No. 5
Federal Reserve Bank of Richmond
PO Box 27622
Richmond, VA 23261
Tel: (804) 697-8000

District No. 6
Federal Reserve Bank of Atlanta
104 Marietta St. NW
Atlanta, CA 30303-2713
Tel: (404) 521-8500

District No. 7
Federal Reserve Bank of Chicago
PO Box 834
Chicago, IL 60690
Tel: (312) 322-5322

District No. 8
Federal Reserve Bank of St. Louis
PO Box 442
St. Louis, MO 63166
Tel: (314) 444-8444

District No. 9
Federal Reserve Bank of Minneapolis
250 Marquette Ave.
Minneapolis, MN 55480
Tel: (612) 340-2345

District No. 10
Federal Reserve Bank of Kansas City
925 Grand Blvd.
Kansas City, MO 64198
Tel: (816) 881-2000

District No. 11
Federal Reserve Bank of Dallas
2200 North Pearl, Station "K"
Dallas, TX 75222
Tel: (214) 922-6000

District No. 12
Federal Reserve Bank of San Francisco
PO Box 7702
San Francisco, CA 94120
Tel: (415) 974-2000

Commercial Banks

These are headquarters listings only—all of these banks have many branches, and many maintain foreign offices.

Banc One Corp.
100 E. Broad St.
Columbus, OH 43271
Tel: (614) 248-5944 Fax: (614) 248-5624

Bank of America, NT&SA
555 California St.
PO Box 37000
San Francisco, CA 94137
Tel: (415) 624-3456 Fax: (415) 624-0412

Bank of Boston
100 Federal St.
Boston, MA 02110
Tel: (617) 434-2200 Fax: (617) 575-2232

Bank of New York
48 Wall St.
New York, NY 10286
Tel: (212) 495-1784 Fax: (212) 495-1246

Bankers Trust Company
280 Park Ave.
PO Box 318, Church St. Station
New York, NY 10015
Tel: (212) 250-2500 Fax: (212) 850-1704

Chase Manhattan Bank
1 Chase Manhattan Plaza
New York, NY 10081
Tel: (212) 552-2222 Fax: (212) 552-3875

Chemical Bank
270 Park Ave.
New York, NY 10017
Tel: (212) 270-6000

Citibank, NA
399 Park Ave.
New York, NY 10043
Tel: (212) 559-1000 Fax: (212) 559-5138

Comerica Bank
100 Renaissance Ctr.
Detroit, MI 48243
Tel: (313) 222-3300

Continental Bank, NA
231 S. LaSalle St.
Chicago, IL 60697
Tel: (312) 828-2345

First Fidelity Bancorporation
550 Broad St.
Newark, NJ 07102
Tel: (201) 565-3200 Fax: (201) 565-2876

First Interstate Bank of California
707 Wilshire Blvd.
Los Angeles, CA 90017
Tel: (213) 614-4111 Fax: (213) 614-4786

First National Bank of Boston
100 Federal St.
Boston, MA 02110
Tel: (617) 434-2200

First National Bank of Chicago
One First National Plaza
Chicago, IL 60670
Tel: (312) 732-4000

First Union National Bank of Florida
225 Water St.
PO Box 2080
Jacksonville, FL 32202
Tel: (904) 361-2265 Fax: (904) 361-6197

First Union National Bank of North Carolina
First Union Plaza
301 S. Tyron St.
Charlotte, NC 28288
Tel: (704) 374-6161 Fax: (704) 374-3425

Hibernia National Bank
PO Box 61540
New Orleans, LA 70161
Tel: (612) 533-5553

Mellon Bank, NA
One Mellon Bank Ctr.
Pittsburgh, PA 15258
Tel: (412) 234-5000 Fax: (412) 234-4025

Morgan Guaranty Trust Co. of New York
60 Wall St.
New York, NY 10260-0060
Tel: (212) 483-2323 Fax: (212) 648-5210

NationsBank of Florida, NA
400 N. Ashley St.
PO Box 31590
Tampa, FL 33631
Tel: (813) 224-5805 Fax: (813) 224-5087

NationsBank of North Carolina, NA
101 S. Tyron St.
PO Box 120
Charlotte, NC 28255
Tel: (704) 386-5000 Fax: (704) 386-6655

NationsBank of Texas, NA
901 Main St.
PO Box 831000
Dallas, TX 75283-1000
Tel: (214) 508-6262 Fax: (214) 880-9074

NBD Bank, NA
611 Woodward Ave.
Detroit, MI 48232
Tel: (313) 225-1000 Fax: (313) 225-2371

Norwest Bank
Sixth and Marquette
Minneapolis, MN 55479
Tel: (612) 667-1234

PNC Bank, NA
Fifth Ave. at Wood St.
Pittsburgh, PA 15222
Tel: (412) 762-2000 Fax: (412) 762-3463

Republic National Bank of New York
452 Fifth Ave.
PO Box 423
New York, NY 10018
Tel: (212) 525-5000

Society National Bank
127 Public Sq.
Cleveland, OH 44114
Tel: (216) 689-8481 Fax: (216) 689-7827

Texas Commerce Bank, NA
712 Main St.
PO Box 2558
Houston, TX 77252
Tel: (713) 216-4865 Fax: (713) 546-7367

Wachovia Bank of North Carolina, NA
301 N. Main St.
PO Box 3099
Winston-Salem, NC 27150
Tel: (910) 770-5000 Fax: (910) 770-5931

Wells Fargo, NA
464 California St.
San Francisco, CA 94163
Tel: (415) 477-1000

Foreign Banks

Only New York addresses have been listed, since New York is the US international banking center. Some of these and other foreign banks maintain offices in other US cities.

Australia and New Zealand Bank Group
120 Wall St.
New York, NY 10005
Tel: (212) 820-9805

Banca Commerciale Italiana
1 William St.
New York, NY 10004
Tel: (212) 607-3500

Banco Central (Spain)
Hispano USA
50 Broadway
New York, NY 10004
Tel: (212) 785-0700

Banco de Santander S.A. (Spain)
375 Park Ave.
New York, NY 10167
Tel: (212) 826-4350, 826-0411

Banco di Napoli (Italy)
277 Park Ave.
New York, NY 10172
Tel: (212) 644-8400, 644-8424

Banco do Brasil
550 Fifth Ave.
New York, NY 10036
Tel: (212) 730-6700, 626-7000

Banco Hispanoamericano (Spain)
245 Park Ave.
New York, NY 10167
Tel: (212) 557-8100

Banco Mexicano
235 Fifth Ave.
New York, NY 10016
Tel: (212) 679-8000

Bank Brussels Lambert
630 Fifth Ave.
New York, NY 10111
Tel: (212) 632-5300/1

Bank of Montreal (Canada)
430 Park Ave.
New York, NY 10022
Tel. (212) 758-6300

Bank of Nova Scotia (Canada)
1 Liberty Plaza
New York, NY 10006
Tel: (212) 225-5000

Banque Indosuez (France)
645 Fifth Ave.
New York, NY 10022
Tel: (212) 408-5600

Banque Nationale de Paris
499 Park Ave.
New York, NY 10022
Tel: (212) 750-1400, 848-0500

Banque Paribas (France)
787 Seventh Ave.
New York, NY 10019
Tel: (212) 841-2000

Barclay's Bank PLC (UK)
75 Wall St.
New York, NY 10005
Tel: (212) 412-4000

Bayerische Vereinsbank, A.G. (Germany)
335 Madison Ave.
New York, NY 10017
Tel: (212) 280-0377, 297-9700, 210-0300

Credit Commercial de France
450 Park Ave.
New York, NY 10022
Tel: (212) 486-3080, 848-0500

Credit Lyonnais (France)
1301 Ave. of the Americas
New York, NY 10036
Tel: (212) 261-7000

Credit Suisse
100 Wall St.
New York, NY 10005
Tel: (212) 612-8000

Dai-Ichi Kangyo Bank Ltd. (Japan)
1 World Trade Center
New York, NY 10048
Tel: (212) 868-1075, 466-0127

Daiwa Bank Ltd. (Japan)
75 Rockefeller Plaza
New York, NY 10019
Tel: (212) 554-7000, 399-2710, 554-7300

Fuji Bank & Trust (Japan)
2 World Trade Center
New York, NY 10048
Tel: (212) 898-2000, 898-2400

Generale Bank (Belgium)
520 Madison Ave.
New York, NY 10022
Tel: (212) 418-8700, 418-8725

Habib Bank Limited (Pakistan)
44 Wall St.
New York, NY 10005
Tel: (212) 422-9720

Hokkaido Takushoku Bank Ltd. (Japan)
2 World Trade Center
New York, NY 10048
Tel: (212) 466-6060

Hong Kong & Shanghai Bank (Hong Kong)
140 Broadway
New York, NY 10005
Tel: (212) 658-5100

Industrial Bank of Japan
245 Park Ave.
New York, NY 10167
Tel: (212) 557-3500, 557-3535

Israel Discount Bank of New York
511 Fifth Ave.
New York, NY 10017
Tel: (212) 551-8500

Kreidietbank (Belgium)
125 W. 55th St.
New York, NY 10019
Tel: (212) 832-7200, 541-0600, 956-5890

Kyowa-Saitamo Bank Ltd.
1 World Trade Center
New York, NY 10048
Tel: (212) 432-6400

Long Term Credit Bank of Japan
1 Liberty Plaza
New York, NY 10006
Tel: (212) 335-4400

Mitsui Trust Bank Ltd. (Japan)
2 World Financial Center
New York, NY 10281
Tel: (212) 416-0400, 644-3832

Multibanco Comermex (Mexico)
One Exchange Plaza, 16th Fl.
New York, NY 10006
Tel: (212) 701-0100 Fax: (212) 422-3559

National Australia Bank
Two World Financial Center
225 Liberty St.
New York, NY 10281
Tel: (212) 916-9500 Fax: (212) 983-1969

National Bank of Canada
125 W. 55th St.
New York, NY 10019
Tel: (212) 605-8800, 632-8500

National Bank of New Zealand
199 Water St., 3rd Fl.
New York, NY 10038
Tel: (212) 607-4307 Fax: (212) 607-5446

National Westminster Bank PLC (UK)
175 Water St.
New York, NY 10007
Tel: (212) 602-2120, 602-1000

Nippon Credit Bank Ltd. (Japan)
245 Park Ave.
New York, NY 10167
Tel: (212) 984-1260, 984-1200

Royal Bank of Canada
1 Financial Square Bldg.
New York, NY 10005
Tel: (212) 428-6200

Sanwa Bank Ltd. (Japan)
55 E. 52nd St.
New York, NY 10055
Tel: (212) 339-6300

Societe Generale of Belgique
12 E. 49th St.
New York, NY 10017
Tel: (212) 319-1622

Standard Chartered Bank PLC (UK)
160 Water St.
New York, NY 10038
Tel: (212) 269-3100

Sumitomo Bank Ltd. (Japan)
1 World Trade Center
New York, NY 10048
Tel: (212) 553-0100

Svenska Handelsbanken (Sweden)
599 Lexington Ave.
New York, NY 10022
Tel: (212) 750-5111, 326-5100

Swiss Bank Corp.
10 E. 50th St.
New York, NY 10055
Tel: (212) 574-3468, 574-3000

Toyo Trust and Banking Co. (Japan)
437 Madison Ave.
New York, NY 10022
Tel: (212) 371-3535

Union Bank of Switzerland
299 Park Ave.
New York, NY 10171
Tel: (212) 715-3000

United Overseas Bank Ltd. (Singapore)
130 Liberty St.
New York, NY 10006
Tel: (212) 775-0560, 912-1328

Yasuda Trust and Banking Co. (Japan)
1 World Trade Center
New York, NY 10048
Tel: (212) 432-2300

INSURANCE COMPANIES

These are headquarters listings only—all of these companies have offices across the US.

Aetna Life and Casualty Company
151 Farmington Ave.
Hartford, CT 06156
Tel: (203) 273-0123 Fax: (203) 275-2677

The Allstate Corporation
Allstate Plaza
Northbrook, IL 60062
Tel: (708) 402-5000 Fax: (708) 402-0045

The Chubb Corporation
15 Mountain View Rd.
PO Box 1615
Warren, NJ 07061-1615
Tel: (908) 903-2000 Fax: (908) 580-2027

CIGNA
One Liberty Place
Philadelphia, PA 19192-1550
Tel: (215) 761-1000 Fax: (215) 761-5515

Connecticut Mutual Life Insurance Co.
140 Garden St.
Hartford, CT 06154
Tel: (203) 987-6500 Fax: (203) 987-6532

The Equitable Companies, Incorporated
787 Seventh Ave.
New York, NY 10019
Tel: (212) 554-1234 Fax: (212) 315-2825

John Hancock Mutual Life Insurance Company
PO Box 111
Boston, MA 02117
Tel: (617) 572-6000 Fax: (617) 572-6451

The Kemper Corporation
One Kemper Dr.
Long Grove, IL 60049
Tel: (708) 320-4700 Fax: (708) 320-4535

Lincoln National Corporation
200 E. Berry St.
Fort Wayne, IN 46802-2706
Tel: (219) 455-2000 Fax: (219) 455-2733

Metropolitan Life Insurance Company
One Madison Ave.
New York, NY 10010
Tel: (212) 578-2211 Fax: (212) 578-3320

The Mutual Life Insurance Company of New York
1740 Broadway
New York, NY 10019
Tel: (212) 708-2000 Fax: (212) 708-2056

New York Life Insurance Company
51 Madison Ave.
New York, NY 10010
Tel: (212) 576-7000 Fax: (212) 576-6794

Northwestern Mutual Life Insurance Company
720 E. Wisconsin Ave.
Milwaukee, WI 53202
Tel: (414) 271-1444 Fax: (414) 299-7022

Principal Financial Group
711 High St.
Des Moines, IA 50392
Tel: (515) 247-5111 Fax: (515) 247-5930

The Travelers Inc.
65 E. 55th St.
New York, NY 10022
Tel: (212) 891-8900 Fax: (212) 891-8909

STOCK & COMMODITY EXCHANGES

American Stock Exchange (AMEX)
86 Trinity Pl.
New York, NY 10006
Tel: (213) 306-1000

Boston Stock Exchange (BSE)
One Boston Pl.
Boston, MA 02109
Tel: (617) 723-9500

Chicago Board of Trade (CBOT)
141 West Jackson Blvd.
Chicago, IL 60604
Tel: (312) 435-3500

Chicago Board Options Exchange (CBOE)
400 La Salle
Chicago, IL 60605
Tel: (312) 786-5600

Chicago Cotton and Rice Exchange (CRCE)
141 West Jackson Blvd.
Chicago, IL 60604
Tel: (312) 341-3078

Chicago Mercantile Exchange (CME)
30 South Wacker Dr.
Chicago, IL 60606
Tel: (312) 786-5600, 930-1000

Cincinnati Stock Exchange, Inc. (CSE)
205 Dixie Terminal Building
Cincinnati, OH 45202
Tel: (513) 621-1410

Citrus Associates of the New York Cotton Exchange
4 World Trade Center
New York, NY 10048
Tel: (212) 938-2702

Coffee, Sugar and Cocoa Exchange (CSCE)
4 World Trade Center
New York, NY 10048
Tel: (212) 938-2800

Commodity Exchange, Inc. (COMEX)
4 World Trade Center
New York, NY 10048
Tel: (212) 938-2900

Financial Instrument Exchange (FINEX)
4 World Trade Center
New York, NY 10048
Tel: (212) 926-2634

Kansas City Board of Trade (KCBT)
4800 Main St.
Kansas City, MO 64112
Tel: (816) 753-7500, 753-1101

Midamerica Commodity Exchange (MidAm)
141 West Jackson Blvd.
Chicago, IL 60604
Tel: (312) 341-3000

Midwest Stock Exchange (MSE)
440 LaSalle St.
Chicago, IL 60603
Tel: (312) 663-2222

Minneapolis Grain Exchange (MGE)
400 S. Fourth St.
Minneapolis, MN 55415
Tel: (612) 338-6212

New York Cotton Exchange (NYCE)
4 World Trade Center
New York, NY 10048
Tel: (212) 938-2650

New York Futures Exchange (NYFE)
20 Broad St.
New York, NY 10005
Tel: (212) 623-4949 (800) 221-7722

New York Mercantile Exchange (NYMEX)
4 World Trade Center
New York, NY 10048
Tel: (212) 938-2222

New York Stock Exchange (NYSE)
11 Wall St.
New York, NY 10005
Tel: (212) 656-8533, (800) 692-6973

Pacific Stock Exchange (PSE)
618 S. Spring St.
Los Angeles, CA 90014
Tel: (213) 977-4500

Pacific Stock Exchange (PSE)
301 Pine St.
San Francisco, CA 94101
Tel: (415) 393-4000

Philadelphia Board of Trade (PBOT)
1900 Market St.
Philadelphia, PA 19103
Tel: (215) 496-5357

Philadelphia Stock Exchange (PHLX)
1900 Market St.
Philadelphia, PA 19103
Tel: (215) 496-5000

Twin Cities Board of Trade (TCBOT)
430 First Ave. North
Minneapolis, MN 55415
Tel: (612) 333-6742

SECURITIES BROKERS & DIVERSIFIED FINANCIAL COMPANIES

These are headquarters listings only—each of these companies has offices across the US.

A.G. Edwards
1 N. Jefferson Ave.
St. Louis, MO 63103
Tel: (314) 289-3000

American Express
American Express Tower
New York, NY 10285
Tel: (212) 640-2000

Bear Stearns
245 Park Ave.
New York, NY 10167
Tel: (212) 272-2000

BT Securities Corp.
1 Bankers Trust Plaza
New York, NY 10015
Tel: (212) 250-5000

Charles Schwab Corp.
101 Montgomery St.
San Francisco, CA 94104
Tel: (415) 627-7000

CIGNA Corporation
900 Cottage Grove Rd.
Bloomfield, CT 06002
Tel: (203) 726-6000

CS First Boston
44 E. 52nd St.
New York, NY 10055
Tel: (212) 909-2000

Daiwa Securities America
1 World Financial Ctr.
200 Liberty St.
New York, NY 10281
Tel: (212) 341-5400

Dean Witter
2 World Trade Ctr.
New York, NY 10048
Tel: (212) 392-2222

Donaldson, Lufkin and Jenrette
140 Broadway Ave.
New York, NY 10005
Tel: (212) 504-3000

Fidelity Investments
21 Congress St.
Boston, MA 02109
Tel: (617) 523-1919

General Electric Financial Services Inc.
260 Long Ridge Rd.
Stamford, CT 06927
Tel: (203) 357-4000

Goldman Sachs & Co.
85 Broad St.
New York, NY 10004
Tel: (212) 902-1000

Kemper Securities Inc.
1221 Ave. of Americas
New York, NY 10020
Tel: (212) 782-3000, (800) 223-0610

Kidder, Peabody & Co.
10 Hanover Sq.
New York, NY 10005
Tel: (212) 510-3000

Merrill Lynch & Co.
250 Vesey St.
New York, NY 10281
Tel: (212) 449-1000

Morgan Stanley Group
1251 Ave. of the Americas
New York, NY 10020
Tel: (212) 703-4000

Nomura Securities International
2 World Financial Ctr., Bldg. B
New York, NY 10281
Tel: (212) 667-9300

Paine Webber Group
1285 Ave. of the Americas
New York, NY 10019
Tel: (212) 713-2000

Piper Jaffray Inc.
Piper Jaffray Tower
Minneapolis, MN 55402
Tel: (512) 342-6000

Prudential Securities
199 Water St.
New York, NY 10292
Tel: (212) 214-1000

Salomon Inc.
7 World Trade Ctr.
New York, NY 10048
Tel: (212) 747-7000

Smith Barney Shearson
1345 Ave. of the Americas
New York, NY 10105
Tel: (212) 399-6000

Yamaichi International (America)
2 World Trade Ctr.
New York, NY 10048
Tel: (212) 912-6360

SERVICES

ACCOUNTING/CONSULTING FIRMS

These are headquarters listings only—all of these companies have offices across the US, and most maintain numerous foreign offices as well.

Altschuler, Melvoin & Glasser
30 South Wacker Dr., Suite 2600
Chicago, IL 60606
Tel: (312) 207-2800 Fax: (312) 207-2954

Arthur Andersen & Co., SC
69 West Washington
Chicago, IL 60602
Tel: (312) 580-0069 Fax: (312) 507-6748

Baird, Kurtz & Dobson
PO Box 1900
Springfield, MO 65801-1900
Tel: (417) 831-7283 Fax: (417) 831-4763

BDO Seidman
15 Columbus Circle
New York, NY 10023
Tel: (212) 765-7500 Fax: (212) 315-1613

Clifton Gunderson & Co.
301 SW Adams, Suite 800
Peoria, IL 61602
Tel: (309) 671-4560

Coopers & Lybrand
1251 Ave. of the Americas
New York, NY 10020
Tel: (212) 536-2000 Fax: (212) 259-1301

Crowe Chizek and Co.
330 East Jefferson Blvd.
PO Box 7
South Bend, IN 46624
Tel: (219) 232-3992 Fax: (219) 236-8692

Deloitte & Touche
10 Westport Rd.
Wilton, CT 06897
Tel: (203) 761-3000 Fax: (203) 834-2231

Ernst & Young
277 Park Ave., 32nd Fl.
New York, NY 10127
Tel: (212) 773-3000 Fax: (212) 773-2821

Grant Thornton
One Prudential Plaza, Suite 700
130 E. Randolph Dr.
Chicago, IL 60601
Tel: (312) 856-0001, 856-0200 Fax: (312) 565-4719

Kenneth Leventhal & Co.
2049 Century Park East, #1700
Los Angeles, CA 90067
Tel: (213) 277-0880 Fax: (310) 284-7970

KMPG Peat Marwick
767 Fifth Ave.
New York, NY 10153
Tel: (212) 909-5000

McGladrey & Pullen
102 W. Second St., 2nd Fl.
Davenport, IA 52801
Tel: (319) 324-0447

Pannell Kerr Forster Worldwide
262 North Belt East #300
Houston, TX 77060
Tel: (713) 999-5134

Price Waterhouse
1251 Ave. of the Americas
New York, NY 10020
Tel: (212) 819-5000 Fax: (212) 790-6620

ADVERTISING AGENCIES

These are headquarters listings only—each of these agencies has many offices across the US and worldwide.

Bates USA
The Chrysler Bldg.
405 Lexington Ave.
New York, NY 10174
Tel: (212) 297-7000 Fax: (212) 986-0270

BBDO Worldwide Inc.
1285 Ave. of the Americas
New York, NY 10019-6095
Tel: (212) 459-5000 Fax: (212) 459-6645

Bozell Worldwide, Inc.
40 W. 23rd St.
New York, NY 10010
Tel: (212) 727-5000 Fax: (212) 727-2436

Chiat/Day Inc. Advertising
340 Main St.
Venice, CA 90291
Tel: (310) 314-5000 Fax: (310) 396-1273

D'Arcy Masius Benton & Bowles, Inc.
1675 Broadway
New York, NY 10019
Tel: (212) 468-3622 Fax: (212) 468-4385

DDB Needham Worldwide Inc.
437 Madison Ave.
New York, NY 10022
Tel: (212) 415-2000 Fax: (212) 415-3562

Foote, Cone & Belding Communications, Inc.
101 E. Erie St.
Chicago, IL 60611-2897
Tel: (312) 751-7000 Fax: (312) 751-3501

Grey Advertising Inc.
777 Third Ave.
New York, NY 10017
Tel: (212) 546-2000 Fax: (212) 546-1495

J. Walter Thompson Co.
466 Lexington Ave.
New York, NY 10017
Tel: (212) 210-7000 Fax: (212) 210-7066, 210-7034

Leo Burnett Company, Inc.
35 W. Wacker Dr.
Chicago, IL 60601
Tel: (312) 220-5959 Fax: (312) 220-3299

Lintas
One Dag Hammarskjold Plaza
New York, NY 10017
Tel: (212) 605-8000 Fax: (212) 838-2331

McCann-Erickson Worldwide
750 Third Ave.
New York, NY 10017
Tel: (212) 697-6000 Fax: (212) 867-5177

Ogilvy & Mather Worldwide, Inc.
309 W. 49th St.
New York, NY 10019
Tel: (212) 237-4000 Fax: (212) 237-5123

Saatchi & Saatchi Advertising
375 Hudson St.
New York, NY 10014-3620
Tel: (212) 463-2000 Fax: (212) 463-9855

Young & Rubicam Inc.
285 Madison Ave.
New York, NY 10017
Tel: (212) 210-3000 Fax: (212) 490-9073

All addresses and telephone numbers are in the United States unless otherwise noted. The country code for the US is [1].

LAW FIRMS

Baker and McKenzie
One Prudential Plaza
130 E. Randolph Drive
Chicago, IL 60601
Tel: (312) 861-8000 Fax: (312) 861-2898
US Branches: Chicago, Dallas, Miami, New York, Palo Alto (CA), San Diego, San Francisco, Washington DC; Foreign Branches: Over 25 worldwide

Cleary, Gottlieb, Steen & Hamilton
One Liberty Plaza
New York, NY 10006
Tel: (212) 225-2000 Fax: (212) 225-3999
US Branches: Washington DC; Foreign Branches: Brussels, Frankfurt, Hong Kong, London, Paris, Tokyo, Moscow

Cravath, Swaine & Moore
825 Eighth Ave.
New York, NY 10019
Tel: (212) 474-1000 Fax: (212) 474-3700
US Branches: White Plains (NY); Foreign Branches: London, Hong Kong

Fulbright & Jaworski
1301 McKinney, Suite 5100
Houston, TX 77010
Tel: (713) 651-5151 Fax: (713) 651-5246
US Branches: Austin, Dallas, Los Angeles, New York, San Antonio, Washington DC; Foreign Branches: London, Hong Kong

Gibson, Dunn & Crutcher
333 South Grand Ave.
Los Angeles, CA 90071
Tel: (213) 229-7000 Fax: (213) 229-7520
US Branches: Century City (CA), Dallas, Denver, Irvine (CA), Menlo Park (CA), New York, Sacramento, San Diego, San Francisco, Seattle, Washington DC; Foreign Branches: Brussels, Hong Kong, Jeddah, London, Paris, Riyadh, Tokyo

Jones, Day, Reavis & Pogue
North Point
901 Lakeside Ave.
Cleveland, OH 44114
Tel: (216) 586-3939 Fax: (216) 579-0212 Fax
US Branches: Atlanta, Chicago, Columbus, Dallas, Irvine (CA), Los Angeles, New York, Pittsburgh, Washington DC; Foreign Branches: Brussels, Budapest, Frankfurt, Geneva, Hong Kong, Kuwait, London, Paris, Riyadh, Taipei, Tokyo

Latham & Watkins
633 W. Fifth St., Suite 4000
Los Angeles, CA 90071
(213) 485-1234 Fax: (213) 891-8763
US Branches: Costa Mesa (CA), Chicago, New York, New Jersey, San Diego, San Francisco, Washington DC; Foreign Branches: Hong Kong, London, Moscow, Warsaw

Mayer, Brown and Platt
190 S. LaSalle St.
Chicago, IL 60603
Tel: (312) 782-0600 Fax: (312) 701-7711
US Branches: Houston, Los Angeles, New York, Washington DC
Foreign Branches: Brussels, London, Tokyo

Morgan, Lewis & Bockius
2000 One Logan Square
Philadelphia, PA 19103
Tel: (215) 963-5000 Fax: (215) 963-5299
US Branches: Harrisburg (PA), Los Angeles, Miami, Newport Beach (CA), New York, Princeton (NJ), Washington DC; Foreign Branches: Brussels, Frankfurt, London, Tokyo.

Morrison & Foerster
345 California St.
San Francisco, CA 94104
Tel: (415) 677-7000 Fax: (415) 677-7522
US Branches: Denver, Irvine (CA), Los Angeles, New York, Palo Alto (CA), Sacramento, Seattle, Walnut Creek (CA), Washington DC; Foreign Branches: Brussels, Hong Kong, London, Tokyo.

O'Melveny & Myers
400 S. Hope St., Suite 1060
Los Angeles, CA 90071
Tel: (213) 669-6000 Fax: (213) 669-6407
US Branches: Century City (CA), Newport Beach (CA), New York, New Jersey, San Francisco, Washington DC; Foreign Branches: London, Tokyo, Hong Kong, Shanghai

Pillsbury Madison & Sutro
225 Bush St.
San Francisco, CA 94104
Tel: (415) 983-1000 Fax: (415) 983-1600
US Branches: Los Angeles, New York, Menlo Park (CA), Orange County (CA), San Diego, San Jose (CA), Washington DC; Foreign Branches: Hong Kong, Tokyo.

Sidley & Austin
One First National Plaza
Chicago, IL 60603
Tel: (312) 853-7000 Fax: (312) 853-7036
US Branches: Los Angeles, New York, Washington DC; Foreign Branches: London, Tokyo.

Skadden, Arps, Slate, Meagher & Flom
919 Third Ave.
New York, NY 10022
Tel: (212) 735-3000 Fax: (212) 735-2000
US Branches: Boston, Chicago, Houston, Los Angeles, Newark (NJ), San Francisco, Washington DC, Wilmington (DE); Foreign Branches: Beijing, Budapest, Brussels, Frankfurt, Hong Kong, Jakarta, London, Moscow, Paris, Prague, Sydney, Taiwan, Toronto, Tokyo

Shearman & Sterling
599 Lexington Ave.
New York, NY 10022
Tel: (212) 848-4000 Fax: (212) 848-7179
US Branches: Los Angeles, San Francisco, Washington DC; Foreign Branches: Abu Dhabi, Beijing, Budapest, Dusseldorf, Frankfurt, Hong Kong, London, Paris, Taipei, Tokyo, Toronto

Sullivan & Cromwell
125 Broad St.
New York, NY 10004
Tel: (212) 558-4000 Fax: (212) 558-3588
US Branches: Los Angeles, Washington DC; Foreign Branches: Hong Kong, London, Melbourne, Paris, Tokyo

Weil, Gotshal & Manges
767 Fifth Ave.
New York, NY 10153
Tel: (212) 310-8000 Fax: (212) 310-8007
US Branches: Dallas, Houston, Miami, Washington DC

White & Case
1155 Ave. of the Americas
New York, NY 10036
Tel: (212) 819-8200 Fax: (212) 354-8113
US Branches: Los Angeles, Miami, Washingon DC; Foreign Branches: 20 worldwide

Vinson & Elkins L.L.P.
2300 First City Tower
1001 Fannin
Houston, TX 77002
(713) 758-2222 Fax: (713) 758-2346
US Branches: Austin, Dallas; Foreign Branches: London, Mexico City, Moscow, Singapore

BAR ASSOCIATIONS

American Bar Association
750 N. Lake Shore Drive
Chicago, IL 60611
Tel: (312) 988-5000

Following is a list of telephone numbers for each state bar association plus those of Washington, DC, Puerto Rico, and the Virgin Islands.

Alabama .... (205) 269-1515
Alaska .... (907) 272-7469
Arizona .... (602) 252-4804
Arkansas .... (501) 375-4605
California .... (415) 561-8200
Colorado .... (303) 860-1115
Connecticut .... (203) 721-0025
Delaware .... (302) 658-5278
Florida .... (904) 222-3729
Georgia .... (404) 527-8700
Hawaii .... (808) 537-1868
Idaho .... (208) 342-8958
Illinois .... (217) 525-1760
Indiana .... (317) 639-5465
Iowa .... (515) 243-3179
Kansas .... (913) 234-5696
Kentucky .... (502) 564-3795
Louisiana .... (504) 566-0930
Maine .... (207) 622-7523
Maryland .... (301) 685-7878
Massachusetts .... (617) 542-3602
Michigan .... (517) 372-9030
Minnesota .... (612) 333-1183
Mississippi .... (601) 948-4471
Missouri .... (314) 635-4128
Montana .... (406) 442-7763
Nebraska .... (402) 475-7091
Nevada .... (702) 382-2200
New Hampshire .... (603) 224-6942
New Jersey .... (908) 249-5000
New Mexico .... (505) 842-6132
New York .... (518) 463-3200
North Carolina .... (919) 828-0561
North Dakota .... (701) 255-1404
Ohio .... (614) 487-2050
Oklahoma .... (405) 524-2365
Oregon .... (503) 620-0222
Pennsylvania .... (717) 238-6715
Puerto Rico .... (809) 721-3358
Rhode Island .... (401) 421-5740
South Carolina .... (803) 799-6653
South Dakota .... (605) 224-7554
Tennessee .... (615) 383-7421
Texas .... (512) 463-1400
Utah .... (801) 531-0660
Vermont .... (802) 223-2020
Virginia .... (804)786-2061
Virgin Islands .... (809) 778-7497
Washington .... (206) 448-0441
Washington DC .... (202) 223-6600
West Virginia .... (304) 342-1474
Wisconsin .... (608) 257-3838
Wyoming .... (307) 632-9061

REAL ESTATE AGENCIES

These are headquarters listings only—each of these companies has many offices across the US.

Allen Tate Company Inc.
6618 Fairview Rd.
Charlotte, NC 28210
Tel: (704) 365-6910

Balcor Co.
4849 Golf Rd.
Skokie, IL 60077
Tel: (708) 677-2900

Beacon Cos. Guest Quarters Hotel L.P.
30 Rowes Wharf
Boson, MA 02110
Tel: (617) 262-9411

Cardinal Industries Inc.
PO Box 32999
Columbus, OH 43232
Tel: (614) 861-3211

Coldwell Banker Real Estate Group Inc.
533 S. Fremont Ave.
Los Angeles, CA 90071
Tel: (213) 613-3242

Cushman and Wakefield Inc.
1166 Ave. of the Americas
New York, NY 10036
Tel: (212) 841-7500

Grubb and Ellis Co.
1 Montgomery St.
San Francisco, CA 94104
Tel: (415) 956-1990

Kennedy-Wilson Inc.
3110 Main St.
Santa Monica, CA 90405
Tel: (213) 452-6664

Koenig and Strey Inc.
999 Waukegan Rd.
Glenview, IL 60025
Tel: (708) 729-5050

Moore and Co.
390 Grant St.
Denver, CO 80203
Tel: (303) 778-6600

Prudential California Realty
9595 Wilshire Blvd.
Beverly Hills, CA 90212
Tel: (310) 271-5001

Prudential Summerson-Burrows Realtors Inc.
8101 College Blvd.
Overland Park, KS 66210
Tel: (913) 491-1550

Realty One Inc.
5035 Mayfield Rd.
Cleveland, OH 44124
Tel: (216) 291-3200

Sentinel Real Estate Corp.
1290 Ave. of the Americas
New York, NY 10104
Tel: (212) 408-2910

Shannon and Luchs Co.
901 15th St. NW
Washington, DC 20005
Tel: (202) 236-1000

TRANSLATORS & INTERPRETERS

There are many translation and interpretation services available in each city—Berlitz is one that has many offices across the US and worldwide.

National
AT&T Language Line
Tel: (800) 628-8486
Professional translators are available by phone for over 140 languages 24 hours a day, 7 days a week.

Atlanta, GA
Berlitz Translation Services
870 Northcliffe Dr. NW
Atlanta, GA 30318-1601
Tel: (404) 350-9966

International Language School Service
5810 Silver Lane NE
Atlanta, GA 30328
Tel: (404) 252-3829 Fax: (404) 851-9303

Baltimore, MD
Berlitz Translation Services
5 Charles Plaza
Baltimore, MD 21201-3933
Tel: (410) 752-0767

Boston, MA
Boston Language Institute
636 Beacon St.
Boston, MA 02215
Tel: (617) 262-3500 Fax: (617) 247-3919

Charlotte, NC
Berlitz Translation Services
5821 Fairview Rd.
Charlotte, NC 28209-3649
Tel: (704) 554-8169

Chicago, IL
Berlitz Translation Services
2 N. La Salle St.
Chicago, IL 60602-3702
Tel: (312) 782-7778

Joan Masters & Sons
875 N. Michigan, Suite 3614
Chicago, IL 60611
Tel: (312) 787-3009 Fax: (312) 787-3434

Cleveland, OH
Berlitz Translation Services
815 Superior Ave. NE
Cleveland, OH 44114-2702
Tel: (216) 861-0907, 861-0950

Dallas, TX
Berlitz Translation Services
17194 Preston Rd.
Dallas, TX 75248-1203
Tel: (214) 380-0404

Denver, CO
Berlitz Translation Services
55 Madison
Denver, CO 80206-5419
Tel: (303) 399-8686

Rocky Mountain Translations
55 Madison St., Suite 175
Denver, CO 80206
Tel: (303) 399-8686 Fax: (303) 333-1035

Honolulu, HI
Berlitz Translation Services
615 Piikoi St.
Honolulu, HI 96814-3116
Tel: (808) 521-9821

Houston, TX
Berlitz Translation Services
520 Post Oak Blvd.
Houston, TX 77027-9405
Tel: (713) 626-7844

Omni Intercommunications
520 Post Oak Blvd., Suite 500
Houston, TX 77027
Tel: (713) 529-3665

Los Angeles, CA
Berlitz Translation Services
3345 Wilshire Blvd.
Los Angeles, CA 90010-1810
Tel: (213) 380-1144

Miami, FL
Berlitz Translation Services
100 Biscayne Blvd.
Miami, FL 33132-2312
Tel: (305) 371-3686

Professional Translating Services
44 W. Flagler St., Suite 540
Miami, FL 33130
Tel: (305) 371-7887 Fax: (305) 381-9824

Minneapolis, MN
6600 France Ave. S
Berlitz Translation Services
Edina, MN 55435-1802
Tel: (612) 920-4100

New York, NY
Berlitz Translation Services
40 W. 51st St.
New York, NY 10019
Tel: (212) 765-1000

Interlingua
551 Fifth Ave.
New York, NY 10176
Tel: (212) 682-8585

Lawyers & Merchants Translation Service
11 Broadway, Suite 1401
New York, NY 10004
Tel: (212) 344-2930 Fax: (212) 422-6877

Translation Aces
29 Broadway, 17th Fl.
New York, NY 10006
Tel: (212) 269-4660 Fax: (212) 269-4662

Philadelphia, PA
Berlitz Translation Services
1608 Walnut St.
Philadelphia, PA 19103-5457
Tel: (215) 735-8500

St. Louis, MO
Berlitz Translation Services
200 S. Hanley Rd.
St. Louis, MO 63105-3415
Tel: (314) 721-1070

San Francisco, CA
Auerbach International Inc.
2031 Union St., Suite 2
San Francisco, CA 94123
Tel: (415) 563-5778 Fax: (415) 563-5770

Washington, DC
Berlitz Translation Services
1730 Rhode Island Ave. NW
Washington, DC 20006
Tel: (202) 331-1163

International Translation Center
1660 L St. NW, Room 613
Washington, DC 20036
Tel: (202) 296-1344 Fax: (202) 452-0978

TRANSPORTATION

AIRPORTS

Anchorage International
PO Box 196960
Anchorage, AK 99519
Tel: (907) 266-2525 Fax: (907) 243-0663

Chicago O'Hare International Airport (ORD)
PO Box 66142
Chicago, IL 60666
Tel: (312) 686-2200, 686-2308 Fax: (312) 686-4980

Dallas/Ft. Worth International Airport (DFW)
PO Drawer 619428
DFW Airport
Dallas, TX 75621
Tel: (214) 574-3197 Fax: (214) 574-3780

Hartsfield Atlanta International Airport (ATL)
Department of Aviation
Atlanta, GA 30320
Tel: (404) 530-6600, 530-6834 Fax: (404) 530-6803

John F. Kennedy International Airport (JFK)
Building #141
Jamaica, NY 11430
Tel: (718) 244-3502 Fax: (718) 244-3505

Los Angeles International Airport (LAX)
One World Way
Los Angeles, CA 90045
Tel: (310) 646-5252 Fax: (310) 646-1893/4

Memphis International Airport
PO Box 30168
Memphis, TN 38130
Tel: (901) 922-8000 Fax: (901) 922-8099

Miami International Airport (MIA)
PO Box 592075, AMF
Miami, FL 33159
Tel: (305) 876-7013/6 Fax: (305) 876-7398, 876-0562

Newark International Airport
Tower Rd., Bldg. 10
Newark, NJ 07114
Tel: (201) 961-2000

San Francisco International Airport (SFO)
PO Box 8097
San Francisco, CA 94128
Tel: (415) 761-0800

PORTS

Port of Long Beach
925 Harbor Plaza
Long Beach, CA 90802
Tel: (310) 437-0041 Fax: (310) 491-0237

Port of Los Angeles
425 South Palos Verdes St.
San Pedro, CA 90731
Tel: (310) 519-3400 Fax: (310) 519-0291

Port of Miami
1015 North America Way
Miami, FL 33132
Tel: (305) 371-7678 Fax: (305) 347-4852

Port of New Orleans
PO Box 60046
New Orleans, LA 70160
Tel: (504) 528-3256 Fax: (504) 524-4156

Port of New York/New Jersey
One World Trade Center, Suite 34S
New York, NY 10048
Tel: (212) 435-6001 Fax: (212) 435-6030

Port of Oakland
530 Water St.
Oakland, CA 94607
Tel: (510) 272-1100 Fax: (510) 839-5104

Port of Seattle
PO Box 1209
Seattle, WA 98111
Tel: (206) 728-3205 Fax: (206) 728-3205

Port of Tacoma
PO Box 1837
Tacoma, WA 98401
Tel: (206) 383-5841 Fax: (206) 593-4534

South Carolina Port Authority
PO Box 817
Charleston, SC 29401
Tel: (803) 723-8651 Fax: (803) 477-8616

Virginia Port Authority
600 World Trade Center
Norfolk, VA 23510
Tel: (804) 683-8500

AIRLINES

AerLingus (Ireland)
Reservations: (800) 223-6537
Cargo: (212) 557-1090, 557-1166 Fax: (212) 984-2000

Aeroflot (Russia)
Reservations: (800) 995-5555
Cargo: (718) 891-2551, 244-0036

Aerolineas Argentinas
Reservations: (800) 327-0276
Cargo: (718) 632-1731/7 Fax: (718) 632-1738

Aeromexico
Reservations: (800) 237-6639
Cargo: (718) 656-6177

Aeronica Airlines (Nicaragua)
Reservations: (800) 323-6422

Aeroperu
Reservations: (800) 777-7717
Cargo: (305) 526-3279

Air Afrique
Reservations: (800) 456-9192
Cargo: (718) 723-5699, (800) 228-4950
Fax: (718) 723-5690

Air Canada
Reservations: (800) 776-3000
Cargo: (718) 656-3407 Fax: (514) 879-7900

Air China
Reservations: (415) 392-2612, 392-2156
Cargo: (415) 877-0750 Fax: (415) 877-0814

Air France
Reservations: (800) 237-2747
Cargo: (718) 553-6900 Fax: (718) 712-2161

Air India
Reservations: (800) 223-2420
Cargo: (212) 407-1441 Fax: (212) 838-9533

Air Jamaica
Reservations: (800) 523-5585
Cargo: (718) 917-6171, 830-0622 Fax: (718) 244-0965

Air Malta
Reservations: (415) 362-2929

Air New Zealand
Reservations: (800) 262-1234
Cargo: (310) 646-8143, (800) 421-5913
Fax: (310) 568-8620

Airborne Express
Cargo: (800) 336-3344, 247-2676

Alaska Airlines
Reservations: (800) 426-0333
Cargo: (907) 789-7378

Alitalia (Italy)
Reservations: (800) 223-5730
Cargo: (212) 903-3466, (718) 656-2828
Fax: (212) 903-3507

All Nippon Airways (Japan)
Reservations: (800) 235-9262
Cargo: (718) 632-6500

ALM Antillean Airlines
Reservations: (800) 327-7230
Cargo: (305) 871-3193

Aloha Airlines
Reservations: (800) 367-5250
Cargo: (808) 935-6490

America West
Reservations: (800) 235-9292
Cargo: (602) 693-2900

American Airlines
Reservations: (800) 433-7300
Cargo: (817) 967-2400 Fax: (817) 967-2406

Argentina Airlines
Reservations: (800) 333-0276
Cargo: (800) 221-6002

Asiana Airlines (South Korea)
Reservations: (800) 227-4262
Cargo: (800) 932-7426

Austrian Airlines
Reservations: (800) 843-0002
Cargo: (718) 481-4650 Fax: (718) 481-4654

Avianca Airlines (Columbia)
Reservations: (800) 284-2622
Cargo: (305) 871-2042 Fax: (305) 871-3371

Aviateca (Guatemala)
Reservations: (800) 327-9832
Cargo: (310) 464-1533

Bahamasair
Reservations: (800) 222-4262
Cargo: (305) 591-0606

British Airways
Reservations: (800) 247-9297
Cargo: (718) 917-5091, 553-5000 Fax: (718) 917-5056

BWIA International (Trinidad & Tobago)
Reservations: (800) 327-7401
Cargo: (301) 434-2066

Burlington Air Express
Cargo: (800) 225-5229

Canadian Airlines International
Reservations: (800) 426-7000
Cargo: (800) 382-1300

Cargolux Airlines International
Cargo: (800) 722-2023

Cathay Pacific Airways (Hong Kong)
Reservations: (800) 233-2742
Cargo: (213) 646-4586 Fax: (213) 646-2512

China Airlines (Taiwan)
Reservations: (800) 227-5118
Cargo: (213) 646-4293 Fax: (213) 646-3206

Continental Airlines
Reservations: (800) 525-0280
Cargo: (713) 443-4400, 443-4411 Fax: (713) 834-6855

Czechoslovak Airlines
Reservations: (800) 223-2365
Cargo: (212) 682-7541

Danzas-Northern Air
Cargo: (800) 426-5962

Delta Airlines
Reservations: (800) 221-1212
Cargo: (404) 714-7000, 765-2095 Fax: (404) 765-2596

DHL Worldwide Express
Cargo: (800) 225-5345

Dominicana Airlines (Dominican Rep.)
Reservations: (800) 327-7240
Cargo: (718) 656-3604

Egypt Air
Reservations: (800) 334-6787
Cargo: (212) 286-2678 Fax: (718) 712-6982

El Al Israel Airlines
Reservations: (800) 223-6700
Cargo: (718) 244-3176, 244-3169 Fax: (718) 244-0500

Emery Worldwide
Cargo: (800) 443-6379

Emirates
Reservations: (212) 758-2786
Cargo: (718) 244-7900 Fax: (718) 244-6881

Ethiopian Airlines
Reservations: (800) 433-9677, 445-2733
Cargo: (212) 867-0095 Fax: (212) 692-9589

EVA Airways (Taiwan)
Reservations: (800) 695-1188
Cargo: (310) 646-9838

Federal Express (FedEx)
Cargo: (800) 463-3339, 247-4747

Finnair
Reservations: (800) 950-5000
Cargo: (718) 656-7570 Fax: (718) 244-0661

Garuda Indonesia
Reservations: (800) 342-7832
Cargo: (800) 422-2746

Gulf Air (Bahrain)
Reservations: (800) 223-1740
Cargo: (212) 986-3950 Fax: (212) 986-3957

Guyana Airways
Reservations: (800) 327-8680
Cargo: (305) 871-1691

Hawaiian Airlines
Reservations: (800) 367-5320
Cargo: (808) 935-0819, 525-5511 Fax: (808) 525-5484

Iberia Airlines (Spain)
Reservations: (800) 772-4642
Cargo: (718) 632-1258, 632-1244 Fax: (718) 632-1251

Icelandair
Reservations: (800) 223-5550
Cargo: (718) 632-1258 Fax: (718) 917-8901

Japan Airlines (JAL)
Reservations: (800) 525-3663
Cargo: (310) 646-2353

KLM Royal Dutch Airlines
Reservations: (800) 777-5553
Cargo: (718) 632-2560

Korean Airlines (KAL)
Reservations: (800) 438-5000
Cargo: (213) 646-9800 Fax: (213) 337-0762

Kuwait Airlines
Reservations: (800) 282-2064
Cargo: (718) 525-0132, 656-6242 Fax: (718) 244-0504

Ladeco Chilean
Reservations: (800) 825-2332
Cargo: (305) 477-5591

LAN Chile Airlines
Reservations: (800) 735-5526
Cargo: (305) 670-1961

Lloyd Aereo Boliviano (LAB Airlines)
Reservations: (800) 327-7407
Cargo: (305) 526-5565 Fax: (305) 871-5760

LOT Polish Airlines
Reservations: (800) 223-0593
Cargo: (718) 656-2674/5 Fax: (305) 656-6063

LTU International Airways (Germany)
Reservations: (800) 888-0200
Cargo: (305) 530-2208

Lufthansa
Reservations: (800) 645-3880
Cargo: (718) 632-7240, (800) 542-2746

Martinair Holland
Reservations: (800) 627-8462
Cargo: (800) 366-3734

Malaysian Airline System
Reservations: (800) 421-8641
Cargo: (800) 233-5597

Mexicana Airlines
Reservations: (800) 531-7921
Cargo: (310) 646-7300, 646-5414 Fax: (310) 646-7301

Middle East Airlines (Lebanon)
Reservations: (415) 397-1834
Cargo: (718) 656-8480

Nippon Cargo Airlines
Cargo: (800) 622-6675

Northwest Airlines
Reservations: (800) 447-4747
Cargo: (612) 726-3456, (800) 692-2746
Fax: (612) 726-4847

Olympic Airways (Greece)
Reservations: (800) 223-1226
Cargo: (212) 735-0273 Fax: (212) 735-0212

Pakistan International Airlines
Reservations: (800) 221-2552
Cargo: (718) 656-4020 Fax: (718) 656-4703

Philippine Airlines
Reservations: (800) 435-9725
Cargo: (415) 877-4818

Polar Air Cargo
Cargo: (800) 828-7652

Qantas Airlines (Australia)
Reservations: (800) 227-4500
Cargo: (415) 445-1440, (800) 227-0290
Fax: (415) 399-0922

Roadway Global Air
Cargo: (800) 742-1742

Royal Air Maroc
Reservations: (800) 292-0081
Cargo: (718) 995-6928 Fax: (718) 244-1246

Royal Jordanian Airlines
Reservations: (800) 223-0470
Cargo: (800) 221-0746

Sabena Belgian World Airlines
Reservations: (800) 955-2000
Cargo: (516) 562-9310, (800) 955-0770
Fax: (516) 562-9315

SAS Scandinavian Airline Systems
Reservations: (800) 221-2350
Cargo: (201) 896-3671, 961-3660 Fax: (201) 896-3728

Saudi Arabian Airlines
Reservations: (800) 472-8342
Cargo: (718) 995-4730 Fax: (718) 244-1668

Singapore Airlines
Reservations: (800) 742-3333
Cargo: (213) 776-2400

South African Airlines
Reservations: (800) 722-9675
Cargo: (212) 917-6258 Fax: (212) 917-6716

Southwest Airlines
Reservations: (800) 435-9792
Cargo: (800) 533-1222

Suriname Airways
Reservations: (800) 327-6864
Cargo: (305) 262-9922 Fax: (305) 261-0884

Swissair
Reservations: (800) 221-4750
Cargo: (718) 244-1050, 481-4737 Fax: (718) 481-4771

TACA International Airlines (Mexico)
Reservations: (800) 535-8780
Cargo: (713) 443-1808, 443-6005

TAP Air Portugal
Reservations: (800) 221-7370
Cargo: (718) 656-7455 Fax: (718) 244-1099

Thai Airways International
Reservations: (800) 426-5204
Cargo: (310) 640-0097

TNT Express Worldwide
Cargo: (800) 558-5555

Tower Air
Reservations: (800) 221-2500
Cargo: (718) 553-4503

TWA International
Reservations: (800) 892-4141
Cargo: (718) 244-2590, 917-8850

United Airlines
Reservations: (800) 241-6522
Cargo: (708) 952-5828, (800) 825-3788, 621-5647
Fax: (708) 952-4674

United Parcel Service (UPS)
Cargo: (800) 742-5877, 782-7892

USAir
Reservations: (800) 428-4322
Cargo: (703) 418-7163 Fax: (703) 418-7168

Varig Brazilian Airways
Reservations: (800) 468-2744
Cargo: (305) 526-5965, 526-6583

VASP Brazilian Airlines
Reservations: (800) 732-8277
Cargo: (310) 646-2793

Viasa Venezuelan Airways
Reservations: (800) 468-4272
Cargo: (305) 871-1580

Virgin Atlantic Airways
Reservations: (800) 877-2537
Cargo: (516) 775-2600 Fax: (516) 354-3760

All addresses and telephone numbers are in the United States unless otherwise noted. The country code for the US is [1].

TRANSPORTATION FIRMS

Headquarters offices only are listed, with information on other locations by state. Services listed are given as a guideline and are not necessarily complete.

A.W. Fenton Co., Inc.
6565 Eastland Road
Cleveland, OH 44142
Tel: (216) 243-5900 Fax: (216) 826-0515
Branches in IL, IN, MD, NY, OH, PA
Services: air/ocean freight forwarder, air cargo agent, customs broker, NVO common carrier, warehousing

A.N. Deringer, Inc.
PO Box 1309
St. Albans, VT 05478-1012
Tel: (802) 524-8110 Fax: (802) 524-5970
Branches in many states across the US
Services: air/ocean freight forwarder, customs broker, air cargo agent, NVO common carrier, warehousing

Air Express Int'l
PO Box 1231
120 Tokeneke Road
Darien, CT 06820
Tel: (203) 655-7900 Fax: (203) 655-5779
Branches in 27 states across the US and worldwide
Services: air/ocean freight forwarder, customs broker, air cargo agent, warehousing

Air-Sea Forwarders, Inc.
PO Box 90637
Los Angeles, CA 90009
Tel: (213) 776-1611 Fax: (213) 216-2625
Branches in CA, GA, IL, MA, NJ, NY, TX and worldwide
Services: air/ocean freight forwarder, customs broker, air cargo agent

Alexander International
PO Box 30209
Memphis, TN 38130
Tel: (901) 345-5420 Fax: (901) 332-6388
Branches in GA, LA, TN, TX
Services: air/ocean freight forwarder, customs broker, air cargo agent, NVO common carrier, warehousing

Alpha International
40 Parker Road, Suite 200
Elizabeth, NJ 07207
Tel: (908) 527-6900 Fax: (908) 527-6940
Branches in CA and NY
Services: air/ocean freight forwarder, customs broker, air cargo agent, NVO common carrier

Amerford International Corp.
8010 Roswell Rd., #300
Atlanta, GA 30350
Tel: (404) 353-4300 Fax: (404) 698-0698
Branches in many states across the US, Puerto Rico, and Israel
Services: air/ocean freight forwarder, air cargo agent, NVO common carrier

American President Lines
1111 Broadway, 9th Floor
Oakland, CA 9607
Tel: (415) 272-7511 Fax: (415) 272-8655
Services: Intermodal shipping and transportation company.

Atlantic Customs Brokers Inc.
PO Box 9622
151 East St.
New Haven, CT 06511
Tel: (800) 446-4751 Fax: (203) 495-7654
Branches in CT, MA, NY
Services: customs broker, ocean freight forwarder

BDP International Inc.
510 Walnut St.
Philadelphia, PA 19106
Tel: (215) 629-8900 Fax: (215) 629-8940
Branches in FL, GA, IL, MD, NY, PA, TX, VA
Services: air/ocean freight forwarder, customs broker, air cargo agent, NVO common carrier

Burlington Air Express
18200 Von Karman Ave.
Irvine, CA 92715
Tel: (714) 752-1212 Fax: (714) 851-1563
Branches in many states across the US and worldwide
Services: air freight forwarder, customs broker, air cargo agent, warehousing

C.H. Powell Company
One Intercontinental Way
Peabody, MA 01960
Tel: (508) 535-7073 Fax: (508) 535-7028
Branches in MD and NY
Services: customs broker, NVO common carrier, ocean freight forwarder

Cargo Brokers International, Inc.
100 Hartsfield Center Parkway
Atlanta, GA 30354
Tel: (404) 559-7200 Fax: (404) 559-6186
Branches in FL, NC, SC
Services: air/ocean freight forwarder, customs broker, air cargo agent, NVO common carrier

Carmichael International Service
533 Glendale Blvd.
Los Angeles, CA 90026
Tel: (213) 250-0186 Fax: (213) 975-0057
Branches in CA, NY, WA
Services: air/ocean freight forwarder, customs broker, NVO common carrier, warehousing

Circle International
260 Townsend St.
San Francisco, CA 94107
Tel: (415) 978-0600 Fax: (415) 978-0699
Internet gopher: circleintl.com
Internet WWW site: http://circleintl.com
52 branch offices across the US and offices worldwide
Services: air freight forwarder, customs broker, NVO common carrier, warehousing, integrated logistics

Clearfreight
8647 Aviation Blvd.
Inglewood, CA 90301
Tel: (310) 568-0600 Fax: (310) 568-9829
Branches in CA and WA
Services: air/ocean freight forwarder, customs broker, air cargo agent, NVO common carrier

Colombia Shipping Inc.
138-01 Springfield Blvd.
Jamaica, NY 11413
Tel: (718) 276-3300 Fax: (718) 712-3622
Branches in CA, IL, PA
Services: air/ocean freight forwarder, customs broker, air cargo agent, NVO common carrier

D.J. Power Company, Inc.
PO Box 9239
Savannah, GA 31412
Tel: (912) 234-7241 Fax: (912) 236-5230
Branches in GA, NC, SC
Services: air/ocean freight forwarder, customs broker, air cargo agent, NVO common carrier

Daniel F. Young, Inc.
17 Battery Place
New York, NY 10004
Tel: (212) 248-1700 Fax: (212) 509-3934
Branches in CA, DC, FL, LA, MD, MI, NY TX
Services: air/ocean freight forwarder, customs broker, air cargo agent, NVO common carrier

Danzas Corporation
3650 131st Ave. SE, #700
Bellevue, WA 98105
Tel: (206) 649-9339 Fax: (206) 649-4911
Branches in many states across the US
Services: air/ocean freight forwarder, customs broker,
air cargo agent, NVO common carrier, warehousing

ELCO Freight International Inc.
6033 W. Century Blvd. #720
Los Angeles, CA 90045
Tel: (310) 641-3900 Fax: (310) 641-0105
Branches in CA, GA, IL, MA, MI, MN, NC, NJ, NY, OR, WA
Services: air/ocean freight forwarder, customs broker,
air cargo agent, NVO common carrier, warehousing

Emery Customs Brokers
100 Port St.
Newark, NJ 07114
Tel: (201) 565-9669 Fax: (201) 589-3360
Branches in 15 states across the US
Services: customs broker, ocean freight forwarder

Eurocontinental Incorporated
Bldg. 9, Hackensack Ave.
Port Kearny, NJ 07032
Tel: (201) 589-5361 Fax: (201) 690-5704
Branches in CA and IL
Services: air/ocean freight forwarder, customs broker,
air cargo agent, NVO common carrier

Expeditors International of Washington, Inc.
PO Box 69620
Seattle, WA 98168-6920
Tel: (206) 246-3711 Fax: (206) 246-3197
Branches in 17 states across the US and worldwide.
Services: air/oceanfreight forwarder, customs broker,
air cargo agent, NVO common carrier

F.X. Coughlin Company
27050 Wick Road
Taylor, MI 48180
Tel: (313) 946-9510 Fax: (313) 946-6945
Branches in FL, GA, IL, OH and Canada
Services: air/oceanfreight forwarder, customs broker,
air cargo agent, NVO common carrier

Fracht FWO Inc.
147-39 175th St.
Jamaica, NY 11434
Tel: (718) 553-7914 Fax: (718) 995-8242
Branches in CA, GA, IL
Services: air/ocean freight forwarder, air cargo agent,
NVO common carrier

Fritz Companies, Inc.
PO Box 7221
San Francisco, CA 94120
Tel: (415) 904-8200 Fax: (415) 904-8661
Branches in many states across the US and worldwide
Services: air/ocean freight forwarder, customs broker,
air cargo agent, NVO common carrier, steamship agent,
warehousing

Global Transportation Services, Inc.
7550 24th Ave. South, Suite 144
Minneapolis, MN 55450
Tel: (612) 727-1091 Fax: (612) 727-1428
Branches in CA, IL, WA
Services: air/ocean freight forwarder, customs broker,
air cargo agent, warehousing

H & M International Transportation, Inc.
75 County Road
Jersey City, NJ 07307
Tel: (201) 216-8400 Fax: (201) 216-8415
Services: warehousing, distribution, trucking,
consolidation and other transportation services.

H.A. & J.L. Wood, Inc.
231 North 3rd St.
Pembina, ND 58271
Tel: (701) 825-6241 Fax: (701) 825-6226
Branches in MN, ND, WA
Services: customs broker, ocean freight forwarder

Harper Group
260 Townsend St.
San Francisco, CA 94107
Tel: (415) 978-0600 Fax: (415) 978-0699
Internet gopher: circleintl.com
Internet WWW site: http://circleintl.com
52 branch offices across the US and offices worldwide
Services: air freight forwarder, customs broker, NVO
common carrier, warehousing, integrated logistics

Hecny Brokerage Services, Inc.
618-622 Glasgow Ave.
Inglewood, CA 90301
Tel: (213) 642-0951 Fax: (213) 642-6658
Branches in CA, FL, IL, IN, NY, OH, TX
Services: air/ocean freight forwarder, customs broker,
air cargo agent, NVO common carrier, warehousing

Hipage Company, Inc.
PO Box 3158
227 E. Plume St.
Norfolk, VA 23514
Tel: (804) 446-1500 Fax: (804) 446-1516
Branches in DC, GA, NC, SC, VA, WI
Services: air/ocean freight forwarder, customs broker,
air cargo agent, NVO common carrier

Intertrans Corporation
125 E. John Carpenter Freeway
Irving, TX 75062
Tel: (214) 830-8888 Fax: (214) 830-7488
Branches in many states across the US
Services: air/ocean freight forwarder, customs broker,
air cargo agent, NVO common carrier

J.E. Lowden & Co.
One Embarcadero Center, Suite 1950
San Francisco, CA 94111-3701
Tel: (415) 781-7040 Fax: (415) 392-3970
Services: air/ocean freight forwarder, customs broker,
air cargo agent, NVO common carrier

J.F. Moran Co., Inc.
1110 Wellington Ave.
Cranston, RI 02910
Tel: (401) 941-7200 Fax: (401) 941-3993
Branches in CA, CT, FL, MA, NY, RI, TX
Services: air/ocean freight forwarder, customs broker,
air cargo agent, steamship agent

Japan Freight Consolidators
1039 Hillcrest Blvd.
Inglewood, CA 90301
Tel: (213) 776-3160 Fax: (310) 215-0789
Branches in CA, IL, MI, NY
Services: air freight forwarder, customs broker, air cargo
agent

John V. Carr & Son, Inc.
PO Box 33479
Detroit, MI 48232-5479
Tel: (313) 222-1121 Fax: (313) 222-1138
Branches across the US and in Canada
Services: air/ocean freight forwarder, customs broker,
air cargo agent, NVO common carrier, warehousing

Karl Schroff & Associates, Inc.
182-16 149th Road
Jamaica, NY 11413
Tel: (718) 244-6340 Fax: (718) 917-8440
Branches in CA, IL, MO
Services: air/ocean freight forwarder, customs broker,
air cargo agent, NVO common carrier

Kenney Transport, Inc.
145-38 157th St.
Jamaica, NY 11434
Tel: (718) 723-1221 Fax: (718) 712-1619
Branches in CA, IL, NJ, TX
Services: air/ocean freight forwarder, customs broker,
air cargo agent, NVO common carrier

L.E. Coppersmith, Inc.
3460 Wilshire Blvd., Suite 700
Los Angeles, CA 90010
Tel: (213) 380-3770 Fax: (213) 380-3987
Branches in CA and TX
Services: air freight forwarder, customs broker, air cargo
agent, ocean freight forwarder

LEP Profit International, Inc.
1950 Spectrum Circle
Marietta, GA 30067
Tel: (404) 951-8100 Fax: (404) 980-8155
Branches in many states across the US
Services: air freight forwarder, customs broker, air cargo
agent, NVO common carrier, ocean freight forwarder,
warehousing

Lykes Bros. Steamship Co., Inc.
17 Battery Place
New York, NY 10004
Tel: (212) 943-6363 Fax: (212) 943-5471
Ocean carrier: containerized, ro-ro, multi-purpose

M.G. Maher & Co., Inc.
One Canal Place, Suite 2100
New Orleans, LA 70130
Tel: (504) 581-3320 Fax: (504) 529-2611
Branches in AL, LA, MS, TN, TX
Services: customs broker, ocean freight forwarder,
steamship agent

Maersk Inc.
Giralda Farms, Maidson Ave.
PO Box 880
Madison, NJ 07940-0880
Tel: (201) 514-5000 Fax: (201) 514-5410
Services: containerized ocean carrier

Matrix International Logistics Inc.
205 S. Whiting St., Suite 500
Alexandria, VA 22304
Tel: (703) 461-8700 Fax: (703) 461-3679
Branches in CA, CT, TX
Services: air/ocean freight forwarder, air cargo agent,
NVO common carrier, warehousing

Meadows Wye & Co., Inc.
2506 Forest Ave.
Staten Island, NY 10303
Tel: (718) 983-9702 Fax: (718) 494-4167
Branch offices in FL, NY, TN, and overseas
Services: customs broker, air cargo agent, NVO common
carrier, ocean freight forwarder

Meston & Brings, Inc./Onan Shipping, Ltd.
PO Box 24363
Seattle, WA 98124
Tel: (206) 625-0404 Fax: (206) 682-9111
Branches in CA, GA, WA
Services: air/ocean freight forwarder, customs broker

Meyer Customs Brokers, Inc.
8100 Mitchell Road
Eden Prairie, MN 55344
Tel: (612) 937-2726 Fax: (612) 937-1227
Branches in FL, IL, MI, WA
Services: air/ocean freight forwarder, customs broker,
air cargo agent, NVO common carrier

MSAS Customs Logistics, Inc.
150-16 132nd Ave.
Jamaica, NY 11434
Tel: (718) 481-5400 Fax: (718) 712-7578
Branches in CA, FL, GA, IL, MA, NY, OH, TX, UT, VA, WA
Services: customs broker, air cargo agent

Myers Group, Inc.
Myers Building
Rouses Point, NY 12979
Tel: (518) 297-2222 Fax: (518) 297-6650
Branches in many states across the US and in Canada
Services: air/ocean freight forwarder, customs broker,
air cargo agent, NVO common carrier, warehousing

Nippon Express USA, Inc.
1 World Trade Center, Suite 1769
New York, NY 10048
Tel: (212) 432-9490 Fax: (212) 938-1932
Branches in many states across the US.
Services: customs broker, NVO common carrier, ocean
freight forwarder, warehousing

Norman G. Jensen, Inc.
3050 Metro Drive, Suite 300
Minneapolis, MN 55425
Tel: (612) 854-7363 Fax: (612) 854-5931
Branches in CA, ID, MI MN, MT, ND, UT, WA
Services: air/ocean freight forwarder, customs broker,
air cargo agent

Page & Jones, Inc.
PO Drawer J
Mobile, AL 36601
Tel: (205) 432-1646 Fax: (205) 433-1402
Branches in AL, FL, GA, LA, MS, NC
Services: air/ocean freight forwarder, customs broker,
steamship agent

Panalpina, Inc.
Harborside Financial Center
Plaza Two, 34 Exchange Place
Jersey City, NJ 07302
Tel: (201) 451-4000 Fax: (201) 451-8572
Branches in many states across the US
Services: air/ocean freight forwarder, customs broker,
air cargo agent, MP, NVO common carrier

PBB USA Inc.
PO Box 950
Buffalo, NY 14213
Tel: (716) 886-0360 Fax: (716) 886-0454
Branches in ME, MA, MI, NY, OH, VT, WA
Services: air/ocean freight forwarder, customs broker,
air cargo agent

Porter International, Inc.
PO Box 81488
San Diego, CA 92138
Tel: (619) 661-4000 Fax: (619) 661-6339
Branches in CA
Services: air/ocean freight forwarder, customs broker,
air cargo agent, warehousing

Quast & Co., Inc.
332 S. Michigan Ave.
Chicago, IL 60604-4406
Tel: (312) 435-3870 Fax: (312) 435-1135
Branches in IL, IN, LA
Services: air/ocean freight forwarder, customs broker,
air cargo agent, NVO common carrier, warehousing

Radix Group International, Inc.
230 Park Ave.
New York, NY 10169
Tel: (212) 697-9141 Fax: (212) 557-4770
Branches in many states across the US
Services: air/ocean freight forwarder, customs broker,
air cargo agent, NVO common carrier, steamship agent,
warehousing

Rogers & Brown Custom Brokers, Inc.
PO Box 20160
Charleston, SC 29413-0160
Tel: (803) 577-3630 Fax: (803) 723-9672
Branches in CA, GA, NC, SC, TX, VA, WA
Services: air/ocean freight forwarder, customs broker,
air cargo agent, warehousing

Samuel Shapiro & Co., Inc.
World Trade Center, Suite 1200
Baltimore, MD 21202
Tel: (410) 539-0540 Fax: (410) 547-6935
Branches in DC, MD, PA, VA
Services: air/ocean freight forwarder, customs broker,
air cargo agent, NVO common carrier

Scanwell Freight Express (USA), Inc.
150-30 132nd Ave.
Jamaica, NY 11434
Tel: (718) 527-1122 Fax: (718) 712-2116
Branches in CA, FL, GA, IL and worldwide
Services: air/ocean freight forwarder, air cargo agent,
NVO common carrier

Schenkers International Forwarders, Inc.
Exchange Place Center
10 Exchange Place, Suite 1500
Jersey City, NJ 07302-3998
Tel: (201) 434-5500 Fax: (201) 434-5600
Branches in many states across the US
Services: air/ocean freight forwarder customs broker,
air cargo agent, NVO common carrier

Sea-Land Service, Inc.
PO Box 2555
Elizabeth, NJ 07207
Tel: (908) 603-2144 Fax: (908) 603-2831
Services: containerized ocean carrier

Seamodal Transport Corp.
221 Main St., Suite 765
San Francisco, CA 94105
Tel: (415) 543-7420 Fax: (415) 543-2137
Branches in CA, IL, MD, SC, VA
Services: air/ocean freight forwarder, customs broker,
air cargo agent, NVO common carrier

Seino America, Inc.
8728 Aviation Blvd.
Inglewood, CA 90301
Tel: (310) 215-0500 Fax: (310) 337-0073
Branches in CA, GA, IL, NY, NC, TX, WA, PR
Services: air/ocean freight forwarder, customs broker,
air cargo agent, NVO common carrier

Southern Overseas Corp.
PO Box 2110
Wilmington, NC 28402
Tel: (919) 392-8300 Fax: (919) 392-8328
Branches in CA, GA, NC, SC, VA
Services: air/ocean freight forwarder, customs broker,
air cargo agent

Tower Group International
128 Dearborn St.
Buffalo, NY 14207
Tel: (716) 874-1300 Fax: (716) 874-4396
Branches in 13 states across the US
Services: air/ocean freight forwarder, customs broker,
air cargo agent, NVO common carrier, warehousing

Unsworth Transport Int'l Inc.
1831 Pennsylvania Ave.
Linden, NJ 07036
Tel: (908) 486-1100 Fax: (908) 925-4833
Branches in NY and worldwide
Services: air/ocean freight forwarder, customs broker,
air cargo agent, NVO common carrier, warehousing

UPS Customhouse Brokerage, Inc.
1930 Bishop Lane
Louisville, KY 40218
Tel: (502) 473-2600 Fax: (502) 473-2731
Branches in AK, CA, HI, NJ
Services: customs broker

W. J. Byrnes & Co./Byrnes Air
PO Box 280205
San Francisco, CA 94128
Tel: (415) 692-1142 Fax: (415) 692-5726
Branches in AZ, CA, CO, WI
Services: air/ocean freight forwarder, customs broker,
air cargo agent, warehousing

W.I.D.E. Corporation
300 Middlesex Ave.
Carteret, NJ 07008
Tel: (908) 969-9600 Fax: (908) 969-9191
Branches in CA, NY
Services: air/ocean freight forwarder, customs broker,
NVO common carrier

W.R. Zanes & Co. of LA, Inc.
PO Box 2330
New Orleans, LA 70176
Tel: (504) 524-1301 Fax: (504) 524-1309
Branches in AL, LA, TX
Services: air/ocean freight forwarder, customs broker,
air cargo agent, warehousing

Wallenius Lines North America, Inc.
PO Box 1232
188 Broadway
Woodcliff Lake, NJ 07675-1232
Tel: (201) 307-1300 Fax: (201) 307-9740
Services: ro-ro ocean carrier.

Western Overseas Corp.
1855 Coronado Ave.
Long Beach, CA 90804
Tel: (310) 985-0616 Fax: (310) 986-1345
Branch Offices in CA, IL, NY, OR, TX, WA
Services: air/ocean freight forwarder, customs broker,
air cargo agent, NVO common carrier, warehousing

Wilson UTC, Inc.
1104 Tower Lane
Bensenville, IL 60106
Tel: (708) 956-3280 Fax: (708) 595-1769
Branches in CA, FL, GA, IL, MI, MD, NY, PA, TX
Services: air/ocean freight forwarder, customs broker,
air cargo agent, NVO common carrier

Wolf D. Barth Co., Inc.
7575 Holstein Ave.
Philadelphia, PA 19153
Tel: (215) 365-8600 Fax: (215) 365-7827
Branches in CA, MD, MA, NJ, NY, NC, PA, SC, TX, WA
and overseas.
Services: air/ocean freight forwarder, customs broker,
air cargo agent, NVO common carrier

World Commerce Services, Inc.
PO Box 66593
Chicago, IL 60666
Tel: (708) 350-0111 Fax: (708) 350-0504
Branches in CA and overseas
Services: air/ocean freight forwarder, customs broker,
air cargo agent, NVO common carrier

Yusen Air and Sea Service (USA), Inc.
60 East 42nd St., Rm. 1915
New York, NY 10165
Tel: (212) 983-1170 Fax: (212) 490-6497
Branches across the US
Services: air/ocean freight forwarder, customs broker,
air cargo agent

MEDIA & INFORMATION SOURCES

DIRECTORIES

Bacon's Directories
Bacon's Publishing Company
332 S. Michigan Ave., Suite 900
Chicago, IL 60604
Tel: (312) 922-2400
Publish media directories: Newspaper/Magazine,
Radio/TV, Media Alerts, Publicity Checker

Commercial News USA-New Products Directory
US Government Printing Office
Superintendent of Documents
Washington, DC 20402
Tel: (202) 512-1800 Fax: (202) 512-2550
A publication of the International Trade Administration

Congressional Quarterly's Washington Information
Directory
Congressional Quarterly Inc.
1414 22nd St. NW
Washington, DC 20037
Tel: (202) 887-8500, (800) 432-2250 Fax: (202) 728-1863

Dun & Bradstreet, Inc.
3 Sylvan Way
Parsippany, NJ 07054
Tel: (201) 605-6000, (800) 526-0651 Fax: (201) 605-6911
Publish a number of directories, including America's
Corporate Families: Billion Dollar Directory, Dun's
Business Rankings, Million Dollar Directory, *and* Who
Owns Whom: North America

Gale Research
PO Box 33477
Detroit, MI 48232-5477
Tel: (312) 961-2242, (800) 877-4253 Fax: (800) 414-5043
E-mail: 72203.1552@compuserve.com
Distribute many directories, including: Business
Rankings Annual, Companies and Their Brands,
Walker's The Corporate Directory of US Public
Companies, Ward's Business Directory, Finance,
Insurance & Real Estate USA, *and* Manufacturing USA,
Service Industries USA

Grey House Publishing
Pocket Knife Square
Lakeville, CT 06039
Tel: (203) 435-0868, (800) 562-2139
Fax: (203) 435-0867
Publish The Directory of Mail Order Catalogs, The
Directory of Business to Business Catalogs, *and* The
Directory of Business Information Sources

Index Products and Services
25 Broadway
New York, NY 10004
Tel: (212) 208-8702, 208-1649
Publish Standard & Poor's Register of Corporations,
Directors and Executives, S&P 500 Directory,
Insurance Rating, Corporate and Register
Biographical

Journal of Commerce
445 Marshall St.
Phillipsburg, NJ 08885
Tel: (908) 454-6879 Fax: (908) 454-6507
Publish the Directory of US Importers *and the*
Directory of US Exporters

Leadership Directories
104 Fifth Ave., 2nd Floor
New York, NY 10011
Tel: (212) 627-4140 Fax: (212) 645-0931
Publish a wide range of government, corporate, and
legal directories.

MacRae's Blue Book, Inc.
817 Broadway
New York, NY 10003
Tel: (212) 673-4700
Publish MacRae's Blue Book *and* MacRae's Industrial
Directories

Manufacturer's News Directories
1633 Central St.
Evanston, IL 60201-1569
Tel: (708) 864-7000 Fax: (708) 332-1100
*Publish a wide range of directories for manufacturers
and services*

Moody's Investors Service, Inc.
99 Church St.
New York, NY 10007
Tel: (212) 553-0300
Tel: (800) 342-5647 x0435
Publish many directories, including Moody's Corporate
Profile, Moody's Handbook of Common Stocks,
Moody's Handbook of OTC Stocks, Moody's Industrial
Manual, Moody's Industry Review, Moody's Municipal
and Government Manual, Moody's Public Utility
Manual, *and* Moody's Transportation Manual.

The NASDAQ Fact Book & Company Directory
National Association of Securities Dealers
1735 K St. NW
Washington, DC 20006
Tel: (202) 728-8267

Reed Reference Publishing
121 Chanlon Rd.
New Providence, NJ 07974
Tel: (908) 464-6800, (800) 521-8110 Fax: (908) 665-6688
Distribute many directories, including The Corporate
Finance Sourcebook, Corporate Meeting Planners, The
Directory of Corporate Affiliations, *and* Martindale-
Hubbell Law Directory

Standard Rate and Data Service
Macmillan Inc.
3004 Glenview Rd.
Wilmette, IL 60091
Tel: (708) 441-2234
*Provide rate and data service for: Business Publications,
Community Publications, Consumer Magazines,
Newspaper Rates, Print Media, Spot Radio*

The Reference Press
6448 Highway 290 East, Suite E-104
Austin, TX 78723
Tel: (512) 454-7778, (800) 486-8666 Fax: (512) 454-9401
Publish the Hoover directories, including Hoover's
Handbook of American Business

Thomas Publishing Company
One Penn Plaza
New York, NY 10119
Tel: (212) 290-7310
Publish the Thomas Register of American
Manufacturers *and* Thomas Register Catalog File

US Industrial Directory
Cahners Publishing Company
1100 Summer St.
Stamford, CT 06905
Tel: (203) 328-2500

Worldwide Directory Products Sales
1000 Des Peres, Suite 220
St. Louis, MO 63131
Tel: (800) 792-2665 Fax: (800) 848-9012
*Sell a variety of national, international, and local
telephone directories, both white and yellow pages*

NEWSPAPERS

Boston Globe
PO Box 2378
Boston, MA 02107
Tel: (617) 929-2000 Fax: (617) 929-3183

Chicago Sun-Times
401 N. Wabash Ave.
Chicago, IL 60611
Tel: (312) 321-3000 Fax: (312) 321-3084

Christian Science Monitor
One Norway St.
Boston, MA 02115
Tel: (617) 450-2000 Fax: (617) 450-2595
National newspaper

Dallas Morning News
508 Young St.
PO Box 655237
Dallas, TX 75265
Tel: (214) 977-8222 Fax: (214) 977-8776

Detroit Free Press
321 W. Lafayette
Detroit, MI 48231
Tel: (313) 222-6400 Fax: (313) 678-6400

Journal of Commerce
110 Wall St.
New York, NY 10005
Tel: (212) 425-1616 Fax: (212) 208-0206
Focuses on trade; not often available in newsstands

Los Angeles Times
Times Mirror Square
Los Angeles, CA 90053
Tel: (213) 237-3000 Fax: (213) 237-4712
Available nationally

Miami Herald
One Herald Plaza
Miami, FL 33132-1693
Tel: (305) 350-2111 Fax: (305) 376-2677

New York Daily News
220 E. 42nd St.
New York, NY 10017
Tel: (212) 210-2100 Fax: (212) 662-2597

New York Times
229 W. 43rd St.
New York, NY 10036
Tel: (212) 556-1234
National coverage; most prestigious daily

Philadelphia Inquirer
400 N. Broad St.
Philadelphia, PA 19101
Tel: (215) 854-2000 Fax: (215) 854-4794

San Francisco Chronicle
901 Mission St.
San Francisco, CA 94103
Tel: (415) 777-1111 Fax: (415) 777-7131

USA Today
1000 Wilson Blvd.
Arlington, VA 22229
Tel: (703) 276-3400 Fax: (703) 558-3955
National newspaper; basic coverage of major events

Wall Street Journal
200 Liberty St.
New York, NY 10281
Tel: (212) 416-2000 Fax: (212) 416-3299
Leading national financial daily

Washington Post
1150 15th St. NW
NW Washington, DC 20071
Tel: (202) 334-6000 Fax: (202) 334-5661
National coverage

COMMERCIAL ONLINE SERVICES

For more background on these services, refer to the "Transportation & Communications" chapter.

America Online (AOL)
8619 Westwood Center Dr.
Vienna, VA 22182-9806
Tel: (703) 448-8700, (800) 827-6364 Fax: (800) 827-4595
One of the three most popular online services.

CompuServe
PO Box 20212
Columbus, OH 43220
Tel: (614) 529-1250, (800) 848-8199
One of the three most popular online services.

DataTimes
14000 Quail Springs Parkway, Suite 450
Oklahoma City, OK 73134
Tel: (405) 751-6400
Provides access to more than 3,500 publications.

Delphi
1030 Massachusetts Ave.
Cambridge, MA 02139
Tel: (800) 544-4005
E-mail: info@delphi.com
Somewhat similar to CompuServe, but provides full Internet access.

Dow Jones News/Retrieval
Dow Jones & Co.
PO Box 300
Princeton, NJ 08543
Tel: (609) 520-4646
Only source for full-text online versions of the Wall Street Journal. Also provides access to many other business and financial publications and reports.

Dun & Bradstreet Information Services
3 Sylvan Way
Parsippany, NJ 07054
Tel: (201) 605-6028
Provides access to information on over 32 million companies in 200 countries.

LEGI-SLATE, Inc.
777 North Capitol St.
Washington, DC 20002
Tel: (202) 898-2300, (800) 733-1131 Fax: (202) 898-3030
E-mail: legislate@gopher.legislate.com
Online information subsidiary of the Washington Post; an excellent source of information for federal legislative and regulatory information.

Knight-Ridder Information Inc.
3460 Hillview Ave.
Palo Alto, CA 94304
Tel: (415) 254-7000, (800) 334-2564
Formerly known as Dialog. Provides access to thousands of publications.

Lexis/Nexis
9443 Springboro Pike
Dayton, OH 45401
Tel: (513) 865-6800, (800) 346-9759 Fax: (513) 865-1666
Provides access to thousands of publications. Nexis is for general business, while Lexis is largly a legal information service.

Prodigy
445 Hamilton Ave.
White Plains, NY 10601
Tel: (914) 993-8000, (800) 776-3449
One of the three most popular online services.

WESTLAW
West Publishing Corp.
610 Opperman Dr.
Eagan, MN 55123
Tel: (612) 687-7000
Aimed at the legal researcher; comparable to Lexis.

All addresses and telephone numbers are in the United States unless otherwise noted. The country code for the US is [1].

GENERAL US BUSINESS, NEWS, & FOREIGN TRADE MAGAZINES

Across the Board
(10 issues/year)
Conference Board
845 Third Ave.
New York, NY 10022
Tel: (212) 759-0900 Fax: (212) 980-7014

Barron's National Business and Financial Weekly
(Weekly)
Dow Jones & Co., Inc.
200 Burnett Road
Chicopee, MA 01020
Tel: (212) 416-2700, (800) 628-9320 Fax: (212) 416-2829

Business Week
(Weekly)
McGraw-Hill, Inc.
1221 Ave. of the Americas
New York, NY 10020
Tel: (212) 512-2000

Congressional Quarterly Weekly Report
(Weekly)
Congressional Quarterly Inc.
1414 22nd St. NW
Washington, DC 20037
Tel: (800) 432-2250 Fax: (202) 728-1863

The Economist
(Weekly)
111 W. 57th St.
New York, NY 10019-2211
Tel: (212) 541-5730 Fax: (212) 541-9378

Financial World (FW)
(Monthly)
1328 Broadway
New York, NY 10001
Tel: (212) 594-5030 Fax: (212) 629-0021

Forbes
(Biweekly)
60 Fifth Ave.
New York, NY 10011
Tel: (212) 620-2200, (800) 888-9896

Fortune
(Biweekly)
Time & Life Building
Rockefeller Center
1271 Ave. of the Americas
New York, NY 10020
Tel: (212) 522-1212 Fax: (212) 522-0003

Global Trade & Transportation
(Monthly)
North American Publishing Co.
401 N. Broad St.
Philadelphia, PA 19108
Tel: (215) 238-5300 Fax: (215) 238-5457

Harvard Business Review
(Bimonthly)
Graduate School of Business Administration,
Harvard University
Boston, MA 02163
Tel: (617) 495-6800 Fax: (617) 495-9933

Foreign Trade
(Monthly)
6849 Old Dominion Drive, Suite 200
McLean, VA 22101
Tel: (703) 448-1338 Fax: (703) 448-1841

Inc.: The Magazine for Growing Companies
(Monthly)
Goldhirsh Group, Inc.
38 Commercial Wharf
Boston, MA 02110
Tel: (617) 248-8000 Fax: (617) 248-8040

Industry Week
(Semimonthly)
Penton Publishing, Inc.
1100 Superior Ave.
Cleveland, OH 44114-2543

Institutional Investor
(Monthly)
88 Madison Ave.
New York, NY 10022
Tel: (212) 303-3300

International Business
(Monthly)
American International Publishing
500 Mamaroneck Ave., Suite 314
Tel: (914) 381-7700

Investor's Business Daily
(Daily)
12655 Beatrice St.
Los Angeles, CA 90066
Tel: (310) 448-6000

Journal of Business and Economic Statistics
(Quarterly)
American Statistical Association
1429 Duke St.
Alexandria, VA 22314
Tel: (703) 684-1221 Fax: (703) 684-2037

Journal of Business Strategy
(6 issues/year)
Faulkner & Gray
11 Penn Plaza, 17th Floor
New York, NY 10001
Tel: (212) 967-7000 Fax: (212) 967-7155

Kiplinger Washington Letter
(Weekly)
Kiplinger Washington Editors, Inc.
1729 H St. NW
Washington, DC 20006-3938
Tel: (202) 887-6400 Fax: (202) 331-1206

Nation's Business
(Monthly)
US Chamber of Commerce
1615 H St. NW
Washington, DC 20062
Tel: (202) 463-5650 Fax: (202) 887-3437

Newsweek
444 Madison Ave.
New York, NY 10022
Tel: (212) 350-4000

Sales & Marketing Management
(15 issues/year)
Bill Communications, Inc.
633 Third Ave.
New York, NY 10017
Tel: (212) 592-6200

Time
Time & Life Bldg.
Rockefeller Center
1271 Ave. of the Americas
New York, NY 10020
Tel: (212) 522-1212

US News & World Report
(Weekly)
2400 N St. NW
Washington, DC 20037
Tel: (202) 955-2000

World Trade
(Monthly)
500 Newport Center Drive, #450
Newport Beach, CA 92660
Tel: (714) 640-7070

US GOVERNMENT PUBLICATIONS

The US Government Printing Office (GPO) is the largest publisher in the United States, with over 12,000 books, periodicals, and electronic information products available. Some of the most interesting are listed below. A catalog entitled "United States Government Information for Business" lists many more. Other catalogs of interest include "US Government Subscriptions," 45 separate subject bibliographies; a complete listing of all publications is available on microfiche or magnetic tape. To order GPO publications or to request catalogs, contact:

US Government Printing Office
Superintendent of Documents
Washington, DC 20402
Tel: (202) 512-1800 Fax: (202) 512-2550

Many government publications are available in electronic form, and some of those can be accessed online via the Federal Bulletin Board. For information on electronic information products, contact:

Office of Electronic Information Dissemination Services
Tel: (202) 512-1530 Fax: (202) 512-1260
Modem: (202) 512-1387
E-mail: help@eids.gpo.gov

The National Technical Information Service (NTIS) also sells many government publications on business and science topics, as well as publications from private publishers and from other foreign governments. To request a catalog or to order from NTIS, contact:

National Technical Information Service (NTIS)
5285 Port Royal Road
Springfield, VA 22161
Tel: (703) 487-4650 Fax: (703) 321-8547
Modem: (703) 321-8020   Telnet: fedworld.gov

Popular publications available from the GPO:

Agriculture Outlook
(11 issues/year)
A US Department of Agriculture publication.

Business America: The Magazine of International Trade
(Monthly)
Information on US export policy, trade opportunities for US exporters, listings of international trade exhibitions.

Census and You
(Monthly)
Newsletter for users of the Census Bureau statistics.

Code of Federal Regulations (CFR)
(Annual)
An annual cumulative codification of rules and regulations published in the Federal Register.

Commerce Business Daily (CBD)
(Daily)
Key information source for businesses interested in selling to the US Government.

Commerce Publications Update
(Biweekly)
Lists all publications and press releases issued by the Department of Commerce.

Compensation and Working Conditions
(Monthly)
Information on wage and benefit changes, statistical summaries, reports on trends in wages, benefits, and collective bargaining.

Construction Review
(Bimonthly)
About 50 pages of statistics plus one or two brief articles per issue.

Customs Bulletin and Decisions
(Weekly)

Economic Indicators
(Monthly)
Published by the Council of Economic Advisors. Tables and graphs on a wide range of US economic indicators.

Export Administration Regulations
(Annual with updates)

Federal Acquisition Regulation (FAR) and the Federal Information Resources Management Regulation
(Quarterly)
Listing of primary regulations used by federal executive agencies requesting supplies and services.

Federal Register
(Daily)
Proposed and final government regulations and rulings in their exact wording, executive directives, proclamations, notices of hearings, and legal notices.

Global Trade Talk
(Bimonthly)
US Customs Service bulletin for the US importer.

Harmonized Tariff Schedule of the United States (HTSUS)
(Annual, with supplements)
Complete tariff schedule with breakdowns on classification and specific duty levels.

Key Officers of Foreign Service Posts: Guide for Business Representatives
(Annual)
US embassies, missions, and consulates.

Statistical Abstract of the United States
(Annual)
Over 1,000 charts and tables with data on population, education, income and expenditures, trade, banking and finance, transportation, and more.

Survey of Current Business
(Monthly)
Features articles and data from the Bureau of Economic Analysis, including general business indicators and statistics for commodities and industries.

United States Government Manual
(Annual)
Information on all agencies, boards, commissions, committees, and other Federal agencies.

US Code on CD-ROM
(Irregular)
Covers federal laws through January 1993.

US Foreign Trade Highlights
(Annual)
Published by the US Department of Commerce. Contains detailed commodity data for exports and imports.

US Industrial Outlook
(Annual)
Analyses of more than 350 US industries and how they will perform both in the short and long term.

The Year in Trade: Operation of the Trade Agreements Program
(Annual)
Published by the US International Trade Commission

Popular items available from NTIS:

National Economic, Social, and Environmental Data Bank (NESE-DB)
(Quarterly)
A CD-ROM incorporating information from more than 50 US Government organizations.

National Trade Data Bank (NTDB)
(Monthly)
A two CD-ROM set from the Department of Commerce with over 90,000 documents relating to US foreign trade.

US GOVERNMENT
COMPUTER BULLETIN BOARDS

There are well over 100 US Government bulletin boards providing a wide variety of information; FedWorld's GateWay System provides access to most of them. Some of the most interesting are listed below. To call any of these bulletin boards, set your modem to 8 bits, no parity, 1 stop bit. Most of these BBSs are free to use, unless otherwise noted. When internet E-mail, gopher, or telnet addresses are available, they have been given. Telephone numbers for further information are given.

Consular Affairs Bulletin Board (CABB)
Tel: (202) 647-1488
Modem: (202) 647-9225
Operated by the Department of State Overseas Office of Consular Affairs. Provides information on international travel for US citizens and visa information for foreigners coming to the US.

Consumer Information Bulletin Board
Modem: (202) 208-7679
Gopher: gopher.gsa.gov

Customs Electronic Bulletin Board
Tel: (703) 440-6236
Modem: (703) 440-6155
Operated by the Customs Service

Economic Bulletin Board (EBB)
Tel: (202) 482-1526
Modem (300/1200/2400 bps): (202) 482-3870
Modem (9600 bps): (202) 482-2584, 482-2167
Telnet: ebb.stat-usa.gov
Operated by the Department of Commerce. There is a subscription charge for this service, although it is relatively low.

Federal Bulletin Board
Tel: (202) 512-1530 Fax: (202) 512-1260
Modem: (202) 512-1387
A service of the US Government Printing Office; users can download and purchase US Government publications.

FedWorld
Tel: 703-487-4608
Modem: (703) 321-8020
E-mail: sysop@fedworld.gov
Operated by the National Technical Information Service (NTIS). Connects users to more than 100 computer bulletin board services operated by departments and agencies of the US government.

Marlinespike Bulletin Board Service
Tel: (202) 366-5807, (800) 9US-FLAG (Information)
Modem: (202) 366-8505
Operated by the Maritime Administration of the Department of Commerce. Includes maritime regulation and legislation, trade event listings, scheduling information on US vessel operators and shipyards.

SBA Online
Modem: (202) 401-9600, (800) 697-4636
Gopher: gopher://www.sbaonline.sba.gov
Operated by the Small Business Administration.

INDUSTRY-SPECIFIC PUBLICATIONS

ABA Journal
(Monthly)
American Bar Association
750 Lake Shore Dr.
Chicago, IL 60611
Tel: (312) 988-5991 Fax: (312) 988-6014
One of many legal publications from the American Bar Association.

Accounting Today
(Biweekly)
Faulkner & Gray
11 Penn Plaza, 17th Fl.
New York, NY 10001
Tel: (212) 967-7000 Fax: (212) 967-7155

Action Sports Retailer Magazine
(Monthly)
Miller Freeman Publications
31652 Second Ave.
S. Laguna, CA 92677
Tel: (714) 499-5374

Adhesives Age
(Monthly)
Argus Business
6151 Powers Ferry Rd. NW
Atlanta, GA 30339
Tel: (404) 955-2500 Fax: (404) 955-0400

Advanced Materials and Processes
(Monthly)
ASM International
Materials Park, OH 44073
Tel: (216) 338 5151 Fax: (216) 338-4634

Advertising Age: The International Newspaper of Marketing
(Weekly)
Crain Communications, Inc.
220 E. 42nd St.
New York, NY 10017-5806
Tel: (212) 210-0100 Fax: (212) 210-0111

Adweek
(Weekly)
BPI Communications
1515 Broadway
New York, NY 10036
Tel: (212) 536-5336 Fax: (212) 944-1719

Aesthetics World Today
(Quarterly)
Aestheticians International Association
4447 McKinney Ave.
Dallas, TX 75205
Tel: (214) 526-0752

Air Conditioning, Heating & Refrigeration News
(Weekly)
Business News Publishing Company
755 West Big Beaver Rd., Suite 1000
Troy, MI 48084
Tel: (313) 362-3700 Fax: (313) 362-0317

Air Transport World
(Monthly)
Penton Publishing
600 Summer St., Box 1361
Stamford, CT 06904
Tel: (203) 348-7531 Fax: (203) 348-4023

American Banker
One State Street Plaza
New York, NY 10004
Tel: (212) 943-6700

American Demographics
(Monthly)
Dow Jones Inc.
PO Box 68
Ithaca, NY 14851
Tel: (607) 273-6343, (800) 828-1133 Fax: (607) 273-3196

American Machinist
Penton Publishing Co.
826 Broadway
New York, NY 10003
Tel: (212) 477-6420

American Metal Market
(Daily)
Chilton Publishing Company
825 Seventh Ave.
New York, NY 10019
Tel: (212) 887-8580 Fax: (212) 887-8522

American Papermaker
MacLean-Hunter Publications
57 Executive Park S., Suite 310
Atlanta, GA 30329
Tel: (404) 325-9153

American Printer
(Monthly)
Maclean Hunter Publishing
29 N. Wacker Dr.
Chicago, IL 60606
Tel: (312) 726-2802 Fax: (312) 726-2574

Apparel Industry Magazine
Shore Communications
180 Allen Road, Suite 300-N
Atlanta, GA 30328
Tel: (404) 252-8831

Appliance
(Monthly)
Dana Chase Publications, Inc.
1110 Jorie Blvd., CS 9019
Oak Brook, IL 60522-9019
Tel: (708) 990-3484 Fax: (708) 990-0078

Appliance Manufacturer
(Monthly)
5900 Harper Road, Suite 105
Solon, OH 44139
Tel: (216) 349-3060 Fax: (216) 498-9121

Athletic Business Magazine
(Monthly)
1846 Hoffman St.
Madison, WI 53704
Tel: (608) 249-0186 Fax: (608) 249-1153

Automotive Industries
(Monthly)
Chilton
Chilton Way
Radnor, PA 19089
Tel: (215) 964-4225 Fax: (215) 964-4251

Automotive News
(Weekly)
Crain Communications
1400 Woodbridge
Detroit, MI 48207
Tel: (313) 446-6000

Aviation Week & Space Technology
(Weekly)
McGraw-Hill
1221 Ave. of the Americas
New York, NY 10020
Tel: (609) 426-5526 Fax: (609) 426-6068

Bakery Production and Marketing
(14 issues/year)
Cahners Publishing
455 N. Cityfront Plaza Dr.
Chicago, IL 60611
Tel: (312) 222-2000 Fax: (312) 222-2026

Best's Review, Life/Health Insurance Edition
Best's Review, Property/Casualty Insurance Edition
(Monthly)
A.M. Best Co., Inc.
Ambest Road
Oldwick, NJ 08858
Tel: (908) 439-2200 Fax: (908) 439-3296

Beverage Industry
(Monthly)
Stagnito Publishing
1935 Shermer Road, Suite 100
Northbrook, IL 60062
Tel: (708) 205-5660 Fax: (708) 205-5680

Beverage World
(Monthly)
Keller International Publishing Corp.
150 Great Neck Road
Great Neck, NY 11021
Tel: (516) 829-9210 Fax: (516) 829-5414

Bobbin Magazine
(Monthly)
Bobbin Blenheim Media Corp.
1110 Shop Rd.
Columbia, SC 29202
Tel: (803) 771-7500 Fax: (803) 799-1461

Business Insurance
(Weekly)
Crain Communications Inc.
740 Rush St.
Chicago, IL 60611-2590
Tel: (312) 649-5286 Fax: (312) 280-3174

Business Marketing
Crain Communications Inc.
740 Rush St.
Chicago, IL 60611-2590
Tel: (312) 649-5260 Fax: (312) 649-5228

Candy Industry
(Monthly)
Advanstar Communications, Inc.
7500 Old Oak Blvd.
Cleveland, OH 44130
Tel: (216) 826-2866 Fax: (216) 819-2651

CDB Interior Textiles
(Monthly)
Columbia Comunications
370 Lexington Ave.
New York, NY 10017
Tel: (212) 532-9290 Fax: (212) 779-8345

Cellular Marketing Communications
Global Communications
Satellite Communications
(All monthly)
Cardiff Publishing Company
6300 South Syracuse Way
Englewood, CO 80111
Tel: (303) 220-0600

Chain Store Age Executive With Shopping Center Age
(Monthly)
Lebhar-Friedman, Inc.
425 Park Ave.
New York, NY 10022
Tel: (212) 756-5000

Chemical Business
(Monthly)
Schnell Publishing Company
80 Broad St., 23rd Fl.
New York, NY 10004
Tel: (212) 248-4177 Fax: (212) 248-4901

Chemical Marketing Reporter
(Weekly)
Schnell Publishing Co., Inc.
80 Broad St.
New York, NY 10004-2203
Tel: (212) 248-4177 Fax: (212) 248-4903

Chemical Week
(Weekly)
Chemical Week Association
888 Seventh Ave.
New York, NY 10019
Tel: (212) 621-4900 Fax: (212) 621-4949

Chilton's Automotive Marketing
(Monthly)
Chilton
Chilton Way
Radnor, PA 19089
Tel: (215) 964-4225 Fax: (215) 964-4251

Chilton's Commercial Carrier Journal
(Monthly)
Chilton
Chilton Way
Radnor, PA 19089
Tel: (215) 964-4225 Fax: (215) 964-4251

Chilton's Distribution
(Monthly)
Chilton
Chilton Way
Radnor, PA 19089
Tel: (215) 964-4225 Fax: (215) 964-4251

Chilton's Electronic Component News
(Monthly)
Chilton
Chilton Way
Radnor, PA 19089
Tel: (215) 964-4225 Fax: (215) 964-4251

Chilton's Hardware Age
(Monthly)
Chilton
Chilton Way
Radnor, PA 19089
Tel: (215) 964-4225 Fax: (215) 964-4251

Chilton's Industrial Maintenance & Plant Operation
(Monthly)
Chilton
Chilton Way
Radnor, PA 19089
Tel: (215) 964-4225 Fax: (215) 964-4251

Chilton's Motor Age
(Monthly)
Chilton
Chilton Way
Radnor, PA 19089
Tel: (215) 964-4225 Fax: (215) 964-4251

Chilton's Food Engineering
(Monthly)
Chilton
Chilton Way
Radnor, PA 19089
Tel: (215) 964-4225 Fax: (215) 964-4251

Computer Industry Almanac
(Annual)
225 Allen Way
Incline Village, NV 89451
Tel: (702) 831-2288 Fax: (702) 831-8610

Computerworld
(Weekly)
IDG
375 Cochituate Rd., Box 9171
Framingham, MA 01701
Tel: (508) 879-0700 Fax: (508) 875-8931

Construction Equipment
(Monthly)
Cahners Publishing Company
1350 E. Touhy Ave.
Des Plaines, IL 60018
Tel: (708) 635-8800 Fax: (708) 390-2690

Consumer Electronic and Appliance News
(Monthly)
Kasmar Publications
3821 W. 226th St.
Torrance, CA 90505
Tel: (408) 294-6390

D & B Reports: The Dun & Bradstreet Magazine for Small Business Management
(Bimonthly)
Dun & Bradstreet Information Services
One Diamond Hill Road
Murray Hill, NJ 07974-0027
Tel: (800) 362-3425 Fax: (212) 593-6596

Datamation
(24 issues/year)
Cahners Publishing
275 Washington St.
Newton, MA 02158-1630
Tel: (617) 964-3030 Fax: (617) 558-4506

Designfax Magazine
(Monthly)
29100 Aurora Road, Suite 200
Solon, OH 44139
Tel: (216) 248-1125 Fax: (216) 686-0214
For design engineers

Direct Marketing
(Monthly)
Hoke Communications
224 Seventh St.
Garden City, NY 11530
Tel: (516) 746-6700 Fax: (516) 294-8141

Discount Merchandiser
(Monthly)
Schwartz Publications
233 Park Ave. S.
New York, NY 10003
Tel: (212) 979-4860 Fax: (212) 474-7431

Drug and Cosmetic Industry (DCI)
(Monthly)
Edgell Communications, Inc.
7500 Old Oak Blvd.
Cleveland, OH 44130
Tel: (216) 826-2839 Fax: (216) 891-2726

EDN (Electronic Design Engineering)
(26 issues/year)
Cahners Publishing
275 Washington St.
Newton, MA 02158-1630
Tel: (617) 964-3030 Fax: (617) 558-4470

Electronic Design
(Fortnightly)
Penton Publishing
San Jose Gateway, Suite 354
2025 Gateway Plaza
San Jose, CA 95110
Tel: (408) 441-0550

Electronic News
(Monthly)
Chilton
Chilton Way
Radnor, PA 19089
Tel: (215) 964-4225 Fax: (215) 964-4251

Electronic Products
(Monthly)
645 Stewart Ave.
Garden City, NY 11530
Tel: (516) 227-1300 Fax: (516) 227-1444

Farm Equipment Guide
(Monthly)
Heartland Communications Group
1003 Central Ave.
Fort Dodge, IA 50501
Tel: (515) 955-1600 Fax: (515) 247-2000

Farmer's Digest
(10 issues/year)
PO Box 624
Brookfield, WI 53008
Tel: (414) 782-4480 Fax: (414) 782-1252

Food Processing
(13 issues/year)
Putnam Publishing
301 Erie St.
Chicago, IL 60611
Tel: (312) 644-2020

Foodservice Equipment and Supplies Specialist
(13 issues/year)
Cahners Publishing Company
1350 E. Touhy Ave.
Des Plaines, IL 60018
Tel: (708) 635-8800

Forest Industries
(Monthly)
Miller Freeman Publications
600 Harrison St.
San Francisco, CA 94107
Tel: (415) 905-2200 Fax: (415) 905-2232

Furniture Design and Manufacturing
(Monthly)
Delta Communications Inc.
400 N. Michigan Ave.
Chicago, IL 60611
Tel: (312) 222-2000 Fax: (312) 222-2066

Furniture/Today
(Weekly)
Cahners Publishing Company
PO Box 2754
High Point, NC 27261
Tel: (919) 605-0121 Fax: (919) 605-1143

Hardware Trade
(Bimonthly)
Master Publications
225 E. Cheyenne Mountain Blvd.
Colorado Springs, CO 80906

Health News Daily
(Daily)
FDC Reports
5550 Friendship Blvd., Suite 1
Chevy Chase, MD 20815
Tel: (301) 657-9830 Fax: (301) 986-6467
Also publish The Pink Sheet and The Green Sheet (on pharmaceuticals), The Grey Sheet (on medical devices), and The Tan Sheet (on nonprescription and nutritional industries)

Industrial Distribution
(Monthly)
Cahners Publishing
275 Washington St.
Newton, MA 02158-1630
Tel: (617) 964-3030 Fax: (617) 558-4327

Industrial Engineering
(Monthly)
Institute of Industrial Engineers
25 Technology Park
Norcross, GA 30092
Tel: (404) 449-0461

Industrial Marketing Management
(Quarterly)
Elsevier Science Publishing Company, Inc.
655 Ave. of the Americas
New York, NY 10010
Tel: (212) 989-5800 Fax: (212) 633-3990

Industrial Photography
Photographic Processing
Photographic Trade News
(Monthly)
PTN Publishing
445 Broad Hollow Rd.
Melville, NY 11747
Tel: (516) 845-2700 Fax: (516) 845-7109

Industrial Product Bulletin
(Monthly)
Gordon Publications
301 Gibraltar Dr.
Morris Plains, NJ 07950
Tel: (201) 292-5100 Fax: (201) 898-9281

Industry Week
(Semimonthly)
Penton Publishing
1100 Superior Ave.
Cleveland, OH 44114
Tel: (216) 696-7000 Fax: (216) 696-8765

InfoWorld
(Weekly)
IDG
155 Bovet Rd., Suite 800
San Mateo, CA 94402
Tel: (415) 572-7341, (800) 227-8365 Fax: (415) 696-8765

Instrumentation & Control Systems
(Monthly)
Chilton
Chilton Way
Radnor, PA 19089
Tel: (215) 964-4225 Fax: (215) 964-4251

Instrumentation & Automation News
(Monthly)
Chilton
Chilton Way
Radnor, PA 19089
Tel: (215) 964-4225 Fax: (215) 964-4251

Intech
Instrument Society of America Services, Inc.
PO Box 12277
Research Triangle Park, NC 27709
Tel: (919) 549-8411

International Advertiser
(Bimonthly)
International Advertising Association
342 Madison Ave.
New York, NY 10017
Tel: (212) 557-1133

International Drug and Device Regulatory Monitor
(Monthly)
Newsletter Services
1545 New York Ave. NE
Washington, DC 20077
Tel: (202) 529-5700

International Journal of Purchasing and Materials
Management
(Quarterly)
National Association of Purchasing Management, Inc.
2055 E. Centennial Circle, PO Box 22160
Tempe, AZ 85285-2160
Tel: (602) 752-6276 Fax: (602) 752-7890

Iron Age
(Monthly)
Hitchcock Publishing Company
191 S. Gary Ave.
Carol Stream, IL 60188
Tel: (708) 665-1000

Jenks Health Care Business Report
Managed Health Care News
Advanstar Communications
PO Box 10460
Eugene, OR 97440-2460
Tel: (800) 949-6525

Journal of Global Marketing
(Quarterly)
The Hayworth Press, Inc.
10 Alice St.
Binghamton, NY 13904-1580
Tel: (607) 722-9678, (800) 342-9678 Fax: (607) 722-1424

Journal of Marketing
(Quarterly)
American Marketing Association
250 S. Wacker Dr., Suite 200
Chicago, IL 60606
Tel: (312) 648-0536 Fax: (312) 993-7542

Machine Design
(28 issues/year)
Penton Publishing
1100 Superior Ave.
Cleveland, OH 44114
Tel: (216) 696-7000 Fax: (216) 696-0177

Machine Design
1100 Superior Ave.
Cleveland, OH 44114-2543
Tel: (216) 248-1125

MacWeek
PCWeek
(Weekly)
Ziff Davis
1 Park Ave.
New York, NY 10016
Tel: (415) 243-3500 Fax: (415) 243-3650

Marketing News
(Biweekly)
American Marketing Association
250 S. Wacker Dr., Suite 200
Chicago, IL 60606
Tel: (312) 648-0536 Fax: (312) 993-7542

Mechanical Engineering
(Monthly)
American Society of Mechanical Engineers
345 E. 47th St.
New York, NY 10017
Tel: (212) 705-7722

Mergers & Acquisitions: The Journal of Corporate
Venture
(Bimonthly)
MLR Publishing Company
229 S. 18th St.
Philadelphia, PA 19103
Tel: (215) 790-7000 Fax: (215) 790-7005

Metal Bulletin
Metal Bulletin Journals, Ltd.
220 Fifth Ave.
New York, NY 10001
Tel: (212) 213-6202

Metal Fabricating News
(Quarterly)
PO Box 1178
Rockford, IL 61105
Tel: (815) 965-4031

Metals Week
McGraw-Hill Publications
1221 Ave. of the Americas
New York, NY 10020
Tel: (212) 512-2823

Mine and Quarry Trader
(Monthly)
Allied Publications
PO Box 603
Indianapolis, IN 46206
Tel: (317) 297-5500 Fax: (317) 299-1356

Minerals Today
(Bimonthly)
US Bureau of Mines
US Department of the Interior
Washington, DC 20241
Tel: (202) 501-9358

Mining Engineering
(Monthly)
8307 Shaffer Parkway
Littleton, CO 80127
Tel: (303) 973-9550 Fax: (303) 973-3845

Modern Materials Handling
(14 issues/year)
Cahners Publishing
275 Washington St.
Newton, MA 02158-1630
Tel: (617) 964-3030 Fax: (617) 558-4402

Modern Plastics
(Monthly)
McGraw-Hill, Inc.
1221 Ave. of the Americas
New York, NY 10020
Tel: (212) 512-6267, (800) 257-9402 Fax: (212) 512-6111

National Underwriter, Life & Health/Financial Services
Edition
National Underwriter, Property & Casualty/Risk &
Benefits Management
(Weekly)
National Underwriter Company
505 Gest St.
Cincinnati, OH 45203
Tel: (513) 721-2140 Fax: (513) 721-0126

Network World
(Weekly)
161 Worcester Rd.
Framingham, MA 01701
Tel: (508) 875-6400 Fax: (508) 820-3467

New Equipment Digest
(Monthly)
Penton Publishing
1100 Superior Ave.
Cleveland, OH 44114
Tel: (216) 696-7000 Fax: (216) 696-8765

NGSA Retail Focus
(Monthly)
National Sporting Goods Association
1699 Wall St.
Mt. Prospect, IL 60056
Tel: (708) 439-4000 Fax: (708) 430-0111

Nonwoven Industry
(Monthly)
Rodman Publishing
17 S. Franklin Turnpike
Ramsey, NJ 07446
Tel: (201) 825-2552 Fax: (201) 855-0553

Oil and Gas Journal
(Weekly)
PennWell Publishing Co.
PO Box 1260
Tulsa, OK 74101
Tel: (918) 835-3161

Oil, Gas and Petrochem Equipment
(Monthly)
PennWell Publishing Company
1421 S. Sheridan St.
Tulsa, OK 74101
Tel: (918) 835-3161 Fax: (918) 831-9497

Packaging
(Monthly)
Cahners Publishing Company
1350 E. Touhy Ave.
Des Plaines, IL 60018
Tel: (708) 635-8800

Packaging Digest
(Monthly)
Delta Communications, Inc.
455 N. Michigan Ave., Suite 1300
Chicago, IL 60611
Tel: (312) 222-2000

Paper Industry Equipment
(Annual)
Hatton-Brown Publishers, Inc.
225 Hanrick St., Box 2268
Montgomery, AL 36104
Tel: (205) 834-1170

Pharmaceutical Executive
(Monthly)
Advanstar Communications
859 Willamette St.
Eugene, OR 97440
Tel: (503) 343-1200

Photo Business
(Monthly)
BPI Communications
1515 Broadway
New York, NY 10036
Tel: (212) 764-7300 Fax: (212) 536-5351

Plant Engineering
(19 issues/year)
Cahners Publishing
1350 E. Touhy Ave.
PO Box 5080
Des Plaines, IL 60017
Tel: (708) 635-8800 Fax: (708) 390-2636

Playthings
Geyer-McAllister Publications, Inc.
51 Madison Ave
New York, NY 10010
Tel: (212) 689-4411

Prepared Foods
(13 issues/year)
Cahners Publishing
455 N. Cityfront Plaza Dr.
Chicago, IL 60611
Tel: (312) 222-2000 Fax: (312) 222-2026

Progressive Grocer
(Monthly)
Progressive Grocer
263 Tressor Blvd.
Stamford, CT 06901
Tel: (203) 977-7600 Fax: (203) 977-7645

Proofs: The Magazine of Dental Sales and Marketing
PennWell Publishing Co.
1421 S. Sheridan
Tulsa, OK 74112
Tel: (918) 835-3161

Public Relations News
(Weekly)
Phillips Business Information
1201 Seven Locks Rd.
Potomac, MD 20854
Tel: (301) 424-3338 Fax: (301) 309-3847

Pulp and Paper
(Semimonthly)
Miller Freeman Publications
600 Harrison St.
San Francisco, CA 94107
Tel: (415) 905-2200 Fax: (415) 905-2232

Purchasing
(Semimonthly)
Cahners Publishing
275 Washington St.
Newton, MA 02158-1630
Tel: (617) 946-3030 Fax: (617) 558-4327

Railway Age
(Monthly)
Simmons-Boardman Publishing Co.
345 Hudson St.
New York, NY 10014
Tel: (212) 620-7200

Randol Buyers Guide
Randol International Limited
18301 West Colfax Ave. #T1B
Golden, CO 80401
Tel: (303) 271-0324 Fax: (303) 271-0334
Information on mines and the mining industry

Restaurant Business
(18 issues/year)
Restaurant Business Magazine
633 Third Ave.
New York, NY 10017
Tel: (212) 592-6200 Fax: (212) 592-6509

Robotics World
Communication Channels, Inc.
6151 Powers Ferry Road NW
Atlanta, GA 30339
Tel: (404) 955-2500

Rubber Directory and Buyer's Guide
Rubber and Plastics News
Plastics News
Crain Communications
1725 Merriman Rd., Suite 300
Akron, OH 44313
Tel: (216) 836-9180

Site Selection
(Bimonthly)
Conway Data, Inc.
40 Technology Park/Atlanta
Norcross, GA 30092
Tel: (404) 446-6996 Fax: (404) 263-8825

Sporting Goods Business
Gralla Publications
1515 Broadway
New York, NY 10036
Tel: (212) 869-1300

All addresses and telephone numbers are in the United States unless otherwise noted. The country code for the US is [1].

Sports Trend
Shore Communications Inc.
Suite 300, N Building
180 Allen Rd. NE
Atlanta, GA 30328
Tel: (404) 252-8831

Stores
(Monthly)
National Retail Federation, Inc.
100 W. 31st St.
New York, NY 10001
Tel: (212) 244-8780

Supermarket Business
(Monthly)
Howfrey Communications
1086 Teaneck Rd.
Teaneck, NJ 07666
Tel: (201) 833-1900 Fax: (201) 833-1273

Telecommunications Reports
Business Research Publications, Inc.
1333 H St. NW, 11th Fl. West
Washington, DC 20005
Tel: (202) 842-3006

Textile World
(Monthly)
Maclean Hunter Publishing Company
29 N. Wacker Dr.
Chicago, IL 60606
Tel: (404) 847-2770 Fax: (404) 252-6150

The Furnishings Digest
Mann, Armistead, & Epperson, Ltd.
121 Shockoe Slip
Richmond, VA 23219
Tel: (804) 782-3297

The Furniture Quarterly
Wheat, First Securities, Inc.
PO Box 1357
Richmond, VA 23211
Tel: (804) 782-3297

Toy and Hobby World International
A4 International Publications
41 Madison Ave.
New York, NY 10010
Tel: (212) 685-0404

Travel Trade
(Weekly)
Travel Trade Publications
15 W. 44th St.
New York, NY 10036
Tel: (212) 730-6600 Fax: (212) 730-7020

Voice Processing Magazine
(Monthly)
Advanstar Communications
3721 Briar Park
Houston, TX 77042
Tel: (713) 974-6637 Fax: (713) 974-6272

Wallcoverings, Windows and Interior Fashion
(Monthly)
Publishing Dynamics Inc.
15 Bank St., Suite 101
Stamford, CT 06901
Tel: (203) 357-0028

Ward's Auto World (Monthly)
Ward's Automotive International (Twice monthly)
Ward's Automotive Reports (Weekly)
Ward's Automotive Yearbook (Annual)
Ward's Communications
28 W. Adams St.
Detroit, MI 48226
Tel: (313) 962-4433 Fax: (313) 962-5593

TELEVISION & RADIO NETWORKS

Television Broadcast Networks

ABC
77 W. 66th St.
New York, NY 10023-6298
Tel: (212) 456-7777

CBS
51 W. 52nd St.
New York, NY 10019
Tel: (212) 975-4321

Fox Broadcasting Company
10201 W. Pico Blvd.
Los Angeles, CA 90035
Tel: (310) 203-3553

NBC (National Broadcasting Co.)
30 Rockfeller Plaza
New York, NY 10112
Tel: (212) 664-4444

PBS (Public Broadcasting Service)
1320 Braddock Pl.
Alexandria, VA 22314-1698
Tel: (703) 739-5000 Fax: (703) 739-0775

Univision
605 3rd Ave., 12th Fl.
New York, NY 10148-0182
Tel: (212) 455-5200 Fax: (212) 867-6710

Television Cable Networks

A&E (Arts & Entertainment Network)
235 E. 45th St.
New York, NY 10017
Tel: (212) 210-1328 Fax: (212) 949-7147

American Movie Classics
150 Crossway Park W
Woodbury, NY 11797
Tel: (516) 364-2222 Fax: (516) 364-2297

ANC/All News Channel
3415 University Ave.
Minneapolis, MN 55414-3327
Tel: (612) 642-4645 Fax: (612) 642-4680

BET (Black Entertainment Television)
1232 31st St. NW
Washington, DC 20007
Tel: (202) 337-5260

BIZ NET/American Business Network
1615 H St. NW
Washington, DC 20062
Tel: (202) 463-5858 Fax: (202) 463-3186

Bravo
150 Crossways Park W.
Woodbury, NY 11797
Tel: (516) 364-2222 Fax: (516) 364-2297

C-SPAN/C-SPAN II (Cable Satellite Public Affairs
Network)
400 N. Capital St. NW, Suite 650
Washington, DC 20001
Tel: (202)737-3220 Fax: (202) 737-3323

CBN/Christian Broadcasting Network
700 CBN Center
Virginia Beach, VA 23463
Tel: (804) 424-7777 Fax: ((804) 523-7959

Cinemax
1100 Ave. of the Americas
New York, NY 10036
Tel: (212) 512-1000

CNBC (Consumer News & Business Channel)
2200 Fletcher Ave.
Fort Lee, NJ 07024
Tel: (201) 585-2622 Fax: (201) 585-6393

CNN (Cable News Network)/Headline News
1 CNN Center
Atlanta, GA 30348-5366
Tel: (404) 827-1503, 523-8517

The Comedy Channel
1100 Ave. of the Americas
New York, NY 10036
Tel: (212) 512-1000

Comedy Central
2049 Century Park E, Suite 4200
Los Angeles, CA 90037
Tel: (310) 201-9500

Country Music Television
2806 Opryland Dr.
Nashville, TN 37214
Tel: (615) 871-5830 Fax: (615) 871-5835

The Discovery Channel
7700 Wisconsin Ave.
Bethesda, MD 20814
Tel: (301) 986-1999

The Disney Channel
3800 W. Alameda Ave.
Burbank, CA 91505
Tel: (818) 569-7500 Fax: (818) 566-1358

E! (Entertainment Television)
5670 Wilshire Blvd., 2nd Fl.
Los Angeles, CA 90036
Tel: (310) 954-2400 Fax: (310) 954-2620

Encore
4700 S. Syracuse Pkwy., Suite 1000
Denver, CO 80237
Tel: (303) 771-7700 Fax: (303) 741-3067

ESPN (Entertainment & Sports Programming Network)
ESPN Plaza
Bristol, CT 06010
Tel: (203) 585-2000

The Family Channel
1000 Centerville Tpke.
Viginia Beach, VA 23463
Tel: (804) 523-7301 Fax: (804) 523-7880

HA! The TV Comedy Network
10 Universal City Plaza, 30th Fl.
Universal City, CA 91608
Tel: (818) 505-7800

Home Box Office (HBO)
1100 Ave. of the Americas
New York, NY 10036
Tel: (212) 512-1000

Home Shopping Network
Box 9090
Clearwater, FL 34618-9090
Tel: (813) 572-8585

The International Channel
12401 W. Olympic Blvd.
Los Angeles, CA 90064
Tel: (310) 826-2429

The Learning Channel
7700 Wisconsin Ave.
Bethesda, MD 20814-3522
Tel: (301) 986-1999 Fax: (703) 524-0237

Lifetime Television
36-12 35th Ave
Astoria, NY 11106
Tel: (718) 482-4000 Fax: (718) 482-1903

The Movie Channel (TMC)
1633 Broadway, 37th Fl.
New York, NY 10019
Tel: (212) 708-1600

MTV (Music Television)/VH-1 (Video Hits One)
1515 Broadway
New York, NY 10036
Tel: (212) 258-7800

Nickelodeon/Nick at Nite
1515 Broadway
New York, NY 10036
Tel: (212) 258-7800

Playboy at Night
8560 Sunset Blvd.
Los Angeles, CA 90069
Tel: (310) 246-4000

QVC Network, Inc.
Goshen Corporate Park
1365 Enterprise Dr.
West Chester, PA 19380
Tel: (215) 430-1000 Fax: (215) 431-6499

The Sci-Fi Channel
2255 Glades Rd., Suite 237W
Boca Raton, FL 33431
Tel: (407) 998-8000 Fax: (407) 998-8006

Shop Television Network
1845 Empire Ave.
Burbank, CA 91504
Tel (818) 840-1400

Showtime
1633 Broadway, 37th Fl.
New York, NY 10019
Tel: (212) 708-1600

Sportschannel America
3 Crossways Park W.
Woodbury, NY 11797
Tel: (516) 921-3764 Fax: (516) 364-1943

TBS
Box 105366
1 CNN Center
Atlanta, GA 30348-5366
Tel: (404) 827-1700 Fax: (404) 827-1593

TNN (The Nashville Network)
250 Harbor Plaza Dr.
Stamford, CT 06904
Tel: (203) 965-6000 Fax: (203) 965-6315

TNT (Turner Network Television)
Box 105366
1 CNN Center
Atlanta, GA 30348-5366
Tel: (404) 827-1647 Fax: (404) 827-1190

Univision
605 3rd Ave., 12th FL.
New York, NY 10158-0180
Tel: (212) 455-5200

USA Network
1230 Ave. of the Americas
New York, NY 10020
Tel: (212) 408-9100 Fax: (212) 408-3600

Viewers Choice
909 3rd Ave., 21st Fl.
New York, NY 10022
Tel: (212) 486-6600 Fax: (212) 688-9497

The Weather Channel
2600 Cumberland Pkwy.
Atlanta, GA 30339
Tel: (404) 434-6800

All addresses and telephone numbers are in the United States unless otherwise noted. The country code for the US is [1].

Radio Networks

ABC Radio Networks
125 West End Ave.
New York, NY 10023-6298
Tel: (212) 456-1000

Associated Press (AP) Network News
1825 K St. NW, Suite 710
Washington, DC 20006
Tel: (202) 736-1100 Fax: (202) 736-1199

Business Radio Network
888 Garden of the Gods Rd.
Colorado Springs, CO 80907
Tel: (719) 528-7040 Fax: (719) 528-5170

CBS Radio Networks
51 W. 52nd St.
New York, NY 10019
Tel: (212) 975-4321 Fax: (212) 975-1519

CNN Radio Network
1050 Techwood Dr. NW
Box 105264
Atlanta, GA 30318-5264
Tel: (408) 827-1500

Dow Jones Network
200 Liberty St., 14th Fl.
New York, NY 10281
Tel: (212) 416-2381 Fax: (212) 416-4195

Financial News Network
2200 Fletcher Ave.
Ft. Lee, NJ 07024
Tel: (201) 585-2622

Gannett Radio
6255 Sunset Blvd.
Los Angeles, CA 90028
Tel: (213) 466-8381 Fax: (213) 466-9330

Global Satellite Network
1458 Ventura Blvd.
Sherman Oaks, CA 91403
Tel: (818) 906-1888 Fax: (818) 906-9736

Mutual Broadcasting System, Inc.
1755 S. Jefferson Davis Hwy.
Arlington, VA 22202
Tel: (703) 413-8300 Fax: (703) 413-8445

National Public Radio (NPR)
2025 M St. NW
Washington, DC 20036
Tel: (202) 822-2300 Fax: (202) 822-2329

NBC Radio Network
1755 S. Jefferson Davis Hwy.
Arlington, VA 22202
Tel: (703) 413-8300 Fax: (703) 413-8445

Unistar Radio Networks
1675 Broadway, 17th Fl.
New York, NY 10019
Tel: (212) 247-1600 Fax: (212) 247-0393

UPI Radio Network
1400 Eye St. NW, 9th Fl
Washington, DC 20005
Tel: (202) 898-8111

USA Radio Network
2290 Springlake Rd., Suite 107
Dallas, TX 75234
Tel: (214) 484-3900 Fax: (214) 243-3489

Westwood One Radio Network
9540 Washington Blvd.
Culver City, CA 90232
Tel: (310) 840-4000

BOOKSTORES

Some of the best-stocked chain bookstores found across the US are Barnes & Noble, Tower Books, Borders, and Doubleday. Look for these chains' "superstores" for the best selection. B. Dalton and Waldenbooks usually have smaller stores with less extensive stock. Those listed below are either particularly large, well-stocked stores or specialize in business and technical publications. Most will ship orders internationally.

Boston
WordsWorth Books
30 Brattle St.
Cambridge, MA 01238
Tel: (617) 354-5201

Chicago
Business Savvy Inc.
50 E. Washington St.
Chicago, IL
Tel: (312) 849-3444 Fax: (312) 849-3445

Los Angeles
OPAMP Technical Books
1033 N. Sycamore Ave.
Los Angeles, CA 90038
Tel: (213) 468-4322, (800) 468-4322

New York
AMA Management Bookstore
135 W. 50th St.
New York, NY 10017
Tel: (800) 553-3210 Fax: (212) 963-4910

Barnes & Noble
105 Fifth Ave.
New York, NY 10003
Tel: (212) 807-0099 Fax: (212) 633-2522

Coliseum Books
1771 Broadway
New York, NY 10019
Tel: (212) 757-8381, (800) 833-1543

McGraw-Hill Bookstore
1221 Ave. of the Americas
New York, NY 10020
Tel: (212) 512-4100

United Nations Bookshop
46th St. and First Ave. Entrance
Department 406
New York, NY 10017
Tel: (800) 553-3210 Fax: (212) 963-4910

Portland
Powell's City of Books
1005 W. Burnside
Portland, OR 97209
Tel: (503) 228-4651, 228-0540, (800) 878-7323

San Francisco
Stacey's Professional Bookstore
581 Market St.
San Francisco, CA 94105
Tel: (415) 421-4687 Fax: (415) 777-5017

Seattle
Elliott Bay Book Company
First and Main Streets
Seattle, WA 98104
Tel: (206) 624-6600 Fax: (206) 343-9558

Washington, DC
Reiter's Scientific, Medical & Professional Books
2021 K St. NW
Washington, DC 20006
Tel: (202) 223-3327, (800) 537-4314 Fax: (202) 296-9103

Index

A

G

N

O